W9-AWW-085

THE LA SCALA ENCYCLOPEDIA OF THE OPERA

GIORGIO BAGNOLI

THE LA SCALA ENCYCLOPEDIA OF THE OPERA

Translated by Graham Fawcett

SIMON & SCHUSTER
NEW YORK LONDON TORONTO SYDNEY TOKYO SINGAPORE

SIMON & SCHUSTER

Rockefeller Center
1230 Avenue of the Americas
New York, New York 10020

Translated by Graham Fawcett

Typeset by Tradespools Ltd, Frome,
Somerset, England

Printed and bound in Spain by Artes
Graficas Toledo.

10 9 8 7 6 5 4 3 2 1

Library of Congress Cataloging-in-Publication Data

The La Scala encyclopedia of the opera.
p. cm.
Includes bibliographical references and index.
ISBN 0-671-87042-4
1. Opera–Dictionaries. I. Teatro alla Scala.
ML 102.08L14 1993
782.1'03–dc20 93-10024
CIP

FOREWORD

Opera means passion, excitement and love, but like all great emotional experiences, it calls for a deeper understanding and needs to be constantly cultivated and nurtured. This is why for some years now I have not concentrated exclusively on performing opera but also on making it more widely known as well as strengthening its roots by searching out new singing talent, setting up new music institutions and becoming involved in operatic events aimed to have widespread public appeal.

People also get to know about opera and those who take part in it through books. This dictionary, for example, is a useful introduction for all those who want to discover more than the pleasure of listening to a beautiful aria or an orchestral prelude.

In these pages the reader will find not only the operas in my own repertoire, like *L'elisir d'amore, Rigoletto, Un ballo in maschera and Tosca* but innumerable others from every period and from most of the countries in the world. Each opera entry includes the plot, the names of those who have sung in it, and a summary of the work's history. The dictionary also traces the development of the art of opera, to which I have been so happy to devote myself on opera-house stages throughout the world and which thrills audiences from East and West alike, establishing the Italian musical tradition as the creator and leading lady, as it were, of the entire genre.

The dictionary we have before us here, with its high-quality illustrations and magnificent photographs from the archives of the great opera houses of the world, offers not only a well-documented journey through the history of opera but also an invitation to the reader to discover contemporary opera, with all the entries devoted to singers of the twentieth century and especially those who are currently forging their careers.

So, alongside my own name and those of my fellow singers like Domingo and Carreras, there are those of the young performers now in the ascendant in the opera world, whose voices will help to keep the flag of opera flying high. The opera lover will also find profiles of the great composers, including Rossini, Donizetti, Puccini and Massenet, as well as of librettists and conductors.

Here, then, is a book which has been needed for some time on the international market: an up-to-date, terminologically accurate dictionary of opera, full of the latest developments and yet concise, able to satisfy everyone's curiosity and – why not? – to enable readers to acquit themselves creditably in company when they go to the opera.

Luciano Pavarotti

A

ABBADO, CLAUDIO

(Milan 1933)
Italian conductor. He studied at the Conservatorio in Milan, and continued his musical training in Vienna with Hans Swarowsky. After winning the Koussevitzky Competition (1958) and the Mitropoulos Prize (1963), he opened the 1967 season at La Scala, Milan, with Bellini's opera *I Capuleti e i Montecchi*. This marked the start of a lasting partnership with La Scala which led to Abbado being appointed principal conductor, music director and then artistic director (1971–79). The conducting posts he has held with some of the great orchestras have been equally important: with the London Symphony Orchestra (principal conductor and music director from 1979 to 1988); with the Vienna Philharmonic Orchestra (principal conductor from 1986); and with the Chicago Symphony Orchestra (principal guest conductor since 1982). Since 1989, following the death of Herbert von Karajan, Abbado has been music director of the Berlin Philharmonic Orchestra. From 1986 to 1991 he was also music director of the Vienna Staatsoper. Alongside his busy concert schedule, Abbado has always shown a very keen interest in opera, and his opera performances have proved to be landmarks in the history of operatic interpretation: the revival of Rossini (*Il barbiere di Siviglia, La Cenerentola*, and *Il viaggio a Reims*), his accounts of Verdi (*Simon Boccanegra* and *Macbeth*) and his approach to Russian opera (*Boris Godunov, Khovanshchina*) and German opera from Schubert's *Fierrabras* to Wagner (e.g. *Lohengrin*) and Berg's *Wozzeck*. His is a vast and increasingly diversified operatic repertoire.

ABU HASSAN

Singspiel *in one act by Carl Maria von Weber (1786–1826) to a libretto by Franz Karl Heimer based on a story from the* Arabian Nights. *First performance: Munich, Hoftheater, 4 June 1811.*

Abu Hassan (tenor) and his wife Fatima (soprano) are besieged by creditors, notably Omar (bass). Hassan hits upon a scheme by which they each claim that the other is dead in order to claim the funeral money and a silk shroud. The trick succeeds and meanwhile Omar has been persuaded by the promises of Fatima's charms to settle the bills. When the Caliph arrives to discover which spouse has died and is confronted with two apparently lifeless bodies, he offers a large sum of money to any who can say who died first. Hassan immediately jumps up, claims that Fatima died first, and explains the story to the Caliph's amusement. Omar is conveyed to prison for immorality and Hassan is promoted to a higher salary.

This *Singspiel* was a resounding success. Written in collaboration with Abbé Wogler, it is in an Oriental style following in Mozart's footsteps.

Left: Claudio Abbado conducting the orchestra of La Scala, Milan.

ACIS AND GALATEA

A two-part masque by George Frederick Handel (1685–1759), to a libretto by John Gay (1685–1732). First performance: Cannons, home of the Earl of Caernarvon (later first Duke of Chandos), in the summer of 1718. A second version, some of it in Italian, was produced at the King's Theater, London on 10 June 1732.

The story of the opera is taken from Ovid's *Metamorphoses*, and is about a nymph, Galatea (soprano), and her love for Acis, a shepherd (tenor). Much of the opera is made up of airs and choruses celebrating the love between the two. The climax of their idyll is shattered by the arrival of the giant Polyphemus (bass), who wants Galatea for himself. His attempts to seduce her are unsuccessful. Watching Acis and Galatea swear undying love for each other, he goes into a rage and hurls a rock at Acis, fatally wounding him. Galatea, in her despair, has no choice but to use her divine powers, and so she turns her beloved Acis into a spring. The final chorus of shepherds appeals to the poor nymph to cry no more and to listen to the trickling water of the spring "still murmuring your sweet song of love."

After the first version of *Acis and Galatea* (in 1708 he had composed a cantata on the same subject), Handel produced an expanded version in three acts to an Italian text, but with the addition of airs and choruses in English, the whole in the form of a *serenata*. Handel then took the first, wholly English version of 1718 and rewrote it during 1739 and 1740, because he wanted to shorten it and so make room for some new pages of purely instrumental music. Other composers who have produced works on the theme of Acis and Galatea are Marc-Antoine Charpentier (1678), Jean-Baptiste Lully (1686), Thomas Augustine Arne (1732) and Franz Joseph Haydn (1763).

ACKERMANN, OTTO

(Bucharest 1909–Wabern, Berne 1960)
Rumanian conductor, naturalized Swiss. He began his musical studies in his native Bucharest, before moving on to Berlin to study with George Szell. After an early career in the major German theaters, he appeared as conductor and producer in theaters in Berne (from 1936) and Zurich (from 1945). A conductor noted for his firm and scrupulous professionalism, Ackermann had an extensive opera repertoire, with particular emphasis on German opera.

ADAM, THEO

(Dresden 1926)
German bass-baritone. He began singing in the Dresden Kreuzchor at a young age, before taking formal singing lessons. He made his debut in 1949 in Weber's *Der Freischütz*, also in Dresden. Most of Theo Adam's appearances have been in German opera houses. His name was especially linked to the Festival at Bayreuth, where he appeared almost every year from 1952, when he sang the part of Ortel in Wagner's *Die Meistersinger von Nürnberg*, and has sung all the major Wagner roles since that time. Adam's interpretations were outstanding in the way they combined musical intelligence and an impressive talent for acting, shown to best advantage in Wagner.

Above: Bass-baritone Theo Adam in *Die Meistersinger von Nürnberg.*

Top: Vincenzo Bellini, the composer of *Adelson e Salvini.*

ADELAIDE DI BORGOGNA

Opera in two acts by Gioachino Rossini (1792–1868), to a libretto by Giovanni Schmidt. First performance: Rome, Teatro di Torre Argentina, 27 December 1817.

The German King Berengario (bass) has stormed the castle of Canosso and deposed the Princess Adelaide (soprano). Prince Ottone (contralto), who loves Adelaide and wants to restore her to the throne, arrives in Canosso at the head of an army. Berengario sends Ottone his son Adelberto (tenor) with the pretense of making peace overtures. Jubilantly acknowledged by the people, Ottone also receives Adelaide's impassioned appeal that she be given justice. He then lets it be known that he wishes to make her his bride. Just as their wedding ceremony is about to begin, however, Berengario bursts in with a group of armed men: Ottone manages to escape, but Adelaide is arrested. Now Berengario's son Adelberto wants to marry Adelaide and is determined to compel her to accept his proposal by announcing that Ottone has been killed. But not only is Ottone not dead, he has drawn up his army and has defeated and imprisoned Berengario. Eurice (mezzo-soprano), Berengario's wife, releases Adelaide in order to save her husband. But Berengario does not want to surrender and takes his forces into battle against Ottone. He is again defeated and taken prisoner with his son. They are both pardoned and set free by Ottone in an act of clemency before he marries Adelaide.

At its first performance, *Adelaide di Borgogna* was not a success, but performances continued nonetheless until the middle of January 1818. It is not a particularly inspiring opera, composed at the end of an exhausting year's work during which Rossini had composed *La Cenerentola, La gazza ladra* and *Armida.*

ADELSON E SALVINI

(Adelson and Salvini)
An opera semiseria *in three acts by Vincenzo Bellini (1801–1835), to a libretto by Andrea Leone Tottola. First performance: Naples, Teatro del Conservatorio di San Sebastiano, between 11 and 15 February 1825.*

The action takes place in Ireland in the eighteenth century. Lord Adelson (baritone) plays host to his Italian friend Salvini (tenor) at his castle. Salvini, a painter with a strange and passionate nature, has fallen madly in love with Nelly (soprano), an orphan and Lord Adelson's ward. The young woman is not unaffected by Salvini's charm, but she is already engaged to Lord Adelson, who has come home to the castle after a long absence to marry Nelly. In despair, Salvini attempts suicide, but is saved by Adelson, who guesses that his friend has tried to kill himself because he has been disappointed in love. He decides to help him so he shows Salvini that he is ready to work for his greater happiness, not realizing that it is his own fiancée whom Salvini loves. Salvini is happy because he thinks his friend has understood the true nature of his love. The fact that Salvini is under this false impression is now exploited by Struley (bass), Adelson's bitterest enemy. Struley suggests to Salvini that the reason why Adelson is so ready to let Salvini take his place in Nelly's affections is that secretly he is already married. Salvini's long-awaited wedding day arrives. When the bride arrives, however, Salvini sees not his beloved Nelly but Fanny (contralto), a servant of Adelson whom the noble Lord believed to be the object of Salvini's passion. Salvini's astonished reaction creates general embarrassment which is suddenly interrupted by the outbreak of a fire, started deliberately by Struley in order to create a diversion so that he can himself more easily kidnap Nelly.

However, this plan fails owing to the intervention of Salvini: he has now understood how he has been deceived by Struley, and, recovered from his passion for Nelly, he returns her to Adelson, declaring himself willing to marry Fanny.

Adelson e Salvini, Bellini's first opera, was described by the composer at the end of the score as a "*dramma, alias pasticcione*" (a drama, and also a huge muddle) and this phrase underlines the fact that the plot fails to hang together in performance. But there is a single "gem" in the score, Nelly's *romanza* "Dopo l'oscuro nembo," which Bellini later used again in *I Capuleti e i Montecchi*, where it becomes Giulietta's aria "Oh, quante volte." Nevertheless, *Adelson e Salvini* did enjoy a modest success, on the strength of which Bellini was commissioned to write *Bianca e Fernando*.

ADINA, OVVERO IL CALIFFO DI BAGDAD

(Adina, or The Caliph of Baghdad)

Opera in one act by Gioachino Rossini (1792–1868), to a libretto by Gherardo Bevilacqua Aldobrandini. First performance: Lisbon, Teatro de San Carlos, 22 June 1826.

The Caliph of Baghdad (bass) is preparing to marry Adina (soprano), his favourite slave. Another slave, Selimo (tenor), aided by Mustafà (bass), the Court gardener, manages to gain entry to the harem and make contact with Adina, whom he loves. Adina has agreed to marry the Caliph because she is grateful to him, but after hearing Selimo's reproaches, she becomes reunited with him. Adina then asks the Caliph if their wedding can be postponed for one day. The Caliph agrees to this request, but then Alí (tenor), custodian of the harem, informs him that Adina has been seen speaking secretly with a male slave. When night falls, Adina, Selimo and Mustafà are about to make their escape when they are surprised by the guards which the Caliph had posted to keep watch on the harem. The would-be fugitives are condemned to death, but at this point there is a *coup de théâtre*: a locket round Adina's neck is recognized, proving her to be the Caliph's daughter from his relationship with Zora, a young Arab woman he had loved many years before. So the opera can end with the marriage of Adina and Selimo.

Composed in 1818, *Adina* was not seen on the stage until 1826, after which it was immediately forgotten. Although described as a *farsa* (i.e. an opera with a strong element of farce in it), the work is really more of a light-hearted comedy, with some finely executed lyrical and sentimental touches.

Sketch for the costume of Adriana Lecouvreur.

ADLER, KURT HERBERT

(Vienna 1905–San Francisco 1988)

Austrian conductor, naturalized American. After studying music in Vienna, he embarked in 1925 on an intensive career involving the major European opera houses, especially in Germany and Italy. In 1938 he emigrated to the United States and lived in Chicago before moving to San Francisco, where he became music director of the San Francisco Opera (1956–81), making a significant contribution to the development of the musical output of that opera house.

ADRIANA LECOUVREUR

Opera in four acts by Francesco Cilèa (1866–1950), to a libretto by Arturo Colautti from the play Adrienne Lecouvreur *by Eugène Scribe and Ernest Legouvé. First performance: Milan, Teatro Lirico, 6 November 1902.*

The action takes place in Paris in 1730. ACT I. The foyer of the Comédie Française. Adriana Lecouvreur (soprano), a celebrated actress at the Comédie, confesses to her old friend Michonnet (baritone), the theater's stage director, that she is in love with a young officer in the retinue of Maurizio, Count of Saxony (tenor), not knowing that the officer is actually Count Maurizio himself. Enter Maurizio, who has come to see the performance. After an impassioned declaration of love, Adriana gives her beloved a small bunch of violets. But the Princesse de Bouillon, too, has designs on the Count. By means of a letter written by Mademoiselle Duclos, who is also an actress at the Comédie and mistress of the Prince de Bouillon (bass), the Princess invites Maurizio to a villa which the Prince himself has placed at the disposal of Mlle Duclos. The letter is intercepted by the Prince, however, who invites the entire company to dinner at his beloved's villa, so that he can unmask his rival there. ACT II. A drawing-room in Mlle Duclos's villa. During a dramatic encounter between Maurizio and the Princesse de Bouillon, she guesses that he is in love with another woman. To calm the Princess's jealousy, Maurizio offers her the bunch of violets Adriana had given him. At that moment, the Prince de Bouillon and the guests arrive, and Maurizio barely has time to hide the Princess in an adjoining room and assure her that he will help her. Adriana enters, and discovers Maurizio's real identity. Maurizio explains to Adriana why he is there and obtains from her the assistance he needs to save from embarrassment the woman in the adjoining room whose name he does not reveal. Left alone together, the two women realize that they are rivals in love for Maurizio. ACT III. A room in the house of the Prince de Bouillon. The Princess welcomes the guests and hopes she will recognize her rival. Adriana also arrives. The Princess and the actress openly confront one another before the assembled gathering. All the cards are now on the table: the Princess invites Adriana to give a recital; Adriana performs the monologue from Racine's *Phèdre*, addressing the final tirade to the Princess herself. ACT IV. A room in Adriana's house. It is Adriana's birthday, but she is unhappy because she thinks Maurizio has left her. A box is delivered to her, containing the violets she had given to Maurizio. But the flowers have been sprinkled with poison—the Princess's ultimate revenge. Adriana smells the flowers and is taken ill. Michonnet alerts Maurizio who comes to the house. The meeting between the two lovers is short-lived. After a brief moment of rapture, Adriana dies from the effects of the poison in Maurizio's arms.

The leading role is based on a real-life person. Adrienne Lecouvreur was a famous actress who performed in the plays of Corneille and Voltaire and lived from 1692 to 1730. Cilèa became interested in Adriana after reading a play which Eugène Scribe and Ernest Legouvé had staged in Paris in 1849. Cilèa's librettist, Antonio Colautti, cut this play and adapted it for opera. The resulting *Adriana Lecouvreur* had a triumphant premiere at the Teatro Lirico in Milan. The opera has enjoyed a lasting success to this day, principally because of the perfection of its melodic line, which is at its most impassioned and vibrant in the writing for Adriana.

ADRIANO IN SIRIA

(Hadrian in Syria)

Opera in three acts by Giovanni Battista Pergolesi (1710–1736), to a libretto by Pietro Metastasio. First performance: Naples, Teatro San Bartolomeo, 25 October 1734.

The Roman Emperor Adriano (tenor) has conquered the Parthians and is in Antioch. As a guarantee of peace, Osroa (tenor), King of the Parthians, Farnaspe (sopranist), Assyrian prince, and Elmirena (soprano), Osroa's daughter, engaged to Farnaspe, have been brought to Adriano's court. Farnaspe asks Adriano to let him marry Elmirena, but she will not agree to it. The Parthian princess, now the object of Adriano's attentions as well, is used as a pawn by the Roman tribune Aquilio (soprano or tenor); he is actually infatuated with Sabina (soprano), Adriano's wife, and wants to arrange things so that Sabina will discover Adriano's desire for Elmirena and leave him. Aquilio is not the only one conspiring against the Emperor: Osroa starts a fire in an attempt to kill Adriano. The bid is unsuccessful, and Farnaspe is arrested on suspicion of being behind the conspiracy. Osroa, disguised as a Roman, makes another attempt on the life of the Emperor. Adriano orders him to be detained, and asks him for Elmirena's hand in exchange for his life. Osroa consents, but wants his daughter to swear undying hatred for her husband-to-be. Adriano condemns Osroa to death. Farnaspe intervenes, his devotion to his king prompting him to relinquish Elmirena, whose love he has won back, if Osroa is spared. In response to this selfless gesture Adriano, who has by now uncovered Aquilio's schemes, pardons Osroa and agrees to the marriage of Farnaspe and Elmirena.

Adriano in Siria was composed by Pergolesi to mark the birthday of the Queen of Spain. It is an example of *opera seria* at its most typical: 17 arias separated by recitatives, a duet, and an ensemble for the opera's finale. All of the arias are structured ABA (the opening material is taken up again at the end after the second subject) and are designed to display how expressively the performers can sing.

AFRICAINE, L'

(The African Maid)

Opera in five acts by Giacomo Meyerbeer (1791–1864), to a libretto by Eugène Scribe. First performance: Paris, Opéra, 28 April 1865.

ACT I. Vasco da Gama (tenor), officer in the King of Portugal's navy, has just returned after being shipwrecked during a voyage of exploration. With him are two prisoners, who belong to an unknown

Poster by A. Barbizet for *L'Africaine* by Giacomo Meyerbeer.

race: Sélika (soprano, the African maid of the title), who is in love with Vasco, and Nélusko (baritone). Before the King's counsellors, Vasco expounds some bold geographical theories which would enable the Portuguese to return to those fabled shores. The Grand Inquisitor (bass) accuses da Gama of heresy and has him put in prison with the two slaves. ACT II. Now behind bars, Vasco is comforted by Sélika. She shows him on a map the correct route to take in order to sail round the Cape of Storms, beyond which, she says, there is a large island where she used to live before a storm washed her ashore on the coast of Africa. Happy now, Vasco embraces Sélika at the very moment when Inès (soprano) is about to enter. Inès was once engaged to Vasco and has now agreed to marry Don Pédro (bass) so as to obtain Vasco's release from prison. Don Pédro, taking advantage of Vasco's plight, has taken command of an expedition due to set out in search of undiscovered countries. ACT III. Vasco is back at sea and catches up with Don Pédro's fleet of ships, with which Inès, Sélika and Nélusko are also travelling. Nélusko, whom Don Pédro has taken on as a pilot, is steering the ship northwards to avoid an approaching storm. Vasco alerts Don Pédro to the unseen dangers of pursuing that course. Don Pédro will not believe him and has Vasco locked in the ship's hold. The storm breaks and the ship is attacked by Nélusko's warriors, who take everyone prisoner. ACT IV. With dancing and singing, the natives celebrate the safe return of their queen Sélika. She swears that she will honour the law of her forefathers and allow no one to set foot on their land. All of the prisoners are therefore condemned to death. In order to save Vasco, Sélika introduces him as her husband and Vasco, overwhelmed by this gesture, promises Sélika that he will always be with her. ACT V. Inès and Vasco are found together. After an outburst of rage, Sélika resolves to say nothing about her own love and lets the two prisoners go free, putting them on board the ship which will take them home. Sélika then climbs a hill where there is a tall manchineel tree. She inhales the scent of its poisonous flowers and falls to the ground delirious. Nélusko hurries to the aid of Sélika, whom he has always loved. He tries to drag her clear of the tree, but Sélika does not want him to: there she has found her happiness, and she dies in his arms. Nélusko is in despair and he too inhales the lethal scent.

Meyerbeer died on 2 May 1864 while he was still revising the score. The work was edited by the composer François-Joseph Fétis, who staged the opera in 1865.

Sketch by K.F. Schnkelper for Spontini's *Agnese di Hohenstaufen.*

AGNES VON HOHENSTAUFEN

Opera in three acts by Gaspare Spontini (1774–1851), to a libretto by Ernst Raupach. First performance: Berlin, 28 May 1827 (first act only). First complete performance: Berlin, Königliches Opernhaus (later the Staatsoper), 12 June 1829.

The action takes place in the German city of Mainz in 1194. Agnes (soprano), daughter of the Emperor Henry VI von Hohenstaufen (bass), loves and is loved by Henry of Brunswick (bass), son of the rebel Duke of Saxony, bitter enemy of the Imperial Household. The Countess Ermengard (soprano), mother of Agnes, attempts to intercede to enable her daughter and the young Henry to marry, as this would signal the end of hostilities between the two families. But the Emperor intends to give his daughter in marriage to Philip Augustus, King of France (tenor), and has Henry arrested for having tried to see Agnes. As a result, tension grows between the two households. The Knights of Brunswick succeed in freeing Henry, but he is then challenged to a duel by Philip of France. The Emperor agrees to the duel taking place. In fact, he has resolved to have the Duke of Saxony's son killed in an ambush. Henry manages to wed Agnes in secret before his duel with the King of France. On the field of combat, the duel is fought between Henry and the bogus Duke of Bourgogne (the name under which the King of France has concealed his true identity). The Duke/King is on the point of losing, but is rescued by French knights who reveal him as their king. The Empress then discloses the fact that Henry and Agnes are already married. The Emperor's fury is interrupted by the arrival of the Duke of Saxony with his army. The situation could get out of hand, but the Duke of Saxony, who has already won control of the city of Mainz, submits to the will of the Emperor, who then gives his blessing to the marriage of Agnes and Henry.

Written by Spontini while he was in Berlin, *Agnes von Hohenstaufen* shows how its composer had attained a new objective in opera, one that would be taken up by the Romantic composers and be particularly attractive to Wagner and Berlioz. In this opera Spontini achieves a dramatic compactness and scenic unity which were extraordinarily modern for the age in which he lived. The remarkable modernity of this opera and the consequent unpopularity of the score were foreseen by Spontini when he wrote: "Perhaps they will publish this score after my death, because just now it is possible that this music will not be understood.

AGRIPPINA

Music drama in three acts by George Frederick Handel (1685–1759), to a libretto by Vincenzo Grimani. First performance: Venice, Teatro San Giovanni Grisostomo, 26 December 1709.

The scheming Empress Agrippina (soprano or mezzo-soprano), believing her Emperor husband Claudio (bass) to have been drowned in a shipwreck, commands her son Nerone (mezzo-soprano) to appear before the people as his father's successor, heir to the imperial throne. Agrippina avails herself of the assistance of two of her admirers, the freedmen Pallante (bass) and Narciso (contralto), in securing power for him. She has, however, reckoned without the return of Claudio, alive and well. He has been saved by Ottone (contralto), whom the Emperor has now proclaimed as the man who will succeed him. Ottone is in love with Poppea (soprano), who is also the object of the attentions of Claudio and of the young Nerone. This situation is exploited by Agrippina, who denigrates Ottone to Poppea, telling her he only wants power, and then repeats this to Claudio to further discredit Ottone. Poppea, for her part, has arranged meetings with her three admirers. Having satisfied herself as to Ottone's loyalty, she reveals to the Emperor that his rival in love is not Ottone but Nerone. Claudio then decides to banish the impudent Nerone, but Agrippina triumphs once again. After justifying her conduct to her husband, who has accused her of conspiracy, by insisting her actions are governed only by the good of Rome, Agrippina discloses to the Emperor that Poppea does not love him either. Claudio thus consents to Poppea's marriage with Ottone, who thereby renounces all claims to the throne, leaving Agrippina the chance to secure both throne and Empire for her son Nerone.

Agrippina, with *Rodrigo*, belongs to Handel's Italian period, and is his first great success as a composer of opera. He creatively transforms Vincenzo Grimani's old libretto and skilfully adapts the outmoded style of Venetian opera, moulding it into the new formula of *opera seria*: arias with reprises abound, underpinned by a richer orchestration which obviously owes much to the Rome tradition.

ÄGYPTISCHE HELENA, DIE

(The Egyptian Helena)

Opera in two acts by Richard Strauss (1864–1949), to a libretto by Hugo von Hofmansthal. First performance: Dresden, Staatsoper, 6 June 1928.

A violent storm on their journey homeward from the Trojan War forces Menelaus (tenor) and Helena (soprano) to beach ship on the island of the witch Aithra (soprano). Menelaus nurses a bitter grievance against Helena and contemplates killing her, but Aithra intervenes with her magic powers, causing Menelaus to think that the woman taken away by Paris was only a ghost, whereas the real Helena had been waiting faithfully for her husband for ten years on this very island. But Menelaus has no time for any perfect, faithful, "real Helena": the only Helena he is interested in is the one who has betrayed him and made him suffer. The Egyptian nobleman Altair (baritone) and his son Da-Ud (tenor) now arrive on the island. These two are enchanted by Helena's beauty, thereby provoking the wrath of Menelaus who, in a fit of jealousy, kills Da-Ud during a hunting contest. Helena then reveals Aithra's trick to her husband. Menelaus's instinct is to kill Helena, but Aithra comes between them and pacifies him. The opera ends with a reconciliation between husband and wife.

Die Ägyptische Helena is a dignified treatment of a favourite theme of Richard Strauss, that of faithfulness and the illusions of married life. Strauss also completed a revised version, which received its premiere in Salzburg in 1933.

AHNSJÖ, CLAES

(Stockholm 1942)

Swedish tenor. He studied singing with Erik Saedén and went on to make his debut in Mozart's *Die Zauberflöte* (The Magic Flute) at the Swedish Royal Opera in Stockholm (1969). He became a member of the resident company of the Munich Opera and has sung in a number of operas by Mozart, Rossini and Britten. Alongside his opera and concert career, which has included appearances at the major international music venues, Ahnsjö has made many major recordings, singing leading roles. These have included the first recordings of operas by Haydn—*Orlando Paladino, La vera costanza, Armida, L'incontro improvviso* and *L'infedeltà delusa*. Here he displays his unique gifts: a sensitivity of interpretation, fine phrasing, and expressive singing.

Above: A performance of *Aida* at La Scala, Milan, directed by Franco Zeffirelli.

Silhouette showing Hugo von Hofmannsthal with Richard Strauss at the piano.

AHRONOVICH, YURY

(Leningrad 1932)

Russian conductor. After completing his musical studies, Ahronovich's conducting career was mainly based in what was then the Soviet Union. He emigrated to Israel in 1972, and began an intensely active period internationally in the main opera and concert houses of Europe and America. A prominent personality, Ahronovich combines sureness and simplicity in his gestures as a conductor with a gift for clarity and sensitiveness of interpretation, well illustrated by his ability to bring out contrasts of colour and rhythm in a score. He is one of the most qualified interpreters of the Slav symphonic and operatic repertoire, particularly late Romantic music.

AIDA

Opera in four acts by Giuseppe Verdi (1813–1901), to a libretto by Antonio Ghislanzoni. First performance: Cairo Opera House, 24 December 1871.

The setting is Memphis and Thebes at the time of the Pharaohs. ACT I. Radames (tenor), captain of the guard, is hoping to be chosen to lead the Egyptian army against the Ethiopian forces threatening Egypt's borders. His dreams of glory are linked to his love for the Ethiopian slave Aida (soprano). She returns Radames's love, unaware that she has a rival in Amneris (mezzo-soprano), daughter of the King of Egypt (bass) who is also in love with the young captain. In the temple of Isis, the high priest Ramphis (bass) presents Radames with the consecrated armour which will bring him victory. ACT II. In giving Aida false news of the death of Radames in battle, Amneris discovers Aida's feelings for him. Radames is welcomed home in triumph, leading his army of troops, war-chariots, banners, and Ethiopian prisoners, among them King Amonasro (baritone), Aida's father, who conceals his identity. He is to remain with Aida in Egyptian hands, while the other prisoners, thanks to Radames's intervention, can be freed. The King of Egypt rewards Radames by offering him the hand of Amneris. ACT III. Radames is persuaded by Aida to leave Egypt for ever. He tells her about a path they can take which will enable them to escape without being detected by the guards. Unseen, Amonasro has overheard their conversation. He now emerges from where he has been hiding and declares that he will lead his army by the same route. In horror, Radames realizes he has given away a military secret and so betrayed his country. The three are then surprised by Amneris and Ramphis, and, while Aida and her father flee, Radames gives himself up to Ramphis. ACT IV. Amneris, driven by her love for Radames, makes a last attempt to save her beloved. But all is in vain. Radames is taken before the court of priests, but offers no defense, not even in response to the charges laid against him. Ramphis and the priests sentence Radames to be buried alive. In the tomb, Radames is reunited with his beloved Aida, and while Amneris, in the temple, laments her lost love, the two lovers in the tomb bid farewell to the world, in each other's arms.

Commissioned to Verdi by the viceroy of Egypt to celebrate the opening of the new opera house in Cairo, *Aida* is a milestone in the development of the composer's musical language. Here Verdi demonstrates his skill both in handling scenes of ensemble on a grand scale with dances, marches and choruses to capture the moments of celebration in the opera, and also in juxtaposing these large set-pieces with the personal drama of the individual characters. Another key innovation in *Aida* is Verdi's use of orchestration: before, he had been concerned largely with writing for the voice; now, in *Aida*, greater stress is laid on the role of highly coloured orchestration to underline the progress of the opera in every detail of the unfolding drama.

Above: A performance of *Aida* at La Scala, Milan, directed by Franco Zeffirelli.

AJO NELL'IMBARAZZO, L'

(The Tutor Embarrassed)
Opera buffa *in two acts by Gaetano Donizetti (1797–1848), to a libretto by Jacopo Ferretti, taken from a play by Giovanni Giraud. First performance: Rome, Teatro Valle, 4 February 1824.*

The Marquis Don Giulio Antiquati (bass) is insistent that his sons Enrico (tenor) and Pipetto (tenor), whose education has been entrusted to the care of a tutor, Don Gregorio (bass), be brought up in a strict, traditional way. While the younger of the brothers, Pipetto, shamelessly pays court to the old maidservant Leonarda (mezzo-soprano), the other brother, Enrico, has actually become secretly married to Gilda (soprano), by whom he has also had a child. Enrico, who is in love with his wife but compelled to be a prisoner in his father's house, asks Don Gregorio to help him by persuading his father to relax his rigid attitude. Gilda, who has in the meantime been smuggled into the Marquis's house, is in hiding in the tutor's bedroom. She is discovered there, however, and the Marquis Don Giulio, scandalized, assumes that she and the tutor are lovers. In the end the truth comes out. The Marquis recognizes the error of his ways, gives his blessing to the marriage of Enrico and Gilda, and entrusts Pipetto to the care of his brother, to help him learn more about the world.

The opera, which has also been produced with the title *Don Gregorio*, is Donizetti's first significant attempt at *opera buffa*. The theme of the comedy, a biting satire on the strict, chaste upbringing of children in very hidebound families, is highlighted by Donizetti's imaginative and dazzling orchestration. The style becomes more personal in the opera's sentimental moments, and Gilda can be seen as the forerunner of the role of Norina in Donizetti's *Don Pasquale*. The *buffo* roles, with syllabic singing taken at great speed, still clearly echo Rossini's style. Donizetti presented a new version of *L'Ajo* at the Teatro Nuovo in Naples on 11 June 1826.

AKHNATEN

Opera in three acts by Philip Glass (b. 1937), to a libretto by the composer and Shalom Goldman, Robert Israel and Richard Riddell. First performance: Stuttgart Opera House, 24 March 1984.

The death of Pharaoh Amenhotep III prepares the way for Amenhotep IV to ascend the throne of Egypt, but when the new Pharaoh appears before his people, he announces that he has taken the name Akhnaten (Spirit of Aten). The new ruler wants to put an end to the influence of the god Amon and Egyptian pantheism and replace them with Aten as the only god. Having repressed and banished the former followers of Amon, Akhnaten (countertenor) proclaims the founding of a new city, Akhetaten (The Horizon of the Aten, or disc of the sun). The Pharaoh is by now living in isolation in his ivory tower, indifferent to the state of chaos into which Egypt has fallen. The priests of Amon incite the people to depose this Pharaoh for turning a blind eye to their sufferings. The enraged crowd bursts into the royal palace, and the Pharaoh and his family are dragged away. The temple of Aten is destroyed, and the old cult of Amon reinstated. With the remains of the city of Akhetaten reduced to a tourist attraction, the shadows of Akhnaten and his family follow the funeral cortège of the old Pharaoh, this being also their own last journey. The era of Aten is over.

Akhnaten is Philip Glass's fifth opera, based on the life of Pharaoh Amenhotep IV. The drama has no plot in the real sense, but is made up of symbolic episodes in the life of this reforming Pharaoh. Central to the opera is the metaphor of the funeral rite, symbolizing the importance of the ancient Egyptians' relationship with the next world. The funeral theme is present throughout, like a continuous thread which links life to death, the moment when human beings come face to face with their divine likeness and remember their mortal existence.

The bass-baritone Simone Alaimo.

ALAIMO, SIMONE

(Villabate (Palermo) 1950)
Italian bass-baritone. His early music studies included singing, piano and organ. Having been paid flattering tributes in numerous singing competitions, he won a lasting reputation as a contestant in the first Maria Callas Competition held by RAI, the Italian radio and television network. He undertook further studies with Gina Cigna and Ettore Camogalliani, before specializing in the *bel canto* repertoire with Rodolfo Celletti. Alaimo has supplemented the work of his early career as a *buffo* bass in Rossini with alternate successes in roles from the baritone repertoire: in Donizetti's *Torquato Tasso* and *L'esule di Roma*, Verdi's *Luisa Miller* and Mascagni's *Cavalleria rusticana*. Alaimo may be counted among the most interesting singers of recent generations, for the delicacy and agility of his singing, and for his considerable acting talent.

ALBANESE, LICIA

(Bari 1913)
Italian soprano who became an American citizen. She made her debut in 1934 at Milan's Teatro Lirico as Cio-Cio-San in Puccini's *Madama Butterfly*. Her triumph in the Italian National Singing Competition in 1933 and her Butterfly at the Teatro Regio in Parma (1935) led to engagements at the major opera houses. Albanese's career from 1940 was mainly based at the Metropolitan in New York, where she sang until 1966. Her expressive gifts, intense, precise phrasing, and fluid singing have made Licia Albanese one of the greatest interpreters of the Puccini repertoire.

ALBERT, EUGENE D'

(Glasgow 1864–Riga 1932)
German composer. He studied at the National Training School in London, where he displayed unusual gifts as a pianist. He was subsequently a pupil of Liszt in Vienna, and became one of the most acclaimed interpreters of Liszt's piano works. His career as a composer began in symphonic and chamber music; it was only from 1893 onwards that Albert devoted himself to writing operas, the most famous example being *Tiefland* (Lowlands, 1903), which has continued to enjoy a degree of popularity in German opera houses. His operas are clearly in the Wagner mould, although they also contain elements of Italian opera.

ALBERT HERRING

Opera in three acts by Benjamin Britten (1913–1976), to a libretto by Eric Crozier taken from Guy de Maupassant's short story

Le rosier de Madame Husson. *Premiered at Glyndebourne, 20 June 1947.*

The action takes place at Loxford in Suffolk, in the spring of 1900. At the house of Lady Billows (soprano), upright, austere, and a self-appointed guardian of public morals, a meeting of prominent members of the community is being held in order to select contestants for the title of "Queen of the May." But none of the young women of Loxford is thought worthy of this honour. So it is decided to make Albert Herring (tenor) a "King of the May" instead. People think of Albert as being retarded, an impression he gives as a result of being brought up in accordance with strict moral principles by Mrs Herring (contralto). Young Albert wants to refuse the honour but his mother forces him to accept. During the coronation ceremony the King of the May, Albert, under the influence of the rum which his friend Sid (tenor) has put in his lemonade, finds the strength to react against the tyranny of his mother, run off with the prize-money he has been given as King of the May, and use it to experience everything which up until then has been denied him. Everyone joins in a desperate search for Albert, who is eventually given up for dead, but then suddenly he reappears, dirty, dishevelled, and drunk. Now, however, he feels really free. While his mother collapses in a fit of hysterics, and the outraged ladies of the May Committee take to their heels, the new Albert is fêted by the young people of the village.

Written by Benjamin Britten for the English Opera Group, a company of artistes which the composer himself had founded, *Albert Herring* was received with great public and critical acclaim at its premiere. As in other works of his, Britten employs a very small orchestra: 12 instruments alone are enough to enable him to achieve a brilliance and theatricality of orchestral colour. The score also reveals the composer's intelligent and subtle characterization.

ALBRECHT, GERD

(Essen 1935)

German conductor. Son of the musicologist Hans Albrecht, he studied in Kiel and Hamburg and began his career as a conductor with the Stuttgart Opera. After conducting for a time in provincial German opera houses, he held the post of musical director at the Deutsche Oper in Berlin from 1972 to 1974. From there he went on to conduct the Tonhalle Orchestra in Zurich (1975–81). Albrecht has been in demand in the major houses and music venues, becoming musical director of the Hamburg Opera in 1988.

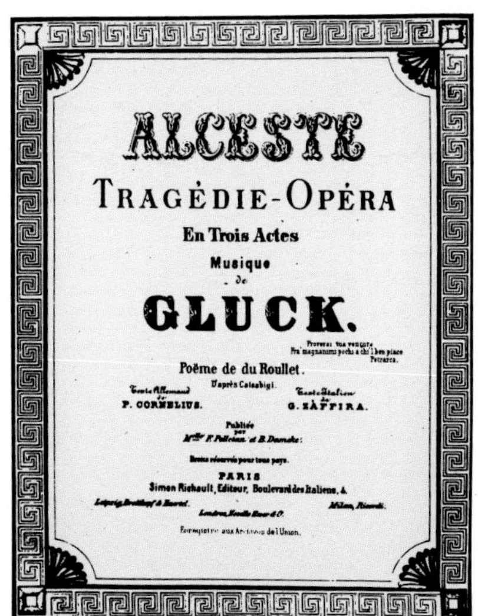

ALCESTE

TRAGÉDIE-OPÉRA

En Trois Actes

Musique de

GLUCK.

Poëme de du Roullet.

D'après Calzabigi.

P. CORNELIUS.

G. ZAFFIRA.

Publiée par

Droits réservés pour tous pays.

PARIS

Simon Richault, Editeur, Boulevard des Italiens, 4.

ALCESTE

Opera in three acts by Christoph Willibald Gluck (1714–1787), to a libretto by Ranieri de' Calzabigi, based on Alcestis, *the tragedy by Euripides. First performance in Italian: Vienna, Burgtheater, 26 December 1767. The French version (text translated and adapted by F. Lebland du Roullet), was performed in Paris at the Académie Royale de Musique (Opéra), 23 April 1776.*

ACT I. Scene 1. In the square before the royal palace in Pherae, Thessaly, the people call on the gods to restore the health of their king Admetus (tenor), now close to death. Queen Alcestis (soprano), accompanied by her children, comes down into the crowd. Moved by the people's demonstration of concern, she begs the gods to show mercy and performs a rite of burnt offerings to Apollo. Scene 2. Inside the temple of Apollo, the High Priest (bass), invokes the god. Suddenly, those present are terrified to hear the voice of the oracle (bass) announcing that the King will have to die unless someone else is sacrificed in his place. Left alone, Alcestis, in despair, decides to offer her life to save her husband. ACT II. In a room in the palace, there is general rejoicing that Admetus has recovered. But the King is sad, because he has learned that he owes his cure to the sacrifice of an unknown well-wisher. Coming face to face with Alcestis, the King discerns an air of deep disquiet in her expression, questions her, and in the end the Queen tells him the truth. Admetus is desperate, and wants to share his wife's fate. ACT III. Scene 1. In the square before the royal palace, Hercules (bass) learns from the crowd of Alcestis's fate and promises to rescue her

K. Macdonald as Albert Herring in the comic opera of the same name.

Left: Title page of the score of the French edition of *Alceste*.

from the Underworld. Scene 2. Alcestis waits for nightfall before entering the Kingdom of Avernus. Admetus wants to follow her, but the infernal spirits require one victim only. While Alcestis and Admetus contend selflessly for the right to be that victim, Hercules arrives, ready to confront the forces of Hell. But, son of Jupiter though he is, he cannot challenge the destiny called for by the gods. Apollo intervenes and, by citing the example of the royal couple's perfect marriage, rules that they should both live and invites the people of Pherae to join in solemn celebration of this felicitous outcome.

Alceste is the second opera on which Gluck and Ranieri de' Calzabigi worked together. After *Orfeo ed Euridice*, *Alceste* is another milestone in the revival of opera. In the preface that he wrote for the first version of this opera, Gluck insisted on the importance of dramatic cohesion between musical expression and literary text which, in a sense, put the music "at the service of the words"–a claim in sharp contrast with the way in which Italian opera traditionally devoted itself to exalting the beauty of the musical form, without reference to the text. Gluck's view meant the abolition of much of the vocal and structural conventions brought in by Italian *opera seria*, placing the emphasis instead on expressive recitative with orchestral accompaniment. Gluck made some major revisions to the score for the Paris version of *Alceste*, but these failed to satisfy the audience. So Gluck, collaborating with the composer François-Joseph Gossec, enlarged the choreographic element in the opera's finale and developed the character of Hercules, which had not appeared in the first French version. This last edition of the opera is the one most often performed.

Sketch for the scenery of *Alceste* by Gluck.

ALCYONE

Tragic opera in five acts and a prologue by Marin Marais (1656–1728), to a libretto by Antoine Houdard de La Motte. First performance: Paris, Académie Royale de Musique (Opéra), 18 February 1706.

In the palace of Ceix, King of Thrace, preparations are underway for the wedding of the monarch to Alcyone, daughter of Aeolus. Pelée, a friend of Ceix, is also in love with Alcyone and only manages with difficulty to hide his feelings for her. The magician Phorbas, a pretender to the Thracian throne and therefore an arch-enemy of Ceix, uses his magic to hold up the wedding ceremony. Ceix, needing to find out what obstacles stand in the way of his marriage to Alcyone, consults Phorbas, not knowing that the magician is his enemy. Phorbas's verdict is that Ceix will lose his beloved Alcyone unless he sets sail at once for Claros to appeal to the god Apollo. When Ceix has departed, Phorbas induces Pelée to tell Alcyone of his love for her, but the young man does not want to betray his friend Ceix. Alcyone is having unhappy premonitions as she awaits the return of her beloved. Phosphore, Ceix's father, also comes to her to announce Ceix's imminent return. A new day dawns. Alcyone catches sight of a body lying lifeless on the seashore. It is Ceix. Overcome with grief, the young woman stabs herself with his still-wet sword. The god Neptune rises from the sea, and transforms the two young people into calm winds who will placate the wrath of the sea-god in time to come.

Alcyone is the last, and musically the most important, of four operas by Marais. Although it contains echoes of Lully's *tragédie-lyrique* style, the refinement and richness of timbre illustrate how Marais has successfully developed the idea of *tragédie en musique*, which he handles differently, by pacing the action more smoothly (using fewer recitatives than Lully) and introducing a boldness of harmony which anticipate Rameau's opera *Hippolyte et Aricie*.

ALER, JOHN

(Baltimore 1949)

American tenor. He studied at Catholic University in Washington, and in 1977 his opera and concert career was launched after he won the Concours Internationale de Chant de Paris. In 1981 he made his debut with the New York City Opera in Mozart's *Don Giovanni* and, the following year, with the Hamburg Opera, he sang the role of Tamino in Mozart's *Die Zauberflöte* (The Magic Flute). He has subsequently made appearances at the principal music venues in Europe and America. Aler has a pleasing voice, with good phrasing and expressiveness. He has proved himself to be particularly suited to the performance of eighteenth-century opera, especially French opera by Gluck and Rameau.

ALESSANDRO STRADELLA

Opera in three acts by Friedrich von Flotow (1812–1883), to a libretto by F. W. Reise. First performance: Hamburg, Stadttheater, 30 December 1844.

The singer and composer Alessandro Stradella (tenor) loves and is loved by Leonora (soprano), a pupil of the rich Venetian Bassi (bass), who will not let the two lovers be together because he has plans for Leonora to marry into wealth. So Stradella persuades Leonora to elope with him. On arrival in a village near

Rome, they decide to marry. Preparations for the wedding are underway. Among the guests are two hired assassins, Barbarino (bass) and Malvolio (tenor), sent by Bassi to kill Stradella and bring Leonora back to Venice. But the assassins play for time: they have been touched by Stradella both as a person and as a composer. Bassi arrives on the scene, and doubles the blood money, inducing Barbarino and Malvolio to accept it, but when they hear Stradella singing a song about the conversion of a man found guilty of a crime, the two bandits are moved once again, so much so that they fall to their knees and ask to be forgiven.

Alessandro Stradella exists in a previous version (1837) by Flotow which he called a *comédie mêlée de chant* (a comedy mingled with song). The work was then revised and this version was completed by Flotow in 1844. These events in the life of the famous seventeenth-century Venetian composer provide Flotow with the starting-point for an opera which is a kind of tribute to Italian *bel canto*.

ALEXANDER, JOHN

(Meridian, Mississippi 1923–1990)

American tenor. He began his career in 1952 singing the title-role in Gounod's *Faust* in Cincinnati. In 1961 he appeared for the first time at the Metropolitan in New York as Ferrando in Mozart's *Così fan tutte*. This performance marked the start of Alexander's 25-year relationship with the Metropolitan (including his Arbace alongside Luciano Pavarotti in Mozart's *Idomeneo*) during which he built up a repertoire in Verdi, Puccini, Wagner, Strauss and others. Alexander is especially remembered as a striking interpreter of Pollione in the first complete recording of *Norma* (1964) with Joan Sutherland. As late as 1983 he was able to create a very intense role of Arindal with June Anderson in a recording of Wagner's *Die Feen*.

ALEXANDER, ROBERTA

(Lynchburg, Virginia 1949)

American soprano. Born into a musical family (her father was a chorus-master and her mother a singer), Alexander made her first stage appearance at the age of eight in the musical *Lost in the Stars* (Weill). After completing her music studies in the United States, Alexander moved in 1978 to Europe, where she began her singing career, making her mark in Amsterdam in 1981 as Pamina in Mozart's *Die Zauberflöte* (The Magic Flute). Since 1984 she has been invited to take part in the Aix-en-Provence festivals, performing more Mozart roles (in *La finta giardiniera* and *Don Giovanni*). In Italy, at La Fenice in Venice, she has sung Vitellia in *La clemenza di Tito* (1986). With engagements in many other opera houses in Europe and America, Alexander devotes part of her time to recital and concert appearances.

ALFANO, FRANCO

(Naples 1875–San Remo 1954)

Italian composer. He studied at the Conservatorio in Naples and in Leipzig with Jadassohn. Admired as a pianist, in 1896 Alfano began to devote himself to the composition of opera. It was not until 1904 that he established himself with his opera *Risurrezione* (Resurrection). Later operas, *L'ombra di Don Giovanni* (1914), *La leggenda di Sakuntala* (1921) and *Cyrano de Bergerac* (1936), illustrate how Alfano distanced himself from the prevailing fashion of realism in opera, and concentrated instead on creating a melody and an expressive atmosphere which were essentially intimate, something he achieved especially in his last work, *Cyrano*, an opera offering a wealth of impressive music. Alfano is best known for having completed Puccini's *Turandot* after the composer's death in 1924.

ALFONSO UND ESTRELLA

Opera in three acts by Franz Schubert (1797–1828), composed between September 1821 and February 1822 to a libretto by Franz von Schober. First performance: Weimar, 24 June 1854.

Mauregato (baritone), after usurping the throne of Troila (baritone), is tormented by the memory of his misdeeds, and his daughter Estrella (soprano) is his only joy. Meanwhile Troila has taken refuge in the mountains in the company of a handful of loyal supporters and his son Alfonso (tenor). Then, by chance, Alfonso meets Estrella, who has lost her way during a hunting expedition, and love grows between them. But Estrella is also the object of the attentions of Adolfo (bass), general to Mauregato. When the King refuses Adolfo's request to marry Estrella, Adolfo, for revenge, conspires against the throne. Mauregato is on the point of yielding, when Alfonso, playing the role of liberator, defeats Adolfo. The throne is restored to Troila, who pardons the wrongs done to him, and Alfonso amid general rejoicing can now marry his beloved Estrella.

Despite the incongruities and negligible literary value in the libretto, Schubert was able to draw enough inspiration from it to compose some wonderful melodies which anticipated German Romanticism at its purest, and to show his great skill in the creation of the opera's most dramatic moments, like the finale of Act 1. *Alfonso und Estrella* was composed between 1821 and 1822, but Schubert never saw it performed, because the score was turned down by every opera house. It was only in 1854, thanks to Franz Liszt who conducted the premiere, that the opera was finally staged.

Above left: The German composer Friedrich von Flotow, composer of *Alessandro Stradella*.

Above: Franz Schubert.

AL GRAN SOLE CARICO D'MORE

See Au grand soleil chargé d'amour

ALÌ BABÀ

Opera in four acts by Luigi Cherubini (1760–1842), to a libretto by Eugène Scribe and Mélesville. First performance: Paris, Opéra, 22 July 1833.

At the foot of a mountain, Nadir (tenor) is suffering because of his love for Delia (soprano), daughter of the avaricious Alì Babà (baritone), who has ordered her to marry the wealthy merchant Aboul Hassan (bass). While Nadir is immersed in his sad thoughts, he notices three men approach the mountain, say a magic word and disappear inside it. When the men have gone, Nadir repeats the formula and finds himself in a large cavern where he discovers vast treasures. In delight, the young man gathers up as much gold as he can and then goes to Alì Babà's house, where the wedding of Delia and Aboul Hassan is about to be held. The ceremony is interrupted, but Alì Babà is suspicious of Nadir's sudden wealth. Having drawn the secret out of him, he has Delia sent away and makes straight for the mountain, only to be captured there by brigands. In the cave Alì Babà finds Delia, who has also fallen into the brigands' clutches: father and daughter are then escorted to the palace to pay a ransom in exchange for their freedom. The three brigands, Alì Babà and Delia, disguised as coffee merchants, arrive at Alì Babà's palace, bearing with them more brigands hidden in the sacks which are supposed to be filled with coffee. At this moment Aboul Hassan providentially and unexpectedly intervenes, avenging himself of the wrongs he has suffered by having the sacks burnt, thus roasting the thieves alive and saving Alì Babà and Delia, who is now free to marry Nadir.

Alì Babà is the last of Cherubini's operas, and is regarded by many as a kind of *Falstaff*, an old man's final flight into the world of fable and whimsicality. It received a lukewarm response at its premiere in Paris.

ALIBERTI, LUCIA

(Catania 1953)

Italian soprano. After receiving her diploma in singing, Aliberti won first prize in the Spoleto Opera Competition and attracted international critical attention for her performance as Amina in Bellini's *La sonnambula* at the opening of the Festival dei Due Mondi in Spoleto in 1979. Her gifts as a singer were immediately in evidence: a good vocal range, agility in the singing of quick passages, and elegant and expressive phrasing.

ALINA, REGINA DI GOLCONDA

(Alina, Queen of Golconda)

Opera semiseria *in two acts by Gaetano Donizetti (1797–1848), to a libretto by Felice Romani. First performance: Genoa, Teatro Carlo Felice, 12 May 1828.*

Alina (soprano), a young peasant woman of Provence who was kidnapped by pirates and brought to the kingdom of Golconda, has married the old King and, on his death, has become Queen of Golconda. Alina now has an admirer in Seide (tenor), who covets the throne. A French ship arrives, bearing Ernesto Volmar (baritone), a young ambassador, and superintendent Belfiore (*buffo* baritone). Alina and her friend Fiorina (soprano), who had also at one time been kidnapped by pirates, discover that Volmar and Belfiore are none other than their long-lost fiancés from France. Seide discovers Alina's love for the Frenchman and incites his followers to revolt. The Queen and her confidante, after a series of tricks, reveal their true identities to the two Frenchmen. Volmar, who has now found his beloved Alina again, saves her from Seide (who had in the meantime thrown her into prison) and gives her back her throne. Alina returns to ruling Golconda, supported by Volmar's love and the affection of her people.

Written by Donizetti for the opening of the 1828 season of opera at the Teatro Carlo Felice in Genoa, *Alina* is one of the most inspired operas in the vast operatic output achieved by this composer. Drawing on the strength of Felice Romani's delightful libretto, Donizetti succeeds brilliantly in combining the genres of *opera seria* and comic opera. His elegant and lively instrumental writing ensures that the music of *Alina* is a perfect accompaniment to the unfolding of events, from the sparkling overture to Alina's arias, not to mention the magnificent Act I quartet between Alina, Fiorina, Volmar and Belfiore. *Alina* is an opera of great theatrical vitality which to this day makes an impact on stage, as was demonstrated at its first twentieth-century revival at the Ravenna Festival in 1987.

ALLEGRA BRIGATA, L

(The Joyful Company)

Six tales in a three-act opera by Gian Francesco Malipiero (1882–1973), to the composer's own libretto. First performance: Milan, La Scala, 4 May 1950.

In a small theater in a park a carefree group of young people with time on their hands are telling each other stories. The first narrator is Violante (soprano): she tells the sad story of the love between a young knight (tenor) and Panfilia (soprano), who is dying of heartbreak.

Top: The Italian sporano Lucia Alberti.

Right: a scene from *Alina, regina di Golconda* by Donizetti.

This is followed by the tale told by Oretta (mezzo-soprano): a painter (tenor), working in a convent, secretly entertains a woman one night in his room. Left alone for a moment, she accidently knocks against a shelf, spilling all her lover's paint-pots over herself, so that when he comes back, he is unable to recognize her, thinks she must be a fiendish apparition, and in terror runs for his life. The monks are soon on the scene and the woman is compelled to escape out of the window. The third story is narrated by Dioneo (tenor): Alfonso di Toledo (tenor) wants to arrange a rendezvous with a woman and offers her all the money he has on him in order to persuade her to meet him. A knight (baritone), while talking with Alfonso, discovers that the woman Alfonso so desires is his own wife. He compels her to return to Alfonso everything he had given her and then kills her. Then Semplicio tells the tale of how Ferrantino degli Argenti (baritone) is infatuated with Caterina (mezzo-soprano), the wife of Francesco da Todi (baritone). Managing to gain entry to her house, he locks the door against her husband after he goes out to report the intruder, and leaves him banging on his own front door in vain. After Semplicio's story, it is the turn of Lauretta (soprano). Her tale is of a woman with a very peculiar brother who fights with his own shadow every night. One night, a lover visiting the woman and dressed in her brother's clothes, bumps into the brother himself, and he, taking the lover for his shadow, kills him with a saber. The final story is told by Beltramo (baritone): Leonora (soprano) is being visited by her lover Pompeo (tenor). When her husband (baritone) appears unexpectedly, Leonora hides her lover under some clothes in a chest. The husband produces a sword he has just bought and, at his wife's suggestion, is on the point of plunging it into the chest to show what a good sword it is, when his wife, at the last moment, stops him. Once out of the chest, Pompeo decides to have his revenge on the woman: he feigns illness and receives a visit from Leonora, accompanied by Barbara (mezzo-soprano), Pompeo's sister. Left alone with Leonora, Pompeo attacks her, tearing her clothes off and leaving her almost naked in his bed. Barbara and a number of knights come to call on Pompeo and find him cured and Leonora naked in his bed, but then Leonora's husband arrives as well and in a fury kills Pompeo. The stage-curtain falls, and the scene shifts to the joyful company: Dioneo, who loves Violante, speaks disapprovingly of the jealous attitude of the husband in the story, provoking a reaction from Beltramo, who is also in love with Violante and now, seized by a fit of jealousy he has kept hidden during the telling of the tale, kills Dioneo. The play within a play finishes with everyone in dismay.

L'allegra brigata was composed in 1943. Free from the stylistic obligations of nineteenth-century opera, it centers on the contrast between the nonchalant approach of the tales the characters narrate, and the heightened real-life drama of the play within a play.

ALLEN, THOMAS

(Seaham Harbour, Durham 1944)

British baritone. He studied at the Royal College of Music in London, and made his debut in 1969 as Figaro in Rossini's *Il barbiere di Siviglia* with the Welsh National Opera. In 1971 he sang the role of Donald in Britten's opera *Billy Budd* at Covent Garden. After many appearances in opera houses across Europe, Allen made his name from 1980 in the major opera venues of America. Allen's is an attractive baritone, soft, supple and varied, with a remarkable zest in phrasing. Coupled with his gifts as an actor, this has made him one of the most sensitive performers in opera today.

ALMEIDA, ANTONIO DE

(Neuilly-sur-Seine 1928)

French conductor, originally from Argentina. After his early music studies in Argentina, he moved to the United States to study in Washington and at Yale. His career as a conductor began in Tanglewood and continued in Boston (1945), New Haven (1947) and Los Angeles (1953). He has held conducting posts in Lisbon (1957–60), Stuttgart (1963–64) and in France, where he was conductor of the Opéra in Paris (1965–67) and *directeur-général* in Nice (1976–78). It is with French opera that Almeida's name is particularly associated: he has to his credit some important interpretations of Bizet's *Le Docteur Miracle*, Halévy's *La Juive*, Ambroise Thomas's *Mignon* and Offenbach's *Les contes d'Hoffmann*.

ALTMEYER, JEANNINE

(La Habra 1948)

American soprano. She studied singing with Martial Singher before completing her studies with Lotte Lehmann. In 1971 she made her debut at the Metropolitan Opera in New York in Bizet's *Carmen* and, a year later, sang the role of Freia in Wagner's *Das Rheingold* in Chicago, a performance which launched her career as an interpreter of Wagner. She appeared in the leading European opera houses, especially in Germany (Munich, Bayreuth from 1979). Although not particularly gifted vocally (her delivery can sometimes be hard in the upper register and rather dull in the lower), Altmeyer is a singer of great personality and musicality, and a sensitive performer.

ALVA, LUIGI

(Lima 1927)

Peruvian tenor. He studied first in Lima and then at the Scuola di Canto at La Scala in Milan (1953), making his debut the following year at Milan's Teatro Nuovo in Verdi's *La traviata.* In 1955 he began his involvement with eighteenth-century opera, when he sang the role of Paolino in Cimarosa's *Il matrimonio segreto* at the Piccola Scala, Milan. From 1960 Alva made many appearances across Europe and the United States. His graceful tenor voice, combined with sensitive musicality and elegant phrasing, helped him become one of the most exquisite performers of Mozart and also of Paisiello, Cimarosa, Piccinni and Fioravanti.

Above: The British baritone Thomas Allen.

ALZIRA

Tragic opera in two acts by Giuseppe Verdi (1813–1901), to a libretto by Salvatore Cammarano based on Voltaire's Alzire ou les Américains. *First performance: Naples, Teatro San Carlo, 12 August 1845.*

Zamoro (tenor), commander of a group of Peruvian guerrillas who are fighting against Spanish oppression, saves the life of the governor, Alvaro (bass), whom his men were on the point of killing. Zamoro's fiancée, Alzira (soprano), believing her beloved to be dead, becomes a Christian in order to be able to marry Gusmano (baritone), Alvaro's son, who has meanwhile taken over the post of governor in his father's place. But Zamoro prevents the wedding from taking place and fatally wounds Gusmano. On the point of death, Gusmano pardons his murderer and gives his consent to the realization of the dream shared by the lovers Alzira and Zamoro.

Alzira is considered the only real failure in Verdi's career, and it was subsequently described by him as a "dreadful piece." He had written it against his own better judgement: the music was due to be completed by the winter of 1844–45, but he was late in finishing it, complaining of illness. Some of the delay was also due to the singer Tadolini, who was about to give birth and, since she was no longer young, there were fears that she might lose her voice. In fact, everything went well for her, but not for *Alzira*.

Alzira, in a performance at the Teatro Regio, Parma.

AMAHL AND THE NIGHT VISITORS

Religious opera-fable in one act by Giancarlo Menotti (b. 1911) to the composer's own libretto, inspired by the famous painting by Hieronymus Bosch, The Adoration of the Magi. *Written to a commission from the National Broadcasting Company of New York, it was televised on 24 December 1951. First stage performance: Bloomington, University of Indiana, 21 February 1952.*

Amahl (speaking role) tells his mother (soprano) that he has seen a fiery comet in the sky. Not believing her son's flights of fancy, the woman makes him get into bed and go to sleep. There is a knock at the door. Amahl and his mother open it to find the three Magi dressed in wonderful clothes. Guided by the comet, Gasper, Melchior and Baldassar are searching for a Baby who is about to be born. During the night, Amahl's mother succeeds in stealing a little of the Magi's gold. But her theft is discovered and the poor woman laments the state of abject poverty in which she lives, adding that her son Amahl cannot walk without crutches. The Magi are understanding and leave the gold with her, while Amahl, who wants to offer the Baby his crutches as a gift, suddenly finds that he is able to walk without them. Everyone is overjoyed and Amahl accompanies the Magi because he wants to meet the Child Jesus.

Amahl and the Night Visitors, which was a remarkable success at its premiere, was the first opera to be televised by NBC, the television network that had commissioned it from Menotti. It became a regular television event on Christmas Eve from then on.

AMARA, LUCINE

(Hartford, Connecticut 1927)

Stage name of Lucine Armaganian, American soprano of Armenian descent. She studied singing in San Francisco with Eisner-Eyn and began her career as a chorus-singer (1945–46). After taking part in various singing competitions, she made her debut, in 1950, in Verdi's *Don Carlos* at the Metropolitan, New York in the first season of Rudolf Bing's reign there. Amara was then offered a place in the Metropolitan Opera Company, and went on to sing in more than 450 productions covering over 40 roles, ranging from Aida to Antonia in *Les contes d'Hoffmann*. Tatyana in *Eugene Onegin* and Ellen in *Peter Grimes*.

AMELIA AL BALLO

(Amelia Goes to the Ball)

Opera buffa *in one act by Giancarlo Menotti (b. 1911), to the composer's own libretto. Preview: Philadelphia, Curtis Institute, 3 March 1937. First performance: New York, Metropolitan Opera House, 1 April 1937.*

Amelia (soprano), with the help of two maidservants (mezzo-sopranos), is preparing to go to the ball. Enter Amelia's husband (baritone) in a rage: he has just found out that Amelia has a lover. Amelia wants to get the argument over with as quickly as possible so that she can go to the ball, so she admits that she is having a relationship with Bubi (tenor), the tenant living on the third floor. Furious, the husband goes out, and in comes the lover who asks Amelia to come away with him, but she is impatient to get to the ball and refuses. Enter the husband, surprising the couple together. The two men get into a row which gradually turns into an exchange of explanations followed by amicable confidences. By now exasperated, Amelia breaks a vase over her husband's head, causing him to faint. People come running, and so do the police, headed by a commissioner (bass). Amelia solves the situation by calling her lover a thief who had broken into their house and struck her husband on the head. Speechless at this, Bubi is taken away by the guards, the husband ends up in hospital, and Amelia can at last go to the ball accompanied by the commissioner.

Amelia al ballo is Menotti's first opera, and yet already the key features of the composer's musical style are visible: his obvious operatic talent within a perfect musical construction brings together the modern experience of American music and the traditional forms of eighteenth- and nineteenth-century opera. Menotti's own libretto displays a firm grasp of theater. These are the strengths that have contributed to the success of *Amelia al ballo.*

AMELING, ELLY

(Rotterdam 1934)

Dutch soprano. She first studied singing in Rotterdam, before going on to complete her training in Paris with Pierre Bernac, one of the most celebrated interpreters of French chamber music. Her encounter with Bernac influenced and shaped Ameling's artistic development. She made her mark immediately – with the sensitivity of her interpretation and great elegance of phrasing – as one of the leading exponents of a very wide repertoire of *Lieder*, chamber music and oratorio from Bach to Britten, and of Mozart, Ravel, Satie and Schubert.

AMICO FRITZ, L'

(Friend Fritz)

Operatic comedy in three acts by Pietro Mascagni (1863–1945), to a libretto by P. Suardon (pseudonym of Nicola Daspuro), based on L'Ami Fritz *by Emile Erckmann and Alexandre Chatrian. First performance: Rome, Teatro Costanzi, 31 October 1891.*

Fritz Kobus (tenor), a young and wealthy land-owner, makes a wager with Rabbi David (baritone): if he succeeds in converting Fritz to the idea of marriage, the Rabbi will receive a vineyard as his reward. In fact, Fritz already has tender feelings for Suzel (soprano), the daughter of his farmer, and the young woman loves her landlord in return, but her caution and the difference in their social background prevent her from telling him so. By means of a trick, David discovers Suzel's secret, and then reveals to Fritz that Suzel is about to marry a young man living locally. Fritz is openly troubled and jealous, and tells Suzel of his own love for her. David has won the bet, but makes a gift of the vineyard to Suzel.

L'amico Fritz is Mascagni's second opera following the triumph of *Cavalleria rusticana*, after which it is his best-known. While reaffirming Mascagni's refined gift for writing melodies, this opera has its limitations, partly due to the composer's attempts at bringing together elements of Italian, French and German music.

AMORE DEI TRE RE, L'

(The Love of the Three Kings)

Poetic/tragic opera in three acts by Italo Montemezzi (1875–1952), to a libretto by Sem Benelli. First performance: Milan, La Scala, 10 April 1913.

The action takes place in a castle in Italy in the tenth century. Fiora (soprano), already engaged to Avito (tenor), has, for political reasons, been compelled to marry Manfredo (baritone), son of Baron Archibaldo (bass), a foreign invader who has taken over the castle and the country round about. Old Archibaldo, who is blind, wanders through the manor-house intent on surprising his daughter-in-law, whom he suspects of being unfaithful. Manfredo, who is deeply in love with his wife, returns to the castle for a short time, and, before leaving again, asks Fiora to wave to him from the battlements until he has disappeared over the horizon. Fiora is moved by this and agrees. Once Manfredo has gone, enter Avito, whom Fiora has continued to meet in secret. Their passion overwhelms the two lovers. Archibaldo, who has overheard their voices, intervenes: Avito manages to escape, but Fiora is strangled by Archibaldo in his fury. In the crypt of the castle, where the body of Fiora is lying, Avito returns to kiss his beloved for the last time, but the chill of death enters his body: Archibaldo has dabbed Fiora's lips with poison so as to discover who her lover is. Manfredo, who has come back because he could no longer make out the figure of his wife on the battlements, kisses her in despair and dies.

Constructed in the manner of the traditional Italian opera, which Montemezzi animated with rich and elaborate orchestral writing very much after the style of Wagner, *L'amore dei tre re* has enjoyed great public acclaim. It was produced at the Metropolitan

Left: *L'Amico Fritz*, in a performance at La Scala, Milan.

Top: Poster for *L'amore dei tre re.*

Opera in New York with Toscanini conducting. Rosa Ponselle, Lucrezia Bori, Ezio Pinza and Giovanni Martinelli are only a few of the most distinguished performers of this romantic opera.

ANACRÉON, OU L'AMOUR FUGITIF

(Fleeting Love)

Opera in two acts by Luigi Cherubini (1760–1842) to a libretto by C. R. Mendouze. First performance: Paris, Opéra, 4 October 1803.

The action takes place in Teos, Ionia. A party for the aged poet Anacréon (tenor) has been organized by his friends and supporters. As he watches the preparations, the poet is aware that, despite his age, his desire to love is more alive than ever. Corinna (soprano), a young singer, loves Anacréon and is loved by him in return. Anacréon recovers his serenity and sings praise to Bacchus and Love, accompanying his song on a lyre. A particularly violent storm breaks, and the poet offers shelter to a young boy (soprano), who tells him he has run away from home because of family intrigues. The boy, who is actually Love, spreads strong feelings of ardour among all the guests at the party. Then a message arrives from Venus, asking that her son be brought back home. Nobody in Anacréon's house is willing to take the child and the goddess thus arrives in person to take Love home with her. The boy, in gratitude to Anacréon, promises to look after his interests for the rest of his life.

Anacréon marked Cherubini's return to the theater at a time of great hardship. The opera, however, was not well received and the music was criticized for being too obviously German. After the first performance, *Anacréon* was not performed again, although a number of excerpts were given in a concert version in Vienna in 1805.

ANDERSON, JUNE

(Boston 1952)

American soprano. After winning her first singing competition when she was only 15, Anderson studied at Yale University, and made her debut in 1978 as the Queen of the Night in Mozart's *Die Zauberflöte* (The Magic Flute) with the New York City Opera. From 1982 onwards, after her performance in *Semiramide* with the Rome Opera, she attracted the attention of the public and critics internationally. She has taken part in major productions of Rossini operas: *Otello* (Venice 1986 and Pesaro 1988), *Armida* (Aix-en-Provence, 1988), *Maometto II* (San Francisco, 1988) and *Riccardo e Zoraide* (Pesaro, 1990). Anderson has also performed operas more closely associated with the *coloratura* repertoire, being particularly outstanding in Bellini's *La sonnambula* and *I puritani*, Donizetti's *Lucia di Lammermoor*, as well as Verdi's *Rigoletto*. Her voice has undoubted qualities of timbre, delivery and compass, and she is especially suited to the elegiac vocal line of Bellini and Donizetti at their most lyrical.

ANDREA CHÉNIER

Historical opera in four acts by Umberto Giordano (1867–1948), to a libretto by Luigi Illica. First performance: Milan, La Scala, 28 March 1896.

The action takes place in France, at the de Coigny castle in 1789, and later in Paris in 1794. Among those invited to a ball by the Contessa de Coigny (mezzo-soprano) is the young poet Andrea Chénier (tenor). At the suggestion of the Contessa's daughter Maddalena (soprano), Chénier recites a poem to love and country which also reprimands the clergy and the aristocracy for their selfishness. Chénier then leaves, and the dancing begins, only to be interrupted when Gérard (baritone), the Contessa's manservant, comes rushing into the ball-room with a troop of peasants. The French Revolution has begun. The scene changes to Paris. Chénier, embittered by the fact that the Revolution has now degenerated into the Terror, is advised by his friend Roucher (bass) to leave Paris, because his life is threatened. Nonetheless Chénier hesitates: for some time he has been receiving letters from an unknown woman. That same evening, he will finally be able to meet her and so he is unwilling to miss the rendezvous. There he discovers that the mystery woman is Maddalena, who has lost her mother and now lives in hiding. The two fall in love,

Top: The American soprano June Anderson.

Right: A scene from *Andrea Chénier.*

but Gérard, who has had Chénier watched, surprises them together. Chénier and Gérard fight, and Gérard is wounded but begs Chénier to escape and to look after Maddalena. A crowd gathers, and Gérard tells them that he does not know who his assailant was. Scene: the Revolutionary Court. Andrea Chénier has been captured. Maddalena, in despair, is ready to offer herself to Gérard if only to save Andrea. Gérard is moved by this and decides to help Maddalena and Chénier. But all is in vain: despite proclaiming his innocence, Chénier is sentenced to death. Maddalena's only choice now is to share her beloved's fate, and so she takes the place of a condemned woman, and mounts the guillotine by Andrea's side.

Of all Giordano's operas *Andrea Chénier* is the one which won the greatest acclaim and to this day is often included in the programme of the world's leading opera houses. The work's success is undoubtedly linked to the composer's confident handling of the melodies, which are impassioned and highly charged with drama, as well as having a certain declamatory quality. The role of Chénier has always attracted the greatest singers.

ANFOSSI, PASQUALE

(Taggia Imperia 1727–Rome 1797)
Italian composer. After studying violin at the Conservatorio di Santa Maria di Loreto in Naples and composition with Francesco Durante, from 1763 Anfossi began composing operas and became known throughout Europe on the strength of his *L'incognita perseguitata* (1773). His output numbered 70 or more operas, among them *La finta giardiniera* (1774), which would later be set by Mozart, and *Il curioso indiscreto* (1777), for which again Mozart wrote some additional arias. The operas of Anfossi deserve diligent revival and reassessment, not least in the light of the influence he had on the development of Mozart's opera composition.

ANGELICI, MARTHA

(Cargèse 1907–Ajaccio 1973)
French soprano of Corsican birth. She studied music in Brussels and began her artistic career in 1934. In 1936 she made her stage debut in Marseilles in Puccini's *La bohème*. Angelici formed an important relationship with the Opéra-Comique in Paris where, from 1939, she appeared for more than 14 years in French and Italian operatic and light-operatic repertoire (singing roles such as Mireille, Micaela and Mimi). From 1953 she sang at the Opéra in Paris, where she consolidated her reputation, becoming one of the French opera audience's best-loved performers. She is especially remembered for her interpretations of Micaela in Bizet's *Carmen* and Pamina in Mozart's *Die Zauberflöte* (The Magic Flute).

ANGÉLIQUE

Farce in one act by Jacques Ibert (1890–1962), to a libretto by Nino. First performance: Paris, Théâtre Femina, 28 January 1927.

Boniface (baritone), a dealer in china, tired of the violent and authoritarian behaviour of his wife Angélique (soprano), decides, on the advice of his friend Charlot (baritone), to put her up for sale. Angélique is attractive and there are plenty of customers. The first to arrive are an Italian (tenor), an Englishman (tenor) and a black (bass); but, after meeting Angélique, these three admirers bow out. In despair, Boniface calls upon the devil himself to take her on. Beelzebub (tenor) miraculously appears, grabs hold of Angélique, and carries her off. Boniface celebrates this turn of events with his friends, but then the devil returns: the woman is "absolute hell," he says, and he will have no more to do with her. Out of his mind, Boniface attempts suicide, but is prevented by Angélique herself, now gentle and submissive. Boniface, although he still has his doubts, resolves to take his wife back but, as soon as the curtain falls, announces that she is still "for sale."

Angélique is one of the greatest and undoubtedly longest-lasting successes of French opera of the first half of the twentieth century. The farcical plot is wonderfully translated into music in Ibert's score which contains a wealth of musical ideas from *opera buffa* in the style of Rossini to the French operetta of Offenbach and Lecocq. *Angélique* to this day retains both its extraordinary brilliance and inexhaustible dramatic energy.

ANNA BOLENA

Opera in two acts by Gaetano Donizetti (1797–1848), to a libretto by Felice Romani. First performance: Milan, Teatro Carcano, 26 December 1830.

Enrico VIII (bass), King of England, has fallen in love with Giovanna Seymour (mezzo-soprano), but in order to be able to marry her he has to rid himself of his wife Anna Bolena (soprano). To this end, Enrico calls upon Lord Riccardo Percy (tenor), a long-time admirer of Anna and still in love with her. Summoned back from exile, Percy asks to meet his beloved Anna. She senses that her position as Queen is in the balance and attempts to resist the amorous advances of Percy, who becomes desperate and wants to kill himself. Enrico VIII bursts into his wife's apartments and has Anna arrested together with Percy and the page Smeton (contralto), who had by chance been present for the conversation between the couple. Giovanna, shocked at having been the involuntary cause of the Queen's downfall, begs the King to show clemency and Anna to forgive her. At first Anna wants to dismiss her request but then, moved by it, does forgive her. Anna's fate, however, is now sealed: after a summary trial, she is condemned to death with her brother Lord Rochefort (bass), Percy and Smeton.

The triumph scored by *Anna Bolena* signalled that Donizetti was now acknowledged as one of the most important composers of his day, and the work is clear evidence of his vigorous operatic personality. *Anna Bolena* was also the first Donizetti opera to be performed all over Europe, and it remained a regular feature of opera house programmes from that time until it disappeared from repertoires at the end of the nineteenth century. It was revived at La Scala, Milan in 1957, with Maria Callas in the leading role, and was a resounding success. Since then, *Anna Bolena* has enjoyed renewed fame.

Giulia Grisi in *Anna Bolena*.

ANSERMET, ERNEST

(Vevey 1883–Geneva 1969)

Swiss conductor. He studied in Lausanne and Paris before training in Munich and Berlin as a conductor. He made his debut in 1914 in Montreux, and subsequently conducted for Diaghilev's famous "Ballets Russes" (1915–16), becoming a close friend of Stravinsky. In 1918, he founded the Orchestre de la Suisse Romande, which he directed until 1966. He was one of the most famous and sensitive interpreters of the twentieth-century repertoire, and took part in some major premieres including Britten's *The Rape of Lucretia* at Glyndebourne in 1946.

ANTIGONAE

Opera in five acts by Carl Orff (1895–1982), from the tragedy by Sophocles translated by Friedrich Hölderlin. First performance: Salzburg, Felsenreitschule, 9 August 1949.

Eteocles and Polynices, sons of Oedipus and nephews of Creon (baritone), King of Thebes, have killed one another. Creon has issued an edict, forbidding, on pain of death, the burial of the body of Polynices, branded a traitor for having tried to invade Thebes. Antigone (soprano) and Ismene (mezzo-soprano), sisters of Eteocles and Polynices, are in despair at their uncle's decree. Nonetheless Antigone defies the wrath of Creon and buries Polynices, but she is discovered and dragged before the King. Antigone defends what she has done, but Creon is adamant and condemns her to death. Creon's son Haemon (tenor), who is engaged to Antigone, tries in vain to dissuade the King from his ruthless decision. Only the voice of the soothsayer Tiresias (tenor), prophesying misfortunes for the house of Creon unless he revokes the death sentence, prevails upon the King to relent. But it is too late. A messenger brings tragic news: Antigone has hanged herself, and Haemon, in despair, has also taken his own life. While Creon, carrying the body of his son in his arms, calls on death, the messenger reveals that Creon's wife Eurydice (soprano) has killed herself too.

The orchestral writing in *Antigonae*, being exclusively for percussion instruments (apart from one double-bass), is, like the German text, wholly suited to the somber and haunting atmosphere of the tragedy. The voices are ideally employed in reproducing the meter and rhythm of the verse. The tragedy of Antigone has inspired many composers, among them Tommaso Traetta (1772) and Arthur Honegger (1927).

ANTONACCI, ANNA CATERINA

(Ferrara 1961)

Italian soprano. She graduated in singing from the Conservatorio Martini in Bologna and went on to complete her training with the soprano Elvira Ramella. In 1986 she made her debut as Rosina in *Il barbiere di Siviglia* in Arezzo. She shared first prize in both the Maria Callas International Singing Competition and the Philadelphia Pavarotti Competition in 1988, and appeared the same year as Elisabetta in Donizetti's *Maria Stuarda*. She was subsequently engaged by leading Italian opera houses, principally in rarely-performed operas such as Cimarosa's *Gli Orazi e i Curiazi* (Teatro dell'Opera, Rome, 1989), Paisiello's *Elfrida* and Manfroce's *Ecuba* (Teatro dell' Opera Giocosa, Savona, 1990) and Mayr's *La rosa rossa e la rosa bianca* (Donizetti Festival, Bergamo, 1990). Her repertoire then concentrated on Rossini operas, mainly of the *opera seria* genre (*Ermione, Elisabetta, regina d'Inghilterra, Mosè* and others).

ANTONY AND CLEOPATRA

Opera in three acts by Samuel Barber (1910–1981) to Franco Zeffirelli's adaptation of Shakespeare's play. First performance: New York, Metropolitan Opera House, 16 September 1966.

Antony (bass-baritone), a Roman general in love with Cleopatra (soprano), Queen of Egypt, has given himself over to the pleasures of life at Cleopatra's palace in Alexandria. The Senate in Rome, however, puts pressure on him to return to the capital. Back in Rome, in order to demonstrate his loyalty to the Empire, Antony has to marry Octavia, the sister of Emperor Caesar Octavian (tenor), although he still loves Cleopatra. Meanwhile, in Egypt, Cleopatra hears of Antony's marriage. She appears to him in a dream, and he sets out again for Egypt. The news that Antony has returned to Egypt angers Octavian and he declares war on the country. Antony is defeated and takes refuge in Cleopatra's palace, where the Queen and her lover have a bitter quarrel. She leaves, goes to her tomb, and from there sends a messenger to Antony to tell him that her last thoughts were of him. Believing Cleopatra to be

Britten, Croziet and Ansermet with the members of the Glyndebourne English Opera Company.

Right: Anna Caterina Antonacci in *Elisabetta, regina d'inghilterra.*

dead, Antony turns his sword upon himself. At the point of death, he is carried to Cleopatra's tomb, where he breathes his last in her arms. Octavian arrives, wishing to take Cleopatra back to Rome as spoils of war. But the Queen will not be separated from her lover. She has an asp brought to her, allows herself to be bitten by it, and dies from its poison.

The opera was staged to mark the opening of the new Metropolitan Opera House in New York. Franco Zeffirelli, who adapted the Shakespeare text, was also the producer and designer, and Alvin Ailey the choreographer. An extensively revised version of the score was introduced later in other theaters.

APE MUSICALE, L'

(The Musical Bee)

Play in two acts by Lorenzo da Ponte (1749–1838), with music by Gioachino Rossini, Wolfgang Amadeus Mozart, Antonio Salieri, Domenico Cimarosa and Nicola Zingarelli. First performance of the final version: New York, February 1829.

Outside a coffee shop in the Isole Fortunate (Isles of Good Fortune, probably Long Island, New York), a group of artists, the singer Narciso (tenor), the poet Mongibello (*buffo* baritone) and Don Nibbio the impresario (*buffo* baritone), are discussing the new play which is due to open in a few days' time. They are all waiting to see the prima donna Lucinda (soprano). Rehearsals for the new play begin: it is called *L'ape musicale* (The Musical Bee), because just as a bee goes from flower to flower collecting nectar, so the poet must gather the best of every singer's repertoire. In front of the composer Don Canario (tenor), Lucinda and Narciso sing a duet from Rossini's *Semiramide*. Don Nibbio and Mongibello join the company and they too sing arias from Rossini. Rossini even supplies the music with which Lucinda brings the new work to a close (the *rondò finale* from *La Cenerentola*), after Nibbio has announced that the opera can be staged as soon as the money has been found to finance it.

Lorenzo da Ponte composed as many as three versions of this musical hotch-potch, in 1789, 1791 and 1792, all three more or less linked to the vagaries of the world of opera. The libretto, in its revised version in Italian and English is more streamlined and coherent than the previous versions. The music represents a sort of journey tracing the development of *opera buffa* from Cimarosa to Mozart and on to Rossini, whose music ends the opera.

APOLLO ET HYACINTHUS, OR HYACINTHI METAMORPHOSIS

Comic opera by Wolfgang Amadeus Mozart (1756–1791), to a Latin text by Rufinus Widl. First performance: Salzburg University, 13 May 1767.

The story is taken from Ovid's *Metamorphoses* and tells of Apollo (contralto) and Zephirus (contralto), who are both smitten with the beautiful Hyacinthus (soprano), son of Ebalus (tenor), King of Laconia. While Apollo and Hyacinthus are having a discus-throwing contest, the jealous and vindictive Zeus uses his powers to alter the discus's flight so that it hits Hyacinthus and mortally wounds him. Apollo, in anguish at the death of his beloved Hyacinthus, changes him into a flower (the hyacinth), while Zephirus is transformed into a wind.

Mozart wrote this opera in 1767, at the age of 11, to mark the end of the University of Salzburg's academic year. *Apollo et Hyacinthus* was presented in the form of nine *intermezzi* interposed in the play *Clementia Croesi* by Rufinus Widl. The Latin libretto, though fragmentary because of the need to divide it up into these *intermezzi*, was seen to good advantage in Mozart's music. Despite a simplicity of resources (the players in this first performance were aged between 12 and 23), the music revealed a sensitivity and imaginative flair well ahead of the purely conventional or workmanlike elements usually found in an opera written to commission.

APOTHECARY'S BELL, THE

See *Campanello dello speziale, Il*

ARABELLA

Comic opera in three acts by Richard Strauss (1864–1949), to a libretto by Hugo von Hofmannsthal. First performance: Dresden, Staatsoper, 1 July 1933.

Vienna, during Carnival, 1860. Count Waldner (bass), a retired captain, lives in a fashionable hotel, although he is grossly in debt. Waldner's only hope is to succeed in arranging good marriages for his two daughters, Arabella (soprano) and Zdenka (soprano). To this end he has sent a portrait of Arabella to an old friend of his, Mandryka, a country land-owner. While they wait for Arabella to be married, her sister Zdenka is made to disguise herself as a boy. But she loves Matteo (tenor), and as she is unable to reveal her face, she writes him passionate letters, signing them in her sister's name. As a result, Matteo declares his love to Arabella, but she rejects him, her romantic feelings being completely taken up with waiting for her "true" love, who then presents himself in the person of the nephew of the now dead old land-owner. This young man's name is also Mandryka (baritone), and he is in love with Arabella. When the two meet, they discover that they were made for one another. But Mandryka feels deceived when he learns

Top left: Antonio Diaz in the first performance of *Antonio e Cleopatra.*

Above: Sketch for *Arabella.*

that Arabella has arranged to see Matteo at night. When Matteo arrives for their assignation, the room he actually enters is Zdenka's. While Arabella is trying to calm the furious Mandryka, Zdenka's sudden appearance resolves the issue. Now there will be two marriages, not one.
Although the plot of *Arabella* is clearly convoluted, the beauty of the opera is all to be found in its most purely lyrical passages. In the duets between Arabella and Zdenka, and even more those of Arabella and Mandryka, Strauss's music brings out the voluptuousness, eroticism and decadence of von Hofmannsthal's libretto.

ARAGALL, JAIME

(Barcelona 1939)
Spanish tenor. After studying singing in Spain and Italy, he made his debut at La Scala, Milan in 1963. Since then he has sung in the main European and American opera houses, drawing on a repertoire which has included the major operas of Verdi and Puccini. Aragall's voice has a fine timbre – resonant and ringing in the upper register.

ARAIZA, FRANCISCO

(Mexico City 1950)
Mexican tenor. He studied with Irma Gonzales and in 1970 made his debut in Beethoven's *Fidelio*. After winning the international singing prize administered by the German radio, he joined the Karlsruhe Opera company in 1975, with whom his first role was Ferrando in Mozart's *Così fan tutte*. He has made appearances since then at the major opera houses and festivals in Europe. In 1981 he sang in the United States (Houston and San Francisco) for the first time. In 1983 came his Metropolitan Opera debut in New York as Belmonte in Mozart's *Die Entführung aus dem Serail* (The Seraglio). In vocal range, agility and luster, Araiza is one of the greatest of Mozart performers (especially in the roles of Tamino, Belmonte and Don Ottavio), although he can also acquit himself impressively singing Rossini (*La Cenerentola, Semiramide, Il viaggio a Reims*).

ARCADIA IN BRENTA, L'

Comic opera in three acts by Baldassare Galuppi (1706–1785), to a libretto by Carlo Goldoni. First performance: Venice, Teatro di Sant'Angelo, 14 May 1749.

The lazy and prodigal Fabrizio Fabroni (*buffo* baritone) has invited a group of idle friends to his villa by the Brenta (the river which links Venice and Padua), for the purpose of worldly pleasure and literary amusement. The plot centers on the individual personality of each character: from Fabrizio himself to his steward, the greedy Foresto (baritone), the conceited fop Count Bellezza (tenor), and the amorous and jealous Giacinto (contralto). Each of these male characters has his equivalent female counterpart: Lauretta (soprano), a pragmatic woman in both word and deed; Lindora (soprano), a hypochondriac; and the pensive Rosanna (soprano), who is given to sighing about love. After a series of love skirmishes, intrigues and misunderstandings, couples begin to emerge: Lauretta with Foresto, Lindora with the count and Rosanna with Giacinto, while the poor, ingenuous Fabrizio has to make do with no more than the grateful thanks of the others.

L'Arcadia in Brenta came as a result of the profitable meeting between Baldassare Galuppi and Carlo Goldoni, and was the first in a large and almost always successful series of operas. Goldoni's libretto, which dates from 1749, is a clever and merciless attack on the Venetian society of the time, with all its decadence, frenzy and capriciousness.

Above: The Spanish tenor Jaime Aragall.

Right: Francisco Araiza in *Lohengrin*.

ARENA, MAURIZIO

(Messina 1935)
Italian conductor. He completed his music studies in Palermo and then moved to Perugia, where he was taught by Franco Ferrara. After working as assistant conductor to Tullio Serafin, Antonio Votto and Gianandrea Gavazzeni, Arena made his debut in 1963 at the Teatro Massimo in Palermo (with Puccini's *La bohème*), a theater in which he continued to conduct until 1971, when he began an active series of engagements in the major opera houses in Italy and elsewhere. Arena has become one of the greatest opera conductors of his time. His interpretations of late nineteenth- and early twentieth-century operas (by Rubinstein, Alfano, Montemezzi and Leoncavallo) are particularly distinguished.

ARIADNE AUF NAXOS

Opera in one act (with a prologue) by Richard Strauss (1864–1949), to a libretto by Hugo von Hofmannsthal. First performance of the opera's first version: Stuttgart, Königliches Hoftheater, 25 October 1912. First performance of the second version: Vienna, Hofoper, 4 October 1916.

The opera is set in the eighteenth century. In a room which has been turned into a theater in the house of a rich Viennese gentleman, feverish preparations for the staging of an *opera seria* are underway. The music-master (baritone) is dismayed to learn that the opera performance will be followed by an entertainment in the form of a farce. The composer (soprano), already displeased, becomes even angrier when the major-domo (speaking role) announces that his master's instructions are that the opera and the farce should be performed simultaneously, to save time. Zerbinetta (soprano), using the weapons of seduction, persuades the composer to adapt the two musical genres so that the opera seria fits in with the *opera buffa*. The performance can now begin. On the

uninhabited island of Naxos, Ariadne (soprano), surrounded by nymphs (sopranos and contralto), is lamenting her cruel fate in having been abandoned there by Theseus. Zerbinetta, Harlequin (baritone), Scaramuccio (tenor), Truffaldino (bass) and Brighella (tenor) try to console Ariadne in her sorrow. But then the nymphs announce the arrival of a god. Ariadne is terrified and, taking him to be the messenger of Death, offers herself to be taken by him to the Underworld. The god, who is Bacchus (tenor), takes her instead to Mount Olympus.

The first version of *Ariadne*, together with Strauss's incidental music for Molière's *Le bourgeois gentilhomme*, came to grief because the performance was too long and the difference between French comedy and German opera too great. Hofmannsthal and Strauss decided on a complete revision of *Ariadne* with an added prologue, which would make it no longer rely on Molière. In its second version, *Ariadne* retained all the musical charm which was the highlight of its success, due more to the intrinsic qualities of the music than to the play-within-a-play device.

ARIANE ET BARBE-BLEUE

(Ariadne and Bluebeard)

Operatic fable in three acts by Paul Dukas (1865–1935), to a libretto taken almost directly from the play by Maurice Maeterlinck. First performance: Paris, Théâtre de l'Opéra Comique, 10 May 1907.

Ariane (soprano), sixth wife of Barbe-bleue (bass), arrives at her husband's castle. The brave young woman wants to find out what happened to his previous wives. Barbe-bleue gives her six keys made of silver and one of gold: with the first six keys she is able to open doors on priceless jewels, amethysts, sapphires, pearls, emeralds, rubies and diamonds. On opening the seventh door, which her husband had forbidden her to do, Ariane hears women's voices coming from a vault below. Barbe-bleue surprises her and, in a rage, is on the point of dragging her down the steps in the direction of the vault, when Ariane screams. Peasants outside the castle hear her and come running to her rescue. Despondently, Barbe-bleue retreats. Ariane, having discovered where his other wives are, climbs down into the vault and frees them, instructing the peasants to guard the castle against Barbe-bleue's return. When he reappears, he is captured by the peasants, who take him, in a sorry state, to face his wives. They have no intention of seeking revenge, however. Instead, they untie him and attend to his wounds. Ariane alone, after vainly appealing to the other women to come with her and regain their freedom, goes out and leaves the castle behind her.

Ariane et Barbe-bleue is the only opera Paul Dukas wrote: it is one of his most successful compositions and an example of a symbolist opera, like Claude Debussy's *Pelléas et Mélisande*, whose librettist was also Maurice Maeterlinck. Although the premiere had no particular impact, later performances built up success for the work.

L'ARIANNA
TRAGEDIA
DEL SIG. OTTAVIO
RINVCCINI,
GENTILOMO DELLA CAMERA
DEL RE CRISTIANISSIMO.
RAPPRESENTATA IN MVSICA
NELLE REALI NOZZE DEL SERENISS.
PRINCIPE DI MANTOVA,
E DELLA SERENISSIMA INFANTA
DI SAVOIA.
IN MANTOVA,
Presso gli Heredi di Francesco Osanna Stampator Ducale. 1608.
Con licenza de' Superiori.

ARIANNA

Tragedy composed by Claudio Monteverdi (1567–1643) for performance to a literary text by Ottavio Rinuccini. First performance: Mantua, Teatro della Corte, 28 May 1608, on the occasion of the celebrations for the wedding of Prince Francesco Gonzaga and Margherita of Savoy.

The setting is the island of Naxos. Venere (Venus) announces that Arianna will be abandoned by Teseo. The goddess calls upon Amore to protect the unfortunate woman. In fact, Teseo, prompted by one of his advisers, does abandon Arianna on the deserted island and sets sail for Athens. The choruses provide comment on what is happening, and tell how Bacco falls in love with Arianna, and comforts her, making her his wife, to general rejoicing.

Staged with great success in 1608, the score of Monteverdi's *Arianna* was subsequently lost, except for part of the sixth scene, the "Lament of Arianna," a passage of exceptional evocative power; for Monteverdi's contemporaries, it became an example of the style to use when expressing in music the feeling of sorrow and of passion without hope. The basic story of what happened to Arianna is here fleshed out by using the choir to give vent to feelings, emotions, doubts and dilemmas. The opera was produced in 1640 to mark the opening of the Teatro Giustiniani di San Moisè when Monteverdi was in Venice. The myth of Ariadne has served as an opera subject for other composers, including Bernardo Pasquini (1685), Benedetto Marcello (1727), Jules Massenet (1906), and Richard Strauss (1912–16).

ARIÉ, RAFFAEL

(Sofia 1920–St. Moritz 1988)

Bulgarian bass. After initially studying the violin, Arié was persuaded to study singing by Christo Brambaroff, first baritone in the Sofia Opera. Arié made his singing debut in a concert in 1939, but his career was

Top: A scene from *Ariadne auf Naxos* by Richard Strauss.

Left: the title page of *Arianna* by Monteverdi.

interrupted by the advent of the Second World War. During the early post-war years, he sang at the opera house in Sofia (in *Eugene Onegin, Boris Godunov* and *Knyaz Igor*). In 1946, after winning the Concours Internationale in Geneva, Arié went to Italy, where his first appearance was in Prokofiev's *The Love for Three Oranges* at La Scala, Milan. A guest artiste in all the major European and American opera houses, he created the role of Truelove in the world premiere of Stravinsky's *The Rake's Progress* (Venice, La Fenice, 1951). Thanks to his *cantabile* bass voice with its gentle delivery, Arié won admiration for his very considerable repertoire of more than 100 operas.

ARKHIPOVA, IRINA

(Moscow 1925)

Russian mezzo-soprano. She studied at the Moscow Conservatory and won special acclaim in 1954 for her singing of the role of Lyubasha in Rimsky-Korsakov's opera *The Tsar's Bride*. After opera and concert appearances in Russian theaters as well as in Poland and Finland, Arkhipova made her debut in 1956 as Carmen at the Bolshoi in Moscow, and within a short time had become the leading mezzo-soprano there. Arkhipova was admired for her performances of the Russian repertoire, in both opera and *Lieder*, in particular for her technique, range and intelligence in interpretation. She has also given persuasive performances of Italian opera (*Aida, Il trovatore* and *Don Carlos*).

ARLECCHINO, ODER DIE FENSTER

(Harlequin, or The Windows)

Theatrical capriccio *in one act by Ferruccio Busoni (1866–1924), to the composer's own libretto. First performance: Zurich, Stadttheater, 11 May 1917.*

The action takes place in Bergamo, northern Italy. Ser Matteo (baritone), a pedantic tailor who is an avid reader of Dante's *Divine Comedy*, is sitting outside his house, working. Arlecchino (speaking role) is busy courting the tailor's wife, Annunziata (silent role). In order to get rid of the husband, Arlecchino tells him that Bergamo has just been invaded by barbarians, and then turns up disguised as an army captain to recruit the terrified Matteo. Colombina (mezzo-soprano), Arlecchino's neglected wife, discovers her husband's latest act of infidelity and allows herself to be courted by Leandro (tenor). Arlecchino pretends to be infuriated and knocks Leandro to the floor with his large wooden sword. In the confusion which results from the wounding of Leandro, Arlecchino takes his chance: he is now free of his wife and uses the key he had taken from Ser Matteo to gain entry to the tailor's house and take Annunziata off with him.

Though reworking the traditional form of *Commedia dell'Arte*, Busoni achieved a libretto and score in *Arlecchino* with a satiric treatment of the standard forms of Italian opera of the past.

ARLESIANA, L'

Opera in three acts by Francesco Cilèa (1866–1950), to a libretto by Leopoldo Marenco, taken from the play L'Arlésienne *by Alphonse Daudet. First performance: Milan, Teatro Lirico, 27 November 1897.*

The action takes place in Provence. Federico (tenor), son of the farmhouse owner Rosa Mamai (mezzo-soprano), has fallen in love with a girl from Arles who he met at the fair, and now wants to marry her. Metifio (baritone), a stableman, reveals to Rosa that the girl Federico wants to marry has been his lover. To prove this, he shows her two letters written by the girl from Arles and leaves them with her so she may show them to her son. Federico is shocked by this discovery and wanders through the Camargue in the grip of a deep depression. Seeing her son so overcome, Rosa tells him she would be willing to invite the girl from Arles to visit them. Federico is moved by this but, knowing he has to cure himself of his infatuation, he marries Vivetta (soprano), a young woman who has always loved him. The scene changes to a room at the farmhouse where preparations are underway for the wedding. Enter Metifio, who has come to collect his two letters, with the announcement that he has decided not to give up the girl from Arles. The sight of Metifio and hearing what he has said throw Federico into a fit of jealousy and he hurls himself at Metifio to strike him. Federico is taken to his room, where he seems to calm down, but after nightfall, he goes to the granary and jumps off the roof to put an end to his despair.

L'Arlesiana was inspired by the famous play by Daudet. Powerfully lyrical, with a wealth of strongly realistic touches, it played a decisive part in launching Enrico Caruso, who created the role of Federico.

ARMIDA

Opera in three acts by Gioachino Rossini (1792–1868) to a libretto by Giovanni Schmidt, taken from the epic poem Gerusalemme Liberata *(Jerusalem Delivered) by Torquato Tasso. First performance: Naples, Teatro San Carlo, 11 November 1817.*

Ariecchino, oder die Fenster by Ferruccio Busoni, in a performance at the Teatro la Fenice, Venice.

The setting is the Christian battleground near Jerusalem during the Crusades. Enter Armida (soprano), with her uncle Idraote (bass). Armida introduces herself to Goffredo (tenor) and tells him a convincing but untrue story of how she has been deposed by her uncle, who has threatened to kill her, and she asks the crusader knights to intervene on her behalf and win back her throne. Goffredo promises to help only after Jerusalem has surrendered, and Armida pretends to be in despair. Eustazio (tenor) and the Paladins, bewitched by Armida, declare themselves on Armida's side. Goffredo therefore appoints Rinaldo (tenor) as Armida's champion. This decision provokes a jealous reaction from the Paladin Gernando (tenor), who breaks in on the meeting between Armida and Rinaldo. Rinaldo, who has already fallen prey to Armida's scheming, responds to Gernando's show of aggression by challenging him to a duel, in which he kills Gernando. Goffredo's anger at what has happened causes Rinaldo to totally surrender to the power of Armida's magic. Rinaldo finds himself on an enchanted island where he abandons himself to the luxuries and pleasures of love. Goffredo sends Carlo (tenor) and Ubaldo (tenor) to find Rinaldo. When Rinaldo has come to his senses and realizes he has been under an illusion, he gladly goes back with Carlo and Ubaldo. Armida tries to stop him, but in vain. In a towering rage, the sorceress calls upon the Furies and, crying out for vengeance, disappears amidst flames astride a winged chariot.

In *Armida*, Rossini uses magic and the world of dreams as the mainstays of the plot, with luxuriant orchestral colours and bold harmonies in the creation of an expressive score.

ARMIDE

(Armida)

Opera in five acts by Christoph Willibald Gluck (1714–1787), to a libretto by Philippe Quinault, freely adapted from Torquato Tasso's epic poem Gerusalemme liberata *(Jerusalem Delivered). First performance: Paris, Académie Royale de Musique (Opéra), 23 September 1777.*

The setting is Damascus. Armide (soprano), niece of King Hydraotes (baritone), has succeeded in seducing all the crusader knights except one, Renaud (tenor), whose failure to succumb to her has wounded her pride. Armide manages to abduct the hero and carry him off to an enchanted island. The sorceress has fallen in love with Renaud, although she is aware that he has been won not by her beauty but by her magic arts. The hero, who now lives as a prisoner on the enchanted island and has forgotten all about his duties as a crusader, is found there by two of his fellow knights. The two have defied the power of Armide's spells and overcome them, and they help Renaud to understand the illusions he has been under. Renaud is freed from the magic power detaining him, and makes ready to leave the island with the knights. Armide is desperate and begs him to stay, but Renaud leaves. The sorceress calls upon the gods of the Underworld, who cause the enchanted island to sink beneath the waves.

Written in 1777, *Armide*, despite the novelty of its structure, does not enjoy the coherence and unity achieved by the composer in better works such as *Orfeo ed Euridice*. *Armide* is most successful in its tragic passages, less so in some of the solo and choral episodes, and contains some ravishing arias for Armide which are among the greatest in all Gluck's operas.

ARMSTRONG, KARAN

(Horne, Montana 1941)

American soprano. She began her music studies at Concordia College, Moorhead (Minnesota) and continued with Lotte Lehmann, Fritz Zweig and Tilly de Garmo. After singing at the Metropolitan Opera and the New York City Opera, Armstrong moved her career to Germany, where she made an impression with a much-admired performance of Richard Strauss's *Salome*, an opera in which she subsequently sang in the leading opera houses of Europe. Armstrong's combined gifts as a singer and actress have also been in evidence in other modern operas (Alban Berg's *Lulu* and *Wozzeck*) as well as in contemporary operas.

Poster for *Armide* by Gluck.

ARMSTRONG, SHEILA

(Ashington, Northumberland 1942)
British soprano. She studied at the Royal Academy of Music in London. In 1965 she won the Kathleen Ferrier Memorial Scholarship, making her debut the same year at London's Sadler's Wells as Despina (*Così fan tutte*). In 1966, she appeared for the first time at the Glyndebourne Festival (as Belinda in Purcell's *Dido and Aeneas*), her Covent Garden debut following in 1973 with the role of Marzelline in Beethoven's *Fidelio*. Armstrong's vocal gifts, sensitivity of interpretation and stage presence made her a celebrated performer with a large opera and concert repertoire, from Purcell and Handel to Delius, Britten, Elgar, Vaughan Williams and many other twentieth-century composers.

AROLDO

(Harold)
Opera in four acts by Giuseppe Verdi (1813–1901), to a libretto by Francesco Maria Piave, which was a reworking of Stiffelio *(1850). First performance: Rimini, Teatro Nuovo, 16 August 1857.*

The action takes place in Scotland in 1200. Aroldo di Kent (tenor) returns from the Crusades to find his wife Mina (soprano) in the grip of a deep sadness. During his absence, Mina had been the mistress of a roving knight, Godvino (tenor), who had been a guest of her father Egberto (baritone). Briano (bass), a hermit and friend of Aroldo, informs him of Mina's unfaithfulness, and encourages him to forgive her. But Aroldo is unable to cope with the wrong he has suffered, and after breaking the marriage-bond with Mina, he leaves to become a hermit himself. The years pass and a storm shipwrecks Mina and Egberto near Aroldo's hermitage. Aroldo and his wife recognize one another, she asks him to forgive her and the old crusader does so. Mina and Aroldo are happily reunited.

Aroldo is a reworking of Verdi's opera *Stiffelio*, which had been heavily censored on account of the delicate subject-matter of its plot (a Protestant pastor betrayed by his wife). So Verdi changed the story's period and also its characters, hoping that his music would in this way be able to achieve fresh vitality. In fact, *Aroldo* also failed to win the acclaim Verdi had wished, and the opera was soon forgotten.

ARROYO, MARTINA

(New York 1936)
American soprano. Her musical education took place at Hunter College, New York, and she made her debut in 1958 in the United States premiere of Pizzetti's *Assassinio nella cattedrale*. Her career became established in 1963 when she took over from Birgit Nilsson in *Aida* at the Metropolitan Opera, New York. On the strength of a warmth of timbre, fine range and flowing delivery, Arroyo was regarded as one of the most interesting Verdi singers internationally. She retired in 1989.

ASCANIO IN ALBA

Serenata teatrale *in two acts by Wolfgang Amadeus Mozart (1756–1791), to a libretto by Giuseppe Parini. First performance: Milan, Teatro Ducale, 17 October 1771.*

The scene is the countryside where the city of Alba Longa will one day be built. To solemnize the foundation of a new city, Venere (Venus) (soprano) wants her grandson Ascanio (male soprano) to marry a young shepherdess, Silvia (soprano), a descendant of Hercules. It is Venere's wish that true love should grow between the two young people and, by means of a dream, she predisposes Silvia to love Ascanio, who meets her without revealing to her who he really is. But Silvia, conscious of being promised to Ascanio, wants the young man to go away. Then Venere explains the misunderstanding and reunites the two lovers. During the wedding, the goddess performs another miracle, transforming trees into columns and branches into lintels, until the city of Alba Longa materializes in all its magnificence. Then Venere asks the young couple to govern justly the people now entrusted to their care.

Ascanio in Alba is an allegorical opera which received its premiere to mark the occasion of the wedding of the Archduke Ferdinand of Austria and Maria Ricciarda Beatrice d'Este and his entry into Milan as governor and captain-general of Lombardy. The mythological figures in the opera are meant to represent Ferdinand, his bride, the Empress Maria Teresa, Ferdinand's mother (in the part of Venus), while Milan becomes the mythical Alba Longa. Mozart was 15 when he composed this musical tribute, which, in spite of some echoes of the Arcadian style, has a good instrumental balance and an elegance of vocal line designed to emphasize the individual vocal talents of the performers.

ASSASSINIO NELLA CATTEDRALE

(Murder in the Cathedral)
Tragic opera in two acts and an intermezzo *by Ildebrando Pizzetti (1880–1968), to the*

Assassinio nella Cattedrale, in a performance at the Basilica di Sant' Ambrogio, Milan.

composer's own libretto based on T.S. Eliot's verse drama Murder in the Cathedral. *First performance: Milan, La Scala, 1 March 1958.*

The action takes place in Canterbury in December 1170. Thomas Becket (bass), Archbishop of Canterbury, has just returned from a seven-year exile imposed on him following his disagreements with the King. Becket is warmly welcomed by his congregation who at the same time are afraid that the Archbishop's reappearance on the scene will trigger off new struggles and hardships for the people. Thomas is visited in his study by four tempters (a tenor and three basses), who try to reawaken old and new desires within him: for pleasure, political power, leadership of a popular uprising, the temptation of martyrdom. Thomas prays to God to keep these temptations away from him. During Christmas Mass, Thomas proclaims himself ready for any sacrifice, even that of his own life, in God's name. Enter four of the King's knights (a tenor and three basses), who accuse Thomas of treason. The Archbishop tenaciously argues his own defense, and the knights issue threats as they take their leave of him. Thomas's priests and congregation sense tragic events in the offing and ask for the cathedral doors to be barred, but Thomas will not agree to it. A short time later, the knights burst in and when Thomas refuses to submit to the will of the King, they kill him with their swords. The assassins then observe ironically that this is the only way to resolve the conflict between Church and State. A chorus of the faithful sing Thomas's praises.

This is one of Pizzetti's last works, and it provides a coherent final chapter to the musical commentary he had developed in *Fedra* and *La figlia di Jorio*. These operas share a common quality of expansiveness and grandiose visions, often dominated by intense religious feeling.

ASSEDIO DI CALAIS, L'

(The Siege of Calais)

Opera in three acts by Gaetano Donizetti (1797–1848), to a libretto by Salvatore Cammarano, taken from Le siège de Calais *by P-L.B. de Belloy. First performance: Naples, Teatro San Carlo, 19 November 1836.*

The action takes place in and around Calais in 1347. Aurelio (mezzo-soprano), son of Eustachio di Saint-Pierre (baritone), governor of Calais, has returned, miraculously unharmed, from a sortie outside the walls of Calais which are surrounded by the English army of the King, Edoardo III (bass-baritone). The city is by now *in extremis*. Aurelio has managed to steal some food for his wife Eleonora (soprano) and their son. The citizens of Calais, incited by an English infiltrator (bass), accuse Eustachio of having brought the city to ruin. The governor unmasks the English spy and offers himself, together with his son Aurelio and other citizens, for execution, the exclusive terms proposed by the English King for saving Calais. Eustachio and the other hostages go to the English camp, accompanied by Eleonora and the other wives, all in tears. Queen Isabella (soprano) and the English soldiers are moved by this, and ask the English King to spare them. This he does, to the disbelief and joy of all those present.

L'assedio di Calais was not particularly successful, largely because of its musical innovations, which Donizetti himself described as representing a "new genre in Italy." The ensemble scenes were nevertheless outstanding, providing moments of eloquent and magnificent theater, like the sextet "O sacre polve" which brings the second act to a truly extraordinary end and prophetically anticipates Verdi's choral writing.

ASTUZIE FEMMINILI, LE

(Feminine Wiles)

Melodramma giocoso *in two acts by Domenico Cimarosa (1749–1801), to a libretto by Giuseppe Palomba. First performance: Naples, Teatro dei Fiorentini, 26 August 1794.*

The action takes place in Rome. Romualdo (baritone) reveals to his ward Bellina (soprano) that she will only

L' ASTUZIE
FEMMINILI
DRAMMA GIOCOSO PER MUSICA
DA RAPPRESENTARSI
NEL REGIO TEATRO
DI VIA DELLA PERGOLA
LA PRIMAVERA DEL MDCCXCV.
SOTTO LA PROTEZ. DELL' A. R.
DI
FERDINANDO III.
ARCIDUCA D' AUSTRIA
PRINCIPE REALE D' UNGHERIA E DI BOEMIA
GRAN-DUCA DI TOSCANA
ec. ec. ec.

IN FIRENZE MDCCXCV.
Nella Stamperia Albizziniana da S.M. in Campo
PER PIETRO FANTOSINI
Con Approvazione.

Top: A scene from *L'assedio di Calais.*

Above: playbill for a 1795 performance of *Le astuzie femminili* by Domenico Cimarosa.

inherit her father's entire estate if she marries Giampaolo (comic bass), an elderly landowner from Naples. But Bellina is in love with Filandro (tenor) and, with the help of her friend Ersilia (soprano) and her governess Leonora (mezzo-soprano), she decides to do everything she can to avoid marrying Giampaolo. Leonora therefore lets Giampaolo know that Romualdo and Filandro are both interested in marrying Bellina. Giampaolo surprises Filandro and Bellina during a tender moment. Flying into a rage, the old man brandishes a gun at Bellina, whereupon she tells him she is ready to marry him there and then. Giampaolo is surprised by Leonora, who takes him for a burglar and screams. This causes such turmoil that the marriage plans of Bellina and Giampaolo are called off. Filandro and Bellina dress up as Hungarians, and arrive separately at the house, each asking after the other and saying they have been deserted because of a certain Filandro and a certain Bellina, whom they have had thrown into prison. Those present introduce the two ''Hungarians'' to each other and they then get married, promising to send Bellina home again. After the wedding, the bride and groom reveal their true identities. Giampaolo and Romualdo are beside themselves with fury at first, and then give in, forgive the couple, and everybody joins in the celebrations.

Written for the court of Vienna in 1792, *Le astuzie femminili* is a mature work full of vitality, in spite of the banal story-line, in which Cimarosa succeeded in creating a treasure-trove of good melodies.

ATLANTIDA, LA

(Atlantis)

Scenic cantata consisting of a prologue and three acts by Manuel de Falla (1876–1946), based on a poem by Jacinto Verdaguer y Santaló. The work was completed by Ernesto Halffter. First concert performance: Barcelona, 24 November 1961. First stage performance: Milan, La Scala, 18 June 1962.

Prologue. Christopher Columbus, while still a boy, is shipwrecked on an island where he meets a wise old man (tenor) who tells him the fabulous history of the oceans and the sinking of the kingdom of Atlantis, of which Spain is the sole surviving trace. ACT I. Hercules discovers Queen Peirene (mezzo-soprano) dying. She has been driven from her realm by the three-headed monster Geryon (two tenors, one bass) who has set fire to the forests and is now heading for Cadiz. Hercules sets out to avenge the Queen. ACT II. Geryon persuades Hercules to go to Atlantis. Hercules travels to the Garden of the Hesperides, where he kills the dragon guarding the tree of golden apples. The Hesperides also die and the gods transform them into the constellation of the Pleiades. The Titans, meanwhile, rise up against the god Neptune, and Hercules, after managing to open up a gap between them and pass through, returns to Cadiz to kill Geryon. Hercules reaches the place where Gibraltar stands now and thinks of a battle-plan against the Titans. The voice of God condemns the rebellion of the Sons of Atlas and sinks Atlantis beneath the waves. The Titans attempt to climb up to heaven by means of a very high tower, but the archangel (tenor) pushes them back with a sword of fire. With the Titans vanquished, Hercules marks the uncrossable frontier of the sea with two pillars. ACT III. Columbus looks out at the ocean and the Pillars of Hercules. Queen Isabella (soprano) dreams of islands rising from the sea. Columbus, with the Queen's help, sails into the unknown. Out of the silence of the unexplored sea, sailors can be heard singing a hymn in praise of the Virgin Mary. While Columbus is looking up at the stars, the land he has longed to see, likened to a ''Spanish cathedral,'' comes into view.

The cantata was left unfinished at his death and was completed by De Falla's pupil Ernesto Halffter.

ATLANTOV, VLADIMIR

(Leningrad 1939)

Russian tenor. Born into a musical family, Atlantov studied at the Leningrad School of Music. After early appearances at the Kirov Theater, he went to Italy to complete his training at the La Scala school in Milan (1964–65). In 1967 he made his debut at the Bolshoi in Moscow. His strong, full voice, ringing and ample in the upper register, has led to his being regarded as one of the leading singers at the Bolshoi, as well as one of the most famous tenors in Russia.

ATOMTOD

(Atomic Death)

Opera in two acts by Giacomo Manzoni (b. 1932), to a libretto by Emilio Jona. First performance: Milan, Piccola Scala, 27 March 1965.

The construction of a great spherical atomic shelter takes place, suggested by video pictures, electronic music and mime. The question of how to use this structure to best advantage is then posed. The builder and the owner select the

A scene from *Atomtod*, in a performance at the Teatro Comunale, Treviso.

people who, in case of necessity, will go with them into the shelter: an attractive woman, a general, a servant, and a minister of religion. The voice of a speaker attempts to calm the people, who are gripped by terror. There are signs of an impending catastrophe. Two men and a woman in full flight try in vain to get inside a spherical shelter. Inside it, the six characters are living an apparently normal life, but little by little their individuality is being broken down. Outside, the people continue to die. The six characters come out of the spherical shelters. By now they have lost all sense of identity: the constant magnetic discharges have eliminated in them all traces of thought and reasoning. Atomic death leaves no sign of life.

Atomtod is Manzoni's second opera, illustrating his chosen course of experimentation with new sounds that express a new musical ideal as well as an ideological one.

ATTERBERG, KURT

(Gothenburg 1887–Stockholm 1974)
Swedish composer and orchestral conductor. He studied at the Stockholm Conservatory, before completing his training in Berlin with the composer Max von Schillings. From 1913 to 1923 he conducted the orchestra of the Royal Dramatic Theater, Stockholm. His output of operas consists of five works: *Härvard Harpolekare* (Härvard the Harpist), 1919; *Bäckahästen* (The River Horse), 1925; *Fanal* (The Burning Land), 1934; *Aladdin* 1941; and *Stormen* (after *The Tempest*), 1948.

ATTILA

Opera in three acts (with a prologue) by Giuseppe Verdi (1813–1901), to a libretto by Temistocle Solera taken from Attila, King of the Huns *by Zacharias Werner. First performance: Venice, Teatro La Fenice, 17 March 1846.*

After destroying Aquileia, Attila (bass) finds among his prisoners a young girl, Odabella (soprano) who impresses him by her indomitable spirit. Attila admires her courage and makes her a gift of his sword. Odabella swears that with this sword she will have her revenge. Enter the Roman General Ezio (baritone), seeking to reach an agreement with Attila: he will give the King of the Barbarians a free hand to conquer the rest of the world if, in return, Attila will let Italy go free. Attila is too proud to agree to this. Meanwhile, the survivors from Aquileia have been rescued by Foresto (tenor) and they now take an oath to rebuild their city. In the vicinity of Attila's camp, Foresto meets Odabella. He believes he has given himself away, but then learns from Odabella that she is resolved to assassinate Attila. While Attila and his forces are preparing to march on Rome, a procession of boys and women appears, led by an old man, Pope Leo I (bass). Attila recognizes him as a figure he has seen in a dream and in terror orders his troops to halt. While a truce with the Huns is still in force, Ezio and Foresto come together to launch an attack on Attila's camp. Their accomplice is Odabella, who is by now completely trusted by Attila. When Attila discovers the plot, it is already too late: the Roman warriors burst into the camp, while Odabella mortally wounds Attila.

Attila, which is one of Verdi's lesser scores, was forgotten by the composer. The rediscovery of the whole of the Verdi repertoire, however, has today given a new lease of life to this opera, with its rich vein of burning patriotism running through the work.

ATTILIO REGOLO

Opera in three acts by Johann Adolph Hasse (1699–1783), to a libretto by Pietro Metastasio. First performance: Dresden, Hoftheater, 12 January 1750.

All of Rome has waited anxiously to hear of the fate of Attilio Regolo since he was taken prisoner five years ago by the Carthaginians. News comes of the unexpected arrival in Rome of the Carthaginian ambassador Hamilcar, who brings with him the hero Attilio himself. Attilio is to be freed as warranty for the current Carthaginian peace proposals, but, having set these out himself in detail before the Senate, he causes widespread consternation by advising the Senators to reject them. This courageous stand by Attilio sends shock waves throughout Rome, with the result that as he prepares to leave the capital again, the people, now in uproar, set their will against the Senate's decision. Attilio addresses the assembled crowds, asking them to remember the ancient Roman tradition: a glorious death is preferable to a life stained by ignominy. The opera ends with a chorus which praises Attilio's virtuousness as the hero leaves for Carthage.

The way Johann Adolphe Hasse approached this unusually epic plot by Metastasio was to remain close to the essential drama of the story, producing passages of richly meaningful lyricism and enthralling power, and shunning all conventions and empty rhetoric. This treatment has earned him a foremost position among those composers who have also made operas of the same story.

The Prologue of *Attila*, in a performance at La Scala, Milan.

ATYS

Tragédie-lyrique consisting of a prologue and five acts by Jean-Baptiste Lully (1632–1687), to a libretto by Philippe Quinault. First performance: Paris, Saint-Germain-en-Laye, 10 January 1676.

Prologue. The Muse Melpomene recounts the story of Atys to King Louis XIV, who is preparing to set out to war. The scene changes to Phrygia where the wedding is about to take place between Sangaride and the King of Phrygia, Célénus. But the young woman actually loves Atys, who will never return her love because he is too obsessed with himself. Enter Atys, who is disturbed to see Sangaride suffering and he tenderly offers her his love. The goddess Cybèle arrives for Sangaride's wedding and burns with desire at the sight of Atys, with whom she is secretly in love. Atys, meanwhile, is confused by his love for Sangaride, which drives him to betray his friendship with Célénus. The young man suddenly falls asleep, the result of a trick by Cybèle to enable her to reveal her love to Atys. Atys wakes suddenly to find himself in the arms of Cybèle, who is embracing him tenderly. Sangaride now appears, in despair: she does not love Célénus and does not want to marry him. As Cybèle watches the two young people together, she instinctively knows how passionately they feel about one another, whereas Sangaride thinks that Atys loves Cybèle. Atys then reassures Sangaride and the two of them pledge undying love to one another; then Atys uses the fact that he is a priest of Cybèle to stop the wedding of Sangaride and Célénus. Célénus is furious and appeals to the goddess to see justice done. Cybèle makes Atys go mad, and he, in the grip of horrifying delusions, kills Sangaride, believing her to be a monster. When Atys comes to his senses and realizes what he has done, he wants to kill himself, but Cybèle stays his hand and turns him into a pine-tree.

This substantial *tragèdie-lyrique* by Lully enjoyed an important revival when it was staged in January 1987 to mark the tercentenary of the composer's death.

A scene from *Atys* by Jean-Baptiste Lully.

AUBER, DANIEL-FRANÇOIS-ESPRIT

(Caen 1782–Paris 1871)

French composer. Despite his prodigious musical gifts, Auber's father sent him to London to gain business experience. On his return to Paris, Auber received encouragement from the composer Boïeldieu, who helped the young man firmly on his way into a career as a composer. After writing instrumental music, Auber transferred his attentions to opera, making his debut in 1805 with *L'erreur d'un moment*, which was relatively unsuccessful. Success eventually came with *La bergère châtelaine* in 1820. From then on, Auber began an intense period of collaboration with the librettist Scribe, who was to provide him with opera libretti for about 40 years, resulting in a long series of serious and comic operas. The most famous of these are: *La muette de Portici* (The Dumb Girl of Portici), 1828; *Fra Diavolo*, 1830; *Le cheval de bronze* (The Bronze Horse), 1835; *Le domino noir* (The Black Domino), 1837; and *Les diamants de la couronne* (The Crown Diamonds), 1841. With *La muette de Portici* Auber brought about the birth of *grand-opéra*, a genre whose great mass scenes, dances and magnificent theatrical effects would influence the French theater of the late nineteenth century. Auber's operatic output is distinguished by the grace, verve and *brio* of his music, which satisfied public taste at the time.

AUDEN, WYSTAN HUGH

(York 1907–Vienna 1973)

British poet and playwright. He studied at Christ Church College, Oxford. Auden had already written for the theater before he began, in 1938, to be associated with the world of music. In 1941 he provided a libretto for Benjamin Britten's opera *Paul Bunyan*, and then, with Chester Kallman, one for Igor Stravinsky's *The Rake's Progress* (1951). Further libretti followed for operas by Hans Werner Henze, *Elegy for Young Lovers* (1961) and *The Bassarids* (1966). Again with Kallman, Auden was responsible for English versions of the libretti of Mozart's *Don Giovanni* and *Die Zauberflöte* (The Magic Flute).

AUFSTIEG UND FALL DER STADT MAHAGONNY

(Rise and Fall of the City of Mahagonny)

Opera in three acts by Kurt Weill (1900–1950), to a text by Bertolt Brecht. First performance: Leipzig, Neues Theater, 9 March 1930.

Leokadja (mezzo-soprano), Begbick (baritone), Fatty (tenor) and Trinity Moses (baritone) are on the run from the police. They are on board a lorry and heading for the Gold Coast to seek their fortune. The lorry breaks down, and Leokadja decides to build a new city, Mahagonny, in that very place. Immediately people begin to arrive there: among those who have moved to Mahagonny are Jenny (soprano) and six other young women, Bill (baritone), Jack (tenor), Jim (tenor) and Joe (bass), who have made money from working as lumberjacks in Alaska. Jim forms a permanent relationship with Jenny. But

THE FRENCH *TRAGÉDIE-LYRIQUE*

It was Jean-Baptiste Lully (1632–1687) and the librettist Philippe Quinault (1636–1686) who transformed the original theatrical genre known as *ballet de cour* (a blend of poetry, music and dance in which dance was easily the strongest element) into *tragédie-lyrique*, or *tragédie-en-musique*, in which the plot, the libretto, the choreography and the orchestra co-exist, each retaining its own unique character and independence. Using the device of lyrical declamation, in which he had clearly been inspired by the way in which actors at the Comédie-Française delivered their lines, Lully nevertheless did not confine himself to extolling the spoken word through having it sung for purely expressive purposes, but wanted to bring out its most delicately dramatic potential. This is why *tragédie-lyrique* resisted the influence of Italian opera, choosing instead to express itself in a musical form which on the one hand, in theory, drew its inspiration from the *recitar cantando* (declaim through singing) of the Florentine School, yet did not attempt to develop the aria in any great extent, with the result that it remained very short in length and offered the singer few opportunities. So it was that the singers of the Académie Royale (the only theater where operas were permitted to be staged) were subjected to a strict discipline, whereby they were to avoid being lionized or indulging in such whims in performance as the use of improvisation, something widely practised by Italian singers. Lully's *tragédie-lyrique* exerted an extremely powerful influence over subsequent French output and ended up as a codified form of national entertainment which the other composers had to adapt to, with the result that Marc Antoine Charpentier (1634–1704), for example, was unable to give full rein to the expression of his artistic personality until after Lully's death. Charpentier was evidently more receptive to Italian influences: he used Italian singers in productions of his own operas which were often even sung in Italian, and while keeping the formal structure of Lully's *tragédie-lyrique* more or less intact (five acts with a prologue, an essentially classical plot, a libretto in verse and a strong dance element), he blended French declamation with Italian lyricism and in so doing gave rise to a style which developed into a kind of vocal *arioso*, more musically elaborate than anything in Lully, but above all concentrating more on dramatic expressiveness. The evolution of the *tragédie-lyrique* reached its peak of accomplishment as an expressive form in the hands of Jean-Philippe Rameau (1683–1764), who was also an outstanding innovator in the area of harmony, as demonstrated by his most famous operas, *Hippolyte et Aricie*, *Les Indes galantes*, *Castor et Pollux* and *Dardanus*. In spite of the inferior literary quality of the libretti he used (compared with Lully's), Rameau proved to be far superior in terms of expressiveness, in view of his more masterly use of the orchestra (given an expansive role in storm scenes and imitations of sounds in nature) and of the *arioso*, which more effectively expressed the feelings in the texts with a much greater clarity.

France could not produce a worthy successor to Rameau's dramatic genius for more than a century and during that time only the German composer Christoph Willibald Gluck (1714–1787) proved capable of developing the *tragédie-lyrique* to realize its full potential as a theatrical form.

Left: Jean-Philippe Rameau.

Above: A scene from *Alceste* by J.B. Lully, performed at Versailles.

the happy atmosphere in Mahagonny starts to change. Many people leave; Leokadja herself wants to go, but is held back by the fact the police are still looking for her. When a warning is issued that a hurricane is on its way, Jim, who is by now bored with living in Mahagonny, announces that everything will be permitted in the city from that day on. Mahagonny falls into chaos and anarchy: Jack dies from indigestion, Joe is killed during a fist-fight with Trinity Moses, and Jim, who is perpetually drunk, gambles away all his gold and ends up in prison for not having paid his bill. A trial is planned, in which Jim is also accused of having thrown the life of the city into confusion and caused the deaths of his friends. With Jim now on his way to the electric chair, everyone is invited to reflect on the situation in which Mahagonny finds itself. The city might have been saved from the hurricane, which had changed direction unexpectedly, but now it is about to be destroyed by a fire. The people file past, as though out of their minds, carrying a series of placards which contradict one another: as they await the end, all sing of death and the ruin of the city.

A first version of *Mahagonny*, in the form of a one-act *Singspiel*, had already been performed in Baden Baden three years before the final version was premiered in 1927. When Brecht and Weill presented this new version of the opera, the reaction of the audience in Leipzig was one of the genuine uproar at what appeared to them to be an opera with a totally subversive message. Initially, the Nazis merely attacked it, but after Hitler's rise to power, *Mahagonny* was banned and in 1938 its parts were destroyed. Only the original score was saved, and this was rediscovered after the war.

AUGER, ARLEEN

(Los Angeles 1939)

American soprano. After graduating from the University of California in 1963, Auger went on to Chicago in 1967 to complete her training. She joined the resident company of the Vienna State Opera (1967–74) and made her debut as the Queen of the Night in Mozart's *Die Zauberflöte* (The Magic Flute). Her international career included appearances in leading opera houses and music venues. Auger's voice had an agreeable timbre, agility in *coloratura* roles, and elegant, refined phrasing. She was particularly distinguished in the eighteenth-century repertoire.

AU GRAND SOLEIL CHARGÉ D'AMOUR

(To the Great Sun Charged with Love)

Scenic action in two parts by Luigi Nono (1924–1990), to texts by Rimbaud, Gorky, Brecht, Pavese, Michel, Bunke, Sanchez, Santamaria, a Vietnam guerrilla, Marx, Lenin, Gramsci, Dimitrov and Che Guevara. First performance: Milan, Teatro Lirico, 4 April 1975.

The action centers on a number of individual women revolutionaries—like Louise Michel of the Paris Commune and the Bolivian guerrilla Tanya Bunke—and the character of the Mother who, as a projection of the ideal, embodies humanity's destiny in love and struggle. Specific historical struggles are also featured, from the 1870 Paris Commune, through the Russian revolutions of 1905 and 1917, to the Latin-American

Above: A scene from *Aufstieg und Fall der Stadt Mahagonny.*

Right: A scene from *Axur, re d'Ormus* by Salieri.

liberation struggles and the Vietnam War: to Nono, these are not simple historical events but processes of liberation. The theatrical element of the work is presented in a fragmentary way, and is in no sense comparable with normal scenic action. Nono and his team of collaborators – director Yuri Lyubimov, conductor Claudio Abbado and designer David Borowsky – have tried to create a language of theater that unites music, words and staging. The texts have been taken from Rimbaud (the title is a line from one of Rimbaud's poems, *Au grand soleil d'amour chargé*), Gorky, Brecht, Cesare Pavese and others. The staging, costumes and choreography become the natural complement of the music by means of an elaborate use of the stage space. Nono's music for the work is in his own recognizable style: it is a musical style that draws on a complex range of resources (vocal soloists, choir, orchestra, electronic equipment) and yet also appears lean, exasperated, sometimes evanescent, charged with lyrical tensions in its continual quest for a vocal language.

AURELIANO IN PALMIRA

Opera in two acts by Gioachino Rossini (1792–1868), to a libretto by Felice Romani. First performance: Milan, La Scala, 26 December 1813.

Aureliano (tenor), Roman Emperor, after reconquering Antioch, declares war on Zenobia (soprano), Queen of Palmyra. The Persian Prince Arsace (mezzo-soprano) sets out at the head of his army to stop the invader; but he is overwhelmed by Roman militias, captured, and taken before Aureliano. Arsace declares himself an ally of Zenobia. She then asks for Arsace to be released, and is ready to take on the Roman army. Aureliano is furious and promises Arsace will die and Zenobia will be defeated, but he is so impressed by the pride of the indomitable Zenobia that he decides to marry her. She refuses him. Arsace, who has meanwhile managed to escape, is put at the head of the remaining troops, and attempts to win Palmyra back, but he is defeated and again imprisoned. Arsace and Zenobia are condemned to death. Confronted with his two courageous prisoners, however, Aureliano shows clemency: Zenobia and Arsace can have their freedom, on condition that they swear a friendship pact with Rome. A chorus of rejoicing seals the new alliance.

Aureliano in Palmira is a genial opera which Rossini was later to treat as something of a musical gold-mine, returning to it to quarry ideas to use in new scores.

AXUR, RE D'ORMUS

(Axur, King of Ormus)

Tragi-comic opera in five acts by Antonio Salieri (1750–1825), to a libretto by Pierre-Augustin Caron de Beaumarchais, translated into Italian by Lorenzo da Ponte from Salieri's opera Tarare. *First performance: Vienna, Burgtheater, 8 January 1788.*

On orders from King Axur (baritone), Altamor (bass) abducts Aspasia (soprano), wife of the army commander Atar (tenor). Not knowing what fate has befallen his wife, Atar seeks an audience with Axur to appeal for justice and help. Seeing the hero humbled, the envious and cruel Axur allows Atar to have a ship so he may set out in search of Aspasia. Biscroma (*buffo* bass), Axur's servant, tells Atar that Aspasia is a prisoner in the King's harem. Enemy troops now threaten to attack the kingdom of Ormus, and the people call on Atar to lead their army out and save the kingdom. Axur announces that the commander is preoccupied with other problems, but Atar, shaking with rage, declares that, on the contrary, he is ready to perform his duties as a soldier and unleash his desire for vengeance. While a party is taking place there, Biscroma smuggles Atar into the harem disguised as a black. Axur bumps into him there, and decides to marry him off to Aspasia, to punish her for being so unfaithful to her husband. A band of armed men led by Urson (tenor) enters the harem, acting on instructions from Axur to kill the black there. When they discover their intended victim's true identity, however, they are all taken aback, but are nonetheless under orders to arrest Atar. Atar is led before the King, where he is reunited with Aspasia and embraces her. The King orders them to be separated, and Atar is taken away to the scaffold. Shouts are heard. The people of Ormus have surrounded the palace and are shouting for Atar to be released. Atar calms the people. At this, Axur, seeing how Atar is more beloved of the people than he is, removes his crown and kills himself. The people then proclaim Atar the new King of Ormus.

The first version of this opera by Salieri was in French: written to a libretto by Beaumarchais, it was entitled *Tarare*, and dates from 1787. On the wave of the tremendous success of *Tarare* wherever it was performed, Salieri prepared a new version to be performed in Vienna, where the tradition was that operas had to be given in Italian. Salieri asked Lorenzo da Ponte to translate the opera from French into Italian, and, in so doing, Da Ponte revised the Beaumarchais libretto, producing a slimmer version of the original. It was performed at the Burgtheater in Vienna, and, now entitled *Axur*, the work achieved such success that the opera became one of those most frequently performed in Vienna.

A scene from *Au Grand Soleil d'amour chargé* by Luigi Nono.

B

BACH, JOHANN CHRISTIAN

(Leipzig 1735–London 1782)
German composer. Eleventh and youngest son (and eighteenth child) of Johann Sebastian Bach. He composed his first opera, *Artaserse* (1760), in Italy, but established his reputation from 1763 in London with the opera *Orione*, in which he introduced clarinets into a British opera orchestra. Five of J. C. Bach's 11 operas were written in London. Ten were based on *opera seria* and five used libretti by Metastasio.

BACQUIER, GABRIEL

(Béziers 1924)
French baritone. He studied at the Paris Conservatoire before making his debut with José Beckmans' Compagnie Lyrique (1950–52). He then sang in Brussels (1953–56). In 1960 he appeared for the first time in Aix-en-Provence, in Mozart's *Don Giovanni*, an opera which made him famous and launched him on an international career. Although Bacquier's voice was not particularly graceful and was technically limited, he has nevertheless gained recognition for his considerable skills in interpretation and phrasing. His repertoire, consisting almost exclusively of French opera, ranged from the Offenbach operettas to Debussy's *Pelléas et Mélisande*.

BADOARO, GIACOMO

(Venice 1602–1654)
Italian librettist. Badoaro came from a noble family and played a very active part in the political and cultural life of the Venetian Republic. He provided the libretto for Monteverdi's *Il ritorno d'Ulisse in patria* (1640). He was one of the first librettists to respond to the then new requirements of compositional style, placing more emphasis on the characterization of roles and exploring ways of increasing the dramatic element.

The French baritone Gabriel Bacquier.

BAILEY, NORMAN

(Birmingham 1933)
British baritone. He began his studies of music in Rhodesia and completed his training in Vienna. His early career centered on opera houses in Austria and Germany. He joined the Sadler's Wells company in London and in 1968 sang his best Wagner role, Hans Sachs in *Die Meistersinger von Nürnberg*. It is as an authoritative interpreter of Wagner that Bailey won acclaim at Bayreuth and in the leading international opera houses, his most admired Wagner roles being Wotan and Amfortas. In addition to Wagner, Bailey's repertoire also includes operas by Mozart (*Le nozze di Figaro*), Prokofiev (*War and Peace*) and Britten (*Peter Grimes*).

BAKER, DAME JANET

(Hatfield, Yorkshire 1933)
British mezzo-soprano. Dame Janet studied singing with Helene Isepp in London. In 1956 she won the Kathleen Ferrier Competition and made her debut in Smetana's opera *Tajemství* (The Secret) with the Oxford Opera Club. Her vast repertoire was principally of works for concert performance, but she also showed herself to the very best account in operas by Purcell (*Dido and Aeneas*), Handel (*Giulio Cesare in Egitto* and *Ariodante*), Berlioz (*Les Troyens* and *Béatrice et Benédict*) and Mozart (*Così fan tutte*), and others by Britten. She gave her farewell stage performances in 1982 in Donizetti's *Maria Stuarda* and Gluck's *Orfeo ed Euridice* at the Glyndebourne Festival.

BALÁZS, BÉLA

(Szeged 1884–Budapest 1949)
Hungarian cinema theoretician, film scriptwriter and librettist. After taking a degree in philosophy, Balázs lived for many years in Austria, where his career concentrated mainly on cinematography. From 1932 he lived in Russia and did not return to Hungary until 1945. For the theater, he wrote two libretti for Béla Bartók, one for the ballet *A fából faragott királyfi* (The Wooden Prince), 1917, and one for the opera *A kékszakállú herceg várá* (Duke Bluebeard's Castle), 1918.

BALFE, MICHAEL WILLIAM

(Dublin 1808–Rowney Abbey, Hertfordshire 1870)
Irish composer and baritone. He studied first in Ireland and then in London, where he made his singing debut. In 1823 he was in Italy, where he composed his first opera, *I rivali di se stessi*. He returned to England in 1835 and embarked on a career as a composer, establishing himself with a work that is regarded as his most famous opera, *The Bohemian Girl*. Balfe had an effortless gift for melody and was admired for the elegance of his compositions, which was appreciated by singers and audience alike. His ballads above all brought him great popularity.

BALLAD OF BABY DOE, THE

Folk opera in two acts by Douglas Moore (1893–1969), to a libretto by John Latouche. First performance: Central City, Colorado, Central City Opera, 7 July 1956.

The action takes place in Leadville and Denver between 1880 and 1893. Horace Tabor (baritone), the wealthiest man in Colorado, is on his way home from an evening at the theater when he meets the young Elizabeth Doe (soprano), a miner's wife known to everyone as Baby Doe. What seems at the outset to be no more than a flirtation between the two turns into a real love affair. A scandal breaks out when Tabor divorces his wife Regina (mezzo-soprano) to marry Baby Doe. The years pass. Tabor, who refused to listen to the advice of Regina when she warned him of an impending crisis in the economy, has now lost everything. Worn out by poverty and illness, he dies in the arms of Baby Doe, who has loved him to the end. The opera's final scene follows Baby Doe, now old and poor, making her way one icy winter's day to Tabor's mine, where she dies of exposure.

Inspired by real events in the lives of Horace Tabor and Baby Doe, Moore's opera was commissioned by the Central City Opera Association and performed with great success in 1956. After the premiere, Moore and

Latouche worked to revise the score (a scene in Act II and an aria for Baby Doe). This version of the opera was performed on 3 April 1958 at the City Center in New York. In the opera's New York performances, the role of Baby Doe was sung by Beverly Sills.

BALLO IN MASCHERA, UN

(A Masked Ball)

Opera in three acts by Giuseppe Verdi (1813–1901), to a libretto by Antonio Somma, based on Gustave III, ou le bal masqué *by Eugène Scribe. First performance: Rome, Teatro Apollo, 17 February 1859.*

The action takes place in Boston at the end of the seventeenth century. Two conspirators, Samuel (bass) and Tom (bass), are plotting against Riccardo di Warwick (tenor), governor of Massachusetts. Riccardo is warned to be on his guard by Renato (baritone), his secretary and the husband of Amelia, with whom Riccardo is in love. The governor invites Renato and the courtiers to visit Ulrica (contralto), a woman accused of witchcraft. In secret, Amelia also comes to see the witch and asks her for a potion which will free her from a love she is afraid of. Ulrica advises her to make use of a herb which can be gathered at midnight near the scaffold. Riccardo overhears this conversation. Ulrica then tells him what the future holds: he will die by a friend's hand. Riccardo catches up with Amelia in the field by the scaffold. They reveal their feelings for one another. Renato arrives, and Amelia covers her face with a veil. A number of conspirators are nearby, ready to assassinate Riccardo. He manages to escape just in time, before the conspirators appear. After recognizing Renato, they ask him who the veiled lady is. His refusal to tell them is about to lead to armed combat, and to prevent this Amelia reveals her identity. The conspirators laugh, but Renato is in despair: realizing Amelia has betrayed him with Riccardo, Renato joins the conspirators to have his revenge. Fate has ruled that he will be the one to kill Riccardo while the masked party is being held at the governor's mansion. During the ball, Amelia pleads with Riccardo to get away from the party. He refuses, and during the festivities Renato fatally wounds Riccardo. The governor frees Amelia from blame, pardons the conspirators and then dies, to the grief of those around him.

Scribe's original play had as its leading character not the governor of an American state but King Gustav III of Sweden, and this was also the case with the opera's original libretto. The intervention of the censor, who would not allow a regicide on stage, meant that the plot had to be altered. Verdi tried to defend his work, but in the end he agreed to transfer the action of *Un ballo in maschera* from Stockholm to Boston and replace the king with a governor. The composer kept very carefully to the drafting of the libretto so as to achieve the same level of elegance and noble feelings even in tragedy and passion.

BALSLEV, LISBETH

(Åbernå 1945)

Danish soprano. She studied at the Opera Academy of the Royal Theater, Copenhagen, where in 1976 she made her debut in Borodin's opera *Knyaz Igor*, singing the role of Yaroslavna. Balslev went on to appear at the leading German opera houses (Hamburg, Dresden, Berlin, Stuttgart and Bayreuth) and established herself as a Wagner performer; her Senta in Wagner's *Der fliegende Holländer* (The Flying Dutchman) brought her international fame, displaying her remarkable stage personality and musical sensitivity.

BALTSA, AGNES

(Lefkas 1944)

Greek mezzo-soprano. She studied in Athens and later in Munich and Frankfurt, where she made her debut as Cherubino in Mozart's *Le nozze di Figaro* (in 1968). After singing in a number of opera houses, including Salzburg (from 1970) and Berlin (from 1973), she started out on a busy international singing and recording career, building up a very large repertoire. Baltsa's high level of professionalism, technical approach, musicianship and interpretative skills, compensates for the limitations of her voice in which the range is more like a soprano, but sounding rather empty in the middle register. She therefore lacks the characteristic timbre of the authentic mezzo-soprano voice.

BÄR, OLAF

(Dresden 1957)

German baritone. After studying music at the Musikhochschule in Dresden and taking part

Left: Luciano Pavarotti in Verdi's *Un ballo in maschera.*

Top: A costume for Riccardo in *Un ballo in maschera.*

Above: The Greek mezzo-soprano Agnes Baltsa.

OPERA AND CENSORSHIP

Like many other expressions of intellectual life and forms of art and entertainment, opera has not escaped from censorship, with the guardians of public order taking a particularly keen interest. It was generally the plots of operas which could not be allowed to offend against prevailing moral, religious and political principles. Verdi was forced to change the settings and characters in *Un ballo in maschera*, because the assassination of a king (Gustavus III) in a European country (Sweden) at a sensitive period in history, 1792 and the French Revolution, was politically dangerous material to represent on stage. As if that was not enough, the censor took a harsh view of any portrayal of moral infringements, such as the adultery of a noblewoman with a monarch, which put into question a concept as sacred as that of marital fidelity, showing the life of a king and his court as immoral. Verdi made strenuous efforts to save his opera and managed to retain the dramatic structure of the plot by turning the figure of King Gustavus III into that of Riccardo, Governor of Boston (making the background a transatlantic one and setting the work a century earlier than the original story) and having him assassinated by a dagger and not the fire-arm featured in Eugène Scribe's play *Gustave III* on which the libretto had been based. The case of *Un ballo in maschera* was undoubtedly the most difficult battle a composer has ever had to wage against censorship, although Verdi clashed with the censor again on a number of other occasions, over works including *Rigoletto*, *La traviata* and *Stiffelio*.

Donizetti had his own battles to fight in this respect, as on the occasion of the Milan premiere of his *Lucrezia Borgia* (1833), when a Milanese family claiming to be descended from the Borgias exerted so much pressure on the Austrian censor that there was a risk of the curtain being brought down on the performance. The censor also intervened in the case of another Donizetti opera, *Poliuto*: a personal decree from the King of Naples himself categorically prohibited the staging of this opera scheduled for production in August 1838, because the plot of *Poliuto* concerned the life of a Christian saint. The same thing happened with *La favorita* (1840): the story of a monk who falls in love with the King's mistress was judged to be absolutely immoral, and consequently, after the Paris premiere, *Poliuto* was transformed and separately re-titled *Elda*, *Daila* and *Riccardo e Matilde*. Censorship was very much in evidence in a number of countries: in England, for instance, operas like Rossini's *Mosè* or Verdi's *Nabucco* were performed with different characters and settings, because the censor would not allow operas about religious subjects. This was the case with Saint Saëns' *Samson et Dalila* which was not seen on the London stage until 1909. Massenet's *Héreodiade* and Strauss's *Salome* also fell foul of British censorship, and several alterations had to be made to *Salome* before it could be produced in London in 1910.

Right: A scene from *Salome* by Strauss.

Above: *Samson et Dalila* by Saint-Saëns.

in numerous singing competitions, Bär made his Covent Garden debut in 1985. This marked the beginning of an international career which has included appearances at the leading European opera houses and festivals: Aix-en-Provence (1986–88), Vienna Staatsoper (1986) and La Scala, Milan (1986). An exquisite Mozart performer (he has sung Papageno and Guglielmo), Bär has also proved himself to be an elegant *Lieder* singer.

BARBAUX, CHRISTINE
(Saint-Mandé 1955)
French soprano. After completing her music studies, Barbaux won the Paris Conservatoire opera prize (1977). This gave her the chance to make her debut as Despina (in Mozart's *Così fan tutte*) at the Opéra du Rhin, where she sang for a three-year period. In 1978 she appeared for the first time at the Opéra in Paris in the role of Barbarina (in Mozart's *Le nozze di Figaro*), a part she went on to sing in Vienna and Salzburg with von Karajan as conductor. Barbaux is a light operatic soprano whose repertoire ranges from Mozart (*Lucio Silla*, *La clemenza di Tito*), to Verdi (*Rigoletto*), Thomas (*Hamlet*), Strauss (*Der Rosenkavalier*) and Poulenc, in whose *Les dialogues des Carmélites* she sang the role of Blanche de la Force in 1989.

BARBER, SAMUEL
(West Chester, Pennsylvania 1910–New York 1981)
American composer. He studied at the Curtis Institute in Philadelphia. In 1935 he won a Pulitzer prize and, a year later, the American Academy's Prix de Rome, which enabled him to travel to Europe for a lengthy stay. Barber did not turn to opera until 1958, when he composed *Vanessa*, to a libretto by Giancarlo Menotti, produced at the Metropolitan Opera, New York. This was followed by *A Hand of Bridge* (Spoleto, 1959) and *Antony and Cleopatra*, which opened the new Metropolitan Opera at the Lincoln Center in 1966. Barber was initially accused of being a post-Romantic conservative, and it was only in the years after his death that his music was again appreciated for its melodic richness and expressive theatrical spontaneity.

BARBIER, JULES
(Paris 1825–1901)
French librettist and dramatist. After initially working (1847) as a playwright, Barbier established himself as an opera librettist. Working with Michel Carré, he became one of the most sought-after and admired writers in this field. Temporary director of the Opéra-Comique (1887), he was a friend and favourite colleague of Charles Gounod, for whom he wrote numerous libretti, including those for *Faust* (1859), *La reine de Saba* (The Queen of Sheba, 1862), and *Roméo et Juliette* (1867). Barbier also wrote the libretti for Meyerbeer's *Dinorah* (1859), for two operas by Ambroise Thomas (*Mignon*, 1866, and *Hamlet*, 1868) and for Offenbach's *Les contes d'Hoffmann* (Tales of Hoffman), 1881.

BARBIER VON BAGDAD, DER
(The Barber of Baghdad)
Opera in two acts by Peter Cornelius (1824–1874), to the composer's own libretto, taken from The Thousand and One Nights, *based on a plot already used in two* Singspiele *by G. André and J. Hattasch. First performance: Weimar, Hoftheater, 15 December 1858.*

Young Nureddin (tenor) is at last able to meet his beloved Margiana (soprano), daughter of the Cadi, a Muslim judge. He summons a barber to the house to cut his hair, and the barber, the garrulous Abul Hassan (bass), entertains Nureddin with his chatter. Finally Nureddin manages to get into his beloved's house. Abul secretly follows him. The unexpected return of the Cadi (tenor) interrupts the lovers' tryst, and Nureddin manages to hide in a chest. Abul fears the worst for the young man and fetches the Caliph (baritone). Nureddin is discovered in the chest, and the Cadi has to give in to pressure from the Caliph and give his consent to the marriage of Margiana and Nureddin. The barber enters the Caliph's service, where he will be able to amuse his new master with his fantastic stories.

Peter Cornelius was unable to enjoy success with this, his first, opera: despite support from Liszt, *Der Barbier von Bagdad* was taken off after the first performance as a result of various intrigues and boycotts. It was only from 1884 onwards, after the opera was performed in Karlsruhe (with a new orchestration by Felix Mottl), that the opera became very popular. *Der Barbier von Bagdad* is full of vigour and is often called the best German comic opera after *Die Meistersinger von Nürnberg*. One of its most famous passages is the *intermezzo*, based on the cry of the muezzin.

BARBIERE DI SIVIGLIA, IL, O LA PRECAUZIONE INUTILE
(The Barber of Seville, or Useless Precaution)
Comic opera in two acts by Giovanni Paisiello (1740–1816), to a libretto by Petrosellini from the comedy of the same name by Beaumarchais. First performance: St. Petersburg, Imperial Theater, 26 September 1782.

In a square in Seville, Count Almaviva (tenor), disguised as Lindoro, confides in Figaro (baritone) that he is in love with Rosina (soprano) but has not succeeded in speaking to her because the young woman is constantly under the watchful eye of Don Bartolo (bass). Figaro, who is Bartolo's barber, tells the Count that the guardian intends to marry his ward. Bartolo, warned by Don Basilio (bass), Rosina's music teacher, does his utmost to discover if Rosina has written a letter and, if so, to whom she has sent it. Enter Almaviva, disguised as a drunken soldier, on the advice of Figaro (who has delivered Rosina's letter to him). At the end of a furious argument, the old man manages to drive away the fake soldier. Almaviva, now dressed as a music teacher and pupil of Basilio, returns to Bartolo's house. Once again the guardian discovers the fraud and chases his intruder away. But Figaro has succeeded in obtaining the key to the balcony. Don Bartolo leaves the house to summon the police and have Lindoro arrested. On his return, however, he finds that Rosina has already married Lindoro (who has now revealed his true identity, and had managed to enter the house with Figaro through a window). The ceremony was performed by the same notary he himself had sent for in order to marry his ward.

A scene from *Il barbiere di Siviglia* by Rossini.

Composed during the period of the composer's sojourn at the court of St. Petersburg (1776–84), this opera enjoyed great popularity, thanks to the elegance of the score and its gentle melodies. Petrosellini's libretto, although faithful to the Beaumarchais play, failed to match its wit and spontaneity, however, and after the opera's initial success, it was forgotten, superseded by Rossini's more brilliant opera (1816) on the same subject.

BARBIERE DI SIVIGLIA, IL
(The Barber of Seville)
Melodramma buffo *in two acts by Gioachino Rossini (1792–1868), to a libretto by Cesare Sterbini, from the play by Beaumarchais. First performance: Rome, Teatro di Torre Argentina, 20 February 1816.*

ACT I. The action takes place in Seville. Count Almaviva (tenor) is in love with Rosina (contralto or soprano), the ward of Don Bartolo (*buffo* bass) who is always kept under strict supervision. In order to get close to Rosina, the Count calls on Figaro (baritone), a local barber, who gives Almaviva the idea of gaining entry to Bartolo's house disguised as a soldier in need of lodgings. But Don Bartolo, who secretly hopes for the hand but most of all for the rich dowry of Rosina, has heard from Don Basilio (bass), an impoverished music teacher, that the Count has arrived in Seville. When Almaviva turns up disguised as a soldier on his doorstep, Bartolo reveals his suspicions at once. Meanwhile the Count, on a pretext, has succeeded in speaking, if only fleetingly, to Rosina. To conceal his noble rank, he tells her his name is Lindoro. After a series of amusing situations, which end in pandemonium, the police arrive, and this puts a stop to Almaviva's bid. ACT II. Being the shrewd man he is, Figaro immediately comes up with another stylish plan for approaching Rosina. The Count will gain entry to Don Bartolo's house that very evening, this time dressed as a music teacher, deputizing for Don Basilio who, he will explain, is indisposed. The ploy appears to have worked, but Don Basilio's arrival, together with an indiscreet reference which the Count happens to let slip, lead once again to the deception being uncovered, and Don Bartolo, in a rage, turns everyone out of the house. Almaviva and Figaro, however, are undaunted: during a storm, they use a staircase to gain access to Don Bartolo's house and carry Rosina off. The young woman has, in the meantime, been duped by her guardian into thinking that Lindoro is a go-between for Count Almaviva. As a result, Rosina refuses to follow the Count, but the misunderstanding is cleared up immediately, and a happy ending is in sight. When the notary arrives, having been summoned by Don Bartolo to perform a hurried wedding for himself and Rosina, he is prevailed upon by Figaro to marry Rosina to Almaviva instead. Don Bartolo can only put on a brave face at the outcome, and console himself with the thought that he need not provide Rosina with a dowry.

Cesare Sterbini wrote the libretto for *Il barbiere di Siviglia* in just 11 days, from 18 to 29 January 1816, and within 20 days Rossini had completed the opera. It is still incredible to think that he was able to create one of the greatest operatic masterpieces ever in such a short space of time. At its premiere in Rome, the opera was a flop; this unfavourable reception for the work had, however, been carefully organized by Paisiello supporters, Paisiello having written an opera based on the same story 16 years before. The unsuccessful premiere was an isolated incident, because in subsequent performances the opera scored the triumph it deserved. The qualities of the opera stem from Rossini's consistently strong composition, the finesse of the instrumental writing and the constant rhythm of the orchestra in support of the vocal line throughout. But then it is impossible not to be swept up by the joyful atmosphere of the work and its irrepressible comedy, guaranteed not least by the subtle and realistic characterization of the individual roles. The role of *Rosina*, written for a *coloratura* muzzo-sporano, has often been performed (with appropriate revisions) by a high *coloratura* soprano.

A popular nineteenth-century print showing a scene from *Il barbiere di Siviglia*.

BARBIROLLI, SIR JOHN
(London 1899–1970)
British conductor of Italian and French parentage. He studied in London, beginning his career as a cellist. In 1927 he conducted his first opera performances (*Aida* and *Madama Butterfly*) at the British National Opera. After his debut at Covent Garden in 1928 (in *Madama Butterfly* and *La bohème*), Barbirolli conducted the leading orchestras of the day, taking in the main European centers, such as Vienna and Rome. It was above all the symphonic repertoire to which Barbirolli devoted his energies most often, with particular success; in the field of opera, as his best-loved works indicate (*La bohème* and *Madama Butterfly*), Barbirolli was a conductor who paid special attention to the relationship between vocal expression and symphonic orchestral colour, one which came happily to fruition in the work of Puccini.

BARENBOIM, DANIEL
(Buenos Aires 1942)
Argentinian pianist and conductor, who later took Israeli citizenship. He studied at the Accademia Nazionale di Santa Cecilia in Rome and with Edwin Fischer and Nadia Boulanger. In 1955 he made his debut in Paris as a pianist, and a busy concert career followed. Barenboim began conducting in 1962 with the English Chamber Orchestra, and went on to conduct some of the most famous international orchestras, including the Berlin Philharmonic, the New York Philharmonic, the Orchestre de Paris (1986–89) and from 1991, succeeding Sir Georg Solti, the Chicago Symphony Orchestra. In 1973 he made his first appearance as a conductor of opera in Mozart's *Don Giovanni* at the Edinburgh Festival. Barenboim has conducted in numerous international opera houses and festivals, including Bayreuth (since 1981). As an opera conductor, he clearly reveals his earlier experience with symphony orchestras, showing an elegant lyrical sensitivity in directing the instrumental accompaniment of singers, while lacking somewhat in vivacity and choice of tempi.

BARSTOW, JOSEPHINE
(Sheffield 1940)
British soprano. She studied in Birmingham and London (at the London Opera Center). In

1967 she made her debut at Sadler's Wells in London as Cherubino in Mozart's *Le nozze di Figaro*. Her first important role was Denise in Tippett's *The Knot Garden* (1970). Barstow has a remarkably strong stage and vocal personality, which has led to distinguished performances in roles whose dramatic content is substantial. Among these are Emilia Marty (Janáček's *The Makropoulos Affair*), the lead in Strauss's *Salome* and Lady Macbeth in Verdi's *Macbeth*. She has also made important contributions to performances of works by contemporary composers like Sir Michael Tippett, Hans Werner Henze and Krzysztof Penderecki.

BARTERED BRIDE, THE

See *Prodana Nevešta*

BARTÓK, BÉLA

(Nagyszentmiklós, Transylvania 1881–New York 1945)

Hungarian composer. His prolific output includes only one opera, an early work in one act, *A kékszakállú herceg vára* (Duke Bluebeard's Castle, 1911) first performed in Budapest in 1918. The extraordinary dramatic power, richness and originality of the score, in which the character of Bluebeard is framed in a gloomy and painful vision, make this one of Bartók's most famous works, as well as one of the most important of the twentieth century.

BARTOLETTI, BRUNO

(Sesto Fiorentino 1926)

Italian conductor. He studied in Florence, and made his first appearance in 1953 in Verdi's *Rigoletto* at the Teatro Comunale, where he subsequently conducted regularly, becoming permanent conductor of the Maggio Musicale Fiorentino orchestra from 1957 to 1964. A large part of his conducting life, which has included engagements in the leading international music venues, is spent in Florence and Chicago, where since 1964 he has been Principal Director. Bartoletti's great professionalism and interpretative rigour have made him one of the most admired opera conductors, not only of the Italian repertoire but also beyond, and above all from the twentieth century: Berg, Britten, Hindemith and Prokofiev.

BARTOLI, CECILIA

(Rome 1966)

Italian mezzo-soprano. She completed her singing studies at the Accademia di Santa Cecilia in Rome and, while still a student, took the minor role of the Shepherd Boy in Puccini's *Tosca* at the Teatro dell'Opera in Rome. After impressing the judges in a singing competition organized by RAI, the Italian broadcasting network, she made her debut in 1987 at the Teatro Filarmonico in Verona in Ciampi's *Bertoldo, Bertoldino e Cacasenno*. In the same year, Bartoli sang the role of Rosina in Rossini's *Il barbiere di Siviglia*, a performance which secured her reputation and took her to other Italian and foreign opera houses (Modena, Cologne, etc.). An exquisite interpreter of Rossini roles, she has since sung in his *La pietra del paragone* in Catania, 1988, *La scala di seta* in Pesaro, 1988, *Le Comte Ory* at La Scala, Milan, 1991 and *La Cenerentola* in Bologna, 1992. As well as Rossini, Bartoli has appeared in Mozart (*Le nozze di Figaro*, Zurich, 1989; *Lucio Silla*, Konzerthaus, Vienna, 1989; and *Così fan tutte*, Naples, 1990 and Florence, 1991). Bartoli's voice possesses an authentic mezzo-soprano timbre (though not very large in volume), musicianship, excellent skills in *coloratura* singing, and stage presence, and she is currently establishing herself both internationally and in the recording studio.

BASSARIDS, THE

(Die Bassariden)

Opera seria *in one act (with an* intermezzo*) by Hans Werner Henze (b. 1926), to a libretto by W. H. Auden and Chester Kallman from* The Bacchae *by Euripides. First performance: Salzburg Festival, 6 August 1966.*

Pentheus (baritone), King of Thebes, announces the end of the worship of Semele, who had a son by Zeus. The King extinguishes the flame on the altar to the goddess and rules that anyone who dares to rekindle it will be put to death. The same penalty will apply to anyone caught worshipping Dionysus. Pentheus, who

Left: The Hungarian composer Béla Bartók.

Above: The Italian mezzo-soprano Cecilia Bartoli.

declares that for him there is only one, universal god, Truth, has the worshippers of Dionysus arrested, among them his own mother Agave (mezzo-soprano). Pentheus attempts to penetrate the world of the Dionysus worshippers and goes to Mount Cythaeron to witness their rites. But he is surrounded and killed by a group of Maenads, including his mother, Agave. When she realizes that under the god's influence she has killed her own son, she is overcome with despair and pleads for death. Dionysus (tenor) appears and, while Thebes burns, he orders Agave and her whole family into eternal exile. The opera ends with the chorus worshipping the statues of Dionysus and his mother, Semele, now transformed into a goddess, Thyone.

Hans Werner Henze, a member of the "historical" avant-garde of contemporary music, has seen in the symbolism of this tragedy a chance to develop his own dramatic and operatic ideas. The result is a grandiose opera, in which the philosophical tension between the rational and the irrational (represented by Pentheus and Dionysus) is expressed through music rich in contrasting tone-colours.

BASSI, CALISTO

(Abbiategrasso, 1800–c. 1860)

Italian librettist and translator. Born into a theatrical family, he inherited from them a great love for the theater. He lived in Milan, where he worked as a poet and stage director at La Scala. He had a good knowledge of French and worked mainly on translations of French operas and operas which had been written by Italian composers in France. Bassi translated Auber's *La muette de Portici* (The Dumb Girl of Portici), Meyerbeer's *Le prophète* and *Robert le diable*, Rossini's *Le siège de Corinthe* (The Siege of Corinth), *Moïse et Pharaon* (Moses and Pharaoh, the enlarged, revised version of *Mosè in Egitto*) and *Guillaume Tell* (William Tell), as well as Donizetti's *La fille du régiment*, *La favorite* and *Les martyres*.

BASTIEN UND BASTIENNE

Singspiel *in one act by Wolfgang Amadeus Mozart (1756–1791), to a libretto by Friedrich Wilhelm Weiskern, from* Le devin du village *by Jean-Jacques Rousseau. First performance: Vienna, in the garden of Dr Anton Mesmer's house, September–October 1768.*

There are only three characters in this opera, the two lovers and a wise old shepherd, Colas (bass). Bastienne (soprano), unhappy because of the fickleness of Bastien (tenor), turns to Colas for reassurance and advice. The shepherd persuades her to feign indifference. When Bastien also turns to Colas for advice, the old man makes Bastienne appear by magic, and the two lovers are reconciled.

Written by Mozart when he was 12 years old, this short opera provided him with one of his first encounters with Viennese high society. It was commissioned by Dr Mesmer, who arranged for *Bastien und Bastienne* to be performed in the garden of his house, a meeting place for the elite of Vienna. The opera consists of simple, graceful arias and duets in *Lied* form, but there are already signs of Mozart's remarkable confidence in the way he handles the small orchestra (strings, two oboes or flutes and two horns) and in the sense of theater.

A scene from *Bastien und Bastienne.*

BASTIN, JULES

(Brussels 1933)

Belgian bass. After studying at the Brussels Conservatoire, Bastin launched his opera career in 1964 at the Liège Opera and the Théâtre de la Monnaie in Brussels, receiving his earliest recognition for performances of French and Italian opera. He has sung in the leading opera houses and concert halls of Europe and took part in the first complete performance of Berg's *Lulu*, at the Paris Opéra in 1979. Bastin is especially noted for his remarkable interpretative skills, which have won him acclaim as a brilliant performer of comic and character roles.

BATTAGLIA DI LEGNANO, LA

(The Battle of Legnano)

Tragic opera in four acts by Giuseppe Verdi (1813–1901), to a libretto by Salvatore Cammarano. First performance: Rome, Teatro di Torre Argentina, 27 January 1849.

The action takes place in Milan and Como, in 1176. The city of Milan is under attack by the troops of Federico Barbarossa (bass). Rolando (baritone), one of the defenders of the city, is reunited with Arrigo (tenor), whom he thought had been killed in battle. Arrigo also sees Lidia (soprano) again: she had once been betrothed to him, but her father had compelled her to marry Rolando. Arrigo places himself in the hands of fate and joins up with the Knights of Death, greatly upsetting Lidia, who writes him a letter to dissuade him. Rolando, who is preparing to go into battle, is approached by Marcovaldo (bass), a German prisoner who is also in love with Lidia. Marcovaldo gives Rolando Lidia's letter. Rolando's fury gives way to jealousy: he comes upon Lidia and Arrigo talking together and shuts Arrigo up in a tower, thus preventing him from assembling with the Knights of Death and bringing dishonour on him. In despair, Arrigo jumps out of the window and plunges into the river below. While Lidia and the women of Milan are praying for the combatants, news arrives that Barbarossa has been defeated. The Lombards return home in triumph, bringing with them Arrigo, who is dying. The young man makes his peace with Lidia and then dies, clasping the battle flag to his chest.

La battaglia di Legnano is regarded as an opera Verdi wrote during a period when he was moving towards more structured and psychologically more complex operas, such as *Luisa Miller*, which was to follow. *La battaglia di Legnano* is a solid and balanced opera, although the subject may have been better served by more bombastic and highly charged music. The work was successful, but, as was often the case with Verdi's work, the censor required alterations to places and characters.

BATTLE, KATHLEEN

(Portsmouth, Ohio 1948)

American soprano. After studying Music at the University of Cincinnati, she made her debut in 1972 at the Spoleto Festival in Brahms' *Ein Deutsches Requiem*, conducted by Thomas Schippers. In 1977 Battle made her first appearance at the Metropolitan Opera House, New York, singing the role of the Young Shepherd in Wagner's *Tannhäuser*. Her artistic career has been linked to the Metropolitan to this day, with further engagements at the Vienna Staatsoper, Covent Garden (since 1985), and the Paris Opéra (1984). As a light operatic soprano, Battle is an elegant Mozart performer (Zerlina, Susanna, Blondchen). She has also won special praise for her Rosina (Rossini's *Il barbiere di Siviglia*) and her Adina (Donizetti's *L'elisir d'amore*), which illustrate her refined and varied phrasing, good control of the voice and flowing delivery.

BEATRICE DI TENDA

Tragic opera in two acts by Vincenzo Bellini (1801–1835), to a libretto by Felice Romani. First performance: Venice, Teatro La Fenice, 16 March 1833.

The scene is the Castle of Binasco, in the year 1418. Filippo Maria Visconti (baritone) has grown tired of his wife Beatrice di Tenda (soprano), widow of the general Facino Cane. Filippo is now in love with Agnese del Maino (mezzo-soprano), a lady-in-waiting to Beatrice. Orombello, Count of Ventimiglia (tenor), reveals to Agnese that he is secretly in love with Beatrice; Agnese, who loves Orombello, is shocked by this confession and decides to have her revenge. She obtains some compromising letters, which are in Beatrice's possession, and offers them to Filippo as the evidence he needs to accuse Beatrice of adultery, evidence reinforced by the discovery of his wife in secret conversation with Orombello. Beatrice and Orombello are arrested and brought before a tribunal. Beatrice pleads her innocence. But Orombello, under torture, has given in, and has accused both himself and Beatrice, though in fact neither are guilty. Beatrice and Orombello are sentenced to death. As Beatrice approaches the scaffold, she has the strength to pardon Agnese, who has now admitted to her mistress the wrong she had done her.

LA
FOLLE JOURNEE,
OU LE
MARIAGE
DE FIGARO,
COMEDIE EN CINQ ACTES
ET EN PROSE.
PAR MR. CARON DE BEAUMARCHAIS.
Représentée, pour la premiere fois, à Paris par les Comédiens ordinaires du Roi, le 27 Avril 1784.
À PARIS, chez les Libraires associés.
M. DCC. LXXXV.

While Agnese faints to the ground, Beatrice proudly and courageously climbs on to the scaffold and the chorus expresses sorrow.

Bellini wrote *Beatrice di Tenda* after a long rest period in the wake of the success of *Norma* in 1831. The opera was composed in haste, and as a result the first performance, at the Teatro La Fenice in Venice, was a fiasco. The negative public response to the opera caused a serious rift between Bellini and his librettist Romani, each blaming the other for the failure, and this quarrel ended their collaboration, which had produced all of Bellini's best operas. *Beatrice di Tenda* subsequently won public acclaim and was performed repeatedly in Italy and elsewhere, though nowadays it is revived only occasionally.

BÉATRICE ET BÉNÉDICT

Opera in two acts by Hector Berlioz (1803–1869), to the composer's own libretto, taken from Shakespeare's Much Ado About Nothing. *First performance: Baden-Baden, Theater der Stadt, 9 August 1862.*

The scene is Messina, Sicily. The townspeople are celebrating the arrival of Don Pedro of Aragon (bass). Héro (soprano), daughter of the governor of Messina, has a special reason for happiness that Don Pedro has come: she will now be able to see her beloved Claudio (baritone), a young officer in the Spanish general's retinue. But while Héro is gladdened by her love, the situation for her cousin Béatrice (mezzo-soprano) is very different: she is distressed by the changeable attitude towards her of Bénédict (tenor), to whom Béatrice is attracted in spite of herself, although marriage is something he shuns. Don Pedro and Claudio try in vain to persuade him, praising the advantages of the married state. The celebrations in Don Pedro's honour are underway at the governor's residence. Béatrice is in a state of agitation; she has had a dream in which she saw Bénédict setting out for battle and falling on the field. Anxious that this vision, which has already made her suffer enough, should not come true, Béatrice decides to return Bénédict's affection. Love triumphs in the end, and the final scene is a predictably happy one.

Béatrice et Bénédict, a comic opera close in style to the Italian repertoire, was Berlioz's last work. It immediately scored an outstanding success, although it never became part of the French repertoire, having to wait until 1890 for its first performance in France.

BEAUMARCHAIS, PIERRE AUGUSTIN CARON DE

(Paris 1732–1799)

French dramatist and amateur composer. Beaumarchais was the son of a clockmaker

Above: Title page of the score for *Le mariage de Figaro* by Beaumarchais.

Left: The American soprano Kathleen Battle.

and initially followed in his father's footsteps, subsequently being appointed as clockmaker to the court of Louis XV. He was a self-taught student of guitar, flute and harp, and composed works for these instruments. He also took lessons from the composers Piccinni and Grétry, counting as his friends other composers of the day such as Sacchini, Martini and Salieri. Beaumarchais also taught the harp to the king's daughters. Despite all these varied activities, his fame rests on his writing for the theater, in particular the trilogy which is regarded as his masterpiece: *Le barbier de Séville, ou La précaution inutile* (1775), *Le mariage de Figaro, ou La folle journée* (1784) and *La mère coupable* (1792). For *Le barbier de Séville* and *Le mariage de Figaro*, he also composed some incidental music. He provided the libretto for *Tarare* (1787), an opera by Salieri.

BECHI, GINO

(Florence 1913)

Italian baritone. He studied singing with Raul Frazzi and Di Giorgi, making his debut in 1936 in Empoli as Germont in Verdi's *La traviata*. Thanks to the exceptional qualities of his voice, (an incredible range, the highest notes sung with rare power, with the timbre of voice equally remarkable in the middle register), Bechi quickly became one of the most famous Italian baritones and sang in the world's leading opera houses: La Scala, Rome, Covent Garden, etc. Bechi performed much of the Verdi repertoire (including *Aida* and *Un ballo in maschera*), and also Leoncavallo's *I pagliacci*, Giordano's *Andrea Chénier* and Mascagni's *Cavalleria rusticana*. He retired from the stage in 1965.

BECHT, HERMANN

(Karlsruhe 1939)

German baritone. He studied in Karlsruhe and Saarbrücken with Josef Greindl. He began his artistic career in the opera houses of Braunschweig and Wiesbaden and appeared at the Deutsche Oper am Rhein from 1974. In 1979 he sang at the Bayreuth Festival for the first of many performances there, immediately proving himself as an impressive interpreter of Wagner. Becht is especially admired for his Alberich in Wagner's *Ring* in the famous version of the work staged by Patrice Chéreau and conducted by Pierre Boulez.

BEECHAM, SIR THOMAS

(St. Helens, Lancashire 1879–London 1961)

British conductor. Beecham did not receive a conventional musical education: after studying at Oxford, he travelled extensively abroad. From 1902 to 1904 he conducted a small touring opera company. In 1910 he gained his first important experience of opera when he conducted the British premiere of Richard Strauss's *Elektra* at Covent Garden. Beecham then introduced British audiences to further Strauss operas: *Salome*, *Ariadne auf Naxos* and *Der Rosenkavalier*. He made a further significant contribution to opera by conducting early performances of *A Village Romeo and Juliet* (1910) and *Irmelin* (1953), both by Frederick Delius. During the Second World War he conducted at the Metropolitan Opera in New York. Beecham was one of the most distinguished British conductors and appeared in all of the leading concert and opera venues in the United Kingdom. His performances were famous for their lively spirit, imagination and musical instinct.

A silhouette showing Ludwig van Beethoven at the piano.

BEESON, JACK

(Muncie, Indiana 1921)

American composer. Beeson studied at the Eastman School of Music in Rochester and completed his training by studying with Béla Bartók. His opera *Lizzie Borden* was commissioned by the Ford Foundation and performed at the New York City Opera in 1965. Other works composed by Beeson for the musical theater are *Jonah* (1950), *Hello Out There* (1954), *The Sweet Bye and Bye* (1957) and *Caption Jinks of the Horse Marines* (1975). Beeson's operas show the influence of the European operatic tradition, although their style also has elements typical of American music and theater. This is also true of the libretti, which habitually employ European literary subject-matter and ideas.

BEETHOVEN, LUDWIG VAN

(Bonn 1770–Vienna 1827)

German composer. Beethoven's vast musical output includes only one complete opera, *Fidelio*, which was commissioned by the Theater an der Wien. Under its original title, *Leonore*, it was performed in 1805 without success, and the following year a somewhat revised version was introduced, likewise to a poor reception. It was not until 1814 that a more extensive revision was put on stage, this time with happier results. In the course of his revisions, Beethoven wrote two additional *Leonore* overtures, finally providing the thematically different *Fidelio* overture, in use today.

BEGGAR'S OPERA, THE

Opera in three acts with music arranged and composed by John Christopher Pepusch (1667–1752) to a text by John Gay. First performance: London, Lincoln's Inn Fields, 29 January 1728.

In the opera's prologue, the Beggar, pretending to be the author of *The Beggar's Opera*, introduces the work and its characters: Captain Macheath (tenor), a well-known thief and libertine, has married Polly (soprano), daughter of the grasping moneylender Mr Peachum (bass). Peachum is worried by the fact that his new son-in-law, who knows too much about him already, is now going to be even closer to him. So he decides to report Macheath to the police and have him arrested. But Macheath knows how to look after himself, even in prison: Lucy (soprano), daughter of the jailer, Lockit (baritone), has been Macheath's mistress and now, after he promises to marry her, she helps him to escape. Further complaints lodged by other women, bribed by Peachum to do so, land Macheath back behind bars again. Now he will have to be put to death, scorned by all his mistresses and admirers. Enter the Beggar at the last minute to tell the condemned man that he has been granted a royal pardon and is free to go.

The Beggar's Opera is the first and most famous of the ballad-operas, a form of theater combining prose, verse and music. At its premiere, it was a triumphant success. Gay's idea was a comedy by beggars for beggars, satirizing the vogue for Italian opera in London and even though it has the air of a serious opera, the setting throughout is a den of thieves, prostitutes and criminals, so the language is loose and sometimes vulgar, laced with topical references. The music consists of adaptations of popular songs and pieces by other composers, skilfully rewritten by Pepusch.

BEHRENS, HILDEGARD

(Varel 1937)

German soprano. Behrens completed her musical studies in Freiburg, embarking on a singing career with the local opera company (1971–72) before moving on to Düsseldorf, where she sang some of the roles which made her famous, especially Marie in Berg's *Wozzeck* and Agathe in Weber's *Der Freischütz*. But it was in Strauss's *Salome* at the Salzburg Festival in 1977 with Herbert von Karajan conducting that Behrens finally attracted international attention. Her Brünnhilde in Wagner's *Ring* in Bayreuth (1983) and at the Metropolitan Opera House, New York, has confirmed Behrens' extraordinary musical and interpretative gifts as one of the greatest performers of Wagner, shown also in *Tannhäuser, Lohengrin, Der fliegende Holländer* (The Flying Dutchman) and *Tristan und Isolde*, and of Richard Strauss (*Ariadne auf Naxos, Die Frau ohne Schatten* and *Elektra*).

BELFAGOR

Comic opera in two acts (with a prologue and epilogue) by Ottorino Respighi (1879–1936), to a libretto by Claudio Guastalla. First performance: Milan, La Scala, 26 April 1923.

The demon Belfagor (baritone) has arrived on earth to find out if it is true that marriage leads men to perdition. He calls at the house of a chemist, Mirocleto (bass), and persuades the man to let him marry one of his daughters and give him a dowry of a hundred thousand ducats. He then turns up again at the house, this time dressed as the wealthy merchant Ipsilonne, and meets Mirocleto's three daughters, Candida, Fidelia and Maddalena (sopranos). Ipsilonne is attracted to Candida, but she loves and is already promised to Baldo (tenor), who is currently away on a journey. Candida marries Ipsilonne, but does not give herself to him, which makes the young demon so desperate that he falls in love with her while he is waiting. Then, when Candida hears that Baldo has come home, she escapes to be reunited with her beloved, and goes with him to seek help from the local priest. Belfagor—now disguised as a tramp—introduces himself to Baldo and, lying, tells him that Ipsilonne has abandoned Candida after completely satisfying his desire for her. Baldo flies into a rage and sends the fake tramp away, but now doubt has begun to assail him. Candida, in despair, prays to God that a miracle may occur to convince Baldo of her faithfulness to him, when the church bells start to ring of their own accord. Belfagor, having finally lost the contest, prepares to return to hell.

Respighi worked for a year drafting the score of *Belfagor* (1921–22), investing it with all his gifts of versatility: the fantastical is juxtaposed with the realistic, and its purely comical passages are set against the most exquisitely lyrical and sentimental ones. *Belfagor* is Respighi's most spontaneous opera, partly on the strength of the composer's excellent collaboration with the librettist Claudio Guastalla, with whose text his music is perfectly in harmony.

BELISARIO

Opera in three acts by Gaetano Donizetti (1797–1848), to a libretto by Salvatore Cammarano based on a number of different sources, principally Belisarius *by E. von Schenk.*

Antonina (soprano), wife of the general Belisario (baritone), harbours an unfounded grudge against her husband, whom she believes has killed one of their two children. The general's enemies take advantage of Antonina's anger against her husband and persuade her to lay before the Emperor Justinian false accusations of treason against Belisario. This she does, and Belisario is sentenced to be blinded and banished. Sightless and in exile, Belisario is comforted by his daughter Irene (mezzo-soprano). On his wanderings Belisario meets a young captain, Alamiro (tenor), who is marching on Byzantium at the head of an army of barbarian troops to avenge the outrage perpetrated against Belisario. Now Belisario recognizes Alamiro as the young son he had believed was dead. In the battle that follows, Belisario is fatally wounded and dies in the presence of Antonina, who has discovered the falsehood of the accusations and informed the Emperor. Then she dies of remorse and despair.

With *Belisario*, Donizetti returned to Venice after an absence of 17 years. The opera was warmly received but could never be counted among the composer's most successful works.

Top: Poster for *The Beggar's Opera* by John Christopher Pepusch.

Left: The German soprano Hildegard Behrens.

BELLINI, VINCENZO

(Catania 1801–Puteaux, Paris 1835)
Italian composer. He studied at the Conservatorio in Naples with Niccolò Zingarelli. His final piece of work there was the score of his first opera, *Adelson e Salvini* (1825), the success of which earned Bellini his first contract, to compose *Bianca e Fernando* (Naples, Teatro San Carlo, 1826). His first major success came in the following year with his opera *Il pirata* (Milan, La Scala), which marked the start of Bellini's important collaboration with the librettist Felice Romani. In 1829 Bellini wrote *La straniera* (Milan, La Scala) and *Zaira* (Parma, Teatro Ducale). The failure of *Zaira* prompted the composer to lift most of the music from that score and use it again in his next opera, *I Capuleti e I Montecchi* (Venice, Teatro La Fenice, 1830). At this point in his career, Bellini composed the two works which are regarded as his masterpieces, *La sonnambula* and *Norma*. The latter work was also the high point of the Bellini-Romani artistic partnership, which ended abruptly after the failure of *Beatrice di Tenda* (Venice, Teatro La Fenice 1833). During this period Bellini began a long series of journeys to London and Paris to attend performances of his operas in those cities. It was in Paris that Bellini's last opera, *I puritani* (Théâtre Italien, 1834) was produced, with enormous success.

BEŇAČKOVÁ-ČÁPOVÁ, GABRIELA

(Bratislava 1947)
Czech soprano. She completed her musical training in Bratislava, graduating in 1971. Her artistic career initially concentrated on performances in opera houses in Prague (from 1970) and Bratislava (1973–74). In 1980 she joined the company of the Vienna Staatsoper, where she distinguished herself by the soft timbre of her voice, supple in its delivery, and by her outstanding qualities as a performer. Beňačková has also appeared in the principal international opera houses. She bases her repertoire on operas by Smetana (*Libuše*), Dvořák (*Rusalka*), Janáček (*Jenůfa*, *Kát'a Kabanová*), Giordano (*Andrea Chénier*) and many others by both Slav and Italian composers.

BENELLI, SEM

(Filettole, (Prato) 1877–Zoagli, (Genoa) 1949)
Italian poet and playwright. He began his studies in Florence, but these were interrupted by the death of his father (1895). Benelli was then obliged to earn a living but continued with his studies by teaching himself. He began writing for the newspapers and then completed his first pieces for the theater. His libretti, often based on his own plays, were set to music by Italian composers of the so-called *post-verismo* (post-realist) school, among them Montemezzi's *L'amore dei tre re* (1913) and Giordano's *La cena delle beffe* (1924).

BENVENUTO CELLINI

Opera in two (and later, in a revised form, three) acts by Hector Berlioz (1803–1869), to a libretto by Léon de Wailly and Auguste Barbier. First performance: Paris, Opéra, 10 September 1838.

The action takes place in Rome during the Carnival of 1532. The goldsmith Benvenuto Cellini (tenor) is in love with Teresa (soprano), daughter of the pope's treasurer, Balducci (baritone), and promised in marriage to Fieramosca. Cellini plans to kidnap Teresa on Carnival night while disguised as a monk. Fieramosca comes to hear of this scheme and prevents Cellini from succeeding, but one of his companions is killed in the attempt. Cellini is accused of murder but manages to escape. Meanwhile, the pope has ordered Cellini to cast a statue of Perseus. He returns to his workshop, only to be met there by Fieramosca and the father of Teresa, who are waiting to have him arrested and sent to the gallows. But a cardinal promises Benvenuto that his life will be saved and Teresa's hand will be his if, before the end of the evening, he is able to cast the statue of Perseus; Cellini's enemies are greatly vexed when he completes the task in time and can at last hold his beloved Teresa in his arms.

Benvenuto Cellini was composed between 1834 and 1837, and its premiere was a spectacular failure. Subsequent productions (Weimar in 1852 and London in 1853) had a similar outcome, and did not boost the fortunes of the opera, which was never included in the permanent repertoire. Although the libretto is inconsistent, and affected in its romanticism, the music, on the other hand, demonstrates that the setting of the opera is no longer treated as merely a backdrop.

BERG, ALBAN

(Vienna 1885–1935)
Austrian composer. Initially self-taught, from 1904 to 1910 he was able to take lessons in advanced composition, with Arnold Schoenberg, who became a close friend, and by whom he was influenced in the development of 12-tone music. Berg wrote only two operas: *Wozzeck* (1925) and *Lulu* (premiered posthumously in 1937), works whose

A scene from *Benvenuto Cellini*.

dramatic content turns on the characters of Wozzeck and Lulu, both of them victims of a tragic personality quirk causing behaviour which veers between the rational and the irrational, to the point of self-destruction. In his dodecaphonic or 12-tone musical language, to which modes of expression deriving from classical forms are added (sonata form, suite, etc.), Berg's admirable achievement was to sculpt these kinds of figure, landmarks in the history of opera.

BERGANZA, TERESA

(Madrid 1935)

Spanish mezzo-soprano. She studied singing with Lola Rodríguez Aragón and made her debut as Dorabella in Mozart's *Così fan tutte* in Aix-en-Provence, creating an immediate impression as one of the most elegant of Mozart performers. In 1958 in Dallas, she sang for the first time the role of Isabella in Rossini's *L'italiana in Algeri* and once again distinguished herself by her phrasing and her natural predisposition to the *coloratura* singing required by Rossini. Apart from Mozart, it is the Rossini of *La Cenerentola*, *Il barbiere di Siviglia* and *L'italiana* that have enabled Berganza to display her polished and at the same time resplendent voice to best advantage. Less convincing, perhaps, is her approach to Bizet's *Carmen* (which she sang in 1977), rather removed from her own style and personality. Berganza's appearances in opera have been more infrequent in recent years, but they have included *Carmen* in London (1984), her debut in Massenet's *Werther* (Zurich, 1977) and Handel's *Ariodante* (Barcelona, 1991). On the other hand, her concert engagements have continued, and in July 1991 she made a triumphant return to Aix-en-Provence, where she first made her name.

BERGONZI, CARLO

(Parma 1924)

Italian tenor. He studied at the Conservatorio in Parma with Grandini and Campogalliani, making his debut in 1948 in Lecce as a baritone in the role of Figaro (Rossini's *Il barbiere di Siviglia*). By 1951 he was singing Andrea Chénier (in Giordano's opera of that name) in Bari. He thus launched himself on a brilliant career which has included leading roles in the world's major opera houses. Bergonzi has a solid vocal technique and remarkable qualities of expression and phrasing, which have made him outstanding in Verdi (*Un ballo in maschera*, *Il trovatore* and *La forza del destino*). His performances in operas by Donizetti, Leoncavallo and Mascagni are equally impressive. On the strength of his technique, tone and style, Bergonzi can claim an extraordinarily long artistic life, which at its end saw him singing the lead in Verdi's *La forza del destino* in Ravenna, Donizetti's *L'elisir d'amore* at the Metropolitan Opera, New York in 1987, and Maurizio in a recording of Cilèa's *Adriana Lecouvreur* with Dame Joan Sutherland (1988).

BERIO, LUCIANO

(Oneglia, Imperia 1925)

Italian composer. He studied at the Conservatorio in Milan with Ghedini and Dallapiccola. In 1955, with Bruno Maderna, he founded a workshop in Milan for the study of electronic music. Berio has taught composition in some of the leading international music institutes, including Harvard University and the Juilliard School in New York. His music for the theater is the product of continuous evolution and elaboration, combining the language of electronic music with total theater, which also finds its expression through pantomime, choreography and recitation. Among Berio's works for the theater are: *Passaggio* (1963), *Laborintus II* (1964), *Recital* (1972), *Opera* (1970–77), *La vera storia* (1982) and *Un re in ascolto* (1984).

BERIO DI SALSA, FRANCESCO

(Naples, end eighteenth century–beginning nineteenth century)

Italian man of letters and librettist. He belonged to the Neapolitan aristocracy and was very active in the cultural life of Naples during the early nineteenth century. He became a librettist by chance, providing his friend Rossini with two texts which he had written specially for him, for the operas *Otello, ossia il moro di Venezia* (1816) and *Ricciardo e Zoraide* (1818).

BERLIOZ, LOUIS-HECTOR

(La Côte-Saint-André, Isère 1803–Paris 1869)

French composer. Almost the whole of Berlioz's output as a composer is based on a dramatic, theatrical notion of music, whether in the form of a symphony (such as the *Symphonie fantastique*) or a concerto (*Harold in Italy*, for viola and orchestra). He therefore had great ability and skill in theatrical composition, but the direct approach he used for opera, evident already in his first opera, *Benvenuto Cellini*, did not find favour with his audience. When he started work on an opera which would take its story from Virgil, Berlioz was not daunted by the obvious practical problems in staging a work on such a large

Above: A scene from *Lulu* by Alban Berg.

Left: The Italian composer Luciano Berio.

scale. *Les Troyens* did not establish itself as an opera, and so was not taken into the normal operatic repertoire, although it contained passages in which the sheer spectacle of the work was reinforced by a precise gift for opera, an originality of musical language and a classical grandeur which no composer had achieved since Gluck.

BERNSTEIN, LEONARD

(Lawrence, Massachusetts 1918–New York 1990)

American conductor, composer and pianist. He studied at Harvard University (1935–39) and at the Curtis Institute in Philadelphia (1939–41). In 1942 he was assistant conductor to Serge Koussevitzky in Tanglewood, where he conducted the American premiere of Britten's *Peter Grimes* (1946). With his outstanding personality as a performer, Bernstein quickly became established as one of the greatest conductors of his time. He had a rather variable relationship with opera, marked by conflicting opinions about his work, as for example in the recordings of *Carmen* (1972) and *La bohème* (1987), which were thought to display an insufficient sense of theater. His interpretations of *Fidelio* (1978) and *Tristan und Isolde* (1981), however, were more in keeping with Bernstein's sympathies for symphonic music. As a composer, he wrote an opera, *Trouble in Tahiti* (1952), an operetta, *Candide* (1956), the celebrated *West Side Story* (1957) and another opera, *A Quiet Place* (1983).

BERRY, WALTER

(Vienna 1929)

Austrian bass-baritone. He studied singing at the Vienna Academy with Hermann Gallos. In 1950 he joined the Staatsoper company in Vienna, where he made his debut in the role of the Count in Mozart's *Le nozze di Figaro*, immediately establishing himself as an elegant interpreter of Mozart. Berry has sung Mozart almost everywhere: from the Salzburg Festival of 1953 to the Metropolitan Opera House, New York in 1966, and in other major international music venues. He has also given distinguished performances in operas of great dramatic substance, such as Richard Strauss's *Die Frau ohne Schatten*, Wagner's *Die Walküre* and Berg's *Wozzeck*.

BERTATI, GIOVANNI

(Martellago 1735–Venice 1815)

Italian librettist. He studied at the Seminary in Treviso under the patronage of a nobleman, A. Grimani. He chose not to take up the religious life, however, preferring to pursue his strong attraction for the theater. He therefore began work as a librettist, first in Venice, where he worked with Galuppi, and then in Vienna, where, between 1790 and 1794, he was appointed poet to the imperial court, replacing Lorenzo da Ponte, who had fallen out of favour. Bertati wrote more than 70 libretti and worked with a number of composers, including Paisiello, Anfossi, Gazzaniga, Salieri and Cimarosa. Among the best-known operas for which he provided a libretto are Giuseppe Gazzaniga's *Don Giovanni ossia Il convitato di pietra*, 1787 and, most important, Domenico Cimarosa's *Il matrimonio segreto*, 1792.

BERTOLO, ALDO

(Turin 1949)

Italian tenor. Ever since singing the role of Elvino (Bellini's *La sonnambula*) at the Festival dei Due Mondi in Spoleto in 1979, he has won great acclaim at a number of international opera houses. Particularly worth noting are his performances in Rossini's *Adelaide di Borgogna* and Bellini's *I puritani* at the Valle d'Itria Festival in 1984 and 1985, and in the first performance in modern times of Piccinni's *Iphigénie en Tauride* at the Teatro Petruzzelli in Bari in 1986. His Ernesto in Donizetti's *Don Pasquale*, which he sang on a number of occasions, was much admired.

BESUCH DER ALTEN DAME, DER

(The Visit)

Opera in three acts by Gottfried von Einem (b. 1918), to a libretto taken from Friedrich

Dürrenmatt's play of the same name. First performance: Vienna, Staatsoper, 23 May 1971.

The people of the Swiss town of Güllen are awaiting the arrival of Claire Zachanassian (mezzo-soprano), an extremely wealthy woman who is making her first visit to her home town in more than 40 years. Her wealth could come to the aid of this impoverished place. Enter Claire, by now incredibly old, surrounded by an entourage. The old lady makes it clear that she is willing to offer Güllen a large sum of money but only on the condition that a certain Alfred Ill is brought to her dead. This Ill, many years before, had made Claire Zachanassian pregnant and then refused to acknowledge his son, helped by a complacent judge who had accepted the testimony of two drunks. Abandoned by Ill, Claire had ended up in a brothel. After much debate, the townspeople, desperate for the money, pass a vote in the town council that Alfred Ill should be killed. Claire gets what she has asked for, and leaves Güllen with her entourage, taking with her the coffin containing the corpse of Alfred which she is going to bury in her garden. The townspeople now have the money she promised them, and are happy.

Der Besuch der Alten Dame is a play about the hypocrisy of the modern world, where a crime of greed is given all the trappings of an act of justice. It has a rich score, abounding in sonorities, with complex contrapuntal textures and a strictly tonal system.

BIANCA E FALIERO, OSSIA IL CONSIGLIO DEI TRE

(Bianca and Faliero, or The Council of Three)

Opera in two acts by Gioachino Rossini (1792–1868), to a libretto by Felice Romani based on Arnaut's Les Venitiens. *First performance: Milan, La Scala, 26 December 1819.*

The action takes place in Venice during the seventeenth century. On his return from a victorious military campaign, General Faliero (contralto) sees his beloved Bianca (soprano) again, only to learn from her that her father, Contareno (tenor), is opposed to their marrying. Bianca has already been promised in marriage to a nobleman, Capellio (bass). On discovering the truth, Faliero accuses Bianca of having betrayed their love pact, but in the course of a secret conversation with Faliero, Bianca reaffirms her love for him. Suddenly Contareno arrives, and Faliero is forced to take refuge in the nearby Spanish embassy next door to Contareno's residence. But then Faliero is arrested on a charge of treason and is brought before the Council of Three, one of whom is Capellio. Faliero is saved by the intervention of Bianca, who tells the judges what happened. Capellio is touched and supports Faliero's defense. Contareno's resistance is finally broken down, and the opera ends with the marriage of Bianca and Faliero.

This was Rossini's 36th opera. It is outstandingly dramatic, with effective and well-varied characterization of the individual roles, to whom Rossini gives richly virtuoso singing parts.

BIANCA E GERNANDO

Opera in two acts by Vincenzo Bellini (1801–1835), to a libretto by Domenico Gilardoni from Carlo Roti's play Bianca e Fernando alla tomba di Carlo duca di Agrigento. *First performance: Naples, Teatro San Carlo, 30 May 1826.*

Fernando (tenor) arrives in Agrigento. He secretly gains entry to the royal palace, where he meets Clemente (bass), with whom he recalls the murder of his father at the hand of Filippo (baritone). Fernando, using the false name of Adolfo, introduces himself to Viscardo (bass), an accomplice of Filippo. The fake Adolfo tells Viscardo that he saw Fernando die. This is good news for Filippo, who meets "Adolfo" and informs him of his forthcoming marriage to Bianca (soprano), Fernando's sister. Then Fernando discovers that his father is not dead, but locked up in the castle dungeons and that it will be his duty, on Filippo's orders, to kill his father. Bianca, who has so far been unaware of the truth, is reunited in the person of "Adolfo" with her brother Fernando, and then, learning from him what had really happened to their father, accompanies him to the dungeons. Filippo, now uncertain of his grasp on power, follows them there and threatens to murder Bianca's child. Clemente intervenes and takes Filippo's weapon from him, and everything ends happily.

Bianca e Gernando was Bellini's second opera, and it received a good response from audience and critics alike at its premiere. The original title of *Bianca e Gernando* (to avoid anyone thinking it referred to the late Bourbon King Fernando, on the instructions of the censor) was changed to *Bianca e Fernando*, but the opera did not enjoy great success.

BILLY BUDD

Opera in four acts by Benjamin Britten (1913–1976), to a libretto by E. M. Forster and Eric Crozier based on the story by Herman Melville. First performance: London, Royal Opera House Covent Garden, 1 December 1951.

On board H.M.S. *Indomitable* during the summer of 1797, heading for the Mediterranean. The ship is short of crew and, when a merchant ship sails close by, a boarding-party is sent across to her to recruit more men for the Royal Navy. Among those newly conscripted is Billy Budd (baritone), a naive young man popular with everyone except the master-at-arms, John Claggart (bass), who works covertly for Billy's downfall, eventually levelling accusations against him in front of Captain Vere (tenor). Vere, an honest man much admired by all, invites Billy to answer his accuser. Seized by a stammer, Billy in frustration involuntarily strikes Claggart, who falls dead. The Captain knows that Billy Budd is not really guilty, but according to martial law, he must bring the young man to trial. Billy is condemned to death, by hanging.

Opposite above: A caricature of Hector Berlioz.

Opposite below: Leonard Bernstein conducting *A Quiet Place*.

Above: A scene from *Bianca e Faliero* by Rossini.

Billy Budd is one of the few operas without female roles. It was commissioned by the Arts Council of Great Britain, and a revision consisting of only two acts was subsequently produced at London's Covent Garden on 9 January 1964.

BIZET, GEORGES

(Paris 1838–Bougival, Paris 1875)

French composer. A pupil of Gounod at the Paris Conservatoire, Bizet devoted his energies to opera composition from the outset of his career. *Don Procopio* (1858–59) reflected his interest in Italian opera, especially Rossini and Donizetti. After his *Ivan IV* (1862–63) came *Les pêcheurs de perles* (The Pearl Fishers, 1863), the first work in which Bizet included features indicating he was composing more freely and creating a musical style of his own. These features are even more in evidence, though lacking in homogeneity, in *La jolie fille de Perth* (The Fair Maid of Perth, 1866). In the years that followed, Bizet wrote *Djamileh* (1871–72) and *Carmen* (1873–74, premiered in 1875). In *Carmen*, which shows the composer at the height of his powers, Bizet expresses the sum of his talent, supported by a congenial libretto which gives him the chance to characterize the individual roles effectively and, above all, to create a power, heat and colour without precedent in *opéra-comique*.

Above: The French composer Georges Bizet.

Right: The American tenor Robert Blake.

BJÖRLING, JUSSI

(Stora Tuna 1911–Stockholm 1960)

Swedish tenor. He studied at the Royal Opera school in Stockholm with John Forsell and Tullio Voghera. He made his debut in Stockholm in 1930 in the role of Don Ottavio in Mozart's *Don Giovanni*. Björling appeared in Vienna, Chicago (1937) and at Covent Garden (1938), but his name is principally associated with the Metropolitan in New York, where, from 1938 until 1960, he was a favourite with the audiences, as an acclaimed performer of Italian and French repertoire. Gifted with a noble timbre, a ringing voice and an excellent technique, Björling's elegant style could be heard in outstanding performances of *Il trovatore, Aida, Tosca, La bohème, Roméo et Juliette* and *Faust*.

BLAKE, ROCKWELL ROBERT

(Plattsburg, New York 1951)

American tenor. After studying music in New York, Blake made his debut at the Kennedy Center in Washington in Rossini's *L'italiana in Algeri* (1976). In 1978 he won the Richard Tucker Award, and this led to an engagement with the New York City Opera in 1979 where he sang Rossini's *Le Comte Ory*. In 1981 he made his first appearance at the Metropolitan Opera House, New York, again in *L'italiana in Algeri*, with Marilyn Horne, and thus established himself as the most accomplished contemporary male performer of Rossini. Blake's extraordinary virtuoso gifts, his noble and expressive phrasing and remarkable vocal range, have enabled him to revive a number of tenor roles – in particular from Rossini's *opera seria* output (*La donna del lago, Ermione, Armida, Zelmira* and *Semiramide*) – and give them their true dramatic breadth, which he heightens with spectacular virtuosity.

BLEGEN, JUDITH

(Missoula, Montana 1941)

American soprano. She studied at the Curtis Institute in Philadelphia and made her concert debut in 1963. The following year, she took part in the Spoleto Festival in Italy and studied Italian opera with Luigi Ricci before making her first appearance in 1968 as Rosina in Rossini's *Il barbiere di Siviglia*. On her return to the United States, Blegen joined the Metropolitan Opera in New York. Her name was associated with many Mozart roles, as well as with Sophie in *Der Rosenkavalier*, Mélisande in *Pelléas et Mélisande* (Debussy) and Adina in *L'elisir d'amore* and Musetta in Puccini's *La bohème*.

BOHÈME, LA

Opera in four acts by Ruggero Leoncavallo (1857–1919), to the composer's own libretto based on the novel by Henry Mürger. First performance: Venice, Teatro La Fenice, 6 May 1897.

It is Christmas Eve. Four friends gather at the Café Momus in Paris. They are Marcello, a painter (tenor), Rodolfo, a poet (baritone), the composer Schaunard (baritone) and a philosopher, Colline (baritone). At the café they meet Musetta (mezzo-soprano) and Mimi (soprano). Marcello makes a passionate declaration of love to Musetta, and she is won over by his words. Between Mimi and Rodolfo, too, a tenderness has also sprung up. During a party, which Musetta has had to hold in the courtyard because creditors have removed everything from her house, the Vicomte Paolo (baritone), who is in love with Mimi, persuades her to come and live with him. Not long after that, Musetta leaves Marcello. Mimi, however, regretting what she has done, asks Marcello if she can come back to him, but the poet feels bitter towards her and turns her away harshly. It is Christmas Eve once again. In Rodolfo's attic, Musetta and Marcello, now together again, have gathered with their other friends to celebrate Christmas. Suddenly Mimi appears. She is seriously ill. Everyone tries to help her but by now it is too late, and Mimi dies in Rodolfo's arms.

Leoncavallo's *La bohème* was performed a year after Puccini's opera of the same name. It found favour with audiences and critics but interest soon waned and it fell from the repertoire.

BOHÈME, LA

Opera in four acts by Giacomo Puccini (1854–1924), to a libretto by Giuseppe Giacosa and Luigi Illica, from the novel by Henry Mürger. First performance: Turin, Teatro Regio, 1 February 1896.

It is Christmas Eve in Paris, in the year 1830. In an attic room, four penniless artists are giving an impromptu party. They are Rodolfo (tenor), a poet; Marcello (baritone), an artist; the composer Schaunard (baritone); and a philosopher, Colline (bass). The celebration is interrupted by the importunate arrival of the landlord, Benoît, who has come to collect the rent. Having sent him away, the friends decide to continue the party at the Café Momus. Rodolfo, however, stays behind to finish some writing. There is a knock at the door. It is Mimi (soprano), a neighbour, asking for a match to light her candle. After an initial awkwardness, the two young people sense an intimacy and gentleness developing between them which quickens into love. The scene changes to the Café Momus, where Rodolfo and Mimi have rejoined their other friends. Out of the crowd appears Musetta, an old flame of Marcello's, now accompanied by the elderly Alcindoro (bass). Musetta still loves Marcello and sends Alcindoro off on an errand so she can throw herself into Marcello's arms. Time passes. It is now February. On a cold morning, Mimi, ill and shivering, tells Marcello that the relationship with Rodolfo is about to end. Rodolfo then tells his friend that Mimi's serious state of health is an opportunity for them to part. Mimi has overheard their conversation, and, overcome with emotion, reveals herself. The two lovers embrace, but the separation is only postponed. Musetta appears and has an argument with Marcello. Time passes. Marcello and Rodolfo remember with regret the times when they were in love. The arrival of Schaunard and Colline lifts their spirits, but, not long after, Musetta bursts in to tell them that Mimi is outside the door, gravely ill. The friends do everything they can to lessen the sufferings of the poor young woman, but it is too late, and Mimi dies in the arms of her beloved Rodolfo.

Puccini took from 1893 until 1895 to complete *La bohème* because collaborating with his librettists proved a long and anguished task. The work was well received, though much less enthusiastically than his *Manon Lescaut* had been. The solid theatrical basis of the opera, the perfect balance between the different theatrical moods of the piece, and the sharp characterization make *La bohème* one of the most original and most often performed operas of all time.

BOHEMIAN GIRL, THE

Opera in three acts by Michael William Balfe (1808–1870), to a libretto by Alfred Bunn. First performance: London, Theater Royal, Drury Lane, 27 November 1843.

The setting is Germany. The story tells of a Polish nobleman, Thaddeus (tenor), and his beloved Arline (soprano), daughter of Count Arnheim (bass). Arline was kidnapped by gypsies as a child and brought up by them. At the time when this story takes place, she has been accused of stealing a jewel from a gentleman, but she is suddenly recognized by her father, the Governor of Pressburg. He is so happy to have found his lost daughter again that he agrees to give her in marriage to Thaddeus, despite the fact that the young man is regarded as politically unacceptable.

The Bohemian Girl is Balfe's most famous work and without a doubt the most successful British opera in the first half of the nineteenth century. The opera was translated into a number of different languages, including Russian.

BÖHM, KARL

(Graz 1894–Salzburg 1981)

Austrian conductor. He began to study music in Graz and completed his studies in Vienna. After his debut in Graz in 1917, he became principal conductor of the Munich Opera (1921–27), moving on to the Vienna Philharmonic from 1933 onwards and later to the Staatsoper in Vienna (1943–45 and 1954–56). He conducted regularly in Salzburg, where his name was associated with the operas of Mozart and Richard Strauss, conducting the first performances at Dresden of *Die schweigsame Frau* (The Silent Woman) in 1935 and *Daphne* in 1938. By virtue of his interpretative rigour in performance, always alert in the exploration of expressive detail while remaining true to the composer's intention, Böhm is remembered as a loyal guardian of tradition.

BOÏELDIEU, ADRIEN

(Rouen 1775–Jarcy, Seine-et-Oise 1834)

French composer. He began to compose operas in Rouen before moving to Paris. His compositions display an agreeable and flow-

Top: A scene from *La bohème* by Puccini.

Above: The Austrian conductor Karl Böhm.

ing gift for melody, and vigorous, vibrant orchestration rich in colour, earning him the nickname of "the French Mozart." Between 1797 and 1800 he wrote *La famille suisse*, *Zoraïme et Zulnar* and *Béniowski*, scoring a particular success with *Le calife de Bagdad*. In 1804 he became chorus-master at the court of the Tsar in St. Petersburg, where he remained until 1807. On his return to Paris, he regained his former popularity with *Jean de Paris* (1812) and with the opera which many consider his masterpiece, *La dame blanche*, 1823.

BOITO, ARRIGO

(Padua 1842–Milan 1918)

Italian poet, librettist and composer. He studied music in Milan with Mazzucato. A scholarship enabled him to travel to Paris, where he met Victor Hugo, Berlioz, Rossini and Verdi. While in Paris, Boito had the idea of composing an opera about Faust and another on the Emperor Nero. On his return to Milan, he wrote *Mefistofele* (1868), which was given a cool reception, and Boito was accused of imitating Wagner. *Mefistofele* was better received in Bologna, a city said to be more open to musical innovation. Under the pen-name Tobia Gorrio (an anagram of his own), Boito wrote the libretto of *La Gioconda* for Ponchielli. As a librettist he also collaborated with Verdi on the revised version of *Simon Boccanegra*, subsequently writing libretti for both *Otello* and *Falstaff*, which are considered among the best libretti in Italian opera. Boito's opera *Nerone* was performed posthumously at La Scala, with Toscanini conducting, in 1924.

Top: Stage design for *Bolivar* by Darius Milhaud.

Above: Arrigo Boito.

BOLIVAR

Opera in three acts by Darius Milhaud (1892–1974) to a libretto by Madeleine Milhaud based on the play of the same name by Jules Supervielle. First performance: Paris, Opéra, 10 May 1950.

The action takes places in various parts of Venezuela, Peru and Colombia during the first 30 years of the nineteenth century. After the death of his wife Maria Teresa (soprano), Bolivar (baritone) begins his struggle to defend the oppressed tenant-farmers against their Spanish masters. It is a long and arduous fight, in which Bolivar has the comfort of another woman by his side, Manuela (soprano). Bolivar crosses the Andes and realizes his dream of liberating South America from Spanish domination. In his honour, Upper Peru takes the name of the Bolivar Republic. But Bolivar the hero refuses any position of power, in keeping with his democratic ideas; nevertheless, he is made the target of plots and assassination attempts by those who look upon him as a dictator. At the end of the opera, Bolivar, now tired and ill, expresses his hope for a federation of all the liberated states, and then dies, comforted by a vision of his beloved wife Maria Teresa.

Bolivar is the third opera in a trilogy dedicated to American history. It was preceded by *Christophe Colomb* (1930) and *Maximilien* (1932). Composed in 1943, it is a tribute to the South American hero Simón Bolivar, but above all it is a declaration of faith in freedom, at a time when Europe was painfully trying to recover from the traumas of war. The opera was not well received at its Paris premiere. It contains echoes of Milhaud's own sojourn in Brazil (1917–18), where he had gone to study and assimilate South American folk music.

BONISOLLI, FRANCO

(Rovereto 1938)

Italian tenor. He established his reputation at the International Competition in Spoleto in 1961, where he made his debut in Puccini's *La rondine*. He subsequently confirmed that early success with appearances at the leading international opera houses, including the Vienna Staatsoper (from 1968), the Metropolitan in New York (from 1971), La Scala, Milan, and many other Italian opera houses. A dramatic tenor of the "realist" school, Bonisolli has given distinguished performances of *Turandot*, *Tosca*, *Il trovatore* and *Aida*.

BONNEY, BARBARA

(Montclair, New Jersey 1956)

American soprano. She studied singing and cello at the University of New Hampshire before completing her training in Europe, where she made her debut in Handel's *Semele* at the Ludwigsburg Festival and scored a considerable success. In 1987 she established her reputation singing Sophie in *Der Rosenkavalier* in Monte Carlo, a role which she has subsequently sung in the main international opera houses under leading conductors, including Solti and Haitinik. Bonney took part in the 1987 season at Geneva's Grand Théâtre and at opera houses in Lausanne (1988), Zurich, and other towns, as well as making her first appearance at the Metropolitan in New York in Johann Strauss's *Die Fledermaus*. Her repertoire also includes operas by Donizetti.

BONYNGE, RICHARD

(Sydney 1930)

Australian conductor and pianist. Bonynge's name is professionally associated with that of his wife, the celebrated soprano Dame Joan Sutherland, whose entire career he has guided. His own work as a conductor has in practice been primarily a collaboration with Dame Joan in opera. In particular, Bonynge has reintroduced a personal performance practice for baroque operas, for example those by Handel, Bononcini and Graun, as well as for the French Romantic and late nineteenth-century opera (such as Delibes and Massenet). He has conducted in the leading opera houses of Europe and America, and from 1976 to 1986 was music director of the Australian Opera Company in Sydney.

BORIS GODUNOV

Opera in four acts, with a prologue, by Modest Mussorgsky (1839–1881), to the composer's own libretto from Pushkin and Karamzin. First performance: St. Petersburg, 27 January 1874.

The action takes place in Russia between 1598 and 1605. Prologue. Inside the monastery at Novodevichy, Boris Godunov (bass), who brought about the assassination, many years before, of Dimitri, the Tsar's heir, pretends he has no desire to ascend the throne. Outside, some of his own men are inciting the crowd to call out the name of Boris as their choice to succeed Tsar Fyodor, who has just died. The scene changes to Kremlin Square, where, to the sound of bells ringing, Boris is crowned Tsar. ACT I. A cell in the monastery of Chudov, five years later. The monk Pimen (bass) is writing the bloody history of his times, while the novice Grigory (tenor) sleeps. Suddenly the young man wakes up. Gripped by visions of power, Grigory, who has learned from Pimen how the Tsar's heir Dimitri had met his end, resolves to avenge him by assuming his identity. An inn on the border with Lithuania. Two mendicant friars arrive, Varlaam (bass) and Missail (tenor), and Grigory is with them: still impersonating Dimitri, he is being followed by the police. They catch up with him at the inn, but he manages to escape. ACT II. The Tsar's apartments in the Kremlin. After spending some time quietly with his children, Boris receives Prince Shuisky (tenor). The Prince has brought Boris news of a revolt stirred up by someone passing himself off as the Tsarevich Dimitri. Boris is terrified, and Shuisky has to assure him again that the real Dimitri did die, but Boris is overcome by remorse and gives himself up to desperate thoughts. ACT III. The castle of Sandomir, in Poland. Princess Marina (mezzo-soprano), who is ambitious for power, seduces the False Dimitri, encouraging him not to falter in his bid for vengeance against Boris. Marina enjoys the support of Rangoni, a Jesuit priest, whom she has promised that she will bring Catholicism to Russia when she becomes Tsarina. ACT IV. In front of the Cathedral of St. Basil in Moscow. News is spreading among the people that troops led by the impostor Dimitri are advancing. A Simpleton (tenor), who has had a coin stolen from him, asks Tsar Boris to mete out to the thieves the same fate which he had once prepared for Dimitri. Boris, while making sure that the culprit is not arrested, entreats the Simpleton to pray for him, but he refuses, lamenting the destiny of Russia. Now the scene changes to a room in the Kremlin. The Duma, presided over by Shuisky, is meeting to assess the progress of the impostor Dimitri. The old monk Pimen is summoned, and tells of miracles taking place at the tomb of the Tsarevich. Boris, who has been listening to this account, is taken seriously ill. Sensing that he is near to death, he calls for his son Fyodor (mezzo-soprano) and, after proclaiming him his successor, he dies. In the forest of Kromy, by night. Crowds of rebels are gathered, waiting for Dimitri. A boyar has been captured and tortured, and two Jesuits singing the praises of Tsarevich Dimitri are chased away. Dimitri arrives, to shouts of exultation. The crowd follows him as though in a frenzy. Left alone on stage, the Idiot sheds tears for Russia's sad fate.

Boris Godunov was begun in 1868 and completed the following year. The score, submitted to the literature committee of the Maryinsky Theater in St. Petersburg, was rejected because it was inappropriate to current taste and the composer's ideas were too bold. Mussorgsky then revised it (the most important change being the addition of the "Polish" act), but the opera was again turned down. After concert performances and productions of individual scenes, *Boris Godunov* was finally staged in 1874, to enormous acclaim. After the composer's death, Nicolai Rimsky-Korsakov took on the task of publishing the score, but most significantly he also reorchestrated it, sometimes smoothing over the composer's more original ideas. The Bolshoi later commissioned the composer Shostakovich to undertake another revision of the work. In recent years the original version has come back into use.

A scene from *Boris Godunov* by Mussorgsky.

BORODIN, ALEXANDER

(St. Petersburg 1833–1887)
Russian composer. The love-child of a prince, Borodin was guided towards the study of science, even though he displayed prodigious musical gifts as a youngster. His meeting with Mussorgsky was a turning-point for Borodin, who then became able to develop his talent for music, in parallel with his scientific career, by joining the Group of Five with Balakirev, Cui, Mussorgsky and Rimsky-Korsakov. As a composer of opera, Borodin completed only one work, *The Bogatyirs*, which was performed in 1867 but without his name. His masterpiece, *Knyaz Igor* (Prince Igor), composed between 1869 and 1887, was finished by Glazunov and Rimsky-Korsakov.

BOUGHTON, RUTLAND

(Aylesbury, Buckinghamshire 1878–London 1960)
British composer. He began studying at the Royal College of Music in London (from 1900), continuing his studies later by himself. Boughton had the idea of creating a school of music in the wake of Wagner's operas, and so in 1914, with the writer Reginald Buckley, he founded the Glastonbury Festival Players, a sort of British Bayreuth. It was in Glastonbury that Boughton composed his operas, all based on events in British history or taken from the cycles of Arthurian legend. His most famous opera is *The Immortal Hour* (Glastonbury, 1914), which enjoyed some popularity in London, too, where it was performed in 1922.

BOULEVARD SOLITUDE

Opera in seven scenes by Hans Werner Henze (b. 1926), to a libretto by Grete Weil from Prévost's novel Manon Lescaut. *First performance: Hanover, Landstheater, 17 February 1952.*

The setting is the entrance hall of a railway station. Manon Lescaut (soprano), accompanied by her brother (baritone), is waiting for a train to take them to a college in Lausanne. Taking advantage of her brother's temporary absence, Manon meets a student, Armand Des Grieux (tenor), with whom she goes to Paris. The scene changes. Manon and Armand are living in poverty in an attic room. Lescaut, who has caught up with his sister since her elopement, persuades her to leave the student and, instead, go and live with a wealthy old man, Lilaque (tenor). Time passes. Manon and her brother have been thrown out of Lilaque's house, accused of theft. Manon finds Armand. He is now addicted to drugs. Lescaut again puts pressure on his sister, this time to accept the advances of Lilaque's son (baritone), who has fallen in love with her. But once more Manon, her brother and Armand are surprised by Lilaque while stealing from his son's house. Manon fires a pistol at Lilaque, wounding him fatally, and she is arrested. Manon avoids looking at Armand as she is taken away, leaving him alone in the square.

Boulevard Solitude was composed in Paris between 1950 and 1951 and successfully conveys the atmosphere and cultural environment of those years. It leaves to the music the job of describing and commenting on the action. Henze makes judicious use of 12-tone music combined with subtle tonalities and a skilful handling of harmony, and in this way manages to make the opera accessible to a wide audience.

BOULEZ, PIERRE

(Montbrison, Loire 1925)
French conductor and composer. From 1944 to 1946 he studied with Messiaen and Leibowitz, and taught himself conducting, which he has always tried to tie in with his composing and musical experimentation. Ever since he began to compose, in 1955, Boulez has been one of the most symbolic and vital figures in modern music. When he conducted *Wozzeck* (1963) and *Lulu*, of which he gave the acclaimed and controversial first complete performance at the Opéra in Paris in 1979, his interpretations of Berg's operas

Right: Sesto Bruscantini in a production of Verdi's *Falstaff* at the Teatro San Carlo, Naples.

Top: The French composer Pierre Boulez.

were seen as authoritative. His approach to Wagner also drew comment, from his first *Parsifal* at Bayreuth (1966) to his again controversial interpretation of the *Ring* with Patrice Chéreau as stage director (1976–1980).

BRAVO, IL

Opera in three acts by Saverio Mercadante (1795–1870), to a libretto by Giovanni Gaetano Rossi. First performance: Milan, La Scala, 9 March 1839.

The setting is sixteenth-century Venice. Foscari (bass), in love with Violetta, has her guardian Maffeo murdered. Pisani (tenor), who has returned secretly from exile to carry his beloved Violetta off with him, asks Il Bravo (tenor) for shelter. Teodora (soprano), Violetta's mother, who regrets abandoning her daughter when she was a child, engages Il Bravo to abduct the young woman. Then Il Bravo reveals that he is Violetta's father, and had no choice but to become a hired assassin for the Republic of Venice in order to save the life of his own father, detained in the Piombi prison. Now Il Bravo has received an order to kill Teodora for offending the Venetian nobility by asking them to leave a party she had given. Teodora reacts by taking her own life just as a messenger arrives to tell Il Bravo that his old father is dead. He is now released from his obligation to work as a state assassin. Meanwhile Violetta has managed to be reunited with her beloved Pisani, and they leave Venice together.

The libretto for the opera is based on James Fenimore Cooper's novel *The Bravo*, with some alterations to names and to the action, and on Bourgeois's play *La vénitienne*.

BRITTEN, BENJAMIN

(Lowestoft, Suffolk 1913–Aldeburgh, Suffolk 1976)

British composer and conductor. He studied at the Royal College of Music with John Ireland and Frank Bridge and heard the leading composers of the day, including Berg and Stravinsky. Britten was immediately drawn to the world of opera, which he looked upon as the most fascinating of all forms of music. His meeting with the poet W. H. Auden and the tenor Peter Pears were crucial, as both had an influence on Britten's approach to the theater. From his first important opera, *Peter Grimes* (1945) to his last, *Death in Venice* (1973), Britten was an increasingly versatile composer, touching on the whole range of music for the theater, from the tragic chamber opera *The Rape of Lucretia* (1946) to the satirical comic opera *Albert Herring* (1947) and the children's opera *Let's Make An Opera* (1949), not to mention the powerful *Turn of the Screw* (1954). Britten's command of many musical genres was the result of a gift for melodic prosody, mastery of a variety of compositional techniques and an instinctive sense of theater.

BRUSCANTINI, SESTO

(Porto Civitanova, Macerata 1919)

Italian baritone. He studied in Rome with Luigi Ricci and made his debut in Puccini's *La bohème* in Civitanova in 1946. He received his first important notices in 1949 when he sang the role of Geronimo in Cimarosa's *Il matrimonio segreto* at La Scala in Milan. Bruscantini, who specialized in the *buffo* repertoire, retired in 1991.

BRUSON, RENATO

(Ganze, Padua 1936)

Italian baritone. He studied singing with Elena Fava-Ceriati. In 1961 he made his debut at Spoleto in *Il trovatore*. After appearances in smaller opera houses, Bruson's career took a decisive turn at the end of the 1960s when his performance in a production of *Lucia di Lammermoor* at the Metropolitan Opera, New York (1968) launched him as one of the greatest baritones of his time, and this reputation was to continue for many years. The character of Bruson's voice is soft and rich in timbres, homogeneous in delivery and associated with the Italian *bel canto*, in particular with Donizetti, many of whose operas Bruson has helped to revive (*Poliuto, Torquato Tasso, Fausta*, etc.). His performances of Verdi are also extraordinarily expressive and abound in psychological insight, from *Macbeth* to *La traviata, Simon Boccanegra* and *Otello*.

BRYDON, RODERICK

(Edinburgh 1948)

British conductor. Brydon began his artistic career as a conductor at Sadler's Wells Opera and Scottish Opera. He then made his Covent Garden debut in Britten's *A Midsummer Night's Dream*. Conducting engagements followed in Hanover (Britten's *Albert Herring*), Karlsruhe (Handel's *Alcina*), Bordeaux (Mozart's *Così fan tutte*), Genoa (Mozart's *La clemenza di Tito*) and Venice (Rossini's *Otello* and Mozart's *Mitridate, re di Ponto*). Brydon has also been a very active conductor of orchestral music (with the Scottish Chamber Orchestra) and is one of the most admired opera conductors of his time.

BUMBRY, GRACE

(St. Louis, Missouri 1937)

American mezzo-soprano and soprano. She studied with Lotte Lehmann (1955–58). After taking part in a number of singing competitions, Bumbry established her reputation on her first appearance at the Paris Opéra, singing Amneris in *Aida*. This success took her to Bayreuth, where she was the first black singer to appear, scoring a triumph as Venus in *Tannhäuser*. Bumbry has given numerous

The Italian baritone Renato Bruson.

concert performances and in opera added to her most admired mezzo-soprano roles (Amneris, Eboli, Carmen) others for the soprano voice (Lady Macbeth, Salome, La Gioconda, Norma, etc.). Bumbry uniquely combines elegance and musicianship of interpretation with powerful stage presence.

BURCHULADZE, PAATA

(Tbilisi 1955)

Georgian bass. He began to study music in his native Tbilisi and completed his studies at the Bolshoi school in Moscow. After his Tbilisi debut in 1976, Burchuladze trained with Simionato in Milan. He took part in a number of singing competitions, sang at the Bolshoi in Moscow (in *Boris Godunov*) and then embarked on a busy career which included appearances in leading opera houses across Europe and the United States. He has sung at La Scala (*Aida* and *Nabucco*) and at the Vienna Staatsoper (*Luisa Miller*, *Il barbiere di Siviglia* and *Khovanshchina*) and has made many recordings.

BURROWS, STUART

(Pontypridd 1933)

Welsh tenor. He studied music in Wales and made his debut in 1963 in Cardiff as Ismaele in Verdi's *Nabucco*. After appearing at Covent Garden as a Prisoner in Beethoven's *Fidelio* (1967), Burrows earned his first major success in the role of Tamino in Mozart's *Die Zauberflöte* (The Magic Flute). It has been as an interpreter of Mozart (in *Don Giovanni*, *Così fan tutte*, *La clemenza di Tito*) that Burrows has appeared in leading international opera houses, as well as giving many concert performances. Burrows has also sung in nineteenth-century Italian opera and is particularly remembered for his Leicester in Donizetti's *Maria Stuarda* alongside Beverly Sills.

BUSONI, FERRUCCIO

(Empoli 1866–Berlin 1924)

Italian composer and pianist. A great devotee and student of Bach, Busoni transcribed for the piano a number of his works. Between 1906 and 1911, Busoni composed his first opera, *Die Brautwahl* (The Marital Lottery), which was premiered in Hamburg in 1912. This work illustrates Busoni's satirical attitude to the operatic tradition, a stance even more in evidence in his subsequent operas, *Arlecchino* and *Turandot*, both given their first performances in 1917. In the same year Busoni started work on his final opera, *Doktor Faust*, which he left unfinished; it was completed by one of his pupils, Philipp Jarnach. *Doktor Faust*, with its austere intellectual quality, is Busoni's most ''Expressionist'' work.

BUSSOTTI, SYLVANO

(Florence 1931)

Italian composer and theatrical avant-gardist. He studied at the Florence Conservatorio, taking lessons in painting and graphic art at the same time. From 1949 to 1956 he devoted himself to the study of composition, developing his own highly individual style. His meeting with John Cage played a major part in his development as a composer. Bussotti has been very active in the theater and is one of the most passionate advocates of a new form of ''total theater,'' to which he has given shape in his own idea of *spettacolo con musica* (literally, a show or performance with music). Among his significant early compositions are *La passion selon Sade* (Palermo, 1965), a work consisting of four *tableaux vivants*, and *Lorenzaccio* (Venice, 1972), a large dramatic fresco which combines opera with dance, recitation and gestural art. His more recent compositions for the theater include *L'ispirazione* (Florence, 1988), *Fedra* (Rome, 1988) and *Bozzetto siciliano* (Catania, 1990). Bussotti is also a noted director and designer of sets and costumes.

BYCHKOV, SEMYON

(Leningrad 1952)

Russian conductor who has taken American citizenship. After studying at the Leningrad Conservatory, Bychkov left Russia to conduct in what was then West Germany and then in America. In 1984 he conducted Mozart's *La finta giardiniera* in Aix-en-Provence, later taking this opera to Lyons (1986) and conducting a concert performance of it in Paris in 1991 with the Orchestre de Paris, whose music director he had become in 1991, succeeding Daniel Barenboim. With the same orchestra Bychkov conducted Berlioz's *La damnation de Faust*, also in 1991.

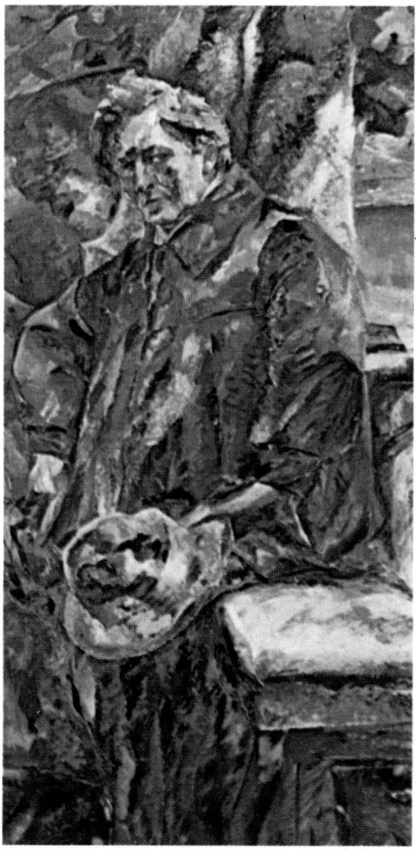

Above: The American mezzo-soprano and soprano Grace Bumbry.

Right: Portrait of the Italian composer and pianist Ferruccio Busoni.

C

CABALLÉ, MONTSERRAT

(Barcelona 1933)
Spanish soprano. She began to study music at the Barcelona Liceu Conservatorio. After her debut in 1956, Caballé appeared in many European opera houses, mainly in supporting roles. In 1965 she gave a sensational performance in Donizetti's *Lucrezia Borgia* at Carnegie Hall. After appearing as Marguerite in Gounod's *Faust* at the Metropolitan Opera House, New York, also in 1965, Caballé saw her name added to the operatic roll of honour as one of the finest *bel canto* singers for two decades. Known throughout the world, Caballé has built up an enormous repertoire, from Handel (*Giulio Cesare in Egitto*) to Rossini (*Elisabetta regina d'Inghilterra* and *La donna del lago*), Verdi (*Aida*, *Il trovatore*, *Un ballo in maschera*, *Luisa Miller*, etc.), Wagner (*Tristan und Isolde*) and Richard Strauss (*Salome*, *Arabella*). This clearly represents a tremendous variety of vocal styles which has certainly not helped the character of her voice. She has a perfect mastery of delivery, always homogeneous, with extraordinary *pianissimi*. These and other qualities were beginning to show signs of hardening and premature wear by the mid 1970s. Nevertheless Caballé remains one of the outstanding figures in operatic history.

CACCINI, GIULIO

(Tivoli 1551–Florence 1618)
Italian singer and composer. He studied singing, harp and lute, then entered the service of Cosimo de' Medici. On the strength of his musical ability, he managed to become part of the artistic life of Florence, gaining admission to the most exclusive cultural circles, in particular the Camerata dei Bardi. The aim of the poets, men of letters and composers who belonged to this society of artists was to look for an alternative to the incomprehensibility of texts in polyphonic compositions by analyzing treatises on Greek music. Caccini started composing in 1589, initially a piece to mark the marriage of Ferdinando de' Medici with Christine of Lorraine, for which Caccini wrote some parts of the *intermezzo, La pellegrina*. In 1600 another marriage, that of Henri IV of France and Maria de' Medici, culminated in an impressive performance of *Il rapimento di Cefalo*, for which Caccini provided the music. At about the same time, Jacopo Peri's *Euridice* was premiered; this work is regarded as the first example of an opera in the history of music. For Peri's opera, Caccini wrote a number of pieces which he then used again in a new *Euridice* he himself composed and which was performed for the first time in December two years later, 1602. In 1602 Caccini published the collection of madrigals and arias *Le nuove musiche*, which provide evidence of the change from the polyphonic to the monodic style. Caccini went to Paris, where he stayed at the court of Henry IV, before returning to Florence, where he died in 1618.

ČAIKOVSKI, PËTR IL'IČ (TCHAIKOVSKY, PETER ILYICH)

(Kamsko-Votkinsk, Viatka 1840–St. Petersburg 1893)
Russian composer. Guided by his family into studying for the judiciary, the young Tchaikovsky took a job with the Ministry of Justice in St. Petersburg in 1859, but resigned in order to devote himself to music. He joined the St. Petersburg Conservatoire and had lessons with Rubinstein and Zaremba. In 1866 he was taken on as a teacher of composition at the Moscow Conservatory, and it was during this period that he composed his first operas: *Voyevoda* (1868), *Undine*, which was never published but Tchaikovsky used part of it in his next opera *The Oprichnik* (1874). *Vakula the Smith* (1876) was subsequently radically revised to become *Cherevichki* (The Slippers, also known as *Les caprices d'Oxane*, 1887). Tchaikovsky's contact with Nadezhda von Meck coincided with the composition of masterpieces like *Eugene Onegin* (1879), his finest opera. He then turned away from Russian themes to write *The Maid of Orléans* (1881), which contains unmistakeable echoes of something of the style of French *grand-opéra*. After this interval, Tchaikovsky returned to exclusively Russian subjects, with *Mazeppa* (1884), *The Sorceress* (1887) and *The Queen of Spades* (1890), a work shot through with tremendous emotional tensions, bordering on hysteria, which are in evidence in the character of Hermann. His last opera, *Iolanta* (1892), is an uneven work which nonetheless displays a typically Tchaikovskyan inspiration and – in some of its purely orchestral passages – anticipates his Sixth Symphony (1893).

CAHUSAC, LOUIS DE

(Montauban 1706–Paris 1759)
French poet, playwright and librettist. Cahusac was from a noble family. One of his achievements was to write a fundamental treatise on dance (1754). He wrote a number of opera libretti for Rameau, including *Zaïs* (1748), *Naïs* (1749) and *Zoroastre* (1749).

Top: The Spanish soprano Montserrat Caballé.

Above: The Russian composer Tchaikovsky (Pëtr Il'ič Čaikovski).

CALDARA, ANTONIO

(Venice c. 1670–Vienna 1736)
Italian composer. Probably a pupil of Giovanni Legrenzi, Caldara began his career in music playing viola and cello and singing in the choir at St. Mark's Basilica in Venice. He was in the service of the Duke of Mantua (1701–7) and then in that of Prince Ruspoli in Rome (1709–11). Caldara's time in Rome was, however, interrupted by a journey to Barcelona, where he was Court Composer to King Carlos III. In 1712 he was at the court in Vienna, although he held no official post there. He returned to Rome, where he stayed until 1716, the year in which he was appointed assistant Kapellmeister in Vienna, as assistant to the composer Johann Joseph Fux. Caldara held this post in Vienna until his death, composing many of his theatrical works there. These amounted to a massive output of 78 operas, written between 1689 and 1736.

CALLAS, MARIA

(New York 1923–Paris 1977)
Stage name of Maria Anna Kalogeropoulos, American-born soprano of Greek parentage. While still a child, she took part in singing competitions and radio broadcasts. When her family moved to Athens, Maria began to study music at the Conservatory there. In 1938 she made her debut at the Athens Opera House in Mascagni's *Cavalleria rusticana*. In the same theater she made further appearances between 1940 and 1945 (in *Tosca*, *Fidelio*, etc.). After specialist training with Elvira De Hidalgo, she returned to the United States (1946) with her father but did not obtain any singing engagements there. In 1947 she arrived in Italy, where she appeared first in Ponchielli's *La Gioconda* in the Arena in Verona. More performances in Italy were to follow: in Venice (*Tristan und Isolde*, *Turandot*, *Aida*, etc.), Rome and Florence (*Norma*, *Les vêpres siciliennes*). In 1949 she embarked on an international career (Buenos Aires, Mexico City, etc.). In 1951 she sang in Verdi's *Les vêpres siciliennes* at La Scala and scored a resounding success. From that moment on, the name of Callas was associated with La Scala: except for a brief interval from 1958 to 1960, she created memorable performances which left her mark on La Scala's golden season. It was here that she sang in *Norma*, *Macbeth*, *Medea*, *La vestale*, *La sonnambula*, *La traviata*, *Anna Bolena*, *Il pirata* and *Poliuto*. In 1965 Callas made her last stage appearance in *Tosca* at Covent Garden. Her final public singing engagements were alongside Giuseppe Di Stefano in a long series of concerts in Europe, America and Japan (1973–74). Maria Callas represented a new direction in the history of singing. Her exceptional vocal gifts (her compass included the range of a mezzo-soprano and that of a light operatic soprano), combined with a truly remarkable technique and rare musicianship, allowed Callas to break through all barriers of style and vocal character. Her extraordinary phrasing assisted her incomparable talents as an actress and enabled her to breathe new life into such roles as Medea, Armida, Lady Macbeth and Anna Bolena and a series of revivals, all invariably distinguished by flawless psychological and stylistic fidelity. These are just some of the many features of Callas that have made her a historic figure in the world of opera and have ensured that her presence continues to be felt.

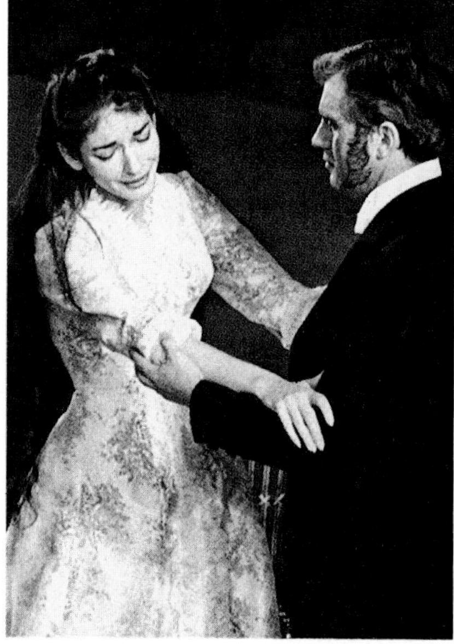

Above: The Italian composer Antonio Caldara.

Top: Maria Callas in *La traviata*.

CALZABIGI, RANIERI DE'

(Livorno 1714–Naples 1795)
Italian man of letters and librettist. While in Naples, where he began working as a librettist between 1747 and 1748, he came into contact with Pietro Metastasio. Around 1750 he went to Paris where, with his brother, he ran a lottery under the patronage of Madame Pompadour. This enterprise, which had begun auspiciously, proved to be disastrous, and Calzabigi was forced to leave Paris for Vienna (1761). There, thanks to Count Durazzo, director of the court theater, he was able to start working with Gluck, who gave Calzabigi much of the credit for his many innovations and new operatic style. Calzabigi's most important libretti were for *Orfeo ed Euridice* (1762), *Alceste* (1767) and *Paride ed Elena* (1770) by Gluck, and *Les Danaïdes* (1774) – a text which was later translated into French and set to music by Salieri – and *Elfrida* (1792), both by Paisiello.

CAMBIALE DI MATRIMONIO, LA

(The Marriage Contract)
Comic opera in one act by Gioachino Rossini (1792–1868), to a libretto by Gaetano Rossi. First performance: Venice, Teatro Giustiniani di San Moisè, 3 November 1810.

Tobias Mill (bass), an elderly shopkeeper, has just come to a profitable arrangement with the wealthy American businessman Slook (comic bass), who is prepared to pay a vast sum of money for a young wife. Tobias immediately thinks of his daughter Fanny (soprano). She is desperate because she is secretly in love with the young Edoardo Milfort (tenor). When the American arrives, he is very pleased with his bride-to-be. Fanny, on the other hand, threatens to scratch his eyes out if he goes through with this marriage. Meanwhile Edoardo appears and asserts his own rights over Fanny. Slook is moved by the feeling the two young people have for each other. So he gives Edoardo the marriage contract and appoints him as his heir. When Tobias finds out that Slook is no longer going to marry his daughter, he flies into a rage and challenges the American to a duel. Before crossing swords, Slook lets Tobias know that Fanny loves Edoardo. The old man is placated by the fact that Edoardo has been made Slook's sole heir, and consents to the marriage. The opera ends in happiness and congratulations from all sides.

THE *BEL CANTO* RENAISSANCE

The revival of *bel canto* singing began on the night of 3 January 1949 at the Teatro La Fenice in Venice when Maria Callas took over from the soprano Margherita Carosio as Elvira in a production of Bellini's opera *I puritani*. It was a role which, like Amina in Bellini's *La sonnambula* and Donizetti's Lucia, had traditionally been given to the light soprano voice. Callas's achievement was a radical transformation of Elvira which restored to the role those historical and psychological qualities of vocal sound which Bellini had originally wanted. Her performances of these roles showed that her demonstration of finely judged insight into the psychology of a character derived from a particularly eloquent use of phrasing, vocal timbres and *coloratura* used for dramatic, i.e expressive ends and not as a pointless exercise in vocal acrobatics. Thanks to this revival of the singing style of the dramatic soprano from the first half of the nineteenth century, Callas made sure that operas which had disappeared from the usual opera-house repertoires again saw the light of day: Rossini's *Armida* and *Il turco in Italia*, Bellini's *Il pirata* and Donizetti's *Anna Bolena* and *Poliuto*. Meanwhile another soprano, Renata Tebaldi, working from a different repertoire, was setting in motion a separate *bel canto* renaissance in such operas as *Aida*, *La forza del destino*, *Andrea Chénier* and *Madama Butterfly* and reintroducing them without the trappings of *verismo*, the realist approach to opera in which the style of singing was totally different from *bel canto*. Tebaldi's example was taken up by Magda Olivero and more recently by Raina Kabaivanska, both authentic restorers of the original vocal sound to operas by Puccini and his contemporaries. No less important in this respect was the contribution of the mezzo-soprano Giulietta Simoniato, who laid the foundations for the revival of the Rossini singing style. The rediscovery of *bel canto* which Callas had started was then advocated and developed by the soprano Joan Sutherland and the mezzo-soprano Marilyn Horne, acknowledged as the most authentic stylists of modern times. They reinstated the way of singing which had been in vogue in the eighteenth century, together with the fashion for variations and cadences to be found in the opera repertoire before Verdi. This marked the beginning of a period during which revivals came thick and fast, with not only Sutherland and Horne but also the sopranos Leyla Gencer, Montserrat Caballé and Beverly Sills championing the cause. The mezzo-soprano Teresa Berganza was responsible with Horne for launching this renewal of specialization in Rossini, followed, in their various ways, by the sopranos Lella Cuberli, Katia Ricciarelli, Luciana Serra, June Anderson, Cecilia Gasdia and Mariella Devia and the mezzo-sopranos Lucia Valentini Terrani, Martine Dupuy, Frederica von Stade and Cecilia Bartoli. Male singers did not exert the same degree of influence as this great flowering of *bel canto* talent among women artistes. Singers like Franco Corelli, Carlo Bergonzi, Alfredo Kraus, Luciano Pavarotti and Renato Bruson played a significant part in the revival of singing, but not of *bel canto* itself. It was left to the bass Samuel Ramey and the tenors Rockwell Blake and Chris Merritt to rediscover *bel canto* (especially in Rossini) in all its glory.

Above: A scene from Rossini's *Il Viaggio a Reims*.

Left: Joan Sutherland.

La cambiale di matrimonio was composed by Rossini when he was 18 years old and still lacked the necessary knowledge and experience to be able to create a new and original opera, so the models he used for *La cambiale* were those of the Italian school of the time. However, in the course of this opera, in which the comic element is combined with moments of feeling, it is already possible to recognize the emerging originality of style which was to be Rossini's hallmark.

CAMBRELING, SYLVAIN
(Amiens 1948)
French conductor. Born into a family of musicians – his sister Frédérique an accomplished harpist and his brother Philippe a conductor – Cambreling completed his music studies at the Conservatoire in Amiens before specializing in conducting with Pierre Dervaux in Paris. After winning the Concours Internationale de Besançon (1974), he took up conducting professionally as assistant conductor in Lyons (1975–81). In 1977 his debut at the Opéra in Paris in *The Rake's Progress* by Stravinsky confirmed Cambreling's success and launched him on a brilliant international career, taking in Glyndebourne (*Il barbiere di Siviglia* in 1981), La Scala, Milan (*Lucio Silla* in 1984) and the Metropolitan Opera House, New York (*Roméo et Juliette* in 1986). In 1981 Sylvain Cambreling was appointed principal conductor at the Théâtre de la Monnaie in Brussels, and in 1987 he took up the post of music director there. He also appears regularly in concert halls. Cambreling has shown himself to be a very persuasive performer with sensitivity and theatrical energy. His accounts of Charpentier's *Louise*, Gounod's *Sapho*, Strauss's *Salome* and Schoenberg's *Moses und Aron* have won particular admiration.

CAMMARANO, SALVATORE
(Naples 1801–1852)
Italian librettist, and the most famous member of a family of artists. He started out as a dramatist and only later (1834) began work as a librettist, eventually becoming one of the most important of Donizetti's collaborators, providing libretti for his *Lucia di Lammermoor* (1835), *Belisario* (1836), *L'assedio di Calais* (1836), *Pia de' Tolomei* (1837), *Roberto Devereux* (1837), *Maria di Rudenz* (1838), *Maria di Rohan* (1843) and *Poliuto* (1848), and, for Verdi, the texts for *Alzira* (1845), *La battaglia di Legnano* (1849), *Luisa Miller* (1849) and *Il trovatore* (1853, this one being completed by Leone Emanuele Bardare). Cammarano also wrote libretti for Mercadante (*Il reggente*, 1843) and Pacini (*Saffo*, 1840).

CAMPANA SOMMERSA, LA
(The Sunken Bell)
Opera in four acts by Ottorino Respighi (1879–1936), to a libretto by Claudio Guastalla based on Gerhardt Hauptmann's dramatic fable Die versunkene Glocke. *First performance: Hamburg, Stadttheater, 18 November 1927.*

The "silver" meadow, home of the Good Witch of the Woods (mezzo-soprano), Rautèndelein the elf (soprano), Ondino, a faun (baritone), nymphs and gnomes, is threatened by Man's incursions. The people of the valley have had a bell cast, but the faun breaks a wheel on the wagon being used to move it and the bell plunges into the lake and sinks to the bottom. The blacksmith Enrico (tenor) is injured attempting to hold on to the bell. Rautèndelein falls in love with him and wants to be with him. The elf kisses Enrico's eyes, whereupon he finds that he sees life in a new way. Enrico, now living with Rautèndelein, is busy building a gigantic temple dedicated to the improvement of mankind. The priest (bass) wants to make Enrico return: Magda, his wife, has in despair thrown herself into the lake, and their family are distraught. The tolling of the sunken bell is heard. Enrico, at his wit's end, turns Rautèndelein away, but his life is now inseparable from that of the elf. Enrico is dying. Rautèndelein appears before him and reproaches him for having left her, then kisses him and helps him as he dies, calling on the sun.

La campana sommersa was universally a great success, although the fantasy and unreality of the subject-matter may have undermined the precision of the opera. Respighi had originally intended to use a German text for the opera, following a request from the publisher, who had been handling negotiations with Hauptmann for the premiere of *La campana sommersa* to be held in Germany, as eventually it was.

CAMPANELLA, BRUNO
(Bari 1943)
Italian conductor. He studied conducting with Piero Bellugi, Hans Swarowsky and Thomas Schippers. He made his debut at the Festival dei due Mondi in Spoleto in 1967. From 1971 onwards, he has conducted regularly in opera houses in Italy and elsewhere, establishing himself as one of the best opera conductors of his day. Campanella is particularly admired for his performances of *opera buffa* and has given brilliant interpretations of *Don Pasquale*, *L'elisir d'amore*, *La fille du régiment* and *Il barbiere di Siviglia*, as well as other operas from the nineteenth-century Italian repertoire.

A scene from *La cambiale di matrimonio* by Rossini.

CAMPANELLO DELLO SPEZIALE, IL, O IL CAMPANELLO DI NOTTE

(The Apothecary's Bell, or The Night Bell)
Opera buffa *in one act by Gaetano Donizetti (1797–1848), to the composer's own libretto, taken from the* vaudeville *by Brunswick, Troin and Lhérie,* La sonette de nuit. *First performance: Naples, Teatro Nuovo, 1 June 1836.*

The action takes place in Naples. A middle-aged apothecary, Don Annibale Pistachio (bass), is holding a party at his home to celebrate his marriage to the young and beautiful Serafina (soprano). The following morning at five o'clock he has to leave for Rome, a journey he must make if he is to qualify for an inheritance. Don Annibale is therefore anxious for his guests to leave so he may be alone with his bride. Enrico (baritone), cousin and one-time admirer of Serafina, has decided to sabotage Don Annibale's wedding-night. So he rings Don Annibale's door-bell, disguised first as a French nobleman with a stomach upset, then, not long after, with another ring at the door, as a singer who has lost his voice and in need of some medicine. Finally somebody (Enrico again) turns up on the apothecary's door-step with a prescription so complicated that it takes ages to prepare, by which time it is five in the morning and poor Don Annibale has to leave for Rome.

The opera, also known as *Il campanello*, was composed in a single week. It was a great success in Italy and elsewhere and is still performed.

CAMPIELLO, IL

(A Venetian Square)
Opera buffa *in three acts by Ermanno Wolf-Ferrari (1876–1948), to a libretto by Mario Ghisalberti, based on the play of the same name by Carlo Goldoni. First performance: Milan, La Scala, 12 February 1936.*

The action takes place in Venice, in the mid eighteenth century: a small square, with assorted houses and an inn. The Neapolitan *cavaliere* Astolfi (baritone), who is very refined but has no money, has left Naples for Venice in an attempt to salvage his finances. Astolfi is courting an affected young lady, Gasparina (soprano), although he also has an eye on two others, Lucieta (soprano), who is betrothed to Anzoleto (bass), and Gnese (soprano), who is in love with Zorzeto (tenor). The old women-residents of the square get themselves involved in this love tangle: Zorzeto's mother Orsola (mezzo-soprano), Pasqua (tenor) and Cate (mezzo-soprano). By courting the young women and flattering the old ones, the fickle Astolfi incurs the jealousy of the fiancés, triggering off a whole series of squabbles and rows in the square. Fabrizio (bass), Gasparina's uncle, is unable to tolerate the increased amount of noise there and decides to move house, but before he goes, he agrees to marry off his niece to Astolfi, even if he is penniless. During a peace-making supper-party held by the residents of the square, Astolfi announces his forthcoming marriage to Gasparina. The young woman bids a last touching and emotional farewell to the little community and to her beloved Venice, which she will now have to leave for far-off Naples with her husband.

Il campiello is one of Wolf-Ferrari's most successful operas. The score achieves a fine balance between melancholy and liveliness, the two key features of this opera. *Il campiello*'s musical setting is an effective complement to the boisterous energy typical of Goldoni's plays.

CAMPRA, ANDRÉ

(Aix-en-Provence 1660–Versailles 1744)
French composer of Italian parentage. He began as a chorus-master in Toulon (1679–81), Arles (1681–83) and Toulouse (1683–94), before becoming music director at Notre Dame in Paris (1694). In 1697 he composed his first opera (an *opéra-ballet*) and one of his best-known works, *L'Europe galante*. In 1700 he left his Notre Dame post to concentrate on writing music for the theater. His

Above: The Italian conductor Bruno Campanella.

Left: A sketch showing a scene from *Il campiello* by Ermanno Wolf-Ferrari.

style blended elements of the French and Italian schools of music with elegance and variety, and very much reflected the French taste of the time, which was still strongly attached to the kind of opera composed by Lully and Charpentier.

CANDIDE

Opera in two acts by Leonard Bernstein (1918–1990), to a libretto by Lillian Hellman and Dorothy Parker, John Latouche and Richard Wilbur. First performance: Boston, Martin Beck Theater, 29 October 1956.

The action first takes place in the castle of Baron Thunder-ten-Tranckh in Westphalia. Here live Cunégonde (soprano) and Maximilien (baritone), children of the Baron, together with their cousin Candide (tenor) and a young maidservant, Paquette (mezzo-soprano). These four live in perfect harmony, thanks to the life philosophy they have been taught by Dr Pangloss (tenor). This harmonious life is disturbed when Candide and Cunégonde begin to fall in love. The relationship is discovered, and Candide is made to leave the castle. In his attempt to rebuild his life, the poor young man sets out on a series of wanderings and adventures, which nonetheless do not shake the faith in life Pangloss had instilled in him. Cunégonde, Maximilien and Paquette are also experiencing difficult times, and after the castle is destroyed by Bulgarian enemy forces, the three are separated. Candide, Cunégonde, Maximilien and Paquette, each having had to cope with adversity and ill-fortune, meet again, only to lose each other once more, first in Portugal, then in France, again in South America and finally in Venice. After innumerable escapades, the four meet up with Dr Pangloss again, and, though reduced to poverty, they return to Westphalia to work the land, their faith in life still unshaken.

Composed by Bernstein between 1954 and 1956, *Candide* had its premiere in Boston before transferring to New York in December of the same year, 1956. The performances on Broadway amounted to 73 nights, too few for a musical. After the final New York performances, in February 1957, *Candide* began to undergo a series of revisions to adapt the show to a variety of different stage situations. Between 1988 and 1989, the conductor John Mauceri and then Bernstein himself produced a definitive version of *Candide*. The sparkle and appeal of Bernstein's score makes *Candide* similar to the genre of classical operetta, on a par with Offenbach's *La belle Hélène* or Johann Strauss II's *Die Fledermaus*.

CANTATRICI VILLANE, LE

Opera giocosa *in two acts by Valentino Fioravanti (1764–1837), to a libretto by Giovanni Palomba. The date of the first performance is uncertain, but it was given at the Teatro dei Fiorentini, Naples in January 1799.*

The setting is Frascati, Italy. The innkeeper Agata (soprano), and two country-women, Giannetta (mezzo-soprano) and Rosa (soprano), are encouraged by Don Bucefalo (bass), a foolish and ignorant chorus-master, to take up singing. Don Bucefalo asks a local squire, Don Marco (bass), to lend him a harpsichord so he may give singing lessons to Rosa, the widow of a young soldier who has died in Spain. But Carlino (tenor), the "dead" husband, comes home sporting a large moustache, and nobody recognizes him. Listening to the local gossip, Carlino suspects his wife of dishonouring his memory. In order to have a better command of the situation, he brandishes a quarter-master's order that he be billeted in Rosa's house. Rosa, now a budding singer, is preparing for her debut with the help of Don Marco, who has become her impresario. This makes the other women jealous, and they take to spreading even more scandal than usual about their friend. Carlino, with the villagers' help, causes an uproar, and the police arrive, at which point Carlino reveals his identity, asking everyone to forgive him, since it was only jealousy and love which drove him to act as he did. The opera ends in general rejoicing.

The date of the first performance of *Le cantatrici villane* is uncertain: Fioravanti wrote in his memoirs that it was staged "at the Carnival of 1798 at the beginning of 1799." An abridged one-act version (in which the text was adapted by Giuseppe Maria Foppa) was performed at the Teatro Giustiniani di San Moisè in Venice on 28 December 1801. *Le cantatrici villane* is the most successful of Fioravanti's numerous operas and was immediately staged throughout Europe, remaining in the repertoire up to the present day.

CANTELLI, GUIDO

(Novara 1920–Orly, Paris 1956)

Italian conductor. He graduated in composition from the Conservatorio in Milan in 1943, having already embarked on a career as a

Right: A scene from *Le cantatrici villane* by Valentino Fioravanti, in a production at the Teatro Mercadante, Naples.

conductor in 1940. After making his mark conducting *La traviata* in Novara in 1943, Cantelli was already being offered engagements with the leading opera houses by 1944 and conducted in the main concert halls of Europe and America. He died in a plane crash at Orly airport while on his way to the United States to conduct the New York Philharmonic. In 1956, the year of his death, Cantelli had been appointed permanent conductor at La Scala. He was looked on as the successor to Toscanini, who had great admiration for him.

CAPECCHI, RENATO

(Cairo 1923)

Italian bass-baritone. After studies in Milan, Capecchi made his debut on Italian Radio in 1948 and in Reggio Emilia the following year in *Aida*. He scored his first major triumph in *Don Giovanni* in Aix-en-Provence (1949) and, as Dulcamara, in a production of *L'elisir d'amore* in Florence in 1950. From then on, Capecchi appeared in *opera buffa* of the eighteenth and also the early nineteenth century (Rossini, Donizetti, etc.), as well as singing dramatic roles (*Rigoletto, I puritani, Wozzeck*, etc.), in opera houses all over the world. A great actor and a sensitive performer, he has used these talents to make up for a voice which is quite pale in timbre and rather restricted in range. He took part in the first performance of Bussotti's *Ispirazione* (Florence 1988), as well as in Donizetti's *Le convenienze ed inconvenienze teatrali* (The Conventions of the Theater, Venice, 1988) and *L'elisir d'amore* (Genoa, 1989) and Puccini's *Manon Lescaut* (Modena, 1990).

CAPPELLO DI PAGLIA DI FIRENZE, IL

(The Florentine Straw Hat)

Musical farce in two acts and five scenes by Nino Rota (1911–1979), to a libretto by the composer and his mother Ernesta from Labiche's play Un chapeau de paille d'Italie *(The Italian Straw Hat). Composed in 1946. First performance: Palermo, Teatro Massimo, 21 April 1955.*

Fadinard (tenor), a young man of means, is about to marry Elena (soprano), daughter of the farmer Nonancourt (bass). Anaide (soprano) and her lover, Lieutenant Emilio (baritone), arrive unexpectedly at Fadinard's house to protest that Fadinard's horse has eaten Anaide's straw hat and completely ruined it. Anaide must have another hat, otherwise she will be in serious trouble with her already very jealous husband. Fadinard therefore has no choice but to go in search of a new hat. It is the start of a whole cavalcade of adventures, from milliners' shops to the house of Anaide's husband, who now has proof of his suspicions about his wife's infidelity. At the point when, in the wake of a string of misunderstandings, Fadinard's wedding plans seem to be ruined, Vézinet (tenor), Elena's uncle, who has unwittingly given his niece a hat identical to the one which Fadinard is desperately trying to obtain, resolves the delicate situation at a stroke. Now that she has her hat, Anaide makes fun of her jealous husband, while Fadinard persuades Elena's father to renew his blessing on the marriage. So the wedding party can begin again.

Il cappello di paglia di Firenze has been staged in different parts of Italy, as well as in other countries. At La Piccola Scala, Milan, it was included in the programme for two consecutive seasons. A typical feature of this *divertissement*, which was turned into a film by René Clair, is its seemingly endless stream of jokes. The score is subtle and elegant, and fits in well with the brisk plot. Nino Rota is best known as a composer of film scores.

CAPPUCCILLI, PIERO

(Trieste 1929)

Italian baritone. He completed his singing studies in Trieste with Luciano Donaggio, making his debut in 1957 at the Teatro Nuovo in Milan as Tonio in Leoncavallo's *I pagliacci*. This launched him on a sparkling career which has included appearances in all the leading international opera houses over several decades. Cappuccilli's name is particularly linked with La Scala, Milan, where, from 1964, he performed in almost every season and had some of his greatest successes, like the now historic Giorgio Strehler production of *Simon Boccanegra* under Claudio Abbąd0 (1971), *Macbeth* (1975), also with Strehler and Abbado, and Zeffirelli's *Otello* (1976) with Carlos Kleiber conducting. Cappuccilli's voice had a warmth of timbre, a very fine range and precise delivery. He always distinguished himself with his considerable skills of interpretation that made him one of the most admired performers of Verdi as well as of the great baritone roles of Italian opera.

CAPRICCI DI CALLOT, I

(The Caprices of Callot)

Opera in a prologue and three acts by Gian Francesco Malipiero (1882–1973), to the composer's own libretto. First performance: Rome, Teatro dell'Opera, 24 October 1942.

Four pairs of masked dancers announce the Carnival. Giacinta (soprano), a dressmaker, prepares to take part in it and makes herself a wonderful dress with which she intends to impress her young fiancé, Giglio (tenor), a penniless actor. Along the Corso in Rome, the Carnival is under way. In the midst of the masked crowd are a little old man and a charlatan who start off by playing a trick on the two

Above: The Italian baritone Piero Cappuccilli in a scene from *Simon Boccanegra* by Verdi, in a production at La Scala in 1971.

lovers and end up joining in their wedding-feast at a sumptuously laid table.

I capricci di Callot is seen by critics as a successful blend of Malipiero's feeling for the whimsical, E. T. A. Hoffmann's *Prinzessin Brambilla* (Princess Brambilla) and Jacques Callot's 24 engravings entitled *Balli di Sfessonia.* Malipiero successfully uses the music to emphasize the action and to give character to the individual roles.

CAPRICCIO

Musical conversation piece in one act by Richard Strauss (1864–1949), to a libretto by Strauss and Clemens Krauss. First performance: Munich, Bayerische Staatsoper, 28 October 1942.

A château near Paris. In her drawing-room, the Countess Madeleine (soprano) is listening to a performance of a sextet for strings (which is used as the overture to *Capriccio*) dedicated to her by the composer Flamand (tenor). He and the poet Olivier (baritone) have started a discussion in which each argues for the supremacy of his own art. La Roche (bass) is going to stage Olivier's tragedy in the château to mark the occasion of the Countess's birthday. The Count (baritone), Madeleine's brother, rehearses the most important scene in the play with the actress Clairon (contralto), whom he loves. Flamand is suddenly inspired and sets the scene to music. A performance by a dancer leads to a reopening of the discussion about the relative merits of the individual arts. The impresario La Roche proclaims that it is he, with his practical showmanship, who makes the arts possible by bringing them together. The Count suggests to Flamand and Olivier that they should make an opera that deals with these arguments and have as its cast everyone present in the room. It is a moment of intense feeling: the barriers between life and the theater have been broken down. All the guests leave for Paris. Madeleine enters the empty room. She has made a rendezvous with both Flamand and Olivier for the following day, and promised that she will marry one of them, but has not yet decided whom. "If I choose one, I lose the other. Is it possible to win without losing?"

Capriccio is Strauss's last opera, and in it he achieves one of his long-cherished aims, to make the words of an opera comprehensible in performance. The main focus of *Capriccio* is the Countess, a personification of opera as the Muse and also the synthesis of poetry and music. Madeleine's final dilemma is, in this sense, the same as Strauss's, and in her honour he has collected together short quotations from the operas he loved most.

CAPTAIN JINKS OF THE HORSE MARINES

Romantic comedy in three acts by Jack Beeson (b. 1921), to a libretto by Sheldon Harnick. First performance: Kansas City, Lyric Theater, 20 September 1975.

Jonathan Jinks (tenor) and his friends Charlie (baritone) and Willie (baritone) are waiting to welcome to America the famous opera singer Aurelia Trentoni (soprano). After the impresario Mapleson (bass) has praised the singer's charm and listed the names of her distinguished admirers, Charlie, who envies Jinks his reputation as a great ladykiller, provokes him with a bet that he cannot seduce Aurelia. Jinks takes him on. When Aurelia and Jinks meet, a strong attraction develops between them. Aurelia agrees to

Above: A scene from *I capricci di Callot* by Malipiero, in the 1942 production at the Teatro dell' Opera, Rome.

Right: A scene from *Capriccio* by Richard Strauss, in a production at the Teatro Comunale, Florence.

see Jinks again. But Jinks is now ashamed of the bet with Charlie, and in his desire to be attentive to Aurelia, he speeds up the customs formalities on her luggage by attempting to bribe an inspector, but picks on the wrong man and is arrested. By the time he is released from prison on bail, Jinks realizes he is hopelessly in love with Aurelia. She loves him too, and the couple become secretly engaged. During a rehearsal for *La traviata*, the opera in which Aurelia will make her American debut, Jinks's mother (mezzo-soprano) advises Aurelia to break off the relationship with her son. Aurelia promises to think it over but also invites Mrs Jinks, who has never been to the opera, to be in the audience for her debut. The increasingly jealous Charlie makes contact with Aurelia, accusing Jinks of being a dowry-hunter and of having put money on his marrying Aurelia. She is stunned by this and no longer has the will to sing, but in the end is persuaded to do so. After Aurelia's triumphant debut in *La traviata*, the story reaches a happy ending. Aurelia sees Jinks and discovers that his love for her is sincere. Jinks's mother, too, moved by the story of Violetta in the opera that evening, gladly gives her blessing to her son's marriage. The opera ends with everyone singing a hymn of praise to the irresistible power of music.

Captain Jinks of the Horse Marines is based on a play by Clyde Fitch written about 1870. Beeson's operatic recipe for the work combines comic elements, which owe something to light opera and stage comedy, translated by the score into the idiom of the American musical, with the romantic element, expressed in more markedly lyrical accents by Aurelia and Jinks. To emphasize the melodramatic nature of Aurelia's character, Beeson intentionally brings together the meeting between Aurelia and Jinks's mother and the duet in Verdi's *La traviata* with Violetta and Germont. Beeson quotes the Verdi work several times in this pleasing score.

CAPULETI E I MONTECCHI, I

(The Capulets and the Montagues)

Tragic opera in two acts by Vincenzo Bellini (1801–1835), to a libretto by Felice Romani based on Shakespeare's sources for Romeo and Juliet. *First performance: Venice, Teatro La Fenice, 11 March 1830.*

The action takes place in Verona in the thirteenth century. Romeo Montecchi (mezzo-soprano), in love with Giulietta Capuletí (soprano), goes incognito to see Capellio (bass), Giulietta's father, with a request for a truce between the two families, between whom a feud of deep hatred exists. The truce could be secured by a marriage between Giulietta and Romeo himself. Capellio contemptuously rejects these proposals and makes it known that Giulietta is soon to marry Tebaldo (tenor), one of his most trusted supporters. Romeo meets Giulietta in secret and asks her to elope with him, but she cannot bring herself to leave her father's house and, by so doing, lose her honour. Romeo tries again to persuade Giulietta to run away with him, but he is surprised by the Capulets and recognized. Only a timely intervention by members of his own family saves him. Giulietta follows the advice of her personal physician and confidant Lorenzo (bass) as to how she can avoid marrying Tebaldo: she must drink from a phial containing a powerful sleeping draught which will give her the appearance of being dead. When she recovers from the effects of it, she can be reunited with Romeo. Meanwhile Romeo is about to fight a duel with Tebaldo when funeral chants are heard issuing from the Capulets' house announcing that Giulietta has died. Stunned by this disaster, both men put down their arms. Romeo goes to the tomb of the Capulets and becomes so desperate from looking at his beloved that he takes poison. Shortly afterwards, Giulietta wakes up, sees Romeo dying and falls dead from grief over the body of her beloved.

Bellini wrote *I Capuleti e I Montecchi* hoping to make up for the failure of his *Zaira* in Parma and, to vindicate himself, he transplanted some of the music from *Zaira* into the new opera. He succeeded totally, scoring a triumph with *I Capuleti*. The exquisitely moving content of the story was by its nature very likely to stimulate the sensibility of Bellini, who reached great lyrical heights in his score, particularly in his writing for the two leading characters.

CARAVANE DU CAIRE, LA

(The Caravan of Cairo)

Opera-ballet in three acts by André Modeste Grétry (1741–1813), to a libretto by Etienne Morel de Chéfdeville. First performance: Fontainebleu, 30 October 1783, in the presence of the King and Queen. First public theater performance: Paris, Académie Royale de Musique (Opéra), 15 January 1784.

A scene from *I Capuleti e i Montecchi* by Bellini.

Husca (bass), a slave trader, is part of a caravan of travellers on its way to Cairo. Among his captives is Zélime (soprano), the daughter of a Nabob, and her husband, Saint-Phar (tenor). During the journey, the caravan is attacked by robbers; Saint-Phar asks Husca to set him free, and then, with great courage, he defends the travellers and drives their assailants away. Husca expresses his gratitude to Saint-Phar by giving him his freedom. Saint-Phar then requests that Zélime be freed instead of him, but Husca refuses, knowing that the young woman will fetch him a handsome price at the Cairo Bazaar. Indeed, the Pasha himself (bass) falls in love with Zélime and has her taken to his harem. Saint-Phar, who has amassed a sum of money as ransom to recover his wife, protests in vain. A few days later, in the Pasha's palace, celebrations are being held in honour of the French navy captain Florestan (baritone) for having provided a safe passage for the Pasha's ship during a storm at sea. The party is interrupted by the eunuch Tamorin (contralto) announcing that a man has just kidnapped Zélime. The young woman and her captor are very quickly overtaken and led into the Pasha's presence. Florestan, who witnesses this scene, recognizes Saint-Phar, Zélime's would-be captor, as the son he has believed to be dead. The Pasha repays Florestan for saving his life by granting Saint-Phar and his wife their freedom, and the opera ends happily.

The music of *La Caravane du Caire* is an elegant match for Morel de Chéfdeville's libretto, offering the Parisian audience of the day a formula that was guaranteed to succeed: an exotic tale, crowd scenes, a battle.

CARDILLAC

Opera in three acts by Paul Hindemith (1895–1963), to a libretto by Ferdinand Lion taken from E. T. A. Hoffmann's story Das Fräulein von Scuderi. *First performance: Dresden, Staatsoper, 9 November 1926. First performance of the wholly revised version: Zurich, Stadttheater, 20 June 1952.*

Paris, in the last decade of the seventeenth century. The city is living in fear because mysterious crimes are being committed all over. A Cavalier (tenor) goes to the workshop of the famous goldsmith Cardillac (baritone). The young man admires the goldsmith's work, in particular a wonderful diadem, which he wants to buy. Cardillac refuses to let him have it, but the young man seizes it and runs off. He then makes for the house of his lover, the Opéra prima donna (soprano) and gives her the priceless diadem, but a masked man climbs into the house, kills the Cavalier and makes off with the diadem. The scene changes. The Gold Merchant (bass) knows that the murderer is Cardillac himself, but he keeps silent because he is in love with Cardillac's daughter (soprano). The Marquis (who remains silent), the prima donna and a group of artists from the Opéra go to Cardillac's shop. The singer sees the diadem and faints. The Marquis buys the diadem. The Gold Merchant, who is himself under suspicion of having committed the murders, warns the prima donna of the risk incurred by anyone who wears the jewel which the Marquis has given her. She is then approached by Cardillac; and, as though in a trance, she hands him the diadem. An Officer who was present throughout has been keeping his eye on the Apprentice. The Officer then snatches up the diadem and escapes. Cardillac madly sets out in pursuit of the Officer. A furious scuffle takes place, and the Officer is wounded. The Gold Merchant confesses the truth and reveals that the goldsmith is the murderer. Customers and passers-by force Cardillac to confess, then kill him. The prima donna, the Daughter and the Gold Merchant weep over him, even though he had allowed himself to be dragged down into madness through his obsession for what he had created.

After the first, 1926 version of *Cardillac*, Hindemith made sweeping changes to the opera in 1952. The music in the opera neither determines nor participates in the emotional state of play. Sometimes Hindemith causes it to become detached from the dramatic content of the words, playing continuously on in a lucid stream of neo-classical polyphony.

CARMEN

Opera in four acts by Georges Bizet (1838–1875), to a libretto by Henri Meilhac and Ludovic Halévy based on the novel Carmen *by Prosper Mérimée. First performance: Paris, Théâtre de l'Opéra-Comique, 3 March 1875.*

The setting is a square in Seville, about 1820. Micaela (soprano), a country girl, is shyly looking for Don José, a corporal in the dragoons. Don José (tenor) arrives just as the girls are coming out of the tobacco factory. Among them is Carmen (mezzo-soprano), who takes a fancy to Don José and attempts to entice him by throwing him a flower. Disturbed by the gipsy girl's shamelessness, he embraces Micaela, who has just brought him news of his mother. A fight breaks out at the factory, and Carmen is arrested for wounding one of the girls. Don José is made to guard her, and she enchants him: completely seduced by her, he helps her to escape. In Lillas Pastia's inn, Carmen is being eyed appraisingly by the bullfighter Escamillo (baritone). But her thoughts are now taken up with José, who arrives shortly afterwards. José is blind with passion and disobeys the orders of

Above: A scene from *Cardillac*, in a production at the Teatro Comunale, Florence.

Captain Zuniga (bass) to return to quarters. This makes him into a deserter from his regiment, and he goes into hiding with Carmen in the mountains. The scene changes to the smugglers' headquarters. Carmen is tired of José and has now fallen in love with Escamillo the bullfighter, who appears at the hide-out. Crazed with jealousy, José hurls himself at Escamillo. The two men confront each other with knives, and Carmen only just manages to keep them apart. Micaela arrives and persuades José to go with her to see his mother, who is dying. Don José follows Micaela, threatening Carmen, who defies him with her shamelessness. In front of the bullring in Seville, the crowd applauds Escamillo on his way to the bullfight with Carmen, who is now his new mistress. Don José roams the square, trying to get close to Carmen. She fearlessly confronts her former lover. José pleads with her to come back to him and show him her love again, but Carmen coldly and disdainfully hurls at his feet a ring José had given her. Mad with jealousy, José falls on Carmen and stabs her to death. Then, sobbing and desperately calling her name, José offers no resistance as he is arrested.

Carmen is Bizet's masterpiece and one of the greatest creative achievements in operatic history. It was nevertheless not understood at its premiere and provoked accusations of immorality, obscenity, poor sense of theater and bad taste. *Carmen* keeps to the time-honoured structure of the *opéra-comique*, into which Bizet breathes new life. Arias, songs, choruses and duets bow to tradition, but the novelty of the work lies in its great emotional impact, with passionate and violent feelings being featured for the first time in French *opéra-comique*, a form of theater greatly restricted by rigid conventions. The score keeps pace with Bizet's new operatic design, injecting a continuous and electrifying stream of musical inventiveness into the action. After the failure of the first night, the opera recovered and eight years later scored a decisive triumph. Bizet was, however, unable to witness the success of his work, as he died three months after the first performance. *Carmen* is thus also his last opera.

CARRÉ, MICHEL

(Paris 1819–Argenteuil 1872)

French playwright and librettist. He wrote a number of libretti for the leading French composers of the time: Meyerbeer (*Dinorah*, 1859), Gounod (*Le médecin malgré lui*, 1858; *Faust*, 1859; *La reine de Saba*, 1862; *Mireille*, 1864; *Roméo et Juliette*, 1867, etc.), Bizet (*Les pêcheurs de perles*, 1863) and Offenbach (*Les contes d'Hoffmann*, 1881).

CARRERAS, JOSÉ

(Barcelona 1946)

Spanish tenor. He made his first appearance at the age of 11 in Manuel de Falla's *El retablo de maese Pedro* (Master Peter's Puppet Show) in Barcelona, and studied music at the Conservatorio in Barcelona with Francisco Puig. In the 1970–71 season he made his debut as Ismaele in *Nabucco*, also in Barcelona. In 1971 Carreras won the "Concorso Verdi" in the Italian composer's birthplace, Busseto. The support and encouragement given to Carreras by the soprano Montserrat Caballé played a significant part in his career, and he sang with her for the first time in the role of Gennaro in *Lucrezia Borgia* (Barcelona, 1970). Between 1971 and 1974, Carreras appeared with the New York City Opera (in *Madama Butterfly*), at the Teatro Colón in Buenos Aires and in Chicago. By 1974 the name of Carreras was becoming increasingly established in the leading international opera houses: the Metropolitan Opera House, New York (*Tosca*), La Scala, Milan (1975), Salzburg Festival (*Un ballo in maschera*, 1976) and Covent Garden (*La traviata*). Carreras took on more and more singing engagements as part of a very busy schedule, as well as scoring some remarkable successes in the recording studio. In 1987 Carreras went down with a sudden, serious illness on the set of Comencini's film of *La bohème*, and he was found to be suffering from leukemia. Carreras gradually resumed his career in 1988, first in concerts only, and then making his comeback in opera (*Carmen* in Vienna, *Samson et Dalila* in London), although to a lesser extent than in the past. Carreras has a very beautiful, resplendent vocal timbre, as well as a tremendously passionate stage temperament. He remains one of the most popular and well-loved singers of his day.

Above: A scene from *Carmen* by Bizet.

Left: The Spanish tenor José Carreras.

CARTERI, ROSANNA

(Verona 1930)

Italian soprano. She studied with Cusinati and Ederle and made her debut in 1949 at the Baths of Caracalla in Rome as Elsa in Wagner's *Lohengrin*. After appearing in Verdi's *Falstaff* in Bologna (1950), Carteri made her name at La Scala, Milan (1951) in a production of Piccinni's *La buona figliola*. Engagements followed with the world's leading opera houses (San Francisco, 1984; Chicago, 1955; Paris, 1956; Salzburg, 1962). With her fine vocal timbre and elegant stage presence, Carteri sang in premieres including Pizzetti's *Il calzare d'argento* (Milan, 1961) and Castelnuovo-Tedesco's *Il mercante di Venezia* (1961), as well as in important revivals such as Puccini's *La rondine* (Naples, 1958) and Rossini's *La donna del lago* (Florence, 1959).

CARUSO, ENRICO

(Naples 1873–1921)

Italian tenor. His modest family background meant he could have no regular singing lessons, learning instead from a number of different teachers whenever the chance arose. His debut is said to have been in November 1894 (others date it as 1895) in Morelli's *L'amico Francesco*. He sang in small theaters and made his first real mark in 1897 in Ponchielli's *La Gioconda* at the Teatro Massimo in Palermo. From this point, Caruso's career took off, extending to engagements abroad (St. Petersburg, Buenos Aires and London). He took part in the first performances of *L'Arlesiana* (1897), *Fedora* (1898) and *Adriana Lecouvreur* (1902). In the 1903–4 season, he made his first appearance at the Metropolitan Opera House in New York, where he sang until the 1920–21 season. During this long period of residency at the Metropolitan, Caruso was seen in a very considerable repertoire, from *L'elisir d'amore* to *Aida*, from *Martha* to *Manon Lescaut*, and from *Faust* to *Samson et Dalila* and *La Juive*. It was during a performance of Halévy's opera that Caruso first complained of symptoms diagnosed as the bronchial pneumonia which forced him to give up singing and led to his death in 1921. To this day Caruso is the very embodiment of the myth of the tenor voice: his vocal splendour, and a delivery that matured naturally until it became almost flawless, are illustrated by the large number of recordings Caruso made over an extended period (1902–20), which crowned him as the first tenor of the gramophone.

Above: Enrico Caruso.

Right: The Italian composer Alfredo Casella.

CASELLA, ALFREDO

(Turin 1883–Rome 1947)

Italian composer. Born to a family of musicians, he began to study the piano at a very young age. In 1896 he moved to Paris, where, besides devoting himself to his studies, he began to give concerts as a pianist. In 1915 he returned to Italy and in the space of a few years had established himself as one of the leading figures in the history of Italian music, both as a composer and as a promoter of initiatives to help revive composers of the past. As an opera composer, Casella wrote *La donna serpente* (Rome, 1932), *La favola di Orfeo* (Venice, 1932) and *Il deserto tentato* (Florence, 1937).

CASKEN, JOHN

(Barnsley, Yorkshire 1949)

British composer. He began to study music at Birmingham University, completing his training in Poland, where he attended courses given by Dobrowolski. His meeting with the Polish composer Witold Lutoslawski proved a decisive influence on his development: from Lutoslawski he assimilated a very sober, clear style in the use of harmony. After his return to England, Casken took part in important reviews of contemporary music, at the Bath Festival (1980), Musica Nova in Glasgow (1984), the Huddersfield Festival (1986) and the Music Today Festival in Tokyo (1990). In 1989 his opera *Golem* was performed in London, winning first prize in the 1990 Britten Award for Composition. John Casken currently teaches music at Durham University.

CASOLLA, GIOVANNA

(Naples 1945)

Italian soprano. A pupil of Michele Lauro at the Conservatorio San Pietro a Maiella in Naples, from where she graduated, Casolla made her debut in 1977 at the Spoleto Festival in the world premiere production of Nino Rota's opera *Napoli Milionaria*. She was then engaged by a number of Italian opera houses, including La Scala, Milan, where she appeared in 1982 in Puccini's *Il tabarro* (revived in 1987). She subsequently sang again at La Scala in Puccini's *La fanciulla del West* (1991) with Lorin Maazel conducting. For her American debut, she gave an outstanding performance as Eboli in Verdi's *Don Carlos* at the Metropolitan, New York in

1986, a role which she repeated at some of the leading opera houses, including Florence's Teatro Comunale (1985), La Fenice in Venice (1992) and the Arena in Verona. She also sang in *Tosca* in Philadelphia with Riccardo Muti conducting. Casolla has appeared at numerous opera houses in Europe (Vienna Staatsoper, Munich, Brussels). Her distinctive dramatic and vocal originality has made her one of the finest interpreters of

Puccini's *Tosca*, *La fanciulla del West* and *Il tabarro*, and of Giordano's *Andrea Chénier*, Mascagni's *Cavalleria rusticana* and other so-called realist operas.

CASSELLO, KATHLEEN

(Wilmington, Delaware 1958)
American soprano, naturalized Italian. She studied with Dan Pressley in Newark, Delaware. In 1984 she won the "Austrian-American" Competition in Wilmington and was able to attend a course of advanced training in Salzburg (1984). Between 1984 and 1985, she won further significant acclaim in a number of different singing competitions, including the "Francisco D'Andrade" in Oporto, the "Francisco Viñas" in Barcelona, the "Pavarotti" in Philadelphia and the "Mozart" in Salzburg. This last award enabled her to make her debut with the Hamburg Opera as the Queen of the Night in Mozart's *Die Zauberflöte* (The Magic Flute) in 1985, a role which she went on to sing with great success in Frankfurt, Berlin (Deutsche Oper), Moscow (Bolshoi) in 1986, Vienna Staatsoper and Geneva. Cassello's voice, essentially a lyric soprano, full-bodied in the middle register, wide-ranging, and particularly well-suited to *coloratura*, has enabled her to tackle not only numerous Mozart roles (Donna Anna, Fiordiligi, Constanze, Vitellia, etc.) but also the leads in *La traviata*, *Rigoletto*, *Lucia di Lammermoor*, *Manon* and others. In 1992 she appeared for the first time in Italy at the Arena in Verona as Musetta (*La bohème*) and in *Lucia di Lammermoor* in Treviso and Palermo.

CASSILLY, RICHARD

(Washington, D.C. 1927)
American tenor. He studied at the Baltimore Conservatory (1946–52) and made his debut in New York in Menotti's opera *The Saint of Bleecker Street* (1955). After singing for a number of seasons at the New York City Opera, Cassilly was invited in 1965 to sing the role of Radamè (*Aida*) at the Hamburg Staatsoper. From this he joined the resident company at the opera house, as well as keeping up his international engagements in the leading European theaters and festivals. Cassilly's dramatic tenor has made its mark in a fairly broad repertoire, consisting of Italian and German operas: *I pagliacci*, *Fidelio*, *Otello*, *Parsifal*, *Tannhäuser* and *Der Freischütz*.

The Italian soprano Giovanna Casolla in Verdi's *Don Carlos.*

CASTOR ET POLLUX

Tragédie lyrique *in five acts (with a prologue) by Jean-Philippe Rameau (1683–1764), to a libretto by Pierre-Joseph Bernard. First performance: Paris, Académie Royale de Musique (Opéra), 24 October 1737.*

Prologue. Minerva (soprano) and Love (tenor) beg Venus (soprano) to put the god of war in chains. The goddess then appears, with Mars (bass), chained, at her feet. The world seems a better place, and everyone is happy that peace has been restored. The Tragedy. Telaire (soprano) is in mourning for the death of her beloved Castor (tenor). Enter, in triumph, Pollux (bass), who announces that he has avenged his brother Castor's death and reveals to Telaire that he loves her. Telaire asks him to go down into the Underworld and bring Castor back to life. Pollux calls on Jupiter (bass) to help him rescue his brother. Jupiter agrees to let Castor return to life on one condition: Pollux must take his place in the realm of the dead. Princess Phoebe (soprano), who is in love with Pollux, tries to prevent him from making the descent into Hades, but when she discovers his love for Telaire, she becomes desperate and incites the demons to stand against him. But Pollux overcomes the forces from beyond the grave and reaches his brother Castor, who does not want to accept life for himself at the expense of his brother's own. Out of love for Telaire, Castor then accepts the life which is being offered to him, but only for a day. The meeting between Telaire and Castor is dramatic, after his revelation that he has returned for a single day only. But then Jupiter intervenes: filled with compassion, and admiring the love and courage of the two brothers, he frees Pollux and reunites him with Castor, inviting them both to take their places among the stars and so live for ever.

Castor et Pollux is Rameau's third opera, after *Hippolyte et Aricie* and *Les Indes galantes*, and, like them, it scored a remarkable triumph: it was performed 254 times between 1737 and 1785, an unusual number at that time. Rameau revived the opera in 1754 in a completely revised version. The change was clearly for the better, strengthening the music and making the whole opera more compact.

CATALANI, ALFREDO

(Lucca 1854–Milan 1893)
Italian composer. After studying at the Liceo Musicale in Lucca, Catalani went to Paris to specialize in piano and composition. On his return to Italy (1873), he continued his studies at the Conservatorio in Milan. Here he composed his first opera, *La falce* (1875), to a libretto by Arrigo Boito. This was followed by *Elda* (Turin, 1880), *Dejanice* (Milan, 1883) and *Edmea* (Milan, 1886). In 1890 Catalani presented *Loreley*, a reworking of *Elda*. These were the years in which his creativity was at its height, culminating in the composition of *La Wally* (Milan, 1892). In this opera Catalani succeeds in finding a perfect balance in his expressive language between his search for a naturalistic timbre (in this case by using Tyrolean melodies), a dramatic intensity in the style of the realist school and a lyrical gift akin to that of Puccini.

CATERINA CORNARO

Opera in a prologue and two acts by Gaetano Donizetti (1797–1848), to a libretto by Giacomo Sacchèro after Vernoy de Saint-Georges' libretto for Halévy's La reine de Chypre. *First performance: Naples, Teatro San Carlo, 18 January 1844.*

- The action takes place in Venice and Nicosia in 1472. In the great hall of Palazzo Cornaro, the wedding is taking place between Gerardo (tenor), a French Cavalier, and Caterina (soprano), daughter of Andrea Cornaro (bass). The ceremony is interrupted by a masked man who reveals himself, in a secret conversation with Andrea, as Mocenigo (bass), a member of the Council of Ten and Venice's ambassador to Cyprus. On orders from the Venetian government, Caterina must marry Lusignano (baritone), the dethroned King of Cyprus. This politically motivated marriage will give Lusignano the support of Venice in his bid to win back his crown, while the Venetian Republic will regain its supremacy over the island. Caterina has to accept, otherwise Gerardo will be put to death. In a dramatic duet, Caterina, to save Gerardo, denies her feelings. Gerardo leaves, cursing this woman, whom he loves. The scene changes to Cyprus. Lusignano has now realized that he is a Venetian pawn. Mocenigo's hired assassins prepare to ambush Lusignano, but he is saved by the timely intervention of a horseman who proves to be Gerardo. He offers the King his friendship and learns from Caterina in person the real reason for their enforced separation. The conspiracy against Cyprus has, however, reached a dramatic turning-point. Venetian ships are about to unleash a decisive attack on the city. Gerardo leads Lusignano's troops to a Cypriot victory. But the King himself is fatally wounded and dies in Caterina's arms as she swears to defend his kingdom.

Although one of Donizetti's minor works, *Caterina Cornaro* abounds in inspired moments and displays great powers of lyrical expressiveness and a fine grasp of theater.

CATONE IN UTICA

Opera in three acts by Antonio Vivaldi (1678–1741), to a libretto by Pietro Metastasio. First performance: Verona, Teatro Filarmonico, spring 1737, in the presence of Charles Albert, Elector of Bavaria.

- Marzia (soprano), daughter of Catone (tenor), is in love with Cesare (soprano) and is herself loved by Arbace (soprano), Prince of Numidia and an ally of Marzia's father. Fulvio (mezzo-soprano), a member of Cesare's political party, is in love with Emilia (mezzo-soprano), the widow of Pompeo and daughter of Scipione. Because of her love for Cesare, Marzia refuses to marry Arbace. Catone holds talks with Cesare, who is laying siege to the city of Utica: in answer to Catone's peace overtures, Cesare says he will grant Rome her freedom from his dictatorial rule. Marzia tries to persuade her father to think well of Cesare, while Emilia attempts to win over Fulvio to the idea of killing Cesare. But Catone, when he comes to learn of his daughter's love for the tyrant of Rome, sends Marzia away. In the meantime, Emilia has tried everything in order to get rid of Cesare. She manages to attack him with a sword which is out of its sheath, but Fulvio appears in time to save him. Meanwhile, Cesare's soldiers have broken down the last barriers of resistance from Utica, and Catone dies in the presence of the victorious general Cesare. But Cesare refuses to accept any honour for his triumph, because the price he has paid is unbearable to him: Catone may have been one of his implacable enemies, but with him dies the last real citizen of Rome, an embodiment of Rome's long-lived strengths.

The second and third acts of Vivaldi's *Catone in Utica* have survived, but the first act has been lost. Metastasio's play had been adjudged too daring, because it featured the death on stage of the leading character. So the poet had to prepare a tasteful happy ending so as not to offend the audience. Although not one of Vivaldi's best operas, it nevertheless contains passages of great musical value.

A scene from *Cavalleria rusticana* by Mascagni.

CAVALIERI DI EKEBÙ, I

(The Knights of Ekeby)

Opera in four acts by Riccardo Zandonai (1883–1944), to a libretto by Arturo Rossato, taken from Selma Lagerlöf's novel Gösta Berlings saga. *First performance: Milan, La Scala, 7 March 1925.*

- The action takes place in Ekeby, Sweden. Gösta Berling, a priest, has been unfrocked and banned from entering the presbytery because of his drinking. After being thrown out of a tavern and rebuked by Anna, the young woman he loves, Berling wants to die. The "commander" (mezzo-soprano), owner of the iron-mines and Lady of the castle of Ekeby, offers him a job with the "Knights," her motley crew of adventurous and bohemian former soldiers. During a Christmas entertainment, Gösta makes a public declaration of his love for Anna. They kiss. The wicked Sintram (bass) insinuates that the "commander" has sold the Knights' souls to the devil, with the result that she is expelled from the community. She comes back later, now ill, after the Knights have already made up their minds to call her home. She pardons everyone and, before dying, bequeaths her worldly goods to Gösta and Anna. The Knights return to their normal work.

This is perhaps Zandonai's most interesting score. The opera was a resounding success, scoring a triumph in Stockholm too, when it was staged there in 1928 to mark the 70th birthday of Selma Lagerlöf.

CAVALIERI, EMILIO DE'

(Rome c. 1550–1602)

Italian composer. Thanks to his father, who was a friend of Michelangelo, Cavalieri was introduced into the most refined circles in Roman cultural life, where he drew attention for his remarkable artistic qualities. Cavalieri also went to Florence, where he was in the service of Ferdinando de' Medici. The work thought to be his masterpiece, *La rappresentatione di anima e di corpo*, was staged in Rome in 1600. This piece cannot be regarded as an opera in the real sense, but rather a kind of "sacred opera," similar to the *sacra rappresentazione* or religious play with music that was the first Roman example of changes in the vocal style and the process of abandoning polyphony in favour of monody.

CAVALLERIA RUSTICANA

Opera in one act by Pietro Mascagni (1863–1945), to a libretto by Giovanni Targioni-Tozzetti and Giovanni Menasci, based on a story by Guido Verga. First performance: Rome, Teatro Costanzi, 17 May 1890.

The setting is a village in Sicily at the end of the nineteenth century. Before setting out on his military service, Turiddu (tenor) had been betrothed to Lola (mezzo-soprano). On his return, however, the young man found she is now married to the cart-driver Alfio (baritone); after trying to console himself with Santuzza (soprano), Turiddu has nonetheless not given up his courting of Lola, and forms an illicit relationship with her. Santuzza, who is deeply in love with Turiddu, attempts to persuade him to come back to her, but he is irritated by her jealousy and violently rejects her. Santuzza curses him and tells Alfio of Lola's unfaithfulness. Alfio swears revenge. While Turiddu is drinking at the inn in the company of Lola and some of the other villagers, Alfio comes up to him, provokes him, and challenges him to a duel. Before going off to fight the duel, Turiddu is filled with compassion for Santuzza and asks his mother Lucia (contralto) to take care of her. He also asks his mother for her blessing. Exit Turiddu. Shortly afterwards, people are heard murmuring in the distance, followed by the women crying out that Turiddu has been killed.

Cavalleria rusticana won first prize in a competition held in 1888 by the publisher Sonzogno, and was a sensational success at its first performance. It continues to receive a warm response to this day. The libretto, one of the most sensitively worked-out combinations of musical and literary language, is supported by a Mascagni score in which the composer's powerful charge of excitable temperament is translated into impassioned singing.

CAVALLI, FRANCESCO

(Crema 1602–Venice 1676)

Italian composer, whose real name was Pier Francesco Caletti Bruni. He was given his first lessons in music by his father, after which, thanks to the patronage of the Venetian nobleman Federigo Cavalli, a former *podestà* (government-nominated mayor) of Crema, Francesco went to Venice in the company of his new benefactor. There he was probably a pupil of Claudio Monteverdi, was admitted to the Cappella of San Marco, and adopted his patron's surname. In 1639 his first opera was staged, *Le nozze di Teti e Peleo*. It was the beginning of a period of the most intense activity for Cavalli, during which he composed operas, mainly for the Venetian theaters but also for Milan (*Orione*, 1653) and for Paris (*Ercole amante*, 1662). Cavalli was, after Monteverdi, the leading exponent of the so-called Venetian school of opera. His works include *Egisto* (1643), *Ormindo* (1644), *Giasone* (1649), *Calisto* (1651), *Serse* (1654) and *Erismena* (1655).

CECCATO, ALDO

(Milan 1934)

Italian conductor. He studied at the Conservatorio in Milan, then completed his training at the Berlin Hochschule and the Accademia Chigiana in Siena (1961–63). In 1964 he made his debut at the Teatro Nuovo in Milan in *Don Giovanni*. After appearing as a conductor in a number of Italian opera houses, including La Scala (1967), Ceccato embarked on an international career in which he made his Covent Garden debut in 1970 (in *La traviata*) and his first appearance at Glyndebourne in *Ariadne auf Naxos* (1971). He has also been conductor of orchestras in Detroit (1973–77), Hamburg (1972–83), and, from 1985, of the Bergen and North German Radio (Hanover) opera companies. More recent performances have included Donizetti's *Maria Stuarda* at a Donizetti festival held in Bergamo, northern Italy, in 1989.

CECCHINA, OSSIA LA BUONA FIGLIOLA

(Cecchina, or The Good-hearted Girl)

Opera in three acts by Niccolò Piccinni (1728–1800), to a libretto by Carlo Goldoni. First performance: Rome, Teatro delle Dame, 6 February 1760.

Cecchina (soprano), a poor girl taken in while still a child has grown up in the house of the Marchese della Conchiglia (tenor). She is in love with the Marchese and he returns her love. Their union is not, however, approved of by Lucinda (soprano), the Marchese's sister, because she is afraid that Cecchina's obscure origins could prove an obstacle to her own marriage to the Knight Armidoro (soprano). So Lucinda tries to obstruct the course of true love between Cecchina and the Marchese, taking advantage, along the way, of the envy felt by two of the maids, Sandrina (soprano) and Paoluccia

A scene from *Cecchina, ossia la buona figliola* by Niccolò Piccinni.

(mezzo-soprano), who spread a slander suggesting that Cecchina is without virtue. Enter Tagliaferro (*buffo* bass) to put a cat among the pigeons: he has been given the job of looking for the daughter of a German baron who had been abandoned as a baby after her mother had died in the war. As a result, it turns out that Cecchina is none other than the young Baroness Marianna. This removes the last barrier to the marriage of the young woman and the Marchese, and leaves the way clear for Lucinda and Armidoro to marry as well.

In his opera *Cecchina*, Piccinni has introduced, alongside the traditional comic types, elements of sentimental drama which give the piece a new spirituality. The opera was an immediate success.

A scene from *La Cenerentola* by Rossini.

CECILIA

Mystery in three episodes and four scenes by Don Licinio Refice (1883–1954), to a libretto by Emidio Mucci. First performance: Rome, Teatro dell'Opera, 15 February 1934.

At the house of the noble Valerio family, preparations are underway for a reception in honour of Cecilia (soprano), the bride-to-be of Valeriano (tenor). A rumour spreads among the slaves that the young woman is a Christian. Tiburzio (baritone), Valeriano's brother, enters, followed by the bridegroom himself, who is given a warm welcome from the crowd; after him come Cecilia and her attendants. At last the pair are left alone together, and Valeriano tells Cecilia of his love for her and all the desire he feels for her. Cecilia reciprocates this feeling, but can also feel an even greater love in her heart, which makes her unable to give herself to Valeriano. He is unable to understand her. An angel appears to defend Cecilia's purity and takes her to the catacombs. A series of miracles removes the last of Valeriano's doubts: he has experienced a conversion to Christianity, and falls to his knees. The bishop, Urbano (bass), baptizes him, and with this heavenly blessing the couple's happiness is now complete. In the final episode of the opera, Valeriano and Tiburzio are put to death. Cecilia is on trial. The Roman prefect, Amachio (baritone), tries to persuade Cecilia to renounce her faith, and even subjects her to torture by fire, but each time her skin is healed by roses raining down on it. Finally Cecilia is brutally killed by a soldier. Her house is subsequently turned into a temple.

Cecilia was Refice's greatest success. Leading singers have sung the part of Cecilia: Renata Tebaldi in 1953, for instance, and Renata Scotto, who sang the role at the opera's American premiere in New York in 1976.

CENDRILLON

(Cinderella)

Fairy-tale opera in four acts and six tableaux by Jules Massenet (1842–1912), to a libretto by Henri Cain taking its inspiration from the fairy-tale by Charles Perrault. First performance: Paris, Théâtre del' Opéra-Comique, 24 May 1899.

Madame de la Haltière (mezzo-soprano) goes to the grand Prince's Grand Ball with her two daughters, Noémie (soprano) and Dorothée (mezzo-soprano), leaving her step-daughter Lucette, who is called Cendrillon (Cinderella), at home. The young woman falls asleep, and in her dream La Fée (the Fairy, light soprano) appears and changes her bedraggled dress into a magnificent ball-gown. Cinderella sets out for the ball as fast as she can, but she must return home by midnight. The scene changes to the ballroom in the Royal Palace, where the Prince (soprano) is completely indifferent to the amorous advances of Cinderella's two step-sisters. But Cinderella's sudden arrival, incognito, stirs him; he is literally enchanted by the beauty and grace of the young woman. In vain does he try to detain her with tender words of love, as midnight strikes and Cinderella hurries away, leaving one of her shoes behind. The step-sisters return from the ball. Both are furious as they tell how some unknown, uninvited female had made a scandalous appearance at Court and create in Cinderella's mind the suspicion that the Prince doubts the young woman is pure of heart. Stunned by this, Cinderella decides to go to the fairies' wood to die. Here she is discovered by the Prince, who is happy to find her again and offers her his heart to show her the sincerity of his love. At this point the fairies make them both fall asleep, so that the whole adventure will seem like a wonderful dream to them. Cinderella has been found unconscious in the wood and has just recovered from a serious illness. A herald's voice is heard out in the street, proclaiming that the Prince will personally receive all the young women who will come and try on the shoe left behind by the mysterious lady. Cinderella is convinced that hers was no dream. The Palace. The fairy is leading Cinderella, who is carrying in her hands the heart of the Prince which he had given to her in the fairies' wood. The Prince can finally hold his beautiful beloved in his arms, and so crown his dream of love.

Some parts of *Cendrillon* are heavy with musical schemes Massenet had used too often. The attempt to emulate Humperdinck's *Hänsel und Gretel* is not entirely successful.

CENERENTOLA, LA, OSSIA LA BONTÀ IN TRIONFO

(Cinderella, or The Triumph of Virtue)

Melodramma giocoso *in two acts by Gioachino Rossini (1792–1868), to a libretto by Jacopo Ferretti. First performance: Rome, Teatro Valle, 25 January 1817.*

The residence of Baron Don Magnifico (*buffo* bass) is home to Angelina (contralto), nicknamed Cenerentola (Cinderella). The Baron, who is Cinderella's stepfather, also has two spoilt daughters of his own, Clorinda (soprano) and Tisbe (mezzo-soprano). They all treat Cinderella like a servant and humiliate her in every imaginable way. She herself has a gentle heart and gives help to a beggar (bass) who is actually Alidoro, court philosopher to Prince Ramiro, while her step-sisters throw him out of the house. Meanwhile, a group of gentlemen-in-waiting have issued a proclamation that Prince Ramiro (tenor) will be holding a reception for the purpose of choosing a bride from the ladies he invites to attend. Part of the preparations involves the Prince himself dressing up as his manservant Dandini (baritone) and Dandini disguised as the Prince calling on the young ladies at their homes first. The Prince admires the grace of Cinderella and immediately falls in love with her. But because the step-sisters are jealous of her, Cinderella is left behind at home. During the ball at the royal palace, a beautiful and mysterious young woman appears. It is actually Cinderella, wearing a splendid dress which Alidoro had given her. All the guests admire her and cannot help noticing how like Don Magnifico's step-daughter she is. Cinderella rejects the advances of the impostor Prince, Dandini in disguise, and tells him she is in love with his manservant, in reality the Prince himself. Ramiro is secretly overjoyed. Meanwhile, Dandini has confided in Don Magnifico that he is not really the Prince, and the Baron angrily leaves, taking Tisbe and Clorinda with him. Cinderella has managed to return home before them, and, having taken off her beautiful dress, is busy doing the housework. Prince Ramiro arrives, introduces himself, and asks for Cinderella's hand in marriage. The scene changes to the throne-room inside the palace, where dignitaries are paying their respects to Cinderella and the Prince. Her step-father and step-sisters are part of this gathering, and Cinderella once again displays her goodness of heart by forgiving them for all the wrongs she had suffered at their hands.

Ferretti's libretto, taken from Perrault's tale, lacks the fantasy elements of the original, because the librettist believed that fairy-tale subjects would not have seemed very credible on the stage. The premiere was not a success, but by the second evening of the run, the response to it was more than positive. To this day, *La Cenerentola* shows extraordinary vitality, and its sparkling characters, like Cinderella herself, further enhance a work already strong in expressive qualities. However, the compactness and balance of the opera are flawed by the difference in the quality of the music between the first act and the second, which is not as good.

CESTI, ANTONIO

(Arezzo 1623–Florence 1669)

Italian composer. In 1637 he entered the Order of the Conventual Franciscan Friars in Volterra. Between 1647 and 1649 he took holy orders, but this did not prevent him from being a member of the cast in the premiere of his first opera, *Orontea* (Venice, 1649), which immediately brought him great fame. In 1659, Pope Alexander VII intervened to enable him to leave the monastic life and become a lay priest. He then led an increasingly busy and adventurous life at the leading courts in Italy, before going on to Vienna, where he was at his most popular. Between 1666 and 1667, he composed his best-known opera, *Il pomo d'oro*, staged on the occasion of the Austrian Emperor's wedding. The heir of Monteverdi and in direct competition with Cavalli, Cesti had a greater gift for melody than his rival, one he expressed particularly well through his wide use of the aria, which for the first time, in Cesti's hands, became an important part of *bel canto* singing.

CHABRIER, ALEXIS-EMMANUEL

(Ambert, Auvergne 1841–Paris 1894)

French composer. Although Chabrier's involvement in music was not continuous, he was keen frequenter of the most important artistic circles in Paris. In 1877 he composed his first opera, *L'étoile*, which was followed by the delightful *Une éducation manquée* (An Unsuccessful Education, 1879). After hearing *Tristan und Isolde* in Munich, Chabrier decided to devote himself full-time to music. Wagnerian influences in his work are obvious in his opera *Gwendoline*, which, after being turned down by the Opéra in Paris, was staged in Brussels in 1887. In the next year, the work regarded as Chabrier's masterpiece, *Le roi malgré lui* (King in Spite of Himself), was also premiered. In 1889, he began to compose *Briséis*, which was left unfinished by the composer after the onset of his final illness. This opera was produced posthumously in Berlin in 1899.

Above: Print showing a scene from *Il pomo d'oro* by Antonio Cesti.

Left: The French composer Alexis-Emmanuel Chabrier.

CHAILLY, LUCIANO

(Ferrara 1920)

Italian composer. He studied music in Ferrara, Bologna and Milan, where he graduated in composition. In 1948 he met Paul Hindemith in Salzburg, whose example would prove to be a decisive factor in the rigour and compactness of style which were hallmarks of Chailly's compositions in the years that followed. Chailly began to write music for the theater in 1955, when his first opera, *Ferrovia sopraelevata* (text by Dino Buzzati), was staged in Bergamo. Two years later, in 1957, *Una domanda di matrimonio*, based on Chekhov, was produced at the Piccola Scala, Milan. Chailly went on to write the following operas: *Il canto del cigno* (Bologna, 1957), *La riva delle Sirti* (Monte Carlo, 1959), *Procedura penale* (Como, 1959), *Il mantello* (Florence, 1960), *Era proibito* (Milan, 1963) and *L'idiota* (Rome, 1970).

CHAILLY, RICCARDO

(Milan 1953)

Italian conductor. Son of the composer Luciano Chailly, he studied music with his father before going on to the Conservatorio in Milan. He completed his studies at the Accademia Chigiana in Siena with Franco Ferrara. In 1972 he made his debut at the Teatro Nuovo in Milan in Massenet's *Werther*. Chailly combined his appointment as Claudio Abbado's assistant at La Scala with a parallel career conducting in leading theater and concert venues. From 1974 he was a guest at the Chicago Opera, and from 1977 at the San Francisco Opera. In 1978 he made his official debut at La Scala, Milan in Verdi's *I masnadieri*. In 1986 he became the music director of the Teatro Comunale in Bologna, where he conducted *Les vêpres siciliennes* (1986), *La traviata* (1987), *Falstaff* (1987), *Die Walküre* (1988) and *Don Giovanni* (1990).

Above: The Italian conductor Riccardo Chailly.

Right: The French composer Gustave Charpentier.

CHARLOTTE CORDAY

Opera in three acts by Lorenzo Ferrero (b. 1951), to a libretto by Giuseppe di Leva. First performance: Rome, Teatro dell'Opera, 21 February 1989.

Paris, 13 July 1793. Charlotte (soprano) arrives in Paris from her native city of Caen at dawn. Here she meets Camille (tenor), a childhood friend, now a deputy at the French National Assembly. Charlotte can see that Camille feels let down by the Revolution and is full of fear and suspicion. Camille takes his leave of Charlotte, arranging to meet her that same afternoon. By now it is daybreak. A group of children are playing a macabre game around the guillotine. Charlotte attracts the attention of Gaston (baritone), bodyguard and confidant to Marat. Their conversation is interrupted by a brawl. Left alone, Charlotte is approached by a tramp (contralto), from whom she buys a shawl and a dagger. Shortly after, Marat (bass) appears. He notices Charlotte's expression at once and is disturbed by it. The scene changes to the parade-ground. Camille and Charlotte meet up again. Charlotte encourages him to overcome his feelings of disappointment by accomplishing deeds which will be an example to others. A drunk (baritone) interrupts their conversation and accuses Camille of treason. This causes an argument which looks as if it is going to get worse when Marat appears unexpectedly and, in a show of leniency, makes light of the accusation with a humorous gesture. He then makes his excuses, complaining of a recurrence of his illness, and goes home. The scene changes to Marat in his bath, where his skin disease compels him to lie. He is waking from a short-lived dream. A few moments later, Charlotte enters. She accuses Marat of having betrayed the Revolution and stained France red with blood. Marat at first boldly defends himself, but soon finds Charlotte's accusations meaningless and loses patience with the situation. At this point Charlotte stabs him with the dagger and in a flash Marat realizes why the expression on her face had so disturbed him.

Charlotte Corday is Lorenzo Ferrara's seventh composition for the theater, written to mark the bicentenary of the French Revolution. For Ferrara serious opera has its own way of communicating a message, by means of traditional devices which he calls "communicative conventions," expressed through a harmony which is linked, as he himself puts it, to the "only true contemporary musical language, which is no more than the complex fusion of other languages, that of rock music."

CHARPENTIER, GUSTAVE

(Dieuze, Lorraine 1860–Paris 1956)

French composer. A pupil of Massenet at the

Paris Conservatoire, in 1887 he won the Prix de Rome with his cantata *Didon*. The work for which he is famous is the opera *Louise* (1900), which was highly successful. The work he wanted to be the successor to this masterpiece, *Julien* (1913), despite being staged in various European theaters and in America, where Enrico Caruso sang the lead, did not manage to win its place in the repertoire. The unique and lasting success of *Louise* led in 1936 to Charpentier supervising the filming of the opera.

CHARPENTIER, MARC-ANTOINE

(Paris 1643–1704)

French composer. At the age of 19 Charpentier went to Italy, where he studied with Carissimi. On his return to Paris in 1670, he made his mark as a composer by working with Molière at the Théâtre Français. His third opera was *David et Jonathas* (1688). His reputation was firmly established after the death of Lully, whom Charpentier succeeded at the Académie Royale de Musique, where his most celebrated opera, *Médée*, was produced in 1693. Charpentier is the most famous opera composer in the period between Lully and Rameau.

CHAUSSON, ERNEST

(Paris 1855–Limay, Seine-et-Oise 1899)

French composer. Chausson originally studied law, and it was only later on that he was able to concentrate on music, becoming a pupil of César Franck. A keen champion of Debussy's music and a passionate Wagnerian, Chausson composed three operas: *Les caprices de Marianne*, 1882–84, *Hélène*, 1883–84 and *Le roi Arthus*, which in 1903 was the only one of the three to be staged, and which demonstrates the affinities between Chausson and Wagnerian theater (in particular *Tristan und Isolde*).

CHERNOV, VLADIMIR

(Krasnodar 1953)

Russian baritone. He began to study music in Stavropol (1974–76) before going on to the Moscow Conservatory (1976–81). As a result of winning the International Tchaikovsky Singing Competition in Moscow in 1982, he was able to attend the La Scala Center for Specialization for a year (1982–83). On his return to Russia, he made his debut in Leningrad as Germont (*La traviata*) at the Maryinsky Theater. He continued to appear there regularly until 1990 in a repertoire which included operas from Italy, such as *Il barbiere di Siviglia* and *Don Pasquale*, from France (*Faust*) and from Russia (*The Queen of Spades* and *Eugene Onegin*). In 1987 he sang with the Leningrad Kirov Opera company in *The Queen of Spades* and appeared in *Eugene Onegin* at Covent Garden, returning there in *Il barbiere di Siviglia* and *Attila* (1991). From 1989 onwards, he appeared regularly in the United States (*La bohème* in Boston) and since 1991 at the Metropolitan Opera, New York (*Luisa Miller*, *La traviata*, *Don Carlos*, *Il trovatore*, *Stiffelio*, etc.) as well as at other major American opera venues (Chicago, San Francisco, Seattle, etc.). He sang at the Teatro dell'Opera in Rome (*Luisa Miller*, 1990), at the Vienna Staatsoper (*Il barbiere di Siviglia* and *The Queen of Spades*, 1991–92), the Théâtre de la Monnaie in Brussels (*Il barbiere di Siviglia*, 1992) and the Arena in Verona (*La bohème* and *Don Carlos*). Chernov has a fine lyric baritone voice, distinguished by its consistency in the different registers, wide range and elegant phrasing, as well as an outstanding stage presence.

CHERUBINI, LUIGI

(Florence 1760–Paris 1842)

Italian composer. He studied in Florence, where he began as a composer of sacred music. In 1779 he wrote his first opera, *Quinto Fabio*, which was performed in 1780. Cherubini's first comic opera had its premiere in 1783: this was *Lo sposo di tre e marito di nessuna*, composed for the Teatro San Samuele in Venice. In 1784 he was in London, where he composed two operas, *La finta principessa*, 1785, and *Giulio Sabino*, 1786. After his time in London, Cherubini moved to Paris (1786), where he lived until his death. In Paris, Cherubini distinguished himself with *Lodoiska* (1791), but his real success came with *Médée* in 1797, the opera now considered to be his finest. It was followed by *L'hôtellerie portugaise* (1798) and *Les deux journées* (1800). The rise of Napoleon, who was hostile to the composer, prompted Cherubini to leave Paris for Vienna in 1805. He eventually returned to Paris, but it was not until 1813, when Napoleon's influence was waning, that the composer could set foot in the Opéra again, where he staged *Les Abencerages*. *Alì Babà* (1833) is Cherubini's last contribution to the theater. Although his music appears to be characterized by rigour and austerity, it displays a great abundance of lyrical and dramatic moments which make it the forerunner of Romantic opera.

The Italian composer Luigi Cherubini.

CHIARA, MARIA

(Piavon di Oderzo, Treviso 1939)

Italian soprano. She attended a course run by

Venice's Teatro La Fenice and in 1965 appeared in a gala performance of Verdi's *Otello* in the courtyard of the Palazzo Ducale in Venice. In the same year, she made her debut with the Rome Opera in the Italian premiere of Henze's *Der junge Lord*. In 1966, also in Rome, she sang for the first time in *La traviata*, of which she then gave further performances in the leading international opera houses. Chiara has also made a name for herself in *Turandot* (Liù), *Madama Butterfly*, *Manon Lescaut*, *La bohème* (Mimi) and *Suor Angelica*. In 1977 she tackled *Aida*, an opera in which she has sung since 1980 at the Arena in Verona and at the opening of the 1985 season at La Scala, Milan. Chiara is a lyric soprano with a beautiful, warm and vibrant timbre and even delivery, especially at low pitches. Her refined, sensitive phrasing was most clearly in evidence in *Aida*, regarded by some as her most accomplished performance.

CHILD AND THE VISIONS, THE

See *Enfant e les sortilèges, L'*

CHRISTIE, WILLIAM

(Buffalo, New York 1944)
American conductor and harpsichord player. After studying piano and organ, he attended Harvard University (1962–66). His meeting in 1967 with the celebrated harpsichordist Ralph Kirkpatrick, whose pupil Christie was, directed his attention towards early music. He taught for two years at the University of Dartmouth, before leaving the United States for Britain. In London, Christie played with the Five Centuries Ensemble (1971–72) with J. Nelson and then joined the Concerto Vocale with J. Nelson and R. Jacobs (1975). From 1978 he was responsible for the setting-up of what is now the vocal and instrumental ensemble Les Arts Florissants, with whom he devoted himself to the revival and performance of early music, especially that of the French baroque. In the opera house, he has conducted important performances of Charpentier's *Médée* and *David et Jonathas* (1986–88) and Hasse's *Cleofide*. He has aroused particular interest with his interpretations of operas by Rameau (*Hippolyte et Aricie*, *Les Indes galantes* and *Castor et Pollux*) and Lully (*Atys*).

CHRISTOFF, BORIS

(Plovdiv 1914)
Bulgarian bass. He began singing in a choir and was then awarded a scholarship which enabled him to go to Italy (1943). Christoff studied in Rome with Stracciari and made his debut in a concert at the Accademia di Santa Cecilia (1946). After a short period during which he appeared in minor roles, in 1947 Christoff was being engaged to sing leading roles on the strength of a voice unique in its range and power, coupled with his own dramatic talents and an extraordinary stage presence. As well as the Russian repertoire (*Khovanshchina*, *Knyaz Igor* and, most particularly, *Boris Godunov*), Christoff scored great successes in Italian opera too, particularly in Verdi (*Don Carlos*, *Ernani*, *Simon Boccanegra*). He appeared in leading opera houses of Europe and America but never at the Metropolitan in New York. Christoff's voice lasted such a remarkably long time that between 1980 and 1984 he gave a number of recitals, and also appeared in *Simon Boccanegra* (Rome Opera) and *Don Carlos* (Teatro Regio, Parma).

CHRISTOPHE COLOMB

Opera in two parts and 27 scenes by Darius Milhaud (1892–1974), to a libretto by Paul Claudel. First performance: Berlin, Staatsoper, 5 May 1930, with a German text by R. S. Hoffmann.

The action takes place between the middle of the fifteenth century and the early years of the sixteenth. The Narrator (played by an actor) begins to read the story of the life of Columbus. The navigator himself, now elderly and poor, is attending a kind of trial which is to examine the events surrounding the discovery of America. Images from Columbus's life appear in turn on a screen: the young boy looking out to sea; the adult trying to make his dream of being a navigator come true. No less important in the opera is the figure of Queen Isabella (soprano): images of her childhood and the most glorious moments of her reign are also shown. After the meeting between Columbus (baritone)

Top: The Italian soprano Maria Chiara.

Right: Boris Christoff in Verdi's *Don Carlos*.

and the Queen, the navigator's adventure begins: from his embarkation, through the difficulties on the voyage, to the discovery of the New World. On his return to Spain, Columbus is hailed as a conquering hero, but the King and his counsellors regard him with suspicion. Columbus does some soul-searching. On to the screen come images of hordes of slaughtered Indians, slaves in chains, sailors asking him to account for their lives. Queen Isabella, who had supported Columbus through his most difficult moments, wants to see him again and sends for him. Columbus is in none of the palaces or the places where the wealthy and powerful meet, but in a humble inn at Valladolid. He sends the Queen his old mule as a gift, and with this creature, caparisoned in magnificent fabrics, the Queen enters the Kingdom of Heaven, walking on a carpet which depicts America. In the background, turning on its axis, the Earth, and up from its surface flies a dove, perhaps the same one which a long time ago a very young Isabella had released into the sky.

This opera is the first of Milhaud's South American trilogy, later followed by *Maximilien* (1932) and *Bolivar* (1950). It is a religious allegory consisting of a free-flowing sequence of scenes unconnected with time or space. The present-day perspective of the Narrator, the images projected on to the screen, and the chorus commenting on the action, are key elements in the drama. *Christophe Colomb* is Milhaud's most mature choral work, standing as a synthesis of his entire artistic output, as if the whole of his musical achievement had been brought together in this single opera.

CHUNG, MYUNG-WHUN

(Seoul 1953)

Korean conductor and pianist who became an American citizen. He began his artistic career as a pianist (1960) before turning to conducting from 1971 onwards as head of the Korean National Symphony Orchestra. He then conducted in the United States, where he was assistant to Carlo Maria Giulini at the Los Angeles Philharmonic Orchestra (1978). In 1986 he made his debut at the Metropolitan Opera House, New York, and, in the following year scored an outstanding success conducting Mussorgsky's *Boris Godunov* at the Teatro Comunale in Florence, returning there in 1988 with Verdi's *Simon Boccanegra* and again in 1990 to conduct Rimsky-Korsakov's *The Legend of the Invisible City of Kitezh*. In 1989 he conducted the inaugural production at the new Opéra Bastille in Paris (Berlioz's *Les Troyens*) and became music director there. Consummately skilful, he conducts with firm, clear gestures. His combination of great analytical talent and theatrical instinct makes him one of the most highly regarded conductors.

Above: The Korean conductor and pianist Myung Whun Chung.

CID, LE

Opera in four acts and ten tableaux by Jules Massenet (1842–1912), to a libretto by Adolphe d'Ennery, Louis Gallet and Edouard Blau, from Corneille's tragedy. First performance: Paris, Opéra, 30 November 1885.

The action takes place in sixteenth-century Spain at the time of the *Reconquista* against the Arabs. In order to avenge a wrong against his father, Don Rodrigue (tenor) fights a duel with and kills Don Gormas (bass), whose daughter Chimène (soprano) is to marry him. As a result, the betrothed couple has to separate, and Chimène appeals to the King (baritone) for vengeance for her father's death. Nevertheless, punishment of the young knight Rodrigue is postponed, since he must leave to fight the Moors. When he returns, victorious, he is acclaimed by everyone as "Cid campeador" (Master warrior). However, the moment has now arrived when the King must see justice done on behalf of the dead Don Gormas, and he decides that the person most fitted to pass sentence is the one who has suffered the greatest wrong, Chimène, the dead man's daughter. The Cid feels he is guilty and resolves to take his own life, but Chimène stays his hand. Saved and forgiven by this young woman's love, the Cid can be reunited with her.

Le Cid, impressive opera of love and glory though it may be, is not one of Massenet's best works: it has an agreeable melodic line but is flawed by a tendency to mannerism and an excessive adherence to the public taste of that time. It does, nonetheless, contain passages of great lyrical sensitivity.

CIESINSKI, KATHERINE

(Newark, Delaware 1950)

American mezzo-soprano. She studied music in Philadelphia, first at Temple University and then at the Curtis Institute. After qualifying in major international singing competitions (1976–77), she made her first appearance in 1978 as Erika in Barber's opera *Vanessa* at the Festival of Two Worlds in Charleston. In the years that followed, Ciesinski sang at the Santa Fe Opera (Berg's *Lulu*), the Lyric Opera in Chicago (*Faust*) and in a number of other theater and concert venues in the United States and Europe: on Radio France (Gounod's *Sapho*, 1979), and in Nancy, Vienna and Spoleto (*Ariadne auf Naxos*, 1984). Ciesinski's is a striking voice with a fine and harmonically rich timbre, and she possesses a remarkable temperament in performance.

CIGNA, GINA

(Angères, Paris 1900)

Italian soprano. Initially self-taught, she went on to study in Paris with Emma Calvé, Hariclea Darclée and Rosina Storchio. Using the stage-name Ginette Sens, she made her debut at La Scala, Milan, in 1927 as Freia (*Das Rheingold*). Two years later, this time as

Gina Cigna and again at La Scala, she sang the role of Elvira (*Ernani*). This marked the beginning of brilliant career in which Cigna established herself as one of the most acclaimed dramatic sopranos of the 1930s and 1940s. Her performances in *Turandot*, *Norma* and *La Gioconda* are famous. In 1948, following a road accident, Cigna retired from the stage to concentrate on teaching.

CILEA, FRANCESCO

(Palmi 1866–Varazze (Savona) 1950)
Italian composer. He studied at the Conservatorio in Naples (1881–1889) and while still a student wrote his first opera, *Gina* (1889), following it with *Tilda* (Florence, 1892), which had been commissioned from him by the Italian music publisher Ricordi. Between 1894 and 1904 Cilea held the chair in counterpoint and theory at the Conservatorio in Florence. It was during this period that he composed the operas *Arlesiana* (Milan, 1897) and *Adriana Lecouvreur* (Milan, 1902), his masterpiece. His opera *Gloria* (1907) was staged with scant success at La Scala with Arturo Toscanini conducting. A later opera, *Il matrimonio selvaggio*, was never performed. Cilea's style while reflecting some aspects of the realist school, was at the same time separate from it, expressing itself more fully at moments of intense lyricism. In this Cilea was clearly more influenced by French composers, especially Massenet, from whom he derived his dramatic dimension, constantly pervading it with a refined lyrical quality.

CIMAROSA, DOMENICO

(Aversa 1749–Venice 1801)
Italian composer. He studied at the Conservatorio di Santa Maria di Loreto in Naples, where he was taught by Gallo, Fenaroli and Carajus. He left in 1772, and made his debut at the Teatro dei Fiorentini in the city with two farces, *Le stravanganze del conte* (1772) and *Le magie di Merlina e Zoroastro* (1772). His working time was then divided between Naples and Rome, and between 1787 and 1791 he was chorus-master at the court of St. Petersburg. After that he was in Vienna, where he composed *Il matrimonio segreto* (1792), with such success that the entire opera was played again as an encore. In 1793 he returned to Naples, and from there went to Venice, where he presented *Gli Orazi e i Curiazi* (1796), his masterpiece of *opera seria*. Cimarosa wrote about 60 operas, as well as sacred music, oratorios and instrumental works.

CINDERELLA

See *Cendrillon*.

CINDERELLA, OR THE TRIUMPH OF VIRTUE

See *Cenerentola, La, ossia La bontà in trionfo* .

CIRANO

Comic opera in two acts by Marco Tutino (b. 1954), to a libretto by Danilo Bramati from Cyrano de Bergerac *by Edmond Rostand. First performance: Alessandria, Teatro Comunale, 18 September 1987.*

After causing a scuffle at the Palais de Bourgogne, Cirano (bass), at the tavern in Ragueneau, is about to write a letter to Rossana (soprano), with whom he is deeply in love, when Rossana herself arrives and confides to Cirano that she loves Cristiano di Neuvillette (tenor), a young cadet. Cirano promises the young woman that he will assist her in her love for Cristiano. When Cirano meets his rival, he encourages him to go to Rossana's house to tell her how he feels. In the garden of Rossana's house, the hesitant cadet uses Cirano's beguiling words and voice to sing of his love to an enraptured Rossana. The idyll is interrupted by the arrival of the governess (mezzo-soprano), who announces that the cadets are to leave for the siege of Arras. The scene changes to the main hall of the Palais de Bourgogne. Rossana is in mourning for the death of Cristiano. Anxiously, the young woman asks for news of Cirano, as she has heard that some of his enemies are planning to set a trap for him. Cirano enters the hall, looking very pale, and with his head bandaged. The ambush has already taken place. By now delirious, he reads out a letter turning towards Rossana, and she immediately realizes the truth, recognizing in Cirano the true author of the beautiful words addressed to her during that by now long past meeting with Cristiano. But now it is too late, and Cirano dies in torment from his wounds.

Cirano is the second opera by Marco Tutino, who could be said in general terms to belong to a "neo-romantic" trend fiercely critical of avant-garde music, accusing it of emptying the concert halls and opera houses of audiences. Tutino seeks primarily to address the audience that loves serious opera. In his own words: "*Cirano* is a popular opera which employs a traditional language (arias, ensemble pieces, etc.) but which at the same time seeks to be an expression of the music of our time. I have put into *Cirano* the music, the sounds, that I truly feel are my own. High-tension music. Very close to rock."

CIRO IN BABILONIA

(Cyrus in Babylon)
Opera in two acts by Gioachino Rossini (1792–1868), to a libretto by Francesco Aventi. First performance: Ferrara, Teatro Comunale 14 March 1812.

Baldassare (tenor), King of Babylon, falls in love with Amira (soprano), the wife of Ciro (contralto), King of Persia, whom he has defeated. While Amira is his prisoner, with her young son, Baldassare attempts to flatter her with his amorous advances. She rejects his offers. Meanwhile Ciro, disguised as an ambassador, makes a bid to free his wife. He is discovered, arrested

Top: The Italian composer Francesco Cilea in a photograph taken in 1913.

Right: The Italian composer Domenico Cimarosa.

and imprisoned. Baldassare has made up his mind to have Amira, even against her will, and orders that the wedding-feast be prepared. But a terrible storm breaks and amid thunder and lightning a mysterious hand appears which traces obscure and threatening words on the wall in letters of fire. The Babylonian King is shocked by it. His wise men and the prophet Daniele (bass) are summoned. Daniele interprets the event as a sign of divine anger, while the wise men advise the King to make a sacrifice to the gods of the three royal Persian prisoners. While Ciro, Amira and their son are waiting to be led to the scaffold, news reaches Baldassare's palace that the Babylonian defenses have been breached by the Persians. Ciro is automatically freed and takes over Baldassare's throne. The people pay homage to their new King.

Ciro may be seen as a step in Rossini's progression towards the masterpieces of his mature period. He regarded *Ciro* as a failure; indeed, it has a very weak, cliché-ridden libretto. The music, on the other hand, contains some unusual arias, which enabled the work to enjoy a degree of success.

CLEMENCIC, RENÉ

(Vienna 1928)

Austrian composer, conductor and virtuoso recorder player. He studied music in Vienna, Berlin and Paris. By 1957 he had already begun to appear as a recorder virtuoso, and from 1958 he performed with an ensemble he founded made up of a group of instrumentalists who took the name Clemencic Consort in 1969. With this group, Clemencic has taken part in a number of modern revivals of medieval and Renaissance music, specializing in the production of operas of the Italian baroque period. From that time, he has brought to light Pietro Andrea Ziani's opera *L'Assalonne punito*, Antonio Sartorio's *L'Orfeo*, Antonio Vivaldi's *L'Olimpiade*, Johann Joseph Fux's *Dafne in Lauro*, Sousa Carvalho's *Testoride Argonauta* and others. Since 1987 he has taught a course on Italian baroque music at the Accademia Chigiana in Siena.

CLEMENZA DI TITO, LA

Opera seria in two acts by Wolfgang Amadeus Mozart (1756–1791), to a libretto by Caterino Mazzolà, taken from Pietro Metastasio's play of the same name. First performance: Prague, National Theater, 6 September 1791.

The plot is characterized by Tito's determination to pardon all who plot against him and the determination of Vitellia – who is in love with Tito and wants to become Empress – to take revenge on him for preferring other women. Tito (tenor) plans to marry Beatrice, and Vitellia (soprano) asks his friend Sesto (mezzo-soprano) to help her in a conspiracy against the Emperor. He agrees, but they learn that Tito has sent Berenice home and now intends to marry a Roman woman, Servilia (soprano), who is in love with, and is loved by, Annio (mezzo-soprano). When Servilia tells Tito of her love for Annio, he decides to take Vitellia as his wife. Unaware of this, Vitellia proceeds with her plot against Tito; it fails, and Tito escapes death. The details of the conspiracy are revealed to him. Sesto is tried by the Senate and condemned to death, and Vitellia also confesses. But the clement Emperor Tito forgives everyone.

Mozart had not composed an *opera seria* for ten years when, at the end of his last summer, he received a commission for an opera to celebrate the coronation of Leopold II, King of Bohemia. He was given very little time in which to write the work, four weeks and no more. Nor was he free to choose the libretto. The characters foisted on him were somewhat conventional, so that Mozart found it difficult to describe them musically and bring them to life. The tight deadline also meant that the orchestration was very simple and straightforward, and obliged Mozart to delegate to Süssmayr the composition of the recitatives. *La clemenza di Tito* is, however, a fine example of a Mozart *opera seria*, a genre in which he never succeeded in bringing out his genius as fully as he did in *opera buffa*.

CLEVER GIRL, THE

See *Kluge, Die*

CLUYTENS, ANDRÉ

(Antwerp 1905–Neuilly, Paris 1967)

Belgian conductor who took French citizenship. Born into an artistic family, he studied in Antwerp, where he made his debut as a conductor (1927–32). He was very active in opera, conducting at the Opéra-Comique in Paris (1947–53) before being appointed to conduct at Bayreuth (*Tannhäuser*), the first French conductor to do so. He returned there to conduct *Die Meistersinger von Nürnberg*, *Parsifal* and *Lohengrin*. He also conducted in other major theaters in Europe and the United States. His theatrical instinct, and his elegant conducting of instrumental accompaniment and tone-colour, made Cluytens a great interpreter of the French repertoire (*Pelléas et Mélisande*, *Les contes d'Hoffmann*) and of Wagner.

COBURN, PAMELA

(Dayton, Ohio 1952)

American soprano. She began her music studies at the University of Indiana, before going on to the Eastman School in Rochester and the Juilliard in New York. After her concert debut, she went to Europe in 1978. In

A scene from *Ciro in Babilonia* by Rossini.

Germany (1980), partly as a result of encouragement from the soprano Elisabeth Schwarzkopf, she received her first real acclaim. Guest artiste at the Munich Opera (from 1982) and at the Vienna Staatsoper (from 1984), Coburn is an admired performer of Mozart (*Le nozze di Figaro, Così fan tutte, Idomeneo*) as well as of Verdi (*Falstaff*), Bizet (Micaela in *Carmen*) and others. Coburn has also made many appearances at leading venues on the international theater circuit. She devotes part of her year to giving recitals and concerts.

COCTEAU, JEAN

(Maisons-Laffitte, Yveslines 1889–Milly-la-Forêt, Essonne 1963).
French poet, novelist, playwright and librettist. He always showed a lively interest in avant-garde movements and was consequently a fervent supporter of "Les Six," a group of composers who wanted to pit themselves against Debussy and Impressionism. Cocteau was an extremely versatile artist who collaborated with a number of different musical figures. Among his output are the libretti for Milhaud's opera *Le pauvre matelot* (1927), Stravinsky's *Oedipus Rex* (1927), Honegger's *Antigone* (1927) and Poulenc's *La voix humaine* (1959).

COLE, VINSON

(Kansas City, Missouri 1950)
American tenor. He studied at the Curtis Institute in Philadelphia, where, in 1975, he appeared in Massenet's *Werther*. In the same year he made his debut at the Santa Fe Opera (*La vida breve*). In 1976 he embarked on an international career in *Acis and Galatea* at the Festival in Angers and *Die Entführung aus dem Serail* (The Seraglio) at Welsh National Opera in Cardiff (1977). Then came engagements in Vancouver (1977), Lyons (1978), Boston (1980), the Salzburg Festival (since 1983) and in other theaters in Europe and America. Cole is a lyric tenor with a very extensive repertoire, including operas by Rossini (*Le Comte Ory*), Cimarosa (*Il matrimonio segreto*), Donizetti (*Don Pasquale* and *Anna Bolena*), Gounod (*Faust* and *Roméo et Juliette*) and others.

COMTE ORY, LE

(Count Ory)
Melodramma giocoso *in two acts by Gioachino Rossini (1792–1868), to a libretto by Scribe and Delestre-Poirson. First performance: Paris, Opéra, 20 August 1828.*

The action takes place in and around the castle of Formoutiers, about the year 1200. Count Ory (tenor), with the help of his friend Raimbaud (baritone), has disguised himself as a hermit, so he can gain entry to the castle and court the Countess Adèle (soprano). Enter Isolier (mezzo-soprano), the Count's page, who fails to recognize his master and confides in him about his own love for Adèle. When the Countess approaches the "hermit," he tells her about the page's feelings, but asks her to stay away from him. While the perplexed Countess is preparing to return to her castle, the Count's tutor (bass) arrives and unmasks Ory, to everyone's dismay. Night falls. A group of poor women on a pilgrimage call at the castle. They tell the Countess they have been threatened by the Count, and so she welcomes them in. The pilgrims turn out to be the Count Ory and some of his knights dressed as women. But then Isolier appears on the scene, realizes the deception, and plans with the Countess to play a trick on his bold rival. So he takes the place of the Countess Adèle and, dressed in her clothes, lets himself be courted by the Count while the bedroom is in darkness. Trumpets announce the return of the Count of Fourmoutiers, Adèle's brother. Ory is forced to flee with his cronies. Adèle goes to meet her brother and the other ladies greet their husbands. Finally Adèle decides she will marry the loyal Isolier, who had succeeded in foiling Count Ory and his schemes.

The libretto of *Le Comte Ory* is an extended version of the play written by the librettist himself, Eugène Scribe. The music that Rossini composed for the opera was partly taken from his *Il viaggio a Reims* (1825), and the impact of its melodic intensity ensured its triumphal success. The humour in *Le Comte Ory* differs from that of *Il barbiere di Siviglia* in being more contained and aristocratic, using a greater degree of subtlety and ambiguity in drawing attention to the comical parts of the libretto. Even though its vigour seems to fall short, the comic quality is certainly on a par with Rossini's masterpieces.

CONI, PAOLO

(Perugia 1957)
Italian baritone. After his early singing studies, he went on to study with Lajos Kozma and Rodolfo Celletti. In 1983 he made his debut in *Lucia di Lammermoor*, followed by Donizetti's *Torquato Tasso* and Mozart's *Don Giovanni* and *Le nozze di Figaro*. In 1986 he made his mark at the Teatro Comunale in Bologna as Guido da Monforte (*Les vêpres siciliennes*). He then made his debut at La Scala, Milan (1987–88) in *La bohème*, returning there to sing the role of Germont in *La traviata*, with Riccardo Muti conducting. Coni appears regularly at London's Covent Garden, the Vienna Staatsoper and the Metropolitan, New York, where his debut was in *L'elisir d'amore* with Luciano Pavarotti. His voice has a fine and extraordinarily expressive timbre, and his delivery is soft and even. He has sung with particular distinction in operas by Donizetti (*Maria di Rohan, La favorite* and *L'assedio di Calais*). His Verdi performances, however, are not always convincing: here Coni has shown signs of forcing in his delivery, revealing a limited range in the upper register. He is nevertheless one of the best Italian baritones of his generation.

Above: A scene from *Le Comte Ory* by Rossini, in a production at the Rossini Opera Festival.

Top: Sketch by Du Fauget for the first performance of *Le Comte Ory*.

CONNELL, ELIZABETH

(Port Elizabeth, South Africa 1946)
Irish soprano who took British citizenship. She studied at the London Opera Center and won the Maggie Teyte Prize in 1972, making her debut at the Wexford Festival as a mezzo-soprano in the same year. In 1973 she appeared, again as a mezzo, with the Australian Opera and the English National Opera. From 1983 she began to sing soprano roles, with engagements at the major theaters in Europe and America. Connell's repertoire includes operas by Mozart (*Così fan tutte*), Verdi (*Macbeth* and *Don Carlos*), as well as Donizetti, Beethoven (*Fidelio*) and Wagner. She won particular acclaim for her recent performances in *Der fliegende Holländer* (The Flying Dutchman, Trieste, 1986), *Oberon* (La Scala, 1989) and *Poliuto* (Rome, 1989).

CONSUL, THE

Opera in three acts by Giancarlo Menotti (b. 1911), to the composer's own libretto. First performance: Philadelphia, Shubert Theater, 1 March 1950.

The action takes place in a European country in modern times. John Sorel (baritone), a patriot fighting to liberate his country from being a police state, is wounded by the police but manages to escape. Magda (soprano), his wife, wants to follow her husband, who intends to seek refuge in a free country, and she calls at the Consulate, where a cold, inhuman secretary (mezzo-soprano) uses petty arguments and documents to create a barrier between the Consul and the wretched people who want to emigrate. For a whole month, Magda tries in vain to speak to the Consul. In the meantime, news of her husband John reaches her: he has not yet left the country and will only cross the frontier if his family can accompany him. Magda is desperate (her child is dead and John's mother is gravely ill), and she goes on calling at the Consulate. She sees a man coming out of the Consul's office and recognizes him as an agent of the secret police who had interrogated her several times, and faints to the ground. John, who has learned of the death of his child and his mother's illness, attempts to reach Magda but is immediately arrested by the police. On hearing that John intends to set foot in the city again, but not knowing that he is already in prison, Magda decides to take her own life, thinking that John will be better able to make a bid for freedom if he no longer has any family ties. So she closes the doors and windows and turns on the gas. With Magda near to death, the telephone rings. Had she been able to answer it, she would have learned of John's arrest and realized that her own death would achieve nothing.

The Consul was an overwhelming success, remaining in the programme at the same theater for eight months and winning a Pulitzer prize and the Drama Critics Award. It has been translated into 12 languages and staged in 20 countries.

CONQUEST OF MEXICO, THE

See *Eroberung von Mexico, Die*

CONTES D'HOFFMANN, LES

(The Tales of Hoffmann)
Fantasy opera in three acts, with a prologue and epilogue, by Jacques Offenbach (1819–1880), to a libretto by Jules Barbier and Michel Carré, based on three tales by E. T. A. Hoffmann. First performance: Paris, Théâtre de l'Opéra-Comique, 10 February 1881.

Nuremberg, at the inn kept by Master Luther (bass or baritone). Councillor

Lindorf (bass or baritone), the first of four evil personas created by the poet Hoffmann (tenor), intercepts and pockets a note which the opera singer Stella (soprano) has sent to Hoffmann to arrange a rendezvous with him. Hoffmann arrives with his friend Nicklausse (mezzo-soprano). The crowd of students at the inn invite Hoffmann to tell them the tales of his escapades in love. Hoffmann's first

Above left: The Italian baritone Paolo Coni.

Left: A scene from *The Consul* by Giancarlo Menotti.

Above: Elizabeth Connell in Verdi's *Macbeth*.

love is Olympia (soprano), whom the poet believes to be the daughter of the scientist Spalanzani (tenor). In fact she is a performing doll made by Spalanzani with the help of Coppélius (bass or baritone). During a reception, Olympia sings and dances divinely, but Coppélius, another of Hoffmann's embodiments of evil, shatters the doll into pieces, and Hoffmann has the painful experience of realizing he has been deceived. The action now moves to Munich. This time Hoffmann is in love with Antonia (soprano), daughter of the lute-maker Crespel (bass). The young woman loves singing, but her father is against it on the grounds that the effort needed to sing could prove fatal to her, as it had to her mother. Enter the diabolical Doctor Miracle (bass or baritone), who induces Antonia to sing a tempting song impossible to resist. At the end, Antonia is exhausted and falls to the ground dead before the despairing Hoffmann. The scene changes to Venice. Hoffmann is in love with Giulietta (soprano), a courtesan who has succumbed to the power of the devilish Dappertutto (bass or baritone) and is now about to tempt Hoffmann to fall under Dappertutto's spell. Hoffmann, who is hopelessly in love with Giulietta, challenges her ex-lover Schlemil (bass or baritone) to a duel. Schlemil has in his possession a key to Giulietta's bedroom. After killing Schlemil and getting hold of the key, Hoffmann discovers that Giulietta has gone away with Dappertutto. The scene returns to the inn, as at the beginning of the opera. Hoffmann has finished telling his stories. Stella comes in and, seeing the poet asleep, leaves with Councillor Lindorf. Hoffmann, in a vision, sees his friend Nicklausse metamorphosed into his Muse of inspiration, who then appeals to Hoffmann to give up worldly passions in favour of his Art.

The orchestration of the opera was left unfinished by Offenbach and completed by Ernst Guiraud (1837–1892), and so the work was not performed until after the composer's death. Although it was Offenbach's most ambitious opera and contains passages of remarkable musical quality, *Les contes d'Hoffmann* was not his most successful one. It does, however, reveal traces of what was to become the new *opéra-comique*, a genre favouring vivid and touching operatic characters.

CONVENIENZE E LE INCONVENIENZE TEATRALI, LE

Opera in one act by Gaetano Donizetti (1797–1848), to the composer's own libretto, based on a farce by Semeone Sografi (1794). First performance: Naples, Teatro Nuovo, 21 November 1827.

The rehearsal room of a provincial theater. The composer Biscroma (comic baritone) and the poet Prospero (*buffo* bass) are awaiting the arrival of the company of singers to begin rehearsals of the new opera. Enter the prima donna Daria (soprano), accompanied by her husband Procolo (baritone), Luigia (soprano), accompanied by her mother Agata Scannagalli (comic bass or comic baritone), and the rest of the company. The atmosphere immediately becomes heated: Daria plays the tyrant and throws tantrums in front of her fellow-singers, the poet and the composer. Not to be outdone, Agata, who "has sung at La Scala" and has had enough of this fuss, intervenes in an attempt to have her daughter's rights recognized. The rehearsal can finally get under way, but by now two of the singers have walked out, plunging the impresario (baritone) into despair. Amid squabbles and hard feelings, the rehearsal starts, but the

Stage design by Alberto Savinio for *The Tales of Hoffmann.*

Right: The American composer Aaron Copland.

impresario announces that owing to the departure of the two singers, the theater director has decided not to proceed with the production, provoking consternation and confusion among the singers.

This is a charming and amusing opera, warmly received whenever it is performed.

COPLAND, AARON

(New York 1900– Westchester 1990)

American composer. He studied with Wittgenstein and Rubin Goldmark in New York before moving to Paris to complete his studies with Nadia Boulanger. He composed two operas: the first, *The Second Hurricane* (1937), has a sparkling, jagged style which owes much to jazz, while the second, *The Tender Land* (1954), is set in the Midwest during the years of the Depression. Here the style is more nostalgic, and its evocative, folksy timbres make it closer to the sound-world of the composer's famous orchestral suite *Appalachian Spring* (1944). Copland is regarded as the "father figure" of American music.

CORBELLI, ALESSANDRO

(Torino 1952)

Italian baritone. He studied singing with Giuseppe Valdengo and Claude Thiolas before specializing at the Accademia Chigiana in Siena (1975). He subsequently scored some remarkable successes in major singing competitions, and this, even though he was still very young, brought him engagements from the leading international opera houses – La Scala, the Paris Opéra, the Vienna Staatsoper, Covent Garden – as well as from Chicago and Philadelphia. Corbelli is gifted with great stage presence and theatrical verve, combined with uncommon musicianship and style. He is one of the best performers of the so-called brilliant repertoire and the so-called *mezzo-carattere* (i.e. neither serious nor comic) roles from the eighteenth and nineteenth centuries, from Paisiello's *Il barbiere di Siviglia* to Mozart's *Così fan tutte* and *Le nozze di Figaro*, Rossini's *La Cenerentola* and Donizetti's *Don Pasquale*.

CORBOZ, MICHEL

(Marsens 1934)

Swiss choral and orchestral conductor. He had no formal music training as such, but one of his uncles, a chorus-master, encouraged him to study piano, singing, accompaniment and harmony. At the age of 20, he was appointed chorus-master at Notre-Dame in Lausanne. In 1961 in Lausanne he founded the Ensemble Vocal, with whom he made his mark in a performance of Monteverdi's *Orfeo*, which earned its status as one of the first performances to grow out of the revival of early performing techniques. In 1969 he became conductor of the chorus of the Gulbenkian Foundation in Lisbon, and here too Corboz made another important contribution to the revival and performance of the sacred compositions of Monteverdi, Bach and Vivaldi. In the field of opera, he has conducted stage productions and gramophone recordings of Cavalli's *Ercole amante* (1979) and Charpentier's *David et Jonathas* (1981).

CORDOVANO, IL

(The Cordoban Rug)

Opera in one act by Goffredo Petrassi (b. 1904), to a libretto by Eugenio Montale based on a text by Miguel de Cervantes. First performance: Milan, La Scala, 12 May 1949.

Lorenza (soprano), young wife of Cannizares (bass), complains to her niece Cristina (light soprano) and her neighbour Hortigosa (contralto) about her husband's tiresome jealousy. The two women persuade Lorenza to overcome her scruples and take a lover. Acting as a procuress, Hortigosa brings a large rolled-up Cordoban rug into Lorenza's house, with a young man hidden inside it. While Cannizares is admiring the rug, the young man slips into Lorenza's room, where they make love, but the husband is made suspicious by his wife's cries and comes into the room. Lorenza welcomes him by throwing a large basin in his face, and in the confusion the young man manages to escape. A policeman arrives to see what all the noise is about, followed by musicians and dancers who pretend to be celebrating the reconciliation of the married couple when in fact they are toasting the start of a piquant liaison. In an aside, Cristina complains that Hortigosa has not found a lover for her too.

Il cordovano keeps faithfully to Cervantes's *intermezzo*, entitled *El viejo celoso* (The Jealous Old Man), of 1615, itself an adaptation for the theater of one Cervantes's own "Novelas ejemplares" (1613) called *Celoso extremeño*. It is one of Petrassi's most

Top: The Italian baritone Alessandro Corbelli.

Above: Stage design for *Il Cordovano* by Goffredo Petrassi.

complex and meaningful operas, rich with allusion and psychological insight expressed in the music.

CORELLI, FRANCO

(Ancona 1921)

Italian tenor. He studied music at the Conservatorio in Pesaro. After winning a competition sponsored by the Maggio Musicale Fiorentino in 1950, he made his debut the following year in Spoleto as Don José (*Carmen*), one of the roles which subsequently made him famous throughout the world. After singing Maurizio di Sassonia (*Adriana Lecouvreur*) at the Rome Opera and taking part in a television production of *I pagliacci*, Corelli made his triumphal first appearance at La Scala (1954), singing alongside Maria Callas in Spontini's *La vestale*. Also with Callas at La Scala, Corelli went on to sing in *Fedora* (1956), *Il pirata* (1958) and *Poliuto* (1960).

CORENA, FERNANDO

(Geneva 1916–Lugano 1984)

Swiss bass. He made his debut in Trieste in 1947 as Varlaam in *Boris Godunov*. His first appearance at La Scala was in the 1949 premiere of Petrassi's *Il cordovano*. He then embarked on a busy international career, and in 1953 began his long association (about 25 years) with the Metropolitan Opera in New York. Corena had great verve and stage presence and was one of the last singers to take on the mantle of the tradition of the *buffo* bass this century.

CORNELIUS, PETER

(Mainz 1824–1874)

German composer. After beginning his artistic career as an actor, Cornelius concentrated on music and became a follower and friend of Liszt and Wagner. Liszt conducted his opera *Der Barbier von Bagdad* in Weimar in 1858. From 1859 to 1864 he lived in Vienna, where he composed the opera *Der Cid*: this was staged in Weimar in 1865.

CORONATION OF POPPEA, THE

See *Incoronazione di Poppea, L'*

CORREGIDOR, DER

(The Magistrate)

Opera in four acts by Hugo Wolf (1860–1903), to a libretto by Rosa Mayreder-Obermayer, based on the story El sombrero de tres picos *(The Three-Cornered Hat) by Pedro de Alarcón y Ariza. First performance: Mannheim, Nationaltheater, 7 June 1896.*

Frasquita (mezzo-soprano), wife of the miller Tio Lucas (baritone), is being courted by the elderly Don Eugenio de Zuniga (*buffo* tenor), a magistrate and an incorrigible womanizer. The Magistrate has Lucas summoned by the mayor, the Alcalde (bass), thus giving himself the chance to pay Frasquita a visit which will not be interrupted. But she resists the old man and threatens him with a gun, causing him to take fright and faint. Frasquita goes in search of her husband. He comes home by a different route and finds Don Eugenio asleep in his bed. Imagining that Frasquita has been unfaithful to him, Lucas decides to have his revenge: he dresses in the Magistrate's clothes and leaves the house. Meanwhile the Alcalde arrives, followed by his usher and his secretary, whom Lucas had made drunk when he had realized that they were holding him on trumped-up pretexts. As soon as the effects of the drink have worn off, the trio charge into Lucas's bedroom and, under the impression it is the miller himself lying in the bed, they rain blows down on Don Eugenio. Enter Frasquita, and everyone sets out in search of Lucas. They then go to the Magistrate's house, where they learn that "Don Eugenio" is already in bed. Frasquita weeps, because she thinks this must mean that her husband is in bed with the Magistrate's wife. In fact, Lucas has simply had an exchange of views with Donna Mercedes (soprano), and the two of them have decided to punish their respective spouses. Lucas and Frasquita assure each other of their faithfulness, while Mercedes leaves the Magistrate under the impression that she has cuckolded him.

Listening to *Der Corregidor* is to be reminded that Wolf was first and foremost a composer of *Lieder*. The entire opera appears to be a sequence of chamber music pieces. It also has some good theatrical moments, combined with subtle characterization of the individual roles, representing those bourgeois figures who also inhabit the world of Wolf's famous *Liederbücher*.

CORSARO, IL

(The Corsair)

Tragic opera in three acts by Giuseppe Verdi (1813–1901), to a libretto by Francesco Maria Piave based on Byron's poem The Corsair. *First performance: Trieste, Teatro Grande, 25 October 1848.*

The Greek pirate Corrado (tenor) manages to infiltrate the camp of the Turks, whose commander is the Pasha Seid (baritone). He is in disguise and so passes unrecognized. But his pirate force attacks the camp before he has given the prearranged signal, and as a result Corrado is discovered, wounded and imprisoned. He is saved by Gulnara (soprano), Seid's concubine. When

Above: The Italian tenor Franco Corelli with Maria Callas and the conductor Victor De Sabata.

Corrado, now on the run, finally reaches his island-refuge, he finds Medora (soprano), his fiancée, dying of grief, after hearing a false report that Corrado has died. Corrado is stunned by this, throws himself into the sea and is engulfed by the waves.

Verdi had initially thought in terms of a parallel between Corrado and Garibaldi, the hero of the Italian Risorgimento, and of patriotism as an underlying theme, represented here by the war waged by Greek pirates against the Turks. On becoming more familiar with the libretto, however, he abandoned the idea.

CORTEZ, VIORICA

(Bucium 1935)

Rumanian mezzo-soprano who became a French citizen. She began her music studies at Iasi, and completed them at the Conservatory in Bucharest. Between 1964 and 1965, she took part in a number of singing competitions and, after winning first prize at the Concours de Chant in Toulouse, she made her debut in that city singing Dalila in Saint-Saëns' opera *Samson et Dalila* (1965). Then came appearances in Bucharest, Paris (Opéra), Milan (La Scala), London (Covent Garden) and a number of other theaters. Cortez's voice has a warm timbre, a natural sensuality and a good range. She won special admiration for her performances in *Carmen*, *Samson et Dalila*, *Aida*, *Don Carlos*, *Il trovatore* and *Werther*.

COSA RARA, UNA, OSSIA BELLEZZA ED ONESTÀ

(A Rare Thing, or Beauty and Honesty)

Opera in two acts by Vincent Martìn y Soler (1754–1806), to a libretto by Lorenzo da Ponte. First performance: Vienna, Burgtheater, 17 November 1786.

The story is based on the amorous intrigues of several couples of country-people and shepherds, either already promised to one another or just in love. The story hinges on Isabella, Queen of Spain (soprano), who is constantly being appealed to in the hope that she can disentangle the disputes and jealousies between these different pairs of lovers. Tita (baritone) and Ghita (soprano) are the targets of continual feelings of jealousy; Lilla (soprano) is in love with Lubino (baritone), but their love is more in dispute than ever; then there is the Queen's concern for her own son, Prince Giovanni (tenor), who is in love with Lilla. The Prince's machinations to have the young shepherdess coincide with the arguments and provocations between Lubino and Tita. In the end, the Queen restores order: the Prince, who is the real cause behind the various rows between the couples, is rescued by his groom, Corrado (tenor), who takes the blame for the Prince. Corrado is duly sent into exile, and the opera ends with the reconciliation of all the couples.

Una cosa rara is Martìn y Soler's second Viennese opera, and also the second on which he worked with Lorenzo da Ponte. It was based on *La luna de la sierra* by Luis Vélez de Guevara (1579–1644), and was one of the most sensational triumphs in the history of opera in Vienna. It was not long before Viennese ladies adopted the fashion of dressing in the style of *Una cosa rara*. The opera made a tour of major European cities and remained in the repertoire (it was still being performed in Paris in 1812). Its success even earned it a quotation by Mozart in the final scene of *Don Giovanni* when the Don is being served at table by Leporello and a small orchestra plays a transcription from the finale of the first act of *Una cosa rara*. When Leporello hears the piece, he recognizes it and exclaims: "Bravi! Cosa rara!"

COSÌ FAN TUTTE, OSSIA LA SCUOLA DEGLI AMANTI

(Women Are All Alike, or The School for Lovers). Opera buffa *in two acts by Wolfgang Amadeus Mozart (1756–1791), to a libretto by Lorenzo da Ponte. First performance: Vienna, Burgtheater, 26 January 1790.*

The action takes place in eighteenth-century Naples. ACT I Scene 1. A café. The old cynic Don Alfonso (bass) presses two young officers, Guglielmo (baritone) and Ferrando (tenor), to place a bet on the fidelity of their fiancées, Fiordiligi (soprano) and Dorabella (mezzo-soprano). The two are so sure of winning that they accept and, for the next 24 hours, they follow Don Alfonso's instructions. Scene 2. A garden overlooking the sea. Fiordiligi and Dorabella pour out their feelings of love as they gaze at portraits of their husbands-to-be. Enter Don Alfonso, who puts the two young women to the test by announcing that their two officers are leaving (not true, in fact) to go off to war. The two sisters, in despair, take leave of their fiancés, while Don Alfonso offers an

Left: A scene from *Così fan tutte* by Mozart.

Top: The Rumanian mezzo-soprano Viorica Cortez.

amused commentary on what is happening. Scene 3. Don Alfonso has prevailed upon the young women's maid, Despina (soprano), who is not exactly a disinterested party, to be his accomplice. She now introduces two new would-be suitors into the house, actually Ferrando and Guglielmo themselves dressed up as Albanians. The two young men immediately start to court Dorabella and Fiordiligi, but their response is one of indignation. Scene 4. A garden. Dorabella and Fiordiligi are lamenting the fact that their fiancés are so far away, when suddenly the two Albanians come rushing up to them, out of breath, having taken poison on being rejected by the young women. Dorabella and Fiordiligi call for help. Enter Despina disguised as a doctor. With a magnet she touches the bodies of the two supposedly poisoned young men, whereupon they make a miraculous recovery and declare their love all over again. ACT II. Scene 1. A bedroom in the house of Fiordiligi and Dorabella. The two sisters, influenced by Despina, are no longer as sure as they were of their love for their fiancés, so they let themselves be persuaded without difficulty to meet their two new suitors in the garden that evening. Scene 2. A garden by the sea. The courting begins: Guglielmo wins the heart of Dorabella, which makes his friend Ferrando feel desperate. Scene 3. The bedroom of the two sisters. Fiordiligi, dressed as a soldier, has decided to go to her fiancé far away. Enter Ferrando, who proceeds to overcome her weakening resistance and so wins Fiordiligi's love. Scene 4. A room with a table laid. Everything is ready for the double wedding: Despina, dressed as a notary, is about to perform the marriage when a sudden roll of drums announces the return of the soldiers. The two sisters hide their Albanians in another room, and then Ferrando and Guglielmo, who have just taken off their Albanian costumes, greet the two young women, realize that they are both about to marry someone else, and pretend to get into a rage against their presumed rivals. At this point Don Alfonso intervenes, explains everything, and makes peace between the couples with the result that they are reunited.

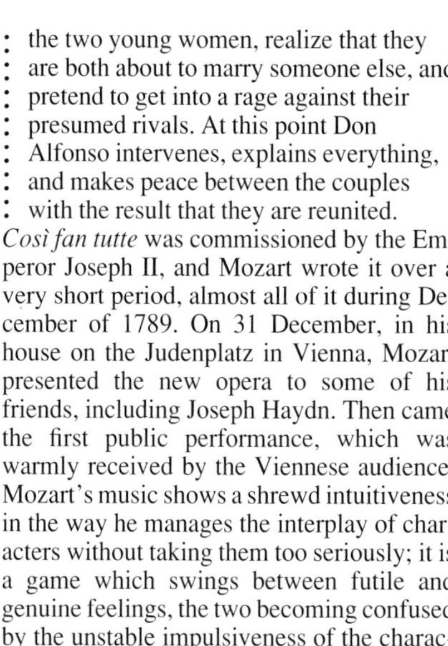

Così fan tutte was commissioned by the Emperor Joseph II, and Mozart wrote it over a very short period, almost all of it during December of 1789. On 31 December, in his house on the Judenplatz in Vienna, Mozart presented the new opera to some of his friends, including Joseph Haydn. Then came the first public performance, which was warmly received by the Viennese audience. Mozart's music shows a shrewd intuitiveness in the way he manages the interplay of characters without taking them too seriously; it is a game which swings between futile and genuine feelings, the two becoming confused by the unstable impulsiveness of the characters, and with the music sometimes revealing the human face behind the mask of pretense.

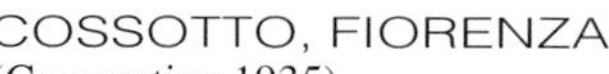

COSSOTTO, FIORENZA

(Crescentino 1935)

Italian mezzo-soprano. She studied at the Conservatorio in Turin, graduating in 1956. She then completed her training at the La Scala school in Milan, subsequently joining the La Scala company and making her debut as Sister Matilde at the premiere in 1957 of Poulenc's *Les dialogues des Carmélites*. She then sang supporting roles until 1961, the year in which she triumphed as Leonora in *La favorita*. Hers is a naturally polished voice, resplendent in the upper register.

Above: A scene from *Così fan tutte* by Mozart.

Top: The Italian mezzo-soprano Fiorenza Cossotto.

COSSUTTA, CARLO

(Trieste 1932)

Italian tenor. Having moved to Argentina while he was still very young, he made his debut in 1958 as Cassio in *Otello* at the Teatro Colón in Buenos Aires. In a short time, he had made his mark as the leading tenor in South America. He sang Cassio again at his first appearance in Italy (Rome, 1962). Engagements followed at Covent Garden (*Il trovatore*, 1964; *Cavalleria rusticana* and *Don Carlos*, 1968), at the Vienna Staatsoper (*Simon Boccanegra* and *Macbeth*) and the Paris Opéra (Verdi's *Requiem* and *Il trovatore*). Cossutta then moved on, gradually so as to avoid harming his voice, from lyric tenor to more markedly dramatic tenor roles. As a result, he achieved a maturity of voice and performance, as illustrated by his memorable Otello in Verdi's opera.

COTRUBAS, ILEANA

(Galati 1939)

Rumanian soprano. She studied music at the Conservatory in Bucharest, and made her debut singing Yniold in Debussy's *Pelléas et Mélisande*, following this with appearances as Oscar (*Un ballo in maschera*) and Cherubino (*Le nozze di Figaro*). After successes in major singing competitions (1965–66), she was contracted by the Théâtre de la Monnaie in Brussels, where she sang Pamina in Mozart's *Die Zauberflöte* (The Magic Flute) and Costanze in *Die Entführung aus dem Serail* (The Seraglio). It is as an exquisite Mozart performer that Cotrubas has won international fame. A performer of sensitivity and refinement, she also excelled in *La bohème*, *La traviata*, and *Manon*. Cotrubas also gave many concerts, concentrating in particular on French chamber music (Debussy, Poulenc, Fauré, etc.). In recent years she has given more preference to this aspect of her career, after retiring from opera in 1990.

COUNT ORY

See *Comte Ory, Le*

CRASS, FRANZ

(Wipperfürth 1928)

German bass-baritone. He studied at the Conservatory in Cologne, making his debut in 1954 at the municipal theater in Krefeld and, two years later, joining the Hanover Opera Company. At the same time he was appearing in major opera houses across Germany, including Bayreuth, where he distinguished himself as an admired interpreter of Wagner, with roles such as the Dutchman in *Die fliegende Holländer* (The Flying Dutchman) and Gurnemanz in *Parsifal*. Equally memorable were his Sarastro in Mozart's *Die Zauberflöte* (The Magic Flute) and Rocco in Beethoven's *Fidelio*.

CRESPIN, REGINE

(Marseilles 1927)

French soprano. After studying at the Paris Conservatoire, she made her debut in Rheims (1948) as Charlotte in Massenet's *Werther*. In 1951 she won acclaim at the Paris Opéra for her performance as Elsa in *Lohengrin*. Also at the Opéra she sang the Marschallin in Strauss's *Der Rosenkavalier* (1956) and took part in the French premiere of Poulenc's *Les dialogues des Carmélites* (1957). With appearances at Bayreuth (*Parsifal* and *Die Walküre*) from 1958 onwards, Glyndebourne (1959), La Scala, Milan (Pizzetti's *Fedra* in 1960) and other leading European and American opera houses, Crespin was regarded as one of the most sensitive and expressive sopranos of the 1960s and 1970s. From the 1970s she gradually took on fewer engagements as a soprano in order to tackle mezzo-soprano roles (Santuzza, Carmen, etc.). In 1989 she undertook an extended tour of farewell concerts but appeared again in the opera house as the Countess in Tchaikovsky's *Pikovaya Dama* (Queen of Spades) in Paris in 1991.

CRISPINO E LA COMARE

(Crispino and the Fairy Godmother)

Opera in three acts by Federico (1809–1877) and Luigi (1805–1859) Ricci, to a libretto by Francesco Maria Piave. First performance: Venice, Teatro Gallo a San Benedetto, 28 February 1850.

The setting is Venice. Crispino (*buffo* bass), a poor cobbler, is at a loss as to how to avoid the abusive behavior of his landlord, Don Asdrubale (bass), who, among other things, is making advances to his wife Annetta (soprano). In despair, Crispino is on the point of throwing himself down a well when a mysterious woman, the Fairy Godmother of the title (mezzo-soprano), stops him and promises that he will become rich and famous. All he has to do is to pretend to be a doctor, and if, while on a visit to a patient, he does not see the Godmother standing at the bedside, his patient will recover. So Crispino establishes himself as a doctor

Left: The Rumanian soprano Ileana Cotrubas.

Above: A scene from *Crispino e la comare* by Federico and Luigi Ricci.

and goes to Don Asdrubale's house to give a professional consultation. The Don's niece, Lisetta (soprano), is gravely ill. Seeing the Godmother standing beside Don Asdrubale, Crispino announces that Lisetta will recover, whereas her uncle will die. And he is proved right. Crispino becomes arrogant as a result of his successes, his fame and his wealth. One day, after he has treated Annetta badly, the Fairy Godmother appears again. Crispino wants to chase her away, but the Godmother strikes him on the shoulder and the little cobbler falls in a dead faint. He is then transported down into an underground place where the Godmother reveals to him that she is Death and his time has come. Crispino repents and asks to be forgiven. The Godmother is touched by this and allows him to return to his family. In a short while, Crispino comes round from his fainting fit to find himself surrounded by Annetta, their children and his friends, and adds to his wife's happiness his own heartfelt promise that he will change his ways.

Crispino e la comare is the most famous opera by the Ricci brothers. Its quality as a piece of theater is probably due to the individual contributions of each of the two brothers, even though it is extremely difficult to establish which brother did what to create this remarkably enjoyable opera, with its well-balanced text and stage action. The music has a melodic vigour typical of the Neapolitan school, as well as plenty of verve, inventive harmonies and an excellent instrumental style.

CRISTOFORO COLOMBO

Opera in three acts and an epilogue by Alberto Franchetti (1860–1942), to a libretto by Luigi Illica. First performance: Genoa, Teatro Carlo Felice, 6 October 1892.

Cristoforo Colombo (baritone) has once again been refused a request to sail the high seas in search of new worlds. Queen Isabella (soprano), who regrets that Colombo has been turned down, feels generously towards him and so removes a diadem she is wearing and offers it to him, to help him equip a fleet of ships for his expedition. Once at sea, there is an air of discouragement and mutiny on board. The sailors are on the point of bearing down menacingly on Colombo when cries of "Land ahoy!" are heard. The scene changes back to Spain, where Colombo's return is awaited. He is to face charges of having seized all the wealth of the New World and proclaimed himself its ruler. Colombo is arrested and put into prison. Years pass. Colombo, now old, ill and impoverished, receives news of the death of Queen Isabella; profoundly distressed by this, he takes to wandering the high seas of his memories, and then turns to his old friend Don Fernando Guevara (tenor), announces in a voice barely audible that his last hour has come, and collapses. Guevara kneels beside Colombo's body.

Cristoforo Colombo was part of the programme for the 400th anniversary celebrations in Genoa of Columbus's discovery of America (1892). The work, and especially its second act, proved difficult to stage, and this was a handicap in the early performances. As a result of differences with the composer, the conductor Luigi Mancinelli handed over the task of conducting the third night of the opera to the young Arturo Toscanini. The opera was recomposed several times. It was staged at La Scala, Milan, on 17 January 1923, with further performances after that in Germany and elsewhere.

CRISTOFORO COLOMBO
DRAMMA LIRICO
di
LUIGI ILLICA
Musica
di
ALBERTO
FRANCHETTI
G. RICORDI & C.
EDITORI

The libretto of *Cristoforo Colombo* by Alberto Franchetti.

CROCIATO IN EGITTO, IL

(The Crusader in Egypt)

Opera in two acts by Giacomo Meyerbeer (1791–1864), to a libretto by Gaetano Rossi. First performance: Venice, Teatro La Fenice, 7 March 1824.

The knight Armando di Orville (mezzo-soprano), sole survivor of a bloody battle between Crusaders and Moors, is living at the court of the Sultan of Egypt, Aladino (bass). Armando, who is using the name Elmireno, enjoys the generous hospitality of the Sultan, whose life he once saved. For this he has become Commander of the Egyptian army and is about to marry the Sultan's daughter Palmide (soprano), with whom he has secretly had a child. In the meantime a delegation of the Knights of Rhodes has arrived, led by Adriano di Monfort (tenor), who recognizes Elmireno as his nephew Armando, whom everyone had believed to be dead. Adriano accuses his nephew of having betrayed the Christian faith and a knight's honour, as well as breaking his promise to Felicia (contralto). Overcome with remorse, Armando swears loyalty to the Knights of Rhodes, and then visits the Sultan to reveal his true identity. Aladino is furious and declares war on the Christian knights. But the opera ends happily: Felicia and Adriano are touched by the love of Palmide (who has meanwhile converted to Christianity) and give their blessing to her marriage to Armando, who wins back the Sultan's trust, thwarts a palace coup and saves the Sultan's life for the second time. Armando and Palmide can now be married amid general rejoicing.

Meyerbeer went to Italy in 1815 to study Italian operatic style and composed a number of operas there, including *Romilda e Costanza* (1817) and, in 1824, *Il crociato in Egitto*. The opera is written in the purest *bel canto* style, and is clearly influenced by Rossini. It contains the last great role (Armando) written for a *castrato*, the famous Giovanni Battista Velluti. The success of *Il crociato in Egitto* was considerable, and the opera was performed in many places within a short space of time. On the crest of this wave of celebrity, Meyerbeer went to Paris, already known there as a distinguished opera composer.

CUBERLI, LELLA

(Austin, Texas 1945)

Stage name of Ellen Cuberli, née Terrell. American soprano, who became an Italian citizen. She studied music at Southern Methodist University in Dallas before moving to Italy and completing her training at the Accademia Chigiana di Siena. After successes in major singing competitions, Cuberli made her debut in *La traviata* in Budapest (1975). In 1978 she scored her first triumph as Constanze in *Die Entführung aus dem Serail* (The Seraglio), in which her gifts as a singer were in evidence. As well as an outstanding stage presence, her vocal and stylistic talents in-

clude elegance and refinement of phrasing, and a consistent delivery whether in even, sustained singing or *coloratura*. These characteristics of *bel canto* have led to Cuberli's name being particularly associated with the operas of Rossini: *Il turco in Italia*, *Tancredi*, *Bianca e Faliero*, *Il viaggio a Reims* and *Semiramide*.

CUNNING LITTLE VIXEN, THE

See *Prihody Lišky Bystroušky*

CUPIDO, ALBERTO

(Portofino 1947)

Italian tenor. He studied at the Centro di Perfezionamento (Center for Specialization) at La Scala, Milan, and the Accademia Chigiana in Siena. After winning singing competitions in Parma (1975) and Busseto (1976), he made his debut in 1976 as Pinkerton (*Madama Butterfly*) at the Teatro Comunale in Genoa. The following year he sang the role of Rodolfo (*La bohème*) in Frankfurt and went on to appear at major German opera houses, including the Deutsche Oper in Berlin (*La traviata*, 1979; *La bohème*, *Luisa Miller*, etc.), the Hamburg Staatsoper (*La bohème*, 1979) and the Bayerische Staatsoper, Munich (*La bohème*, 1980). Cupido was a guest artist at the Opéra in Paris from 1983 and his name has also been associated with La Scala (since 1984, with *Lucia di Lammermoor*), the Vienna Staatsoper (since 1981, *Gianni Schicchi*), the San Francisco Opera (since 1983, *La traviata*), Covent Garden (*Tosca*, 1992) and with all the other main Italian and European opera houses. Drawing on the Italian Romantic opera repertoire and also the French (*Faust*, *Werther*, *Manon*, etc.), Cupido boasts an extremely attractive vocal timbre as well as remarkable facility in the upper register and naturally incisive phrasing.

CURTIS, ALAN

(Mason, Michigan 1934)

American harpsichord-player and conductor. He graduated from the Universities of Michigan (1955) and Illinois (1956) and then began to appear in the dual role of conducting from the harpsichord. A teacher at the University of California at Berkeley, Curtis is also involved in the revising of scores, both in the harpsichord repertoire (works by Couperin, Balbastre and C. P. E. Bach) and in the revival of baroque opera. He has edited and conducted important revivals of Handel's operas *Admeto* and *Agrippina*.

CYRANO DE BERGERAC

Opera in four acts and five tableaux by Franco Alfano (1876–1954), to a text by Henri Cain, from the play by Rostand. First performance: Rome, Teatro Reale, 26 January 1936.

The setting is Paris, around the year 1640. Cyrano (tenor), a penniless nobleman from Gascony, is secretly in love with his cousin Rossana (soprano). After discovering that she loves one of his comrades-in-arms, Cristiano (tenor), who does not have the courage to reveal his feelings, Cyrano sacrifices himself for the happiness of the couple and, one night, imitating Cristiano's voice, asks Rossana for a kiss. Rossana is willing, whereupon Cristiano takes Cyrano's place. Cristiano and Rossana get married. Cristiano and Cyrano go to war, and Cyrano writes his friend's love letters home to Rossana, who then makes the journey to the battlefield to embrace such a beloved husband; but Cristiano is fatally injured in battle, and his dying request to Cyrano is that he should tell Rossana who had really written the letters. Cyrano, however, does not want to disappoint Rossana in her love. Fifteen years later, Cyrano, who has been seriously injured by unknown assailants, is being cared for in the convent where Rossana has lived since Cristiano died, and he speaks to her in burning and passionate words of love. Rossana thus discovers the truth and realizes that what she has always loved in Cristiano was really the spirit of Cyrano. The hero then dies in Rossana's arms.

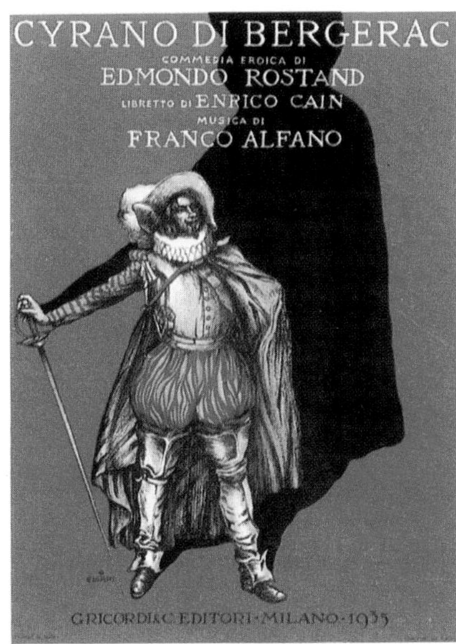

Cyrano de Bergerac was Franco Alfano's last work. After its premiere in Rome, it was staged in French at the Opéra-Comique in Paris on 29 May 1936. Both these productions were a success, but the opera was not included in the repertoire.

CYRUS IN BABYLON

See *Ciro in Babilonia*

Top left: The soprano Lella Cuberli.

Left: The Italian tenor Alberto Cupido.

Above: The libretto of *Cyrano di Bergerac* by Franco Alfano.

D

DAFNE, LA

Dramatic fable in a prologue and six scenes by Jacopo Peri (1561–1633) in collaboration with Jacopo Corsi (1561–1602), to a text by Ottavio Rinuccini. First performance: Florence, at the home of Jacopo Corsi, during the Carnival of 1598.

The story comes from Ovid's *Metamorphoses* and is preceded by a prologue in which the character playing the Latin poet bids the audience welcome. As the curtain rises, the chorus presents the god Apollo, who has killed the Python and declares that he attaches no importance to the skills of Love. The latter quickly takes his revenge. When the nymph Dafne appears, Apollo is overwhelmed by her beauty and falls in love with her. The nymph escapes, with the god in pursuit. Love sings of his triumph over Apollo, and the chorus echoes his words. A messenger tells how Dafne was about to be caught by Apollo when she called on the gods for help and they changed her into a laurel-tree. From that moment, the laurel would be sacred to Apollo and its leaves would be used to make garlands to crown the heads of poets and kings. The fable ends with the chorus praising love and hoping that everyone who loves will be loved by their beloved in return.

Probably composed between 1594 and 1595, Peri's *La Dafne* is generally considered the first opera. Its score has almost all been lost, and the brief excerpts that have survived are not enough evidence on which to base an assessment of the whole. However, by looking at these fragments alongside the libretto, it can be said that *Dafne* is the first example of "singing" speech, modelled on the style of delivery used by actors of tragedies in Ancient Greece. Rinuccini's play was subsequently set by Marco da Gagliano (Mantua, 1608) and, in Martin Opitz's German translation, by the composer Heinrich Schütz in 1627, making it the first opera to be composed in Germany.

DALLAPICCOLA, LUIGI

(Pisino d'Istria 1904–Florence 1975)

Italian composer. He began to study music in Pisino but during the First World War moved to Austria with his family. On his return to Italy, he continued his musical studies in Pisino and then in Trieste and Florence

Top: The soprano Toti Dal Monte as Lucia in *Lucia di Lammermoor.*

Above: The composer Luigi Dallapiccola in a drawing by Colacicchi.

(1922). Florence's Conservatorio was the focus of Dallapiccola's life as a composer and teacher between 1934 and 1967. His compositions for the theater are the three operas *Volo di notte* (Florence, 1940), *Il prigioniero* (Florence, 1950) and *Ulisse* (Berlin, 1968), and the sacred music-drama *Job* (Rome, 1950), works which, like the whole of Dallapiccola's musical output, are landmarks in musical history and not only that of Italy. Dallapiccola's writing for the theater is inspired by a profound interest in human drama, with all its deep anxieties and continual search for truth.

DAL MONTE, TOTI

(Mogliano Veneto 1893–Pieve di Soligo 1975)

Stage name of Antonietta Meneghel. Italian soprano. After being encouraged to study piano, Dal Monte injured her hand and then concentrated on singing, taking lessons from Barbara Marchisio. She made her official debut at La Scala, Milan (1916), as Biancafiore in Zandonai's *Francesca da Rimini*. After further specialist training with the baritone Pini-Corsi, Dal Monte sang the role of Gilda in *Rigoletto* in Turin (1918), a role in which she appeared at La Scala (1922) and subsequently in all the leading opera houses of Europe and America. As well as her performance of Gilda, Dal Monte won fame for her Lucia, Amina and Rosina, roles to which she later added those of Mimi and Cio-Cio-San. Dal Monte, or La Toti (as she came to be known), was one of the last prima donnas of the pre-Callas era. Although hers was a typically light soprano voice and therefore not so full-bodied, she never limited her singing to mere displays of virtuosity, and characterized her roles with subtle yet personal interpretative skill.

DAME BLANCHE, LA

(The White Lady)

Opera in three acts by François-Adrien Boïeldieu (1775–1834), to a libretto by Eugène Scribe, from Sir Walter Scott. First performance: Paris, Théâtre de l'Opéra-Comique, 10 December 1825.

Scotland, 1759. Dickson (tenor), a landowner in the county of Avenel, welcomes into his home Georges (tenor), a young officer who has asked for hospitality. The young man knows nothing of his own family and is searching for a young woman who had recently tended his wounds and with whom he has fallen in love. Gaveston (bass), formerly steward to the last Count of Avenel, has handled his master's affairs in such a way as to create an inheritance for himself, a sum he plans to use in order to buy the castle, which has been put on sale owing to pressure from creditors. All the local landowners have come to an agreement that they will buy the holding in order to retain it for its owner, and Dickson is entrusted with this task. The castle has a ghost, the White Lady, and she herself makes an appointment with Dickson for midnight. Dickson is terrified, so Georges offers to take his place. Meanwhile, Anna (soprano) has also arrived at the castle. She is a young orphan whom the Counts of Avenel had brought up and is now Gaveston's ward. The young woman intends to use some hidden treasure to save the castle. Dressed as the White Lady, Anna meets Georges and persuades him to buy the castle for her. So he does. In a spiralling sequence of twists and intrigues, it is discovered that Georges is none other than the young Julien, son of the deceased Count. A happy ending is in sight: Anna is the mysterious young woman Georges has been looking for, so as the two young people find happiness, everything becomes clear and ends.

La dame blanche is Boïeldieu's masterpiece. His music for the opera is light, effortless, graceful and clear, and had an enormous success which led to its great popularity. For decades, the work was the showpiece of the leading French opera houses (in 1826 alone it was performed at least 150 times). Its 1,000th performance was given in Paris on 16 December 1862.

DAMNATION DE FAUST, LA

(The Damnation of Faust)

Dramatic legend in four acts and ten scenes by Hector Berlioz (1803–1869), to a libretto by the composer and Almire Gandonnière, based on Goethe's Faust. *First concert performance: Paris, Théâtre de l'Opéra-Comique (Salle Favart), 6 December 1846. First stage performance: Monte Carlo, Théâtre du Casino, 18 February 1893.*

The action takes place in Hungary. It is dawn. The life-weary old philosopher Faust (tenor) witnesses the awakening of the happy village. Faust can no longer tolerate his solitary life and decides to poison himself. Méphistophélès (baritone) appears to him offering him youth and the pleasures of life. Faust is uncertain, and puts Méphistophélès to the test by asking him to carry out his promises. Méphistophélès transports Faust first to a tavern in the midst of a joyful company of students and soldiers, and then to a wood where the philosopher, now rejuvenated, falls asleep and dreams of Marguerite (soprano), with whom he falls in love. With the aid of Méphistophélès, Faust manages to gain entry to his beloved's house. Faust makes his presence known to Marguerite, tells her that he loves her, and seduces her. But immediately Méphistophélès intervenes and leads Faust away. Overwhelmed with love, Marguerite weeps for her lost serenity as she awaits Faust, who has abandoned her. In a forest, Faust, now tired of the pleasures of life, asks Nature to grant him peace. Méphistophélès, afraid of losing Faust's soul, warns him that Marguerite is about to be executed after being found guilty of killing her mother. Faust begs him to help Marguerite and Méphistophélès agrees, asking Faust for his soul by way of exchange. While Faust is plunging into Hell, Marguerite who, having repented, accepts her punishment and rejects Méphistophélès's help, is ascending into Heaven amid a host of angels glorifying God.

At the end of 1828, Berlioz had composed a cantata for soloists, chorus and orchestra entitled *Huit scènes de Faust op. 1*, the embryo of a new work, which he began to compose in 1845. A year later, he gave this the title *La damnation de Faust*. The work's premiere received a decidedly negative response, and the second performance, which was rehearsed with the greatest attention to detail, was a total fiasco. This absolute failure had a profound effect on the composer, bringing him close to a serious breakdown. Several decades later, the opera scored an extraordinary triumph and to this day remains the only truly popular opera that Berlioz wrote.

DANAÏDES, LES

Tragic opera in five acts by Antonio Salieri (1750–1825), to a libretto by du Roullet and von Tschudi. Partly based on Ranieri de' Calzabigi's text for Ipermestra. *First performance: Paris, Académie Royale de Musique (Opéra), 26 April 1784.*

Danaus (bass), hounded and persecuted by his brother Aegyptus, wants his revenge and asks his 50 daughters, who are about to marry Aegyptus's 50 sons, to make good the offense he has suffered. After the weddings, the daughters fulfil their father's wishes by killing their husbands. Only one bride, Hypermestra (soprano), does not obey her father's will and helps her beloved Lynceus (tenor) to escape. At their father's bidding, the

Top: A scene from *La damnation de Faust* at the Paris Opéra.

Above: An illustration for Goethe's *Faust*, the work which inspired Berlioz to compose *La damnation de Faust*.

Danaïds pursue the fugitive relentlessly across Mount Thyrsus. Meanwhile Lynceus, with a group of armed men, returns to the palace. Danaus, who now has no way out, searches for Hypermestra in order to be avenged on her, but he is confronted by Pelagus (baritone), who kills him. Lynceus escapes with his bride to Memphis in the land of Isis. A flash of lightning destroys the palace of Danaus, the earth opens and, out of a sea of blood, the rock to which Danaus has been chained rises up: lightning flashes continuously above his head and a vulture eats his entrails. The Danaïds, who have all been chained together, are being tormented by demons, serpents and Furies, while being deluged by fire.

In this opera, Salieri's masterpiece, there are a number of features that herald the Romantic era, conveyed by the emphasis on dramatic expressiveness. The Paris premiere took place as a result of the support and encouragement of Gluck. Salieri's name was given as Gluck's collaborator, and it was only after the work's great success that he was revealed as the sole composer.

DANCO, SUZANNE

(Brussels 1911)

Belgian soprano. She began to study music at the Brussels Conservatoire and in 1936 won a singing competition in Vienna. She continued her studies in Prague with Fernando Carpi. In 1941 Danco made her theatrical debut in Genoa as Fiordiligi in Mozart's *Così fan tutte*. She subsequently appeared in many Italian opera houses, including La Scala, Milan (*Peter Grimes* and *Oedipus Rex*). In the years that followed, Danco's name was linked with the festivals of Edinburgh, Glyndebourne and Aix-en-Provence, where she proved a most sensitive Mozart performer. She also appeared at Covent Garden, at the Vienna Staatsoper and in leading American opera houses. After retiring from the stage, she concentrated on teaching and has held specialized courses at the Accademia Chigiana in Siena.

Above: A scene from *Les Danaïdes*, Antonio Salieri's masterpiece.

Right: The Italian poet Gabriele D'Annunzio, the author of several libretti.

DANIELS, BARBARA

(Newark, Ohio 1946)

American soprano. She studied with Tajo and Markova, later specializing with famous conductors like Thomas Schippers and James Levine. In 1974 she made her debut in Cincinnati, as Musetta in *La bohème*, and then moved to Europe where, between 1975 and 1984, she made appearances in Innsbruck (*Così fan tutte*), at the Staatstheater in Kassel, and at the opera house in Cologne. In 1978, she appeared for the first time at Covent Garden in *La bohème*, with subsequent roles there in *Don Giovanni*, *Die Fledermaus* and *Falstaff*. In 1983, Daniels sang for the first time, again as Musetta, at the Metropolitan Opera House in New York where she has appeared regularly, notably as Minnie in *La fanciulla del West*.

D'ANNUNZIO, GABRIELE

(Pescara 1863–Gardone Riviera 1938)

Italian poet, novelist and playwright. Throughout his life, D'Annunzio maintained close links with the world of music; there was a deep rapport between music and his literary style, which expressed a "musicality" in words. He was also especially interested in helping to increase the popularity in Italy of the music of Claude Debussy and Richard Strauss. He was in close touch and collaborated with the composers of the so-called "young school." This resulted in his libretti for *La nave* (1908) and *La pisanella* (1913) for Ildebrando Pizzetti and for *La Parisina* (1913) for Pietro Mascagni. D'Annunzio adapted a number of texts for the opera, including *Fedra* and *La figlia di Jorio*, again for Pizzetti, *Sogno di un tramonto d'autunno* for Malipiero, and others. He wrote the text for *Le Martyre de Saint Sébastien*, a mystery play with incidental music by Debussy.

DANTONS TOD

(Danton's Death)

Opera in two parts by Gottfried von Einem (b. 1918), to a libretto by the composer Boris Blacher, based on the play of the same name by Georg Büchner. First performance: Salzburg Festival, 6 August 1947.

The action takes place in Paris in 1794, at

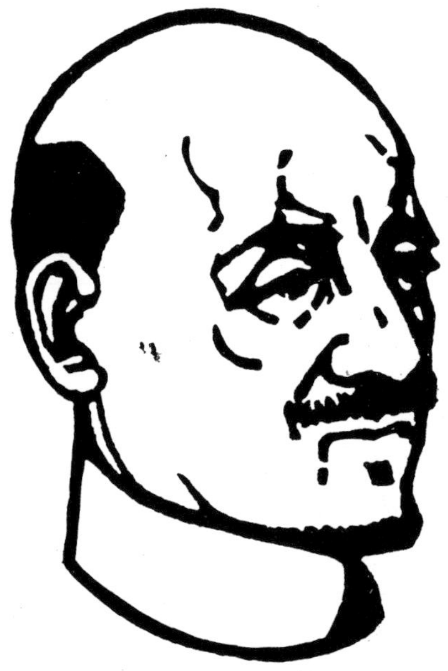

the house of Hérault de Séchelles (tenor). Among the guests are Georges Danton (baritone), his wife Julie (mezzo-soprano) and the deputy Camille Desmoulins (tenor). De Séchelles, Danton and Desmoulins are worried about the serious situation in which France finds herself; only by the destruction of the status quo and reorganization can the Republic be built. But Danton has no illusions about the real possibility of changing the present course of events. While demonstrations against the bourgeoisie and the intellectuals take place in the streets, Robespierre (tenor) harangues the crowd with his demogogic speeches about the power of the people. Danton, who has witnessed this event, encourages Robespierre to adopt a more realistic vision. Robespierre realizes he will have to get rid of Danton and his supporters. Danton and Desmoulins are duly arrested. During the trial, Danton strenuously defends his ideas and warns against the imminent danger of dictatorship. The Revolutionary Tribunal condemns both men for seeking to undermine the authority of the law. Danton and his comrades make their way to the scaffold singing the *Marseillaise* but their voices are drowned by the shouts of the crowd. When all is over and the square is deserted, Lucile (soprano), Desmoulins' wife, now out of her mind, sits weeping on the steps of the guillotine.

The opera had a great success at the Salzburg Festival not least because it was being presented there not long after the collapse of the Nazi regime. Büchner's text, which originally comprised 29 scenes, was condensed into six scenes for the opera without being unfaithful to the original. In 1950 the composer produced a new version of the work.

DAPHNE

Opera in one act by Richard Strauss (1864–1949), to a libretto by Joseph Gregor. First performance: Dresden, Staatsoper, 15 October 1938.

A feast in honour of Dionysus is being prepared. Young Daphne (soprano), daughter of Gaea (mezzo-soprano) and Peneios, is completely absorbed in her contemplation of nature and asks the sun not to set so she can go on looking at the trees, the flowers and the stream. She has nothing but blank looks for the shepherd Leukippos (tenor), who is in love with her; she rejects him and is reproached by Gaea for doing so. Apollo (tenor) appears in human form, and Daphne, who has been asked by her father to look after the newcomer, is struck by his noble appearance, calls him brother and embraces him. Apollo, who has halted the chariot of the sun for Daphne, kisses her. Daphne flees in turmoil. During a shepherd's celebration, Leukippos, in disguise, offers her a Dionysiac drink and invites her to dance, but Apollo, who is jealous, unmasks Leukippos and reveals himself for the god that he is. Leukippos curses him, and the god responds by killing him with an arrow but, faced with Daphne's despair (she believes she is responsible for the young man's death), Apollo recognizes that he has usurped the rights of Dionysus and prays to Zeus to change the young woman into a laurel.

Strauss's *Daphne* is seldom performed. In common with his other late operas, the work is Olympian in character, and its setting is outside space and time. Its most beautiful passages are the symphonic interlude which accompanies Apollo's kiss and Daphne's final aria as she is transformed into a laurel.

DA PONTE, LORENZO

(Ceneda, now Vittorio Veneto 1749–New York 1838)

Stage name of Emanuele Conigliano, Italian man of letters and librettist. After converting from Judaism to Christianity in 1763 (he took the name of Da Ponte in honour of the Bishop of Ceneda), he studied at a seminary and took holy orders in 1773. He then embarked on a wandering life filled with scandal, arriving in Vienna in 1781 where, thanks to the support of Antonio Salieri, he became Court Poet to the Imperial theaters. It was in Vienna that Da Ponte met Mozart, for whom he wrote libretti for *Le nozze di Figaro* (1786), *Don Giovanni* (1787) and *Così fan tutte* (1790). Also while in Vienna, he provided libretti for Martín y Soler (*Una cosa rara*, 1786), Salieri (*Axur, re d'Ormus*, 1788) and other musicians. On the death of Emperor Joseph II, he left Vienna to settle in London (1793), and moved from there to America. He held the chair of Italian at Columbia University in New York (1826–37). With Manuel Garcia, he was one of the first to introduce Italian opera into the United States.

DARA, ENZO

(Mantua 1938)

Italian bass. He studied singing and piano and in 1960 made his debut at Fano (on the Italian Adriatic) as Colline in *La bohème*. In 1966, Dara sang for the first time the role of Dulcamara (*L'elisir d'amore*) in Reggio Emilia. One of his first important successes was in 1969 when he appeared as Mustafà in Rossini's *L'italiana in Algeri* at the Spoleto Festival with Thomas Schippers conducting. Dara confirmed his qualities as a singer in his performance of Bartolo (*Il barbiere di Siviglia*) at La Scala, Milan in 1971 in the famous production by Ponnelle directed by Abbado, and was recognized as the finest comic bass in Italy. Dara is a subtle actor complementing the vocal precision of a real master of style with his powerful stage presence. As a result, he has been acclaimed in the leading opera houses of the world as the most authentic performer of all Rossini's comic operas, as well as those of Cimarosa and Donizetti.

Above: The Italian bass Enzo Dara.

DARDANUS

Tragic opera in a prologue and five acts by Jean-Philippe Rameau (1683–1764), to a libretto by Charles-Antoine Le Clerc de la Bruyère. First performance: Paris, Académie Royale de Musique (Opéra), 19 November 1739.

In the prologue, Amour finds Jalousie disturbing and upsetting the Pleasures and dismisses her. Without her, however, the Pleasures fall asleep, and Vénus has to call her back to wake them up again. The tragedy tells the story of Iphise (soprano), daughter of Teucer (bass), King of Phrygia. Against her father's wishes, Iphise loves Dardanus (tenor), her country's enemy. Teucer has promised her hand to Prince Antenor (bass-baritone). In anguish, Iphise decides to consult the wizard Isménor (bass). Dardanus, who returns Iphise's love, obtains from Isménor a magic wand which he uses to take on the physical appearance of the wizard. In this way, he is able to listen as Iphise confides in him, learns of her love for him and, finally, happily reveals his identity to her, whereupon the young woman flees in confusion. Dardanus is captured by his enemies, but Jupiter causes a monster to rise out of the sea, and Antenor sets out to fight it. He is, however, saved by Dardanus, who has been freed by Vénus (soprano) and, failing to recognize him, promises him undying friendship and offers him his sword as a token. Neptune's oracle has prophesied that Iphise will be given in marriage to whoever kills the monster. Dardanus, in the presence of Teucer and his joyful people, is honoured for his achievement and Antenor, in keeping with his promise of friendship, renounces his love for Iphise in favour of Dardanus.

Dardanus was revised so many times that the final version was completed only in 1760. The above story follows the original version. With the fantastic and miraculous features omitted (for example, the episode with the monster), some delightful melodies that appeared in the original version are lost, but this is made up for by the way in which the music plays its own dramatic part in the final version.

DARGOMYZHSKY, ALEXANDER

(Troitskoye, Tula 1813–St. Petersburg 1869)

Russian composer. His first opera, *Esmeralda* (1847), based on Victor Hugo's *Notre-Dame de Paris*, shows clear signs of French influence. After travelling for some years abroad, Dargomyzhsky set to work on his opera *Rusalka* (1856). His musical language is fully expressed in his last opera, *Kamenniÿ Gost* (The Stone Guest), staged posthumously in 1872.

DAVID ET JONATHAS

Tragédie en musique *in a prologue and five acts by Marc-Antoine Charpentier (1634–1704), to a libretto by Père Bretonneau. First performance: Paris, Collège Louis-Le-Grand, 28 February 1688.*

Saül (bass), King of Israel, at war against the Philistines, senses the absence of God's support and consults a witch (contralto). She calls up the ghost of Samuel (bass) and prophesies to Saül that his end is near and David will accede to the throne. After conquering the Amalekites, David (contralto) goes to the Philistines' camp. The Philistine king, Akish (bass), receives David with full honours and informs him that he is going to meet Saül, with whom he will seek to make a treaty. During this truce, awaiting resolutions which will either put an end to the war between the Israelites and the Philistines or prolong it, David is reunited with Jonathas (soprano), Saül's son and David's friend, whom he loves as a brother. Meanwhile Joab (tenor), jealous of David, puts the idea into Saül's head that David is using the truce as a pretext to conspire against Israel and bring about her ruin. Saül, who had been waiting for an opportunity to rid himself of David, immediately believes Joab's false accusations. David is accused of treason and is defended by Akish, who provokes Saül to an even greater wrath, which leads him to wage battle against the Philistines once more. David, who has found shelter in the enemy camp, meets Jonathas and tells him that he will never lift his sword against Saül. Not long after, Saül is defeated in battle and Jonathas, who has been mortally wounded, dies in David's arms; Saül himself, fleeing from the Philistines, falls upon his own sword and is close to death. While Akish is announcing that David will be the new King of Israel, David, badly affected by the death of his friend, walks away.

Composed in 1687–88, immediately after the death of Lully, *David et Jonathas* is the first sign of a break with Lully's supremacy in the theater. Charpentier's opera, staged as an *intermezzo* for the Latin tragedy *Saul* by Père Charmillat, is a major step forward in the evolution of the *tragédie lyrique*. The prologue is no longer separate.

Right: The British conductor Sir Colin Davis.

DAVIES, RYLAND

(Cwm Ebbw Vale, Monmouthshire 1943)

Welsh tenor. While he was still studying at the Royal College of Music in Manchester, he took part in a number of performances of *Il barbiere di Siviglia*, *L'italiana in Algeri*, *Fidelio* and *Paride ed Elena*. During the 1964–65 season, he made his official debut with Welsh National Opera in the role of Almaviva (*Il barbiere di Siviglia*). His career then centered on London's Sadler's Wells and Covent Garden, where he appeared in a number of productions of operas by Britten (*Gloriana*, 1967), Berlioz and Mozart.

DAVIS, SIR COLIN

(Weybridge, Surrey 1927)

British conductor. After studying the clarinet, he turned to conducting. He co-founded the Chelsea Opera Group in 1950, and it was here that he gained his first experience as a conductor. Davis appeared in the Royal Festival Hall in London (1959) and with the BBC Scottish Orchestra (1957–59) before becoming music director at London's Sadler's Wells in 1959. In 1967, he made his debut at the Metropolitan Opera, New York (with Britten's *Peter Grimes*) and, in the same year, he was appointed principal conductor of the BBC Symphony Orchestra, a post he held until 1974. Since then he has appeared with the leading international orchestras. Davis has also been very active in the theater. He was music director at Covent Garden (1971–86), and conducts there regularly. He was the first British conductor to be invited to appear at the Bayreuth festival (1977). His remarkable and vigorous sense of theater and his analytical clarity have brought him distinction as a conductor of Mozart and of French opera (especially Berlioz), and for his performances of operas by Britten and Tippett.

DAWSON, LYNNE

(York 1956)
British soprano. After working initially as an interpreter, Dawson studied singing at the Guildhall School of Music in London. She began her career by giving concert performances, winning acclaim as a singer of early and baroque music. From 1985 she appeared with Trevor Pinnock's English Concert, as a soloist with the Monteverdi Choir and with other distinguished British music groups, with whom she has undertaken a number of foreign tours. As an opera singer, Dawson has appeared at the festival in Aix-en-Provence (*Iphigénie en Aulide*, 1987), at the Brighton Festival (*Le nozze di Figaro*), on Radio France (*Arabella*), in Naples at the Teatro Mercadante (*Così fan tutte*, 1990) and in Amsterdam (*Benvenuto Cellini*).

DEATH IN VENICE

Opera in two acts by Benjamin Britten (1913–1976), to a libretto by Myfanwy Piper from Thomas Mann's story, Der Tod in Venedig. *First performance: Aldeburgh Festival, 17 June 1973.*

Munich. The great writer Gustav von Aschenbach (tenor), in a futile search for beauty, youth and the illusion of perfect love, comes, after much soul-searching, to a decision to leave Munich for Venice. On arriving at a hotel on the Venice Lido, Aschenbach is deeply affected by the sight of a woman and her three sons, and especially by one of these, young Tadzio, whom the writer looks upon as a "masterpiece" he himself would like to have created. Venice becomes oppressive and is in the grip of an epidemic. Aschenbach drifts into a fantasy world, in which he sees Tadzio and his friends engaged in play on a sun-drenched beach. As his imagination continues to wander, Aschenbach loses all touch with the real world. Now alone, because all the other guests at the hotel have left in a hurry at the news that a cholera epidemic is spreading through the city, Aschenbach, in a vision, sees Tadzio playing on the beach again. But this time the young man is thrown to the ground and humiliated by one of his friends. Aschenbach cries out. He would like to help Tadzio, but the youth gets to his feet and walks towards the sea, deaf to the voices of his friends calling him. Aschenbach, too, calls out the name he loves so much and, as Tadzio appears to turn back and look in his direction, the old man dies, slumped in his chair.

Britten's opera is faithful to the original story, transferring Aschenbach's drama into an almost mythological world. With it, Mann's *Death in Venice* found its place in opera as well, after Luchino Visconti's successful film version, which used Mahler's music for the sound track.

DEBORA E JAELE

Dramatic opera in three acts by Ildebrando Pizzetti (1880–1968), to a libretto by the composer after the Book of Judges. *First performance: Milan, Teatro alla Scala, 16 December 1922.*

The subject is taken from the Old Testament, Book of Judges, Chapters IV and V. Act I. The tribes of Nephthali, Zebulun and Issachar are gathered in a square in Kedesh waiting for Deborah (soprano), the prophetess of Israel, to speak. They are ready to fight Sisera (tenor), the cruel King of Canaan, but want the prophetess to advise them about strategy and predict the outcome of the battle. She tells them they will win if they attack the enemy in the open. Jaele (soprano), wife of the spy Hever (baritone), is falsely accused of returning Sisera's love. Deborah takes up Jaele's

Left: A scene from *Death in Venice* by Benjamin Britten

Above: A drawing of Claude Debussy (see page 98).

cause, and sends her on a special mission to Sisera: it is she who must persuade him to lead his army into the open field, where Barak (bass) Commander of the Jewish forces, will overcome him. Act II. The terrace of Sisera's palace at Harosheth. Sisera, contradicting his cruel reputation, punishes the servant of one of his captains for abducting two young slaves from their parents. Hever betrays his own people by advising Sisera to ambush them where they can easily be defeated, but Sisera, disliking this traitorous behaviour, has him arrested. A veiled woman enters. It is Jaele, whom Sisera has loved for a long time. She advises the King to lead this people to Mount Tabor, where she tells him there are only a few hundred Israelites. Her trickery is soon discovered. She admits her guilt and asks Sisera to pass judgement over her, but instead of punishment, he declares his love. She is moved by his words, and is attracted towards him, but, on the point of relenting, she hears a lullaby sung by the mother of children killed by Sisera's soldiers. Mindful of her duty, she returns to Israel. Act III. The Israelites win the battle as prophesied. All their enemies are killed, except Sisera, who takes refuge in Jaele's tent. The prophetess Deborah orders her to give him up to the people, but she kills him herself rather than allow him to fall into the hands of his victorious enemies.

Deborah and Jaele. composed between 1915 and 1921, is generally regarded as Pizzetti's masterpiece. It is a good illustration of his conception of music drama, based on an exact and balanced relationship between text and music, a reaction against both *verismo* and post-romantic opera.

DEBUSSY, CLAUDE

(Saint-Germain-en-Laye, Yvelines 1862–Paris 1918)

French composer. From 1872, he studied at the Paris Conservatoire, where he proved to be a fairly rebellious student who took badly to academic discipline. In the summer of 1880 he went to Russia, where until 1883 he was employed as a pianist by Nadezhda von Meck, the patroness of Tchaikovsky. In 1884 Debussy won the Gran Prix de Rome with his cantata *L'enfant prodigue*. He then completed his studies in Rome, where he met Verdi and Liszt. Between 1887 and 1888 he composed *La demoiselle élue*, his second major vocal work. In 1890 he became interested in the play *Rodrigue et Chimène*, by Catulle Mendès, out of which grew his first, abortive, attempt at an opera. But in 1892, when Maurice Maeterlinck staged his play *Pelléas et Mélisande* in Brussels, Debussy was immediately interested by the text and asked Maeterlinck if he could make an opera out of it. The writing of Debussy's *Pelléas et Mélisande* spanned no less than nine years (1893–1902) and the work is his only experiment in the field of opera.

DE CAROLIS, NATALE

(Anagni 1957)

Italian bass-baritone. After winning the Concorso di Spoleto (1983), he made his debut as Don Basilio in *Il barbiere di Siviglia*. He then sang in a number of Italian opera houses (Bologna, Florence, Naples, etc.). He finally made his mark in 1987, singing the role of Masetto in the production of *Don Giovanni* which opened that year's season at La Scala, Milan with Riccardo Muti conducting. This led to an international career for De Carolis, taking in the leading opera houses and festivals from New York to Salzburg. De Carolis is an admired Mozart performer.

Right: The Italian bass-baritone Natale de Carolis.

DE GAMERRA, GIOVANNI

(Livorno 1743–Vicenza 1803)

Italian poet, playwright and librettist. He worked first in Milan (1765–70) and then in Vienna, where he became Imperial Court Poet (1775). On his return to Italy, he was called to Naples (1786) by Ferdinand IV and developed his "Plan for the Establishment of the New Musical Theater" which in the end did not win royal approval. He then lived in Pisa for a while before returning to Vienna as Poet of the Imperial Theater (1793–1802). He wrote a number of libretti, including that for the opera *Lucio Silla*, set to music by Mozart and by J. C. Bach.

DELIBES, CLÉMONT-PHILIBERT-LÉO

(Saint-Germain-du-Val, Sarthe 1836–Paris 1891)

French composer. He studied organ and composition with Benoist and Adam at the Paris Conservatoire. In 1853 he was engaged as a pianist at the Théâtre-Lyrique in Paris and after that as chorus-master at the Opéra. By 1852 Delibes had already started writing operettas, and in 1857 he presented his first *opéra-comique*, *Maître Griffard*. This was followed by *Le jardinier et son seigneur* (1863), *Le roi l'a dit* (1873) and *Jean de Nivelle* (1880). His masterpiece, *Lakmé*, appeared in 1883. His ballets *Coppélia* (1867) and *Sylvia* (1876) are equally famous.

DELIUS, FREDERICK

(Bradford, Yorkshire 1862–Grez-sur-Loing, Fontainebleau 1934)

British composer. In spite of his family's opposition to the idea, Delius devoted himself to the study of music. After moving to Florida, he studied with T. F. Ward and on his return to Europe completed his musical training in Leipzig. Between 1890 and 1892, Delius composed his first opera, *Irmelin*, which received its premiere in Oxford in 1953. This was followed by *Koanga* (1895–97), which was staged in 1904. Between 1900 and 1901 he wrote his most famous opera, *A Village Romeo and Juliet* (1907), which was followed by *Fennimore and Gerda* (1908–10), produced in 1919. Delius also composed *The Magic Fountain* (1893) and *Margot-La-Rouge* (1902), which were not performed in his lifetime.

DELLA CASA, LISA

(Burgdorf, Berne 1919)

Swiss soprano. At the age of 15 she began to study singing in Zurich with Margarete Haeser. In 1941, she made her debut in Solothurn in *Madama Butterfly*. From 1943 until 1950 she sang at the Stadttheater in Zurich, where she scored considerable success in the title role of Strauss's *Arabella*, considered to be her most accomplished performance. In 1947 she began to appear at the Staatsoper in Vienna, then at major theaters and festivals across the world: Salzburg, Glyndebourne, Bayreuth, and the Metropolitan Opera, New York (1953). Della Casa had an impeccable technique of delivery, soft timbre and elegant phrasing. She has been one of the most highly acclaimed performers of Richard Strauss (*Der Rosenkavalier* and *Capriccio*) and Mozart. She retired from the stage in 1974.

DEL MONACO, MARIO

(Florence 1915–Mestre 1982)

Italian tenor. He studied at the Conservatorio in Pesaro. After his debut in Pesaro in 1940, singing the role of Turiddu in *Cavalleria rusticana*, he scored his first major success, in the same year, at the Teatro Puccini in Milan as Pinkerton in *Madama Butterfly*. By 1946 Del Monaco's name was attracting attention in a number of opera houses in Italy and other countries (the Arena in Verona, Covent Garden, etc.). In 1949 he made his debut at La Scala in *Manon Lescaut* and continued to sing there until 1963. In 1950 he gave his first performance as Otello, the role which, more than any other, is associated with this singer (he sang it 427 times up until 1972). The robust and ringing character of his voice and his aggressive and dramatic personality in performance made Del Monaco famous not only in *Otello* but also in *Andrea Chénier*, *La fanciulla del West*, *La forza del destino*, *I pagliacci* and *Samson et Dalila*, operas in which his vocal and interpretative gifts are seen to fullest advantage. In 1975, after a number of performances of *I pagliacci* in Vienna, Mario Del Monaco retired from the stage.

DE LOS ANGELES, VICTORIA

(Barcelona 1923)

Stage name of Victoria Lopez Garcia, Spanish soprano. In 1940 she began to study singing and piano at the Barcelona Conservatory. After graduating from there in 1942, she took part in a number of singing competitions, winning nearly all of them. In 1945, she made her debut at the Liceo in Barcelona (*Le nozze di Figaro*) and by 1948 was singing the role of Salud in De Falla's opera *La vida breve* (one of her most touching performances) for the BBC in London. A year later, she appeared as Marguerite (*Faust*) at the Opéra in Paris. These were the first stages in a brilliant international career which in subsequent years brought De Los Angeles to Covent Garden (*La bohème*), La Scala (*Ariadne auf Naxos*), to the Metropolitan Opera House (*Faust*, *Madama Butterfly*) and to Bayreuth (*Tannhäuser*). There was outstanding purity in the character of her voice, and her delivery was soft and highly disciplined. These qualities have also been in evidence in her concert performances, to which De Los Angeles has been particularly dedicated, especially during the most recent years of her career. She has also made many recordings, including admirable performances in *Faust*, *Manon*, *La bohème*, *Madama Butterfly*, *Il barbiere di Siviglia* and *La traviata*.

DEMETRIO E POLIBIO

Opera in two acts by Gioachino Rossini (1792–1868), to a libretto by Vincenzina Viganò Mombelli. First performance: Rome, Teatro Valle, 18 May 1812.

The action takes place in the capital of the Parthians' kingdom. King Polibio (bass) announces the marriage of his daughter Lisinga (soprano) to Siveno (contralto), a young man who grew up at court and whom Polibio loves like a son. Enter Eumene, ambassador of the King of Syria, Demetrio (tenor), actually the King himself posing as an ambassador. He asks Polibio if Siveno, the son of a dear friend of the Syrian King, may return with him to Demetrio's court. Polibio refuses this request because he loves Siveno too much to be separated from him. Eumene/Demetrio then decides to kidnap Siveno, but when he enters the royal apartments, he discovers that he is in Lisinga's apartment by mistake. Realizing this, he decides to kidnap the young woman instead and use her as a hostage. Siveno and Polibio catch up with the kidnappers. At this moment of high tension, Demetrio recognizes a medallion being worn by Siveno which proves that the young man is actually his son. Lisinga is immediately released while Siveno, although very distressed, follows his long-lost father. In despair at being separated from him, Lisinga wants to win back Siveno, if necessary by force, so she returns to the King of Syria's camp intending to kill Demetrio. As she is about to raise the dagger, however, Siveno stays her hand. Demetrio takes this gesture as a sign that Siveno has now acknowledged him as his father, and so reunites the two lovers and offers King Polybius his friendship.

Demetrio e Polibio was Rossini's first composition for the theater, written between 1808 and 1809 to a commission from the Mombelli family. Domenico Mombelli, a tenor, sang the role of Demetrio, while his daughters Ester and Marianna played the parts of Lisinga and Siveno. The opera's libretto was written by Vincenzina Mombelli, Domenico's wife. The opera was very warmly received by the audience at its first performance: there was an encore for the Lisinga-Siveno duet "Questo cor ti giura amore," the only moment in the work that heralds the lyricism that would reappear in Rossini's later operas in duets for soprano and contralto.

Above: A scene from Mozart's *Lucio Silla*, to a libretto by Giovanni De Gamerra.

DEMON

(The Demon)

Opera seria *in three acts by Anton Grigor'yevich Rubinstein (1829–1894), to a libretto by Pavel Alexandrovich Viskovatov based on Lermontov's poem. First performance: St. Petersburg, Imperial Theater, 25 January 1875.*

The Demon (baritone), portrayed as an ordinary human being with demonic characteristics, looks sorrowfully down from the peak of Kazbec on the world stretched out beneath him. Melancholy and full of regret for his misspent youth, he now longs for the comfort of a woman's love. He meets Tatyana (soprano), who is dancing with other young women on the eve of her wedding. The Demon falls in love with her and has her husband-to-be, Prince Sinodal (tenor), attacked and killed by brigands. To escape the Demon's clutches, Tatyana takes refuge in a convent, but the Demon finds her there, and during a long love-duet he celebrates his triumph. But then Sinodal, who has been transformed into an angel, appears. Heavenly voices call to Tatyana, who wrestles free from the Demon's arms and falls dead. While Tatyana, now redeemed, ascends to Heaven, the Demon is left alone and in despair.

The Demon, a sensational success at its premiere, is still seen as Rubinstein's masterpiece. The themes of passion and redemption recall elements of Wagnerian opera, but the music of this Russian composer has no real connection with that of Wagner.

DÉMOPHOON

Opera in three acts by Luigi Cherubini (1760–1842), to a libretto by Jean-François Marmontel from the Italian original by Pietro Metastasio. First performance: Paris, Académie Royale de Musique (Opéra), 1 December 1788.

Démophoon, King of the Chersonnesus in Thrace, must sacrifice every year a virgin from among his own people, and he asks the oracle of Apollo when he will be able to put an end to this horrific ritual. The oracle's answer is: "When the innocent usurper of a kingdom realizes that this is what he is." Démophoon has sent away his own daughters to spare them from being chosen as the sacrificial victim and his minister, Matusio, intends to do the same with his daughter, Dircé. The King is infuriated by this and condemns Dircé to be sacrificed, not knowing that Dircé is secretly married to Timante, his son and heir to the throne, who is destined to marry Creusa, daughter of the King of Crete. She, however, is loved by Cherinto, second son of Démophoon. Timante refuses to marry Creusa, and Démophoon, whose suspicions are now aroused, discovers that Timante and Dircé are already married. His first reaction is to condemn them both to death, but then he pardons them. At this point Matusio finds out that Dircé is actually Démophoon's daughter, while Timante proves to be his own son. This means that Timante is no longer heir to the throne, and so the oracle's prophecy has come true, now that the innocent usurper or would-be king has become aware that he was, unintentionally, in the wrong. As a result, the sacrifices can cease and Démophoon will be able to give Cherinto, his sole heir, the hand of Creusa in marriage.

Démophoon is Cherubini's first French opera. To write it he abandoned the Italian style of his earlier operas which had been produced in Italy and in London. Cherubini also made every effort to bring his strengths as a composer of harmony into play in the dramatic expression of the opera, but the audience of the day did not understand these changes. Other composers carried out Cherubini's ideas more successfully in ensuing years. *Démophoon* thus failed to win acclaim and ran for only eight nights.

Above: The tenor Anton Dermota as Florestano in Beethoven's *Fidelio.*

DERMOTA, ANTON

(Kropa, Slovenia 1910–Vienna 1989)

Yugoslav tenor who became an Austrian citizen. After studying organ and composition at the Ljubljana Conservatory, he devoted his energies to singing, in which he was trained by Marie Rado. In 1936 he appeared in Vienna in *Die Zauberflöte* (The Magic Flute) and at the Salzburg Festival with Arturo Toscanini conducting. Much of Dermota's career would be concentrated in either Salzburg or Vienna. The light lyric tenor character of his voice enabled him to excel in Mozart (Ferrando, Tamino, Belmonte, etc.), but as a result of having an excellent technique and vigorous phrasing, Dermota ventured into a much larger repertoire, including *Fidelio*, *Les contes d'Hoffmann* and *La bohème*, roles which he sang, in addition to Mozart, in the great opera houses of the world.

DERNESCH, HELGA

(Vienna 1939)

Austrian soprano and mezzo-soprano. After completing her musical studies at the Conservatory in Vienna, she joined the resident company of the Berne Stadttheater (1961), where her first appearance was in the role of Fiordiligi (*Così fan tutte*), after which she sang in *Simon Boccanegra* and *Les contes d'Hoffmann*. Engagements followed in Wiesbaden and, from 1965, Bayreuth, where, in 1967, she scored her first major success as Elisabeth (*Tannhäuser*). As a Wagner performer, Dernesch has appeared in Vienna, Berlin and Salzburg with von Karajan (*Tristan und Isolde*, 1969). She has sung in Edinburgh, London, Hamburg, New York (from 1973) and Chicago. At the end of the 1970s, she began to take on mezzo-soprano parts. In 1985 she was Marfa (*Khovanshchina*) and Herodias (*Salome*) at La Scala, Milan (1987) and the Metropolitan Opera House, New York (1990).

DESSÌ, DANIELA

(Genoa 1957)

Italian soprano. She graduated from the Conservatorio in Parma and went on to further training at the Accademia Chigiana in Siena. In 1980 she won the Italian Radio and Television "Concorso Auditorium" and was a finalist in the first year of the "Concorso Maria Callas." Dessì began her career as a soloist with chamber concert and oratorio appearances, making her operatic debut in Savona in *La serva padrona*. Engagements followed with the major opera houses in Italy and other countries. Dessì's is a lyric soprano voice with a richness of timbre and is tonally very beautiful. She has a very large and stylistically very varied repertoire. Among her more recent performances are *Mefistofele* and *Don Giovanni* (Florence 1990).

DEUTEKOM, CRISTINA

(Amsterdam 1932)
Stage name of Christine Engel. Dutch soprano. She studied with Johan Thomas and Coby Riemersma at the Amsterdam Conservatory. She joined the Netherlands Opera as a member of the chorus and between 1965 and 1966 sang supporting roles. In 1967 she made her mark as The Queen of the Night in *Die Zauberflöte* (The Magic Flute) at the Munich Staatsoper. Deutekom's qualities were immediately apparent: her range, and her eminent suitability to sing *coloratura*.

DEUX JOURNÉES, LES, OU LE PORTEUR D'EAU

(The Two Days, or The Water-Carrier)
Opera in three acts by Luigi Cherubini (1760–1842), to a libretto by Jean Nicolas Bouilly. First performance: Paris, Théâtre Feydeau, 16 January, 1800.

The action takes place in Paris, about 1640. A water-seller, Daniel Micheli (baritone), has concealed in his house Count Armand (tenor) and his wife Constance (mezzo-soprano), who are wanted by the police for having offended Cardinal Mazarin. Old Daniel has recognized Armand as the man who once, in Berne, saved him from dying of starvation, and wishes to repay the debt. His children, Antoine (tenor) and Marcelline (soprano), appear, having just obtained passes enabling them to travel to the village where Antoine is to marry Angélique (soprano), a farmer's daughter. Together they concoct a plan to get the two fugitives out of the city. A captain of the guard arrives, with orders to requisition the house. Daniel immediately puts the Count to bed and pretends that he is his old sick father. The next day Constance manages to get through the cordon by using Marcelline's pass. She is joined by Daniel with his cart and water-barrel, inside which the Count is hiding. The water-seller tells the guards he has seen the fugitives elsewhere and then opens his barrel so that the Count can leave his hiding place and escape. In the village where his fiancée lives, Antoine helps Count Armand to conceal himself in the hollow trunk of a tree, while Constance takes refuge in Angélique's house. Some soldiers appear and settle down at the foot of the very tree where Armand is hidden. Constance, who has brought her husband food, is arrested for her suspicious behaviour and faints. When she recovers she calls to her husband by name, causing him to be recognized and arrested. Fortunately, Daniel arrives with a royal decree which exonerates and frees Armand.

Les deux journées was given 200 successive performances but was later almost completely forgotten. The libretto is complex and rather threadbare, but Cherubini's music stems from his greatest creative period.

DEVIN DU VILLAGE, LE

(The Village Fortune-Teller)
Musical intermezzo *in one act by Jean-Jacques Rousseau (1712–1778), to the composer's own libretto. First performance: Fontainebleau, Court Theater, 18 October 1752.*

Colette (soprano) is upset at having been abandoned by Colin (tenor). She decides to visit a fortune-teller (bass) in the village to find out if she will succeed in persuading her beloved to return to her. Colette learns from the fortune-teller that Colin has left her for another woman but still loves her, and he will be the one to take the initiative, come back, and kneel before her. Meanwhile, she would be well advised to pretend that she is no longer in love with him. When Colin does actually want to come back to Colette, the fortune-teller tells him that Colette is in love with a man from the city. In despair, Colin asks for a spell to be cast, but the meeting between the two young people does not seem to go very well for Colin. In the end, however, everything comes right and the fortune-teller and villagers help celebrate the reunion of the two lovers.

Rousseau was influenced by *opera buffa*, in particular by Pergolesi's *La serva padrona*, which was staged in Paris at the beginning of 1752. Pergolesi's opera had triggered off the

Left: The soprano Daniela Dessì in a scene from Mozart's *Così fan tutte*. She is pictured with the bass Luigi Desderi.

famous *querelle des bouffons*, a confrontation between supporters of French opera (Lully, Rameau) and those who favoured Italian opera. Rousseau sided with the Italian factions and *Le devin du village* demonstrates his passion for Italian music.

DEVINU, GIUSY

(Cagliari 1960)
Italian soprano. In 1982 she made her debut as Violetta in *La traviata*, the opera which has a special place in her repertoire and one which she has performed in a number of Italian opera houses (including La Scala under Riccardo Muti). Her strong lyric soprano voice, with its particularly fine range, well suited to singing at speed, and her innate musicianship and refinement, have made Devinu one of the most gifted sopranos of her day. She won special acclaim for her performances in *Rigoletto* (Bologna, 1990), *L'occasione fa il ladro* (Pesaro, 1989), *Don Pasquale* (Venice, 1990) and *Le nozze di Figaro* (Venice, 1991).

Above: The Italian soprano Giusy Devinu

Top: A scene from *Les dialogues des Carmélites*, in a production at La Scala.

DIALOGUES DES CARMÉLITES, LES

Opera in three acts by Francis Poulenc (1899–1963), to the composer's own libretto based on the play of the same name by Georges Bernanos. First performance: Milan, La Scala, 26 January 1957.

Paris 1789. In a room in his palace, the Marquis de La Force (baritone) waits for his daughter Blanche (soprano). When she arrives, deeply upset and agitated, she tells him she intends to enter a convent so as to find peace and rediscover a sense of inner balance. Some time later, in the Carmelite convent, Blanche befriends Constance (soprano), a young nun with a carefree disposition. One day Constance confides in Blanche that by a miraculous intuition she knows that they will meet their deaths together. Blanche is very disturbed by this news and forbids Constance to mention death again. Meanwhile, the Mother Superior (mezzo-soprano), who is seriously ill, is enduring her last agony, but is unable to accept death with equanimity and confesses her anguish to Blanche. Blanche is deeply affected. A few days later, the convent is attacked by a mob in full cry; the nuns decide not to flee but to accept martyrdom. Only Blanche escapes and returns to her home. The other nuns are arrested and condemned to death. They are led to the place of execution, and one by one they climb the scaffold singing the *Salve Regina*. When it comes to Constance's turn, Blanche suddenly appears out of the crowd which has gathered to watch the executions. She is transfigured by a mysterious joy which has dispelled all fear and makes her way to the scaffold.

In *Les dialogues des Carmélites*, Poulenc draws together the most exquisitely feminine features of the play by Bernanos, while choosing to avoid the tangled philosophical arguments that underlie the play.

DÍAZ, JUSTINO

(San Juan, Puerto Rico 1940)
American bass-baritone. After attending the University of Puerto Rico, he completed his music studies at the New England Conservatory (Boston). He gave his first performances with the New England Opera Theater (1963–64), and made his mark singing the male lead in Samuel Barber's opera *Antony and Cleopatra*, which opened the new Lincoln Center of the Metropolitan Opera House, New York in 1966. This launched Díaz on an international career, which included the roles of Escamillo in *Carmen* at the Salzburg Festival, with Herbert von Karajan conducting, and Maometto in the famous La Scala production of Rossini's *L'assedio di Corinto*. He then sang in Vienna, Hamburg, Paris and London but has devoted much of his time to the Metropolitan and other American opera houses and festivals. His remarkable vocal range has enabled him to tackle many baritone roles, and recently he sang Iago in the film version of Verdi's *Otello* directed by Franco Zeffirelli (1986), a role which he also performed at the Metropolitan under Carlos Kleiber (1990).

DIDO AND AENEAS

Opera in three acts by Henry Purcell (1659–1695), to a libretto by Nahum Tate. First known performance: London, Mr Josias Priest's Boarding House for Girls, Chelsea, before December 1689.

The Royal Palace in Carthage. Belinda (soprano) begs her confidante Queen Dido (mezzo-soprano) to be calm, but in vain, because Dido's heart is tormented by her love for Aeneas (tenor). The Trojan prince enters with his retinue, confesses his love for Dido and implores the Queen to return his feelings. The scene ends with a solemn chorus and dance. The witches' cavern. A Sorceress (mezzo-soprano) summons the witches and reveals to them her plan to take Aeneas away from Dido and lead

Carthage to destruction. The Sorceress sends one of her Spirits (soprano), disguised as Mercury, with a false message from Jupiter telling Aeneas that he must leave Carthage and pursue his pioneering destiny. While Aeneas, Dido and Belinda are hunting with their retinue, they are caught up in a storm unleashed by the Sorceress to make the Queen return to her palace. While everyone is leaving the wood, the Spirit impersonating Mercury appears to Aeneas and tells him to leave Carthage that very night. With Aeneas's fleet ready to set sail, the hero has a final dramatic meeting with Dido. He is so deeply affected by Dido's reproaches that for a moment he reconsiders whether to depart or not, but the broken-hearted Queen declares she is ready to confront her fate and proudly commands Aeneas to go. Left alone with Belinda, Dido sings her own funeral lament, asking that her mistakes not be a source of grief to anyone. The opera ends with a chorus inviting Love to sprinkle rose-petals on the hapless dead Queen.

Dido and Aeneas is the only opera to have been written by Purcell, and was performed only once during his lifetime. It is something of a flawed masterpiece. Having been written with a view to being staged with only the most basic theatrical resources, and lasting little more than an hour, it demonstrates the disadvantages of a plot which consists of a hurried sequence of events. As a result, the character of Aeneas appears rather weak, whereas that of Dido is real and psychologically convincing. The opera is halfway between an English masque and an Italian opera. The main value of the work is Purcell's unprecedented achievement in measuring up to the complex requirements of an *opera seria* and overcoming the limitations imposed by the subject, reduced, in duration and action, to a tableau equivalent to no more than one act of an opera.

DIMITROVA, GHENA

(Beglej, Pleven 1941)

Bulgarian soprano. She studied with Christo Brumbarov at the Conservatory in Sofia and graduated there. During the 1965–66 season, she joined the permanent company of the opera house in Sofia. After early appearances in supporting roles, Dimitrova sang Abigaille (*Nabucco*) for the first time. In 1970 she won Sofia's international singing competition, and this enabled her to go to Italy (1972–73) for advanced training at the La Scala school in Milan. In 1972, after winning first prize in Treviso's "Concorso Internazionale," she opened the season at the Teatro Regio in Parma as Amelia in *Un ballo in maschera* alongside José Carreras, who was also making his debut. In 1975 she appeared as Turandot, a role which, together with those of Abigaille and Lady Macbeth, produced one of her most highly acclaimed performances. Dimitrova has sung *Turandot* in the major international opera houses including La Scala, the Metropolitan in New York (1987) and Covent Garden (1984). She has an exceptional voice, unparalleled in its power, and is one of the very few dramatic sopranos of the present day. In addition to *Nabucco*, *Macbeth* and *Turandot*, her repertoire includes *Tosca*, *La Gioconda*, *Norma* and *La fanciulla del West*.

DINORAH, OU LE PARDON DE PLOËRMEL

Opera comique *in three acts by Giacomo Meyerbeer (1791–1864), to a libretto by Jules Barbier and Michel Carré. First performance: Paris, Théâtre de l'Opéra-Comique, 4 April 1859.*

The action takes place in Brittany. Dinorah (soprano), mad with grief at having been abandoned on the day of her

Left: A scene from *Dido and Aeneas*, in a 1986 production at Reggio Emilia.

Above: The Bulgarian soprano Ghena Dimitrova in a scene from *Nabucco*.

BRITISH OPERA

The birth of opera in Britain dates from the year 1656 and the staging in London of *The Siege of Rhodes*. Various composers had a hand in writing it (the music has since been lost) and it was an example of a ''masque,'' a typically English genre combining singing, dancing, pantomime and recitation, which derives from the French *ballet de cour* and the Italian *intermedio*. The first important examples of opera proper were *Venus and Adonis* (c. 1685) by John Blow (1649–1708) and above all *Dido and Aeneas* (1687) by Henry Purcell (1659–1695), in which French influences are evident, while works like *King Arthus* (1691) and *The Fairy Queen* (1692), described as operas at the time, are actually composite works, in which singing is certainly not of secondary importance although the dramatic ingredients of the masque are still playing their part. The eighteenth century saw the advent of Italian opera: *Camilla* by Giovanni Bononcini (1670–1747), which was staged in English in 1706, was the first Italian *opera seria* to be performed in Britain. From 1716 to 1731 Bononcini had a rival in this genre, George Frederick Handel (1685–1759), who, after the success of *Rinaldo* (1711), his first English opera, wrote his operas in Italian for Italian singers. Only in his oratories (in which he uses arias in a theatrical way) does Handel compose in English. The first reactions to the supremacy of Italian opera in Britain come with *The Beggar's Opera* (1728) by John Gay (1685–1732) with music drawn from popular tunes and from opera and adapted by Johann Christoph Pepusch (1667–1732), marking the rise of the ballad opera, and *Artaxerxes* (1762) by Thomas Augustine Arne (1710–1778). A prominent figure in the world of opera in Britain in the early nineteenth century is Henry Bishop (1786–1855), whose works, especially *Clari*, his most famous opera, reveal a simple but effective lyrical gift. The first performance of Carl Maria von Weber's *Oberon* (1826) was very much a moving force in stimulated the beginnings of Romantic opera in Britain. Leading composers in this period are Michael Balfe (1808–1870), who wrote *The Bohemian Girl* (1843) and William Wallace (1812–1865). Not until the early part of the twentieth century do the first authentically British achievements in opera emerge, with Rutland Boughton (1878–1960) and Josef Holbrooke (1878–1958), the first significant participants in the development of British opera as such, even though it bears the stamp of Wagner.

Frederick Delius (1862–1934), Gustav Holst (1874–1934) and Ralph Vaughan Williams (1872–1958), who wrote the first genuine British operas *A Village Romeo and Juliet* (1907), *Savitri* (1916) and *Hugh the Drover* (1924) respectively, are the most eminent opera composers of the period from 1900 to 1920, before the appearance of Benjamin Britten (1913–1976). Alongside Britten is Sir Michael Tippett (1905), whose operas include *The Midsummer Marriage* (1955), *King Priam* (1962) and *The Knot Garden* (1970). Other important names in British music are Sir Arthur Bliss (1891–1975), Sir William Walton (1902–1983), Sir Lennox Berkeley (1903), Sir Peter Maxwell Davies (1934) and John Taverner (1944).

Right: Henry Purcell, in a portrait by Closterman.

Above: A scene from Benjamin Britten's *Albert Herring*.

wedding, roams the countryside in search of her beloved Hoël (baritone). She comes to the hut of the shepherd Corentin (tenor) and falls asleep. Hoël also comes by, but Dinorah fails to recognize him and sets out again on her wanderings. Hoël tells Corentin how a terrible storm had destroyed his own hut on the day of the wedding and, not wanting Dinorah to have to live a life of hardship with him, he had gone in search of a treasure he had been told about. Corentin now joins in the search, and together they reach the place where the treasure is. But neither of them wants to be the first to touch it, because the elves who guard it have the power to cause the death of anyone who dares to do so. Suddenly Dinorah arrives. Hoël believes her to be a magic apparition and runs away. Corentin exploits this situation by persuading Dinorah to touch the treasure. Whereupon Dinorah faints to the ground and Hoël, who has now realized she is who she seems to be, rushes to help her and saves her. The shock Dinorah has just experienced turns out to have been providential, because she can no longer remember being abandoned or the year spent searching for Hoël. Hoël sees that this is what has happened and so hastens to convince Dinorah that nothing is wrong or ever has been. The two happy young people set out for the church of Ploërmel, where they are to be married.

Dinorah may not belong to the historical type of opera which Meyerbeer liked best, but it was nonetheless composed with taste and finesse, the thinness of the libretto and of the musical structure of the work being compensated for by charming arias which have lost none of their appeal today.

D'INTINO, LUCIANA

San Vito al Tagliamento, Pordenone 1959

Italian mezzo-soprano. She graduated from the Conservatorio Benedetto Marcello in Venice in 1983, the year in which she won the Spoleto Singing Competition. On the strength of this, she made her debut as Azucena (*Il trovatore*). In the years immediately following, she sang in *Il barbiere di Siviglia* in Macerata and Naples (1984 and 1986), *Aida* (Cagliari, Trieste), *Luisa Miller* (Opera di Roma, 1990) and at other opera houses. From 1987 she appeared at La Scala, Milan, where she sang in *Nabucco*, *Guillaume Tell*, Pergolesi's *Lo frate 'nnamurato*, Jommelli's *Fetonte* and Cilèa's *Adriana Lecouvreur*. D'Intino's reputation also rests on her appearances at theaters in Venice, Pesaro, Turin, Naples and Florence, as well as at major international opera houses like the Metropolitan, New York, where she sang for the first time in 1991 (*Luisa Miller*). Her fine timbre and the consistency of her voice across the entire range, reinforced by an outstanding technique, have made her one of the finest mezzo-sopranos of her day.

DIRINDINA, LA

Comic opera in two parts by Domenico Scarlatti (1685–1757), to a libretto by Girolamo Gigli. First performance scheduled for the Teatro Capranica in Rome at Carnival time, 1715, to be performed with the opera Amleto, *also by Scarlatti, but the premiere was cancelled owing to the intervention of the papal censors.*

The simple plot centers on the young and attractive Dirindina (soprano): she has an ambition to become an opera singer and goes to have singing lessons from Don Carissimo (*buffo* baritone), a cunning chorus-master with a dubious reputation. He shows more interest in the young woman's physical rather than artistic attributes. While the elderly Don is courting Dirindina in between vocal exercises, the *castrato* musician Liscione (soprano) entices her with the prospect of a possible singing contract. Before an astonished Don Carissimo, Liscione puts Dirindina's qualities as a performer to the test. The aspiring prima donna then takes on the persona of a tearful Dido and accuses her Aeneas (Liscione) of infidelity and desertion. At the end of the "test," Dirindina and Liscione sing that they are well satisfied ... and also in love. Don Carissimo joins in their happiness despite his surprise, and with a touch of irony blesses the couple's marriage and wishes them prosperity.

This delightful score, which was rediscovered by the musicologist Francesco Degrada in 1968, is one of the most successful examples of that tradition in music known as the *opera in berlina*, or parlour-game opera. The characters of the worldly-wise Dirindina, the old chorus-master Don Carissimo, and the shady *castrato* Liscione are skilfully drawn, and the scene between Dido and Aeneas, an obvious parody of Metastasian *opera seria*, is especially brilliant.

DI STEFANO, GIUSEPPE

(Motta Santa Anastasia (Catania) 1921)

Italian tenor. He made his debut in 1946 in the role of Des Grieux (*Manon Lescaut*) in Reggio Emilia. During the same year he appeared at La Fenice in Venice (Bizet's *Les pêcheurs de perles*), at the Teatro Comunale in Bologna (*La sonnambula*) and in Barcelona (*Rigoletto*). In 1947 he sang at La Scala for the first time (*Manon*), and this launched him on a career which brought engagements at the Metropolitan Opera House, New York (*Rigoletto*, *L'elisir d'amore*, etc.), Mexico City, the Paris Opéra (*Faust*), Berlin (*Lucia di Lammermoor*), etc. His voice is remarkable for the beauty of its timbre. His technical skill, especially during the first part of his career up until the early 1950s, enabled him to achieve a controlled delivery, while singing *pianissimo*, which produced a particularly soft, expressive sound. After the mid 1960s, he substantially reduced his engagements, appearing at La Scala (Monteverdi's *L'incoronazione di Poppea*), in Montreal, Vienna (Léhar's *Das Land des Lächelns*) and at the Teatro San Carlo in Naples in 1969.

Above: A scene from *La Dirindina* by Scarlatti.

DJAMILEH

Comic opera in one act by Georges Bizet (1838–1875), to a libretto by Louis Gallet, based on the poem Namouna *by Alfred de Musset. First performance: Paris, Théâtre de l'Opéra-Comique, 22 May 1872.*

The opera is set in Egypt. Haroun (tenor), a wealthy and bored young man, changes his mistress every month and each time gives his secretary Splendiano (baritone) the task of purchasing him a new one at the bazaar. Haroun would no doubt have treated Djamileh (mezzo-soprano) in the same way, and she too would have been abandoned, had she not fallen in love with him. The young slave-girl then hatches a plan with Splendiano which enables her to return to Haroun in disguise. In this way, and with a combination of shrewdness, love and devotion, Djamileh wins Haroun's heart.

Djamileh is set in a foreign country and is a rich tapestry of Oriental colour. The work, which hints at the later, mature Bizet, was not a success, being judged excessively Wagnerian. It ran for only 11 performances and was not seen in Paris again until 27 October 1938.

DOHNÁNYI, CHRISTOPH VON

(Berlin 1929)

German conductor. He completed his music studies in Munich, where he won the Richard Strauss prize for conducting (1951). A year later, his artistic career began with an invitation from Georg Solti to go to the Frankfurt Opera as chorus-master. He subsequently became the company's conductor. Next came appointments as music director, first in Lübeck (1957–63), then in Kassel (1963–66), and in 1968 von Dohnányi took up the post of director and manager at the Frankfurt Opera, where he remained until 1977, accepting a similar dual appointment with the Hamburg Opera from 1975. In 1984 he accepted the music directorship of the Cleveland Orchestra and is particularly admired in the opera world as a conductor of twentieth-century and contemporary music. He conducted the first performances of Hans Werner Henze's operas *Der Junge Lord* (The Young Lord, 1965) and *The Bassarids*, 1966, Gottfried von Einem's *Kabale und Liebe* (Love and Intrigue, 1976) and *Baal* by Friedrich Cerha. Von Dohnányi is married to the soprano Anja Silja, with whom he has recorded Berg's operas *Lulu* (1978) and *Wozzeck* (1980), performances that have earned unanimous praise from the critics.

DOKTOR FAUST

Opera in two preludes, an intermezzo *and three scenes by Ferruccio Busoni (1866–1924), to the composer's own libretto based on popular legends about Faust and on Christopher Marlowe's play* The Tragical History of Doctor Faustus. *First performance: Dresden, Staatsoper, 21 May 1925.*

The action takes place in the first half of the sixteenth century. In Wittenberg, Doctor Faust (baritone) is visited by three students (tenor and baritone), all strangers to him, who offer him a book which will enable him to harness the powers of darkness to his own use. At midnight Faust carries out the ritual instructions in the book, and Mephistopheles (tenor) appears to him. Mephistopheles says he will give Faust everything he wants until the day he dies, when Faust must become his slave. Faust signs the agreement. Marguerite's brother has sworn to kill Faust for having seduced her. Mephistopheles causes a group of soldiers to mistake him for a brigand, and they kill him. Already well-known there as a scientist, Faust arrives at the palace of the Duke of Parma (baritone). Here he falls in love with the Duchess (soprano), seduces her and takes her to Germany. Some time later, Mephistopheles brings Faust news of the Duchess's death and throws the body of a new-born baby on to the floor to incriminate Faust before transforming the infant corpse into a bundle of straw and setting it alight. Out of the smoke rises the figure of a woman, Helen of Troy. But when Faust comes closer, the apparition vanishes. The three students who had given Faust the magic book reappear. They have come to collect the book and to tell Faust that his death is near. Faust, in anguish, tries to perform an act which might redeem him. On the steps of the church sits a beggar-woman with a baby in her arms. The beggar-woman is the Duchess of Parma, and she is holding the corpse of the newborn child. Then the ghost of Marguerite's brother appears, while the face on the church's crucifix changes into that of Helen of Troy. In despair, Faust covers the dead baby with his cloak and then performs a magic spell.

Above: H.W Henze with Christoph von Dohnányi during a rehearsal for the premiere of *The Bassarids.*

Right: A sketch by Sironi for Act II of *Doktor Faust* by Ferruccio Busoni.

Faust dies, but a young man materializes from under the cloak with a flowering branch in his hand and walks away.

Doctor Faust was left unfinished when Busoni died, and it was completed by Philipp Jarnach. It is not only Busoni's last opera but also the high point of his output, in view of the maturity and completeness of the work.

DOKTOR FAUSTUS

Scenes from the novel by Thomas Mann, with text and music by Giacomo Manzoni (b. 1932). First performance: Milan, La Scala, 16 May 1989.

Composer Adrian Leverkühn (bass-baritone) meets a prostitute to whom he gives the name Esmeralda (soprano). They have a relationship, even though she has warned him against it. Later, Adrian goes to see Doctor Erasmi (speaking role), who diagnoses a venereal infection. Adrian meets Satan, who gradually changes into three different people. The first (bass) tells him of a contract Adrian can sign, which would give him 24 hours of extraordinary experiences, after which, however, his body and soul would be damned to perdition. The second (light tenor) describes how this will actually happen: the infectious disease which he has caught from Esmeralda will cause him to go mad and then die. The third (soprano) explains what Hell and eternal damnation are like. Finally all three remind Adrian of the conditions of the contract and its final stipulation, that it will not now be possible for him to love anyone at all. Adrian accepts. The scene changes. Adrian welcomes to his home his little nephew Nepomuk Schneiderwein, nicknamed Echo. Adrian's love for Echo proves fatal for the child, who dies of meningitis. Adrian is distraught with grief and a sense of guilt for having given in to his feelings, which the pact with Satan forbade him to do. So he decides to wipe out all that is good and noble and magnanimous in the world. Adrian comes to the end of his life. In the presence of a number of his friends, he confesses his pact with Satan, which was sealed by his encounter with Esmeralda. He relives the sad experience of his childhood, and as the hallucinating images become stronger in his mind, he goes mad. Serenus Zeitblom (speaking voice), Adrian's friend since childhood, tells the story of the last years of Adrian's life, his death and burial.

Doktor Faustus, Mann's complex and powerful novel, had already provided material for Manzoni when he wrote his *Scene sinfoniche per il Doktor Faustus* (1984) and *Studio finale del Doktor Faustus* (1984–85). These early musical responses to Mann's novel came together in Manzoni's dramatic and musical development of his opera on the Faust story. The composer has noticeably cut down the number of characters and scenes featured in the novel and has focused his interest on the role of Adrian, presenting the key moments in his human and inner drama.

DOMINGO, PLACIDO

(Madrid 1941)

Spanish tenor who took Mexican citizenship. After his earliest appearances in small roles in Mexico City, where his family had settled, Domingo scored his first success in the United States, in Dallas, where he made his debut as Arturo in *Lucia di Lammermoor* (1961). Domingo sang mainly for Israel Opera until about 1966, when he embarked on an international career which took him to the leading opera houses of Europe. Since then he has appeared all over the world, made records, and sung leading roles in opera films (*La traviata*, *Cavalleria rusticana*, *I pagliacci*, Franco Zeffirelli's *Otello* and Francesco Rosi's *Carmen*). He is one of the most distinguished tenors of his day, with a unique voice, unmistakeable for the colour and intensity of its timbre, but also with an elegance of style, incisive and noble in performance. Domingo has great warmth as a performer, drawing on a wealth of immediacy and spontaneity which enable him to always be convincing on stage. He has an extremely wide repertoire, from Weber to Wagner, but has given his best performances of all in late Romantic and realist opera (Puccini and his generation).

DOMINGUEZ, ORALIA

(San Luiz Potosí 1927)

Mexican mezzo-soprano. She studied music at the Conservatorio Nacional de Música in Mexico City, making her debut in 1950 at the Palacio de Bellas Artes. She then moved to Europe. After a series of concert appearances in England, France, Spain and Germany, Dominguez sang for the first time at La Scala in the role of the Princesse de Bouillon (*Adriana Lecouvreur*). She then sang at the Teatro San Carlo in Naples and at the Opéra in Paris. In 1955 she took part in the first performance of Tippett's opera *The Midsummer Marriage* at Covent Garden. In addition to the most famous mezzo-soprano roles (Amneris, Azucena, Carmen, etc.), her repertoire included operas by Monteverdi (*Orfeo*, *L'incoronazione di Poppea*), Handel (*Giulio Cesare*) and Rossini. Dominguez possessed elegant phrasing supported by an excellent technique and a soft, controlled delivery, which equipped her with a persuasive combination of style and interpretation in the performance of early vocal music.

Above: Placido Domingo in Verdi's *Otello*.

DON CARLOS

Opera in five acts by Giuseppe Verdi (1813–1901), to a libretto by François-Joseph Méry and Camille Du Locle, based on the tragedy of the same name by Friedrich Schiller. First performance: Paris, Opéra, 11 March 1867.

The action takes place in France and Spain in 1560. The Spanish Infante Don Carlos (tenor) meets Elisabeth de Valois (soprano), who has been promised to him in marriage, but the news that the King of France has offered Elisabeth's hand to Carlos's father, Philip II, King of Spain (bass), shatters the love between the two. In the cloister at the monastery of San Yuste, Don Carlos reveals his heartache to his friend Rodrigo (baritone), who suggests that Carlos leave Spain for Flanders. With Rodrigo's help, Carlos meets Elisabeth for the last time before he departs. He confesses his continuing love, but Elisabeth, although in turmoil, remains true to her pledge to Philip II, to whom she is now married. No sooner has Carlos gone than the King enters. He is annoyed to find his Queen unattended and is quick to show Rodrigo his jealousy of a possible love between Elisabeth and his own son. Later, in the Queen's garden, Carlos has a meeting with a lady whom he believes to be Elisabeth. She is in fact Princess Eboli (mezzo-soprano), who is in love with him, and when she discovers what his true feelings are, she decides to have revenge. In the square of Our Lady of Atocha, during an *auto-da-fé*, Carlos appears in the company of a Flemish delegation and joins their protest against the King. In his study, Philip receives the Grand Inquisitor (bass), who asks the King to condemn Carlos and Rodrigo for heresy, because he is afraid they will foster an open revolt. Meanwhile, Princess Eboli has set her revenge in motion: she has handed over to the King a casket belonging to Elisabeth and containing a portrait of Carlos. The King, now convinced that he has been betrayed, has his son arrested. In prison, Carlos is visited by Rodrigo. He has taken on himself all the blame for the revolt against the King. Suddenly a hired assassin fires an arquebus at Rodrigo, and he is mortally wounded. Carlos is released from prison and meets Elisabeth in the cloister at the monastery of San Yuste. Then the King and the Grand Inquisitor come upon them there, and Carlos is about to be arrested when the tomb of Carlos V opens up and a monk appears, saying that peace from the trials and tribulations of this earthly life will only be won in the world to come, and offering Carlos his protection. Philip, the Inquisitor and Elisabeth all believe they have seen Carlos V himself.

Don Carlos is the third work to have been commissioned from Verdi by the Opéra in Paris, after *Jerusalem* (a reworking of *I lombardi*) and *Les vêpres siciliennes*. Verdi composed the work in five acts out of respect for French operatic tradition. He was not especially satisfied with this form, however. In order to adapt the work to the *grand-opéra* style, he was obliged to include a certain amount of sub-plot, as well as the inevitable ballet, which increased the spectacle of the opera but made the development of the plot slower and more muddled. After *Don Carlos* had been performed in Bologna, Verdi made a number of cuts in the score, reducing the opera from the original five acts to four, and it was in this version that the work was performed at La Scala in 1884.

Above: A scene from Verdi's *Don Carlos*, in a 1985 production at the Teatro Comunale, Florence.

DON GIOVANNI, OSSIA IL CONVITATO DI PIETRA

(Don Juan, or The Stone Guest)

Comic opera in one act by Giuseppe Gazzaniga (1743–1818), to a libretto by Giovanni Bertati. First performance: Venice, Teatro Giustiniani di San Moisè, 5 February 1787.

Don Giovanni (tenor) takes advantage of the dark night to seduce Donna Anna (soprano) but is surprised by the Commendatore (bass), Donna Anna's father. Don Giovanni mortally wounds him and then slips away. Donna Anna asks her fiancé, Duke Ottavio (tenor), to avenge her father's death, then decides to take refuge in a convent until the vendetta has been carried out. Don Giovanni, now searching for new adventures, meets Donna Elvira (soprano), an old flame of his. To liberate himself from her, he leaves her in the capable hands of his servant Pasquariello (bass), who is so affected by Donna Elvira's distress that he pours out the story about his master's adventures in love. Having sidestepped Donna Elvira, Don Giovanni concentrates on another of his conquests, Donna Ximena (soprano), to whom he swears to be eternally faithful. This promise is very short-lived: after taking his leave of Donna Ximena, the Don finds himself in the midst of a village festival celebration. Here he runs into Pasquariello, who is getting on nicely with Maturina (soprano), a young country-woman. Maturina's intended, Biagio (bass), is annoyed because she is dancing with Pasquariello. Don Giovanni calms everyone down, but only so as to have the chance himself to seduce Maturina after issuing threats to Biagio and making him go away. Shortly after this, Donna Ximena, who has begun to have her doubts about Don Giovanni's real feelings, asks Pasquariello the truth about the Don. While the servant is busy singing his master's praises, enter Don Giovanni, followed by Donna Elvira hurling abuse at him. Donna Ximena asks

Don Giovanni to explain himself and he, with his usual cunning, succeeds in convincing both women as to the sincerity of his feelings. The next scene is set in the cemetery which houses the Commendatore's tomb. The statue of Donna Anna's father is insolently offered an invitation to dinner by Don Giovanni, whereupon it comes to life and accepts. A little later, at home, Don Giovanni and Pasquariello are dining happily. They are interrupted by the arrival of the Commendatore's statue, which drags Don Giovanni to hell. Pasquariello, Duke Ottavio, Elvira, Ximena and Maturina do not offer any moral to the tale but decide to put Don Giovanni out of their minds in order to take part in the Carnival festivities.

Gazzaniga's music, while remaining true to the tradition of Italian *opera buffa*, displays uncommon dramatic and musical gifts, which make this *Don Giovanni* an opera of considerable interest.

DON GIOVANNI, OSSIA IL DISSOLUTO PUNITO

(Don Juan, or The Libertine Punished)

Dramma giocoso *in two acts by Wolfgang Amadeus Mozart (1756–1791), to a libretto by Lorenzo Da Ponte. First performance: Prague, National Theater, 29 October 1787.*

The action takes place in Seville. Don Giovanni (baritone), a dissolute knight, has gained entry, wearing a mask, to the house of the Commendatore (bass) in order to seduce the man's daughter, Donna Anna. The father comes running when he hears his daughter's cries, only to be killed in a brief duel with the Don. Later, Don Giovanni has a chance meeting with Donna Elvira (soprano), whom he had seduced and then deserted some time before. To get rid of her, the Don leaves to his servant Leporello the task of revealing to Elvira the true nature of his cynical and dissolute character. Meanwhile, Don Giovanni falls for a young country-woman, Zerlina (soprano). Zerlina is flattered by the knight's attentions and is about to give in to him when Donna Elvira intervenes. This does not stop Zerlina and her fiancé Masetto (bass) from taking part in a celebration organized by Don Giovanni. Three masked figures enter the ballroom: they are Donna Elvira, Donna Anna (who has identified Don Giovanni as her father's killer by the sound of his voice) and her fiancé, Don Ottavio (tenor). While the dancing is in progress, Don Giovanni draws Zerlina aside, and she calls for help. The masked trio reveal their identities, confront Don Giovanni with all his misdeeds, and predict that he will soon be punished. Later still, Don Giovanni, dressed in Leporello's clothes, tries to seduce Donna Elvira's maid. Masetto, who is looking for the Don in order to have revenge on him, catches him in the act but fails to recognize him in Leporello's clothes. Don Giovanni gets rid of the countrymen who have turned up to give Masetto their support, and then beats up the unfortunate Masetto before escaping. The Don takes refuge in the cemetery where the Commendatore is buried. Here he meets Leporello and, as he is regaling him with his latest amorous exploits, he hears a menacing voice coming from the statue of the Commendatore. When Don Giovanni realizes that it is the statue itself that has spoken to him, the fearless reprobate gets Leporello to invite the Commendatore to dinner. Not long after, during the meal, Donna Elvira rushes into the room in a last attempt to make Don Giovanni repent, but she is greeted with scorn and derision, and she leaves. At the door she runs into the statue of the Commendatore, who has accepted Don Giovanni's invitation to dinner. The statue invites the Don to repay the visit and offers him his hand: as he takes it, Don Giovanni feels himself turn to ice and, as the statue disappears, an abyss opens and the Don is swallowed up.

Legend has it that Mozart wrote the overture the day before the first performance. The score challenges the structure of a particular operatic genre: *Don Giovanni* cannot be described as an *opera buffa giocosa* in the real sense, but a perfect blend of comic elements with others that are genuinely tragic and are conveyed by dark and realistic music. The complexity of the opera lies in precisely this combination of contrasting ingredients, and it is rightly regarded as one of the great operatic masterpieces.

Above: A scene from Mozart's *Don Giovanni*.

Left: Mozart composing *Don Giovanni* in Prague.

DON PASQUALE

Opera buffa *in three acts by Gaetano Donizetti (1797–1848), to a libretto by the composer and Giovanni Ruffini. First performance: Paris, Théâtre des Italiens, 3 January 1843.*

The action takes place in Rome. Don Pasquale (comic bass) is furious because his nephew and heir Ernesto (tenor) will not agree to a marriage of convenience which has been arranged for him with a staid and wealthy lady. Doctor Malatesta (baritone), a friend of Ernesto, pretends to be on Don Pasquale's side. He cunningly suggests that Don Pasquale should punish his young nephew by taking a wife himself, and recommends his own sister. The idea appeals to the old man, and he begs his friend to introduce him to her. Malatesta then issues instructions to Norina (soprano), a young and beautiful widow with whom Ernesto is in love. Norina's job is to play the part of the non-existent sister, Sofronia, charm Don Pasquale and then, once a fake marriage contract has been signed, drive him mad with her caprices. The old man is conquered by the sweetness of the alleged Sofronia and asks if he can sign the contract straightaway. No sooner has this been done than Norina begins her transformation: she becomes shameless and arrogant and throws Don Pasquale into despair. On one occasion, Don Pasquale tries to stop his wife from going to the theater, whereupon Norina simply gives the poor old man a slap on the face and then, as she goes out, drops one of Ernesto's visiting-cards, on which is written a rendezvous with her for that evening in the garden. Don Pasquale sends for Doctor Malatesta to help him surprise his wife. When Don Pasquale arrives, Ernesto escapes without being recognized, and the old man is furious. At this point Malatesta suggests Pasquale tell his wife that Norina, Ernesto's wife-to-be, will be arriving to stay at their house the next day. Sofronia declares that she will not tolerate such an affront and will be leaving, but, fearing a trick, asks to come to the wedding. Don Pasquale agrees.

DON PASQUALE

DRAMMA BUFFO IN TRE ATTI

POSTO IN MUSICA DAL MAESTRO

GAETANO DONIZETTI

da rappresentarsi

NEL TEATRO CARLO FELICE

L'Autunno del 1843.

GENOVA

Tipografia dei Fratelli Pagano.

Canneto il lungo, n.° 800.

Above: The libretto for *Don Pasquale*, printed for the 1843 performance at the Teatro Carlo Felice, Genoa.

Now the whole conspiracy is revealed to him. At first Don Pasquale is angry but then feels happy to be rid of Sofronia and gives his blessing to the marriage of Norina and Ernesto.

When Donizetti composed *Don Pasquale*, he was already at the height of his career. He composed it over a period of 11 days in November 1842, although it took much longer to write the orchestral parts and meet the individual needs of the different performers. The work was a sensational success with audience and critics, and *Don Pasquale* was an immediate triumph in opera houses throughout the world. It is Donizetti's last great success, and remains popular to this day.

Right: Portrait of Gaetano Donizetti by G. Carnevali.

DON PERLIMPLIN, OVVERO IL TRIONFO DELL'AMORE E DELL'IMMAGINAZIONE

(Don Perlimplin, or The Triumph of Love and Imagination)

Opera for radio in one act by Bruno Madera (1920–1973), adapted by the composer from Lorca's play. First performance: RAI (Italian Radio), 12 August 1962.

This is a fairy tale which uses dialogue to tell the enchanting tale of Don Perlimplin, elderly husband of Belisa, and how he kills the young knight in the red cloak who is in love with Belisa and loved by her. The knight in the red cloak is none other than the gentle Don Perlimplin himself, who is killing himself, or rather the darker side of his own nature, in order that Belisa may acquire a soul.

This is Maderna's first opera, and he wrote it for radio. *Don Perlimplin* is a music-comedy in which the characters have speaking parts. Only Belisa sings, and she has only two numbers. The lead, Don Perlimplin, is played by the sound of a flute.

DON PROCOPIO

Opera buffa *in two acts by Georges Bizet (1838–1875), to an original Italian text by Carlo Cambiaggio translated into French by Paul Collin and Paul Bérel. First (posthumous) performance: Monte Carlo, Théâtre du Casino, 10 March 1906.*

The country-house of Don Andronico, in Italy, around 1800. Don Andronico (bass) has decided to give the hand of his niece Bettina (soprano) in marriage to Don Procopio (baritone), a rich and greedy old man. All of the other members of the family are scheming to prevent the wedding from taking place. So Bettina, with the support of Eufemia (soprano), the wife of Don Andronico, and of her own brother Ernesto (baritone), lets the old man believe that she intends to squander all his money and not let him have another moment's peace. Dumbfounded and alarmed, Don Procopio gives up his marriage plans with a flurry of excuses. Bettina is delighted and gets married instead to her beloved Odoardo (tenor), the young officer who has been courting her.

Don Procopio is an imitation of Italian *opera buffa* and dates back to the period when Bizet was studying in Rome. It has links with Donizetti's *Don Pasquale*, but also shows that Bizet already displayed a good technique and unusual expressive vigour.

DON QUICHOTTE

Opera in five acts by Jules Massenet (1842–1912), to a libretto by Henri Cain, based on Jacques Le Lorrain's novel Le chevalier de la longue figure *which drew its inspiration from Cervantes. First performance: Monte Carlo, Théâtre du Casino, 19 February 1910.*

The story of Don Quichotte as narrated by Le Lorrain is freely based on the original by Cervantes. In his version, Lorrain has changed Dulcinea into Dulcinée, a chambermaid, Don Quixote himself into Don Quichotte, a bombastic preacher, while the wise Sancho Panza becomes a kind of socialist propagandist.

This *Don Quichotte* is one of Massenet's minor late works. The libretto is of little value, and the music is inferior to that of the other works for which Massenet is famous.

DON SANCHE, OU LE CHÂTEAU D'AMOUR

Comic opera in one act by Franz Liszt (1811–1886), to a libretto by Théaulon de Lambert and De Rancé. First performance: Paris, Théâtre de l'Opéra-Comique, 17 October 1825.

The castle of love is a kind of "happy isle" where pairs of lovers from both the nobility and the lower class sing in homage to the joys of love. Don Sanche (tenor) presents himself at the castle gates but he is denied entry, because only pairs of lovers are allowed free access. Don Sanche laments his wretched state: he loves the Princesse Elzire (mezzo-soprano), but she is in love with the knight Romuald de Navarre. The lord of the castle of love, the wizard Alidor (baritone), comes to Don Sanche's aid. With the help of a magic spell, Alidor sees the Princesse en route for Navarre and then causes a storm to break, which compels the Princesse and her retinue to change direction. Elzire arrives at the castle, and asks for hospitality, but is refused because she does not have a lover, and so she cannot enter. The castle page-boy (soprano) invites Elzire to accept Don Sanche's love, as then she will be able to enter the castle. But the Princesse haughtily refuses. A chorus announces the arrival of the knight Romuald. The proud knight wants to marry Elzire at all costs. Faced with Romuald's arrogance, Don Sanche decides to fight him on behalf of Elzire, whom he loves hopelessly. In the duel Don Sanche is seriously wounded, and at this point Elzire realizes that she loves him. In despair, the Princesse asks to enter the castle, and offers her life in exchange for that of Don Sanche. The gates of the castle open and Alidor appears. The wizard reveals the truth: Alidor had taken on the form and semblance of Romuald, and the duel and Don Sanche's wound were nothing less than a test of love. Elzire and Don Sanche swear eternal love.

The score of *Don Sanche* had been lost but was rediscovered in 1900 by Jean-Philippe Chantavoine. It is Liszt's only opera, written when he was only fourteen years old. It is rightly considered to be a work of little importance.

DONAT, ZDISLAVA

(Posen/Poznan 1936)

Polish soprano. She studied music at the Conservatory in Warsaw before going on to train in Italy. She then took part in a number of singing competitions and began to appear with the Poznan Opera (1964–71) and the Warsaw Opera (1971), going on to sing in a number of opera houses in Europe and America. Donat's name, however, is most associated with theaters in the German-speaking world: Munich, Salzburg and Bregenz in particular, where she made her mark as the Queen of the Night in *Die Zauberflöte* (The Magic Flute) and Constanze in *Die Entführung aus dem Serail* (The Seraglio).

DONATH, HELEN

(Corpus Christi, Texas 1940)

American soprano, née Helen Erwin. At the age of 18 she began to sing in concerts. In 1961 she moved to Europe, joining the resident company at the Cologne Opera, where she made her debut as one of the Rhinemaidens in Wagner's *Das Rheingold.* This was followed by appearances with the Hanover Opera (1963–66) and in Munich (1967). She sang on several occasions at the Salzburg Festival from 1964 and in many other international opera houses. Donath has also made many recordings and had a busy concert-hall career. She had a fine lyric soprano voice and attracted attention for her exquisite Marzelline in *Fidelio*, as Gretel in *Hänsel und Gretel*, Pamina in *Die Zauberflöte* (The Magic Flute), Zerlina in *Don Giovanni* and Sophie in *Der Rosenkavalier*.

Above: A scene from *Don Quichotte* by Massenet.

DONIZETTI, GAETANO

(Bergamo 1797–1848)

Italian composer. He studied in Bergamo and began composing while still a student, scoring his first success with his opera *Enrico di Borgogna* (1818). Between 1818 and 1829 he wrote nearly 30 operas, including *Zoraide di Granata* (1822), *L'ajo nell'imbarazzo* (1824), *Emilia di Liverpool* (1824), *Gabriella di Vergy* (1826), *Le convenienze e le inconvenienze teatrali* (1827), *L'esule di Roma* (1828) and *Elisabetta al castello di Kenilworth* (1829). It was in 1830 that Donizetti's gifts were confirmed beyond doubt with *Anna Bolena*, which also marked an artistic turning-point in his career as a composer. In the years that followed, Donizetti wrote another masterpiece, *L'elisir d'amore* (1832), then *Lucrezia Borgia* (1833), *Rosamonda d'Inghilterra* and *Maria Stuarda* (both 1834). In 1835, now at the height of his fame, Donizetti began to compose for the Paris opera houses, making his debut at the Théâtre des Italiens with *Marin Faliero*, and in the same year he produced another of his masterpieces, *Lucia di Lammermoor*. After the delightful *Il campanello dello speziale* (1836), Donizetti passed through a particularly distressing year (1837) in which his wife Virginia died. Overcoming his grief, he managed to stage *Roberto Devereux*. In 1839 the censors in Naples prevented the production of his *Poliuto*. Donizetti was bitter about this and took the opera to Paris, where it was performed in 1840 with a new title, *Les martyres*. Also for the Parisian stage he wrote *La fille du régiment*, *La favorite* and *Don Pasquale* (1843). Another of Donizetti's masterpieces was *Linda di Chamounix*, which he composed for Vienna in 1842. He was intensely busy during these years of his life, too, though already undermined in body and spirit: mental disorders brought on by syphilis were turning to madness. His last operas were written while he was suffering from increasing exhaustion, and he died on 8 April 1848.

DONNA DEL LAGO, LA

(The Lady of the Lake)

Opera seria *in two acts by Gioachino Rossini (1792–1868), to a libretto by Andrea Leone Tottola, based on the poem by Sir Walter Scott. First performance: Naples, Teatro San Carlo, 24 October 1819.*

The action takes place during the period when the inhabitants of the mountain area of the county of Stirlingshire in Scotland were rising up against Giacomo V (James V) of Scotland, who sought to invade their territory. Elena (soprano), the daughter of the rebel chieftain Douglas d'Angus (bass), opens her heart to the waves as she crosses the lake. She is in love with Malcolm (contralto), but her father has promised her to Rodrigo (tenor). King Giacomo (tenor) comes to hear of Elena's beauty; so he disguises himself as a knight by the name of Uberto of Snowdon and asks the young woman for hospitality, immediately falling in love with her. On learning of the love which binds her to Malcolm, the King takes his leave of her and, as he says goodbye, gives her a ring which will enable her to have her every wish granted by the King of Scotland. Elena takes this precious gift to Giacomo's court, is astonished when she recognizes the King as none other than Uberto the knight,

Above: Donizetti in Paris, helped by his nephew Andrea.

Right: A scene from *La Donna del Lago* by Rossini.

Opposite above: Sir Walter Scott.

Opposite below: A scene from *Ernani* by Verdi.

ITALIAN OPERA AND THE LITERATURE OF ROMANTICISM

The historical novel played a vital role in nineteenth-century European culture. Sir Walter Scott's *The Bride of Lammermoor*, now almost forgotten, became enormously popular when it first appeared in 1819, and the sad adventures of its Scott's heroine had already been drawn upon by a number of writers from far and wide who adapted the story for the theater and the opera-house before it was immortalized in Donizetti's opera *Lucia di Lammermoor*. Before him, Rossini had been captivated by the melancholy Scottish settings described by Sir Walter Scott in his novel *The Lady of the Lake*. In *La donna del lago* (1819), Rossini, a complete stranger to the Romanticism of Northern Europe, becomes animated in his use of languid melodies and the martial songs of Scottish clansmen. But the enchantment and the passions unleashed from the pages of Scott's novels are made more real in *Lucia di Lammermoor*: building on an excellent libretto by Salvatore Cammarano, Donizetti perfectly recreates the mysterious, nocturnal and Gothic atmosphere of the story. Dramas and passions, in historical settings, are among the ingredients in the literary works of Friedrich Schiller (1759–1805), whose *Wilhelm Tell* (1804) inspired Rossini's *Guillaume Tell* (1829). Schiller was also the source for the libretto of Donizetti's *Maria Stuarda* (1834) and his plays *Die Jungfrau von Orleans* (The Maid of Orleans, 1801), *Die Räuber* (The Robbers, 1782), *Kabale und Liebe* (Intrigue and Love, 1784) and *Don Carlos* (1787) were also a source of inspiration for opera composers. Whereas in *Giovanna d'Arco* (1845, from *Die Jungfrau von Orleans* play) and *I Masnadieri* (1847, based on *Die Räuber*), Verdi's music reflects the mediocrity of the libretti, in *Luisa Miller* (1848, taken from *Kabale und Liebe*) and *Don Carlos* (1867), he reveals a mastery of Schiller's favourite themes:

love to which a father is opposed (to be found not only in his *Don Carlos* but also in von Einem's opera *Kabale und Liebe*) and, at the same time, the feelings of veneration which the male lead has for his father, and it is the conflict between these two elements which creates the drama. To these may be added a new ingredient, featured in *Don Carlos*, friendship: it is out of friendship for Posa that Carlos renounces his longing for happiness. The works of Victor Hugo (1802–1885) proved equally inspiring to composers. His plays and novels, strongly imbued with political ideas which prized equality and liberty, were a phenomenon of the very greatest importance in the literature of Romanticism both in France and beyond, and provided a considerable stimulus to librettists (and to censors, who reacted against operas inspired by Hugo with some ferocity). Donizetti turned to Hugo for his *Lucrezia Borgia* (1833), just as Bellini had, attracted by his play *Hernani* (1830) until the pressures brought to bear on Bellini by the censor made him change his mind and he started on something else instead, the less fraught *La Sonnambula*. *Hernani* was consequently taken up by Verdi who remained steadfast in the face of protests from Hugo himself (who denounced the libretto for Verdi's *Ernani* as a crude imitation of his work) and discovered in this Hugo play, and above all in another of his plays, *Le roi s'amuse* (1832) – which was the inspiration for *Rigoletto* (1851), "the greatest subject and possibly the greatest play of modern times." It was in *Rigoletto* that Verdi, following the version of the libretto to the letter, achieved a flawless operatic equivalent of Hugo's play while avoiding some of the *longueurs* which are a hallmark of Hugo's dramatic language. The French playwright's *Angelo, tyran de Padoue* (1835) was the basis for Saverio Mercadante's opera *Il giuramento* (1837) and Amilcare Ponchielli's famous *La Gioconda* (1876).

shows him the ring and asks for her father's release from captivity. Faithful to his promise, the King not only grants Douglas his freedom but completes Elena's happiness by giving his blessing to her marriage with Malcolm.

Rossini was in the habit of writing his opera scores very quickly, and *La donna del lago* was no exception. The music is not only spontaneous and original but complex in structure, and features some completely new ideas which anticipate some of the themes and cadences of Romantic opera.

DONNA SERPENTE, LA

(The Snake Woman)

Fairy-tale opera in a prologue and three acts by Alfredo Casella (1883–1947), to a libretto by Cesare Lodovici based on the fairy-story of the same name by Carlo Gozzi. First performance: Rome, Teatro dell'Opera, 13 April 1932.

The action takes place in the Caucasus during the mythical age of the fairies. Miranda (soprano), favourite daughter of the fairy King Demogorgòn (baritone), has asked if she may go and live among human beings in order to marry King Altidòr (tenor). But she will have to abide by a number of conditions: she will have to stay with her husband for nine years and a day without telling him who she really is; if, during this time, Altidòr has not cursed her, despite the terrible things that Miranda will cause to happen, Miranda will become mortal and be able to remain with her husband. If Altidòr retaliates, Miranda will be turned into a snake for 200 years. After nine years and a day of happy life together, with the added joy of two children born to them, Altidòr discovers Miranda's true identity. But she and the children have disappeared. Altidòr searches desperately for them in the desert, accompanied by his old tutor Pantùl (baritone). All of a sudden the desert is transformed into the garden of a royal palace. Miranda appears and warns Altidòr that in order to be reconciled with her he will have to remain in the desert and endure the difficult tests to which he will be subjected without ever saying a word against her. Shortly after that, there is a violent earthquake and Miranda appears on top of a rock. Flames are burning round a stake, and Miranda orders their children to be thrown into the fire. Altidòr is distraught but does not utter a word against Miranda. On his return to Tiflis, Altidòr finds the city suffering from famine, while the Tartar army is about to launch its definitive attack. A final deadly report reaches Altidòr: the enemy troops are under orders from Miranda. Altidòr can stand no more and curses the wife who forced him to leave his country at a time of danger. Whereupon Miranda appears to tell him she knows he has cursed her, but he may nevertheless still be able to revoke it if he performs an exceptional act of courage. Miranda is then turned into a snake and slides away. Enter the fairy Farzana (soprano). Altidòr learns from her that Miranda is at the summit of a high mountain in the Caucasus. In order to rescue her, he must face some arduous tests. The King sets out to rescue his wife. Among the crags is a level open space and a sepulcher. Altidòr kills three monsters and then, drawing near to the sepulcher, hears Miranda's voice calling to him. He rushes towards the sepulcher, but a wall of fire rises up to stop him. Without hesitation, the King hurls himself through the flames. He has won. The sepulcher fades, and in its place is Miranda's palace, Miranda herself and the children.

By avoiding the temptations of a realistic narrative, and being more concerned with music rather than dramatic effect, Casella displays in *La donna serpente* all his best qualities as a composer, recalling both the comic tradition of *Falstaff* and the style of seventeenth-century stage-opera.

Above: A scene from *Donnerstag aus Licht* by Stockhausen.

DONNERSTAG AUS LICHT

(Thursday, from the cycle *Licht*)

Opera in three acts. Libretto, dance and action by Karlheinz Stockhausen (b. 1928). First performance: Milan, La Scala, 15 March 1981.

Michael, son of Eve and Lucifer, displays extraordinary artistic gifts as he grows up. His parents experience personal tragedies: his mother goes mad and ends up in a lunatic asylum, where she is killed by one of the doctors; and his father, an alcoholic, leaves for the war, never to return. Now completely changed, Eve and Lucifer come to Michael. They are to be his examiners. Michael does brilliantly in these exams in singing, trumpet and dance and is admitted to the school. He then begins a fantastic journey round the Earth. At the South Pole, in the company of musicians dressed as penguins, Michael, with two clarinettists, performs some comic clown-like acrobatics. On his return to his home in heaven, he is welcomed with a hymn which is interrupted by the devil-Lucifer, against whom Michael fights a difficult battle. He wins, and so is able to continue enjoying himself. In the end, the young man recalls the story of Lucifer, the arrogant angel, from the Bible, whereas he, Michael, has wanted to become a man in order to "bring heavenly music to humankind, and human music to the celestials."

Donnerstag aus Licht is the first instalment in Stockhausen's monumental opera cycle about the seven days of the week. Three main characters feature in the cycle. In this episode, Michael is associated with Thursday, day of Thor-Donner-Jove. Stockhausen is the overall creator of the work, including its text, choreography and production.

DORÁTI, ANTAL

(Budapest 1906–Gerzensee 1988)

Hungarian conductor and composer who became an American citizen. He studied music in Budapest, and Kodály and Bartók were among his teachers. After embarking on his career as a conductor in Hungary and Germany, Dorati went on to conduct the famous Monte Carlo Ballets Russes from 1933 onwards and the American Ballet Theater (1938–41). In 1948 he took American citizenship and continued his conducting career with a number of international orchestras: the Minneapolis Symphony (1949), the BBC Symphony (1962), the Stockholm Symphony (1966), the National Symphony of Washington, the Royal Philharmonic (1976) and, from 1977 to 1981, the Detroit Symphony. Dorati made invaluable recordings of Haydn's operas.

DORIA, RENÉE

(Perpignan 1921)
French soprano. By the age of 18 she was already appearing in concerts. In 1942 she made her triumphant theater debut at the Opéra in Marseilles as Rosina in *Il barbiere di Siviglia.* She followed this with Olympia (*Les contes d'Hoffmann*) and the lead role in *Lakmé*, with which she made her debut at the Opéra-Comique (1944). In 1947 she made her first appearance at the Opéra in Paris as the Queen of the Night in *Die Zauberflöte* (The Magic Flute) before turning to *Rigoletto, La traviata, Les dialogues des Carmélites*, and others. Doria sang in Italy and Holland, adding to her repertoire the roles of Marguerite (*Faust*), Lucia (*Lucia di Lammermoor*) and Juliet (*Roméo et Juliette*).

D'ORMEVILLE, CARLO

(Rome 1840–Milan 1924)
Italian playwright, librettist and theatrical impresario. Founder and leading spirit of periodicals devoted to the theater, D'Ormeville's working life was in opera houses, first as stage director at La Scala, then as impresario (he put on the premiere of *Aida* in Cairo in 1871). He wrote about 80 libretti for operas.

DOWNES, SIR EDWARD

(Birmingham 1924)
British conductor. After studying at the University of Birmingham (1941–44), he went on to attend the Royal College of Music in London. He won a scholarship in 1948, and was able to take advanced lessons in conducting with Hermann Scherchen. In 1950 he began conducting and from 1952 appeared at Covent Garden where, among other posts he held, he was assistant to Georg Solti. He was the first British conductor after the Second World War to conduct Wagner's *Ring* cycle (1967). From 1972 to 1976 he was music director of Australian Opera in Sydney, and from 1980 principal conductor of the BBC Philharmonic Orchestra in Manchester.

DREIGROSCHENOPER, DIE

(The Threepenny Opera)
Music drama in a prologue and three acts by Kurt Weill (1900–1950), to a libretto by Bertolt Brecht freely adapted from The Beggar's Opera *by John Gay. First performance: Berlin, Theater am Schiffbauerdamm, 31 August 1928.*

London, about 1900. The prologue introduces the opera's cast. Polly (soprano), the daughter of dealer J. J. Peachum (bass), has gone against her parents' wishes and married a thief called Mack the Knife. In order to rid themselves of their undesirable new son-in-law, Polly's parents decide to report Mack the Knife to the police. They are sure that he will be found in a brothel. Mrs Peachum bribes the prostitutes, promising them a reward if they call the police the moment Mack arrives. And so it turns out: Sea-Pirate Jenny (mezzo-soprano) calls Mrs Peachum and Constable Smith. Mack tries to escape but is arrested. In prison, Mack has a visit from Lucy (soprano), the daughter of police commissioner Brown (bass), nicknamed Tiger Brown. With Lucy's help, Mack gets away. When Peachum finds out that Mack has vanished, he puts the blame on Brown, telling him that if he does not deal with this escape with uncompromising determination, he will organize a demonstration by the beggar community to obstruct the procession at the Queen's coronation. Brown manages to arrest Mack once again, and he is sentenced to death. Polly rushes to the prison to bid him a last farewell. Mack attempts to scrape together some money to bribe a policeman and escape again and is unsuccessful. He asks everyone's forgiveness and sets out for the gallows. At the last moment a royal messenger arrives on horseback: the Queen has pardoned Mack, given him a castle, made him a peer of the realm and sends her best wishes to the happy couple. Peachum's comment on all this? "Unfortunately," he says, "real life is very different, as we know. Messengers rarely arrive on horseback, if the downtrodden dare to resist."

Die Dreigroschenoper is a political and social opera which develops the ideas later expanded by Brecht and by Weill in *Mahagonny*. It confronts the audience and involves them, forcing them to think about the conditions of the society in which they live. The music draws on cabaret, jazz, serious opera and folk music. The score is not an accompaniment, but openly participates in the action. The opera is made up of 22 separate items, a sort of *Singspiel* with speaking and singing parts in the form of ballads, recitatives, popular songs, and fox-trot and shimmy dance rhythms. The music noticeably improves on the text, which is not one of Brecht's most effective libretti.

Above: The Hungarian conductor and composer Antal Doráti.

DROT OG MARSK

(King and Marshal)

Tragic opera in four acts by Peter Heise (1830–1879), to a libretto by Christian Richardt. First performance: Copenhagen, 25 September 1878.

The action takes place in Denmark in 1246. King Erik V (tenor) has a reputation for being a ruthless womanizer. During a military campaign against the Swedes the King sends out his loyal marshal Ingeborg (baritone) at the head of his forces and, while he is waiting for them to return, wastes no time in seducing the marshal's wife. When the marshal returns from the war, he finds that his wife has been the victim of a rape and is ready to ask that the outrage she has suffered be avenged. The marshal appears before the Crown High Court. In front of the people, nobles, and King Erik himself, Ingeborg accuses the King of having betrayed his honour as a knight, and consequently he renounces all oaths of loyalty to the crown. The marshal's courageous accusations find support among a number of nobles of the Danish court, who join forces with the marshal in having his revenge. The plot is carried out on Saint Cecilia's day, 22 November 1286, when the King is assassinated in a hay-loft, dying from 56 stab wounds, administered, as legend has it, by each of the conspirators in turn.

The story of the opera is based on a number of Danish legends which recount the events leading up to the murder of King Erik V. The main source of inspiration for Peter Heise's *Drot og marsk*, however, was a tragedy by Carsten Hauch produced in 1849. The young Heise undoubtedly attended one of the performances of Hauch's play, because in the years that followed he began writing music on the theme of the tragedy; this phase of his work then found a real focus, thanks to Heise's collaboration with his librettist and friend Christian Richardt, in this opera, which was such a resounding success at its premiere that it ran for more than 100 performances.

Above: The Czech composer Antonín Dvořák

DU LOCLE, CAMILLE

(Orange, Avignon, 1832–Capri 1903)

French librettist. In 1856 he made his debut as a librettist, and in 1869 he was appointed Secretary at the Opéra, then assistant director and finally director at the Opéra-Comique (1870–74). It was during these years that Du Locle commissioned Bizet to write *Carmen.* He enjoyed a particularly happy friendship and collaboration with Verdi, for whom, with F. J. Méry, he wrote the libretto for *Don Carlos.* He also translated into French the libretti for *Aida, Simon Boccanegra, La forza del destino* and *Otello.*

DUE BARONI DI ROCCA AZZURRA, I

(The Two Barons of Rocca Azzurra)

Opera buffa *in one act by Domenico Cimarosa (1749–1801), to a libretto by Giuseppe Palomba. First performance: Rome, Teatro Valle, Carnival 1783.*

Baron Demofonte (*buffo* baritone) and his nephew Totaro (baritone) are waiting anxiously for Laura, Totaro's bride-to-be. Franchetto (tenor) arrives and introduces himself as an ambassador from the bride. He wants his sister Sandra (soprano) to become a baroness and so has replaced the portrait of Laura (soprano) with that of his sister. But when the sister arrives, she finds that the reception she is given is inappropriate to her position as a future baroness. When it is revealed that there are two brides-to-be, the puzzle as to which of the two is the real Laura has to be worked out. This leads to a series of situations involving disguises, squabbles and fits of jealousy in order to find out the truth. In the end Franchetto confesses that he was behind the deception and that Laura is the true bride. Everyone is left satisfied: Laura marries Totaro, while Demofonte marries Sandra, who can now become a baroness after all.

Despite a number of weak points in the libretto, which was to some extent careless in creating situations and introducing characters, *I due baroni di Rocca Azzurra* enjoyed success and was performed in a number of different theaters.

DUE FOSCARI, I

(The Two Foscari)

Tragic opera in three acts by Giuseppe Verdi (1813–1901), to a libretto by Francesco Maria Piave based on the tragedy The Two Foscari *by Lord Byron. First performance: Rome, Teatro di Torre Argentina, 3 November 1844.*

Venice, in the fifteenth century. Francesco Foscari (baritone) is the Doge of Venice from 1423 to 1457. After a period in exile brought about by his disorderly life, the Doge's son Jacopo (tenor) returns to Venice in secret. But word reaches Jacopo Loredano (tenor), an enemy of the Foscari, and he reports the Doge's son to the Council of Ten. The Doge has no choice but to do his duty, which means having to send his son back into exile. Leaving his wife Lucrezia (soprano) and his children behind, Jacopo dies on board the ship which is taking him to the island of Crete. The Doge abdicates, and then he too dies, worn down by grief.

When Verdi first read through Byron's play, he found it "full of passion, and ideal for an opera." But when the opera did not turn out to be a perfect success, the composer wrote that it "read more like a funeral" than a tragedy. In any case, the composer was later able to turn this experience to good use: his study of the tension between the interests of the state and love of family in the plot of *I due Foscari* served him well for his next opera, *Simon Boccanegra.*

DUKAS, PAUL

(Paris 1865–1935)

French composer. He studied at the Paris Conservatoire. In 1888 he came second in the Grand Prix de Rome with his cantata *Velléda.* He had a success with his orchestral scherzo *L'apprenti sorcier* (The Sorcerer's Apprentice) in 1897, and this remains his most famous composition. In 1892 he first attempted to write an opera but only managed to complete one, *Ariane et Barbe-Bleu* (to a libretto by Maeterlinck), in 1907. This is almost certainly the first opera to have come under the influence of Debussy's *Pelléas et Mélisande*, but unlike Debussy's opera, *Ariane* has a more clear-cut style, especially in the emotional shaping of the narrative.

DUKE BLUEBEARD'S CASTLE

See *Kékszákallú Herleg Vára, A*

DUNN, SUSAN
(Malvern, Arkansas 1954)
American soprano. She made her debut as Aida in Peoria (Illinois) in 1982. She then won a number of singing competitions, including the 1983 Richard Tucker Award. In 1985 she gave an impressive performance in the first act of *Die Walküre* at New York's Carnegie Hall, and this launched her on a brilliant career, with appearances at the principal American opera houses (Chicago, San Francisco, Houston, Washington, etc.), making her mark as an outstanding exponent of Verdi. Dunn won tremendous acclaim in the role of Elena in Verdi's *Les vêpres siciliennes* at the Teatro Comunale in Bologna (1986), where she also sang in *Don Carlos* (1988) and *Giovanna d'Arco* (1990). More engagements to sing Verdi came from the Vienna Staatsoper (*Un ballo in maschera*, 1988) and for her debut at the Metropolitan Opera House in New York (*Il trovatore*, 1989), where she subsequently appeared in *Luisa Miller* (1991).

DUPUY, MARTINE
(Marseilles 1952)
French mezzo-soprano. After studying at the Marseilles Conservatoire, she began to sing in minor roles at the opera house in Marseilles (1973). She entered a number of singing competitions, including the "La voix d'or Ninon Vallin" (1973) and the "Premio Lauri-Volpi" in Peschiera del Garda. Dupuy trained in Italy with Rodolfo Celletti, who encouraged her in the direction of the *bel canto* repertoire, and before long she was appearing at the principal opera houses in Italy and receiving engagements from across Europe and America. Her extraordinary skill in vocalization, style and expressiveness have ensured Dupuy her place as one of the authentic *bel canto* singers of today.

DUVAL, DENISE
(Paris, 1921)
French soprano. She studied music at the Conservatoire in Bordeaux and made her debut at Bordeaux's Grand Théâtre. A turning-point in her career came when she met the composer Francis Poulenc, who created some of his most famous operatic roles for her in *Les mamelles de Tirésias* (Paris Opéra, 1953), *Les dialogues des Carmélites* (Opéra, 1947) and *La voix humaine* (Opéra-Comique, 1959). She appeared at a number of opera houses across Europe, including La Scala, Milan and the Théâtre de la Monnaie in Brussels and won particular renown as one of the most accomplished exponents of twentieth-century French music theater.

DVOŘÁK, ANTONÍN
(Nelahozeves, Bohemia 1841–Prague 1904)
Czech composer. At a very young age he played the violin and sang in the choir in the chapel of his native city. From 1854 he specialized in organ and music theory and also studied singing, piano and viola. After moving to Prague in 1857, he played violin in the Prozatimni theater orchestra (1861). By this time he had already started composing, to which he devoted all his time from 1871. Within a few years, Dvořák's compositions had made him famous not only in Europe but also in the United States, where he was invited to become director of the New York Conservatory, a post he held from 1892 to 1895. He began to write operas in 1870: the first was *Alfred*, followed by *Kráhl a uhlír* (The King and the Charcoal Burner, 1871), *Tverdé palice* (Hard Heads, composed in 1874 and staged in 1881), *Vanda* (1876), *Selma sedlák* (The Cunning Countryman, 1878) and *Dimitrij* (1881–82). Particularly outstanding are the operas *Jakobin* (The Jacobin, 1889) and *Čert a Káča* (The Devil and Catherine, 1899), which abound in musical motifs associated with Bohemian folklore. Then came *Rusalka* (1901), Dvořák's masterpiece, while his last opera, *Armida*, was staged in 1904. Its failure so affected Dvořák that he suffered a stroke and subsequently died.

DVORSKÝ, PETER
(Horná Ves 1951)
Czech tenor. Immediately after completing his studies at the Conservatory in Bratislava, and still not yet 20, Dvorsky joined the company of the Bratislava National Theater, where he made his debut in 1972. After winning the Tchaikovsky Prize in Moscow in 1974, he completed his training at La Scala, Milan. From 1976 he appeared at the Vienna Staatsoper, and in 1977 he embarked on an international career, which took him to the Metropolitan Opera House in New York (*La traviata*), La Scala (*La bohème*, *Adriana Lecouvreur* and *Manon Lescaut*), Covent Garden and other theatrical venues Dvorský has a very fine lyric tenor voice and in recent years has concentrated increasingly on dramatic tenor roles.

Above: A sketch for one of the scenes in *Dimitrij* by Dvořák.

Left: The tenor Peter Dvorsky.

E

ÉCHO ET NARCISSE

Opera in a prologue and three acts by Christoph Willibald Gluck (1714–1787), to a libretto by Ludwig Theodor von Tschudi. First performance: Paris, Académie-Royale de Musique (Opéra), 24 September 1779.

Young Narcisse (tenor) spends his life contemplating his own reflection, while his beloved, Écho (soprano), whose voice can only repeat the sounds she hears, does not know how to distract him from his exclusive self-love. Amour (soprano), who had encouraged the growth of love between these two, tries to do what he can to help it survive. Unfortunately prayers, sacrifices and the laments of shepherds and naiads fail to alter the situation. In her despair, Écho sees death as the only way to escape from her unhappy love. When Narcisse discovers that Écho is dying, he realizes what love is and, overcome by despair, he wants to take his own life. But Amour intervenes to reunite Écho and her beloved Narcisse, while the shepherds and woodland deities sing a hymn of praise for the happy marriage of the couple.

Unlike its predecessor, *Iphigénie en Tauride* (Iphigenia in Tauris), *Écho et Narcisse*, which was Gluck's last opera, was a fiasco. After making substantial alterations to the score, Gluck allowed *Écho et Narcisse* to be staged again in 1781. It stands somewhat apart from Gluck's other works, the pastoral setting having nothing in common with the baroque operas of a composer like Lully or Rameau, imbued as it is with a subtle melancholy expressing suffering and a desire for death.

ÉDA-PIERRE, CHRISTIANE

(Fort-de-France, Martinique 1932)

French soprano. After studying music at the Paris Conservatoire, Éda-Pierre made her debut in 1958 at the opera house in Nice in Bizet's *Les pêcheurs de perles* (The Pearl Fishers). She was engaged by the Opéra-Comique and the Paris Opéra (1960), and gave outstanding performances of a repertoire which included French opera, such as *Lakmé*, *Les Indes galantes* and *Dardanus*, and Italian opera such as *Lucia di Lammermoor*, *Rigoletto* and *La traviata*. Éda-Pierre was a very musical, elegant and stylistically versatile performer who also excelled in Mozart operas as well as in operas by contemporary composers such as Capdevielle, Amy, Milhaud, Chaynes and Messiaen. She was appointed to the Chair of Singing at the Paris Conservatoire in 1977.

EDELMANN, OTTO

(Vienna 1917)

Austrian bass-baritone. He studied music at the Vienna Academy of Music and made his debut in Gera in 1937 (*Le nozze di Figaro*). His career was interrupted by the war and he resumed it in 1947, the year in which he appeared for the first time at the Vienna Staatsoper in *Der Freischütz*. Edelmann sang at Bayreuth (1951–52), the Metropolitan Opera House, New York (1954), the Salzburg Festival (1948–64), and La Scala, Milan (1951–54). His greatest roles included Rocco in *Fidelio*, Hans Sachs in *Die Meistersinger von Nürnberg* and Baron Ochs in *Der Rosenkavalier*, which he recorded in 1956 with Herbert von Karajan.

EDGAR

Opera in four acts by Giacomo Puccini (1858–1924), to a libretto by Ferdinando Fontana from Alfred de Musset's play La coupe et les lèvres. *First performance: Milan, La Scala, 21 April 1889.*

The opera is set in Flanders in the year 1302. Edgar (tenor) is torn between pure love for Fidelia (soprano) and a sensual attraction to Tigrana (mezzo-soprano), a black boy abandoned as a baby by gipsies and brought up by Fidelia's father. Frank (baritone), Fidelia's brother, loves Tigrana, but she does not return his love. Tigrana is accused of scandalous conduct by the villagers, and Edgar comes to her defense. Frank challenges his rival, but is wounded. Edgar and Tigrana run away together. Edgar joins a group of soldiers who happen to be marching through and recognizes one of them as Frank. The two men settle their differences, and Edgar admits that he regrets leaving Fidelia. Tigrana swears that she will be avenged on him for having left her. The scene changes to the ramparts of a fortress near Courtray. A Mass is being celebrated for Edgar, who is believed to have fallen on the battlefield. A monk appears and eventually turns out to be Edgar himself. Fidelia throws herself into his arms, only to be stabbed by Tigrana. The murderess is led away to be executed.

Edgar was Puccini's first full-length opera. The critics decided that it was a failure, and after its premiere, the opera was given only two more performances. The theme did not appeal to Puccini and had been imposed on him by the publisher Ricordi, which undoubtedly had a negative effect on the outcome of the opera. Puccini subsequently

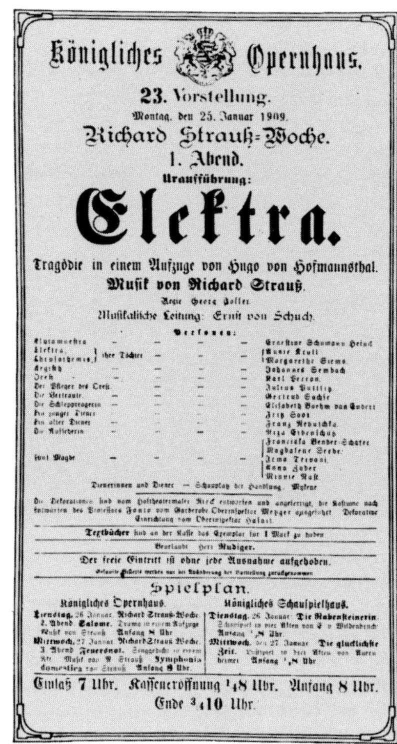

Above: The title page of Puccini's opera, *Edgar*.

Top: Playbill for the first performance of *Elektra* by Richard Strauss.

revised the opera, reducing it from four acts to three. The new version was produced in Ferrara on 28 February 1892.

EICHHORN, KURT

(Munich 1908)

German conductor. After studying at the Conservatory in Würzburg, he began conducting professionally at the Stadttheater in Bielefeld. He played an active role as conductor with the Dresden Opera (from 1941) and the Munich Opera (from 1946), where he spent much of his career. Eichhorn conducted many symphony concerts and was particularly distinguished for his performances of German music, as well as winning special acclaim from the critics for his recordings of the operas of Carl Orff (*Die Kluge*, 1970, and *Der Mond*, 1974).

EINEM, GOTTFRIED VON

(Berne 1918)

Austrian composer. He began by studying piano, and then in 1983 became a *Korrepetitor* (coach) at the Berlin Staatsoper, dividing his time between this post and a job as music assistant at the Bayreuth Festival. Between 1941 and 1942 he studied composition with Boris Blacher. His first opera, *Dantons Tod* (Danton's Death), was staged in 1947 at the Salzburg Festival of which he was a member of the board. Von Einem was director of the Konzerthausgesellschaft in Vienna and also a composition teacher at the Hochschule. His operas include *Der Prozess* (The Trial, 1953), *Der Zerrissene* (The Casualty, 1964), *Der Besuch der Alten Dame* (The Visit, 1971), *Kabale und Liebe* (Love and Intrigue, 1976) and *Jesu Hochzeit* (1980).

EINSTEIN ON THE BEACH

Opera in four acts by Philip Glass (b. 1937), to a text by Chris Knowles and Sam Johnson. First performance: Avignon Festival, 25 July 1976.

Although described as an opera, *Einstein on the Beach* is completely different from the normal concept of opera. The entire work focuses on three recurring images, each of which is characterized differently by the music. Among these images are trains, recalling the toy trains Einstein used to play with when he was a boy, but also the trains which the adult Einstein used as examples to demonstrate his theory of relativity. Next to appear is a bed, on which Einstein probably used to reflect on the threat of atomic catastrophe that his work had helped to make possible. Here Glass includes a scene in which it seems as though modern science itself is being put on trial. The third image is a continual reminder of the implications of the Atom, a force for freedom and transcendence which Einstein has unleashed. The symbol of this final vision is a spaceship, which the composer links with the nuclear apocalypse suggested by the works's title, taken from Nevil Shute's novel about the nuclear holocaust, *On the Beach*. These images, here given in outline, are actually much more complex and abstract. There is also an appearance by Einstein himself, raising a violin to his shoulder (he used to play one for relaxation) and watching events unfold like a latter-day Nero.

Einstein on the Beach is one of the most representative examples of minimalist composer Philip Glass's compositions for the theater. In this opera, he uses a variety of forces: four actors, a group of 12 voices and dancers, and an instrumental ensemble consisting of a solo violin, two flutes, four saxophones and three electric organs.

ELEKTRA

Tragic opera in one act by Richard Strauss (1864–1949), to a libretto by Hugo von Hofmannsthal, based on his own play which was inspired by Sophocles. First performance: Dresden, Königliches Opernhaus, 25 January 1909.

The setting is the courtyard of the palace of the sons of King Atreus. Elektra (soprano) is tormented by the memory of her father Agamemnon, treacherously murdered by his wife Klytämnestra (mezzo-soprano) and her lover Aegisth (tenor). Chrysothemis (soprano), Elektra's sister, warns her that their mother and Aegisth want to imprison her in a tower. It is not long before Klytämnestra enters, decked in jewels and talismans: she is hoping to use propitiatory sacrifices as a way of ridding herself of the nightmares that haunt her every night. Elektra accuses her mother of having driven her brother Orest out of the house for fear that he will exact vengeance. Klytämnestra threatens Elektra, then asks her to suggest a remedy to cure her of these dreadful dreams. "You will dream no more," answers Elektra, "when the rightful victim falls beneath the axe," meaning Klytämnestra herself. A maid enters with the news that Orest is dead. Klytämnestra is jubilant. Elektra decides to press ahead with her plan of revenge, and asks her sister to help her, but Chrysothemis is terrified and runs away. Left alone, Elektra is approached by one of the strangers who had announced the death of Orest. When the man realizes it is Elektra who stands before him, he reveals his true identity. It is Orest himself (baritone) and he has spread the news of his own death to make it easier for him to strike against his father's killers. He enters the palace. Shortly after that, Klytämnestra is heard uttering an inhuman cry. Aegisth appears, accompanied by Elektra, who lights his

Above: Sketch by L. Sievert for the production of *Elektra* which opened at La Scala on 26 May 1954.

way across the courtyard with a flaming torch. Aegisth disappears inside the palace. There is a moment's silence, then Aegisth reappears at a window calling out for help. Vengeance has been taken. Like a worshipper of Bacchus, Elektra goes into a frenetic dance of joy, then suddenly falls to the ground and lies motionless. Chrysothemis throws herself on Elektra's body, then rushes to the palace door. She knocks, but there is no answer.

Strauss's music is less disturbing here than in his opera *Salome*, in spite of the larger orchestral forces and a wider range of effects. From the dramatic point of view, the high points of the score are the encounter between Klytämnestra and Elektra, where the music moves from polytonality to the extremes of atonality to convey a sense of the Queen's torment, and the scene where Elektra and Orest recognize each other, in which the tension reaches its climax.

ELISABETTA AL CASTELLO DI KENILWORTH

(Queen Elizabeth at Kenilworth Castle)

Opera in three acts by Gaetano Donizetti (1797–1848), to a libretto by Andrea Leone Tottola, based on the novel Kenilworth *by Sir Walter Scott, and also known as* Il castello di Kenilworth. *First performance: Naples, Teatro San Carlo, 6 July 1829.*

Preparations are underway at Kenilworth Castle for the arrival of Queen Elizabeth (soprano). Albert, Earl of Leicester (tenor), who knows that the Queen loves him, tells his friend Lambourne (bass) that he has actually found true love with someone else, Amelia (soprano), whom he has secretly married. A hiding-place is found for Amelia by Warney (baritone), Leicester's squire, in a secret apartment in the castle, but Warney, who is himself in love with Amelia, attempts to part the couple by telling Amelia that her husband has been unfaithful to her. Amelia manages to escape from her prison and unexpectedly meets Elizabeth, to whom she reveals her relationship with Leicester and the alleged betrayal. Elizabeth indignantly takes Amelia with her and goes to see Leicester, but Warney lies to the Queen that Amelia is his wife. Later, Warney tries to drag Amelia away. When she resists, Warney pretends to offer her a drink; in fact it is a poisoned chalice. But Amelia is saved by her close friend Fanny (mezzo-soprano). Enter Leicester, followed by Elizabeth. The Queen has learned the truth, and after ordering Warney's arrest, she pardons Leicester and Amelia.

The events covered by Sir Walter Scott's novel *Kenilworth* gave Rossini the idea for his opera *Elisabetta, regina d'Inghilterra*, also premiered in Naples (1815) and given several more performances in 1829, a few months before the first night of Donizetti's *Elisabetta al castello di Kenilworth.* This all clearly influenced Donizetti, whose opera bears the hallmarks of Rossini's style. In particular, the display of *fioriture* (vocal flourishes) which Donizetti gives his Queen Elizabeth to sing has clear parallels with the part Rossini wrote for his own Elizabeth.

ELISABETTA, REGINA D'INGHILTERRA

(Elizabeth, Queen of England)

Opera in two acts by Gioachino Rossini (1792–1868), to a libretto by Giovanni Schmidt based on the play by Carlo Federici. First performance: Naples, Teatro San Carlo, 4 October 1815.

The Earl of Leicester (tenor), commander of the English army, has returned from winning a victory against the Scots. Queen Elizabeth (soprano), who is in love with Leicester, awaits his arrival with trepidation. Among the Scottish hostages is Matilda (soprano), the young daughter of Mary Stuart, whom Leicester has secretly married. Fearing Elizabeth's wrath, Leicester takes his friend the Duke of Norfolk (tenor) into his confidence, but Norfolk, who is jealous of Leicester's successes, tells Elizabeth that her favourite has betrayed her. After making the marriage public knowledge, the Queen orders the arrest of Leicester, Matilda and Matilda's brother Henry (mezzo-soprano). In prison, Leicester is visited by Norfolk, whom he continues to think of as his friend. Norfolk warns Leicester that the people are ready to rise up and rescue him, but Leicester does not want any conflict over the decisions taken by the Queen. Shortly after that, Elizabeth herself offers Leicester a chance to escape, but he rejects it and asks instead for the release of Matilda and Henry. But the Queen insists that Matilda and Henry be tried. This leads to the discovery that the real traitor is Norfolk, as he has overheard the conversation between the Queen and Leicester and now emerges from his hiding-place and threatens Elizabeth, but Henry and Matilda intervene and restrain him. After the guards have dragged the traitor away, Elizabeth grants everyone a royal pardon, while the people sing in praise of the Queen's generosity of spirit.

Right: A scene from *Elisabetta, regina d'Inghilterra* in a performance at the Teatro San Carlo Napes during the 1991–92 season.

It was with *Elisabetta, regina d'Inghilterra* that Rossini made his debut at the Teatro San Carlo in Naples. Rossini worked on the score with particular care and the end result represented a significant step forward in the development of the composer's *opera seria* style. The sung recitatives have been replaced by others with orchestral accompaniment and the chorus takes more part in the action.

ELISIR D'AMORE, L'

Opera in two acts by Gaetano Donizetti (1797–1848), to a libretto by Felice Romani, which was a revised version of Le Philtre *written by Eugène Scribe for Auber in 1831. First performance: Milan, Teatro alla Canobbiana, 12 May 1832.*

The action takes place in a village in the Netherlands. Nemorino (tenor), a shy young peasant, is in love with Adina (soprano), the wealthy owner of a farm. He tells her of his feelings, but she does not reciprocate them, being fickle and capricious and apparently preferring the company of the arrogant garrison sergeant, Belcore (baritone). Meanwhile, Doctor Dulcamara (comic bass), a charlatan who offers cures for all ills, has arrived in the village square. Nemorino loses no time in asking Dulcamara for a potion which might cause Adina to love him. After drinking the elixir (which is actually an ordinary bottle of wine), the ingenuous Nemorino has such faith in its effect that he has a complete change of mood and attitude towards Adina. Surprised and irritated by this, Adina accepts Belcore's proposal of marriage out of spite. Now desperate, Nemorino asks Dulcamara for another bottle of elixir, but as he has no more money to pay for it, he agrees to Belcore's suggestion that he join up as a soldier on the spot, then he can use his enrolment fee to pay for the elixir. In the meantime, word gets around of a large inheritance which Nemorino has just been left by an uncle. Nemorino does not yet know anything about this and suddenly finds himself being surrounded and courted by the young women of the village. This convinces him that the elixir has begun to work. Adina has meanwhile learned of the elixir of love and the sacrifice Nemorino made by joining the army. Touched, she realizes that she loves him and buys back his enlistment papers. So there is a happy ending: Nemorino, now rich and no longer bound by his obligations as a soldier, is in a position to marry Adina, while Dulcamara once again sings the praises of his amazing and extraordinarily effective elixir.

The premiere of *L'elisir d'amore* was a triumphant success, and the opera had a run of 32 performances. Together with *Don Pasquale* and *Il barbiere di Siviglia*, it can be seen as a glorious example of nineteenth-century comic opera at its finest. The score brims over with ravishing melodies, revealing Donizetti's great comic talent, whereby laughter can turn into a smile and the smile cloud over with melancholy, as in the famous aria "Una furtiva lagrima" (A furtive tear).

ENFANT ET LES SORTILÈGES, L'

(The Child and the Visions)

Opera-ballet in two acts by Maurice Ravel (1875–1937), to a libretto by Colette. First performance: Monte Carlo, Théâtre du Casino, 21 March 1925.

The scene is the interior of an old house in Normandy. The principal character, a young boy (mezzo-soprano), is trying to do his homework, but his mind keeps straying to forbidden pleasures such as pulling the cat's tail or even making his mother (contralto) stand in a corner for being naughty. When she comes in again and finds that the boy has not even started his homework, he is punished. Alone again, the boy vents his rage by destroying everything round him. Then, exhausted, he throws himself into a large armchair, which suddenly comes to life and pushes him off. This is the beginning of his magical experiences, as the objects he has destroyed protest at the way he has treated them. The boy is afraid and goes to sit by the hearth, but the fire (soprano) threatens him, while shepherds and shepherdesses begin to step down off the tattered wall-paper on the wall and dance to the sound of soft music, lamenting the fact that they can never be together again. Out from the pages of a story-book steps a princess (soprano), whom the boy asks for help. The princess calms him with her

Top left: Doctor Dulcamara in an engraving by De Valentini for *L'elisir d'amore*.

Above: A scene from *L'enfant et les sortilèges* by Ravel.

gentleness but then vanishes, and her place is taken by an old man who looks rather frightening: he is Arithmetic, and the boy runs off, terrified, into the garden. But here too the animals and trees have something to reproach the boy for. Finally left alone, the boy finds an injured squirrel and cares lovingly for it. The other animals witness this good-natured gesture by the boy and begin to doubt that he has a spiteful nature. In the end, they escort him back into the house and leave him in his mother's safe-keeping. Alone in front of her, the boy realizes how much harm spitefulness can do.

The first performance of *L'enfant et les sortilèges* unleashed a tide of controversy among the critics. It was staged again in Paris in 1926 and continued to arouse conflicting views. Final recognition of its quality came when it was performed in New York, London and Brussels, where the imaginativeness of Ravel's music was at last appreciated: the score owes nothing to the canons of traditional opera and is unique of its kind.

ENTFÜHRUNG AUS DEM SERAIL, DIE

(The Seraglio)

Singspiel *in three acts by Wolfgang Amadeus Mozart (1756–1791), to a libretto by Gottlob Stephanie jr., based on Christoph Friedrich Bretzner's* Belmont und Constanze. *First performance: Vienna, Burgtheater, 16 July 1782.*

The action takes place in Turkey in the eighteenth century. Outside the palace of Pasha Selim (speaking role), Belmonte (tenor), a young Spaniard, is searching for his bride-to-be, Constanze (soprano), who has been kidnapped by pirates and sold to the Pasha together with Belmonte's servant Pedrillo (tenor) and Pedrillo's fiancée Blonde (soprano). After asking unsuccessfully for information from Osmin (bass), the palace overseer, Belmonte manages to meet Pedrillo, who has been appointed palace gardener. Delighted to see each other again, the two quickly set to work on an escape plan. In the meantime, Selim is trying to win the love of his young woman prisoner Constanze, but she would rather die than be unfaithful to Belmonte. When Selim has taken his leave of Constanze, Pedrillo introduces him to Belmonte, who is promptly engaged as a garden designer. On the evening of the following day, Blonde tries to comfort Constanze in her deep dejection at the thought of now having to face death. Pedrillo is able to get word of the escape plan to Blonde, but first he must be rid of Osmin. He has no trouble in persuading Osmin to drink some wine. Osmin falls into a deep sleep, and Pedrillo puts a ladder up against the wall for Constanze and Blonde to climb down, which they soon do. The two couples are reunited. Meanwhile, Osmin has woken up, and comes after them, swearing revenge. The four young people are arrested and taken before the Pasha. Belmonte is then recognized by Selim as the son of one of his bitterest enemies, which makes things look even worse for the four, but Selim surprises everybody by releasing the two couples and allowing them to return home despite protests from Osmin. The opera ends with a *vaudeville*.

Mozart attempted to catch the true spirit of a fairy-tale, and to blend comic, tragic and fantastic elements. The orchestration, with timpani, triangles, trumpets, octave flutes and cymbals, created a strongly Eastern flavour, things Oriental being much in fashion at that time.

Above: A scene from *Die Entführung aus dem Serail* (The Seraglio), in a production at La Scala during the 1971–72 season.

ERCOLE AMANTE

(Hercules the Lover)

Opera in five acts by Francesco Cavalli (1602–1676), to a libretto by Abbot Francesco Buti. First performance: Paris, Théâtre des Tuileries, 7 February 1662, in the presence of King Louis XIV, resplendently dressed as the Sun King.

The allegorical prologue to the opera, added for the occasion by Camille Lilius, was a homage to the 15 leading royal families of the Western world, particularly the French one. They were introduced to the audience from heaven by Diana (soprano), their parts played by a number of ladies of the court together with the King and Queen. Diana commands Ercole (bass) to continue with his Labours and promises him the hand of Beauty (soprano) in marriage. The next part of the action tells the story of the loves of Ercole and Iole (soprano), the intrigues of Juno (contralto) and the love of Hyllo (tenor), Ercole's son, for Iole. The finale sees Ercole taking Beauty as his wife and Hyllo being married to Iole.

Ercole amante was composed by Cavalli to mark the occasion of the marriage of Louis XIV to the Infanta Maria Teresa (1660), but was not staged until two years later. The score was not successful because of the opposition of French composers towards Italian opera.

EREDE, ALBERTO

(Genoa 1908)

Italian conductor. He studied first in Genoa and Milan, then with Weingartner (1929–31) and Fritz Busch (1930). He made his debut in 1930 at the Accademia Nazionale di Santa Cecilia in Rome and went on to conduct Wagner's *Ring* cycle for the first time in Turin (1935). He then appeared at the Glyndebourne Festival and also at the Salzburg Festival, where he was music director from 1935 to 1938. In the years following the Second World War, Erede became music director of the New London Opera Company

(1946–48). From 1950 to 1955 he conducted at the Metropolitan Opera House, New York, and from 1956 at the Deutsche Oper am Rhein, where he was appointed music director in 1958. He made numerous appearances at leading Italian opera houses (particularly La Scala, Milan and the Teatro San Carlo in Naples), and from 1975 he was the artistic director of the Concorso Paganini in Genoa. He conducted with particular distinction at the Bayreuth Festival, including *Lohengrin* in 1968.

ERKEL, FERENC

(Gyula, Békés 1810–Budapest 1893)
Hungarian composer, conductor and pianist. He began studying music with his father, and then at the age of 12 was sent to Bratislava, where he took piano and composition. He began his career as a pianist (1834), but around 1836 he was appointed director of the German Municipal Theater in Pest, where he made his debut conducting Bellini's *La straniera*. In 1840 he put on his own first opera, *Bátori Mária*. Of the ten operas Erkel wrote, the most famous (still frequently performed nowadays) are *Hunyadi László* (1844), *Bánk-Bán* (1861) and *Brancovics György* (1874). The founder of the Budapest Philharmonic Orchestra (1840) and a teacher at the Budapest Academy of Music, he encouraged the development of a Hungarian musical tradition.

ERMIONE

Tragic opera in two acts by Gioachino Rossini (1792–1868), to a libretto by Andrea Leone Tottola based on Racine's tragedy Andromache. *First performance: Naples, Teatro San Carlo, 27 March 1819.*

Princess Ermione (soprano) is in love with King Pirro (tenor), who has pledged to make her his bride but has fallen in love with Andromaca (mezzo-soprano) and is breaking his pledge to Ermione. Prince Oreste (tenor) from Greece, whose love for Ermione is not returned, is being used by her as a go-between in order to exact revenge. Pirro is approaching the altar with Andromaca when he is killed by Oreste. But Ermione has had a change of heart about the order to kill Pirro, which she had given Oreste when she was in despair, and now she curses Oreste for what he has done. Oreste escapes as a result of the intervention of his soldiers.

The opera is important in Rossini's development. His aim here was to go beyond the use of "separate numbers," which he now replaced with large-scale scenes of "music drama". The second act, for example, consists of only four numbers: Ermione's *scena*, "Di che vedesti piangere," magisterially guides the action in the direction Rossini wants, making it a kind of "expanded" aria into which he inserts recitatives and other dramatic material which do not interrupt the forward movement of the action. The extraordinary modernity of this structure was not understood by the audience in Naples, whose response led to *Ermione* being taken off after the first night.

ERNANI

Opera in four acts by Giuseppe Verdi (1813–1901), to a libretto by Francesco Maria Piave, based on Victor Hugo's play Hernani. *First performance: Venice, Teatro La Fenice, 9 March 1844.*

The action takes place in Spain and Aix-la-Chapelle in 1519. Ernani (tenor) is planning an uprising to dethrone Don Carlos (baritone), the King of Spain. Ernani loves Elvira (soprano), who has been promised in marriage to the elderly Don Silva (bass), and goes to Don Silva's castle to take her away with him. Elvira is also loved by Don Carlos, who is at the castle. Ernani, Elvira and Don Carlos meet in the young woman's apartment. Don Silva arrives in a rage, but recognizes Don Carlos, who then saves Ernani by passing him off as a royal messenger. Shortly after that, Ernani, pursued by soldiers, takes refuge in Don Silva's castle. The wedding between Don Silva and Elvira is about to take place. In despair, Ernani reveals his identity and puts himself in Don Silva's hands. Enter Don Carlos in pursuit of the rebel Ernani, but the rules of hospitality oblige Don Silva not to hand his rival over. So Don Carlos leaves the castle taking Elvira with

Left: A scene from *Ermione*, in the production at the 1987 Rossini Opera Festival.

Above: A scene from *Ernani*, in a 1970 production at the Teatro dell'Opera, Rome.

him. Ernani then tells the jealous Don Silva that Don Carlos is also in love with Elvira. Ernani invites Don Silva to join him in taking revenge on Don Carlos and leaves him a hunting-horn. After the act of vengeance has been carried out, Don Silva will be entitled to order Ernani's death by a single blow of the horn. Not long after that, at Aix-la-Chapelle, in the vault beneath Charlemagne's tomb, Don Carlos, who has in the meantime become Emperor, has a group of conspirators arrested, among them Ernani and Don Silva. He is in a position to put the conspirators to death, but wanting to be magnanimous, he pardons all of them and offers Ernani Elvira's hand in marriage. While the wedding celebrations are taking place, the sound of a hunting-horn is heard, and Don Silva appears. Ernani keeps his word to Don Silva by stabbing himself in the chest with a dagger.

Victor Hugo's well-known play lent itself well to adaptation into an opera, and Verdi's music is full of Romantic energy. In his deft handling of the interplay between characters, Verdi has been able to accommodate a dramatic role for the chorus, particularly powerful in "Si ridesti il leon di Castiglia," which was destined to become one of the best-loved hymns of the Italian Risorgimento.

Above: A scene from Act III of *Ernani*.

Right: The soprano Janis Martin in a scene from *Erwartung*, produced at La Scala for the 1979–80 season.

EROBERUNG VON MEXICO, DIE

(The Conquest of Mexico)

Opera in one act by Wolfgang Rihm (b. 1952), to the composer's own libretto based on Antonin Artaud's Théâtre de Seraphine. *First performance: Hamburg, Opernhaus, 2 February 1992.*

Although the opera features two characters, Montezuma (dramatic soprano) and Fernando Cortez (baritone), there is no real action. The composer has divided the work into four scenes: 1) Omens. Mexico waits; it senses the storm is approaching. 2) Profession of faith. Mexico seen through Cortez's eyes. 3) Upheaval. Rebellion spreads throughout the country. 4) Abdication. Total chaos.

Rihm does not tackle his subject by showing the clash between the two civilizations or the genocide of a people, but by using the elaborate symbolism of Artaud's *Théâtre de Seraphine*. Out of this text there emerges a conflict of the masculine and feminine principles, seen here in terms of three elements, "Neuter, Feminine and Masculine," which are made to recur throughout the work as a *leitmotiv* (thus justifying the fact that the role of Montezuma is given to a female voice). Musically Rihm's idea was to create an environment of sound inside the auditorium, so he asked that 47 instrumentalists (percussion being most in evidence) be stationed in various parts of the theater; the chorus, on the other hand, is recorded on magnetic tape, while the interplay on stage is between the two characters and other "voices" who express no need to communicate and are given no individual psychological identity. Despite the complexity of the work, *Die Eroberung von Mexico* has been hailed as one of the greatest successes of contemporary German theater.

ERWARTUNG

(Expectation)

Monodrama for soprano and orchestra by Arnold Schoenberg (1874–1951), to a text by Marie Pappenheim. First performance: Prague, Neues Deutsches Theater, 6 June 1924.

On the edge of a wood, a woman (soprano) is on her way to a rendezvous with her lover. She is aware of a hidden menace in the night's still air, but plucks up courage and makes her way into the wood. The woman is conscious of mysterious presences in the darkness, brushing against her, preventing her from going on. She thinks she hears weeping.

She is frightened by rustlings and the cry of a night bird, and starts to run. She comes into a clearing lit by the moon. The woman tries to calm herself and stops to listen. She thinks she can hear her lover calling to her but again is overcome by the fear that a hundred hands are clutching at her and large, fixed eyes are staring at her in the dark. Exhausted, the woman comes out on to the road leading to the house of her rival. While she is looking for somewhere to sit down and rest, her foot catches against something on the ground. It is the body of her lover, still bleeding. He has been murdered. The woman cannot believe her eyes. Then, as though in a trance, she covers his lifeless body with kisses, bitterly reproaches him for his betrayal of her, and is overwhelmed by disconnected and inexpressible memories. The dawning of a new day separates the lovers, this time forever.

Schoenberg wrote the score for *Erwartung* during his "atonal" period. The music is composed in a continuous stream highlighted by sudden flashes of sound which vanish as quickly as they have come, as though the vocal part is a recitative interspersed with explosions of melody.

ESCLARMONDE

Opera in four acts by Jules Massenet (1842–1912), to a libretto by Blau and de Gramont. First performance: Paris, Théâtre de l'Opéra-Comique, 15 May 1889.

In front of the basilica in Byzantium, the Emperor Phorcas (baritone), who is also a magician, is abdicating in favour of his daughter Esclarmonde (soprano). The young woman, who has been initiated into the magic arts, will only be able to retain the throne and her magical powers if she keeps her face hidden until her twentieth birthday. On that day a tournament will take place, and the winner will have her hand in marriage. Phorcas entrusts his other daughter, Parséis (mezzo-soprano), with the task of looking after Esclarmonde. Before long Esclarmonde tells her sister of her feelings for the French knight Roland (tenor), whom she has loved from a distance without his knowledge. Parséis then advises her sister to use her magic powers to make Roland come to her. So Esclarmonde calls upon the spirits of air, water and fire to lead the knight to an enchanted island, where she will go to meet him. Once on the island, Esclarmonde declares her love to Roland but warns him that he must never attempt to find out who she is. Then Esclarmonde presents the knight with the sword of St. George, with which he must free the city of Blois from the besieging Saracens. Roland routs the enemy forces and, as a reward, King Cléomer (baritone) offers him the hand of his daughter. To the astonishment of all present, Roland refuses this honour. Later, the Bishop of Blois (bass) presses Roland to tell him why he has turned down the King's offer. Roland finds himself having to speak about the mysterious woman who comes to him every night. The Bishop puts Roland on his guard, believing him to be the victim of sorcery, and then takes his leave of him. After a while, Esclarmonde arrives, but at that same moment the door bursts open and the Bishop appears with a group of monks. While the Bishop and the monks are uttering prayers of exorcism, Esclarmonde, cursing the fact that her love has been betrayed, escapes on her fiery chariot. In the forest of Ardennes, a herald announces the tournament which will take place in Byzantium, for which the hand of Esclarmonde will be the prize. Parséis goes to see Phorcas and tells him what has happened. The old Emperor summons Esclarmonde and decides that in return for her disobedience, she must forfeit the throne and her magical powers, and that Roland will die if Esclarmonde does not give up her love for him. So Esclarmonde meets Roland and tells him that she can no longer love him. Roland, now desiring only death, goes to the tournament in Byzantium. But the young knight wins the tournament and presents himself before the veiled young woman who will be the winner's bride. At this point, Esclarmonde reveals her true identity to Roland, and there is general rejoicing for the two lovers.

Esclarmonde, while clearly influenced to some extent by Wagner, shows how Massenet is already using his own particular musical language and has a distinct personality.

ESPERIAN, KALLEN

(Waukegan, Illinois 1961)

American soprano of Armenian descent. She studied music at the University of Illinois and began her artistic career as a mezzo-soprano,

Above: The soprano Kallen Esperian

Left: Another scene from *Erwartung*, performed by the soprano Kallen Esperian.

appearing in theaters and concert halls in America. In 1985 she won first prize in the Pavarotti Competition in Philadelphia. This led to Esperian being engaged to sing Mimi with Pavarotti on a tour of China with the orchestra and chorus of Genoa's Teatro Comunale. Esperian received considerable further acclaim as Mimi at the Vienna Staatsoper (1986), the Deutsche Oper Berlin (1986), Lyric Opera of Chicago (1987) and the Metropolitan Opera House, New York (1989). In 1989 she took over from Katia Ricciarelli in *Luisa Miller*, and in the following year scored a personal triumph as Desdemona in Verdi's *Otello* at the Opéra Bastille in Paris.

ESTES, SIMON

(Centerville, Iowa 1938)

American bass-baritone. He studied singing at the Juilliard School in New York and subsequently in Europe, where he embarked on his artistic career at the Hamburg Opera. Engagements followed at the Deutsche Oper in Berlin and other opera houses in Europe and the United States (including Rome, San Francisco, and Chicago), and from 1978 he appeared at the Bayreuth Festival in Wagner's Der fliegende Holländer (The Flying Dutchman) and *Parsifal*. Since 1982 he has been a regular guest with the Metropolitan Opera, New York, where his roles have included Wotan, Boris, Orest, Porgy, etc.

Above: Bass-baritone Simon Estes in a scene from *Don Carlos*.

ESULE DI ROMA, L'

(The Exile from Rome)

Opera in two acts by Gaetano Donizetti (1797–1848), to a libretto by Domenico Gilardoni based on Caigniez's Androclès. *First performance: Naples, Teatro San Carlo, 1 January 1828.*

The action takes place in Rome during the reign of Tiberius. Murena (bass), a senator, has caused Settimio (tenor), the bridegroom-to-be of his daughter Argelia (soprano), to be condemned and sent into exile. In order to be able to see his beloved again, Settimio secretly returns to Rome, but he is discovered and sentenced to death. At this point the implacable Murena is overcome with remorse: he exonerates Settimio, publicly declares him innocent and consents to his marriage to Argelia.

Thanks to the strong cast of singers who took part in the Naples premiere, *L'esule di Roma* was a sensational success. Audiences were equally positive when the work was subsequently performed at a number of other opera houses.

ETOILE, L'

(The Star)

Opéra-comique *in three acts by Emmanuel Chabrier (1841–1894), to a libretto by Eugène Leterrier and Albert Vanloo. First performance: Paris, Théâtre des Bouffes-Parisiens, 28 November 1877.*

King Ouf I (tenor), goes among his people in disguise to find some of his opponents to execute, a spectacle to which he treats his subjects every year. Meanwhile, and also incognito, Laoula (soprano), daughter of King Mataquin, and King Ouf's bride-to-be, arrives with the retinue of Prince Hérisson de Porc-Epic. Laoula is actually in love with Lazuli (soprano), a young pedlar, with whom she has lost all contact. Lazuli has been imprisoned for speaking against King Ouf. This provides Ouf with an offender to put to death, but Siroco (bass), the court astrologer, warns the King that if Lazuli were to die, the King would meet the same fate the next day. The young pedlar, having now become the object of constant attention, wishes to regain his freedom and attempts to escape but is mortally wounded by a guard. In despair, Ouf compels Laoula to marry him so that he may have an heir before he dies. The wedding ceremony is about to begin. Although the clocks have all been put back to postpone the hour foretold for King Ouf's death, the moment finally comes. But nothing happens. Suddenly, Lazuli appears, miraculously restored to life. Lazuli marries his beloved Laoula amid general rejoicing.

Despite the rather cool reception given to the work at its first performance, *L'etoile*, Chabrier's first composition for the theater, is an opera rich in verve and ingenious in its ideas, particularly in the comic passages.

ETOILE DU NORD, L'

(The North Star)

Opera in three acts by Giacomo Meyerbeer (1791–1864), to a libretto by Eugène Scribe. First performance: Paris, Théâtre de l'Opéra-Comique, 16 February 1854.

The subject of the opera is the story of Katherine (soprano), a Russian countrywoman, who, disguised as a man, takes the place of her own brother in the army of Tsar Peter (baritone). This gives her the opportunity of informing the Tsar of a plot being hatched against him. The Tsar falls in love with the young woman, marries her and makes her his Tsarina.

In *L'etoile du nord*, Meyerbeer introduced a number of passages from a previous *Singspiel*, *Ein Feldlager in Schlesien* (An Encampment in Silesia), written specially for the famous singer Jenny Lind. The opera was later revised and renamed *Wielka.*

ETRANGER, L'

(The Outsider)

Opera in two acts by Vincent d'Indy (1851–1931), to the composer's own libretto. First performance: Brussels, Théâtre de la Monnaie, 7 January 1903.

The Outsider (L'Etranger) is an individual who has sacrificed all human feelings in the interests of his ideal, without having understood that human endeavour is useless if driven by selfish individualism. He sails the oceans on a never-ending voyage, managing always to dominate the power of the sea thanks to an emerald in his possession, which had once belonged to St Paul. The Outsider is in love with Vita, a young woman who does not understand his apparently cold and insensitive behaviour and so attempts to make him jealous and persuades him to reveal the secret of the emerald. As a result, however, the emerald loses its power. So Vita throws the amulet into the sea, unleashing a tempest which capsizes the boat. No one dares to come to the aid of the shipwrecked pair, and though The Outsider, with Vita at his side, courageously faces up to the raging sea, their vessel sinks beneath the waves.

There are clear echoes of Wagner in the mysterious and symbolic atmosphere of this opera (as found in *Der fliegende Holländer*, The Flying Dutchman) and in its romantic mysticism, which recalls *Lohengrin*. The best passages are to be found in the second act, where d'Indy gives full reign to his creative talents. Debussy's view of *L'Etranger* was very positive: "This opera is an object lesson for those who believe in the crude imported aesthetics which would have us smother the music under mountains of realism."

EUGENE ONEGIN

See *Evgenij Onegin*

EURIDICE

Musical fable in a prologue and six scenes by Jacopo Peri (1561–1633), to a text by Ottavio Rinuccini. First performance, Florence, Palazzo Pitti, 6 October 1600, on the occasion of the wedding of Maria de' Medici and Henri IV of France.

After a prologue in which Tragedy (contralto) announces the subject of the opera and extends a greeting to the royal spectators, shepherds and nymphs celebrate the wedding-day of Orfeo (tenor) and Euridice (soprano). They are joined by Euridice herself, who leads them in a dance of joy. Orfeo sings of his own happiness and prays to the gods that it may last. After Euridice has gone away, the messenger Dafne (soprano) arrives with the sad news that the young bride has died from a poisonous snake-bite; Orfeo is overcome with despair and wants to kill himself, but Venus (contralto) appears and encourages him to make the descent into Hades to ask Plutone to give him back his beloved. On his arrival in the Underworld, Orfeo touches the hearts of Plutone (bass) and Proserpina (contralto) with his sorrowful singing. Euridice is restored to him unconditionally. Back on earth, the nymphs and shepherds are waiting anxiously. Then the young couple appear and there are dances and choruses to celebrate their happiness.

The opera is based on recitative and highlighted by melodic passages in which the melody itself, while not actually amounting to an "aria," adopts an unusual beauty of line, and the precise way in which the music punctuates the words conveys the impression of true feeling.

EURYANTHE

Romantic opera in three acts by Carl Maria von Weber (1786–1826), to a libretto by Helmina von Chézy based on the medieval story Histoire de Gérard de Nevers et de la belle et vertueuse Euryanthe de Savoie. *First performance: Vienna, Kärntnertortheater, 25 October 1823.*

The action takes place at the castles of Premery and Nevers around the year 1100. At the court of Louis VI (bass), Count Adolar (tenor) is singing the praises of his young wife, Euryanthe of Savoy (soprano). The jealous Count Lysiart (baritone) raises doubts as to the possibility that there is such a person as a truly virtuous woman. Adolar challenges him to a duel, but Lysiart gets out of it and launches a different kind of challenge: if he does not succeed in seducing Euryanthe, he will forfeit everything he possesses, whereas if Adolar loses, then he will have to give up everything instead. Meanwhile, Euryanthe confides in her friend Eglantine (soprano), who is secretly in love with Adolar, revealing to her a distressing family secret: Adolar's sister, Emma, had taken her own life. Lysiart despairs of ever succeeding in his ambition to seduce Euryanthe but finds support from an unexpected quarter when Eglantine tells him Adolar's secret and hands him a ring which Adolar had once given to Euryanthe. As a result of this, Adolar's joy on his return at being reunited with his wife is short-lived: Lysiart shows Adolar the ring, explaining that he has been given it by Euryanthe as a pledge of her love. Adolar imagines he has been betrayed and abandons Euryanthe in the forest. In her desperate plight, Euryanthe happens to meet the King, who is out hunting, and tells him about the shameful wager of which she has been made the target. The King believes her story and promises that she will have justice. Meanwhile, Lysiart marries Eglantine. A chance remark from Eglantine leads Adolar to understand that he has been misled about Euryanthe. He challenges Lysiart to a duel, but the King arrives with the news that Euryanthe has died of grief. Eglantine is overcome with remorse and admits to the deception; thus unmasked, Lysiart kills her and is arrested. Euryanthe, who is not really dead but has only fainted, returns and embraces her husband.

Euryanthe was a triumph. The work is a heroic grand opera, praised by Beethoven but criticized by Schubert as unmusical.

Above: Jacopo Peri as Orfeo in the first performance of his opera, *Euridice*.

DER EVANGELIMANN

(The Evangelist)

Opera in two acts by Wilhelm Kienzl (1857–1941), to a libretto by the composer, based on the story by Leopold Florian Meissner (1894). First performance: Staatsoper, Berlin, 4 May 1895.

Johannes Fredhofer, a teacher at the Benedictine Monastery of St. Othmar, loves Martha, the daughter of the provost, and is jealous of his brother, Mathis, a chancellor at the same monastery, with whom the girl is in love. When he is not able to separate the two lovers he tells the authorities of their relationship and has Mathis expelled from the monastery. He then causes a fire, for which Mathis is blamed and sentenced to twenty years in prison. Magdalena, Martha's friend, meets him thirty years later. Mathis tells her that when he came out of prison and learned that Martha had been unable to get over her grief and had killed herself, he had become an evangelist preacher. Magdalena is looking after Johannes, who is stricken with remorse and near to death. She persuades the two brothers to meet. Although he does not recognize him, Johannes confesses his guilt to his brother, who absolves him.

Of the composer's operas *Der Evangelimann* was the only one to meet with lasting success.

EVANS, SIR GERAINT

(Pontypridd 1922–Aberaeron 1992)

Welsh baritone. After musical training at the Guildhall School of Music, he went on to study in Hamburg and Geneva. He made his debut at Covent Garden in *Die Meistersinger von Nürnberg* in 1948. Even though his name was particularly associated with Covent Garden, Sir Geraint had a busy international career which, between 1949 and the mid 1960s, included appearances at the leading opera houses and festivals of Europe and the United States. His vast operatic repertoire ranged from Mozart to Donizetti (*L'elisir d'amore* and *Don Pasquale*), Verdi (*Falstaff*) and Berg (*Wozzeck*), Tippett and Britten, and he sang in the world premiere's of Britten's operas *Billy Budd* (1951), *Gloriana* (1953) and *Troilus and Cressida* (1954).

Above: A scene from *Evgenij Onegin*, in a production at the Bolshoi.

EVGENIJ ONEGIN

(Eugene Onegin)

Opera in three acts by Peter Ilyich Tchaikovsky (1840–1893), to a libretto by K. S. Shilovsky and Modest Ilyich Tchaikovsky based on the poem of the same name by Pushkin. First (student) performance: the theater of the Moscow Conservatory, 29 March 1879. Official first performance: Moscow, Bolshoi Theater, 23 April 1881.

The action takes place in St. Petersburg at the beginning of the nineteenth century. In her garden, the widow Làrina (mezzo-soprano), together with her two daughters Olga (contralto) and Tatyana (soprano), celebrates the completion of the harvest. Lensky (tenor), Olga's fiancé, and a friend of his, Eugene Onegin (baritone), a stylish, educated, skeptical and egotistical young man, arrive on a visit. Onegin makes an impression on Tatyana, who falls in love with him. That same night, Tatyana writes Onegin a long, impassioned letter, in which she reveals her feelings. At their next meeting, Onegin is polite but cool: he does not feel suited to marriage and begs Tatyana to forget about him. Not long after, during Tatyana's birthday celebrations, Onegin irritates Lensky by flirting with Olga. Lensky challenges him to a duel. At dawn the following day, the two rivals appear to hesitate as their encounter draws near, because of the ties of friendship they had enjoyed until the previous day. But the rules of honour prevail, and Lensky falls, fatally wounded by the first shot. A few years later, during a party at the palace of Prince Gremin (bass) in St. Petersburg, Onegin sees Tatyana again: she is now the wife of the Prince, and he discovers a great passion for her. In response to Onegin's requests, Tatyana receives him in private. Faced with Onegin's passionate declarations of love, Tatyana, though inwardly hesitating, stays firm in her faithfulness to her husband, resolutely rejects Onegin's proposals that they run away together, and bids him farewell forever.

This is undoubtedly Tchaikovsky's theatrical masterpiece. The music is effortless and spontaneous, typical of Tchaikovsky, and contains all the European musical influences (French, Italian and German) The result is a musical score that is a perfect reflection of the inherent sentiment of opera.

EWING, MARIA

(Detroit 1950)

American mezzo-soprano and soprano. She studied with Eleanor Steber in Cleveland and Jennie Tourel in New York and earned her first major success as Cherubino in *Le nozze di Figaro* with the Metropolitan Opera, New York. She then appeared at La Scala in Milan (*Pelléas et Mélisande*, 1976) and the Salzburg Festival (*Le nozze di Figaro*), and from 1978 she sang at the Glyndebourne Festival in the roles of Dorabella, Rosina (*Il barbiere di Siviglia*), the Composer (*Ariadne auf Naxos*), Poppea (*L'incoronazione di Poppea*) and Carmen. In 1988 she made her first appearance at Covent Garden as Salomé in a sensational production of Strauss's opera by her then husband Sir Peter Hall. Ewing is gifted with vocal skills but above all with extraordinary talents as a performer, and these qualities were in evidence again the first time she sang the lead in *Tosca* in Los Angeles in 1990.

F

FALLA, MANUEL DE

(Cadiz 1876–Alta Gracia, Argentina 1946) Spanish composer. Born into a wealthy family, he received his earliest musical education from his parents. He then attended the Madrid Conservatory, where he studied piano with Jose Tragó and composition with Felipe Pedrell. His career as a composer was very active from the outset, and he quickly completed works for piano and five *zarzuelas*, among them *Los amores de la Inés* (1902). He made his mark immediately as one of the most important figures in Spanish music. In 1905, his one-act opera *La vida breve* won the Real Academia de Bellas Artes prize. As well as his famous ballets, *El amor brujo* (1915) and *El sombrero de tres picos* (1919), de Falla wrote an opera for puppets, *El retablo de Maese Pedro* (1923), and in 1927 he began to compose *Atlantida*, a work he never finished. This opera, or rather "scenic cantata," was completed by his pupil Ernesto Halffter and given a concert performance in Barcelona in 1961 and at La Scala, Milan, in 1962.

FALSTAFF

Comic opera in three acts by Giuseppe Verdi (1813–1901), to a libretto by Arrigo Boito, from Shakespeare, in particular The Merry Wives of Windsor. *First performance: Milan, La Scala, 9 February 1893.*

• The action takes place in Windsor in the fifteenth century. The old knight John Falstaff (baritone), convinced that he is still irresistibly attractive to women, writes two identical letters, one to Alice Ford (soprano), the other to Meg Page (mezzo-soprano), in which he asks each to meet him. The two women receive the letters and, after taking Mistress Quickly (contralto) into their confidence, decide to play a practical joke on Falstaff. Alice Ford lets Falstaff know that she will see him between two and three o'clock. So Falstaff goes to Alice's house. Alice accepts the knight's attentions, but keeps him at arm's length. In rushes Mistress Quickly to announce the arrival of Meg Page, who in turn announces the arrival of Alice Ford's husband (baritone). The women hide Falstaff in a laundry basket while the jealous Ford, certain that his wife has betrayed him, searches the house from top to bottom. Meanwhile the women tip the laundry basket, with Falstaff inside it, into the Thames. Later, while Falstaff is still boiling with rage from this treatment, Mistress Quickly arrives and, begging Falstaff's pardon, informs him that Alice will be waiting for him at midnight in the royal park. Meanwhile, Ford, who is now sure that his wife has remained faithful to him, decides to take part in this new hoax. More than that, he decides that that very evening he will hold the wedding of his daughter Nannetta (soprano) to the elderly Doctor Cajus (tenor), taking advantage of the fact that everyone will be in disguise. But Mistress Quickly overhears this and runs to warn Nannetta to enable her to thwart these plans. Falstaff keeps his appointment in the park, and Alice pretends to accept his declarations of love. Suddenly Meg appears and announces a witches' sabbath, whereupon a horde of people dressed as goblins jump on Falstaff, torment him and give him a good beating. When he realizes that he has been duped, the old knight repents. At this point, Ford blesses the couples who are about to be married, but at the last minute it is realized that Nannetta is marrying her beloved Fenton (tenor) and that the "bride" of Doctor Cajus is Bardolfo (tenor), Falstaff's servant disguised as the Queen of the Fairies. By now it is too late to change things, and the opera ends with the message that "All the world's a jest."

Falstaff was Verdi's last opera, in which, thanks not least to the literary consistency of Boito's libretto, the composer was able to convey an extraordinary freshness of inspiration as well as exceptional vitality of expression. Verdi's masterly orchestration in this opera took him almost a year to compose. A meticulous work, it was immediately and enthusiastically acclaimed by the audience at the premiere.

Left: A portrait of the Spanish composer Manuel De Falla by Picasso.

Above: A scene from Verdi's *Falstaff.*

FANCIULLA DEL WEST, LA

(The Girl of the Golden West)

Opera in three acts by Giacomo Puccini (1858–1924), to a libretto by Carlo Zangarini and Guelfo Civinini, from David Belasco's play The Girl of the Golden West. *First performance: New York, Metropolitan Opera House, 10 December 1910.*

The action takes place at a camp for prospectors during the Gold Rush in California about 1850. The prospectors gather at the Polka Saloon, which is run by Minnie (soprano). Among the customers is the sheriff, Jack Rance (baritone): he is trying to attract the attention of Minnie, with whom he is in love. A stranger by the name of Dick Johnson (tenor) arrives; he is none other than the notorious bandit Ramerrez, who has come to steal the gold which the prospectors have handed over to Minnie for safe-keeping. Minnie, who has previously met Johnson, protects him from Rance's searching and jealous questions. Johnson/Ramerrez inwardly gives up the idea of the robbery which he had planned. Minnie invites him to continue their conversation at her house. Later, while Minnie and Johnson are declaring their love to each other, the sheriff and his men, by now on the bandit's trail, arrive on the scene. Minnie has found Johnson somewhere to hide and tells them she is alone in the house. No sooner has Rance gone away than Johnson reveals his true identity to Minnie. She is furious at having been deceived and insists that he leave. Johnson goes out, but a few minutes later drags himself back to Minnie's door with a gun-shot wound. She takes pity on him, helps him inside and hides him in the attic. Rance returns and discovers the wounded bandit. In desperation, Minnie persuades the sheriff to gamble with her for Johnson's life. She cheats and wins. Not long after, however, Johnson is captured and about to be hanged. Minnie bursts in, brandishing a pistol, and makes an impassioned speech in which she pleads with the prospectors to spare the bandit's life. Despite protests from Rance, Johnson is freed. After bidding farewell to the crowd, Johnson and Minnie set off together.

La fanciulla del West scored a triumph with its American audience, whereas the critics were not so enthusiastic, praising only the composer's masterly technique. The opera is undoubtedly seen as "different" from the rest of Puccini's output, in view of its obviously bold use of harmony in the manner of Strauss and Debussy. For these reasons, it is not as popular as *Tosca* or *La bohème* and is one of the least often staged of Puccini's operas.

Above: A scene from *La fanciulla del West* by Puccini.

Right: The American soprano Carole Farley.

FARLEY, CAROLE

(Le Mars, Iowa 1946)

American soprano. She studied first in the United States, then in Europe, where she was taught by Marianne Schech in Munich. After making her debut in Linz in 1969, she quickly made her name from performances at leading opera houses in Germany and subsequently in Belgium and France. In 1975 she appeared for the first time at the Metropolitan Opera House, New York, in the role of Mimi in *La bohème*, and sang in Offenbach's *La belle Hélène* at the New York City Opera. As well as fine vocal qualities, Farley is gifted with great musicianship and performance skills combined with a striking stage presence, which have contributed to her outstanding accounts both of traditional roles such as Violetta and Manon, etc., and less typical ones, such as Lulu in Berg's opera and the lead in Poulenc's *La voix humaine*.

FARNACE, IL

Opera in three acts by Antonio Vivaldi (1678–1741), to a libretto by Antonio Maria Lucchini. First performance: Venice, Teatro di Sant'Angelo, Carnival 1727.

The action takes place in the city of Heraclea, the capital of Pontus. Farnace (alto *castrato*), usurper of the throne of Pontus after the death of King Ariarte, has married the dead King's daughter, Tamiri (contralto). Berenice (contralto), widow of Ariarte and Tamiri's mother, had fled to Rome to seek assistance against the usurper and has now returned to Heraclea with an army commanded by Pompeo (alto *castrato*). The city falls into Roman hands, and Selinda (soprano), Farnace's sister, is taken prisoner and escorted to the enemy camp. Here the Roman captain Gilade (soprano *castrato*) falls in love with her. Selinda hopes to enlist Gilade's help in support of her brother Farnace. Tamiri, taken before Pompeo and Berenice, refuses to hand over her son to the enemy. In order to appease the vengeful fury of her mother, Tamiri shows her the child, but Berenice, remaining implacable, turns down all gestures of peace. Meanwhile, with Gilade's help, Selinda attempts to have her brother, Tamiri and their son set free, but Farnace refuses to give in. Selinda has also been assured of the support of Aquilio (alto *castrato*), another Roman captain. In response to a plea by Tamiri, Pompeo frees the child, but at that very moment comes the news that Farnace has also been imprisoned. The prisoner tries to conceal his true identity but is recognized by Berenice. Farnace is condemned to death but is saved by the intervention of Gilade and his soldiers. Farnace then orders that Pompeo be spared, but not Berenice. Seeing all her plans of revenge evaporate, Berenice, armed with a sword, pounces on Tamiri and threatens to kill her. Pompeo arrives just in time and manages to calm both women, as a result of which Berenice and Farnace are reconciled. Selinda marries Gilade, and the opera ends happily.

As with many eighteenth-century scores, there are two different versions of *Il Farnace* in existence. The first is the one performed in Venice in 1727, and subsequently revived in Ferrara. The second version was probably prepared by Vivaldi for a performance in Prague in 1730. In this second score, Vivaldi made some changes, the most significant of which involved adapting the vocal parts to suit a new cast of singers: the role of Selinda was to be sung by a mezzo-soprano instead of a soprano, while Farnace, in a move fairly unusual at that time, was altered to a tenor voice instead of an alto *castrato*.

FARRELL, EILEEN

(Willimantic, Connecticut 1920)

American soprano. She studied singing in New York with Merle Alcock and Eleanor McLellan and made her debut in a concert on CBS (1940), continuing to sing for this network in broadcasts over the next five years. In 1950 and 1955 she took the lead in two concert performances of Berg's *Wozzeck* at Carnegie Hall and in Cherubini's *Medea* at the New York City Town Hall. Her proper theater debut was in 1956, the year in which she sang Leonora in *Il trovatore* in San Francisco. Engagements followed in Chicago (*La Gioconda*) and at the Metropolitan Opera House, New York (1960–65). After retirement from the stage, she concentrated on teaching. The character of Farrell's voice, which has a Wagnerian quality (although she never performed Wagner on stage), won her acclaim above all in the Italian repertoire, especially for her majestic Elisabetta in the recording of Donizetti's *Maria Stuarda* with Beverly Sills (1971).

Above: The German mezzo-soprano Brigitte Fassbaender.

FASSBAENDER, BRIGITTE

(Berlin 1939)

German mezzo-soprano. She studied music with her father, Willi Domgraf-Fassbaender, and at the Conservatory in Nuremberg. In 1961 she made her debut as Nicklausse in *Les contes d'Hoffmann* at the Bayerische Staatsoper in Munich and then joined the resident company there. She made successful appearances at leading opera houses in Germany and across Europe and America. Fassbaender has had a very active career as a recording artist, and, thanks to her outstanding musical gifts and stylistic elegance, she has earned particular distinction as Cherubino in *Le nozze di Figaro*, Octavian in *Der Rosenkavalier*, Hänsel in *Hänsel und Gretel* and Countess Geschwitz in *Lulu*, as well as in leading Wagnerian roles (Fricka, Brangäne, etc.). She is also a concert artist, with impressive performances in oratorio and *Lieder* recitals to her name.

FAURÉ, GABRIEL

(Pamiers, Ariège 1845–Paris 1924)

French composer. Prodigiously gifted in music, he was only nine when he started attending Niedermeyer's school (1854–66). He also studied with Saint-Saëns and in 1866 became the organist in Rennes, subsequently being appointed organist at the church of Notre-Dame de Clingancourt in Paris (1870). After the Franco-Prussian war, he was the organist at Saint-Sulpice (1871) and from 1877 choirmaster and then official organist at the Madeleine (1896). In the same year he was elected to the chair of composition (succeeding Massenet) at the Paris Conservatoire, where his pupils included Ravel, Enescu, Koechlin, Boulanger and other important composers of the twentieth-century French school. His remarkable output of sacred and secular vocal music included a famous *Requiem* (1877) as well as the song cycles *La bonne chanson* (1891) and *Le jardin clos* (1915). He wrote two operas, *Prométhée* (1900) and *Pénélope* (1913), the latter being considered his masterpiece.

FAUST

Opera in five acts by Charles Gounod (1818–1893), to a libretto by Jules Barbier and Michel Carré, based on Goethe's Faust. *First performance: Paris, Théâtre Lyrique, 19 March 1859.*

The action takes place in Germany during the sixteenth century. The aged philosopher Faust (tenor) ponders with deep regret his solitary life and how devoid it is of youthfulness and love. He is about to take poison when Méphistophélès (bass) appears to him dressed as a gentleman and offers him youth and pleasures in exchange for his soul. Faust hesitates, but when he sees a vision of Marguerite conjured up by Méphistophélès he agrees to the pact. Not long after, there is a public holiday. Valentin (baritone), Marguerite's brother, is leaving to go to war and entrusts his sister to the care of Siebel (mezzo-

soprano), a student who is in love with her. Faust, now transformed into a young knight, approaches Marguerite and asks if he may escort her home. The young woman refuses and sets off on her own, but Méphistophélès reassures Faust, promising him that Marguerite will be his. In Marguerite's garden, Faust is deeply moved by her charm. He no longer wants to seduce her, but Méphistophélès urges him not to delay. In the night, Marguerite appears on her balcony and calls to Faust. He hurries to her side. Later, Marguerite, who is now expecting a child, cannot even pray anymore because Méphistophélès prevents her from doing so. Now back from the war, Valentin learns that Faust has seduced his sister, challenges him to a duel but is mortally wounded. Marguerite, now in prison awaiting execution, has gone mad and has killed Faust's child. Faust comes to see her. He attempts to persuade her to escape with him, but Marguerite becomes delirious, and after calling on God to forgive her, she dies. A choir of angels accompanies Marguerite's soul to heaven, while Faust is left praying on his knees.

Gounod gave everything he had to the composition of this work, but it was not warmly received and only earned the recognition it deserved after being performed in Germany and Italy. To this day, *Faust* is regarded as Gounod's best opera.

Above: A scene from *Faust* in a performance at the Paris Opéra.

Right: A drawing of J.-B. Faure as Méphistophélès in *Faust*.

FAUSTA

Opera consisting of an introduction and two acts by Gaetano Donizetti (1797–1848), to a libretto by Domenico Gilardoni, Andrea Tottola and the composer himself. First performance: Naples, Teatro San Carlo, 12 January 1832.

The action takes place in Rome in 326 B.C. In Piazza del Campidoglio, the Emperor Costantino (baritone), his second wife Fausta (soprano) and the whole of Rome are celebrating the return of the Emperor's son Crispo (tenor) from a victorious campaign in Gaul. Among the prisoners-of-war is the Princess Irella (mezzo-soprano), who is in love with Crispo. Crispo, who returns Irella's love, asks his father if he may marry her, and Costantino agrees. But Fausta, who is secretly in love with her stepson, asks that the wedding be postponed for the time being. Later, in a dramatic encounter, Fausta tells Crispo of her feelings. The young man is initially horrified but then throws himself at Fausta's feet and asks for her compassion. Costantino enters and finds Crispo in this position, whereupon Fausta, out of revenge, accuses Crispo of having attempted to seduce her. In great indignation, the Emperor sends his son into exile. At nightfall, Crispo has a secret meeting with Irella and discovers a gathering of conspirators led by Massimiano (bass), the ousted emperor and Fausta's father, who are plotting Costantino's downfall. They leave the scene, and the Emperor and his retinue arrive. They come upon Crispo in possession of weapons, and he is accused of attempted patricide. Massimiano himself, who is also leader of the Roman Senate, condemns Crispo to death. Only when the sentence has been carried out does Costantino discover Massimiano's plot. Fausta, after vainly attempting to save Crispo, is overcome with remorse, takes poison and, before dying, reveals her guilt to a despairing Costantino.

After the great triumph of *Anna Bolena* (1830) in Milan, which firmly established Donizetti's reputation, he returned to Naples, where he composed *Francesca di Foix* and *La romanziera e l'uomo nero* in 1831 and *Fausta* in 1832. *Fausta* provides clear evidence of Donizetti's maturity as a dramatist in his masterly characterization of the individual roles, especially those of Fausta and Costantino.

FAVORITE, LA

(The Favourite)

Opera in four acts by Gaetano Donizetti (1797–1848), to a libretto by Alphonse Royer, Gustav Vaëz and Eugène Scribe, from Baculard d'Arnaud's play Le Comte de Comminges. *First performance: Paris, Académie Royale de Musique (Opéra), 2 December 1840.*

The action takes place in Castile in 1340. ACT I. The monastery of St. James of Compostela. Fernand (tenor), a novice, confesses to the Father Superior, Balthazar (bass), that he is in love with a woman whose name he does not know. In spite of Balthazar's warnings, Fernand decides to leave the monastery and become acquainted with the woman. Fernand arrives on the shore of the island of León, accompanied by Inez (soprano), the unknown woman's confidante. Then the woman loved by Fernand, Léonore (mezzo-soprano), appears and orders him not to try to see her any more. The sudden announcement of the arrival of the King makes Léonore hurry away. Fernand decides to go in search of glory and honour in order to be able to win the hand of his beloved. ACT II. The gardens of the Alcazar. King Alphonse XI (baritone) is more determined than ever to marry his mistress, Léonore de Gusman, now that he has left his wife. But Léonore feels humiliated by the position that she occupies at court. Enter Don Gaspare (tenor), an official to the King, who has intercepted a love letter addressed to Léonore, and Alphonse wants to discover who has written it. The scene changes to a banqueting room in the royal palace, where celebrations are being held in honour of Fernand, who has just returned from a decisive victory over the Arabs. Meanwhile, Father Balthazar has arrived to ask the King for an explanation of his undignified behaviour. As a gesture of defiance, Alphonse introduces him to his new bride, Léonore. Balthazar then publicly serves Alphonse with a writ of papal excommunication and curses the couple. ACT III. As a reward for Fernand's courage, Alphonse agrees that he should marry the woman he loves. When Fernand reveals that she is Léonore, the King gives his consent just the same. In anguish, Léonore does not want to deceive Fernand and sends Inez to tell him the truth about her; but Inez is arrested on the King's orders. The wedding celebrations begin. The King decorates Fernand for his honourable achievements. Don Gaspare and the knights comment ironically on Fernand's wedding. He takes offense at this and challenges all of them to a duel. Balthazar intervenes and tells Fernand the truth, that he has just married the King's mistress. Enraged, Fernand breaks his sword in two, throws his decorations on the ground and storms out, followed by Balthazar. ACT IV. In front of the Church of St. James of Compostela. Balthazar, Fernand and the monks are praying among the tombs. A pilgrim approaches Fernand and collapses from exhaustion: it is Léonore,

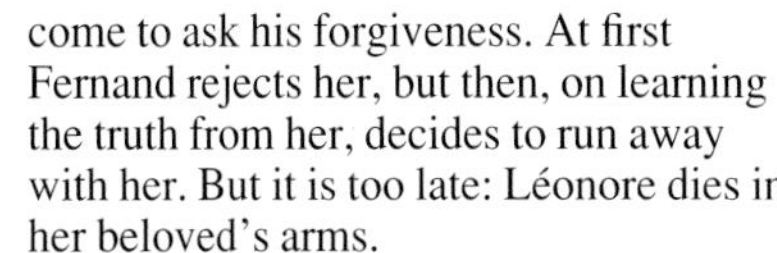

come to ask his forgiveness. At first Fernand rejects her, but then, on learning the truth from her, decides to run away with her. But it is too late: Léonore dies in her beloved's arms.

This opera was due to be performed in three acts at the Théâtre de la Renaissance under the title *L'angelo di Nisida*. But the theater was then closed, and so *La favorite* was transferred to the Académie Royale de Musique. For this performance, Donizetti added a fourth act, on which he worked with Scribe. Despite the poor quality of the libretto, Donizetti managed to turn *La favorite* into the opera which, together with *Lucia di Lammermoor*, is his most accomplished tragic creation. The first three acts are markedly inferior to the fourth, in which Donizetti achieves moments of great inspiration. The opera's success was enormous and enduring.

FEDORA

Opera in three acts by Umberto Giordano (1867–1948), to a libretto by Arturo Colautti, based on the play of the same name by Victorien Sardou. First performance: Milan, Teatro Lirico, 17 November 1898.

The action takes place around the end of the nineteenth century. Count Vladimir Andreyevich, engaged to be married to the Princess Fedora Romanov (soprano), is killed in St. Petersburg under mysterious circumstances. Suspicion falls on Loris Ipanov (tenor), who has unaccountably left the city. Fedora vows to trace him in order to be avenged. The scene changes to Paris and Fedora's house where a reception is being held at which Loris is one of the guests. Fedora has managed to make Loris fall in love with her in order to make him confess to the crime. Loris admits to having struck Vladimir, but the motive was one of honour, and he promises her that he will bring her proof within two hours. In the meantime, Fedora reports Loris to the police and accuses Loris's brother of having taken part in an attempt on the Tsar's life. When Loris returns, he tells Fedora that Vladimir had been his wife's lover for some time, and shows her the evidence, a number of letters written by

Left: A scene from *La favorite* by Donizetti.

Vladimir to his beloved. Fedora is astonished and feels all the love she has had for Vladimir's memory turning to hatred. At the same time, she senses that Loris is winning her heart, and she prevents him from being arrested by the police. Loris and Fedora live happily in Switzerland. But then comes the sad news that Loris's brother has been arrested and has died in prison, and his mother has died of grief. Loris also finds out that the accusations made against his brother came from a woman whose identity was never revealed. Loris curses the unknown accuser and swears that he will discover her identity so that he can kill her. In vain Fedora asks him to forgive "that woman." But Loris will not hear of it. Now afraid that she will be unmasked, Fedora takes poison. Loris realizes too late that he has been the cause of her suicide, and Fedora dies asking him to forgive her.

Fedora was Giordano's most successful work after *Andrea Chénier*. The Italian composer Pizzetti thought the opera showed an "extraordinary sense of theater."

FEDOSEYEV, VLADIMIR

(Leningrad 1932)

Fedoseyev was principal conductor of the Soviet Radio and Television Orchestra from 1974. He pursued an active international career which took him to the leading European countries and the United States, and established his reputation as one of the greatest interpreters of the Russian symphonic and operatic repertoire.

FEDRA

Tragic opera in three acts by Ildebrando Pizzetti (1880–1968), to a libretto by Gabriele D'Annunzio, based on his play of the same name. First performance: Milan, La Scala, 20 March 1915.

In Greece, the mothers of the heroes who have fought at Thebes are awaiting the arrival of King Teseo (baritone), bearing the ashes of the battle-dead. A false rumour tells of the King's death. Fedra (mezzo-soprano), his wife, is secretly glad to hear this news: she is in love with her stepson, Ippolito (tenor), and hopes to be able to win the young man's heart now that her husband is dead. But Teseo reappears in the city, and among the gifts he has brought for Ippolito is a very beautiful slave-girl, Ippanoe (soprano). Fedra is jealous of the young woman, initially flatters her, then threatens her, and finally drags her to the altar of Jupiter, where she kills her. It is not long before Ippolito is asking Fedra about the cause of Ippanoe's death, but he soon falls asleep from the fatigue of a long ride on horseback. Fedra then approaches him and kisses him, whereupon Ippolito wakes up and tells his stepmother to go away. Fedra is maddened by the pain of this rejection and longs first to have her revenge and then to take her own life. When Teseo arrives, Fedra accuses Ippolito of having raped her. The King is furious and calls upon the god of the sea to kill his son. Not long afterwards, Teseo is summoned to the seashore and is overwhelmed by the sight of his son's body: he had been thrown from his horse and the animal had become wild and torn him to pieces. Fedra arrives. She has already drunk poison and admits that she alone is to blame. Now Ippolito is hers. Fedra collapses over her stepson's body and dies.

The first performance of the opera was cancelled at the publisher Sonzogno's request and replaced with *Parisina*, another opera with a libretto by D'Annunzio and music by Mascagni.

FEEN, DIE

(The Fairies)

Romantic opera in three acts by Richard Wagner (1813–1883), to the composer's own libretto based on Carlo Gozzi's play La donna serpente. *First performance: Munich, Königliches Hof- und Nationaltheater, 29 June 1888.*

During a shooting party, Prince Arindal (tenor) dives into a river and finds himself in a mysterious kingdom. Here he falls in love with the enigmatic and beautiful Ada (soprano) and becomes her husband, but he must not ask her who she is or where she comes from until eight years have passed. At the end of the eighth year, Arindal can no longer resist questioning her. She answers that she is a fairy, whereupon she, the castle, and their children vanish. Arindal is determined to defeat the law governing the fairy world

Above: A sketch by N. Benois for Umberto Giordano's *Fedora*.

Right: The Russian conductor Vladimir Fedoseyev.

which, he being human and they immortal, he cannot accept. But first he has to face some difficult challenges. Arindal remains steadfast. With the help of the magician Groma (bass), he goes down into the Underworld and overcomes monsters and evil spirits before reaching the hallowed place of the fairies, where he finds Ada has been turned to stone. He frees her with the power of his singing, but Ada cannot become a human woman. Then Arindal, driven by the strength of his love for her, himself aspires to immortality and can now share with Ada the joys of living together in the fairies' world.

Die Feen is Wagner's first opera, and he made several attempts to have it put on in Leipzig, but failed. The score, which obviously belongs to Wagner's formative period, contains clear parallels with German Romantic music (Beethoven and Weber), but also with the operatic style of Meyerbeer and Italian composers.

FERNAND CORTEZ, OU LA CONQUÊTE DU MEXIQUE

(Fernando Cortez, or The Conquest of Mexico)

Tragédie lyrique *in three acts by Gaspare Spontini (1774–1851), to a libretto by Etienne de Jouy and Joseph Alphonse Esménard, based on the tragedy by Alexis Piron. First performance: Paris, Opéra, 28 November 1809.*

Mexico City. The high priest (bass) is about to perform the sacrifice of two Spanish prisoners inside an Aztec temple. King Montezuma (bass) interrupts the rite on the advice of Prince Telasco (baritone). Telasco's sister Amazily (soprano), who has been converted to Christianity and is in love with Cortez (tenor), goes to the Spanish camp. Amazily is acting as a peace-maker and so has asked the Spaniards for a truce. She is welcomed lovingly by Cortez, but his fellow Spaniards are suspicious of her, believing her to be a spy. Then Telasco also arrives at the camp, bearing valuable gifts, and proposes that the life of Alvaro (tenor), who is Cortez's brother and one of the prisoners awaiting sacrifice, be exchanged for Mexico's safety. Cortez will not agree to this and sets fire to his own fleet to prevent anyone from leaving the country. Telasco is taken hostage, but Cortez releases him in an act of good will. Telasco, however, implacable in his hatred of the enemy, stirs up the people and takes over custody of the Spanish prisoners, whose release he then barters for the safe return of Amazily. After leaving Cortez, Amazily goes to King Montezuma with a peace overture in the hope of preventing the Mexican people from being massacred. This gesture convinces Montezuma of Cortez's noble intentions, whereupon the King gives him the hand of Amazily in marriage and enters into an alliance with him.

The Italian composer Gaspare Spontini, composer of *Fernand Cortez.*

Spontini had been commissioned to write an opera Napoleon had asked for which would celebrate his military victories. Now Emperor, Napoleon was on the point of embarking on a new military campaign in Spain. *Fernand Cortez*, though an enormous success, did not turn out as Napoleon had wished: audiences were openly more sympathetic to the victims than to the conquerors. As a result, the opera was taken off.

FERNANDEZ, WILHELMENIA

(Philadelphia 1949)

Stage name of the American soprano Wilhelmenia Wiggins. She began to study music in Philadelphia before moving on to the Juilliard School in New York (1969–73). She made her debut on Broadway as Bess in *Porgy and Bess* (1977). A remarkable stage performer, she then divided her time between America and Europe, including roles in *La bohème*, *Don Giovanni*, *Turandot* and *Carmen*. She appeared in the film *Diva* (1981), directed by Jean-Jacques Beineix.

FERNE KLANG, DER

(The Far-off Sound)

Opera in three acts by Franz Schreker (1878–1934), to the composer's own libretto. First performance: Frankfurt-am-Main, Opernhaus, 18 August 1912.

Fritz (tenor), a young composer, bids farewell to his beloved, Greta Graumann (soprano). Greta tries in vain to persuade him not to go, but Fritz, although sad, is firm in his resolve and can no longer postpone his departure, because he must realize his dream, as an artist, to trace a far-off sound whose echo vibrates in his head. Not long after Fritz has left, Greta's mother (mezzo-soprano) and father (bass) arrive. Her father is a former army officer who is perpetually drunk and now heavily in debt. He is being pursued by a group of drinkers from the local inn: he has just lost again while gambling with them, and in this latest game he has gambled away his daughter, losing her to the inn-keeper. Greta pretends to accept the situation but then secretly leaves the house to go to Fritz. Ten years pass, and the scene changes to Venice, where Greta is now "The Lovely Greta," a high-class prostitute. During a party at a rich man's palace, she is trying to escape from the persistent attentions of a Count (baritone) who reminds her of Fritz when a man in travelling clothes comes into the room. It is Fritz. He recognizes Greta and asks her to forgive him for having abandoned her. For a moment, Fritz and Greta recapture their love, but then Fritz's eyes are opened by Greta's revelation of her new way of life. Fritz is horrified and hurries away. Greta pretends to be happy with the idea of leaving with the Count, which she does. Five more years pass. The scene is now an inn near the theater where *The Harp*, composed by Fritz, is being staged. A member of the chorus comes into the inn and reports that the opera is being very well received by the audience. A policeman (bass) enters and helps a woman to a table. It is Greta, who, overcome by the emotional power of the music, feels faint. She is recognized by Doctor Vigelius (high bass), whose house is near the inn. Meanwhile, the audience is leaving the theater, and it appears that the third act of the opera has been a failure. Greta begs Vigelius to take her to Fritz's house. She finds him, aged and ill, absorbed in listening for the far-off sound he has not heard for a long time. When he sees Greta, the two lovers embrace ecstatically. Fritz is overwhelmed by a growing sense of elation on finding love again and now being able to hear the far-off sound more and more clearly, until the two experiences create one emotion inside him. But his physical condition has been so weakened by illness that he can take no more, and after expressing his desire to rewrite the last act of his opera, Fritz collapses and dies in Greta's arms.

Der ferne Klang was Schreker's first major operatic success. The positive acclaim it received, and the beauty and richness of its orchestral colours, confirmed him as one of the important opera composers of his day, in a direct line from the Wagnerian school but also demonstrating his awareness of more recent innovations in music, especially those of Debussy.

FERRARINI, ALIDA

(Villafranca, Verona 1947)

Italian soprano. She studied music at the Conservatorio in Verona and made her first public appearances in the chorus at the Arena in Verona. She made her debut in 1974 as Mimi in Puccini's *La bohème* at the Teatro Comunale in Treviso. In 1975 she sang the role of Mercédès in Bizet's *Carmen* at the Arena in Verona, where she appeared frequently in the years that followed, scoring a big success as Micaela (*Carmen*), Oscar (*Un ballo in maschera*) and Gilda (*Rigoletto*), a role she has performed in a number of opera houses in Italy and abroad, including at the Teatro Regio in Parma (1987), the Paris Opéra (1988) and the Teatro Arriaga in Bilbao (1990). She gave a particularly distinguished performance as Micaela at La Scala, Milan, in a cast which also included Placido Domingo and Shirley Verrett.

FERRERO, LORENZO

(Turin 1951)

Italian composer. A pupil of Massimo Bruni and Enore Zaffiri, he specialized in the study of electronic music at the Experimental Studio in Bourges (1972–73) and with the Musik-Dia-Licht Film Galerie in Munich (from 1974). His operas include *Rimbaud* (1978), *Marilyn* (1980), *La figlia del mago* (1981), *Mare nostro* (1985), *Night* (1985), *Salvatore Giuliano* (1986), *Charlotte Corday* (1989) and *Le Bleu-Blanc-Rouge et le Noir* (1990). From 1980 to 1984 he was adviser to the Puccini Festival at Torre del Lago, and in 1991 he was appointed artistic director to the resident opera company at the Arena in Verona.

Above: A scence from *Fidelio* in a production at La Scala.

Right: The Italian soprano Alida Ferrarini.

FERRIER, KATHLEEN

(Higher Walton, Lancashire 1912–London 1953)

British contralto. She graduated in piano in 1928 and was a pianist for about ten years. During this time she also took singing lessons, making a debut in 1943 as a soloist in Handel's *Messiah*. Ferrier's career was almost exclusively that of a concert artist. In 1946 she appeared for the first time in opera in the premiere of Benjamin Britten's *The Rape of Lucretia* at Glyndebourne, and the following year she was warmly acclaimed for her performance in another Glyndebourne production, Gluck's *Orfeo ed Euridice*, an opera she sang in again in Amsterdam and at London's Covent Garden in 1953.

FERRO, GABRIELE

(Pescara 1937)

Italian conductor. From 1964 Ferro appeared at leading opera houses and concert halls in Italy. He conducted in the La Scala season of orchestral concerts from 1974, and was appointed music director of the Sicily Symphony Orchestra and permanent conductor of the RAI Symphony Orchestra in Rome.

FEUERSNOT

(Fire-Famine)

Singedicht *in one act by Richard Strauss (1864–1949), to a libretto by Ernst von Wolzogen. First performance: Dresden, Königliches Opernhaus, 21 November 1901.*

The action takes place in Munich on the feast of St. John some time in medieval history. In keeping with ancient custom, fires are lit using wood which the children have collected from house to house. Kunrad (baritone) throws a large armful of wood on to the pyre. Then he glimpses Diemut (soprano), daughter of the local burgomaster (bass), coming out of a near-by house, rushes up to her and shocks everyone present by kissing her. Diemut then joins with the other young women in deciding that Kunrad should be punished for his presumption. So, when Kunrad asks Diemut if he may come into her house, she pretends to welcome him, invites him to climb into a basket, and then hoists the basket off the ground and leaves him hanging in mid-air. Everyone laughs at the young man, but when he manages to get back down, something mysterious happens: all the fires in the city go out. With a single leap, Kunrad reaches Diemut's side, and she leads him into her bedroom. It is not long before the fires of St. John rekindle themselves of their own accord, and the crowd cries out for joy at the union of the two lovers.

The subject of *Feuersnot* was decidedly scabrous for public taste at that time and caused something of a sensation. The influence of Wagner and Bruckner is clearly present in Strauss's score.

FIAMMA, LA

(The Flame)

Opera in three acts by Ottorino Respighi (1879–1936), to a libretto by Claudio Guastalla based on the play The Witch *by G. Wiers Jenssen. First performance: Rome, Teatro dell'Opera, 23 January 1934.*

The action takes place in Ravenna in the seventh century. Silvana (soprano), the wife of Basilio (baritone), exarch of the city, has given shelter to a citizen, Agnese di Cervia (mezzo-soprano), who is accused of sorcery and is being pursued by the enraged populace. During celebrations in the exarch's house in honour of the safe return of Donello (tenor), Basilio's son by his first marriage, a posse of people who have been let in by Basilio's cruel mother Eudossia (mezzo-soprano), search the house, find Agnese and remove her forcibly. Convinced that she has been betrayed by Silvana, Agnese prophesies that she will meet with the same fate. Later, Donello tells his father that before she died, Agnese had accused Silvana's mother of sorcery, and that the woman had used magic spells to make Basilio marry her daughter. Basilio confirms the allegation by saying that he too feels he has been the victim of witchcraft. Silvana is stunned by this revelation, and so she decides to find out if she, like her mother, has the power to dominate people. In the dead of night, she calls out the name of Donello, with whom she is in love. The young man suddenly appears and kisses her. Shortly after this, Basilio, who is by now suspicious of his wife, sends Donello to Byzantium. Silvana becomes desperate and screams at Basilio that she wants him dead, whereupon the man falls lifeless to the ground. Eudossia then accuses her daughter-in-law of sorcery. At her trial, Silvana confesses her love for Donello but pleads not guilty to the other charges against her. However, when she sees that Donello himself is beginning to believe the idea that he too has been the victim of a spell, she gives way to despair, refuses to offer any further defense and allows herself to be led to the stake.

The setting in Byzantium, and the somber and magical nature of the plot were a tremendous spur to Respighi's imagination. In *La fiamma* the composer succeeded in conveying a strong emotional and dramatic quality he had never achieved before.

FIDELIO, ODER DIE EHELICHE LIEBE

(Fidelio, or Conjugal Love)

Opera in two acts by Ludwig van Beethoven (1770–1827), to a libretto by Joseph von Sonnleithner and Friedrich Treitschke. First performance: Vienna, Theater an der Wien, 20 November 1805.

The action takes place in a fortress which serves as a state prison, near Seville, some time in the seventeenth century. Leonora (soprano), the wife of Florestan (tenor), who has been unjustly imprisoned by the treacherous Don Pizarro (bass), has disguised herself as a man and, calling herself Fidelio, has been taken on as an assistant jailer in the prison where her husband is confined. Don Pizarro receives news that an inspection is due to be carried out at the prison and decides that Florestan must be got rid of. So he leads Rocco (bass), the jailer, to believe that the prisoner Florestan must be executed at once by order of the King, and that a grave will have to be dug to put the body in. Rocco feels he cannot refuse to do this, but Leonora has overheard everything and, determined to save her husband, goes down into the dungeons with Rocco, on the pretext of helping him to dig the grave. Leonora attempts to comfort her husband, whose sufferings have exhausted him, when suddenly Pizarro enters. He is armed with a dagger and is on the point of killing Florestan when Leonora comes between them, shielding her husband, and points a pistol at Pizarro. At that moment, a fanfare of trumpets announces the arrival of the Minister. Pizarro is forced to flee. A few moments later, the Minister, Don Fernando (bass), announces that the King has granted an amnesty for all political prisoners. He then recognizes Florestan among them, whom he had believed to be dead. Don Fernando gives orders for Pizarro to be punished for his misdeeds while Leonora, happy at last, loosens her husband's chains and all those present praise the ideals of freedom and love.

The first performance of *Fidelio* on 20 November 1805 could hardly have been received with less enthusiasm by the audience. The same thing happened when the second version of the opera was staged, again at the Theater an der Wien, on 9 March 1806. Beethoven was bitterly disappointed and withdrew the work after only a few performances. It was several years before the composer completed a new revised version of *Fidelio*, eventually produced at the Kärntnertortheater in Vienna on 23 May 1814, and this time the opera was a success. This third version is the one that continues to be performed all over the world.

FIERRABRAS

Opera in three acts by Franz Schubert (1797–1828), to a libretto by Josef Kupelwieser. First performance: Karlsruhe, Hoftheater, 9 February 1897.

The action takes place in southern France and Spain at the time of Charlemagne.

A scene from *Fierrabras*, by Schubert, which was first performed in Karlsruhe in 1897.

The Emperor Charlemagne (bass) has returned to his castle after a battle against the Spanish Moors. Among his prisoners is Fierrabras (tenor), son of the Moorish prince Baland (bass). The paladin Roland (baritone) is presented by Charlemagne's daughter Emma (soprano) with the victor's crown. Fierrabras recognizes Emma as the young woman he had met a few years before in Rome and secretly loved, and confides his feelings to Roland, since they are good friends. Roland, for his part, confesses that he too was in Rome and remembers the occasion because he had met Florinda (soprano), Fierrabras's sister, there and is in love with her. Meanwhile the Emperor decides to send the paladins as his ambassadors to Baland's camp. Among their number is a knight by the name of Eginhard (tenor), whose love for Emma, which is reciprocated by her, must be kept secret because Eginhard is not well thought of by Charlemagne. Fierrabras is distressed to learn of this relationship but decides to help the two young lovers. Eginhard leaves, and Fierrabras, on being surprised by Charlemagne while talking with Emma, is taken into custody. At the Moors' camp, Baland, furious to discover that his son Fierrabras has converted to Christianity since being taken prisoner, has all the paladin ambassadors arrested. Florinda, who has recognized Roland among the prisoners, helps them all to escape, but they are caught by the Moors and forced to fight. Eginhard manages to get away, reaches Charlemagne, and assembles an army to go to the aid of the paladins. In the meantime, Emma has told her father that she is in love with Eginhard and that Fierrabras has protected her. So Fierrabras is set free and joins forces with Eginhard's paladins, who succeed in rescuing Roland. The opera can now have a happy ending: Eginhard is reunited with his beloved Emma, Roland finds Florinda again and Baland, the Moorish prince, is converted to Christianity, thus setting the seal on Charlemagne's victory.

Fierrabras, Schubert's last stage work, was composed between May and October 1823. It was finally staged in Karlsruhe in 1897, but it was not until 1988 at the Wiener Festwochen in Vienna that the opera was produced in its entirety for the first time.

Above: A sketch by Renato Guttuso for *La figlia di Iorio* by Ildebrando Pizzetti.

FIERY ANGEL, THE

See Ognennyi Angel

FIGLIA DI JORIO, LA

(The Daughter of Jorio)

Pastoral tragedy in three acts by Ildebrando Pizzetti (1880–1968), to the composer's own libretto based on the tragedy of the same name by Gabriele D'Annunzio. First performance: Naples, Teatro San Carlo, 4 December 1954.

The action takes place in Abruzzo, Italy. Mila di Codro (soprano), the daughter of Jorio, the magician, is being pursued by a group of men who have been working on the harvest. She is given shelter from them in the house of the shepherd Aligi (tenor), where preparations are underway for his wedding to Vienda di Giave. Aligi falls in love with Mila and goes to live with her in a cave. One day Lazaro di Roio (baritone), Aligi's father, comes to the cave when Mila is alone and attempts to rape her. Aligi comes running but is dragged away by two countrymen Lazaro had brought with him. Aligi is, however, eventually freed by his sister Ornella (soprano), and in a blind fury he kills his father. Aligi is tried for his father's murder, and his sentence is that his hand be cut off and that he then be tied up in a sack containing a mastiff and thrown into the river. Enter Mila, who tells everyone that she alone is responsible for the crime: she had, she says, used her magic powers to make Aligi think he was his father's murderer, but in fact it was she who had killed Lazaro. Aligi is stunned by this revelation, but believes Mila and curses her. The crowd sets Aligi free and prepares to burn Mila at the stake. The young woman walks calmly to the pyre, convinced that she has saved her love. Only Ornella knows the truth of Mila's sacrifice and weeps for her.

Together with *Assassinio nella cattedrale*, *La figlia di Jorio* is Pizzetti's most famous opera.

FILLE DU RÉGIMENT, LA

(The Daughter of the Regiment)

Opera in two acts by Gaetano Donizetti (1797–1848), to a libretto by Jules Vernoy de Saint-Georges and Jean Bayard. First performance: Paris, Théâtre de l'Opéra-Comique (Salle Favart), 11 February 1840.

The action takes place in Switzerland. The young foundling Marie (soprano) has been brought up by French soldiers, and much of the responsibility for her care has been taken by the brusque sergeant Sulpice (bass). A young Swiss by the name of Tonio (tenor) has been following the troops and wants to enlist, but he is arrested as a spy. Marie intervenes and tells the soldiers that Tonio once saved her life. Tonio and Marie are in love, but Sulpice does not want Marie to marry a foreigner. Not long after this, the Marquise de Birkenfeld (mezzo-soprano) takes refuge in the French camp; while there, she realizes that Marie is actually her niece, and decides to take the young woman home with her to her castle. Meanwhile Tonio has enlisted, to make himself more eligible to marry Marie, but much to everyone's dismay, she leaves with the Marquise. At the castle Marie lives in luxury but is sad because she is obliged to perform many tedious tasks, and she regrets having left her life with the regiment. She is filled with despair when she finds out that the Marquise wants her to marry the Duke de Krakentorp. But when Sulpice and Tonio come to the castle, the Marquise reveals

to them that she is actually Marie's mother, not her aunt. She asks Sulpice if he will break this news to Marie and persuade her to agree to marry the Duke. However, when she sees how deeply unhappy Marie and Tonio have been made by this arranged marriage, she has compassion on them and gives her blessing for them to be married.

La fille du régiment is Donizetti's first Paris opera and to this day one of the most frequently performed, thanks to the freshness of its score, in which Donizetti has captured the light style of the *opéra-comique*.

FINTA GIARDINIERA, LA

(The Make-believe Gardener)

Opera buffa *in three acts by Wolfgang Amadeus Mozart (1756–1791), to a libretto by Giuseppe Petrosellini. First performance: Munich, Residenztheater, 13 January 1775.*

The foolish old *podestà* (tenor) (a mayor appointed by the government) is in love with Sandrina (soprano), a young woman gardener. Sandrina is really the Marchesa Violante and is going about in disguise to make it easier for her to retrace Count Belfiore (tenor). She is engaged to be married to the Count, but he had wounded her in a fit of jealousy and then left her, under the impression she was dead. Belfiore goes to see the *podestà* to ask to marry his niece Arminda (soprano), who promptly rejects her beloved Ramiro (mezzo-soprano). When Sandrina realizes Belfiore is just a few yards away from her, she faints with emotion. Belfiore thinks he must be seeing things and kisses Sandrina, thereby arousing Arminda's jealousy. Sandrina, however, denies to Belfiore that she is really Violante. Only when Ramiro arrives (he now knows that his rival Belfiore has been accused of murdering Violante) does Sandrina reveal her true identity, to him, but when Belfiore reappears, she denies it again. The vindictive Arminda has Sandrina removed to a forest and abandoned there. Everybody begins to wander through the glades, and in the general confusion Belfiore and Sandrina are at their wits' end, but all turns out for the best: Arminda accepts Ramiro's love, while Belfiore is reunited with his Violante.

An outstanding feature of Mozart's version is the clear separation between comic and serious characters. Mozart was not entirely successful in blending the two, and as a result of this the opera lacks consistency.

FINTA SEMPLICE, LA

(The Make-believe Simpleton)

Opera buffa *in three acts by Wolfgang Amadeus Mozart (1756–1791), to a libretto by Marco Coltellini based on Carlo Goldoni. First performance: Salzburg, Archbishop's Palace, 1 May 1769.*

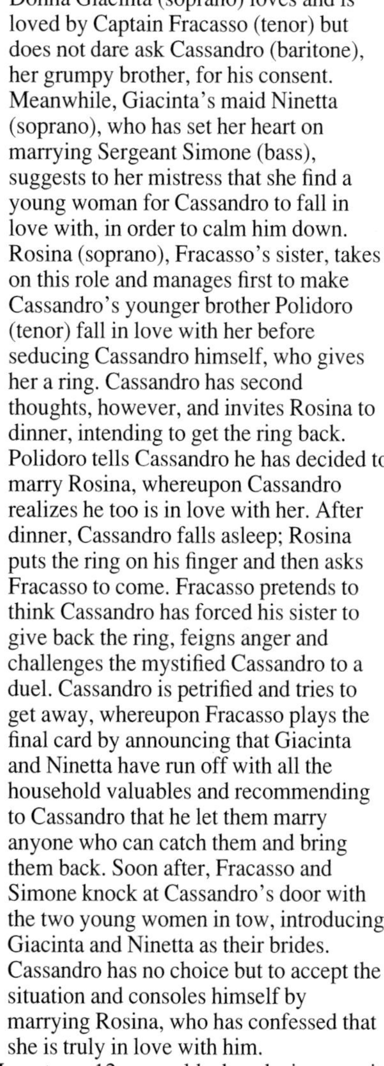

Donna Giacinta (soprano) loves and is loved by Captain Fracasso (tenor) but does not dare ask Cassandro (baritone), her grumpy brother, for his consent. Meanwhile, Giacinta's maid Ninetta (soprano), who has set her heart on marrying Sergeant Simone (bass), suggests to her mistress that she find a young woman for Cassandro to fall in love with, in order to calm him down. Rosina (soprano), Fracasso's sister, takes on this role and manages first to make Cassandro's younger brother Polidoro (tenor) fall in love with her before seducing Cassandro himself, who gives her a ring. Cassandro has second thoughts, however, and invites Rosina to dinner, intending to get the ring back. Polidoro tells Cassandro he has decided to marry Rosina, whereupon Cassandro realizes he too is in love with her. After dinner, Cassandro falls asleep; Rosina puts the ring on his finger and then asks Fracasso to come. Fracasso pretends to think Cassandro has forced his sister to give back the ring, feigns anger and challenges the mystified Cassandro to a duel. Cassandro is petrified and tries to get away, whereupon Fracasso plays the final card by announcing that Giacinta and Ninetta have run off with all the household valuables and recommending to Cassandro that he let them marry anyone who can catch them and bring them back. Soon after, Fracasso and Simone knock at Cassandro's door with the two young women in tow, introducing Giacinta and Ninetta as their brides. Cassandro has no choice but to accept the situation and consoles himself by marrying Rosina, who has confessed that she is truly in love with him.

Mozart was 12 years old when the impresario of the Imperial Theaters in Vienna, Afflisio, invited him to write this opera. The commission had originally been the idea of the Empress Maria Theresa herself, who had been impressed by the extraordinary musical gifts of the child prodigy. Mozart took only a few weeks to compose the opera, but the fuss created by the singers and instrumentalists involved, who did not want to be conducted by

Left: A scene from *La fille du régiment* by Gaetano Donizetti, in a production at the Teatro Comunale, Florence.

Above: A silhouette of Mozart.

a child, prevented *La finta semplice* from being staged. Only later, after the Archbishop of Salzburg showed an interest, was it possible for the opera to be performed in his own court theater.

FIORAVANTI, VALENTINO

(Rome 1764–Capua 1837)
Italian composer. He studied in Rome and Naples, where he had an active career until 1803, the year he was invited to Lisbon to be the director of the São Carlos theater (until 1807). After spending a few years in Paris, Fioravanti returned to Italy in 1816. He settled in Rome and took over from Giuseppe Jannacconi as chorus-master at St. Peter's, his own compositions at the time being mostly of sacred music. His operatic output consists of more than 70, mostly comic, works written between 1784 and 1824, the best-known of which are *Le cantatrici villane* (1798–99) and *I virtuosi ambulanti* (1807).

FISCHER-DIESKAU, DIETRICH

(Berlin 1925)
German baritone. He was educated in Berlin and gave his first concert in 1947. In 1948 he made his theater debut as Posa (*Don Carlos*) at the Städtische Oper in Berlin, where he was engaged as first baritone. He appeared at Bayreuth from 1954, in Salzburg from 1957, at the Vienna Staatsoper from 1957 and in Munich, London and New York. Fischer-Dieskau's is a voice with a clear and not especially full-sounding timbre. He has a gift for phrasing and the ability to catch exactly the right expressive accent, consistently placing this in its proper stylistic context. These musical qualities, combined with remarkable skills as a stage performer, have enabled Fischer-Dieskau, despite the naturally "hybrid" character of his voice (between lyric baritone and bass-baritone), to tackle a very wide range of vocal styles, including those of great dramatic substance (Verdi, Wagner and Strauss).

FLAMINIO, IL

Music comedy in three acts by Giovanni Battista Pergolesi (1710–1736), to a libretto by Gennarantonio Federico. First performance: Naples, Teatro Nuovo, Autumn 1735.

Giustina (mezzo-soprano), a young widow, lives in a house on the outskirts of Naples with her faithful maid Checca (soprano). Giustina would like to get married and has chosen Polidoro (tenor), a young Neapolitan with a reputation for being a libertine. To show Giustina how serious his intentions are towards her, Polidoro takes up residence in her house with his sister Agata (soprano). Agata is engaged to be married to Ferdinando (tenor) but is in love with Giulio (soprano), her brother's secretary. Giulio is actually Flaminio, who loves Giustina but had been rejected by her, and now Giustina is clearly somewhat agitated and curious by the presence of Giulio/Flaminio, whereas he pretends not to have recognized Giustina and withdraws from her when she presses her attentions on him. The plot steers its way through arguments, jealousy and misunderstandings to a happy ending: Giulio has finally revealed his true identity and marries Giustina, who has broken off with Polidoro; Agata goes back to Ferdinando; while Bastiano (bass), Polidoro's servant, marries Checca.

Il Flaminio was Pergolesi's last work for the theater and also one of his most important compositions. He dispenses with dialect in the *buffo* or comic part of the work, which he makes more conventional and bourgeois, so that it even takes on the mood of an *opera seria* conveyed by the poetic handling of the love interest through arias imbued with *bel canto*.

DIE FLEDERMAUS

(The Bat)
*Operetta in three acts by Johann Strauss II (1825–99), to a libretto by Meilhac and Halévy (*Le Réveillon*, based on a German comedy by Roderich Benedix (*Das Gefängnis*, 1851), and adopted by Karl Haffner and Richard Genée. First performance: Vienna, Theater an der Wien, 5 April 1874.*

The action takes place in Vienna, in the second half of the nineteenth century. The house of Gabriel von Eisenstein, a wealthy man about town. His wife, Rosalinde (soprano), is surprised to hear the voice of an old admirer, Alfred, an opera singer (tenor), serenading her from the garden. He hides while the maid Adele (soprano) asks for the evening off to visit a sick aunt. Rosalinde refuses, flustered as she is by Alfred's appearance and the fact that her husband is to begin a

Above: The German baritone Dietrich Fischer-Dieskau.

Right: A scene from *Il Flaminio* by Pergolesi.

short prison sentence that very evening. Adele bursts into tears, because in fact her sister, a ballet dancer called Ida (soprano), had secured her an invitation to a ball given by the wealthy Russian Prince Orlofsky. Alfred announces that he will return as soon as Eisenstein has gone to prison and Rosalinde allows Adele to go out. Eisenstein (tenor) enters, blaming his lawyer, Dr Blind (tenor), for failing to extricate him from the mess in which he finds himself. His annoyance is dispelled when his friend Dr Falke (baritone) produces an invitation for him (and unknown to him for Rosalinde) to Prince Orlofsky's ball. So he leaves for prison in evening dress. Alfred takes his place at the supper table and in Rosalinde's arms. They are together when Frank, the prison governor (baritone), unexpectedly arrives to escort his distinguished prisoner to his cell. Rosalinde persuades Alfred to pretend to be her husband and go to prison for her sake. Then she is free to dress, as Falke has instructed, as a Hungarian Countess and to leave for the ball. Act II. Prince Orlofsky's palace. The Prince (mezzo-soprano) begs Falke to amuse him. Falke explains he has already arranged an entertainment. His plan is to obtain an elaborate revenge on Eisenstein for once leaving him after a party to walk home, in broad daylight, in fancy dress as a bat. Eisenstein (under the assumed name of Marquis Renard) recognizes Adele. He is then introduced to the "Chevalier Chagrin" (actually Frank) and their halting French exchanges cause much merriment, until the arrival of a masked Hungarian beauty quickly attracts his attention. He sets about charming her with a chiming pocket watch. Everyone sits back to enjoy a performance of the Imperial Ballet before joining in a chorus in praise of Champagne, brotherhood and sisterhood. Realizing that it is six o'clock and time to report to the prison, the Marquis and the Chevalier hurry away. Act III. The prison. Frosch (speaking part) the jailer, is tipsy and complains about the noise which his prisoner has been making and the nuisance of having to call a lawyer for him. Frank arrives, closely followed by Ida and Adele. They ask him to promote Adele's career on the stage and she sings a quick coloratura aria to prove her abilities. He bundles them into the only spare cell when another visitor rings the bell. It turns out to be Eisenstein, who is unnerved to hear that someone calling himself Eisenstein has been under lock and key all night. Frank leaves the room for a moment to greet a further arrival and Eisenstein takes the opportunity to borrow Blind's wig and gown so as to be in a position to see the prisoner. The new arrival is Rosalinde, and Eisenstein takes a high moral tone when interviewing her with Alfred. Shortly, however, his own disguise is perceived and Rosalinde produces the incriminating chiming watch. As if by magic, all Prince Orlofsky's other guests arrive and they resume the chorus with a toast to champagne.

Despite a brilliant première the operetta was not immediately successful in Vienna and there were only 16 performances. It triumphed in Berlin, Hamburg and even Paris before it returned to be welcomed ecstatically by the Viennese. It has remained the supreme masterpiece and epitome of Viennese operetta ever since.

FLIEGENDE HOLLÄNDER, DER

(The Flying Dutchman)

Opera in three acts by Richard Wagner (1813–1883), to the composer's own libretto, based on Aus den Memoiren des Herrn von Schnabelewopski *by Heinrich Heine. First performance: Dresden, Hofoper, 2 January 1843.*

The action takes place on the Norwegian coast at an unspecified time. The Dutchman (bass) is given no rest by a curse which has condemned him to a life wandering the oceans of the world; except that, every seven years, he is allowed to put to shore and look for a woman who will swear to be faithful to him forever and, by making such a pledge, free him from the curse. During a storm at sea, the Dutchman lands on the coast of Norway, where he meets an old sailor, Daland (bass), and tells him about his wretched destiny. Daland's greed is aroused by the Dutchman's wealth, and he invites him to his home, where Daland's daughter Senta (soprano) is waiting for him. The young woman is deeply impressed by their visitor, who she realizes is the legendary Flying Dutchman, and swears she will be eternally faithful to him. While preparations are underway for their wedding, Senta is approached by Erik (tenor), a young hunter who had been engaged to her. Erik tries to win back Senta's love while, unseen by them, the Dutchman is a witness to their conversation. Imagining that he is being betrayed by Senta, the Dutchman becomes desperate and decides to set sail. Senta vainly tries to make him stay, protesting her innocence, and then takes what seems like the only step left to her by climbing on to the cliff and throwing herself into the sea. This is the proof of her faithfulness. The Dutchman has been saved and, as his ship sinks, the souls of

Above: A drawing showing three characters from *Der fliegende Holländer.*

Left: The American tenor Bruce Edwin Ford.

the two lovers are seen, transfigured, on the horizon.

The opera features Wagner's favourite themes: a curse, redemption, and death seen as the achievement of an inner stability. These are all elements which Wagner would be developing in his subsequent operas, along with the use of the *leitmotif*, which played an important role for the first time in this work.

FORD, BRUCE EDWIN

(Lubbock, Texas 1956)

American tenor. He studied singing at West State University, Canyon, and at the Texas Tech University in Lubbock, before going on to the Houston Opera to train with John Gillas and Elena Nicolai. He began his career at Houston in minor roles. From 1983, Ford concentrated his career mainly in Europe, especially in Germany and Austria. A Mozart performer of some refinement, Ford has also acquitted himself with distinction in the operas of Rossini.

FORZA DEL DESTINO, LA

(The Force of Destiny)

Opera in four acts by Giuseppe Verdi (1813–1901), to a libretto by Francesco Maria Piave, based on Don Alvaro, o la Fuerza del Sino *by Angel Saavedra, Duke of Rivas. First performance: St. Petersburg, Imperial Theater, 10 November 1862.*

The action takes place in Spain and Italy around the middle of the eighteenth century. Donna Leonora (soprano), daughter of the Marquis of Calatrava (bass), has agreed to elope with her beloved Don Alvaro (tenor), so as to escape her father, who is opposed to their marrying. But the couple are caught by the Marquis. Don Alvaro is willing to face up to the Marquis's rage and, to show that he is unarmed, throws his pistol on to the floor. But the weapon goes off accidentally and kills the Marquis. Leonora, in shock at her father's death, takes refuge in a monastery to hide from her brother Don Carlo (baritone), who has sworn to kill her in revenge for their father's murder. Meanwhile, Don Alvaro, who has no news of Leonora and believes her to be dead, has enlisted in the Spanish army now fighting in Italy. Don Alvaro's intervention saves the life of an army captain, who in turn saves Don Alvaro's life after he is wounded in battle. The two men take an oath of friendship, but the captain, who is really Don Carlo, discovers Don Alvaro's identity and challenges him to a duel. The night-patrol comes by and separates them. To keep out of Don Carlo's way, Don Alvaro goes to a monastery – unknown to him, the same one where Leonora had sought refuge. Don Carlo traces him there and challenges again. The duel takes place near the cave where Leonora is now living, and Don Alvaro fatally wounds Don Carlo. Leonora hears cries for help and runs to the scene but, as she leans over her brother to attend to him, Don Carlo, just before he dies, runs his sister through with his sword. Leonora dies in Alvaro's arms.

La forza del destino was commissioned from Verdi by the director of the Imperial Theater in St. Petersburg. The work was an outstanding success, but Verdi decided to make some radical changes. In particular, he altered the finale: in the first version, Don Carlo had died on stage and Don Alvaro had taken his own life by throwing himself off a precipice, whereas in the revised score Don Alvaro survives and Don Carlo kills his sister but dies off stage. The second version had a triumph at La Scala, Milan, on 27 February 1869.

FOSS, LUKAS

(Berlin 1922)

Adopted name of Lukas Fuchs, German pianist, composer and conductor who took American citizenship. He studied in Berlin and Paris (from 1933). After moving with his family to the United States, he completed his music studies at the Curtis Institute in Philadelphia and went on to train under Koussevitzky at the Berkshire Music Center and with Hindemith at Yale University. From 1944 he embarked on a career as a pianist, turning later to teaching, conducting and composing. It was as a composer that Foss succeeded in blending his European musical origins (on which the German late Romantic tradition had been a particularly strong influence) and the more typically American ones. His musical output includes orchestral and choral music and oratorios and an opera, *The Jumping Frog of Calaveras County*, 1950.

FRA DIAVOLO, OU L'HÔTELLERIE DE TERRACINE

(Fra Diavolo, or The Inn at Terracine)

Opéra-comique *in three acts by Daniel Auber*

A scene from *La forza del destino*, in a production at La Scala, Milan during the 1965–66 season.

Right: Zoe Prevost as Zerlina in *Fra Diavolo* by Daniel Auber.

(1782–1871), to a libretto by Eugène Scribe and Casimir Delavigne. First performance: Paris, Théâtre de l'Opéra-Comique, 28 January 1830.

The action takes place in the Italian province of Latium at the end of the eighteenth century. Lorenzo (tenor), young commander of the Carabinieri army corps, is in love with Zerlina (soprano), but her father, Matteo (bass), an innkeeper, wants her to marry a wealthy property-owner. Meanwhile, a British couple have arrived in the village, Lord Cockburn (baritone) and his wife Lady Pamela (mezzo-soprano), who have been robbed of their jewellery by bandits. Lorenzo is convinced that this is the work of Fra Diavolo, a brigand currently terrorizing the area, and sets out with his men to capture the outlaw. After he has left, the Marchese di San Marco arrives at the inn; this is none other than Fra Diavolo himself (tenor) in disguise. The "Marchese" pays court to Lady Pamela, from whom he finds out that a large sum of money was missed when she was robbed. Determined to have this money, Fra Diavolo attempts to steal it but is interrupted by the return of Lorenzo, who has put Fra Diavolo's men to flight and recovered the jewels. Still disguised as the Marchese, Fra Diavolo explains his behaviour as an escapade in the name of love. But he loses none of his resolve: while preparations are in progress for Zerlina's wedding to the wealthy old property-owner, Fra Diavolo's henchmen Beppo (tenor) and Giacomo (bass) are to give him the signal when the inn is empty. These two bandits are, however, identified by Lorenzo, who then uncovers Fra Diavolo's plan. So he gets his men into position and orders Beppe and Giacomo to give the prearranged signal. Fra Diavolo is duly arrested, and Lorenzo can at last marry Zerlina.

Fra Diavolo is Auber's best-known *opéra-comique* and one which continues to be admired. The score offers clear evidence of Auber's brilliant and attractive style, which captured the prevailing tastes of his day.

FRANCESCA DA RIMINI

Tragic opera in four acts by Riccardo Zandonai (1883–1944), to a libretto arranged by Tito Ricordi from the tragedy of the same name by Gabriele D'Annunzio. First performance: Turin, Teatro Regio, 9 February 1914.

The action takes place in Ravenna and Rimini during the twelfth century. Guido da Polenta (tenor), Lord of Ravenna, has promised his sister Francesca (soprano) in marriage to Gianciotto Malatesta (baritone), Lord of Rimini, but as a precaution in case Francesca rejects her husband-to-be, who is lame, he has led her to believe that she will actually be marrying Gianciotto's brother, the handsome Paolo (tenor). When Francesca meets Paolo, she is immediately attracted to him and, lost in a reverie, gives him a rose. Some time later, during a battle between the Malatesta and Parcitadi families, Francesca climbs to the top of a tower to watch. When Paolo is slightly wounded, Francesca, who has never stopped loving him despite having been obliged to marry Gianciotto, is on the point of confessing her love to Paolo when Gianciotto arrives and tells his brother to leave for Florence, where he has been appointed Captain of the People. Paolo and Francesca meet again two months later. While reading together of the passionate adventures of Guinevere and Lancelot, the flame of love is kindled between them. Not long after that, Malatestino (tenor), Gianciotto's younger brother, who is fascinated by Francesca, offers her his love. Francesca is indignant, whereupon Malatestino, for revenge, tells Gianciotto that Paolo and Francesca are lovers. Gianciotto pretends to set out for Pesaro, then suddenly bursts into the room, surprising the lovers, and kills them both.

Francesca da Rimini is Zandonai's masterpiece. The richness of its orchestration and operatic inspiration enabled the composer to create some beautifully-drawn roles, making this opera one of the most important in the twentieth-century Italian repertoire.

FRANCHETTI, ALBERTO

(Turin 1860–Viareggio 1942)

Italian composer. His musical output was particularly influenced by composers of the German school, especially Wagner. His greatest operatic successes were *Cristoforo Colombo* (1892) and *Germania* (1902). He was also active as a teacher and served as director of the Conservatorio in Florence from 1926 to 1928.

FRANCI, FRANCESCA

(Rome 1962)

Italian mezzo-soprano. Born into a musical family (her grandfather was the baritone Benvenuto Franci, and her sister Raffaella is a pianist), Franci was a pupil of Rodolfo

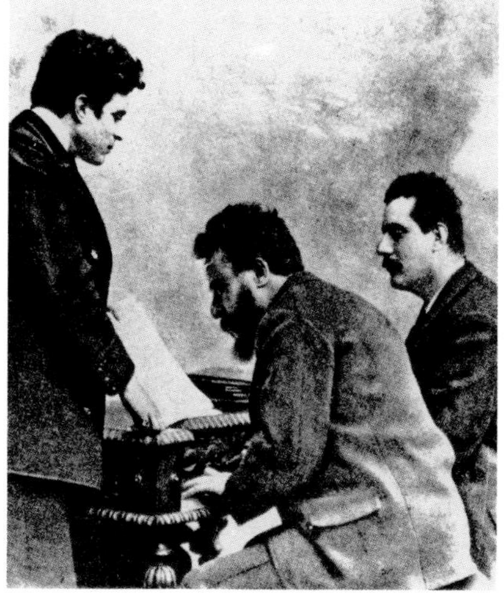

Top left: A scene from *Francesca da Rimini* by Riccardo Zandonai.

Above: The Italian composer Alberto Franchetti with Mascagni, on the left, and Puccini.

Celletti and made her debut at a concert in the Teatro Filarmonico in Verona in 1985. In the years that followed, she made her name as Maddalena (Verdi's *Rigoletto*) at the Teatro Comunale in Genoa (1987), Rosina (Rossini's *Il barbiere di Siviglia*) at the Teatro Petruzzelli in Bari (1988), and Suzuki (Puccini's *Madama Butterfly*) at the Teatro Comunale in Bologna (1988), where she appears regularly. Also in 1988 she was guest artist at the Valle d'Itria Festival (in Donizetti's *Maria di Rohan*) and at La Scala, Milan (in Rossini's *Guillaume Tell*). Franci has sung at the Teatro dell'Opera in Rome (from 1987), the Teatro San Carlo in Naples (from 1987), the Teatro Comunale in Florence (from 1992) as well as at the Opéra in Paris, Wiesbaden, and a number of other theaters.

FRATE 'NNAMURATO, LO

(The Brother in Love)

Opera in three acts by Giovanni Battista Pergolesi (1710–1736), to a libretto by Gennarantonio Federico. First performance: Naples, Teatro dei Fiorentini, 30 September 1732.

Capodimonte, in the year 1730. Carlo (tenor), a wealthy man of property, wants to forge stronger links with the family of his bride-to-be, Lucrezia (contralto). So he decides to marry off his two nieces, Nina (mezzo-soprano) and Nena (soprano), one to Lucrezia's father, Marcianello (bass), and the other to Don Pietro (bass), Lucrezia's brother. The two young women are not keen on the husbands who have been chosen for them, because they are both in love with Ascanio (soprano), a young foundling who has been brought up in Marcianello's house. Ascanio is courting not only Nina and Nena but also Lucrezia, who tells him of her love. Ascanio uses the pretext of his obscure origins to inform Lucrezia that he cannot marry her. The truth is that he is attracted to both Nina and Nena and is at a loss to know which of them to choose. Meanwhile, the two sisters attempt to get rid of their husbands-to-be: Nena catches Pietro making advances to the maid Vannella (soprano), pretends to be jealous and tells him that the wedding cannot take place. Nina takes the same course of action: she sees Marcianello amusing himself with Vannella, pretends to take offense, and raises doubts over her being able to marry him. All the wedding plans are consequently going up in smoke when jealousy breaks out between the women as to which of them will marry Ascanio. Marcianello, indignant at all this confusion, wants Ascanio out of the house but then calms down and forgives the young man. Pietro, on the other hand, has decided to get rid of Ascanio once and for all, so he follows him with drawn sword and wounds him in one arm. Carlo hurries to the scene and, while treating Ascanio's wound, notices a mark on his arm which identifies him as a nephew of Carlo's who had been abducted as a baby. This means that Ascanio is actually the brother of Nena and Nina. So Ascanio can marry Lucrezia, Marcianello agrees, and Carlo, who is happy to have found his lost nephew, willingly steps aside to let his bride-to-be marry Ascanio instead.

Written when the composer was 22 years old, this work has freshness and verve, and cleverly combines Italian with a "cultured" form of Neapolitan dialect.

FRAU OHNE SCHATTEN, DIE

(Woman without a Shadow)

Opera in three acts by Richard Strauss (1864–1949), to a libretto by Hugo von Hofmannsthal. First performance: Vienna, Staatsoper, 10 October 1919.

The Emperor (tenor) has married the daughter of Keikobad, Lord of the Spirits. The young fairy-Empress has no shadow, and this indicates that she is barren: being a spirit, she has no need to reproduce. A messenger (baritone) from Keikobad announces to the Empress (soprano) that unless she can find a shadow for herself within three days, she will have to return to the kingdom of the Spirits and the Emperor will be turned to stone. In desperation the Empress sets out with her Nurse (mezzo-soprano) to search for someone who will sell her a shadow. On her way, she comes to the house of Barak (bass-baritone). He is unhappy because after three years of marriage his Wife (soprano) has not yet been able to give him any children. The Nurse wins the Wife's confidence, flatters her, and then offers to make all her dreams come true if she will part with her shadow. The woman is unwilling to do this; she is forever in the grip of a crying need to escape from her wretched existence, but here is the Nurse persuading her to deceive her husband. After seeing a tempting vision, the Wife shouts at Barak that she has cuckolded him. Barak hurls himself at his Wife but is stopped in his tracks as he sees in the firelight that she has no shadow. He is about to kill her when the Empress intervenes: she has now realized that she has done wrong, and no longer wants the shadow. The Wife immediately insists she has done nothing at all and everything has been a dream. Suddenly the ground opens and Barak and his Wife are engulfed. The messenger says that the Empress must get hold of the woman's shadow. The Emperor has already been turned to stone, but the Empress repeats that she will not do it: she cannot save her husband if this

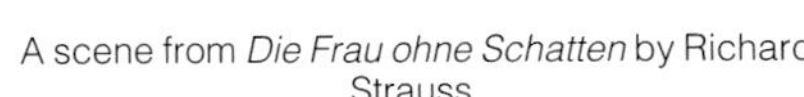
A scene from *Die Frau ohne Schatten* by Richard Strauss.

means condemning two other human beings. This sacrifice of hers performs the miracle: the Emperor comes back to life and there is a shadow on the ground at the Empress's feet. Barak and his Wife are also reunited after climbing out of the abyss into which they had fallen.

Hofmannsthal's libretto for *Die Frau ohne Schatten* was inspired by Oriental legends and by the fairy-tales of Carlo Gozzi and the Brothers Grimm. The text seems to be full of symbols, and their meaning is often hard to determine. Strauss's music abounds in orchestral colour and refinement, the individual roles are all marvellously characterized, and voices and orchestra are united with an intense expressive energy.

FREISCHÜTZ, DER

(The Marksman with Magic Bullets)

Romantic opera in three acts by Carl Maria von Weber (1786–1826), to a libretto by Friedrich Kind based on a story by Johann Apel and Friedrich Laun. First performance: Berlin, Schauspielhaus, 18 June 1821.

A village in Germany, in the seventeenth century. Kilian (baritone) beats the young gamekeeper Max (tenor) in an archery competition. Max is jeered at by everyone and is about to attack Kilian when the chief huntsman Cuno (bass) and Caspar (bass) arrive on the scene and get both men to calm down. Cuno promises Max that if he wins the contest due to be held in the presence of Prince Ottakar (tenor), he can marry the Prince's daughter Agathe (soprano). Max is then approached by Caspar, who guarantees him victory as long as he places his trust in the power of the "Dark Hunter," who is none other than the devil Samiel (speaking role). Max accepts and is soon on his way to the Wolf's Glen, where the pact will be sealed. Caspar, who has already sold his own soul to Samiel, proposes the annulment of the pact between them in exchange for the soul of Max. Samiel agrees. When Max arrives, the magic bullets are forged: there are seven of them, but one of these Samiel will direct at a victim of his choice. On the day of the contest, Max wins. The Prince asks that the victor use his final bullet to shoot down a dove flying among the tree-tops. But Samiel has put Agathe's soul inside the dove. As Max takes aim to fire, he hears Agathe's voice asking him to be merciful. The gun goes off nonetheless, but the bullet hits Caspar. Ottakar questions Max closely, and Max tells him the truth. Ottakar rules that if Max can show for a whole year that he is an honest man, then he will be able to marry Agathe.

Der Freischütz was conceived in the form of a *Singspiel*, that is with sung and spoken sections interspersed, and its first performance was not a resounding success. But when, in October of the same year, it was staged in Vienna, the opera was a triumph. It became the touchstone of German Romantic opera.

FRENI, MIRELLA

(Modena 1935)

Stage name of the Italian soprano Mirella Fregni. After studying at the Conservatorio in Bologna and in Mantua, Freni made her debut as Micaela in *Carmen* in Modena (1955). Two years later, she won the "Concorso Viotti" in Vercelli, going on in 1959 to score a sensational triumph, again as Micaela, at the Teatro Massimo in Palermo. By 1960 Freni was already launched on a brilliant international career (Glyndebourne, Covent Garden, etc.), singing Mozart (*Le nozze di Figaro*, *Don Giovanni*), Donizetti (*L'elisir d'amore*), Puccini (*La bohème*, *Turandot*) and Verdi (*Falstaff*). It was in fact as Nannetta in *Falstaff* that she made her first appearance at La Scala, Milan, in 1962, returning in the 1963 season to sing Mimi in the famous production of *La bohème* by Franco Zeffirelli with Herbert von Karajan conducting. Freni's very fine, deeply musical, lyric soprano voice and her expressive use of phrasing, combined with a remarkable sensitivity in performance, have enabled her to

Left: A drawing for *Der Freischütz* by Carl Maria von Weber.

Above: The Italian soprano Mirella Freni.

THE CHARACTER OF THE VOICE IN GERMAN ROMANTIC OPERA

German opera began on 18 June 1821 with the premiere of Weber's masterpiece *Der Freischütz*, which immediately became the model for future generations of composers. The historical significance of *Der Freischütz* is principally due to its popular setting (which would later influence Wagner in his writing for *Die Meistersinger*), and the presence of nature as something real but also fantastical and tending to the supernatural. It was in this opera that Weber devised the vocal and psychological prototypes which would later be used extensively by other German composers. The part of Agathe, a symbol of purity and gentleness, is scored for a lyric soprano: the ecstatic vocal line refrains from virtuoso display. and the role itself clearly inspired that of Elisabeth in Wagner's *Tannhäuser*. The diabolical Kaspar paves the way for the bass voice to be more commonly used for "negative" roles (Pizarro in Beethoven's *Fidelio* could be seen as a precedent here) and Weber takes full advantage of the bass register for its ability not only to sound somber but also to express vehemence. From then on, bass roles were to acquire a certain ambivalence in German opera, and this becomes clear in Wagner's handling of them. In fact his greatest bass parts are actually scored for bass-baritones, for example the Dutchman, Amfortas, Wotan, Hagen and Alberich, while his true bass roles – the Landgrave in *Tannhäuser*, the King in *Lohengrin* or King Marke in *Tristan und Isolde* – are, it could be argued, less significant and psychologically less well characterized than the others. In Weber's *Der Freischütz* too, the role of Max is vocally that of a baritone in many ways: not especially extended in the upper register and with no virtuoso touches; whereas Weber's other two best-known operas, *Euryanthe* and *Oberon*, reveal some very different features. In *Euryanthe*, particular interest is generated by the "negative" figures of Eglantine and Lysiart, whose scourging, declamatory vocal style looks forward to the roles of Ortrud and Telramund in Wagner's *Lohengrin*. In addition, Eglantine and Lysiart are the most prominent roles scored by Weber for mezzo-soprano and baritone soloists, at least in his major operas (in *Oberon*, Fatima and Sherasmin are actually supporting roles), while in Wagner these voices are evidently treated as hybrids – Ortrud, for instance, can actually be sung just as effectively by a mezzo-soprano (with the necessary extra range) or by a soprano. German composers almost invariably favoured high soprano and tenor voices, and it remained for Wagner to give bass and baritone, and to a lesser extent mezzo-soprano, roles their due in his own idiosyncratic way but no less adequately for that. In *Oberon*, the atmosphere of chivalry and imagination is such that the voices of the individual characters are imbued with it: consequently Huon and Reiza, although their roles are essentially lyrical, unleash sudden surges of energy. The tendency towards a "heroic" quality of voice becomes more accentuated in Wagner, reaching its height in Wagner's scoring of the roles of Tannhäuser, Siegmund, Siegfried, Tristan and Parsifal for *Heldentenor*. Some of Wagner's writing for soprano is more lyrical in quality, e.g. Elisabeth (*Tannhäuser*), Elsa (*Lohengrin*), Eva (*Die Meistersinger*) and Sieglinde (*Die Walküre*); whereas more dramatic features are already in evidence in the case of Senta (*Der fliegende Holländer*) and recur later in the roles of Brünnhilde, Isolde and Kundry.

Right: An illustration for the score of *Tristan und Isolde*, published by Ricordi in 1907.

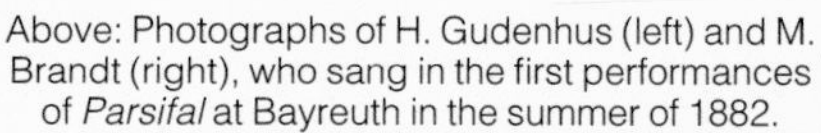

Above: Photographs of H. Gudenhus (left) and M. Brandt (right), who sang in the first performances of *Parsifal* at Bayreuth in the summer of 1882.

maintain her vocal resources almost intact over the years. She has therefore been able to tackle successfully roles associated with a different character of voice such as Manon Lescaut, Tosca, Aida and Elisabeth de Valois. She has given impressive performances as Tatyana (*Eugene Onegin*) and Lisa (*Queen of Spades*), roles which she has sung in the great opera houses of the world. Mirella Freni is one of the most highly regarded sopranos in international opera.

FREY, PAUL

(Toronto 1942)

Canadian tenor. He began to study music in 1963, and became a pupil of the baritone Louis Quilico in Toronto. His early career was in Canada, where he sang minor roles in opera and oratorio. After scoring his first success as the lead in Massenet's *Werther* in Toronto, Frey moved to Basle, Switzerland, where he specialized in the German repertoire. He was particularly admired for his performance in Wagner's *Lohengrin*, which he has sung in many different places, including Germany (at Bayreuth from 1987) and France. He has also appeared in *Parsifal* and *Die Meistersinger von Nürnberg*. In addition to Wagner, Frey has established a reputation as a Strauss performer (*Ariadne auf Naxos*, *Daphne*, *Die Liebe der Danae* and *Capriccio*), and his repertoire also includes operas by Mozart, Weber (*Oberon*) and Beethoven (*Fidelio*).

FRICK, GOTTLOB

(Ölbronn, Württemberg 1906)

German bass. He studied music in Stuttgart, where he began his career in 1927. In 1934 he made his debut as Daland in *Der fliegende Holländer* (The Flying Dutchman) in Coburg. From 1940 he sang with the Dresden Staatsoper and joined the Berlin Staatsoper in 1950. He also made appearances in Vienna, Munich, London, Salzburg and Bayreuth. Frick's reputation rests in particular on a number of Wagner roles (Hunding, Hagen, Fasolt and Gurnemanz), as well as Caspar (*Der Freischütz*) and Rocco (*Fidelio*).

FRICSAY, FERENC

(Budapest 1914–Basle 1963)

Hungarian conductor who took Austrian citizenship. Fricsay, a pupil of Kodály and Bartók in Budapest, began his conducting career with the Szeged Symphony Orchestra and the Szeged Opera (1934–44). A crucial turning-point came with his involvement in the Salzburg Festival, where he conducted the world premiere of Gottfried von Einem's opera *Dantons Tod* (1947). Here too he conducted the first staged performances of Frank Martin's *Le vin herbé* and Carl Orff's *Antigonae* (1949). Fricsay was engaged as a conductor by the principal German and Austrian theaters and concert halls (Deutsche Oper in Berlin, Vienna Staatsoper, Bayerische Staatsoper in Munich, etc.). He was also an active opera conductor, earning particular distinction in the Mozart repertoire.

FRIEDENSTAG

(Peace Day)

Opera in one act by Richard Strauss (1864–1949), to a libretto by Joseph Gregor. First performance: Munich, Bayerische Staatsoper im Nationaltheater, 24 July 1938.

The action takes place on 24 October 1648 in a city under siege during the Thirty Years' War. The Emperor has ordered his people to resist to the end, but they are weary and beg him to surrender. The Commandant (baritone) decides that he is going to blow up the citadel and die in the explosion. Maria (soprano), his fearless wife, wants to share her husband's fate. The fuse is ready to be lit when three bursts of cannonfire give the signal that the war is over. The Commandant, who suspects a trap, is still armed when he receives the commander-in-chief of the besieging army. But Maria intervenes and manages to avert a tragic confrontation. The opera ends with a hymn to peace.

The meager quality of Gregor's libretto, based on Pedro Calderón's *La rendición de Breda* is, despite being revised by Stefan Zweig, the weakest point in *Friedenstag*. The subject did not inspire Strauss greatly, and consequently the music is somewhat conventional and at variance with the composer's true spirit.

FULTON, THOMAS

(Memphis, Tennessee 1950)

American conductor. He began to study piano when he was very young and made his debut as a soloist at the age of 14. He then studied at the Curtis Institute in Philadelphia, where he started his conducting career as assistant conductor (1975–77), a position he went on to occupy in Hamburg (1977–78) and with the Metropolitan Opera, New York (from 1978). After his official debut in 1981, Fulton appeared in a number of American and European opera houses, winning particular acclaim for his performances of the French repertoire such as *Robert le diable* by Meyerbeer at the Paris Opéra and *Manon* in Parma, as well as conducting the first recordings of Adam's *Le postillon de Longjumeau* and Auber's *La muette de Portici*.

FURIOSO ALL'ISOLA DI SAN DOMINGO, IL

(The Madman on the Isle of San Domingo)

Opera in two acts by Gaetano Donizetti

Above: A scene from *Friedenstag* by Richard Strauss.

Left: The Italian soprano Mirella Freni.

(1797–1848), to a libretto by Jacopo Ferretti, based on an episode from Cervantes' Don Quixote. *First performance: Rome, Teatro Valle, 2 January 1833.*

Driven mad by the infidelity of his wife Eleonora (soprano), Cardenio (baritone) roams the island of San Domingo, bleeding and dishevelled, terrifying the people. A boat comes ashore. In it is Eleonora, who had set out to search for her husband and been forced back by a storm. Further severe weather at sea causes another boat to end up on that stretch of coast-line: Fernando (tenor), Cardenio's brother, had also put to sea in search of him. Eleonora and Fernando meet, discover that the Madman is none other than their Cardenio, and, with the help of some of the residents of San Domingo, resolve to find him and restore him to sanity. After a series of adventures, during which Cardenio is about to kill his wife as a prelude to taking his own life, he finally comes to his senses. Eleonora regrets her infidelity, and he forgives her.

At its first performance, *Il furioso all'isola di San Domingo* was an outstanding success. This was partly due to an excellent cast of singers dominated by the then 22-year-old baritone Giorgio Ronconi, who already displayed the remarkable artistic talents which later led him to create the principal role in Verdi's *Nabucco*.

FURLANETTO, FERRUCCIO

(Sacile 1949)

Italian bass. After his university studies, Furlanetto concentrated on training as a singer from 1972. He took part in a number of competitions and in 1974 made his debut in the role of Sparafucile (*Rigoletto*), going on to sing Colline (*La bohème*) in Trieste in the same year. He then embarked on an international career, with appearances in the main opera houses: La Scala, Milan (*Macbeth*, *Don Giovanni*, *Les vêpres siciliennes*), San Francisco (*La Gioconda*), Covent Garden (*Don Giovanni*) and Salzburg (*Don Carlos* and *Don Giovanni*). Not particularly gifted vocally, he has nevertheless distinguished himself principally in Mozart operas, displaying considerable talents as a performer.

Above: The Italian bass Ferruccio Furlanetto.

FURTWÄNGLER, WILHELM

(Berlin 1886–Baden Baden 1954)

German conductor and composer. He studied first in Munich with Joseph Rheinberger and Max von Schillings, then in Berlin. He began his career as a conductor in Munich (1906) before taking up conducting posts in Zurich and Lübeck (1915–20). He was engaged by principal orchestras and opera houses in Germany and Austria: the Leipzig Gewandhaus, Berlin Philharmonic (1922–28), Vienna Philharmonic (1927–30), Bayreuth and Salzburg Festivals. He returned to the Berlin Philharmonic in the mid 1930s. After the war he resumed his career, conducting at the leading opera houses and festivals of Europe. As an opera conductor, Furtwängler gave outstanding performances of Beethoven's *Fidelio*, Weber's *Der Freischütz* and Wagner's *Ring* cycle.

FUX, JOHANN JOSEPH

(Hirtenfeld, Styria 1660–Vienna 1741)

Austrian composer. Born into a modest country family, he studied at the Jesuit University in Graz (1680). He then almost certainly went to Italy, where he continued his studies. From 1696 he was in Vienna, where he worked as organist at the Schottenkirche (1696–1702). He was appointed Court Composer (1698) and then devoted his energies to music at St. Stephen's Cathedral, where he was chorus-master to Wilhelmine Amalia, the Emperor's widow. As well as his vast output of instrumental works, Fux composed oratorios, sacred music and operas, establishing himself as one of the greatest exponents of baroque music in Austria.

Right: A scene from *Il Furioso all' Isola di San Domingo* by Donizetti.

G

GALUPPI, BALDASSARE (KNOWN AS IL BURANELLO)

(Burano, Venice 1706–Venice 1785)
Italian composer. He began to study music with his father and made his composing debut at the age of 16 with the opera *Gli amici rivali*, which was not a success. With the encouragement of Benedetto Marcello, however, young Galuppi continued his studies with Antonio Lotti. In 1726 he was active in Florence. Then he returned to Venice before going on to Turin, where, between 1737 and 1740, he composed his operas *Issipile e Adriano* and *Adriano in Siria*. His intensely active career was based mainly in Venice, where he was chorus-master at St. Mark's and choirmaster at the Ospedale degli Incurabili (1762). He also spent time in London (1741) and St. Petersburg (1765–67). Galuppi's prolific output included opera, instrumental music and oratorio, and he made his mark as one of the most vital and original composers of the eighteenth century. His operas include *Scipione in Cartagine* (1742), *Il filosofo di campagna* (1754) and *Il re pastore* (1762), and a number of others in both the *opera seria* and the *opera buffa* genres, many of them in collaboration with Carlo Goldoni as librettist.

GAMBILL, ROBERT

(Indianapolis, Indiana 1955)
American tenor. He studied music in Europe, at Hamburg's Hochschule für Musik (1976–81). His earliest appearances were in Geneva, Frankfurt and Wiesbaden, and he made his La Scala debut in 1981 in the world premiere of Stockhausen's *Donnerstag aus Licht*, which he went on to perform at the Holland Festival, in Stuttgart, and at the Maggio Musicale Festival in Florence. He joined the resident companies of the opera houses in Wiesbaden (1981–83) and Zurich (1984–87), then took part in the leading European festivals, including Glyndebourne and Aix-en-Provence, as well as appearing at the major international opera houses. Gambill's repertoire mainly consists of operas by Mozart, Rossini and Donizetti.

GAMBLER, THE

See *Igrok*

GANZAROLLI, VLADIMIRO

(Piacenza d'Adige 1932)
Italian bass-baritone. He studied singing with Adami Corradetti and made his debut at the Teatro Nuovo in Milan in Gounod's *Faust*. This launched him on a brilliant career, in which he specialized in the *opera buffa* repertoire of the eighteenth and nineteenth centuries. An admired Mozart performer, Ganzarolli has made some highly regarded recordings of *Don Giovanni*, *Le nozze di Figaro*, *Così fan tutte* (1970–73) and Haydn's *La vera costanza* (1977).

GARCISANZ, ISABEL

(Madrid 1934)
Spanish soprano. She studied at the Conservatory in Madrid and, after winning a scholarship, went on to train in Vienna where she made her debut in Rossini's opera *Le Comte Ory*. She was then engaged by the Staatsoper in Vienna and sang in operas by Donizetti and Ravel. Her performance in the role of Serpetta in Mozart's *La finta giardiniera* in Strasbourg led to her becoming internationally established as a Mozart singer (Susanna, Cherubino, the Countess, etc.). Her repertoire, which is very extensive, includes operas like Cavalli's *L'Ormiolo*, Rameau's *Zéphire* and Chabrier's *Le roi malgré lui*.

GARDELLI, LAMBERTO

(Venice 1915)
Italian conductor. He studied music in Pesaro and Rome, where he was an assistant to Tullio Serafin. He made his conducting debut with the Opera di Roma in 1945 (*La traviata*). He then acted as permanent conductor at the Royal Swedish Opera in Stockholm (1946–55), and also took up appointments in Budapest as conductor of the Budapest Opera House and Magyar Radio (Budapest) orchestras from 1960. He appeared regularly at Glyndebourne (from 1964), at the Metropolitan Opera House, New York (from 1966), at Covent Garden (1969) and at a number of other international concert venues and opera houses. Gardelli came to fame through his controversial recordings of early Verdi operas (*Un giorno di regno*, *I Lombardi*, *Attila*, *I masnadieri*, *I due Foscari*, *Il corsaro*, *Stiffelio* and *Alzira*). He devoted a number of years to conducting operas by Respighi, three of which, *La fiamma* (1984), *Belfagor* and *Maria Egiziaca* (1989), he also recorded.

GARDINER, JOHN ELIOT

(Fontmell Magna, Dorset 1943)
British conductor. He studied music with Thurston Dart and George Hurst in London, and with Nadia Boulanger in Paris. He then founded the Monteverdi Choir, with whom he made his debut in 1966. Specializing in the repertoire of the seventeenth and eighteenth centuries, Gardiner prepared and performed some important revised editions of operas such as Monteverdi's *Orfeo*, Rameau's *Dardanus* and *Les fêtes d'Hébé*, Leclair's *Scylla et Glaucus* and Gluck's *Iphigénie en Tauride*, which he conducted in many festivals as well as European and American opera houses (Covent Garden, Sadler's Wells, Aix-en-Provence, etc.). He founded the English Baroque Soloists in 1978, performing with them numerous instrumental, sacred and oratorio works by Monteverdi, Handel, Bach and other baroque composers.

GARINO, GÉRARD

(Lancon de Provence 1949)
French tenor. Garino studied singing at the Bordeaux Conservatoire while reading medicine at university at the same time. After training in Italy he won two important singing competitions (1973 and 1977) and made his debut at the Grand Théâtre in Bordeaux as Almaviva in Rossini's *Il barbiere di Siviglia*. Garino went on to appear regularly at this opera house, in Boïeldieu's *La dame blanche*, Délibes' *Lakmé* and Gounod's *Mireille*. He

Left: The composer Baldassare Galuppi.

tecchi (1989), *Rigoletto* and *Un ballo in maschera* (1990), and *Mosè in Egitto* (1991). Gatti has also been active as a conductor of symphonic music and as a teacher (he has taught conducting at the Conservatorio in Parma), and enjoys a growing reputation in the international opera world, with appearances with Lyric Opera of Chicago, Covent Garden and a number of other venues. He is one of the most gifted Italian conductors of the new generation.

then sang in Toulouse in Mozart's *Così fan tutte*, in Aix-en-Provence (Bizet's *Les pêcheurs de perles*) and at other provincial French opera houses (Nice, Nantes, Toulon, etc.). In 1984 Garino appeared for the first time at the Paris Opéra (in Cimarosa's *Il matrimonio segreto*) and also sang in other countries such as at the Opéra in Liège, in Treviso, Rovigo and Madrid. His fine vocal gifts and evident sensitivity of phrasing are displayed in his recordings.

GARNER, FRANÇOISE
(Nérac 1933)
French soprano. She studied music first at the Paris Conservatoire and then in Rome at the Accademia Nazionale di Santa Cecilia and in Vienna. In 1963 she made her debut in Menotti's *L'ultimo selvaggio* at the Opéra-Comique in Paris and subsequently specialized in *coloratura* roles (Lakmé, Rosina, Olympia, Lucia, Gilda, etc.). In the mid 1970s she extended her repertoire to include lyric soprano and dramatic soprano roles (Marguerite, Juliette, etc.). Garner has concentrated her career mainly in Italy and also sung in *Madama Butterfly*, *I puritani*, *Norma* and *Guillaume Tell*.

GASDIA, CECILIA
(Verona 1959)
Italian soprano. She studied music at the Conservatorio in Verona, graduating in piano in 1980. In 1981 she won the first "Concorso Maria Callas" staged by RAI, the Italian radio and television network. After making her debut in *Luisa Miller* in Pavia, Gasdia won tremendous acclaim at La Scala, Milan, when she took over from Montserrat Caballé in *Anna Bolena* (1982). This performance launched her on a brilliant career which, in the years that followed, led to leading roles in important musical and operatic events, including Ken Russell's production of Stravinsky's *The Rake's Progress* (Florence, 1982), *Mosè in Egitto* and *Moïse et Pharaon* in Pesaro and at the Paris Opéra (1983), and in Franco Zeffirelli's production of *La traviata* (Florence, 1985). Gasdia has made many appearances at major international opera houses, devoting much of her energy to Italian *bel canto* repertoire, especially Rossini.

GATTI, DANIELE
(Milan 1961)
Italian conductor. A pupil of Corghi for composition and Bellini for conducting at the Conservatorio in Milan, Gatti won the 1987 "Laboratorio Lirico" prize in Alessandria and then made his debut conducting Verdi's Giovanna d'Arco. In 1988 he conducted at the Teatro Petruzelli in Bari (*Il barbiere di Siviglia*) and at La Scala (*L'occasione fa il ladro*). From 1989 he was a guest artiste at the Rossini Opera Festival in Pesaro, where he conducted *Bianca e Faliero* and *Tancredi* (1991). He had a particularly important association with the Teatro Comunale in Bologna, conducting *I Capuleti e i Mon-*

GAVANELLI, PAOLO
(Monselice 1959)
Italian baritone. He made his debut as Leporello (*Don Giovanni*) in 1985 at the Teatro Donizetti in Bergamo. During the 1988–89 seasons he scored his first big successes at the Liceu in Barcelona (Gounod's *Faust*) and at the Teatro La Zarzuela in Madrid, where he sang Marcello in *La bohème*, a role he went on to perform in 1989 at La Fenice in Venice, at the Teatro Comunale in Bologna (1991), the Munich Bayerische Staatsoper (1991) and the Vienna Staatsoper (1991). The other significant milestones in his brilliant career include his debut (1990) in *Il trovatore* at the Metropolitan Opera House in New York, where he was to return in 1991 to sing in *I puritani* and *La traviata*; engagements with the San Francisco Opera (*Andrea Chénier*, 1992), the Chicago Opera (*Un ballo in maschera*), and at Stuttgart (*Andrea Chénier*, 1989); and appearances at the leading Italian opera houses – La Scala, Milan (from 1991), the Teatro dell'Opera in Rome (from 1990), the Teatro Carlo Felice in Genoa (from 1991), the Rossini Opera Festival in Pesaro (from 1989).

GAVAZZENI, GIANANDREA
(Bergamo 1909)
Italian conductor, composer, critic and musicologist. He studied piano with Lorenzoni and composition with Pizzetti at the Conservatorio in Milan. After graduating, he embarked on a brilliant and intensive career as a conductor, specializing in nineteenth-century and contemporary Italian opera and conducting the premieres of Pizzetti's *La figlia di Jorio* (1954) and *Assassinio nella cattedrale* (1958). Gavazzeni's name is particularly associated with La Scala, where he started conducting in 1948.

GAZZA LADRA, LA
(The Thieving Magpie)
Opera in two acts and four scenes by Gioachino Rossini (1792–1868), to a libretto by Giovanni Gherardini from the play La pie voleuse *by D'Aubigny and Caigniez. First performance: Milan, La Scala, 31 May 1817.*

: A French village at the end of the
: seventeenth century. Giannetto (tenor),

son of the wealthy property-owner Fabrizio (bass), has come home after completing his military service. Everyone celebrates his return, especially Ninetta (soprano), a young maidservant at the house, who loves Giannetto and is loved by him in return. Then Fernando (bass), Ninetta's father, pays a secret visit to Fabrizio's house and tells his daughter that the authorities want to arrest him for being a deserter. Being short of money, Fernando gives Ninetta a silver fork and asks her to sell it in order to raise some money. Not long after that, a magpie gets into the house and flies away with one of Fabrizio's silver spoons in its beak. His wife Lucia (mezzo-soprano) notices that the spoon has disappeared, and then hears that Ninetta has just sold an item of silverware to the pedlar Isacco (tenor), so she accuses Ninetta of stealing the spoon. Ninetta is arrested by the *podestà*, who wants revenge on her because she rejected his advances. During her trial, in which Ninetta is sentenced to death, Fernando tries to intervene, only to be arrested himself. Meanwhile Pippo (contralto), one of Fabrizio's manservants, discovers that the real thief was the magpie. So Ninetta is released and Fernando is pardoned with her. The opera ends with general rejoicing.

La gazza ladra, not particularly successful at its Milan premiere, was acclaimed in Paris. Apart from its overture, the opera received no further performances and was soon forgotten. Its revival is comparatively recent, enabling audiences to rediscover and revalue this Rossini *opera semiseria*.

GAZZANIGA, GIUSEPPE

(Verona 1743–Crema 1818)

Italian composer. He studied in Naples, where two of his teachers (1761–1770) were Nicola Porpora and Niccolò Piccinni. He made his debut as a composer of opera at the Teatro Nuovo in Naples with *Il barone di Trocchia* (1768), an *intermezzo*. He then went to Rome and Venice, where he was commissioned to write an opera for the Imperial Court theater in Vienna, *Il finto cieco* (1770), which was poorly received and yet set this composer on the road to success. On his return to Italy in 1771, Gazzaniga embarked on a period of intense activity. He went to Munich and Dresden, then held the post of chorus-master in Urbino (1775–76) and in Crema (1791), where he remained until his death.

GAZZETTA, LA

(The Gazette)

Opera buffa *in two acts by Gioachino Rossini (1792–1868), to a libretto by Giuseppe Palomba. First performance: Naples, Teatro dei Fiorentini, 26 September 1816.*

The naive Don Pomponio (bass) has placed an advertisement in "La Gazzetta" to find a husband for his daughter Lisetta (soprano). Lisetta is against this, being determined to marry the inn-keeper Filippo (tenor). One who reads the advertisement in the newspaper is Alberto (tenor). He turns up at Filippo's inn and tells the inn-keeper he is sure that the young woman advertised as looking for a husband is Lisetta. With Filippo's support, Lisetta flatly denies this. Perplexed, Albert then asks Doralice (mezzo-soprano), a young woman who is staying at the inn with her father Anselmo (bass), in the hope that she is the one. Doralice dismisses him indignantly. But this time Alberto is not going to give up: he has fallen for Doralice and decides to speak directly to her father. The only trouble is that instead of speaking to Anselmo, he reveals all his feelings to Don Pomponio by mistake, making a formal request for permission to marry and then boasting about his noble origins, which date back even as far as Philip of Macedon. Pomponio is completely satisfied by all this and informs his daughter Lisetta that he has decided to offer her hand in marriage to a man called Filippo. Lisetta imagines he must be talking about her fiancé and so readily agrees, but, when confronted by Alberto, it is the real Filippo she wants, while Alberto really wants Doralice. A whole series of misunderstandings and confusion ensues, but all ends happily, with everybody getting married to the right person: Lisetta to Filippo, and Alberto to Doralice.

Above: A scene from *La gazza ladra* (The Thieving Magpie) by Rossini.

Left: The conductor Gianandrea Gavazzeni

Apart from variations to the story here and there, the plot of *La gazzetta* is taken from Carlo Goldoni's comedy *Il matrimonio per concorso* (Marriage by Competition) of 1762. This fresh and amusing score is preceded by an overture which Rossini used again for *La Cenerentola* (1817).

GEDDA, NICOLAI

(Stockholm 1925)

Stage name of the Swedish tenor Nicolai Ustinov. Born of a Russian father and a Swedish mother, Gedda studied singing in his native Stockholm, initially with his father and then with Carl Martin Oehmann. In 1952 he made his debut in the role of Chappelou in Adam's *Le postillon de Longjumeau*, which launched him immediately on a brilliant and intensive international career: he sang at La Scala in the premiere of Carl Orff's *Il trionfo d'Afrodite*, at the Paris Opéra (1952), Aix-en-Provence (1954), Covent Garden and the Metropolitan Opera House, New York. With a repertoire of more than 60 roles, Gedda's sensitivity, technique and phrasing enabled him to give outstandingly distinguished performances of French opera (Faust, Roméo, Benvenuto Cellini, Enée, Werther, Des Grieux). He also had some particularly notable successes in the Russian repertoire as one of the finest interpreters of the roles of Lensky (*Eugene Onegin*), and Dimitri (*Boris Godunov*). Gedda kept a very busy schedule of concerts, recitals and recordings.

GELMETTI, GIANLUIGI

(Rome 1945)

Italian conductor. After studying music at the Accademia Nazionale di Santa Cecilia in Rome, where he graduated in conducting in 1965, Gelmetti completed his training with Franco Ferrara (1962–67), Sergiu Celibidache and Hans Swarowsky. From 1976 he began to conduct in major Italian opera houses, particularly making his mark in important revivals of opera from outside the normal repertoire, such as Donizetti's *Les martyrs* at La Fenice in Venice (1978), Piccinni's *La buona figliola* at the Teatro dell'opera, Rome (1981), Janáček's *Výlet pana Broučka do mesíce* (The Excursions of Mr Brouček) in Genoa (1987), Mascagni's *Le maschere* at the Teatro Comunale in Bologna (1988) and Salieri's *Les Danaïdes* at the Ravenna Festival (1990). Also active internationally, Gelmetti was appointed permanent conductor of the Süddeutsche Rundfunk Symphony Orchestra in Stuttgart and in 1990 music director of the Orchestre Philharmonique de Monte Carlo.

GEMMA DI VERGY

Opera in two acts by Gaetano Donizetti (1797–1848), to a libretto by Giovanni Emanuele Bidera based on Charles VII chez ses grands vassaux *by Alexandre Dumas* père. *First performance: Milan, La Scala, 26 December 1834.*

The action takes place in France in 1428. Everyone at the Château de Vergy is waiting for the return of the Count (baritone). News comes that he has disowned his wife Gemma (soprano) and is now preparing to marry Ida di Greville (mezzo-soprano) in order to ensure that he has a son and heir to continue the family line. Tamas (tenor), a young Arab and the Count's favourite servant, defends the rights of Gemma, with whom he is secretly in love. When Ida reaches the Château, Gemma, dressed as a lady-in-waiting, gains entry to her apartments in a bid to kill her. She is stopped by Tamas, who tells Gemma of his love for her and asks her to elope with him. But Gemma is deaf to his words and, in her despair, curses the husband who has betrayed her. After Tamas has left, she is overcome with remorse and prays to God that the Count may live happily with his

Above: The Swedish tenor Nicolai Gedda

Right: A scene from *La Gazzetta* by Rossini.

new wife. At that moment, cries are heard: the Count has been murdered during his wedding ceremony by Tamas, who then takes his own life. The opera ends with a great aria in which Gemma also calls upon death.

After its first performance at La Scala in 1834, *Gemma di Vergy* enjoyed enormous popularity: it was staged all over Europe and also in America (1843) and Russia (1847). It was then forgotten for a time, but thanks to the involvement of Montserrat Caballé, the opera returned to the stage of the Teatro San Carlo in Naples (1975) and to Carnegie Hall in New York (1976), also with Caballé, for its first performances since 1901. In 1987 it was again revived in Bergamo as part of the Donizetti Festival.

GENCER, LEYLA

(Istanbul 1928)

Turkish soprano. A pupil of Giannina Arangi-Lombardi at the Istanbul Conservatory, she made her debut in 1950 in Ankara as Santuzza in *Cavalleria rusticana*. Her first appearance at the Arena Flegrea in Naples was in the same Mascagni opera (1953), and she went back to Naples in 1954 to sing in *Madama Butterfly* and *Eugene Onegin* (1954). She sang in San Francisco (from 1956 onwards), Buenos Aires (from 1961), Vienna (from 1956) and Glyndebourne (1962). Gencer had a truly remarkable technique and great fluency in fast passages, and her musicianship and extraordinary skills in phrasing has enabled her to explore a range of operas whether as part of the traditional repertoire (*Lucia di Lammermoor*, *La forza del destino* and *Don Carlos*) or using her resources as a dramatic soprano to specialize in the revival of forgotten operas of the early nineteenth century. Her last stage appearance was in 1983, in Gnecco's *La prova per un'opera seria* at La Fenice in Venice, after which she gave a series of recitals.

GENESI

Opera in three acts by Franco Battiato (b. 1945), to ancient texts translated from Sanskrit, Persian, Greek and Turkish collected and adapted by the composer, and original texts by Tommaso Tramonti and Battiato. First performance: Parma, Teatro Regio, 29 April 1987.

The Gods, distressed by the chaos of the human race, decide to send four Archangels to Earth to help the inhabitants overcome the grave state of emergency prevailing there. In human form, the Archangels make contact with people who have been able to carry on the teachings and practices of the ancient esoteric tradition: a singer who lives a life of research and meditation; the monks of a monastery, cut off from the world, where ancient rites are celebrated; and a fraternity who devote themselves to Sacred Dance. These are the individuals who will ensure the salvation of the planet. The singer and his people set off on a voyage in a vast spaceship in order to reach a new understanding. After this journey they attain insight into the origins of the world. In a trance, the singer calls upon the names of famous composers in alphabetical order and then a hymn of glory is sung in honour of the Archangels before they depart.

Genesi is the first ''serious'' work by the celebrated Sicilian singer-composer Franco Battiato. It expresses themes dear to the composer concerning the world of Eastern mysticism.

GENOVEVA

Opera in four acts by Robert Schumann (1810–1856) to a libretto by Robert Reinick based on Tieck's tragedy Das Leben und Tod der heiligen Genoveva *and Hebbel's* Genoveva. *First performance: Leipzig, Stadttheater, 25 June 1850.*

Before leaving to join the armies of Charles Martel in the war against the Saracens, Count Siegfried (baritone) entrusts the care of his wife Genoveva (soprano) to his loyal friend Golo (tenor). But Golo falls in love with Genoveva. She firmly rejects him. So, with the help of Margareta (mezzo-soprano), a witch who was once also his nurse, he devises a plot to accuse Genoveva publicly of being unfaithful to her husband. Margareta makes contact with Siegfried in Strasbourg, where he has been taken to recover after being wounded, and binds him with her spell. As a result, he becomes convinced of Genoveva's infidelity, is beside himself with anger, and rushes home to the castle. Meanwhile, Genoveva has been taken to the forest to be put to death. Once again Golo tries to persuade her to run away with him, in return for her life, but Genoveva still refuses. Horns are heard, announcing the arrival of Siegfried. The Count has learned the truth, hurries to rescue his wife, and takes her back to the castle with him in triumph.

Genoveva was Schumann's only composition for the theater. The first performance was poorly received, and this made Schumann very bitter. *Genoveva* contains some fine passages, but the inadequate libretto is a burden on the opera.

Top: A scene from *Genesi*, in its first performance at Parma.

Above: Robert Schumann, who composed *Genoveva*.

GERMANIA

Opera in a prologue, two scenes and an epilogue by Alberto Franchetti (1860–1942), to a libretto by Luigi Illica. First performance: Milan, La Scala, 11 March 1902.

Carlo Worms (baritone), one of the students opposed to Germany submitting to Napoleon, is awaiting the return of his friend Federico Loewe (tenor). Worms is consumed by anguish and remorse for having betrayed Federico by seducing his girlfriend Ricke (soprano). Ricke wants to tell Federico everything, but Worms begs her to keep quiet about it so as not to break up the friendship between the two men. Not long after this, Ricke and Federico marry; Worms finds out about it after escaping from an enemy prison and immediately wants to be far away from them. Unable to keep the truth from Federico any longer, Ricke writes him a brief note and then vanishes. During a conspirators' meeting, Federico accuses Worms of being a coward. Worms offers no defense but is ready to give his life in battle. Ricke roams the battlefield on the plain of Leipzig looking for Federico. She finds him dying. After recognizing Ricke, Federico asks her to forgive Worms and to go in search of him. Ricke discovers Worms's body, covers him with a flag, and then goes back to Federico, who dies in her arms, happy that Germany has been victorious.

Germania was given a positive reception at its premiere and, together with *Cristoforo Colombo*, is Franchetti's most famous opera. The composer uses orchestral sonorities from German music and handles the dramatic and musical organization of the piece in a typically realistic way.

GERSHWIN, GEORGE

(Brooklyn, New York 1898–Beverly Hills 1937)

American composer. The son of Russian-Jewish parents (his original surname was Gershovitz) who emigrated to the United States in 1893, the young Gershwin had a remarkable musical instinct. He initially studied piano. In 1915 he was engaged as a pianist by Remick's, the music publishers. He went on to work for another publishing company, Harms (from 1918 onwards), and his own compositions started becoming quite well-known. His reputation increased as a result of the operetta *La, La, Lucille* (1919). In 1922 he wrote his music-theater piece, *Blue Monday*, published in a new version in 1925 with the title *135th Street*. In 1924 *Rhapsody in Blue* was premiered. At the height of his fame in 1928, Gershwin went to Paris, where he composed *An American in Paris*. The first festival devoted to performances of his works was held in 1929 at the Lewisohn Stadium, and from 1931 he started writing music for the first "talkies." His operatic masterpiece, *Porgy and Bess*, was staged in 1935.

GESZTY, SYLVIA

(Budapest 1934)

Hungarian soprano. She studied music at the Budapest Conservatory and made a very successful debut at the Budapest National Opera in 1959. In the early 1970s Geszty completed her training in Berlin, then began a series of appearances in which she sang the most famous *coloratura* roles, especially The Queen of the Night in *Die Zauberflöte* (The Magic Flute), in major European opera houses, including Munich, the Salzburg Festival and the Vienna Staatsoper. She also won particular acclaim for her recordings of *Così fan tutte* in 1969, *Die Zauberflöte* in 1968 and for *Ariadne auf Naxos* in 1967.

GHEDINI, GIORGIO FEDERICO

(Cuneo 1892–Nervi 1965)

Italian composer. He studied cello and composition at the Liceo Musicale in Turin. After graduating in composition (1916), Ghedini worked as a deputy conductor at Turin's Teatro Regio. In 1918 he began to concentrate on teaching, first in Turin and then in Parma (1938) and Milan (1941). From 1951 to 1962 he was director of the Milan Conservatorio. As a composer, Ghedini came to fame in about 1940. He made his theater debut with the opera *Maria d'Alessandria* (Bergamo, 1937). This was followed by *Re Hassan* (Venice, 1939), of which he presented a second version in 1961, *La pulce d'oro* (Genoa, 1940), *Le baccanti* (Milan, 1948), *Billy Budd* (Venice, 1949) and *L'ipocrita felice* (a reworking of his radio opera *Lord Inferno*, Milan, 1956).

GHIAUROV, NICOLAI

(Lydjene, near Velingrad 1929)

Bulgarian bass. After studying music at the Sofia and Moscow Conservatories, he made his debut in Sofia in *Il barbiere di Siviglia* (1956). This was followed by appearances at

Above: George Gershwin.

Top: The Bulgarian bass Nicolai Ghiaurov.

Right: The composer Giorgio Federico Ghedini.

the Bolshoi in Moscow, and at the Vienna Staatsoper. In December 1957 Ghiaurov made his debut in *Faust* at the Teatro Comunale in Bologna. His dazzling career was now underway, and it was not long before he was singing at the major international opera houses, including the Paris Opéra (1958), La Scala, Milan (1960), the Teatro Comunale in Florence, the Salzburg Festival (1962) and Covent Garden. His vocal gifts, great musicianship, and qualities of style and interpretation have led to outstanding performances in the Russian, Italian and French repertoires.

GHIUSELEV, NICOLA

(Pavlikeni 1936)

Bulgarian bass. After studying painting and music at the State Conservatory for the Arts in Sofia, he concentrated on singing and took lessons from Brambarov. He made his debut in 1960 as Timur (*Turandot*) at the Sofia National Opera. He won a number of singing competitions and then in 1965 set out on a long tour with the Sofia National Opera Company, during which he performed some of the great roles of the Russian repertoire. In this same year, he appeared for the first time at the Metropolitan Opera House, New York, as Ramfis (*Aida*) and embarked on what was to prove a brilliant international career. Ghiuselev has made guest appearances at the major opera houses, including La Scala, Milan, the Paris Opéra, the Vienna Staatsoper and the Teatro del Liceu in Barcelona. On the strength of his fine vocal timbre, musicianship and qualities of interpretation, he has distinguished himself in the Russian, Italian and French repertoires as well as in concerts, especially of songs by Mussorgsky, Tchaikovsky and Dargomyzhsky.

GHOSTS OF VERSAILLES, THE

Grand opera buffa *in two acts by John Corigliano, to a libretto by William Hoffmann based on Beaumarchais's* La mère coupable. *First performance: New York, Metropolitan Opera House, 19 December 1991.*

In a prologue, the ghosts of Louis XVI (bass), Marie Antoinette (soprano) and all their court are getting ready to attend a new play by Beaumarchais (bass-baritone). With this new work, Beaumarchais wants to distract the Queen, whom he loves deeply, from the painful memory of her death, which she has not yet managed to come to terms with. Beaumarchais, however, has decided to use his play and a diamond necklace belonging to the Queen in order to change the course of history. Up goes the curtain of the Petit Trianon theater, and the story moves to 1793, on the eve of the Terror. Louis XVI has already been guillotined and Marie Antoinette is in prison. Also in Paris is Count Almaviva (tenor), with his wife Rosina (soprano) and their faithful servants Figaro (baritone) and Susanna (soprano). With them too is Léon (tenor), the son born from the relationship between Rosina and Cherubino (mezzo-soprano), and Florestine (soprano), the Count's love-child. The two young people are in love, but Almaviva has promised Florestine to Patrick Bégearss (tenor), a mysterious Irish colonel and Revolutionary spy. Almaviva has an important mission to carry out: at a reception at the Turkish embassy he will sell the diamond necklace to the British ambassador (baritone) and use the money to save Marie Antoinette's life. Figaro also turns up at the embassy in order to save the Count from being betrayed by Bégearss, who intends to get hold of the necklace and then have Almaviva and his family arrested. By means of a subtle ploy the cunning servant obtains the necklace. But when Almaviva asks Figaro to give it to him, Figaro refuses, on the grounds that he has no intention of saving an arrogant Queen. At this point Figaro steps out of the story and Beaumarchais has a word with him. The playwright manages to persuade Figaro to save the Queen after all. The plot then resumes its former course. Enter Bégearss, who, after obtaining the necklace, does indeed have Almaviva and his family arrested. But Figaro succeeds in escaping, and he and Beaumarchais, disguised as undertakers, get into the prison to set the prisoners free. At first the plan seems to be working, but then Bégearss appears, followed by guards. Figaro is quick to react, however, and reports Bégearss to the revolutionaries for having acquired the necklace and not handed it over to his superiors. The traitor is arrested and immediately guillotined, whereas Figaro and the Almavivas are able to make good their escape. Beaumarchais is left behind. He intends to release Marie Antoinette, who is being kept in the same prison. The voice of the Queen's ghost is heard: she has realized the depth of Beaumarchais's love for her and so wants to stay with him. As a result, history must take its course. Thus, whilst Marie Antoinette is being guillotined, her ghost is reunited with her beloved Beaumarchais, while Figaro, Susanna and the Almavivas fly away in a hot-air balloon.

Corigliano's opera was supposed to be staged to mark the centenary of the Metropolitan Opera during the 1983–84 season, but the score was not finished in time. *The Ghosts of Versailles* eventually went into production in 1991 and was a great success. The work is theatrically very complex, because of the large number of characters involved.

Left: The Bulgarian bass Nicola Ghiuselev

GIACOMINI, GIUSEPPE

(Veggiano di Padova 1940)
Italian tenor. Initially self-taught in singing, he went on to have lessons with Elena Fava Ceriati at the Conservatory in Padua. Giacomini made his debut in 1966 in Vercelli as Pinkerton (*Madama Butterfly*); he then took part in a number of singing competitions and appeared in *La traviata* with the Bratislava Opera. At the beginning of the 1970s, his career became international, with appearances at the Deutsche Oper Berlin, the Vienna Staatsoper (1972) and in Munich (1973). In 1975 he appeared for the first time in the United States (*La fanciulla del West* with the Connecticut Opera), and in 1976 he scored a great success on his debut at the Metropolitan Opera House, New York, in the role of Alvaro (*La forza del destino*). As well as making regular guest appearances at the Metropolitan, Giacomini performed at the leading international opera houses. His dramatic tenor voice, with its polished timbre and supreme in the upper register, has made him an ideal interpreter of operas like *Andrea Chénier*, *La forza del destino*, *Tosca*, *Cavalleria rusticana* and *I pagliacci*. In 1987 in New Orleans he sang Verdi's *Otello* for the first time and gave subsequent performances of this in major opera houses.

Above: A scene from *Gianni di Parigi* by Donizetti.

Right: The Italian bass Bonaldo Giaiotti as Filippo II in Verdi's *Don Carlos*.

GIAIOTTI, BONALDO

(Ziracco (Udine) 1932)
Italian bass. He studied music first in Udine and later in Milan and New York. After winning several international singing competitions, he made his debut in Milan in 1958 with *La bohème* and *Manon*. By 1959 he was singing in the United States, where he made his debut during the 1960–61 season at the Metropolitan Opera House, New York, as Zaccaria in *Nabucco*, and he continued to appear there regularly until the 1986–87 season. His career at the same time included appearances at the major European opera houses. Giaiotti's is an authentic bass voice which, together with his outstanding musicianship and sensitivity of phrasing, has enabled him to give excellent accounts of himself on record too, as Ramfis in *Aida* (1966), Ferrando in *Il trovatore* (1966), Wurm in *Luisa Miller* (1975) and the Father Superior in *La forza del destino* (1976).

GIANNI DI PARIGI

Opera in two acts by Gaetano Donizetti (1797–1848), to a libretto by Felice Romani. First performance: Milan, La Scala, 10 October 1839.

The heir to the throne of France, who has been promised the hand of the Princess of Navarre (soprano) in marriage, has assumed the identity of a wealthy citizen by the name of Gianni (tenor). The young Prince has disguised himself in this way in order to become acquainted with the Princess without being recognized. With his page Oliviero (mezzo-soprano) and a stylish retinue, Gianni installs himself at the inn of Pedrigo (bass). Taking advantage of the innkeeper's greed, Gianni offers to pay a considerable sum so as to be allocated the apartments and provisions already booked by the Princess for herself and her own retinue. When the Princess arrives, Gianni gallantly offers her his hospitality. The Princess has realized the true identity of this obliging gentleman but does not reveal this and plays along with him. The time the two young people spend together leads to their falling in love, and this provides the opera with its happy ending: Gianni reveals who he really is and shows that he is more willing than ever to marry the Princess.

Donizetti began to compose *Gianni di Parigi* around 1828 and later made a number of changes to the work, especially to the leading role. He wanted to give the part to the famous tenor Rubini, who turned it down. The opera was consequently staged, more or less unbeknown to the composer, at La Scala, Milan, in 1839.

GIANNI SCHICCHI

See *Trittico, Il*

GIGLI, BENIAMINO

(Recanati 1890–Rome 1957)
Italian tenor. After studying at the Accademia Nazionale di Santa Cecilia in Rome, he made his debut in 1914 at the Teatro Sociale in Rovigo, singing the role of Enzo in Ponchielli's opera *La Gioconda*. He soon established his reputation at major opera houses such as the Teatro San Carlo in Naples (1915–16), the Teatro Real in Madrid (1917) and La Scala, Milan (*Mefistofele* 1918). From the 1920–21 season onwards, Gigli became well-known at the Metropolitan Opera House, New York, where he appeared every year until 1935. After that his career was mainly centered in Europe: at Covent Garden, in Berlin, and at the leading Italian opera houses. He appeared in public for the last time at a concert in Washington on 25 May 1955. Gigli was, with Caruso, the most famous tenor of the twentieth century. His exceptional vocal gifts and outstanding personality as a performer (although less as an actor) were seen to particular effect in lyric operas such as *Lucia di Lammermoor*, *Mefistofele* and *La bohème*, but his complete control over

voice and phrasing made it possible for him to give persuasive performances of roles suited to voices of a more dramatic character, such as *Tosca*, *Cavalleria rusticana*, *Andrea Chénier* and *Aida*.

GIMÉNEZ, RAÚL

(Carlos Pellegrini 1951)
Argentinian tenor. He studied music at the Fondación del Teatro Colón in Buenos Aires and made his debut at the same theater in the role of Ernesto (Donizetti's *Don Pasquale*) during the 1980–81 season. From 1984 onwards, he embarked on an international career, appearing at the Wexford Festival in Ireland (as Filandro in Cimarosa's *Le astuzie femminili*). A specialist in the Italian *bel canto* repertoire, Giménez has appeared in

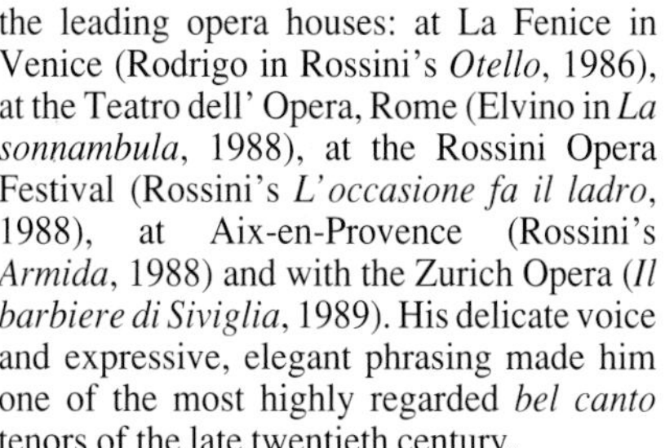

the leading opera houses: at La Fenice in Venice (Rodrigo in Rossini's *Otello*, 1986), at the Teatro dell' Opera, Rome (Elvino in *La sonnambula*, 1988), at the Rossini Opera Festival (Rossini's *L'occasione fa il ladro*, 1988), at Aix-en-Provence (Rossini's *Armida*, 1988) and with the Zurich Opera (*Il barbiere di Siviglia*, 1989). His delicate voice and expressive, elegant phrasing made him one of the most highly regarded *bel canto* tenors of the late twentieth century.

GIOCONDA, LA

Dramatic opera in four acts by Amilcare Ponchielli (1834–1886), to a libretto by Tobia Gorrio (anagrammatic pseudonym for Arrigo Boito) from Victor Hugo's novel Angelo, tyran de Padoue. *First performance: Milan, La Scala, 8 April 1876.*

The action takes place in Venice in the seventeenth century. Gioconda (soprano), a travelling ballad-singer, has rejected the love of Barnaba (baritone), a spy for the Council of Ten. For revenge, Barnaba accuses Gioconda's blind mother (contralto) of witchcraft. Enzo Grimaldo (tenor) springs to the lady's defense. Gioconda is in love with Enzo, whom she believes to be a sailor. In fact, he is a nobleman from Genoa who has been sent into exile by the Republic of Venice and has now returned to that city to see once again his fiancée Laura (mezzo-soprano), who has been forced to marry Alvise Badoero (bass), head of the Inquisition. Barnaba has recognized Enzo and promises to help him to escape with Laura, but then he sends an anonymous letter to the authorities disclosing Enzo's whereabouts. That same evening, Gioconda, who has heard that Enzo is eloping with another woman, hides near the ship in order to kill her rival, only to recognize Laura as the woman who had helped to save her mother, so she does not carry out her plan. Alvise's guards arrive. Laura and Gioconda escape together, while Enzo, after setting fire to the ship, throws himself into the sea. At the Palazzo Ca' d'Oro, Alvise accuses Laura of treason and orders her to take poison. Gioconda breaks into the Palazzo and

Left: The Argentinian tenor Raúl Giménez.

Above: Beniamino Gigli.

exchanges the poison for a narcotic, which she persuades Laura to drink so she can pretend to be dead. Shortly after this, at the end of a sumptuous party, Alvise shows his appalled guests Laura's apparently dead body. One of those present is Enzo: assuming that Laura really is dead, he attacks Alvise and is arrested. Gioconda begs Barnaba to save the young man's life, promising him herself in return. Gioconda then has Laura (who is still asleep) carried to her house on the island of Giudecca. Enzo arrives, realizes the extent of Gioconda's generosity and runs off with Laura. Barnaba then appears, and Gioconda, rather than give in to a love she finds repugnant, kills herself.

Ponchielli's most famous opera, *La Gioconda* was a sensational success at its first performance and continued to be popular throughout the twentieth century. The composer made a large number of changes to the score in order to eliminate some of the complexities in the plot and music. By the time the work was staged in Rome (1877) and in Genoa (1879), it already seemed different from its first production. The definitive version was the one seen at La Scala, Milan, on 12 February 1880.

GIOIELLI DELLA MADONNA, I

Opera in three acts by Ermanno Wolf-Ferrari (1876–1948), to a libretto by E. Golisciani and C. Zangarini. First performance, in the German version by H. Liebstöckl: Berlin, Kurfürstenoper, 23 December 1911.

The action takes place in Naples at the end of the nineteenth century. Gennaro (tenor), a blacksmith, is anguished by his love for Maliella (soprano), an orphan who has been brought up in his household. The young woman shamelessly allows herself to be courted by all the young men, including a ruffian by the name of Raffaele (baritone), who is prepared to steal for her the jewels of the Madonna, which at that moment are being carried through the streets as part of a procession. Maliella is frightened but at the same time flattered by this. On returning home, she is reproached by Carmella (mezzo-soprano), Gennaro's mother; while Gennaro himself, on learning that Maliella wants to leave home, once again declares his love for her. Maliella rejects him, insisting that she will give her love to the man who steals the jewels of the Madonna for her. Now desperate, Gennaro carries out the theft himself, then brings the jewels to Maliella. Now she must surely be his. At the hide-out of the Camorristi (a band of gangsters), Maliella (pursued by Gennaro, who does not want her to get away) asks Raffaele for help, but Raffaele, who has heard that Maliella has been with another man, rejects her with contempt and horror because she is wearing the jewels of the Madonna. At this point Gennaro is dragged in by some of the Camorristi. Maliella flings the jewels down at his feet and runs away. The Camorristi also beat a hasty retreat, so as not to be accused of complicity in the sacrilegious theft. Left alone, Gennaro picks up the necklace, goes to the statue of the Madonna, places it at her feet, and stabs himself.

The first performance was given in German. Only later, when the work was staged at the Metropolitan Opera House in New York, with Toscanini conducting, was Wolf-Ferrari able to hear it in Italian.

GIORDANO, UMBERTO

(Foggia 1867–Milan 1948)

Italian composer. After graduating in 1890, Giordano made his debut at the Teatro di Torre Argentina in Rome with his opera *Mala vita* (1892). This was followed by *Regina Diaz* (1894), a failure. He was fortunate, however, with *Andrea Chénier* (1896), a success he then built on with *Fedora* (1898). These are thought of as being Giordano's masterpieces for the theater. They were followed by works which enjoyed the same degree of public acclaim but left the critics divided: *Siberia* (1903), *Marcella* (1907), *Mese Mariano* (1910), *Madame Sans-Gêne* (1915), *La cena delle beffe* (1924) and *Il re* (1929).

GIORNO DI REGNO, UN, OSSIA IL FINTO STANISLAO

(King for a Day, or the Impostor Stanislaus)

Opera in two acts by Giuseppe Verdi (1813–1901), to a libretto by Felice Romani based on Le faux Stanislas *by A. V. Pineau-Duval. First performance: Milan, La Scala, 5 September 1840.*

Stanislao, King of Poland, is under threat from enemy plotting and calls upon the Cavalier di Belfiore (baritone) to impersonate him. In his new role, the Cavalier also has to keep up this pretense with his former mistress, the Marchesa del Poggio (soprano), who plays along and pretends not to recognize him. Belfiore finds himself caught up in a series of love intrigues which involve Giulietta (mezzo-soprano), the Marchesa's niece: she is in love with Edoardo (tenor) but is required to marry the elderly Treasurer, La Rocca. Eventually news arrives that the King is safe and has appointed the Cavalier di Belfiore as his Marshal for services

Above: A scene from *La Gioconda*, in a 1963 production at the Arena in Verona.

Right: Umberto Giordano, in a portrait by Rietti painted in 1937.

rendered to his country. The opera has a happy ending, with Belfiore marrying the Marchesa and Giulietta her beloved Edoardo.

This was Verdi's second opera and first failure in his career as a composer. The young man was scarcely in the right frame of mind to compose a comic opera, having lost his wife and two of his children within the space of two years. As a result, the music is formal and devoid of real verve, as is the rather mannered libretto by Felice Romani. Stung by this experience, Verdi steadfastly refused to write another comic opera until *Falstaff*, near the end of his life.

GIOVANNA D'ARCO

(Joan of Arc)

Opera in a prologue and three acts by Giuseppe Verdi (1813–1901), to a libretto by Temistocle Solera based on Schiller's Die Jungfrau von Orleans. *First performance: Milan, La Scala, 15 February 1845.*

The action takes place in France. With the French army about to be overrun by the sheer numbers of the British army, King Carlo VIII (tenor) has a vision which prompts him to go and lay his sword at the feet of a miraculous image of the Virgin Mary. Also there he finds Giovanna (soprano), a young shepherdess, to whom the Virgin has entrusted a mission to save France. The young woman takes the King's sword and urges Carlo not to surrender. France is victorious. Everyone sings the praises of Giovanna for having saved her country. Their joy is overshadowed, however, by the arrival of Giacomo (baritone), Giovanna's father. He is convinced his daughter is in league with the devil and has the King under her spell. Giovanna does not understand her father's accusations and offers no defense. She is put in prison, where she calls on the Virgin Mary. Giacomo overhears his daughter praying, realizes the truth, asks her forgiveness and has her released. Giovanna returns to the fight, saves France again and its King, but this time is mortally wounded. Before she dies, with King Carlo, Giacomo and the people at her side, Giovanna, in ecstasy, gives France her blessing.

Solera's absurd and inconclusive libretto clearly played some part in the failure of this opera, which is seen as one of Verdi's weakest, both musically (with the exception of some passages in Giovanna's music) and theatrically.

GIRL OF THE GOLDEN WEST

See *Fanciulla del West, La*

GIULIETTA E ROMEO

(Romeo and Juliet)

Tragic opera in three acts by Riccardo Zandonai (1883–1944), to a libretto by Antonio Rossato. First performance: Rome, Teatro Costanzi, 14 February 1922.

The action takes place in Verona and Mantua during the thirteenth century. One night, some supporters of Tebaldo, a Capulet (baritone), clash with a group of armed members of the rival family of the Montagues. The arrival of the night patrol breaks up the fight. The street is now deserted. Romeo, a Montague (tenor), and Giulietta, a Capulet (soprano), who has appeared on her balcony, exchange passionate words of love. The hatred between their families prevents them from being together, and the two lovers are thus forced to meet in secret. Tebaldo, who has discovered these secret meetings between Romeo and Giulietta, reminds the young woman of her obligation to marry the Count of Lodrone. While Giulietta is protesting her love for Romeo, news arrives that two of the Capulets have been killed by a group of Montagues led by Romeo. Tebaldo hurries away. Romeo enters the garden of the Capuleti, and Giulietta tries to persuade him to come with her to a safer place, but then Tebaldo arrives. He hurls himself at Romeo, who, attempting to defend himself, kills his adversary. To avoid being arrested under the law that makes armed fighting illegal, Romeo takes refuge in Mantua. Some time after this, a minstrel (tenor) sings a sad song mourning the death of Giulietta. This is the first that Romeo has heard of it, and he sets out at once for Verona. In the mausoleum of the Capulets, Romeo is confronted with Giulietta's body and takes poison. Giulietta, who had only drunk a narcotic in order to pretend to be dead and avoid marrying the Count of Lodrone, wakes up at that moment: the sight of Romeo dying fills her with despair, and she falls dead.

Rossato's libretto is indebted less to Shakespeare's play than to the tale by Luigi da Porto, reworked by Matteo Bandello. One significant difference concerns the death of Giulietta: in Shakespeare's play, she stabs herself. The music is confirmation of Zandonai's remarkable gift for melody.

GIULINI, CARLO MARIA

(Barletta 1914)

Italian conductor. He graduated in viola and composition from the Conservatorio in Rome and studied for his diploma in conducting in 1941 with Bernardino Molinari. From 1945 to 1952, Giulini was musical director for the RAI (Italian Radio) Orchestra in Milan and Rome, and from 1955 he conducted the Chicago Symphony Orchestra. His conducting debut was in Bergamo in 1950 (*La traviata*). He then conducted at La Scala, Milan, and at Florence's Maggio Musicale Festival (*L'italiana in Algeri*, *Alceste*, *La traviata*, *La Wally*), Glyndebourne, the Edinburgh Festival (*Falstaff*, 1955) and London's Covent Garden (*Don Carlo*, *Falstaff*). Giulini devoted most of his career to conducting the orchestral repertoire, appearing with the leading international orchestras including the Vienna Philharmonic (1973–76), the Chicago Symphony (1969–72) and the Los Angeles Philharmonic (1978–84). He has made many recordings of opera, including live performances which illustrate his strength of personality and gifts as a conductor, including Donizetti's *Don Sebastiano* (1955), *Don Giovanni* (1959), *Le nozze di Figaro* (1960) and *Don Carlos* (1970).

Above: Poster by L. Metlicovitz for *Giulietta e Romeo* by Riccardo Zandonai.

GIULIO CESARE IN EGITTO

(Julius Caesar in Egypt)

Opera in three acts by George Frederick Handel (1685–1759) to a libretto by Nicola Haym, adapted from the original by Francesco Bussani. First performance: London, Haymarket Theater, 20 February 1724.

After being decisively defeated by Cesare's troops, Pompeo asks the King of Egypt for asylum. His wife Cornelia (mezzo-soprano) and son Sesto (contralto) plead with their conqueror to show clemency. Enter Achilla (bass), captain to Tolomeo (contralto), who has brought Cesare (contralto) the head of Pompey. Cesare is angry at this and orders that his dead enemy be given all due honours. Meanwhile, Cleopatra (soprano) attempts to ally herself with Cesare in order to ensure her succession to the throne of Egypt. At the same time, Tolomeo, her brother, is planning with Achilla to kill Cesare. A few days later, Cleopatra, who has won Cesare's love, is about to reveal her feelings to him when a number of hired assassins burst in and Cesare is forced to escape by throwing himself into the sea. Achilla tells the King that Cesare is dead and asks for the hand of Cornelia, with whom he is in love, but the King will not agree, because he too is in love with her. Then the Roman troops are defeated by the Egyptians. When Cesare arrives, he finds that his army has been completely routed. Achilla is mortally wounded and hands over to Sesto (who had managed to escape from Tolomeo's harem) a seal with which he will be able to enlist the help of a hundred soldiers hostile to Tolomeo. Cesare gains possession of the seal and, having assembled his men, confronts the Egyptians and defeats them. Sesto kills Tolomeo, thus avenging his father's death. Cornelia is freed, and citizens and soldiers alike rejoice at Cleopatra's coronation, as Cesare escorts her to the throne.

The plot of this opera was so complicated that during the performances the theater management used to keep the auditorium lights lit or provide the public with candles so they could follow the printed libretto. From the musical point of view, *Giulio Cesare* is one of Handel's most finely balanced operas. The alternation between recitatives and arias is beautifully judged, and the arias themselves are all excellently constructed, especially those he gives to Cleopatra, some of the loveliest to be found anywhere in baroque opera.

Above: The Russian composer Mikhail Ivanovich Glinka.

Opposite: Carlo Broschi, known as Il Farinelli, in a painting from the period.

GIURAMENTO, IL

(The Oath)

Opera in three acts by Saverio Mercadante (1795–1870), to a libretto by Giovanni Gaetano Rossi. First performance: Milan, La Scala, 11 May 1837.

Elaisa (soprano) and Bianca (mezzo-soprano) are in love with Viscardo (tenor). Bianca's husband, Manfredo (baritone), has discovered his wife's adultery and decides to punish her by making her drink poison. Elaisa, who owes Bianca a debt of gratitude, exchanges the poison for a sleeping draught. Viscardo, seeing Bianca apparently lifeless, assumes that it is Elaisa who has done the deed and kills her with his sword. At that very moment Bianca wakes up.

The plot, based on Victor Hugo's novel *Angélo, tyran de Padoue*, was later used by Cui and Ponchielli for their operas *Angelo* and *La Gioconda*, both dating from 1876. *Il giuramento* is considered to be Mercadante's best opera: it contains passages of outstanding lyricism, although its dramatic element and characters are fairly conventional.

GLASS, PHILIP

(Baltimore 1937)

American composer. He began to study music at the Conservatory in Baltimore, going on to the University of Chicago and the Juilliard School (1957–61). He then took advanced lessons in composition with Nadia Boulanger at the Paris Conservatoire (1964–66). His meeting in 1966 with the celebrated composer and sitar virtuoso Ravi Shankar stimulated Glass to become involved with the stylistic elements of Indian music, which he adapted for a new style of composition often called minimalism. Using the minimalist musical language, which is made up of short, repetitive melodies over a static or gradually, subtly shifting harmonic pattern, Glass has composed a great deal of instrumental music and film scores as well as his operas *Einstein on the Beach* (1976), *Satyagraha* (1980), *Akhnaten* (1985), *Hydrogen Jukebox* (1990) and *The Fall of the House of Usher* (1991).

GLINKA, MIKHAIL IVANOVICH

(Novospasskoye, Smolensk 1804–Berlin 1857)

Russian composer. His obvious talent for music at a very early age was encouraged by his paternal uncles, who were excellent amateur musicians. From 1817 to 1822 he attended boarding-school in St. Petersburg. His father's opposition to the idea of a career in music meant that young Glinka had to take a job with the foreign service. He soon left it, however, and in 1830 set out to travel in Western Europe. In Italy he was in close contact with leading figures in the Italian opera world, notably Bellini and Donizetti. On his return to Russia in 1834, enriched by the experience of this journey, he soon renewed his contacts with the intellectual circles of St. Petersburg, especially Pushkin and Zhukovsky, who gave him the idea for the plot of his first work, *Ivan Susanin* (A Life for the Tsar, 1836) which, though influenced by Italian opera, also incorporates Russian folklike idioms and represents one of the first examples of home-grown opera in Russia. Of equal importance is Glinka's other work for the theater, *Ruslan and Ludmilla* (1842).

THE GOLDEN AGE OF THE CASTRATO

It was because women were not allowed to sing in performances of sacred music that castrati were first used. To begin with, the parts for female voices were given to boy trebles, but this meant that the singers were continually having to be replaced once the boys' voices broke and they could no longer sing the notes, and the use of artificial falsetto singers turned out to have major disadvantages in view of the fact that their delivery did not produce a consistently pleasant sound. So the practice of castration became more widespread. The idea had been imported from Spain (having originated in the East) and the first castrati to come to Italy were actually from Spain, – Francisco Soto (who from 1562 was active at the Pontifical Chapel) and Hernando Bustamente (who was at the Court in Ferrara some twenty years later). It was therefore around the end of the sixteenth century – not least as a result of a decree by Pope Sixtus V in 1588 which forbade women to appear on stage anywhere in the Papal State – that castrati started to make their mark in the theaters. The first great castrato to be seen in an Italian theater was G. Francesco Grossi, known as Siface. The extraordinary boldness of the castrato voice, its flawless delivery and outstanding virtuosity, were the key to the splendour of baroque opera: castrati sang not only the female roles but also played the troop commander, the lover and the tyrant to the detriment of the male voices which, in all but a few isolated instances, were given secondary roles. Among the most important castrati of the eighteenth century was Giovanni Appiani, known as Appianino, one of the first pupils of Nicolò Porpora, the composer and one of the greatest singing teachers of his generation. Other famous castrati who attended his school were Antonio Hubert, known as Il Porporino, who in 1741 was in the service of Frederick II of Prussia, Gaetano Majorana, known as Il Caffarelli, whose appearances included Handel's *Faramondo* and *Serse*, and finally Carmelo Broschi, known as Il Farinelli and regarded as the greatest singer in the history of opera. Il Farinelli was a cultured man for whom popes, emperors and monarchs would compete, so overpowered were they all by his prodigious singing. One only has to reflect that his voice had such a soothing effect on King Philip of Spain that the king wanted to retain him at Court in Madrid and offered him 50,000 francs a year to stay. Other celebrated castrati included Francesco Bernardi, known as Il Senesino, for whom Handel composed a number of operas, among them *Floridante*, *Flavio*, *Giulio Cesare*, *Tamerlano*, etc.; Domenico Cecchi, known as Il Tortona; and Gioacchino Conti, known as Il Gizziello, who became famous on the strength of his particular talent for singing about love and his exceptional range (up to five octaves above middle C) as demonstrated by his performances in the operas *Atalanta* and *Sigismondo* which Handel wrote for him. The first half of the eighteenth century was unquestionably the golden age of the castrato, because once Gluck's reforms of opera had come into effect, the use of the castrato voice gradually diminished, disappearing altogether at the onset of first the Enlightenment and then the French Revolution.

After further prolonged travels throughout Europe, Glinka died in Berlin on his way home.

GLORIANA

Opera in three acts by Benjamin Britten (1913–1976), to a libretto by William Plomer based on the biographical novel Elizabeth and Essex *by Lytton Strachey. First performance: London, Royal Opera House, Covent Garden, 8 June 1953.*

Queen Elizabeth (soprano) interrupts a duel between her favourite, the Earl of Essex (tenor), and Lord Mountjoy (baritone), reproaching both men and bidding them to make peace with one another. In her apartments, the Queen receives her adviser, Lord Cecil (bass), who insists she chooses someone to marry, but the Queen tells him she is wedded to the realm. Then Essex comes in, sings a sweet melody, and asks the Queen to appoint him as commander-in-chief of the English forces being sent to Ireland. The scene changes to a garden where Lord Mountjoy and Lady Penelope Rich (mezzo-soprano) are plotting a coup d'état. During a court ball in Whitehall, Lady Essex (soprano), who has been urged by her husband to attend the occasion ostentatiously dressed, is afraid her display of elegance will anger the Queen. When the ladies retire to change, the Queen dons the gown which Lady Essex has just removed and thus publicly humiliates her. Elizabeth then appoints Essex to command the military expedition to Ireland. Essex returns defeated, bursts into the Queen's bedroom (even though her ladies-in-waiting try to prevent him) and finds Elizabeth without her wig. Elizabeth's initial reaction is simply to show displeasure, but later she orders Lord Cecil to arrest Essex on a charge of insurrection. As Essex makes his way to the scaffold, his wife and friends beg the Queen to show mercy, but in vain. Left alone, Elizabeth sits on her throne weeping and calling on God to help her.

Gloriana was staged to mark the coronation of Queen Elizabeth II. The inclusion of dances, large-scale ensemble scenes and lush orchestration reinforce the celebratory aspect of this opera, which also confirmed Britten as England's leading composer.

GLOSSOP, PETER

(Sheffield 1928)

British baritone. He studied singing with Leonard Mosley and made his debut at London's Sadler's Wells Theater, where his first appearance was as a member of the chorus (1952). His career then focused on Covent Garden, where for more than ten years he sang leading baritone roles, especially those of the Italian repertoire (Rigoletto, Rodrigo, Scarpia, Tonio, etc.), roles which also brought him international renown. Glossop was active as a recording artist and took part in the first performances on record of Berlioz's *Les Troyens* (1969) and Donizetti's *Roberto Devereux* with Beverly Sills, besides winning particular acclaim as Iago in Verdi's *Otello*, with Herbert von Karajan conducting (1974).

GLUCK, CHRISTOPH WILLIBALD

(Erasbach, Upper Palatinate 1714–Vienna 1787)

German composer. His father was opposed to his taking up music, and in 1731 he ran away from home to Prague, where he had his first direct experiences of opera. In 1736 he went to Vienna, moving on from there in the same year to Milan as a member of the retinue of Prince Antonio Maria Melzi. Here Gluck's first opera, *Artaserse* (1741), was staged; it was an outstanding success, effectively launching him on an intensive career as a composer of opera, which took him to a number of Italian cities and then to England (1745). In 1752 he settled permanently in Vienna, where he met Count Giacomo Durazzo, who was in charge of Vienna's theaters. It was through Durazzo that Gluck was first exposed to the influence of French opera, which he made to blend marvellously with the style of Italian *opera seria*. From 1754 to 1764, Gluck was Kapellmeister at the Archduchess Maria Theresia's Imperial Music Theater. This is the most important period in the composer's career, during which he also met the poet Raniero De Calzabigi, who provided the libretti for *Orfeo ed Euridice* (1762), *Alceste* (1767) and *Paride ed Elena* (1770). The modernity of these operas was not immediately appreciated in Vienna, and consequently Gluck turned his interest to French opera, composing *Iphigénie en Aulide* (1774), *Armide* (1777), *Iphigénie en Tauride* (1779) and *Echo et Narcisse* (1779). After suffering a slight stroke, Gluck returned in 1780 to Vienna, where he spent the last years of his life.

GLÜCKLICHE HAND, DIE

(The Lucky Hand)

Drama with music in four scenes for baritone, mixed chorus and orchestra by Arnold Schoenberg (1874–1951), to the composer's own text. First performance: Vienna, Volksoper, 14 October 1924.

Above: A scene from *Gloriana*, in a 1966 production at London's Sadler's Wells Theater.

Right: The German composer Christoph Willibald Gluck.

The Man (baritone) is being held down by a monster who has embedded its teeth in his neck, while mysterious voices are urging him to give up his unobtainable dreams. The scene changes. The Man and the Woman (mimed role) love each other, but then the Woman allows herself to be carried off by the Lord, who symbolizes the stark reality of this world. The Man climbs a rocky slope, which represents life's struggles. Suddenly a cave is lit up, in which the Man sees a group of busy workmen. Unaffected by the contempt and hostility they show towards him, the Man sets a piece of gold on an anvil and with a single hammer-stroke fashions a magnificent diadem. A storm blows up, and the workshop disappears, to be replaced by another cave, in which the Man finds the Woman again. He wants to win her back, but she runs away, dislodging a rock, which rolls down on to him: this sequence represents the truth that when we go in search of unobtainable happiness we are always overwhelmed with anguish. As at the beginning, so now the Man is pinned down by the monster's teeth, while once again the voices, now in mocking tones, repeat their message to him that it is useless to concentrate one's desires on fleeting, abstract imaginings.

The short text of *Die glückliche Hand* was written in 1910, while the score was completed three years later. This is a complex, richly symbolic, expressionist opera: except for two short passages, the Man uses mime, and there are only a few moments where he actually sings. His dramatic experiences are a kind of allegory of the isolation of the human being, whose "happiness" is only a passing illusion.

GOBBI, TITO

(Bassano del Grappa 1913–Rome 1984)
Italian baritone. He studied singing with Giulio Crimi in Rome and made his debut in 1935 in Gubbio as Count Rodolfo (*La sonnambula*). After winning first prize in 1936 in both a singing competition in Vienna and one held by La Scala, Milan, Gobbi appeared for the first time in the role of Germont (*La traviata*) at the Teatro Adriano in Rome in 1937. He went on to perform this role at the Teatro dell' Opera, Rome (1939), where in 1942 his singing of Wozzeck in the Italian premiere of Berg's opera gave immediate prominence to his unique talents. Also in 1942 he made his first appearance at La Scala (as Belcore in *L'elisir d'amore*). In the years that followed, he embarked on an intensive international career including venues such as San Francisco (from 1948), the Salzburg Festival (1950), London's Covent Garden, Chicago and the Metropolitan Opera, New York (1956). This schedule continued more or less without a break until 1977, the year of his retirement from the stage. Gobbi drew on an exceptionally large repertoire, from Mozart to Rossini, all the leading Verdi roles, Puccini, Leoncavallo, etc. He also left an equally extensive range of recordings (the last dating from 1977) which illustrate his skill in phrasing and interpretation, despite obvious vocal limitations. After retirement, he devoted his energies to opera production (1982).

GOLDBERG, REINER

(Crostau, near Bautzen, Saxony 1939)
German tenor. He studied singing with Schellenberg at the C. M. von Weber Academy in Dresden (1962–67). His initial appearances were as a chorus member, and he went on to join the company of the Dresden Staatsoper (1973). Engagements followed in Berlin (1977), Hamburg and Munich, and soon he was singing at major international opera houses. Goldberg's repertoire consists mainly of operas by Wagner and Richard Strauss. His recordings of Wagner's *Parsifal* and Strauss's *Daphne*, both of which he made in 1981, are particularly worth noting and illustrate the authentic *Heldentenor* qualities of his voice and interpretative skills.

GOLDMARK, KARL

(Keszthely 1830–Vienna 1915)
Austrian composer of Hungarian birth. After studying in Vienna, he embarked in 1844 on a career in music as a violinist and conductor

The German tenor Reiner Goldberg in Wagner's *Tannhäuser.*

Above: The Italian baritone Tito Gobbi.

first in Budapest and then in Vienna and other cities. In 1860 he settled permanently in Vienna, where he won considerable renown. Of his operas, clearly influenced by Wagner, the most famous is *Die Königin von Saba* (The Queen of Sheba), 1875.

GOLEM

Opera in two parts, Prelude and Legend, by John Casken (b. 1949), to the composer's own libretto in collaboration with Pierre Audi, based on Jewish folklore. First performance: London, Almeida Theater, 28 June 1989.

The Prelude opens in a deserted place. The Maharal (baritone), now an old man, recalls the time when he created the Golem. A mysterious chorus, later joined by the voice of Ometh (counter-tenor), stirs up the Maharal's feelings as he relives those tragic events in his mind. In the Legend, the young Maharal makes a creature out of clay from the bank of a river. He calls the creature Golem and then tries to teach it to live like a human being. The Golem (bass-baritone) discovers desire when he meets the young Miriam (soprano), and this makes the Maharal angry. Ometh, a man of ambiguous character, wants the Golem to join him, because together, he says, they will be able to eliminate evil from the Earth. Once again the Maharal intervenes to keep the Golem away from Ometh, whom he looks upon as a fraud. The scene changes to an encampment where a number of men are planning to rebel against the wretchedness of their lives. One of them, Stoikus (tenor), believes that the coming of a prophet is near at hand. While involved with the others in reading the Tarot, Stoikus, overcome by an uncontrollable frenzy, wants to ask the Golem a question, but it becomes irritated and kills him. After once again separating the Golem from Ometh's negative influence, the Maharal comes to realize that creating it has caused nothing but harm.

Commissioned by the Almeida International Festival of Contemporary Music in London, *Golem* confirmed John Casken's position as one of the most representative composers of the British contemporary music scene.

Above: The Spanish tenor Dalmacio Gonzales.

Top: The Austrian composer Karl Goldmark.

GOMES, ANTÔNIO CARLOS

(Campinas Sao Paolo 1836–Belém Pará 1896)

Brazilian composer. He studied with his bandmaster father before going on to take advanced lessons at the Imperial Conservatory of Music in Rio de Janeiro, where in 1860 he founded the National Opera. As the result of winning a scholarship, Gomes was able to travel to Italy and studied in Milan (1864–66) before embarking on a profitable career as a composer, which aroused the interest of Verdi. Of his compositions for the theater, which include *Fosca* (1873), *Salvator Rosa* (1874) and *Maria Tudor* (1879), the most famous is *Il Guarany* (1870).

GOMEZ, JILL

(New Amsterdam, British Guyana 1942)

British soprano. She studied singing in London, at the Royal Academy of Music and the Guildhall School of Music. After a first appearance in a supporting role in Weber's *Oberon* with the Cambridge University Opera, she joined the Glyndebourne Festival chorus in 1967. The following year she sang the lead in *L'elisir d'amore*, and in 1969 she made her debut at Glyndebourne as Mélisande in Debussy's opera. At Covent Garden she sang the role of Flora in the premiere of Tippett's *The Knot Garden* (1971). Gomez has specialized in the baroque and general eighteenth-century repertoire, winning acclaim for recordings of Handel's *Acis and Galatea* (1978) and *Admeto* (1979).

GOMEZ-MARTINEZ, MIGUEL-ANGEL

(Granada 1949)

Spanish conductor. An infant prodigy, he went on to take advanced lessons in the United States and in Vienna, where he was a pupil of Hans Swarowsky. Gomez-Martinez won a number of important competitions for young conductors and was subsequently acclaimed with great enthusiasm in Lucerne (1972), Berlin (*Fidelio*, 1973), Hamburg, Frankfurt and Munich. Resident conductor at the Vienna Staatsoper (1977–82), he was appointed conductor of Radiotelevisión Española in Madrid in 1984.

GONZALES, DALMACIO

(Olot, Catalonia 1946)

Spanish tenor. He studied in Barcelona and subsequently in Salzburg and then won international singing competitions in Barcelona (1972) and at the Salzburg Mozarteum (1975). After making his debut at the Liceu in Barcelona (1978), he scored important successes in Nice (Donizetti's *Parisina*), at the

New York City Opera (*La traviata*, 1979), at the Metropolitan Opera House, New York (*Don Pasquale*, 1980) and at La Scala, Milan (*Ariodante*, 1981). His elegant style, grace of expression and softness of delivery have made Gonzales an admired interpreter of Rossini.

GOODALL, SIR REGINALD

(Lincoln 1901–London 1990)
British conductor. He studied piano and violin with Arthur Benjamin and W. H. Reed and conducting at the Royal College of Music in London. From 1936 to 1939 he worked as a répétiteur at Covent Garden and, after that, first with the Royal Choral Society and then for Furtwängler with the Berlin Philharmonic. He went on to conduct at Sadler's Wells (from 1944) and at Covent Garden (from 1947). Goodall conducted the premieres of *Peter Grimes* in 1945 and *The Rape of Lucretia* in 1946. His name came to be associated mostly with the operas of Wagner and his performances were much admired. Between 1973 and 1977 he conducted the *Ring* cycle (in English) with English National Opera, while for Welsh National Opera he conducted *Tristan und Isolde* and *Parsifal*, all of them subsequently recorded.

GORR, RITA

(Ghent 1926)
Stage name of Marguerite Geirnaert, Belgian mezzo-soprano. In 1949 she made her debut as Fricka (*Die Walküre*) in Antwerp. She went on to take advanced lessons with R. Lalande and F. Adam (1949–52) before joining the Strasbourg Opera, where, after appearing in supporting roles, she gradually established herself as a principal (Carmen, Amneris, Orfeo, etc.). Winning first prize in the Lausanne International Singing Competition in 1952 paved the way for her to be engaged by major international opera houses, from the Opéra in Paris to Bayreuth, Covent Garden and La Scala. With her authentic mezzo-soprano voice and great dramatic temperament, Gorr has given outstanding performances as Amneris (*Aida*), Dalila (*Samson et Dalila*), Charlotte (*Werther*), Mother Marie (*Les dialogues des Carmélites*), Ortrud (*Lohengrin*) and Kundry (*Parsifal*). In 1990 she sang the role of Marthe in a recording of *Faust*.

GOUNOD, CHARLES

(Paris 1818–Saint-Cloud, Paris 1893)
French composer. His first music teacher was his mother, and he went on to study at the Paris Conservatoire, where he was a pupil of Halévy, Le Sueur and Paer. In 1839 he won the Prix de Rome, which enabled him to spend three years in Italy (1840–43). On his return to France, his friendship with the celebrated singer Pauline Viardot helped him to overcome a difficult period in his personal and artistic life. With Viardot's encouragement, Gounod composed in 1851 his opera *Sapho*, which marked the beginning of his brilliant career. It was to be followed by numerous other successful operas, including *Faust* (1859), *Mireille* (1864) and *Roméo et Juliette* (1867). Gounod was also active as a teacher and a conductor of orchestras and choirs. After spending some time in London (1870–74), he returned in 1874 to settle permanently in Paris, concentrating on the composition of sacred music, in which he was particularly prolific.

Above: The Belgian soprano Rita Gorr.

Left: The French composer Charles Gounod.

GOYA

Opera in three acts; text and music by Giancarlo Menotti (b. 1911). First performance: Washington, Kennedy Center, 15 November 1986.

In an inn on the outskirts of Madrid, the young painter Francisco Goya (tenor), who has just arrived in the city, is attracted by a mysterious veiled lady sitting nearby, who is behaving coquettishly with some bullfighters. Goya approaches the woman and, after being introduced to her as the greatest painter in Spain, invites her to pose for him. She agrees but asks him to come to the Palacio de Alba, where she is working as a maid. The next day Goya keeps their appointment, entering the palace by the tradesman's entrance. The young woman reassures the shy painter, then leaves to dress for the sitting. She reappears surrounded by a number of courtiers and ladies: the maid is in fact Cayetana, the Duchess of Alba (mezzo-soprano). At first Goya appears confused, but then the Duchess encourages him to begin work on her portrait. As he prepares to paint the lips of the Duchess, Goya is filled with strong feelings, puts down his brushes and kisses her passionately. The relationship between the two causes a scandal among the courtiers. During a lavish reception, Cayetana continues to behave provocatively, even going so far as openly challenging the Queen (soprano) by presenting at court two new ladies wearing the same dress as the Queen, who immediately wants revenge. Goya reproaches Cayetana for these excesses, but she scorns him, accusing him of opportunism. At that moment, the painter is suddenly taken ill, maddened by a whistling sound in his head which makes him rush out, to general amazement. Some time later, the Duchess is on the point of death, having been struck down by an equally mysterious sudden illness. Knowing she has been poisoned, in the presence of the Queen, who has come to visit her, she expresses all her contempt for the Spanish court. Then she dies. Goya arrives too late and is in despair for not having had the courage to defend his beloved. In his studio, years later, Goya, old and alone, lives tormented by nightmares which have seriously affected his state of mind. His spirit is then calmed by a vision of his dearest Cayetana, and he is able to die at peace with himself.

Giancarlo Menotti composed *Goya* at the request of the tenor Placido Domingo, who sang the lead at the first performance. After its American premiere, Menotti made a number of changes, especially to the vocal line in the role of Goya and to the third act. In this new version, *Goya* was staged at the Festival dei Due Mondi in Spoleto, Italy, in June 1991.

Above: The Spanish composer Enrique Granados.

Top: The French composer André-Ernest-Modeste Grétry

GOYESCAS

Opera in three acts by Enrique Granados (1867–1916), to a libretto by Fernando Periquet y Zuaznabar. First performance: New York, Metropolitan Opera House, 28 January 1916.

The action takes place in a Madrid suburb at the end of the nineteenth century. The toreador Paquito (baritone), though in love with the beautiful Pepa, is not unwilling to make advances to Rosario (soprano), a wealthy lady who is herself loved by Fernando (tenor), a young officer. During a public celebration, the jealousy between these four suddenly comes to the surface: Fernando rejects Rosario, believing her to have been unfaithful to him, and then challenges Paquito to a duel. Fernando is mortally wounded and dies in the arms of his beloved Rosario.

Goyescas was Granados's last work for the theater and also the most famous. It is simply a stage version of the collection of piano pieces of the same name, inspired by the paintings of Goya. The first performance of the work at the Metropolitan in New York was a notable but temporary success.

GRANADOS, ENRIQUE

(Lérida, Catalonia 1867–drowned at sea, English Channel 1916)

Spanish composer and pianist. He studied piano and composition in Barcelona, where he made his debut as a pianist in 1883. From 1887 to 1889 he continued his piano studies in Paris. On his return to Spain, he embarked on an intensive career as a concert pianist, which he combined with composing. His *Goyescas* for piano, a series of piano pieces inspired by Goya's art, was a sensational success in Paris in 1914. His opera of the same name, largely inspired by the piano composition, was due to be performed for the first time in Paris, but the outbreak of the First World War meant that the premiere had to be transferred to New York (1916). Sailing back from the United States, Granados lost his life in the sinking of the ship *Sussex*.

GREINDL, JOSEF

(Munich 1912)

German bass. A pupil at the Munich Academy (1932–36), Greindl made his debut in Krefeld in 1936 as Hunding in *Die Walküre*. He then appeared with Düsseldorf Opera (1938–42), at Bayreuth (from 1943) and in Berlin (1948). His international career began at the end of the Second World War, when he started appearing at major opera houses: Salzburg, London's Covent Garden, La Scala, Milan and the Metropolitan Opera House, New York (1952–53) Greindl drew on a vast repertoire, from Mozart to Verdi (including a memorable Sparafucile in a 1944 recording of *Rigoletto*). His name is particularly associated with Wagner roles, notably Daland in *Der fliegende Holländer* (The Flying Dutchman), Hagen in *Götterdämmerung* (Twilight of the Gods), and Fafner in *Das Rheingold*.

GRÉTRY, ANDRÉ-ERNEST-MODESTE

(Liège 1741–Montmorency, Paris 1813)

French composer of Belgian birth. Encouraged to study music by his father, who was a church violinist, Grétry began as a choirboy in the church of St Denis in Liège, then concentrated on studying violin, thoroughbass and composition. A scholarship awarded to him in 1759 enabled him to travel to Italy. In 1766 he left Italy for Geneva, where he made friends with the composer Monsigny and with Voltaire, both of whom encouraged him to compose for the theater. After settling in Paris (1767), he made his debut as an opera composer with *Le huron*, staged at the Comédie Italienne. This was the first of a long series of successes in the theater which not even the turmoil of the French Revolution could affect. Among his operas, in which he established a perfect balance between the Italian style and the strict French tradition, are *Zémire et Azor* (1771), *La caravane du Caire* (1783), *Richard Coeur-de-Lion* (1784) and *Guillaume Tell* (1791).

GRISELDA, LA

Opera seria *in three acts by Alessandro Scarlatti (1660–1725), to a libretto by Apostolo Zeno. First performance: Rome, Teatro Capranica, Carnival 1721.*

Gualtiero, King of Sicily (baritone), disowns Griselda (soprano), the shepherdess he has married, to satisfy the wishes of his people, who want only royal blood heirs on the throne of their kingdom. Gualtiero's marriage had produced a daughter, Costanza (soprano), who has been brought up at the court of Corrado (tenor), prince of Puglia, and has never known her real parents. Costanza loves and is loved by Roberto (tenor), Corrado's son. But Costanza has been told she must marry Gualtiero, unaware that he is her father. Only Corrado knows the truth, but he keeps silent so as to help Gualtiero save his throne. Griselda has now returned to her life in the woods. Here she meets the young Costanza, and an affectionate relationship immediately develops between them, which results in Costanza asking Griselda to be her maid. At court, Griselda resists the amorous advances of Ottone (baritone), a grandee of the realm who had on a number of occasions attempted to win her love. Now, after yet another rejection, Ottone admits that it was he who turned the people against Griselda so that they would reject her and he could then marry her. The opera can thus have a happy ending, with Griselda—reunited with her husband and daughter—appearing to the people, who acclaim their shepherdess queen now that she has been seen to possess great qualities.

La Griselda was Alessandro Scarlatti's last composition for the theater. It is considered his greatest achievement and, together with *Il Mitridate Eupatore* and *Il Tigrane*, one of his musical masterpieces. The story of Griselda has been turned into an opera by a number of other eighteenth-century composers.

GRISÉLIDIS

Opera in three acts by Jules Massenet (1842–1912), to a libretto by Silvestre and Morand based on medieval legend. First performance: Paris, Théâtre de l'Opéra-Comique, 20 November 1901.

The Marquis de Saluce (baritone), who has married the beautiful Grisélidis (soprano), daughter of poor country folk, is about to go to war against the Saracens. Before leaving he is willing to place a bet, even with the Devil himself, on the fidelity and obedience of his wife. The Devil appears, and the Marquis, agreeing to the bet, leaves the Devil (baritone) his wedding-ring as security. When the Marquis has gone, the Devil and his wife Fiamina (mezzo-soprano) arrive at the château, he disguised as a slave-trader and she as a slave-girl with whom the Marquis is apparently in love, and whose freedom he has bought. Fiamina shows Grisélidis the Marquis's wedding-ring, adding that from now on, at the express command of the Marquis, she is to be lady of the house. Grisélidis obeys her husband's wishes, leaves the château and finds shelter in a forest. The Devil, intent on causing the young woman to surrender her virtue, sends Alain (tenor) to her, a shepherd who had previously wanted to marry her. He then abducts her young son Loys. Disguised as an old man, the Devil appears to Grisélidis and suggests that she come with him to meet the person who has stolen her child. He will give the boy back to her in exchange for a kiss. Eventually, Grisélidis agrees. The Devil then appears to the Marquis, who has in the meantime returned to the château, and conjures up for him the sight of Grisélidis on her way to the rendezvous. At first the Marquis is furious, but then he notices his own ring on the old man's finger and realizes he is talking to the Devil. Later, the Marquis and Grisélidis come to understand the deceptions to which they have been subjected and pray for the safe return of their son. St. Agnes then miraculously appears, holding little Loys in her arms.

A minor opera in Massenet's output, *Grisélidis* nonetheless confirms the composer's gift for melody, *Grisélidis* also achieves a successful balance between libretto and music.

GRIST, RERI

(New York 1932)

American soprano. She sang in Leonard Bernstein's *West Side Story* in 1957, and Bernstein engaged her as soprano soloist for a performance of Mahler's Fourth Symphony. After being under contract to the Santa Fe Opera, Grist moved to Europe and the Cologne Opera, where she made her debut as the Queen of the Night in *Die Zauberflöte* (The Magic Flute). She went on to sing with the Zurich Opera and at major international opera houses, including La Scala, Milan, Covent Garden, the Munich Bayerische Staatsoper, San Francisco and the Metropolitan Opera House, New York. As well as having a typical light soprano voice, Grist made her name through a certain brilliance particularly suited to Mozart (Susanna, Zerlina, Despina, Blonde) and Richard Strauss (Zerbinetta). Especially worthy of note were her performances of Stravinsky's *Le rossignol* (1961) and the role of Oscar (*Un ballo in maschera*), which she also recorded for Riccardo Muti (1975).

Above: Nineteenth-century print of the Italian composer Alessandro Scarlatti.

Left: The American soprano Reri Grist.

GRUBEROVA, EDITA
(Bratislava 1946)
Czech soprano. A pupil of Medvecká and Boesch at the Bratislava Conservatory, she made her debut in Bratislava as Rosina in *Il barbiere di Siviglia* (1968). Engaged under contract by the Vienna Staatsoper (1970), the opera house in which she made her name and appeared most frequently, Gruberova scored her first major success as the Queen of the Night in *Die Zauberflöte* (The Magic Flute), a role which she subsequently sang at Glyndebourne (1973), at the Salzburg Festival (from 1974 onwards) and in Munich (1978). Her career was finally assured in 1976 with Zerbinetta in *Ariadne auf Naxos* at the Vienna Staatsoper, which she went on to sing with great success at the Florence Maggio Musicale Festival (1977), the Metropolitan Opera House, New York (1979), La Scala, Milan (1984), and Covent Garden (1987). The natural richness of Gruberova's voice, with its remarkable virtuosity and expressiveness, has enabled her not only to tackle roles in the vocally more substantial light lyric soprano repertoire but also to work her way gradually towards operas such as *La traviata*, *Lucia di Lammermoor*, *Maria Stuarda*, *Roberto Devereux* and *Norma*.

GRÜMMER, ELIZABETH
(Diedenhofen, Alsace-Lorraine 1911–Warendorf 1986)
German soprano. A pupil of Schlender, she made her debut at Aix-la-Chapelle in 1941 (*Parsifal*). In the years that followed, she appeared in Duisburg and Prague, and from 1946 she was a member of the Berlin Städtische Oper, singing operas by Mozart and Wagner, a repertoire which, within a short time, she began to perform internationally, at Covent Garden (from 1951), La Scala (from 1952), the Vienna Staatsoper (1953), the Salzburg Festival (1954–61) and Bayreuth (1957–59). Grümmer had a very fine lyric soprano voice of great elegance and expressiveness. She is particularly remembered for *Don Giovanni*, *Così fan tutte*, *Lohengrin*, *Tannhäuser* and *Der Freischütz*. From 1965 she taught at the Berlin Conservatory, in Hamburg, and at the Paris Opéra School of Singing.

Above: The German baritone Franz Grundheber.

Top: The Czech soprano Edita Gruberova.

GRUNDHEBER, FRANZ
(Trier 1937)
German baritone. He studied music in the United States. On his return to Europe, he began his career singing with Hamburg Opera, where he was a member of the company and then made regular guest appearances. In 1984 he sang *Macbeth* at the Opéra in Paris and was invited back for Mandryka (*Arabella*), one of his most acclaimed roles. Further Strauss was to follow: he sang Olivier in *Capriccio* (Salzburg Festival, 1985–87), and Orest in *Elektra* (1989). Equally significant were his interpretations of Wagner, in *Lohengrin*, *Das Rheingold*, *Götterdämmerung* (Twilight of the Gods) and *Der fliegende Holländer* (The Flying Dutchman) at Salzburg, the Florence Maggio Musicale Festival and the Deutsche Oper Berlin. His performance of Wozzeck in Berg's opera at the Vienna Staatsoper with Claudio Abbado conducting (1987) won widespread public and critical acclaim, and the vocal and performing skills he brought to this difficult role established him as one of its greatest exponents.

GUADAGNO, ANTON
(Castellammare del Golfo 1925)
Italian conductor. He studied music at the Conservatories of Parma and Palermo and at the Accademia di Santa Cecilia in Rome before going on to the Salzburg Mozarteum (1948). He made his debut as an opera conductor in South America and Mexico, joining the Metropolitan Opera in New York in 1958. From 1966 to 1972 he was music director of Philadelphia Lyric Opera, and in subsequent years he appeared in a number of other opera houses in America (Cincinnati, the Metropolitan, Palm Beach, etc.) and Europe, most notably the Vienna Volksoper. He regularly conducted at the Arena in Verona from 1977 (*Aida*, *Rigoletto*, *La forza del destino*).

GÜDEN, HILDE
(Vienna 1917–Munich 1988)
Stage name of the Austrian soprano Hilde Herrmann. She studied with Wetzelberger in Vienna and first appeared in operetta (1939). Two years later she sang the role of Cherubino (*Le nozze di Figaro*) in Zurich and from 1946 appeared at the Vienna Staatsoper, which became her favourite opera house. Güden also sang at Covent Garden (from 1947), La Scala, Milan (1948), the Metropolitan Opera House, New York (from 1950), and at other important international opera houses and festivals. With her vocal and interpretative gifts, Güden was one of the most highly acclaimed exponents of Mozart (Zerlina, Susanna, etc.) and Richard Strauss (Sophie, Zerbinetta, Daphne, etc.).

GUERRA, LA
Music drama in one act by Renzo Rossellini (1908–1982) to the composer's own libretto. First performance: Naples, Teatro San Carlo, 25 February 1956.

The action takes place in modern times. The scene is a city in a country ruled by a foreign power. Marta (mezzo-soprano), an old lady who is paralyzed and lives in a basement with her daughter Maria (soprano), is anxiously awaiting the return of her younger son Marco (speaking role), who had fled three years earlier in order to avoid falling into the enemy's clutches. The old postman (bass), who is also their neighbour, brings Marta the latest news on the withdrawal of the army of occupation and warns her that Maria, who is having a relationship with an enemy officer, Erik (tenor), may be in danger of reprisals as soon as the city is liberated. That same evening, while Marta is asleep, Erik tries to persuade Maria to leave with him, but she is expecting a child and is unable to decide. Marta has overheard their conversation and implores Maria not to abandon her. They are suddenly interrupted by people crowding into their basement in terror. In the confusion, Maria slips away to join Erik. Then Marco returns. He has been blinded in combat, and his mother is so overwhelmed by the sight of him that she collapses and dies. Outside the house, the people are heard shouting for joy as they learn that their freedom has been won back.

Renzo Rossellini, who made his name principally as a composer of film scores, succeeded in imbuing *La guerra* with an extraordinary vitality more often associated with the cinema. The modernity of the subject-matter of this opera invites comparison with the neo-realism of which the composer's brother, Roberto, the famous film director, was one of the greatest exponents.

GUGLIELMO RATCLIFF

Tragic opera in four acts by Pietro Mascagni (1863–1945), to a text by Heinrich Heine in an Italian translation by Andrea Maffei. First performance: Milan, La Scala, 16 February 1895.

The action takes place in Scotland in 1820. Conte Douglas (baritone) arrives at the castle of MacGregor, where he is to marry Maria (soprano), MacGregor's daughter. Douglas tells of how he has been attacked by brigands but, thanks to the intervention of a mysterious knight, has escaped with his life. Maria's father (bass) then tells the Conte that Guglielmo Ratcliff (tenor), a suitor rejected by Maria, had already killed two of her previous fiancés in duels. Douglas too receives a challenge to do combat at the Black Rock. There he recognizes Guglielmo as the knight who had saved his life. Douglas has already called upon the spirits of the dead fiancés to come to his aid and gets the better of Ratcliff but does not kill him. Meanwhile, Maria's nurse Margherita (mezzo-soprano) tells Maria that some time ago Maria's mother Elisa had rejected Edvardo, Guglielmo's father, in order to marry MacGregor, but had continued to love Edvardo, who then died in mysterious circumstances when the relationship was discovered by MacGregor. At this point in the story Guglielmo suddenly appears. He begs Maria to go away with him. She is still shocked by the story she has just heard and, though she feels that she is in love with Guglielmo, she implores him to go away. Ratcliff, maddened by having to endure yet another rejection, throws himself upon Maria and kills her. Immediately after that, he also kills MacGregor, who has come running to his daughter's aid, and then, holding the body of his beloved in his arms, he shoots himself.

While still a student at the Conservatorio, Mascagni had become fascinated by Heine's tragedy. He worked on the composition of the first version of *Guglielmo Ratcliff* from 1888 to 1890. After *Cavalleria rusticana* (1890), he took up the *Ratcliff* score again and made a number of changes to it. This second version was produced in 1895.

GUI, VITTORIO

(Rome 1885–Florence 1975)

Italian conductor and composer. He began to study music with his mother and then attended the Accademia Nazionale di Santa Cecilia in Rome. In 1907 he made his debut at the Teatro Adriano in Rome, following it up straightaway by embarking on his first series of conducting engagements at a number of Italian opera houses (Teatro Regio in Turin, Teatro San Carlo in Naples, etc.). In 1923 he was invited by Toscanini to open the season at La Scala, Milan, conducting Richard Strauss's *Salome*. In 1933 he took part in the founding of Florence's Maggio Musicale festival. Music director and artistic adviser to the Glyndebourne Festival (1952–69), Gui was also involved in the revival of Rossini's operas.

GUILLAUME TELL

(William Tell)

Tragic opera in four acts by Gioachino Rossini (1792–1868), to a libretto by Etienne de Jouy and Hippolyte Bis based on Schiller's play of the same name. First performance: Paris, Opéra, 3 August 1829.

The action takes place in Switzerland in the sixteenth century. Guillaume Tell (baritone), a skilled archer, helps a shepherd, Leuthold (bass), to safety while he is being pursued by the soldiers of the Austrian governor Gesler (bass), then oppressing the region. In retaliation, the

Above: The Italian conductor Vittorio Gui during a rehearsal.

Left: The Austrian soprano Hilde Güden.

soldiers torch the village and take as their hostage Melchthal (bass), one of the most influential villagers. A few days later, Arnold (tenor), Melchthal's son, meets Mathilde (soprano), an Austrian princess with whom he is in love. After they pledge their love, Mathilde urges Arnold to become one of Gesler's supporters, because in this way he will gain fame and fortune. Then Guillaume brings Arnold news that his father, Melchthal, has been put to death, and Arnold vows to fight alongside the patriots. On the main square in Altdorf, Guillaume and his son Jemmy (soprano) are arrested. Rodolphe (tenor), one of Gesler's men, accuses Tell of having aided Leuthold's escape. In order to save his son's life, Guillaume is forced to prove his skill by shooting a single arrow at an apple placed on top of Jemmy's head. Guillaume hits the target, but turns out to have a second arrow he could have used: he proudly explains that this arrow had been intended for Gesler, if he had not hit the apple. Gesler gives orders for Tell and Jemmy to be arrested, but the boy is saved by Mathilde, who has him entrusted to her care. Meanwhile Jemmy gives the agreed signal for the revolt to begin. Guillaume and Gesler are on a boat heading for the castle of Kusmac. A storm breaks, and Tell manages to steer the boat to the bank, leaps out and fires an arrow at Gesler, which kills him. Arnold and the conspirators arrive. The fortress of Altdorf has fallen, and Switzerland has been liberated.

The score generates an extraordinary Romantic atmosphere which was decidedly novel at the time and was undoubtedly the reason for the opera's failure. In addition, *Guillaume Tell* did not provide the audience with the typical ingredients of a Rossini opera which they had come to expect. The *bel canto* element and other features are here replaced by a new expressiveness, abounding in lyricism and dramatic pathos.

GULYAS, DENES

(Budapest 1954)

Hungarian tenor. At the age of ten, he joined the choir of Hungarian radio as a treble. He then entered the Budapest Academy of Music. After winning the prestigious Hungarian Radio Prize (1977), he became a member of the Budapest State Opera Company (1978).

Above: A scene from *Guillaume Tell*, in a production at La Scala.

GUNTRAM

Opera in three acts by Richard Strauss (1864–1949), to the composer's own libretto. First performance: Weimar, Hoftheater, 10 May 1894.

The action takes place in medieval Germany. The League of the Champions of Love sends Guntram (tenor), a knight, to liberate the peoples being oppressed by the regime of Duke Robert (baritone). Freihild (soprano), Robert's wife, who has also fallen victim to the cruelty of her husband, is on the point of taking her own life when she is saved by Guntram. He falls in love with her, and when Robert arrives, accompanied by the old Duke, his father (bass), Guntram asks if he may take part in a singing competition between the Minnesingers at court. During the contest, Guntram sings of the joys of peace and good government, contrasting these with the horrors of war and tyranny. Robert feels that Guntram's words are directed at him and challenges Guntram to a duel. Robert is killed, and the old Duke has Guntram arrested, but he is freed again by Freihild. Guntram must now appear before the Counsel of the Champions of Love and submit to the judgement of the elders. Inwardly, however, he has already understood that his action has not only been prompted by a hunger for justice but because he wished to see dead the husband of the woman with whom he was in love. Having already passed judgement on himself, Guntram refuses to appear before the Council and condemns himself to a life of solitude.

Guntram was Richard Strauss's first opera, and its failure was at least partly due to the difficulties of the leading role. Clearly influenced by Wagner, the work nonetheless contains moments that hint at the great operatic Strauss scenes to come, such as the broad sweep of the finale.

GWENDOLINE

Opera in three acts by Emmanuel Chabrier (1841–1894), to a libretto by Catulle Mendès. First performance: Brussels, Théâtre de la Monnaie, 10 April 1886.

The action takes place in the eighth century during the war between the Saxons and the Danes. Harald, King of the Vikings (tenor), is in love with Gwendoline (soprano), daughter of Armel (bass), the Saxon chieftain. Armel consents to their marriage but has a clear purpose in doing so: he is going to use the occasion of the wedding celebrations to attack the Danes and kill Harald. Gwendoline, who loves Harald, wants to avoid being made an accomplice of Armel's treacherous plans and so tries to persuade Harald to flee, but it is already too late. Gwendoline dies with Harald when Armel comes to kill him.

The Paris Opéra refused to stage *Gwendoline* because of the excessive Wagnerian influence in the work. As a result, it was performed in Brussels, with great success. Chabrier's choice of a northern setting for the opera and his introduction of a *leitmotiv* are among the first French instances of Wagnerism. However, Chabrier's use of these features is only external to the action, because it is his own personality that has left the clearest mark on the score.

H

HADLEY SCHEDULE, JERRY

(Princeton, Illinois 1952)

American tenor. He made his first appearance with New York City Opera as Arturo in *Lucia di Lammermoor* (1979). Within a short time he had become established on the international opera scene, at the Metropolitan Opera House, New York, where he made his debut as Des Grieux (*Manon*) and continued to sing regularly, at the Vienna Staatsoper (from 1982) and at the Glyndebourne Festival (1983). He has also been very active as a concert soloist. Thanks to his remarkable vocal gifts, combined with impressive qualities of performance and musicianship, Hadley is an elegant interpreter of a repertoire ranging from Mozart to Verdi.

HADRIAN IN SYRIA

See *Adriano in Siria*

HAENDEL, GEORG FRIEDRICH

(Halle 1685–London 1759)

German composer, naturalized British. After his studies and early days as an organist in Halle, in 1703 he moved to Hamburg, where he came into contact with the opera world for the first time and found work with the Hamburg Opera, then directed by the composer Reinhard Keiser. In Hamburg, Handel had his first operas, *Almira* and *Nero* (subsequently lost), produced in 1705, and *Florinda e Dafne* (later divided into two parts, *Florinda* and *Dafne*, because it was so long) in 1706, the year in which he set out on the journey to Italy that was to prove so crucial to his development. The operas Handel composed during his stay in Italy, *Rodrigo* (c. 1707) and particularly *Agrippina* (1709), illustrate how completely he succeeded in absorbing the style of Italian opera, but are also early examples of his own compositional style, already on display in *Rinaldo* (1711), the first opera he wrote after leaving Italy and coming to London in 1710. The whole of his subsequent output as a composer of opera, though he kept to the structure of Italian *opera seria*, shows Handel more and more interested in using effective means of expression and exploiting more fully the potential of the orchestra by scoring for a richer variety of instruments. Operas such as *Tamerlano* (1724) or *Rodelinda, regina de'Longobardi* (1725) show how Handel increasingly experimented with the dramatic element in opera and constructed scenes that were much more musically elaborate and effective as theater, a trend that can also be seen in Orlando's great mad scene from the opera of the same name (1733). Here Handel employs linked movements that symbolize the crazed state of mind of the character, and for perhaps the first time in history a tempo of 5/8 was used. The rediscovery of Handel's operas in the period between 1970 and 1990 directed the spotlight on his dramatic and theatrical strengths, and he is now regarded as the greatest composer of opera between 1700 and 1730.

HAGEGÅRD, HÅKAN

(Karlstad 1945)

Swedish baritone. He studied music at the Stockholm Royal Academy of Music and later had lessons with Tito Gobbi in Rome, Gerald Moore in London and Erik Werba in Vienna. He made his debut in 1968 at the Stockholm Royal Opera as Papageno in Mozart's *Die Zauberflöte* (The Magic Flute), a role he went on to sing at a number of other opera houses, including La Scala, Milan, in

Above: The Dutch conductor Bernard Haitink.

Left: Jerry Hadley Schedule as Tonino in Mozart's *Die Zauberflöte* (The Magic Flute).

1985 and the Paris Opéra in 1986, and immortalized in the film version of the opera directed by Ingmar Bergman (1974). Hagegård appeared at the Drottningholm Festival (from 1970) and the Glyndebourne Festival (from 1973) as well as at the Metropolitan Opera House in New York (from 1978, in Donizetti's *Don Pasquale*), at the Grand Théâtre in Geneva (Mozart's *Così fan tutte*, 1985, and Verdi's *Don Carlos*, 1988), and Covent Garden (Wagner's *Tannhäuser*, 1987). Hagegård's voice, with its fine, essentially lyric, timbre, soft delivery and his elegant phrasing, has brought him fame principally as a Mozart singer, although his performances as a concert artist, and particularly in *Lieder*, are equally important.

HAGER, LEOPOLD

(Salzburg 1935)

Austrian conductor. He studied organ, piano, harpsichord, conducting and composition at the Salzburg Mozarteum. After beginning his music career as a chorus-master (1957), he rapidly established his reputation as a conductor in Linz (1962–64), Cologne (1964–65), Freiburg (1965–69) and from 1969 to 1981 in Salzburg, where he conducted the Mozarteum orchestra, concentrating on the performance and recording of Mozart's early operas. These were not always favourably received by the critics but were in every case acknowledged as significant premieres of otherwise forgotten operas.

Above: The Swedish baritone Håkan Hagegård.

Top: The French composer and teacher Fromental Halévy.

HAITINK, BERNARD

(Amsterdam 1929)

Dutch conductor. He studied violin and conducting at the Amsterdam Conservatory and began his music career as a violinist. Haitink became a conductor in 1955. From 1957 onwards he conducted the Netherlands Radio Philharmonic Orchestra and in 1961 was appointed music director, and subsequently (1967–79) principal conductor, of the Amsterdam Concertgebouw orchestra. He went on to appear with the London Philharmonic Orchestra (1967–77) and in 1977 was appointed music director at the Glyndebourne Festival, a prestigious post which, from 1987, he also held at Covent Garden. Haitink's extensive repertoire in opera ranges from Mozart to Verdi, Wagner and Strauss.

HALÉVY, FROMENTAL

(Paris 1799–Nice 1862)

French composer and teacher. He studied at the Paris Conservatoire, where he became Cherubini's favourite pupil. In 1819 he won the Grand Prix de Rome, which enabled him to travel to Italy in 1820. After returning to France (1823), he managed to have his first opera, *L'Artisan*, staged in 1827; this was followed by *Clari* in 1828 and *Le dilettante d'Avignon* in 1829. His success from these works launched Halévy on his career as an opera composer, which he combined with that of teacher (from 1827). He composed more than 30 operas, of which the most famous to this day is *La juive* (1835). He was an outstanding teacher, and his numerous pupils included Gounod, Bizet and Lecocq.

HALÉVY, LUDOVIC

(Paris 1833–1908)

French librettist. Nephew of the composer Fromental Halévy, he worked with Henri Meilhac and Hector Crémieux on a number of opera libretti for Offenbach, including *La belle Hélène*, *La vie parisienne*, *La grande-duchesse de Gérolstein*, and *Orphée aux enfers*, and also for Lecocq, Delibes and Bizet (*Carmen*).

HALKA

Opera in four acts by Stanislaw Moniuszko (1819–1872), to a libretto by Wlodzimierz Wolski based on K. W. Wójcicki's story Gorálka. *First concert performance: Vilnius, Müller Palace, 20 December 1848. First stage performance: Wilna, 16 February 1854. Revised version, Warsaw, Imperial Theater, 1 January 1858.*

The action takes place on a Polish country estate at the end of the eighteenth century. A party is in progress to celebrate the betrothal of Zofja (mezzo-soprano), daughter of Stolnik (bass), to Janusz (baritone), a young nobleman who had, some time before, seduced Halka (soprano), a young country-woman. Halka is in love with Janusz and is unaware that he is to marry another woman. Jontek (tenor), whose love for Halka has been rejected by her, tries in vain to reason with her and make her face the reality of the situation. Only when she hears the guests in Stolnik's house singing in celebration of Zofja's forthcoming wedding to Janusz does Halka despairingly realize the truth. Halka wanders round the small village church in which the wedding is taking place. She is now out of her mind with grief and wants to take revenge by setting fire to the church, but then reflects on the number of innocent lives that would be lost by such an act and forgives Janusz for his infidelity. Shortly after, as the wedding procession is about to emerge from the church, Halka, who has lost all reason for living, throws herself into the river.

Halka is Moniuszko's first *opera seria*, and the work is considered to be his musical masterpiece as well as the first outstanding example of national theater in Poland. The composer drew his inspiration from Polish folk culture: the mazurka in the first act and the Dance of the Mountain-Dwellers in the third have become popular in their own right and are often performed as concert pieces.

HAMARI, JULIA

(Budapest 1942)

Hungarian mezzo-soprano. After studying at the Budapest Conservatory (1961–66), she completed her training in Stuttgart (1966–67), where she made her debut in Bach's *St Matthew Passion*. She immediately established herself as an elegant performer of concert repertoire and was very soon combining this with roles in opera. She first appeared in 1967 in Salzburg as Mercédès (*Carmen*), with Herbert von Karajan conducting. Within a short space of time she had won international acclaim at major opera houses in an extensive repertoire ranging from Handel to Gluck, Mozart, Haydn, Rossini and Wagner.

HAMLET

Opera in five acts by Ambroise Thomas (1811–1896), to a libretto by Jules Barbier and Michel Carré based on Shakespeare's tragedy. First performance: Paris, Opéra, 9 March 1868.

Hamlet (baritone), Prince of Denmark, has a dream in which the ghost of his father (bass) tells him that his death was caused by his brother Claudius (bass), who has now become King in his place and married his widow Gertrude (mezzo-soprano). Hamlet vows to avenge his father and, in order to hide his longing for vengeance, pretends to be mad and treats his beloved Ophélie (soprano) so cruelly that she comes to believe that Hamlet hates her and kills herself in despair. King Claudius has realized that Hamlet knows his secret and so attempts to kill him, first with a poisoned chalice (which Gertrude drinks from instead and dies), then by arranging a duel between Hamlet and Laërte (tenor), Ophélie's brother, in which Laërte's sword will have poison on it. The two combatants are both mortally wounded but, before he dies, Hamlet reveals Claudius's misdeeds and kills him with his sword, thus avenging his father's death.

Next to *Mignon*, *Hamlet* is Thomas's best-known opera, although its fame is due to a number of excerpts from the work remaining in the repertoire: Hamlet's toast in the second act and the mad scene of Ophélie in the fourth, a challenge for *coloratura* sopranos. In spite of the limitations imposed on it by the requirements of *grand-opéra* (such as choreographic and ballet interludes) which slowed up the action, *Hamlet* is musically outstanding, thanks to the composer's extraordinary skill in the handling of the vocal parts. Hamlet's is one of the most dramatic baritone roles.

HAMPSON, THOMAS

(Washington, D.C. 1955)

American baritone. He took music lessons from a very early age and went on to study at the Music Academy of the West. As a result of winning a competition organized by the Metropolitan Opera, New York (1980), Hampson moved to Europe in 1981 and joined the resident company of the Deutsche Oper am Rhein. He then appeared with the Zurich Opera (from 1984) and established himself as a Mozart performer. It was as the Count in *Le nozze di Figaro* that he made his debut at the Metropolitan, where he continued to appear regularly, drawing on a repertoire which, in addition to operas by Mozart, included Rossini (*Il barbiere di Siviglia*), Gounod (*Faust*) and Tchaikovsky (*Eugene Onegin*). Hampson also established a reputation as a concert artist (Schumann, Mahler, etc.) and in musicals. He is regarded among the foremost international singers.

HANDEL, GEORGE FREDERICK

See *Haendel, Georg Friedrich*

HANS HEILING

Romantic opera consisting of a prologue and three acts by Heinrich August Marschner (1795–1861), to a libretto by Edward Devrient. First performance: Berlin, Hofoper, 24 May 1833.

Hans (baritone), son of the Queen of the Spirits (soprano) and a mortal father, abandons his supernatural state and takes on human form, because he is in love with Anna (soprano). But Anna discovers his true identity and leaves him for Konrad (tenor). Distraught, Hans tries to kill first his rival and then the entire human race. The Queen of the Spirits intervenes and urges her son to be forgiving. He is persuaded and, now resigned to what has happened, returns to his own world, resolving never to set foot in the mortal world again.

Hans Heiling, which was based on popular legend, enjoyed great success throughout Germany and Austria. In Vienna and Magdeburg, the opera was conducted by Richard Wagner, who was particularly influenced by the romantic atmosphere in Marschner's work.

HÄNSEL UND GRETEL

Musical fairy-tale in three acts by Engelbert Humperdinck (1854–1921), to a libretto by Adelheid Wette from the story by the Brothers Grimm. First performance: Weimar, Hoftheater, 23 December 1893.

Two children, Hänsel (mezzo-soprano) and Gretel (soprano), have driven their mother (mezzo-soprano) to despair: while running after them to scold them, she has upset a cup of milk, which is the only food the poor family has. She hurriedly sends them off into the forest to pick strawberries. Hänsel and Gretel look for the strawberries but eat them all, forgetting what their mother had asked them to do. Night falls, and the two children, having lost their way home, are faced with the terrors of spending the night in the forest. The Sandman (soprano) appears and throws some grains of sand in their eyes. Hänsel and Gretel fall into a deep sleep, guarded by angels. The next morning, when they wake up, they are astonished to see a little house made of marzipan, biscuits and sugar. Curious, they approach the house, only to fall under the spell of the witch (mezzo-soprano), who locks them up with the intention of eating them. Hänsel is shut in a hen-house to be fattened up and then cooked. But Gretel, taking her chance while the Witch is looking the other way, succeeds in setting her brother free. The two of them then push the old woman into the oven. When the oven explodes, the house is destroyed and the spell broken. In the end their parents arrive, and then a number of other children appear who had fallen victim to the Witch and now thank Hänsel and Gretel for freeing them.

The German composer George Frederick Handel (see page 171).

Hänsel und Gretel, which is clearly Romantic in style, was seen as a kind of reaction to the music of Wagner. It contains echoes of Wagner's own expressive musical language, although Humperdinck filtered this influence in his own personal and original way. The score contains musical ideas derived from nursery rhymes and popular songs, whose simplicity makes the opera accessible to a wide and varied audience. As a result, *Hänsel und Gretel* has won great acclaim ever since.

HAPPY DECEPTION, THE
See *Inganno felice, L'*

HARLEQUIN, OR THE WINDOWS
See *Arlecchino, oder Die Fenster*

HARNONCOURT, NIKOLAUS
(Berlin 1929)
German conductor and cellist, naturalized Austrian. He grew up in a family of musicians and studied at the Vienna Academy of Music, starting his career as a cellist with the Vienna Symphony Orchestra (1952–69). In 1953 he founded the Concentus Musicus, with whom he began to concentrate on Early Music. By the early 1960s he had established a reputation for performances of Bach's vocal and instrumental music, and he won distinction for his interpretations of operas by Monteverdi (*Orfeo*, *Il ritorno di Ulisse in patria* and *L'incoronazione di Poppea*). Alongside his performances with the Concentus Musicus, known throughout Europe and the United States, Harnoncourt has conducted the leading international orchestras.

HAROLD
See *Aroldo*

HARPER, HEATHER
(Belfast 1930)
British soprano. She studied singing at Trinity College of Music, London, and made her first public appearances with the Ambrosian Singers and the BBC Chorus. In 1954 she made her stage debut with the Oxford University Opera Club. From 1957 she appeared at the Glyndebourne Festival: her debut there was as First Lady in *Die Zauberflöte* (The Magic Flute). In 1961 Harper made her first appearance at Covent Garden, where she subsequently sang numerous roles in operas by Bizet, Offenbach, Wagner, Richard Strauss and Poulenc. She distinguished herself in performances of the contemporary repertoire, particularly the music of Benjamin Britten.

HARWOOD, ELIZABETH
(Barton Seagrave, Northamptonshire 1938–London 1990)
British soprano. She studied at the Royal Manchester College of Music (1956–60). After winning the Kathleen Ferrier Memorial Prize (1960), she made her Glyndebourne Festival debut as Second Boy in *Die Zauberflöte* (The Magic Flute). From 1961 she appeared at Sadler's Wells Theater in London in a repertoire from Mozart to Rossini, Massenet (*Manon*) and Strauss (*Ariadne auf Naxos*). Her Covent Garden debut dates from 1967 (*Arabella*), and it was here that she earned the kind of acclaim which would bring her to the attention of the international opera world. At the beginning of the 1970s she sang at the Salzburg Festival, at La Scala, Milan (1972), and the Metropolitan Opera (1975).

Above: A scene from *Il ritorno di Ulisse in patria* by Monteverdi, conducted by Nikolaus Harnoncourt in Zurich.

Right: The conductor Nikolaus Harnoncourt.

HÁRY JÁNOS
Opera in two acts by Zoltán Kodaly (1882–1967) to a libretto by Béla Paulini and Zsolt Harsányi, based on the comic poem Az obsitos *by János Garay. First performance: Budapest, Hungarian Royal State Opera House, 16 October 1926.*

In the inn of the Hungarian village of Grob-Abony, the elderly Háry János (baritone) spins yarns to his companions about the adventures he supposedly had when he was young. On the border between Russia and Galicia, a slow-witted guard had held up the sledge on which Mária Lujza (mezzo-soprano), daughter of the Austrian Emperor, was travelling. Cunning János intervened, picked up the man's sentry-box and carried it across the frontier. This brilliant solution to the problem earned him an invitation to court, where the jealous chamberlain Ritter von Ebelasztin (speaking role) challenged him to ride Lucifer, a firebrand of a horse. On this occasion too our hero emerged triumphant: not only did he tame the fiery steed but even won the personal approval of the Emperor Franz (speaking role) by curing him of gout with a pot of his miraculous ointment. Then János set out to fight against Napoleon (bass), once again displaying his courage. He captured Napoleon and succeeded in winning the heart of Mária Lujza, who had in the meantime become Napoleon's wife. She promptly left the Emperor of France to marry János, but he rejected her in order to remain faithful to his fianceée Örzse (mezzo-soprano). Everybody in the inn is left open-mouthed by János's amazing adventures.

Háry János is one of the masterpieces of modern opera. The freshness of Kodály's music, drawing on national folk melodies, reinforces the humour of the action, which is based on Hungarian popular legend.

HASSE, JOHANN ADOLF

(Bergedorf, Hamburg 1699–Venice 1783)
German composer. Hasse came from a family of organists. After singing as a treble in the choir in his native city, he began, around 1718, to appear as a tenor with the Hamburg Opera. The following year, he moved to Brunswick, where he presented his first opera, *Antioco*, in which he also sang the leading role. He then went to Italy to train as an opera composer, studying with Porpora and Alessandro Scarlatti in Naples, where he scored his first major successes. From there he moved to Venice (1727), where he became chorus-master at the Ospedale degli Incurabili and also met and married the famous singer Faustini Bordoni, who supported him during his brilliant career as a composer of opera. He was active in Dresden, where he scored a triumph with *Cleofide* (1731). Over a period of 30 years, Hasse wrote for Italian opera houses (especially Venice) but also for London, Vienna and Munich. He composed his last opera, *Ruggiero*, in Milan in 1771, and then returned to Venice (1773), where he lived until his death. Hasse was a master of Italian *opera seria*: in his most important compositions for the theater – *Cleofide* (1731), *Didone abbandonata* (1742), *Ipermestra* (1744) and *Semiramide riconosciuta* (1744) – he obeyed almost to the letter the formal language of the genre (the three-movement *sinfonia*, three-part arias, etc.) but also revealed a definite personality of his own in the music and displayed great skill in expressive use of the orchestra.

HAUGLAND, AAGE

(Copenhagen 1944)
Danish bass. He studied music in Copenhagen, began his career at Den Norske Opera in Oslo and went on to appear in Bremen (1970–73) and Copenhagen (from 1973). In 1975 he made his debut at Covent Garden as Hagen in Wagner's *Götterdämmerung* (Twilight of the Gods), and in 1977 he sang with the English National Opera in *Die Walküre* and *Götterdämmerung*. In 1979 he appeared for the first time at the Metropolitan Opera House in New York as Baron Ochs in Richard Strauss's *Der Rosenkavalier*, a role he went on to sing at leading international opera houses. He returned to the Metropolitan to sing mainly Wagner but also won acclaim there for his performance in Mussorgsky's *Khovanshchina*. Haugland appeared at the Vienna Staatsoper, where he scored a success as the Doctor in Berg's *Wozzeck* (1987), and at the Opéra in Paris, where he sang another of his favourite roles, Varlaam in *Boris Godunov*.

HAYDN, FRANZ JOSEPH

(Rohrau 1732–Vienna 1809)
Austrian composer. At the age of eight he sang as a treble in the St Stephen's Singschule in Vienna, where he remained for about ten years. From 1750 he began to concentrate on composition, and as early as 1751 he was commissioned to write his first work for the theater, *Der krumme Teufel* (The Lame Devil), staged in 1752. Haydn was employed in the service of Baron von Fürnberg (1755–59) and then worked for Count Morzin (1759–60). He married in 1760 and in 1761 entered the service of Prince Paul Anton Esterházy in Eisenstadt, where he was deputy chorus-master and then (in 1766) director. From 1790 onwards, while retaining the title of chorus-master, Haydn was released from his direct commitments to the court of Esterházy and was able to return to Vienna. He was invited to England and set out for London in 1791, returning there in 1794. In 1795 he went back to Vienna, where he was honoured as the most famous living composer, and died there in 1809 while the city was under occupation by Napoleon's troops. A feature of Haydn's compositions for the theater was his blend of comedy with other elements more typical of *opera seria*. This characteristic was developed in *Il mondo della luna* (1777), *La vera costanza* (1779) and, even more markedly, in *L'isola disabitata* (1779). Another important ingredient was his use of vocal ensemble at the end of an act (concertato), which takes on an increasingly prominent role as Haydn's dramatic and theatrical skills developed. By the time of *La fedeltà premiata* (1780), Haydn's use of the mixed comic and serious genre was somewhat in decline, while *Armida* (1784) and *Orfeo ed Euridice, ovvero l'anima del filosofo* (1791) fall into the category of *opera seria* again, the latter also displaying links with Gluck's *opera seria* style.

HEGER, ROBERT

(Strasbourg 1886–Munich 1978)
German conductor. His musical education was in Strasbourg and in Munich with Max von Schillings. In 1907 he made his debut as a conductor in Strasbourg. He was active at the Munich Staatsoper (1920–25), where from 1950 he was principal conductor, at the Vienna Staatsoper (1925–33), at the Berlin Opera (1935–50) and in other major opera houses especially in Germany and Austria. In the 1950s and 1960s Heger made a significant contribution as an interpreter of the German repertoire and has to his credit some outstanding recordings of operas by Weber, Lortzing, Nicolai, Flotow and Wagner.

Top: Portrait of Franz Joseph Haydn.

Above: The German conductor Robert Heger

HEISE, PETER ARNOLD

(Copenhagen 1830–Tårbæk 1879)
Danish composer. He studied music in Copenhagen and Leipzig (1852–53). From 1858 to 1865 he concentrated on teaching in Soro. He then returned to Copenhagen before moving to Italy, where he met and became friends with Giovanni Sgambati, for whom he wrote several works. Heise's operatic output includes *Paschaens Datter* (The Pasha's Daughter, 1869), and *Drot og Marsk* (King and Marshal, 1878).

HENDRICKS, BARBARA

(Stephens, Arkansas 1948)
American soprano. A pupil of Jennie Tourel at the Juilliard School, she made her debut in 1976 in Monteverdi's *L'incoronazione di Poppea* and in the same year sang Amor in Gluck's *Orfeo ed Euridice* at the Holland Festival. In the years that followed, Hendricks appeared at the Glyndebourne Festival (*Fidelio*), at the Deutsche Oper Berlin (1978) and at the Salzburg Festival (1981). As a result of coming into contact in the early 1980s with famous conductors like Giulini (for whom she sang Nannetta in Verdi's *Falstaff*), Abbado, Bernstein and especially von Karajan (Puccini's *Turandot*, Brahms' *A German Requiem*, Mozart's *Mass in C minor*, etc.), Hendricks became one of the most celebrated of international operatic and concert sopranos. Although her light lyric soprano voice is not particularly wide-ranging in timbre, Hendricks has shown elegant phrasing, a softness of delivery and a certain talent for pathos in expression especially well suited to the French repertoire, in which she has given her most persuasive performances.

HENRY VIII

Opera in four acts by Camille Saint-Saëns (1835–1921) to a libretto by Léonce Détroyat and Armand Silvestre. First performance: Paris, Opéra, 5 March 1883.

Henry VIII (baritone), King of England, is in love with Anne Boleyn (mezzo-soprano), lady-in-waiting to the Queen. Anne loves Don Gomez de Feria (tenor), the Spanish ambassador, but her ambition to become Queen of England prompts her to agree to marry Henry VIII. The

Vatican refused to grant the King a divorce so Parliament proclaims the Church of England's independence from that of Rome and the King disowns his legitimate wife Catherine of Aragon (soprano). However, Catherine has in her possession a letter which provides evidence of the relationship between Anne Boleyn and Gomez. To retrieve this letter, Anne goes to Kimbolton, where Catherine is dying. Anne pretends to be repentant, but the Queen is not deceived. Henry and Gomez try unsuccessfully to obtain the letter, but Catherine resists them and eventually throws the incriminating evidence into the fire. After Catherine's death, Henry, who still has his suspicions about Anne, threatens her with death if the truth about her relationship with Gomez should ever emerge.

Henry VIII came up against a number of difficulties before it was produced: after several postponements and revisions of the libretto by its two authors, the work was staged at the Opéra, with the critics viewing it favourably as a well-structured and compact work.

HENZE, HANS WERNER

(Gütersloh, Westphalia 1926)
German composer. He studied at the State Conservatory in Brunswick (1942) and at the University of Heidelberg (1946). During the years following the Second World War, Henze continued his musical education in Paris with René Leibowitz (1947–49). He spent a year (1948–49) at the Deutsche Theater in Konstanz as music director, and from 1950 to 1952 he was artistic director at the Staatstheater in Wiesbaden. In 1953 he settled in Italy, where he concentrated mainly on composing but also worked as a conductor, producer and in the field of education. Henze consistently showed a special interest

Right: The American soprano Barbara Hendricks

Above: The German composer Hans Werner Henze.

in opera: after his earliest experiments in writing for the theater, he had his first major operatic success with *Boulevard Solitude* (1952), followed by *Der Prinz von Homburg* (1960), *Elegy for Young Lovers* (1961), *Der junge Lord* (1965), *The Bassarids* (1966) and, more recently, *Pollicino* (1980), *Die englische Katze* (1983) and *Das Verratene Meer* (1990).

HERCULES THE LOVER

See *Ercole Amante*

HERMANN, ROLAND

(Bochum, Westphalia 1936)

German baritone. He studied music in a number of countries, including his native Germany, Italy, and the United States. He made his debut in 1967 in Trier as the Count in Mozart's *Le nozze di Figaro*. The following year, he joined the resident company of the Zurich Opera, going on to appear in Frankfurt (1979) and Hamburg (1982). At the same time, his career developed internationally, leading to engagements with a number of opera houses in Europe, the United States and Japan. Hermann proved himself to be an extremely versatile artist, at ease both in the great roles of the traditional repertoire (from Mozart to Verdi and Wagner) and in those of twentieth-century and contemporary opera, as is illustrated by some of his outstanding recordings: Schoeck's *Penthesilea* (1973), Carl Orff's *Prometheus* (1973) and Egk's *Peer Gynt* (1981).

HÉRODIADE

Tragic opera in four acts by Jules Massenet (1842–1912), to a libretto by Angelo Zanardini based on Gustave Flaubert's story Hérodias. *First performance: Brussels, Théâtre de la Monnaie, 19 December 1881.*

Salomé (soprano), whom her mother, Hérodiade (mezzo-soprano), has abandoned in order to marry Hérode (baritone), has become a follower of the prophet Jean (John the Baptist, tenor) and has fallen in love with him. But Hérode, enchanted by the beauty of Salomé, makes no secret of his own desire for her, and Hérodiade, by now his wife, decides to exploit his passion for the young woman in order to have Jean (who is hostile to her) put to death. Although Jean and his followers provide Hérode with effective weapons of opposition to the Romans' oppressive rule, Jean refuses to be manipulated by him, so Hérode, who has in the meantime discovered Salomé's love for the prophet, has him thrown into prison. Salomé wants to die with Jean and insists on having herself imprisoned with him. Moved by Salomé's self-sacrifice in wanting to join him in prison, Jean no longer rejects her love, which he now considers pure. But Salomé is taken away from him in order to take part in an orgiastic celebration held in honour of the Romans. Desperate, Salomé begs Hérode to have mercy. Hérodiade now recognizes Salomé as the daughter she had once abandoned and joins her in her appeal to save Jean. But it is too late: the prophet has already been beheaded, and Salomé kills herself in her mother's presence.

Hérodiade is a lyrical and richly melodic opera which also offers a wealth of passionate feelings and clearly delineates the sharp contrasts between the characters.

HÉROLD, LOUIS-JOSEPH FERDINAND

(Paris 1791–1833)

French composer. He began to study piano with his father, a respected teacher, before entering the Paris Conservatoire (1802). In 1812 he won the Prix de Rome, which enabled him to travel to Italy. He stayed in Rome and then in Naples, where he met Paisiello and Zingarelli. While in Naples he composed his first opera, *La gioventù di Enrico V* (1815), which was a modest success. In the same year he went to Vienna, where he met Salieri and Hummel. He then returned to Paris and was appointed *maestro* at the Théâtre des Italiens, after which his career as a composer began to flourish. His considerable output of works for the theater includes the operas *Les rosières* (1817), *La clochette* (1817), *L'asthénie* (1823), *Marie* (1826), his greatest success *Zampa* (1831), *Le pré-aux-clercs* (1832) and *Ludovic*, which he left unfinished.

HEURE ESPAGNOLE, L'

Comédie musicale *in one act by Maurice Ravel (1875–1937), based on the comedy by Maurice Etienne Legrand, who wrote the libretto under the pseudonym Franc-Nohain.*

A scene from *L'heure espagnole* by Ravel, first performed in Paris in 1911.

OPERA AND EXOTICISM

The *opera seria* of the eighteenth century depicted the heroes and heroines of ancient times, from its various different roles for Achilles, Agamemnon, Alcestis and Iphigenia from Ancient Greece to the emperors of the Roman world. The choice of classical antiquity corresponded to an enormous interest (which had become more widespread in the course of the century) in archaeology, together with a curiosity to know more about the Orient, first Turkey and Persia, and then India and America too. As a result the operas with classical heroes were soon joined by others featuring Darius, Tamburlaine, Xerxes, Genghis Khan and Montezuma. The plots changed but not the style of the music, which remained as before except that staging and costumes became more magnificent and imaginative. So it was that in the ''Oriental'' operas of Vivaldi, Handel, Hasse and Graun there were no significant changes at all; in others, however, such as Rameau's *Les Indes galantes* (1735) or Gluck's *Le Cinesi* (1754) and above all in Mozart's *Die Entführung aus dem Serail* (The Seraglio, 1782), the composers used so-called Turkish-style music which they scored for instruments like the bass drum, cymbals, triangle and piccolo. In this opera Mozart also gave a new lease of life to a theme which had already been extensively used before, that of the harem and abduction. The French musical world was particularly susceptible to the appeal of the East and the exotic. Even before Rameau's time, Jean-Baptiste Lully (1632–1687) had composed his celebrated and very entertaining *Cérémonie des Turcs* for Molière's *Le Bourgeois Gentilhomme*, an indication that French composers were already interested in the exotic, as indeed they continued to be in the centuries that followed. And although Grétry and Boieldieu still turned for inspiration to the Middle East for some of their operas such as *La caravane du Caire* and *Le calife de Bagdad*, the first performance in 1828 of Auber's opera *La muette de Portici* (the moment at which *grand-opéra* officially arrived) marked a broadening of the concept of ''the exotic'' into the notion of ''local colour.'' Consequently· barcarolles are featured in Auber's opera to conjure up images of Naples and the sea, while Meyerbeer, the greatest exponent of *grand-opéra*, also paints a picture of Russia in his opera *Le' étoile du nord* (1854) and Bizet achieves yet another kind of exoticism in the wealth of colour with which he creates his marvellous portrait of Spain in the famous *Carmen* (1875). The attraction of the East for composers remained unchanged, Bizet himself having already been drawn to it for his earlier operas *Les pêcheurs de perles* (1863) and *Djamileh* (1872) and many other composers with him. Among the best-known of these were Jules Massenet who was following a particular literary fashion of the day then at its height when he composed operas like *Hérodiate* (in 1881, in which the plot, based on a story by Flaubert, combines history and the Bible with a hint of the exotic), *Le roi de Lahore* (1878), *Thais* (1894), from the novel by Anatole France, and *Le Cid* (1885), where the ''local colour'' comes in the form of some exceptionally fine dances each bearing the title of a Spanish province: ''Castillane,'' ''Andalouse,'' ''Aragonaise''. Another work which has remained famous to this day is Camille Saint-Saëns' *Samson et Dalila*, in which the evocative power of the East is in evidence in the great ''Bacchanale'' of Act III, a series of dances which, as well as recalling Oriental musical themes, unleashes the force and violence of a pagan orgiastic rite.

Above: Print showing the scene of the destruction of the temple in *Samson et Dalila* by Saint-Saëns.

Valent Adamberger

Catarina Cavalieri

Right: The silhouettes of Valent Adamberger and Catarina Cavalieri, the first to perform *Die Entführung aus dem Serail* (The Seraglio) by Mozart.

First performance: Paris, Théâtre de l'Opéra-Comique, 19 May 1911.

The action takes place in a clock-maker's shop in Toledo during the eighteenth century. Ramiro (baritone), a muleteer, has brought Torquemada (tenor) an old watch to mend. The clock-maker's wife, Concepción (soprano), reminds her husband that today being Thursday, he must go and check the public clocks in the town. Torquemada sets out, asking Ramiro to wait for him to return. Concepción is expecting her lover, the poet Gonzalve (tenor), and so tries to get rid of the muleteer by asking him to carry a heavy clock up to the next floor. When Gonzalve appears, Concepción can at last be alone with him. Enter Ramiro, who has now taken the clock upstairs. Concepción persuades him to go and bring the clock back again, because there is another one she would like him to take upstairs instead of the first clock. The muleteer agrees, and Concepción has just enough time to hide Gonzalve inside the second clock, which Ramiro will soon be coming to take upstairs. Inigo Gomez (bass), a wealthy banker and another of Concepción's admirers, arrives. While Ramiro is carrying the clock with Gonzalve inside it upstairs, Gomez decides to play a trick on Concepción by hiding inside the clock which Ramiro has just brought back downstairs. Then Ramiro comes down again, followed by Concepción. She is furious: Gonzalve is a great one for fine words but not good at following them up with actions. After persuading poor Ramiro to swap the clocks yet again, Concepción, who has by now lost interest in the banker, has her eye on Ramiro. With Gonzalve and Gomez both safely inside the clocks, Concepción, irritated by both lovers, begins to see the muscular muleteer in a different light. But the two lovers finally climb out of the pendulum-cases and linger so long in the shop that Torquemada finds them there when he comes home. The clock-maker is pleased to have two customers in his shop and takes advantage of their moment of confusion to sell each of them a clock, then tells his wife he has no clocks left. She replies that she will always be able to tell the time, because every morning Ramiro will be passing under her window "as regularly as clockwork."

Ravel finished *L'heure espagnole* in 1907, but it was not until 1911 that the work was staged at the Opéra-Comique. It was quite well received but nevertheless disappeared from French theater programmes after a few performances and was not seen again until 1938.

H. H. ULYSSE

Opera in two parts by Jean Prodromidès (b. 1927), to a text by Serge Ganzl. First performance: Strasbourg, Opéra du Rhin 4 March 1984.

The plot is a sort of inner journey by Howard Hamilton Jr. (baritone) in the footsteps of the legendary Ulysses. H. H. J. retraces the adventures of Ulysses and, in a rapid succession of images somewhere between reality and fantasy, he releases Ulysses' sailors from the spell in which they had been trapped by the sorceress Circe (soprano) for 2,000 years. Accompanied by Hélas (counter-tenor), who acts as his divine protector, the young traveller meets the Cyclops Polyphemus (bass), who comes to life in the form of an imaginary character from fable, like an ogre, a monster which had appeared in H. H. J.'s story-books when he was a child. Then it is the turn of Calypso (soprano), the symbol of wisdom and knowledge in the opera. Calypso wants to communicate her knowledge to the young stranger and thus render him immortal. But for H. H. J. this would be impossible: the shock of encountering Calypso's world brings him to the edge of madness, but he is snatched to safety by Hélas. Sucked in through the Gate of Hell, H. H. J. enters the underworld, a vast hall which resembles a Las Vegas casino. Escorted by Cerberus (tenor), H. H. J. meets a number of Hell's "clients," including Agamemnon and Clytemnestra, but also Circe, Calypso and Nausicaa, who appear in the form of three film-stars with whom H. H. J. was once in love. He must then resume his wandering journey. Driven on by a violent storm unleashed by Poseidon (bass-baritone), H. H. J. has a dream in which he relives his meeting with Nausicaa, together with images of the lost paradise of his youth and childhood. A group of young men and women tell the story of the stranger's adventures and ask, "is he H. H. J. or Ulysses?" While the young people are miming the traveller's return to Ithaca and the massacre of Penelope's suitors, Poseidon violently interrupts H. H. J.'s dream. The young traveller finds himself alone, powerless, defeated, and overcome by a sense of futility at his inner journey, which seems to be leading nowhere. In the end, however, truth dawns, and he feels suddenly enlightened. The words that had prompted him to attempt his long journey return to echo in his ears: "Set out, do not hold back, you are the man whose life you still have to live."

In this opera, the composer Prodromidès does not simply reproduce the famous events of Homer's epic poem *The Odyssey* but creates a dream-like voyage in which the boundaries of time and space vanish: this is a modern-day man (inspired by the semi-legendary figure of Howard Hughes) making a journey in the world of imagination and identifying himself with Ulysses. The score of *H. H. Ulysse* is for an ensemble of eight instrumentalists, a group of 12 voices, chorus, large orchestra, stage orchestra and magnetic tape.

HINDEMITH, PAUL

(Hanau 1895–Frankfurt-am-Main 1963)
German composer. In 1921 his second string quartet won him international fame. In the same year he wrote his first one-act operas,

A scene from *L'heure espagnole* by Ravel (see page 177).

Above: A scene from *Cardillac* by Hindemith, in a production at La Scala during the 1986–87 season.

Mörder, Hoffnung der Frauen (Murder, the Hope of Women) and *Nusch-Nuschi*, followed by *Sancta Susanna* in 1922. In 1927 Hindemith, by now considered the most important composer of the new generation, was appointed professor of composition at the Hochschule für Musik in Berlin. He had just completed *Cardillac* (1926), which he subsequently revised. His Berlin period produced *Neus vom Tage* (News of the Day) in 1929, and he also composed *Mathis der Maler* (Mathis the Painter), although the first performance of this opera was banned in 1934 by the Nazi authorities. In 1937, Hindemith left Germany for Switzerland. It was in Zurich in 1938 that *Mathis der Maler* had its successful premiere. In 1940 Hindemith moved to the United States, where he taught at Yale University School of Music from 1941 until 1953. After taking American citizenship (1946), he settled again in Switzerland in 1953, teaching in Zurich (1951–55). Other significant works in Hindemith's remarkable operatic output are *Hin und Zurück* (There and Back), 1927, *Die Harmonie der Welt* (The Harmony of the World), 1957, and *Der lange Weihnachtsmahl* (The Long Christmas Dinner), 1961.

HINES, JEROME

(Hollywood 1921)

Stage name of Jerome Heinz, American bass. After making his debut with the San Francisco Opera in 1941, singing Monterone (*Rigoletto*), Hines made his first important appearances in 1946, the year in which he performed for the first time at the Metropolitan Opera House, New York (*Faust*) after winning first prize in the Caruso singing competition. The distinctive fullness and resonance of his voice established a reputation for Hines further afield than the Metropolitan (where his appearances continued almost uninterrupted) at other leading international houses. His repertoire centered mainly on the important bass roles (*Boris Godunov*, *Don Carlos*, *Khovanshchina*, *Parsifal*).

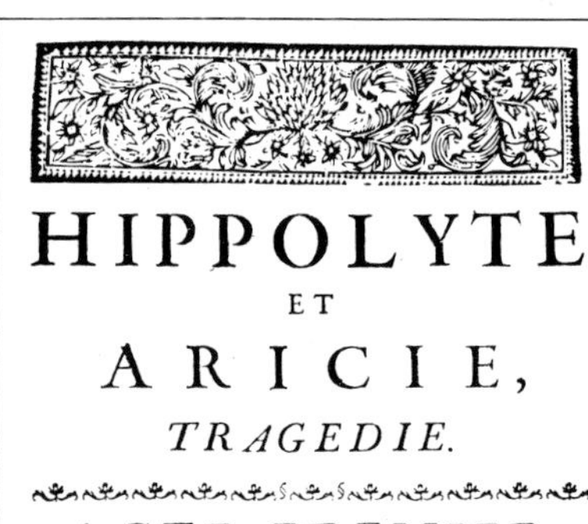

HIPPOLYTE

ET

ARICIE,

TRAGEDIE.

ACTE PREMIER.

Le Théâtre repréſente un temple conſacré à Diane: On y voit un Autel.

SCENE PREMIERE.

ARICIE.

Emple ſacré, ſéjour tranquille,
Où Diane aujourd'hui doit recevoir mes vœux,
A mon cœur agité, daigne ſervir d'azile
Contre un amour trop malheureux.

Right: The title page to the libretto of *Hippolyte et Aricie* by Rameau.

HIPPOLYTE ET ARICIE

Tragic opera in five acts and a prologue by Jean-Philippe Rameau (1683–1764), to a libretto by S. J. Pellegrin. First performance: Paris, Académie Royale de Musique (Opéra), 1 October 1733.

In the prologue, Diane (soprano) and L'Amour (soprano), with Jupiter (baritone) as their arbiter, fight to win the support of those who live in the forest. Aricie (soprano) receives from Hippolyte (tenor) a confession of his love for her. The two young people provoke the anger and jealousy of Phèdre, the wife of Thésée (bass), who is in love with her stepson Hippolyte and wants to have Aricie consecrated to the worship of Diane. Thésée has gone down into the underworld and manages to return to earth, thanks to the protection of his father, Neptune; but everyone has by now given him up for dead, and Phèdre, imagining herself to be a widow, declares her love to Hippolyte, who rejects her. Thésée appears, to the delight of his people. He unjustly believes his son is guilty of having loved his step-mother and asks Neptune to bring about the young man's death. During the games staged in honour of Diane, a terrible monster rises out of the sea. Hippolyte confronts it, vanishing with it amid flames and smoke. Phèdre kills herself in despair. But Diane pulls Hippolyte to safety and he is carried off by the Zephyrs to be reunited with his beloved Aricie. The young couple are married.

The work's first performance caused controversy among the supporters of Lully's style of opera, while the more progressive circles of Parisian life hailed it an outstanding success.

HOFFMANN, ERNST THEODOR AMADEUS

(Königsberg 1776–Berlin 1822)

German poet, writer and composer. After studying law in Berlin, he began a career in government as an official of the Prussian administration in Poland. The limited nature of this job increasingly prompted Hoffmann to concentrate on his music studies, which he did with great energy. He left Poland for Bamberg, where he was music director of the theater (1808). From 1810, Hoffmann led an intensely active life as a conductor (in Leipzig and Dresden, 1813–14) and as the composer of some ten operas, including *Die Maske*, 1799, *Scherz, List und Rache* (Jest,

Cunning and Revenge), 1801, *Die lustigen Musikanten* (The Merry Musicians), 1805, *Aurora*, 1811 and *Undine*, 1816. His literary output was remarkable and provided the inspiration for many operas, the most famous of which are Offenbach's *Les contes d'Hoffmann*, 1880, Busoni's *Die Brautwahl* (The Choice of a Bride), 1910, Hindemith's *Cardillac*, 1926, and Malipiero's *Capriccio di Callot*, 1942.

HOFMANN, PETER

(Mariánske Lázne 1944)

German tenor. He studied music at the Staatlische Hochschule für Musik in Karlsruhe and with Seiberlich. He made his debut in Lübeck in 1972 as Tamino in *Die Zauberflöte* (The Magic Flute). In 1974 he tackled the Wagnerian repertoire for the first time, singing the role of Siegmund (*Die Walküre*) in Wupperthal. Two years later he appeared in Stuttgart as Parsifal, repeating this role with distinction within the space of a few months at some of the major German opera houses, including Bayreuth, where he also sang the role of Siegmund again (1976). A member of the Vienna Staatsoper from 1977, Hofmann was at the same time embarking on an international career which took him to the Opéra in Paris (from 1976), Covent Garden, La Scala, the Salzburg Easter Festival and other opera venues. Hofmann's Wagner roles were particularly outstanding for their musicianship and elegant, expressive phrasing.

HOFMANNSTHAL, HUGO VON

(Vienna 1874–Rodaun, Vienna 1929)

Austrian poet, playwright and librettist. Hofmannsthal's was a complex and many-sided personality. He is known in the field of opera for his long friendship and collaboration with Richard Strauss, for whom he wrote libretti for *Elektra* (1906–8), *Der Rosenkavalier* (1909–10), *Ariadne auf Naxos* (first version

1911–12, second version 1915–16,) *Die Frau ohne Schatten* (1914–17), *Die ägyptische Helena* (1924–27), subsequently revised in 1933, and *Arabella* (1930–32).

HOLLREISER, HEINRICH

(Munich 1913)

German conductor. He studied at the Akademie der Tonkunst in Munich and with the conductor Karl Elmendorff. He began his career in 1932 in Wiesbaden before moving on to Darmstadt, Mannheim (1938), Duisburg and Munich (1942–45). From 1945 to 1951, Hollreiser was general musical director in Düsseldorf, and in the years that followed he devoted much of his time and energy to the opera houses of Vienna (1952–61) and Berlin (1961–64) where, in addition to the usual repertoire of Wagner, Verdi and Strauss, he conducted many twentieth-century operas, such as Milhaud's *Orestie* (1963) and von Einem's *Der Prozess*. He was also active at Bayreuth from 1973 to 1975, conducting *Tannhäuser* and *Die Meistersinger von Nürnberg*. He conducted the first performance on record of Wagner's *Rienzi* (1975).

HOLLWEG, WERNER

(Solingen 1936)

German tenor. He began to study music at the age of 20, going on to take advanced lessons in Munich and Lugano, and made his debut with the Vienna Kammeroper in 1961 in Mozart's *Il re pastore*. This was followed by a series of contracts which took Hollweg to Bonn, Florence's Maggio Musicale Festival, Hamburg, Munich, Berlin, the Salzburg Festival and New York. An outstanding singer with elegant phrasing (also in the *Lieder* repertoire), Hollweg is especially renowned for his Mozart performances, but also for those in operas by Rossini (*Tancredi*) and Wagner (*Tannhäuser*).

HONEGGER, ARTHUR

(Le Havre 1892–Paris 1955)

Swiss composer. He studied at the Conservatory in Zurich (1909–1911) and at the Paris Conservatoire (1911–15). After settling permanently in Paris, between 1917 and 1921 he founded the group of composers known as "Les Six" with Milhaud, Satie, Auric, Durey, Poulenc and Tailleferre. In 1921 he wrote a dramatic oratorio, *Le roi David*, which established him as a composer of the first rank. His operas were *Antigone* (1927), the biblical opera *Judith* (1926), *Amphion* (1931), the operetta *Les aventures du roi Pausole* (1930) and the stage oratorio *Cris du monde* (1930–31). His most famous work was *Jeanne d'Arc au bûcher* (Joan of

Above: The German conductor Heinrich Hollreiser.

Top: Costume design for *Der Rosenkavalier* by Richard Strauss, to a libretto by Hugo von Hofmannsthal.

Left: The poet, playwright and librettist Hugo von Hofmannsthal.

Arc at the Stake), composed in 1936 to a text by Paul Claudel.

HONOUR OF THE INDIES

See *Indes galantes, Les*

HOPF, HANS

(Nuremberg 1916)
German tenor. A pupil of Paul Bender, he made his debut in 1936 with the Bayerische Landesbühnen. From 1939 to 1942 he joined the resident company of the Municipal Theater in Augsburg before moving on to Dresden, Berlin (1946–49) and Munich from 1949. He appeared regularly at the Vienna Staatsoper and in Salzburg (from 1954) and also sang at leading international opera houses, including Covent Garden (1951–53), the Metropolitan Opera House, New York (from 1952) and Bayreuth (1951). During the 1960s Hopf built his reputation in *Heldentenor* roles: Siegfried, Tristan, etc. Of equal importance were his performances as the Emperor (*Die Frau ohne Schatten*) and as Max (*Der Freischütz*), which enabled him to assert his authoritative personality as a singer.

HORENSTEIN, JASCHA

(Kiev 1898–London 1973)
Russian conductor, naturalized American. He left Russia at the age of six when his family moved to Königsberg in Germany. There he completed his music studies before going in 1920 to Berlin, where he embarked on his professional music career with the Berlin Philharmonic Orchestra (1925–28). Chief conductor and later director of music at Düsseldorf Opera (1928–30), Horenstein went to the United States in 1933 and taught at the New School for Social Research in New York in 1940. He went on numerous tours, conducting major orchestras in Australia, New Zealand (1936–37), Palestine and Scandinavia. In opera, he conducted the French premieres of Berg's *Wozzeck* in 1950 and Janáček's *Z mrtvého domu* (From the House of the Dead) in 1951, and the first performance in America of Busoni's *Doktor Faust* in 1964.

The American soprano Marilyn Horne.

HORNE, MARILYN

(Bradford, Pennsylvania 1929)
American mezzo-soprano. She studied singing with her father, an amateur tenor, and made her debut in Los Angeles (1954) in Smetana's *Prodaná nevěsta* (The Bartered Bride). The following year, she recorded the singing soundtrack for Dorothy Dandridge in the film *Carmen Jones*. Horne's voice at that time seemed soprano, and it was as a soprano that she appeared between 1957 and 1960 with the Gelsenkirchen Opera company in Germany, singing roles in *La bohème*, *La fanciulla del West*, *Simon Boccanegra*, *Wozzeck* and others. On her return to the United States, she met the conductor Richard Bonynge and his wife, the soprano Joan Sutherland. Horne appeared with Sutherland for the first time in 1961 in a concert performance of Bellini's *Beatrice di Tenda*, and this proved to be the beginning of a close artistic collaboration between them which was soon to include *Norma* (1963) and *Semiramide* (1964), high points of the *bel canto* revival. Horne had an active career in the world of international opera, at Covent Garden (from 1964), La Scala, Milan (from 1969) and the Metropolitan Opera House, New York (from 1970). She drew on a wide-ranging repertoire which featured operas by Verdi (*Il trovatore*, *Aida*, *Don Carlos*, *Falstaff*) and Bizet (*Carmen*), but her tremendous skills in technique and expression enabled her to concentrate mainly on the *bel canto* repertoire, from Vivaldi (*Orlando Furioso*) to Handel (*Rinaldo*, *Orlando*, *Semele*) and especially Rossini, in both *opera seria* (*Tancredi*, *La donna del lago*, *Semiramide*) and *opera buffa La Cenerentola*, *Il barbiere di Siviglia*, *L'italiana in Algeri*) and, with this repertoire, to play a major part in the renaissance of Rossini's operas.

LES HUGUENOTS

Opera in five acts by Giacomo Meyerbeer (1791–1864), to a libretto by Eugène Scribe (1791–1861) after Emile Deschamps (1791–1871). First performance: Paris, Opéra, 29 February 1836.

France, August 1572. Act I. To comply with the King's wishes – that the bitter religious hostilities cease – the Catholic Count de Nevers (baritone) invites to a banquet at his château in Touraine the Huguenot Raoul de Nangis (tenor) with fellow Catholics. A toast of love is suggested and Raoul begins with a vow to an unknown girl whom he had defended from an attack in the street by some young men. A young woman comes to speak with the Count. Raoul recognizes her as the unknown lady whom he now loves and assumes that she is the Count's mistress. She is, in fact, Valentine de Saint-Bris (soprano), who has been sent by the Queen to beg the Count to free her from her promise of marriage. Urbain (mezzo-soprano), the Queen's page, invites Raoul to meet a lady who wishes to remain anonymous and he leaves blindfolded for the mysterious meeting. Act II. The gardens of Chenonceaux. To consolidate the peace, Marguérite de Valois (soprano) wants Valentine (whose father, de Saint-Bris, is a Catholic leader) to marry Raoul. Valentine is happy, for she admired Raoul's courage and has fallen in love with him. When Raoul's blindfold is removed, Marguérite offers to receive him at court if he will marry Valentine. The Count de Saint-Bris (baritone) presents his daughter to Raoul who, believing her to be Nevers' mistress, refuses to marry her. The Catholics are incensed. Act III. Paris. The wedding of Valentine and Nevers is about to be celebrated. Raoul's servant, Marcel (bass), gives Saint-Bris a note from his master challenging him to a duel. Valentine overhears a plot to ambush Raoul at the duel and warns Marcel, who calls his followers. Fighting breaks out between Catholics and Huguenots until the arrival of the Queen quells the disturbance. Raoul now realizes the truth about Valentine's meeting with Nevers. Act IV. Paris, the house of the Count de Nevers. Raoul questions Valentine, but he is forced to hide with Saint-Bris and Nevers arrive. Saint-Bris wants to exterminate the Huguenots, but Nevers will not take part in the conspiracy and is arrested. The Catholics are to wear white scarves and at the tolling of a bell they will begin the massacre of the Huguenots. Priests bless their swords. When the bell begins to ring, Raoul, who has heard the terrible plan from his hiding place, frees himself with difficulty from Valentine's embrace and runs to warn his follows. Act V, Scene I. Raoul calls the Huguenots, who have gathered to celebrate the marriage of the King and Queen, to arms. Scene II. A Hugenot churchyard. Marcel lies wounded and Raoul, nearby, is determined to await death beside him. Valentine appears with the news that Nevers has been killed and that the Queen is prepared to pardon him if he will give up his faith. Raoul refuses and Valentine, deeply affected, resolves to accept the Protestant faith of her beloved. They die together, killed by her father's men.

The story is based on the massacre of the Huguenots in Paris on the night of St. Bartholomew, 24 August 1572. This is one of Meyerbeer's most beautiful operas and it enjoyed a huge success. He was an innovator of lyric opera, the creator and best exponent of grand opera, and in his *Huguenots* we find the merits and defects of all his finest productions: pages of true poetry and fine dramatic insight contrast with romantic and spectacular stage effects.

HUGH THE DROVER, OR LOVE IN THE STOCKS

Ballad opera in two acts by Ralph Vaughan Williams (1872–1958), to a libretto by Harold Child (1869–1945). First performance: London, Perry Memorial Theater, Royal College of Music, 4 July 1924.

England, the beginning of the nineteenth century. Mary's father, the Constable (bass), wants his daughter (soprano) to marry the rich but oafish John the Butcher (bass-baritone). She falls in love, however, with Hugh the Drover (tenor), who is regarded with suspicion by the townspeople because he loves the freedom of the countryside, animals and the open road. John continues to press his suit with Mary's father, convinced that his wealth will prove irresistible. The two men fight a boxing match to decide which shall marry Mary, and Hugh wins. Then John accuses Hugh of being a Napoleonic spy. Hugh is locked into the village stocks. None of Mary's stratagems to release him are successful and Hugh has to spend the night there, and endure the taunts of John and his friends. In the morning, however, Mary appears with her father's key to the stocks and unlocks them. The lovers are about to escape, when Mary's absence is noticed at home, and the villagers are surprised to find her sitting beside Hugh – in the stocks. John declares that he cannot marry one who behaves in this undignified way, but Mary's friends sympathize with her. A Sergeant (baritone) arrives to take the suspected spy away, but he recognizes Hugh as an old comrade and cheerfully releases him. Instead, he marches off with John, determined to "make a man" of him. Hugh and Mary happily set off together for the open road.

Although the character of John the Butcher has been criticized as a dull creation arousing neither sympathy nor dislike, the opera as a whole has great delicacy. Mary is a surprisingly passionate character for an English opera and the music underlines this throughout. The opera, composed between 1911 and 1914, has never been a great international success.

HUMPERDINCK, ENGELBERT

(Siegburg 1854–Neustrelitz 1921)

German composer. He studied at the Conservatory in Cologne (1872–76) and in Munich (1877–79). During a trip to Italy in 1880 he was introduced to Richard Wagner, whom he followed to Bayreuth, helping him prepare *Parsifal* for the stage. A tireless traveller, Humperdinck taught at the Conservatory in Barcelona from 1885 to 1887 before moving back to Germany to teaching posts at the Conservatories of Cologne and Frankfurt (1890–96). In 1900 he was appointed as a member of the Akademie der Künste in Berlin and as a professor at the Berlin Musikhochschule (until 1920). Of Humperdinck's remarkable output for the theater, his first opera, *Hänsel und Gretel* (1893), is the only one which has remained well-known. His other operas include *Dornröschen* (The Sleeping Beauty in the Wood), 1902, *Die Heirat wieder Willen* (A Marriage not of One's Choosing), 1905, *Die Marketenderin* (The Vivandière), *Königskinder*, 1910, and *Gaudeamus*, 1919.

The German composer Engelbert Humperdinck.

HUNYADI LÁSZLÓ

Opera in three acts by Ferenc Erkel (1810–1893), to a libretto by Béni Egressy. First performance: Budapest, Pest Hungarian Theater, 27 January 1844.

In the fortress of Nandorférvar, the commanding officer László Hunyadi (tenor) is awaiting the arrival of King László V (tenor), to whom he intends to hand over the keys of the castle as a mark of his devotion. The nobles, Hunyadi's supporters, are critical of this, as they have their doubts about the King, known to be weak and easily led, especially after the discovery of a clandestine plot in which the King's counsellor Ulrik Czilley (baritone) was supposed to assassinate Hunyadi and his younger brother Matyas (contralto). When the King and his retinue arrive, Hunyadi confronts Czilley in a bid to show that he is behind the plot. Czilley reacts by making an attempt on Hunyadi's life, but his supporters intervene and kill the traitor. The King asks Hunyadi for his forgiveness and swears that he will not avenge Czilley's death. But László V's innate dishonesty soon reveals itself: after falling in love with Maria (soprano), Hunyadi's fiancée, the King wants to be rid of his rival for her love, and therefore heeds the advice of the ambitious palatine Gara (baritone) and accuses the Hunyadi brothers of being disloyal to the throne. As a result, the King's bodyguards burst in on the celebrations of the engagement between Hunyadi and Maria, arrest him, and drag him away. He is condemned to death. The scene changes to St. George's Square in Buda, where Hunyadi is about to be beheaded. The executioner's axe falls three times on to Hunyadi's neck without striking his head from his body. Erzsébet Szilágy (soprano), Hunyadi's mother, calls for the honouring of a sacred tradition whereby, should the third blow of the axe not kill the condemned man, a fourth should not be attempted. But Gara, heedless of the appeals from Erzsébet and the crowd, orders the executioner to bring down the axe again.

Hunyadi László represents the highest point in Ferenc Erkel's artistic development towards the creation of an authentic Hungarian opera. The work also contains clear influences from Italian and French opera (performances of operas by Verdi and other composers were conducted by Erkel in Hungary), though these have been combined here with the Hungarian tradition, which provides the primary ingredient, not least in the choice of an authentically Hungarian subject for the plot.

Right: The Finnish baritone Jorma Hynninen.

Above: The Russian baritone Dimitri Hvorostovsky.

HVOROSTOVSKY, DIMITRI

(Krasnoyarsk, Siberia 1962)

Russian baritone. He studied music in his native city with Ekaterina Yofel (1982). After graduating, he began to appear at the opera house in Krasnoyarsk (1986) in operas from the Russian repertoire but also from the Italian (*I pagliacci*) and the French (*Faust*). He went on to distinguish himself in major singing competitions like the BBC's Cardiff Singer of the World Competition (1989), through which he made his name with audiences and critics in the West. His enormously successful debut as a concert artist was at the Wigmore Hall in London (1989), Alice Tully Hall in New York (1990) and subsequently in Washington. As a performer of opera, he sang at the opera house in Nice in Tchaikovsky's *Queen of Spades* in 1989, at La Fenice in Venice (*Eugene Onegin*) in 1991 and at Covent Garden (*I puritani*) in 1992. His recordings have also brought him fame, among them Mascagni's *Cavalleria rusticana*.

HYNNINEN, JORMA

(Leppavirta 1941)

Finnish baritone. After studying with Matti Tuloisela and Antti Koskinen at the Sibelius Academy in Helsinki, he went on to have lessons in Rome with Luigi Ricci and in Essen with Clemens Keiser-Breme. In 1969 he made his debut as Silvio (*I pagliacci*) with Finnish National Opera in Helsinki, which became the initial focus of his career before he moved on to the Royal Opera in Stockholm. Outside Finland, Hynninen sang at the Opéra in Paris (*Pelléas et Mélisande*, 1980), at the Metropolitan Opera House in New York (*Don Carlos*, 1984, followed by *Le nozze di Figaro*, *Tannhäuser* and *Eugene Onegin*), the Liceu in Barcelona (*Tannhäuser*, 1988), the Chicago Lyric Opera (*Don Carlos*, 1989) and numerous other theaters. He has appeared frequently at the Savonlinna Festival, of which he became artistic director in 1992, after serving in a similar capacity for Finnish National Opera. Hynninen has also been a very active concert artist and taken part in a number of world premieres of operas by contemporary composers: Sallinen's *Punainen Viiva* (The Red Line, 1978) and *The King Goes Forth to France* (1984), Merikanto's *Juha* (1987) and Rautavaara's *Thomas* (1986) and *Vincent* (1990). Among recordings he made in the late 1980s are Mozart's *Le nozze di Figaro* (1986) with Riccardo Muti conducting and Richard Strauss's *Elektra* with Seiji Ozawa (1988).

I

IDOMENEO, RE DI CRETA

Opera seria *in three acts by Wolfgang Amadeus Mozart (1756–1791), to a libretto by Giovanni Battista Varesco. First performance: Munich, Hoftheater, 29 January 1781.*

The action takes place in Crete at the time of the Trojan War. Ilia (soprano), a young princess and daughter of King Priam and prisoner of Idomeneo (tenor), King of Crete, is in love with Idamante (mezzo-soprano), who is ruling the island while his father Idomeneo is at war in Troy. News arrives of the King's imminent return to Crete. But a terrible storm wrecks Idomeneo's ship. In order to placate Neptune, Idomeneo promises that he will sacrifice to the god the first living creature he sees after setting foot on dry land, but is speechless with horror when it is his son Idamante he catches sight of on the shore. He does not have the courage to fulfil his terrible pledge to Neptune and decides to send Idamante to Greece as escort for the Princess Elettra. A monster rises out of the sea and prevents the pair from setting sail. Idomeneo is consequently compelled to acknowledge that destiny has chosen his son as the sacrificial victim. Shortly after this, with Idamante about to be sacrificed, Ilia bursts in and offers to take the young prince's place. At this point Neptune's oracle (bass) stops the sacrifice and allows Ilia and Idamante to marry, calling upon Idomeneo to abdicate in his son's favour.

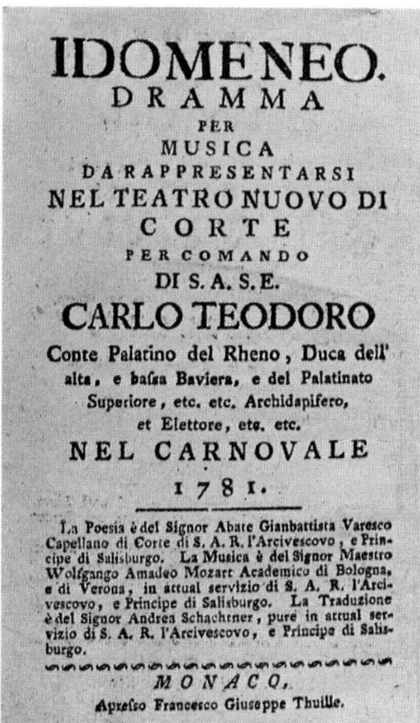

IDOMENEO.
DRAMMA
PER
MUSICA
DA RAPPRESENTARSI
NEL TEATRO NUOVO DI
CORTE
PER COMANDO
DI S. A. S. E.
CARLO TEODORO
Conte Palatino del Rheno, Duca dell' alta, e bassa Baviera, e del Palatinato Superiore, etc. etc. Archidapifero, et Elettore, etc. etc.
NEL CARNOVALE
1781.

La Poesia è del Signor Abate Gianbattista Varesco Capellano di Corte di S. A. R. l'Arcivescovo, e Principe di Salisburgo. La Musica è del Signor Maestro Wolfgango Amadeo Mozart Academico di Bologna, e di Verona, in attual servizio di S. A. R. l'Arcivescovo, e Principe di Salisburgo. La Traduzione è del Signor Andrea Schachtner, pure in attual servizio di S. A. R. l'Arcivescovo, e Principe di Salisburgo.

MONACO,
Apresso Francesco Giuseppe Thuille.

The premiere of *Idomeneo* was an outstanding success, providing Mozart with the encouragement he needed to leave his native city of Salzburg in favour of the more open and culturally richer environment of Vienna, which was to become his adoptive city. The story of Idomeneo was turned into an opera by several other composers, including Campra (1712), Gazzaniga (1790) and Paër (1794).

IGROK

(The Gambler)

Opera in four acts by Sergei Prokofiev (1891–1953), to the composer's own libretto from the story by Dostoevsky. First performance: Brussels, Théâtre de la Monnaie, 29 April 1929 (in French, with the title Le joueur*).*

Far from his native country, Alexei Ivanovich (tenor) becomes a tutor in the house of a stupid and incompetent General (bass) and falls in love with his sister-in-law Polina (soprano). One day she sends Alexei in her place to play roulette. This proves to be a decisive experience for Alexei; after winning a tidy sum, he tries his luck again and loses everything. On returning to the house, he finds a nightmarish situation: the General is being visited by two adventurers, Degrieux (tenor) and Mademoiselle Blanche (contralto), who wish to secure a sizeable bequest from an old Aunt which the family expects at any moment. Instead, the Aunt (mezzo-soprano) turns up in person, determined to rid the house of the atmosphere of corruption which the gamblers are causing there. But she too is overwhelmed by gambling fever and loses almost everything at the tables. Degrieux and Mademoiselle Blanche vanish, while Alexei goes back to gambling again. Mademoiselle Blanche uses various wiles and subterfuges to make him into a professional gambler and leads him to ruin. Polina, who is in love with Alexei, tries to save him, but it is too late: Alexei is no longer capable of giving up roulette.

Composed between October 1915 and March 1916, the opera is faithful to the text and spirit of Dostoevsky's original story. When Prokofiev took up the score again 11 years later, he found it tediously lengthy and cut it down.

Left: The libretto for Mozart's *Idomeneo.*

Top: A scene from *Idomeneo.*

Above: The Russian composer Sergei Prokofiev.

This shortened version was the one seen at the first performance in Brussels.

IMMORTAL HOUR, THE

Opera in two acts by Rutland Boughton (1878–1960), to a libretto by Fiona Macleod (pseudonym of William Sharp). First performance: Glastonbury, 26 August 1914.

Dalua (baritone), the Lord of Shadow, is gifted with the fatal touch of death and has the power to know the thoughts of both mortals and immortals. He knows that Etain (soprano), princess of the fairies, has left her happy land of youth and of heart's desire to travel into the alien world of mortals in search of something nameless, some joy or new experience which she vaguely and obscurely senses is possible. Dalua also knows that the mortal king Eochaidh (baritone) has abandoned war and the struggle for power, the luxury and ceremonial of court, prompted by the wish for a new experience – the "immortal hour." Eochaidh has also asked the fairies to send him a girl more beautiful than any other mortal so that he can win her love and make her his bride. Dalua decides to allow him to meet Etain, although the outcome can only be unlucky since marriage between a mortal and an immortal is impossible. He casts a spell which makes Etain forget all about her past. The two then meet and marry. After an idyllic year Etain has changed. She is anxious and troubled by dreams and confused memories of her past. During the festival to celebrate the first anniversary of their wedding, a stranger asks for a hearing. It is Midir, prince of fairies, who had loved Etain in the land of youth and of heart's desire. He has come to take her back to her people. As soon as the stranger looks at Etain she suddenly remembers everything and follows him out of the palace as if in a trance, deaf to her husband's entreaties. This is Dalua's moment. At his fatal touch the king falls dead at the foot of his throne.

The opera was first performed in London in 1920. On 13 October 1922 it opened at the Regent Theater, where it had a highly successful run of 216 performances.

Above: A scene from *Igrok* (The Gambler) by Prokofiev (see page 185).

Right: The French composer Vincent d'Indy.

INCORONAZIONE DI POPPEA, L'

(The Coronation of Poppea)

Opera in three acts and a prologue by Claudio Monteverdi (1567–1643), to a libretto by Gian Francesco Busenello. First performance: Venice, Teatro di San Giovanni e Paolo, possibly on Boxing Day 1642.

In the prologue, Virtù (Virtue, soprano), Fortuna (Fortune, soprano) and Amore (Love, soprano) argue about which of them exerts the most influence over mankind. Amore proves supreme, bending human beings to her will. Ottone (contralto), a young Roman patrician, is in despair because of the infidelity of his beloved Poppea (soprano): he has discovered that she is the mistress of Nerone (the Emperor Nero, soprano or mezzo-soprano). At the Imperial palace, Ottavia (soprano), Nerone's wife, has discovered that her husband is betraying her and laments her fate as a deserted wife. The philosopher Seneca (bass) tries in vain to console her and to persuade Nerone not to leave his wife. Poppea, seeing Seneca as an obstacle to her ambition to become Empress, sows the seed of suspicion in Nerone's mind that Seneca is influencing him, a thought which so irritates Nerone that he sentences Seneca to death. The philosopher receives with great dignity the order instructing him to take his own life. Ottone, who has by now lost Poppea's love, cannot be at peace with himself, and Ottavia exploits his mood by urging him to kill her rival (Poppea). Ottone dresses in the clothes of Drusilla (soprano), a young woman who is in love with him, and without being recognized gains entry to Poppea's apartments. But his bid fails, and Ottone is taken for Drusilla. As a result, Drusilla herself is arrested and condemned to death. Ottone intervenes and tells the Emperor the truth. Nerone sentences him to be exiled, allowing Drusilla to go with him, then disowns Ottavia and banishes her from Rome. The Emperor can now marry Poppea, who is duly acknowledged as Empress by the people and the Senate.

The two manuscript versions of *L'incoronazione di Poppea* that are in existence differ in important ways. One is kept in the Biblioteca Marciana (the library of St. Mark's) in Venice, the other in the library of San Pietro a Maiella in Naples. The Naples manuscript appears to be older and more like Monteverdi, whereas the Venetian one has been simplified and abridged by the composer Francesco Cavalli. *Poppea*, Monteverdi's last opera, conveys a painfully realistic sense of the crisis of Renaissance man, tempered

by affectionate tolerance. The characters are motivated by passion in politics and in love, feelings symbolized triumphantly by Nerone and Poppea in the opera, while the other characters are reduced almost to ciphers who are there simply to praise them. The libretto is the first to handle a historical theme and, as such, the opera is a prototype.

INDES GALANTES, LES

(The Honour of the Indies)

Opéra-ballet *in three entrées and a prologue by Jean-Philippe Rameau (1683–1764), to a libretto by Louis Fuzelier. First performance: Paris, Académie Royale de Musique (Opéra), 23 August 1735. First performance with four entrées: Paris, Académie Royale de Musique (Opéra), 10 March 1736.*

The young people of four allied nations (France, Spain, Italy and Poland) have been dragged into war by Bellone, the Goddess of War (bass) and have to leave behind Hébe (soprano) and L'Amour (soprano). Les Amours, disappointed at having been abandoned by Europe, leave for distant shores. In the first entrée, entitled *The Generous Turk*, Osman (bass), Pasha of a Turkish island in the Indian Ocean, is in love with Émilie (soprano), his Provençal slave, who has been taken away from her fiancé Valère (tenor), an officer in the navy. Valère is shipwrecked on the island and taken prisoner by the Pasha. Osman recognizes him as the man who had once saved his life and generously sets both young people free, thus giving up his claim to Émilie. Second entrée: *The Incas of Peru.* Don Carlos (tenor), a Spanish officer, is in love with Phani (soprano), a young Peruvian princess, who returns his love. The Inca Huascar (bass) is jealous and, during a feast, causes a volcano to erupt, only to be caught in the lava while Carlos flees with his beloved Phani. Third entrée: *The Flowers. Persian Festival.* On the day of the flower festival, Tacmas (tenor), a Persian prince and King of the Indies, enters the gardens of his favourite, Ali, disguised as a merchant. Tacmas is in love with Ali's slave, Zaire (soprano), while Fatime (soprano), Tacmas's slave, is in love with Ali. Fatime appears dressed as a Polish male slave, and Tacmas, taking her for an enemy, attacks her. In the end the confusion is resolved: Tacmas and Ali exchange slaves and all go off to the festival together. Fourth (additional) entrée: *The Savages.* The action takes place in America somewhere between the French and Spanish colonies. Adario (tenor), with his Indian warriors, is treating for peace with the Europeans. Two officers, the French Damon (tenor) and the Spanish Don Alvar (bass), are competing for the love of Zima (soprano), but she marries Adario. Enraged at being rejected, Don Alvar is calmed down and helped to see reason by Damon. The opera ends with the celebration of festivities in the name of Peace.

Les Indes galantes is one of Rameau's masterpieces. There is a great fluency about the way in which his music keeps pace with the different episodes in the plot as well as shaping individual characters and clearly expressing the differences and contrasts between them. The opera was initially a dubious success. Rameau had it performed again a year later, after making a number of changes and adding the fourth entrée. This second performance was a triumph.

INDY, VINCENT D'

(Paris 1851–1931)

French composer, conductor and teacher. During the Franco-Prussian war (1870) he met Henri Duparc, who referred him to César Franck, with whom he took lessons in composition (1872–80). His career as a composer (begun in 1869) was particularly influenced by the musical world of Wagner, whose disciple he became in 1876 during a journey to Germany. There are clear echoes of Wagner in d'Indy's most famous opera, *Fervaal* (1897).

INFEDELTÀ DELUSA, L'

(Unfaithfulness Frustrated)

Comic opera in two acts by Franz Joseph Haydn (1732–1809), to a libretto by Marco Coltellini. First performance: Eszterháza Castle, 26 July 1773.

The action takes place in a rural community in Tuscany. The opening quintet introduces all the characters in the opera: old Filippo (tenor), father to Sandrina (soprano), wants to marry his daughter to the wealthy Nencio (tenor); Sandrina, however, is in love with Nanni (bass), who feels the same way about her; Nanni's sister Vespina (soprano), is in love with Nencio. Nanni suspects he has a rival and is afraid of losing his beloved: he prefers to die, hoping that the man who will take Sandrina away from him will suffer a thousand torments. Sandrina does not know how to rebel against her father's will. It falls to Vespina to handle the intricate situation with great skill, realizing that if Nanni and Sandrina are able to marry, Nencio's heart will be free again and he will be sure to yield to her desires. Astute young woman that she is, Vespina manages to achieve her objectives with a cavalcade of pretense and disguise, appearing first as a mother deserted by her husband, then as a wealthy Marquis and finally as a notary. The opera ends happily with the weddings taking place exactly as she had intended.

Haydn's music, partly on the strength of the brilliant libretto by the distinguished Coltellini, is intended to be something of a parody. In this way, Haydn plays his part in opening up what was to prove a very rich vein for composers of comic operas (*opera buffa*) in years to come.

Above: A scene from *L'incoronazione di Poppea* by Monteverdi.

INGANNO FELICE, L'

(The Happy Deception)

Opera in one act by Gioachino Rossini (1792–1868), to a libretto by Giuseppe Maria Foppa. First performance: Venice, Teatro Giustiniani di San Moisè, 8 January 1812.

The setting is a valley, near the entrance to a mine and the house of Tarabotto (bass), the miners' leader. Ten years previously, Tarabotto had taken into his household, and passed off as his niece, a poor young woman called Nisa (soprano). Nisa is actually Isabella, wife of the Duke (owner of the mine). Isabella, as a consequence of an act of deception by Ormondo (tenor) and Batone (bass), is believed to be dead. The Duke (tenor) remarried, but his second wife has since died. Enter the Duke, Ormondo and Batone. Batone thinks Nisa may be the former Duchess. Tarabotto causes the Duke and young Nisa to come face to face, a meeting which leaves them feeling equally uneasy. Tarabotto then overhears Ormondo and Batone plotting to abduct Nisa, whose resemblance to the Duchess, until then presumed dead, is too striking to be a coincidence. Batone almost repents but does not want to reveal too much under Tarabotto's skilful interrogation. Eventually the miners' leader tells the Duke that someone is plotting to harm his niece. Ormondo wants to take his own life in order to atone for his misdeeds. But Isabella, now finally recognized and happily married again, stays his hand, and the opera ends amid general rejoicing.

Although described as a farce, *L'inganno felice* is actually an *opera semiseria* which clearly demonstrates Rossini's skill in portraying characters and alternating between comic and dramatic moments. The opera was a tremendous success and, until the appearance of *Tancredi*, was the one that numbered the most performances.

INSPIRATION

See *Ispirazione, L'*

INTERMEZZO

"Bourgeois comedy" with symphonic interludes in two acts by Richard Strauss (1864–1949) to the composer's own libretto. First performance: Dresden, Staatsoper, 4 November 1924.

The conductor Robert Storch (baritone) is leaving for Vienna. Christine (soprano) bewails her lot as the wife of a celebrity. Left behind on her own, she does not discourage the attentions of the young Baron Lummer (tenor) and goes out dancing with him. But it is not long before she realizes that all the Baron wants is her money. A letter arrives addressed to Storch. Christine opens it and is horrified to see that it has been written in rather intimate terms by someone called Mieze Meier. In a fury, Christine sends a telegram to her husband, threatening him with divorce. The telegram is delivered to Storch, who is in the company of his friends, among them the conductor Stroh (tenor), for whom the letter opened by Christine had actually been intended. Storch returns home, preceded by Stroh, who has agreed to be the one to explain the misunderstanding to Christine. But she, although sure that Robert is innocent, receives him coldly, because she is convinced that sooner or later something like that will really happen between them. Robert loses his head, whereupon Christine realizes how terrible life would be without him. The two reconcile, and Christine is finally convinced that theirs is a truly happy marriage.

Intermezzo was directly inspired by an episode in the marriage of Richard Strauss and his wife Pauline. Strauss has calculated the psychological and instrumental richness of this opera perfectly: the "conversation in music" technique, achieved by an extraordinarily accomplished use of *parlando*, the tragi-comic developments of the action, and the interludes, all help to deepen the psychology of the characters and the feelings which prompt them to act as they do.

INTOLLERANZA 1960

(Intolerance 1960)

Scenic action in two acts by Luigi Nono (1924–1990). The subject, based by the composer on an idea by Angelo Maria Ripellino, draws on texts by Brecht, Paul Eluard, Mayakovsky, Sartre, Fucik and Ripellino himself. First performance: Venice, Festival Internazionale di Musica Contemporanea, 1961.

Above: A sketch for Gluck's *Iphigénie en Aulide*, drawn by Boquet.

Right: A scene from *Iphigénie en Aulide*.

An emigrant miner runs away because he is homesick, leaving behind the woman he loves. She does not understand his feelings and turns against him. Alone and known to no one, he finds himself by chance caught up in a political demonstration, is arrested, tortured, brainwashed, and finally sent to a labour camp. After all this institutionalized brutality and so much futile suffering, the miner finds that the companionship of his fellow-prisoners has helped him to rediscover humanity, comradeship and love, all feelings which the "system" had sought to eradicate from people's hearts. Finally, the earth is invaded by the waters of a purifying flood which flows over everything and everyone. The work ends with the Brechtian chorus "An die Nachgeborenen" (To the Newly Born), spreading a sense of faith in something new which will revive the relationship between people and give a fresh meaning to life.

Intolleranza 1960, dedicated to Arnold Schoenberg, was revised several times by the composer. When it first appeared, its markedly political content succeeded in unleashing a good deal of controversy. The complex musical language in this score requires an 80-strong orchestra, large mixed chorus, 50 solo singers, various narrators, and magnetic tape. Nono's intention was to give voice, through this work, to a universal dramatic statement which would ideally reflect the spirit of Expressionist theater in the 1920s as well as that of contemporary American theater. For Nono, the opera was an expression of the awakening of the conscience of a man who rebels and then seeks a reason and a human basis for living.

IPHIGÉNIE EN AULIDE

(Iphigenia in Aulis)

Tragic opera in three acts by Christoph Willibald Gluck (1714–1787), to a libretto by F. Leblanc du Roullet after Racine. First performance: Paris, Académie Royale de Musique (Opéra), 19 April 1774.

The action takes place in the Greek camp in Aulis. Calchas (bass) reveals to King Agamemnon (bass) that the irate goddess Artemis wants the King's daughter Iphigénie (soprano) to be sacrificed before the Greeks are able to set sail for Troy. In his anguish, Agamemnon seeks to avoid a sacrifice by sending Arcas (bass) to Mycenae to prevent Iphigénie and her mother Clytemnestre from coming to the camp, instructing him to spread the false rumour that Achille has been unfaithful to his bride-to-be Iphigénie. But Iphigénie and Clytemnestre (mezzo-soprano) have already arrived in Aulis. Achille defends himself against the charges and convinces Iphigénie of his faithfulness. Then Achille learns that Agamemnon will have to sacrifice his daughter. The hero rises up against so cruel a father and, after a dramatic encounter with Agamemnon, compels him to order that his wife and daughter be taken back to Mycenae. Meanwhile, the soldiers, who are afraid of the anger of the gods, obstruct Iphigénie's departure. She has actually stepped forward to be sacrificed when Achille springs on to the altar, determined to prevent such a terrible act from taking place, and disarms Calchas. Clytemnestre also pleads with Jupiter to spare the victim he has asked for. At this point Artemis (soprano) intervenes: she has been placated by Iphigénie's heroism, her weeping mother and the people's sorrow, and now takes Iphigénie into her care, leaving Agamemnon able to set out for Troy.

Iphigénie en Aulide is an opera essentially in the Gluck mould and was for its composer a key stage in his reaffirmation of a "reforming" approach to which he had already set his seal in 1762 with *Orfeo ed Euridice*. This opera is one of those rare cases in which drama and music constitute a single entity. Even though the dramatic content of the libretto is somewhat limited, the power, grandeur and delicacy of the music are an example of Gluck's talents and innovations.

IPHIGÉNIE EN TAURIDE

(Iphigenia in Tauris)

Tragic opera in four acts and five scenes by Christoph Willibald Gluck (1714–1787), to a libretto by Nicolas-François Guillard from the tragedy by Euripides. First performance: Paris, Académie Royale de Musique (Opéra), 18 May 1779.

Iphigénie (soprano), having become a priestess of Artemis in Tauris, is ordered by King Thoas (bass) to sacrifice to the goddess all foreigners who set foot in that country. Two Greeks, Oreste (baritone) and Pylade (tenor), survivors of a shipwreck, have been taken prisoner. Thoas orders them to be sacrificed. Oreste laments his sad fate: the Furies are pursuing him, and his mother Clytemnestre, killed by him in order to avenge his father, whom she had murdered, appears before him. Iphigénie meets Oreste, questions him, learns of the sad deaths of his parents, and decides to save this stranger who vaguely reminds her of her brother. So she outlines a plan of escape, but Oreste refuses to be saved and wants Pylade to be the one who is spared. Pylade vows that he will save his friend or die with him. Then, at the sacrificial altar, Iphigénie and Oreste recognize each other as brother and sister. Meanwhile, Thoas has discovered that one of the prisoners, Pylade, has escaped. His anger mounts when he realizes that the other one, Oreste, is Iphigénie's brother and he orders that Iphigénie too be put to death. At that moment, however, Pylade bursts in at the head of a force of Greek warriors, and Thoas is killed in the ensuing conflict. The voice of Artemis (mezzo-soprano) encourages the Scythians to abandon their barbaric rituals and tells Oreste that he has now atoned for his mother's murder and can go back to Mycenae with his sister.

Iphigénie en Tauride was Gluck's last opera but one. It enjoyed a robust success, confirming the triumph of operatic reform and

A scene from *Iphigénie en Tauride*, in a production at La Scala.

Gluck himself as a classical composer in the fullest sense of the term, in that he could fuse idea and form into a single unity. In this opera, in which the action has been humanized to such an extent that it dominates what is left of the mythological element, the concept of form that Gluck had been aiming at for many years is fully implemented.

IRIS

Opera in three acts by Pietro Mascagni (1863–1945), to a libretto by Luigi Illica. First performance: Rome, Teatro Costanzi, 22 November 1898.

The action takes place in a village in Japan. Osaka (tenor), a wealthy but morally suspect young man, is in love with Iris (soprano), an ingenuous young girl. Osaka hires Kyoto (baritone), the owner of a tea-house, to kidnap her. With this in mind, the two men stage a play about the troubled love-life of Dhia and Ior, daughter of the Sun. Iris is standing in the crowd watching the play when she is seized and dragged away. Kyoto leaves and then sends a letter saying that Iris has gone to live in the red-light district of her own accord. Iris's blind father (bass) asks to be taken to where his daughter is, so that he can curse her. In Osaka's house, Iris resists his enticements and amorous advances. He becomes bored with her and passes her on to Kyoto. Kyoto makes her display herself to the crowd, where her blind father happens to be standing. He is led to her and curses her, throwing mud in her face. In despair, Iris wants to die and throws herself into a ravine. Her body is found at the bottom by a number of rag-merchants who attempt to steal her clothes, but they flee when they realize that the young woman is still alive. The light of the rising sun reveals Iris dying and seems to comfort her in her final moments of anguished self-questioning about her sad fate. With flowers opening all around her, Iris dies in a blaze of light.

Iris is clearly an opera in the *art nouveau* manner, and although the critics voiced their reservations, it was a sensational success with the public. The opera is a perfect example of Mascagni's melodic style which blends in beautifully with the symbolism of the libretto. The overall effect reveals a quest for new modes of expression and an attempt to achieve consistency.

ISABEAU

Dramatic legend in three parts by Pietro Mascagni (1863–1945), to a libretto by Luigi Illica. First performance: Buenos Aires, Teatro Coliseo, 2 June 1911.

The action takes place in an imaginary city at a legendary time. It is announced that a contest will be held at the castle of King Raimondo (bass): the knight who can inspire feelings of love in Princess Isabeau (soprano) will be given her hand in marriage. At that moment Giglietta (mezzo-soprano) and her nephew Folco (tenor) arrive at the castle bearing gifts for the Princess. Isabeau appears to appreciate their offerings and engages Folco as her falconer. Shortly after this, the contest takes place: Isabeau shows no feeling towards the contenders, with the exception of a mysterious knight for whom she feels sympathy. The knight is Ethel, the King's nephew, who had been banished. The people hail him as the Princess's husband-to-be, but Isabeau refuses their choice, and thus goes against her agreement with her father. The King's minister Cornelius (bass) advises him to punish the Princess, and she is condemned to ride naked through the streets of the city to atone for her proud insistence on remaining chaste. But the

Above: Title page of the score to Mascagni's *Iris*.

Right: Poster by G. Palanti for *Isabeau* by Mascagni.

people ask the King to proclaim that anyone who attempts to watch the Princess go by will be blinded. Covered only by her wonderfully long hair, Isabeau emerges from the palace. Folco, unaware of the proclamation, throws bunches of flowers down from a garden and into her path. He is attacked by the crowd and arrested. The next day, Isabeau, troubled with guilt at being the involuntary cause of the sentence passed on Folco, asks if she may speak to the prisoner. The young man seems calm and happy to go to the scaffold, because he will carry with him the vision of the Princess. To save Folco, with whom she has fallen in love, the Princess offers herself to him as his bride. Cornelius has overheard their conversation, opens the prison door, and then throws Folco to the hostile crowd. Isabeau hurries to tell the King what has happened; when she returns, there is no sign of her beloved, and so she hastens to face death with him.

The opera was composed almost entirely between June and September 1910 in close collaboration with the librettist. It was initially intended to be premiered in New York but, after various obstacles, ended up being staged in South America. It was also performed simultaneously at La Fenice in Venice and La Scala, Milan. The opera is an attempt by Mascagni to come up with a new kind of music drama using a superficial treatment in the style of Gabriele D'Annunzio which was very much in vogue at the time. It was not well received, however, and fell far short of the composer's expectations.

ISOLA DISABITATA, L'

(The Desert Island)

Opera in one act by Franz Joseph Haydn (1732–1809), to a libretto by Pietro Metastasio. First performance: Eszterháza Castle, 6 December 1779.

Following a shipwreck, two sisters, Silvia (soprano) and Costanza (mezzo-soprano), have lived for ten years on an uninhabited island. The younger one, Silvia, who knows nothing of the world, is quite happy living in the midst of nature on the island, whereas Costanza misses her life back home and especially the love of her fiancé Gernando. A boat lands on one of the island's beaches. On it are Gernando (tenor) and his friend Enrico (baritone). Gernando recognizes the island as the place where he had left the two sisters to go for help, only to be captured by pirates. Stepping ashore, Gernando finds a message of despair from Costanza scratched on a rock and is so disturbed by it that he wants to die. Enrico takes control and orders the sailors to help poor Gernando back to the boat. Enrico remains on the island and comes upon Silvia. Never having seen a man before, she takes fright and runs away. Not long after this, Gernando finally meets his Costanza, but she is unable to cope with the emotion of seeing him again and after accusing him of betraying and abandoning her, she collapses in a dead faint. Gernando goes back to the boat for help, but on his way he runs into the sailors, who are under strict instructions from Enrico to bring him back on board by force. Meanwhile, Enrico has come upon Costanza, and as soon as she has recovered, he describes to her everything that had happened to Gernando ten years before. Silvia arrives out of breath. She tells the others that she has seen Gernando being dragged away by some men. Enrico calms the two women. In the end all four of the young people are reunited and, overjoyed by their new-found happiness, set sail for home.

In this work Haydn adopts the genre of "reformed" *opera seria* originating from Gluck. The style concentrates particularly on the psychological development of the action, and as such forges a direct link with the sobriety at the heart of Gluck's operas.

ISPIRAZIONE, L'

(Inspiration)

Opera in three acts by Sylvano Bussotti (b. 1931) from an outline by Ernst Bloch, to the composer's own text. First performance: Florence, Teatro Comunale, 26 May 1988.

In the year 2031 a spaceship takes off amid violent sounds which fill the stage. Harno Lupo (bass), Time Lord, and Futura (singer and actress), Mistress of Space, are on a voyage heading towards the Realm of Music Theater. The spaceship reaches the year 2750. Here a chorus of computers and a robot orchestra conducted by a chorus-master (*buffo* bass) are rehearsing a new opera. In a break from rehearsals, a man is heard snoring: he is Maestro Wolfango (baritone), an old violinist who cannot bear the music in the new opera and is fiercely critical of it. His attitude gets Wolfango dismissed from the orchestra. His wife Argià (dramatic soprano) is furious, and her daughter Serena (lyric soprano) and Futura try to calm her. Serena is a great believer in her father's skill as a composer and secretly writes out the parts of an opera composed by him. Wolfango suddenly reappears, surprises his daughter and, jumping to the conclusion that she is stealing some money, treats her harshly. He then sits down to get on with his composing. The scene changes. In a future age, the world is portrayed as having been reduced to an arid wilderness. Wolfango is living in a ghetto. Harno Lupo tells him that his daughter has become a famous opera singer. The old violinist is much displeased by this news and declares his aversion to consumer music. A number of people invite Wolfango to go to the theater, but he refuses, only to be dragged there by force. When he comes into the auditorium, the sound he hears is of his own music, his opera *Syrena*, and this brings the old composer and his daughter success.

The plot of *L'ispirazione* provided Bussotti with the starting-point for yet another stage

Above: A scene from *L'ispirazione* by Sylvano Bussotti.

work displaying his many-sided career as librettist and designer of sets and costumes. Bussotti does not hesitate to quote his own music in the score, as well as melodies from his childhood and the music of Dallapiccola.

ITALIANA IN ALGERI, L'

(The Italian Girl in Algiers)
Dramma giocoso *in two acts by Gioachino Rossini (1792–1868), to a libretto by Angelo Anelli. First performance: Venice, Teatro Gallo a San Benedetto, 22 May 1813.*

Mustafà, the Bey of Algiers (bass), no longer loves his wife Elvira (soprano) and plans to step aside so she can be married to Lindoro (tenor), a young Italian slave. The Bey's pirates have boarded an Italian vessel and captured both crew and passengers, among them Isabella (mezzo-soprano). She had set out from Italy with an old admirer, Taddeo (*buffo* bass), in search of her fiancé, whom the pirates had previously abducted. Isabella bewitches the Bey and undermines his plans: he remains with his wife, while Lindoro, whom Isabella has recognized as her fiancé, becomes her personal slave. Later, Lindoro and Isabella devise a plan of escape. Enter Mustafà, longing to seduce Isabella, but the skilful young woman manages to avoid being alone with him. Mustafà is furious, but Lindoro calms him and reassures him that Isabella loves him so much that she has nicknamed him her "*pappataci*" (literally, one who eats greedily and keeps silent). The Italian slaves, dressed as *pappataci*, give Mustafà clothes like theirs to wear. A boat appears, which had been made ready to help the two young people to escape. Taddeo discovers that Isabella is going to run off with Lindoro and he tells Mustafà of their plan. But Mustafà, who has taken the oath of the *pappataci* (eat, drink, sleep, and keep quiet), does not respond. Only when the boat has left does the Bey realize that he has been duped. Railing against the cunning of Italian women, he goes back to his wife, who forgives him for having been so gullible.

L'italiana in Algeri is one of Rossini's masterpieces, which he wrote in only 20 days. At the premiere, its sensational success left the composer amazed. The vitality of the work is unprecedented, Rossini creating his individual characters by using the music to impose particular kinds of rhythm on the action. They are caricatures but also have a psychological depth and refinement which make them into a new kind of figure in comic opera.

A scene from *L'italiana in Algeri* by Rossini, which was first performed in Venice in 1813.

IVAN IV

Opera in five acts by Georges Bizet (1838–1875), to a libretto by François-Hippolyte Leroy and Henri Trianon. First performance: Bordeaux, Grand Théâtre, 12 October 1951.

The action takes place in the sixteenth century. Marie (soprano), daughter of Temrouk (bass), the King of the Caucasus, meets two strangers who have lost their way and shows them the right road. These travellers are in fact Tsar Ivan IV (baritone) and his young Bulgarian servant (mezzo-soprano). Then a group of Russian soldiers arrives and threatens a massacre if Temrouk does not hand over his daughter to them. In order to avoid the deaths of innocent people, Marie surrenders to them voluntarily. The scene changes to the Kremlin, during the celebrations of Tsar Ivan's victory over the Tatars. The Tsar, eager to find himself a wife, has a group of women prisoners brought to him. Among them is Marie. The two recognize each other, but she flatly rejects his proposal of marriage and seeks the protection of Princess Olga (mezzo-soprano), the Tsar's sister. In the end, however, Marie does agree to become Ivan's wife, not least because she has realized that she loves him. In the meantime, the boyar Yorloff (baritone), who had wanted one of his daughters to marry the Tsar, forms an alliance with Temrouk and his son Igor (tenor) with a view to assassinating him. But when Igor discovers that Ivan's bride is none other than his own sister, and that she is ready to sacrifice her own life for that of her royal husband, he withdraws from the conspiracy. Yorloff then stakes everything on accusing Marie and Igor of plotting to harm the Tsar, an idea given credence by the fact that Temrouk's troops are at that moment threatening to attack the Kremlin. The Tsar condemns the two traitors to death, but then, unable to cope with the sorrow this brings him, appears to lose his reason. Yorloff exploits this by proclaiming himself Regent. But Temrouk has exposed Yorloff's treacherous intention to have his children put to death; he succeeds in shaking the Tsar out of the apathy into which he had fallen, as a result of which Ivan regains command of the situation, sentences Yorloff to death, and is restored to the throne with his beloved Marie.

The libretto of *Ivan IV* had been written for Gounod, but he set it aside and offered it to Bizet, who revised the score and almost completed it, leaving only the fifth act unfinished. The opera was lost, however, to be rediscovered only in the 1920s. It was then revised, and the premiere was given posthumously. One of the more recent revivals of *Ivan IV* took place at the Montpellier Festival in 1991.

OPERA IN RUSSIA

Opera made its debut in Russia between 1729 and 1731, when the first touring companies came to St. Petersburg from Italy, France and Germany. In 1731 Tommaso Ristori staged an *opera buffa* by his son Giovanni Alberto Ristori, *Calandro*. In 1735 the Neapolitan composer Francesco Araja settled in St. Petersburg and an *opera seria* of his, *La forza dell' amore e dell' odio* (The Power of Love and Hate), was performed there the following year. It was Araja too who wrote the first opera to be composed in Russian, *Tsefal i Prokris* (Cephalus and Procris, 1755) to a libretto by Sumarakov. After Araja, Italian composers were very much in evidence in Russia, especially during the reign of the Empress Elizabeth Petrovna, who was a fervent admirer of Italian culture: they included Manfredini, Galuppi, Traetta, Paisiello, Cimarosa and Martìn y Soler, to name only the most famous. With the accession of Catherine II, French *opéra-comique* came back into fashion alongside Italian opera. A great deal of interest was aroused by the staging of a version in Russian of Jean-Jacques Rousseau's *Le devin du village* (1777), which inspired a number of other operas in this genre, among them *Mel' nik-koldun* (The Miller-Magician) by the Russian composer Evstigney Fomin (1786). The second half of the eighteenth century witnessed the success of several important Russian composers, notably Matinsky, Pashkevich (one of the early pioneers of Russian opera), Bortnyansky and Fomin, who was almost certainly the most representative composer of his generation (and wrote a celebrated melodrama, *Orfey i Evridika*, dating from 1792). The development of a Russian musical identity was given fresh stimulus in 1824 with the first performance in Russia of Weber's opera *Der Freischütz*, which provided Russian composers with the incentive to turn to folk traditions in search of a national identity. Verstovsky played a particularly significant role here: his opera *Askol' dova mogila* (Askold's Grave, 1835) used material inspired by Russian folk legends. This opera, which has since been completely forgotten, paved the way for the creative output of Glinka, who is regarded as the father of Russian music. One year after the premiere of Verstovsky's opera came Glinka's *Ivan Susanin* (1836), in which the historical setting of the plot and scenes involving the people provided key precedents for subsequent generations of opera composers, as did the ingredients taken from fable in *Ruslan and Lyudmila* (1842), Gluck's other most influential work. All of these elements were brought to perfection in the operas of Dargomyzhsky and even more so by Mussorgsky (*Boris Godunov*, *Khovanshchina*), Rimsky-Korsakov (*Sadko*, *The Golden Cockerel*, *Tsar Saltan*, etc.), Borodin (*Prince Igor*), Cui (*William Ratcliff*, *Angelo*, *The Captain's Daughter*, etc.) and Tchaikovsky (*Eugene Onegin*, *The Maid of Orleans*, *The Queen of Spades*, etc.). However, there are clear signs in the works of Cui and Tchaikovsky of links with Western music, something which would be found again later on in composers like Rachmaninov, Taneyev and Stravinsky. The more recent leading names in Russian opera, Prokofiev and Shostakovich, espoused the ideas of "Soviet realism" as well as using plots drawn from history and legend. Two such examples are Prokofiev's *The Story of a Real Man* and Shostakovich's *Lady Macbeth of Mtsensk* (1934 and 1959).

Above: The cover of the libretto to *A Life for the Tsar* by Glinka.

Right: The Russian composer Rimsky-Korsakov.

J

JACOB LENZ

Chamber opera in one act by Wolfgang Rihm (b. 1952), to a libretto by Michael Fröhling, from the story Lenz *by Georg Büchner. First performance: Hamburg, Staatsoper, 8 March 1979.*

The opera tells of an episode in the life of the German poet Jakob Lenz (baritone). In 1778, when he was on the verge of madness, Lenz stayed for a while in Waldach at the house of the pastor Fiedrich Oberlin (bass), where he met Christoph Kaufmann (tenor), a passionate advocate of philanthropic ideas. The action centers on these individuals' vain attempts to establish common ground between them when they have no point of contact. The alienation and poetic negativity of Lenz who, in the name of a realistic credo, rejects any kind of illusion, clash with Oberlin's sermonizing rhetoric and the pragmatic enthusiasm of Kaufmann, with his belief in "harmony and reality." The consequences of this prove fatal. Undermined also by his obsession with women, represented here by Fiederike (soprano), by the end of the opera Lenz no longer has control over his madness and is violently overtaken by it. He is placed in a straitjacket and left completely alone mouthing meaningless words.

"Chamber opera" is a perfect description of *Jakob Lenz*: there are just three main characters, joined by a chorus made up of only six voices. The musical language in which the voices sing harks back to the classical forms of polyphony, the motet, the madrigal and the chorale. Rihm uses this vocal ensemble to "double" for the character of Jakob Lenz himself. He also employs a reduced orchestra of only 11 instruments, which the composer has chosen for their ability to create the somber sound-world he wants. The structure of the opera is very simple: a sequence of 12 scenes, which links back to the theater of Expressionism, like a metaphor of the Via Crucis, which here represents Jakob Lenz's own Stations of the Cross on his way to madness.

JACOBS, RENÉ

(Ghent 1946)

Belgian counter-tenor and conductor. He studied singing, specializing in the Early Music repertoire, at the same time as studying philology at the University of Ghent. He made a name for himself as a counter-tenor in performances of baroque opera and oratorio under renowned baroque specialists like Gustav Leonhardt, Nikolaus Harnoncourt and Alan Curtis. From 1977 he conducted the Concerto Vocale, with whom he was responsible for some important revivals of operas by Antonio Cesti (*L'Orontea*) and Francesco Cavalli (*Xerse*). He has also conducted performances of operas by Monteverdi (*L'incoronazione di Poppea*, *Il ritorno di Ulisse in patria*), Handel (*Flavio*) and Gluck (*Le cinesi*).

JAKOBIN

Opera in three acts by Antonín Dvořák (1841–1904), to a libretto by Marie Červinková-Riegrová. First performance: Prague, Czech National Theater, 12 February 1889.

The story centers on the life of Bohus of Harasov (baritone), a Jacobin who has returned from political exile and tries to

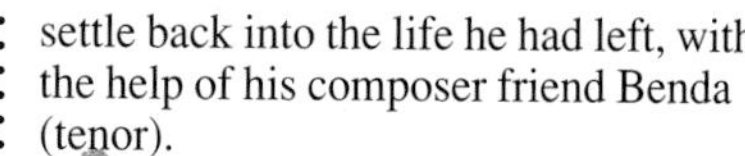

settle back into the life he had left, with the help of his composer friend Benda (tenor).

Jakobin, a work in which Dvořák was influenced by *grand-opéra*, was very successful in Czechoslovakia, where it has been frequently performed to this day.

JANÁČEK, LÉOŠ

(Hukvaldy, Northern Moravia 1854–Ostrava 1928)

Czech composer. The son of a schoolmaster and organist, he received his earliest musical education at the school of the Augustinian "Queen's" Monastery in old Brno (from 1865) and then at the Prague Organ School (1874–75). He already had experience as a choral and orchestral conductor and had begun composing when he joined the Leipzig Conservatory in 1879, moving on from there to the Vienna Conservatory in 1880. On his return to Czechoslovakia, he became director of the Brno Organ School (1881–1919), which changed to a State Conservatory in 1919. Janáček's mastery of ethnological studies earned him the position of president of the Committee for Folk Song in Moravia and Silesia (1905) and of the State Institute for Folk Song in Brno (1919). In 1887 Janáček began writing opera: his first was *Šárka*, and his remarkable subsequent output included *Jenůfa* (1894–1903), in which there are still elements of folk realism, *Kát'a Kabanová* (1919–21), *Prihody Lišky Bystroušky* (The Cunning Little Vixen, 1921–23), *Vec Makropulos* (The Makropoulos Case, 1923–25), and *Z mrtvého domu* (From the House of the Dead, 1927–28).

Right: The Czech composer Léoš Janáček.

Above: The German soprano Gundula Janowitz.

JANOWITZ, GUNDULA

(Berlin 1937)

German soprano. She joined the company of the Vienna Staatsoper, where she made her debut as Marzelline in Beethoven's *Fidelio* (1960). In the same year she appeared for the first time in Bayreuth (as a Flower Maiden in *Parsifal*) and this launched her on a brilliant career with engagements at the Salzburg Festival (from 1963), Glyndebourne (1964) and many other venues. Janowitz has been an elegant performer of the *Lieder* and general concert repertoire (oratorios, etc.). Her mobility of timbre and expressive singing has enabled her to give particularly distinguished performances of the Mozart repertoire as well as to win acclaim for her roles in operas by Weber, Wagner and Richard Strauss. During the 1980s her appearances were restricted to *Lieder* recitals. In 1988 she was appointed *Operdirektorin* in Graz.

JANOWSKI, MAREK

(Warsaw 1939)

German conductor of Polish origin. He studied music at the Hochschule in Cologne and in Siena, where he completed his training. He began his conducting career as a coach in Aix-la-Chapelle, Cologne and as Kapellmeister at Düsseldorf. In 1969 he was appointed first Kapellmeister at the Cologne Opera (until 1974) and then musical director in Freiburg (1973–75) and in Dortmund (1975–80). He worked with the Dresden Staatskapelle (with whom, from 1980 to 1983, he recorded Wagner's *Ring* cycle), the Royal Liverpool Philharmonic Orchestra (1983–87) and the Nouvel Orchestre Philharmonique de Radio France, who engaged him as their musical director in 1988. In the field of opera, Janowski's name has been mainly associated with the German repertoire.

JEANNE D'ARC AU BÛCHER

(Joan of Arc at the Stake)

Dramatic oratorio consisting of a prologue and eleven scenes by Arthur Honegger (1892–1955), to a libretto by Paul Claudel. First performance: Basle, Basel Kammeroper, 12 May 1938.

The action takes place in France at the time of the Hundred Years War. A chorus bewails the sad state of France now that it has fallen into enemy hands, and a voice (bass) announces the advent of a young woman who will set the country free. Jeanne d'Arc (speaking role) appears on stage, the stake burning beneath her feet. Frère Dominique (speaking role), who has come down from Heaven, shows Jeanne the book in which the charges against her have been written, and comforts her. Jeanne relives her trial and her sentence that she be burned for heresy and witchcraft. Dominique tells her how the rulers of France, Burgundy and England, attended by their wives Foolishness, Arrogance and Avarice, played a game of cards with Death. They then divided the winnings between them and handed Jeanne over to the Duke of Bedford. Jeanne hears once again the voices of St. Marguérite (soprano) and St. Catherine (contralto), while the people cheer the King on his way to Rheims to be crowned. Jeanne recalls the time when "voices" urged her to save France and the crown. She is afraid of the stake, but the Virgin (soprano) reassures her: she will endure the torments of the flames with joy, because she herself is a flame of France and will finally ascend into Heaven, her innocence acknowledged by the crowd, her chains broken in pieces.

Claudel's poetic text conveys a poetic vision of the medieval world by concentrating on elements of mystery and magic which were typical of the age in which Joan of Arc (Jeanne) lived. He gives ample space to allegory, and one of the magical elements he creates is to make Joan appear at the stake from the beginning and, while there, relive the events of her life. Honegger skilfully translates into music the mystical, lyrical and dramatic aspects of the text. The work stands apart from traditional forms of opera: some of it is sung and some, including the leading role, only spoken.

JENŮFA

(Original title: *Jeji pastorkyna*, Her Stepdaughter)

Opera in three acts by Léoš Janáček (1854–1928), to a libretto by Gabriela Preissová. First performance: Brno, Czech Provisional Theater, 21 January 1904.

The action takes place in Bohemia at the end of the nineteenth century. At the house of old Buryja (contralto), her granddaughter Jenufa (soprano) is anxiously waiting for Števa (tenor), whom she loves and whose child she is expecting, to return from the military recruitment office. Enter Laca (tenor), Števa's brother. Laca, who is secretly in love with Jenufa, accuses Buryja of having made Števa her favourite and turned a blind eye to his dissolute life. Then Števa comes in drunk. He behaves casually towards Jenufa, and she reproachfully reminds him of his obligations, but Števa does not want to commit himself and simply praises Jenufa for her beauty. Left alone with Jenufa,

A scene from *Jenůfa* by Janáček, which was first performed at Brno in 1904.

Laca tells her of his love. But when she rejects him, he tries to embrace her and wounds her in the face with a knife. Time passes and Jenufa, having now had her baby, lives a life confined to the house. Števa has abandoned her and become engaged to Karolka (mezzo-soprano), the burgomaster's daughter. Kostelnička (soprano), Jenufa's stepmother, decides to kill the child by throwing it into the river, and then persuades Laca, who still loves Jenufa, to marry her. Believing that her child died while she lay delirious with fever, Jenufa agrees to marry Laca. On the day of the wedding, halfway through the ceremony, a young shepherd announces that the river has thawed and the body of a baby has been found. Jenufa recognizes the corpse as that of her child, and everyone accuses her of having killed it, whereupon Kostelnička admits her own guilt and is arrested. Alone with Laca, Jenufa tells him to leave her, but he refuses, and Jenufa is so moved by his feelings that she feels she has experienced true love for the first time.

Jenůfa represents a turning-point in Janáček's career as a composer: here he is finally able to devise a language of his own, which dominates both the melodic and the vocal line with unmistakeable originality.

JÉRUSALEM

Opera in four acts by Giuseppe Verdi (1813–1901), to a libretto by Alphonse Royer and Gustave Vaez. First performance: Paris, Opéra, 26 November 1847.

Before setting out for the Crusades, the Count of Toulouse (bass) overlooks long-standing family feuds and consents to the marriage of his daughter Hélène (soprano) to Gaston (tenor), Count of Béarn. Roger (baritone), the Count's brother, is against the marriage and hires an assassin to kill Gaston, but fate rules that the victim of the assassin's knife is not Gaston but his brother, the Count of Toulouse. Roger promptly summons up old hatreds between the two families and lays blame for the murder on Gaston, who is duly sent into exile. Time passes, and the scene changes to Palestine. Full of remorse, Roger lives in solitude and poverty to atone for his guilt. Hélène, who has come to Palestine looking for Gaston, is the prisoner of the Emir of Ramla and discovers Gaston in the same prison. The armies of the Crusaders, led by the Count of Toulouse, who in fact has miraculously survived the attempted assassination, set Hélène free but imprisoned Gaston. He pleads his innocence but is publicly degraded and condemned to death. As Gaston prepares to be led to the scaffold, he is set free by Roger (whose true identity is known to no one there) and given a sword with which he can go and fight. The Crusaders are victorious, and Gaston, who has been the first to breach the walls of Jerusalem, gives himself up to the Count of Toulouse, to whom he declares that he is ready for his sentence to be carried out. Again Roger intervenes: now dying, he reveals his identity and clears Gaston of the charges unjustly laid against him. The Count is moved to pardon his dying brother and reunite Hélène with Gaston.

In August 1847 Verdi was contracted by the Paris Opéra to put on a new version of his opera *I Lombardi alla prima Crociata*, which had never been staged in France. Two of Eugène Scribe's collaborators, Royer and Vaez, had the task of preparing the libretto in French. *Jérusalem* proved to be a more consistent and musically substantial opera than *I Lombardi*.

JERUSALEM, SIEGFRIED

(Oberhausen 1940)

Stage name of Siegfried Salem, German tenor. He was first bassoon in the Hofer Symphoniker and then in the Schwäbische Symphoniker in Reutlingen (from 1961) and the Stuttgart Süddeutschen Rudfunks orchestra. He made his debut at the opera house in Stuttgart in 1975. From 1976 he appeared in Darmstadt (*Madama Butterfly*) and Hamburg, among other venues, where he tackled his first Wagner roles. He joined the company of the Deutsche Oper Berlin in 1978, having already made his first appearance at Bayreuth the previous year as Walter in *Die Meistersinger von Nürnberg*. Jerusalem became acknowledged as a heroic Wagner tenor (he sang Parsifal from 1979) and also won an international reputation for *Fidelio*, *Die Zauberflöte* (The Magic Flute) and *Martha*.

JESSONDA

Opera in three acts by Ludwig Spohr (1784–1859), to a libretto by Edouard Heinrich Gehe, after the drama La veuve de Malabar *by Antoine Lemierre. First performance: Kassel, 28 July 1823.*

The action takes place in the Indian city of Goa. The old Rajah, whom Jessonda (soprano) had married against her will, has just died, and, in accordance with the law of the land, she is to be burned alive

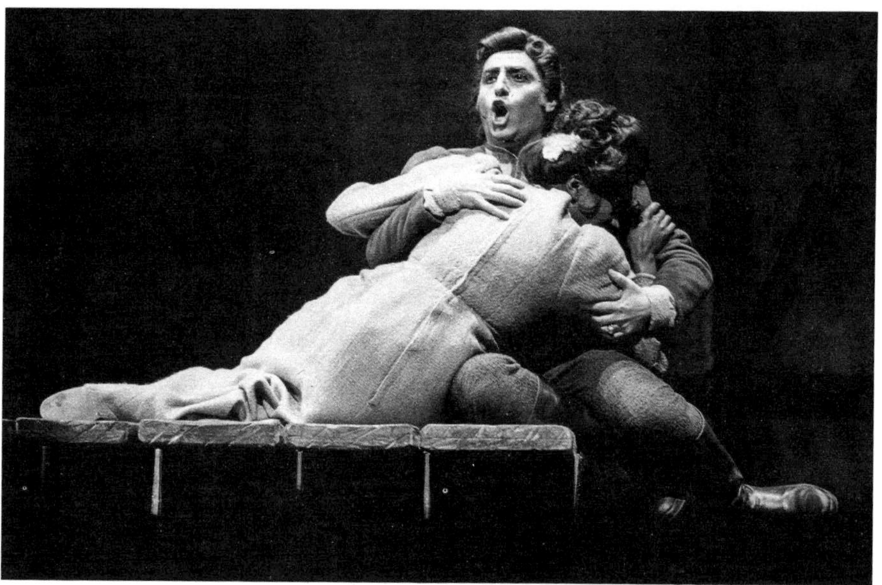

Above: A scene from *Jenůfa* by Janáček.

Right: The German composer Ludwig Spohr.

on the funeral pyre of her dead husband. Nadori (tenor), the young Brahmin, who has come to tell Jessonda of the tragic fate now awaiting her, meets her sister Amazili (soprano), falls in love with her and promises her that he will save Jessonda. Meanwhile, Jessonda is hoping to be rescued by the Portuguese general Tristan d'Acunha (baritone), to whom she was once engaged, unaware that a truce has been reached between the city of Goa and the Portuguese forces who have been laying siege to it, with the result that it is no longer within Tristan's power to demand that she be spared. But when the truce is broken after two spies have set fire to the Portuguese ships, Tristan attacks Goa and intervenes just in time to save Jessonda from immolation. Nadori secretly takes Jessonda to the temple, where she can be finally reunited with Tristan, while Nadori himself wins the hand of Amazili.

Jessonda was Spohr's greatest success, and has since been revived on a number of occasions up to this day. In this opera the composer adopts a thoroughly Romantic format, turning his back for the first time on classical opera and its separate arias and recitatives in favour of dramatic and musical continuity.

JEWESS, THE
See *Juive, La*

JOAN OF ARC
See *Giovanna d'Arco*

JOCHUM, EUGEN
(Babenhausen 1902–Munich 1987)
German conductor. Between 1922 and 1925 he studied in Munich with von Hausegger. He embarked on his conducting career while still very young, winning critical acclaim for his performances at the opera house in Munich with the Berlin Radio Orchestra (1932) and with the Hamburg Opera (from 1934). In 1949 he founded the Munich Radio Orchestra and was its conductor until 1960, when he began to share with Bernard Haitink the post of principal conductor of the Amsterdam Concertgebouw orchestra (until 1969). Between 1969 and 1973 he conducted the Bamberg Symphony Orchestra and also won renown for appearances at Bayreuth from 1953 to 1973 and as guest conductor of the leading orchestras of Europe and the United States. Jochum was acknowledged as a fine interpreter of late Romantic repertoire (Bruckner, Brahms, etc.), and in the field of opera he gave outstanding performances of Mozart's *Così fan tutte* and Wagner's *Lohengrin, Die Meistersinger von Nürnberg* and *Tristan und Isolde*.

JOHANNSSON, KRISTJAN
(Akureyri Du 1950)
Icelandic tenor. He began to learn music in Iceland and in 1978 moved to Italy, where he studied singing at the Conservatorio Nicolini in Piacenza. He then took advanced lessons with Campogalliani, and with Poggi and Tagliavini. In 1981 he made his debut at the National Theater in Iceland as Rodolfo in Puccini's *La bohème*. His career continued in Italy where, among other roles, he sang Pinkerton (*Madama Butterfly*) at the Spoleto Festival dei Due Mondi (1983) in Ken Russell's production. He went on to appear in a number of British and American opera houses and by the end of the 1980s was being engaged by leading international venues, including Lyric Opera of Chicago, La Scala, Milan, the Teatro Comunale in Florence, the Vienna Staatsoper and the Metropolitan Opera, New York. Johannsson's remarkably resonant and ringing *lirico spinto* tenor voice brought him distinction in, among others, *Aida, La forza del destino, Cavalleria rusticana, Tosca, Turandot* and *La fanciulla del West*.

JOLIE FILLE DE PERTH, LA
(The Fair Maid of Perth)
Opera in four acts and five scenes by Georges Bizet (1838–1875), to a libretto by Saint-Georges and Adenis based on the novel The Fair Maid of Perth *by Sir Walter Scott. First performance: Paris, Théâtre Lyrique, 26 December 1867.*

The opera is set in Perth, Scotland, at the end of the fourteenth century. Le Duc de Rothsay (baritone) takes advantage of the fact that Carnival celebrations are in progress to arrange for the abduction of Catherine Glover (soprano), a young woman of Perth with whom he is in love. Meanwhile, Henri Smith (tenor) and Ralph (bass) are awaiting St. Valentine's Day, when, according to tradition, Catherine will decide which of them she wants to marry. Mab (mezzo-soprano), a young gipsy-woman who is in love with Henri, thwarts the attempt to abduct Catherine, but when Catherine chooses young Henri as her husband-to-be, he rejects her, believing her to have been the Duc's mistress. The Duc overhears this conversation and feels he is being mocked, so, out of revenge, he decides not to say that Catherine is innocent. Ralph comes to Catherine's defense and is challenged to a duel by Henri, the intention being to follow the popular belief that fate should be left to decide whether Catherine is guilty or not. The Duc arrives just in time to save Henri, who had made up his mind to let himself be killed, and declares Catherine innocent. Catherine has meanwhile been so distraught that she lost her mind, but she regains her sanity with the help of Mab, and the opera ends happily.

In *La jolie fille de Perth* Bizet made every effort to respond to the current fashion in opera, so much so that he ended up actually seeming behind the times and provoked a reaction from those who were expecting something

Top: The German conductor Eugen Jochum.

Above: The Icelandic tenor Kristjan Johannsson.

different from him. Nevertheless, this is his only opera to be favourably received in the opera house.

JOMMELLI, NICCOLÒ

(Aversa 1714–Naples 1774)
Italian composer. In 1737 his first opera, *L'errore amoroso*, was staged, launching him on a successful career as an opera composer. He began to write for the opera houses in Rome (1740), Bologna (1741) and Venice (1741) and was director of the Conservatorio degli Incurabili in Venice (1743–47). With his reputation now established, he worked in Vienna (1749) and Stuttgart (1753–69), where he became court Kapellmeister and reached the height of his fame. His vast operatic output includes *Didone abbandonata* (1746 and 1749), *Fetonte* (1753), *La clemenza di Tito* (1753) and *Armida abbandonata* (1770).

JONES, DAME GWYNETH

(Pontnewynydd 1936)
Welsh soprano. She studied at the Royal College of Music in London and completed her training at the Accademia Chigiana in Siena and with Maria Carpi in Geneva. After making her debut as a mezzo-soprano with Zurich Opera (1962–63), she appeared for the first time at Covent Garden in 1964, where she had a personal success the following year as Sieglinde (*Die Walküre*). This launched her on a brilliant career, which from 1966 included distinguished performances at major international opera houses: Vienna, Munich, Berlin, and Bayreuth (where she triumphed again as Sieglinde). She continued to appear regularly at Bayreuth. From 1972 onwards she was a member of the Metropolitan Opera, New York. Dame Gwyneth is renowned as a singer capable of great vocal impact and stage presence. She has performed from an extremely wide-ranging repertoire which includes a number of Italian operas, although her most distinguished performances have been in Wagner and Richard Strauss.

JONGLEUR DE NOTRE-DAME, LE

(The Juggler of Our Lady)
Opera in three acts by Jules Massenet, to a libretto by Maurice Léna. First performance: Monte Carlo, Théâtre du Casino, 18 February 1902.

The action takes place in the fourteenth century. On the market-square in Cluny, Jean (tenor), a juggler, is introducing his act with an Alleluia in praise of wine. At this, the Prior (bass) comes out of the abbey, orders the crowd to disperse and reproaches Jean for singing a blasphemous song. Jean shows how sorry he is and the Prior is so moved that he pardons him and invites him to dinner. Inside the abbey, Jean realizes that the life of a monk is not so bad, with its regular meals and monastic activities often involving the arts, so he decides to stay on. Some time later, in the abbey chapel, the monks are singing a hymn to the Virgin. Jean, now dressed as a monk, asks the Virgin to allow him to honour her in his own way, with a juggling act. This said, he takes off his habit and launches into his routine. The Painter Monk (baritone) alerts the rest of the community, and, unseen, all of the monks come to watch. The Prior is on the point of condemning Jean's sacrilegious behaviour when he is stopped by the monk in charge of the kitchens, Boniface (bass). A miracle takes place: the statue of the Virgin comes to life, and angels' voices sing their approval of Jean the juggler. The monks are astonished, whereas Jean, unaware that any miracle has occurred, asks the Prior to pardon him for his spontaneous act. Suddenly a halo appears above Jean's head, and he collapses, as though from heart failure. The Virgin ascends into Heaven bearing Jean, who dies happy in her arms.

A minor opera, *Le jongleur de Notre-Dame* is nonetheless a fine example of Massenet's work. The same graceful melodic line, to be found in many of his other compositions, is applied here to a religious context, although this is not used in a dramatic, passionate way, Massenet opting instead for the lyrical and elegiac.

Top: The Italian composer Niccolò Jommelli.

Right: The Welsh soprano Gwyneth Jones.

JONNY SPIELT AUF

(Johnny Strikes Up)

Jazz opera in two acts by Ernst Krenek (b. 1900), to the composer's own libretto. First performance: Leipzig, Opernhaus, 11 February 1927.

The action takes place in modern times. Max (tenor), a composer with a difficult and introverted personality, falls in love with Anita (soprano), a young singer. At her hotel, Anita is reluctantly packing her bags to leave for Paris, where she is due to sing in one of Max's operas. Also staying at the hotel is Daniello (baritone), a violinist who owns an extremely valuable violin. Jonny (baritone), a young black musician in the hotel dance-band, steals Daniello's violin and, after trying to seduce Anita, conceals the instrument in her banjo-case. Daniello, who has also fallen for Anita's charms, discovers he has been robbed and has the hotel turned upside down in order to find his violin. The search yields nothing. To have revenge on Anita for wanting to end their brief relationship, Daniello entrusts Anita's maid Yvonne (soprano) with a ring Anita had given him and asks her to deliver it to Max. When Max receives it, he understands everything and leaves. Yvonne, Jonny's fiancée, hears the true story from Jonny about the theft of the violin and, shocked and confused by the revelation, tells Anita of the episode involving the ring, which had clearly prompted Max's sudden departure. Meanwhile, Max has gone to the mountains, climbed on to a promontory of ice and is on the point of jumping off when he hears mysterious voices coming from the glacier, which give him new feelings of hope in his life. Down below at the hotel, Daniello hears Jonny playing the stolen violin and calls the police, but Jonny has fled to the railway station, intending to escape to Amsterdam. Also at the station is Anita, on her way to America. Anita is being escorted by Max, and Jonny hides the stolen violin in Max's luggage. Max is arrested, and Yvonne, who would have been able to tell the true story, is stopped by Daniello. Then Daniello falls under a train and dies. In the end Jonny confesses to having stolen the violin. Max is released, reunited with Anita, and the two leave for America. The symbolic journey to a new world represents Max's rediscovered faith in life. The opera ends with everybody asking Jonny to play for them.

Jonny spielt auf was an international success. In it, jazz elements marry happily with passages reminiscent of Puccini.

JO, SUMI

(Seoul 1963)

Korean soprano. She came to fame when Karajan invited her to sing at the Salzburg Festival (*Le nozze di Figaro*, 1988, and *Un ballo in maschera*, 1989–90). She has appeared at La Scala, Milan (Jommelli's *Fetonte*, 1988), the Teatro dell'Opera in Rome (Strauss's *Ariadne auf Naxos*, 1991), the Teatro San Carlo in Naples (Matilde in Rossini's *Elisabetta regina d'Inghilterra*, 1991–92) and the Metropolitan Opera in New York (*Rigoletto*, 1990, and *Lucia di Lammermoor*, 1992–93). Her typical *coloratura* soprano voice is tender in delivery, and she shows great skill in achieving very high notes.

JOSEPH EN ÉGYPTE

Opera in three acts by Etienne Nicholas Méhul (1763–1817), to a libretto by Alexandre Duval. First performance: Paris, Théâtre de l'Opéra-Comique, 17 February 1807.

The action takes place in Memphis at the time of the great famine recorded in the Bible. Joseph (tenor), governor of Egypt, has saved his country from hunger by using reserves of grain amassed during the years of the fatted calf. Joseph wants to have his father Jacob and his brothers near him, to make sure they do not die of starvation. Then, quite by chance, they arrive and, not knowing who he is, ask him for hospitality. Joseph offers it, without revealing his identity. Siméon (tenor), the brother who had once, unbeknown to his father and brothers, sold Joseph as a slave and then given him up for dead, is consumed with remorse. No longer able to bear the burden of guilt, Siméon makes his confession to Jacob. The old man is so enraged that he utters a terrible curse on him. But Joseph begs his father to forgive Siméon and then tells the old man who he really is. In an atmosphere charged with emotion, Siméon is forgiven, and the opera ends with songs of thanks to God.

La légende de Joseph en Égypte is Méhul's most famous opera. The music, lyrical and melodious, does not always seem in keeping with the dramatic situations. Nonetheless, there is a consistent richness of harmony and counterpoint, as well as moments of simple yet striking inspiration.

JOUY, ETIENNE DE

(Jouy-en-Josas, Seine-et-Oise 1764–Saint-Germain-en-Laye 1846)

French librettist. He initially took up a military career but abandoned it in 1797 to con-

Top: A sketch for the character of Joseph in *Joseph en Egypte* by Méhul.

Above: A scene from *Guillaume Tell*, the libretto to which was written by Etienne de Jouy.

centrate on politics and literary activities, and on the strength of these he was admitted to the Académie Francaise (1815). Jouy was the Paris Opéra's official librettist and wrote some 20 libretti, among them texts for: *La vestale* in 1807 and *Fernand Cortez* in 1809 for Spontini; *Les abencérages* in 1813 for Cherubini; the Paris version of Rossini's *Moïse et Pharaon* in 1827 and the same composer's *Guillaume Tell* in 1829, the latter co-written with Florent Bis.

JOYFUL COMPANY, THE

See *Allegra brigata, L'*

JUGGLER OF OUR LADY

See *Jongleur de Notre Dame, Le*

JUIVE, LA

(The Jewess)

Opera in five acts by Jacques Fromental Halévy (1799–1862), to a libretto by Eugène Scribe. First performance: Paris, Opéra, 23 February 1835.

The action takes place in Constance in the fifteenth century. Ruggiero (tenor), provost of the town of Constance, announces that public celebrations are to be held following the victory of Prince Léopold against the Hussites. Ruggiero then orders the arrest of the Jewish goldsmith Éléazar (tenor) after it is discovered that he has not stopped work on this most solemn day. Éléazar and his daughter Rachel (soprano) would have been put to death, were it not for the intervention of Cardinal Brogni (bass). Brogni recalls meeting Éléazar before becoming a priest, when his own wife and daughter had died in tragic circumstances, and he now orders the goldsmith's release. Meanwhile, in her father's workshop, Rachel is visited by Léopold, whom she takes to be a painter and fellow Jew, and invites him to celebrate Passover with her. Shortly after this, Éléazar and Rachel are attacked by the crowd, and Léopold comes to the defense of both father and daughter as the guards, who have arrived to put down the disturbance, are on the point of arresting them. On the eve of Passover, Léopold reveals to Rachel that he is a Christian and explains that he had lied to her out of love but wants Rachel to elope with him. However, Éléazar comes upon them while they are making their escape, and Léopold, in despair, declares that he is unable to marry Rachel. The scene changes to the Emperor's garden, where celebrations in Léopold's honour are in full swing. Enter Éléazar bearing a gold chain which the Princesse Eudoxie (soprano) had ordered from him. The Princesse offers the chain to Léopold, calling him her husband. Rachel rushes up to the Prince, tears the chain from his neck and announces that Léopold has had a relationship with her. Léopold does not defend himself and, for having had relations with an unbeliever, is condemned to death with Rachel and her father. Eudoxie pleads with Rachel to proclaim Léopold's innocence in order to save him, and Rachel agrees. For his part, Cardinal Brogni wants to persuade Éléazar to give up his faith, as in this way he will be able to save his daughter. The goldsmith refuses and tells the cardinal that his own daughter, whom Brogni was under the impression had died at the same time as her mother, had actually been saved by a Jew, but he refuses to reveal more than that. Then Éléazar and his daughter are condemned to death, whereas Léopold, thanks to Rachel's intervention, is released. As the Jew and his daughter are on their way to execution, Brogni begs him to disclose his lost daughter's whereabouts, and Éléazar points to Rachel.

La Juive is the first opera to use a religious conflict from history as its plot. The score is particularly demanding on the voice.

Above: Costume design for Rachel, the heroine of *La Juive* by Halévy.

JUMPING FROG OF CALAVERAS COUNTY, THE

Opera in one act by Lukas Foss (b. 1922), to a libretto by Jean Karsavina, based on the short story by Mark Twain. First performance: Bloomington, University of Indiana, 18 May 1950.

A stranger with a large moustache (bass) challenges a jumping frog by the name of Daniel Webster, belonging to Smiley (tenor), to a contest. While the boys are busy placing bets on whose frog will win, the stranger fills Daniel's gullet with lead shot. The stranger makes advances to Lulu (mezzo-soprano) in the town square, arousing the jealousy of the local lads. As might be expected, Daniel loses the contest, but it is only after the stranger has left with all the winnings that everyone realizes he has tricked them. The frog is rid of the lead shot, while all the spectators run after the stranger, bring him back, force him to return all their money to them, and then report him to the police. After that, Lulu starts smiling at Smiley again.

In *The Jumping Frog of Calaveras County*, Lukas Foss reveals his brilliant musical and dramatic talent.

JURINAC, SENA

(Travnik 1921)

Stage name of Srebrenka Jurinac, Bosnian soprano. In 1942 she made her debut with the Zagreb Opera as Mimi (*La bohème*). She was contracted by the Vienna Staatsoper and scored a sensational success on her first appearance there in 1945 as Cherubino (*Le nozze di Figaro*). In the space of a few years, Jurinac had made her name as a Mozart performer at leading international opera houses: the Salzburg Festival (Dorabella, 1947), La Scala, Milan (Cherubino, 1948), Covent Garden (1948) and Glyndebourne. Her vocal gifts, sure technique and exceptional stylistic sensitivity gradually enabled Jurinac to tackle a wide-ranging repertoire, including Octavian in *Der Rosenkavalier*, Leonora (*Fidelio*), Elisabetta (*Don Carlos*) and Cio-Cio-San (*Madama Butterfly*).

K

KABAIVANSKA, RAINA

(Burgas 1934)

Bulgarian soprano, naturalized Italian. After studying music in Bulgaria and Italy, she made her debut in 1959 in Puccini's *Il tabarro* in Vercelli. In 1961 came her first appearance at La Scala as Agnese in Bellini's *Beatrice di Tenda* (the cast also included Joan Sutherland), and the following year she was Desdemona to Mario Del Monaco's Otello in Verdi's opera. During this part of her career, Kabaivanska tackled an extremely wide repertoire, based exclusively on Italian opera from Bellini to Verdi and Puccini. During the 1970s her rigour, expressiveness and refinement were seen at their best in the operas of Puccini (*Madama Butterfly*, *Manon Lescaut*, *Tosca*), Cilèa (*Adriana Lecouvreur*) and Zandonai (*Francesca da Rimini*), in which she appeared at major international opera houses under the most celebrated conductors. In these performances she succeeded marvellously in combining two great strengths: a manner of singing consistently attentive to the composer's wishes, and equally striking and charismatic talents as an actress which brought her acclaim as a most accomplished interpreter of this repertoire.

KALUDOV, KALUDI

(Varna 1953)

Bulgarian tenor. He began to study singing with Zafirova before moving on to the Conservatory in Sofia, where he had lessons with Jablenska, graduating in 1976. In 1978 he joined the Sofia Opera, appearing there while still a student. Simultaneously he embarked on an international career, singing at numerous opera houses in Europe and America (including *Boris Godunov* in Houston and Chicago with Claudio Abbado conducting). He recorded Mussorgsky's *Khovanshchina* in 1986 (Golitsyn) and Borodin's *Knyaz Igor* (Vladimir) in 1987, both conducted by Emil Tchakarov.

KAMENNÏY GOST'

(The Stone Guest)

Opera in three acts by Alexander Dargomyzhsky (1813–1869), to a libretto based on Pushkin's play of the same name. First (posthumous) performance: St. Petersburg, Maryinsky Theater, 28 February 1872.

The action takes place in Spain. Don Juan (tenor), banished after being found guilty of killing the Knight Commander, has secretly returned to Madrid with his servant Leporello (bass). The Don calls at the house of Doña Laura (mezzo-soprano), an actress whom he has seduced. After supper, Don Juan fights a duel with Laura's fiancé, Don Carlos (baritone), and kills him. The next day, near the Knight Commander's tomb, Don Juan, using the alias Don Diego de Calvido, approaches Doña Anna (soprano), widow of the murdered Knight. After persuading her to agree to a rendezvous, Don Juan, feeling pleased with the way things are going, invites the statue of the Knight Commander to join him and Doña Anna when they meet the next day. The scene changes to Doña Anna's bedroom, where Don Juan has managed to break down her defenses and also obtained her forgiveness for having concealed his true identity. There is knocking at the door. Enter the statue (bass), and, as Doña Anna faints, it crushes Don Juan to death.

Kamennïy Gost' was left unfinished by the composer on his death and was completed by Rimsky-Korsakov and Cui. The opera was not exactly a resounding success, but it nevertheless entered the repertoires of Soviet opera houses. In this work Dargomyzhsky perfected the melodic recitative that is the hallmark of his particular operatic language. This style had considerable influence on Russian composers.

KARAJAN, HERBERT VON

(Salzburg 1908–Anif, Salzburg 1989)

Stage name of Heribert Ritter von Karajan, Austrian conductor. He began studying piano in 1912 at the Salzburg Mozarteum and then went on to Vienna, where he attended Schalk's courses in conducting. Between 1926 and 1928 he continued his studies at the Vienna Musikhochschule and also began conducting at the Ulm State Theater (1927–34). He then became director of the Aachen Opera House (1935–42), and in the meantime his reputation as a conductor was strengthened by the great success of his debut at the Vienna Staatsoper in 1936 with *Tristan und Isolde* and of a number of concert appearances with the Berlin Philharmonic. In 1939 he was appointed Staatskapellmeister at the Berlin Opera, having already made his mark at the leading concert halls and opera houses of Europe (La Scala, Florence, Paris, etc.). The next and crucial phases of his artistic career came immediately following

Left: The Bulgarian soprano Raina Kabaivanska

Above: Herbert von Karajan

the Second World War, when in the space of a few years he appeared for the first time at the Salzburg Festival (1948), relaunched the Bayreuth Festival (1951) and was appointed conductor-for-life of the Berlin Philharmonic (1955–89). He was artistic director at Salzburg (where he founded the Easter Festival in 1963), at the Vienna Staatsoper and of the Philharmonia Orchestra. These are only some of the numerous artistic appointments held by Karajan, one of the major figures in the world of the arts in the twentieth century. His artistic discipline and personality as a performer, combined with a keen originality, also left their mark on opera.

KÁT'A KABANOVÁ

Opera in three acts and six scenes by Léoš Janáček (1854–1928), to the composer's own libretto based on The Thunderstorm *by Alexander Ostrovsky. First performance: Brno, National Theater, 23 November 1921.*

The action takes place in the second half of the nineteenth century in the small Russian city of Kalinov on the banks of the Volga. Boris Grigorjevic (tenor) unburdens himself to his friend Vána Kudrjás (tenor): he is in love with Katerina Kabanová (soprano), the wife of Tichon Ivanyc Kabanov (tenor), and his family life has been overshadowed by difficulties in his relationship with his uncle Dikoj (bass), a wealthy merchant. Enter Kát'a (Katerina), accompanied by her husband Tichon and Marfa (known as Kabanicha, mezzo-soprano), her mother-in-law, who reproaches her son for loving her less than he does his wife. In the Kabanov household, Kát'a too is unhappy, feels oppressed by her mother-in-law and is disappointed in her husband, who treats her coldly. While Tichon is away travelling, Kát'a, after having refused repeatedly to meet Boris, agrees to a rendezvous with him. Not long after, she is consumed with remorse, interprets the approach of a violent storm threatening the city as a warning from heaven, and confesses her guilty feelings to Tichon. She bids farewell to Boris, and throws herself into the Volga. Kabanicha coldly thanks the towns people who have helped retrieve the body.

This opera, composed between 1919 and 1921, represents one of the peaks of Janáček's operatic output. It abounds in passages of high drama alongside other sections marked by a typically Slav lyricism.

Above: A scene from *Kát'a Kabanová*, in a production at the Berlin Komische Oper.

KAVRAKOS, DIMITRI

(Athens 1946)

Greek bass. He studied singing in Athens, where he made his debut in 1970 as Zaccaria (*Nabucco*). He then sang in Spoleto (Verdi's *Requiem*) and in 1976 appeared for the first time in the United States (Refice's *Cecilia*). Engagements followed as guest artiste at leading American opera houses, especially at the Metropolitan in New York (where his first appearance was in *Don Carlos*) and at Lyric Opera of Chicago (from 1980). Kavrakos's career then took in the major international opera venues, including Covent Garden, the Paris Opéra and La Scala, Milan.

Right: The German conductor Joseph Keilberth

KEILBERTH, JOSEPH

(Karlsruhe 1908–Munich 1968)

German conductor. He studied music in Karlsruhe, where he began his conducting career as corrépétiteur at the local opera house (1935–40). He went on to be conductor of the German Philharmonic Orchestra, Prague (1940–45), and the Dresden Opera (1945–51), artistic director of the Hamburg Philharmonic Orchestra and the Munich Bayerische Staatsoper (1959–68), and founder of the Bamberg Symphony Orchestra. He conducted at the Bayreuth Festival (1952–56), where the reinforcing of his reputation as one of the most important conductors of his day was borne out by his recordings, in particular of *Der Freischütz*, *Lohengrin*, *Der fliegende Holländer* (The Flying Dutchman), *Arabella* and *Cardillac*.

KÉKSZAKÁLLÚ HERCEG VÁRA, A

(Duke Bluebeard's Castle)

Opera in one act by Béla Bartók (1881–1945), to a libretto by Béla Balázs. First performance: Budapest, Királyi Operház, 24 May 1918.

The setting is a castle in the world of fable. Duke Bluebeard (bass) enters his castle with Judith (soprano), his new bride. The great hall has seven doors leading off it, but no windows. Out of curiosity, and so as not to have to linger in darkness, Judith asks her husband if she can open the seven doors. After hesitating, Bluebeard gives her the keys one by one. Judith discovers that the first chamber contains instruments of torture covered in blood; in the second, she finds weapons of battle; the third reveals a treasure-chest sparkling with jewels stained with blood. The fourth door opens on a lush garden resplendent with roses but when Judith picks one, she sees blood dripping from the stem. She opens the fifth door on to an expanse of land, where a crimson cloud veils the horizon. Bluebeard pleads with her not to open the remaining doors, but Judith will not listen to him. The sixth reveals a dark lake of tears. Behind the seventh stand three life-like, luminous figures, the ghosts of Bluebeard's previous wives, transformed because they uncovered their husband's secrets. After Bluebeard has told her the story of his wives, Judith crosses the threshold of the seventh room, and all the other doors close together. Bluebeard is left standing in the darkness.

Bartók's opera is now regarded as the masterpiece of Hungarian opera, but its success was not immediate. When it was completed in 1911, the Hungarian Commission of Fine Arts ruled that it was unstageable. Rediscovered in 1918 by the Italian conductor Egisto Tango, however, the work was seen to condense the entire range of Bartók's musical achievements until 1911.

KENNY, YVONNE

(Sydney 1950)
Australian soprano. She began her career with an appearance at the Queen Elizabeth Hall in London (1975) singing the lead in Donizetti's opera *Rosamunda d'Inghilterra*. In the same year she won the Kathleen Ferrier prize, enabling her to make her debut at Covent Garden, where her roles included Ilia (*Idomeneo*), Marzelline (*Fidelio*), Susanna (*Le nozze di Figaro*) and Liù (*Turandot*), and she also sang in Handel's *Semele*. Kenny went on to appear at a number of international opera houses, including Aix-en-Provence, Glyndebourne and Munich. With her pleasant timbre, precise delivery and good technique, she has developed a repertoire focusing mainly on operas by Handel and Mozart. In Italian opera, besides *Rosamunda d'Inghilterra*, she has taken part in other important revivals of operas by Donizetti: *Elisabetta al castello di Kenilworth*, *Ugo*, *Conte di Parigi* and *Emilia di Liverpool*.

KERTÉSZ, ISTVÁN

(Budapest 1929–Kfar Saba, Tel Aviv 1973)
Hungarian conductor. He studied composition and conducting at the Franz Liszt Academy, Budapest. His conducting career began in Györ (1955–57) and Budapest (1955–57).

He then went to live in Germany, where he worked in Augsburg (1958–63) and Cologne (1964–73). His international appearances were as conductor of the London Symphony Orchestra (1965–68), Vienna Philharmonic and Israel Philharmonic. Noted for his elegant handling of the expressive possibilities of timbre, Kertész was also a vigorous conductor of opera and gave some incomparable performances of Bartók's *A Kékszakállú herceg vára* (Duke Bluebeard's Castle), Kodály's *Háry János*, and Mozart's *La clemenza di Tito*, *Die Entführung aus dem Serail* (The Seraglio) and *Die Zauberflöte* (The Magic Flute).

KHOVANSHCHINA

See *Kovàncina*

KING, JAMES

(Dodge City, Kansas 1925)
American tenor. He studied violin and piano at the University of Louisiana and Kansas, and subsequently singing under the tutelage of Martial Singher and Max Lorenz. After winning the American Opera Auditions in Cincinnati, he embarked on a singing career which then took him from the United States to Europe. He made his debut at Florence's Teatro La Pergola in *Tosca* (1961) and sang with the Deutsche Oper in Berlin the following year. Also in 1961 came his first performance at Salzburg in Gluck's *Iphigénie en Aulide*. In the years that followed, King appeared at the Vienna Staatsoper, the Bayreuth Festival (1965–75), La Scala, Milan (from 1968) and the Paris Opéra, and made his debut with the Metropolitan Opera, New York, in 1966 (*Fidelio*), where he returned in 1988 to sing the role of Bacchus in *Ariadne auf Naxos*. His best performances have been mainly in German opera, in particular Richard Strauss and Wagner.

KING AND MARSHAL

See *Drot og Marsk*

KING ARTHUR OR THE BRITISH WORTHY

Musical play by Henry Purcell (1659–1695), to a libretto by John Dryden. First performance: London, Dorset Gardens Theater, May or June 1691.

Arthur (tenor), King of the Britons, and Oswald (tenor), Saxon King of Kent, both wish to marry Emmeline (soprano), daughter of the Duke of Cornwall. Oswald abducts Emmeline while Arthur, who has been resisting the charms of two sirens (sopranos), breaks the spells binding him. On St. George's Day there is a decisive struggle between the two rivals: the wizard Osmond (bass) and a Spirit of the Earth (bass) are supporting Oswald, while Merlin (bass) and a Spirit of the Air (soprano) are on the side of Arthur's Britons. Arthur meets Oswald in hand-to-hand combat and, after disarming him, grants him his life. Emmeline marries Arthur, while Merlin proclaims the King "the foremost Christian hero." Then, using magic, Arthur causes the islands of Britain to rise up out of the sea. The opera ends with a hymn to St. George.

Top: The Hungarian conductor István Kertész.

Above: The American tenor James King.

King Arthur is a play with incidental music, a genre very much in vogue with English audiences at the time. The score, not published until after the composer's death, is not complete. Nevertheless, the music plays an important role in this work and is rich in colour, especially in the instrumental sections.

KING FOR A DAY, OR THE IMPOSTER STANISLAUS

See *Giorno di regno, Un, ossia Il finto Stanislao*

KING PRIAM

Opera in three acts by Sir Michael Tippett (b. 1905), to the composer's own libretto based on Homer's Iliad. *First performance: London, Coventry Theater, 29 May 1962.*

Queen Hecuba (soprano), wife of Priam (baritone), King of Troy, has been deeply disturbed by a dream which seems to prophesy that Priam will die by the hand of his son Paris (tenor). In great sorrow, Priam decides to have his son put to death, but the young man is saved by shepherds. Many years later, during a hunt, Paris meets his father again. Priam is happy that his son has survived and takes him back to Troy. Time passes, and Paris, who has been absent from the kingdom to attend the marriage of his brother Hector (baritone) to Andromache (soprano), returns to Troy with Helen (mezzo-soprano), whom he has taken away from her husband, Menelaus, King of Greece. It is to win Helen back that the Greeks lay siege to Troy. This is the beginning of a time of ill-fortune for Priam and his family. After Patroclus (baritone) has been killed by Hector, Hector himself dies at the hands of Achilles (tenor). Hector's death devastates Priam, and the old man goes to plead with Achilles to return his son's body. His request is honoured, and while the two are drinking wine together, each predicts the other's death: Achilles will be killed by Priam's son, Priam himself by Neoptolemus, son of Achilles. At the palace, Priam bids farewell to Hecuba, Andromache and Helen, to whom he shows particular tenderness. He then kneels at the altar. At that moment the Greeks burst in, and the old King is killed by Neoptolemus.

With this opera, Tippett exchanged the contemporary situations in his previous works for an intentionally rarefied atmosphere, employing modern techniques which are at the same time close to the world of classical tragedy; the use of the Chorus, for example, is here transformed by the composer, who brings it on in dramatized interludes in which the actual characters in the opera are given an abstract role, introducing to the audience the emotions which are then turned into actions as the plot unfolds. Tippett also makes broad use of a declamatory vocal style perfectly in keeping with the characters and their final tragic catharsis.

KING ROGER

See *Król Roger*

KLEIBER, CARLOS

(Berlin 1930)

German conductor. Son of the conductor Erich Kleiber, he began his music studies in Buenos Aires, where his family had emigrated. On his return to Europe, he initially studied chemistry in Zurich but then concentrated on music. In 1954 he started conducting in Potsdam and subsequently in Düsseldorf, Zurich, Stuttgart, and Munich (from 1968). In 1974 he made his debut at Bayreuth (in *Tristan und Isolde*), going on to appear at other major international opera houses such as Covent Garden (1974) and La Scala (from 1976). His opera repertoire included *Wozzeck*, *Der Rosenkavalier*, *La bohème* and *Otello*. His recordings earned considerable critical acclaim, especially *Der Freischütz* in 1973 (Kleiber's recording debut), *La traviata* in 1977 and *Tristan und Isolde* in 1981, the latter with fascinating orchestral brilliance and sensitivity of interpretation.

KLEIBER, ERICH

(Vienna 1890–Zurich 1956)

Austrian conductor. After studying at the Prague Conservatory, his career began in Darmstadt (1912) and continued in Wuppertal (1919), Düsseldorf (1921) and Mannheim (1922). In 1923 his performance of *Fidelio* at the Berlin Staatsoper was a great success. With his reputation already established at that opera house, he was appointed *Generalmusikdirektor* at the age of 33, a post he held for 12 years. During this period he directed the premieres of Berg's *Wozzeck* (1925) and Milhaud's *Christophe Colomb* (1930). In 1935 he left Germany because of the political situation and settled in Argentina, where from 1936 he conducted at the Teatro Colón in Buenos Aires. After the war, he returned to Europe, appearing as a regular guest conductor at Covent Garden (1950–53) and the Berlin Staatsoper (1954–55). His outstanding mastery as a conductor is illustrated by his recordings of *Der Rosenkavalier*

Top: *The Polovtsians' Dance* from *Knyaz Igor* (Prince Igor) by Borodin.

Right: The German conductor Carlos Kleiber.

(1953) and *Le nozze di Figaro* (1955), remarkable for Kleiber's penetrating grasp of the score and impassioned interpretation.

KLEMPERER, OTTO

(Breslau 1885–Zurich 1973)
German conductor. He began his music studies in Frankfurt (1901) and continued them in Berlin, where the composer Hans Pfitzner was one of his teachers. He made his debut in Prague in 1907 and developed his career in opera houses and concert halls in Hamburg (1910), Barmen (1913), Strasbourg (1914), Cologne (1917), Wiesbaden (1924), and from 1927 at the Kroll Opera in Berlin, where he conducted operas by Janáček (*Z mrtvého domu*, From the House of the Dead), Hindemith (*Cardillac*), Schoenberg (*Erwartung*) and others. The advent of Nazism forced Klemperer to leave Germany for the United States, where he conducted the Los Angeles Philharmonic Orchestra from 1933 until 1939. During the period immediately after the Second World War, Klemperer returned to Europe, where he resumed his international career even though a serious illness had left him partially paralyzed. He conducted at the Budapest State Opera (1947–50) and the Philharmonia Orchestra in London (of which he became conductor-for-life in 1955) and also conducted at Covent Garden from 1961. In the field of opera, Klemperer's art, at once disciplined and powerfully enriched by emotion and dramatic tension, is exemplified by his recordings of *Der fliegende Holländer* (The Flying Dutchman) in 1968 and *Così fan tutte* in 1971.

KLUGE, DIE

(The Wise Woman)
Opera in one act by Carl Orff (1895–1982), to the composer's own libretto based on a fairy-tale by the Brothers Grimm. First performance: Frankfurt, Städtische Bühne am Main, 18 February 1943.

A countryman (baritone) sits in prison lamenting his fate. While he was working in the fields, he had found a mortar made of gold and, believing this to be his duty, took it to the King. But his daughter (soprano), being gifted with great insight, predicted that the King would accuse him of theft and throw him into prison. The King (baritone) is so moved by the countryman's protestations that he has him brought before the throne and, on learning of his daughter's great wisdom, commands that she be brought to the palace. To put the young woman's wisdom to the test, the King sets her three riddles, which she solves, and as a result he decides to marry her, after setting her father free. Some time later, a muleteer (baritone) appears before the King and asks him to resolve a dispute: a man (tenor) with a donkey has accused him of theft. They had both slept in a stable and, on waking at dawn, had found that a donkey foal had been born during the night. The foal had been claimed by the muleteer on the grounds that it was lying closer to his donkey. With the help of three criminals (tenor, baritone and bass) who had been paid to give false evidence, the muleteer convinces the King that he is in the right. The wise young woman consoles the donkey-owner by deciding to help him. Shortly after this, the man sits down at the road-side with a fishing-net and pretends to be fishing on dry land. The King, imagining that the donkey-

owner has gone mad, questions him. The donkey-owner's blatant response is that the verdict the King had reached in his case was misguided, and the King realizes that such a comment could only have come from the wise young woman. He is offended by it and demands that she leave the castle but allows her to take with her a chest containing all her dearest possessions. She gives the King a sleeping-draught and shuts him inside the chest. When he wakes up, he forgives his wife, praises her wisdom, and has the foal given back to the donkey-owner.

The fable-based plot of *Die Kluge* makes an ideal subject for the expressive and dramatic style of Carl Orff, described by the musicologist Karl Heinz Ruppel as a language of "immediacy, stylization, elementary and at the same time symbolic. A theater of reality and comedy and the uplifting of the spirit, vital as well as spiritual, mimetic and magical."

KMENTT, WALDEMAR

(Vienna 1929)
Austrian tenor. After studying under Adolf Vogel, Elisabeth Rado and Hans Duhan at the Vienna Academy of Music, he made his debut in 1950 in a performance of Beethoven's Ninth Symphony. A year later, he appeared at the Vienna Staatsoper and in 1955 began to take part in the Salzburg Festival. These two centers were the focus of much of his career, although he also gave some performances at Bayreuth (1968–70) and La Scala, Milan (1968). Kmennt's name is principally associated with Mozart's operas, and his recordings of *Così fan tutte* in 1955, *Idomeneo* in 1961 and *Die Zauberflöte* (The Magic Flute) in 1964 reveal him as a refined and sensitive performer who is also vigorous in characterization.

KNAPPERTSBUSCH, HANS

(Elberfeld 1888–Munich 1965)
German conductor. He began as an assistant at the Bayreuth Festival (1910–12) and went on to conduct in Mülheim an der Ruhr (1912), Elberfeld (1913–18), Leipzig (1918) and Dessau (1919). In 1922 he succeeded Bruno Walter as conductor of the Munich Bayerische Staatsoper. His appearances at the Salzburg and (from 1951) Bayreuth Festivals carried great prestige.

KNIGHTS OF EKEBY, THE

See *Cavalieri di Ekebù, I*

KNYAZ IGOR

(Prince Igor)
Opera in four acts and a prologue by Alexander Borodin (1833–87), to the composer's own libretto, based on an anonymous twelfth-century Russian poem The Song of Igor. *First performance (posthumous): St. Petersburg, Maryinsky Theater, 4 November 1890.*

The action takes place in the Russian city of Putivl in 1185. Putivl is under attack by the Polovtsians, and Prince Igor (baritone) has decided to go out and join battle with them in the open. As he prepares to set out, an eclipse of the sun takes place, which is seen as a bad omen, but Igor decides to go nonetheless and takes with him Vladimir (tenor), his son

The German conductor Hans Knappertsbusch

by his first wife. Only two musicians, who have been conscripted against their will, Skula (bass) and Eroshka (tenor), manage to desert and join the forces of Prince Galitsky (bass-baritone), Igor's brother-in-law. Time passes. The dissolute Galitsky has now decided to replace Igor on the throne and, in pursuit of this aim, Skula and Eroshka set about winning popular support. In her apartments, Yaroslavna (soprano), Igor's wife and the sister of Galitsky, is deeply worried as to what might have happened to her husband and Vladimir, of whom she has heard no more news. She reproaches her brother for his profligate way of life, but Galitsky reacts with arrogance. Then the boyars bring news that Igor has been defeated, the army destroyed, and Igor and Vladimir taken prisoner. The enemy is now poised to attack Putivl. Meanwhile, in the Polovtsian camp, young Vladimir has fallen in love with Kontchakovna (mezzo-soprano), the daughter of Khan Kontchak (bass). With the Polovtsians preparing for victory, rumour circulates among the prisoners that Putivl has already fallen into enemy hands. As a result, the sentries begin to dance and drink themselves into a stupor. Seeing his chance, Igor manages to escape, but Vladimir is stopped by the guards and saved from death only by the intervention of Kontchak, who then proceeds to give him his daughter's hand in marriage. Shortly after this, Igor reaches Putivl, where Yaroslavna is overjoyed to have him back. Skula and Eroshka have seen Igor arrive and, afraid that they will be punished, assemble the crowds to celebrate his safe return. They are pardoned, and everyone is left in no doubt of a victory over the Polovtsians.

Borodin worked on *Knyaz Igor* until his death but left the work unfinished. The other composers in the Group of Five to which Borodin belonged took it upon themselves to complete the score: Glazunov finished the third act and drafted the overture, while Rimsky-Korsakov tackled the orchestration, obeying Borodin's instructions. The opera was warmly received at its first performance.

KÓDALY, ZOLTÁN

(Kecskemet 1882–Budapest 1967)
Hungarian composer. From 1903 he concentrated on the study of Hungarian folk-music. In this regard, his meeting with Béla Bartók was a turning-point, as the two men went on to found the New Hungarian Music Society in 1911. He made a number of journeys abroad (1928, to England and the Netherlands, and subsequently also to Italy), where he was widely acknowledged as a scholar and composer. In opera his name is associated with *Háry János* (1926, revised in 1960), one of the masterpieces of Hungarian national opera. His other operas are *Székely fonó* (The Transylvanian Spinning Room) 1932 and *Czinka Panna*, 1948.

KOLLO, RENÉ

(Berlin 1937)
Stage name of René Kollodzievski, German tenor. In 1965 he made his debut in Brunswick, and from 1967 to 1971 he sang with Cologne Opera. In 1969 he appeared for the first time at the Bayreuth Festival as the Steersman in *Der fliegende Holländer* (The Flying Dutchman). He returned to Bayreuth in the years that followed and sang Erik, Lohengrin, Walther, Parsifal, Siegfried and Tristan, etc., as well as developing a busy international career which took him to La Scala, the Vienna Staatsoper (from 1971), the Metropolitan Opera, New York (1976), and Covent Garden.

KÖNIG HIRSCH

Opera in three acts by Hans Werner Henze (b. 1926), to a libretto by Heinz von Cramer, based on Carlo Gozzi's fairy story Il re Cervo *(1762). First performance: (original version) Berlin, Städtische Oper, 23 September 1956; (renamed* Il re Cervo*) Cassel 1963.*

Act I. In an imaginary kingdom, the Governor (bass-baritone) tries to seize power from the young boy King (tenor) by arranging for him to be abandoned in the forest. Brought up by the forest animals, the King returns after some years and regains his throne. Two speaking statues, Truth and Wisdom (contraltos), tell him it is time he took a wife, and point out the virtues and defects of all the girls who parade before him. He falls in love with one maiden (soprano) and, fearful lest the statues advise against his love, he smashes them. The Governor accuses the maiden of wanting to kill the King, and she is condemned to death. The King realizes that it is his duty to save her; he pardons her and then, renouncing his kingdom, returns to the forest to live

Above: A scene from *Knyaz Igor* (Prince Igor) in a production at La Scala during the 1964–65 season.

Right: The Hungarian composer Zoltán Kódaly.

close to nature and in search of peace. A parrot (ballerina) who accompanies him will put him in touch with the world of nature. Act II. Hoping to kill the King, the Governor organizes a hunt in the forest. The parrot and Nature defend the King, who is changed into a stag, but a message from the parrot to the King is intercepted by Checco, the young dreamer (tenor), who reveals the King's new shape and so the hunters chase the stag. The whole forest protects the King stag and drives the hunters away. The King's metamorphosis is only apparent, however; time passes and he feels once more the call of the real world. He returns to the city to seek the love of a woman. Act III. The Governor has meanwhile made himself King, but fearful that the real King might return, he lives in continual fear. With the return of the legitimate King the Governor is killed by the same assassin he had hired to kill the King. The King, restored to the form of a man once again, marries the maiden he loves.

King Stag, written in Italy, is an act of homage to Italy. Influenced by the avant-garde twelve-tone technique from Schönberg to Webern, Henze has always taken up an intermediate position with regard to the more extreme and severe forms, preferring to incorporate avant-garde elements within a musical framework that has its roots in Berg and Stravinsky, and is sometimes coloured by shades of jazz or popular music. The score of *King Stag* exemplifies this approach: the music has a fundamentally modern structure, but there are also explicit concessions to a non-operatic language, influenced by popular and traditional Italian songs and tunes.

KÖNIGIN VON SABA, DIE

(The Queen of Sheba)

Opera in four acts by Karl Goldmark (1830–1915), to a libretto by Salomon Hermann Mosenthal. First performance: Vienna, Hoftheater, 10 March 1875.

The action, which recalls the story in the Bible, centers around the visit of the Queen of Sheba (soprano) to King Solomon (baritone). Assad (tenor), the King's favourite son, promised in marriage to Sulamith (soprano), daughter of the High Priest (bass), falls in love with the Queen at first sight. Although Assad declares his love for the Queen, Solomon demands that the wedding to Sulamith take place as planned. The Queen is jealous and, after talking with Assad during the night, makes an appearance at the temple where the wedding ceremony is taking place. In a sudden moment of madness, Assad curses religion and the temple he is standing in and runs out. Only as a result of Sulamith's entreaties is his sentence of death for this sacrilege commuted to one of exile. Meanwhile, Assad is wandering in the desert. The Queen has been following him, catches up with him and tries to seduce him, but he rejects her. He is finally found by Sulamith and dies embracing her.

Die Königin von Saba was Goldmark's first opera. Its first performance was remarkably successful and made the composer's name. The music, rich in colour and Oriental touches, is clearly influenced by Wagner.

KOVĂNCĬNA

(Khovanshchina)

National music drama in five acts by Modest Mussorgsky (1839–1881), to the composer's own libretto based on ancient chronicles of the schismatic "Old Believers" sect. First performance: St. Petersburg, Kononov Theater, 21 February 1886.

The action takes place in Moscow in 1682. In Red Square, Prince Ivan Khovansky (bass), commander of the *streltsy* (undisciplined troops who had changed their allegiance from the Regent Sophia to Prince Khovansky himself) is organizing a conspiracy aimed at seizing power. He passes among the crowd, inciting them to riot. Then a young Lutheran woman, Emma (soprano), comes into the square pursued by Andrey (tenor), Ivan's son, who professes to be in love with her. She is rescued by the arrival of Marfa (mezzo-soprano), a mystic and Old Believer who once was Andrey's mistress. Enter Khovansky. Struck by Emma's beauty, he orders his soldiers to conduct her to his palace. Dosifey (bass), leader of the Old Believers (who represent Russian spirituality and the country's pre-European culture), arrives in time to lead

Top: The German tenor René Kollo.

Above: A scene from *Khovanshchina* by Mussorgsky.

Emma to safety. A few days later, Prince Golitsin (tenor), one of Khovansky's allies and a supporter of reforms that are bringing Russia closer to the West, receives a letter from the Regent Sophia, whose lover he has been but whom he does not trust because of her overriding ambition. Meanwhile, Ivan Khovansky arrives, and a dispute arises between the two men about Golitsin's new interventionist acts. Dosifey comes in and calls upon the two princes to settle their differences in the name of the old Russia. At that moment the boyar Shaklovity (baritone) appears and announces that young Tsar Peter (later Peter the Great) has uncovered the conspiracy, which he has described as a *khovanshchina*, or ''Khovansky business'', and has launched an investigation. Shortly after this, and even though he has been put on his guard by Golitsin, Prince Khovansky is assassinated in his palace by the boyar Shaklovity, a supporter of Peter. Meanwhile, Golitsin has been sentenced to exile for his own machinations, and Dosifey receives news that the Council has ordered the extermination of the Old Believers. On hearing of his father's death, now fearing for his own life, Andrey Khovansky takes refuge in a hermitage in the forest where Dosifey and his followers are making ready to bear witness to their faith by burning themselves on a pyre. Marfa comforts Andrey, kisses him for the last time, and then pulls him on to the pyre before putting a torch to it. The Tsar's soldiers arrive, only to recoil in horror when they see the pyre ablaze.

Left unfinished by the composer on his death, this opera (like *Boris Godunov*) was orchestrated and completed by Rimsky-Korsakov. As had been the case with *Boris*, Rimsky-Korsakov's edition was criticized in some quarters, above all on the grounds that Mussorgsky's music had often been altered and forced to fit the framework of Rimsky's own aesthetics. Stravinsky and Ravel produced a new finale for *Khovanshchina* for a performance in Paris in June 1913, and this led to discussions of Rimsky's score. The work was revised by Shostakovich in 1960.

KRAUS, ALFREDO

(Las Palmas 1927)

Stage name of Alfredo Kraus Trujillo, Spanish tenor. He made his debut in 1956 as the Duke of Mantua (*Rigoletto*) at the Cairo Opera House. In the same year he appeared at La Fenice in Venice (Malipiero's *Passione* and Verdi's *La traviata*) and then in a number of other Italian opera houses. In 1959 he sang with Joan Sutherland in *Lucia di Lammermoor* at Covent Garden, a performance which launched him on a particularly brilliant international career, including appearances at La Scala (*Falstaff*, 1961), Lyric Opera of Chicago (*L'elisir d'amore*, 1963), the Metropolitan Opera, New York (*Rigoletto* and *Don Giovanni*, 1965) and the Salzburg Festival (*Don Giovanni*, 1968). This career, distinguished by Kraus's excellent technique, refinement and style, continued into the 1990s with performances of some of his charismatic roles, notably Werther and Des Grieux in Massenet's operas.

KRAUSE, TOM

(Helsinki 1934)

Finnish bass-baritone. He studied music at the Vienna Academy of Music (1956–59) and made his first public appearance in a concert in Helsinki (1957). His career as an opera singer began in 1958, first with the Berlin State Opera and then in Hamburg. In 1962 he made his debut at Bayreuth in *Lohengrin* and a year later sang the role of the Count in Richard Strauss's *Capriccio* at Glyndebourne. In 1967 he appeared for the first time in the United States with the Metropolitan Opera, New York (*Le nozze di Figaro*) and then in Chicago and San Francisco. A regular guest artist at the Salzburg Festival (since 1968), Krause established his reputation on the strength of an agreeable, well-modulated voice with a soft delivery and an excellent style in singing recitatives.

KRAUSS, CLEMENS

(Vienna 1893–Mexico City 1954)

Austrian conductor. He studied music at the Conservatory in Vienna, graduating in 1912. He made his debut in Riga and then went on to conduct in Nuremberg (1915–16), Stettin (1916–21) and Graz (1921–22). From 1922 onwards he conducted at the Vienna Staats-

Above: An 1897 poster for *Khovanshchina*.

Right: The Spanish tenor Alfredo Kraus.

oper, subsequently becoming music director in Frankfurt (1924–29), Berlin (1935–36) and Munich (1937–44). He was a distinguished interpreter of Mozart, Wagner and Richard Strauss, conducting the first performances of Strauss's *Arabella* in 1933, *Friedenstag* in 1938, *Capriccio* (of which he also wrote the libretto) in 1942 and *Die Liebe der Danae* in 1952. He also conducted the Viennese premiere of Berg's *Wozzeck* (1930).

KRENEK, ERNST

(Vienna 1900–Palm Springs 1991)
Austrian composer. He was a pupil of Franz Schreker at the Vienna Academy of Music (1916–20) and at the Berlin Hochschule für Musik. Krenek became famous for his opera *Jonny spielt auf* in 1927. He settled in Vienna in 1928 and began a prolific career as a composer. In 1937 he emigrated to the United States, taking American citizenship in 1945, and developed a busy career as a teacher. His operatic output includes *Leben des Orest* (Life of Orestes), 1930, *Karl V*, 1938, and *Der Zauberspiegel* (The Magic Mirror), 1966.

KRENN, WERNER

(Vienna 1943)
Austrian tenor. He studied bassoon and began his career in music with the Vienna Symphony Orchestra, at the same time taking singing lessons with Elisabeth Rado in Vienna. He made his debut in 1966 at the Berlin Festival in Purcell's *The Fairy Queen*. In 1967 he appeared for the first time in Salzburg and went on to sing in Aix-en-Provence (*Don Giovanni*, 1969), at the Vienna Staatsoper and a number of other music venues. Krenn is an admired interpreter of Mozart as well as of the concert and oratorio repertoire. He made fine recordings of Mozart's *La clemenza di Tito* (1967) and *Don Giovanni* (1969).

KRIPS, JOSEF

(Vienna 1902–Geneva 1974)
Austrian conductor. He studied in Vienna and embarked on a career as a violinist at the Volksoper (1918–21). He began conducting at the opera house in Aussig (1924–25), from where he went on to Dortmund (1925–26) before becoming music director in Karlsruhe (1926–33). From 1933 onwards, he appeared regularly at the Vienna Staatsoper, and from 1947 he was often guest conductor at the Salzburg Festival. He conducted the London Symphony Orchestra (1950–54), the Buffalo Symphony Orchestra (1954–63), the San Francisco (1963–70) and the Vienna Symphony (1970–73) as well as working with a number of other leading orchestras and at international opera houses. Famous for his interpretations of Mozart, Krips concentrated particularly on operas from the German repertoire, including an important revival of Wagner's *Rienzi* at the Bayreuth Festival (1960).

KRÓL ROGER

(King Roger)
Opera in three acts by Karol Szymanowski (1882–1937), to a libretto by the composer and Jaroslaw Iwaszkiewicz. First performance: Warsaw, Grand Theater, 19 June 1926.

The action takes place in Palermo, Sicily, in the twelfth century. A solemn mass is being held in the cathedral. King Roger II (baritone) arrives and is exhorted by the church authorities to condemn a Shepherd who has been preaching heresy. But when the Shepherd (tenor) appears, the King and his wife, Roksana (soprano), are impressed by the young man and invite him to their palace that evening. The second act takes place at the palace, where the Shepherd's charismatic preaching exerts a hypnotic effect on all except the King, who does not follow when Roksana and the courtiers go off with the stranger. Despite his own rational reservations, however, Roger eventually leaves to find his wife. In the third act, he reaches an ancient amphitheater where the new converts have performed rituals. Roksana appears, and the two start a sacrificial fire, in whose light the Shepherd shows himself as Dionysus, the classical god of beauty and sensual abandon. Other followers join Roksana in the form of Greek Maenads. When Dionysus leads them off, Roger remains alone to hail the rising sun, feeling an overwhelming sense of liberation and exaltation.

Composed between 1920 and 1924, *Król*

Above: Alfredo Kraus in *Werther* by Massenet.

Left: The Finnish bass-baritone Tom Krause.

Roger was inspired by an anonymous German poem from the middle of the twelfth century. Szymanowski bathes the music in an atmosphere that combines unreal elements and motifs which have the aura of being pagan yet purified by religious feeling. In this respect, the first act of the opera, set in the cathedral, is the most successful.

KUBELIK, RAFAEL

(Bychory 1914)

Czech conductor, naturalized Swiss. The son of violinist Jan Kubelik, he studied composition and conducting at the Prague Conservatoire. He made his debut in 1934 with the Czech Philharmonic, which he continued to conduct until 1948. Kubelik was music director of the Brno Opera (1939–41). He went on to appear with the Chicago Symphony (1950–53), held the post of artistic director at Covent Garden (1955–58) and conducted the Bavarian Radio Orchestra (1961–79). During the 1973–74 season, he served as music director at the Metropolitan Opera, New York, where he conducted the company's first production of *Les Troyens*. In 1985 he retired from conducting for health reasons. In the opera house, Kubelik gave particularly outstanding performances (which he also recorded) of Hindemith's *Mathis der Maler* (1979), Pfitzner's *Palestrina* (1973), Verdi's *Rigoletto* (1971) and Weber's *Der Freischütz* (1980).

KUBIAK, TERESA

(Lódz 1937)

Polish soprano, whose original name was Woytaszek. After studying music at the Conservatory in Lódz, she made her debut at the theater in that city in 1967 as Micaela in Bizet's *Carmen*. After joining the permanent company of the Warsaw Opera, she embarked on a brilliant international career: this led to appearances first at the main opera houses of Europe and then in the United States, in Chicago, Houston, San Francisco and above all with the Metropolitan Opera in New York. Kubiak appeared there from 1973, making her debut as Lisa in Tchaikovsky's *Queen of Spades*, and sang from a wide-ranging repertoire including operas by Wagner (*Tannhäuser*), Puccini (*Tosca*, *Il tabarro*, etc.), Janáček (*Jenůfa*) and numerous others.

KUHLMANN, KATHLEEN

(San Francisco 1950)

American mezzo-soprano. After studying music, she made her debut as Maddalena (*Rigoletto*) with Lyric Opera of Chicago (1979). By the following year she was singing the role of Meg (*Falstaff*) at La Scala, Milan. Also in Italy, she sang at the Teatro Regio in Parma in *Il barbiere di Siviglia* (1983), *Orfeo ed Euridice* (1987) and *La donna del lago* (1989), and at the Teatro San Carlo in Naples in Rossini's *Semiramide* with Montserrat Caballé (1987). Her outstanding qualities as a *bel canto* singer, combined with a fine timbre and consistency of delivery, have also been displayed in other Rossini operas, such as *Tancredi* and *La Cenerentola*, as well as in Vivaldi's *Orlando Furioso* (San Francisco 1990), in which she sang the role of Alcina in a cast which also included Marilyn Horne.

KUHN, GUSTAV

(Turrach 1947)

Austrian conductor. He began his music studies at the Salzburg Mozarteum (from 1964), and completed his training as a conductor with Bruno Maderna and Herbert von Karajan, and under Hans Swarowsky at the Vienna Musikhochschule. In 1970 he began his conducting career in Istanbul, continuing in Enschede (Netherlands) and Dortmund (1975–77). From the beginning of the 1980s, Kuhn appeared at leading international opera houses, where he combined conducting with opera production.

KUNDLAK, JOSEF

(Bratislava 1956)

Polish tenor, born in Slovakia. He studied at the Conservatory in his native city and completed his training at the European Opera Center in Belgium. In 1983 he joined the resident company of the Pressburg State Opera, with whom he has often toured. After winning numerous singing competitions, including the Luciano Pavarotti (1985) in Philadelphia, he began his international career by appearing at Bologna's Teatro Comunale in *L'elisir d'amore* in 1987, with further performances at La Scala, Milan, in *Così fan tutte* in 1989 and *Die Meistersinger von Nürnberg* in 1990, and in 1991 at the Donizetti Festival in *Elisabetta al castello di Kenilworth*, the Teatro San Carlo in Naples and the Bayerische Staatsoper in Munich.

KUNZ, ERICH

(Vienna 1909)

Austrian bass-baritone. He made his opera debut in Troppau in 1933 in Mozart's *Die Entführung aus dem Serail* (The Seraglio). He went on to appear at opera houses throughout the German provinces before joining the resident company of the Vienna Staatsoper in 1941. Kunz sang at the Glyndebourne Festival (1935) as well as Salzburg and Bayreuth. Despite limited vocal resources, he was an intelligent, effective onstage performer, particularly in comic roles in Mozart, Richard Strauss (*Ariadne auf Naxos*) and Wagner (*Die Meistersinger von Nürnberg*).

Above: The Polish tenor Jozef Kundlak in a scene from *Farnace*.

Right: The Czech conductor Rafael Kubelik

L

LABORINTUS II

Scenic opera by Luciano Berio (b. 1925) for chamber orchestra, electronic music, one contralto voice, two soprano voices; spoken text taken from passages from Dante's La Vita Nuova, Il Convivio *and* La Divina Commedia *and from writings by T.S. Eliot, Ezra Pound, Edoardo Sanguineti, biblical texts etc. Composed between 1963 and 1965 to a commission by ORTF to mark the 700th anniversary of Dante's birth.*

In this opera, using that word in its broadest sense, the composer rejects not only the traditional elements that make up the conventional opera (singing, music, scenic action, etc.) but also the traditional structuring of the text and its purpose. As Berio himself wrote: "*Laborintus II* is a scenic opera and may be treated as a 'performance', like a story, an allegory, a document, a dance etc. It can therefore be performed at school, in a theater, on television, in the open air, etc." This is thus an "open work", the fruition of which is not objective and not pre-determined by the composer. It is, rather, extremely subjective and influenced by the spectator as well as by conductor and the producer. Structurally speaking, *Laborintus II*, which takes its name from a collection of poems by Edoardo Sanguineti called *Laborintus*, is a montage of different "sound materials" which, by being juxtaposed not continuously but sporadically, generate a comprehensive challenge to formal structures by the drastic ways in which it breaks away from the genre of theater music. The choice of literary texts is not a random one and reveals the refined artificiality of the music by skilfully emphasizing it.

LADY MACBETH OF THE MTSENSK DISTRICT, OR KATERINA ISMAILOVA

See *Ledi Makbet Mtsenskova Uezda*

LAFONT, JEAN-PHILIPPE

(Toulouse 1951)

French baritone. He began his music studies in Toulouse, and then went on to the Opéra-Studio in Paris, where he made his debut in 1974 as Papageno in Mozart's *Die Zauberflöte* (The Magic Flute). He continued in Mozart, singing *Così fan tutte* in Toulouse and *Le nozze di Figaro* in Strasbourg. With appearances in the major Parisian opera houses, as well as in leading theaters and festivals in the French- and German-speaking countries of Europe, Lafont has performed from a vast and versatile repertoire including numerous French opera roles as well as operas by Rossini, Verdi and Puccini. He has recorded Rameau's *Les Boréades* (1981), Adam's *Le postillon de Longjumeau* (1986) and Auber's *La muette de Portici* (1986).

LAKES, GARY

(Woodward, Oklahoma 1950)

American tenor. He graduated from Southern Methodist University in Dallas and went on to study with William Eddy at the University of Southern California. After establishing a name for himself in a number of important singing competitions, he made his debut in Seattle (1981) in Wagner's *Das Rheingold.* Contracts followed in rapid succession in Mexico City (1983), at Covent Garden (1985), in Stuttgart and at the Metropolitan Opera, New York, where he made his debut in 1986 and has appeared regularly, mainly in Wagner roles (Siegmund, Erik, etc.). He has also sung Dimitri in *Boris Godunov*, Bacchus in *Ariadne auf Naxos*, Floristan in *Fidelio* and Samson in *Samson et Dalila*. He sang the role of Siegmund (*Die Walküre*) in James Levine's recording of Wagner's *Ring*.

Poster for *Lakmé* by Delibes.

LAKI, KRISZTINA

(Erd 1944)

Hungarian soprano. After studying at the Bartók Conservatory in Budapest, she made her debut as Gilda in *Rigoletto* in Berne, where she joined the resident opera company (1971–74). She subsequently appeared as a member of the Düsseldorf Deutsche Oper am Rhein (1974–79) before embarking on an international career which took her to Glyndebourne (1979), Salzburg (1980), Covent Garden, Munich and other major venues. In the early 1990s, Laki sang with the permanent companies of the Cologne and Stuttgart Operas. Renowned for her performances of Mozart and Richard Strauss, she has also drawn on a wide-ranging concert repertoire. She recorded von Einem's *Dantons Tod* (Danton's Death) in 1983, Paisiello's *Il barbiere di Siviglia* in 1984, Mozart's *Der Schauspieldirektor* (The Impresario) in 1986 and Mysliveček's *Il Bellerofonte* in 1987.

LAKMÉ

Opera in three acts by Léo Delibes (1836–1891), to a libretto by Edmond Gondinet and Philippe Gille based on Pierre Loti's Le mariage de Loti. *First performance: Paris, Théâtre de l'Opéra-Comique, 14 April 1883.*

The action takes place in India around the middle of the nineteenth century. A British officer, Gérald (tenor), gains entry to the house of the Brahmin Nilakanha (bass), curious about its mysterious atmosphere and by Lakmé (soprano), the Brahmin's daughter, who is famed for her beauty. Lakmé herself appears. Her allure makes a deep impression on Gérald, and she too is much affected by their meeting. Nilakanha arrives, and Gérald rushes away. When the Brahmin realizes that the sanctity of his house has been violated by a stranger, he vows revenge. The next day Nilakanha persuades Lakmé to sing in a public square, convinced that her voice and presence will compel the stranger to reveal himself. This is indeed what happens. Left alone with Gérald, Lakmé pleads with him to run away with her to a safe place, but Gérald refuses, because he does not want to be a deserter from the army. Shortly after this, during a procession, Nilakanha comes up to Gérald and stabs him. The wound is not serious, however, and Lakmé has Gérald taken to a hut in the forest where she can look after him. While she is fetching water from a spring with miraculous properties, Frédéric (baritone), a friend of Gérald's who has managed to trace him, arrives and urges him to return to the garrison. When Lakmé comes back, she realizes Gérald is wracked with doubt as to whether he should choose his duty or his love for her. In despair, Lakmé picks a leaf from a poisonous plant and swallows it. But Gérald has overcome his uncertainty and drinks from the cup of the spring-water of eternal love. Nilakanha rushes in, but Lakmé stays her father's hand by revealing to him that Gérald has now become sanctified by drinking with her from the cup. Then Lakmé dies in her beloved's arms.

Lakmé, Delibes' most famous opera, was an enormous success, with 200 performances at the Opéra-Comique in 1895, reaching a total of 1,000 in 1931. To this day *Lakmé* continues to be staged by the leading international opera houses. Its celebrated "Bell Song" has remained firmly established in the *coloratura* soprano repertoire.

LALLI, DOMENICO

(Naples 1679–Venice 1741)

Alias of Niccolò Sebastiano Biancardi, Italian poet and librettist. He left Naples in 1706 after being accused of theft, changed his name and wandered through Italy before settling in Venice, where he began a busy literary career. While in Venice he enjoyed the patronage of Apostolo Zeno and the friendship of Pietro Metastasio and Carlo Goldoni. He was director of the Teatro San Samuele (1735) and the Teatro San Giovanni Crisostomo (1737). He was also poet at the Court of the Elector of Bavaria (1727–40). He wrote many libretti for Vivaldi (*Ottone in villa*), Albinoni, Alessandro Scarlatti (*Il Tigrane*), Galuppi, Hasse and others.

LALO, ÉDOUARD VICTOR ANTOINE

(Lille 1823–Paris 1892)

French composer. Initially a pupil at the Lille Conservatoire, he continued his music studies at the Conservatoire in Paris and privately with Julius Schulhoff and J-E. Crèvecoeur. He began his career in music as a violinist and did not establish his reputation as a composer until after 1870, when he scored a first success with his *Symphonie espagnole* (1875). He wrote only three operas, one of which, *Fiesque* (1886), was never staged, while another, *La Jacquerie* (1895) was left unfinished. *Le roi d'Ys* (1888) was well received, however, and continues to be performed to this day.

LANGRIDGE, PHILIP

(Hawkhurst, Kent 1939)

British tenor. He studied violin at the Royal Academy of Music and started singing lessons in 1962, first with Bruce Boyce and then with Celia Bizoni. He made his debut in 1964 at Glyndebourne and has performed there on a number of occasions, principally in Mozart roles. He has also sung with the English National Opera and at Covent Garden, and has made guest appearances at numerous international opera houses and music venues, including Aix-en-Provence (1976), the Metropolitan Opera, New York, La Scala and the Vienna Staatsoper. Langridge draws on an extremely wide repertoire, from the baroque to contemporary music, and has taken part in a number of world premieres. He has been equally prolific as a recording artist in operas ranging from Handel and Rameau to twentieth-century works (Holst, Ravel, Berg, Stravinsky and Schoenberg).

Above: The French composer Edouard Lalo.

Right: The Italian tenor Vincenzo La Scola

LA SCOLA, VINCENZO

(Palermo 1958)

Italian tenor. After winning a number of singing competitions, he made his debut in Parma in 1983 as Ernesto in Donizetti's *Don Pasquale*. In 1985 he had a great success in the role of Nemorino (*L'elisir d'amore*) in Brussels, followed by further acclaimed performances in Paris in *Gianni Schicchi* and *La fille du régiment* in 1987–88. La Scola has appeared regularly at major Italian opera houses and made his debut at La Scala, Milan in 1988 (*L'elisir d'amore*), returning there in 1991 to sing in *La traviata* and in 1992 for *Lucia di Lammermoor*. He has recorded Bellini's *Beatrice di Tenda*, Mascagni's *Le maschere*, and Verdi's *Rigoletto* with Riccardo Muti conducting. He is regarded as one of the finest lyric tenors of the new generation.

LATHAM-KOENIG, JAN

(London 1953)

British conductor. He began his career in music as a pianist but always had a strong interest in conducting, to which he devoted his energies from 1981 onwards. His first appearances were in Denmark and Sweden, and he has been a regular guest conductor with leading international orchestras, including the Los Angeles Philharmonic, the Royal Philharmonic and the Orchestre Philharmonique de Radio France. Much of Latham-Koenig's career has been concentrated on opera, especially the Italian repertoire. He has conducted important revivals of operas by Donizetti – *Il diluvio universale* (Genoa, 1985), *Poliuto* (Rome, 1989) and *Elisabetta al castello di Kenilworth* (Bergamo, 1989) – as well as premiere productions of Bussotti's *Fedra* (Rome, 1988) and *L'ispirazione* (Florence, 1988). He has been guest conductor at the Teatro dell'Opera in Rome and at the Vienna Staatsoper (from 1989) and has recorded operas of Kurt Weill.

LATTUADA, FELICE

(Caselle di Morimondo, Milan 1882–Milan 1962)

Italian composer. Initially self-taught, he subsequently attended the Conservatorio in Milan where he graduated in 1912. He was director of the Civica Scuola di Musica in Milan from 1985 until his death. His operas include *La tempesta* (1922), *Le preziose ridicole* (1929) and *Don Giovanni* (1929).

LAUBENTHAL, HORST

(Eisfeld 1939)

Stage name of Horst Neumann, German tenor. After studying music in Munich he became the only pupil of the tenor Rudolf Laubenthal (1886–1972), whose surname he adopted. He appeared for the first time at the Würzburg Mozart Festival as Don Ottavio (*Don Giovanni*) in 1967. The following year he joined the resident company of the Stuttgart Opera, with which he embarked on a brilliant and increasingly international career. An admired Mozart performer, Laubenthal subsequently added Wagner operas to his repertoire. In 1988 he took part in the world premiere recording of Franz Schmidt's *Notre-Dame*.

LAURI-VOLPI, GIACOMO

(Lanuvio, Rome 1892–Valencia 1979)

Stage name of Giacomo Volpi, Italian tenor. He studied at the Accademia Nazionale di Santa Cecilia in Rome with Antonio Cotogni and made his debut in Viterbo with *I puritani* and *Rigoletto* in 1919. The following year he had a sensational success in Massenet's *Manon* at the Teatro Costanzi in Rome. This was immediately followed by appearances at Buenos Aires and Madrid, and with La Scala, Milan (1922), the Metropolitan Opera, New York (1923), and other major international opera houses until 1959. Lauri-Volpi was a romantic tenor in both phrasing and temperament, and the boldness of his range, as well as his ringing tone and softness of delivery, enabled him to triumph in *Il trovatore*, *Gli Ugonotti*, *Aida*, *Turandot*, etc. His only recordings of complete operas (*Luisa Miller*, *Les Huguenots*, *Il trovatore*, *La bohème*) date from the early 1950s, when Lauri-Volpi was nearly 60 years old, and are not of the same standard as the performances he gave in his finest years.

LEAR

Opera in two parts by Aribert Reimann (b. 1936), to a libretto by Claus Henneberg, from Shakespeare's tragedy King Lear. *First performance: Munich, Bayerische Staatsoper, 9 July 1978.*

With the duties of a monarch weighing heavily upon him, King Lear (baritone) has decided to divide his kingdom between his three daughters, Goneril (dramatic soprano), Regan (soprano) and Cordelia (soprano). Whichever daughter can give him the finest demonstration of her love for him will receive the largest part of the realm. Goneril and Regan vie with one another to say what devoted daughters they are, whereas Cordelia, who finds it natural that she should love her father, remains silent. Furious at this, Lear duly parcels out the kingdom between Goneril and Regan and their respective husbands, the Duke of Albany (baritone) and the Duke of Cornwall (tenor), while Cordelia leaves the country to be the wife of the King of France (bass-baritone), who loves her for her honesty and not for the inheritance she might have received. Goneril and Regan lose no time in devising schemes to rid themselves of their father as quickly as possible, behaving towards him with increasingly ferocious cruelty as he gradually goes out of his mind. The King of France's army comes to Lear's assistance. Cordelia comforts her father and promises him a peaceful old age, reassuring him too about the future of his kingdom, presently ravaged by the bitter war between Edmund (tenor) and Edgar (countertenor), sons of the Duke of Gloucester (bass-baritone). But Lear and Cordelia are taken prisoner by Edmund, who is in league with Regan. Then Edgar appears and challenges his step-brother to a duel, in which Edmund is killed. Regan dies with him as a result of being given poison by her sister. Goneril then takes her own life as Lear enters, carrying the body of Cordelia (put to death by Edmund) in his arms. For the old King such sorrow is impossible to bear, and, by now completely mad, he falls dead to the ground.

Henneberg's libretto is a faithful transposition of Shakespeare's play, for which Reimann has succeeded in composing a complete musical equivalent emphasizing every moment of the story's tragic events. The solo roles were created for the talents of singers of such caliber as the baritone Dietrich Fischer-Dieskau, who sang Lear. The opera was staged at the Munich Festival in a magnificent production by Jean-Pierre Ponnelle and scored an extraordinary success. *Lear* is one of the greatest contemporary German operas.

LEAR, EVELYN

(Brooklyn 1928)

American soprano. She studied singing at the Juilliard School in New York and then in Berlin, where she made her debut in 1959 in *Ariadne auf Naxos*. In the same year she made her concert debut in London and also sang the Composer in *Ariadne auf Naxos* at the Deutsche Oper Berlin. A regular guest artiste at the opera houses of Munich, Vienna (*Lulu*, 1962), Salzburg and Covent Garden, Lear is particularly remembered for her performances as Marie (*Wozzeck*) and Lulu (*Lulu*) in Berg's operas, which she recorded

Above: Philip Langridge, British tenor, in a scene from *Boris Godunov*.

Left: Giacomo Lauri-Volpi, Italian tenor in the role of Alfredo (*La Traviata*).

in 1964 and 1967, displaying great gifts both as a singer and as an actress. She married the baritone Thomas Stewart.

LEDI MAKBET MTSENSKOVO UEZDA

(Lady Macbeth of the Mtsensk District or Katerina Ismailova)

Opera in four acts by Dmitry Dmitrievich Shostakovich (1906–75), to the libretto by the composer and Alexander Preis, based on the story by Leskov. First performance: Leningrad, Maly Theater, 22 January 1934.

The wealthy merchant Zinovi Borisovich Ismailov (tenor) takes as his wife Katerina (soprano), who is young and beautiful but comes to him with no dowry. Katerina does not love her husband and, after the wedding, finds herself beset by the tedium of the Ismailov household, where she also has to cope with her father-in-law Boris (bass), a domestic tyrant. Katerina looks for an escape through her passion for Sergei (tenor), her husband's new assistant. But Boris discovers their intrigue and orders that Sergei be flogged by his workmates. To have her revenge, Katerina poisons her father-in-law and then, not yet satisfied, also kills her husband and conceals the corpse with her lover's help. The couple decide to marry, but their wedding is interrupted by the arrival of the police after the discovery of Zinovi's body. While the guilty pair are on their way to labour camps in Siberia, Sergei, now tired of Katerina's love, which has ruined his life, turns his attention to a young female prisoner, Sonyetka (mezzo-soprano). Katerina throws her rival into a lake before following her to meet the same fate.

This was Shostakovich's second and last opera, composed between 1930 and 1932. The premiere and subsequent performances brought the composer success but this was abruptly ended in 1936 in Moscow when the censors banned the work. It was re-staged in Moscow on 8 January 1963 in a new version, entitled *Katerina Ismailova*, in part an attempt to tone down the harshness of the original.

LEECH, RICHARD

(Hollywood 1956)

American tenor. He studied music at Binghamton, New York. He began singing as a baritone but became a tenor and made his debut at the age of 21 in a student production of Offenbach's *Les contes d'Hoffmann*. After being among the winners of the Enrico Caruso Prize in Milan in 1980, Leech embarked on a career in the United States, where he appeared in a number of cities, including Cincinnati, Baltimore, and Pittsburgh. In 1984 he appeared for the first time with New York City Opera and at Carnegie Hall as Rodolfo in *La bohème*, one of his most acclaimed roles. In 1987 he established his reputation at the Deutsche Oper Berlin singing Raoul in Meyerbeer's *Les Huguenots*. In the years that followed, he returned to sing in Berlin (*L'elisir d'amore* and *Lucia di Lammermoor*, 1988–89), as well as at the Vienna Staatsoper (*Rigoletto*), La Scala, Milan (*Madama Butterfly*, 1990; *La bohème*, 1991) and from 1989 at the Metropolitan Opera, New York, where his debut was in *La bohème* and he went on to appear in *Faust* (1990) and *Un ballo in maschera* (1992). He has sung at numerous other international opera houses and concert halls, and his outstandingly beautiful lyric tenor voice and equally remarkable stage presence have made him one of the most highly acclaimed American tenors.

LEGGENDA DI SAKÚNTALA, LA

(The Legend of Sakuntala)

Opera in three acts by Franco Alfano (1876–1954), to the composer's own libretto. First performance: Bologna, Teatro Comunale, 10 December 1921.

The action takes place in India at an unspecified time. During a hunting party, the King (tenor) meets a beautiful young woman, Sakúntala (soprano), who is the daughter of a wood-nymph and has been brought up by the hermit Kanva (bass). At first Sakúntala resists but finally yields to the young King's passionate advances. Shortly after this, a pilgrim, Durvasas (bass), knocks at the door of the hermitage, yet no one opens it so as not to violate the rule decreeing that only Sakúntala herself should do so. But the

A scene from *Lady Macbeth of the Mtsensk District* by Shostakovich in a production at the Teatro Verdi, Trieste.

young woman is so taken up with her love that she does not hear the pilgrim knocking. In a fury, he curses her and prophesies that when the King meets her again, he will no longer remember who she is, unless Sakúntala shows him the ring he had given her. Sakúntala is expecting a child, so two hermits accompany her to the King's court. But the prophecy is fulfilled when the King loses his memory. In vain does Sakúntala remind him of their love. She wants to show him the ring but cannot find it. In despair, Sakúntala leaves. Shortly after this, the palace guards bring in a fisherman (tenor) who has found a jewel on the river-bank. It is Sakúntala's ring. When he sees it, the King's memory is restored and he calls for the young woman to be brought back. But by now Sakúntala has already thrown herself into the wood-nymphs' pond and vanished in a cloud of fire. Yet her voice can still be heard comforting her beloved and telling him that the child they are expecting is destined to become a great ruler.

La leggenda di Sakúntala is considered one of Alfano's most successful operatic achievements. The composer encountered several difficulties in abridging the original text of the Indian legend on which the libretto is based. During the Second World War, the only copy of the complete score was destroyed, and Alfano had to reconstruct it from a version he had made for voice and piano. The revised work was staged at the Teatro dell'Opera in Rome in 1952 under the title *Sakúntala*. There is a wealth of chromatic harmony in this score, whereas its orchestration and general technique reveal Alfano's search for new expressive means and a more modern symphonic style.

LEINSDORF, ERICH

(Vienna 1912)

Professional name of Erich Landauer, Austrian conductor, naturalized American. A pupil of the University and State Academy in Vienna (1931–33), he made his debut in 1933 with the Vienna State Academy Orchestra. From 1934 to 1937 he was assistant to Bruno Walter and Arturo Toscanini in Salzburg and New York. Under contract to the Metropolitan Opera, he was first a répétiteur and then assistant conductor there, and from 1939 onwards he was in charge of the German section of the repertoire. He conducted the orchestras of Cleveland (1943–46), Rochester (1947–56) and Boston (1962–69). From 1969 he conducted in many opera houses and concert halls across Europe, including the Bayreuth Festival (1972). He made a number of opera recordings, including *Madama Butterfly* (1958), *Macbeth* (1958), *Ariadne auf Naxos* (1960), *Salome* (1968), *Aida* (1970) and *Il tabarro* (1970).

LEITNER, FERDINAND

(Berlin 1912)

German conductor. A pupil of Artur Schnabel and Franz Schreker, he went on to train as a conductor with Karl Muck. He embarked on his conducting career in 1943 in Berlin, subsequently conducting in Hanover (1945–46), Munich (1946–47) and Stuttgart (1947). In 1951 he was joint conductor with Igor Stravinsky for the world premiere of *The Rake's Progress* in Venice. From 1956 he conducted at the Teatro Colón in Buenos Aires, held music director posts at the Zurich Opera (1969–84) and the Residentie Orchester in The Hague (1976–80), and from 1988 he was principal guest conductor of the Italian Radio and Television Symphony Orchestra in Turin. A renowned opera conductor, Leitner was in charge of the first recordings of Carl Orff's *Antigonae* (1961) and Busoni's *Doktor Faust*.

LEONCAVALLO, RUGGERO

(Naples 1857–Montecatini 1919)

Italian composer. He studied music at the Conservatorio in Naples from 1866. He started courses in law in Bologna but also attended the Italian poet Giosuè Carducci's literature classes, graduating with a degree in letters in 1878. There followed a fairly adventurous time in his life, during which he travelled between Egypt, Marseilles and Paris. Thanks to the baritone Victor Maurel, he was then able to meet the music publishers Ricordi and Sonzogno. The success of Mascagni's *Cavalleria rusticana* inspired Leoncavallo, and he wrote *I pagliacci* within the space of five months. The opera was staged in 1892 and was a sensational success. Leoncavallo's subsequent operas, *I Medici* (1893), *Chatterton* (1896), *La bohème* (1897), which was overshadowed by Puccini's opera of the same name produced the previous year, *Zazà* (1900) and *Edipo re* (1920), were enthusiastically received at first but soon disappeared as none managed to achieve the dramatic and melodic immediacy of *I pagliacci*.

LEONI, FRANCO

(Milan 1864–London 1949)

Italian composer. He studied at the Conservatorio in Milan and in 1892 moved to England, where he taught singing and pursued a career as a conductor until 1917. He then divided his time between France and Italy before settling permanently in England, where in 1905 he scored a notable success with his opera *L'oracolo*. Leoni's output was almost exclusively operatic, including *Raggio di luna* (1890), *Rip van Winkle* (1897), *Ib and Little Christina* (1901), *Tzigana* (1910), *Francesca da Rimini* (1914) and *Le baruffe chiozzotte* (1920).

Above: The Italian composer Ruggero Leoncavallo.

Left: The Austrian conductor Erich Leinsdorf.

LEONORA, OSSIA L'AMOR CONIUGALE

(Leonora, or Conjugal Love)

Opera in two acts by Ferdinando Paër (1771–1839), to a libretto by Giovanni Schmidt, from the original French version by Jean Nicolas Boully. First performance: Dresden, Court Theater, 3 October 1804.

In a prison near Seville, Giachino (bass), the prison warder, tries to convince Marcellina (soprano), daughter of the jailer Rocco (bass), to accept his love. But Marcellina rejects him, because she is in love with Fedele, her father's assistant. Marcellina does not realize that young Fedele is really Leonora (soprano) in disguise, the wife of Florestano (tenor), who has been secretly imprisoned by the governor Pizzarro (baritone). On hearing the announcement of an imminent inspection by Don Fernando (baritone), Minister and Spanish grandee, Pizzarro resolves to have Florestano killed. Leonora manages to save her husband's life, and Pizzarro, now exposed, is imprisoned in Florestano's place. The opera ends in general rejoicing. Marcellina, saddened at having lost her Fedele, consoles herself by accepting a marriage proposal from Giachino.

Staged a year earlier than Beethoven's *Fidelio*, on the same subject, Paër's *Leonora* was an enormous success. Naturally any comparison with Beethoven's work is unfair to Paër, whose score is well-balanced in dramatic terms, the music perfectly matching the action. The most successfully characterized roles are those of Leonora and Marcellina, the latter much more important than Marzelline (her equivalent) is in *Fidelio*.

LEONORE 40/45

Opera semiseria with a prologue and prelude and two acts by Rolf Liebermann (born 1910), to libretto by Heinrich Strobel. First performance: Basle, Stadttheater, 26 March 1952.

The story develops between 1939 and 1947 in France and Germany. During the prologue, Emile (baritone), a guardian angel living on earth, tells us that we are about to see a love story enacted, and that he will only intervene when needed by the participants. In 1939 Alfred (tenor), a German living with his father on the French border, is listening to Beethoven's *Fidelio* on the radio when the programme is interrupted to announce that the country is mobilizing for war: he must leave. In the house opposite, a Frenchwoman, Germaine (contralto), asks her daughter Yvette (soprano) for news of the political situation. Her husband had been killed in the First World War, and she declares that only through peace and goodwill will men be able to solve their problems. Yvette, on the other hand, is convinced that France is in the right, and she is excited by these events. Two years later, in occupied Paris, Yvette and Alfred meet at a concert. They get to know one another and fall in love. In August 1944, however, Alfred has to leave Paris with the retreating German army. Yvette wants to hide him in her house, but he refuses to allow her to run such a risk; they bid farewell as the people of France celebrate their liberation. At this point Emile appears, explaining that it is time for him to intervene in order that the story should have a happy ending. The war is over and Yvette has lost trace of her fiancé and is desperately searching for him. Emile approaches her and, to test her love, tells her that Alfred must be punished for his part in the German atrocities. Yvette defends him and eventually the angel leads her to Alfred, arranging for her to be taken on by the factory where he is employed. After a time, Yvette and Alfred decide to get married and present themselves before a tribunal that symbolizes the machinery of bureaucracy. The judges declare that it is impossible to arrange a marriage between two persons whose countries are enemies. At this point the guardian angel appears again: to the strains of *Fidelio*, he says that, like Leonora, the heroine of the Beethoven opera, Yvette has won love by her faith, and he joins the two young people in matrimony.

The opera received a mixed reception by both public and critics. It is the embodiment of Liebermann's liking for drama constructed on two levels: the realistic level and the surrealist-symbolic level. On the one hand the opera represents a condemnation of war and tyranny, and on the other it extols the new music, symbol of a renewed and free humanity.

The American conductor James Levine.

LEPPARD, RAYMOND

(London 1927)

British conductor and harpsichord player. He was a pupil of Hubert Middleton and Boris Ord at Cambridge University (1948–52) and made his debut at Wigmore Hall in London in 1952. He was a lecturer at Trinity College for about ten years, during which time he also appeared as a conductor at leading British music venues, including Covent Garden (from 1959) and Glyndebourne (from 1962), as well as with the English Chamber Orchestra and the BBC Northern Symphony Orchestra (1973–80). Particularly admired as an interpreter of the late seventeenth- and eighteenth-century repertoire, Leppard's achievement in this field has included important revivals (also preserved in recordings between 1968 and 1971) of Francesco Cavalli's operas *L'Ormindo* and *La Calisto* and operas by Monteverdi (*Orfeo*, *Il ritorno di Ulisse in patria*, etc.), Handel (*Ariodante*) and Rameau (*Dardanus*) and others. From 1984 to 1986 he was principal conductor of the St. Louis Symphony Orchestra.

LE SUEUR, JEAN-FRANCOIS

(Drucat-Plessiel, Abbeville 1760–Paris 1837)

French composer. He was a choirboy in Abbeville (1767) and Amiens (1774), subsequently becoming a chorus-master in Sées and at the Saint-Innocents church in Paris, the city where he completed his music studies. He also held posts as a chorus-master in Dijon, Le Mans, Tours and at Notre Dame in Paris (1786). From 1795 he was an inspector of teaching at the Paris Conservatoire, where he taught composition from 1818 to 1825 and where such famous composers as Gounod, Berloiz and Ambroise Thomas were students. He was also Court chorus-master (from 1804). His output as an opera composer includes *La caverne* (1793), *Paul et Virginie* (1794) and *Télémaque* (1796).

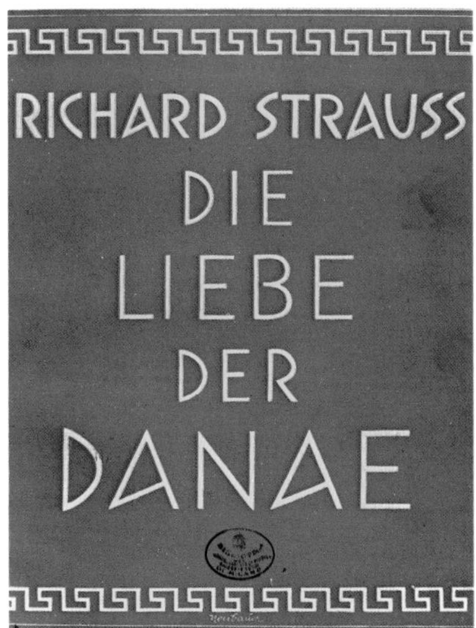

LEVINE, JAMES

(Cincinnati 1943)

American conductor and pianist. He studied with Walter Levine and at the Juilliard School in New York with Rosina Lhévinne and Jean Morel. After completing his training with Rudolf Serkin, Alfred Wallenstein, Max Rudolf and Fausto Cleva, Levine became assistant conductor of the Cleveland Orchestra at the age of 21, combining this responsibility with conducting and teaching at the Aspen Music School and Festival and at Meadow Brook. In 1970 in San Francisco he conducted *Tosca*, the opera in which he made his debut, the following year, with the Metropolitan Opera, New York, where much of Levine's career has been associated: he was principal conductor there from 1973 and music director from 1975, mainly conducting works from the Italian and German repertoires. Levine's career has also taken him to leading European concert halls and opera houses, including the Salzburg Festival, the Vienna Staatsoper and Bayreuth, where he conducted *Parsifal* in 1982, the centenary of the opera's premiere. A conductor of considerable artistic gifts, Levine made numerous recordings of operas including Mozart, Verdi, Puccini, Richard Strauss and Wagner.

LEWIS, HENRY

(Los Angeles 1932)

American conductor. He began his artistic career in 1948 as an instrumentalist, playing double-bass in the Los Angeles Philharmonic. He went on to found the Los Angeles Chamber Orchestra and at the same time held the post of assistant conductor of the Philharmonia Orchestra in Los Angeles (1961–65). He made his debut as a conductor in 1963, subsequently taking on the posts of music director of the Los Angeles Opera (1965–68) and the New Jersey Symphony (1968–75). Lewis also appeared as guest conductor at a number of American and European opera houses. He was married to the mezzo-soprano Marilyn Horne, whom he often conducted in concerts and operas as well as in performances on record of Massenet's *La Navarraise* (1974) and Meyerbeer's *Le prophète* (1976).

LIBUŠE

Festival opera in three acts by Bedřich Smetana (1824–1884), to a libretto by Joseph Wenzig. First performance: Prague, National Theater, 11 June 1881.

Bohemia is under the rule of the Princess Libuše (soprano), who is much loved and respected for her wisdom. A serious conflict breaks out between two young and powerful brothers over the division of their father's legacy, threatening to undermine national stability. Krasava (soprano), a young woman who is in love with Chrudós (bass), one of the two brothers, believes her love is not returned and so pretends to love the other brother, Stáhlav (tenor). This makes the discord between the brothers all the more bitter. Libuše's solution to the brothers' conflict is to quote ancient law, whereby the inheritance would be divided into equal parts. Chrudós, dissatisfied with this verdict, publicly insults the Princess by telling her that a woman cannot properly control the fortunes of a state. Libuše, offended by this, chooses for her husband a simple, wise man, Premysl (baritone). Meanwhile Krasava has confessed her true feelings to Chrudós and gets him to promise to make peace with his brother. In the presence of Libuše and her husband-to-be, the brothers are reconciled, while the people sing the praises of the wise Libuše. In a prophetic vision, the Princess then declares that "the Czech nation will never perish."

The first performance of *Libuše* coincided with the inauguration of the Prague National Theater and the marriage of Archduke Rudolf to Archduchess Stephanie. Smetana felt strongly about these events, and to this day the Czech nation sees *Libuše* as a hallowed opera, performed on all the great occasions in Czech life.

LIEBE DER DANAE, DIE

(The Love of Danae)

Opera in three acts by Richard Strauss (1864–1949), to a libretto by Joseph Gregor. First performance: Salzburg Festival, 14 August 1952.

Pollux (tenor), King of Eos, is burdened by debts and wants to marry his daughter Danae (soprano) to Midas (tenor), King of Lydia. Danae is visited in a dream by Jupiter (bass), who appears to her as golden rain, and she vows she will belong to the man who will be able to give her not only gold but also the pleasures of love. Disguised as the messenger Chrysopher, Midas tells Danae her suitor has arrived and accompanies her to the harbour to welcome him. Out of the ship

Top: A playbill for the opera *Die Liebe der Danae* by Richard Strauss.

Above: The British conductor Raymond Leppard.

steps Jupiter. Danae is dazzled and faints. Jupiter discovers that Midas loves Danae and curses him. In his ardour, Midas embraces Danae, changing her into a golden statue. Jupiter reappears, and Midas suggests that the choice between the two of them be left to the statue. Danae chooses Midas, whereupon the blood in her veins begins to flow again. Midas, now stripped of all power by Jupiter, reveals to Danae that he is reduced to poverty. Danae is nevertheless happy to be united with the man she loves. Jupiter wants to win Danae back and goes to see her, disguised as a tramp, but she is implacable and throws herself into the arms of her beloved Midas.

The virtuosity in *Die Liebe der Danae* and the orchestral splendour which Strauss lavished on the score are unable to conceal the longueurs and incongruities in an opera that has never become established in the repertoire. It nevertheless contains a moment of real beauty in the prelude to the third act when Jupiter tries for the last time to persuade Danae to return to him.

LIEBERMANN, ROLF

(Zurich 1910)

Swiss composer. He studied music first in Zurich and subsequently with Hermann Scherchen in Budapest. He completed his training with Wladimir Vogel, with whom he developed his use of 12-tone music. He scored a major success with his first opera, *Leonore 40/45* (1952), followed by *Penelope* (1954) and *Die Schule der Frauen* (School for Wives, 1957), inspired by Molière's *L'école des femmes*. Liebermann was artistic director of the Hamburg Staatsoper (1959–73) and of the Paris Opéra (1973–80). In 1987 he won great acclaim for the first performance of his opera *La forêt* at the Grand Théâtre in Geneva.

LIEBESVERBOT, ODER DIE NOVIZE VON PALERMO, DAS

(The Ban on Love, or The Novice of Palermo)

Opera in two acts by Richard Wagner (1813–1883), to the composer's own libretto based on Shakespeare's Measure for Measure. *First performance: Magdeburg, Stadttheater, 29 March 1836.*

Friedrich (baritone), governor of Sicily, takes advantage of the Duke's absence to impose a harsh regime on the life of the island. All entertainments are forbidden, and the death sentence is to be passed on anyone found guilty of committing adultery. The Sicilians laugh at the governor's new decrees until a young man, Claudio (tenor), is unjustly condemned to death for having broken the law. Isabella (soprano), a novice and the condemned man's sister, implores Friedrich to show clemency, but he will only do so on condition that she give herself to him. Isabella consents, but devises a plan whereby Marianna (soprano), Friedrich's rejected lover and herself a novice, will go to the governor in Isabella's place. The ruse is successful, and Friedrich's hypocritical behaviour is duly exposed for all to see. His own law rules that he should now be put to death. The Sicilians abolish this law and condemn the governor to march at the head of the Carnival procession and then wed Marianna. Isabella marries Luzio (tenor), a close friend of Claudio, who has always loved her.

The first performance of *Das Liebesverbot* was a failure. As a consequence, Wagner, together with a large number of colleagues (including Minna Planer, the actress who married him), moved from Magdeburg to Königsberg. Italian and French opera are the main influences on the style of this work.

LIFE FOR THE TSAR, A

(Ivan Susanin)

Opera in four acts and an epilogue by Mikhail Glinka (1804–1857), to a libretto by Georgy Rosen. First performance: St. Petersburg, Imperial Theater, 27 November 1836.

In the village of Domnin, the inhabitants are celebrating the Russians' victory over the Polish invasion forces. Among the Russian soldiers returning home in triumph is Bogdan Sobinin (tenor), who is greeted by Antonida (soprano), daughter of Ivan Susanin (bass). Susanin is worried: he still fears for Russia's safety and pleads with his daughter to put off her wedding for the time being. Then Sobinin announces that, to secure the peace, a new Tsar, Mikhail Romanov, has been elected. Susanin feels reassured and agrees to the wedding going ahead. Meanwhile the Poles have emerged from their defeat determined to strike back, and they decide to send a detachment of men to abduct the new Tsar. So while Susanin, Vanya (mezzo-soprano), a young orphan he has brought up, Antonida and Sobinin are praying to God to bless the forthcoming marriage with his protection, Polish soldiers burst in and force Susanin to take them to the Tsar's hide-out. Susanin pretends to do as he is told but manages covertly to instruct Vanya to warn the

Above: A scene from *Linda di Chamounix* by Gaetano Donizetti.

Right: The Argentinian tenor Luis Lima.

Tsar of this imminent threat while he tries to play for time by taking the Poles the wrong way. He bids farewell to his daughter and tells her not to delay her wedding if he does not return in time. At the Tsar's palace, Vanya tells the soldiers of the plot against the Tsar's life. Meanwhile, Susanin and the Poles have pitched camp for the night in a forest. Susanin realizes that his end is near, so, as dawn breaks, believing that now the Tsar must be safe, he reveals to the Poles that he has taken them the wrong way. The Poles realize they are lost, turn on Susanin and kill him. The opera ends in the Square of the Kremlin with the jubilant crowds hailing the Tsar and Russia's liberation from the invader.

The plot, based on the historical figure of Ivan Susanin who had given his life in 1612 to save Russia, had already been turned into an opera before, but Glinka's version gave it fresh status as a work which provided a link between the international musical culture and that of Russia. The first performance was received enthusiastically, although there were dissenting voices among those who wanted opera to remain Italian. A significant feature of the score is the use of the chorus, which represents an important stage in the development of Russian opera.

LIMA, LUIS

(Cordoba 1950)

Argentinian tenor. He began to study music in 1970 at the school of the Teatro Colón in Buenos Aires, and then won a scholarship which enabled him to complete his training at the Conservatory in Madrid. He won much praise in a number of important international singing competitions, making his debut in Lisbon in 1974 as Turiddu (*Cavalleria rusticana*). The first stage of his career centered on opera houses in Stuttgart, Hamburg, Munich and Berlin. In 1975 he made his debut at La Scala, Milan, and in 1978 at the Metropolitan Opera, New York, and gradually added further first appearances at the most prestigious international opera houses. Lima has great stage and vocal presence and is famous for his performances in *Don Carlos* and *Carmen*.

LINDA DI CHAMOUNIX

Opera in three acts by Gaetano Donizetti (1797–1848), to a libretto by Gaetano Rossi. First performance: Vienna, Kärntnertortheater, 19 May 1842.

The action takes place in France around the year 1670. The Marquis of Boisfleury (*buffo* baritone) is in love with Linda (soprano), daughter of Antonio (baritone) and Maddalena (soprano), poor country people of Chamounix. He promises to help this poor family, who are threatened with eviction, and to have Linda educated at his château. Shortly after this, Carlo (tenor), a young painter, comes to see Linda, with whom he is in love. Carlo is really the Viscount of Sirval, nephew of the Marquis, but he does not dare reveal his identity to Linda, because he fears his family will oppose his marrying a countrywoman. The village Prefect (bass), aware of the underlying motive in the Marquis's offer, advises Linda's parents to send the young woman away to Paris for a while, to stay with the Prefect's brother. The scene changes to Paris, where, as a result of the death of the Prefect's brother, Linda is staying with Carlo, who is waiting for permission from his mother to marry Linda. Antonio has also come to Paris and is trying to locate his daughter. When he sees her dressed in fine clothes, he spurns her, believing that she is now a kept woman, and treats her with contempt. At that moment, Pierotto (contralto), a young friend of Linda, brings news that the Viscount is about to marry a noblewoman. This is too much for Linda, and she becomes distraught. Some time later, the Viscount arrives, looking for Linda: he has rejected the marriage imposed on him by his mother and now wants to marry Linda. Then Linda appears, accompanied by Pierotto. She no longer recognizes anyone, but slowly, with a song he used to sing, the Viscount succeeds in restoring Linda to her former self. She feels alive again and, in this atmosphere of deep feelings and embraces, the opera comes to the happiest of endings.

Linda di Chamounix is the first of the operas composed by Donizetti for the Court in Vienna. Its success was such that the Emperor appointed him Court Composer and imperial Kapellmeister, posts previously held by Mozart.

LINDENSTRAND, SYLVIA

(Stockholm 1941)

Swedish mezzo-soprano. She studied at the Stockholm Royal Academy of Music and made her debut with the Stockholm Royal Opera, where she sang in *Don Giovanni*, *Le nozze di Figaro*, *Boris Godunov* and *Carmen*. Lindenstrand appeared at the Drottningholm Castle Theater and was a guest artist at a number of opera houses in Europe, including Aix-en-Provence and the Grand Théâtre in Geneva. She also performed in contemporary operas and sang the lead in Börtz's *The Bacchae*, staged in November 1991 in Stockholm in a production by Ingmar Bergman.

LIPOVŠEK, MARJANA

(Ljubljana 1957)

Mezzo-soprano from the former Yugoslavia. After studying music in Ljubljana, she went on to train at the Academy of Music in Graz and at the Opera Studio in Vienna (1978). She joined the Vienna Staatsoper in 1979 and made her debut at the Salzburg Festival in the world premiere of Cerha's *Baal* in 1981, the year in which she became a member of the Hamburg Staatsoper. Since then, she has appeared at major international opera houses, including La Scala, Milan, Covent Garden, Munich and the Deutsche Oper Berlin. Lipovšek is one of the major singers of her generation and, as well as in the leading roles of the German, Italian and French repertoires, has also distinguished herself as Marfa in *Khovanshchina* (Vienna, 1989) and

Top: The mezzo-soprano of former Yugoslavia Marjana Lipovšek.

Above: The Hungarian composer and pianist Franz Liszt.

Marina in *Boris Godunov* (Vienna, 1991), both with Claudio Abbado conducting.

LISZT, FRANZ

(Raiding 1811–Bayreuth 1886)
Hungarian composer and pianist. Encouraged by his father to study music while still very young, he was awarded a scholarship which enabled him to study in Weimar and Vienna. In 1823 he was in Paris, where he studied composition with Paër, and during this period he made his only attempt at writing an opera, *Don Sanche* (Don Sancho). Staged in Paris in 1825, it was taken off after only three performances and completely forgotten. The idea of writing music for the theater remained with Liszt all his life. His output includes numerous transcriptions for piano of operas by Rossini, Donizetti, Bellini, Verdi, Beethoven, etc. There was also his fundamental contribution to opera as a conductor: he directed a number of first performances or important revivals, for example the successful production of *Tannhäuser* in 1849, then the premieres of *Lohengrin* in 1850, *Der fliegende Holländer* (The Flying Dutchman) in 1853, Schubert's *Alfonso und Estrella* in 1854 and Cornelius's *Der Barbier von Bagdad* in 1858. His oratorio *Die Legende von der heiligen Elisabeth* has been staged as an opera.

LIVIETTA E TRACOLLO

Intermezzo in two parts by Giovanni Battista Pergolesi (1710–1736), to a libretto by T. Mariani. First performance: Naples, Teatro San Bartolomeo, 25 October 1734.

Livietta (soprano) and her friend Fulvia (mime), both dressed as men, intend to catch Tracolio (bass), a vagrant thief, and his accomplice Faccenda (mime), who have robbed Livietta's brother. Disguised as a pregnant woman, and under the name of Baldracca, Tracollo appears before Livietta and Fulvia, who pretend to be asleep. The brigand glimpses a little chain around Fulvia's neck and attempts to steal it, but Livietta exposes the rogue. To avoid being arrested, Tracollo even tries to seduce Livietta, declaring himself madly in love with her but she is not swayed by the rascal's protestations. In the second intermezzo, Tracollo, disguised as an astrologer, feigns madness in order to move Livietta. She in turn pretends to be dead. In the end, moved by the knave's distress, she gets to her feet and grants him her hand in marriage, having made him promise that he will henceforth change his way of life.

Performed between the acts of *Adriano in Siria*, also by Pergolesi, *Livietta e Tracollo*, like *La serva padrona*, is an intermezzo of some considerable significance in that it marks the start of the eighteenth- and nineteenth-century tradition of Italian comic opera. The music is light and joyful, rich in delightful comic effects.

LJUBOV K TRYOM APELSINAM

(The Love for Three Oranges)
Opera in a prologue, four acts and ten scenes by Sergei Prokofiev (1891–1953), to the composer's own libretto taken from the fairy-tale by Carlo Gozzi. First performance: Chicago, Opera House, 30 December 1921.

In the prologue, Tragedians, Comedians, Lyricists and Empty Heads argue over what makes the best theater. Ten Eccentrics chase them off the stage and announce a performance of *The Love for Three Oranges*. The King of Clubs (bass), aided by his jester Truffaldino (tenor), prime minister Leandro (baritone) and his confidant Pantalone (baritone), are organizing games and entertainments to amuse the Prince (tenor), who is suffering from melancholy. Against a backcloth covered in cabalistic emblems stand the magician Celio (bass), the King's protector, and Fata Morgana (soprano), protector of Leandro. Fata Morgana beats the magician at cards. In the palace, Leandro tells his accomplice Clarissa (contralto) of an effective way to get rid of the Prince – by reading extremely dreary books to the wretched man. During festivities designed for the Prince's entertainment, Fata Morgana arrives. Her presence turns the atmosphere icy. Truffaldino argues with her, and she ends up falling over backwards. The Prince at last bursts out laughing, but Fata Morgana has revenge by ordering that the Prince set out in search of three oranges, with which he will fall in love. Off goes the Prince, accompanied by Truffaldino. The pair reach the castle of the witch Creonta, where the oranges await them. Here the Prince bribes the Cook (bass) by giving her a ribbon and manages to obtain the three oranges. The scene changes to a desert. While the Prince is asleep, Truffaldino becomes thirsty and cuts open two of the oranges, causing the deaths by thirst of the two Princesses inside them. The Prince wakes up and opens the third orange: out steps the Princess Ninetta (soprano), saved from death thanks to the intervention of the Eccentrics, who bring water on stage in a fire bucket. The Prince rushes off to tell his father that he wants to marry Ninetta. On arriving at Court, he finds that Fata Morgana has replaced the King with Smeraldina (mezzo-soprano). The cabalistic backdrop returns. Celio and Fata Morgana are having an argument. The Eccentrics manage to shut Fata Morgana away. Back in the throne-room, to everyone's horror, it is discovered that the Princess has been turned into a mouse by Fata Morgana. Enter Celio, who changes her back again

A scene from *Livietta and Tracollo* by Giovanni Battista Pergolesi, performed for the first time at Teatro San Bartolomeo in Naples.

into beautiful Ninetta. The traitors Smeraldina, Leandro and Clarissa flee from Fata Morgana, while the rest of the Court toast the happy couple.

A mixture of satire, fable and comedy, created as a reaction against the prevailing naturalism, this opera caused controversy when it was first staged. The rich, varied and imaginative score is ideally suited to bringing out the atmosphere of fable in Gozzi's play. Prokofiev uses soloists and chorus, dividing the latter into groups (tragedians, comedians, cynics, etc.) whose task it is to underline each episode of the action, and this makes for a strikingly bold and innovative opera.

LLOYD, ROBERT

(Southend, Essex 1940)

British bass. After studying music at Oxford and the London Opera Center, he made his debut with Sadler's Wells Opera in 1969. In 1972 he joined the company at the Royal Opera House, Covent Garden, where he has continued to appear regularly. In 1975 came his debut in the United States, singing Sarastro in Mozart's *Die Zauberflöte* (The Magic Flute) in San Francisco. He went on to appear at the Opéra in Paris (*Don Giovanni*), in Aix-en-Provence, Glyndebourne, Munich and other major opera venues. His repertoire also includes Gurnemanz (*Parsifal*) and Boris (*Boris Godunov*), roles in which he won considerable acclaim at the Metropolitan Opera in New York (March 1991) and the Vienna Staatsoper (October 1991).

LODOÏSKA

Opera in three acts by Luigi Cherubini (1760–1842), to a libretto by Claude-François Fillette-Loraux, based on Les amours du Chevalier de Faublas *by J.-B. Louvet de Couvrai. First performance: Paris, Théâtre Feydeau, 18 July 1791.*

The action takes place in Poland in 1600. The young Count Floreski (tenor), accompanied by his equerry Varbel (baritone), is searching for his fiancée, Princess Lodoïska, whose father will not allow her to marry him. Floreski and Varbel are within sight of the gloomy castle of Count Dourlinski (baritone) when they are set upon by a band of Tartars, led by Titzikan (tenor). The two overcome their adversaries, and Titzikan offers the hand of friendship to the young Count. Just at that moment, someone throws stones down from the tower. Floreski picks them up and discovers a message from Lodoïska, now a prisoner in the castle. Varbel suggests that he and Floreski enter the castle, pretending to be Lodoïska's brothers come to take her home. Shortly after this, while Dourlinski is trying to persuade Lodoïska to marry him, the two "brothers" arrive. After their request that Lodoïska be released falls on deaf ears, they ask if they may spend the night at the castle. Dourlinski agrees. He then attempts to poison Floreski and Varbel, but Varbel realizes what is happening and is able to swap the glasses. The pair try to make their way to Lodoïska, but the Count overtakes them and has them put under lock and key. With the situation now apparently desperate, cannon-shots are heard: the Tartars are storming the castle. While the battle is raging, a fire breaks out. Floreski saves Lodoïska before the tower collapses and is saved in his turn by Titzikan, who wrests a dagger from Dourlinski's hand. The two lovers are finally reunited, amid general rejoicing.

Lodoïska, Cherubini's second opera, was a sensation, enjoying an unbroken run of 200 performances, the greatest success in the French theater at the height of the Revolution. The praise Cherubini received for it made up for the failure of his first Paris opera, *Démophoon*. *Lodoïska* is a forerunner of Romantic opera, in terms of both its musical style and its adventure-story plot.

LODOLETTA

Opera in three acts by Pietro Mascagni (1863–1945), to a libretto by Giovacchino Forzano. First performance: Rome, Teatro Costanzi, 30 April 1917.

The action takes place in about 1850 in a Dutch village. The French painter Flammen (tenor), compelled to flee from the police for political reasons, takes refuge in a Dutch village, where he meets a young woman, Lodoletta (soprano), recently orphaned by the death of her father. The two find they have a strong liking for one another which soon turns into love. Flammen assures Lodoletta he will not desert her but, having obtained a permit to return to France, he cannot resist the temptations of the capital and leaves the village. Lodoletta catches up with him in Paris, where Flammen, eaten up by remorse and his memory of her, feels unable to join in the carefree atmosphere of the New Year's Eve

Above: A sketch for *The Love for Three Oranges* by Sergei Prokofiev.

Left: The British bass Robert LLoyd.

celebrations. Without being seen, Lodoletta looks in through a window and catches sight of Flammen dancing. Overcome by despair and fatigue, she collapses from exhaustion and lies in the snow, too weak to move. Flammen comes out into the garden. He has realized too late what has happened and weeps as he gathers up the body of Lodoletta in his arms.

The story of *Lodoletta* is taken from *Two Little Wooden Shoes* by Ouida (pen-name of Marie Louise de la Ramée). Puccini had asked first Roberto Bracco and then Giuseppe Adami to adapt it for the theater, only to abandon the project later. Mascagni's score shows some lack of cohesion between, on the one hand, Acts I and II, whose fresh, idyllic atmosphere is reminiscent of Mascagni's *L'amico Fritz*, and Act III, in which there is heightening of the drama.

LOHENGRIN

"Invisible action" for soloist, instruments and voices by Salvatore Sciarrino (b. 1947) to the composer's own text after Jules Laforgue. First performance (with the Italian subtitle melodramma, *serious opera): Milan, Piccola Scala, 15 January 1983. First performance in the final version: Catanzaro, 9 September 1984.*

Laforgue's *Moralités légendaires*, on which the text of Sciarrino's *Lohengrin* is based, lays great dramatic emphasis on the figure of Elsa. She is a patient in a psychiatric hospital suffering from hallucinations as a result of taking heroin. Elsa relives the knight Lohengrin's act of desertion by clasping to her a cushion, which then changes into a swan, thus acting out the wedding-night she never had and her all too improbable hope that her knight would return. Sciarrino's intention was to carve out "a monstrous landscape of the soul" and explore the "endless night" of Elsa's mind.

The deeply internalized plot unfolds in a dream-like atmosphere in keeping with Sciarrino's musical language, basically consisting of elaborate yet motionless figures which produce sounds very similar to noise.

LOHENGRIN

Romantic opera in three acts by Richard Wagner (1813–1883), to the composer's own libretto. First performance: Weimar, Hoftheater, 28 August 1850.

The action takes place in Antwerp during the first half of the tenth century. In the presence of King Heinrich der Vogler (King Henry the Fowler, bass), Friedrich von Telramund (baritone), Count of Brabant, spurred on by his wife Ortrud (mezzo-soprano), accuses Elsa (soprano), daughter of the Duke of Brabant, of having killed her brother. Telramund calls for her to be punished and asserts his own claim to succeed to the Duchy of Brabant. On being pressed by the King, Elsa says she has dreamed of a champion who will defend her. Heinrich leaves it to God to pass judgement in the case, whereupon, to the amazement of all those present, a small boat approaches drawn by a white swan and out of it steps a knight (tenor) in silver armour. He declares himself ready to defend the honour of Elsa, but she must never ask his name or where he comes from. Telramund is defeated and banished from the kingdom. Hungry for revenge, Ortrud feigns concern for Elsa's well-being, warning her not to put blind faith in this unknown knight, and thus sows the seeds of suspicion in Elsa's mind. The next day, the marriage of the knight to Elsa is about to take place. As the wedding procession prepares to ascend the steps of the church, Ortrud accuses the mysterious knight of having defeated Telramund by magic. Telramund himself demands that his opponent reveal who he is and where he comes from. The knight refuses: only to Elsa, he says, will he be obliged to answer if she asks him such questions. Shortly after, in the wedding chamber, Elsa, now beset by doubt, can no longer hold back from questioning him, and the knight endeavours in vain to allay her suspicions. Suddenly, Telramund and his henchmen burst into the room to kill him, but he overwhelms them in one stroke. However, his fate is sealed: since Elsa wishes it, he will reveal his mysterious identity in the presence of the King and the nobles and then bid farewell to his bride. At the same spot where he had arrived on the previous day, he makes his speech: he comes, he says, from Monsalvat, a sanctuary where a brotherhood of chaste heroes guards the Holy Grail, the chalice used by Jesus at the Last Supper. These knights are given superhuman powers when they come down to earth to defend innocent people from danger, but if their secret is revealed, then they must return to Monsalvat. I, he says, am Lohengrin, son of Parsifal, King of the Grail. Elsa desperately tries to prevent him from leaving. But already the swan who will take Lohengrin back to Monsalvat has

Above: A nineteenth-century print depicting Richard Wagner's *Lohengrin*.

Right: A costume model for Elsa, the protagonist of *Lohengrin*.

reappeared on the waters of the Scheldt. Ortrud steps forward and with cruel glee reveals that the swan is none other than Elsa's brother Gottfried, whom she, Ortrud, had transformed by witchcraft. Lohengrin kneels in prayer, and suddenly the swan disappears and Gottfried steps out of the river. Lohengrin departs, and Elsa falls lifeless into her brother's arms.

The composition of this opera took from 1845 until 1848. Wagner regarded *Lohengrin* as a significant milestone in achieving the reforms he had been working towards for some time. The score shows all the signs of his efforts to break up the restrictive format of arias in favour of a recitative which attains new heights of expressiveness in the music written for Ortrud.

LOMBARD, ALAIN

(Paris 1940)

French conductor. He initially studied the violin with Line Talluel and subsequently attended the Paris Conservatoire, where he studied piano and conducting. He was already conducting at the age of 11 and by 18 had started a career as a conductor. He conducted at the opera house in Lyons (1961–65) and in 1963 he made his debut in the United States at the American Opera Society (*Hérodiade*). His first appearance with the Metropolitan Opera in New York was in 1967 (*Faust*). Lombard was artistic director of the Opéra du Rhin (1974–80), music director at the Opéra in Paris (1981–83), and from 1988 conductor of the Orchestre Nationale de Bordeaux-Aquitaine. Among his finest performances of opera on record are Delibes' *Lakmé* (1971) and Puccini's *Turandot* (1977).

LOMBARDI ALLA PRIMA CROCIATA, I

(The Lombards on the First Crusade)

Opera in four acts by Giuseppe Verdi (1813–1901), to a libretto by Temistocle Solera, based on the poem of the same name by Tommaso Grossi. First performance: Milan, La Scala, 11 February 1843.

The action takes place at the end of the eleventh century. Pagano (bass) had wounded his brother Arvino (tenor) after Viclinda (soprano) had passed him over and decided to marry Arvino instead. For this he had been sentenced to exile, and now he was returned to Milan. The two brothers forgive one another, but Pagano is inwardly still considering ways of taking revenge. He hires a group of thugs to abduct Viclinda. On the night planned for the abduction, however, Pagano kills his father by accident. In despair he tries to take his own life but is prevented from doing so. Many years later, Arvino takes part in the first Crusade. His daughter Giselda (soprano), held prisoner by Acciano (bass), tyrant of Antioch, is loved by Acciano's son Oronte (tenor). Meanwhile, Arvino is within sight of Antioch. A hermit, who is actually Pagano (he has withdrawn from the world to live in a cave so as to expiate the murder of his father), shows himself willing to be an accomplice of the Crusaders in their campaign to conquer the city. Giselda is set free, but thinking that Oronte has been killed she curses the unjust God who allowed this carnage to take place. However, Oronte is not dead: he was wounded, and now, dressed as a Crusader, finds Giselda in the Lombard camp. The young couple take refuge in the hermit's cave. Oronte is baptized and dies in the arms of his beloved Giselda. Pagano reunites Giselda with her father just as the Crusaders are about to conquer Jerusalem. In the last and decisive battle, the hermit is mortally wounded. He is carried to Arvino's tent, where he reveals that he is Pagano. His brother forgives him, and Pagano dies peacefully in sight of the Christian flags now flying over the conquered city of Jerusalem.

Verdi's romantic penchant for the medieval world and its ballads is the key feature of *I Lombardi alla prima crociata*, the composer's first successful attempt at writing a broadly popular kind of opera.

LONDON, GEORGE

(Montreal 1919–Armonk, New York 1985)

Stage name of George Burnstein, Canadian bass-baritone of Russian origin. He studied in Los Angeles and, as George Burnson, made his debut in the role of the Doctor (*La traviata*) at the Hollywood Bowl in Los Angeles in 1942. He then completed his training in New York, where he sang in musicals and operetta until 1949, when he was engaged by Karl Böhm to appear at the Vienna Staatsoper. His first role there was Amonasro (*Aida*). By 1950 he was singing at Glyndebourne (*Le nozze di Figaro*) and in 1951 made his debut at Bayreuth, where he became established as one of the finest Wagner singers (Amfortas, the Dutchman, Wotan). Within a short time, London had won for himself a huge international reputation and made appearances at the major opera houses such as La Scala, Milan, Covent Garden, the Bolshoi in Moscow and Metropolitan Opera in New York. His unusual vocal gifts, rich-

Left: A scene from Verdi's *I Lombardi alla prima crociata.*

ness of timbre and remarkable range, combined with an extraordinary presence as a performer, enabled him to shine not only in Mozart and Wagner, but also in operas by Mussorgsky (*Boris Godunov*), Richard Strauss (*Arabella*), Puccini (*Tosca*). He retired from the stage in 1967 and concentrated on production. From 1975 to 1980 he was director of the Washington Opera Society. He left an outstanding body of recordings which bear witness to his great personality as an artist.

LONG CHRISTMAS DINNER, THE

Opera in one act by Paul Hindemith (1895–1963), to the composer's own libretto, taken by the eponymous one-act play by Thornton Wilder. First performance: Mannheim, 17 December 1961 (in the German version, under the title Das Lange Weihnachtsmahl*).*

In the dining room of the Bayard family, everything is ready for Christmas dinner. The story spans ninety years: ninety Christmas meals. It begins with the infirm Mother Bayard, her son Roderick and his wife Lucia. The old lady recalls times past. Cousin Brandon enters and five

years have elapsed. As the conversation proceeds, the mother's wheelchair rolls towards a black door which represents death. The conversations proceed, virtually identical. A nanny enters with

the son of Roderick and Lucia, followed by his little sister Genevieve. The years go by: Charles is now the head of the family, because his father is seriously ill and soon after dies. Charles marries Leonora Banning. From their union, a child is born, who only lives a short time. Brandon and Lucia also die. Genevieve is distraught. Twins are born, then another child. Cousin Ermengarda joins the family. She will announce, among other events both happy and sad, that she is building a new house for the new generation.

The Long Christmas Dinner was Hindemith's last work for the theater. He had already displayed a degree of staleness in *Die Harmonie der Welt* and here shows a tendency to be rather academic as well as a weariness of inspiration.

LOPARDO, FRANK

(New York 1958)

American tenor of Italian origin. He studied in New York, winning his first significant acclaim in 1984 in St Louis as Tamino in *Die Zauberflöte* (The Magic Flute). He became immediately successful in the Mozart repertoire, performing at La Scala, Milan (*Don Giovanni*, 1986), the Glyndebourne Festival (*Così fan tutte*, 1987) and Aix-en-Provence (*Don Giovanni*). Also noted as a performer of Rossini (*Il barbiere di Siviglia*, *Il viaggio a Reims*) and of Donizetti (*L'elisir d'amore*, *La sonnambula*), he appears regularly at Covent Garden, the Chicago Lyric Opera, the Metropolitan Opera House, New York and the Vienna Staatsoper.

LORELEY

Azione romantica *(romantic action) in three acts by Alfredo Catalani (1854–1893), to a libretto by Carlo D'Ormerville and Angelo Zanardini. First performance: Turin, Teatro Regio, 16 February 1890.*

The action takes place in Germany around the year 1300. Walter (tenor), a wealthy man from Oberwesel who is due to marry Anna di Rebberg (soprano), niece of the Margrave of Biberich (bass), has fallen in love with Loreley (soprano), a young orphan. When Loreley learns that Walter has made up his mind to marry Anna, she calls on the King of the Rhine to help her. Loreley then throws herself into the river and emerges transformed into a magnificent creature with the powers to win forever the fickle heart of Walter. The next day, while the wedding of Walter and Anna is in progress, Loreley appears, and her singing so enchants Walter that, despite Anna's attempts to stop him, he leaves the church to follow her. When Walter hears that Anna has died of grief, in despair he feels like throwing himself into the river, but the river spirits and Loreley prevent him. Loreley is about to take Walter in her arms when the Spirits of the Air remind her that she has sworn to be faithful to the King of the Rhine. So she bids farewell forever to Walter and vanishes into the depths of the river. In desperation, Walter throws himself into the river.

Loreley is a reworking of Catalani's first opera, entitled *Elda*, composed ten years previously. The new work was very successful at first and was often performed throughout the world. Catalani's star faded, however, with the rise of the verismo movement.

LORENGAR, PILAR

(Saragossa 1929)

Spanish soprano. She studied music at the Conservatory in Barcelona and made her debut in 1949 as a mezzo-soprano, appearing as a soprano in 1952. At first she concentrated on zarzuelas and concert repertoire,

Top: A scene from *Loreley* by Alfredo Catalani.

Above: The American tenor Frank Lopardo.

then won her earliest international recognition at the Festival of Aix-en-Provence, where she sang Cherubino (*Le nozze di Figaro*) in 1955. The next year it was as Pamina in *Die Zauberflöte* (The Magic Flute) at Glyndebourne that Lorengar established her reputation. She subsequently appeared at Covent Garden (*La traviata*), the Metropolitan Opera, New York (*Don Giovanni*, 1963), and the Deutsche Oper Berlin (from 1959 onwards). Her vast repertoire was initially based on Mozart, but she soon added to it operas by Verdi, Puccini and Wagner.

LORENZACCIO

Romantic opera in five acts and 23 scenes (with a further two off-stage) by Sylvano Bussotti (b. 1931) with acknowledgements to the play of the same name by Alfred de Musset. Text by the composer. First performance: Venice, Teatro La Fenice, 7 September 1972.

The action takes place in Florence. At night a number of young thugs, acting on instructions from Duke Alessandro de' Medici, are preparing to kidnap Uliva. Maffio, Uliva's brother, is outraged and organizes a popular uprising against the Medici. While the characters of Alfred de Musset and George Sand discuss art, the story of Lorenzo de' Medici begins to unfold in a series of conspiracies and duels. Allegorical representations of the State and Church, with de Musset and Sand alongside them, act as spectators and judges of the various episodes in the story, leading to the finale, in which all the characters join in a procession of sad funeral songs and dances as they are escorted by Eros, Majesty and Death to the grave.

Composed between 1968 and 1972 and presented as part of the 35th Venice Festival of Contemporary Music, *Lorenzaccio* is one of Bussotti's most interesting works, bringing together all the resources of music theater, refined here by the composer's imaginative poetics to create an opera that is both grandiose and stylistically original.

LORENZI, GIOVANNI BATTISTA

(Naples 1721–1807)

Italian abbot, erudite academic, connoisseur of contemporary French literature and librettist. In 1763 he joined the company of the Teatro di Corte in Naples, becoming its director and royal literary inspector in 1769. In 1768 he had begun to provide story-lines to numerous composers of his day, among them Domenico Cimarosa (*L'apparenza inganna*, *Il marito disperato*), Giovanni Paisiello (*L'idolo cinese*, *Don Chisciotte*, *Il Socrate immaginario*, *Nina ossia la pazza per amore*, etc.) and Niccolò Piccinni (*Gelosia per gelosia*, *La corsara*, etc.), thus making an important contribution to the development of *opera buffa* in Naples.

LORTZING, GUSTAV ALBERT

(Berlin 1801–1851)

German composer, actor, singer and conductor. Born into an acting family, Lortzing made his acting and singing debut while teaching himself music. He also played the cello in various orchestras. In 1833 he was engaged by the Opera in Leipzig, where he appeared as a singer and actor, making his conducting debut there in 1844. As a conductor he worked at the Theater an der Wien in Vienna (1846–48) and in Berlin (1850–51). His popular output included the operas *Zar und Zimmermann*, 1837, *Der Wildschütz*, 1845, and *Undine*, 1845, regarded as his finest works.

LOTT, FELICITY

(Cheltenham 1947)

British soprano. She studied at the Royal Academy of Music, London, making her debut as Pamina in *Die Zauberflöte* (The Magic Flute) with English National Opera (1975). In 1976 she took part in the world premiere of Henze's opera *We Come to the River* at Covent Garden. She returned there to sing the Marschallin in Strauss's *Der Rosenkavalier*, as well as roles in operas by Britten and Wagner. A regular guest artiste at the Glyndebourne Festival, where she won admiration for her singing in the operas of Mozart and Richard Strauss, Lott has also appeared in New York, Chicago and at numerous other venues in the United States and Europe as a distinguished performer of concert repertoire.

The Spanish soprano Pilar Lorengar.

LOUISE

Roman musical *in four acts and five scenes by Gustave Charpentier (1860–1956), to the composer's own libretto, incorporating contributions from numerous others, notably Saint-Pol-Roux. First performance: Paris, Théâtre de l'Opéra-Comique, 2 February 1900.*

The action takes place in Paris, at the end of the nineteenth century. Louise (soprano), a beautiful dressmaker from a working-class family, is in love with Julien (tenor), a penniless young poet. Louise's mother (mezzo-soprano) surprises the pair, interrupts their conversation and takes her daughter sternly to task. Louise's father (baritone) also intervenes but, while appearing to share his wife's opinion, proves to be more understanding. Louise promises not to see Julien again, but then, reading in a newspaper about the marvellous life people live in Paris, she bursts into floods of tears. A few days later, Julien comes up to Louise while she is on her way to work and tries to persuade her to leave her family and live with him. Shortly after this, Louise hears, over the dressmakers' chatter at the workshop, Julien's voice singing a serenade. Pretending to feel unwell, Louise leaves work and goes away with Julien. The couple settle in Montmartre and appeal to the spirit of the city of Paris to be the guardian angel of their love and free and happy life. During a Bohemian ceremony, Louise is crowned Muse of Montmartre, but the party is interrupted by the arrival of her mother, who begs Louise to come home because her father is seriously ill and asking for her. Louise leaves with her mother, who promises to allow her to return to Julien

whenever she likes. Louise's father recovers, but he and her mother continue to keep their daughter with them. Louise misses the happy existence she has left behind. After a violent clash with her parents, she flees from the house to live the life she wants, while her father curses Paris for having lured away that which he has held most dear.

Louise, the most successful of French naturalistic operas, was a sensational success and became extremely popular. The reason for this was a combination of musical simplicity, concrete realism, openness to social issues and the affirmation of freedom and pleasure in a way that was congenial to free spirits of the time. The work is also full of autobiographical references to Charpentier's life in Montmartre and his socialist ideas.

LOVE FOR THREE ORANGES, THE

See *Ljubov k Tryom Apelsinam*

LOVE OF DANAE, THE

See *Liebe der Danae, Die*

LUCHETTI, VERIANO

(Tuscania 1939)

Italian tenor. After private singing lessons, he made his debut at Spoleto's Teatro Nuovo (in Giordano's *Fedora*) and went on to score an important early success, again at Spoleto, at the 1967 Festival dei Due Mondi, in Donizetti's *Il furioso all'isola di San Domingo*. He won great acclaim for his performance in Meyerbeer's *L'Africaine* at the Maggio Musicale Festival in Florence (1971) alongside Jessye Norman. This launched him on a brilliant career which led to appearances at international opera houses throughout the world in a comparatively wide-ranging repertoire incorporating operas by Verdi, Puccini and Bizet. Particularly worth noting are his recordings of *Nabucco* (1977) and *Macbeth* (1986) conducted by Riccardo Muti and Riccardo Chailly, respectively.

LUCIA DI LAMMERMOOR

Opera in three acts by Gaetano Donizetti (1797–1848), to a libretto by Salvatore Cammarano based on Sir Walter Scott's novel The Bride of Lammermoor. *First performance: Naples, Teatro San Carlo, 26 September 1835.*

The action takes place in Scotland at the end of the sixteenth century. In the grounds of Ravenswood Castle, Lord Enrico Ashton (baritone), worried that the political struggles in which he is involved have undermined his family, plans to marry his sister Lucia (soprano) to Lord Arturo Bucklaw (tenor). But Normanno (tenor), commander of Enrico's guard, suspects Lucia of having a secret love for a man who once saved her life from a mad bull, only to discover that the man in question is Enrico's hereditary enemy, Edgardo di Ravenswood (tenor). Shortly after this, Lucia has a secret rendezvous with Edgardo, during which he tells her he has to leave for France. Edgardo would like to ask Enrico if he can marry Lucia, but she, all too aware of her brother's deep hatred for Edgardo, dissuades him, at the same time swearing undying love for him. In order to compel Lucia to fall

in with his own wishes, Enrico shows her a fake letter that Edgardo is supposed to have sent to another woman. Lucia does not doubt her brother, assumes the letter is genuine and agrees with much sadness to marry Arturo. The scene changes to a hall in the castle filled with guests who witness Lucia signing the marriage contract. Suddenly Edgardo bursts in, accuses her of infidelity and, in despair, curses the entire Ashton family. Later, at the tower on Wolf's Crag, Enrico challenges Edgardo to a duel, to be fought near the tombs of the Ravenswoods. Meanwhile, at the castle, while the wedding celebrations are underway, Raimondo (bass), a friend of Lucia's, announces she has gone mad and killed Arturo. Enter Lucia. In her madness she recalls past events, conjures up ghosts and imagines she is at the altar marrying Edgardo. Unaware of what has happened, Edgardo is waiting for Enrico to arrive for the duel and has decided to let his opponent kill him, as life no longer has

Top: Donizetti's *Lucia di Lammermoor* in a cartoon.

Above right: Portrait of Salvatore Cammarano, the Italian librettist.

Right: The Italian tenor Veriano Luchetti.

THE THEME OF MADNESS IN OPERA

The great ''mad scene'' in Donizetti's *Lucia di Lammermoor* is undoubtedly the most famous moment of the work, as well as being the highest point of expressiveness in romantic Italian opera before Verdi, in which scenes of madness and folly provided a focus, or even the crucial element, of most of the plots. The importance a composer would give to dramatic scenes of this kind can be gathered from the scale on which they were conceived (not least in terms of length) and the care lavished on them. In the mad scene from *Lucia di Lammermoor*, for example, there is a choral passage in which a bass soloist describes how the heroine's reason has been clouded and prepares the audience for her entrance, so that when she does finally appear, all attention is concentrated on her. In an extended recitative (''Il dolce suono''), Lucia pieces together and relives the story of her love. This leads to the aria, which in *Lucia* is closer to an arioso (''Ardon gli incensi''), a kind of expansion of the recitative. At this lyrical moment Lucia herself, by now completely transported on to a otherwordly plane, believes that her dream of love is coming true. Then, after a linking scene the portrayal of ''madness'' ends with a *cabaletta* (''spargi d'amaro pianto''), in which Lucia, in a moment of painful clarity, bids farewell to life on earth.

Mad scenes are usually given to female characters and express the situation of the heroine in which as a victim she not only confronts the fact that her love cannot ever be realized, but also finds a way of having revenge on her persecutors. Donizetti had already shown in the operas he wrote before *Lucia di Lammermoor* that he possessed good judgement – both dramatically and musically – in handling this kind of scene, as in the finale of *Anna Bolena*, with its especially beautiful aria ''Ah dolce guidami castel natio,'' one of the composer's finest achievements and one of the most superlative passages ever written for a romantic heroine.

Before Donizetti, another great composer, Vincenzo Bellini, had included scenes of raving, delirium, fainting and sleepwalking in his operas: the anguished frenzy of Imogene at the end of *Il pirata*, the subtle suggestion of madness which pervades the character of Amina in *La sonnambula* and most notably Elvira in *I puritani*, where Bellini's extraordinary lyrical gift enables him to portray the heroine as her mind wanders because she is faced with the agonizing memory of lost love. This profusion of operatic representations of madness stemmed from the poetics of pera composition in the early romantic period, contained within the *bel canto* tradition which shrinks from tragedy. Imogene, Elvira, Anna Bolena, Lucia and others are prisoners of their dream-like and pathetic utterances, so that for them there can be no catharsis. The only way of escape for the heroines is madness, which becomes the victim's search for the reasons that will explain why their personal drama cannot be resolved. The kind of singing that conveys the heroines' dismay and delirium is made up of tormented melodies and *coloratura* passages. It was not until the operas of Giuseppe Verdi were seen in Italian opera houses that singing was given a truly dramatic dimension.

Right: Costume for the role of Elvira in Bellini's *I puritani*.

Above: The Italian soprano Mariella Devia in *Lucia di Lammermoor*, by Donizetti.

any meaning for him. Raimondo appears and tells Edgardo that Lucia is dead. Edgardo is devastated and, invoking the spirit of his beloved, dies by his own dagger.

The libretto of *Lucia di Lammermoor* is faithful to the novel by Sir Walter Scott. The score was composed by Donizetti in only 36 days, winning for him the further honour of a place in the first rank of composers of *opera seria* and marking the beginning of his mature period. The first performance of the work was an outstanding success with audience and critics alike, and it continues to be staged to enormous acclaim.

LUCIO SILLA

Opera in three acts by Wolfgang Amadeus Mozart (1756–1791), to a libretto by Giovanni de Gamerra. First performance: Milan, Teatro Ducale, 26 December 1772.

The action takes place in ancient Rome. The dictator Silla (tenor) has an unrequited love for Giunia (soprano), daughter of Mario. She is betrothed to Cecilio (soprano), then living in exile but firmly resolved to make her his bride. Cecilio comes back secretly to Rome and meets Giunia. The main purpose of his return is to hatch a plot against Silla in which his fellow-conspirator is Cinna (tenor), who is sentimentally involved with Celia (soprano), Silla's sister. The plot is uncovered, and Cecilio is condemned to death. Giunia does not hesitate to face his destiny with him and, now ready for anything, confronts Silla, before the Senate and the Roman people, with his abuse of political power and arrogant actions. Silla is forced to admit his wrong-doings, Cecilio and the plotters are freed, and two marriages then take place, that of Giunia to Cecilio and Cinna to Celia.

This is the last opera Mozart wrote for Italy. For the first performance, the role of Silla was given to the tenor Bassone Morgnone, but since he lacked the necessary experience and did not inspire great confidence, Mozart only gave him two very straightforward arias and instead devoted all his energies to the solo parts for Giunia and Cecilio, roles to be played by singers of great distinction. However, *Lucio Silla* failed to enjoy the success which had been hoped for.

The German mezzo-soprano Christa Ludwig.

LUCREZIA BORGIA

Opera in a prologue and two acts by Gaetano Donizetti (1797–1848), to a libretto by Felice Romani after the tragedy of the same title by Victor Hugo. First performance: Milan, La Scala, 26 December 1833.

The action takes place at the beginning of the sixteenth century in Venice. While attending a masked banquet, Maffio Orsini (contralto) relates the story of an old man who has prophesied that he and a friend of his will die by the hand of Lucrezia Borgia. At that moment a masked lady enters. This is Lucrezia (soprano) herself, who shows particular interest in a young man, Gennaro (tenor), who is asleep in a corner. Lucrezia leans over him and kisses him. When Gennaro wakes, he tells Lucrezia his life story, revealing that he never knew his mother. Their conversation is interrupted by the arrival of Gennaro's young companions, who recognize Lucrezia and remind her of her past crimes. Some time later, in Ferrara, Duke Alfonso (bass), Lucrezia's husband, has become jealous of the attention his wife is paying Gennaro, who has recently arrived with a delegation from Venice. Alfonso has Gennaro arrested on a charge of defacing the name-plate on the main door of the palace, erasing the "B" of Borgia to leave the word "*orgia*" (orgy). Lucrezia implores her husband to be lenient with Gennaro, but Alfonso is adamant and demands that Gennaro be made to take poison. Lucrezia saves him by giving him an antidote and helps him escape by a secret exit. Before leaving Ferrara, Gennaro is persuaded by Orsini to accompany him to a party at Princess Negroni's palace. During the feast, Gubetta (bass), one of the Duke's spies, provokes Orsini, and he reacts unflinchingly. The ladies withdraw while Gennaro calms everyone down. A toast is proposed, but then a funereal song is heard and the lights go out. Lucrezia has had all the doors locked behind her and now announces to the guests that, in revenge for the insults she received in Venice, she has had their wine poisoned. Then she notices Gennaro and begs him to drink the antidote, but this time he refuses, preferring to die with the others. In desperation, Lucrezia reveals to him that he too is a Borgia and her son, but it is too late: Gennaro dies in the arms of his mother as, overcome with grief, she sobs out his name.

Lucrezia Borgia was initially given a chilly reception, despite its cast of excellent singers. For the first performance, Donizetti had to write a final *cabaletta* (at the insistence of Henriette Lalande) which he intended to excise from later editions of the score. More changes were made following the intervention of the censor, whose repeated insistence that the title be changed was due to the fact that the Borgia family had produced several popes.

LUDWIG, CHRISTA

(Berlin 1928)

German mezzo-soprano. Born into a musical family (her parents sang at the Vienna Opera), she studied music with her mother and with Felice Hüni-Mihacek, making her debut in 1946 in Frankfurt in *Die Fledermaus*. She then appeared in a number of cities in Germany until 1954, the year in which she sang for the first time at the Salzburg Festival (Cherubino in *Le nozze di Figaro*). In 1955 she was engaged by the Vienna Opera (again in *Le nozze di Figaro*). Ludwig went on to sing at the Metropolitan Opera, New York (from 1959), Lyric Opera of Chicago, La

Scala, Milan (from 1960), Bayreuth (1966), Covent Garden (1968), and at a number of other opera houses. She had by then emerged as a performer of Mozart (*Così fan tutte*) and Richard Strauss (*Der Rosenkavalier*) on the strength of her obvious vocal, stylistic and technical gifts, which enabled her to tackle an extremely wide-ranging repertoire, including operas by Verdi and Beethoven. Ludwig is a fine exponent of the *Lieder* repertoire and has had a long career as a recording artist.

LUISA MILLER

Opera in three acts by Giuseppe Verdi (1813–1901), to a libretto by Salvatore Cammarano based on the tragedy Kabale und Liebe *by Friedrich Schiller. First performance: Naples, Teatro San Carlo, 8 December 1849.*

The action takes place in the Tyrol during the first half of the eighteenth century. Luisa Miller (soprano) and Rodolfo are in love. The young man is the son of Count Walter (bass), who wants him to marry the Duchess Federica (mezzo-soprano). But Rodolfo does not intend to desert Luisa and threatens that, unless he is allowed to marry Luisa, he will expose his father for having assassinated the lawful Count and usurped his title and estates. Miller (baritone), Luisa's father, has been arrested for refusing to tolerate Count Walter's continual abuses. Wurm (bass), the castle administrator and in love with Luisa, forces her to write a letter in which she declares that she does not love Rodolfo and only accepted his advances out of ambition. As a result, Miller is released from prison. Wurm then has Luisa's letter delivered to Rodolfo. He is devastated by it and decides to go ahead with the marriage to the Duchess, in accordance with his father's wishes. But instead he goes to see Luisa, pours poison into two glasses and drinks with her. Faced with death, Luisa reveals how she was blackmailed into writing as she did. Rodolfo curses his father, kills the treacherous Wurm and dies alongside his faithful Luisa.

Luisa Miller is considered the first opera of Verdi's maturity. At the time, it was said to mark the beginning of the composer's personal style, a judgement based on the fact that *Luisa Miller* was a middle-class heroine, itself something quite new. Verdi uses the psychological refinement of the Luisa character as a starting-point from which to focus on the figure of Violetta, heroine of *La traviata* (premiered less than four years later).

LULLY, JEAN-BAPTISTE

(Florence 1632–Paris 1687)

Adopted name of Giovanni Battista Lulli, Italian composer, naturalized French. Little or nothing is known of his musical education up the time of his arrival in Paris in 1646, when at the age of 14 he was taken into the service of the Princesse d'Orleans. He began to compose arias and took advanced violin lessons, entering the court of Louis XIV in 1652. This marked the beginning of an artistic career which reached its height with his appointments to the posts of "Maître de la Chambre du Roi" (1657), "Surintendant de la Musique" (1661) and "Maître de la musique de la famille royale" (1662). He worked with Molière, for whom he wrote numerous scores of incidental music, among them the music for *Le bourgeois gentilhomme* (1670). Lully's real debut dates from 1673 and his opera *Cadmus et Hermione*. This was followed by *Alceste* (1674), *Thésée* (1675), *Atys* (1676), *Roland* (1685) and *Armide* (1686), a masterpiece of *tragédie-lyrique*, the genre that Lully himself created and developed to its highest point of achievement.

LULU

Opera in a prologue and three acts by Alban Berg (1885–1935), to the composer's own libretto based on Frank Wedekind's plays Erdgeist *and* Die Büchse der Pandora. *First performance: Zurich, Stadttheater, 2 June 1937.*

The action takes place about 1930. In the prologue, an Animal Tamer (*buffo* bass) introduces the cast of the opera as if they were animals. The most dangerous is Lulu, a snake with a woman's face. Ludwig Schön (baritone), editor of a leading newspaper, who had previously

Above: A scene from *Lucrezia Borgia* in a production at Teatro San Carlo, Naples.

Left: Marble bust of Jean-Baptiste Lully.

taken Lulu (soprano) in off the streets and made her his mistress, now wants her to marry an elderly friend of his, Dr Goll (baritone). But Lulu is encouraging the advances of a painter (lyric tenor), and when the old Doctor discovers this relationship, he is devastated and dies of heart failure. Lulu then marries the Painter but is irritated to hear that Schön has decided to marry a virtuous woman and confronts him. The Painter intervenes and accuses Schön of wanting to upset his wife, whereupon Schön tells the Painter about Lulu's dissolute past, and the Painter in despair kills himself. Some time later, Lulu, now a famous dancer, catches sight of Schön and his fiancée in the audience during a performance. Pretending to have been taken ill, Lulu goes to her dressing-room. Schön comes to see her there, and the sight of her rekindles his love, so he decides to leave his fiancée. Lulu becomes Frau Schön but does not stop seeing her dubious friends, among them Countess Geschwitz (mezzo-soprano), who is in love with her. Alwa (dramatic tenor), one of Schön's sons by a previous marriage, has also fallen madly in love with his new step-mother. Schön surprises them together and threatens his wife with a gun, but in the ensuing argument, Lulu grabs the weapon and kills Schön, is arrested and then, struck down with cholera, ends up in a house for the diseased poor, from which she is helped to escape by Countess Geschwitz. Years later, Lulu has become a prostitute in the service of the Marquis Casti-Piani, who wants to sell her to an Egyptian. To avoid this fate, Lulu runs away to London with Alwa and the Countess. Now living in a miserable attic and reduced to poverty, Lulu has no choice but to return to prostitution. She meets Jack the Ripper, who murders her and then kills the Countess, the name of her beloved Lulu on her lips.

Berg worked on *Lulu* from 1928 until his death in 1935. The opera was left partly unfinished, as the composer had not been able to orchestrate and revise the third act. It was consequently staged in two acts, incorporating two excerpts from the third act that Berg had included in his *Symphonische Stücke*. It was not until 24 February 1979 that the complete version of *Lulu* was staged, at the Opéra in Paris, after the orchestration had been finished by Friedrich Cerha from Berg's piano score.

A scene from *Lulu*, an opera in a prologue and three acts by Alban Berg.

LUSTIGEN WEIBER VON WINDSOR, DIE

(The Merry Wives of Windsor)

Comic-fantastic opera in three acts by Otto Nicolai (1810–1849), after Shakespeare's play The Merry Wives of Windsor *in an adaptation by S. H. Mosenthal. First performance: Berlin, Hofoper, 9 March 1849.*

The elderly Sir John Falstaff (bass) is courting Mistress Fluth (soprano) and Mistress Page (mezzo-soprano) at the same time. The two ladies want to play a hoax on their suitor and invite him to a tryst at Mistress Fluth's house while her husband (baritone) is away. They have made sure to tell the husband about the assignation in an anonymous letter. He flies into a fury and bursts in on the tryst, obliging Falstaff to save himself by hiding in a basket of dirty laundry. ACT II. Unaware that he is talking to Mistress Fluth's husband, Falstaff tells him how his adventure turned into a misadventure, which makes the husband even more furious and jealous, with the result that once again he turns up unexpectedly, ruining Falstaff's attempts at seduction and forcing the old knight to make good his escape disguised in the clothes of an old maid-servant. ACT III. After disabusing her husband of his futile feelings of jealousy, Mistress Fluth teaches Falstaff an even sterner lesson by inviting him to a rendezvous in Windsor Forest, where he is set upon by a pack of elves and goblins who beat the living daylights out of him.

Die lustigen Weiber von Windsor was Nicolai's last and most important opera before his untimely death. It combines the best aspects of German musical Romanticism and the Italian operatic tradition. To this day, the work's irony and wit and the freshness of its melodies have led to it being regularly performed in Germany and Austria, where it is even more popular than Verdi's *Falstaff*.

LUXON, BENJAMIN

(Redruth, Cornwall 1937)

British baritone. He studied at the Guildhall School of Music in London and began his career with the English Opera Group, winning his first real acclaim in the leading role of Britten's *Owen Wingrave* in 1970. From 1972 he sang at Glyndebourne, making his debut there in Monteverdi's *Il ritorno di Ulisse in patria*, subsequently appearing in Mozart's *Le nozze di Figaro* and *Don Giovanni*. Also in 1972 Luxon made his debut at Covent Garden in Maxwell Davies's *Taverner*. He returned to sing in a number of other productions, scoring a particular success in *Eugene Onegin*. He also appeared with English National Opera and at other major music venues in Europe and the United States as well as pursuing a very active career as a concert artist.

M

MAAG, PETER

(St. Gallen 1919)

Swiss conductor. After studying music in Zurich, he went on to complete his training in Geneva and made his debut at the Biel-Solothurn civic theater (1943–51), where he was appointed conductor. His career then concentrated on the Düsseldorf Opera (1952–54), and until 1959 he was Generalmusikdirektor of the opera house in Bonn. From 1964 until 1967 he was first conductor at the Vienna Volksoper and then music director of the opera houses in Parma (1971–77), Turin (1977) and of the Berne Symphony Orchestra and Opera House (from 1984). Maag was also an active teacher, as evidenced by his involvement in the Bottega del Teatro Comunale di Treviso (from 1988), a workshop for young opera singers, where he conducted new productions of operas by Mozart (*Don Giovanni*, *Le nozze di Figaro*), of whom he is an admired interpreter, and Verdi (*Il trovatore*, *Falstaff*).

MAAZEL, LORIN

(Neuilly-sur-Seine 1930)

American conductor and violinist. He studied in Pittsburgh with Vladimir Bakaleinikov and earned a reputation as an infant prodigy, conducting at the New York World's Fair and also, on the invitation of Toscanini, the NBC Symphony (1941). He went on to complete his music studies in the United States and in Europe, where he began to appear at leading music and opera venues (Vienna 1955, Berlin 1956, etc.). In 1960 he became the first American to conduct at Bayreuth (*Lohengrin*) and he then conducted at the Metropolitan Opera in New York (*Don Giovanni*, 1962) and the Salzburg Festival (*Le nozze di Figaro*, 1963). From 1965 until 1975 he was music director at the Deutsche Oper Berlin, where in 1968 he conducted the world premiere of Dallapiccola's *Ulisse*. Appointed music director at the Vienna Staatsoper in 1982 (until 1984), he conducted the first performance of Berio's *Un re in ascolto* at the Salzburg Festival in 1984. He also appeared at La Scala, Milan, conducting *Falstaff* (1981), *Turandot* (1983), *Aida* (1985), *Fidelio* (1990), *La fanciulla del West* (1991) and *Manon Lescaut* (1992). His performances of Puccini's operas in particular were distinguished by attention to orchestral and dramatic colour. He conducted the soundtracks of Joseph Losey's film *Don Giovanni* (1979), Francesco Rosi's *Carmen* (1983) and Franco Zeffirelli's *Otello* (1985).

MACBETH

Opera in four acts by Giuseppe Verdi (1813–1901), to a libretto by Francesco Maria Piave, based on the tragedy by William Shakespeare. First performance: Florence, Teatro alla Pergola, 14 March 1847.

On their way home from victory in battle, the Scottish generals Macbeth (baritone) and Banquo (bass) come upon three witches who prophesy their future: Macbeth will become Thane of Glamis and Cawdor and King of Scotland, and Banquo's children will one day be sovereigns there. Shortly after this, messengers bring news to Macbeth that he has been made Thane of Cawdor. At Macbeth's castle, the arrival of King Duncan is awaited. Lady Macbeth (soprano) incites her husband to murder the King during the night. The King's son Malcolm (tenor) flees to England. Macbeth is now King of Scotland, and his wife also wants to have Banquo and his son Fleance killed. Banquo is murdered, but Fleance manages to escape. During a feast at the castle, Banquo's ghost appears and strikes fear into Macbeth. He returns to consult the witches, but their verdict is puzzling: he will remain ruler of Scotland until Birnam Wood "shall come against him." Lady Macbeth prevails on her husband to kill the wife and children of Macduff (tenor), who is in England with Malcolm gathering an army to march against Scotland. Having reached Birnam Wood, Macduff's soldiers tear branches from the trees to use as camouflage before marching towards Macbeth's castle. Lady Macbeth is now prey to nightmares and walks in her sleep. While preparing himself to face the invading forces, Macbeth receives the news that his wife is dead, and he is then challenged and killed by Macduff. The opera ends with general rejoicing as the people hail their new King, Malcolm.

After its opening performances in Florence, *Macbeth* was staged in Paris in 1865 with substantial revisions: Lady Macbeth's aria in the second act ("La luce langue"), the Macbeth-Lady Macbeth duet in the third act ("Vi trovo alfin") and the opera's finale. Considered one of Verdi's most expressive and powerful operas, *Macbeth* has in recent times been seen as a major step forward in Verdi's musical development. His orchestration here reached new heights of accomplishment, which would prove of enormous benefit in the scoring of his later operas.

MCCRACKEN, JAMES

(Gary, Indiana 1926–New York 1988)

American tenor. A pupil of Walter Ezekiel and Mario Pagano, McCracken made his debut in Central City, Colorado. He appeared with the Metropolitan Opera in New York and from 1957 he was a member of the permanent company of Bonn Opera. Much of his career, however, centered on the Metropolitan, where from 1963 he appeared regularly in such operas as *Fidelio*, *Carmen*, *I pagliacci*, *Aida*, *Samson et Dalila* and *Otello*. His finest recording performances include

Top: The American conductor Lorin Maazel.

Above: The American tenor James McCracken.

Florestan in *Fidelio*, Verdi's *Otello* and Jean in Meyerbeer's *Le prophète*.

MCINTYRE, DONALD

(Auckland 1934)
New Zealand bass-baritone. He studied at London's Guildhall School of Music and made his debut with Welsh National Opera in Cardiff in 1959 singing Zaccaria in Verdi's *Nabucco*. From 1960 to 1967 he was a member of the Sadler's Wells company in London, and in 1967 he appeared for the first time at Covent Garden (as Pizarro in *Fidelio*). The same year brought his Bayreuth Festival debut, as Telramund in *Lohengrin*, and he returned there to sing in *Der fliegende Holländer*, *Parsifal* and *Tristan und Isolde*, as well as taking the role of Wotan in the famous and controversial Chéreau/Boulez *Ring* (1976–80). He also sang with Hamburg Opera (from 1971), at La Scala, Milan, the Paris Opéra (1973–74), the Metropolitan Opera in New York (from 1975) and at many other international music venues. In addition to his reputation as one of the most distinguished interpreters of Wagner, McIntyre has won acclaim for his performances in operas by Richard Strauss, Berg (*Wozzeck*) and Weber.

MACKERRAS, SIR CHARLES

(Schenectady, New York 1925)
Australian conductor. He studied at the Conservatory in Sydney and at the Academy of Fine Arts in Prague (1947–48), where he first became interested in the operas of Janáček, subsequently becoming a tireless advocate. He made his debut at London's Sadler's Wells, where he conducted from 1948 to 1954, and was music director from 1970 to 1977. He was conductor at the Hamburg Opera (1966–70) and of the BBC Symphony (1977–79), as well as at numerous other international music venues. Mackerras is regarded as one of the greatest interpreters of Janáček in *Jenufa, Príhody Lisky Bystrousky* (The Cunning Little Vixen), *Vec Makropulos* (The Makropoulos Case), *Kát'a Kabanová* and *Z mrtvého domu* (From the House of the Dead), of which he made impressive recordings. He is also known as a conductor of Purcell's *The Indian Queen* and *Dido and Aeneas*, Martinu's *Griechische Passion* (The Greek Passion) and Delius's *A Village Romeo and Juliet*.

MCLAUGHLIN, MARIE

(Lanarkshire 1954)
Scottish soprano. She studied in Glasgow and at the London Opera Studio. After her debut in 1978, she appeared regularly at Covent Garden, first 1981 as Zerlina in *Don Giovanni*. It is as a Mozart performer that McLaughlin scored her greatest successes and displayed fine vocal timbre and sensitivity in performance. Nor should her abilities as an actress be overlooked, as can be seen from video recordings of Jonathan Miller's 1982 production of Verdi's *Rigoletto* at the English National Opera and of the Glyndebourne 1987 *La traviata* production by Sir Peter Hall. These performances also drew attention to the limitations of McLaughlin's technique, particularly in the upper register, which have prevented her from attempting nineteenth-century Italian opera.

MACNEIL, CORNELL

(Minneapolis 1922)
American baritone. After studying at the Julius Hartt School and completing his training with Friedrich Schorr, he made his debut in the role of John Sorel in the world premiere of Menotti's *The Consul* in Philadelphia (1950). He then appeared with New York City Opera (1953–55) and in San Francisco (1955) and Chicago (1957). In 1959 he won international fame for his Verdi performances of Carlo V (*Ernani*) and Rigoletto at La Scala, Milan, and with the Metropolitan Opera House in New York respectively. Much of his career was to center on the Metropolitan, especially in Verdi roles, of which he proved to be an outstanding interpreter. In 1982 he sang Germont in Franco Zeffirelli's film of *La traviata*.

MADAMA BUTTERFLY

Opera in three acts by Giacomo Puccini (1858–1924), to a libretto by Giuseppe Giacosa and Luigi Illica, from the play Madame Butterfly *by David Belasco, based on a story by John Luther Long. First performance: Milan, La Scala, 17 February 1904.*

The action takes place in Nagasaki around the time the opera was written. A wedding is taking place between Pinkerton (tenor), a lieutenant in the U.S. Navy, and Cio-Cio-San, a geisha (Madama Butterfly) (soprano). Pinkerton sees this marriage as simply a game he can walk away from when he becomes bored, and the American consul Sharpless (baritone) reproaches him in a paternal way for his attitude. Three years have

Above: The New Zealand bass-baritone Donald McIntyre.

Right: The soprano Rosetta Pampanini as Butterfly.

Opposite above: Giacomo Puccini with Elsa Szamosi in the role of Butterfly.

Opposite right: A scene from *Madame Sans-Gêne* by Umberto Giordano.

gone by since Pinkerton's departure, and Butterfly continues to wait for him. Then one day the sound of cannon announces the arrival of Pinkerton's ship. Accompanied by his new American wife Kate (soprano) and by Sharpless, Pinkerton calls at Butterfly's house. The Consul has told him that, unbeknown to him, a son has been born to him in his absence. Consumed with remorse, Pinkerton feels unable to face Butterfly and leaves without seeing her. Then the unhappy Butterfly sees Kate with the Consul and guesses the terrible truth: Kate has come to take the child away. After bidding a heart-rending farewell to her son, Butterfly stabs herself through the heart. Pinkerton appears in the doorway, but all he can do is to gather up the lifeless body of poor Butterfly in his arms.

Madama Butterfly, Puccini's own favourite opera, marks (together with *La bohème*) a return to psychological drama, intimate stories, a careful observation of the workings of the heart and the poetry of everyday life. The opera focuses exclusively on the character of Butterfly and her path to tragedy. The first performance caused an uproar, a fiasco engineered by factions hostile to the composer. But Puccini altered the score, making it smoother and more balanced: the original version was in two acts, and the composer now divided the second act into two acts. This new version, staged at the Teatro Grande in Brescia on 28 May 1904, was a triumphant success.

MADAME SANS-GÊNE

Opera in three acts by Umberto Giordano (1867–1948), to a libretto by Renato Simoni, based on the comedy of the same name by Victorien Sardou and Emile Moreau. First performance: New York, Metropolitan Opera House, 25 January 1915.

The action takes place in Paris on 10 August 1792, the day of the storming of the Tuileries. Caterina Hubscher (soprano), a beautiful young woman from Alsace who is known as Madame Sans-Gêne, has offered her laundry-room as a hiding place to a wounded Austrian officer, the Conte de Neipperg (tenor). Sergeant Léfebvre (tenor), Caterina's fiancé, helps her to arrange the Conte's escape. Many years later, Léfebvre, having won great distinction in the battle of Danzig, has been made Marshal and Duke of Danzig, and Madame Sans-Gêne, now married to him, has become the Duchess. Caterina's easy-going conduct causes irritation at Court, and Napoleon (baritone) himself orders Léfebvre to divorce her and marry someone more suited to his social position. But the couple have no intention of separating: Caterina reacts by causing a scandal at a reception and then appears before Napoleon. The Emperor orders her to divorce, but Caterina reminds him of the days in her laundry-room when she helped a penniless young officer by the name of Napoleon Bonaparte. The Emperor is moved by this revelation and Caterina takes advantage of the situation to ask him for clemency for her friend Neipperg, who had been caught entering the Empress's apartments. Napoleon duly intervenes in the case, showing his admiration of Caterina's intelligence and generosity. To the amazement of the assembled gathering, Caterina leaves on the arm of the Emperor to start the hunt.

Madame Sans-Gêne was initially very successful, but as the years passed, it was performed increasingly less often (the last time being in 1967 at La Scala). It nonetheless illustrates how Giordano could bring the same vigorous instinct for theater to bear on an opera with a historical plot which he had already demonstrated in *Andrea Chénier*.

MADERNA, BRUNO

(Venice 1920–Darmstadt 1973)
Italian composer and conductor, naturalized German. He studied at the Conservatorio di Santa Cecilia in Rome, where in 1940 he graduated in composition. He then continued his studies in Venice with Malipiero and in Vienna with Hermann Scherchen. His first work for the theater was the radio opera *Don Perlimplin* (1962), and this was followed by *Hyperion* (1964), *Von A bis Z* (From A to Z, 1970) and *Satyricon* (1973). As a conductor, he concentrated on contemporary music, conducting the world premieres of Nono's *Intolleranza* (1960) and Berio's *Passaggio* (1963) as well as operas by Richard Strauss, Mercadante, Mozart and Monteverdi, whose *Orfeo* he revised in 1967.

MALFITANO, CATHERINE

(New York 1948)
American soprano. After studying at the Manhattan School of Music, she made her debut in 1972 as Nannetta (in Verdi's *Falstaff*) at the Central City Festival. She was under contract to New York City Opera from 1974 to 1979 and at the same time embarked on an intensive career which took her to leading opera houses in America and to Europe (from 1974 onwards), where she sang at the Holland Festival (Susanna in *Le nozze di Figaro*). Malfitano went on to appear at the Salzburg Festival (*La clemenza di Tito* in 1976), Covent Garden (*Le nozze di Figaro* and *Don Giovanni* in 1976), the Teatro Comunale in Florence (*Les contes d'Hoffmann* in 1980 and, later, in a number of other roles, including the lead in Monteverdi's *L'incoronazione di Poppea* in 1992) at other leading opera venues. With an extremely wide-ranging and versatile repertoire and outstanding performance talents, she has in recent years been acclaimed for her singing of Puccini's *Madama Butterfly* and Richard Strauss's *Salome*. In 1992 she was Tosca in the multi-media event transmitted throughout the world by Italian television.

MALGOIRE, JEAN-CLAUDE

(Avignon 1940)
French conductor and oboist. He studied music first at the Conservatoire in Avignon and from 1956 at the Paris Conservatoire, beginning his career as a solo and orchestral oboist. In 1967, with a group of friends, he founded an orchestral ensemble of players using original instruments, "La Grand Ecurie et la Chambre du Roy." As conductor of "La Grand Ecurie," he was responsible for a number of performances from the baroque repertoire, from Monteverdi to Handel (*Rinaldo*, *Serse*, *Tamerlano*) and particularly featuring the major French opera composers – Lully, Charpentier, Rameau – which he conducted at leading Early Music festivals as well as at numerous opera houses, especially in France. His more recent performances have included Gluck's *Alceste* and Lully's opera of the same name at the Opéra in Paris (1991) and his own pastiche reconstruction of Vivaldi's *Montezuma* in Monte Carlo (1992).

Above: The Italian contralto Bernadette Manca di Nissa.

MALIPIERO, GIAN FRANCESCO

(Venice 1882–Treviso 1973)
Italian composer. He studied at the Conservatory in Vienna and in Venice and Bologna, where he graduated in composition (1904). In a full career spanning 70 years, he composed more than 30 works for the opera house, among them the three Goldoni plays (*La bottega da caffè* and *Sior Todero Brontolon*, composed in 1922, and *Le baruffe chiozzotte* in 1926), performed in Darmstadt in 1926; *Orfeo* (1925); *Torneo notturno* (1931); his most famous opera, *La favola del figlio cambiato* (1934); *Giulio Cesare* (1936); *I capricci di Callot* (1942); and *L'allegra brigata* (1950). Malipiero's theatrical language is decidedly anti-romantic, emphasizing a vocal element, which shows the influence not only of Gregorian chant and the music of the sixteenth century but also of the twentieth century. Studies and books written by Malipiero about leading figures in the history of musical theory and innovation – *Monteverdi* (1930), *Stravinsky* (1945) and *Vivaldi* (1958) – illustrate a particularly important part of his musical vision.

MANCA DI NISSA, BERNADETTE

(Cagliari 1954)
Italian contralto. She studied singing privately before going on to the Salzburg Mozarteum. In 1981 she won the International Bel Canto Competition in Pesaro and then made her debut as Isaura in *Tancredi* at the Rossini Festival in Pesaro in 1982, returning there to sing in *Il viaggio a Reims* 1984 and *La gazza ladra* 1989. From 1983 (when she was again Isaura in *Tancredi*), she appeared regularly at La Fenice in Venice, where she sang in Albinoni's *Il nascimento dell'Aurora*, Mozart's *Mitridate, re di Ponto* (1984 and 1991), Handel's *Semele* (1991) and Rossini's *L'italiana in Algeri* (1992). From 1985 she was engaged by La Scala, Milan, in operas including Jommelli's *Fetonte* (1988), Pergolesi's *Lo frate 'nnamurato* (1989) and, most notably, Gluck's *Orfeo ed Euridice* (1989), conducted by Riccardo Muti, in which she sang the lead. Also very active as a concert artiste and drawing on an extensive repertoire ranging from the baroque of Handel and Pergolesi to contemporary music and Luigi Nono (*Prometeo*, 1984), Manca Di Nissa has established a reputation as a Rossini singer on the strength of her authentic contralto voice, with its consistent delivery and finely-placed technique, and her skill in *bel canto*.

MANON

Opera in five acts and six scenes by Jules Massenet (1842–1912), to a libretto by Henri Meilhac and Philippe Gille, based on the novel Histoire du chevalier des Grieux et de Manon Lescaut *by Antoine-François Prévost. First performance: Paris, Théâtre de*

Right: The composer Gian Francesco Malipiero.

l'Opéra-Comique, 19 January 1884.

The action takes place in France in 1721. The stage-coach from Arras draws up in the courtyard of a tavern in Amiens, and from it steps Manon (soprano). She is met by Sergeant Lescaut (baritone), her cousin, who has been entrusted with the task of accompanying her to a convent school. Left alone for a moment, Manon is approached by the young Chevalier Des Grieux (tenor). Love blossoms quickly

between the two, and they run away together to Paris. Some time later, Lescaut pays his cousin Manon a visit. With him is a friend, De Brétigny (baritone). While Des Grieux is talking to Lescaut, De Brétigny offers Manon his wealth and warns her that Des Grieux's father has been so irritated by his son's conduct that he is going to have him abducted. He is indeed carried away and, while Manon becomes De Brétigny's mistress, Des Grieux, now disillusioned with life, decides to join the priesthood. Manon visits him at the seminary of Saint-Sulpice, and Des Grieux, seduced once again by her charms, runs away with her. The scene changes to the Hôtel de Transylvanie, where Des Grieux is forced to gamble in order to obtain the money he needs to satisfy Manon's every whim, but during a game of cards, the two of them are accused of cheating and arrested. The old Comte Des Grieux (bass) has his son released, but Manon is treated as a prostitute and deported to America. With the help of Lescaut, Des Grieux attempts to help Manon to escape, but the plan fails. Manon, weak from struggling with hardship, dies in her beloved's arms.

Manon is the most famous and most musically accomplished of Massenet's operas. In it the composer skilfully blended several different musical genres, from serious to comic opera and from the lyrical through the intimate to the tragic, demonstrating his art at its best in a work which represents the highest achievement of French musical Romanticism.

MANON LESCAUT

Opera in four acts by Giacomo Puccini (1858–1924), to a libretto (revised by the composer) by Giuseppe Giacosa, Luigi Illica, Ruggero Leoncavallo, Marco Praga and Domenico Oliva from the novel Histoire du chevalier des Grieux et de Manon Lescaut *by Antoine-François Prévost. First performance: Turin, Teatro Regio, 1 February 1893.*

The action takes place in France during the second half of the eighteenth century. The stage-coach from Arras stops in the square at Amiens and Manon (soprano) steps down from it. Against her wishes, she is on her way to the convent school, and her brother Lescaut (baritone) is accompanying her. Des Grieux (tenor), a student, has caught sight of Manon and, enchanted by her beauty, approaches and speaks to her. For both, it is love at first sight. Another student, Edmondo (tenor) warns Des Grieux that Geronte de Ravoir (bass), a wealthy old treasury official and one of Manon's travelling companions, is plotting to abduct her to Paris. Des Grieux thwarts the abduction and persuades Manon to go to the city with him. Some time later, Manon, after deserting Des Grieux, has become the mistress of Geronte and is living in his luxurious house. But this luxury does not satisfy her, and she asks her brother for news of Des Grieux. He arrives, and a passionate love scene is played out between the two. Geronte surprises the lovers together and, in a rage, goes to call the police. The couple decide to run away, but Manon lingers to collect money and jewellery. The police arrive, and she is arrested on charges of theft and prostitution. She is then sentenced to be deported. Des Grieux and Lescaut attempt to help her to escape, and when this fails, Des Grieux obtains permission from the Captain of the ship to travel with her. The scene changes to a desolate landscape. The two lovers have fled from New Orleans and, weak and exhausted, they head into the wilderness. Manon, worn out, dies shortly afterwards in the arms of her beloved. Crazed with grief, Des Grieux collapses over Manon's body.

Manon Lescaut is Puccini's third opera but the first in which he fully discovered his identity as a composer. The strongest features of the score are romantic feelings and the urgency of passion. Puccini expresses these with a wealth of melodic ideas he was never able to recreate in his later operas. The work was composed between March 1890 and October 1892. This long gestation period was principally due to difficulties with the libretto, which was co-written by five writers as well as the publisher Ricordi. The wait was, however, more than rewarded by the success the opera enjoyed at its first performance.

MANUGUERRA, MATTEO

(Tunis 1924)

French baritone. He began to study singing in Buenos Aires, where he made his debut as the tenor soloist in Mozart's *Requiem*. In 1962 he began to appear as a baritone in France, at the Opéra in Lyons and the Paris Opéra (from 1966). Manuguerra was engaged by leading

A scene from *Manon Lescaut* by Giacomo Puccini, performed for the first time in Turin in 1893.

international opera houses, particularly in the United States, and his performances were mainly of the Italian repertoire. His reputation also rests on recordings of *Nabucco* (1977), *La battaglia di Legnano* (1978), *Stiffelio* (1979), *I puritani* (1979), *Cavalleria rusticana* (1979) and *I masnadieri* (1982).

MAN WHO MISTOOK HIS WIFE FOR A HAT, THE

Chamber opera in one act by Michael Nyman, to a libretto by Michael Morris, Christopher Rawlence and the composer, based on a clinical case described by Oliver Sacks in his book of the same name. First performance: London, Institute of Contemporary Arts, 27 October 1986.

The action centers on Doctor S. (tenor), neurologist, and one of his patients, Doctor P. (baritone), a singer. P.'s is an extremely unusual clinical case: he sees objects in a distorted way, mistakes parking-meters for human beings, and even mistakes his wife, Mrs. P. (soprano), for his hat. Doctor S. begins a long series of visits to P.'s house and comes to the conclusion that P. is suffering from a serious condition of visual agnosia (loss of the faculty of recognition), which prevents his brain from making coherent visual sense of something his eye sees, so that its parts never add up to a whole. Mrs. P. helps by providing a normal daily routine, but as soon as these habits are interrupted, P. withdraws into silence and complete immobility. Doctor S. observes that his wife's love and his passion for the music of Schumann are the only sources of equilibrium in P.'s fragmented visual world. In the end, Doctor S. realizes it is these two things alone that have for years enabled Doctor P. to lead an active life.

It was after writing numerous works of instrumental music and film scores (especially with the director Peter Greenaway) that the British composer Michael Nyman first tried his hand at opera with *The Man Who Mistook his Wife for a Hat*.

MAOMETTO II

Opera in two acts by Gioachino Rossini (1792–1868), to a libretto by Cesare Della Valle. First performance: Naples, Teatro San Carlo, 3 December 1820.

The action takes place in Negroponte, a Venetian colony in Greece besieged by the Turkish forces of Maometto II. The commanding officer Paolo Erisso (tenor), after reaching a decision with his captains to fight to the death, entrusts his daughter Anna (soprano) to a young warrior, Calbo (contralto). He is in love with Anna, but she admits to her father and to Calbo that she loves another man, whom she knows as Uberto di Mitilene. Their conversation is interrupted by the announcement that Maometto's troops have succeeded in forcing their way into the city. Maometto (bass) puts Erisso and Calbo in prison. Anna is distraught and pleads for clemency, but at that moment she recognizes the troops' leader as the man with whom she is in love. Maometto releases the two prisoners but asks for Anna's hand in marriage. She is taken to Maometto's tent, struggling between her duty towards her father and country and her love for the man who is also her enemy. In the end she decides to share the fate of her own family, goes to her father and asks him to allow her to marry Calbo. Erisso and Calbo go off to fight, leaving Anna to pray fervently, while from far off can be heard the sounds of a Venetian victory over the Muslim forces. Maometto arrives, and Anna reveals to him that she has married Calbo. Maometto, who had believed Calbo to be Anna's brother, hurls himself at her in a rage. Clinging to her mother's tomb, Anna stabs herself.

Maometto II represents a crucial stage in the development of Rossini's dramatic skills. He attempts to dispense with the usual *opera seria* structure of separate items in order to accelerate the progress of the action. With this in mind, he devotes special attention to both the recitatives and the *bel canto* passages, which are given precise theatrical role, linked not only to the requirements of the singers but also to a particular dramatic situation. Rossini makes prominent use of the chorus as the narrator of events.

MARIA DI ROHAN, O IL CONTE DI CHALAIS

Opera in three parts by Gaetano Donizetti (1797–1848), to a libretto by Salvatore Cammarano, based on the play Un duel sous le cardinal Richelieu *by Lockroy and Badon. First performance: Vienna, Kärntnertortheater, 5 June 1843.*

The action takes place in Paris around the year 1630. Enrico di Chevreuse (baritone) has killed a nephew of Cardinal Richelieu in a duel. Thanks to the intercession of Count Riccardo di Chalais (tenor), Maria

Above: A scene from *Maometto II* by Giacomo Rossini, performed for the first time in Naples in 1820.

Right: Portrait of Gaetano Donizetti

di Rohan (soprano), a lady-in-waiting to the Queen, is able to win clemency for Chevreuse, whom she has secretly married. Shortly after this, Armando di Gonde (contralto) makes some malicious insinuations about Maria, and Riccardo challenges him to a duel. Meanwhile, there is a rumour that Richelieu has been deposed, and consequently Chevreuse, now out of prison, feels he is in a position to reveal that he has married Maria. On the day of the duel, Riccardo, afraid he is going to be killed, writes a letter to Maria in which he confesses that he loves her. But then Maria arrives to warn him that Richelieu has regained power and could avenge himself on Riccardo in return for the clemency Riccardo had obtained for Chevreuse. Enter Chevreuse himself, who is Riccardo's godfather, to remind him that the hour appointed for the duel is drawing near. Maria, on the unexpected arrival of her husband, has hidden in another room and now lingers with Riccardo. The Visconte di Suze (bass), a friend of Riccardo, brings news that Chevreuse has taken his place in the duel and has been wounded. Riccardo hastens to his friend's side and learns that Richelieu's guards have been searching his house. Worried by this, he returns home and is unable to find the letter to Maria, which he had left in a drawer. The letter is handed to Chevreuse shortly after on the Cardinal's instructions. In his fury, Chevreuse cannot believe Maria's protestations of innocence nor Riccardo's word when he swears she is telling the truth. Chevreuse wants a duel, and the two men go out to fight, but Chevreuse returns soon after to say that Riccardo has been killed trying to resist arrest by Richelieu's guards.

Maria di Rohan belongs to the last period of Donizetti's creative life. It was a modest success but soon disappeared from the repertoire. Revived for the first time in Bergamo in 1957, the opera was subsequently staged at the Teatro San Carlo in Naples (1962), in Lisbon (1968), at La Fenice in Venice (1974) and at the Valle d'Itria Festival (1988).

MARIA STUARDA

Opera in three acts by Gaetano Donizetti (1797–1848), to a libretto by Giuseppe Bardari based on Schiller's tragedy. First performance with the censored title of Buondelmonte*: Naples, Teatro San Carlo, 18 October 1834. First performance with the original title but with substantial revisions: Milan, La Scala, 30 December 1835.*

At the Palace of Westminster in 1587, Roberto, Earl of Leicester (tenor), delivers to Queen Elisabetta (mezzo-soprano) a letter from Maria Stuarda (soprano), the Scottish Queen being held prisoner at Fotheringhay. In the letter Maria asks for an audience with her cousin Elisabetta, and the Queen, moved by this request but also jealous of Leicester's interest in her rival, eventually agrees. But their meeting turns into a clash when Maria, no longer able to endure Elisabetta's humiliating insinuations, summons up all her pride to express her contempt for her. Angered, and prompted by her minister, Lord Cecil (bass), Elisabetta signs Maria's death sentence. Maria prepares to die, and after making her confession to Talbot (bass) and saying her farewells, she is supported by Leicester as she approaches the place of execution.

The Spanish soprano Montserrat Caballé in the role of Maria Stuarda in Donizetti's opera of the same name.

The censor took exception to the idea of two Queens hurling powerful insults at one another on stage, particularly if one of them was to be the very Catholic Mary Stuart, and ordered that the opera's characters and settings be changed. The libretto was revised by Pietro Salatino, and this version of the original was staged with the title *Buondelmonte*.

MÂROUF, SAVETIER DU CAIRE

(Mârouf, The Cobbler of Cairo)

Comic opera in five acts by Henri Rabaud (1873–1949), to a libretto by Lucien Népoty based on a story from The Thousand and One Nights. *First performance: Paris, Théâtre de l'Opéra-Comique, 15 May 1914.*

Mârouf (tenor), an out-of-work cobbler, has the misfortune of having a wife, Fattoumah (soprano), whose exploits are a catalogue of disasters. One day her loud shouting is overheard by the Cadi (bass) himself, who imagines the noise is due to Mârouf beating his wife and orders that he be thrashed for it. Distraught and aching all over, Mârouf decides to leave home. The scene changes to the city of Khaitan, where Mârouf is welcomed in fine style by Ali (bass), an old school friend. The festivities in honour of Mârouf arouse the curiosity of the Sultan (bass). He assumes that this Mârouf is a wealthy foreign nobleman and not only invites him to his palace but offers him the hand of his daughter, Princess Saamcheddine (soprano), in marriage. Enchanted by the Princess, Mârouf nonetheless tells her who and what he really is. When the Sultan also discovers that Mârouf is not wealthy at all, the Princess, who is in love with the cobbler, leaves Khaitan with him. The two find shelter in the hut of a fellah (tenor). One day Mârouf comes across a stone covering a stairway that leads down to an underground vault. The Princess wants to explore it, but Mârouf dissuades her, because he does not want the fellah to know about the vault. As he tries to push the stone back into place, the ring on it breaks. The Princess rubs it on her dress, and lo and behold the fellah turns into the guardian of the treasure and genie of the ring. After gathering up large quantities of riches, Mârouf is saved from execution and is free to live happily with his Princess.

Mârouf is Rabaud's most famous opera. Its premiere was a resounding success and it enjoyed an unbroken run of 200 performances.

MARRINER, SIR NEVILLE

(Lincoln 1924)

British conductor and violinist. He studied at the Royal College of Music in London and began his career as a violinist, first with the Philharmonia Orchestra (from 1952), then with the London Symphony (1956–68). In 1959 he founded the Academy of St. Martin-in-the-Fields Orchestra, which he directed for many years. He also conducted the Los Angeles Chamber Orchestra (1969–79), the Minnesota Orchestra (1979–86) and the symphony orchestra of Süddeutsche Rundfunk, Stuttgart (1983–89). Marriner's name remains most closely associated with the Academy of St. Martin-in-the-Fields, with whom he has also given important performances of opera, especially Mozart's *Così fan tutte*, *Don Giovanni*, *Le nozze di Figaro* and *Die Zauberflöte* (The Magic Flute) and Rossini's *Il barbiere di Siviglia* and *La Cenerentola*.

Top: The German composer and conductor Heinrich Marschner.

Above: The British conductor and violinist Sir Neville Marriner.

MARSCHNER, HEINRICH

(Zittau, Saxony 1795–Hanover 1861)

German composer and conductor. He displayed a prodigious gift for music and abandoned his law studies at the University of Leipzig in order to study it full-time. His career centered mainly on Dresden (from 1821), Leipzig (from 1827) and Hanover (1831–59). Marschner had a considerable reputation as both composer and conductor at leading German opera houses. His own operas include *Der Vampyr* (1828) and *Hans Heiling* (1833).

MARSHALL, MARGARET

(Stirling 1949)

Scottish soprano. She studied at the Royal Scottish Academy in Glasgow and in Munich with Hans Hotter. In 1974 she won the Munich International Singing Competition, after which she developed a career as a concert artiste until 1976, the year in which she made her debut with Scottish Opera in Glasgow and sang Euridice in Gluck's *Orfeo ed Euridice* at the Maggio Musicale Festival in Florence with Riccardo Muti conducting. She returned to Florence in 1979 as the Countess in Mozart's *Le nozze di Figaro*, having established a reputation as an exquisite Mozart performer. She has performed at Covent Garden (*Le nozze di Figaro*), the Salzburg Festival (*Così fan tutte*, 1982–86) and La Scala, Milan, as well as making many concert appearances, especially in Bach, Handel, Vivaldi and Pergolesi.

MARTHA, ODER DER MARKT ZU RICHMOND

(Martha, or Richmond Market)

Opera in four acts by Friedrich von Flotow (1812–1833), to a libretto by Friedrich Wilhelm Riese, after S. H. Vernoy de Saint-Georges' ballet-pantomime Lady Henriette, ou la servante de Greenwich, *set to music by Flotow with Burgmüller and Deldevez (1844). First performance: Vienna, Hofopertheater, 25 November 1847.*

The action takes place in England around 1710. Lady Harriet (soprano), lady-in-waiting to Queen Anne, decides to solve the problem of her boredom by dressing up as a country-woman and, with her friend Nancy (mezzo-soprano), joining a group of servant-girls who are going to Richmond in search of work. The two accept an offer of employment by Plunkett (baritone) and his friend Lionel (tenor). But when, in their new posts, they are asked to prepare supper or use a spinning-wheel, Martha (Harriet's new name) and Betsy (as Nancy now calls herself) show themselves to be considerably lacking in expertise. That night, Harriet's cousin Sir Tristram (bass) arrives in a carriage, and the two young women take to their heels. A few days later, Harriet and Nancy are part of the entourage accompanying the Queen on a hunting expedition, and they are recognized by Plunkett and Lionel. Lionel goes up to Harriet, with whom he is in love, but she feels ashamed of the feeling she also has for the young countryman and makes a show of pushing him away. Lionel is arrested, but then, thanks to a ring he has in his possession, which Harriet gets Plunkett to hand to the Queen, he is not only released but recognized as the heir to the Earl of Derby, who had been unjustly deprived of his title. Plunkett asks Nancy to marry him, while Harriet offers her heart and hand to Lionel.

Martha is Flotow's most successful and popular opera and has continued to be performed fairly frequently. It is very much in the tradition of *opéra-comique*, with an eclectic style and Franco-Italian influences.

MARTIN, ANDREA

(Klagenfurt 1949)

Austrian baritone. He studied at the Vienna Musikhochschule, at the Wiener Staatsopernstudio, with Hans Swarowsky, and finally at the Accademia di Santa Cecilia in Rome. After early performances in Austria and Germany, he was a finalist in the first year of the Maria Callas Competition (1980), which enabled him to establish his reputation at La Fenice in Venice (1981) in the role of Corrado in Donizetti's *Maria di Rudenz*. He went on to sing in some of the leading houses in Italy and elsewhere. Martin became known as an elegant performer of the nineteenth-century Italian repertoire and especially of the operas of Donizetti, taking part in the first performances in modern times of Donizetti's *Alina, regina di Golconda* (1987) and *Imelda de' Lambertazzi* (1989).

MARTIN, JANIS

(Sacramento, California 1939)
American soprano. A pupil of Julia Monroe in Sacramento, she went on to complete her training in New York with Lili Wexberg and Otto Guth. She made her debut in San Francisco as Annina (*La traviata*) in 1960. Two years later, thanks to a competition, she was able to join the Metropolitan Opera in New York, where she spent three seasons. From 1965 to 1969 she became a member of the opera house in Nuremberg, where she sang mezzo-soprano roles. From 1970 she tackled the soprano repertoire, forging a reputation as a singer of Wagner and Richard Strauss. She went on to appear in leading international opera houses, including La Scala, Milan, the Vienna Staatsoper, the Deutsche Oper Berlin and Lyric Opera of Chicago. Martin became known as a singer of powerful incisiveness and great vocal impact, powered by a triumphantly secure upper register, gifts very much in evidence in her performances of Richard Strauss's *Elektra* (Toulouse, 1992) and Wagner's *Der fliegende Holländer* (The Flying Dutchman, Teatro San Carlo, Naples, 1992).

MARTÌN Y SOLER, VICENTE

(Valencia 1754–St. Petersburg 1806)
Spanish composer. A choirboy at Valencia Cathedral, he went on from there to Madrid, where in all probability he made his debut as a composer. Chapel-master to the Infante Carlos, later Carlos IV, he then moved to Italy, where between 1779 and 1785 a number of his operas and ballets were staged, particularly in Naples. From 1785 he was in Vienna, where he worked with Lorenzo da Ponte, the librettist for Martìn y Soler's best-known opera, *Una cosa rara* (1786). He then entered the Court of Catherine II of Russia (from 1788), where he wrote another opera, *Gore Bogatyr' Kosometovic* (The Wicked Knight, 1789), to a libretto by the Empress Catherine. After a sojourn in London (1794–96), he settled permanently in St. Petersburg, holding important court posts.

MARTINŮ, BOHUSLAV

(Polička 1890–Liestal, Basle 1959)
Bohemian composer, naturalized American. He studied the violin at the Conservatory in Prague (1906–13), and began his music career in the Czech Philharmonic Orchestra (1913–23). He then studied composition in Prague (1922), went on to complete his training in Paris (from 1923) with Roussel and came into close contact with Stravinsky, Honegger and other composers. He left France in 1940 and settled in the United States (1941), becoming an American citizen in 1952. In 1957, however, he settled in Switzerland, where he remained until his death. Martinů is regarded as one of the greatest Czech composers of the twentieth century. He composed about 15 operas, including *Veselohra na moste* (Comedy on the Bridge, 1937), *Julietta* (1938) and *Griechische Passion* (The Greek Passion, performed posthumously in 1961).

MARTINUCCI, NICOLA

(Taranto 1941)
Italian tenor. He began to study singing in adult life, with the encouragement of the famous tenor Mario Del Monaco. He studied in Milan with Marcello Del Monaco, the tenor's brother, and made his debut at the Teatro Nuovo in Milan (1966) as Manrico (*Il trovatore*). His performance as Calàf (*Turandot*) won him the 1966 Viotti prize in Vercelli, and this brought him further important debuts in Italy and beyond. His reputation was substantially increased in 1980 when he sang Radamès (*Aida*) at the Arena in Verona, a performance which showed him to be one of the finest tenors of his generation. In the years that followed, Martinucci was a guest artist at leading European and American opera houses, from La Scala, Milan (from 1983), where he sang in *Andrea Chénier*, *I Lombardi*, *Aida*, *Turandot* and *Il tabarro*, to Covent Garden (from 1985), the Metropolitan Opera House, New York (*Turandot*, 1988) and many others. Martinucci's is a vigorous lyric tenor voice. He is famous for his performances in *Aida* and *Turandot*, but his repertoire also includes *Tosca*, *Norma*, *La Gioconda*, *I pagliacci* and *Il trovatore*.

MARTON, EVA

(Budapest 1943)
Hungarian soprano. She studied with Endre Rösler and Jenö Sipos at the Franz Liszt Music Academy in Budapest. After graduating in 1968, she was under contract to the opera house in Budapest (1968–72), where she sang in Rimsky-Korsakov's *Zolotoy Pyetushok* (The Golden Cockerel), Handel's *Rodelinda*, Puccini's *Tosca* and the Countess in Mozart's *Le nozze di Figaro*. From 1972 to 1977 she was a member of the resident company at the Frankfurt Opera and quickly established her reputation at the leading German opera houses, in *Don Giovanni* (Munich, 1974); *Die Frau ohne Schatten* (Hamburg, 1976); *Tannhäuser* (Bayreuth, 1977) and *Tosca* (Vienna Staatsoper, 1973). From 1976 she sang regularly at the

Top: The Italian tenor Nicola Martinucci as Radames in Verdi's *Aida*.

Above: The Bohemian composer Bohuslav Martinů.

Metropolitan Opera in New York, appearing in *Die Meistersinger von Nürnberg*, *Elektra*, *Die Frau ohne Schatten*, *Lohengrin*, *La Gioconda*, *Fidelio*, and *Turandot*, an opera she has sung throughout the world. Marton was engaged to join the opera houses in Chicago (from 1980) and San Francisco (from 1984), and at the Salzburg Festival (from 1982). With her powerful dramatic soprano voice and great stage presence, she won particular acclaim as an interpreter of Wagner and Richard Strauss.

MARTY, JEAN-PIERRE

(Paris 1932)

French conductor and pianist. After embarking on a brilliant career as a pianist, muscle trouble forced him to give up the instrument. He then took up conducting in New York, becoming principal conductor at the American Ballet Theater (1963). On his return to France, he began to concentrate on opera conducting (from 1965), appearing as guest conductor at various opera houses (1965–73). From 1973 to 1980 he was in charge of opera at Radio France, and in 1979 he resumed his career as a pianist. In 1987 he became director of the American Conservatory at Fontainebleu. Marty also conducted the first recording of Auber's opera *Manon Lescaut* (1975).

MARTYRDOM OF ST. MAGNUS, THE

Chamber opera in nine scenes by Sir Peter Maxwell Davies (b.1934), to the composer's own libretto, based on George Mackay Brown's novel Magnus. *First performance: Kirkwall (Orkney), St. Magnus Cathedral, 18 June 1977.*

The action takes place in the twelfth century. The battle of Menai Strait is about to be fought between the King of Norway (first baritone), reinforced by contingents from Orkney and the Shetland Isles, and the Earl of Shrewsbury, who has the support of Wales. Earl Magnus (tenor), a pacifist, refuses to fight, lays down his arms, and begins to pray while the battle is raging. The Norwegians, Magnus's men, are victorious, and no arrow has hit Magnus. The scene changes to Orkney. The King of Norway entrusts Magnus and Earl Hakon (bass) with the government of the Orkney Isles. But rivalries quickly spring up between these two. Blind Mary (mezzo-soprano), whose role in the opera is that of narrator, describes the distressing events of the civil war. Magnus's longing for peace eventually leads to the calling of a peace conference. Magnus sets out for the island of Egilsay to meet Hakon, making light of a sense of foreboding he now feels. Hakon not only rejects Magnus's every overture of peace but throws him into prison and condemns him to death. At this point the narration switches to our own time. Hakon is now an official, Magnus a political prisoner. Hakon orders Lifolf the Butcher (first baritone) to execute the prisoner, a fate that awaits anyone who opposes Hakon's oppressive regime and is prepared to face death for their beliefs. The action then returns to the twelfth century. Blind Mary is praying at the tomb of St. Magnus and asking that, in his name, "the peace of Christ be brought into the world."

The Martyrdom of St. Magnus was commissioned by the BBC to mark the 50th birthday of Queen Elizabeth II. The score shows the composer's love of a chamber style, which in this work creates a sacred atmosphere close to the spirit of a mystery play. Maxwell Davies employs a small instrumental ensemble of about ten players and a correspondingly modest vocal ensemble of only five soloists (mezzo-soprano, tenor, two baritones and a bass). These five cover as many as 26 roles between them, as in the original story by George Mackay Brown.

MARY, QUEEN OF SCOTS

Opera in three acts by Thea Musgrave (b. 1928), to the composer's own libretto, based on Amalia Elguera's play Moray. *First performance: Edinburgh Festival, September 1977.*

The action takes place in Edinburgh between 1561 and 1668. Mary Stuart (soprano), widow of the King of France, has made a triumphant return to Scotland and become Queen. James, Earl of Moray (baritone), Mary's step-brother, and the Earl of Bothwell (tenor) immediately begin to compete with one another for the new sovereign's favour. The two noblemen are openly hostile to Lord

Above: The Hungarian soprano Eva Marton (see page 239).

Right: Pietro Mascagni among the cast of *Cavalleria rusticana* at its premiere in Rome.

Darnley (tenor), Mary's true favourite. The Queen wants to be left to bestow her affections as she wishes and, after dismissing Bothwell from her Court, she marries Darnley. The marriage proves to be a complete failure. Darnley leads a dissolute life and is not capable of being a king. Mary, now expecting a child, feels that the burden of power rests wholly on her shoulders and asks Moray for support. Meanwhile Darnley, who has been led to believe that the child about to be born is not his but the offspring of a relationship between the Queen and the musician David Riccio (bass-baritone), murders Riccio in a drunken fit of jealous rage. Mary accuses Moray of having incited Darnley to commit the murder in order to win the crown for himself, and as a result Moray is banished from Scotland. Moray then marches on Edinburgh at the head of an army. Lord Gordon (bass), Earl of Huntly, advises Mary to flee from Scotland and not to place too much trust in Lord Bothwell, whom she has recalled to Court. Now undermined and afraid, Mary accepts Bothwell's advances in the interests of protecting her newborn child. Furious at what is happening, Moray attacks and wounds Bothwell and accuses Mary of having allowed herself to be seduced by him. The people call for Mary to abdicate, and she takes refuge in England. Lord Gordon ensures the safety of her child, and no sooner has Moray taken power than Gordon kills him. Lord Morton (baritone), a friend of Moray, now comes forward as the guardian of Mary's child and assumes power in Scotland.

Mary, Queen of Scots is Thea Musgrave's most important opera. It demonstrates the composer's remarkable sense of theater as well as a perfect blend of music and words, illustrating how Musgrave had conceived text and music together and consequently created a work of impressive dramatic unity.

MASCAGNI, PIETRO

(Livorno 1863–Rome 1945)

Italian composer and conductor. He began to study music at the Conservatorio in Livorno (1876). After overcoming the disapproval of his father, who wanted him to be a lawyer, he devoted all his energies to music and became a student at the Conservatorio in Milan (1882). He was dismissed for breach of discipline, joined an operetta company and embarked on a career as conductor. In 1890 he won a competition run by the music publishers Sonzogno. His entry was the opera *Cavalleria rusticana*, which scored a tremendous success and made the composer's name. His subsequent operas were not so well-received. He attempted various genres, ranging from the idyllic (*L'amico Fritz*, 1891, and *Lodoletta*, 1917) to the romantic (*Guglielmo Ratcliff*, 1895), to using flowers as an exotic symbol (*Iris*, 1898), *Commedia dell'Arte* (*Le maschere*, 1901) and the medieval world (*Isabeau*, 1911, and *Parisina*, 1913), but they did not achieve the dramatic and musical completeness of *Cavalleria rusticana*. Alongside his work as a composer, Mascagni continued to conduct (until 1943) as well as holding important posts in various musical institutions: he was director at the Conservatorio in Pesaro (1895–1902), artistic director of the Teatro Costanzi (1909–10) and academician at the Accademia di Santa Cecilia (1922). He was one of the founders of the Accademia d'Italia (1929).

MASCHERE, LE

Opera in three acts by Pietro Mascagni (1863–1945), to a libretto by Luigi Illica. First performance: given simultaneously in Milan, Venice, Verona, Turin, Genoa and Rome, 17 January 1901 and two days later in Naples, 19 January 1901.

Young Florindo (tenor) is in love with Rosaura (soprano), daughter of Pantalone (bass), who reciprocates his love. But her father has decided to marry her to Captain Spaventa (baritone). Colombina (light soprano), maid to Doctor Graziano (baritone), and Brighella (tenor) help and

Top: A poster for Mascagni's *Le Maschere.*

Above: The composer Pietro Mascagni.

protect the young couple so they can continue their idyll. To this end, Brighella obtains a special powder for them that when poured into the wine at Rosaura and Spaventa's wedding, causes complete chaos among the guests, which results in the drawing-up of the marriage contract being postponed. With the aid of Arlecchino (tenor), Spaventa's servant, and Colombina, the lovers try to get the marriage cancelled for good. Arlecchino promises that he will provide them with a suitcase containing documents that are compromising for the Captain, but this suitcase falls into the hands of Doctor Graziano, who promptly joins forces with Brighella, disguised as a policeman, in reporting Spaventa to the authorities for fraud and bigamy. Pantalone then gives in and allows Florindo to marry Rosaura.

Le maschere was very favourably received in Rome (where it was conducted by Mascagni himself) but simultaneous performances in the other Italian cities brought no success, probably as a result of public expectations being too high in the wake of an exaggerated publicity campaign. The freshness and vitality of the work and the popular character of its music, however, enabled the work to be reassessed later on.

Scene from *I masnadieri* by Giuseppe Verdi.

MASINI, GIANFRANCO

(Reggio Emilia 1937)
Italian conductor. He studied music at the Conservatories of Parma and Bologna before going on to complete his training in Vienna with Hermann Scherchen. After his debut in 1973, he pursued a busy career, particularly in opera. Music director at the Teatro Guiseppe Verdi in Trieste, where his appearances were as conductor of *Linda di Chamounix* (1989), *L'elisir d'amore* (1990), Bellini's *La straniera* (1991) and Smareglia's *Pittori fiamminghi* (1991), Masini has been principal guest conductor of the Berlin Symphony Orchestra since 1987.

MASNADIERI, I

(The Thieves)
Opera in four parts by Giuseppe Verdi (1813–1901), to a libretto by Andrea Maffei, based on Schiller's tragedy Die Raüber. *First performance: London, Queen's Theater, 12 July 1847.*

The action takes place in Germany at the beginning of the eighteenth century. Carlo (tenor) receives a letter from his brother Francesco (baritone) in which he learns that his father, Massimiliano, Count of Moor (bass), has refused to forgive him for deserting his family. Embittered and disappointed, Carlo turns to life as an outlaw and becomes the leader of a gang of thieves. The letter is actually part of Francesco's plan to get rid of his brother and then do the same to his old father by lying to him that Carlo has died. Massimiliano cannot bear so much sorrow, and he dies. Francesco now has a completely free hand and proposes to Amalia (soprano), his cousin and engaged to Carlo. But Amalia refuses, flees from the castle, meets Carlo in a wood and tells him of his father's death and Francesco's treachery. However, Massimiliano was not dead. He had merely fainted and, on Francesco's orders, had been locked up in an old tower. Carlo sets him free and with the rest of his gang makes a move against Francesco, who now has no way out and hangs himself. As a result, Carlo is reunited with his father and Amalia, but his happiness is short-lived. The thieves remind him of the oath which binds him to them. Amalia, unable to bear life without him, begs him to kill her. Carlo stabs her and then goes off to face his destiny.

By 1847, the year of the premiere of *I masnadieri*, Verdi had already consolidated his reputation as a composer. On the strength of it, he was commissioned by Mr Lumley, manager of Her Majesty's Theater in London, to produce this work.

MASSARD, ROBERT

(Pau 1925)
French baritone. One of the greatest French baritones of his generation, he made his name at the Paris Opéra in 1951 as the High Priest in Saint-Saëns' *Samson et Dalila*. He went on to appear in Aix-en-Provence in Gluck's *Iphigénie en Tauride* (1952), at La Scala, Milan, the Glyndebourne Festival (Ravel's *L'heure espagnole*, 1955) and Chicago. In 1957 he sang the role of the Count in the first French performance of Richard Strauss's *Capriccio* at the Opéra-Comique.

MASSENET, JULES

(Montaud, St. Étienne 1842–Paris 1912)
French composer. At the age of 11 he became a student at the Paris Conservatoire where, from 1861, he studied composition with Ambroise Thomas. In 1863 he won the Grand Prix de Rome, receiving considerable encouragement from Franz Liszt. On his return to Paris, he made his operatic debut in

1867 with *La Grand'-tante*, the first in a long line of operas which included *Le roi de Lahore*, 1877; *Hérodiade*, 1881; *Manon*, 1884; *Le Cid*, 1885; *Esclarmonde*, 1889; *Werther*, 1892; *Thaïs*, 1894; *La Navarraise*, 1894; *Sapho*, 1897; *Cendrillon*, 1899; *Le jongleur de Notre-Dame*, 1902; and *Don Quichotte*, 1910. From 1878 until 1896 he held the chair of composition at the Paris Conservatoire, where his pupils included Gustave Charpentier. Also in 1878 he became a member of the Académie des Beaux-Arts, and he was elected its president in 1910.

MASSIS, RENÉ

(Lyons 1947)
French baritone. He studied at the Conservatoire in Lyons and went on to complete his training in Milan from 1970 to 1976. He made his debut as Silvio in *I pagliacci* in Marseilles in 1976. He subsequently appeared at all the leading French opera houses and took part in the first performance in modern times of Piccinni's *Iphigénie en Aulide* at the Teatro Petruzzelli in Bari in 1986. This was followed by roles in *Benvenuto Cellini* at the Teatro Comunale in Florence in 1987, at the Teatro Massimo in Palermo in Respighi's *Semirama* in 1987, in Poulenc's *Les dialogues des Carmelites* at the Teatro dell' Opera in Rome in 1991, and appearances in numerous other opera houses in Italy, Spain (the Liceu in Barcelona, etc.) and Holland (Amsterdam). Drawing on a wide-ranging repertoire of French and Italian operas, Massis has come to be regarded as one of the most famous of French baritones.

MASTERSON, VALERIE

(Birkenhead 1937)
British soprano. She studied in Liverpool and at the Royal College of Music in London with Eduardo Asquez. She made her debut at the Landestheater in Salzburg in 1963 as Frasquita in *Carmen* and subsequently became a member of the D'Oyly Carte Opera Company, with whom she sang Nannetta in *Falstaff* and Fiorilla in *Il turco in Italia*. At the beginning of the 1970s her career centered on the Sadler's Wells Theater and English National Opera, for whom she sang in Mozart's *Die Entführung aus dem Serail* (The Seraglio), Rossini's *Le Comte Ory*, Handel's *Giulio Cesare*, among others. In 1974 Masterson appeared for the first time at Covent Garden where she sang in the first performance of Hans Werner Henze's *We Come to the River*. In 1975 she gave a distinguished performance as Matilde in Rossini's *Elisabetta regina d'Inghilterra* alongside Montserrat Caballé. She was engaged by the Opéra in Paris (*Faust*) and went on to sing at many other French opera houses, as well as in Geneva, Milan (at the Piccola Scala in Handel's *Ariodante*, 1978) and elsewhere throughout Europe and the United States. Particularly admired for her performance of French repertoire (*Mireille*, *Romeo et Juliette*, *Manon*) Masterson also earned a reputation for roles in Verdi operas, especially *La traviata*, which she has sung many times.

MASUR, KURT

(Brieg, Silesia 1927)
German conductor. He studied in Breslau (1942–44) and Leipzig (1946–48). He made his debut at the Landestheater in Halle (1948) and went on to conduct in Erfurt (1951–53), Leipzig (1953–55) and Dresden (1955–58). He then held the posts of music director at Schwerin (1958–60) and at the Komische Oper in Berlin (1960–64). In the years that followed, he conducted the Dresden Philharmonic (1967–72), the Leipzig Gewandhaus Orchestra (from 1970), and in 1992 he succeeded Zubin Mehta at the helm of the New York Philharmonic. Masur's reputation rests in particular on his performances of German opera from Mozart to Beethoven, Wagner, Richard Strauss and Berg.

The French composer Jules Massenet in his study.

MATAČIĆ, LOVRO VON

(Susak, Rijeka 1899–Zagreb 1985)
Croatian conductor. After studying in Vienna and Cologne, he embarked on a career in music in Yugoslavia, where he conducted the Belgrade Opera from 1926 to 1931, while from 1932 until 1938 he was conductor of Zagreb Opera. After a period conducting the Vienna Staatsoper (1942–45), he worked in Croatia, organizing the Festivals of Split and Dubrovnik. From 1954 he conducted in Italy and Germany, at the East Berlin Opera and as *Generalmusikdirektor* in Dresden (1956–58) and Frankfurt (1961–66). In Italy, his numerous appearances in Florence, Rome and Bologna earned him a reputation as an interpreter of Wagner and Richard Strauss.

MATHIS DER MALER

(Matthias the Painter)
Opera in seven scenes by Paul Hindemith (1895–1963), to the composer's own libretto. First performance: Zurich, Stadttheater, 28 May 1938.

The action takes place during the Peasants' Rebellion of 1542, which followed in the wake of the Lutheran schism. Hans Schwalb (tenor), leader of the peasant uprising, and his daughter Regina (soprano) take refuge in a monastery where the painter Mathis Grünewald (baritone) is painting in the cloister. Mathis decides to come to the aid of Schwalb and his daughter and offers them his horse to help them on their way. Shortly afterwards, the guards arrive in pursuit of Schwalb. Mathis admits to having helped them escape but insists in answering only to his patron, Cardinal Albrecht of Mainz, for this action. The following day in Mainz, after attending a turbulent meeting at which Cardinal Albrecht (tenor) is put under pressure by both Catholics and Protestants, Mathis sees Ursula (soprano). Ursula and Mathis love each other, but she reproaches him for having neglected her. Enter Sylvester von Schaumberg (tenor), Captain of the Guard, who publicly accuses Mathis of having been an accessory to Schwalb's escape. Mathis reveals that he is on the side of the oppressed and resigns from the service of the Cardinal, who is willing to let him be relieved of his duties. Some time later, Mathis tells Ursula that, although he loves her, he must turn his back on love and art in these troubled times in order to help the oppressed. After joining forces with the rebellious peasants, Mathis, Schwalb and Regina try to dissuade them from futile pillaging and violence. Mathis rescues the Countess of Helfenstein (contralto) from the rebels' fury. The arrival of the army leads to the peasants being routed: Schwalb is killed,

but Mathis is saved, thanks to the intervention of the Countess, and escapes with Regina. The couple take refuge in a wood, and while Regina is asleep, Mathis has a vision in which he imagines himself as St. Anthony being tempted by riches, power, lust, knowledge and authority. Then the vision fades, to be replaced by St. Paul, in the guise of the Cardinal, who urges him to return to painting. In his studio in Mainz, Mathis is exhausted after painting for a long time, while Regina, attended by Ursula, is dying. The Cardinal appears and offers Mathis his house, but the painter refuses. He senses that his work is now at an end, and he is finally alone with the memory of his art and achievements.

Mathis der Maler, regarded as Hindemith's greatest opera, is a reconstruction of the life of the mysterious and gifted painter Mathis Grünewald and a tribute to his greatest work, the Isenheim altarpiece in the city of Colmar. Staged in Zurich, the opera was a triumphant success and was seen as Hindemith adopting a stance against the Nazis, who had forced the composer to seek refuge abroad.

MATHIS, EDITH

(Lucerne 1938)

Swiss soprano. After studying music at the Conservatories in Lucerne and Zurich, she made her debut at the Stadttheater in Lucerne in 1956 as Second Genie in Mozart's *Die Zauberflöte* (The Magic Flute). Engaged by the Cologne Opera (1959–63) and the Berlin Opera (1963), she also appeared during that period at the Salzburg Festival (1960) and Glyndebourne (1962) and, within a short time, was being acclaimed in all the major cities as an exquisite Mozart performer. As well as being active with Hamburg Opera (1961–72), she also sang with the Metropolitan Opera in New York in Mozart's *Die Zauberflöte* (1970), Covent Garden in *Le nozze di Figaro* (1970), at the Vienna Opera in *Don Giovanni* (1972) and in Munich (since 1977). In addition to her Mozart roles, Mathis has given excellent performances in Debussy's *Pélleas et Mélisande*, as Marzelline in Beethoven's *Fidelio*, as Sophie and more recently as the Marschallin in Strauss's *Der Rosenkavalier*. Her outstanding musicianship and versatility have enabled her to excel in concert repertoire, from Bach to Schubert, Schumann and Mahler. She is married to the conductor Bernhard Klee.

MATRIMONIO SEGRETO, IL

(The Clandestine Marriage)

Opera in two acts by Domenico Cimarosa (1749–1801), to a libretto by Giovanni Bertati, based on two plays, The Clandestine Marriage *by George Colman and David Garrick and* Sophie, ou le Mariage Caché *by Marie-Jeanne Riccoboni. First performance: Vienna, Burgtheater, 7 February 1792.*

Carolina (soprano), the younger daughter of Geronimo (*buffo* bass), a wealthy merchant from Bologna, has secretly married Paolino (tenor), a young man employed by her father, who only wants his daughters to marry titled suitors. Having arranged a marriage with Count Robinson (baritone) for his other daughter, Elisetta (soprano), Elisetta's father tells Carolina that he has a good match arranged for her too. Things become more complicated when Count Robinson announces that he prefers Carolina to Elisetta, but Carolina sidesteps the Count's continual declarations. Geronimo is unable to understand what is happening in all the confusion. In order to save his marriage, Paolino asks for help from Fidalma (mezzo-soprano), Geronimo's sister, but she confesses that she loves him and is certain that Geronimo will not oppose their marriage. Paolino faints in Fidalma's arms and is surprised by Carolina, who imagines she has been betrayed by her. The misunderstanding is soon cleared up, but in the meantime Fidalma and Elisetta, both jealous of Carolina, persuade Geronimo to have her sent to a convent. At this point, the young couple decide to confess that they are already married, after which Count Robinson says he is willing to marry Elisetta. Geronimo forgives them, and everything ends happily.

Il matrimonio segreto is the most successful and most representative of Cimarosa's operas and a perfect example of eighteenth-century Italian comic opera. Its premiere was a sensational success. At the end of the per-

Above: The Swiss soprano Edith Mathis.

Right: A scene from *Il matrimonio segreto* by Domenico Cimarosa.

formance, the Austrian Emperor invited the composer and the entire cast to dinner. After dinner, he asked that the company go back to the theater and perform the entire work all over again, something which had never happened before in the history of opera.

MATTEUZZI, WILLIAM
(Bologna 1957)
Italian tenor. He began to study singing at the age of 17 with the tenor Paride Venturi and went on to have lessons with Rodolfo Celletti, who encouraged him to specialize in the *bel canto* repertoire, in particular Rossini. Winner of the Italian ENAL and AS.LI.CO. singing competitions in 1979, he made his debut as Des Grieux in Massenet's *Manon*. In 1980 he won the first year of the biennial Enrico Caruso competition for solo tenors, and this enabled him to be admitted to the La Scala Centro di Perfezionamento (Center for Advanced Training). He then began to tackle an extremely broad-based repertoire, ranging from Vivaldi (*Orlando Furioso*) to Mozart (*Così fan tutte*, *Don Giovanni*, *Idomeneo*, etc.), Bellini (*La sonnambula*, *I puritani*), Donizetti (*La fille du régiment*), Offenbach, Stravinsky (*Mavra*) and others. His light lyric tenor voice, with its remarkable range (up to a high F and G), and his talents as a seasoned performer of fast passage-work, a high degree of musicianship and consistent phrasing, have fully qualified him for admission to that inner circle of performers associated with the "Rossini renaissance," in both the *buffo* repertoire.

MATTILA, KARITA
(Somero 1960)
Finnish soprano. She studied singing with Liisa Linko-Malmio and Kim Borg at the Sibelius Academy in Helsinki and made her debut as the Countess in *Le nozze di Figaro* at the Finnish National Opera in 1982. On the strength of winning the Voices of the World international singing competition in Cardiff in 1983, she was engaged by leading European and American opera houses, including the Théâtre de la Monnaie in Brussels, the Opéra in Paris, Covent Garden, Lyric Opera of Chicago and the Metropolitan Opera in New York. She is an outstanding performer of the Mozart repertoire and has recorded *Don Giovanni* and *Così fan tutte* under the direction of Sir Neville Marriner. Other operas in which she has sung are Schubert's *Fierrabras*, conducted by Claudio Abbado, and Weber's *Der Freischütz* with Sir Colin Davis, works that displayed her fine lyric soprano.

MAUCERI, JOHN
(New York 1945)
American conductor. After studying music at Yale, he began his conducting career with the Yale Symphony Orchestra (1968–74). Two years later he made his first appearance at the Metropolitan Opera in New York (conducting Beethoven's *Fidelio*), after which he went on to conduct at New York City Opera (1977–82) as well as other major American opera houses. He conducted the American Symphony from 1984 to 1987, the year in which he was appointed music director of Scottish Opera in Glasgow. Mauceri is well-known for excellent performances (also recorded) of the operas of Kurt Weill.

MAVRA
Opera buffa *in one act by Igor Stravinsky (1882–1971), to a libretto by Boris Kochno after Pushkin's short story in verse,* Domik v Kolomne *(The Little House at Kolomna). First performance: Paris, Opéra, 3 June 1922.*

From the window of her house, young Parasha (soprano) is engaged in a romantic conversation with Vassily (tenor), a hussar. The couple are trying to find a way to meet. Vassily goes away, and along comes Parasha's mother (contralto). Their old servant has just died, and the mother is sending Parasha to look for a replacement. Left on her own, the mother mourns the loss of her servant in the company of a neighbour (contralto). Then Parasha returns with the new maid, Mavra, a healthy and robust young woman. Mavra is actually the young hussar, enterprisingly dressed up as a woman. Mavra gets to work, and Parasha's mother leaves, only to return unseen to observe the new maid's conduct. She is astonished to see this pleasant young woman shaving. This leads to a tremendous uproar: the hussar climbs out a window and runs off as fast as his legs will carry him, leaving Parasha desperately calling out to him.

This short opera was inspired by the music of Glinka and Tchaikovsky and pays tribute to both composers. At the same time, however, it displays the many facets of Stravinsky's style, one which brings together extremely dissimilar musical elements and consequently makes *Mavra* much more than a straightforward homage to nineteenth-century opera. It was not particularly successful at its first performance, mainly as a result of an inadequate production and the fact that the Opéra stage was too large for it.

MAXWELL DAVIES, SIR PETER
(Manchester 1934)
British composer. He studied at the Royal Manchester College of Music and later in Rome with Goffredo Petrassi and in Princeton with Roger Sessions. Maxwell Davies pursued a very active career writing for the theater, approaching it with a considerable freedom of expression, in contrast with traditional criteria of opera composition. This quality is in evidence in his *Eight Songs for a Mad King* (1969); *Taverner* (1972), the work whose distinguishing features most closely resemble traditional opera; *Miss Donnithorne's Maggot* (1974); *Le jongleur de Notre-Dame* (1978); and *The Martyrdom of St. Magnus* (1977).

Top: The Italian tenor William Matteuzzi.

Above: The Finnish soprano Karita Mattila.

MAYR, GIOVANNI SIMONE

(Mendorf über Kelheim, Bavaria 1763–Bergamo 1845)

Italian composer, teacher and musicologist of German origin. A choirboy at the monastery of Weltenberg, he won admiration as a harpsichord player at a young age. He studied theology and canon law in the city of Ingolstadt, where he came into close contact with cultural circles. In 1787 he moved to Italy, staying in Bergamo and Venice, where he continued his music studies and made his theatrical debut with the opera *Saffo* (1794). In 1802 he became *maestro di cappella* in the church of Santa Maria Maggiore in Bergamo, where in 1805 he instituted "charitable music lessons," in which Donizetti was one of the participants from 1806 to 1815. As a composer of opera, Mayr earned an international reputation for *Lodoïska* (1796), *Ginevra di Scozia* (1801) and *Medea in Corinto* (1813). His career as a composer ended with *Demetrio* in 1824, and by 1826 he was already showing signs of the illness which would eventually rob him of his sight.

Top: A scene from Tchaikovsky's *Mazeppa*.

Above: The composer Giovanni Simone Mayr.

Opposite: A scene from Cherubini's *Médée*.

MAZEPPA

Opera in three acts by Peter Ilyich Tchaikovsky (1840–1893), to a libretto by the composer and V. P. Burenin based on Pushkin's epic poem Poltava. *First performance: Moscow, Bolshoi Theater, 15 February 1884.*

The action takes place in the Ukraine at the beginning of the eighteenth century. In the garden of the house belonging to Kochubey (bass), the Ukrainian Minister of Justice, celebrations are being held in honour of the heroic Mazeppa (baritone), military commander of the Ukraine. Kochubey's daughter, Maria (soprano), although much younger than Mazeppa, is in love with him. She confides her feelings to Andrey (tenor), a young man who has been her friend since childhood and is secretly in love with her. Andrey goes away sadly. Mazeppa asks Kochubey for Maria's hand in marriage. Kochubey is surprised and vigorously rejects the proposal. But Maria wants to be with Mazeppa, and they leave together while her parents curse him for having taken their daughter away from them. Shortly after this, Kochubey learns that Mazeppa has made an alliance with the King of Sweden and is plotting against the Tsar, so he sends Andrey to Moscow to warn of the danger. The Tsar does not believe this charge against Mazeppa, in whom he has the greatest confidence, and orders Kochubey to be arrested. Under torture, he confesses that his accusation was false. Kochubey is sentenced to death, and Mazeppa is at a loss to know how to tell Maria that her father's execution is imminent. She finds out about his tragic predicament from her mother, Lyubova (mezzo-soprano), and then goes with her to try to see her father, but the two women arrive just as he is being beheaded. Crazed with grief, Maria collapses. After the battle of Poltava, a victory for Tsar Peter the Great against the Swedes, Mazeppa, who has been betrayed by King Charles XII, takes refuge in Kochubey's house. Andrey draws his sword and hurls himself at Mazeppa but is fatally wounded when Mazeppa produces a gun and fires at him. Maria, now completely out of her mind, gathers up Andrey in her arms and cradles him, singing a children's lullaby. Still on the run, Mazeppa hurries away as Andrey dies with Maria deliriously clasping him to her.

Inspired by the historical figure of Ivan Mazeppa, the Cossack ataman who attempted to set up a Ukrainian state independent from Russia by forging an alliance with King Charles XII of Sweden, *Mazeppa* marked Tchaikovsky's return to Russian themes, which he had set aside when he wrote his opera *The Maid of Orleans*.

MAZUROK, YURI

(Krasnik, Lublin 1931)

Russian baritone. A pupil of Sveshikovaya at the Moscow Conservatoire, he began his career at the Bolshoi Theater (1962), where he appeared in the great baritone roles of Russian and Italian opera. He went on to sing at some of the leading opera houses and festivals in the West, including Covent Garden (1975), the Vienna Staatsoper, the Festival of Aix-en-Provence and, from 1978, the Metropolitan Opera in New York.

MAZZARIA, LUCIA

(Gorizia 1966)

Italian soprano. After beginning her music studies at the Conservatorio in Trieste, she continued them privately there and in Rome. She made her debut as a concert artiste in

Fauré's *Requiem* in Trieste (1986) and went on to appear at La Fenice in Venice, where she took over from Renata Scotto in *La bohème* in 1987. She returned to La Fenice to sing Liù (*Turandot*, 1987–88, 1992), Mimi (Leoncavallo's *Bohème*, 1989), Tatyana (Tchaikovsky's *Eugene Onegin*, 1991) and Maria (Verdi's *Simon Boccanegra*, 1991). Mazzaria's international appearances as Liù and Mimi included La Scala (1988), Monte Carlo (1990), Covent Garden (1990), the Vienna Staatsoper (1991), Lyric Opera of Chicago (1991), the San Francisco Opera (1992) and others. Also featuring in her repertoire are Bizet's *Carmen*, Gounod's *Faust*, and Verdi's *La traviata* and *Don Carlos*.

MAZZUCCATO, DANIELA

(Venice 1946)

Italian soprano. She studied at the Conservatorio Benedetto Marcello in Venice, making her debut as Gilda (*Rigoletto*) at La Fenice. Engagements followed at La Scala and other opera houses in Italy (the Teatro Verdi in Trieste, the Teatro San Carlo in Naples, Palermo's Teatro Massimo, etc.), as well as at the Opéra in Paris, Covent Garden (*L'elisir d'amore*) and opera houses in Marseilles, Hamburg and Frankfurt.

MEDEA IN CORINTO

Opera in two acts by Giovanni Simone Mayr (1763–1845), to a libretto by Felice Romani. First performance: Naples, Teatro San Carlo, 28 November 1813.

The action takes place in Corinth. A wedding is about to take place between Creusa (soprano), daughter of King Creonte (baritone), and Giasone (Jason), the Argonaut. Medea (soprano), daughter of the King of Colchis, who helped Giasone to succeed in his quest for the Golden Fleece and has borne him two children, has now been rejected by him. With the assistance of Egeo (tenor), King of Athens and previously engaged to Creusa, Medea interrupts the wedding and accuses Giasone of breaking his vow to her. Using magic she then sprinkles poison on a robe she proceeds to offer as a present to Creusa and has Egeo, imprisoned by Creonte, set free so that he can pursue their vendetta. Meanwhile, Creusa and Giasone are married, but their happiness is short-lived: Creusa has donned the robe she was given by Medea and is now in her death throes. Devastated, Giasone goes in search of Medea to seek revenge. The sorceress confronts him, brandishing a dagger bespattered with blood, and tells Giasone she has just killed his children. As huge flames leap upwards from the burning palace, Medea is seen for the last time in a chariot drawn by two dragons, vanishing into the fire.

This was the first opera composed by Mayr for the Teatro San Carlo in Naples and it was a tremendous success, receiving numerous performances in Naples as well as being staged at several other opera houses.

MÉDÉE

Opera in three acts by Luigi Cherubini (1760–1824), to a libretto by François Benoît Hoffmann, based on the tragedy by Corneille. First performance: Paris, Théâtre Feydeau, 13 March 1797.

The action takes place in Corinth, and the curtain rises to reveal the main gates of the Palace. It is the eve of the wedding of Glauce (soprano), daughter of King Créon (bass), to Jason (tenor), the hero who had gone to Colchis and returned with the Golden Fleece. But Glauce fears the revenge of Médée (soprano), who for Jason's sake betrayed her father and her people and killed her brother Absyrtus. Médée appears at the Palace gates, uttering dark threats. Driven away by Créon and rejected by Jason, she cannot be comforted by her maid Néris (mezzo-soprano) and hatches her plan of vengeance. After obtaining permission from Créon to stay in Corinth with her children for one more day, Médée tells Néris to take Glauce a magic robe and necklace (given to her by Apollo) as a wedding gift. As she is dragging her children out of the Palace, cries are heard signalling the death of Glauce. Pursued by an angry crowd, Médée takes refuge in the temple with her children and Néris, only to emerge shortly after, holding the bloody dagger with which she has killed the children. Jason is devastated by grief, and Médée promises that her ghost will be waiting for him in the Underworld. With the temple now on fire, Médée vanishes among the flames.

Médée, Cherubini's most famous opera, did not have a very successful premiere and immediately disappeared from the repertory of the Paris theaters. But it opened the way to nineteenth-century opera, distancing itself from eighteenth-century models with its atmosphere of tragedy brilliantly captured by the composer. In keeping with the tradition of the Théâtre Feydeau, the opera's recitatives were spoken. These were set to music by Franz Lachner for a performance of *Médée* in Frankfurt in 1855 and have since become an integral part of the score. The myth of Medea has inspired numerous composers to write operas, including Cavalli (1649), Giannettini (1675), Kusser (1692), Charpentier (1693), Benda (1775), Pacini (1843), Milhaud (1939) and, most recently, Theodorakis (1991).

MEDIUM, THE

Opera in two acts, text and music by Giancarlo Menotti (b.1911). First performance: New York, Barrymore Theater, 8 May 1946 (private performance). From 18 February 1947 it appeared on Broadway in a double-bill with The Telephone.

Madame Flora (contralto), assisted by her daughter Monica (soprano) and by Toby, a young mute, makes a living by presenting herself to gullible people as a medium. During a séance, Flora pretends to be in a trance while Monica, dressed in flowing white veils, appears to Mrs Nolan (mezzo-soprano), who has lost a daughter. Then, from behind a curtain, she mimics the sweet laughter of a little girl, which Mr Gobineau (baritone) and his wife take to be that of their dead daughter. The session has just ended when Flora jumps up screaming that an icy hand has clasped her throat. When the clients have left, Flora accuses Toby of having played a cruel trick on her. Later, however, Flora imagines she can hear a child crying out and laughing. Monica calms her by singing her a lullaby. A few days later, while Monica and Toby are playing happily together, Flora bursts in on them, the worse for drink: she again accuses Toby and beats him unmercifully. The clients are arriving, but Flora does not want to go on pretending, so she

Top: Scene from Boito's *Mefistofele*.

Right: The Indian conductor Zubin Mehta.

Opposite: Sketch for Wagner's *Die Meistersinger von Nürnberg*.

confesses to being a fraud and sends them away. She wants to get rid of Toby as well, but Monica comes to his defense. Flora sinks into some kind of delirium, sees a curtain moving, picks up a gun and fires. A blood-stain spreads on the curtain, and the body of Toby falls to the ground lifeless. Monica flees in terror while Flora, by now out of her mind, is left convinced she has killed the ghost.

Composed in response to an invitation from Columbia University's Alice M. Ditson Fund, *The Medium* was enormously successful, and the composer himself directed a film version.

MEFISTOFELE

Opera in a prologue, four acts and an epilogue by Arrigo Boito (1842–1918), to the composer's own libretto, based on Goethe's Faust. *First performance: Milan, La Scala, 5 March 1868.*

In heaven, Mefistofele (bass) makes a defiant wager with God that he can become the master of Faust's soul. So he goes down to earth and, introducing himself to Faust (tenor) as the Child of Darkness, sets out the deal he is offering: all the pleasures and joys of life now, in return for Faust's soul after death. Faust agrees. Transformed into a young man again and calling himself Enrico, Faust courts and seduces Margherita (soprano). Mefistofele then prevails on Faust to attend a sabbath of witches, wizards and goblins. But Faust is disturbed by a vision of Margherita in chains, guesses that her life has turned to tragedy and asks Mefistofele to enable him to reach her. In prison, Margherita is grimly delirious: she has poisoned her mother and drowned the child she had with Faust. Faust enters the prison, accompanied by Mefistofele, and urges her to come away with him, but Margherita is horrified when she sees the Devil standing beside him, calls on God to forgive her and falls dead. A voice from on high proclaims her salvation. The scene changes to Greece, where Faust has expressed the wish to meet the legendary Helen of Troy (soprano), with whom he falls hopelessly in love. She is not unmoved by Faust's admiration and they go off together in search of the tranquil valley of Arcadia. Time passes, and Faust, now old and tired, is in his study, beset by disillusionment as he thinks back over everything he has experienced and comes to the realization that only the love of God could have filled the emptiness inside him. He then calls upon the Lord and, grasping the Gospel, dies redeemed like Margherita, while Mefistofele, defeated, sinks into the earth.

The first performance of *Mefistofele* ended in a barrage of whistling. After this fiasco, Boito reviewed the score and made improvements and cuts (the original version lasted more than five hours). With these changes, the opera was staged at the Teatro Comunale in Bologna on 4 October 1875. This time it was a success and came to be regarded as an operatic masterpiece.

MEHTA, ZUBIN

(Bombay 1936)

Indian conductor. His first music lessons were with his father, Mehli Mehta, a violin-

ist, conductor, and founder of the Bombay Symphony. He went on to attend the Vienna Academy of Music (1954–60) and studied conducting there with Hans Swarowsky. He completed his training at the Accademia Chigiana in Siena and at Tanglewood. It quickly became clear, after he had won first prize in the International Conductors Competition in Liverpool, that Mehta's gifts included exceptional technical flair, elegance and sensitivity of interpretation. Music director of the orchestras of Montreal (1961–67), Los Angeles (1962–78), New York (1978–91) and Israel (for life from 1981), he has also made memorable appearances at major international opera venues.

MÉHUL, ÉTIENNE-NICOLAS

(Givet, Ardennes 1763–Paris 1817)

French composer. He arrived in Paris in 1778 as a student. Gluck's help and patronage then enabled him to begin a career as an opera composer. Success was slow, but he subsequently became one of the most highly acclaimed composers of his time. A firm advocate of the ideas of the Revolution, in 1795 he was appointed inspector of the Paris Conservatoire. Among his compositions for the theater are *Une folie* (1802), *Uthal* (1807) and most notably *Joseph* (1807), considered his masterpiece.

MEIER, JOHANNA

(Chicago 1938)

American soprano. She studied singing with John Brownlee at the University of Miami and subsequently at the Manhattan School of Music in New York. She made her debut with New York City Opera in 1969 as the Countess in Richard Strauss's *Capriccio*. She appeared for the first time at the Metropolitan Opera in New York in 1976, where she specialized in roles from the German repertoire. Since 1981 she has performed at the Bayreuth Festival, becoming the first American soprano to sing the role of Isolde there.

MEIER, WALTRAUD

(Würzburg 1956)

German mezzo-soprano. After studying music in Cologne, she made her debut at the Stadttheater in Würzburg in 1976 as Cherubino (*Le nozze di Figaro*). She then joined the company of the Mannheim Opera (1978–80), where she sang a number of Wagner roles. From 1980 to 1983 she sang with the Dortmund Opera and during this period appeared as Fricka in *Die Walküre* at the Teatro Colón in Buenos Aires. In 1984 she appeared for the first time at the Bayreuth Festival singing Kundry (*Parsifal*), a role she also sang at Covent Garden, the San Francisco Opera (1988) and at the opening of the 1991–92 season at La Scala, Milan.

MEILHAC, HENRI

(Paris 1831–1897)

Librettist and dramatist. After leaving school, he worked in a bookshop, at the same time contributing to *Le journal pour rire* and to *La vie parisienne* (1852–55). From 1856 he began a busy career in the theater, writing vaudevilles, comedies and opera libretti. As a librettist he frequently collaborated with Ludovic Halévy. He wrote the libretti for *Carmen* (1875) and *Manon* (1884) for Massenet, *La belle Hélène* in 1864 and *La vie parisienne* in 1866.

MEISTERSINGER VON NÜRNBERG, DIE

(The Mastersingers of Nuremberg)

Opera in three acts by Richard Wagner (1813–1883), to the composer's own libretto. First performance: Munich, Hoftheater, 21 June 1868.

The action takes place in Nuremberg around 1550. Walther von Stolzing (tenor), a young knight, is in love with Eva (soprano), daughter of the goldsmith Veit Pogner (bass). Eva returns Walther's love but her father proposes to give her in marriage to the winner of a singing competition being held by the Mastersingers the following day. In order to qualify to take part in the competition, Walther has an audition to become a Mastersinger, during which he bursts into a passionate hymn in praise of spring, but Beckmesser (baritone), a pedantic clerk who also wants to marry Eva, has noted down all the mistakes Walther has made and maliciously announces at the end that Walther's song has not observed the rules. The cobbler Hans Sachs (bass-baritone) admires the boldness and beauty of Walther's ode, but his intervention is to no avail, and Walther fails. Shortly afterwards, Eva, who has now heard of the disastrous outcome of Walther's audition, goes to see Hans Sachs and tells him of her feelings for the young man. The cobbler promises to help the lovers. Later, Walther persuades Eva to elope with him, but Beckmesser suddenly appears and sings a serenade under Eva's window. To distract Beckmesser's attention, Maddalena (mezzo-soprano), Eva's nurse, appears at the window dressed in Eva's clothes. David (tenor), her fiancé, recognizes her despite her disguise, imagines that Beckmesser's serenade is intended for Maddalena, and the two men come to blows. This leads to chaos: Eva and Walther, hiding behind a lime-tree, try once again to get away but are wisely stopped by Sachs. The next day in Sachs's workshop, Walther tells the cobbler about a wonderful dream he has had. Sachs writes down everything he says, offers him some advice, and this

Sketch for Wagner's *Die Meistersinger von Nürnberg.*

leads to the composition of a magnificent love song. Then Beckmesser enters the workshop while the others are out, sees Walther's love song and walks off with it. Sachs surprises him and cleverly gives him permission to use the song as if it were his own. The scene changes to the day of the competition. The contest opens, and Beckmesser is chosen to sing first. Everyone laughs at the grotesque performance he gives of Walther's love song. Beckmesser rails against Sachs, who, after relating the story of how the poem had been set to music, calls on Walther to sing it the way it had been composed. The audience is immediately captivated, and the Masters, deeply impressed, proclaim him the winner.

Die Meistersinger is the only comedy in Wagner's output. The historical figure of Hans Sachs symbolizes both the importance of tradition and the necessity of renewal in art. The opera can be seen to represent a tribute to the highest achievements of the German musical tradition by an artist whose revolutionary restlessness had until then only enabled him to present an image of himself as a brilliant amateur.

Top: The American mezzo-soprano Susanne Mentzer.

Above: The Italian composer Giancarlo Menotti.

MENASCI, GUIDO
(Livorno 1867–1925)

Italian man of letters and librettist. He began to take an interest in the theater at the suggestion of his friend Giovanni Targioni-Tozzetti, who invited him to collaborate with him on the libretto for Mascagni's *Cavalleria rusticana*. The same team were responsible for further libretti for Mascagni operas, *I Rantzau* (1892) and *Zanetto* (1896).

MENDÈS, CATULLE
(Bordeaux 1841–Saint Germain-en-Laye 1909)

French poet, dramatic critic and librettist. He moved to Paris in order to pursue a literary career and founded *La revue fantaisiste*, the news-sheet of the Parnassians, as well as contributing to the publication of *Le Parnasse contemporain* (1866). Mendès was also very active in theater and music and wrote libretti for Chabrier's *Gwendoline* in 1886, Massenet's *Ariane* in 1906 and *Bacchus* in 1909, and others for operas by Messager and d'Indy.

MENOTTI, GIANCARLO
(Cadegliano, Varese 1911)

Italian composer, longtime American resident. He started to study music at the Conservatorio in Milan and at the age of 16 emigrated to the United States, where he studied at the Curtis Institute in Philadelphia with Rosario Scalero. His first opera, *Amelia al ballo* (1937), was outstandingly successful. Menotti's reputation was then firmly reinforced by his subsequent operas, *The Medium* (1946), *The Telephone* (1947) and *The Consul* (1950). These were followed by his opera for television, *Amahl and the Night Visitors* (1951) and *The Saint of Bleecker Street* (1954). Menotti continued to compose with unflagging energy, producing a number of other operas, of which the most typical examples are *Maria Golovin* (1958), *The Last Savage* (1963) and *Goya*. Written for Placido Domingo, *Goya* was staged in Washington in 1986 before being radically revised and performed in its new version at the Spoleto Festival in 1991. Menotti then announced that this work was to be his swansong as a composer.

MENTZER, SUSANNE
(Philadelphia 1957)

American mezzo-soprano. A pupil of Norman Newton at the Juilliard School in New York, she made her debut in 1981 at the Houston Opera in the role of Albina in Rossini's *La donna del lago*. She went on to appear at a number of opera houses across America (Dallas, Chicago, San Francisco, Philadelphia, etc.). In 1983 she appeared for the first time in Europe, as Cherubino in Mozart's *Le nozze di Figaro* with the Cologne Opera, where she was subsequently to enjoy great personal acclaim singing the lead in Massenet's *Cendrillon* (1985). She then took part in the Rossini Opera Festival in Pesaro (1986) as Isolier in *Le Comte Ory* and the opening production of the 1987–88 season at La Scala, Milan, as Zerlina in Mozart's *Don Giovanni*. She sang Cherubino at the Metropolitan Opera in New York, at the Vienna Staatsopera, in Hamburg, at the Opéra in Paris (1984) and at many other houses. Mentzer's repertoire has been further enhanced by the addition of the roles of Adalgisa in Bellini's *Norma*, Rosina in Rossini's *Il barbiere di Siviglia*, Octavian in Strauss's *Der Rosenkavalier*, Jane Seymour in Donizetti's *Anna Bolena* and Marguerite in Berlioz's *La damnation de Faust*.

MERCADANTE, GIUSEPPE SAVERIO RAFFAELE
(Altamura 1795–Naples 1870)

Italian composer. He studied at the Royal College of San Sebastiano in Naples and made his debut with a comic ballet, *Il servo balordo* (1818), following it with his opera *L'apoteosi di Ercole* (1819), produced at the Teatro San Carlo in Naples. In 1821 he had his first big success with the opera *Elisa e Claudio* in Milan. After living for a while in Spain and Portugal (1827–29), where some of his operas were staged, he returned to Italy and settled in Novara, where he occupied the post of *maestro di cappella* at the cathedral (1833–40). In 1840 he was appointed director of the Conservatorio di San Pietro a Maiella in Naples, the city where he was to spend the rest of his life. Mercadante's considerable output of works for the theater included *I briganti* (1836), *Il giuramento* (1837), *Le due illustri rivali* (1838), *Elena da Feltre* (1838), *Il bravo* (1839), *Il reggente* (1843), *Gli Orazi ed i Curiazi* (1846) and *Virginia* (1866).

MERRILL, ROBERT

(Brooklyn, New York 1917)
American baritone. His earliest singing lessons were with his mother, a respected concert artiste, after which he went on to train with Samuel Margolis in New York. In 1944 he made his debut as Amonasro in *Aida* in Trenton. After further appearances in Dayton and Detroit, Merrill won a competition held by the Metropolitan Opera in New York in 1945 and made his debut as Germont in *La traviata*, following this with Enrico in *Lucia di Lammermoor* and Escamillo in *Carmen*. He joined the permanent company at the Metropolitan and sang leading roles in more than 900 performances there. He concentrated mainly on Italian repertoire and maintained a consistently high standard of solid professionalism.

MERRITT, CHRIS

(Oklahoma City 1952)
American tenor. He was educated at the University of Oklahoma City, where he made his first appearance at the age of 21, singing the lead in Offenbach's *Les contes d'Hoffmann*. He was then engaged by Santa Fe opera, where he made his official debut (1975) as Fenton in Verdi's *Falstaff*. He appeared at the Landestheater in Salzburg as Lindoro in *L'italiana in Algeri* in 1978 and subsequently in *Gianni Schicchi*, *Faust*, *L'elisir d'amore* and *Idomeneo*. After taking part in the Metropolitan Opera auditions, he scored a triumph in his first role, Arturo in *I puritani* (1981), which brought him to the attention of international critics and audiences. Merritt set out to specialize in *bel canto* repertoire, particularly Rossini: he sang at Carnegie Hall in *Tancredi* (1983), at the Opéra in Paris in *Moïse et Pharaon* (1983), with the Opera Orchestra of New York in *Guillaume Tell* (1984) and most notably at the Rossini Opera Festival in Pesaro, where from 1985 he sang in *Maometto II*, *Bianca e Faliero*, *Otello* and *Ermione*. His name has also featured in the programmes of a number of other opera houses in Italy and elsewhere, such as the Châtelet in Paris in *La donna del lago*, at Lyric Opera of Chicago in Donizetti's *Anna Bolena*, at the Maggio Musicale Festival in Florence in *Benvenuto Cellini* in 1987, at La Scala, Milan, in *Il viaggio a Reims* (1985), *Guillaume Tell* (1988) and *Les vêpres siciliennes* (1989), at the Teatro dell' Opera in Rome in *Ermione* (1991), at Geneva's Grand Théâtre in *Benvenuto Cellini* in 1992, and others. With Rockwell Blake and William Matteuzzi, Merritt has been a corner-stone of the "Rossini renaissance," as a result of which long-forgotten roles like Pirro in *Ermione*, Antenore in *Zelmira*, Leicester in *Elisabetta, regina d'Inghilterra*, Rinaldo in *Armida* and Arnoldo in *Guillaume Tell* have been given new life, thanks to the majestic character of his voice.

MESPLÉ, MADY

(Toulouse 1931)
French soprano. She graduated from the Toulouse Conservatoire and then made her debut as Lakmé in the opera by Delibes in Liège (1953), returning to the same house to sing in *Il barbiere di Siviglia*, Ambroise Thomas's *Mignon* and Offenbach's *Les contes d'Hoffmann*. Engagements followed at the Théâtre de la Monnaie in Brussels (1954), at the Opéra-Comique in Paris (*Lakmé*, 1956) and in Aix-en-Provence (Grétry's *Zémire et Azor*). Her reputation became firmly established when she took over from Dame Joan Sutherland as Lucia at the Paris Opéra, a performance which launched her on a brilliant international career singing the great *coloratura* soprano roles. She also took part in the French premieres of Menotti's *The Last Savage* (1963) and Henze's *Elegy for Young Lovers* (1965).

METASTASIO, PIETRO

(Rome 1698–Vienna 1782)
Italian poet and librettist, born Pietro Trapassi. His prodigious early gifts for singing and poetry attracted the attention of the Arcadian poet Gravina, who took charge of his cultural education. In 1717 he published his first tragedy, *Giustino*, written when he was 14, and then moved to Naples (1719), where he enjoyed the patronage of the celebrated singer Marianna Benti Bulgarelli, known as La Romanina. She put him in touch with the leading composers then working in Naples – Sarro, Alessandro Scarlatti, Vinci and Porpora – of whom the last two were also responsible for completing his musical education. His first big success came in 1924 with his libretto for Sarro's *Didone abbandonata*. He moved to Vienna in 1730, succeeding Apostolo Zeno as imperial court poet, a post which he retained until his death. In Vienna Metastasio wrote most of his plays and libretti, many of which were set to music

Above: The American tenor Chris Merritt.

Left: The Italian composer Giuseppe Mercadante.

by more than one composer, such as *Artaserse* (1730), with more than 40 different operas called by that name. The reason for his enormous success was the fluency and elegance of his verses, which were in harmony with the taste of the period, and his intricate plot-lines, based on mythology and the Roman world. His was a static form of theater, in which characters expressed stylized emotions and feelings, and it was in reaction to this limitation of dramatic scope that Gluck and Calzabigi devised their reforms. Among his most important libretti are *Catone in Utica* (1728), *L'Olimpiade* (1733), *Demofoonte* (1733), *Achille in Sciro* (1736), *Attilio Regolo* (1740) and *Il re pastore* (1751).

MEYERBEER, GIACOMO

(Tasdorf, Berlin 1791–Berlin 1864)
German composer, born Jakob Liebmann Beer. Of a wealthy Jewish family (he added the surname Meyer in honour of a relative who had made him his sole heir), he was brought up in an atmosphere congenial to the development of his artistic gifts. He began to study composition in 1807, and his theater debut was marked by the opera *Jephtas Gelübde* (1812). His time in Italy between 1816 and 1824 was a turning-point producing his successful *Il crociato in Egitto* (1824), the opera which made his name throughout Europe. He returned to Berlin and lived there until the death of his father in 1829, when he moved to Paris. Here he enjoyed a triumph with his opera *Robert le Diable*, which made him the most popular opera composer of his time. He scored another major success with *Les Huguenots* in 1836, while from 1842 to 1849 he was *Generalmusikdirektor* in Berlin. But Meyerbeer's name was most consistently associated with the Paris stage, where he was hailed as the greatest exponent of *grand-opéra* for *Le prophète* (1849). Other celebrated Meyerbeer operas are *L'étoile du nord* (1854), *Dinorah* (1859) and *L'Africaine*, staged posthumously in 1865.

MICHEAU, JEANINE

(Toulouse 1914–Paris 1976)
French soprano. She studied at the Toulouse Conservatoire and in Paris, making her debut in 1933 at the Théâtre de l'Opéra-Comique as Cherubino in *Le nozze di Figaro*. Her career then centered for the most part on the two leading opera houses in Paris, the Opéra-Comique and the Opéra, where in 1940 she sang the lead in the first performance of Milhaud's *Médée*. Micheau took another Milhaud role when she sang Manuela in the world premiere of *Bolivar* (Opéra, 1950). She drew on both lyric and *coloratura* soprano repertoires (*Manon*, *Lakmé*, *La bohème*). Her performances in Debussy's *Pelléas et Mélisande* and Ravel's *L'enfant et les sortilèges* were particularly memorable.

MIDSUMMER MARRIAGE, THE

Opera in three acts by Sir Michael Tippett (b.1905), to the composer's own libretto. First performance: London, Royal Opera House, Covent Garden, 27 January 1955.

Mark (tenor) and Jenifer (soprano) love each other and want to get married, but they have decided that, before taking this step, they must become completely mature. Another couple, Bella (soprano), a secretary, and Jack (tenor), a mechanic, do not see maturity as the issue: for them the important thing is to find happiness. The plot alternates between everyday reality, represented by King Fisher (baritone), a wealthy financier and Jenifer's father, and a magical world set in old England, symbolized by the clairvoyant Sosostris (contralto) and wise priests (bass and mezzo-soprano). At the end of their inner journey, Mark and Jenifer find truth and are consequently able to marry.

The Midsummer Marriage is Tippett's first opera. It draws its inspiration from Mozart's *Die Zauberflöte* (The Magic Flute), which Tippett reworks in psychoanalytical terms, exploring the theme of the quest with a wide-ranging use of symbolism.

MIDSUMMER NIGHT'S DREAM, A

Opera in three acts by Benjamin Britten (1913–1976), to a libretto by the composer and Peter Pears, based on Shakespeare's comedy. First performance: Aldeburgh, 11 June 1960.

The action takes place in a wood near Athens. Puck (speaking role), messenger to Oberon (counter-tenor) and Tytania (soprano), King and Queen of the Fairies, looks on as his master and mistress quarrel. Tytania refuses to be separated from her page-boy, and Oberon threatens revenge. He then decides to sprinkle Tytania's eyes with the sap from a magic flower while she is asleep. When she wakes up again, the Fairy Queen will fall in love with the first creature she sees. Into the wood come Hermia (mezzo-soprano) and Lysander (tenor). These two young people are in love, but fate is against them, because Hermia is betrothed to Demetrius (baritone). He too enters the wood, chased by Helena (soprano), who adores him, but whom he cannot abide. Oberon decides to help the unfortunate Helena and commands Puck to anoint Demetrius's eyes with a little of the magic sap. Now the wood becomes increasingly lively, with the arrival of six artisans looking for a quiet place to rehearse a play they intend to perform in honour of the marriage of Theseus (bass), Duke of Athens. In the meantime, while Hermia and Lysander, are asleep, Puck makes the mistake of anointing Lysander's eyes with the magic sap. Enter Helena, who wakes Lysander, only to be overwhelmed by his sudden protestations of love for her. Confused, Helena runs off, with Lysander in hot pursuit. A few moments later, as Tytania is drifting into sleep, Oberon himself uses the magic sap on his wife. The artisans begin their

Top: The Italian librettist Pietro Metastasio.

Above: The German composer Giacomo Meyerbeer.

Opposite above: The American soprano Julia Migenes.

Opposite : A poster for Thomas's *Mignon*.

rehearsal, and no sooner has one of them, Bottom (bass-baritone), retired behind a bush than Puck exploits the situation by using magic on him and giving him an ass's head. The other artisans take to their heels in terror, while Tytania, awakened by the din, falls madly in love with Bottom. Meanwhile, even though Oberon has put Puck's blunders to rights, misunderstandings continue to reign between the two pairs of lovers. Oberon gets his page-boy back, releases Tytania from the spell and is reconciled with her, while poor Bottom still does not understand what has happened to him. The two original pairs of lovers are finally reunited, and the opera ends with their weddings, after the artisans have performed their play to the Duke and his bride, Hippolyta (contralto).

This is one of Britten's most elegant scores, in which he captures the whimsical atmosphere of Shakespeare's play.

MIGENES, JULIA

(New York 1945)

American soprano. In 1965 she made her opera debut in Menotti's *The Saint of Bleecker Street* with New York City Opera. She sang in San Francisco, Houston and at the Metropolitan Opera in New York, where she was given an enthusiastic reception as Lulu in Berg's opera, displayed her outstanding gifts as a performer, as did her appearance in the leading role in Francesco Rosi's film *Carmen* (1985).

MIGNON

Opera in three acts by Ambroise Thomas (1811–1896), to a libretto by Michel Carrée and Jules Barbier, based on Goethe's Wilhelm Meister. *First performance: Paris, Théâtre de l'Opéra-Comique, 17 November 1866.*

Lothario (bass), an elderly travelling musician, is wandering the world in search of his daughter, who has been missing for many years. In front of an inn, he tries to help a young woman belonging to a band of gypsies but Wilhelm Meister (tenor), a young adventurer, gets to her before he does and brings her to safety. She reveals that her name is Mignon (mezzo-soprano) and she is an orphan, but she knows nothing else about her life. Touched by this, Wilhelm decides to take her with him and help her to find her family. He has, however, already fallen for the charms of Philine (soprano), an actress, and decides to go with her to the castle where the actors are on their way to perform a play. Mignon follows them, disguised as a page-boy. At the castle she gives way to temptation and dons one of Philine's costumes, but cannot entice Wilhelm, with whom she is in love. In despair, she wants to take her own life but is comforted by Lothario, who believes he has recognized her as his lost daughter. Mignon curses Philine and prays that fire from Heaven will fall upon her. Confused in his thoughts, Lothario attempts to carry out her wish and sets fire to the conservatory where the play had been performed, unaware that Mignon has just entered it. Wilhelm rushes in and saves her. Time passes, and the scene changes to Italy, where Lothario and Wilhelm have taken Mignon so that she

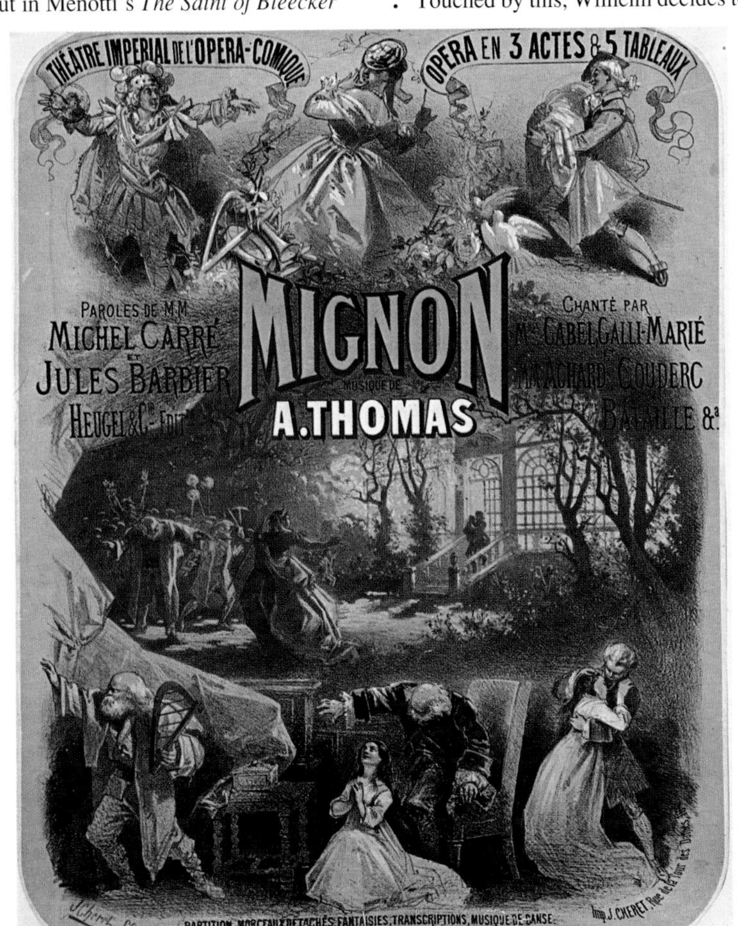

may regain her health. The three stay in Palazzo Cipriani, an old deserted building. The setting, on the shore of a lake, and the palazzo itself, awaken far-off memories in Lothario, and he realizes he is actually Count Cipriani, owner of the palazzo, while a number of his daughter's possessions bring him to the certain knowledge that Mignon is his lost daughter. Overcome with emotion, Mignon faints in the arms of Lothario and Wilhelm, who revive her and speak to her lovingly. Mignon is reunited with her father and with Wilhelm, who confesses that he loves her.

Mignon is unquestionably Thomas's finest opera and the only one to have remained in the repertoire of many of the world's opera houses. The music is enriched by a powerfully expressive energy. In order to give full rein to his preference for a story that is not tragic, the composer turned the tragic outcome of Goethe's play into a happy ending.

MILANOV, ZINKA

(Zagreb 1906–New York 1989)

Stage name of Zinka Kunc, Croatian soprano who became a naturalized American. A pupil of Milka Ternina, she completed her training with Fernando Carpi in Prague and made her debut as Leonora (*Il trovatore*) in Ljubljana in 1927. She was leading soprano with Zagreb Opera (1928–35) and earned an international reputation as a result of her performances in Verdi's *Aida* at the Vienna Staatsoper and his *Requiem*, conducted by Toscanini, at the Salzburg Festival in 1937. In the same year, Milanov made her first appearance at the Metropolitan Opera House in New York (*Il trovatore*). She continued to sing there until 1966, when she retired from the stage. She was engaged by a number of other European and American opera houses, including Covent Garden, La Scala, Milan, and the Teatro Colón in Buenos Aires. From 1977 onwards she taught at the Curtis Institute in Philadelphia.

MILASHKINA, TAMARA

(Astrakhan 1934)

Russian soprano. She studied singing with Elena Katul'skaya and then joined the company at the Bolshoi in Moscow (1958), where she performed the great roles of Russian opera, in particular Lisa in Tchaikovsky's *Queen of Spades* and Tatyana in *Eugene Onegin*. She toured with the Bolshoi in Europe and the United States (1975). In 1962 she was the first Russian soprano to be engaged by La Scala, Milan (as Lidia in Verdi's *La battaglia di Legnano*), and she subsequently appeared at the Vienna Staatsoper (*Queen of Spades*) and at the Deutsche Oper Berlin (*Tosca*, 1974).

The French composer Darius Milhard in a painting.

MILCHEVA-NONOVA, ALEKSANDRINA

(Shumen 1934)

Bulgarian soprano. She studied at the Conservatory in Sofia and made her debut with the Varna Opera as Dorabella (*Così fan tutte*) in 1961. After winning the Toulouse International Singing Competition in 1966, she became a member of the resident company of the opera house in Sofia. At the same time she embarked on a busy international career which took her to the Vienna Staatsoper, the Opéra in Paris, Covent Garden and the Salzburg Festival. Milcheva-Nonova's reputation rests on her performances of the great mezzo-soprano roles in the traditional repertoire (Carmen, Amneris, Azucena, Eboli, Dalila, Santuzza, etc.), but she has also given particularly distinguished performances of the great roles of Russian opera.

MILHAUD, DARIUS

(Marseilles 1892–Geneva 1974)

French composer. His family's comfortable circumstances helped develop his interest in music and so he enrolled at the Paris Conservatoire in 1909. He took an active part in the cultural and musical life of the city, becoming a member of "Les Six." Milhaud was a tireless composer who tackled the widest possible range of musical genres, from symphonies to ballets, incidental music, film scores and opera. His first ventures into writing for the theater included *Les malheurs d'Orphée* (1926), *Christophe Colomb* (1930), *Maximilien* (1932) and *Médée* (1939). He then moved to the United States, where he taught, and in 1943 he composed what may be regarded as his major opera, *Bolivar* (Paris Opéra, 1950). After returning to France in 1947, he began teaching in the same year at the Paris Conservatoire.

MILLER, LAJOS

(Szombathely 1940)
Hungarian baritone. After studying at the Budapest Academy of Music he made his debut at the Opera House in Budapest in the Hungarian composer Szokolay's *Hamlet*. His international career reached a turning-point after successfully taking part in three singing competitions, the Gabriel Fauré in Paris (1974), the Toti dal Monte in Treviso (1975) and the Budapest Liszt prize (1975). He then appeared at a number of opera houses in Germany (Munich, Cologne, etc.), in France – including Aix-en-Provence (in Donizetti's *Il campanello*), the Paris Opéra (Leoncavallo's *I pagliacci*, 1982, Berio's *La vera storia*, 1985, etc.) and Radio France (Mercadante's *Il giuramento*, Bellini's *Beatrice di Tenda*, etc.) – and at a number of other Italian opera houses (Teatro Comunale in Florence, La Scala, etc.) as well as the Vienna Staatsoper. Miller's notable timbre and fine qualities of phrasing and interpretation enabled him to give convincing performances of many operas from the Italian repertoire, from Donizetti (*Lucia di Lammermoor*) to Verdi (*Il trovatore*, *Luisa Miller*, *Un ballo in maschera*, etc.) and Puccini (*Tosca*).

MILLO, APRILE

(New York 1958)
American soprano of Italian origin. She was taught by her parents, who were both respected opera singers. In 1978 she won the Verdi Competition in Busseto and was awarded the Giuseppe Verdi prize in the Francisco Viñas Competition in Barcelona. In 1980 she made her debut as Aida with Utah Opera in Salt Lake City, where she subsequently appeared in 1981 as Santuzza in Mascagni's *Cavalleria rusticana*. In Europe, Millo sang for the first time in Karlsruhe in 1982, again as the lead in *Aida*. She was engaged by La Scala, Milan and her debut there, as part of the 1982–83 season, was as Elvira (in Verdi's *Ernani*), a role she went on to sing with Welsh National Opera in Cardiff in 1984. Also in 1984 she made her first appearance in New York in two concert performances of *Ernani* and Rossini's *Guillaume Tell* with the Opera Orchestra of New York, also making her Metropolitan Opera House debut as Amelia in Verdi's *Simon Boccanegra*. From then on, Millo's name was associated with many of the productions at the Metropolitan, where she appeared in *Ernani* (1985), *Don Carlos* (1986), *Otello*, *Aida* (opening production of the 1989–90 season), *Andrea Chénier* (1990) and *Un ballo in maschera* (1990). She also participated in the seasons of the Opera Orchestra of New York from 1984 onwards (*I Lombardi*, *La battaglia di Legnano*, *Il pirata*, *La Wally*), appearing abroad at the Vienna Staatsoper (*Aida*, 1986), the Arena in Verona (*Aida* and *Don Carlos*, 1988, 1989, 1992), at the Baths of Caracalla, the Teatro dell' Opera in Rome (*Luisa Miller*, 1990), the Teatro Regio in Parma (1991), Lyric Opera of Chicago (*Mefistofele*, 1991), Munich (*La forza del destino*, 1992) and the Opéra Bastille in Paris (*Un ballo in maschera*, 1992). Millo has won numerous international prizes (the Richard Tucker award for 1985, the Maria Callas in Frankfurt in 1986). Her consistent and extensive lyric soprano voice with its particularly fine timbre, plus an outstanding personality in performance, built her reputation as one of the finest Verdi singers of the late twentieth century.

MILNES, SHERRILL

(Downers Grove, Illinois 1935)
American baritone. He studied singing at Drake University in Des Moines, Iowa, and began his career in the chorus of the Chicago Symphony. He first appeared as a soloist with Boris Goldousky's touring company, for which he sang more than 15 roles. He was then engaged by New York City Opera, appearing as Germont in *La traviata*, Valentin in *Faust* and Rupprecht in the American premiere of Prokofiev's *The Fiery Angel* in 1964. In 1965 he appeared for the first time at the Metropolitan Opera in New York (*Faust*), continuing to sing there into the 1990s. He made his European debut in 1970 singing the lead in Verdi's *Macbeth* at the Vienna Staatsoper and went on to appear at other major opera houses. Milnes's is a wide-ranging lyric baritone with a ringing quality in the upper register and a fine timbre. In the 1970s and the beginning of the 1980s, he was one of the most highly acclaimed performers of a vast repertoire, particularly featuring Italian opera (Rossini, Donizetti, Verdi, Giordano, Leoncavallo, etc.) and French (Massenet, Thomas, etc.), all of which is preserved in a large number of recordings.

MINTON, YVONNE

(Sydney 1938)
Australian mezzo-soprano. She studied music in Sydney and in 1961 won the Kathleen Ferrier prize in Holland. She made her debut in London at the City Literary Institute in 1964 singing the lead in Britten's opera *The Rape of Lucretia*. After appearing with the Handel Opera Company and New Opera Company, she sang for the first time at Covent Garden in 1965 (as Lola in *Cavalleria rusticana*), returning to win acclaim as Marina (*Boris Godunov*), Ascanio (Berlioz's *Benvenuto Cellini*), Orfeo (*Orfeo ed Euridice*) and in many other roles. In the early 1970s Minton sang in Chicago, at the Metropolitan Opera in New York in *Der Rosenkavalier* (1973) and the Bayreuth Festival (1974–77). In 1976 she appeared as the Countess in the first performance of the complete version of Berg's *Lulu* at the Opéra in Paris, a role which she went on to sing at La Scala, Milan (1977–78). She was Leokadja

Above: The American soprano Aprile Millo.

Left: The American baritone Sherrill Milnes.

in Kurt Weill's *Aufstieg und Fall der Stadt Mahagonny* at the Maggio Musicale Festival in Florence in 1990. Minton's fine timbre and intense personality have contributed to her reputation as an admired Wagner singer, but she has an equally notable record as a concert artiste, drawing on a vast repertoire from Monteverdi to Schoenberg.

MIREILLE

Opera in three acts and four scenes by Charles Gounod (1818–1893), to a libretto by Michel Carré, based on Mistral's Provençal poem Mireio. *First performance: Paris, Théâtre Lyrique, 19 March 1864 in the five-act version and 16 December 1864 in the three-act version.*

The setting is spring-time in Provence. Mireille (soprano), beautiful daughter of Maître Ramon (bass), loves and is loved by the impoverished Vincent (tenor). Mireille reveals her feelings for Vincent to her best friend Taven (mezzo-soprano). Taven warns Mireille that her father intends to give her in marriage to the wealthy Ourrias (baritone). She must not despair, however, but place her faith in the Virgin Mary. Mireille confesses to her father that she is in love with Vincent. His response is that he will never allow her to marry him. Ourrias, jealous of Vincent, seriously wounds him. Taven finds Vincent and takes him home to look after him while Ourrias, consumed with remorse, dies while crossing the river on a ferry-boat that capsizes. Taven informs Mireille that Vincent has been wounded. She goes to the church of Les Saintes Maries in a wilderness in the region of Crau to offer up everything she possesses in return for Vincent's recovery. While there she suffers sunstroke, but nevertheless manages to reach the church, where she dies in Vincent's arms.

After the final version of the opera was staged in December 1864, *Mireille* was always performed with a happy ending. It is only since 1939 that the original version, with its tragic finale, has returned. Gounod's music is a marvellous recreation of the legendary charm of Provence, using early and medieval songs.

MIRICIOIU, NELLY

(Adjud 1952)

Rumanian soprano. At the age of five she sang on the radio, and she began to study singing at the Conservatory in Bucharest when she was 14 (her teacher gave her the name of Nelly, in memory of Nelly Melba). After her debut in Bucharest as the Queen of the Night in Mozart's *Die Zauberflöte* (The Magic Flute), she moved to England, where she began her career. After singing roles from the lyric and *coloratura* repertoires, she moved on to more dramatic parts, from Donizetti's *Lucrezia Borgia* to Elena (in Verdi's *Les vêpres siciliennes*), Puccini's *Manon Lescaut* and *Tosca*, and particularly Violetta in *La traviata*, which she has sung at major international opera houses.

MITCHELL, LEONA

(Enid, Oklahoma 1949)

American soprano. She studied at the University of Oklahoma and in Santa Fe and San Francisco. In 1972 she made her debut as Micaela (*Carmen*) in San Francisco, repeating this role in 1975 when she joined the Metropolitan Opera in New York. Here she sang roles from the lyric repertoire, including *La bohème* and *Gianni Schicchi*, as well as appearing at a number of European opera houses. From the 1980s onwards she tackled more demanding lyric and also dramatic soprano roles, highlighting her fine timbre and effective dramatic presence.

MITRIDATE, RE DI PONTO

(Mithridates, King of Pontus)

Opera in three acts by Wolfgang Amadeus Mozart (1756–1791), to a libretto by Vittorio Amedeo Cigna-Santi, from Racine's tragedy Mithridate. *First performance: Milan, Teatro Ducale, 26 December 1770.*

Mitridate (tenor) returns home after being defeated by the Romans. Despite his old age and feelings of bitterness at having lost the war, Mitridate is fired with youthful love for Princess Aspasia (soprano). He has two rivals, however, in his two sons: Sifare (soprano), who is honest and loyal, and Farnace (contralto), a man bordering on wickedness and cruelty. The King does not hesitate to fight it out, and this rivalry gives rise to some psychologically complex situations. The story ends with the death of Mitridate in battle after he has made peace with his sons and drawn comfort from seeing the happiness of Sifare and Aspasia, who have married with his blessing, while Farnace returns to his previous love for Ismene (soprano).

This is the finest *opera seria* libretto ever set to music by Mozart, thanks to the quality of the tragedy by Racine on which it was based. Unfortunately the 14-year-old composer was

Above: The Australian mezzo-soprano Yvonne Minton.

Right: The American soprano Leona Mitchell.

too young and inexperienced to make full use of the opportunity the opera offered. Consequently, *Mitridate* consists entirely of an alternating sequence of mostly stylized recitatives and arias, designed to display the singing ability of the performers. In spite of this, there are some passages in which Mozart's dramatic involvement feels sincere and impassioned. The opera was a great success and earned him a commission to write a new work, *Ascanio in Alba*.

MITROPOULOS, DIMITRI

(Athens 1896–Milan 1960)

Greek conductor, naturalized American. He began to study music in Athens and completed his training in Brussels (1920–21) and Berlin (1921–24). Appointed assistant by the Deutsche Oper Berlin (1921–24), he then moved back to Athens to become conductor of the orchestra at the Conservatory (1927–30) and teach composition (1930). His extraordinary originality, coupled with equally exceptional mastery of technique and performance, led to his quickly gaining an international reputation and becoming one of the greatest conductors of modern times. Permanent conductor of the orchestras of Minneapolis (1947–49) and New York, first in collaboration with Leopold Stokowski (1949) and then in his own right (1951–57), Mitropoulos conducted at the Metropolitan Opera in New York from 1954 to 1960, as well as appearing at La Scala, Milan, the Teatro Comunale in Florence and the Vienna Staatsoper, where he gave memorable performances of operas by Verdi, Puccini and Strauss, preserved in numerous live recordings. He died following a heart attack during an orchestral rehearsal at La Scala.

MÖDL, MARTHA

(Nuremberg 1912)

German soprano and mezzo-soprano. She began to study singing at the age of 21 at the Conservatory in Nuremberg and with Otto Müller in Milan. In 1942 she made her debut in Remscheid (as Cherubino in *Le nozze di Figaro*) and went on to appear as a mezzo-soprano with the Düsseldorf Opera (1945–49). From there she moved to the Hamburg Opera (1949) and began to sing soprano roles, particularly in operas by Wagner, enjoying major successes in Vienna, Berlin, London, Bayreuth (Kundry in *Parsifal*, 1951, and subsequently as Brünnhilde, Isolde, etc.) and at the Metropolitan Opera in New York (1956). From the 1970s she appeared in character roles (giving a famous performance as Albert's mother in Britten's opera *Albert Herring*) and again displayed her artistic gifts of exceptional dramatic intensity and equally powerful stage presence.

MOFFO, ANNA

(Wayne, Pennsylvania 1932)

American soprano of Italian origin. She studied with Euphemia Giannini-Gregory at the Curtis Institute in Philadelphia and then at the Accademia di Santa Cecilia in Rome, where she completed her training with Luigi Ricci. After her debut at the Teatro Nuovo in Spoleto (1955–56), when she sang Norina in Donizetti's *Don Pasquale*, Moffo came to fame singing the lead in a television production of Puccini's *Madama Butterfly*. She then appeared at the Aix-en-Provence Festival (Zerlina in *Don Giovanni*, 1956), La Scala, Milan, the Salzburg Festival, the Chicago Lyric Opera (1957) and, from 1959, at the Metropolitan Opera in New York, where her debut role was Violetta (*La traviata*) and where she appeared for several seasons in a wide-ranging repertoire (*Manon*, *Rigoletto*, *I pagliacci*, *Faust*, etc.). Her essentially lyric soprano, well-suited to *coloratura*, has not always measured up to her considerable performing skills in many demanding roles, and by the 1970s there were clear signs of deterioration in the voice. A sensitive and elegant singer, Moffo has made many recordings, which include excellent performances of operas by Mozart (*Le nozze di Figaro*), Donizetti (*Lucia di Lammermoor*), Verdi (*La traviata* and *Falstaff*) and Puccini (*La rondine*).

MOÏSE ET PHARAON, OU LE PASSAGE DE LA MER ROUGE

(Moses and Pharaoh, or The Crossing of the Red Sea)

Opera in four acts by Gioachino Rossini (1792–1868), to a libretto by Etienne de Jouy and Luigi Balocchi. First performance: Paris, Opéra, 26 March 1827.

Submitting to divine will, Pharaon (baritone) stands aside to let the Israelites, led by Moïse (bass), leave for the promised land. This saddens Pharaon's son Aménophis (tenor), who is secretly in love with Anaï (soprano), a young Hebrew woman and daughter of Marie (mezzo-soprano), Moïse's sister. In an attempt to delay Anaï's departure, Aménophis suggests to his father that the Israelites may join forces with the

Top: A portrait of Mozart.

Above: The Greek conductor Dimitri Mitropoulos.

Midianites to declare war on Egypt. The Israelites are consequently not allowed to leave. After a moment's anxiety, Moïse confronts Pharaon and demonstrates the power of his God: those present are left standing in terror as darkness covers the sun. Greatly disturbed by this chilling darkness, Pharaon summons Moïse and renews his promise. The sun immediately comes out again. Before their departure, Osiride (bass), the High Priest, rules that the Israelites must pay tribute to the Goddess Isis. Moïse refuses. Enter the captain of the guard, Ophide (tenor), who recalls the terrible divine plagues, caused by Moïse, which had devastated Egypt. Pharaon orders that the Israelites be sent away from Memphis in chains. The scene changes to the desert, where the fleeing Israelites have reached the shores of the Red Sea. Aménophis, who had abducted Anaï, delivers her back to her own people as conclusive proof of his love. But, after a moment of indecision, she decides to stay with them. Aménophis is furious and threatens revenge. Moïse calls upon his people not to be afraid and, after he has offered up a prayer to God, the waters of the Red Sea miraculously part and the Israelites cross to the other side. Aménophis arrives, leading his Egyptian troops in pursuit, but with a thunderous roar the waters come crashing back down on them and they disappear. The sun comes out again and shines over the pacified sea.

Moïse is the French revised version of *Mosè in Egitto* (1818). The alterations made to the music and libretto enhanced Rossini's style with great majesty and touches of the sublime.

MOLINARI-PRADELLI, FRANCESCO

(Bologna 1911)

Italian conductor. A pupil at the Conservatorio in Bologna and the Accademia di Santa Cecilia in Rome, he made his debut in Brescia and Bergamo (1939) and went on to appear at the great Italian opera houses. He then conducted at Covent Garden (1951), San Francisco, Chicago (1957 and 1959) and the Metropolitan Opera in New York (from 1966). Molinari-Pradelli's reputation rests on his rigorous professionalism as a conductor in a career devoted almost exclusively to opera, and especially the great Italian repertoire.

MOLL, KURT

(Buir, Cologne 1938)

German bass. He studied cello and then singing at the Conservatory in Cologne and made his debut in 1961 in Aachen as Lodovico in Verdi's *Otello*, joining the company there until 1965. After appearing at a number of different theaters in Germany and Austria, Moll sang for the first time at Bayreuth in 1968, where he embarked on a career as a Wagner singer in *Tristan und Isolde*, *Parsifal*, *Lohengrin* and *Der fliegende Holländer* (The Flying Dutchman), a repertoire which made him famous throughout the world. As well as for Wagner, Moll has received great critical acclaim for his Mozart roles and concert repertoire.

MOND, DER

(The Moon)

Opera in two acts by Carl Orff (1895–1982), to the composer's own libretto after a story by the Brothers Grimm. First performance: Munich, Nationaltheater, 5 February 1939. A new version was staged at the same theater in 1950.

The narrator (tenor) tells how once upon a time the earth was not completely illuminated during the night: one hemisphere remained entirely in darkness, while in the other the night was lit up by a shining round sphere which hung from an oak tree. Four young men (tenor, two baritones and bass) are travelling the world when they come upon this light in the tree. A countryman (baritone) tells them this is the moon and he is paid to keep the moon's tank full, so that its light retains its brightness. The four young men steal the moon and take it back to their dark country. Many years go by. Throughout their lives the four have kept the light of the moon shining, and now, close to death, each of them wants to take part of the moon with him to the grave. As a result, their country goes back to having dark nights. After waking up in the next world, the four friends decide to put the moon together again and hang it up, but its light awakens all the other dead, and within a short time they are celebrating and making merry. The uproar causes St. Peter (bass) to intervene: once the dead, now drunk, tired and sleepy, have returned to their coffins, St. Peter picks up the moon and takes it with him to Heaven, where he hangs it to a star and it lights the whole earth.

In *Der Mond*, Orff once again uses his characteristically expressive and musical language to present a perfect blend between archaic music and modern music.

MONDO DELLA LUNA, IL

Opera in three acts by Franz Joseph Haydn (1732–1809), to a libretto by Polisseno Fegejo Pastor, adapted from Carlo Goldoni's play of the same name. First performance: Esterháza Castle, 3 August 1777.

The elderly Buonafede (bass) has two daughters, Flaminia (soprano) and Clarissa (soprano). Flaminia is in love with Ernesto (contralto), while Clarissa

Above: The Italian conductor Francesco Molinari-Pradelli.

Right: The German bass Kurt Moll.

loves Eclittico (tenor). But Buonafede stands in the way of the two couples being together. So Eclittico, together with Ernesto and his servant Cecco (tenor), who is in love with Lisetta (mezzo-soprano), Buonafede's maid and courted by her master, decides to exploit Buonafede's naivety and pretends to be an astrologer. Through a trick telescope Buonafede sees the wonders of the moon, and when a mysterious emperor of the moon invites Eclittico to come to his planet, the credulous Buonafede begs him to take him there. After falling asleep under the influence of a powerful sleeping-draught, Buonafede wakes up under the impression that he is on the moon, whereas in fact he has been moved into the garden of Eclittico's house, cleverly transformed to resemble a lunar landscape. Enter Cecco, disguised as the emperor of the moon, followed by the two sisters, who have been well-briefed by their lovers. When Cecco, Eclittico and Ernesto ask to marry Lisetta, Clarissa and Flaminia, the naive Buonafede ends up by consenting. When the hoax is admitted to him, he is enraged but has to give in and forgives everyone. The three couples can be happy with the way things have worked out, and the opera ends in general rejoicing.

Il mondo della luna is a real *divertissement*. Haydn develops Goldoni's story and brings the different characters very much to life. The opera was painstakingly put together with great care over every detail. In particular it demonstrates Haydn's flair for parody, which enables him to transcend the stereotyped comedy made fashionable by the *opera buffa* of the time. *Il mondo della luna* is also an opera by Giovanni Paisiello, which originally had the title *Il credulo deluso* (1774) and later adopted Goldoni's original title (1783).

MONIUSZKO, STANISLAW

(Ubiel, Minsk 1819–Warsaw 1872)

Polish composer. His musical education took place in Warsaw, Minsk and Berlin (1837–40), where he studied composition with Rugenhagen. On his return to Poland, he began a dual career as a composer and conductor. After writing various operettas, he tackled opera, and his *Halka* (final version, 1858) was the first significant example of a national Polish opera. Moniuszko's subsequent output for the theater, although concentrating on the comic genre, demonstrated his deep commitment to the development of national opera. After *Halka*, Moniuszko's most celebrated score is *Straszny dwór* (1865). Both operas have continued to be included in the repertoires of Polish opera houses.

MONNA LISA

Opera in two acts by Max von Schillings (1868–1933), to a libretto by Beatrice Dovsky. First performance: Stuttgart Hoftheater, 26 September 1915.

In a prologue, set in Florence in modern times, a lay brother (tenor) prevails upon two travellers, a husband (baritone) and wife (soprano), to visit a monastery of Carthusians which at one time had been the palace of Francesco del Giocondo, a wealthy merchant, and his third wife, Fiordalisa Gherardini, whom Leonardo Da Vinci immortalized in his portrait *Mona Lisa*. The action then transfers to 1492 and recreates the tragic life of the young Mona Lisa. On the last day of the carnival in that year, a young papal emissary, Giovanni de' Salviati (tenor), comes to the house of Francesco (baritone) to acquire a pearl of great price for the pope. While there, Giovanni sees Fiordalisa (soprano) again, the woman he has been in love with. She has meanwhile been forced to marry the elderly Francesco and now lives in a state of dejection. Francesco discovers the pair kissing but pretends to have seen nothing and steals away again before making it clear that he is about to enter. Hearing him approaching, Giovanni has to hide in a closet while Fiordalisa takes to her apartments. Francesco enters the room, assumes that Giovanni has taken refuge in the closet and locks it. Fiordalisa comes in and asks him for the keys, but Francesco declares that none of the pearls in that closet is more precious to him than his wife and throws the key out of the window into the river Arno below. Fiordalisa cries out and faints. The next day, Ash Wednesday, Fiordalisa regains consciousness and finds herself exactly where she had been when she fainted. At first she is bewildered, but then she realizes what has happened and, like a woman possessed, hurls herself at the closet door, calling out Giovanni's name. But he has already died of suffocation. At that moment Dianora (mezzo-soprano), Francesco's daughter, comes in: she has found the key in the bottom of her boat. Left alone, Fiordalisa is so distraught that she does not have the courage to open the door. As she stands there, Francesco comes in and tells her that he has been to see Giovanni de Salviati to give him the pearl but has not found him. Fiordalisa

A scene from *Il mondo della luna* by Franz Joseph Haydn.

looks at her husband with a devilish smile and shows him the key, leading him to believe that Giovanni is safe and sound, before asking him to open the closet to take out some jewels. Perturbed by Fiordalisa's enigmatic smile, Francesco opens the closet, whereupon as quick as lightning Fiordalisa shuts the door, trapping him inside. In the epilogue, which brings us back to modern times, the novice has finished his story. The woman has been profoundly affected by it, while the husband, astonished at his wife's reaction, goes out. The young novice looks at the wife in consternation: the three of them are the reincarnation of the three characters in the story.

At its first performance, *Monna Lisa* was a moderate success, and this grew in subsequent years as a result of it being given a number of performances in Europe, the United States and Russia. It was revived at Karlsruhe in 1983 to mark the 50th anniversary of the composer's death.

MONTAG AUS LICHT
(Monday, from "Light")
Opera in three acts, a Greeting and a Farewell by Karlheinz Stockhausen (b. 1928), libretto, actions and movements by the composer. First performance: Milan, La Scala, 7 May 1988.

Montag represents another "day" in the operatic cycle of seven days begun by Stockhausen in 1981 with *Donnerstag aus Licht* (Thursday, from "Light"). The composer has given this cycle three main characters: Michael, associated with Thursday (the day of Thor-Donner-Jove), Lucifer (linked to Saturday, the day of Saturn) and Eva (Monday, day of Selene, the moon). On this day, the composer celebrates femaleness, and the birth and rebirth of man. The score, a mosaic of sight and sound, is somewhat complicated by its level of dramatic clarity and the fact that the performance of the music requires a considerable number of players as well as prerecorded, particularly electronic, material.

MONTARSOLO, PAOLO
(Naples 1925)
Italian bass. He first studied singing in Naples with Enrico Conti and then moved to Milan's La Scala school. The direction he was going to take was already clear from his debut in Cherubini's *L'hôtellerie portugaise* in 1951 at La Scala. As a *buffo* bass Montarsolo won acclaim at major international opera houses for his performances of a repertoire ranging from eighteenth-century Neapolitan opera to Rossini and Donizetti, in particular *La Cenerentola* and *Don Pasquale*.

Above: The Italian bass Paolo Montarsolo.

Right: The Italian composer Claudio Monteverdi in a drawing by Grevenbroeck.

MONTEMEZZI, ITALO
(Vigasio, Verona 1875–1952)
Italian composer. He studied at the Conservatorio in Milan, where he graduated in 1900. He made his debut in opera with *Giovanni Gallurese* (1905), which earned him a commission from the Ricordi publishing house to write two more operas: *L'amore dei tre re* (1913), his most famous opera, and *La nave* (1918). In 1939 he moved to the United States, where he composed his last opera, *L'incantesimo* (1942). He returned to settle permanently in Italy in 1949.

MONTEVERDI, CLAUDIO
(Cremona 1567–Venice 1643)
Italian composer. He studied music with Marco Antonio Ingegneri, *maestro di cappella* at the Cathedral in Cremona. Between 1590 and 1592 he was in the service of Duke Vincenzo I Gonzaga in Mantua and was appointed *maestro di cappella* in 1601. In 1607 Monteverdi's *Orfeo* was staged, marking a crucial turning-point in his career. This was followed in 1608 by *Arianna*, the score of which has been lost, and, in the same year, *Il ballo delle ingrate*. Differences of opinion with the Duke led to Monteverdi being dismissed from the Court in Mantua in 1612. The following year he became *maestro di cappella* in St. Mark's Cathedral, Venice. During this Venetian period, the opening of the public theaters prompted Monteverdi to compose many operas, of which only two have survived, *Il ritorno di Ulisse in patria* (1641) and *L'incoronazione di Poppea* (1643).

MOORE, DOUGLAS
(Cutchogue, New York 1893–Green Point 1969)
American composer. He began his music studies in the United States and continued them in Paris (1919) with Vincent d'Indy and Nadia Boulanger. He taught at Barnard College and Columbia University (1926–62), at the same time pursuing a busy career as a composer of orchestral, chamber and choral music and opera. His best-known operas are *The Devil and Daniel Webster* (1939) and *The Ballad of Baby Doe* (1956).

MORINO, GIUSEPPE
(Assisi 1950)
Italian tenor. He made his debut as Faust in Spoleto (1981) and specialized in the *bel canto* repertoire. From 1984 he sang at the

Martina Franca Festival in Italy, where he gave particularly distinguished performances in Bellini's *Il pirata* (1987) and Donizetti's *Maria di Rohan* (1988) and *La favorita* (1990). A parallel international career brought engagements at the Vienna Staatsoper (*Rigoletto*, 1986) as well as at La Scala, Milan (from 1987) and the Donizetti Festival in Bergamo (*Gianni di Parigi*, 1988). Morino's voice, though not possessing an especially fine timbre, has considerable range and the support of good technique. After an early interest in Bellini and Donizetti, he subsequently turned to the Romantic repertoire and *opéra-lyrique*.

MORRIS, JAMES

(Baltimore 1947)

American bass-baritone. He began to study music at the Peabody Conservatory and then attended the University of Maryland, where he was a pupil of Rosa Ponselle. He joined the Baltimore Opera as a member of the chorus and quickly distinguished himself in solo roles. After completing his training, Morris was engaged in 1971 by the Metropolitan Opera in New York, where in 1975 he enjoyed his first major success as Don Giovanni in Mozart's opera. Much of his career has centered on the Metropolitan, where he has drawn on an extensive repertoire of bass and baritone roles in operas from Mozart to Verdi and Wagner. His reputation as a Wagner singer rests on some highly acclaimed performances as Wotan in the *Ring* cycle at the Metropolitan conducted by James Levine (and subsequently recorded) and in the role of the Dutchman in *Der fliegende Holländer* (The Flying Dutchman), which he also sang at La Scala, Milan (1988), with Riccardo Muti conducting. On the international opera scene, Morris appeared at all the leading opera venues, including the Salzburg Festival (from 1982), the Vienna Staatsoper (from 1984) and Munich.

MOSÈ IN EGITTO

(Moses in Egypt)

Opera in three acts by Gioachino Rossini (1792–1868), to a libretto by Andrea Leone Tottola. First performance: Naples, Teatro San Carlo, 5 March 1818.

Egypt has been plunged into a great darkness, divine retribution because Pharaoh (bass) has not obeyed the Word commanding him to release the Israelites from slavery. So Pharaoh summons Mosè and promises him freedom for his people. At this, Mosè (bass) calls upon God and the darkness vanishes. Word that the Israelites are about to leave is a source of despair to Osiride (tenor), Pharaoh's son, who is secretly in love with Elcia (soprano), a young Hebrew woman. With the help of the High Priest Mambre (tenor), Osiride incites the people to rise up in protest against the proclamation by which the Israelites are to be freed, and then convinces his father that Mosè is plotting against him. The departure of the Israelites is suspended. But once again the Egyptians have failed to respect the Word, and this time they are punished with a deluge of fire. Pharaoh orders the expulsion of the Israelites from the land of Egypt. Osiride, in desperation, abducts Elicia and drags her into an underground vault. Discovered there by the Queen, Amaltea (soprano), and Aronne (tenor), the young couple are separated and forcibly returned to their own people. Meanwhile Pharaoh, still beset by doubts, has Mosè arrested, because he fears an alliance between the Israelites and the Egyptians' enemies. Mosè is outraged and prophesies the most terrible retribution, the death of all first-born boys in Egypt, but Pharaoh does not believe him and orders that Osiride be consecrated as Pharaoh with powers equal to his own. Enter Elcia to plead for Mosè to be freed. Osiride will not be moved and demands the death penalty for him. The response to this latest outrage against divine authority is a thunderbolt from Heaven, which strikes Osiride dead. Having left Egypt, the Israelites reach the shores of the Red Sea. Pharaoh's army is in pursuit, but Mosè breathes new courage into his people and, after calling on God, lifts up his staff, whereupon the Red Sea opens up, and the Israelites pass safely and reach the opposite shore. The Sea then closes behind them, and its waters sweep the Egyptian army away.

Mosè in Egitto evolved on two distinct levels: on the one hand there is the drama of the Israelites people conveyed by an extraordinary use of the chorus, and on the other the love relationship between Elcia and Osiride. The most prominent and significant strand in this opera is unquestionably its description of the drama of a people, an ingredient which would later influence Verdi when he came to compose *Nabucco* and *I Lombardi*.

MOSER, EDDA

(Berlin 1941)

German soprano. Daughter of the musicologist Hans Joachim, she studied singing with Hermann Weissenborn and Gerty König in Berlin. After her debut as Kate Pinkerton in *Madama Butterfly*, she made a number of appearances at opera venues in Germany, including Hamburg, the Salzburg Festival (as Wellgunde in *Das Rheingold*) and Frankfurt. An acclaimed interpreter of the contemporary repertoire (Henze, Zimmermann, Nono, etc.), Moser was able to use her considerable vocal range and *coloratura* skill in powerful performances as the Queen of the Night in *Die Zauberflöte* (The Magic Flute) and as Constanze in *Die Entführung aus dem Serail*

Scene from *Mosè in Egitto* by Goachino Rossini, performed for the first time in Naples in 1818.

(The Seraglio). Her career then expanded as she took on engagements at the world's major opera houses, from the Metropolitan Opera in New York (from 1968) to the Vienna Staatsoper (1971), Aix-en-Provence (1972), the Opéra in Paris (from 1977) and the Maggio Musicale Festival in Florence (1981). In more recent years she enjoyed great success for her appearances as Reiza in Weber's opera *Oberon* (Catania, 1987), as Salome in Richard Strauss's opera of the same name (Teatro dell' Opera in Rome, 1988) and as Marie in Berg's *Wozzeck* (Modena, Parma and Reggio Emilia, 1989), this last a role that displayed her intuitive musicianship combined with her acting qualities, which were also impressively in evidence in her performance as Donna Anna in Joseph Losey's 1979 film version of *Don Giovanni*.

MOSER, THOMAS

(Richmond, Virginia 1945)
American tenor. He studied singing in the United States with Lotte Lehmann, Gérard Souzay and Martial Singher. He made his debut at the Opernhaus in Graz (1975), then went on to sing in Munich and at the Vienna Staatsoper, where he became a member of the resident companies (from 1976), drawing on an extensive repertoire from Mozart (*Idomeneo*, *Così fan tutte*, *Don Giovanni*, etc.) to Richard Strauss (*Capriccio*, *Salome*, etc.). In 1979 he sang for the first time at the Salzburg Festival (as the messenger in *Aida*) and at New York City Opera (in *La clemenza di Tito*). From the 1980s Moser has appeared in the leading European opera houses. He is especially admired as a performer of Mozart and Strauss and of the concert repertoire.

MOSES UND ARON

Opera in three acts by Arnold Schoenberg (1874–1951), to the composer's own libretto. First performance (posthumous): Zurich, Stadttheater, 6 June 1957.

It has fallen to Moses (bass speaking role) to free the Israelites from slavery and lead them out of Egypt to the Promised Land. With him on this mission will be his brother Aaron (tenor), who will act as his mouthpiece, just as Moses will interpret the thought of God. Aaron's task is to convince the incredulous Israelites, who waver between diffidence, hope and scepticism. Moses is exhausted and discouraged, but when Aaron seizes the staff from his brother's hand and performs miracles with it, the people are won over, kneel down and place themselves in the hands of the new God. Moses withdraws to climb Mount Sinai. After 40 days the Israelites are still waiting at the foot of the mountain for Moses to descend bearing the tablets of the Law, and the uncertainty leads to disorder and violence. Aaron tries to calm the angry crowd but then is himself so beset with doubt that he eventually gives in. After building a golden calf, the people indulge in an unbridled orgy which culminates in the sacrifice of four virgins and leads to suicides and acts of destruction. Moses reappears, and his fury is terrifying. Appalled by what he sees, Moses utters a curse and makes the golden calf disappear. Moses and Aaron are left alone to confront one another. A dispute flares up between them, and it seems as though Aaron almost has the upper hand over Moses, who is so overcome with doubt that he smashes the tablets of the Law. But then he manages to impose his moral authority and the power of his faith. Aaron is arrested, accused by Moses with having prevented the Israelites from being lifted up to God and of having persuaded them instead to put their trust in him. Moses orders that he be allowed to go free, but at that moment Aaron is struck dead.

A scene from *Moses und Aron*, an opera in three acts by Arnold Schoenberg.

The music of the first two acts of *Moses und Aron* was written between 1930 and 1932, while the third act was never scored. The reason for this may perhaps be guessed at from the anguished words that Moses speaks at the end of the second act: "Thus all was but madness that I believed before, and can and must not be given voice. O word, thou word that I lack!" The opera is one of the finest achievements in twentieth-century music, as well as marking the fruition of Schoenberg's artistic development. Of particular significance is the composer's characterization of the two leading roles: Moses, who can think but not speak, expresses himself through the medium of *Sprechgesang* (speech-song), while Aaron sings in the conventional way.

MOZART, WOLFGANG AMADEUS

(Salzburg 1756–Vienna 1791)
Austrian composer. His father Leopold, an excellent musician, completely devoted himself to his son's musical education. The young Wolfgang also had the opportunity of visiting Johann Christian Bach, having les-

sons in Bologna and above all deepening his knowledge and studies of Italian opera. After his first two attempts at writing for the theater – his sacred play *Die Schuldigkeit des ersten Gebotes* (1767) and his Latin comedy *Apollo et Hyacinthus* (1767) – Mozart's first opera was *La finta semplice* (1768, performed 1769), followed by his *Singspiel* of 1768, *Bastien und Bastienne*. It was during his frequent journeys to Italy that productions were staged of his *Mitridate, re di Ponto* (1770), *Ascanio in Alba* (1771) and *Lucio Silla* (1771), all conceived in the style of the contemporary *opera seria*. Then came *La finta giardiniera*, partly composed in Salzburg and performed in Munich in 1775, followed by other Salzburg works, *Il re pastore* (1775), the incidental music for Gebler's *Thamos* (1779) and the unfinished *Zaide* (1779). The climax of these compositions was *Idomeneo, re di Creta*, successfully staged at the Burgtheater in Munich (1781). In Vienna, where he had settled in 1782, Mozart continued his exploration of opera composition. After *Die Entführung aus dem Serail* (The Seraglio, 1782), the first important example of German opera, a number of minor works (the unfinished *L'oca del Cairo*, 1783, and *Lo sposo deluso*, 1784) and *Der Schauspieldirektor*, 1786, Mozart began his fruitful collaboration with the librettist Lorenzo Da Ponte, which led to the Italian trilogy masterpieces – *Le nozze di Figaro* (1786), *Don Giovanni* (1787) and *Così fan tutte* (1790) – after which he returned to *Singspiel* with *Die Zauberflöte* (The Magic Flute, 1791), high point of this musical genre. At the same time he was engaged on the composition of *La clemenza di Tito*, a commission from Bohemia to mark the coronation of Leopold II. In this score, based on an old libretto by Metastasio revised by Caterino Mazzolà, Mozart achieved a perfect stylization of Italian *opera seria*.

MRTVÉHO DOMU, Z

(From the House of the Dead)

Opera in three acts by Léoš Janáček (1852–1928), to the composer's own libretto, after Dostoevsky's novel Zapiski iz mertogo doma (The House of the Dead). *First performance: Brno, National Theater, 12 April 1930.*

The action takes place in a Siberian prison on the banks of the river Irtysh. On an icy winter's morning, the prisoners emerge from their cells. A political prisoner arrives, Alexander Petrovich Goryanchikov (baritone). His appearance and behaviour irritate the camp Commandant (bass), who orders that he be punished. Meanwhile the guards herd the convicts off to work. Goryanchikov reappears. He has decided to escape and lays an ambush for the guards, but his bid fails and he is captured. While the prisoners are at work on the river bank, Goryanchikov gives a reading lesson to Alyeya (soprano), a young Tartar who has told him all about his family. When the work period is over, the convicts put on a play. After the curtain has fallen, the dismal life of the prison camp resumes. Alyeya, wounded by a prisoner who picked a quarrel with him, is being given assistance. In the infirmary, while Goryanchikov is visiting Alyeya, the other prisoners relate the circumstances that led to their being incarcerated. The commandant then summons Goryanchikov and tells him that he is free to go. Goryanchikov embraces Alyeya affectionately while the other prisoners release an eagle that had made its home in the camp, a symbol of the inviolable freedom of the human spirit.

From the House of the Dead was Janáček's last opera, composed between 1927 and 1928 and produced posthumously. The work, in which the leading role is played by the crowd, represents the summit of Janáček's dramatic art, which he had attained through the development of a strongly expressionist language.

MUETTE DE PORTICI, LA

(The Mute Young Woman of Portici)

Opera in five acts by Daniel François Auber (1782–1871), to a libretto by Eugène Scribe and Casimir Delavigne. First performance: Paris, Opéra, 29 February 1828.

The action takes place in Naples and Portici in 1647. Alphonse (tenor), son of the Duke of Arcos, is shortly to marry the Spanish princess Elvire (soprano) when he confesses to his friend Lorenzo (tenor) that he has seduced and deserted Fenella (mime and dancer), a mute young commoner. Shortly after this, Fenella enters. She has just escaped from the prison in which the Duke of Arcos had had her detained in order to keep her away from his son. Fenella uses sign language to ask Elvire to help her, and Elvire promises to give her protection. After the wedding of Alphonse and Elvire, Fenella meets the young couple, recognizes the bridegroom as her former

Top: Wolfgang Amadeus Mozart.

Above: A scene from Auber's *La muette de Portici.*

lover and arouses the jealousy of the princess, who rejects her new husband. On her return home, Fenella explains to her brother, Masaniello (tenor), a fisherman, what has happened to her. Masaniello, with the support of his fellow fishermen, swears to avenge his sister. Meanwhile, Elvire, who has forgiven Alphonse, sends the knight Selva (bass) to look for Fenella. When he finds her, he compels her to accompany him, fending off Masaniello when he comes to his sister's defense. Masaniello then incites the people to rise up. Portici is thrown into turmoil by the rebellion. Elvire and Alphonse are forced to flee. Chastened by the resulting bloodshed, Masaniello offers to help the two fugitives himself. A few days later, troops are regaining control of the city. Masaniello leads the population against the soldiers but he is slain by his own comrades in the act of saving Elvire's life. Fenella is tormented by grief at the death of her brother and throws herself from the palace balcony.

Almost certainly Auber's most famous opera and one of the most outstanding successes at the Opéra in Paris, *La muette de Portici* received as many as 500 performances between 1828 and 1880 in Paris alone. It is one of the rare instances of an opera in which the leading role, being a mute, is played by a mime or dancer. Of all his operas, only in *La muette* was Auber able to create a real sense of drama. It was also the first time – another significant feature – that he had used the crowd as chorus, giving them a key role in the development of the plot. These ingredients make *La muette de Portici* the first important model for the *grands-opéras* to come.

MURRAY, ANN

(Dublin 1949)

Irish mezzo-soprano. A pupil of Frederick Cox at the Royal College of Music in Manchester, she subsequently attended the London Opera Center and made her theater debut as Zerlina in *Don Giovanni* with Scottish Opera. Murray went on to appear with English National Opera in Rossini's *Le Comte Ory* and *La Cenerentola* and in Purcell's *Dido and Aeneas*. In 1976 she was engaged by Covent Garden, where her first role was as Cherubino (*Le nozze di Figaro*). In the years that followed, she pursued an international career with appearances at the Aix-en-Provence Festival (Handel's *Alcina*, 1978), Cologne Opera (Rossini's *La Cenerentola*), New York City Opera (Mozart's *La clemenza di Tito*), the Salzburg Festival and La Scala, Milan (*Lucio Silla*, 1984, and Donna Elvira in Mozart's *Don Giovanni*, 1987). Murray's reputation also rests on her many concert performances, but she is known above all as a Mozart singer of considerable refinement. She is married to the tenor Philip Langridge.

MUSSORGSKY, MODEST

(Karevo, Pskov 1839–St. Petersburg 1881)

Russian composer. Obliged by his father to pursue a military career, he subsequently left the army (1859) to concentrate on music. After obtaining a modest position as a civil servant in St. Petersburg, he came into close contact with the composers Balakirev, Cui, Borodin and Rimsky-Korsakov, with whom he formed the Group of Five. By 1856 he was already writing music for the theater, including the incomplete *Salammbô* (1863–64), based on Flaubert's novel, and the first act of *Jenitha* (The Marriage) after Gogol (1868). In the same year he began to compose *Boris Godunov*, which, after a painful gestation period, was finally staged in 1874. Meanwhile, he set to work on *Khovanshchina* (1872–80), the orchestration of which remained unfinished. This second masterpiece by Mussorgsky was initially completed by Rimsky-Korsakov and then, for a production in Paris in 1913, given a new final scene by Ravel and Stravinsky. It was not until 1960 and Shostakovich's version that *Khovanshchina* appeared in a form that was more faithful to the original. Only fragments of *Pugačevščina* (1877), Mussorgsky's last work for the theater, survive.

MUTI, RICCARDO

(Naples 1941)

Italian conductor. He studied music in Naples (piano) and Milan (composition and conducting). Winner of the 1967 Guido Cantelli prize, he made his opera debut in 1969 conducting Verdi's *I masnadieri* in Florence. He then became permanent conductor of Florence's Maggio Musicale Festival orchestra (1971–81), during which time he conducted a number of important productions: Meyerbeer's *L'Africaine* (1971), Rossini's *Guillaume Tell* (1972), Spontini's *Agnes von Hohenstaufen* (1974), Gluck's *Orfeo* (1976), Verdi's *Les vêpres siciliennes* (1978), *Otello* (1980) and others. In 1971 he made his debut at the Salzburg Festival (*Don Pasquale*), returning to conduct there regularly from 1982 onwards (*Così fan tutte*). Other engagements have included the Vienna Staatsoper (from 1973), Munich (from 1976) and Covent Garden (from 1977). From 1986 onwards he was music director at La Scala in Milan, where he became recognized as a rigorous, impassioned interpreter of the Mozart and Verdi repertoires, as well as of Rossini, Wagner and operas outside the repertoire such as Pergolesi's *Lo frate 'nnamurato* (1989) and Cherubini's *Lodoïska* (1991). Conducting the Philadelphia Orchestra (principal conductor 1981–92), Muti won enormous acclaim for his account of Leoncavallo's *I pagliacci* with Luciano Pavarotti, a production marking the centenary of this opera's first performance (1892–1992).

Above: The Irish mezzo-soprano Ann Murray.

Right: The Italian conductor Riccardo Muti.

N

NABUCCO

Opera in four parts by Giuseppe Verdi (1813–1901), to a libretto by Temistocle Solera. First performance: Milan, La Scala, 9 March 1842.

The action takes place in Babylon and Jerusalem. The Hebrews have been defeated by the Babylonian forces of Nabucco (baritone). The High Priest, Zaccaria (bass), attempts to lift their spirits by revealing to them that he has a card up his sleeve, having managed to take prisoner Nabucco's daughter Fenena (soprano). But Ismaele (tenor), nephew of the King of Jerusalem, falls in love with her. While he is trying to set her free, the slave-girl Abigaille (soprano) and Nabucco himself appear on the scene. Zaccaria wants to have Fenena executed, but Ismaele's intervention stays Zaccaria's hand and the Hebrews curse him as a traitor of the people. Some time later, during Nabucco's absence, Fenena is acting as regent. Abigaille plots to kill her and win power. While Fenena is being converted by Zaccaria, Abigaille is on the verge of achieving her objective after exploiting a false rumour that Nabucco is dead. Suddenly, however, Nabucco himself reappears and, to the horror of the Hebrews, proclaims himself God. He is promptly struck by a thunderbolt from Heaven and loses his mind. Abigaille therefore deposes Nabucco and decides to put Fenena to death together with all the Hebrews. Nabucco calls upon the God of the Hebrews and, after being restored to sanity, places himself at the head of an army which has remained loyal to him and arrives just in time to save his daughter. Abigaille takes her own life but, before dying, asks for forgiveness from Fenena and intercedes with Nabucco for his consent to Fenena marrying her beloved Ismaele.

Nabucco, Verdi's third opera, was his first real success. Imbued with patriotic spirit, the work was given as many as 57 performances over four months, as a result of which it found its way into the opera houses' usual repertoire, where it has remained one of the most popular of all operas. *Nabucco* also provided Verdi with his first chance to meet the soprano Giuseppina Strepponi, who created the role of Abigaille and was to retire from the stage only a few years later.

NAFÉ, ALICIA

(Buenos Aires 1947)

Argentinian mezzo-soprano. She studied music at the Manuel De Falla Conservatory and the Teatro Colón in Buenos Aires. After being awarded a scholarship, she was able to complete her training in Madrid. In 1975 she made her debut in Toledo in Verdi's *Requiem*. Her reputation grew as a result of engagements at major opera houses in Spain (Seville, Madrid, Barcelona) and South America, followed by roles in France and Germany. She sang with the Hamburg Opera Company from 1977 to 1981 and also appeared at the Bayreuth Festival (1976–77), the Paris Opéra and many other opera houses. Nafé is famous for her performance as Carmen in Bizet's opera but enjoyed considerable success too in Mozart's *Così fan tutte* and *La clemenza di Tito*, and as Charlotte in Massenet's *Werther*.

NAVARRAISE, LA

Opera in two acts by Jules Massenet (1842–1912), to a libretto by Jules Claretie and Henri Cain. First performance: London, Royal Opera House, Covent Garden, 20 June 1894.

The action takes place in a Basque village in 1874 during the Carlist war. Anita (soprano), an orphan from Navarre, is in love with and loved by Araquil (tenor), a young sergeant, son of the wealthy Remigio (baritone). The father is opposed to this relationship and insists on a large dowry, which the poor Anita has no way of amassing. Anita goes to see General Garrido and declares she is ready to kill the Carlist leader Zuccaraga for a reward of "2,000 douros." But this desperate gesture by Anita proves fruitless: Araquil has become jealous as a result of Anita's behaviour and has pursued her to the Carlist camp. During the shooting which follows the murder of Zuccaraga by Anita, Araquil is mortally wounded and dies shortly afterwards in Anita's arms, at which point she goes out of her mind with grief.

La Navarraise may be taken as Massenet's acknowledgement of the emerging realist style of opera.

Top: The Argentinian mezzo-soprano Alicia Nafé.

Above: A scene from the fourth act of Verdi's *Nabucco*.

NEBLETT, CAROL
(Modesto, California 1946)
American soprano. After studying violin and piano, she concentrated on singing. She had lessons first with William Vennard and subsequently with Pierre Bernac and Lotte Lehmann. In 1969 she made her debut as Musetta (Puccini's *La bohème*) at New York City Opera, where she appeared for a number of seasons. She went on to sing at Lyric Opera of Chicago in the role of Chrysothemis in Richard Strauss's *Elektra* (1975), at Dallas Civic Opera as Antonia in Offenbach's *Les contes d'Hoffmann*, and as Minnie in *La fanciulla del West*, one of her most outstanding performances, in the production which opened the 1974–75 season at the Teatro Regio in Turin. Great interest was aroused by her interpretation of Senta in Wagner's *Der fliegende Holländer* (The Flying Dutchman) at the Metropolitan Opera in New York during the 1978–79 season. She also won acclaim at Covent Garden in *La fanciulla del West*, at the Vienna Staatsoper in Korngold's *Die tote Stadt*, another of her celebrated performances, at the Salzburg Festival in *La clemenza di Tito* and at other leading opera houses. She displayed not only unquestionable vocal gifts but also a strong performing temperament and considerable charm. More recent appearances have included the lead role in Respighi's *Semirama* (Palermo, 1987), the Lady in Hindemith's *Cardillac* (Florence, 1991) and Queen Isabella in Franchetti's *Cristoforo Colombo* (Miami, 1992).

NELSON, JUDITH
(Chicago 1939)
American soprano. Her interest in Early Music took her to Munich, where she studied singing with Andrea von Ramm. She then completed her training with Martial Singher in California. Within a short time she was being hailed as one of the most distinguished singers of the seventeenth- and eighteenth-century repertoires and appeared with the leading performers in this genre, including Christopher Hogwood, Alan Curtis, René Jacobs and William Christie. In opera, she sang in Monteverdi's *L'incoronazione di Poppea* and Purcell's *Dido and Aeneas* and *The Fairy Queen*.

NERONE
Opera in four acts by Arrigo Boito (1842–1918), to the composer's own libretto. First performance (posthumous): Milan, La Scala, 1 May 1924.

In a cemetery on the Appian Way, Simon Mago (baritone) and Tigellino (bass) are digging a hole in which Nerone (tenor) will be able to place the funerary urn containing the ashes of Agrippina, his mother, whom he has killed. Like a ghost, Asteria (soprano) appears. She is in love with Nerone and hopes that, with Simon Mago's help, she will be able to win his love. Then Simon Mago comes upon a gathering of Christians in another part of the same cemetery. Fanuel (baritone), one of the Christians' leaders, confronts Simon Mago, while Rubria (mezzo-soprano), a young vestal virgin who has been converted to Christianity, hurries away to warn her fellow Christians that they have been discovered. Simon Mago offers Fanuel a chance to join forces with him, kill Nerone and seize control of the Empire, and when Fanuel refuses, Simon Mago vows to have his revenge. Some time later, Simon Mago endeavours to ingratiate himself still further with Nerone and exploit his credulity by causing Asteria to appear before him dressed as a divine protectress of the dead. But Nerone uncovers the hoax and angrily orders his Pretorian guards to destroy the altar in the temple. He also decrees that Simon Mago should be forced to throw himself from one of the towers in the Circus during the next festival and amuse the crowds by trying to fly. Having survived the destruction of the temple, Asteria warns Fanuel and the Christians that Simon Mago has revealed the whereabouts of their meeting-place to Nerone. But it is too late: Simon Mago arrives with the Pretorian guards, and Fanuel is arrested. At the Circus, Tigellino tells Nerone that Simon Mago's followers are planning to start a fire during the spectacle to save their leader from his fate. Nerone is unconcerned by this and comments that if Rome goes up in flames, he will have the glory of rebuilding it. Clouds of smoke and cries of terror signal that the fire has been started. In the underground passages beneath the Circus, Asteria and Fanuel come upon the body of Simon Mago and find Rubria wounded. Rubria confesses to being a vestal virgin who was converted to Christianity without abandoning the worship of Vesta. Fanuel pardons her. Meanwhile, fire spreads, and the roof of the Circus collapses, burying Rubria and the other Christians beneath it.

The Russian bass Evgeny Nesterenko in Mozart's *Magic Flute*.

The composition of *Nerone* was very protracted, with intervals of ten years and more in between, and at the time of Boito's death it was still unfinished. The score was completed by Vincenzo Tommasini and Antonio Smareglia under the supervision of Arturo Toscanini. In *Nerone*, Boito achieves a greater degree of dramatic intensity than in his opera *Mefistofele*, once again focusing on the antithesis of good and evil, represented here by the contrast between the Pagan world and the advent of the Christian way of life.

NESTERENKO, EVGENY
(Moscow 1938)
Russian bass. He studied music at the Conservatory in Leningrad and made his debut in that city at the Maly Theater as Gremin in a production of Tchaikovsky's *Eugene Onegin* as part of the theater's 1962–63 season. He went on to sing at Leningrad's Kirov Theater (from 1967) and at the Bolshoi Theater in

Moscow (from 1971), where he was acknowledged as a performer of the great Russian operatic repertoire (*Boris Godunov*, *Prince Igor*, *Mazeppa*, etc.) as well as of Gounod's *Faust*, Rossini's *Il barbiere di Siviglia* and others. At the same time, he was emerging as an international artist, with successful debuts at the Vienna Staatsoper, La Scala, Milan (a memorable Filippo II in Verdi's *Don Carlos* conducted by Claudio Abbado in 1978) and Covent Garden. Between the end of the 1970s and well into the 1980s, Nesterenko became established as one of the world's greatest basses on the strength of his vocal range, qualities of timbre and phrasing, and remarkable gifts as an actor.

NEUMANN, VÁCLAV

(Prague 1920)

Bohemian conductor. A graduate of the Conservatory in Prague (1940–45), he made his debut in 1948 in a concert with the Czech Philharmonic. After conducting at Karlový Ṽáry (1951–54) and Brno (1954–56) and appearing as conductor of the principal orchestral ensembles in Prague (1954–63), Neumann was engaged by the Komische Oper in East Berlin (1956–64) and gave distinguished performances of the operas of Léoš Janáček (which he also recorded). From 1964 to 1968 he was *Generalmusikdirektor* of the Leipzig Gewandhaus Orchestra, moving on to become music director at Stuttgart Opera (1969–72). In 1968 he returned to his native Prague to conduct the Czech Philharmonic.

NICOLAI, CARL OTTO EHRENFRIED

(Königsberg 1810–Berlin 1849)

German composer and conductor. He studied in Berlin from 1827 to 1833, the year in which he moved to Italy to continue his studies in Rome. He then went to Vienna, where in 1837 he was appointed Kapellmeister and singing teacher at the Court of Vienna. In 1838 he made his debut as a composer of opera with *Rosmonda d'Inghilterra*, staged in Trieste in 1839 under the title *Enrico II*. His career then switched from Vienna to Berlin (1848), where he took on the post of Kapellmeister to the Berlin Opera, scene of the premiere of his operatic masterpiece *Die lustigen Weiber von Windsor* (The Merry Wives of Windsor), a work which has retained its popularity in Germany and Austria.

NICOLESCO, MARIANA

(Gaujani 1948)

Rumanian soprano. A pupil of Jolanda Magnoni at the Accademia di Santa Cecilia in Rome, she won the 1972 Rossini International Singing Competition, on the strength of which she made her debut as Mimi (*La bohème*) in Cincinnati with Thomas Schippers conducting. Schippers then asked for her to sing Violetta in *La traviata*, again in Cincinnati, a role in which she made her debut at New York City Opera (1977) and at the Metropolitan Opera House in New York (1978). After this, her career developed internationally with appearances at La Fenice in Venice (Bellini's *Beatrice di Tenda*, 1975), La Scala (first performance of Berio's *La vera storia*, 1982), the Paris Opéra (Dargomyzhsky's *Kamenniy Gost'*, The Stone Guest, 1985) and other major opera houses.

NIELSEN, INGA

(Holboek 1946)

Danish soprano. After studying music in Vienna and Stuttgart, she received her first engagements from opera houses in Münster and Berne. She then concentrated her career in Germany (from 1975), singing at a number of opera venues there, including the Bayreuth Festspielhaus (1977). In 1978 she made her debut at the Vienna Staatsoper singing Adele in Johann Strauss's *Die Fledermaus*, a role she also sang in Paris (1983). Her international reputation rests on appearances at New York City Opera, the Salzburg Festival, the Teatro Colón in Buenos Aires (Mozart's *Idomeneo*), the Schwetzingen Festival (the first performance of Henze's *Die Englische Katze*, 1983) and at numerous other houses.

NILSSON, BIRGIT

(Karup, Kristianstad 1918)

Swedish soprano. She studied at the Royal Academy of Music, Stockholm, with Joseph Hislop and Arne Sunnegaardh. In 1946 she made her debut as Agathe in Weber's *Der Freischütz* at the Royal Opera in Stockholm. By 1948 she was already tackling her first Wagner role, appearing as Senta in *Der fliegende Holländer* (The Flying Dutchman), also at the Royal Opera. Within a few years, her international career was underway. After early appearances at the Glyndebourne Festival in 1951 in Mozart's *Idomeneo* and at the

Top: The Rumanian soprano Mariana Nicolesco.

Above: The Swedish soprano Birgit Nilsson in Puccini's *Turandot*.

Vienna Staatsoper in *Die Walküre* and *Lohengrin*, Nilsson's reputation became firmly established between 1954 and 1955 at all the most prestigious opera venues. Acclaimed as a Wagner singer, Nilsson frequently sang Turandot in Puccini's opera and Leonore in Beethoven's *Fidelio*, as well as appearing in Mozart's *Don Giovanni*, Verdi's *Macbeth*, *Un ballo in maschera* and *Aida*, and Richard Strauss's *Elektra*, *Die Frau ohne Schatten* and *Salome*.

NIMSGERN, SIEGMUND

(St. Wendel, Saar 1940)
German baritone. He studied music in Saarbrücken and Wiesbaden. In 1967 he made his debut in Saarbrücken as Lionel in Tchaikovsky's *The Maid of Orleans*. In 1971 he moved to the Deutsche Oper am Rhein in Düsseldorf (where he stayed until 1975). By 1973 he was already singing at La Scala, Covent Garden, the Opéra in Paris (Amfortas in *Parsifal*) and San Francisco. Acclaimed for his roles in Wagner (*Tristan und Isolde*, the *Ring* cycle and *Lohengrin*) and Strauss (*Salome* and *Arabella*), Nimsgern's reputation also rests on his performances of a very extensive repertoire including Verdi's *Macbeth* and *Simon Boccanegra*, Bizet's *Carmen*, Berlioz's *La damnation de Faust*, Mozart's *Le nozze di Figaro* and *Don Giovanni*, and Hindemith's *Cardillac*.

NINA, OSSIA LA PAZZA PER AMORE

(Nina, or The Woman Mad for Love)
Opera in two acts by Giovanni Paisiello (1740–1816), to a libretto by Benoît-Joseph Marsollier, translated into Italian by Giuseppe Carpani, with additions by Giambattista Lorenzi. First performance: Caserta, Gardens of the Royal Palace, 25 June 1789.

Nina (soprano), daughter of the Count (bass), had been promised in marriage to Lindoro (tenor), but the Count has subsequently chosen a richer and nobler candidate as his prospective son-in-law. Lindoro has been caught in Nina's company by the new fiancé and is killed by him in a duel. When she hears of her beloved Lindoro's death, Nina goes out of her mind and begins to wait for her beloved to return. One day, while the Count is thanking Susanna (soprano), Nina's governess, for the care she has shown towards his daughter, the old servant Giorgio (*buffo* bass) enters with news that Lindoro is alive: he has been discovered trying to get into the garden by climbing over the wall. The Count asks Lindoro for his forgiveness and welcomes him like a son. He then tells him of Nina's sad state. Lindoro goes in to see his beloved, but Nina does not know who he is and seems very disturbed. Little by little she regains her sanity. She recognizes Lindoro, and when she learns that her father is no longer against their getting married, her happiness is complete. The opera ends with general rejoicing that the two lovers can be united.

Nina demonstrates Paisiello's skill in transforming French *comédie larmoyante*, his starting-point here, into the Romantic pathos that would characterize early nineteenth-century opera, such as Bellini's *La sonnambula*. This is well illustrated by Nina's famous *cavatina* "Il mio ben quando verrà," which reveals clear links with the delicate melodies sung by Bellini's Amina.

NIXON IN CHINA

Opera in three acts and six scenes by John Adams (b.1947), to a libretto by Alice Goodman. First performance: Houston Grand Opera, 22 October 1987.

The action takes place in Peking in February 1972. The President of the United States, Richard Nixon (baritone), accompanied by his wife, Pat (soprano), and his Secretary of State, Henry Kissinger (bass), is welcomed on his arrival at Peking airport by Premier Chou En-lai (baritone). An hour later, Nixon meets Mao Tse-Tung (tenor), and they engage in a conversation that blends philosophy and politics. A banquet is held to establish the friendship between China and the United States. The next day, the First Lady talks to the press and visits the key sites of Imperial China. In the evening, the Nixons attend a ballet devised by Chiang Ch'ing (soprano), Mao's wife. The finale of *Nixon in China* shows the leading characters in their different bedrooms. Nixon, his wife and their entourage are clearly tired after their busy schedule of talks and official visits; only Mao seems full of energy, evidently as convinced of his revolutionary ideals

Above: The German baritone Siegmund Nimsgern.

Right: A frieze opening the first act of Paisiello's *Nina*.

as can be guessed from the expression on his face in the portrait hanging on the wall behind him.

With *Nixon in China*, John Adams reveals his preference for topical subjects, a priority which he was to return to in his 1991 opera on the hijacking of the cruise liner *Achille Lauro*, *The Death of Klinghoffer*. The freedom of expression that Adams brings to his subject is paralleled by the stylistic freedom of his essentially tonal musical language, which incorporates elements as diverse as jazz, rock and traditional opera. The result is captivating and, most important, easy to listen to. Although in some respects belonging to the Minimalist school, Adams ploughs his own expressive furrow, one quite distinct from the formal rigidity of a composer like Philip Glass, the most famous exponent of Minimalism.

NONO, LUIGI

(Venice 1924–1990)

Italian composer. He studied at the Conservatorio in Venice with Gian Francesco Malipiero and subsequently with Bruno Maderna (1946–48) and Hermann Scherchen. By the early 1950s, Nono's musical philosophy, like those of Maderna, Pierre Boulez and Karlheinz Stockhausen, was clearly indebted to the Second Viennese School, particularly Webern. Nono developed his own musical style by means of experiments with serial, electronic and concrete music. Nono never separated his artistic expression from his social and revolutionary commitment, a powerful presence in his first composition for the theater, *Intolleranza 1960*. There are already traces in this score of the perfect blend between music, image and scenic action that Nono was to achieve most fully in *Au grand soleil chargé d'amour* (To the Great Sun Charged with Love, 1975). Here the composer shows considerable skill in representing the literary text in all its evocative power. Nono's last composition for the theater was *Prometeo*, the first version of which was staged in Venice in 1984 and the final version under the auspices of Ansaldo in Milan in 1985. In this "tragedy of listening," he resorted to a complex use of live electronics and a computer alongside traditional instruments and solo voices, thus revolutionizing previous ways of thinking about composition and form in his quest for "sound" and "space."

NORMA

Opera in two acts by Vincenzo Bellini (1801–1835), to a libretto by Felice Romani, based on Alexandre Soumet's play Norma, ou l'infanticide. *First performance: Milan, La Scala, 26 December 1831.*

The action takes place in Gaul during the period of Roman domination. Pollione (tenor), the Roman proconsul, is on his way through the sacred forest of the Druids to meet Adalgisa (soprano), a young priestess with whom he is in love, and confides in his friend Flavio (tenor) that he no longer loves the Druid chief priestess, Norma, who has borne him two children. No sooner have the two Romans left the scene than warriors and Druids appear, led by Norma (soprano) and her father, Oroveso (bass). Divinely inspired, Norma announces that the gods do not yet favour a war against Rome. When everyone else has gone, Pollione meets Adalgisa and tries to get her to elope with him to Rome. Adalgisa goes to Norma to ask if she may be released from her vows and discloses her feelings. Norma seems sympathetic at first, but when Pollione appears and she realizes that he is the object of Adalgisa's love, her fury explodes. During the night, at the height of her despair, Norma calls upon death and, fearing that Pollione may want to take their children to Rome with him, decides to kill them. But she lacks the courage to go through with it. So she calls Adalgisa and, being under the impression that she will be Pollione's new wife, entrusts the children to her care. But Adalgisa refuses, goes to Pollione herself and begs him to return to Norma. The following day, Oroveso announces to his warriors that Pollione is about to be replaced by a more ruthless proconsul. In spite of everything, Norma is still talking peace, but it is not long before she comes to learn from her maid Clotilde (mezzo-soprano) that Adalgisa has failed in her attempt to persuade Pollione to return, and that Pollione himself is more determined than ever to run away with the young priestess. In a towering rage she calls the people and her warriors together and declares war, massacre and the extermination of the Roman people. Pollione himself is dragged into the temple, where Norma pleads with him for the last time to renounce his love for Adalgisa. Pollione refuses, and Norma, in the presence of her father and the people, announces that a priestess has broken her sacred vows. Then, amid general consternation, she reveals that the priestess is herself, making public her relationship with Pollione. Pollione finally realizes the strength of Norma's love for him, asks her forgiveness and follows her to the place of execution.

Bellini's most famous opera enjoyed extraordinary success at its first performance and has continued to do so, wherever it is staged, to the present day. It is one of the most important milestones in the history of opera and may be regarded as the apotheosis of pure

An engraving by A. Sanquirico for the premiere of Bellini's *Norma*.

singing, whether lyrical (e.g. ''Casta Diva'') or tragic (the finale of the first act).

NORMAN, JESSYE

(Augusta, Georgia 1945)
American soprano. Having grown up in a family where music was much encouraged and played, she began to study music regularly at the University of Michigan (1967–68) with Pierre Bernac and from there went on to have lessons with Alice Duschack at the Peabody Conservatory in Baltimore. In 1968 she won first prize in the German Radio International Singing Competition, on the strength of which she was offered a contract for three seasons at the Deutsche Oper Berlin. It was here that in 1969 she made her debut as Venus in Wagner's *Tannhäuser*, and she followed this by singing the Countess in Mozart's *Le nozze di Figaro*. In 1971 she appeared as Sélika in Meyerbeer's *L'Africaine* at the Maggio Musicale Festival in Florence. 1972 saw her at La Scala in Verdi's *Aida* and also marked her Covent Garden debut as Cassandre in Berlioz's *Les Troyens*. Her many appearances as a concert artist have taken her to the major concert venues in Europe, the United States, Australia and Canada. She is a frequent visitor to France, where she is particularly popular, winning acclaim there in 1983 at the Aix-en-Provence Festival as Phèdre in Rameau's *Hippolyte et Aricie* and in 1985 as Ariadne in Richard Strauss's *Ariadne auf Naxos*, as well as appearing at the Opéra-Comique in 1984 in Purcell's *Dido and Aeneas* and in Lyons in Charpentier's *Médée*. It was during these years that Norman returned to opera, having concentrated on concert and recital engagements, and appeared with the Metropolitan Opera in New York (*Les Troyens*, *Ariadne auf Naxos*, *Parsifal*), Lyric Opera of Chicago (Gluck's *Alceste*, 1990) and elsewhere. Her operatic career as a recording artiste has been much more consistent, with a particular emphasis on Wagner as well as performances of Bizet's *Carmen* and Mascagni's *Cavalleria rusticana*. Having a sumptuous timbre of great beauty and richness of colour, especially in the middle-to-lower register, Norman possesses a supreme elegance of phrasing which is both noble and extremely expressive.

The American soprano Jessye Norman.

NOS

(The Nose)
Opera in three acts by Dmitry Dmitrievich Shostakovich (1906–1975), to the composer's own libretto in collaboration with Yevgeni Zamyatin, Georgi Ionin and Aleksander Preis after the short story by Gogol. First performance: Leningrad, Maly Theater, 18 January 1930.

Platon Kovalyov (baritone), a police inspector, wakes up one morning and is surprised to find that his nose is no longer there. While the poor man is beside himself with worry, his barber, Ivan Yakovlevich (bass) is having his breakfast when he is no less surprised to discover the missing nose in his loaf of bread. He recoils in horror, sees it as incriminating evidence against himself and hurries off to throw it into the river Neva. Meanwhile Kovalyov has started looking for his nose. He comes across it in the street dressed up as a top official (tenor) but immediately loses sight of it again. Then the police become involved in the search for the mischievous nose. Heartrending advertisements appear in the newspapers, but to no avail. Finally comes the day when the nose is returned to its rightful owner. A surgeon (bass) is urgently summoned to sew the nose back again, but complications occur and the operation is not a success. Kovalyov is becoming increasingly desperate now and has really lost all hope of ever having his nose put back again properly. At last, one fine morning, the nose comes home as unexpectedly as it had left and quietly reattaches itself to Kovalyov's face.

Shostakovich was about 21 when he composed *Nos* between 1927 and 1928. He gave the opera a youthful energy and spontaneity in an attempt to convey the qualities of caricature in the plot.

NOTRE DAME

Opera in two acts by Franz Schmidt (1874–1939), to the composer's own libretto in collaboration with Leopold Wilk based on the novel by Victor Hugo. First performance: Vienna, Imperial Court Theater, 1 April 1914.

The action takes place in Paris in the Middle Ages. Captain Phoebus (tenor) is in love with Esmeralda (soprano), an enchanting gipsy woman, and will not listen to the advice of one of his officers (baritone) who has warned him that Esmeralda is married, so his feelings could prove very dangerous. The scene changes to the Place de Notre Dame, where Esmeralda comes to the aid of Quasimodo (bass), the Cathedral's hunchback bell-ringer, rescuing him from the crowd who were on the point of lynching him. Taking advantage of the confusion, Phoebus persuades Esmeralda to meet him that night. Her husband Gringoire (tenor) has noticed Phoebus's interest in his wife, follows Phoebus to the rendezvous, stabs him and runs away. Esmeralda is accused of wounding Phoebus and is duly imprisoned and then sentenced to death. The Archdeacon of Notre Dame comes to visit her. He is also in love with her, but he leaves her to her fate so as to preserve his integrity as a priest. In the Place de Notre Dame Esmeralda is about to mount the scaffold when Quasimodo appears and, to the crowd's amazement, snatches her away and carries her off into the Cathedral. It is not long, however, before the Archdeacon intervenes and Quasimodo is forced to hand Esmeralda over to the guards. The Archdeacon watches Esmeralda's execution from the ledge between the two bell-towers where the hunchback has taken refuge. Consumed with rage, Quasimodo, who has now discovered the Archdeacon's hypocrisy and cruelty, pushes him off the ledge to his death.

Notre Dame is one of some 30 scores inspired by Hugo's novel. Schmidt began work on his opera on 30 August 1904 and finished it on 10 August 1906. The marvellous music in *Notre Dame* (especially a most beautiful theme for Esmeralda) leads one to overlook the limitations of a rather weak libretto.

NOZZE DI FIGARO, LE

(The Marriage of Figaro)
Opera in four acts by Wolfgang Amadeus Mozart (1756–1791), to a libretto by Lorenzo Da Ponte from Beaumarchais' play La folle journée ou le mariage de Figaro. *First performance: Vienna, Burgtheater, 1 May 1786.*

The action takes place in Spain in the

eighteenth century, at the house of Count Almaviva. Susanna (soprano), maid to the Countess (soprano), is preparing for her wedding in a few hours' time to Figaro (bass-baritone), servant to the Count (bass-baritone). Susanna tells Figaro the Count has been making eyes at her. Figaro confidently sets about upsetting his master's ploys, but he too has his problems: Marcellina (mezzo-soprano), the ageing housekeeper of Doctor Bartolo (*buffo* bass), has arrived to demand that Figaro now fulfil his side of the bargain and marry her, something he once agreed to in writing in the event of his being unable to repay money he had borrowed from her. Then the page, Cherubino (soprano), comes in and confesses to Susanna that he is in love with the Countess. When the Count appears too – he has come to see Susanna to arrange a meeting with her – and casually picks up one of the Countess's dresses from an armchair, he discovers Cherubino hiding under it. Pandemonium breaks out, and then Figaro arrives to ask if the wedding can be brought forward. Cherubino is to be punished by being sent off to join the army in Seville. Then Figaro and Susanna tell the Countess about her husband's love ambitions and decide to play a joke on him: Susanna will send him a letter in which she will pretend to agree to meet him and then get Cherubino to dress up as a woman and keep the rendezvous in her place. The transformation of Cherubino begins, but the Count turns up at a particularly crucial moment, unaware that the letter he has received is a trick or that the Countess is quietly panicking as a result of having just hidden Cherubino in an adjoining closet. Suddenly suspicious, the Count wants to enter the closet, from which Cherubino has escaped by jumping out of a window, and which now contains Susanna. The Count, after fetching some tools to force the door that the Countess was unwilling to open, finds himself face to face with a smiling Susanna. In comes Figaro too, and then the situation is further confused by the arrival of Marcellina and Bartolo to demand what is owing to them. The plan proceeds, and Susanna pretends to agree to meet the Count, but then the Countess keeps the appointment dressed in Susanna's clothes. Meanwhile, Marcellina recognizes Figaro as the love-child she had from her relationship with Bartolo. That evening in the garden, Susanna waits for the Count. But by chance Figaro has found out about the rendezvous and goes to the appointed place himself to expose her infidelity. There then follows a whole series of misunderstandings, triggered off by the Countess and Susanna having changed places, and Figaro and the Count come out the worst. Eventually everything becomes clear and the story ends joyfully, to everyone's satisfaction.

It was with *Le nozze di Figaro* that Mozart began his productive collaboration with Da Ponte. Here the composer is completely successful in conveying the psychological intricacies which Da Ponte had suggested the main characters should reflect; the roles of the Count and Figaro in particular serve to dramatize an underlying socio-political issue, the contrast between the aristocracy that is tied to the past and the shrewd servant class seeking to better itself.

NUCCI, LEO

(Castiglione dei Pepoli 1942)

Italian baritone. He studied singing in Bologna and in Milan with Giuseppe Marchesi; and he made his debut at Spoleto's Teatro Lirico as Figaro in Rossini's *Il barbiere di Siviglia* (1967), one of his finest roles and one in which he appeared in more than 100 performances throughout the world. For family reasons he then interrupted his career and joined the chorus at La Scala, Milan (1969–75), but in 1975 he resumed training with Ottaviano Bizzarri and made his return as a principal, again as Figaro, in Padua in 1975. He repeated this role at La Scala in 1976, and this was the beginning of a brilliant and busy international career. Nucci's is a fine baritone with a capacity for excellent phrasing. He also has unusual gifts as a performer (for example his Macbeth in the film of the opera by Claude d'Anna, 1987). His considerable repertoire (about 50 roles) concentrated more recently on Verdi.

Top: A scene from Mozart's *Marriage of Figaro.*

Above: The Italian baritone Leo Nucci.

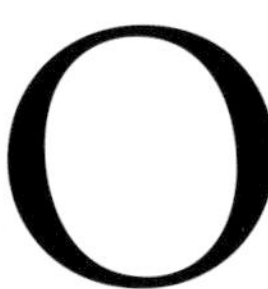

OBERON, OR THE ELF KING'S OATH

Opera in a prologue and three acts by Carl Maria von Weber (1786–1826), to a libretto by James Robinson Planché, based on the epic poem by Christoph Martin Wieland. First performance: London, Royal Opera House, Covent Garden, 12 April 1826.

Oberon (tenor), King of the Elves, has been arguing with his wife Titania (soprano) as to whether it is men or women who are more inclined to be unfaithful, and he announces that he will not make peace with Titania until he has found a truly faithful couple. The long search for this couple proves unsuccessful. Then Puck (contralto) tells his master about Sir Huon of Bordeaux (tenor): he had apparently killed the son of Charlemagne, but the Emperor, on learning that his son's death had occurred during a formal duel, showed clemency towards Sir Huon, at the same time ordering him to go to the Court of the Sultan Haroun el Raschid, kill the Turkish Prince Babekan (speaking role), who was betrothed to the Caliph's daughter Reiza (soprano), and abduct her. Oberon decides that the loyal and courageous Sir Huon sounds like the sort of man who would also be capable of experiencing great love, and so, using magic, he makes him dream of Reiza and Reiza dream of Huon and fall in love with him. At the Caliph's Court, accompanied by his faithful servant Scherasmin (baritone), to whom Puck has given a magic horn that will bring Oberon to their rescue no matter what the danger, Huon kills Babekan and elopes with Reiza. Guards pursue the couple, but Scherasmin sounds the enchanted horn, whereupon Oberon appears and Huon, Scherasmin, Reiza and her maid Fatima (mezzo-soprano) are whisked away on to a ship and set out to sea. The King of the Elves wants to put the two young people's love to the test and gets Puck to unleash a violent storm during which the ship is wrecked when it runs aground on an island. Reiza is seized by pirates, who take her to Tunis, where she is shut away in the Emir's harem. Huon, although wounded, has managed to escape. Puck looks after him and then goes with him to Tunis. There Huon attempts to gain entry to the harem but is surprised by Roxane (contralto), the Emir's wife, who is so impressed by this stranger's audacity that she falls in love with him. Huon rejects her, but just at that moment the Emir himself, Almansor (bass), arrives and condemns Huon to die at the stake because he has profaned the harem. Reiza intervenes to save him, only to be sentenced to death herself. Now Oberon and his magic take control of the situation: the two young people are brought to safety, and their love serves to reunite the King of the Elves and his wife Titania. The reward for Huon and Reiza will be to receive Charlemagne's appreciation and favour.

A direct commission by Covent Garden, *Oberon* is a *Singspiel*, or a composition that alternates between sung passages and recitatives. Weber began work on the opera, the original libretto of which was in English, in January 1825, but ill-health delayed the completion of the score until early 1826, and he continued to revise it during rehearsals. The audience received the opera with great enthusiasm, while the critics, in a futile comparison, judged it inferior to *Der Freischütz*.

OBERTO
CONTE DI S. BONIFACIO
DRAMMA IN DUE ATTI
DA RAPPRESENTARSI
NELL' I. R. TEATRO ALLA SCALA
L' AUTUNNO 1839.
Milano
PER GASPARE TRUFFI
M.DCCC.XXXIX

Libretto of *Oberto, Conte di San Bonifacio*, an opera in two acts by Giuseppe Verdi.

OBERTO, CONTE DI SAN BONIFACIO

Opera in two acts by Giuseppe Verdi (1813–1901), to a libretto by Antonio Piazza, revised by Bartolomeo Marelli and Temistocle Solera. First performance: Milan, La Scala, 17 November 1839.

The action takes place in Bassano del Grappa (northern Italy) in 1228. Count Riccardo di Salinguerra (tenor) is about to marry Cuniza (mezzo-soprano). But he has previously seduced Leonora (soprano), daughter of Count Oberto di San Bonifacio (bass), and now Leonora, accompanied by her father, goes to see Cuniza and tells her what happened. Cuniza resolves to sacrifice her own love and compel Riccardo to make reparation for the wrong he had done by marrying Leonora. But Oberto wants to defend his honour in a duel. Riccardo tries to avoid this confrontation but eventually does fight and kills him. Overcome with remorse, he flees in despair, while Leonora, who feels responsible for what has taken place, decides to enter a convent.

Oberto, Conte di San Bonifacio marked Verdi's debut as an opera composer. In it there are already signs of the particular dramatic elements that Verdi would develop in his later compositions. The work was commissioned by Bartolomeo Merelli and the first performance was a success. This earned Verdi a contract for a further three operas.

OBRAZTSOVA, ELENA

(Leningrad 1939)

Russian mezzo-soprano. She first studied music at the Conservatory in Leningrad. In 1964 she made her debut as Marina (*Boris Godunov*) at the Bolshoi Theater in Moscow, where she subsequently became a member of the permanent company. She took part in a number of tours in Canada and the United States and was successful in major singing competitions. From the early 1970s, she began to earn an international reputation, singing in San Francisco (*Il trovatore*, 1975), and La Scala (*Werther*, 1975), where she returned in subsequent years in *Don Carlos*, *Khovanshchina*, *Cavalleria rusticana* and *Boris Godunov*. A celebrity with the Metropolitan Opera in New York, where she sang for a number of seasons, as well as at the Vienna Staatsoper and several other houses, Obraztsova owes her reputation mainly to the great impact of her authentic mezzo-soprano voice combined with an equally impressive stage presence.

OCCASIONE FA IL LADRO, L', OVVERO IL CAMBIO DELLA VALIGIA

(Opportunity Makes the Thief, or The Wrong Suitcase)

Opera in one act by Gioachino Rossini (1792–1868), to a libretto by Luigi Prividali. First performance: Venice, Teatro Giustiniani di San Moisè, 24 November 1812.

The action takes place in the outskirts of Naples. Don Parmenione (baritone), with his servant Martino (*buffo*) and Count Alberto (tenor), find themselves sheltering at the same inn during a severe storm. The Count is on his way to meet Berenice (soprano), a marchioness who has been left an orphan and entrusted to the care of her uncle Eusebio (tenor). Before he died, Berenice's father had revealed his plan for her to marry Count Alberto. Once the storm has died down, the travellers resume their journey, but Don Parmenione accidentally takes Alberto's suitcase, and when he realizes his mistake, his curiosity gets the better of him. He opens the suitcase and finds inside it a beautiful portrait of Berenice. He immediately falls in love with her and decides to take Alberto's place. Meanwhile Berenice, with her uncle's agreement, plans to test the sincerity of her husband-to-be and asks her friend Ernestina (mezzo-soprano) to act the part of her mistress, while she will dress up as her maid. When Alberto arrives, he falls in love with the maid. Then Parmenione appears and declares that he is the husband-to-be, despite Alberto's protests. This leads to a series of misunderstandings, but in the end everything is resolved for the best, with Berenice marrying Alberto and Parmenione proposing to Ernestina.

L'occasione fa il ladro was very poorly received by audiences in Venice, despite being a lively work of great brilliance with a fast-moving story. Its merits have been vindicated by the success of more recent performances in Pesaro (1987) and at La Scala (1988).

OCHMAN, WIESLAW

(Warsaw 1937)

Polish tenor. He studied singing in Krakow, Bytom and Warsaw. In 1959 he made his debut with Bytom Opera as Edgardo (*Lucia di Lammermoor*) and then went on to sing in Krakow and Warsaw, where he made his name in performances of *Eugene Onegin*, *Boris Godunov* and *Tosca*. From 1967 his career developed, taking him, among other venues, to the Deutsche Oper Berlin, the Hamburg Staatsoper, the Glyndebourne Festival and the Paris Opéra (*Les vêpres siciliennes*, 1974). His exquisitely lyrical voice, with its gentle delivery and elegant phrasing, has brought him particular distinction in the operas of Mozart.

OEDIPUS REX

Opera-oratorio in two parts by Igor Stravinsky (1882–1971), to a text by Jean Cocteau, based on Sophocles and translated into Latin by Jean Daniélou. First performance: Paris, Théâtre Sarah Bernhardt, 30 May 1927.

The population of Thebes has been decimated by plague. The oracle of Apollo, consulted by Créon (baritone), the brother-in-law of King Oedipe (tenor), reveals that Thebes will be delivered from the plague on condition that the death of its former King Laius, assassinated many years before, is avenged. Oedipe therefore summons the soothsayer Tirésias (bass) who discloses that the perpetrator of the crime is a member of the royal family. Oedipe is disturbed by this news, but Jocaste (mezzo-soprano), Laius's widow and now married to Oedipe, puts his mind at rest by saying that often in the past the oracles had been wrong when foretelling the future and that in any case, according to them, King Laius was supposed to have been killed by his own son, whereas in fact he died by the hand of an unknown stranger. But Jocaste's words do not even begin to reassure Oedipe, who has not forgotten how, in the past, he himself killed an old man. Enter a Shepherd (tenor) and a Messenger (baritone). The Messenger announces that Oedipe's father, Polybus, is dead. At this point the Shepherd reveals that Oedipe is Laius's son: Polybus found the child abandoned and took him in. The hapless King now realizes the terrible truth: he has killed his father and married his own mother. Jocaste commits suicide by hanging, while Oedipe blinds himself rather than ever seeing the light of day again.

This opera-oratorio combines the formal structure of *opera seria* and a modern organization of the plot. A speaker provides a commentary on the events as they happen, while the characters from the Greek myth become realistic through a kind of tragic immobility as they confront their fates.

OFFENBACH, JACQUES

(Cologne 1819–Paris 1880)

German composer and conductor, naturalized French. To begin with, he studied both the violin and the cello and then concentrated solely on the cello, completing his training in this instrument in Paris, where he had moved

Above: A scene from *L'occasione fa il ladro* by Gioachino Rossini.

Left: *Oedipus Rex* by Igor Stravinsky, first performed in Paris in 1927.

in 1833. At the end of his studies, he joined the orchestra at the Opéra-Comique (1849) as a cellist. He was soon appointed conductor at the Théâtre Français (1850–55) where he had his first works for the theater staged. Once his growing reputation had become established, he took over the Théâtre Marigny in the Champs-Elysées in 1855 and renamed it the Bouffes-Parisiens. Here, for more than a decade, he had productions of his own works put on. From 1872 to 1876 he was director of the Théâtre de la Gaîté and went on tours of Europe and America (1875). The last years of his life were spent in Paris, where he left *Les contes d'Hoffmann* unfinished at his death. His output for the theater consists of more than 100 operettas, including *La belle Hélène*, 1864, *La vie parisienne*, 1866, *La Grande-duchesse de Gerolstein*, 1867 and *La Périchole*, 1868. Offenbach was one of the most gifted composers of the light comic genre, his music at the same time bearing witness to the frivolity and decadence of the French bourgeoisie of the Second Empire.

OGNENNYI ANGEL

(The Fiery Angel)

Opera in five acts and seven acts by Sergei Prokofiev (1891–1953), to the composer's own libretto, based on the novel by Valery Bryusov. First performance: Venice, Teatro La Fenice, 14 September 1955.

The action takes place in Germany during the sixteenth century. After a long journey in the Americas, Ruprecht (baritone) is resting at a modest inn when he hears the cry of a woman coming from an adjoining room. He hurries to the scene and finds Renata (soprano), a young woman, distraught with fear because of some danger she cannot see. A calmer Renata tells Ruprecht her story: ever since childhood, she has been visited by the angel Madiel, who had promised he would take on human form and become her lover. Renata subsequently believed that her angel was Count Heinrich, so she became his mistress. Since that time, she has come to be tormented by terrible visions. Ruprecht decides to help her to contact Count Heinrich. After consulting a fortune-teller (mezzo-soprano) and the magus Doctor Agrippa von Nettelsheim (tenor), Renata finally traces Heinrich, only to be rejected by him. To have her revenge, Renata wants Ruprecht to fight Heinrich in a duel, but then she sees her former lover transformed into an angel and changes her mind. By then the duel has already taken place and Ruprecht has been wounded. So Renata promises her love to Ruprecht, but grows to feel that such a feeling would be sinful and runs away. Healed from his wound, Ruprecht wanders through the city of Cologne and meets some strange characters, among them Mephisto (tenor) and Faust (bass), to whom he gives a guided tour of the city. Meanwhile, Renata has taken refuge in a convent. She is still experiencing hallucinations, and all the other nuns are suffering from diabolical anxiety. In the wake of some wild scenes of hysteria, Renata is condemned to be burned at the stake as a witch.

The opera was composed between 1922 and 1925 at a particularly critical moment for Prokofiev, after the failure of his opera *The Love for Three Oranges* and he applied himself with passionate energy to its composition. Despite his efforts, it fell into complete oblivion. Rediscovered by chance in Paris in 1952, the work was staged in Paris in 1955 and is now acknowledged as Prokofiev's finest opera, in which his handling of the complex and tortuous story of Renata is nothing short of masterly.

OLIMPIE

Opera in three acts by Gaspare Spontini (1774–1851), to a libretto by Joseph Dieulafoy and Charles Brifaut, based on Voltaire's tragedy. First performance: Paris, Opéra, 22 December 1819.

At the temple of Diana at Ephesus, Antigone (bass), King of Asia Minor, and Cassandre (tenor), King of Macedonia, successors to Alexander the Great, are celebrating peace after years of being enemies. Cassandre is supposed to have unknowingly caused the death of Alexander and is now in love with his

Above: The German composer and conductor Jacques Offenbach.

Right: Set design for Prokofiev's *Ognennyi angel.*

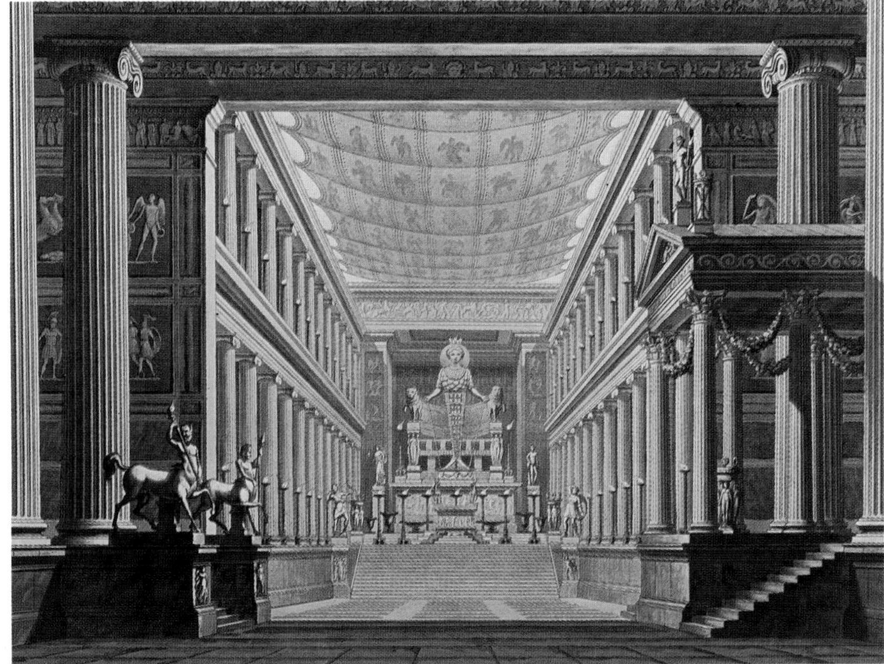

daughter Olimpie (soprano), Antigone's slave and known by the name of Aménais. Cassandre has decided to marry her, but the priestess Arzane, whose real identity is Statira (mezzo-soprano), Alexander's widow, is horrified when she believes she has recognized in Cassandre her husband's murderer. It is not long before she reveals who she and her daughter really are. Hailed by the people as their queen, Statira does not accept Cassandre's story when he claims that it was he who had saved them on the day of Alexander's death and requires that Olimpie have nothing more to do with Cassandre. Antigone then proposes that he marry Olimpie, but Olimpie rejects both Antigone's offer of marriage and Cassandre's plan that she elope with him. In the end Antigone, after being mortally wounded during a battle with Cassandre's troops, confesses that it was he who killed Alexander. Now above suspicion, Cassandre is free to marry Olimpie.

The original version of this Spontini opera ended with the death of the heroine, the suicide of Statira and an appearance by Alexander to welcome them both among the gods. The operatic conventions of the period were such that those elements of *Olimpie* which were too obviously tragic were cut out. Nevertheless, it remains one of the composer's most successful and inspired operas.

OLIVERO, MAGDA

(Saluzzo 1912)

Italian soprano. After graduating in piano, composition, and later in singing at the Conservatorio in Turin, she made her debut in 1933 as Lauretta in Puccini's *Gianni Schicchi* at the Teatro Vittorio Emanuele in Turin. Engagements quickly followed for her to appear at La Scala, the Teatro Reale dell'Opera in Rome, the Teatro Massimo in Palermo and the Teatro Regio in Turin. Having started her career as a light lyric soprano, Olivero then turned her attention to more dramatically substantial challenges like Violetta (*La traviata*), Margherita (*Mefistofele*), Francesca (*Francesca da Rimini*) and Adriana (*Adriana Lecouvreur*, Rome, 1939), one of her strongest roles. In 1941 she retired from the theater, following her marriage, and it was not until 1951 that she returned, again in *Adriana Lecouvreur*, at the Teatro Grande in Brescia. From here her career developed with appearances at all the major opera houses in Italy, Europe and the United States, and continued until the beginning of the 1980s (although she was still giving concerts in 1991). Olivero's phrasing was richly inventive and sensitive, and she was an intense and consummate actress. She won acclaim as one of the greatest exponents of the operas of Puccini (*La bohéme*, *Tosca*, *Manon Lescaut*), Cilèa (*Adriana Lecouvreur*) and Giordano (*Fedora*).

O'NEILL, DENNIS

(South Wales 1948)

Welsh tenor. He studied singing in London with Frederic Cox and in Italy with Ettore Campogalliani. After taking part in a number of singing competitions, he made his debut in Perth (Australia) in 1977. He then joined the permanent company of Scottish Opera, with whom he sang almost continuously until 1989. At the same time he was appearing at major British opera houses, including Covent Garden, where he sang in *La bohème*, *Rigoletto*, *Madama Butterfly* and *Lucia di Lammermoor*. O'Neill has also appeared at the Metropolitan Opera in New York (*La traviata* and *La bohème*), Chicago, San Francisco (*Mefistofele*, 1989–90) and several other opera houses.

ORACOLO, L'

Opera in one act by Franco Leoni (1864–1949), to a libretto by Camillo Zanoni, based on The Cat and the Cherub *by C. B. Fernald. First performance: London, Royal Opera House, Covent Garden, 28 June 1905.*

The action takes place in San Francisco's Chinatown in the early years of the twentieth century. It is the Chinese New Year. Ah-Joe (soprano), daughter of the wealthy merchant Hu-Tsin (bass), loves and is loved by Uin-San-Lui (tenor), son of the doctor and sage Uin-Scì (bass). Ah-Joe is also the object of desire of Cim-Fen (baritone), owner of a gaming-house and opium-den. But Hu-Tsin has refused to let Cim-Fen marry his daughter, and consequently Cim-Fen is planning revenge. To this end he takes advantage of the general commotion surrounding the traditional ceremony of the Procession of the Dragon and the momentary distraction of the maid Hua-Quî (contralto) to abduct Hu-Cî, Hu-Tsin's younger son. When it is discovered that the boy is missing, Cim-Fen goes to see the distraught Hu-Tsin and offers to bring him his son back in exchange for the hand of Ah-Joe. Then Hua-Quî tells San-Lui that Cim-Fen had seduced her and placed her at the mercy of his every whim, but that he now wants Ah-Joe. Cim-Fen has overheard the conversation between these two and confronts San-Lui at the entrance to his house. There is a struggle, and San-Lui is mortally wounded. Ah-Joe is overcome with grief, while Uin-Scì, drawing on his powers of insight, perceives that little Hu-Cî is being held prisoner in the cellar of Cim-Fen's house. Uin-Scì sets the boy free and then confronts Cim-Fen on his return from the gaming-house and kills him with an axe.

L'oracolo is the masterpiece of Franco Leoni, an Italian composer who became a

Set design for the first act of *Olimpie*, an opera in three acts by Gaspare Spontini.

British citizen. The opera's plot may be somber and very much in the realist style, but the music and orchestration are rich in colour, reflecting the exotic setting as well as the darkness of the story. Among the characters, it is the sinister figure of Cim-Fen that predominates, a role Leoni specifically created for the unusual dramatic and vocal talents of the baritone Antonio Scotti. A great success at its premiere, *L'oracolo* was subsequently performed at a number of other opera houses, particularly in the United States.

ORAZI E I CURIAZI, GLI

(The Horatii and the Curiatii)

Opera in three acts by Domenico Cimarosa (1749–1801), to a libretto by Antonio Simeone Sografi. First performance: Venice, Teatro La Fenice, 26 December 1796.

The action takes place in Rome. Alba Longa is at war with Rome. Sabina (soprano), a member of the Curiatius family, has married Marcus Horatius (tenor) in Rome and now finds herself having to suppress her true feelings for her homeland of Alba Longa and her own family there. Her brother-in-law Publius Horatius (tenor) tells her that a truce has been negotiated between the two cities. As a result, it is possible for Horatia (mezzo-soprano) and Curiatius (soprano) to marry. During the wedding ceremony, the two young people express their wish that they may never be separated for political reasons. Publius Horatius brings news that the Kings of Rome and Alba Longa have agreed to let the final outcome of the war be decided by combat between three champion fighters from either side. By chance, and much to the dismay of Sabina and Horatia, it falls to three Horatii and three Curiatii to be the combatants. The scene changes to the Campus Martius (field of Mars), where the fighting is about to commence. The chief augur (bass) intervenes to rule that the gods may not approve of combat between relatives, so it will be necessary to consult the oracle. In the temple of Apollo, the voice of the oracle (bass) proclaims that combat between the Horatii and the Curiatii must go ahead. In a Roman square, Marcus Horatius appears in a triumphal chariot and is hailed by an excited crowd. At his feet lie the corpses of the three dead Curiatii. Horatia is devastated when she sees the body of her husband. She rails against her brother and calls down the curse of the gods upon Rome. In his fury, Horatio draws his sword and kills his sister.

At its premiere, *Gli Orazi e i Curiazi* was an unqualified success, resulting in an unbroken run of 48 evening performances. Particularly outstanding among the opera's supremely expressive arias is Curiatius's "Quelle pupille tenere" in the first act, described by Stendhal as the most beautiful aria of the entire eighteenth century.

Top: A scene from Cimarosa's *Gli Orazi e i Curiazi.*

Above: A scene from *L'Orfeo* by Monteverdi in a production by Zurich Opera.

OREN, DANIEL

(Tel Aviv 1955)

Israeli conductor. He began to study music (flute, cello, piano, and also singing and composition) at a very young age. In 1967 he turned his attention to conducting and went on to take courses of advanced training with Ahlendorf in Berlin and with Franco Ferrara in Italy. In 1975 he won first prize at the Herbert von Karajan International Competition for conductors and then embarked on a fast-moving career, which quickly revealed him as one of the most accomplished opera conductors of his day. His remarkable creative instinct has been particularly in evidence in the operas of Puccini (*Tosca*, *Manon Lescaut*), Verdi (*Nabucco*) and other composers, mainly of the twentieth century.

ORFEO, L'

Opera in a prologue and five acts by Claudio Monteverdi (1567–1643), to a libretto by Alessandro Striggio. First performance: Mantua, Accademia degli Invaghiti, 24 February 1607.

In the prologue, Music (mezzo-soprano) introduces the plot and extols the marvellous effects that the art of music has on the human spirit. In a lush country landscape, Orfeo (tenor), surrounded by nymphs and shepherds, sings of his love for the beautiful Euridice (soprano). All those present go to the temple to give thanks to the gods. While Orfeo, with great emotion, is relating the story of his love, the messenger Silvia (contralto) appears, bearing the terrible news that Euridice has died after being bitten by a snake while picking flowers for her wedding garland. Fighting back his despair, Orfeo declares he will go down into the underworld to fetch Euridice back. Accompanied by Hope (mezzo-soprano), he reaches the banks of the river Styx, but from there he will have to cross to the other side alone. Enter the ferryman Caronte (bass). He wants to send Orfeo back, but with the power of his singing and the help of the gods Orfeo makes the guardian of the underworld fall asleep. Now he is able to continue on his

OPERA IN THE UNDERWORLD

The first performance of Jacopo Peri's *Euridice* in the year 1600 heralded the birth of opera. It also launched the character of Orpheus, who was to play a leading part in an incredible number of operas up until the early twentieth century, and introduced "scenes in the underworld" in which operas would increasingly be set, especially during the Baroque period. Orpheus's journey into Hades in search of his beloved Eurydice was the cue for composers to express themselves in a more impassioned way through both the words and the music.This innovative feature of opera was already in evidence in the "Intermedi" (intermezzos) from *La Pellegrina* performed in Florence in 1589 to mark the occasion of the marriage of Ferdinando de' Medici to Christine of Lorraine. In the fourth "Intermedio" there is an underworld scene on a par with Dante's *Inferno* for its power to create atmosphere (with the stage-set playing a key role). So, even before the official birth of opera, this genre, derived from the miracle plays of olden times, had a high profile. The scope for spectacle offered by scenes from the underworld became a prominent feature of French opera. In almost all of the *tragédies-lyriques* from the seventeenth century, the underworld was very much in vogue – in Act IV of Lully's *Alceste* (1674), for instance, set in Pluto's kingdom where a "fête infernale" is being held, or in the third act of the same composer's opera *Armide* (1686), where the sorceress calls upon Hatred, Revenge, Cruelty and the other underworld deities. After Lully, underworld scenes figured in the operas of Marc-Antoine Charpentier, for instance, in Act III of his *Médée* (1693), in the first act of Cavalli's *Giasone* (1649) and in works by numerous other composers of the seventeenth century. In both *Médée* and *Giasone*, the leading female character is Medea, a sorceress who may be compared here with that other famous weaver of spells possessing supernatural powers, Armida. These roles are among the most recurrent in *opera seria* of the eighteenth century and beyond: in *Medea in Corinto* (1813), Medea is involved in a scene where she summons up the spirits of the underworld, played by the chorus (something which Cherubini does not include in his famous *Medea* of 1797). There are plenty of underworld scenes in Rameau's operas, too: in the third act of *Castor et Pollux* (1737), equipped, like so many French operas, with a "danse des démons"; and we find Pluto with an escort of "divinités infernales" and Fates in the second act of *Hippolyte et Aricie* (1733). Envy and the Furies play prominent roles in the Prologue to *Le Temple de la gloire* (1745), while demons and Furies appear in various scenes in *Zoroastre* (1756). The potential of this aspect of theater even attracted the attention of a composer like Verdi, who showed a certain predilection not for demons or Furies but for the occult, from the witches in his *Macbeth* to the witch Ulrica in *Un ballo in maschera*, a character portrayed by the composer to great dramatic effect. In German romantic opera, there are further examples of scenes from the underworld, from Weber's *Der Freischütz* (1821) to Marschner's *Der Vampyr* (1828), operas on which the literature of the period, with its typical penchant for the fantastic, had had its influence.

GIASONE
Drama Musicale,
DEL
D. HIACINTO ANDREA
CICOGNINI,
Academico Instancabile.
Da Rappresentarsi in Venetia nel Theatro
di San Cassano,
Nell'Anno 1649.
All'Illustriss. e Reuerendiss.
Signor
ABATE UITTORIO
GRIMANI CALERGI.
IN VENETIA, M. DC.XLIX.
Con Licenza de Superiori, e Priuilegio.
Si Vende in Frezzaria [illegible] Giacomo Batti.

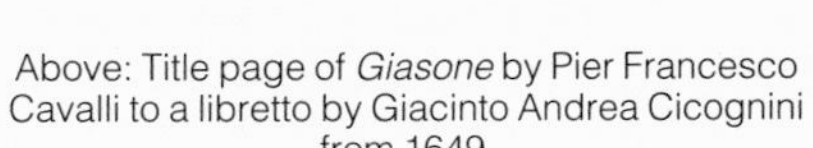
Above: Title page of *Giasone* by Pier Francesco Cavalli to a libretto by Giacinto Andrea Cicognini from 1649.

Right: The witch Ulrica in *Un ballo in maschera*. opera *Orfeo ed Euridice*.

journey. At last he finds himself in the presence of Proserpina (mezzo-soprano), wife of Pluto (bass), the King of Hades. She intercedes with her husband and asks him to restore Euridice to the ill-starred Orfeo. Pluto consents, setting one condition: in leading his bride out of Hades, he must not turn round to look at her until they are safely back in the world again. But Orfeo cannot control his impatience and turns his head just once. Later, deep in the woods of Thrace, Orfeo weeps for the bride he has lost. Apollo (tenor) comes down from heaven and offers him immortality. Together they ascend to the celestial spheres, where Orfeo will be able to contemplate for ever the vision of his Euridice.

Monteverdi's *Orfeo*, one of the first extant operas, is a cornerstone of music history. His composition of the vocal parts in the score is thorough and precise, whereas the instrumental line, as was the practice at that time, has been more thinly scored, using a figured bass that leaves ample space for improvisation. Another interesting feature of this opera is its purely instrumental sections, for which Monteverdi indicates in the score (published in 1609) the exact combination of the fairly large orchestral forces he requires. Its dramatic tension, responding perfectly to the demands of Striggio's text, made *Orfeo* a point of reference for every composer writing music for the theater in ensuing centuries.

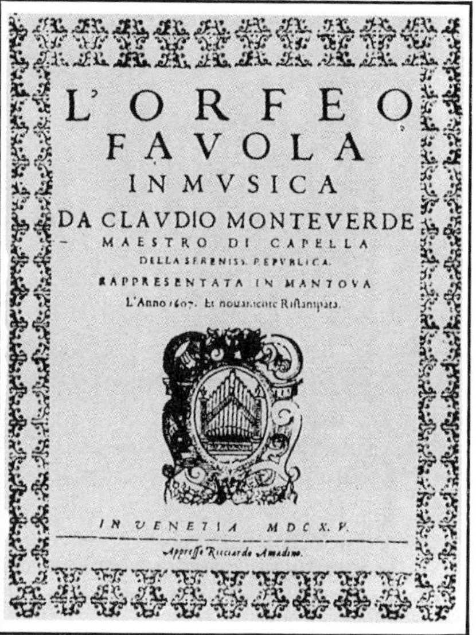

L' ORFEO
FAVOLA
IN MVSICA
DA CLAVDIO MONTEVERDE
MAESTRO DI CAPELLA
DELLA SERENISS. REPVBLICA.
RAPPRESENTATA IN MANTOVA
L'Anno 1607. Et nouamente Ristampata.
IN VENETIA MDCXV.
Appresso Ricciardo Amadino.

Top: Title page of the 1615 edition of Monteverdi's *L'Orfeo*.

Above: The German composer Carl Orff.

ORFEO ED EURIDICE

Opera in three acts by Christoph Willibald Gluck (1714–1787), to a libretto by Ranieri de' Calzabigi. First performance: Vienna, Burgtheater, 5 October 1762.

Beside the tomb of Euridice, Orfeo (contralto), surrounded by nymphs and shepherds, mourns the death of his young bride. Enter Amore (soprano), Jove's messenger. Moved by Orfeo's sorrow, Jove will grant him the chance to descend into the underworld and fetch Euridice, but on one condition: as he leads his young wife back towards the world of light, Orfeo must not turn round and look at her, nor must he disclose this fact to her. Conscious of the difficult task that lies ahead, Orfeo makes his way first into the shadowy recesses of Avernus, where his sweet singing, charged with the passion of despair, placates the infernal spirits. He then comes to the Elysian Fields, where he finds Euridice (soprano). Without looking at her, Orfeo takes her by the hand and guides her along the path of their return journey. But Euridice is disturbed by her beloved's strange conduct and declares she would rather die than live without his love. On hearing these words, Orfeo no longer can contain himself and looks round at her. In that moment, Euridice falls dead. Once again it is Amore who comes to Orfeo's aid in his grief, and the gods are so touched that they restore Euridice to him, so that she can go on living by his side.

Orfeo ed Euridice marked the starting-point of Gluck's reforms, which were of fundamental significance to the history of opera. This was the first time that a composer of *opera seria* in the eighteenth century had involved himself so closely in the emotions expressed both by the music and the drama, the music itself being used vigorously to create character. The opera's performances in Vienna were not an unqualified success, partly because of its novelty, and Gluck revised the score before the work was seen in Paris. Not only had this new version been translated into French, but the role of Orfeo, originally written for the *castrato* Guadagnini (a contralto), had been transcribed to be sung by a tenor.

ORFF, CARL

(Munich 1895–1982)

German composer. He studied in Munich with Beer-Walbrunn and Zilcher. Répétiteur and then conductor in Munich, Mannheim and Darmstadt, he subsequently concentrated on teaching and began to develop his *Schulwerk*, which was to become one of the fundamental teaching texts in music education, based on his own method. In 1937 his name became internationally known as a result of the success of his scenic cantata *Carmina Burana*. This was followed by *Catulli Carmina* (1943) and *Il trionfo di Afrodite* (1953), which, with *Carmina Burana*, made up a triptych Orff entitled *I trionfi*. His other distinguished compositions include the trilogy based on Greek tragedy, *Antigonae* (1949), *Oedipus der Tyrann* (1959) and *Prometheus* (1966), as well as his operas *Der Mond* (The Moon, 1939), *Die Kluge* (The Wise Woman, 1943), *Die Bernauerin* (The Young Woman of Berne, 1947) and *De Temporum fine Comoedia* (1973, revised 1979).

ORLANDO FURIOSO

Opera in three acts by Antonio Vivaldi (1678–1741), to a libretto by Grazio Braccioli, based on Ariosto's poem. First performance: Venice, Teatro Sant'Angelo, Autumn 1727.

The knight Orlando (contralto) sings of his courage: it will ensure that he triumphs whenever fate is against him and also enable him to find his beloved Angelica (soprano). But Angelica is mourning the death of *her* beloved, Medoro (tenor). Medoro then reappears after surviving a shipwreck. He is injured, but the sorceress Alcina (contralto) cures him and protects both lovers from Orlando (who is consumed by jealousy and wants to kill Medoro) by leading him to believe that Medoro is Angelica's brother. Left alone, Alcina sees a winged horse being ridden by Ruggiero (contralto). The sorceress falls in love with him and persuades him to drink from her magic fountain; its effect is such that when Bradamante (contralto), who is betrothed to Ruggiero, appears, Ruggiero does not recognize her, preoccupied as he now is by his love for Alcina. Astolfo (bass), who is also in love with the sorceress but has been rejected by her, promises he will have his revenge. In the meantime, Angelica seeks to free herself from Orlando, because he is an obstacle to her love for Medoro. So she asks Orlando to fetch her a magic potion which has the power to grant everlasting youth but which is guarded by a terrible monster. When Orlando goes down into the cave to confront the monster, a voice reveals to him that he is a prisoner of Alcina. He realizes he has been duped but manages to get away and eventually finds himself in a forest, where the wedding between Angelica and Medoro has just taken place. The bride and groom have engraved their names on a tree trunk. Orlando reads this inscription and goes mad with rage and despair. Astolfo, Ruggiero – now released from the sorceress's magic clutches – and Bradamante want to avenge Orlando by defeating Alcina. Meanwhile Orlando's madness has driven him to commit senseless acts, and he mistakes the statue of Merlin for his beloved Angelica, which angers Aronte, guardian of the temple of Hecate, Alcina's dominion. Orlando disarms Aronte and tears down the statue from its pedestal. In so doing, he breaks the spell, and Alcina's power vanishes. With the sorceress defeated, Orlando regains his sanity and, to the delight of everyone, consents to the wedding of Angelica and Medoro and gives them his blessing.

Vivaldi had previously composed an opera entitled *Orlando finto pazzo* (1714), also to a libretto by Braccioli, but its failure prompted him to set to work on a fresh version of the opera and make various changes to the libretto. This new score was a triumphant success, as indeed it was to be again in 1978, the year in which *Orlando Furioso* was restaged at the Teatro Filarmonico in Verona, with Marilyn Horne singing the lead, to mark the 300th anniversary of Vivaldi's birth. A number of other operas have been inspired by the characters from Ariosto's poem, among them Handel's *Orlando* (1733), Haydn's *L'Orlando paladino* (1782) and works by Steffani (1691), Scarlatti (1711), Anfossi (1778) and many others.

ORLEANSKAYA DYEVA

(The Maid of Orleans)

Opera in four acts by Peter Ilyich Tchaikovsky (1840–1893), to the composer's own libretto based on Zukovsky's translation of Schiller's tragedy Die Jungfrau von Orleans. *First performance: St. Petersburg, Maryinsky Theater, 13 February 1881.*

Thibaut (bass), father of Joan of Arc (soprano or mezzo-soprano), urges his daughter to marry a young man called Raymond (tenor). But Joan cannot agree to this, because a voice from heaven has called upon her to undertake the task of freeing France from the English invader. The French King Charles VII (tenor) lacks the will to respond and take his troops into battle, because he does not want to leave his favourite, Agnès Sorel (soprano). Enter Dunois (baritone), the King's adviser, and the Cardinal (bass) to announce that a girl has led the French troops and put the enemy to rout. On the battlefield Joan saves the life of Lionel (baritone), a knight from Burgundy, and gradually enmity gives way to mutual love between these two. The scene changes to Rheims. Here, in front of the cathedral on the day of Charles VII's coronation, Thibaut charges Joan with witchcraft. She feels guilty of loving Lionel, who is shortly to fall mortally wounded in battle against the English, while Joan will atone for her faults by being burned at the stake and then, summoned by a choir of angels, ascends in glory to heaven.

With this opera, Tchaikovsky turned his back on Russian themes to concentrate on a story popular with composers in the West. After the premiere of *Orleanskaya Dyeva* had proved unsuccessful, Tchaikovsky made a number of changes, most notably transcribing the role of Joan to the mezzo-soprano register.

ORONTEA, L'

Opera in three acts by Antonio Cesti (1623–1669), to a libretto by Giacinto Andrea Cicognini. First performance: uncertain, although it is known to have been performed in Venice at the Teatro SS. Giovanni e Paolo during Carnival 1666.

Creonte (bass), guardian of Orontea (mezzo-soprano), Queen of Egypt, urges the sovereign to choose a husband for herself. But Orontea is in love with Alidoro (contralto), a young man of humble background, who has narrowly escaped being murdered and has now found refuge, together with his mother, Aristea (mezzo-soprano), at Orontea's court. There follows a series of complicated episodes involving Silandra (soprano), a lady-in-waiting, who is falling in love with Alidoro, while Aristea in turn loves the knight Ismero, who is really Giacinta (soprano) in disguise and also secretly in love with Alidoro. It was Giacinta who had attempted to murder Alidoro on the instructions of the Queen of Phoenicia. At the end of the opera, it is

A scene from *Orlando Furioso*, an opera in three acts by Antonio Vivaldi.

discovered that Alidoro is actually Floridano, rightful heir to the Phoenician throne, who had been abducted by pirates as a boy and brought up by Aristea. Alidoro is therefore free to ask Orontea to marry him.

Cesti's *L'Orontea* is one of the most vigorous and enduring successes in the history of seventeenth-century Italian opera. From 1660 to 1683 it was staged in numerous cities in Italy and elsewhere in Europe. Recent studies show that a performance thought to have occurred in 1649 in Venice did not take place, as the opera presented there in that year was not by Cesti but by Francesco Lucio. Cesci's score therefore dates from between 1657 and 1662, that is, while the composer was travelling between Austria and Italy. A score found in Innsbruck, which was written between those years, has been acknowledged as the original, preceding subsequent editions.

ÖSTMAN, ARNOLD

(Malmö 1939)

Swedish conductor, pianist and organist. He studied organ and piano in Stockholm and Paris, then began his career in music as the organist at the Klara Church in Stockholm and as a teacher at the School of Music and Drama there. Appointed director of the Vadstena Academy (1969), he started to devote his energies to detailed research in the field of baroque music. After appearing also as an accompanist, he founded the Norreland Opera in Umea in 1974. A turning-point in his career was his appointment to the music directorship of the Drottningholm Festival (a post which, until 1984, he shared with the British conductor Charles Farncombe), where he specialized in conducting Mozart operas performed on period instruments. Internationally Östman appeared at the Opéra in Paris, at Covent Garden and with the Cologne Opera.

OTELLO

Opera in four acts by Giuseppe Verdi (1813–1901), to a libretto by Arrigo Boito, based on Shakespeare's tragedy. First performance: Milan, La Scala, 5 February 1887.

The action takes place during the sixteenth century in Cyprus, at a time when that island was a Venetian dominion. Otello (tenor), the island's governor, returns to Cyprus after a triumphant campaign against the Turks. Jago (baritone), Otello's ensign, loathes the Moor – because Otello has promoted Cassio (tenor) instead of Jago to the rank of Captain – and is planning his revenge. Jago has a word with Roderigo (tenor), who loves Otello's wife Desdemona (soprano), and treacherously insinuates to him that Cassio feels the same way as he does for Desdemona. Then he succeeds in turning Roderigo and Cassio against each other, but the resulting duel ends up in a brawl. Acting on false information from Jago, Otello intervenes, punishes Cassio and strips him of his rank. Jago's plot progresses as he sows the seeds of jealousy in Otello's mind, leading him to suspect a secret love affair between Cassio and Desdemona. To reinforce these allegations, Jago says he has seen Cassio in possession of a handkerchief that Otello had given to his wife. Now mad with jealousy, the Moor swears he will kill Desdemona. But in the meantime, ambassadors of the Venetian Republic have arrived in Cyprus to announce that Otello has been summoned to Venice and Cassio will be taking over in his absence. As Jago sets in motion the final part of his devilish plan by inciting Roderigo to kill Cassio, Otello shocks everyone by pushing Desdemona to the ground and cursing her. Shortly afterwards, in Desdemona's bedchamber, Otello wakes his wife up. She tries to defend herself, but he suffocates her. Emilia (mezzo-soprano), Jago's wife, comes in, bringing news that Roderigo has been killed by Cassio. When she finds Desdemona dead, Emilia accuses Jago of masterminding the sequence of events. Otello, in great distress and aware at last of the deception to which he has fallen victim, kisses his wife for the last time and then stabs himself.

A French drawing for Verdi's *Otello*.

The collaboration of Verdi and Boito proved difficult, but it was actually as a result of the continual disagreements between these two that the work took shape as it did. The plot of *Otello* unfolds with a single core of dramatic meaning and unprecedented expressive energy.

OTELLO, OSSIA IL MORO DI VENEZIA

(Othello, or The Moor of Venice)

Opera in three acts by Gioachino Rossini (1792–1868), to a libretto by Francesco Berio di Salsa, based on Shakespeare's tragedy. First performance: Naples, Teatro del Fondo, 4 December 1816.

Surrounded by Senators and the people, the Doge of Venice (tenor) welcomes Otello (tenor), commander of the fleet of the Venetian republic, on his triumphant return from a victorious campaign against the Turks. Roderigo (tenor) and Jago (tenor), two of the Moor's officers, hate Otello; Roderigo particularly, as Jago has led him to suspect that Desdemona (soprano), with whom he is in love, actually loves Otello. By way of proof, Jago shows Roderigo a love letter from Desdemona addressed to Otello. The scene changes to a celebration, during which Elmiro (bass), Desdemona's father, announces that his daughter is soon to be married to Roderigo. Otello also appears on the scene and, to everyone's shock, calls on Desdemona to honour her vow of love for him. Then Desdemona announces to the assembled gathering that she has for some time been keeping faith with Otello. Elmiro curses his daughter and drags her away. These events lead Otello to doubt that his love will continue to be a happy one. Seeing how upset Otello is, Jago goes up to him, gives him to understand that his doubts are well-founded and shows him Desdemona's love letter, pointing out that it was intended for Roderigo. This is the evidence of Desdemona's unfaithfulness. Otello challenges Roderigo to a duel and then goes to see Desdemona in her room. She protests her innocence, but in vain. Otello flings himself upon her and stabs her. Then Elmiro, the Doge and his retinue enter. They bring news that Jago has been unmasked, but by now it is too late, and Otello in desperation turns the dagger on himself.

Rossini wrote *Otello* for Naples's Teatro del Fondo, as the city's Teatro San Carlo had burned down a few months before. Despite the fact that the libretto by Berio di Salsa had distorted Shakespeare's plot, Rossini succeeded in composing a score of the highest quality, especially in the third act where the heights of the music make the tragedy what it is. *Otello* represents the apotheosis of Rossini as a composer of *opera seria* and looks forward to Romantic opera.

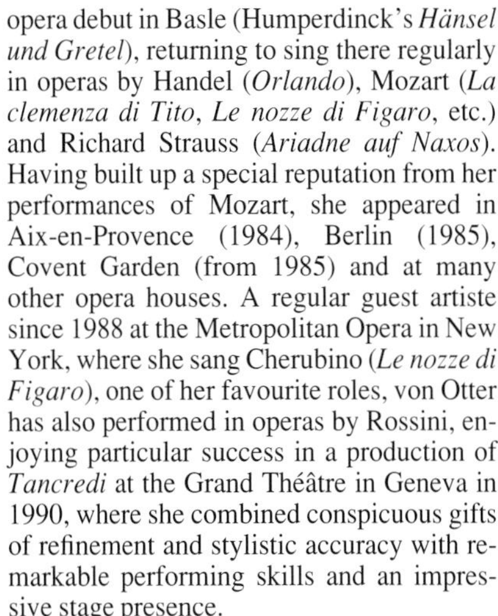

OTTER, ANNE SOPHIE VON

(Stockholm 1955)

Swedish mezzo-soprano. She began her music studies at the Conservatory in Stockholm before moving on to complete her training in Vienna with Erik Werba and in London with Geoffrey Parsons and Vera Rosza (from 1981). She began her career as a *Lieder* singer at the Festivals of Drottningholm and Vadstena (1981–82). In 1982 she made her opera debut in Basle (Humperdinck's *Hänsel und Gretel*), returning to sing there regularly in operas by Handel (*Orlando*), Mozart (*La clemenza di Tito*, *Le nozze di Figaro*, etc.) and Richard Strauss (*Ariadne auf Naxos*). Having built up a special reputation from her performances of Mozart, she appeared in Aix-en-Provence (1984), Berlin (1985), Covent Garden (from 1985) and at many other opera houses. A regular guest artiste since 1988 at the Metropolitan Opera in New York, where she sang Cherubino (*Le nozze di Figaro*), one of her favourite roles, von Otter has also performed in operas by Rossini, enjoying particular success in a production of *Tancredi* at the Grand Théâtre in Geneva in 1990, where she combined conspicuous gifts of refinement and stylistic accuracy with remarkable performing skills and an impressive stage presence.

OZAWA, SEIJI

(Hoten, Manchuria 1935)

Japanese conductor. A pupil of Saito at the Toho School of Music in Tokyo, he went on to train as a conductor in the United States and in Berlin with Herbert von Karajan in 1959. In the same year he won the international competition in Besançon and, in 1960, the Mitropoulos Prize in New York, on the strength of which he was appointed assistant conductor to Leonard Bernstein (1961–62 and 1964–65), quickly establishing himself by conducting the leading international symphony orchestras. Preeminently a conductor of symphonic music, Ozawa made his opera debut in *Così fan tutte* in Salzburg in 1969. He then appeared at Covent Garden (conducting *Eugene Onegin* in 1974), the Paris Opéra (*Oedipus Rex*, *L'enfant et les sortilèges* and *Turandot*, 1981) and at La Scala, Milan, where he conducted Tchaikovsky's *Pikovaya dama* (The Queen of Spades, 1990). An active recording artist, particularly of symphonic music, Ozawa conducted Berlioz's *La damnation de Faust* in 1974 and a controversial performance of Bizet's *Carmen* in 1989.

Above: The Japanese conductor Seiji Ozawa.

Left: A set design for Rossini's *Otello*.

P

PACINI, GIOVANNI

(Catania 1796–Pescia 1867)
Italian composer. His father, Luigi, had created the role of Geronio in Rossini's *Il turco in Italia.* After his debut in Milan with *Annetta e Lucindo* (1813), Pacini rapidly became established as one of the most highly acclaimed composers of his day, alongside Bellini, Donizetti and Verdi. As well as for his most famous opera, *Saffo* (1840), he is remembered for *Furio Camillo* (1839), *Medea* (1843) and *Maria Tudor* (1843).

PADMÂVATÎ

Opéra-ballet *in two acts by Albert Roussel (1869–1937), to a libretto by Louis Laloy, inspired by Oriental poems. First performance: Paris, Opéra, 1 June 1923.*

Ratan-Sen (tenor), King of Tchitor, is married to the strikingly beautiful and virtuous Padmâvatî (soprano or mezzo-soprano). A Brahmin (tenor) falls in love with the Queen, but she rejects him. Expelled from the kingdom, the Brahmin plans his revenge and asks for the assistance of Alaouddin (baritone), King of Delhi, who also falls in love with Padmâvatî and asks that she be given to him before he will agree to the alliance which is being sought by Ratan-Sen. Ratan-Sen refuses, and this sparks off a war between the two kingdoms, during which he is mortally wounded. While the Brahmin is being condemned to death by the outraged people, Padmâvatî has the dying Ratan-Sen put out of his agony, orders his funeral pyre to be built and throws herself on to it alongside his body.

Roussel's opera recalls the French tradition of *opéra-ballet*, in which dancing played a prominent part in the structure of the opera, but he manages to avoid the temptation of a self-consciously exotic style and achieves instead a score which is alive to the developments in music in the early twentieth century.

Top: The Italian composer Ferdinando Paër in a print from a drawing by G. Bossi.

Right: A German caricature from 1911 of Ruggero Leoncavallo.

PAËR, FERDINANDO

(Parma 1771–Paris 1839)
Italian composer. He studied in Parma, where he made his debut in 1791 with the opera *Orphée et Euridice.* After his early major successes, he was appointed Kapellmeister at the Court of Vienna (1798), was at the Dresden Hoftheater (1802) and subsequently became *maître de chapelle* to the Emperor Napoleon in Paris (1807) and director of the Théâtre des Italiens (1812–27). His best-known operas include *Griselda* (1798), *Camilla* (1799), *Ginevra degli Almieri* (1802), *Leonora* (1804), in which he used the same story that Beethoven would turn to a year later, and *Le maître de chapelle* (1821).

PAGLIACCI, I

(The Clowns)
Opera in two acts and a prologue by Ruggero Leoncavallo (1857–1919), to the composer's own libretto. First performance: Milan, Teatro Dal Verme, 1 May 1892.

In the prologue, Tonio (baritone), an actor in a company of travelling players, announces to the audience that the show they are about to see is drawn from real life. The action takes place in a village in Calabria, where the arrival of a company of travelling players is welcomed with great enthusiasm by all the inhabitants. While Canio (tenor) and the other players are on their way to the inn, Nedda (soprano), Canio's wife, is approached by Tonio. He tells her he is in love with her, but she violently rejects him. Tonio wants revenge and when, shortly afterwards, he comes upon Nedda talking to Silvio (baritone), one of the villagers and her lover, he hurries to inform Canio. Canio appears on the scene, but Silvio manages to get away without Canio recognizing him, and Nedda refuses to reveal his name. Tonio persuades Canio to wait: the lover will reappear during his show. Left alone, Canio laments that he must play the clown while his heart his breaking. Later, when the performance begins, Peppe (tenor), dressed as Harlequin, has a love-tryst with Nedda, who is Columbine. In bursts Canio, playing the part of Pagliaccio, Columbine's husband, and Harlequin runs off. Canio, finding himself in a situation identical to that of his own life, rushes up to Nedda like a madman and demands the name of her lover. When she refuses to speak, he stabs her to death. Silvio clambers on to the stage to help Nedda, whereupon Canio kills him too. Then he turns to the audience with the words "The play is over."

I pagliacci, based on a real-life event that took place in Montalto in Calabria, was an immediate success and within a short time was playing in opera houses throughout the world. It is regarded as the realist opera *par excellence.*

PAISIELLO, GIOVANNI

(Roccaforzata, Taranto 1740–Naples 1816)
Italian composer. He studied in his home town before moving on to the Conservatorio di Sant'Onofrio in Naples, where he was a pupil of Durante and Abos. He became music director of the company at Bologna's Teatro Marsigli-Rossi. His debut as an opera composer came about 1764, and he immediately earned a reputation, principally in *opera buffa.* On returning to Naples (1783), he composed a number of operas, among them *L'idolo cinese* (1767), *Don Chisciotte* (1769) and *Socrate immaginario* (1775). He accepted an invitation to the Court of Catherine II of Russia in St. Petersburg, where he wrote his famous opera *Il barbiere di Siviglia* (1762). Eight years later, Paisiello was once again back in Naples and took up the post of chorus-master and court composer to Ferdinand IV. This was the beginning of an ex-

tremely productive period for him, during which he wrote, among other operas, *La grotta di Trofonio* (1785), *La Molinara* (1788) and *Nina, pazza per amore* (1789). Napoleon, who greatly admired Paisiello, invited him in 1802 to Paris, where he became the Emperor's director of chapel music. In 1803, although by now honoured and sought after, he returned to settle permanently in Naples and died there in near-poverty in 1816.

PÁL, TAMÁS

(Gyula 1937)

Hungarian conductor. He studied piano, composition and conducting at the Liszt Music Academy in Budapest. His career as a conductor began at the opera house in Budapest in 1960, where he has continued to conduct regularly ever since. From 1987 onwards, Pál conducted the Budapest Music Weeks. Internationally, he has been a regular guest conductor at opera houses in Marseilles, Trieste and throughout Europe. He has won acclaim for the recovery of forgotten scores and for his performances of Salieri's *Falstaff* (1984), Liszt's *Don Sanche* (1985) and Cimarosa's *Il pittor parigino* (1988).

PALACIO, ERNESTO

(Lima 1946)

Peruvian tenor. He began to study music in Lima and then moved to Italy, where he completed his training in Milan. He made his debut in San Remo in Rossini's *Il barbiere di Siviglia*, and it is in the operas of this composer that the most important achievements of Palacio's international career have taken place. He has been equally committed to the eighteenth-century repertoire and composers including Vivaldi, Cimarosa and Paisiello. His credits as a prolific recording artist include distinguished performances of Rossini's *Tancredi*, *Maometto II*, *Ermione* and *Mosè in Egitto*, which revealed his gifts of musicianship and fidelity to a composer's style.

PALESTRINA

Opera in three acts by Hans Pfitzner (1869–1949), to the composer's own libretto. First performance: Munich, Residenztheater, 12 June 1917.

Silla (mezzo-soprano), a pupil of Palestrina (tenor), is playing on his violin a melody different in style from that of his teacher and reveals his aspirations to Ighino (soprano), Palestrina's son. Enter Cardinal Borromeo (baritone), followed by Palestrina himself. The Cardinal invites Palestrina to compose a Mass for the closing ceremony of the Council of Trent, but Palestrina, now feeling old and tired, turns down the commission. Left alone, Palestrina sees, as though in a vision, faces of composers of the past and hears their voices urging him to persevere with his work. These images are followed by choirs of angels singing a *Kyrie eleison* and finally by his dead wife Lucrezia. Palestrina experiences a sensation of peace and sets to work. The scene changes to Trent, where everything is ready for the opening of the Council. It is rumoured that Palestrina has been imprisoned for refusing to compose the Mass. No sooner is the Council in session than disagreements begin to surface. All the participants are concerned about the ritual of the Mass, and Cardinal Borromeo attempts to calm everyone down, but when the session is suspended at midday a furious row breaks out between their Italian, German and Spanish servants. Soldiers appear and open fire. The action now moves to Palestrina's house. Ighino is telling his obviously debilitated father that his Mass is about to be performed: it had been collected and kept by Silla when he was arrested. Enter the singers from the papal chapel to announce that the performance of the Mass has been a triumph. Pope Pius IV (bass) congratulates Palestrina in person, and Cardinal Borromeo asks the composer for his forgiveness. Old Palestrina realizes that he has already given his all as a composer. Now at peace, he sits down at the organ and offers thanks to God.

The Italian tenor Enrico Caruso as Tonio in Leoncavallo's *I pagliacci*.

Palestrina, clearly influenced by Wagner, had a wide circle of admirers among more conservative German opera-goers, who objected to the new trends in music represented by Strauss, Schoenberg and Busoni. Pfitzner's opera is a tribute to the Italian composer whose *Missa Papae Marcelli* is said to have saved the art of counterpoint in sixteenth-century church music.

PALMER, FELICITY

(Cheltenham 1944)

British soprano. She studied at the Guildhall School of Music in London. After making her debut as a concert artist and winning the prestigious Kathleen Ferrier Memorial Prize (1970), she sang for the first time in the opera house as Susanna in *Le nozze di Figaro* at Houston Opera (1973). Much of her career has been devoted to oratorio, chamber music and concerts. As an opera singer, Palmer has appeared in Gluck's *Armide*, Holst's *Sāvitri*, Tippett's *King Priam*, Lully's *Alceste*, Mozart's *Idomeneo* and *Le nozze di Figaro*.

PANERAI, ROLANDO

(Campi Bisenzio, Florence 1924)

Italian baritone. He studied in Florence with Vito Frazzi and in Milan with Giacomo Armani and Giulia Tess. He made his debut in 1947 at the Teatro San Carlo in Naples as Faraone in Rossini's *Mosè* and appeared for the first time at La Scala in 1951 (as Sharpless in Puccini's *Madama Butterfly*). In 1955 he was Ruprecht in the first performance of Prokofiev's *The Fiery Angel* at La Fenice in Venice. Drawing on an extensive repertoire, Panerai's reputation particularly rests on his performances in comic opera of the eighteenth century (Mozart, Cimarosa, Paisiello, etc.) and the nineteenth (Rossini, Donizetti, Verdi and Puccini) at major international opera venues such as Salzburg, Aix-en-Provence and Covent Garden.

PANNI, MARCELLO

(Rome 1940)

Italian composer and conductor. He studied in Rome at the Conservatorio and the Accademia Nazionale di Santa Cecilia. He completed his training in Paris and then embarked on a career as a composer and conductor. As well as his particular interest in twentieth-century and contemporary music, Panni was involved in reviving rare operas, including Cavalli's *Giasone* (Genoa, 1972), *Il Flaminio* (Naples, 1982), Pergolesi's *Adriano in Siria* (Florence, 1985), Handel's *Giulio Cesare* (Martina Franca, 1989), Paisiello's *Nina, pazza per amore* (Savona, 1987) and Piccinni's *Iphigénie en Tauride* (Rome, 1991). From the 1990–91 season onwards, Panni has frequently appeared with Luciano Pavarotti in various performances of *Rigoletto* and *L'elisir d'amore* at the Metropolitan Opera in New York and in several European cities, including Vienna and London.

PARIDE ED ELENA

Opera in five acts by Christoph Willibald Gluck (1714–1878), to a libretto by Ranieri de'Calzabigi. First performance: Vienna, Burgtheater, 3 November 1770.

Paride (soprano or tenor), son of the King of Troy, lands on the coast of Sparta with his retinue. He is welcomed by Amore (soprano) who, disguised as Erasto, offers the Trojan prince his help in winning Elena (soprano), the beautiful Queen of Sparta. Paris seeks an audience with the Queen, at which he presents her with magnificent gifts, but she behaves with cold indifference towards the young man, having decided that he would be too unreliable to love. Paride, however, puts his trust in Venere (Venus) and Amore, and gradually they help him to touch Elena's heart, although she continues to resist and does not dare to show her own feelings to Paride, preferring to implore him to forget her. Then Amore gives Elena the false news that Paride has left. The Queen is disheartened and thus reveals her love for him. Suddenly Paride reappears before her. Elena finally gives in to love and sets sail for Troy with Paride, while the goddess Atena (soprano) prophesies that this love will lead to misfortune for Greece.

The soprano Mariella Devia as Parisina in Donizetti's opera of the same name.

The static plot was certainly one of the reasons why *Paride ed Elena* had so little success at its first performance. In the absence of any dramatic content (a key feature of Gluck's previous operas *Orfeo ed Euridice* and *Alceste*), this opera is mainly distinguished by its delicately lyrical arias, the elegant instrumental writing of its dances and the beauty of the chorus passages.

PARISINA

Opera seria *in three acts by Gaetano Donizetti (1797–1848), to a libretto by Felice Romani, based on the poem of the same name by Lord Byron. First performance: Florence, Teatro della Pergola, 17 March 1833.*

Duke Azzo d'Este (baritone) has become suspicious about the faithfulness of his wife, Parisina (soprano). She harbours tender feelings for Ugo, a childhood friend, but is trying to restrain herself. Watched by Ernesto (bass), the Duke's general, Ugo distinguishes himself on the battlefield and again in a tournament, where he is presented with the victor's crown by a visibly affected Parisina. Azzo is consumed with jealousy, enters Parisina's bedroom during the night, overhears her speaking her beloved's name in her sleep and swears revenge. Ernesto then breaks the news to Azzo that Ugo is actually his son and had been entrusted to him for safe-keeping by Azzo's first wife, Matilde, before she died. This revelation does not dissuade Azzo from his desire for revenge. He orders Ernesto to take Ugo a long way away from Ferrara. But when Azzo comes upon Ugo and Parisina bidding a tender farewell to each other, he becomes angrier than ever, has Ugo arrested and condemned to death, and then shows the young man's dead body to Parisina, causing her to die of grief.

Parisina was unfavourably received at its first performance, though it contains passages of obvious quality. The opera fell into oblivion, to be revived for the first time in 1964, as part of the Siena Music Weeks, with Marcella Pobbè singing Parisina. In 1974, as a result of Montserrat Caballé taking the role, *Parisina* enjoyed renewed popularity.

PARSIFAL

Sacred festival drama in three acts by Richard Wagner (1813–1883), to the composer's own libretto, based mainly on Wolfram von Eschenbach's poem Parzival. *First performance: Bayreuth, Festspielhaus, 26 July 1882.*

The action takes place in the Pyrenees, in and around the castle of Monsalvat, which houses the Holy Grail, the sacred chalice from which Jesus drank at the Last Supper. King Amfortas (baritone), suffering from a wound that seems as if it will never heal, is being borne to the nearby lake, where he hopes the water will be soothing. Suddenly Kundry (soprano or mezzo-soprano) appears, a wild and beautiful young woman, who has brought the King balsam to alleviate his suffering. The King accepts it, even though he knows he can only be healed by a hero who has been made pure through pity, a "Pure Fool." Then the knight Gurnemanz (bass) tells the squires of the King's tragic story: carrying the spear which had been thrust into Christ's side at the crucifixion, Amfortas had set out to storm the castle of the magician Klingsor (bass), who had been using his diabolical craft to ensnare the knights of the Grail. But Amfortas, seduced by the charms of a woman in the pay of the magician, had fallen into sin. Klingsor seized the spear and wounded Amfortas, and the wound has not stopped bleeding since. Gurnemanz's tale is interrupted by the arrival of Parsifal (tenor). He has been brought in after killing one of the sacred swans of Monsalvat, and he now destroys his weapons as an act of penitence. When Gurnemanz asks him who he is, the young man is unable to answer. Gurnemanz senses that this may be the Pure Fool destined to heal Amfortas and leads him to the castle so that he can attend the solemn ritual of displaying the Grail. Parsifal witnesses the ceremony but does not understand what is going on. Gurnemanz, annoyed at this, reproaches Parsifal for his indifference and tells him to leave. The scene changes to Klingsor's magic castle. Klingsor summons up Kundry and commands her against her will to seduce Parsifal, who in the meantime has already resisted the advances of the Flower-maidens. Kundry goes to Parsifal and reminds him of his mother's love for him, which she says he can recapture in her. Then she kisses him. At this point Parsifal realizes what is happening. The insight he now has into the sin which has caused Amfortas's suffering fills him with horror, and he pushes Kundry away. Overwhelmed by his rejection she calls on Klingsor, who hurls Amfortas's spear from the top of the tower, but the spear miraculously stops in mid-air. Castle and garden vanish, and Kundry is left lying on the ground. Time passes. Near the mountain of the Grail, Gurnemanz revives Kundry. Parsifal appears, wearing armour. Gurnemanz asks him to take off his armour because it is Good Friday. Gurnemanz then recognizes Parsifal and tells him the knights of the Grail have been dejected ever since Amfortas refused to celebrate the solemn ritual of displaying the Grail, and Titurel (bass), the King's father, has died of grief. Parsifal is beset with anguish, but Gurnemanz nevertheless anoints him king of the Grail and asks him to accompany him to the castle, where the funeral of Titurel is taking place. Parsifal enters and touches Amfortas's wound with the spear, healing it. Then he unveils the Grail and renews the ritual. From high in the sky a white dove descends and hovers above the heads of Parsifal and the knights, while Kundry, now redeemed, dies.

Wagner spent the last years of his life working on *Parsifal*, from 1877 to 1882, although he had been studying legends, including that of the Holy Grail, many years earlier and had composed the first drafts of the opera then. The work contains fascinating sequence of *leitmotiv* and is pervaded by mysticism.

PASTOR FIDO, IL

(The Faithful Shepherd)

Opera in three acts by George Frederick Handel (1685–1759), to a libretto by Giacomo Rossi, based on the poem by Battista Guarini. First performance: London, Queen's Theater, 22 November 1712.

The shepherd Mirtillo (contralto) loves and is loved by the nymph Amarilli (soprano), and yet when she is with him, she is cold and disdainful towards him. In despair, Mirtillo confides in Eurilla (mezzo-soprano), who secretly loves him. She promises, falsely, that she will try to win Amarilli over for him. Silvio (tenor) now appears, whom the goddess Diana has pledged to Amarilli as a husband. But Silvio wants to enjoy his freedom and steps back from Dorinda (mezzo-soprano) when she opens her heart to him and hopes for his love. In the ensuing action, Eurilla arouses Amarilli's jealousy, and Mirtillo believes he has at last succeeded in touching her heart. Mirtillo and Amarilli marry, and Silvio's attitude towards Dorinda is mollified.

Il pastor fido was revised several times and three versions of the opera survived. Rossi's libretto is clearly inferior to the poem by Guarini which had first inspired him, but Handel responded with a score very much in keeping with the Arcadian spirit of the story.

PATANÈ, GIUSEPPE

(Naples 1932–Munich 1989)

Italian conductor. He studied music (piano

A scene from *Parsifal*, an opera in three acts by Richard Wagner.

and composition) at the Conservatorio San Pietro a Maiella in Naples, the city where he made his conducting debut in *La traviata* (1953). The key points of his career were the posts he held as conductor at the Landestheater in Linz (1961–62), at the Deutsche Oper Berlin (1963–68) and at the Opera House in Budapest (1980–89). Patanè was one of the most highly acclaimed Italian opera conductors, and his credits included appearances at the major international opera houses. He died after suffering a heart attack while conducting Rossini's *Il barbiere di Siviglia* in Munich.

PAVAROTTI, LUCIANO

(Modena 1935)

Italian tenor. His debut in 1961 as Rodolfo in Puccini's *La bohème* in Reggio Emilia immediately led to appearances at numerous opera houses in Italy, as well as at Covent Garden (*La bohème*, 1963), the Glyndebourne Festival (Mozart's *Idomeneo*, 1964) and other international opera venues. In 1965 he sang for the first time at La Scala in *La bohème*, the opera in which he made his debut with the Metropolitan Opera in New York (1967). Further engagements took him to Tokyo, Hamburg, Berlin and Barcelona. In 1973 in the United States he gave the first of the recitals which were to become such a prominent feature of his career. A singer of enormous popularity, thanks not least to the large number of records, videos and publications in which he has appeared, Pavarotti possesses great gifts, including a beauty and brilliance of timbre and a consistency throughout the entire range, culminating in a supreme and splendid upper register. His repertoire, which initially centered almost exclusively on early romantic operas such as *I puritani*, *La favorita* and *La fille du régiment*, was gradually enhanced by more dramatic roles such as *Tosca*, *Luisa Miller* and *Un ballo in maschera*.

PEARS, SIR PETER

(Farnham, Surrey 1910–Aldeburgh 1986)

British tenor. He studied at the Royal College of Music in London (1933–34) and with Elena Gerhardt and Dawson Freer. In 1936 he met Benjamin Britten, with whom he subsequently undertook a series of tours as a duo in Europe and America. The key achievements in his career came through his association with Britten's music. He created the lead roles in *Peter Grimes* (1945) and *Albert Herring* (1951), as well as that of the Male Chorus in *The Rape of Lucretia* (1946), and gave numerous other first performances, including *Death in Venice* (1973), Britten's last opera. A performer of rare musical intelligence and refinement, Pears was also a distinguished performer of the chamber repertoire.

PÊCHEURS DE PERLES, LES

(The Pearl Fishers)

Opera in three acts by Georges Bizet (1838–1875), to a libretto by Eugene Cormon and Michael Carré. First performance: Paris, Théâtre Lyrique, 30 September 1863.

Luciano Pavarotti.

On the island of Ceylon, Zurga (baritone), chief of a tribe of fisher-folk, and Nadir (tenor), a pearl fisher, are recalling the past, in particular how they had once loved the same woman, a dancer priestess, and had renounced that love so as not to risk losing each other's friendship. Then a boat comes to the island bearing a veiled woman whose task in life is to sail the ocean and calm stormy weather with her singing. She is none other than Léila (soprano), the dancer with whom Nadir and Zurga had been in love. In an old abandoned temple, Léila tells the High Priest Nourabad (bass) of the time she risked death to save the life of a fugitive and had been rewarded by him with a necklace. Later, Nadir is reunited with Léila, and they decide to see each other every evening. But Nourabad discovers them together and reports them. When Zurga recognizes Léila, he becomes blindly jealous and sentences them both to death. Léila tries to defend Nadir, but to no avail. Before being led to the scaffold, she gives a fisherman a necklace and asks him to deliver it to her mother. But Zurga has seen this necklace before and realizes it was Léila who had once saved his life. So he decides to help her, sets fire to the village and releases Nadir and Léila. As the couple make their escape, Zurga himself is caught by Nourabad and sentenced to be burned at the stake.

Les pêcheurs de perles only became a great success many years after Bizet's death. It was subsequently forgotten and then revived in 1938 at a production at La Scala, Milan. This popular work and *Carmen* are the only Bizet operas to have entered the repertoire. The score abounds in enchanting melodies and demonstrates Bizet's great lyrical gift as well as his striking originality as an artist. Another prominent feature in this work is his use of orchestral colours to evoke landscape as well as situation and character.

PELLÉAS ET MÉLISANDE

Drame lyrique *in five acts and 12* tableaux *by Claude Debussy (1862–1918) from the play of the same name by Maurice Maeterlinck. First performance: Paris, Théâtre de l'Opéra-Comique, 30 April 1902.*

Golaud (baritone), grandson of King Arkel (bass), loses his way in a forest, then comes upon a young woman weeping. Her name is Mélisande (soprano), and she speaks only vaguely about where she is from or who has wronged her. Golaud takes Mélisande

with him, and she agrees to stay with him and be his wife. At the castle, Genèvieve (contralto), mother of the step-brothers Golaud and Pelléas (tenor), reads the King a letter from Golaud to his brother Pelléas, in which he asks if he can come home with his bride. He adds that he will reach the castle within three days and, before crossing the threshold, will need to be assured that Mélisande is going to be welcomed; if this is the case, he asks that a lamp be left burning at the top of the tower. The day arrives, and Pelléas does indeed welcome his brother and new sister-in-law, but then he announces he will be leaving the next day. The scene changes to the park, where Mélisande is sitting with Pelléas beside a fountain known to have miraculous properties. As she plays with the ring which Golaud had given her, it falls in the water. Confined to bed after a fall from his horse, Golaud is being cared for by Mélisande when he notices the ring is missing. She tells him she lost it in a grotto by the sea-shore. He sends her to look for it and, as night has now come, asks Pelléas to accompany her. These two are standing in front of the grotto when a shaft of moonlight reveals three beggars lying asleep, a sight that terrifies both of them. Back at the castle, Mélisande is combing her long hair out of the tower window. Pelléas, about to leave, comes to the foot of the tower to say goodbye. As Mélisande leans to reach out her hand, her hair cascades down around Pelléas's face like the leaves of a willow tree. Golaud comes upon them like this and is consumed with jealousy. He warns Pelléas it would be better if he stayed away from Mélisande now that she is expecting a child. In front of the castle, Golaud, whose suspicions are growing, asks little Yniold (soprano), his son by his first marriage, to tell him what Pelléas and Mélisande do when they are together. Then he lifts the boy up to the window to spy on them. Yniold says he can see them sitting quietly. When his father presses him for details, the boy becomes frightened and starts to cry. In a corridor of the castle, Pelléas, now determined to leave the castle, asks Mélisande if he can meet her once more by the fountain. Golaud appears, gets hold of Mélisande by the hair and throws her to the ground, without explaining his actions. King Arkel intervenes and calms the angry Golaud. Pelléas and Mélisande keep their appointment by the fountain. They confess their love for each other and embrace for the first and last time. Golaud finds them there, stabs his brother with his sword and wounds Mélisande. Back in her bed-chamber, Mélisande is dying after giving birth to a girl. Golaud, overcome with remorse, is still so jealous that he asks if her love for Pelléas had ever been consummated. Mélisande looks sadly at her newborn child and dies without answering.

Pelléas and Mélisande, Debussy's only completed opera, is not only considered his masterpiece but one of the greatest works in the history of opera. The blending of the symbolism in Maeterlinck's text and Debussy's insistence on the importance of colour in music required a long process, from 1893 until 1901, but the result was perfection.

PEPUSCH, JOHANN CHRISTOPH

(Berlin 1667–London 1752)

German composer, naturalized English. He settled in England around 1700, became a harpsichordist at the Drury Lane Theater and made his name on the strength of *The Beggar's Opera* (1728), to a text by John Gay, the first example of a ballad-opera.

PERGOLESI, GIOVAN BATTISTA

(Jesi, Ancona 1710–Pozzuoli 1736)

Italian composer. He studied in Naples (from 1723), where he was a pupil of Greco and Durante. In 1732 *Lo frate 'nnamurato*, an *opera buffa*, brought him his first success in the theater. The intermezzo *La serva padrona* from his next opera, *Il prigionier superbo* (1733), enjoyed a resounding success all its own. Pergolesi's last operas, *L'Olimpiade*

A scene from Debussy's *Pelléas and Mélisande*, performed for the first time in Paris in 1902.

and *Il Flaminio*, were staged in 1735, and a year later he died, at the age of only 26, after completing his *Stabat Mater*.

PERI, JACOPO
(Rome 1561–Florence 1633)
Italian composer and singer, known as "Zazzerino." He studied with Cristofano Malvezzi in Florence, where he became one of the leading composers at the court of the Medici. In 1589, to mark the occasion of the wedding between Ferdinand I and Christine of Lorraine, he contributed to the composition of the *intermedi* performed during Bargagli's play *La pellegrina*. A member of the Camerata Fiorentina, Peri collaborated with the poet Ottavio Rinuccini in 1598 on *Dafne*. This is regarded as the first opera, but only a few fragments have survived. The marriage of Marie de Medicis with Henri IV of France in 1600 provided the occasion for the staging of his *Euridice*, which marked the birth of serious opera as we know it today.

PERRY, JANET
(Minneapolis 1947)
American soprano. A pupil of Euphemia Gregory at the Curtis Institute in Philadelphia, she completed her training in Europe and made her debut in Linz in 1969 as Zerlina in Mozart's *Don Giovanni*. As well as appearing at major German and Austrian opera houses, especially in Munich and Cologne, Perry has sung at the Opéra in Paris (*Don Giovanni*, 1981, and Johann Strauss's *Die Fledermaus*, 1983), at La Fenice in Venice (Mozart's *Die Zauberflöte*, The Magic Flute, 1987) and at numerous other theaters. She was Nannetta in Verdi's *Falstaff* and Sophie in Richard Strauss's *Der Rosenkavalier* with Herbert von Karajan conducting (1980 and 1983).

PERTILE, AURELIANO
(Montagnana 1885–Milan 1952)
Italian tenor. He made his debut in Vicenza (1911) in Flotow's *Martha*, then completed his training in Milan. His career reached its height at La Scala, Milan, during the 1920s, when he was one of Toscanini's favourite singers. His farewell stage performance was in a production of Boito's *Nerone* in 1946. Pertile had an exceptional technique, coupled with extremely refined and elegant phrasing. His repertoire was remarkably wide-ranging and included operas by Rossini, Donizetti and Wagner.

The bass Michele Pertusi (at center) in Rossini's *Semiramide*.

PERTUSI, MICHELE
(Parma 1965)
Italian bass. He made his debut in 1984 in Pistoia as Monterone in Verdi's *Rigoletto*. His distinctive vocal and performing gifts immediately made an impression, so that within a few years he had become one of the most admired and sought-after singers of his generation. His earlier reputation rests particularly on his performances as Alfonso (Donizetti's *Lucrezia Borgia*) at the Liceu in Barcelona with Dame Joan Sutherland and Alfredo Kraus (1989), as Edoardo III (Donizetti's *L'assedio di Calais*) at the Donizetti Festival in Bergamo (1990), Don Alfonso (Mozart's *Così fan tutte*) at the Teatro Comunale in Florence with Zubin Mehta conducting, and as Assur (Rossini's *Semiramide*) at the Rossini Opera Festival in Pesaro (1992). It was in his performance of the role of Assur that Pertusi's outstanding talents as a *bel canto* singer were displayed to full effect. He has also revealed great musicianship, incisive phrasing and fine command of the stage.

PESKÓ, ZOLTÁN
(Budapest 1937)
Hungarian conductor. He studied at the Liszt Academy in Budapest, where he graduated in composition (1962). He went on to train as a conductor in Siena and at the Accademia di Santa Cecilia in Rome. He also attended Pierre Boulez's music courses in Basle (1965) and began his conducting career as assistant to Lorin Maazel at the Deutsche Oper Berlin (1966), where he became resident conductor from 1969 to 1973. Much of Peskó's career centered on Italy, conducting the major orchestras and appearing at the main opera houses, while from 1983 onwards he also conducted regularly throughout Europe and the United States. As well as taking a keen interest in contemporary music, Peskó is committed to reviving forgotten scores, for example Mussorgsky's *Salammbô* (Italian Radio and Television, Milan, 1980) and Mysliveček's *Bellerofonte* (Budapest, 1987).

PETER GRIMES
Opera in three acts with a prologue by Benjamin Britten (1913–1976), to a libretto by Montagu Slater, based on George Crabbe's poem The Borough. *First performance: London, Sadler's Wells Theater, 7 June 1945.*

The action takes place in a fishing village on the coast of East Anglia around the year 1830. In the town-hall, the magistrate, Swallow (bass), having concluded the inquest on a boy who had died while working for Peter Grimes (tenor), returns a verdict of accidental death but advises Peter not to take on any more apprentices. Not long after this, Peter tells Captain Balstrode (baritone) that, as a way of winning back the trust of the villagers, who have viewed him with suspicion since the boy's death, he intends to marry the village schoolmistress, Ellen Orford (soprano). The scene changes to the inn, where a number of fishermen have brought news that the storm raging in the area has caused the road to cave in below Peter Grimes's house. Enter Peter himself, looking pale and distraught. He is assumed to be drunk, and the fisherman Bob Boles (tenor) calls him a murderer. Peter rushes out into the storm, dragging with him the new apprentice whom Ellen has brought to the inn. Some weeks later, Peter wants to take a boat and go out to sea on a fishing trip. Ellen asks him to leave the new boy behind to rest. Several individuals witness the ensuing argument, as a result of which they decide to carry out an inspection inside Peter's house. As the villagers arrive at his humble abode, Peter forces the boy to leave by the back door, which overlooks the cliff edge. The boy is so frightened and anxious that he slips, falls and is killed. The villagers find everything in order inside the house. For several days Peter is not seen in the village, and Mrs Sedley (mezzo-soprano), the town gossip, says she is convinced that Peter has killed another boy. While enquiries are launched, Ellen and Balstrode come upon Peter in the fog, wandering about like a madman. Balstrode advises Peter to take the boat out to sea, sink it and go down with it. At dawn on the next day, someone mentions that there is a boat foundering out in the bay, but no one takes any notice.

Peter Grimes was the opera that established Britten's reputation and has continued to be regarded as one of his most important compositions as well as having renewed the profile of British music in the world.

PETERS, ROBERTA
(New York 1930)
Stage name of the American soprano Roberta Petermann. She studied singing with William Hermann in New York, making her debut there at the Metropolitan Opera in 1950 as Zerlina (Mozart's *Don Giovanni*). Becoming a permanent member of the Metropolitan Opera Company, she was acclaimed for her performances of the *coloratura* repertoire. She also appeared at, among other venues, Covent Garden (from 1951) and the Salzburg Festival (1963–64). With her outstanding light soprano voice, she won distinction for her roles in Donizetti's *Lucia di Lammermoor*, Mozart's *Die Zauberflöte* (The Magic Flute), Rossini's *Il barbiere di Siviglia*, Richard Strauss's *Ariadne auf Naxos* and Verdi's *Rigoletto*, operas which she has also recorded.

PETRASSI, GOFFREDO
(Zagarolo, Rome 1904)
Italian composer. He studied at the Conservatorio Santa Cecilia in Rome, where he later taught. He was the Intendant at La Fenice in Venice from 1937 to 1940. He composed two operas, *Il Cordovano* (1949) and *Morte dell'aria* (1950), regarded as landmarks in contemporary Italian theater.

PETRELLA, ERRICO
(Palermo 1813–Genoa 1877)
Italian composer. He studied in Naples with Zingarelli, Ruggi and Vincenzo Bellini and, while still a youth, made his debut in 1829 with *Il diavolo color di rosa*. Petrella composed 24 operas, among them *Le precauzioni* (1851), *Marco Visconti* (1854), *Jone* (1858), *La contessa di Amalfi* (1864) and *I promessi sposi* (1896), all forgotten.

PETROSELLINI, GIUSEPPE
(Corneto, now Tarquinia, 1727–Rome 1799)
Italian librettist. As an abbot, he lived in Rome at the papal court and was a member of numerous academies. A prolific librettist, he wrote plots for operas by Piccinni, Cimarosa (*L'italiana in Londra*, 1779, *Il pittor parigino*, 1781, etc.), Paisiello (*Il barbiere di Siviglia*, 1782) and others.

PFITZNER, HANS ERICH
(Moscow 1869–Salzburg 1949)
German composer. After studying music in Frankfurt and Wiesbaden, he embarked on an intensive conducting career, which included posts in Mainz (1894–96), Berlin (1903–6), Strasbourg (1908–19) and in teaching. The Nazi regime ruthlessly exploited his rejection of the musical avant-garde and adoption of prominently nationalistic stances closely aligned to Wagner's style of composition. His most famous opera is *Palestrina* (1917).

PIAVE, FRANCESCO MARIA
(Murano, Venice 1810–Milan 1876)
Italian librettist. He was the official poet at La Fenice in Venice (1848–59) and at La Scala, Milan (1859–67). He wrote about 60 libretti, the most memorable being those for Verdi's operas *Ernani* (1844), *I due Foscari* (1844), *Macbeth* (1847 and 1865), *Il corsaro* (1847), *Stiffelio* (1850, later restaged as *Aroldo*, 1857), *Rigoletto* (1851), *La traviata* (1853), *Simon Boccanegra* (1857) and *La forza del destino* (1862, revised in 1865). He also supplied the libretto for the Ricci brothers' *Crispino e la comare* (1850).

PICCINNI, NICCOLÒ
(Bari 1728–Passy, Paris 1800)
Italian composer. He made his debut as an opera composer with *Le donne dispettose* (1754) in Naples and quickly became well-known. He then moved to Rome where, in 1760, his opera *Cecchina, ossia la buona figliola* was produced, scoring a sensational success which led to performances throughout Europe. He moved to Paris in 1776, where he clashed with those who championed Gluck's French operas. The events of the French Revolution prompted Piccinni to return to Naples (1791), but he went back to Paris in 1798 where, despite all the recognition he had received, he died in poverty. As well as his masterpiece, *Cecchina* (better known as *La buona figliola*), Piccinni's prolific output of operas includes *L'Olimpiade* (1768), *Alessandro nelle Indie* (1758 and 1774), *I viaggiatori* (1775), *Roland* (1778), *Iphigénie en Tauride* (1781) and *Didon* (1783).

Above: The Italian composer Niccolò Piccini.

Left: The Italian composer Goffredo Petrassi.

PICK-HIERONIMI, MONICA

(Cologne 1948)

German soprano. She studied singing with Dietger Jacob and made her debut in 1975 at the Oberhausen Theater in Cologne in Nicolai's opera *Die lustigen Weiber von Windsor* (The Merry Wives of Windsor). She went on to join the resident companies at the Staatstheater am Gärtnerplatz in Munich (1977–78) and at the Nationaltheater in Mannheim (1978–88), where she sang roles from a wide-ranging repertoire including Mozart, Verdi, Wagner and Richard Strauss. Her international engagements have included Barcelona, Vienna and Paris. In 1992 she appeared for the first time at Carnegie Hall in New York, singing the role of Irene in Wagner's *Rienzi*.

PIDÒ, EVELINO

(Turin)

Italian conductor. He studied bassoon, piano and composition at the Conservatorio in Turin. He then specialized in conducting and went on to complete his training in Vienna with Karl Österreicher. In 1986 he conducted Puccini's *Madama Butterfly* in the controversial Ken Russell production at the Spoleto Festival, which immediately acknowledged him as one of the most accomplished opera conductors of the new generation. He won particular acclaim for his performances of the Rossini operas *Zelmira* (Teatro dell' Opera, Rome, 1989), *Ermione* (Teatro dell'Opera, Rome, 1991), *Guillaume Tell* (Teatro Filarmonico, Verona, 1992) and *Adina* (Teatro dell'Opera, Rome, 1992).

PIEROTTI, RAQUEL

(Montevideo 1950)

Uruguayan mezzo-soprano of Italian origin. She studied piano (from 1968) and singing (from 1971) at the Conservatory in Montevideo, making her debut in 1973 in Mozart's *Le nozze di Figaro*. She then moved to Spain, where her first appearance was as a soprano in Rossini's *Elisabetta, regina d'Inghilterra* (1980). She changed to mezzo-soprano, establishing her reputation with performances at La Scala, Milan (*Le nozze di Figaro*, 1980), and at a number of other international opera houses. Pierotti is known as an elegant stylist and a particularly distinguished singer of Handel (*Giulio Cesare*), Mozart (*Così fan tutte*), Donizetti (*Maria Stuarda*) and above all Rossini (*Il barbiere di Siviglia* and *La Cenerentola*).

PIETRA DEL PARAGONE, LA

(The Touchstone)

Opera in two acts by Gioachino Rossini (1792–1868), to a libretto by Luigi Romanelli. First performance: Milan, La Scala, 26 September 1812.

The action takes place in the luxurious house of Count Asdrubale (bass), where a group of his friends have gathered. They include the Marchesa Clarice (contralto), who is secretly in love with Asdrubale; the poet Pacuvio (*buffo*); the journalist Macrobio (*buffo*); Aspasia (soprano) and Fulvia (mezzo-soprano), both of whom entertain aspirations towards the Count and his wealth; and Giocondo (tenor). Assisted by his servant Fabrizio (bass), who is disguised as a Turk, Asdrubale decides to test the sincerity of these friends of his. So he announces despairingly that a foreign creditor is demanding a promissory note from him in respect of a huge sum of money which he does not possess. His guests' reaction is to protect their own interests, saying they are unwilling to get involved in his affairs. Only Clarice and Giocondo are prepared to help their friend out of trouble. But then enter Fabrizio: he has a plan which will happily solve the problem. Shortly afterwards, Clarice puts on a "performance" of her own, in which she pretends to receive a letter from her twin brother, Lucindo, announcing that he is due to arrive soon. Lucindo then appears (it is actually Clarice dressed up) in officer's uniform and declares that he has come to take his sister away with him. At this point Asdrubale shows his feelings and asks Lucindo for permission to marry Clarice, whereupon Clarice reveals her true identity, everything is made clear, and the opera ends with the wedding of Clarice and Asdrubale, while Fulvia and Aspasia console themselves by marrying Macrobio and Pacuvio.

It was with *La pietra del paragone* that Rossini, not yet 21, made his debut at La Scala, Milan. The opera was a triumphant success, one of the most convincing of his entire ca-

Above: The Italian conductor Evelino Pidò.

Right: A scene from Tchaikovsky's *The Queen of Spades.*

reer as a composer – after its first performance, it had an unbroken run of 50 nights. Although this work was one of Rossini's most successful *buffo* operas, nowadays it is rarely staged.

PIKOVAYA DAMA

(The Queen of Spades)

Opera in three acts and seven scenes by Peter Ilyich Tchaikovsky (1840–1893), to a libretto by his brother Modest Ilyich, based on the story by Pushkin. First performance: St. Petersburg, Maryinsky Theater, 19 December 1890.

The action takes place in St. Petersburg around the year 1800. In a public garden, a young officer, Herman (tenor), confesses to his friend Count Tomsky (baritone) that he is in love with a young woman whose name he does not know. He subsequently discovers – as other characters arrive – that her name is Lisa (soprano) and she is the grand-daughter of an old Countess and engaged to Prince Yeletsky (baritone). Tomsky tells Herman that the Countess (contralto), a compulsive card-player whose nickname is 'The Queen of Spades,' is said to hold the secret to a combination of three cards which will never fail to win, but whoever succeeds in discovering this secret will also be the cause of her death. That same night, Herman manages to gain entry to Lisa's bedroom and declares his love for her. Their conversation is interrupted by the arrival of the Countess, and Lisa has to conceal Herman's presence. The old lady eventually goes out, and Lisa, sad at having to marry a man she does not love, falls into Herman's arms. The scene changes to a magnificent masked ball, at which Prince Yeletsky unsuccessfully tries to win Lisa's heart, while Lisa secretly hands Herman the key to her house and arranges to meet him that night. Herman enters the house but is by now obsessed with the secret of the three cards and cannot resist the temptation to await the arrival of the Countess. She comes in, tired after the ball, gets ready for bed, and falls asleep in an armchair. Herman goes up to her and insists on knowing the secret. The Countess is stricken with shock at seeing this intruder and dies. Enter Lisa, who orders Herman out of the house, accusing him of having wanted not her love but only the Countess's secret. The ghost of the Countess appears to Herman in his room in the garrison and tells him the winning combination: three, seven, ace. On the banks of the river Neva, Herman meets Lisa, but he is in a state of dreamy excitement and can think of nothing but the next card game. After he rushes away, she becomes desperate, throws herself into the Neva and drowns. At the gaming-table Herman is winning after successfully bidding on the three and the seven, but instead of the Ace the Queen of Spades is played. The card then changes into the ghost of the Countess, and Herman, now completely out of his mind, takes his own life.

In this opera Tchaikovsky immersed himself in the atmosphere of the story and the personalities of his characters, concentrating particularly on the psychological development of Herman. The powerfully dramatic elements in Tchaikovsky's score, which may be seen as unique in his oeuvre, led to this opera being given an enthusiastic reception at its premiere. Together with *Eugene Onegin*, it is the most frequently staged of Tchaikovsky's operas.

PILOU, JEANNETTE

(Alexandria 1931)

Stage name of Joanna Pilós, Greek soprano naturalized Italian. She studied music in Italy and made her debut in 1958 in *La traviata* at the Teatro Smeraldo in Milan. She went on to receive considerable acclaim at the Vienna Staatsoper, the Metropolitan Opera in New York (1967–72), La Scala and Covent Garden (Mozart's *Le nozze di Figaro*). Her agreeable lyric soprano and striking stage presence helped her to build a particular reputation as Violetta (Verdi's *La traviata*), Mimi (Puccini's *La bohème*), Juliette (Gounod's *Roméo et Juliette*) and Mélisande (Debussy's *Pelléas et Mélisande*).

PIRATA, IL

Opera in two acts by Vincenzo Bellini (1801–1835), to a libretto by Felice Romani. First performance: Milan, La Scala, 27 October 1827.

The action takes place in Sicily during the thirteenth century. A violent storm at sea has led to the wrecking of a pirate ship, captained by Gualtiero (tenor), on the coast near the castle of Caldora. Having survived the fury of the ocean, the shipwrecked pirates are graciously welcomed by Imogene (soprano), wife of Ernesto, Duke of Caldora (baritone) and a particularly bitter enemy of Gualtiero. Once inside the castle, Gualtiero reveals his identity to Imogene, who had once been betrothed to him. He reproaches her for betraying his love and marrying Ernesto, the very man who had forced him into exile. In despair, Imogene explains to Gualtiero that she had had to demur before Ernesto's acts of violence and blackmail. Gualtiero's presence at the castle causes deep feelings of turmoil in Imogene, arousing the Duke's suspicions. Then he discovers his rival in his wife's apartments and challenges him to a duel. They fight, Ernesto is killed, and Gualtiero, condemned to death, mounts the scaffold while Imogene is left crazed by grief.

The first performance of *Il pirata* at La Scala was a triumph, its success at least partly due to the presence in the cast of two of the greatest singers of the time, the soprano Henriette Méric-Lalande and the tenor Giovanni Battista Rubini, for whom Bellini created the difficult role of Gualtiero. Although drama is more prevalent than lyricism in *Il pirata*, passages like Imogene's mad scene nonetheless anticipate Bellini's later, supremely lyrical achievement in *Norma*.

PIZZETTI, ILDEBRANDO

(Parma 1880–Rome 1968)

Italian composer. He studied in Parma with

A sketch by Sanquirico for Bellini's *Il pirata*.

Tebaldini and showed an enthusiastic interest in theater early on. His meeting with the Italian poet Gabriele D'Annunzio in 1905 provided the impetus for his most important composition for the theater, the incidental music to *La nave* (1908). D'Annunzio also provided the subject for his first opera, *Fedra* (1915). After this, Pizzetti was to write his own libretti for operas such as *Dèbora e Jaéle* (1922), *Fra Gherardo* (1928), *Lo straniero* (1930), *Orsèolo* (1935), *La figlia di Jorio* (after D'Annunzio, 1954), *Assassinio nella cattedrale* (after T. S. Eliot, 1958) and *Clitennestra* (1965), operas that represent a key chapter in the history of Italian opera even if more recently they have been seldom staged.

PLASSON, MICHEL
(Paris 1933)
French conductor. He studied piano, percussion and conducting at the Paris Conservatoire. In 1962 he won first prize in the Besançon International Competition and consequently went to the United States to complete his training with Erich Leinsdorf, Pierre Monteux and Leopold Stokowski. He was principal conductor at the opera house in Metz (1965–68), then permanent conductor at the Théâtre du Capitole in Toulouse (from 1968) where he was also general music director (1973–82). Plasson's reputation also rests on appearances at leading French and international opera houses and numerous recordings, mainly of French repertoire, including Massenet's *Werther*, Gounod's *Faust* and several Offenbach operettas.

PLATÉE
Opéra-ballet *in a prologue and three acts by Jean-Philippe Rameau (1683–1764), to a libretto by Jacques Autreau and Adrien Joseph Le Valois d'Orville. First performance: Versailles, 31 March 1745.*

The prologue depicts the birth of Comedy. In a vineyard in Greece, Thespis (tenor), inspired by satyrs and maenads and assisted by Thalie (soprano), Momus (baritone) and Amour (soprano), proposes to create a special type of performance with the aim of correcting the defects in the human race and at the same time showing how absurd the gods are. The plot chosen is the stratagem once used by Jupiter (bass) to cure Junon (soprano) of jealousy. Here the play begins. In order to confuse Junon, Jupiter, with the help of King Cithéron and Mercure, pretends to be in love with Platée (tenor), a vain and ridiculous nymph. Then he appears to her and declares his tender feelings for her. Junon is furious and watches, unseen, Jupiter's courting of Platée. Next comes the wedding ceremony itself: satyrs, maenads and country-folk, led by La Folie (soprano), join in the procession, at the front of which is a coach, drawn by two frogs, bearing Platée, her face hidden by a veil. Just as Jupiter is about to take his wedding vow, Junon arrives in a rage, hurls herself at Platée, tears off the veil and starts to laugh. Jupiter and Junon are reunited and return to heaven while Platée returns to her pool.

The text and music of *Platée* make it unique among the operas of the eighteenth century. The libretto by the ingenious Autreau was later revised, transforming the opera into a true *comédie-ballet*.

PLISHKA, PAUL
(Old Forge, Pennsylvania 1941)
American bass. He studied singing in New Jersey and began his career with the opera company in Paterson, New Jersey (1961–66). He then moved on to the Metropolitan Opera in New York (1967), where he appeared regularly, drawing on an extensive repertoire which included the principal bass roles of Italian opera (Filippo II, Oroveso) as well as Russian opera (Boris, Varlaam). Plishka's reputation also rests on his performances at numerous international opera houses and on his many recordings, featuring him in distinguished performances as Oroveso (Bellini's *Norma*), Giorgio Valton (Bellini's *I puritani*), Enrico VIII (Donizetti's *Anna Bolena*), Méphistophélès (Gounod's *Faust*) and the Padre Guardiano (Verdi's *La forza del destino*).

PLOWRIGHT, ROSALIND
(Worksop, Nottinghamshire 1949)
British soprano. She studied at the Royal College of Music in Manchester and at the London Opera Center and made her debut with the English National Opera in 1975. After winning first prize at the International Singing Competition in Sofia (1979), she began her international career with the opera company in Bern (1980–81) and went on to appear at numerous other opera venues, including the Torre del Lago Festival (Puccini's *Manon Lescaut*), La Scala (from 1983, with Puccini's *Suor Angelica*), Covent Garden (*Andrea Chénier* and *Otello*, 1984) and the Arena in Verona (*Il trovatore*, 1985). Plowright's reputation rests on her remarkable vocal gift, as demonstrated in particular

Above: The British soprano Rosalind Plowright.

Right: A scene from *Poliuto* by Gaetano Donizetti.

by her interpretations of Verdi, such as her outstanding Elisabetta in *Don Carlos* at the Coliseum in London in 1992.

POLIUTO

Opera seria *in three acts by Gaetano Donizetti (1797–1848), to a libretto by Salvatore Cammarano, after Corneille's tragedy* Polyeucte. *First performance (posthumous): Naples, Teatro San Carlo, 30 November 1848.*

The action takes place in Mytilene, Armenia, during the third century A.D. The Roman magistrate Poliuto (tenor) has secretly converted to Christianity, and his wife Paolina (soprano), having discovered this, fears for his life. The latest edict has ruled that all Christians be put to death. The arrival of the new proconsul, Severo (baritone), in Mytilene is deeply worrying to Paolina: she had been betrothed to Severo but had subsequently come to believe he had died in battle, so she had married Poliuto. His wife's state of mind arouses Poliuto's suspicions, and he doubts she is being faithful to him. Paolina has a clandestine meeting with Severo, in which she tells him that there can never again be anything between them. Their conversation is overheard by Poliuto, who is now convinced his wife is betraying him. Then Nearco (tenor), leader of the Christians in Armenia and arrested on orders from Severo, refuses to reveal the name of the latest Christian convert to be baptized. This is none other than Poliuto, who promptly announces publicly that he has embraced the Christian faith and turns on Paolina in a fury, disowning her as his wife. The scene changes to the prison where Poliuto has been confined. Paolina comes to see her husband and swears she has never betrayed him. Reunited with his wife, Poliuto can now die at peace. Paolina pleads with him to save himself by renouncing Christianity, but when she sees how resolute he is and experiences the presence of God's grace for herself, she declares herself ready to face martyrdom at her husband's side. Severo tries in vain to rescue Paolina, but she clings to Poliuto, and together they go off to meet their destiny in the arena.

The censor found the plot of *Poliuto* "too sacred," and as a result the first performance, scheduled for Naples in 1838, had to be cancelled. In Paris, Donizetti worked with Eugène Scribe on a French version, entitled *Les martyrs*, staged at the Opéra in Paris on 10 April 1840. It was only after the composer's death that the original *Poliuto* was finally performed, at the Teatro San Carlo, where it had been due to be premiered ten years earlier. It was revived with great success at La Scala in 1960 with Maria Callas, Franco Corelli and Ettore Bastianini in the cast. The same story exists in another version, in French, with a libretto by Barbier and Carré, set to music by Gounod as *Polyeucte* and premiered in 1878.

Above: The Italian composer Amilcare Ponchielli.

PONCHIELLI, AMILCARE

(Paderno, Cremona 1834–Milan 1886)

Italian composer. He was encouraged to study music by his father and attended the Conservatorio in Milan (1843–54). After graduating, he embarked on a career in music as an organist in Cremona, scene of the premiere in 1856 of his first opera, *I promessi sposi*, which was staged again, in a revised version, in 1872. Two further Ponchielli operas also received first performances in Cremona, *La Savoiarda* in 1861 (this too was later revised and the new version produced in Milan in 1877) and *Roderico, re dei Goti* (1863). The staging in Milan of the new version of *I promessi sposi*, in which the lead role was sung by the soprano Teresa Brambilla (who later became the composer's wife), demonstrated Ponchielli's gift for theater. It was to a commission from the music publisher Ricordi that he went on to write *I Lituani* (1874), then *La Gioconda* (1876), the opera which was to bring him fame. Ponchielli taught composition at the Conservatorio in Milan from 1883 to 1886, and his pupils included Puccini and Mascagni. After *Il figliuol prodigo* (1880) came *Marion Delorme* (1885), unfavourably received by audiences. This response plunged him into a deep depression, from which he was unable to recover, and he died of pneumonia a year later.

PONS, JUAN

(Ciutadella, Minorca 1946)

Spanish baritone. He studied in Barcelona, where he made his debut as a tenor. Advised by the tenor Richard Tucker to resume his study of singing, he discovered that his true voice was a baritone. He won the acclaim of international audiences and critics in 1980 as Falstaff in Verdi's opera, a role which he went on to sing on numerous occasions at leading international opera houses. This launched Pons on a busy career, which took him to the Metropolitan Opera in New York (Verdi's *Il trovatore*, 1983) and the Opéra in Paris (*Falstaff* and Leoncavallo's *I pagliacci*, 1982). His voice has a fine timbre and is soft, supple and wide-ranging. He is an excellent performer of Verdi and Puccini, as illustrated by his more recent successes at La Scala (where he sings regularly) in Puccini's *La fanciulla del West* and Verdi's *La traviata* (1991).

POPP, LUCIA

(Uhorská, Ves 1939)

Austrian soprano of Slovak origin. In 1963 she made her debut with Bratislava Opera as the Queen of the Night in Mozart's *Die Zauberflöte* (The Magic Flute). In the same year she moved to Vienna, where she completed her training and then appeared at the Theater an der Wien as Barbarina in Mozart's *Le nozze di Figaro*, at the Staatsoper (as the Queen of the Night) and at the Salzburg Festival (as one of the three Genii in *Die Zauberflöte*). Her international appearances included engagements at Covent Garden (Oscar in Verdi's *Un ballo in maschera*, 1966), the Metropolitan Opera in New York (as the Queen of the Night, 1967) and at numerous other opera houses. She has also been active as a concert artiste. Popp's shining timbre, expressiveness and stage presence initially earned her a reputation as an exquisite Mozart singer, although she went on to distinguish herself in the roles of Sophie (Richard Strauss's *Der Rosenkavalier*) and Marzelline (Beethoven's *Fidelio*). In more recent years Popp tackled more markedly lyrical Wagner and Strauss roles, such as Elsa, Elisabeth (*Lohengrin* and *Tannhäuser*), the Marschallin (*Der Rosenkavalier*), Arabella and the Countess (*Capriccio*).

PORGY AND BESS

Opera in three acts by George Gershwin (1898–1937), to a libretto by Du Bose Heyward and Ira Gershwin, after Heyward's novel Porgy. *First performance: Boston, Colonial Theater, 30 September 1935.*

The action takes place in Catfish Row, the black district of Charleston, South Carolina. An argument breaks out, during which Crown (bass), a strong and violent stevedore, kills his friend Robbins and has to flee. Bess (soprano), Robbins's girlfriend, is left alone and turns for protection to the lame beggar Porgy (baritone), who had always been in love with her. Some time later, Bess is living happily with Porgy when Crown reappears and puts pressure on Bess to go away with him. But it is not long before Bess, ill and frightened, returns to Porgy. He welcomes her back, looks after her and promises to protect her. When Crown appears again, Porgy strangles him. He is arrested and stays in prison for several days before being released through lack of evidence. During his absence, Bess has been on her own. Sporting Life (tenor), a small-time drug pusher, takes advantage of her situation and persuades her to come with him to New York. When Porgy returns home from prison and finds Bess is no longer there, he sets out to follow her and bring her back.

The early performances of *Porgy and Bess* were given a mixed response, but later on the opera was received with great enthusiasm, both in the United States and other countries, including Russia, where it was staged in 1955. *Porgy and Bess* is scored for black singers and makes dramatic use of popular musical idioms, including spirituals. As a result, it departs from European models of opera and is justifiably regarded as the American opera *par excellence*.

POSTILLON DE LONGJUMEAU, LE

(The Coachman of Longjumeau)

Opéra-comique *in three acts by Adolphe-Charles Adam (1803–1856), to a libretto by Adolphe de Leuven and Léon Lévy Brunswick. First performance: Paris, Théâtre de l'Opéra-Comique, 13 October 1836.*

The Marquis de Corcy (baritone), director of the royal opera house, has to make an unscheduled stop in the village of Longjumeau, where he is deeply impressed by the singing voice of a coachman, Chapelou (tenor), and persuades the young man to accompany him to Paris. Madeleine (soprano), Chapelou's young wife, now abandoned by her husband on what was their wedding day, wants revenge for this. A large inheritance enables her to transform herself into wealthy Madame Latour. Time passes, and Chapelou, who has become famous and now goes by the stage name of Saint-Phar, arrives with his opera company at Madame Latour's château. The tenor does not recognize his wife and pays court to her. She plays along with this, even going so far as to win a proposal of marriage from him. Their wedding duly takes place, but then the Marquis, who had himself been planning to marry Madame Latour, discovers that Saint-Phar is not the widower he had claimed to be and denounces him as a bigamist. At the end, however, everything becomes clear, Madame Latour reveals her true identity and is reunited with her husband.

Le postillon de Longjumeau is seen as Adam's operatic masterpiece and brought him international fame. The decline in popularity of the *opéra-comique*, however, meant that it disappeared from the repertoire, together with Adam's other operas, and nowadays it is performed only rarely.

POULENARD, ISABEL

(Paris 1961)

French soprano. She studied music at the Maitrise de Radio France and at the École d'Art Lyrique of the Opéra in Paris (1979–81). She was engaged by Early Music conductor Jean-Claude Malgoire and made her debut in a number of productions with the

Above: A costume model for *Le postillon de Longjumeau* by Adolphe-Charles Adam.

Right: A scene from *Porgy and Bess* by George Gershwin.

AMERICAN OPERA

Opera arrived in the United States in the eighteenth century in the form of the Ballad Opera and the most famous example of this genre, *The Beggar's Opera*, was staged in New York in 1750. "Travelling" companies also put on performances of Italian operas, but one of the first examples of an opera originating in the United States was *The Disappointment, or The Force of Credulity*, to a libretto by Andrew Barton (published in 1797), while the music, composed anonymously, was made up of popular tunes. Also in the eighteenth century we find operas like *The Temple of Minerva* (1781) composed by F. Hopkinson (although the music has since been lost) or *Tammany* (1794) by J. Hewitt, from which none of the music has survived either. The first American opera of which some of the musical items have come down to us is *The Archers* (1796) by the British composer B. Carr. For much of the eighteenth century British composers played an active role in the United States. The French also exercised their influence – V. Pelissier, for instance, wrote an opera called *Edwin and Angelina* (1796) – as did the Italians (P.A. Corri adopted the pseudonym Arthur Clifton and composed the opera *Enterprise* in 1822). The first opera to be written by an American composer is thought to have been *The Saw Mill, or a Yankee Trick* (1824) by M. Hawkins. Even in the nineteenth century, American opera continued to be obviously influenced by that of Europe, and especially of Italy, staged by famous names like M. Carcin Jr. who, in 1825, brought operas by Rossini to New York, and Lorenzo Da Ponte who moved to the United States in 1806 and put on *L'ape musicale*, a pastiche of music by various composers (New York, 1830). Composers in whose music there is clear evidence that they have been influenced by Italian opera include W.H. Fry and his opera *Leonora* (1845). The musical form which was typically American was the musical comedy, associated with names like Richard Rodgers, who wrote *Oklahoma!, South Pacific and The King and I*, Frederick Loewe, with his *My Fair Lady*, and Jerome Kern with the celebrated *Show Boat*. The American opera *par excellence* is *Porgy and Bess* (1935) by George Gershwin, while during the 1930s new generations of composers came to the fore who brought about a fresh and significant development in music theater, among them Marc Blitsztein (*The Cradle Will Rock*, 1937; *Regina*, 1948); V. Thomson (*Four Saints in Three Acts*, 1934); Aaron Copland (*The Tender Land*, 1954); Deems Taylor (*The King's Henchman*, 1927) and Louis Gruenberg (*The Emperor Jones*, 1934).

Other prominent figures are Giancarlo Menotti, one of the most prolific and admired of composers; Douglas Moore (*The Devil and Daniel Webster*, 1939; *The Ballad of Baby Doe*, 1956; Lukas Foss (*The Jumping Frog of Calaveras County*, 1950); S. Barber (*Vanessa*, 1953; *Antony and Cleopatra*, 1966); C. Floyd (*Susannah*), 1955; Leonard Bernstein (*Trouble in Tahiti*, 1952; *Candide*, 1956; *A Quiet Place*, 1983). Outstanding among contemporary composers is Philip Glass, whose works include *Einstein on the Beach* (1976), *Akhnaten* (1984), and *The Voyage* (1991), staged at the Metropolitan Opera House in New York as part of the Columbus Quincentenary celebrations.

Top: A scene from *A Quiet Place* by Leonard Bernstein.

Left: A scene from Gershwin's *Porgy and Bess* in a 1955 production at La Scala.

Atelier Lyrique in Tourcoing, Northern France (1981–86). With the same conductor she took part in recordings of Rameau's *Le temple de la gloire* (1982) and Handel's *Tamerlano* (1984). she appeared with the Amsterdam Baroque Orchestra conducted by Ton Koopman (Queen of the Night in Mozart's *Die Zauberflöte*, The Magic Flute, 1982) and Sigiswald Kuijken (Handel's *Alessandro*, 1984). She has appeared in Nice in Vivaldi's *L'incoronazione di Dario* (1985), at the Opéra-Comique in Paris in Rameau's *Hippolyte et Aricie* (1986), at the Innsbruck Festival in Cesti's *Orontea* conducted by René Jacobs (1985–86) and at a number of other venues. She has also given many concerts, appearing as soloist in oratorios and cantatas.

POULENC, FRANCIS

(Paris 1899–1963)
Professional name of French composer, Jean Marcel Poulenc. He studied composition with Charles Koechlin and piano with Ricardo Viñes. He became a member of "Les Six" with Auric, Durey, Honegger, Taillefer and Milhaud and in 1921 made his debut as a composer for the theater with his incidental music for Cocteau and Radiguet's *Le gendarme incompris*. It was not until immediately after the Second World War, however, that Poulenc's operas, *Les mamelles de Tirésias* (1947), *Les dialogues des Carmélites* (1957) and *La voix humaine* (1959) began to arouse interest and since then they have come to be considered among the masterpieces of opera history.

PRATICÒ, BRUNO

(Aosta 1958)
Italian bass-baritone. He studied with the baritone Giuseppe Valdengo and went on to complete his training at La Scala and with Rodolfo Celletti. After winning the Riccardo Stracciari singing competition, he made his debut in 1982 as Dr Bartolo in Rossini's *Il barbiere di Siviglia* in Bologna. A year later, he established his reputation in the role of Mustafà in Rossini's *L'italiana in Algeri* with Claudio Abbado conducting. Praticò's indubitable gifts as a singer, coupled with outstanding stage technique, have led to his being acknowledged as one of the most accomplished performers of the *buffo* repertoire, from Cimarosa and Paisiello to Rossini and Donizetti, composers in whose operas he has appeared at many leading venues.

PRÊTRE, GEORGES

(Waziers, Douai, 1924)
French conductor. He initially studied music at the Conservatoire in Douai and then moved to Paris. In 1946 he made his debut by taking over as conductor for a performance of Lalo's *Le roi d'Ys* in Marseilles. During the years that followed, Prêtre conducted at a number of different opera houses in the French provinces, eventually coming to Paris in 1956 to conduct Richard Strauss's *Capriccio* at the Opéra-Comique. At the same theater he conducted the world premiere of Poulenc's *La voix humaine* in 1959, the year in which he appeared for the first time at the Opéra (Gounod's *Faust*), returning to conduct there regularly and becoming music director for the 1970–71 season. In the meantime his busy international career had also been developing: he conducted Massenet's *Thaïs* at Lyric Opera of Chicago (1959) as well as productions at Covent Garden (Puccini's *Tosca* with Maria Callas, 1961), the Metropolitan Opera (Saint-Saëns' *Samson et Dalila*) and La Scala, Milan (1964). Prêtre is an acclaimed interpreter of French and Italian repertoire (*Pelléas et Mélisande*, *Faust*, *Lucia di Lammermoor*, *Don Carlos*, *La bohème*). His appearances as a conductor of opera became more infrequent, as he preferred to conduct more symphony concerts.

Top right: The French conductor Georges Prêtre.

Right: The Welsh soprano Margaret Berenice Price.

PREVITALI, FERNANDO

(Adria 1907–Rome 1985)
Italian conductor. He studied cello and composition at the Conservatorio in Turin. After his time as a cellist at the Teatro Regio in Turin, he was appointed assistant to Vittorio Gui at the Teatro Comunale in Florence. From there he went on to Genoa (1935–36) and then became music director of the Radio Italiana Orchestra, which he was to conduct more or less continuously until 1972. Previtali appeared at leading opera houses in Italy and the United States (including *Anna Bolena* in Dallas, with Renata Scotto). One of the greatest opera conductors, he is particularly remembered for his interpretations of Verdi.

PREY, HERMANN

(Berlin 1929)
German baritone. He studied at the Musikhochschule in Berlin with Günther Baum and Harry Gottschalk. After making his concert debut in 1951, he appeared for the first time in opera as a Prisoner in Beethoven's *Fidelio*. He was a member of the permanent company of the Hamburg Opera (1953–60) and at the same time embarked on an international career which included regular appearances at the Vienna Staatsoper (from 1956), the Städtische Oper in Berlin (from 1956), the Salzburg Festival in Richard Strauss's *Die schweigsame Frau* (1959), the Metropolitan Opera in New York in *Tannhäuser* (1960), the Bayreuth Festival (from 1965), Covent

Garden, and La Scala from 1973 (Rossini's *Il barbiere di Siviglia*) and at numerous other theater and concert venues. He is considered to be one of the greatest *Lieder* singers. An impeccable stylist gifted with a voice that has a fine timbre and is soft and resplendent in the upper register, Prey also owes his reputation to outstanding gifts as an actor, which enabled him to take on not only dramatic roles but also, and mainly, comic parts like Papageno in *Die Zauberflöte* (The Magic Flute) or Eisenstein in Johann Strauss's *Die Fledermaus*.

PRICE, JANET

(Abersychan, Pontypool 1938)
Welsh soprano. She specialized in the French repertoire with Nadia Boulanger in Paris and made her debut in 1971 in Rossini's *Le Comte Ory* with Welsh National Opera. In the years that followed, Price's fine vocal gifts, combined with supreme skill in *coloratura* singing, brought her acclaim in performances of a number of forgotten operas by Donizetti (*Maria Padilla*, *Elisabetta al castello di Kenilworth*, *Torquato Tasso*, etc.), Meyerbeer (*Il crociato in Egitto*, *L'étoile du nord*) and Offenbach (*Robinson Crusoe*), which she sang principally at the Camden Festival but also elsewhere.

PRICE, LEONTYNE

(Laurel, Mississippi 1927)
American soprano. She studied at the Juilliard School of Music in New York, graduating in 1952. After her concert debut in 1950, she appeared on stage for the first time in 1951 in Virgil Thomson's *Four Saints in Three Acts*. She sang this opera and Gershwin's *Porgy and Bess* in a number of European cities between 1952 and 1954. After a notable personal success in the American premiere of Poulenc's *Les dialogues des Carmélites* in San Francisco in 1957, she firmly established her reputation in the role of Aida in Verdi's opera. Again as Aida, she appeared at the leading international opera houses, including the Vienna Staatsoper (1958), Covent Garden (1958–59) and La Scala, Milan (1960). Further performances followed at the Salzburg Festival (Mozart's *Don Giovanni*, 1960) and at the Metropolitan Opera in New York, where she made her debut in 1961 in Verdi's *Il trovatore* and went on to appear in a number of Verdi and Puccini operas. She created the role of Cleopatra in Samuel Barber's *Antony and Cleopatra*, the inaugural production at the Lincoln Center, home of the Metropolitan Opera, in 1966. It was in this theater in 1985 that Price returned to the role of Aida for her farewell stage performance, although she went on giving concerts. On the strength of the beauty and richness of her timbre and the brilliance of her voice in the upper register, Price came to be acknowledged as the greatest Verdi soprano of her generation. She also gave notable performances in Puccini's *Tosca*, *Madama Butterfly* and *Il tabarro*.

The American soprano Leontyne Price.

PRICE, MARGARET BERENICE

(Tredegar 1941)
Welsh soprano. After studying at Trinity College of Music in London, she made her debut with Welsh National Opera as Cherubino in Mozart's *Le nozze di Figaro* (1962), the role in which she was to appear again in 1964 at Covent Garden when she took over from Teresa Berganza, establishing herself as one of the finest of Mozart singers. She went on to enjoy great success in Mozart operas at the Glyndebourne Festival (1966), San Francisco (1969), Cologne (1971), the Paris Opéra (1973) and La Scala, Milan (from 1976). Her lyric soprano voice, with its sonorous timbre, excellent delivery technique and expressiveness, have gradually enabled her to tackle more dramatic roles, including operas by Verdi, Cilèa and Richard Strauss.

PRIGIONIERO, IL

(The Prisoner)
Opera in a prologue and one act by Luigi Dallapiccola (1904–1975), to the composer's own libretto, inspired by one of the Contes cruels *by Villiers de l'Isle-Adam and Charles de Coster's* La légende d'Ulenspiegel et de Lamme Goedzac. *First (concert) performance: Italian Radio, 1 December 1949. First stage performance: Florence, Teatro Comunale, 20 May 1950.*

The action takes place around the year 1570 in Saragoza. In the prologue, the Mother (soprano) relates how each night she is tormented by the same dream, in which she is terrified by the ghost of Philip II coming towards her and then being transformed into an image of death. The scene changes to the Official's somber cell. The Prisoner (baritone) describes to his Mother the tortures he has undergone and how he regained hope and faith when the Gaoler (tenor) called him "brother." When the Mother has left, the Gaoler returns. Still referring to him as "brother," the Gaoler tells him that in Flanders a rebellion has broken out and, with increasing fervour, encourages him to hope. The Prisoner is deeply affected by this and, shortly afterwards, notices that the Gaoler, on his way out, has left the cell door open. The Prisoner staggers out of his cell and down a long corridor, frightened that he is going to be discovered. He passes a monk and two priests (tenor and baritone) discussing theology, and they seem not to be aware of him. The Prisoner comes out into a garden and here finds himself face to face with the Grand Inquisitor, whom he recognizes as the Gaoler and who then proceeds to reproach him gently with having wanted to escape his just deserts. The Prisoner realizes he has undergone the ultimate torture, the illusion of freedom. He allows himself to be led to the scaffold laughing like a madman and saying the word "Freedom" over and over again, almost to himself.

Dallapiccola began work on *Il prigioniero* in 1944, the year in which Florence was liberated from Nazi occupation, and he finished it at the beginning of 1948. The opera's historical setting is the liberation of Flanders, but in fact it is a tribute to the Resistance against all dictatorship. At its premiere in Florence, *Il prigioniero* was well received by the audience, but the rather negative response of the Italian critics led to enormous controversy, focused mainly on the ideological implications of the libretto. Outside Italy the opera was acknowledged as a masterpiece, and performances followed in many countries.

PRIHODY LIŠKY BYSTROUŠKY

(The Cunning Little Vixen)
Opera in three acts by Leóš Janáček

A scene from Janáček's *Prihody lišky bystroušky* (The Cunning Little Vixen), performed for the first time in Brno in 1924.

(1854–1928), to the composer's own libretto, based on the story Liška Bistruška *by Rudolf Tésnohlídek. First performance: Brno, National Theater, 6 November 1924.*

A Gamekeeper (baritone) catches a little Vixen (soprano) and takes it home, to the delight of his children. He tries to domesticate the animal, but to no avail. One night the creature escapes and heads back to the woods. The Gamekeeper makes futile attempts to recapture it, behaving for all the world like a lover resentful at having been abandoned, because to him the little Vixen has come to represent Térynka, "a wild and beautiful creature" whom he had loved in his youth but who has subsequently been courted, unsuccessfully, by the local Schoolmaster (tenor). When Térynka finally marries Harasta (baritone), a drifter living a free life like hers, Harasta kills the Vixen so that he can make Térynka a gift of its fur. But the Vixen's death takes on the same significance in the Gamekeeper's life as Térynka's having left him. The cycle seems to have reached its end, but when spring comes around again, the Gamekeeper, in the same clearing where he had caught the little Vixen, sees another vixen cub looking at him with eyes just like her mother's, transfixing him with exactly the same longing for life.

This is one of the most important operas by Janáček and indeed in twentieth-century Czech music.

PRITCHARD, SIR JOHN

(London 1921–Daly City, California 1989) British conductor. Born into a musical family, he initially had music lessons with his violinist father and then went on to study piano, viola and conducting in Italy. He made his debut as a conductor in 1943 with the Derby String Orchestra, which he continued to conduct until 1947. This was the year in which he took up an appointment as répétiteur at Glyndebourne, where he subsequently became chorus-master and assistant to Fritz Busch. In 1949 Busch's sudden indisposition meant that Pritchard was called upon to take his place in the Festival. He conducted regularly at Glyndebourne from 1951 onwards, including the British premiere of Henze's *Elegy for Young Lovers*. He conducted, at Covent Garden, the first performances of Britten's *Gloriana* (1953), and Tippett's *The Midsummer Marriage* (1955) and *King Priam* (1962). Pritchard made many appearances at leading international opera venues, among them the Edinburgh Festival (from 1951), the Vienna Staatsoper (from 1952) and Aix-en-Provence. From 1985 he was music director of San Francisco Opera.

PRINCE IGOR

See *Knyaz Igor*

PRODANA NEVĚSTA

(The Bartered Bride)

Opera in three acts (the first version being in two acts) by Bedřich Smetana (1824–1884), to a libretto by Karel Sabina. First performance: Prague, Provisional Theater, 30 May 1866.

The action takes place in a Czech village. Kecal (bass), a local marriage-broker, is offering the parents of the beautiful Mařenka (soprano) a prize candidate for their daughter's hand. He is Vašek (tenor), younger son of the wealthy Tobias Micha (bass). Mařenka promptly turns him down, admitting she is already attached to Jeník (tenor), a poor young man from an obscure background from whom she will never part. But Kecal has every intention of pressing on with his marriage plan, so he suggests to Jeník that he give up his beloved Mařenka in exchange for a large sum of money which happens to be on offer because the prospective replacement bridegroom is wealthy Micha's son. Jeník readily agrees to this. When Mařenka learns that she has been bartered by her dearest Jeník, she is so enraged that she decides to behave in accordance with her parents' wishes and marry Vašek. However, Vašek has come to the conclusion that Mařenka is disloyal, and he refuses to sign the marriage contract, not least because he has fallen in love with Esmeralda (soprano), a dancer with a company of acrobats. At the end everything turns out for the best: Jeník goes to see Tobias Micha and his wife Háta (mezzo-soprano), who are astonished when they recognize him as Micha's son from his first marriage. Jeník produces the contract, signed by Kecal, which shows that Mařenka has been sold to Micha's son and then walks off with her on his arm.

The composition of this opera occupied Smetana from 1863 to 1866, when it was first performed. But he continued to revise the score, and it was not until 1870 that he produced the final version in three acts, which was staged on 25 September of that year. Despite the fact that alterations and revisions had been made over a long period, the work retained its stylistic unity and became one of the most celebrated of Czech operas.

PROKOFIEV, SERGEI SERGEIEVICH

(Sontsovka, Ukraine 1891–Nikolina Gora, Moscow 1953)

Russian composer. His prodigious musical gifts were encouraged by his mother, as a result of which he had already begun to compose two operas by the age of nine. He went to Moscow, where he often visited Taneyev and Glière and became a student at the Conservatory in St. Petersburg. He quickly established a reputation as a pianist and composer and had his first success in the theater with the opera *Igrok* (The Gambler, 1915–17, revised in 1927–29). In 1918 he toured extensively in the United States, where his opera *Ljubov k tryom apelsinan* (The Love for Three Oranges) was produced in a French version in Chicago in 1921. Prokofiev then settled in Paris and continued with the composition of *Ognennyi Angel* (The Fiery Angel, 1919–27), which received its first stage performance posthumously in Venice in 1955. The first opera he wrote after his return to the Soviet Union in 1933 was *Semyon Kotko* (1939–40). This was followed by *Obrucheniye v monastïre* (Betrothal in a Monastery) which he composed in 1940–41 and was premiered in 1946. The great tapestry of *Voina i mir* (War and Peace, 1941–52) was Prokofiev's most ambitious operatic undertaking. His final opera, *Povest'o nastoyashchem/cheloveke* (The Story of a Real

Man) was composed in 1948 but not given a first performance until 1960. Based on the ideological precepts of Socialist Realism, it is not a particularly remarkable work.

PROMETEO

Opera by Luigi Nono (1924–1990), to texts compiled by Massimo Cacciari. First performance (first version): Venice, the Church of San Lorenzo, 25 September 1984. Final version: Milan, on factory premises belonging to Ansaldo, 25 September 1985.

Verso Prometeo, Tragedia dell'ascolto (Towards Prometheus, A Tragedy of Listening) is the complete title of this work by Nono, for which the composer and philosopher Massimo Cacciari evolved a text described as "musical-philosophical, on the subject of listening, of attention to listening, a text capable of breaking the idolatrous chains forged by images, narration, and passage after passage made up of words and mere talk." It is a challenging work that dispenses with any visual setting, which might connect the sound to a visual correlative, and replaces it with a real acoustic structure. The performance and audience space, designed by the architect Renzo Piano in the shape of a ship's keel, acts as a large container of sounds which in the Milan version of *Prometeo* gave even greater prominence to Nono's later experiments with the orchestra and a formidable battery of electronic apparatus. The texts, which range from Aeschylus to Hölderlin and Rilke, retain a value of their own, into which sounds are fed and superimposed on one another in an elaborate interweaving of polyphony.

PROPHÈTE, LE

(The Prophet)

Opera in five acts by Giacomo Meyerbeer (1791–1864), to a libretto by Eugène Scribe. First performance: Paris, Théâtre de l'Opéra, 16 April 1849.

The action takes place in Holland and Germany during the revolt of the Anabaptists. Jean de Leyde (tenor) and Berthe (soprano) ask the Count d'Oberthal (bass) to allow them to marry. But the Count will not do so, because he is in love with Berthe. This abuse of position by the Count comes to the attention of the Anabaptists, who then invite Jean to join them and prophesy that he will be crowned. Berthe attempts to reach her fiancé, but the Count forces her to return to his castle, threatening that otherwise Fidès (mezzo-soprano), mother of Jean (who has become the Anabaptists' prophet), will be condemned to death. The Anabaptists, led by Jean, conquer the Count's castle, and Berthe and Fidès both manage to escape. Under the impression that her son is dead, Fidès curses the Anabaptists, while Berthe vows to kill their prophet. Meanwhile, Jean, under siege in a castle at Munster, has been

Above: The Russian composer Sergei Prokofiev.

Left: A scene from *Prometeo* by Luigi Nono, performed in the final version for the first time in Milan in 1985.

IL PROFETA

OPERA IN CINQUE ATTI

Parole di Eugenio Scribe, recate in italiano da F. M. di Santo-Mango

MUSICA DI

GIACOMO MEYERBEER

Riduzione per Canto con accompagnamento di Pianoforte di A. Garaudé

Opera completa Fr. 50

Proprietà dell' Editore che si riserva il diritto della stampa di tutte le riduzioni, traduzioni e composizioni sopra quest' Opera. — Reg. all' Arch. dell' Unione.

MILANO

I. R. Stabilimento Naz.e Privileg.e

DI CALCOGRAFIA, COPISTERIA E TIPOGRAFIA MUSICALI DI

GIOVANNI RICORDI

Contrada degli Omenoni N. 1720 e sotto il portico a fianco dell' I. R. Teatro alla Scala.

FIRENZE, Ricordi e Jouhaud. — MENDRISIO, C. Pozzi. — PARIGI, Brandus e C. — LONDRA, Cramer e C.i — LIPSIA, Breitkopf e Härtel.

BIBLIOTECA DEL R. CONSERVATORIO DI MUSICA MILANO

betrayed by his own followers. Berthe arrives on her mission of murder, but when she learns that Jean is the prophet, she takes her own life. Rather than surrender, Jean sets fire to the stores of gunpowder and blows up the castle, killing himself and Fidès, who had forgiven both him and the enemies who had come to capture him.

Le prophète, based on a real-life episode during the revolt of the Anabaptists, is one of Meyerbeer's most successful compositions for the theater. The choral scenes are impressive, as is the orchestral writing (the ballets in Act III and the Coronation March in Act IV), while the roles of Jean and Fidès are among the finest Meyerbeer created.

PROSPERINA Y EL EXTRANJERO

(Prosperina and the Stranger)

Opera in three acts by Juan José Castro (1895–1968), to a libretto by Omar del Carlo. First performance: Milan, La Scala, 13 March 1952.

The setting is a quarter of ill repute in Buenos Aires. Prosperina has just been brutally treated for the umpteenth time by Porfirio Sosa, the lover who has brought her here, taking her from her mother who lives on a farm in the pampa. Porfirio has been arrested for this and all his other unsettled accounts with the law. Marcial Quiroga, a sinister local character, has designs on Prosperina, who is now alone: he would not mind having her as his mistress, and she could earn money for him too. But his plans are foiled by the arrival of a stranger who takes lodgings in the same house. The stranger intervenes to protect Prosperina, and she is able to leave with her mother, who comes to take her home again to the pampa. Her mother wants to find a respectable husband for her, but Prosperina is obsessed by the memory of the stranger. She runs away to Buenos Aires again and flings herself into his arms. Suddenly the stranger, mindful of something, pushes her away as the shade of the dead wife appears. He comes from a distant world that nobody knows. He has suffered greatly, perhaps too much. Porfirio returns from prison, thirsting for revenge, having been told by Marcial of Prosperina's love affair. Porfirio and Marcial kill the stranger. Prosperina gathers up the stranger's few belongings and goes away, while Porfirio tries in vain to make her stay.

In 1952 *Prosperina and the Stranger* won the prize offered by La Scala, Milan, to mark the 50th anniversary of the death of Giuseppe Verdi.

PUCCINI, GIACOMO

(Lucca 1858–Brussels 1924)

Italian composer. He was born into a musical family who saw to it that he entered the world of music at a very early age, initially as a chorister and then as an organist. He studied music in Lucca and at the Conservatorio in Milan (1880–83). After graduating in composition (1883) he entered a one-act opera competition run by *Il teatro illustrato*, the in-house journal of the music publishers Sonzogno. Puccini's winning entry, *Le Villi* (1884), brought the young composer his first taste of fame as well as arousing the interest of the music publisher Ricordi. Although his second opera, *Edgar* (1889), was not a success, encouragement from Ricordi prompted Puccini to continue writing operas, and in 1893 came *Manon Lescaut*, his first masterpiece. In *La bohème* (1896), Puccini's compositional style was clearly at its height, while *Tosca* (1900) revealed his capacity for translating the dramatic intensity of a story into music and for powerful characterization in the three leading roles of Tosca, Cavaradossi and Scarpia. *Madama Butterfly* (1904) was a large-scale composition in which Puccini was exploring how to devise an exotic setting. This kind of experiment is yet more in evidence in *La fanciulla del West* (1910), notable for the modernity of Puccini's musical language, and in the unfinished *Turandot* (1926). After as fragile a work as *La rondine* (1917), which gave rise to a great deal of controversy (more recently, it has been revalued), Puccini worked between 1914 and 1918 on his *Trittico*, a triptych of one-act operas, *Il tabarro*, *Suor Angelica* and *Gianni Schicchi*, which illustrate his consid-

Above: Title page of *Le prophète* by Giacomo Meyerbeer.

Right: The Italian composer Giacomo Puccini.

erable skill in creating characters of dramatic and psychological depth.

PURCELL, HENRY

(London 1659–Westminster, London 1695) English composer. His father and uncle were both well-known musicians and members of the Chapel Royal, and it was in this atmosphere that the young Purcell grew up. The increasing success of his career led to his appointment in 1685 as Court harpsichordist alongside John Blow, composer to the Chapel Royal. Purcell's prestige was at its height during the reign of William III, especially as a composer for the theater. To this period belong his masterpiece *Dido and Aeneas* (1689), in which Purcell achieves a high degree of tragic expressiveness, and also his notable *ambigues* or ''semi-operas'' *King Arthur* (1691), *The Fairy Queen* (1692) and *The Indian Queen* (1695). The considerable amount of incidental music he wrote for some of Shakespeare's plays serves to illustrate his remarkable feeling for the theater.

PURITANI, I

Opera in three parts by Vincenzo Bellini (1801–1835), to a libretto by Carlo Pepoli, after the play Les têtes rondes et les cavaliers *by Jacques d'Ancelot. First performance: Paris, Théâtre Italien, 24 January 1835.*

The action takes place in England during the seventeenth century. Colonel Sir Riccardo Forth (baritone) tells Sir Bruno Robertson (tenor) of his sadness: he wants to marry his beloved Elvira (soprano), daughter of the governor of the fortress, Lord Walton (bass), but his proposal has been rejected because the intention is that she should marry Lord Arturo Talbo (tenor), a Cavalier and supporter of the Stuarts. The scene changes to the great *salle d'armes*. Arturo enters and declares his love to Elvira. Lord Walton gives Arturo a permit which will enable him to leave the occupied fortress and entrusts his daughter to Arturo's care, adding that he will not be able to come to their wedding himself, as he has to attend the trial of a woman prisoner accused of being a Stuart spy. Walton leaves, and Arturo, now alone with this unknown woman, discovers that she is actually Queen Enrichetta (mezzo-soprano), widow of the French King Charles I. Arturo does not hesitate: he will help her to flee. He gives her Elvira's wedding veil to wear and uses the permit to get her clear of the fortress. On their way out, the two meet Riccardo, who lets them pass though he is aware that he is damaging his own interests by allowing a prisoner to escape. Elvira takes leave of her senses when she learns that Arturo has left with another woman, and the Puritans set out in pursuit of both fugitives. Act II opens in the Walton fortress, where Sir Giorgio Walton (bass), Elvira's uncle, tells the assembled gathering of Elvira's madness and expresses his sorrow at what has happened to her. Arturo has been condemned to death in absentia, but Sir Giorgio, who has guessed at the part played by Riccardo in the escape of Arturo and Enrichetta, tries to persuade him, for Elvira's sake, not to carry out the death penalty on Arturo. Sir Giorgio and Riccardo then vow to fight and die together for the Puritan cause. Aware that the Puritans are still on his trail, Arturo looks about him as he draws near to the fortress. When she appears, he throws himself at her feet, explains why he has been away so long, and once again declares his love for her. Their conversation is interrupted by a drum-roll, which causes Elvira to panic. The Puritans burst on to the scene and capture Arturo. He is about to be executed when a messenger brings news of Cromwell's victory and announces that clemency has been granted to all Stuarts. As a result, Arturo can marry Elvira, and her anguish turns to joy.

I puritani is Bellini's last opera, the one to which he clearly devoted the most time and attention, with the prospect of its Paris premiere. His hard work was rewarded by a sensational success on the first night, but he was not able to enjoy the full fruits of this achievement, as he died in Puteaux only eight months later on 24 September 1835. *I puritani* went on to be performed throughout the world, especially in more recent years as a result of tenors like Aldo Bertolo, Salvatore Fisichella, William Matteuzzi, Rockwell Blake and Chris Merritt who have been able to master the dauntingly difficult role of Arturo, which Bellini composed for the legendary Giovanni Battista Rubini.

ELVIRA WALTON

Dramma Serio

IN TRE PARTI

DA RAPPRESENTARSI

NEL NOBILE

TEATRO DI APOLLO

Nel Carnevale dell' Anno 1836.

Musica del Maestro Cav. Vincenzo Bellini.

ROMA

Tipografia Puccinelli a Torre Sanguigna n.º 17.

Con approvazione.

PUTNAM, ASHLEY

(New York 1952)

American soprano. A pupil of Elizabeth Mosher and Willis Patterson at the University of Michigan, she made her debut in 1976 with Virginia Opera in Norfolk, Virginia, singing the lead in Donizetti's *Lucia di Lammermoor*. In 1978 she sang for the first time at Glyndebourne as Musetta in *La bohème*. She appeared with the New York City Opera (*La traviata*, 1978) and with the Metropolitan Opera House in New York, with which she toured the United States in *Lucia di Lammermoor*. At the same time, Putnam was developing an international career which led to engagements in Europe, including an appearance in Aix-en-Provence in Mozart's *Mitridate, re di Ponto* as Sifare. After her earlier performances as a *coloratura* soprano, she went on to sing more specifically lyrical and dramatic parts, including Vitellia in Mozart's *La clemenza di Tito* (Catania, 1989) and Káťa in Janáček's *Káťa Kabanová* (Florence, 1989) as well as in Hindemith's *Cardillac* (Florence, 1991).

Above: The English composer Henry Purcell.

Left: Title page of *I puritani* by Vincenzo Bellini, performed in Rome in 1836 under the title Elvira Walton

Q

I QUATRO RUSTEGHI, OR DIE VIER GROBIANE

(The School for Fathers)

Operatic comedy in three acts by Ermanno Wolf-Ferrari (1876–1948), libretto by Giuseppe Pizzolato, from I Rusteghi *by Carlo Goldoni (1707–93) German version by H. Teibler. First performance: Munich, Hoftheater, 19 March 1906.*

Venice, the eighteenth century. Act I. Lucieta (soprano), daughter of Lunardo (bass), and Margarita (mezzo-soprano), her stepmother, complain about her father's strictness. He will not allow her to take any part in the Carnival. Lunardo informs Margarita that he has arranged a marriage for Lucieta with Maurizio's son Filipeto (tenor), but that, as is only proper, the engaged pair are not to meet until the wedding day. Filipeto, anxious that he should not be made to marry a woman he has not even seen, calls on his aunt, Marina (soprano), to ask for help. His uncle Simon (bass-baritone) arrives and sends him away. Shortly afterwards, Marina has another caller, Felice (soprano), accompanied by her husband Canciano (bass) and a visitor to Venice, Count Riccardo (tenor), and the women begin to plan how the young people can be given at least a glimpse of each other. Act II. The women meet at Lunardo's house and Felice explains her scheme. Since it is Carnival time, Filipeto is to enter the house disguised as a woman, in the company of Count Riccardo. The young couple look, and no sooner look than love. But now the old gentlemen make an untimely appearance. Filipeto and Riccardo hide, and the head of the household announces the betrothal. Maurizio goes off to fetch Filipeto, but discovers that he left home with Riccardo. In the ensuing discussion Canciano remarks that he always suspected the foreigner and Riccardo erupts indignantly. Filipeto is also found and the whole plot is uncovered. Lunardo is furious and orders all his guests to leave. The wedding is off! Act III. Lunardo, Canciano and Simon debate what should be done with such presumptuous women. They are joined by Felice who, instead of defending herself, attacks them with spirit, beginning with her own husband, Canciano, and then accusing the others of infecting him with their silly ideas. Riccardo goes to talk to Filipeto's father Maurizio, who has sulked at home since his awful experience; Lucieta and Margarita beg Lunardo's pardon, thus affording him some slight satisfaction; the wedding is arranged without delay, and everything ends in a delightful supper-party.

This opera has been compared to fine patterned lace, enriched with polyphonic passages, songs, repetitions and subtle instrumental melodies. Although the work as a whole may suggest an attempted musical echo of the eighteenth century, it also has echoes of Verdi's *Falstaff.*

QUIET PLACE, A

Domestic drama in three acts by Leonard Bernstein (1918–1990), to a libretto by the composer and Stephen Wadsworth based on Bernstein's own earlier opera Trouble in Tahiti. *First performance: Houston, Grand Opera, 17 June 1983.*

The story begins in the 1980s. Relatives and friends have gathered to attend the funeral of Dinah. They are Bill (baritone), Dinah's brother; Susie (mezzo-soprano), her closest friend; the Analyst (tenor); Doc (bass), the family doctor; his wife Mrs Doc (mezzo-soprano); Sam (baritone), Dinah's husband, and his two children, Dede (soprano) and Junior (baritone). Dinah's sudden death as the result of a road accident has the effect of uniting the family, while at the same time revealing that there is no real contact between any of them. After the funeral, as he sorts through Dinah's possessions, Sam relives his complex relationship with her. The scene then changes to the 1950s, and this flashback provides an insight into how relations grew to be so difficult between each of the members of the family. Sam, Didie and Junior read Dinah's diary and come to the realization that they have to learn to communicate with one another.

The first performance of *A Quiet Place* was given a rather negative reception by the critics. Bernstein then worked with Wadsworth and conductor John Mauceri on an extended revision. He turned the original one-act format into three acts by incorporating into the score his previous opera *Trouble in Tahiti*, to which *A Quiet Place* had provided the sequel, the two works having originally been staged as a double-bill at the Houston premiere. The revised version received its first performance at La Scala in Milan in June 1984 and was subsequently seen at the Vienna Staatsoper (1986) and in Bielefeld and Maastricht (1987), winning the acclaim of audiences and critics.

QUINAULT, PHILIPPE

(Paris 1635–1688)

French playwright and librettist. One of the greatest exponents of French theater and a contemporary of Racine, Quinault worked closely with Jean-Baptiste Lully, for whom he wrote the libretti for *Alceste* (1674), *Thésée* (1675), *Atys* (1676), *Proserpine* (1680), *Armide* (1686) and others. Many of his libretti were later taken up and turned into operas by other composers, among them Paisiello and Gluck.

Set design by Zuffi for *Alceste* composed by Jean-Baptiste Lully to a libretto by Philippe Quinault.

R

RABAUD, HENRI-BENJAMIN

(Paris 1873–1949)

French composer. He studied composition with Massenet at the Paris Conservatoire. In 1884 he won the Prix de Rome, which enabled him to go to Italy, where he discovered the operas of Verdi, Mascagni and Puccini, and to Bayreuth. The year 1904 marked his debut as a composer with *La fille de Roland*, and he went on to establish his reputation with *Mârouf* (1914), which was to remain his best-known opera. He also wrote *L'Appel de la mer* (1924), *Rolande et le mauvais garçon* (1934), *Martine* (1947) and the unfinished *Le jeu de l'amour et du hasard* (1954).

RAFFANTI, DANO

(Lucca 1948)

Italian tenor. A pupil of Rodolfo Celletti in Milan, he made his debut at La Scala, Milan, in 1976 as Rodrigo in Verdi's *Otello*. From 1977 he appeared at the Valle d'Itria Festival. His performances there in Auber's *Fra Diavolo*, Bellini's *I Capuleti ed i Montecchi* and Rossini's *Il barbiere di Siviglia* were well-received and he displayed a quality of timbre and technical and stylistic gifts later confirmed by his Medoro (in Vivaldi's *Orlando Furioso* at the Teatro Filarmonico in Verona in 1978 and elsewhere) and Rodrigo (Rossini's *La donna del lago*). He also appeared in Donizetti's *Parisina* at the Teatro Comunale in Florence (1990) and the French version of *Don Carlos* at the Teatro Regio in Turin (1991).

RAIMONDI, GIANNI

(Bologna 1923)

Italian tenor. He studied singing in Naples with the tenors Melandri and Barra Carracciolo and made his debut in Budrio in 1947 (Verdi's *Rigoletto*). At the beginning of the 1950s he appeared at several opera houses in his native Italy and beyond, including La Scala, Milan, in 1956 (*La traviata*), the Vienna Staatsoper in 1958 (*Rigoletto*) and the Metropolitan Opera in New York (*La bohème*, *Rigoletto*, *La traviata*, *Tosca*). Raimondi's repertoire was essentially that of a lyric tenor, but his remarkable vocal range, beauty of timbre and elegant delivery enabled him also to tackle operas in the early nineteenth-century repertoire, such as Rossini's *Armida* and *Guillaume Tell*, Bellini's *I puritani* and Donizetti's *La favorita*, *Linda di Chamounix* and *Anna Bolena*. He retired from the stage in 1979.

RAIMONDI, RUGGIERO

(Bologna 1941)

Italian bass-baritone. He studied in Rome with Ghibaudo, Pediconi and Piervenanzi and made his debut at the Sperimentale (an association that helps to launch singers on their careers) in Spoleto in 1964 as Colline (*La bohème*). In the same year he appeared as Procida (*Les vêpres siciliennes*) at the Teatro dell'Opera in Rome. His rise to fame in the Italian and international opera world was rapid, including engagements at La Scala, Milan (from 1968), Glyndebourne (*Don Giovanni*, 1969) and the Metropolitan Opera in New York (*Ernani*, 1970). Raimondi's outstanding performing ability and exceptional range as a singer have enabled him to take on a whole range of contrasting roles, from Mozart to *Boris Godunov* and *Don Carlos* and (as a baritone) the roles of Scarpia, Escamillo and Falstaff. His reputation also rests on several performances of opera on film (in particular as Don Giovanni in Joseph Losey's 1978 film version). Other successful performances include *Don Chisciotte* and *Il viaggio a Reims* (Don Profondo).

RAKE'S PROGRESS, THE

Opera in three acts by Igor Stravinsky (1882–1971), to a libretto by W. H. Auden and Chester Kallman, after engravings by William Hogarth. First performance: Venice, Teatro La Fenice, 11 September 1951.

The Italian tenor Ruggiero Raimondi.

The action takes place in England in the eighteenth century. In the garden of a country house, a dubious character called Nick Shadow (baritone) reveals to the young Tom Rakewell (tenor) that the latter has inherited a huge fortune. After bidding farewell to his fiancée, Anne, Tom sets out for London, accompanied by Nick, who has offered to be at his service on an unpaid basis. They come to an agreement that they will settle up with each other in a year and a day. At the brothel run by Mother Goose (mezzo-soprano), Tom abandons himself to a life of corruption and debauchery. In the meantime, Anne having heard no news of her husband-to-be, goes to London to look for him. By now Tom has grown tired of having one love affair after another, and Nick persuades him to marry Baba the Turk (mezzo-soprano), a monstrous but very wealthy woman. Anne appears and is distraught to see the level of depravity to which Tom has sunk. She expresses bitter regret at the way he is living and then goes. Soon disgusted by the awfulness of his new wife, Tom decides to try his hand at business and obtains from Nick a machine which is supposed to turn stones into bread. As might be expected, Tom's "business" fails, and Baba, in a last attempt to help him, tells Anne (who has come back again) that Tom still loves her and that she alone can save him. During the night, close by the fountain in a cemetery, Tom discovers that Nick Shadow is actually the Devil and wants his soul. Tom asks to play him at cards, with his immortality as the prize, and in the end he wins the game. In a fury Nick makes him go out of his mind and pushes him headlong into a ditch. When Tom regains consciousness, he thinks he is Adonis. Now completely mad, Tom is visited in the madhouse by his ever-faithful Anne. She lovingly indulges his delusions by pretending to be Venus and sends him gently to sleep with a tender lullaby. Then she leaves. When

Tom wakes up, he calls out the names of gentle Venus and Orpheus, then lies back on his bed and dies.

The idea for *The Rake's Progress* came to Stravinsky when he saw the set of eight engravings by the eighteenth-century artist William Hogarth entitled *The Rake's Progress*, portraying the adventures of a libertine. Auden and Kallman made a perfect job of transforming these Hogarth images into an elegant and atmospheric text, inspiring Stravinsky to respond in the same spirit and write a score in which he was obviously using tonality, characteristic features and also form (like plain recitative and arias with solo instrumental accompaniment) to recreate the sounds of eighteenth-century music.

RAMEAU, JEAN-PHILIPPE

(Dijon 1683–Paris 1764)

French composer. The son of an organist, Rameau followed in his father's footsteps and also became a chorus-master. In 1706 he moved to Paris. His early experiences in the theater were by no means easy, as his first important composition, *Hippolyte et Aricie* (1733) met with mixed reactions, and the same thing happened to *Les Indes galantes* (1735). But his enriching of the *tragédie-lyrique* style and the *opéra-ballet* soon made its mark, although not without difficulty. Rameau's most outstanding works for the theater include *Castor et Pollux* (1737), *Dardanus* (1739), *La Princesse de Navarre* (1745), *Platée* (1745), *Zoroastre* (1749), *Les Paladins* (1760) and *Les Boréades* (1764).

RAMEY, SAMUEL

(Colby, Kansas 1942)

American bass. He made his debut as Zuniga (*Carmen*) with New York City Opera in 1973, later joining the permanent company as well as appearing at the major American opera houses (Philadelphia, Santa Fe, Houston and the Metropolitan Opera) in a varied repertoire ranging from Mozart to Donizetti, Verdi and Boito. In Europe he sang, among other venues, at the Glyndebourne Festival in *Le nozze di Figaro* and *The Rake's Progress* (1976–77) and in Bordeaux (*Don Giovanni*, 1976). In 1980 he scored a sensational success as Assur (*Semiramide*) in Aix-en-Provence, establishing himself as one of the finest *bel canto* basses of his day. The faultless character of Ramey's voice, coupled with an equally outstanding stage presence, enabled him to find the right style for Argante in Handel's *Rinaldo* and the great Rossini roles in *L'italiana in Algeri*, *Il turco in Italia*, *Maometto II*, *Il viaggio a Reims* and *La donna del lago* (which he performed at the Rossini Opera Festival in Pesaro from 1981 onwards). His reputation also rests on his appearances in French opera, notably the historic production of *Robert le Diable* at the Opéra in 1985.

RANDOVÁ, EVA

(Kolin 1936)

Czech mezzo-soprano. She studied singing at the Conservatory in Prague and made her debut in Ostrava, where she went on to appear in major mezzo-soprano roles. She sang in Prague in 1969 and at the opera houses in Nuremberg and Stuttgart (where she was a member of the permanent company from 1971). International engagements at principal venues followed, such as Bayreuth (where she appeared regularly from 1973), the Salzburg Easter Festival (also from 1973) and the Opéra in Paris (from 1975). Randová is regarded as one of the great Wagner singers, as can be heard in her Ortrud in the Solti recording of *Lohengrin* (1985–86), and she gave a distinguished performance in the role of Kostelnička in Janáček's *Jenůfa* (1982).

Above: A sketch for the first performance in Venice in 1951 of Stravinsky's *The Rake's Progress.*

Right: The American bass Samuel Ramey performing in *The Marriage of Figaro.*

RAPE OF LUCRETIA, THE

Opera in two acts by Benjamin Britten (1913–1976), to a libretto by Ronald Duncan based on André Obey's Le viol de Lucrèce. *First performance: Glyndebourne, 12 July 1946.*

The action takes place during the siege of Ardea. In a tent, the Etruscan and Roman generals are in high spirits. They tell how a series of surprise visits to their wives in Rome the night before revealed that only Lucretia (mezzo-soprano), the wife of Collatinus, was being virtuous and chaste. Tarquinius (baritone) is prompted by this story to slip away from the tent unseen and set out for Rome on horseback. He calls unannounced at Lucretia's house and asks for hospitality, only to exploit the situation by entering her room during the night and raping her. The following morning, Lucretia sends for her husband and tells him what has happened, then stabs herself. Her death leaves the Romans feeling outraged, and they vow to have their revenge against the Etruscans.

The enormous success of *The Rape of Lucretia* at its premiere in July 1946 resulted in a total of 80 performances by October. In this work Britten uses a chamber-opera structure for the first time, with only eight singers and an instrumental ensemble of 15.

RAVEL, MAURICE

(Ciboure, Basses Pyrenées 1875–Paris 1937)

French composer. He wrote only two operas, *L'heure espagnole* (1911) and *L'enfant et les sortilèges* (1925), but both are good examples of his style and musical art. Two further operas were planned but never came to fruition, one on the theme of the sunken bell, the other about Joan of Arc.

RE PASTORE, IL

(The Shepherd King)

Opera in two acts by Wolfgang Amadeus Mozart (1756–1791), to a libretto by Pietro Metastasio. First performance: Salzburg, Archbishop's Palace, 23 April 1775.

After freeing the kingdom of Sidon from a tyrant, Alessandro Magno (Alexander the Great, tenor) wants to hand back the throne to its rightful heir, Aminta (soprano), who is living the life of a humble shepherd and is in love with the nymph Elisa (soprano). The story also involves another pair of lovers, Tamiri (soprano), daughter of the deposed tyrant, and Agenore (tenor), a member of the kingdom's nobility. Alessandro wants to give Tamiri in marriage to Aminta as a way of resolving internal political differences, but this move turns out to be devastating for the feelings of those involved. In the end, however, Aminta becomes a Shepherd King with his beloved Elisa by his side, while Tamiri and Agenore are sent to rule over another territory, bestowed on them by Alessandro.

Il re pastore is one of Metastasio's last libretti and not one of his best. Mozart handles the static plot by giving prominence to the instrumental writing. As a result, *concertante* arias, accompanied by solo instruments (flute and violin), are a constant feature, in which the soloists compete with the singer. In *Il re pastore*, Mozart displays a more clearly developed artistic personality than in his early operas. The same Metastasio libretto has also been used by Hasse, Gluck, Jommelli and Piccinni.

REFICE, LICINIO

(Patrica, Frosinone 1885–Rio de Janeiro 1954)

Italian composer. Ordained priest in 1910, he taught at the Scuola Pontificia di Musica Sacra from 1910 to 1950 and was *maestro di cappella* at the Church of Santa Maria Maggiore (1911–47). He also composed the operas *Cecilia* (1934) and *Margherita da Cortona* (1938).

RENDALL, DAVID

(London 1948)

British tenor. He studied at the Royal Academy of Music in London and in Salzburg. In 1974 he made his debut at Covent Garden in Richard Strauss's *Der Rosenkavalier* and Mozart's *Don Giovanni*. He sang at New York City Opera (Puccini's *La bohème*, 1978), the Metropolitan Opera in New York (Donizetti's *Don Pasquale*, 1980) and at a number of other opera houses. His recordings include Mozart's *Così fan tutte*, Handel's *Ariodante* and Puccini's *La rondine*.

RENZETTI, DONATO

(Torino di Sangro 1950)

Italian conductor. He studied at the Conservatorio in Milan and the Accademia Chigiana in Siena. After impressing the judges at prestigious competitions for young conductors, he made his debut at the Teatro Comunale in Bologna in 1977 conducting Rossini's *Il Signor Bruschino*. Renzetti's reputation rests particularly on his performances at important international festivals and opera houses as a Rossini conductor, including the Rossini Opera Festival in Pesaro (*L'italiana in Algeri*, 1981, and *La cambiale di matrimonio*, 1991), Glyndebourne (*La Cenerentola*, 1983) and the Teatro Petruzzelli in Bari (*Il turco in Italia*, 1985). He also conducted at the Opéra in Paris (Verdi's *Jerusalem*, 1984) and at the Metropolitan Opera in New York (*La bohème*, 1990).

RESNIK, REGINA

(New York 1922)

American mezzo-soprano. She studied in New York and embarked on her career as a soprano in 1942 with the New York Opera Company in Verdi's *Macbeth*. She made her debut at the Metropolitan Opera in New York as Leonora (*Il trovatore*), returning there in the role of Ellen Orford in the American premiere of Britten's *Peter Grimes* (1945). After appearing at Bayreuth in 1953 as Sieglinde in *Die Walküre*, Resnik made the decision to become a mezzo-soprano. There followed a period of training with Giuseppe Danise, after which she returned to the stage of the Metropolitan to sing Marina in *Boris Godunov*. A remarkably creative performer, she went on to make her name in the roles of Eboli, Amneris, Carmen, Klytämnestra and Herodias. In 1958 she created the role of the Baroness in the first performance of Samuel Barber's opera *Vanessa*.

Above: The French composer Maurice Ravel.

Left: A scene from *The Rape of Lucretia* by Benjamin Britten.

RESPIGHI, OTTORINO

(Bologna 1879–Rome 1936)

Italian composer. A pupil of Torchi and Martucci at the Liceo Musicale in Bologna, he embarked on a career as a violinist, which took him to Russia and Germany. After the operas he composed between 1905 and 1910, Respighi did not return to opera until 1923 when he wrote *Belfagor*. This was followed by *La campana sommersa* (1927), *Maria Egiziaca* (1932), *La fiamma* (1934) and *Lucrezia*, which he left unfinished. It was eventually staged at La Scala, Milan, in 1937 in the version completed by his wife.

RICCIARDO E ZORAIDE

Opera in two acts by Gioachino Rossini (1792–1868), to a libretto by Francesco Berio di Salsa. First performance: Naples, Teatro San Carlo, 3 December 1818.

The action takes place in the Nubian city of Duncala. King Agorante (tenor) has defeated the army of King Ircano (bass) and taken prisoner Zoraide (soprano), Ircano's daughter. Agorante wants to marry her and is ready to confront his rival, the knight Ricciardo (tenor), with whom Zoraide is already in love. Ricciardo arrives in disguise, accompanied by the Christian ambassador Ernesto (tenor), and devises a ploy whereby he is able to meet Zoraide and reassure her. Ircano, also incognito, then appears on the scene and challenges Agorante to a duel, the outcome of which will decide whether Zoraide is to be freed. Ricciardo, similarly unaware that the man who has challenged him is actually King Ircano, duly fights his opponent and beats him, with assistance from Zomira (mezzo-soprano), betrothed to Agorante. Ricciardo is about to flee with Zoraide when they are discovered and condemned to death by Ircano, whose real identity has now been revealed. A contingent of Franks commanded by Ernesto storms the place where the execution is about to be carried out and releases the prisoners. Agorante is spared, and the opera ends happily.

Ricciardo e Zoraide, though a great success at its premiere in Naples, was not well received in the other cities where it was performed. This can be explained by the presence of some fairly unusual features not found elsewhere in Rossini's works. Here he has written music that is more recognizably pre-Romantic, playing down the *bel canto* style people expected from him, replacing it with a more emotionally lyrical score which looks forward to Bellini and Donizetti.

RICCI, LUIGI

(Naples 1805–Prague 1859)

Italian composer. He studied at the Conservatorio in Naples, where he was a pupil of Zingarelli and Generali. He had his first success in 1822 with the opera *L'impresario in angustie*, followed by *Chiara di Rosemberg* (1831), *Un'avventura di Scaramuccia* (1834) and *La festa di Piedrigotta* (1852). He collaborated with his brother Federico (1809–77), himself a composer, on what was to become their most famous opera, *Crispino e la comare* (1850).

RICCIARELLI, KATIA

(Rovigo 1946)

Italian soprano. She graduated from the Conservatorio in Venice and made her debut in Mantua in 1969 as Mimi (*La bohème*). Her reputation was firmly established in the following year after her appearance in Cherubini's opera *Anacréon* in Siena, but more especially on the strength of her performance in the Italian Radio's New Verdi Voices Competition, which led to engagements during the 1972–73 season in Trieste (*Il corsaro*), the Teatro dell'Opera in Rome (*Giovanna d'Arco*) and Chicago (*I due Foscari*). She went on to sing at La Scala, Milan (*Suor Angelica*, 1973), Covent Garden (*La bohème*, 1974) and the Metropolitan Opera, New York (*La bohème*). Ricciarelli's repertoire was extremely wide-ranging, from Gluck, Mozart and Cherubini to Rossini, Donizetti and numerous operas of Verdi, Bellini and Puccini. But this clearly did not benefit her angel-like soprano voice, with its exceptionally beautiful timbre, especially well-suited to elegiac singing, with the result that by the early 1980s the voice was already showing signs of premature strain, mainly in the upper register.

RICHARD COEUR DE LION

(Richard the Lion-Heart)

Opera in three acts by André Grétry (1741–1813), to a libretto by Michel-Jean Sedaine. First performance: Paris, Théâtre de la Comédie-Italienne, 21 October 1784.

King Richard (tenor) is a prisoner in the castle of Linz. Blondel (tenor), one of his trusty servants, arrives in the nearby village posing as a blind minstrel to find out if the prisoner in the castle actually is his master. Then Marguerite (soprano), Countess of Flanders, in love with Richard, also appears in the village. Blondel stands beneath the castle walls and plays on his violin the melody of a song Richard had written for Marguerite,

Above: The Italian composer Ottorino Respighi.

Right: A scene from *Ricciardo e Zoraide* by Gioachino Rossini.

whereupon Richard's voice is heard from his cell in the tower, picking up the tune and singing the words to it. Blondel can now be sure the prisoner is Richard, and Marguerite helps him to devise a plan to free his king. After locking up the prison governor, Marguerite's knights and soldiers surround the castle. Richard is released and can be reunited with his beloved.

Richard Coeur de Lion is the most interesting of Grétry's operas. The score is deeply expressive, with arias pre-romantic in tone and accent. The orchestra's role in this opera is given a particular importance by the richness and originality of Grétry's instrumental writing.

RIDDERBUSCH, KARL

(Recklinghausen 1932)

German bass. After studying singing and music at the Conservatory in Duisburg, he made his debut in Munster in 1961 as Filippo II (*Don Carlos*). Engagements followed at opera houses in Essen (1962–65) and Düsseldorf, and in 1967 he appeared for the first time at the Bayreuth Festival as Heinrich in *Lohengrin*. This launched his international career, which was to include regular guest appearances at Bayreuth up until 1977, the Salzburg Easter Festival (from 1967), the Metropolitan Opera in New York and Covent Garden. Ridderbusch's reputation rests mainly on Wagner but also on Baron Ochs (Richard Strauss's *Der Rosenkavalier*), Boris (Mussorgsky's *Boris Godunov*) and Rocco (Beethoven's *Fidelio*).

RIENZI DER LETZE DER TRIBUNEN

(Rienzi, Last of the Tribunes)

Opera in five acts by Richard Wagner (1813–1883), to the composer's own libretto, based on Edward Bulwer Lytton's novel. First performance: Dresden, Hoftheater, 20 October 1842.

The action takes place in Rome during the fourteenth century. The city has been abandoned by the popes, now in exile in Avignon, and is torn by conflicts between rival families. While the tribune Rienzi (tenor) is away, Paolo Orsini (bass) and his associates set out to abduct Orsini's sister Irene (soprano). An attempt to foil them is made by Adriano Colonna (soprano), who loves Irene, with the help of his family and the people of Rome. The quarrel between the Colonna and the Orsini is resolved by the sudden return of Rienzi, who restores calm. The fact that Rienzi clearly enjoys public support antagonizes the Colonna and Orsini, who join forces with the intention of killing him. After the first assassination bid fails, the noble families sow discontent among the people by telling them his unrestrained ambition will lead Rome to ruin. This is followed by a papal bull excommunicating him, and Rienzi soon realizes that he has been deserted by everyone. The angry crowd marches on the Capitol, which Adriano vainly tries to guard. Rienzi pleads with Irene to look to her own safety and then perishes in the blaze engulfing the palace.

This early Wagner opera, written for the Paris stage, has all the hallmarks of *grand-opéra*: marches, great ensemble scenes, ballets and a spectacular operatic finale portraying the Capitol in flames. Enthusiastically received in Dresden, *Rienzi* subsequently enjoyed little success and was seldom revived in the twentieth century. The opera's best-known moments include the overture and Rienzi's prayer in the fifth act.

RIGOLETTO

Opera in three acts by Giuseppe Verdi (1813–1901), to a libretto by Francesco Maria Piave, based on Victor Hugo's play Le roi s'amuse. *First performance: Venice, Teatro La Fenice, 11 March 1851.*

The action takes place in the Duchy of Mantua during the sixteenth century. The Duke (tenor) is an unscrupulous libertine and his servant, Rigoletto (baritone), is a physically deformed jester, forever playing tricks on the noblemen at Court. They decide to get revenge by abducting Gilda (soprano), whom they believe to be Rigoletto's mistress. In reality, however, she is the daughter he fathered in his youth. Meanwhile, the Duke, disguised as a student, has courted Gilda. The nobles abduct her and take her to court, where the Duke seduces her. Reunited with her father, she reveals the outrage that has been perpetrated on her. Rigoletto vows revenge and turns to Sparafucile (bass), a killer hired to murder the Duke. The assassin's sister, Maddalena (mezzo-soprano), lures the Duke to a sordid tavern in the suburbs of Mantua. But the victim of Sparafucile's dagger is not the Duke but Gilda, who chooses to sacrifice herself for the man she still loves. When the sack containing the corpse is delivered to Rigoletto, he discovers the chilling truth. Gilda is still alive, but nothing more can be done for her and she dies in her father's arms.

Rigoletto, the first opera in Verdi's popular trilogy, which includes *La traviata* and *Il trovatore*, marks something of a revolution in opera, in that the leading role is a grotesque figure far removed from the usual operatic character types. As well as demonstrating exceptional psychological insight into the personality of Rigoletto and contrasting this with the superficiality of the Duke, Verdi reaches beyond the classical tradition of opera as a sequence of separate items, instead moving towards the kind of dramatic unity he would display so impressively in *Otello* and *Falstaff*.

RIMSKY-KORSAKOV, NIKOLAI

(Tikhvin, Novgorod 1844–Lyubensk, St. Petersburg 1908)

Russian composer. Encouraged to study music at an early age, he decided instead to carry on the family tradition and take up a career as an officer in the navy. He made his debut as an opera composer with *Pskovityanka* (The Maid of Pskov), which he revised three times, and this was followed by *Mayskaya noch'* (May Night, 1877–79) and *Snegurockha* (The Snow Maiden, 1880–81) in which Rimsky-Korsakov reveals his fondness for traditional Russian popular legends as well as for the works of the great Russian poets and playwrights, from Gogol to Pushkin. His most distinguished operas include *Motsart i Sal'yeri* (Mozart and Salieri, 1897), *Tsarskaya nevesta* (The Tsar's Bride, 1898–99), *Tsare Saltane* (The Tale of Tsar Saltan, 1899–1900), *Zolotoy pyetushok* (The Golden Cockerel, 1906–17) and *Skazaniye o*

The soprano Katia Ricciarelli.

nevidimom grade Kitezhe i deve Fevronii (Legend of the Invisible City of Kitezh and the Maiden Fevroniya, 1907).

RINALDI, ALBERTO

(Rome 1939)
Italian baritone. He made his debut singing the lead in Verdi's *Simon Boccanegra* in Spoleto (1963). The following year, he was Figaro (*Il barbiere di Siviglia*) at La Fenice in Venice. In 1966 he made his first appearance at La Scala (*L'incoronazione di Poppea*), where he returned to sing regularly. A guest artiste at numerous international opera houses (including the Vienna Staatsoper, Covent Garden, the Paris Opéra, the Metropolitan Opera in New York and Lyric Opera of Chicago), Rinaldi draws on an extensive repertoire ranging from Mozart to the *opere buffe* of Rossini, Donizetti and Verdi.

RINALDI, MARGHERITA

(Turin 1935)
Italian soprano. She made her debut in Spoleto in 1958 in *Lucia di Lammermoor*. In 1965 she appeared for the first time at La Scala, Milan (*Rigoletto*), and went on to sing in Chicago, San Francisco and at other major international opera houses. An exquisite Mozart singer, Rinaldi also won acclaim for her roles in Rossini, Donizetti and Bellini as well as Meyerbeer and Strauss.

RING DES NIBELUNGEN, DER

(The Ring of the Nibelung)
Stage-festival play over three days, with a prologue, by Richard Wagner (1813–1883), to the composer's own libretto, based on the Nibelung Saga. First performance of the complete cycle: Bayreuth, Festspielhaus, 13, 14, 16 and 17 August 1876.

RHEINGOLD, DAS

(The Rhinegold)
Prologue and one act. First performance: Munich, Hoftheater, 22 September 1869.

Somewhere on the Rhine's rocky riverbed, the Rhinegold is being guarded by Woglinde (soprano), Wellgunde (soprano) and Flosshilde (mezzo-soprano), the three Rhine maidens. The dwarf Alberich (baritone), risen from the dark caverns of Nibelheim, tries to win the love of the three maidens, but when a gleam of sunlight makes the Rhinegold shine and the three women unwisely tell him about its treasure's magic power, Alberich is so eager to make that power his own that he curses love, seizes the Gold and flees. Meanwhile the giants Fasolt (bass) and Fafner (bass) have just finished building the magnificent castle of Valhalla for Wotan (bass-baritone), king of the Gods, his wife Fricka (mezzo-soprano) and the other gods. Wotan had promised the builders that their reward would be Freia (soprano), goddess of beauty and youth, but now he refuses to hand her over. The row that develops is interrupted by the arrival of Loge (tenor), god of fire. He tells about Alberich, his immense wealth and the power he has acquired, and his story has exactly the effect he wanted: the giants relinquish their claim on Freia in exchange for the Nibelung gold. So Wotan and Loge descend into Nibelheim, where Alberich has enslaved the Nibelungs and is forcing them to mine the earth for precious metals. Wotan succeeds in regaining the gold as well as a magic ring forged from it. Devastated at being robbed of his dream of power, Alberich utters a terrible curse: the ring will bring misfortune to anyone who comes by it. The curse is quick to take effect. No sooner has Wotan entrusted the ring to the giants than they begin quarrelling, and Fafner kills Fasolt. A thunderbolt is unleashed by Donner (bass), god of storms, and then the majestic structure of Valhalla appears. The gods, standing on a rainbow, can now make their way to their new home, while the song of the Rhine maidens is heard lamenting the loss of the gold.

WALKÜRE, DIE

(The Valkyries)
First Day
Opera in three acts. First performance: Munich, Hoftheater, 26 June 1870.

One stormy night, Siegmund (tenor), wounded, with enemies pursuing him, is looking for shelter in the forest when he comes upon the hut belonging to Hunding (bass), husband of Sieglinde (soprano). Hunding returns home, finds Siegmund there (whom he has never seen before), and questions him. Siegmund explains that after his father disappeared, hostile people killed his mother and abducted his twin sister. When he goes on to say he has just come from battling to save a bride from a forced marriage, Hunding realizes he is talking to an enemy of his own clan. He tells Siegmund that while the rules of hospitality will ensure him a roof for the

Above: Title page of the first edition of *Rigoletto* by Giuseppe Verdi.

Right: The Russian composer Nikolai Rimsky-Korsakov

"A STORM IN THE HEAVENS, A MURDER HERE ON EARTH!"

With these words, in the third act of Verdi's *Rigoletto*, Rigoletto himself, overcome with horror, connects the tragic event in his own life with the unleashing of the powers of nature. This quotation from Verdi is a signpost to ways in which various aspects of the natural world, extensively explored in painting and Romantic literature, are also fully represented in music, where nature comes to express the psychological dimension in a situation. But its links are not only with Romanticism, because as early as the *opera seria* of the eighteenth century the Elements played a leading part in arias which drew on nature to provide a moral, and went on to assume an increasingly important role when Gluck's opera reforms came along (for example, the aria "Che puro ciel" in *Orfeo ed Euridice*.) The earliest significant examples of storm-scenes in opera were in Mozart's *Idomeneo*: in Act One, for instance, he achieves a marvellous description of the sea at storm, a veritable termult in Nature which involves the characters, and builds up a tremendouly strong interplay between terror as a psychological symptom and as something Nature inspires. In nineteenth-century Italian opera there are the Rossini "storms," from the famous one in his *Il barbiere di Siviglia* (which the composer had already used in another of his operas, *La pietra del paragone*), where the storm serves as a theatrically effective "intermezzo," to *Guillaume Tell*, where, in the opera's finale, Rossini describes a storm on the Lake of Lucerne during which William Tell kills the tyrant Gessler. Here nature seems almost to be an accomplice to the hero in his efforts to free Switzerland from oppression. The intermezzo in *Il barbiere* comes a long time before the storm in *Tell*, whereas there are only six years between the premiere of *Guillaume Tell* and that of Bellini's *I puritani* and Donizetti's *Lucia di Lammermoor*. In the third act of Bellini's opera, where Arturo is looking for somewhere to hide from the Puritans by whom he is being hunted on suspicion of being guilty of betrayal, he is caught in a storm. Bellini's handling of the storm-music serves to heighten the atmosphere of hostility surrounding Arturo. In Donizetti's *Lucia di Lammermoor*, too, there is a storm at the beginning of the third act (a scene which is often, and without justification, cut from productions in the opera-house): "Orrida è questa notte, come il mio destino," sings Edgardo, while the orchestral accompaniment underlines the romantic quality of his role in all its desperation and longing for death. This romantic view of the storm, intensifying a moment of impulse and rebellion, also appears in Bellini's *Il pirata*, where the storm which causes Gualitero to be shipwrecked draws attention to his psychological state and to his tormented life as a pirate. Something similar happens in Verdi's *Il corsaro*: in the opera's third act, Corrado, the corsair of the title, is a prisoner in a tower. As the heavens are about to open and unleash the full force of the storm, he calls upon "lightning in all its horror" to put and end to his "wretched existence." This example of a Verdi "storm-scence" is nonetheless far removed from the tragic power he generates in Act III of *Rigoletto*. Closer to the spirit of *Il pirata* and *Il corsaro*, and creating a very different sort of impact, is the storm which opens Verdi's *Otello*. Like Gualitero and Corrado, Otello is the military commander who challenges Nature and emerges the victor, just as he has over his enemies, but the storm through from which he has come acts as a kind of premonition of a very different storm, that of human passion which he will not survive.

Above: A scene from Mozart's *Idomeneo*.

night there, the next morning they will face each other in mortal combat. Sieglinde, strongly attracted to Siegmund, pours a sleeping-draught into Hunding's drink. Alone with Siegmund, she shows him a sword which a mysterious traveller (Wotan in disguise) had embedded in the trunk of an ash-tree, wagering that only the strongest of warriors would be able to pull it out. With a mighty effort, Siegmund extracts the sword and names it Nothung (born of necessity). By now consumed with passion, Siegmund and Sieglinde, who have also realized that they are actually twin brother and sister, run off into the spring night. Wotan commands Brünnhilde (soprano), whom he loves best of all his Valkyrie daughters, to defend Siegmund against the vengeful Hunding. But Fricka (mezzo-soprano), as goddess of marriage, demands that Wotan condemn such adulterous love by bringing about Siegmund's death. Wotan eventually is left with no alternative but to change his original command to Brünnhilde. So Brünnhilde comes to Siegmund and tells him that he will have to die, but the hero declares that, rather than abandon Sieglinde, he is ready to kill both himself and her. Deeply moved, Brünnhilde resolves to protect them both. Hunding appears, and there is a duel, in the course of which Siegmund's sword is shattered by Wotan and as a result he is mortally wounded. Then, with supreme disdain, Wotan kills Hunding with a single glance and sets off in pursuit of Brünnhilde, who has escaped with Sieglinde. Sieglinde has to find refuge before she can give birth to Siegfried, Siegmund's son and the pure hero whose task it will one day be to reforge the magic sword Nothung. She will be going to a cave in the forest where Fafner is guarding the treasure and will have her child there. Sieglinde hurries away, just before Wotan arrives. In a fury, he announces Brünnhilde's punishment: she will lose her immortality, be plunged into a deep sleep, surrounded by a curtain of fire, and only the bravest of heroes will be able to reach her and make her his own. In great distress, Wotan slowly kisses Brünnhilde's eyes and sends her to sleep. Then he covers her with his shield while the god Loge builds a barrier of flame.

Above: A scene from *Die Walküre* by Richard Wagner.

Right: The tenor G. Unger as Siegfried in the *Twilight of the Gods* production in Bayreuth, 1876.

SIEGFRIED

Second day

Opera in three acts. First performance: Bayreuth, Festspielhaus, 16 August 1876.

In a cave in the forest, Mime (tenor), the Nibelung, is making a vain attempt to recast the fragments of the magic sword Nothung, which Wotan's spear had broken. Mime has seen to the upbringing of Siegfried (tenor) ever since Sieglinde died while giving birth to him. Now Mime is hoping that with Siegfried's strength to help him he will be able to gain possession of the ring, which will enable him to rule the world. None of Mimi's attempts to forge another sword worked, each one breaking as soon as Siegfried wields it. Siegfried orders Mime to repair Nothung and then he will leave him forever. Realizing he lacks the skill, Mime becomes desperate. A Wanderer (bass) enters the cave. It is Wotan. He prophesies to Mime that only a man who knows no fear will be able to temper the sword. As Wotan takes his leave of Mime, he warns him to be on guard in the face of such boldness. Siegfried reappears, and Mime tries to prevent Wotan's prophecy from coming true by treating Siegfried to a terrifying description of the dragon Fafner, guardian of the Rhinegold. But Siegfried pays no heed and reforges Nothung himself, while Mime is preparing a poisoned potion to bring about the hero's death after he has killed the dragon. Deep in the forest, Alberich (baritone), Mime's Nibelung

brother, keeps anxious watch outside the cave of Fafner (bass). He is approached by the Wanderer, who prophesies that Mime will avail himself of the young man's strength to kill the dragon and gain possession of the Rhinegold. As dawn breaks, Siegfried, followed by Mime, reaches Fafner's cave. He blows into his hunting-horn, wakes the dragon and kills him. Drawing his sword out of Fafner's side, Siegfried splashes himself with the dragon's blood. As though by magic, he is now able to understand the meaning of the song of the Woodbird (soprano), which tells him that Fafner's cave contains the ring with which it will be possible to rule the world, and also that Mime intends to poison him. When Mime comes up and offers him the potion to drink, Siegfried kills him. Then, with the Woodbird as his guide, he makes his way towards the mountain where, he is told, the most beautiful of women lies asleep inside a circle of fire and has been promised to the hero with a pure heart who will be able to overcome the flames and win her. At the foot of the mountain Wotan summons Erda (contralto), the seer, and she offers him a veiled prophecy that the gods will die: on that day, she says, the ring will be returned to the Rhinemaidens and the world will be freed from Alberich's curse. When Siegfried appears, Wotan holds up his spear in an attempt to bar the way to the mountain-top. Siegfried breaks the spear in two, destroying the god's power, and then presses on towards the summit. When he reaches it, the flames surrounding Brünnhilde (soprano) die down. Siegfried draws near to her and wakens her with a kiss. After an intense love duet, the two embrace passionately.

GÖTTERDÄMMERUNG

(Twilight of the Gods)
Third day
Opera in three acts. First performance: Bayreuth, Festspielhaus, 17 August 1876.

On the mountain where Siegfried has awakened Brünnhilde, the three Norns (soprano, mezzo-soprano and contralto) are weaving the destinies of humankind and gods when suddenly their thread breaks. This is the sign that the end of the gods is nigh. Now ready to undertake fresh tasks, Siegfried (tenor) embraces Brünnhilde before setting out on a journey to the kingdom of the Gibichungs. At the palace of Gunther (bass), Hagen (bass), Gunther's step-brother and the son of Alberich, is so determined to regain the ring for his father that he decides to use Gunther for his own ends. When Siegfried arrives, Hagen prompts Gunther's sister Gutrune (soprano) to offer him a magic draught which will make him forget Brünnhilde and suddenly fall in love with Gutrune instead. Siegfried drinks and falls under the spell, whereupon the image of Brünnhilde fades from his mind. To be able to marry Gutrune, Siegfried is ready to brave the curtain of fire a second time and abduct Brünnhilde. Siegfried goes to fetch Brünnhilde, his appearance having been transformed so that he resembles Gunther. On his return to the palace of the Gibichungs, Siegfried announces that Brünnhilde and Gunther will shortly be arriving. Preparations must now be made for a double wedding. When Brünnhilde enters, she furiously charges Siegfried with having betrayed her, but the hero's mind is still dulled by the magic draught, he dismisses her accusations. Longing for revenge, Brünnhilde wants Siegfried's death and confides to Hagen that Siegfried's back is the only vulnerable part to his body. On the banks of the Rhine, Siegfried, Hagen and Gunther are resting after a long day's hunting. While Siegfried is telling the others the story of his life, Hagen restores his memory with another potion. With increasing emotion he remembers how he won the heart of Brünnhilde, and at that moment Wotan's two ravens fly by. Siegfried turns to watch them, whereupon Hagen seizes his chance to plunge his spear between the hero's shoulders. Gunther accuses Hagen, and Hagen kills him. He is drawing near to Siegfried's body in order to remove the magic ring from his finger when, to everyone's horror, the hand is raised threateningly. Brünnhilde comes forward, suffering anguish because she had not understood that Siegfried was the victim of a magic spell, takes the ring from his finger, places it on her own hand, then puts a blazing torch to the pyre where Siegfried's body has been laid. Brünnhilde mounts her horse and throws herself into the flames, now burning so high they reach to heaven and set light to Valhalla where the gods await their end.

The poems of the twelfth-century, *Edda* and the *Nibelungenlied* (the medieval German epic poem), are the sources of Wagner's inspiration for his monumental *Ring* tetralogy,

Above: A page from the original score of *Siegfried*.

Left: A scene from *Götterdämmerung* (Twilight of the Gods).

on which he worked for 28 years, from 1848 to 1876. After the libretto of the whole cycle had been completed in 1853, he began to draft the score following the chronological order of events in the story. *Das Rheingold* was completed in 1854, *Die Walküre* in 1856. In the same year Wagner started *Siegfried*, which he finished in 1869; he went on to complete *Götterdämmerung* in 1874. The cycle was staged in its entirety in Bayreuth between 13 and 17 August 1876 as the opening production at the Festspielhaus, the new theater that Wagner had created. The musical revolution brought about by the *Ring* was the direct result of the free flow of its music (uninhibited by the stop and start of separate items) and the superimposition and combination of *leitmotivs*, the recurring musical features which Wagner uses to provide thematic links by their associations with particular characters, events and feelings.

RINUCCINI, OTTAVIO

(Florence 1563–1621)

Italian librettist and poet. Official poet at the Court of the Medici, he wrote libretti that made a significant contribution to the rise of opera. Among the operas for which he wrote texts were Peri's *Dafne* (1594), *Euridice* (1600) by Peri and Caccini, and Monteverdi's *Arianna* (1608) and *Il ballo delle ingrate* (1608).

RITORNO DI ULISSE IN PATRIA, IL

(Ulysses's Homecoming)

Opera in three acts by Claudio Monteverdi (1567–1643), to a libretto by G. Badoaro, based on the last books of Homer's Odyssey. First performance: Venice, Teatro San Cassiano, Spring 1640.

In the palace on Ithaca, Penelope (soprano) is lamenting her solitary state as she endures bitter years of waiting for her husband, Ulisse, and her Suitors exert increasing pressure on her. With the help of Minerva (soprano), Ulisse has meanwhile landed secretly on the island. Disguised as a beggar, he reveals his true identity only to his faithful servant Eumete (baritone) and his own son Telemaco (mezzo-soprano) before making his way to the palace, where the Suitors are preparing to undergo a test to see if they can string Ulisse's bow. Whoever succeeds will marry Penelope. Ulisse himself is the only one present to pass the test. Penelope recognizes him, whereupon he kills all the Suitors and is reunited with his beloved wife.

A scene from *Il ritorno di Ulisse in patria*, an opera in three acts by Claudio Monteverdi.

This Monteverdi opera was believed lost, but the score was rediscovered in Vienna's National Library in 1881. Although the libretto was fairly mediocre, Monteverdi managed to overcome its limitations with considerable mastery and musical inventiveness, illustrated most clearly in his wonderful characterization of the individual roles. *Il ritorno di Ulisse in patria* has been given numerous performances that have sought to recreate the authentic Monteverdi sound on instruments of the period. In 1984 Hans Werner Henze made a controversial modern transcription of the work, staged at the Salzburg Festival and revived for the Maggio Musicale Festival in Florence in 1987.

ROARK-STRUMMER, LINDA

(Tulsa, Oklahoma 1949)

American soprano. She attended Southern Methodist University in Dallas and made her debut with a touring company from San Francisco Opera in *Le nozze di Figaro* and *Les contes d'Hoffmann* (1974–76). She then moved to Europe and joined the resident companies of the Heidelberg (1978–80) and Linz Opera (1980–87), specializing in the Italian repertoire. In 1985 she enjoyed an important personal success as Odabella in Verdi's *Attila* at New York City Opera, the role in which she made her Italian debut in the same year at La Fenice in Venice, returning there in 1987 as Lina in Verdi's *Stiffelio*. She sang at La Scala, Milan (*Nabucco*, *I due Foscari*), took the role of Abigaille in *Nabucco* at the Arena in Verona (from 1988) and appeared, among other venues, at the Teatro San Carlo in Naples, the Vienna Staatsoper, and the Teatro Colón in Buenos Aires. Her repertoire also includes *Norma*, *Macbeth*, *Medea*, *Jenůfa* and *Tosca*, operas in which she displayed musicianship and great natural ability in stage performance.

ROBERT LE DIABLE

(Robert the Devil)

Opera in five acts by Giacomo Meyerbeer (1791–1864), to a libretto by Scribe and Delavigne. First performance: Paris, Opéra, 21 November 1831.

The action takes place in Palermo during the thirteenth century. Robert (tenor), Duke of Normandy, learns from the minstrel Raimbaut (tenor) that he was apparently born as the result of his mother falling in love with the Devil. Outraged at this, Robert is about to kill Raimbaut but stops himself when he recognizes him as the husband of Alice (soprano), his foster-sister. At the invitation of Isabelle (soprano), the woman with whom Robert is in love, he agrees to enter a tournament in her honour. But then a knight comes on to the scene and challenges Robert to a duel which, he says, is to take place in a wood. Robert keeps the appointment and gets lost in the wood. The knight, on the other hand, remains at Court and appears as a combatant at the tournament in Isabelle's honour. In dismay, Robert seeks help from his friend Bertram (bass), who is actually the Devil and his own father. Bertram advises him to go to the cemetery and cut a magic branch which will give him the power to win Isabelle's heart. After taking Bertram's advice, Robert arrives at Isabelle's palace, whereupon the magic branch causes everyone to fall into a deep sleep. But before the magic takes effect on her too, Isabelle finds the strength to reproach Robert for his disloyalty. Consumed with remorse, Robert breaks the branch, at which everyone wakes up and Robert is arrested. He is released by Bertram, whose aim is to win his son's soul, and is about to swear allegiance to him when Alice enters with the news that Isabelle has forgiven him. At the same moment, the time allotted by the powers of darkness for the conquest of Robert's soul expires. Robert is released from Bertram's hold on him and is free to go to Isabelle, while Bertram himself returns to the underworld.

Robert le diable is the first opera in Meyerbeer's French period and marks the beginning of his collaboration with Eugène Scribe. This *grand-opéra* enjoyed enormous success and firmly established Meyerbeer as one of the greatest opera composers of his day. The work contains many inspired passages, and its dramatic insight is remarkable, but its complexity and sheer scale have meant that it is very seldom performed. It was revived in 1968 at the Maggio Musicale Festival in Florence but was not seen again in its complete version at the Paris Opéra until 1985, when the cast included Samuel Ramey, Alain Vanzo and June Anderson.

ROBERTO DEVEREUX

Opera in three acts by Gaetano Donizetti (1797–1848), to a libretto by Salvatore Cammarano, based on J. Ancelot's tragedy Elisabeth d'Angleterre. *First performance: Naples, Teatro San Carlo, 29 October 1837.*

The action takes place in London at the end of the sixteenth century. Roberto Devereux (tenor), Earl of Essex, is accused of treason by his enemies. Queen Elisabetta (soprano), who is in love with him, has no intention of authorizing that he be condemned. But then Roberto behaves somewhat coldly towards her, and the discovery of a scarf, an obvious love token, makes the Queen realize that Roberto no longer loves her. The new object of Roberto's love is Sara (mezzo-soprano), Duchess of Nottingham. These two had been in love before, but during Roberto's absence Sara's father had died and the Queen had obliged her to marry the Duke of Nottingham (baritone). Elisabetta is now convinced of Roberto's guilt and signs the death sentence, fully expecting him to give her back the ring on his finger which she herself had given him, with which he would be able to win clemency. In fact Roberto entrusts the ring to Sara and asks her to take it to the Queen. But Nottingham is so angry that he delays his wife's departure on her mission of mercy. Not until the death sentence has been carried out does Sara deliver the ring to the Queen. Distraught at the fatality of this delay, the Queen accuses the Duke and Duchess of the death of her beloved Roberto.

Roberto Devereux enjoyed great success and was performed regularly until 1882. Revived at the Teatro San Carlo in Naples in 1964 with the soprano Leyla Gencer in the lead, it was subsequently staged quite frequently.

ROI DE LAHORE, LE

Opera in five acts by Jules Massenet (1842–1912), to a libretto by Louis Gallet. First performance: Paris, Opéra, 27 April 1877.

The action takes place in India at the time of Sultan Mahmoud's invasion in the eleventh century. Scindia (baritone), prime minister to the King of Lahore, loves the priestess (soprano) and asks the High Priest, Nair Timour (bass), to release the young woman from her vows, but his request is dismissed. Scindia has discovered, however, that Nair has been meeting a man at night, and he publicly denounces her for doing so. Nair's secret lover turns out to be Alim (tenor), King of Lahore. In order to atone for his sin, Alim goes off to war against the Moslems. The scene changes to the battlefield, where Alim's army has been defeated. Scindia announces that he must now take command of the army, as the King has been mortally wounded. In reality the King has been vilely betrayed and thrown into prison, where he dies in Nair's arms. The Paradise Garden of the god Indra. Indra (bass) invites Alim to tell his story and is so moved by the sadness of Alim's experiences that he allows him to return to life among the living, as long as he understands that he will die exactly at the same moment as the woman he loves. Alim makes his reappearance in Lahore, dressed as a beggar, just as Scindia is about to be crowned king. There is a confrontation between them, and Alim accuses Scindia of having betrayed and murdered him. Scindia is taken aback for a moment, but then declares that Alim is an impostor. Alim manages to escape by taking refuge in the temple, where he is reunited with Nair. But Scindia hunts them down and threatens them both, whereupon Nair cheats Scindia by stabbing herself, and Alim dies with her as the god Indra had prophesied.

Le roi de Lahore is one of Massenet's most representative operas. Although earlier than both *Manon* and *Werther*, it already shows clear signs of the musical gifts that would later make Massenet one of the most important opera composers in the second half of the nineteenth century.

ROI D'YS, LE

Opera in three acts by Édouard Lalo (1823–1892), to a libretto by Édouard Blau after a Breton legend. First performance: Paris, Théâtre de l'Opéra-Comique, 7 May 1988.

Costume design for *Robert le diable*, an opera in five acts by Giacomo Meyerbeer.

The King of Ys (bass) has decided to bring a particularly bloody war to an end by offering the hand of his daughter Margared (mezzo-soprano) in marriage to Prince Karnac (baritone). But Margared and her sister Rozenn (soprano) are both secretly in love with young Mylio (tenor), who disappeared in mysterious circumstances many years previously. While celebrations in honour of Margared's marriage are taking place, Mylio suddenly reappears and announces that he loves Rozenn. Margared's reaction is to refuse to marry Karnac. Karnac is so enraged that he throws down the gauntlet and challenges the king. But the challenge is taken up instead by Mylio, who asks for the hand of Rozenn as his prize. He is successful and can therefore marry his beloved. Margared, consumed with jealousy, forms an alliance with the defeated Karnac. She tells him of a dyke which protects the city of Ys from the sea. If it were breached, she says, the entire population would be drowned. Then St. Corentin, patron saint of Ys, appears and attempts to dissuade them from this terrible idea. Margared is deeply affected by his appeal and wants to withdraw, but Karnac is adamant that the plan will go ahead and prepares to demolish the dyke. The sea engulfs the city and its terrified people find refuge on high ground. Mylio kills Karnac, leaving a repentant Margared. She waits until the waters have almost reached the higher ground before calling out to St. Corentin to forgive her and then throwing herself into the torrent. The saint appears, whereupon the sea rapidly recedes. The people pray for Margared's soul.

Lalo's opera received enormous public and critical acclaim and remains popular in France.

ROLANDI, GIANNA

(New York 1952)

American soprano. She studied music at the Curtis Institute in Philadelphia. In 1975 she joined the resident company of the New York City Opera, where she made her name as a *coloratura* soprano in *I puritani*, *Lucia di Lammermoor* and *Rigoletto*. Her reputation rests on her appearances at the Metropolitan Opera in New York, where she made her debut in 1979 in *Der Rosenkavalier* and at numerous European opera houses and festivals, including Glyndebourne, the Grand Théâtre in Geneva, the Paris Opéra and the Teatro dell'Opera in Rome.

The soprano Adelina Patti in Gounod's *Roméo et Juliette.*

ROLFE JOHNSON, ANTHONY

(Tackley, Oxfordshire 1940)

British tenor. A pupil at the Guildhall School of Music, he made his debut in 1973 with the English Opera Group and then began to appear regularly with English National Opera and Welsh National Opera. Also a concert soloist and known throughout the world for his singing of oratorio, Rolfe Johnson has won particular acclaim for his performances of Mozart in Aix-en-Provence and at La Scala, Milan, Salzburg and other major opera venues.

ROMANI, FELICE

(Genoa 1788–Moneglia 1865)

Italian librettist, poet and critic. One of the leading librettists of the early nineteenth century, he made his start with *La rosa rossa e la rosa bianca* and *Medea in Corinto* by Mayr (1813). His many libretti include those for Rossini's *Il turco in Italia* and *Bianca e Faliero*, Bellini's *Il pirata*, *La straniera*, *I Capuleti ed i Montecchi*, *La sonnambula* and *Norma*, Donizetti's *Anna Bolena*, *L'elisir d'amore*, *Parisina* and *Lucrezia Borgia*, and Verdi's *Un giorno di regno*.

ROMÉO ET JULIETTE

Opera in five acts by Charles Gounod (1818–1893), to a libretto by Jules Barbier and Michel Carré, from the play by Shakespeare. First performance: Paris, Théâtre Lyrique, 27 April 1867.

During a ball at the Capulets' house, Roméo (tenor), a member of the Montague family, the Capulets' bitterest enemies, enters wearing a mask. He meets Juliette (soprano), and they immediately fall in love. They manage to see each other again after the ball and decide to marry in secret, despite the hatred that divides their two families. The following day, in the cell of Frère Laurent (bass), Juliette's confessor, they are married. Shortly afterwards, a fight breaks out near the Capulets' house between rival Capulet and Montague supporters. Roméo intervenes to stop the fighting and is challenged by Tybalt (tenor), Juliette's cousin. Roméo does not accept the challenge at first, but when he sees his friend Mercutio (baritone) mortally wounded by Tybalt, his sense of outrage spurs him on to avenge his friend. Roméo kills Tybalt and is duly banished from Verona. After bidding Juliette a last desperate farewell, he leaves for Mantua. Juliette's father (bass) informs her that he has arranged for her to marry Count Pâris (baritone). Juliette is left alone with Frère Laurent and agrees to his idea that she drink a potion which will send her into such a deep sleep that everyone will believe she is dead, except Roméo, who will have been let into the secret. But Roméo does not receive Frère Laurent's message and is left thinking that Juliette really is dead. He goes to the Capulets' tomb to see his beloved wife again. He lies beside her and drinks poison. Juliette wakes up and finds Roméo dying. She stabs herself with his dagger and dies with him in a last passionate embrace.

One of the many operas inspired by the tragic story of the two young lovers of Verona, *Roméo et Juliette* was a great success at its premiere and enjoyed many repeat performances. What emerges most clearly from this score is Gounod's great lyrical gift, illustrated by the arias and duets sung by Roméo and Juliette.

RONDINE, LA

Opera in three acts by Giacomo Puccini (1858–1924), to a libretto by Giuseppe Adami. First performance: Monte Carlo, Théâtre du Casino, 27 March 1917.

SHAKESPEARE IN OPERA

The plays of William Shakespeare (1564–1616) have inspired many composers, providing them with an unparalleled and inexhaustible source of ideas for operas. By the end of the seventeenth century, the English composer Henry Purcell had already written *The Fairy Queen* and *The Tempest* as well as incidental music for *A Midsummer Night's Dream* and *The Tempest*. During the eighteenth century many operas were based on Shakespeare's *Romeo and Juliet* – Niccolò Zingarelli's *Romeo e Giulietta*, for instance (1796) was performed at the leading opera houses of Europe over a long period. The tragic story of the young lovers from Verona was a favourite among Romantic composers, among them Vaccai (in 1825), Bellini (1830) and Gounod (1867). In the twentieth century it continued to appeal, resulting in the opera by Zandonai and the dramatic oratorio *Romeo und Julia* (1947) by the German composer Boris Blacher. The nineteenth century saw Shakespeare's *Henry IV* providing the source material for operas by Pacini (staged in 1824) and Mercadante (in 1834), the latter being one of the first composers to write an opera based on *Hamlet* (1832), although the most celebrated opera from this play is the one by the French composer Ambroise Thomas (1868). *Othello*, *King Lear*, *Macbeth* and *Antony and Cleopatra* have inspired undisputed masterpieces in music, from Rossini's *Otello* (1816) to Verdi's powerful version of the same play (1887) and the German composer Reimann's *Lear*. The young Verdi composed an opera of great intensity from Shakespeare's *Macbeth*, and something of the same dramatic energy can also be found in Bloch's *Macbeth* (1910) which has the added feature of keeping strictly to the original text, even using Shakespeare's own words. The tragic events in the life of the Queen of Egypt, which Shakespeare had immortalized in *Antony and Cleopatra* (1606–7), have led to operas by, among others, Samuel Barber, whose *Antony and Cleopatra* was the inaugural production at the new Metropolitan Opera House in New York in 1966. Not only Shakespeare's tragedies but also his comedies have aroused the interest of many opera composers: the play *Much Ado About Nothing* was transformed by Berlioz into his 1862 *opéra-comique* of 1862, *Béatrice et Bénédict*; while *The Merry Wives of Windsor* has also received a good deal of attention, not least from Karl Ditters von Dittersdorf (1796) and Antonio Salieri, whose brilliant *Falstaff* was staged in 1799. To these should be added Michael Balfe's *Falstaff*, (1838), Nicolai's *Die lustigen* Weiber von Windsor (1849) and Adolphe Adam's *Falstaff* (1856), but the most famous opera with this title is unquestionably Verdi's, written by him at the age of 79 after 55 years as a composer and distinguished by a truly extraordinary originality and innovative style. Richard Wagner drew on Shakespeare's *Measure for Measure* for his opera *Das Liebesverbot* (1823) and Benjamin Britten's 1960 opera, *A Midsummer Night's Dream*, is one of his most imaginative and poetic works.

Above: A scene from *Otello* by Gioachino Rossini in a print of the time.

Right: Portrait of William Shakespeare.

The action takes place in Paris during the Second Empire and opens in the luxurious house of Magda de Civry (soprano), mistress of the banker Rambaldo (baritone). She tells her guests of the time she went to Chez Bullier and met a young student who gave her her first experience of love. While the poet Prunier (tenor) is making remarks about Magda's sentimental notions of romance, a new guest comes in. This is young Ruggero Lastouc (tenor), who has come up from the country to meet Rambaldo. As it is his first time in Paris, Lisette (soprano), Magda's maid, suggests he spend an evening at Chez Bullier. Magda decides she wants to be there too, incognito. The scene changes to Chez Bullier where Magda, dressed in her maid's clothes, is sitting at the same table as Ruggero, and he has not recognized her. Overwhelmed by the memory of her first love, Magda gives in to the passion she is beginning to feel for the young man. Time passes. Magda and Ruggero are living together in a little house on the Côte d'Azur. Ruggero tells Magda that he wants to marry her, and that they have his mother's blessing. But Magda has convinced herself that her past makes her unworthy to be Ruggero's wife. So she tells him who she really is and then leaves him to return to Paris and her ''gilded-cage'' life.

The idea of writing a romantic comic operetta in the Viennese style appealed to Puccini, but he had a fairly difficult time composing *La rondine*. Having signed the contract in 1914, he took until 1916 to finish the work. The first performance was an enormous success, and although subsequent revivals of the opera were not always well received, it has remained quite popular and is still performed.

ROSENKAVALIER, DER

(The Knight of the Rose)

Opera in three acts by Richard Strauss (1864–1949), to a libretto by Hugo von Hofmannsthal. First performance: Dresden, Königliches Opernhaus, 26 January 1911.

The Princess of Werdenberg, known as the Feldmarschallin (soprano), is entertaining her young lover, Count Octavian (mezzo-soprano), in the privacy of her bedroom, when sounds from the antechamber startle them into thinking that the Marschallin's husband has returned earlier than expected. Octavian has just enough time to dress up as a woman before the door bursts open, revealing Baron Ochs (bass), a boorish and conceited individual who has come to tell his cousin the Marschallin that he is engaged to Sophie (soprano), daughter of the wealthy burgher von Faninal (baritone). Ochs asks the Marschallin who she thinks would be the best person to deliver the traditional symbolic silver rose to his fiancée. The Marschallin suggests Count Octavian as a possible messenger and shows the Baron a portrait of him. Ochs is satisfied and leaves. Alone again with Octavian, the Marschallin is overwhelmed by a melancholy, foreboding that he will desert her for a younger woman. The scene changes to von Faninal's house. Octavian arrives, goes up to Sophie and presents her with the rose. The two of them immediately feel attracted to each other. While they are exchanging tender feelings, they are discovered, whereupon Octavian confronts the Baron and nicks him with his sword. An uproar ensues, and the situation is complicated even further when a message is handed to the Baron informing him that the maid (actually Octavian in disguise) he had seen that morning in the Marschallin's bedroom was hoping for a private rendezvous with him. The meeting is arranged to take place at a tavern. Baron Ochs keeps the appointment and is preparing to enjoy this adventure with the ''maid'' when a woman suddenly appears and claims that she is the Baron's abandoned wife and the children she has brought with her are his children. This causes more confusion, made worse by the arrival of a Police Officer who starts an investigation. Everything is resolved when Octavian reappears dressed as a man and the deception is brought to light. The Marschallin comes in to confirm Octavians identity. Then she realizes that Sophie and Octavian love each other and sadly, but with dignity, accepts the fact that the laws of life will often show no mercy.

Der Rosenkavalier is Richard Strauss's creative *tour de force*. Unlike in his previous operas *Salome* and *Elektra*, he dispensed with somber settings and chose the heady atmosphere of a ''comedy for music.'' In the composer's words, ''The libretto is bathed in a delightful rococo atmosphere, which I have done my best to translate into music ...'' Alongside the fascinating soliloquies, which resemble refined conversations, Strauss has created an orchestral sound well endowed with colour and a richness of timbre so exceptional that in the ensemble scenes the music can even drown out von Hofmanns-

Above: A scene from *Der Rosenkavalier* by Richard Strauss, in a 1989 production at Florence's Teatro Comunale.

Right: A costume model by Roller for the first performance of *Der Rosenkavalier* at Dresden's Königliches Opernhaus in 1911.

thal's words. It is in this symphonic quality of *Der Rosenkavalier*, and Strauss's way of employing it to filter and illuminate the psychology of his characters, that the opera's greatness is to be found.

ROSSELLINI, RENZO
(Rome 1908–Monte Carlo 1982)
Italian composer and music critic. The brother of the film director Roberto Rossellini, he composed numerous film scores. He made his opera debut in 1956 with *La guerra*. This was followed by *Il vortice* (1958), *Uno squardo dal ponte* (1961), *Il linguaggio dei fiori* (1963), *La leggenda del ritorno* (1966), *L'avventuriero* (1968), *L'annonce faite à Marie* (1970) and *La reine morte* (1973).

ROSSI, GAETANO
(Verona 1774–1855)
Italian librettist. He worked at La Fenice in Venice and as stage-manager at the Teatro Filarmonico in Verona. A prolific and admired librettist (he produced about 120 in all), he provided texts for Rossini's *La cambiale di matrimonio*, *La scala di seta*, *Tancredi* and *Semiramide*, Donizetti's *Linda di Chamounix*, Meyerbeer's *Il crociato in Egitto* and Mercadante's *Il bravo*.

ROSSI-LEMENI, NICOLA
(Istanbul 1920–Bloomington, Indiana 1991)
Italian bass. He studied singing with his mother, the Russian singer Xenia Lemeni Makedon, and in Verona with Cusinati. After his 1946 debut at La Fenice in Venice (as Varlaam in *Boris Godunov*), Rossi-Lemeni appeared at leading international opera houses and within a few years made his name as one of the finest singing actors since the war. Acclaimed for his performances in *Boris Godunov*, *Don Carlos*, *Anna Bolena* and *La forza del destino*, he also earned a reputation for his commitment to twentieth-century opera, appearing in operas by Berg, Falla and Bloch as well as in world premieres, such as Pizzetti's *Assassinio nella cattedrale* (1958).

ROSSINI, GIOACHINO
(Pesaro 1792–Passy, Paris 1868)
Italian composer. Born into a musical family (his father was a horn player and his mother a singer), young Gioachino taught himself music before going on to attend the Liceo Musicale in Bologna (1806). During this period he composed his first opera, *Demetrio e Polibio* (1812). But his official debut had already taken place in Venice (1810) with *La cambiale di matrimonio*. This was followed by *L'equivoco stravagante* (1811), *L'inganno felice*, *Ciro in Babilonia*, *La scala di seta*, *La pietra del paragone* and *L'occasione fa il ladro*, all dating from 1812, of which *La pietra del paragone* was especially important as Rossini's first major success at La Scala, Milan. In 1813 he continued to write for the Venetian theaters (for whom he composed *L'inganno felice*, *La scala di seta* and *L'occasione fa il ladro*), completing *Il signor Bruschino* and *Tancredi*, the latter firmly establishing his reputation and leading to the overwhelming and irresistible *L'italiana in Algeri*. The year 1814 began with a failure, *Aureliano in Palmira* at La Scala, but the same opera house would shortly witness the success of his next opera, *Il turco in Italia*. *Sigismondo* turned out to be another fiasco, but then Rossini had written it for Venice, where he was on the Austrian police's list of prime suspects for his openly republican sympathies. So it was at the age of 23 and already at the height of his fame that Rossini left Venice for Naples, where in 1815 he won acclaim for *Elisabetta, regina d'Inghilterra*. During 1816 he spent some time in Rome, during which he produced *Torvaldo e Dorliska* and, most notably, *Il barbiere di Siviglia* (The Barber of Seville), followed in 1817 by *La Cenerentola* (Cinderella) and, for La Scala, *La gazza ladra* (The Thieving Magpie). But it was in Naples that Rossini composed his most important *opere serie*: *Otello* (1816), *Armida* (1817), *Mosè in Egitto* (1818), *Ricciardo e Zoraide* (1818), *Ermione* (1819), *La donna del lago* (1819), *Maometto II* (1820) and *Zelmira* (1822). Other operas belonging to these years include *Adelaide di Borgogna* (Rome, 1817), *Adina* (composed in 1818, but not staged until 1926 in Lisbon), *Bianco e Faliero* (Milan, 1819) and *Matilde di Shabran* (Rome, 1821). *Semiramide* was premiered in Venice in 1823 and marked the end of Rossini's career as a composer in Italy. He moved to France, settling in Paris in 1824, and made his Paris theater debut in 1825 with *Il viaggio a Rheims* (1825), written in honour of the coronation of Charles X. As he adapted to French taste in opera, Rossini radically revised *Maometto II* and *Mosè in Egitto*, transforming them into *Le siège de Corinthe* (1826) and *Moïse et Pharaon* (1827). After the exquisite *Le Comte Ory* (1828), an opera which would have no little influence on French opera in the years that followed, Rossini himself composed in 1829 what was to be his swan song in opera, *Guillaume Tell*, a work which Berlioz hailed as "Rossini's masterpiece" and included everything Rossini had achieved as an opera composer.

ROTA, NINO
(Milan 1911–Rome 1979)
Italian composer. He studied in Milan, Rome and Philadelphia. He came to fame as the composer of film scores for the Italian director Federico Fellini. He also wrote music for the theater, including the operas *Ariodante* (1942), *Il cappello di paglia di Firenze* (1955), *La notte di un nevrastenico* (1959), *Aladino e la lampada magica* (1968) and *La visita meravigliosa* (1970).

ROTHENBERGER, ANNELIESE
(Mannheim 1924)
German soprano. She studied at the Conservatory in Mannheim and made her debut in 1943 in Koblenz. She then joined the Hamburg Opera Company (1946–56), as well as appearing regularly at the Vienna Staatsoper (from 1953), at the Salzburg Festival (from 1954) and at the world's leading opera houses. An excellent performer in Mozart (especially as Pamina and Constanze) and

Above: Gioachino Rossini.

Left: The German soprano Anneliese Rothenberger.

Richard Strauss (Sophie, Zdenka), Rothenberger also came to be acknowledged as an outstanding operetta singer on the strength of her radiant agile lyric soprano voice, coupled with impressive performing gifts.

ROUSSEL, ALBERT

(Tourcoing 1869–Royan 1937)
French composer. He gave up his career in the navy to concentrate on music, studying with Gigout and D'Indy, and then became a professor at the Schola Cantorum in Paris (1902–13). He wrote three operas: *La naissance de la lyre* (1925), *Le testament de tante Caroline* (1936), and *Padmâvatî* (1923), which is regarded as his masterpiece.

RUBINSTEIN, ANTON GRIGOR'YEVICH

(Podolsk 1829–St. Petersburg 1894)
Russian composer and pianist. He came to be acknowledged as one of the greatest pianists of his generation. In 1848 he settled in St. Petersburg, where he pursued concertizing and composition and founded the Conservatory, of which he was director from 1862 to 1867 and from 1887 to 1890. His output as a composer was prolific, and the most important of his operas is *Demon* (1875).

RUDEL, JULIUS

(Vienna 1921)
Austrian-born conductor, naturalized American. He began studying music at the Vienna Academy of Music and then in 1938 moved to the United States where he attended the Mannes School of Music in New York. His debut as a conductor was at City Center in 1944 in Johann Strauss's *Der Zigeunerbaron* (The Gipsy Baron). He was artistic and music director of New York City Opera (1957–79) and had an active international career. He made numerous recordings of Italian operas, including *I puritani*, *Mefistofele*, *Anna Bolena*, *Rigoletto*, and also French operas like *Louise*, *Les contes d'Hoffmann*, *Thaïs*, *Manon* and *Cendrillon*, in many of which the soprano Beverly Sills sang the leading role.

RUFFINI, ALESSANDRA

(Milan 1958)
Italian soprano. She studied at the Conservatorio Giuseppe Verdi in Milan, and completed her training at La Scala (1983–85). She made her debut in 1985 in Vivaldi's *Giustino*. Ruffino specializes in the eighteenth-century repertoire and has performed in many operas, including several revivals: Sacrati's *La finta pazza*, Gluck's *Paride e Elena* and Salieri's *La locandiera*. Her excellent voice and technical skill, together with her impressive stage presence, have also earned her praise in the operas of Rossini (*Il barbiere di Siviglia, Adina*), Bizet (*Les pêcheurs de perles*), Delibes (*Lakmé*), Gounod (*Romeo et Juliette*), Verdi (*Rigoletto*) and Puccini (*La bohème*).

Above: The Italian soprano Alessandra Ruffini.

RUSALKA

Lyrical fairy-tale in three acts by Antonín Dvořák (1841–1904), to a libretto by Jaroslav Kvapil. First performance: Prague, Czech National Theater, 31 March 1901.

On the shores of a lake, the nymph Rusalka (soprano) confides to the old Water Spirit (bass) that she is in love with a Prince (tenor) and wants to be changed into a human being. The Water Spirit makes a vain attempt to dissuade Rusalka but then gives in and advises her to go and see the witch Ježibaba (contralto). Ježibaba agrees to turn her into a human, but on certain conditions: Rusalka will no longer be able to speak, and should she lose the Prince's love, she will change back into a nymph and he will be damned with her. No sooner has Rusalka been transformed than the Prince appears and leads her to his castle. But very soon the Prince grows tired of this young woman who does not speak, and he surrenders to the love of a Foreign Princess (soprano). Rusalka plunges into the lake, where she is changed into a will-o'-the-wisp and only the Prince's death can save her, the very idea of which she rejects, as she still loves him. The young Prince has not forgotten Rusalka and, consumed by remorse, searches for her in desperation. When he finds her again, he clasps her in a passionate embrace, despite the warning that to do so will prove fatal for him, which it does, leaving Rusalka to make her own sad way back into the waters of the lake.

Rusalka is, with Smetana's *Prodaná nevěsta*, the most popular opera in the Czech repertoire, as well as being Dvořák's best-known work. In it the composer creates character and dramatic situation by an exquisite use of *leitmotiv* and inspired lyricism.

RYDL, KURT

(Vienna 1947)
Austrian bass. He studied at the Vienna Academy of Music and the Moscow Conservatory. After successes in major singing competitions, he made his debut in 1973 in Stuttgart as Daland in *Der fliegende Holländer* (The Flying Dutchman). From 1977 onwards he was a permanent member of the Vienna Staatsoper company. Rydl's considerable repertoire includes Italian, French, German and Russian operas. He has appeared at major international opera houses, including Bayreuth, La Scala, Milan, and San Francisco, and sang the role of the Grand Inquisitor (*Don Carlos*) at the Arena in Verona in 1992.

RYSANEK, LEONIE

(Vienna 1926)
Austrian soprano. A pupil of Alfred Jerger and Rudolf Grossmann at the Vienna Conservatory, she made her debut in 1949 as Agathe in Weber's *Der Freischütz*. In 1951 she had her first important success as Sieglinde in *Die Walküre* at the Bayreuth Festival, where she was to appear regularly until the 1980s. Engagements followed in Munich (from 1952), Covent Garden (from 1953), the Vienna Staatsoper (from 1954) and the Metropolitan Opera in New York (from 1959). A distinguished Wagner and Strauss singer, Rysanek was an equally persuasive Verdi performer (*Macbeth*, *Un ballo in maschera*, *Otello*). Her firm voice and excellent technique enabled her to sustain her career over many years, and in 1992 she sang the Countess in Tchaikovsky's *Pikovaya Dama* (The Queen of Spades) in Barcelona, Klytämnestra in Strauss's *Elektra* in Paris and Kostelnička in *Jenůfa* in New York.

S

SADKO

Romantic opera in seven scenes (three or five acts) by Nicolay Rimsky-Korsakov (1844–1908), to a libretto by the composer and Vladimir I. Bielsky, based on an old anonymous Russian poem. First performance: Moscow, Solodovnikov Theater, 7 January 1898.

Scene I. At a banquet of the merchants of Novgorod, two players on the *gousli*, a type of guitar, entertain. Najata (contralto) sings of the glories of old Kiev, but Sadko (tenor) irritates the merchants by suggesting that they lack the spirit of adventure. If he had as much money as they have he would not be content until his ships had sailed out of the lake into the the open sea in search of unknown treasures. They laugh at him and continue their merrymaking. Scene II. At night. Sadko sings on the shore of lake Ilmen and the daughters of the sea appear. The Sea King's daughter, Volkhova (soprano), falls in love with him and, before she leaves at dawn, makes him three promises: he will catch three golden fishes, he will journey to a far distant land and she will wait for him faithfully. Scene III. Lubava (mezzosoprano), Sadko's wife, is anxious lest Sadko may have left her and gone on an expedition. Scene IV. The harbour. Sadko bets the assembled crowd of merchants that he can catch golden fishes in the lake. He does, and the merchants agree that their wealth is forfeit. Sadko chooses to take only their ships and invites the adventurous among them to join him. Three foreigners describe their homelands for him – a Viking (bass), an Indian (tenor) and a Venetian (baritone) – and Sadko resolves to set sail for Venice. Scene V. Twelve years have passed. Sadko is again bound for Novgorod with a cargo of treasure. His ship is becalmed, and he remembers that he has not paid tribute to the King of the Ocean. The sailors throw pearls and gold overboard to no avail and Sadko realizes that he must sacrifice himself. He watches his ship sail away as he stands on a bare plank floating on the sea, strumming his *gousli*. Volkhova bids him descend to the seabed. Scene VI. At the Court of the King of the Ocean, he is presented to Volkhova's parents and the King celebrates his marriage to the Princess. Suddenly a legendary hero, dressed as a pilgrim, appears: he announces that Volkhova must immediately return to Novgorod, for she is to be transformed into a river. The old King's reign is over. Sadko and his bride set sail in a sea shell. Scene VII. The shore of lake Ilmen at dawn. Volkhova leaves Sadko asleep and becomes the river which joins the lake to the sea. When he awakes, he finds his wife Lubava standing beside him joyful at his return. He suspects that he has dreamed his adventures until he recognizes his ship sailing into the harbour and discovers that he is welcomed home as the wealthiest merchant in the city.

Rimsky-Korsakov made his first draft in 1867, in the form of a symphonic poem, and in it was condensed the musical substance of the opera that was to be composed almost 30 years later. The range of the subject, the fantastic theme and the possibility of introducing the grandeur of the sea onto the stage by expressing the sounds of it, all captured the ardent imagination of the composer.

SAINT OF BLEECKER STREET, THE

Opera in three acts and five scenes by Giancarlo Menotti (b. 1911), to the composer's own libretto. First performance: New York, Broadway Theater, 27 December 1954.

The action takes place in a poor street in the Italian quarter of New York, home to Annina (soprano), a young healer regarded as a saint, and her brother, Michele (tenor), who thinks his sister is a fanatic. During a wedding ceremony, Annina and Don Marco (bass), a priest supportive to Annina, reproach Desideria (soprano), Michele's lover, for her immoral conduct. Desideria is infuriated and reacts by accusing Michele of being secretly in love with his sister. Michele kills Desideria and runs away. Annina meets her brother again in a subway station and pleads with him to give himself up, but he refuses and instead implores her to leave the city with him. A few days later, Annina is dying and expresses a long-cherished desire to become a nun. While the religious ceremony is taking place, Annina loses consciousness, and as Don Marco slips the consecrated ring on her finger, she dies.

The Saint of Bleecker Street illustrates Menotti's preference for stories of everyday life and, in this case, his wish to portray Italian immigrant life in New York, which is bound up with human passions and a fanatical, mystical religious faith, challenged by contact with the new reality of America.

Above: Sketch for *The Saint of Bleecker Street* by Giancarlo Menotti.

Left: The French composer, organist and pianist Camille Saint-Saëns (see page 320).

SAINT-SAËNS, CAMILLE

(Paris 1835–Algiers 1921)

French composer, organist and pianist. A child prodigy, he was already appearing in public by the age of ten. He went on to study organ and composition with Benoist and Halévy. He made his debut as an opera composer in 1864 with *Le timbre d'argent*. His most famous work is *Samson et Dalila*, which was first performed in German in Weimar (1877) and at the Paris Opéra in 1892. He also wrote *Étienne Marcel* (1879), *Henry VIII* (1884), *Proserpine* (1887), *Ascanio* (1890), *Phryné* (1893), *Les barbares* (1901), *Hélène* (1904), *L'ancêtre* (1906) and *Déjanire* (1911).

SALIERI, ANTONIO

(Legnago 1750–Vienna 1825)

Italian composer. He was first encouraged in music by his brother and went to study in Venice with Pescetti, Pacini and particularly Leopold Gassmann, music director to the Imperial Chapel in Vienna, who persuaded him to move to Vienna. Here he made his debut as an opera composer with *Le donne letterate* (1770). This was followed by further operas which brought him much fame. His *Europa riconosciuta* was the work chosen to mark the opening of La Scala in Milan in 1778. For Paris he wrote *Les Danaïdes* (1784) and *Tarare* (1787), to a libretto by Beaumarchais, which Da Ponte transformed into *Axur, re d'Ormus*, the version staged in Vienna in 1788. Salieri's other operas for Vienna included *La grotta di Trofonio* (1785), *Prima la musica, poi le parole* (1786) and *Falstaff* (1799).

SALOME

Opera in one act by Richard Strauss (1864–1949), from Oscar Wilde's play in Hedwig Lachmann's German translation. First performance: Dresden, Königliches Opernhaus, 9 December 1905.

The action takes place at the palace of Herodes (tenor) in Tiberias. Narraboth (tenor), Captain of the Guard, watches entranced as Salome (soprano), Herodes's daughter, appears on the terrace. She in turn is fascinated by the voice of Jochanaan (John the Baptist, baritone), which she can hear coming up from the well below, where he has been imprisoned by Herodes. He is proclaiming the coming of the Messiah. Salome orders that the prisoner be brought before her, even though Narraboth tries to dissuade her. As soon as he is out of the well, Jochanaan unleashes a tirade against Herodes and his wife, Herodias (mezzo-soprano). Salome is overwhelmed by the sight of Jochanaan and uses all her powers of seduction on him. Narraboth becomes desperate and kills himself. Jochanaan rejects Salome and goes back down to his cell. Herodes appears and is shocked to see Narraboth lying dead, with the dark words of the prophet still audible from below. Herodes, inflamed with lust, asks Salome to dance for him, promising her that afterwards he will grant her dearest wish. Salome dances. When she has finished, she asks for the head of Jochanaan. Herodes is appalled and tries to persuade her to change her mind, but eventually he has to give in. The executioner brings Jochanaan's head up from the well on a silver platter. Ecstatically Salome seizes hold of it. Consumed with passion, she gazes at the bleeding head and then kisses it on the lips. This horror proves too much for Herodes, and he cries out to the guards to kill her.

Above: The Italian composer Antonio Salieri.

Right: Title page to an Italian translation of the libretto of *Salome* by Richard Strauss.

Despite the sensitive nature of the story and the atrocity of the final scene, *Salome* was an immediate triumph: the singers, conductor and composer took 38 curtain-calls. The work became an international success and at once entered the repertoires of opera houses everywhere. The opera expresses great dramatic tension, reinforced by an extremely lavish orchestration in the style of Strauss's symphonic poems, which can be seen as a new departure the composer would develop in his subsequent operas.

SAMSON ET DALILA

Opera in three acts and four scenes by Camille Saint-Saëns (1835–1921), to a libretto by Ferdinand Lemaire after the Bible story and Voltaire. First performance: Weimar, Hoftheater, 2 December 1877.

The action takes place in Gaza, Palestine, in about 115 B.C. The people of Israel are crying out against their oppression by the Philistines. Samson (tenor), a Hebrew warrior, urges the people to give themselves wholly to God, and then, as though inspired from Heaven, goes up to the satrap Abimélech (bass), who had been treating the Israelites with contempt, and kills him. Samson puts himself at the head of rebels and wins back control of the city, but while he is kneeling at prayer with his people, he is approached by Dalila (mezzo-soprano), priestess of Dagon, who invites him to her house. He falls under her spell and agrees to come. The High Priest (baritone) persuades Dalila to find out the secret of Samson's strength. Samson is seduced by Dalila into revealing his secret. Dalila then deprives him of his supernatural power by cutting off his hair, and Samson is taken

prisoner and blinded. In chains, Samson calls upon God to forgive him for his transgression and is then led through the midst of the dancing Philistines to the center of the temple and made to humble himself before the god Dagon. Samson asks a young boy to guide him towards two pillars which support the roof of the temple, then calls upon God to restore his old strength for just long enough to enable him to exert such colossal pressure on the columns that they give way. The Philistines are left screaming as the temple caves in, burying them beneath the rubble.

Samson et Dalila is Saint-Saëns' most famous work. Its vocal line and the sensuality of the music, imbued with the rich incandescence of its Wagnerian orchestration, have contributed to its continuing prominence in world opera.

SANTI, NELLO

(Adria 1931)

Italian conductor. He studied composition and singing at the Conservatorio Pedrollo in Padua. He made his debut at Padua's Teatro Verdi conducting *Rigoletto* in 1951. From 1958 to 1969 he conducted the Zurich Opera. He went on to conduct at Covent Garden (*La traviata*, 1960), the Vienna Staatsoper (1960), the Arena in Verona and at numerous other opera houses. His reputation also rests on his association with the Metropolitan Opera in New York and regular conducting appearances there since 1962 in Italian opera, more recently *Manon Lescaut* (1990), *Luisa Miller* (1991), *Cavalleria rusticana* and *I pagliacci* (1993). Specializing mainly in Verdi, Santi is acclaimed for his skill in combining solid professionalism with precision in his support and accompaniment of singers.

SAPHO

Pièce lyrique *in five acts by Jules Massenet (1842–1912), to a libretto by Henri Cain and Arthur Bernède from the novel by Alphonse Daudet. First performance: Paris, Théâtre de l'Opéra-Comique, 27 November 1897.*

The action takes place in Paris. The sculptor Caoudal (baritone) has arranged a gathering of artists at his house, among them the young painter Jean Gaussin (tenor) who has just arrived from the country. Bewildered by his first experience of Parisian society, Jean is no less fascinated by the beautiful Fanny Legrand (soprano), a celebrated model who goes by the name of Sapho. Then Jean is visited by his father, Césaire (bass), his mother, Divonne (mezzo-soprano), and Irène (soprano), a young orphan who loves him. But the young painter is by now completely taken up with his love for Fanny, who returns these feelings. Fanny and Jean live happily together in the country in Ville-d'Avray, but this peaceful scene is interrupted by the arrival of Caoudal and a bunch of his dissolute friends. Jean learns from Caoudal that Sapho has a past which was anything but pure. He then has a furious quarrel with her, leaves, and returns to Provence. There he tries to forget her by accepting Irène's love. Fanny's sudden arrival (she has been unable to bear losing Jean) promises to bring the two together again, but Jean's parents ask Fanny to leave. It is winter. Back at their house in Ville-d'Avray, Fanny rereads Jean's love letters. She looks up and sees him. He cannot live apart from her, but at the same time he is tormented by Fanny's past. She realizes that although there is still love between them, something has been destroyed which can never be restored. Jean eventually falls asleep, tired after his journey and the emotional turmoil of the situation. Fanny goes away, leaving him.

Although not often performed in recent

Above: A scene from *Samson et Dalila* by Saint-Saëns.

times, *Sapho* – which in some respects recalls *La traviata* – is one of Massenet's most successful operas. The two main characters are portrayed with an intuitiveness that beautifully conveys the dramatic and lyrical qualities in their natures, especially Fanny, in whom Massenet has created one of the most attractive and intense figures in French opera.

SARDINERO, VICENTE

(Barcelona 1937)
Spanish baritone. He studied at the Conservatory in Barcelona and began his career singing *zarzuelas*. After completing his training in Milan with Badiali, he made his name after taking part in two singing competitions, the Francisco Viñas in Barcelona (1965) and the Verdi in Busseto (1966). His debut came in 1967 at the Liceu in Barcelona when he sang Germont (*La traviata*). In the same year he embarked on an international career, which took him to La Scala (*Lucia di Lammermoor*), New York City Opera (*I pagliacci*, 1970) and other leading opera houses. More recently, Sardinero appeared at the Opéra in Paris (*I puritani*, 1987) and at the Teatro dell'Opera in Rome (*Roberto Devereux*, 1987).

SASS, SYLVIA

(Budapest 1951–1991)
Hungarian soprano. A pupil of Olga Revhegyi at the Liszt Academy in Budapest, she made her debut at the Budapest State Opera in 1971 as Frasquita (*Carmen*). After impressive results in major singing competitions, she quickly established an international reputation with appearances at Covent Garden (*I Lombardi*, 1976), the Metropolitan Opera in New York (*Tosca*, 1977), La Scala (*Manon Lescaut*, 1978), and other leading revues. Her decisive dramatic presence prompted her too soon to perform a repertoire of roles that were too dramatic for her voice, given that it was at its most successful and expressive when delivering a *pianissimo*. Among her best performances (which she also recorded) are Bartók's *A Kékszakállú herceg vára* (Bluebeard's Castle), Erkel's *Hunyadi László*, Mozart's *Don Giovanni* and Verdi's *Ernani* and *Stiffelio*.

Above: A scene from *La Scala di seta* by Rossini.

SĀVITRI

Opera in one act by Gustav Holst (1874–1934) to the composer's own libretto. First performance: London, Wellington Hall, 5 December 1916.

The action takes place in a forest in India. Sāvitri (soprano) is worried because her dreams have been warning her that a disaster is about to occur. Enter Death (bass) with the intention of taking Satyavan (tenor), Sāvitri's husband, away with him. Satyavan collapses lifeless into Sāvitri's arms, and she desperately vows eternal love. Death, moved by her selflessness, offers to grant Sāvitri anything she desires except giving Satyavan back his life. Sāvitri then asks for life, the life she receives from love, and says that for her life has only one name, the name of her husband. Death, won over by Sāvitri's heart-felt prayer, restores Satyavan to her.

Right: The Italian composer Domenico Scarlatti.

Sāvitri was composed in 1908 but had to wait until 1916 for its successful premiere. The opera draws its inspiration from an episode in the Indian epic poem, the *Mahabharata*.

SAWALLISCH, WOLFGANG

(Munich 1923)
German conductor. He studied at the Munich Academy and made his debut in Aachen in 1947 (Humperdinck's *Hänsel und Gretel*), continuing to conduct there until 1953. He rapidly became established and was appointed *Generalmusikdirektor* in Aachen (1953–57), Wiesbaden (1957–59), Cologne (1959–63) and the Bayreuth Festival (1957–62) before moving on to an equivalent post with the Munich Opera in 1971 (he became *Intendant* in 1982). During this time Sawallisch had been conducting internationally as well as appearing as an accompanist at *Lieder* recitals. A frequent guest at La Scala, Milan, since his debut there in 1965, he returned in 1992 to conduct Strauss's *Arabella*. Sawallisch is regarded as one of the greatest conductors of his generation and has won particular acclaim for his interpretations of Wagner and Richard Strauss.

SCALA DI SETA, LA

(The Silken Ladder)
Opera in one act by Gioachino Rossini (1792–1868), to a libretto by Giuseppe Maria Foppa after François-Antoine-Eugène de Planard. First performance: Venice, Teatro Giustiniani di San Moisè, 9 May 1812.

Giulia (soprano) has secretly married Dorvil (tenor), but her guardian, Dormont (tenor), wants her to become the wife of Blansac (baritone), with whom Giulia's cousin Lucilla (mezzo-soprano) is in love. Every night Dorvil comes to Giulia by climbing a silken ladder to her window. Through a misunderstanding, the servant Germano gives Blansac the impression that Giulia is waiting for him that night. Lucilla discovers this intrigue and finds herself a hiding-place from which she can surprise them. Germano does the same, and so, last but not least, does Dormont, who ends up surprising Lucilla, Germano and Blansac. At first there is outrage, but then Dorvil and Giulia appear and admit to being married. They are forgiven by Dormont, who also gives his blessing to the marriage of Lucilla and Blansac.

The libretto for *La scala di seta*, taken from a French farce, is clearly similar to the story of Cimarosa's *Il matrimonio segreto*. Its premiere in Venice was a success, but the reception was mixed. Nevertheless the opera is a masterpiece, carried along by a brilliant energy, especially in the spacious final scene, which demonstrates Rossini's immense sense of theater.

SCALCHI, GLORIA

(Trieste 1956)

Italian mezzo-soprano. Born into a family of musicians which had produced a famous Rossini contralto during the nineteenth century, Sofia Scalchi (1850–1922), she was first taught to sing by her father. She specializes in the *bel canto* repertoire, particularly Rossini, and the Rossini roles she has sung include Emma (*Zelmira*, Teatro dell'Opera, Rome, 1989), Zomira (*Ricciardo e Zoriade*, Pesaro, 1990), Sinaide (*Mosè*, Teatro Comunale, Bologna, 1991), Andromaca (*Ermione*, Teatro dell'Opera, Rome, 1991), and Arsace (*Semiramide*, Pesaro, 1992), the role in which she made her debut with the Metropolitan Opera in New York (1992). Scalchi has also appeared in Donizetti's *La favorita* (Bergamo, 1991), Massenet's *Werther* and Donizetti's *Roberto Devereux* (Teatro Comunale, Bologna, 1991–92).

SCANDIUZZI, ROBERTO

(Maserada sul Piave 1958)

Italian bass. After graduating in singing from the Conservatorio in Treviso (1981), he made his debut in 1982 at the Teatro Comunale in Bologna as Brander in Berlioz's *La damnation de Faust* and at La Scala, Milan, as Bartolo in Mozart's *Le nozze di Figaro* with Riccardo Muti conducting. Within a short time, Scandiuzzi was making successful appearances at the major Italian opera houses. In 1985 came his Covent Garden debut (*Lucia di Lammermoor*), and he returned in 1991 to score a personal success as Fiesco (*Simon Boccanegra*) under Sir Georg Solti. His first appearance at the Vienna Staatsoper was in 1992 in *La forza del destino*, an opera in which he also sang at the Teatro San Carlo in Naples and Florence's Teatro Comunale (for Zubin Mehta). Scandiuzzi's voice has a particularly fine timbre, range and softness in delivery, and these qualities, combined with the elegance and vigour of his phrasing and an impressive stage presence, have led to his being acknowledged as one of the greatest Italian basses of his time. An acclaimed Verdi singer (*Don Carlos*, *Nabucco*, *Simon Boccanegra*, etc.), he has also given distinguished performances of the concert repertoire (Rossini's *Stabat Mater* and Verdi's *Requiem*), as well as appearing with some of the world's greatest conductors, including Giulini, Haitink, Ozawa and Sinopoli.

SCARLATTI, ALESSANDRO

(Palermo 1660–Naples 1725)

Italian composer. One of the greatest and most prolific opera composers of his day (he wrote nearly 150 operas), he was the founder of the Neapolitan School of opera. His debut came in 1679 with *Gli equivoci nel sembiante*. Scarlatti was responsible for establishing the three-part or Italian overture and the *da capo* aria as staple ingredients of baroque opera. His own most famous operas include *Mitridate Eupatore* (1707), *Il Tigrane* (1715), *Il trionfo dell'onore* (1718) and *La Griselda* (1721).

SCARLATTI, DOMENICO

(Naples 1685–Madrid 1757)

Italian composer, son of Alessandro. Remembered mainly as a composer for the harpsichord, he also composed some 50 operas, among them *Tetide in Sciro* (1712), *La dirindina* (1715) and *Il narciso* (1720).

SCHAUSPIELDIREKTOR, DER

(The Impresario)

Komödie mit Musik *in one act by Wolfgang Amadeus Mozart (1756–1791), to a libretto by Gottlieb Stephanie the younger. First performance: Vienna, Schönbrunn Palace, 7 February 1786.*

An impresario (speaking role) who has to put together a new opera company holds auditions for singers and actors. Two sopranos, Madame Herz and Madame Silberklang, are among those who sing for him. A vociferous argument breaks out between these two as to which is the prima donna. The tenor Monsieur Vogelsang intervenes and tries to calm them. Peace is eventually restored in the final vaudeville.

Many composers have written operas about the trials and tribulations of an opera impresario. Mozart took Stephanie's coarse libretto for this musical comedy and wrote a fine overture, two beautiful arias and a vaudeville. *Der Schauspieldirektor* was premiered in a double-bill with Salieri's opera *Prima la musica, poi le parole*, which proved the more successful of the two.

SCHIKANEDER, EMANUEL

(Straubing 1751–Vienna 1812)

German librettist, composer, actor, theatrical agent and singer. Schikaneder was a versatile character who wrote about 100 opera libretti, of which the most famous is *Die Zauberflöte* (The Magic Flute) by Mozart, with whom he enjoyed a close friendship.

SCHMIDT, ANDREAS

(Düsseldorf 1960)

German baritone. He studied organ, piano, conducting and then singing with Ingeborg Reichelt. He completed his training with Dietrich Fischer-Dieskau in Berlin and made his debut in 1984 as Malatesta in Donizetti's *Don Pasquale* with the Deutsche Oper Berlin. His fine voice, excellent technique and elegant phrasing rapidly established him as an artist of international stature, with appearances at Covent Garden (*Faust*, 1986, *Cosí fan tutte*, 1989), Munich (*Così fan tutte*, 1986); the Vienna Staatsoper (*Tannhäuser*, 1988–89) and the Metropolitan Opera, New York (*Le nozze di Figaro*, 1991). Also a highly acclaimed concert soloist, Schmidt

Above: Emanuel Schikaneder.

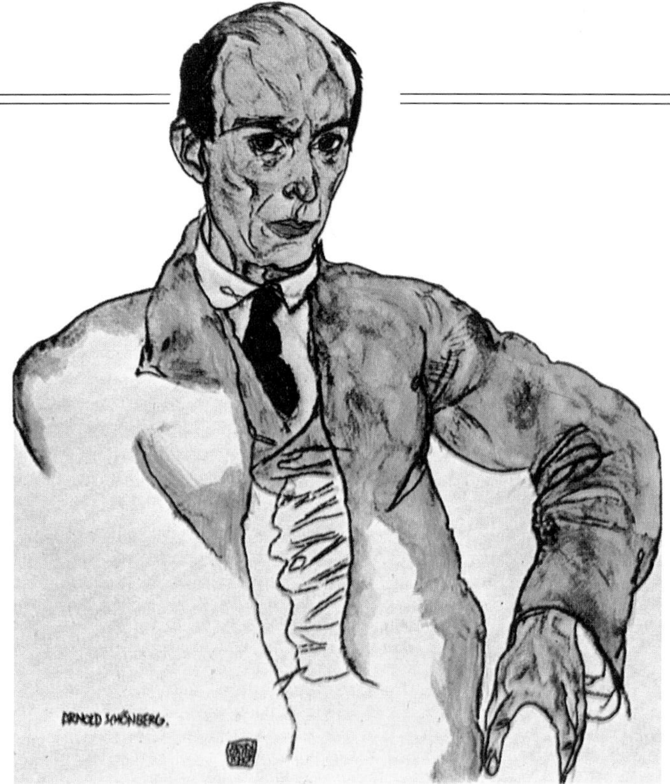

has come to be regarded as one of the most impressive baritones of the new generation.

SCHOENBERG, ARNOLD
(Vienna 1874–Los Angeles 1951)
Austrian composer. He was initially self-taught and then studied with Zemlinsky, who later became his brother-in-law. Schoenberg's completely new musical language is also given full expression in his four operas. *Erwartung* (Expectation, 1924) was followed by *Die glückliche Hand* (The Favoured Hand, 1924), in which the composer used *Sprechgesang* for the first time. Adopting the twelve-tone technique, Schoenberg wrote *Von Heute auf Morgen* (From Day to Day, 1930) and finally *Moses und Aron* (Moses and Aaron, 1954), which, although unfinished, is the high point of Schoenberg's achievement in opera.

SCHUBERT, FRANZ
(Lichenthal 1797–Vienna 1828)
Austrian composer. He showed exceptional artistic gifts at a very early age and began studying music with Michael Holzer, Kapellmeister in Lichenthal. In 1812 he became a pupil of Salieri, who taught him for about five years. His output for the theater had no success, and almost all his operas were premiered after his death. Schubert's interest in opera is demonstrated by the numerous scores he left unfinished or barely started. After his first attempt, *Der Spiegelritter* (The Looking-Glass Knight), composed between 1811 and 1812 but never completed, Schubert's most important theater works are *Claudine von Villa Bella* from 1815 (the overture and first act survive), *Die Freunde von Salamanka* (1815), *Alfonso und Estrella* (1821–22) and *Fierrabras* (1823).

Above: The Austrian composer Arnold Schoenberg.

SCHWARZ, HANNA
(Hamburg 1943)
German mezzo-soprano. She studied at the Hanover Musikhochschule, making her debut as Siegrune in *Die Walküre* in Hanover in 1970. Three years later, she joined the permanent company of the Hamburg Opera (1973). In 1975 she sang for the first time at the Bayreuth Festival (Erda in the *Ring*) and went on to appear regularly in such roles as Fricka (in the Boulez-Chéreau *Ring* cycle) and Brangäne (*Tristan und Isolde*) as well as in *Der Rosenkavalier* and *Die Frau ohne Schatten*, ideal operas for displaying the abundant vocal gifts for which Schwarz has won international acclaim.

SCHWARZKOPF, ELISABETH
(Jarocin, Poznan 1915)
German soprano, naturalized British. She studied in Berlin with Lula Mysz-Gmeiner and Maria Ivogün and she made her debut in 1938 with the Berlin Städtische Oper as one of the Flower Maidens in Wagner's *Parsifal*. Initially she concentrated on the *coloratura* repertoire. By the end of the Second World War, she had become a distinguished *Lieder* singer and then began to appear in Mozart operas and as an exceptional interpreter of Strauss roles in *Der Rosenkavalier*, *Capriccio* and *Arabella*. After retiring from the stage in 1971, Schwarzkopf gave concerts and recitals (her performances of *Lieder* by Schubert, Wolf, Strauss and Mahler are historic) until 1979, when she ended her singing career and turned instead to teaching and opera production (*Der Rosenkavalier* in Brussels, 1981).

SCHWEIGSAME FRAU, DIE
(The Silent Woman)
Comic opera in three acts by Richard Strauss (1864–1949), to a libretto by Stefan Zweig, after Ben Jonson's play Epicoene, or The Silent Woman. *First performance: Dresden, Staatsoper, 24 June 1935.*

The action takes place in the eighteenth century. The old sea-dog Sir Morosus (bass), who miraculously survived after his ship exploded, cannot endure noise of any kind. Henry Morosus (tenor), his nephew and sole heir, moves into the house with a group of friends who belong to an opera company, and they create chaos. Morosus is so enraged by this that he sends these unwanted guests away, disinherits his nephew, and asks his barber (baritone) to find him a wife. The barber, who is on Henry's side, introduces Morosus to Timida, a wise and silent woman who is actually Henry's wife, the singer Aminta, in disguise. After a mock wedding, Timida turns into a fiendish chatterbox. Morosus is in the depths of despair. At this point Henry and Aminta confess their hoax to Morosus, who reacts with apoplectic rage but then discovers his own inner peace after becoming reunited with them.

The score of *Die schweigsame Frau* is one of the richest and most elaborate Richard Strauss ever wrote. Its fast-moving, brilliant dialogues and near-virtuoso orchestration ensured the opera a triumphant premiere.

SCIMONE, CLAUDIO
(Padua 1934)
Italian conductor. He studied with Carlo Zecchi, Dimitri Mitropoulos and Franco Ferrara, and in 1959 founded the chamber orchestra I Solisti Veneti, with whom he rapidly won considerable fame for performances of eighteenth-century instrumental music, especially Vivaldi. In 1979 he made his opera debut

conducting Vivaldi's *Orlando Furioso* (which he had rediscovered) at the Teatro Filarmonico in Verona and repeating it at the Aix-en-Provence Festival in 1981. Scimone returned to operatic Vivaldi in 1984 when he conducted *Catone in Utica*, but he also became known for his performances (often backed up by recordings) of Rossini operas, including *L'Italiana in Algeri*, *La donna del lago*, *Mosè in Egitto*, *Maometto II*, *Ermione*, *Zelmira* and *Armida*.

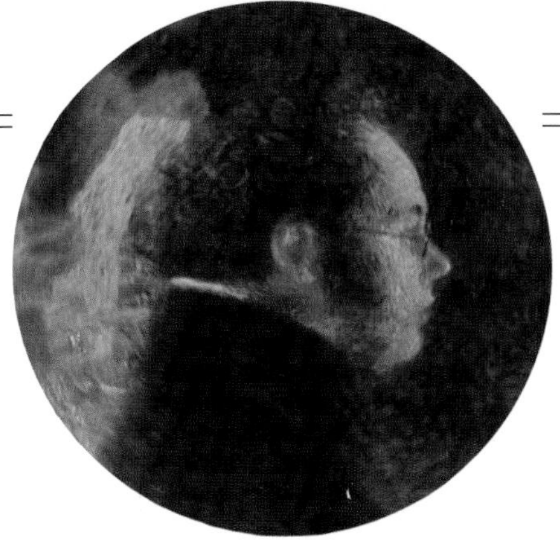

SCOTTO, RENATA

(Savona 1934)

Italian soprano. A pupil of Ghirardini, Merlini and Llopart, she made her debut in Savona in 1952 singing the lead in Verdi's *La traviata*, a role in which she returned a year later at the Teatro Nuovo in Milan. Also in 1953 she appeared for the first time at La Scala, Milan (as Walter in Catalani's *La Wally*). She then embarked on a brilliant career with engagements at the major Italian opera houses and became firmly established in 1957 when she replaced Maria Callas in a production of *La sonnambula* in Edinburgh. Appearances followed at the world's leading opera venues, although her name was particularly associated with the Metropolitan Opera, New York (1965–87), where she also made her opera production debut in *Madama Butterfly*, revived for the Arena in Verona in 1987. Her *coloratura* lyric soprano voice brought her fame as Mimi, Amina, Lucia, Gilda and Butterfly, and at the end of the 1960s she began gradually to enlarge her repertoire so that her many Verdi roles (*I Lombardi*, *Les vêpres siciliennes*, *Il trovatore*, *Macbeth*, etc.) were complemented by others from the operas of Puccini, Giordano and Mascagni, without diminishing the prominence of her extraordinary qualities in phrasing. In 1992 Scotto made her first appearance as the Marschallin in Richard Strauss's *Der Rosenkavalier* at the Teatro Massimo Bellini in Catania, Sicily.

SCOVOTTI, JEANETTE

(New York 1933)

American soprano. She studied singing with Margit Schey-Kux at the Third Street Music School and at the Juilliard School. She made her debut in 1959 at New York City Opera in Menotti's *The Medium*. In the 1962–63 season she appeared for the first time as Adele in Johann Strauss's *Die Fledermaus* with the Metropolitan Opera in New York, where she spent four seasons singing the major *coloratura* soprano roles. In 1966 she was engaged by Rolf Liebermann to join the permanent company of the Hamburg Opera. She then appeared at leading international opera venues and started making recordings. Scovotti's reputation also rests on her fine timbre and impeccable technique, leading to excellent performances and recordings of Offenbach's *Les contes d'Hoffmann*, Rameau's *Castor et Pollux*, Handel's *Rinaldo* and Richard Strauss's *Die schweigsame Frau*.

SECUNDE, NADINE

(Cleveland, Ohio 1951)

American soprano. One of the greatest interpreters of the Wagner and Strauss repertoires, she sang in the Munich Opera production of *Das Rheingold* in 1987, *Lohengrin* at Covent Garden in 1988, *Elektra* at the Boston Symphony Hall in 1988, *Tannhäuser* at Lyric Opera of Chicago in 1988, and *Lohengrin* at La Fenice in Venice in 1990.

SEGRETO DI SUSANNA, IL

(Susanna's Secret)

Opera in one act by Ermanno Wolf-Ferrari (1876–1948), to a libretto by Enrico Golisciani. First performance, with the German title Susannens Geheimnis, *Munich, Hoftheater, 4 December 1909.*

Count Gil (baritone) is jealous of his wife, Susanna (soprano). She has taken to leaving the house at unusual times, and there is a smell of tobacco in the house. These things have made the Count suspicious, and he believes she has a lover. He questions her, and when she denies everything, he accuses her of hiding something. Susanna admits she is, but will not enlighten him further. The Count makes a scene and breaks things. Susanna shuts herself in her room, only to reemerge and suggest to her husband that he might like to go out to his club. The

Left: A scene from *Die schweigsame Frau* by Richard Strauss.

Above: Portrait of Franz Schubert.

Count goes out, and Susanna, now alone, lights a cigarette. But the Count is so sure that his wife has a lover in the house that he climbs back in again through the window . . . and discovers his wife's innocent secret. He asks to be forgiven and even promises that he will smoke too, to keep her company.

Composed along the lines of an eighteenth-century *intermezzo*, Wolf-Ferrari's opera, since its premiere in Munich, has been well-received wherever staged, such as at the Teatro Costanzi in Rome with Toscanini conducting (1911), at the Metropolitan Opera in New York, or at Covent Garden.

SEMIRAMIDE

Opera in two acts by Gioachino Rossini (1792–1868), to a libretto by Gaetano Rossi, after Voltaire's Sémiramis. *First performance: Venice, Teatro La Fenice, 3 February 1823.*

In the temple of Belus, Queen Semiramide (soprano) has to choose the man who will accede to the throne following the assassination of her consort, King Nino. But the ceremony is interrupted by a thunderbolt from heaven, taken as a sign that the gods want the assassin to be punished. Oroe (bass), the chief magus, summons Arsace (contralto), commander of the army, to return to Babylon. Semiramide is in love with Arsace and wants him as her husband. So she orders that Azema (soprano), the Assyrian princess whom Arsace loves, be given in marriage to the Indian King Idreno (tenor) and then, before Nino's tomb, announces that the name of her new husband-to-be is Arsace. At that moment, amid thunder and lightning, the ghost of Nino (bass) appears and utters a mysterious prophecy: Arsace will become king, but only after avenging him. Later, at the royal palace, Prince Assur (bass), Semiramide's accomplice in the murder of Nino, recalls with her the moment of the assassination. Meanwhile, Oroe has disclosed to Arsace the names of the King's killers. Arsace is horrified, and then Oroe reveals that Arsace is actually Nino's son, who had been believed dead. Now that he has discovered the whole truth, Arsace confronts Semiramide with the news that he is her son, but he is very worried by the fact that he is bound to avenge his father's murder. Assur, Arsace and Semiramide have, without each other's knowledge, entered Nino's tomb. In the darkness Arsace mistakes his mother for Assur and kills her. When he realizes what he has done, he wants to take his own life, but the priests and people will not allow him to do so and instead hail him as the new king of Babylon.

Semiramide, the last opera Rossini wrote for the Italian stage, was received with great enthusiasm at its Venice premiere, a success repeated in Naples and Vienna. The score is majestic (in some ways anticipating French *grand-opéra*) in its ensemble scenes, but also original in its dramatic intensity and the beauty of the singing.

Right: The Colombian mezzo-soprano Martha Senn.

Above: A scene from *Semiramide* by Rossini.

SENN, MARTHA

(St. Gallen 1949)

Colombian mezzo-soprano. Her stylistic competence, sensitive interpretation and enchanting stage presence led to her being chosen to deputize for Lucia Valentini Terrani in the production of *Carmen* which opened the Teatro San Carlo season in 1986. This opened the doors of the leading Italian opera houses to her, including the Teatro dell'Opera in Rome (*L'Italiana in Algeri*, 1987), the Teatro Comunale in Bologna (*Falstaff*, 1987), the Teatro Massimo in Palermo (*La belle Hélène*, 1988), La Fenice in Venice (Leoncavallo's *La bohème*, 1990), the Rossini Opera Festival in Pesaro (Rossini's *L'Atelier Nadar*, 1990), La Scala (*Fra Diavolo* 1992), as well as other leading international venues.

SERRA, LUCIANA

(Savona 1943)

Italian soprano. She appeared for the first time in 1966 at the Erkel Theater in Budapest and went on to sing with Tehran Opera (1969–76). In 1979 she appeared at the Teatro Comunale in Bologna (as Amina in *La sonnambula*) and from there embarked on her international career. Engagements included Covent Garden (*Les contes d'Hoffmann*, 1980), Lyric Opera of Chicago

(*Lakmé*, 1983), the Vienna Staatsoper (1988) and the Metropolitan Opera, New York (*Die Zauberflöte*, The Magic Flute, 1990). Serra's outstanding virtuosity and equally admirable command of the upper register made her one of the finest performers of the *coloratura* repertoire.

SERSE

(Xerxes)

Opera in two acts by George Frederick Handel (1685–1759), to a libretto adapted from one written by Minato for Cavalli, revised by Stampiglia. First performance: London, King's Theater, 15 April 1738.

Serse (contralto), King of Persia, falls hopelessly in love with the Princess Romilda (soprano), forgetting all about Amastre (contralto), whom he is supposed to marry. But Romilda is already attached to Arsamene (contralto), Serse's brother. When Serse is rejected by Romilda, he sends his brother into exile. Arsamene is also loved by Atalanta (soprano), Romilda's sister, who does everything she can to encourage Romilda to marry the King. She intercepts a letter from Arsamene addressed to Romilda and leads the King to believe that he has written it to her, at the same time urging him to move forward the date of her wedding to Arsamene. For his part, Serse uses the letter in an attempt to convince Romilda that Arsamene is being unfaithful to her. This deception is uncovered, but Serse will not be deterred from his purpose and goes to see Ariodate (bass), Romilda's father. He explains the situation in so ambiguous a way that Ariodate is left with the impression that he should give Romilda to Arsamene. By the time Serse realizes he has been misunderstood, the two lovers are already married, and he has no choice but to accept things as they now are and return to Amastre's love for him.

Serse is one of the most important of Handel's works. Its premiere was preceded by a performance in the form of an oratorio on 28 March 1738. Serse's largo in Act 1, "Ombra mai fu," is particularly successful and has become famous as "Handel's Largo." But there is much else to be appreciated here too, indeed a mark of originality with which Handel imbued the entire work.

SERVA PADRONA, LA

(The Maid Mistress)

Intermezzo *in two parts by Giovan Battista Pergolesi (1710–1736), to a libretto by Gennaro Federico. First performance, as an* intermezzo *in another opera by Pergolesi,* Il prigionier superbo*: Naples, Teatro San Bartolomeo, 28 August 1733.*

The maid Serpina (soprano) rules the roost in the house of Uberto (bass), an elderly bachelor. Tired of putting up with her high-handedness, Uberto announces that he intends to get married and asks his servant Vespone (mimed role) to find him a wife, adding that it does not matter how unprepossessing she looks as long as she is submissive. Serpina, who is in no doubt at all that she has a special place in the old man's heart, disguises Vespone as Captain Tempesta, her fiancé. He gives Uberto some withering glances, and Serpina explains that her fiancé will only marry her if Uberto will provide her with a large sum of money as a dowry. She then adds that the Captain will only give her up if Uberto marries her himself. Uberto is relieved and accepts the second solution, while Serpina, who could have wished for nothing better, is no longer maid but mistress in her own house.

La serva padrona marks the birth of comic opera, which would enjoy its period of greatest growth throughout the eighteenth century and culminate in the operas of Rossini. In this work Pergolesi has created new musical forms and brought a fresh approach to the psychological shaping of character, both of which will prove fundamental to the development of *opera buffa. La serva padrona* also sparked off a heated debate when it was staged in Paris in 1752, giving rise to the famous *querelles des bouffons*, a war of taste between the champions of French and Italian opera.

SHICOFF, NEIL

(New York 1949)

American tenor. He studied singing in Delaware and at the Juilliard School in New York, making his debut as Narraboth (Strauss's *Salome*) at the Kennedy Center in Washington. He made his first appearance with the Metropolitan Opera in New York in 1976, as Rinuccio in *Gianni Schicchi*, a performance which led to regular engagements there (*La traviata*, *Faust*, 1989–90; *Tosca*, 1991). He went on to appear at Covent Garden (*Madama Butterfly*, *La bohème*, *Macbeth*), at the Vienna Staatsoper (*Rigoletto*) and at La Scala, Milan (*Eugene Onegin*). His voice has a silvery timbre. He shows qualities of musicianship, elegant phrasing and acting ability, especially in evidence in his most celebrated roles, as Hoffmann in Offenbach's opera and Lensky in Tchaikovsky's *Eugene Onegin.*

SHIMELL, WILLIAM

(Ilford, Essex 1952)

British baritone. He made his debut at the English National Opera in 1980 (Masetto in *Don Giovanni*). He then appeared at the Glyndebourne Festival (*Le nozze di Figaro*, 1984 and 1989) and at the Welsh National

Left: The British baritone William Shimell at the Ravenna Festival in 1991.

Opera in Cardiff. In 1987 he was well received for Count Almaviva (*Le nozze di Figaro*) in his debut appearance at La Scala, Milan, under Riccardo Muti (with whom he recorded both *Le nozze di Figaro* and *Don Giovanni*).

SHIRLEY, GEORGE

(Indianapolis 1934)
American tenor. He made his debut in 1959 in Woodstock, New York, as Eisenstein in Johann Strauss's *Die Fledermaus*. In 1961 he appeared for the first time with the Metropolitan Opera in New York (*Così fan tutte*) and went on to sing at the Spoleto Festival, Glyndebourne (1966) and Covent Garden (*Don Giovanni*, 1967). An outstanding Mozart singer, Shirley also owes his reputation to his distinguished performances in Debussy's *Pelléas et Mélisande* and Stravinsky's *Oedipus Rex*.

SHIRLEY-QUIRK, JOHN

(Liverpool 1931)
British baritone. A pupil of Roy Henderson, he made his debut in 1961 at the Glyndebourne Festival in Debussy's *Pelléas et Mélisande*. He sang with the English Opera Group (1964–73) and from 1973 onwards at Covent Garden. His repertoire included Britten's operas *Owen Wingrave* (1971) and *Death in Venice* (1973).

SHOSTAKOVICH, DIMITRI DMITRIEVICH

(St. Petersburg 1906–Moscow 1975)
Russian composer. He became an active member of the avant-garde alongside Prokofiev and focused his attention on the whole range of contemporary European music. He was appointed director of the Young Workers' Theater and made his debut with the satirical opera *Nos* (The Nose, 1930), followed by the darkly sardonic *Lady Macbeth of Mtsensk* (1934), which he revised in 1959 and had produced with the new title of *Katerina Ismailova*. His opera based on Gogol, *Igrok* (The Gambler), was left unfinished, but he did complete important orchestrations of Mussorgsky's *Boris Godonov* and *Khovanshchina*.

SIEBEN TODSÜNDEN DER KLEINBÜRGER, DIE

(The Seven Deadly Sins)
Ballet with singing in seven scenes and a prologue by Kurt Weill (1900–1950); text by Bertolt Brecht. First performance: Paris, Théâtre des Champs-Elysées, 7 June 1933.

In the prologue, set in Louisiana, Anna I (soprano), a straightforward and practical woman, and Anna II (ballerina), an idealist and dreamer, leave home and family life to seek their fortune. The seven scenes that follow depict the seven deadly sins. While still in Louisiana, Anna II encounters Sloth and wants to go to sleep, but Anna I asks her to reflect on the example of a blackmailer, who cannot allow himself to be lazy. In Memphis, Anna II has to become a striptease artist and realizes that if people are prepared to pay to watch a striptease, then it is better to forget about Pride. In Los Angeles, Anna I warns her sister to control her Anger at the injustices of society, because it makes her undesirable. In Philadelphia, Anna II has trouble with greed: Gluttony is causing her to lose her figure, and therefore her clients too. On arrival in Boston, the two sisters come across Lust, which Anna II likens to altruistic love, because there is no money in it. From here they move on to Baltimore. Anna II has become famous but is showing signs of Avarice, which is affecting her relations with her clients. The last part of their journey takes the sisters to San Francisco. Tired after all their travelling, they experience Envy of those who feel free to live their passions fully. In the end, they manage to overcome all moral scruples and learn to accept the rules of the game imposed by bourgeois society, and this spurs them on to obtain the money they need to build a house for their family.

This is the last work on which Weill collaborated with Brecht, a partnership which had begun in 1927 but which by 1933 was already at breaking-point. Nevertheless, the opera is one of Weill and Brecht's greatest successes. The score contains several echoes of their previous works and makes use of violent and melancholy songs to illustrate how the main characters pass through various stages of their growth as individuals.

SIGNOR BRUSCHINO, IL

Opera in one act by Gioachino Rossini (1792–1868), to a libretto by Giuseppe Maria Foppa, based on Le fils par hasard, ou Ruse et folie *by de Chazet and Ourry. First performance: Venice, Teatro Giustiniani di San Moisé, January or February 1813.*

On the death of his father, Florville (tenor) tells Sofia (soprano) that he is finally in a position to marry her. But

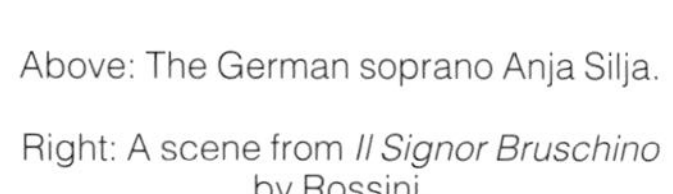

Above: The German soprano Anja Silja.

Right: A scene from *Il Signor Bruschino* by Rossini.

Gaudenzio (*buffo*), the young woman's guardian, has already promised her to someone by the name of Bruschino (tenor), whom no one has ever heard of. When he discovers that Filiberto (baritone), an inn-keeper, is holding Bruschino until he pays his debts, Florville, posing as Bruschino, goes to see Gaudenzio. But then Bruschino senior (bass or baritone) arrives and, not surprisingly, is not fooled by Florville's impersonation of his son. Everyone else, however, thinks he is pretending not to recognize Bruschino the younger because the young man's conduct is so unseemly. Bruschino senior then discovers Florville's hoax, but when he learns that this is the son of Senator Florville, an implacable enemy of Gaudenzio, he joins in the conspiracy, recognizes Florville as his own son and consents to his marrying Sofia. When Gaudenzio realizes he has been tricked, he has no choice but to give in and accept the *fait accompli*.

Il Signor Bruschino is a slightly earlier work than Rossini's *Tancredi* and comes a few months before *L'italiana in Algeri*. It already shows signs of the daring harmonies and comic realism of the mature Rossini and is famous for its overture, in which the violinists can be heard tapping their bows on their music-stands.

SILJA, ANJA
(Berlin 1940)
Stage name of Anja Silja Regina Langwagen, German soprano. She was born into an artistic family and studied with her grandfather Egon von Rijn. After singing in a concert in Berlin at the age of ten, she made her debut in 1956 as Rosina (*Il barbiere di Siviglia*) at the Berlin Städtische Oper. She appeared regularly at the opera houses in Stuttgart (from 1958) and Frankfurt (from 1959) and went on to sing at the Bayreuth Festival in 1960, where her Senta in *Der fliegende Holländer* (The Flying Dutchman) caused a sensation. She became Wieland Wagner's favourite singer and so began her association with Bayreuth, appearing as Elsa, Elisabeth, Freia, Venus, Isolde and Brünnhilde. She also won acclaim in the international opera world and, on the strength of her outstanding gifts as a singer and actress, came to be acknowledged as one of the greatest performers of Strauss's *Salome* and *Elektra*, Berg's *Wozzeck* and *Lulu* and Weill's *Mahagonny*.

SILLS, BEVERLY
(Brooklyn, New York 1929)
Stage name of Belle Silverman, American soprano. A pupil of Estelle Liebling in New York, she made her debut in Philadelphia in 1947 as Frasquita in *Carmen*. In 1955 she joined New York City Opera, with whom her name was to be associated until she retired from the stage in 1980, thereafter serving for a time as general manager of the company. In 1965 she made her European debut in Lausanne in *Die Zauberflöte* (The Magic Flute). She was at La Scala, Milan, in 1969 to sing in Rossini's *Le siège de Corinthe* and returned there to take part in the following season's *Lucia di Lammermoor*. In 1975 she made her first appearance with the Metropolitan Opera, New York, again in *Le siège de Corinthe*, and continued to sing there until the 1978–79 season. Sills' reputation rests on her technique and interpretative gifts and particularly in Handel's *Giulio Cesare*, Donizetti's *Roberto Devereux*, *Maria Stuarda*, *Anna Bolena* and *Lucia di Lammermoor*, Bellini's *I puritani* and Massenet's *Manon*, all of which she recorded.

Left: The American soprano Beverly Sills in a scene from *L'assedio di' Corinto* by Rossini.

SIMON BOCCANEGRA
Opera in a prologue and three acts by Giuseppe Verdi (1813–1901), to a libretto by Francesco Maria Piave, from the play Simón Bocanegra *by Antonio García Gutiérrez. First performance: Venice, Teatro La Fenice, 12 March 1857.*

The action takes place in Genoa during the fourteenth century. The sometime corsair Simon Boccanegra (baritone), a commoner, is about to be elected Doge of Venice as a result of maneuvering by fellow-plebeians Paolo (baritone) and Pietro (bass) Albiani. Boccanegra hopes this will enable him to marry Maria, whose father is the patrician Jacopo Fiesco (bass). But Maria dies, and the daughter she had from her relationship with Boccanegra has disappeared in mysterious circumstances. Twenty-five years later, the foundling girl whom Fiesco has brought up – nobody suspecting she is actually Doge Simon's daughter – bears the name Amelia Grimaldi, and the patrician Gabriele Adorno (tenor) is in love with her. Simon sees a portrait of Maria which Amelia (soprano) has had in her keeping and realizes that she is his own daughter. Then Adorno is arrested on a charge of having killed a man who had attempted to abduct Amelia (whose real name is Maria, after her mother). Amelia/Maria alleges that her would-be abductor was Paolo Albiani, to whom Simon had at one time promised her in marriage, cancelling the wedding after realizing that Amelia was his daughter. Having failed in his bid to abduct her, Paolo convinces Gabriele that an impure liaison exists between Amelia/Maria and the Doge. In a fury, Gabriele tries to murder Simon, but then Simon tells him everything. Meanwhile, Paolo has secretly poisoned Simon. Gabriele, who now has Simon's blessing to marry Maria, puts down a popular revolt which Albiani had whipped up, and Albiani is imprisoned. Before he dies, Simon sees Fiesco again, tells him that Amelia/Maria is his own daughter, and then proclaims Gabriele as his successor.

The Venice premiere of *Simon Boccanegra* was a failure. In 1880 the music publisher Ricordi suggested to Verdi that he revise the score and Verdi asked Boito to carry out substantial alterations to Piave's libretto. The opera's new version was produced at La Scala, Milan, on 24 March 1881, where it was an outstanding success.

SINOPOLI, GIUSEPPE

(Venice 1946)

Italian composer and conductor. He studied at the Conservatorio in Venice with Bruno Maderna and Karlheinz Stockhausen. In 1972 he moved to Vienna, where he completed his training as a conductor with Hans Swarowsky. In 1978 he made his debut as an opera conductor at La Fenice in Venice in Verdi's *Aida*. He went on to conduct at Covent Garden (Puccini's *Manon Lescaut*), the Metropolitan Opera in New York (*Tosca*, 1985) and the Bayreuth Festival (*Tannhäuser*, 1985), where he has since appeared regularly. Among the best performances in his active recording career are Verdi's *Nabucco* (1982) and Puccini's *Manon Lescaut*.

SKAZANIYE O NEVIDIMOM GRADE KITEZHE I DEVE FEVRONII

(Legend of the Invisible City of Kitezh and the Maiden Fevroniya)

Opera in four acts by Nikolai Rimsky-Korsakov (1844–1908), to a libretto by Vladimir Belsky. First performance: St. Petersburg, Maryinsky Theater, 20 February 1907.

Vsevolod (tenor), Prince of the city of Kitezh, is wounded during a hunt in the forest. Fevronia (soprano), young sister of a woodcutter, who lives near Little Kitezh, on the outskirts of the city, goes to his aid, whereupon the Prince falls in love with her and asks her to marry him. As a magnificent bridal procession is escorting Fevronia through Little Kitezh, the drunkard Kutierma (tenor) calls out unkindly to her, reminding her of her humble origins. She answers him modestly, and the people are touched. Suddenly everything is interrupted by the arrival of the Tartars, who put the city to fire and sword. The survivors find refuge in Greater Kitezh, while Fevronia, who has been taken prisoner, prays for the city's salvation. It is not long before a thick fog envelops the city so that it can no longer be seen. The Tartars are on the shores of Lake Yar, looking across at where the city used to be. Kutierma, who has acted as a guide to the invading forces, lets out a cry as he catches sight of the invisible city's reflection on the water of the lake. The Tartars are terrified by this wonder and take flight. Kutierma escapes with Fevronia, but she becomes exhausted and finds herself alone in the forest. In the delirium of her last moments alone, she sees herself surrounded by flowers while Prince Vsevolod, her husband-to-be, who died defending Kitezh, leads her to the invisible city. And Kitezh is revealed again, a city shining in eternity. The bridal procession begins again, and the two young people are united in the world beyond the grave.

Composed between 1903 and 1904, this opera draws its inspiration from legend. The score is a perfect blend of melodies taken from Russian folk-song and the composer's own music.

Right: Bedřich Smetana.

Above: A scene from *Simon Boccanegra* by Verdi, in a production at the Teatro Communale, Florence.

SMETANA, BEDŘICH

(Litomyšl 1824–Prague 1884)

Czech composer. He could play the violin by the age of four, the piano at six, and very soon after that began to compose. His sensitivity to the historical and cultural roots and traditions of Czechoslovakia, at a time when his people were particularly aware of their national heritage, inspired him to write his first opera, *Branibori v Cecháс* (The Brandenburgs in Bohemia), composed in 1862–63 and staged in 1866. But the opera of his that was to become the symbol of Czech nationalism is *Prodaná Nevesta* (The Bartered Bride, 1866), which is regarded as his masterpiece. *Dalibor* (1868) and *Libuše* (1881), on the other hand, are operas with a romantic theme, especially *Libuše*, which is still traditionally performed to mark important days in the nation's calendar. These two were followed by *Dvě vdovy* (The Two Widows, 1874), *Hubička* (The Kiss, 1876), *Tajemství* (The Secret, 1878) and *Čertova stěna* (The Devil's Wall, 1882), which combine romance with comedy and recreate Czech folk settings and traditions.

SMITH, JENNIFER
(Lisbon 1945)
British soprano. She studied at the Conservatory in Lisbon and became acknowledged as one of the finest singers of the Early Music and baroque repertoires. Her reputation rests on appearances at the Aix-en-Provence Festival (Rameau's *Les Boréades* and *Hippolyte et Aricie*), the Opéra in Paris (Lully's *Atys*, 1987) and other leading music venues in roles from operas by Handel (*Amadigi di Gaula* and *Hercules*), Purcell (*The Fairy Queen*, *The Indian Queen* and *King Arthur*) and Rameau (*Castor et Pollux* and *Les Indes galantes*).

SÖDERSTRÖM, ELISABETH
(Stockholm 1927)
Swedish soprano. She attended the Royal Academy of Music and Opera School in Stockholm, making her debut at Drottningholm Court Theater in Mozart's *Bastien und Bastienne* (1947). She joined the Swedish Royal Opera, at the same time embarking on a brilliant international career, in which her name was particularly associated with the Glyndebourne Festival (from 1957). She also sang at the Metropolitan Opera, New York (from 1959) and Covent Garden (from 1960). A singer of refinement with considerable gifts as a performer, Söderström drew on an extremely wide repertoire ranging from Monteverdi to Mozart and Debussy, Richard Strauss and Janáček.

SOLERA, TEMISTOCLE
(Ferrara 1815–Milan 1878)
Italian librettist and composer. He studied music and letters in Vienna. His libretti include the ones he wrote for Verdi's operas *Oberto*, *Nabucco*, *I Lombardi*, *Giovanna d'Arco* and *Attila*. He also worked as a theater impresario in various cities in Spain and wrote five operas to his own libretti.

SOLTI, SIR GEORG
(Budapest 1912)
Hungarian conductor, naturalized British. He studied at the Liszt Academy in Budapest with Dohnányi and Bartók as his teachers for piano and Kodály and Leo Weiner for composition. Répétiteur with the Budapest Opera from 1933 to 1939, he made his debut in 1938 in Budapest with *Le nozze di Figaro*. He was music director at the Bayerische Staatsoper (1946–52) and at the Frankfurt Opera (1952–61), *Generalmusikdirektor* at the Salzburg Festival (from 1951) and held the music directorship at Covent Garden (from 1959). In 1952 he appeared for the first time in the United States, then was music adviser to the Paris Opéra (1973–74) and in 1982 conducted a new production of Wagner's *Ring* at Bayreuth. Conductor of leading international orchestras, Solti is acknowledged as one of the most important artistic figures of modern times, particularly noted for his performances of Mozart, Wagner and Richard Strauss. His many recordings include the first integral stereo version of Wagner's *Ring* cycle and the first *Arabella* of Richard Strauss.

SONNAMBULA, LA
(The Sleepwalker)
Opera in two acts by Vincenzo Bellini (1801–1835), to a libretto by Felice Romani, based on a vaudeville by Scribe and Delavigne. First performance: Milan, Teatro Carcano, 6 March 1831.

The action takes place in a Swiss village. Celebrations are under way for the wedding of the wealthy land-owner Elvino (tenor) and Amina (soprano), an orphan adopted by Teresa (mezzo-soprano). Lisa (soprano) the inn-keeper, is consumed with jealousy because she loved Elvino and has been rejected by him. The festivities are interrupted by the arrival of a carriage bringing Count Rodolfo (bass), son of the late lord of the village, who has been away for some time. To keep his identity a secret, Rodolfo decides to stay at Lisa's inn. While he is in his room, Amina appears, dressed in white and walking in her sleep. She keeps on calling to her husband and talks about her wedding, but then becomes tired and lies down on the couch. Lisa has witnessed this scene unnoticed and now runs to tell Elvino. When he comes into the room, Amina tries desperately to protest her innocence, but Elvino is overcome with jealousy and disowns her. Lisa takes advantage of Amina's disgrace and is about to marry Elvino, who has ignored Rodolfo's repeated assurances that Amina is innocent. Enter Teresa, who accuses Lisa of being unfaithful just like Amina and declares that she has found one of Lisa's handkerchiefs in the Count's room. Elvino is stunned by this revelation, but then attention is distracted from him to Amina, who has just appeared and is obviously walking in her sleep. She sings of her desperate love for Elvino. He realizes he has been wrong about her,

Above: A scene from *Skazaniye o Nevidimom Grade Kitezhe I Deve Fevronii* by Rimsky-Korsakov.

takes her in his arms and wakens her, to everyone's delight.

The premiere of *La sonnambula* was an enormous success and was followed by numerous performances in opera houses in Italy and other countries, with the result that it entered the normal opera house repertoires. Bellini poured all his melodic and lyrical fervour into this work, and passages such as Elvino's *cavatina* "Prendi l'anel ti dono" and Amina's romance "Ah, non credea mirarti" are masterpieces of their kind. A gentle pastoral tone is marvellously sustained throughout the score, in which the apparently plain orchestration perfectly matches the opera's atmosphere. The role of Amina has consistently attracted great sopranos, more recently Maria Callas, Renata Scotto, Dame Joan Sutherland, June Anderson and Mariella Devia.

SOVIERO, DIANA
(Jersey City, New Jersey 1942)
American soprano. After completing her music studies, she made her debut at the Chautauqua Festival as Mimi (*La bohème*) and went on to sing at the major American opera houses in San Francisco, Philadelphia and Chicago, and at the Metropolitan Opera in New York, where her regular appearances included *Suor Angelica* (1989), *La traviata* and *Faust* (1990), *Madama Butterfly* (1992), *La bohème* and *I pagliacci* (1992–93). Engagements in Europe took her to Zurich (*La bohème*, 1982), the Paris Opéra (*La traviata*, 1984), the Teatro dell'Opera, Rome (Massenet's *Manon*, 1984), La Scala, Milan (*I pagliacci*, 1987) and the Teatro Comunale in Florence (*Suor Angelica*, 1988). Soviero combines a fine lyric soprano voice with a remarkable natural ability in stage performance.

SOYER, ROGER
(Thiais 1939)
French bass-baritone. He studied at the Paris Conservatoire and made his debut at the Opéra in 1963. In 1965 he scored his first personal success as Plutone (Monteverdi's *Orfeo*) at the Aix-en-Provence Festival, where he made several return visits. He went on to sing at all the leading international opera houses and built a reputation not only for of French opera but also as a Mozart singer of considerable refinement, especially in the role of Don Giovanni.

Above: A scene from *La sonnambula* by Bellini, first performed in Milan in 1831.

Right: The Russian composer Dimitri Shostakovich (see page 328).

SPACAGNA, MARIA
(Providence, Rhode Island 1946)
American soprano of Italian origin. After studying at the New England Conservatory, she began her career in the mid 1960s with appearances at various American opera houses (Dallas Opera, 1977; New York City Opera, 1978; St. Louis Opera, 1982). In the 1989–90 season she made her debut with the Metropolitan Opera in New York (*Rigoletto*), returning there during the 1990–91 season to sing in *Le nozze di Figaro*, *Otello* and *Luisa Miller* and in 1992–93 for *La bohème*. Her reputation also rests on a number of European engagements, including Raffaello De Banfield's *Lord Byron's Love Letter* at the Teatro G. Verdi in Trieste in 1987, the Spoleto Festival (Traetta's *Antigone*, 1988), La Scala, Milan (*Madama Butterfly*, 1988), La Fenice, Venice (1989), and Cologne Opera (*La traviata*, 1989–90). The elegance of Spacagna's phrasing, coupled with a voice that is consistent across the range and great sensitivity of interpretation, led to her being acclaimed as one of the great singers of her generation.

SPONTINI, GASPARE
(Maiolati, Ancona 1774–1851)
Italian composer. He studied with Sala and Tritto at the Conservatorio della Pietà dei Turchini in Naples, but made his debut as an opera composer in Rome with *Li puntigli delle donne* (1796), which was a remarkable success. From 1799 to 1801 he was in Palermo before moving to Paris (1803). There in 1807 his opera *La vestale* was a triumph. He became official composer to the Court of Napoleon and wrote *Fernand Cortez* (1809). He was director of the Théâtre Italien from 1810 to 1812 and again from 1814 to 1820. He took French nationality in 1817 and in 1819 composed and staged *Olympie*, which had very little success. This disappointment prompted Spontini to leave France and move to Berlin, on the invitation of the Emperor Friedrich Wilhelm III (1820). There he composed *Lalla Rookh* (1821), *Alcidor* (1823) and most notably *Agnes von Hohenstaufen* (1829, revised 1837), the atmosphere of which was already openly Romantic.

STADE, FREDERICA VON

(Somerville, New Jersey 1945)

American mezzo-soprano. She began to study singing at the age of 20, under the tutelage of Sebastian Engelberg, Paul Berl and Otto Guth in New York. She made her debut in 1970 as the Third Genie in Mozart's *Die Zauberflöte* (The Magic Flute) at the Metropolitan Opera House in New York, where she remained for three seasons. She returned to the Metropolitan regularly, more recently in *Le nozze di Figaro* (1991), *Il barbiere di Siviglia* (1992) and *Der Rosenkavalier* (1992–93). After appearing at various American opera houses (San Francisco, Santa Fe), she became firmly established in 1973 following her performance as Cherubino (*Le nozze di Figaro*) at the Paris Opéra, which launched her international career. Von Stade's voice is distinctive for its fine, rather bright timbre, its range (she has also sung soprano roles), and its proven skills in passages requiring agility. It is most naturally suited to interpreting a lyrical or elegiac vocal line. Her finest roles (in addition to that of Cherubino) have included the lead in Massenet's *Cendrillon* and *Chérubin* and Debussy's *Pelléas et Mélisande*.

STEINBERG, PINCHAS

(Tel Aviv 1945)

Israeli conductor who took American nationality. After learning the violin in Israel, he moved to the United States, where he continued his music studies at the University of Indiana and Roosevelt University. He became first violin in the Chicago Lyric Opera orchestra and made his debut as a conductor when he took over from Ferdinand Leitner during a performance of *Don Giovanni*. In 1971 he settled in Berlin and studied composition with Boris Blacher, as well as developing a brilliant career as conductor of some of the leading orchestras. From 1979 onwards he again concentrated on opera, conducting at the Liceu in Barcelona (Wagner's *Götterdämmerung*, 1987), the Vienna Staatsoper (*Il trovatore*, 1988) and the Arena in Verona (*Aida*, 1989).

STEWART, THOMAS

(San Saba, Texas 1928)

American bass-baritone. He studied at Baylor University and with Mack Harrell at the Juilliard School, where, while still a student, he made his debut as La Roche (Richard Strauss's *Capriccio*). He joined New York City Opera and was awarded a study bursary which enabled him to complete his training in Europe. His first appearance there was in Berlin as Escamillo (*Carmen*, 1958), the role he sang at his Covent Garden debut in 1960. Also in 1960, he made his Bayreuth debut (Amfortas in *Parsifal*), continuing to appear there every year until 1975. Stewart established an international reputation as a Wagner singer with performances at the Opéra in Paris (1967), the Salzburg Easter Festival (1967–73) and the Metropolitan Opera in New York. He married the soprano Evelyn Lear.

Above: The American bass-baritone Thomas Stewart.

STIFFELIO

Opera in three acts by Giuseppe Verdi (1813–1901), to a libretto by Francesco Maria Piave, based on the play Le pasteur, ou L'évangile et le foyer *by Eugène Bourgeois and Emile Souvestre. First performance: Trieste, Teatro Grande, 16 November 1850.*

The action takes place in Germany at the beginning of the nineteenth century. Stiffelio (tenor), a Protestant pastor who is being persecuted for his beliefs, takes refuge in the castle of his follower Count Stankar (baritone) and marries Lina (soprano), the Count's daughter. While Stiffelio is away, Lina is unfaithful to him with Raffaele di Leuthold (tenor), a nobleman. Stankar is on the point of killing Raffaele to vindicate the family's honour when Stiffelio intervenes, insisting that a Christian is bound to forgive, and he accepts his young wife's contrition.

Stiffelio had several brushes with the censor, who balked at the rather delicate nature of the subject and also at a scene in which Stiffelio himself is heard quoting from the Holy Gospel. Verdi changed the settings, but the opera was still not particularly well received. In 1857 he almost completely revised the score and gave it the new name, *Aroldo*.

STILWELL, RICHARD

(St. Louis, Missouri 1942)

American baritone. He began studying music at the University of Indiana and then in Bloomington and New York. He made his debut with New York City Opera in 1970 as Pelléas in Debussy's *Pelléas et Mélisande*. Stilwell's considerable range as a light baritone enabled him to tackle this role successfully, and he went on to sing Pellías, among other venues, at La Scala, Milan, La Fenice in Venice, Covent Garden and the Paris Opéra. He also recorded it in 1978 for Herbert von Karajan. He has appeared at the Metropolitan Opera in New York (from 1975), the Glyndebourne Festival and the Vienna Staatsoper. His repertoire ranges from Monteverdi to Mozart, Donizetti, Verdi, Strauss and Britten.

STOCKHAUSEN, KARLHEINZ

(Mödrath, Cologne 1928)

German composer. He studied with Frank Martin at the Musikhochschule in Cologne (1947–51) and went on to complete his training in Paris with Darius Milhaud and Olivier Messiaen (1952–53). In 1953 he joined the Cologne Electronic Music Studio and was its director from 1963 to 1973. One of the greatest exponents of contemporary music, Stockhausen embarked in 1977 on a seven-day cycle of operas under the title *Licht* (Light). *Donnerstag aus Licht* (Thursday, from "Light"), the first day of the cycle, was premiered at La Scala, Milan in 1981, also the venue for the first performances in 1984 and 1988 of *Samstag aus Licht* (Saturday, from "Light") and *Montag aus Licht* (Monday, from "Light").

STRANIERA, LA

(The Stranger)

Opera in two acts by Vincenzo Bellini (1801–1835), to a libretto by Felice Romani, after d'Arlincourt's L'étrangère. *First performance: Milan, La Scala, 14 February 1829.*

The action takes place in Brittany, at and around the castle of Montolino, during the fourteenth century. Arturo, Conte di Ravenstal (tenor), who is to marry Isoletta (mezzo-soprano), daughter of the Lord of Montolino (bass), has fallen in love with a mysterious veiled woman, Alaide (soprano), "la straniera" (the stranger). But Alaide tries to distance herself from Arturo's passion for her. Arturo confides to his friend the Barone di Valdeburgo (baritone) his desire to break off his engagement to Isoletta. Valdeburgo impresses upon Arturo the importance of not seeing Alaide again, but Arturo takes this to mean that there is some kind of secret liaison between Valdeburgo and Alaide. Overwhelmed by jealousy, Arturo challenges Valdeburgo to a duel. Valdeburgo is wounded and falls into the lake. Alaide comes running. She reveals to Arturo that Valdeburgo was her brother, but when some of the local people arrive on the scene and find Alaide holding the bloodstained sword, they accuse her of murder. At her trial, Alaide and Arturo are found guilty and sentenced to death. But then Valdeburgo appears, having mysteriously survived, and exonerates both defendants. He commands Arturo to relinquish all hope of winning the heart of Alaide. Out of respect for Alaide's peace of mind, Arturo agrees to marry Isoletta. But during the wedding ceremony, Arturo is overwhelmed by feelings of anguish and hurries from the church in pursuit of the veiled Alaide, who had been attending the ceremony. He implores her to come away with him. But now the truth is uncovered. Alaide is actually Queen Agnès, who had been sent away from court and has now been summoned back to the throne. This revelation shows Arturo that his love has no hope, and he kills himself.

The romantic and mysterious setting of the story, much to the taste of audiences at that time, is adequately served by Bellini's music. Although Romani's libretto had its limitations, the score contains passages of the most inspired lyricism, on a par with Bellini at his best, such as the duet in the first act between Arturo and Alaide and Alaide's final scene.

Above: A scene from *La Straniera* by Bellini.

Right: The German composer Richard Strauss.

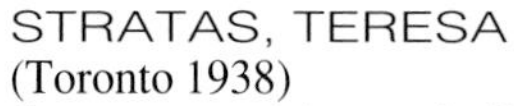

STRATAS, TERESA

(Toronto 1938)

Stage name of Anastasia Strataki, Canadian soprano of Greek origin. She studied at the Conservatory in Toronto and made her debut in that city in 1958 as Mimi (*La bohème*). A year later, she appeared for the first time at the Metropolitan Opera, New York, as Poussette in Massenet's *Manon*, and within a short time she established herself as a performer of leading roles at the Metropolitan in a considerable repertoire ranging from Mozart to Verdi, Puccini and Debussy. Later performances included *Suor Angelica* and *Gianni Schicchi* (1989), *Tosca* (1991) and Marie Antoinette in the world premiere of John Corigliano's opera *The Ghosts of Versailles* (1991–92). Her international career took her to La Scala, Milan (De Falla's *Atlantide*, 1962), the Deutsche Oper Berlin (*La traviata*, 1966) and Covent Garden (*La bohème*, 1961). Perhaps her most outstanding role is that of Lulu in Berg's opera, which she sang in the first performance of the three-act version at the Opéra in Paris (1979). Stratas has a moderate voice but remarkable gifts of interpretation, which she shows to full effect in the films of *La traviata* and *I pagliacci* directed by Franco Zeffirelli.

STRAUSS, RICHARD

(Munich 1864–Garmisch-Partenkirchen 1949)

German composer and conductor. His father was an excellent horn player in the orchestra at the Munich Opera, and Richard began to study piano at the age of four and violin when he was six. He started composing symphonic music at an early age too and became a conductor, one of the most celebrated of his generation. Already famous for his symphonic poems, Strauss made a first attempt at opera with *Guntram* (1894, revised in 1940). This was followed by *Feuersnot* (Fire-peril, 1901). Both operas were given a lukewarm reception. Strauss established himself as an opera composer in 1905 with *Salome*. In 1909 came *Elektra*, the first fruit of Strauss's collaboration with the poet and playwright Hugo von Hofmannsthal. After the tragic atmosphere of these two works, Strauss immersed himself in the rococo world of *Der Rosenkavalier* (1911). The year 1912 saw the first version of *Ariadne auf Naxos* (final version 1916), offering an early glimpse of that Straussian blend of extremely varied artistic treatments which was to be such a distinctive feature of *Die Frau ohne Schatten* (Woman without a Shadow, 1919). This opera represents the peak of Strauss's musical and dramatic achievement. Then came *Die aegyptische Helena* (1928) and *Arabella* (1933), the last operas on which Strauss had worked with von Hofmannsthal (the poet died in 1929). The blend of different kinds of atmosphere found in *Ariadne* returns in *Die schweigsame Frau* (The Silent Woman, 1935). After his not particularly happy experience with *Friedenstag* (Peace Day, 1938), Strauss returned to the classical world and created the evanescent settings of *Daphne* (1938) and *Die Liebe der Danae* (The Love of Danae, first performed posthumously in 1952). In his last opera, *Capriccio* (1942), he once again explored the mysteries of artistic creation, in particular the relationship between music and poetry.

STRAVINSKY, IGOR

(Oranienbaum, now Lomonosov 1882–New York 1971)

Russian composer. Although his family was not particularly in favour of his taking up music, he became a pupil of Rimsky-Korsakov in 1903. In 1907 he began to compose his first opera, *Le rossignol* (The Nightingale), completing it in 1914. He wrote only two more operas, *Mavra* (1922) and *The Rake's Progress* (1951). Some of his other compositions are closely related to opera, however, among them *Renard* (1916–22), *Oedipus Rex* (1927) and *Perséphone* (1934).

STREIT, KURT

(Itazuke, Japan 1959)

American tenor. Born in Japan to American parents, he studied in the United States at Albuquerque and Cincinnati with Marilyn Tyler. In 1985 he made his debut at the Santa Fe Festival in Strauss's *Die Liebe der Danae*. He then moved to Europe and in 1986 joined the Hamburg Opera. He appeared at the Schwetzingen Festival in 1987 in Gluck's *Echo et Narcisse*, at the Glyndebourne Festival in *Die Entführung aus dem Serail* (The Seraglio, 1988) and *Die Zauberflöte* (The Magic Flute 1990), as well as in Aix-en-Provence (1989), Covent Garden (1990) and San Francisco. A member of the Vienna Staatsoper company since 1988, Streit is regarded as one of the greatest Mozart singers of his generation. His repertoire also includes operas by Rossini (*Il barbiere di Siviglia*), Donizetti (*L'elisir d'amore* and *Don Pasquale*), Beethoven (*Fidelio*) and Puccini (*Gianni Schicchi*).

STUDER, CHERYL

(Midland, Michigan 1955)

American soprano. After studying music in Midland and then at the Interlochen Arts Academy and the Berkshire Music Center at Tanglewood (1975–77), she went on to complete her training at the Hochschule für Musik in Vienna and with Hans Hotter (1978). She made her debut as the First Lady in *Die Zauberflöte* (The Magic Flute) at the Munich Opera, where she was to become a member of the resident company for two seasons. Appearances followed at various opera houses in Germany (Darmstadt, Berlin, Hanover, etc.), and in 1984 she sang professionally for the first time in the United States (Micaela in *Carmen*) in Chicago. She was in *Lohengrin* in San Francisco and *Carmen* at the Metropolitan Opera in New York (1988), becoming a regular visitor to the Metropolitan with more recent performances in *Don Giovanni* (1990) and *La traviata* (1992–93). Studer's name is also associated with the Bayreuth Festival (since the 1985 *Tannhäuser*) and with Salzburg (Strauss's *Elektra*, 1989). In 1987 she made her La Scala debut in *Don Giovanni* with Riccardo Muti and returned to sing in *Les vêpres siciliennes* (1989–90) and *Attila* (1991), also conducted by Muti. One of the most highly regarded international opera singers, Studer has a fine lyric soprano voice with a considerable range and shows some natural talent for singing passages that require vocal agility. These gifts have enabled her to tackle a considerable variety of roles in operas from Mozart's *Die Zauberflöte* (The Magic Flute), *Die Entführung aus dem Serail* (The Seraglio) and *Idomeneo* to Rossini (*Semiramide*), Donizetti (*Lucia di Lammermoor*), Verdi, Wagner and Richard Strauss (*Salome*, *Die Frau ohne Schatten*, *Elektra*). It is in the German repertoire that she has given her most convincing performances.

SUMMERS, JONATHAN

(Melbourne 1946)

Australian baritone. He studied music in London and made his debut in 1975 with Kent Opera in *Rigoletto*. In 1976 he sang the role of Tonio in *I pagliacci* at the English National Opera in London. He then joined the Covent Garden company while developing his international career with appearances at opera houses in Paris in *Lohengrin* (1982), *Die Fledermaus* (1983) and *La traviata* (1986), with Australian Opera in Sydney (*La traviata* and *Il trovatore* with Dame Joan Sutherland, 1981 and 1983), the Grand Théâtre in Geneva (1984) and La Fenice in Venice (Leoncavallo's *La bohème*, 1990).

SUOR ANGELICA

See *Trittico, Il*

Above: A drawing of Stravinsky by Picasso.

Left: The American soprano Cheryl Studer.

SURJAN, GIORGIO

(Rijeka 1954)

Italian bass of Slav origin. He completed his training at La Scala, Milan (1979–81), where he made his debut in Verdi's *Ernani* and continues to sing regularly. His more recent appearances there include *Guillaume Tell* (1988), *La clemenza di Tito* (1989) and *Iphigénie en Tauride* (1992), all with Riccardo Muti conducting. His international career has taken him to the Paris Opéra (*Macbeth*, 1984–87, *I puritani*, (1987), Covent Garden and Aix-en-Provence (*Les vêpres siciliennes*), the Liceu in Barcelona (*Norma*, with Dame Joan Sutherland) and other important theater and concert venues. His vast repertoire contains eighteenth-century operas as well as the leading composers of nineteenth-century Italian opera.

SUTHERLAND, JOAN

(Point Piper, Sydney 1926)

Australian soprano. After early singing lessons from her mother, she attended the Sydney Conservatory and made her first concert appearances. In 1951 came her stage debut in Goossens' *Judith* in Sydney, and in the same year she moved to London, completing her training at the Royal College of Music and privately with Richard Bonynge, whom she married in 1954. In 1952 she made her Covent Garden debut as the First Lady in *Die Zauberflöte* (The Magic Flute), and it was there that she appeared most often, scoring a triumphant success in 1959 as Lucia in Donizetti's *Lucia di Lammermoor*, a performance which launched her international career. In 1961 she sang in *Lucia di Lammermoor* at La Scala, in San Francisco, at the Metropolitan Opera in New York and eventually at all of the world's leading opera houses. Dame Joan's exceptional vocal gifts, combined with an equally outstanding technique, brought the renaissance of *bel canto* to its peak. In her, opera discovered one of the greatest performers for works like Handel's *Alcina*, *Acis and Galatea* and *Rodelinda*, Bellini's *La sonnambula*, *Norma* and *I puritani*, and Donizetti's *Lucia di Lammermoor*, *La fille du régiment* and *Maria Stuarda*. Her repertoire also featured operas by Verdi (*La traviata*, *Rigoletto*, *Il trovatore*, etc.), Puccini (*Suor Angelica* and *Turandot*, the latter recorded) and many French composers (Delibes, Meyerbeer, Massenet, Thomas). In October 1990, Dame Joan gave her farewell stage performance in Meyerbeer's *Les Huguenots* at the Sydney Opera House.

SWEET, SHARON

(New York 1951)

American soprano. She studied at the Curtis Institute in Philadelphia and completed her training with Margaret Harshaw and Marinka Gurewich. After making her concert debut on a European tour (1985–86), she made her stage debut in Dortmund singing Elisabeth in Wagner's *Tannhäuser* (1986), followed by appearances at the Opéra in Paris (*Don Carlos*, 1987), the Deutsche Oper Berlin (where she joined the resident company) and the Vienna Staatsoper. In 1990 she sang for the first time at the Metropolitan Opera in New York (*Il trovatore*), moving on to roles in various operas, especially Verdi (*Un ballo in maschera*, 1992–93).

SYLVESTER, MICHAEL

(Noblesville, Indiana 1951)

American tenor. After studying music, he made his debut in Hamilton as Riccardo (*Un ballo in maschera*). He went on to appear in a number of American cities, including Memphis, Syracuse, Indianapolis (Bacchus in *Ariadne auf Naxos*), Cincinnati (*Madama Butterfly*) and Los Angeles (*La bohème*). His debut at the Metropolitan Opera in New York was in 1991 in *Luisa Miller*, and he returned there in 1992 for *Madama Butterfly*. Appearances in Europe have included the Opéra in Paris (*Norma*, 1987), La Fenice in Venice (*Don Carlos*, 1991) and Covent Garden (*Simon Boccanegra*, 1991).

Right: The Italian bass Giorgio Surjan.

SZÉKELY FONÓ

The Transylvanian Spinning-Room)

Opera in one act by Zoltán Kódaly (1882–1967), to a libretto by Bence Szabolcsi. First performance: Budapest, Hungarian Theater, 24 April 1932.

The action takes place one evening in a spinning-mill. The proprietress, a young widow (contralto), bids a sorrowful farewell to her lover (baritone), who has to leave the country following some unspecified trouble with the authorities. A group of girls comes by and tries to cheer her with a folk-song, to which she responds by singing something melancholy. The sad atmosphere is broken into by the arrival of a noisy group of boys. They play the game of "Ilona Görög," a popular acted-out version of a love story in which a young man called László pretends to die for love of the beautiful Ilona. At the end of the performance, in comes Long-Nosed Flea (baritone), an unpleasant masked figure from whom everyone immediately recoils. He starts making fun of the onlookers, but then an old woman manages to have him led away. Left alone, the young widow sinks back into her depressed state, but then her lover returns unexpectedly. The trouble has finally been cleared up, and he is now free.

Székely Fonó is made up of a series of songs, choruses and national dances, in which the dramatic element is not particularly significant. The story has been conceived as a kind of tapestry, bringing together the events that the folk-songs are about.

T

TABARRO, IL

See *Trittico, Il*

TADDEI, GIUSEPPE

(Genoa 1916)

Italian baritone. He made his debut at the Teatro dell'Opera in Rome in 1936 as the King's Herald (*Lohengrin*). In the years that followed he sang at a number of opera houses, but his real career began in 1946, when he was engaged by the Vienna Staatsoper, with which he remained until 1990. From 1948 he sang at the Salzburg Festival (*Le nozze di Figaro*) and La Scala, Milan (*Andrea Chénier*). In 1957 he made his United States debut in San Francisco (*Macbeth* and *Tosca*), followed by his Covent Garden debut in 1960 (*Otello*) and his first appearance with the Metropolitan Opera in New York in 1985 (*Falstaff*). Taddei is remembered for an extremely adaptable voice, rich in timbres. He performed a very wide range of roles from eighteenth-century *opera buffa* to Wagner and realist opera. His extraordinarily long career as a singer continued into the early 1990s with appearances in opera (as Dr Bartolo in *Il barbiere di Siviglia* in Bonn, 1991) and concert.

TAILLON, JOCELYNE

(Doudeville 1941)

French mezzo-soprano. A pupil of Suzanne Balguérie at the Grenoble Conservatoire, she made her mark in the Voix D'Or singing competition in Luchon. Her first appearances were in concerts, and from 1965 she studied with Germaine Lubin. In 1968 came her stage debut in Bordeaux (Dukas's *Ariane et Barbe-bleue*). The following year she sang Geneviève (*Pelléas et Mélisande*) at the Glyndebourne Festival and repeated this role at other leading international opera houses, together with appearances in numerous other operas, including Monteverdi's *L'incoronazione di Poppea*, Verdi's *Falstaff* and Britten's *Peter Grimes*.

TAKÁCS, KLARA

(Budapest 1945)

Hungarian mezzo-soprano. She began singing with the Budapesti Madrigálkórus in Budapest and continued her music studies at the Liszt Academy. In 1973 she joined the Budapest State Opera, where she has continued to sing as first soprano. She also appears at leading international opera houses in a repertoire that includes Orfeo (Gluck's opera), Cherubino (Mozart's *Le nozze di Figaro*), Rubria (Boito's *Nerone*), Suzuki (Puccini's *Madama Butterfly*), Eudossia (Respighi's *La fiamma*) and Aristea (Vivaldi's *L'olimpiade*).

TALVELA, MARTTI

(Hiitola, Karelia 1935–Juva, Mikkeli 1989)

Finnish bass. He studied with Öhmann in Stockholm and made his debut there at the Swedish Royal Opera in 1961 as Sparafucile in Verdi's *Rigoletto*. In 1962, at the invitation of Wieland Wagner, he appeared for the first time at the Bayreuth Festival, where he sang the great Wagner roles until 1970. He also came to prominence with performances at the Salzburg Easter Festival (1967), the Metropolitan Opera in New York (from 1968), Covent Garden (from 1970) and the Opéra in Paris (1974). From 1973 to 1979 he was director of the Savonlinna Festival. During the 1970s Tavela was one of the most famous interpreters of Boris Godunov and the roles of Sarastro (*Die Zauberflöte*, The Magic Flute), the Grand Inquisitor (*Don Carlos*) and Hagen (Wagner's *Götterdämmerung*).

TAMERLANO

Opera in three acts by George Frederick Handel (1685–1759), to a libretto by Nicola Haym. First performance: London, King's Theater, 31 October 1724.

Tamerlano (contralto), Emperor of the Tartars, has defeated and taken prisoner Bajazet (tenor), Emperor of the Turks, and is in love with his daughter Asteria. But Asteria loves and is loved by Andronico (contralto), a Greek prince and ally of Tamerlano. In order to be in a position to marry Asteria, Tamerlano wants to be free of his bride-to-be, Irene, (soprano) by giving her in marriage to Andronico. This leads to a complex web of stormy confrontations between the different characters, and eventually Asteria, who had agreed to marry Tamerlano, reveals that she had done so in order to be able to murder him. Asteria is imprisoned, but then Tamerlano releases her and rediscovers his desire to make her his wife. However, he finds out about the love of Asteria and Andronico and swears to have revenge. During a banquet Asteria tries to poison Tamerlano, but Irene saves him. Bajazet takes his own life, while Tamerlano, who has come to realize how much Irene loves him, consents to the marriage of Asteria and Andronico.

Tamerlano was a great success as an opera. There is clearly a strong dramatic dimension to the work (anticipating Gluck's reforms), as in the great scene where Bajazet dies, in the third act. Other operas on the Tamerlaine story were written by Porpora (1730) and Vivaldi (1735).

Top: The Italian baritone Giuseppe Taddei.

Above: The Finnish bass Martti Talvela.

A scene from *Tancredi*, an opera in two acts by Gioachino Rossini.

TANCRÈDE

Tragédie-lyrique *in a prologue and five acts by André Campra (1660–1744), to a libretto by Danchet, taken from Torquato Tasso's* Gerusalemme Liberata. *First performance: Paris, Académie Royale de Musique (Opéra), 7 November 1702.*

Tancrède (baritone), a Christian knight, loves Clorinde (contralto), an indomitable Saracen warrior-princess. She secretly returns his love, but the hatred dividing Christian and Muslim creates a barrier between them. The situation is further complicated by a tangled web of emotions: the Saracen King Argant (bass) is in love with Clorinde, while Herminie (soprano), herself a Saracen princess, loves Tancrède; and the magician Isménor (bass) feels passionately towards Herminie. In the end Clorinde decides that she will have nothing more to do with love and would rather die; so she puts on Argant's armour and confronts Tancrède, who assumes he is staring his rival in the face and kills him. When Tancrède discovers the truth, he becomes desperate and calls on Death to come to him.

Tancrède keeps to the structure of Lully's *tragédie-lyrique*, with its allegorical prologue and considerable number of ballets and fantasy scenes. But Campra shows more expressive variety than Lully, especially in the opera's most lyrical passages. The harmonies he uses in the score are of great interest for their obvious parallels with the Italian style.

TANCREDI

Opera in two acts by Gioachino Rossini (1792–1868), to a libretto by Gaetano Rossi based on Voltaire's tragedy Tancrède. *First performance: Venice, Teatro La Fenice, 6 February 1813.*

The action takes place in Syracuse, Sicily, in the tenth century. Argirio (tenor), Lord of Syracuse, has promised his daughter Amenaide (soprano) to Orbazzano (bass), leader of an enemy faction, as a way of uniting all parties against the Saracen army, which is laying siege to the city. Amenaide is desperate: she loves Tancredi (contralto), son of the deposed King of Syracuse. Amenaide sends a letter to her beloved in which she calls on him to help her. Tancredi, banished from the city after being charged with treason, secretly returns to Syracuse. When he meets Amenaide, she begs him to flee and does not tell him that she is about to marry. But then, in her father's presence, she firmly rejects Orbazzano. He, however, has obtained the letter Amenaide had sent to Tancredi, although it does not bear his name. The letter, intercepted near the Saracen camp, is widely assumed to have been intended for the Saracen leader, Sultan Solamir. Amenaide is wrongly arrested on a charge of treason. Having disguised himself so as to leave no chance of being recognized, Tancredi challenges Orbazzano to a duel and kills him. He then abandons Amenaide, by whom he believes he has been betrayed, launches an attack on the Saracens, defeats them and saves Syracuse. Eventually it is discovered that Amenaide's letter was intended for Tancredi and not Solamir. Tancredi, mortally wounded, is happy to learn that Amenaide was not to blame and asks Argirio to unite them in marriage before he dies in Amenaide's arms.

For its original performances in Venice, *Tancredi* had a happy ending. But when the opera was revived in Ferrara in March of the same year, 1813, Rossini had substituted the tragic ending to be found in Voltaire's play. The audience did not appreciate this change, and the first version was readopted. The extraordinary modernity of this part of the work makes it easy to see why the audience of that time did not approve, but it also shows how much importance Rossini attached to the second finale. When *Tancredi* was revived at the Teatro dell'Opera in Rome in 1977 the tragic finale was restored, and the opera is now performed with this ending. *Tancredi* is Rossini's first operatic masterpiece and marked the beginning of his enduring fame.

TANNHÄUSER UND DER SANGERKRIEG AUF WARTBURG

(Tannhäuser and the Singing Competition in the Valley of the Wartburg)

Opera in three acts by Richard Wagner (1813–1883), to the composer's own libretto. First performance: Dresden, Hoftheater, 19 October 1845.

The action takes place in Thuringia in the early thirteenth century. In the underground world of the Venusberg, the goddess Venus (soprano or mezzo-soprano) tries in vain to dissuade the poet Tannhäuser (tenor) from his desire to return to earthly life, now that he is sated with her love. In a valley in Thuringia near the Castle of Wartburg, Tannhäuser is reunited with the Landgrave Hermann (bass) and his friend Wolfram von Eschenbach (baritone) with the other minstrel noblemen. These are Tannhäuser's old companions, and he is glad to be with them again, above all because he longs to see the Landgrave's daughter Elisabeth (soprano) again, who occupies a very special place in his heart. Elisabeth, who is still in love with him too, feels both troubled and happy as she receives him. But then, during a grand singing competition (in which she is sure Tannhäuser will triumph and be granted her hand in marriage as his prize), he impulsively sings a song in praise of sensual love in the name of Venus, revealing that he had been living at her court. These words are an outrage to the assembled knights, and they are ready to put this pagan to death when Elisabeth intervenes: she has been wounded in love, but she asks Christian forgiveness for Tannhäuser, making them stay their hand. Moved by Elisabeth's action, Tannhäuser accepts the Landgrave's verdict that he make a pilgrimage to Rome to seek absolution from his sin. Many months later, exhausted and in rags, Tannhäuser returns to the castle. He confides despairingly to Wolfram that the pope has refused to absolve him, saying he can no more win forgiveness than the pope's staff can flower. Resigned to eternal damnation, Tannhäuser calls out to Venus, and the goddess appears, but Wolfram tells Tannhäuser that Elisabeth has died after praying for him for a long time. At the mention of Elisabeth's name, Venus disappears and a procession emerges from the castle bearing Elisabeth's bier. The pilgrims declare a miracle: the pope's staff has burst into flower. Repentant and now redeemed, Tannhäuser embraces her body and dies.

Wagner began writing the libretto for *Tannhäuser* at the end of the spring of 1842 and completed it in May 1843; composition then took until April 1845. In October of that year, the work was premiered in Dresden, where the audience gave it a lukewarm reception. It met with the same response in Paris when it was staged there in 1861, even though Wagner had added a bacchanal to satisfy the French. But the richness of the music in *Tannhäuser* was soon recognized, and it has come to be regarded as one of Wagner's most important early works.

TAPPY, ERIC

(Lausanne 1931)

Swiss tenor. A pupil of Fernando Capri at the Conservatory in Geneva, Ernst Reichert at the Salzburg Mozarteum, and Eva Liebenberg in Hilversum, he made his debut in a concert in Strasbourg in 1959 (in Bach's *St. John Passion*). In the same year came his opera debut in Milhaud's *Les malheurs d'Orphée* in Zurich. He went on to sing the leading role in Rameau's *Zoroastre* at the Opéra Comique in Paris (1964), a performance that launched him on his career.

TCHAIKOVSKY, PETER ILYCH

See Čaikovski, Pëtr Il'ič

TCHAKAROV, EMIL

(Burgas 1948–Paris 1991)

Bulgarian conductor. He was a child prodigy, conducting for the first time at the age of 11. He studied at the Conservatory in Sofia. In 1972 he won the Herbert von Karajan award for conductors. After serving as Karajan's assistant in Berlin and Strasbourg, he completed his training with Franco Ferrara (1972) and Eugen Jochum (1974). Within a short time he had established himself as a leading international conductor.

TEAR, ROBERT

(Barry, Glamorgan 1939)

Welsh tenor. A chorister at King's College, Cambridge (1957–60) and at St. Paul's Cathedral in London, he made his stage debut with the English Opera Group in Britten's *The Rape of Lucretia* in 1963. He also took part in the first performances of Britten's *The Burning Fiery Furnace* (1966) and *The Prodigal Son* (1968), as well as in productions of other contemporary operas, including Gordon Crosse's *The Grace of Todd* (1969), Tippett's *The Knot Garden* (1970) and Taverner's *Thérèse* (1979).

TEBALDI, RENATA

(Pesaro 1922)

Italian soprano. She studied in Parma with Brancucci and Campogalliani and in Pesaro with Carmen Melis. She made her debut as Elena (Boito's *Mefistofele*) in Rovigo in 1944. In 1946 she was chosen by Toscanini

Above: Stage design for the first performance of *Tannhäuser* by Richard Wagner.

Left: The Italian soprano Renata Tebaldi.

to sing in the concert held to mark the re-opening of La Scala in Milan, where in the same year she sang Elsa in *Lohengrin*. She was to return to La Scala regularly for nine seasons, between 1947 and 1960 and in two concerts in 1974 and 1976. Engagements followed for her to appear at the other leading Italian opera houses, and then, from 1950 onwards, at Covent Garden, the San Francisco Opera, the Metropolitan Opera in New York (*Otello* in 1955 and then almost uninterruptedly until 1973) and in Chicago (*Manon Lescaut*, 1957). Her lyric soprano voice is remembered for its sheer musicality and particularly fine timbre. Tebaldi's best performances were as Aida, Leonora, Margherita (*Mefistofele*), Wally (in Catalani's opera), Mimi, Butterfly, Liù and Maddalena di Coigny in Giordano's *Andrea Chénier*.

TE KANAWA, DAME KIRI

(Gisborne, Auckland 1944)

New Zealand soprano. She began to study singing with Maria Leo in Auckland and continued with Vera Rosza in London. She made her debut at the Camden Festival as Elena in Rossini's *La donna del lago*. In 1970 she sang for the first time at Covent Garden (as one of the Flower Maidens in Wagner's *Parsifal*), returning there in 1971 as the Countess in Mozart's *Le nozze di Figaro*. It was as a Mozart singer that she began her rapid rise to international celebrity, with appearances in Lyons (1972), San Francisco (1972) and at Glyndebourne (1973). In 1974 came her debut with the Metropolitan Opera in New York (Verdi's *Otello*), and she was to return there in *Don Giovanni* and *Le nozze di Figaro*. She had a triumphant success in *Don Giovanni* at the Opéra in Paris in 1975. Dame Kiri has also won acclaim in operas by Richard Strauss (*Der Rosenkavalier*, *Arabella* and *Capriccio*) and in Italian opera (*La bohème*, *Tosca*, *La traviata*, *Simon Boccanegra*, etc.). An elegant singer of great charm (she was Donna Elvira in Joseph Losey's film version of *Don Giovanni*), Dame Kiri is one of the most noted sopranos in international opera.

Above: The New Zealand soprano Dame Kiri Te Kanawa.

Right: Title page to the score of *The Telephone* by Giancarlo Menotti.

TELEPHONE, THE

Opera in one act by Giancarlo Menotti (b. 1911), to the composer's own libretto. First performance: New York, Heckscher Theater, 18 February 1947.

Ben (baritone) is about to leave town, but first he goes to see Lucy (soprano) to take her a gift, which she accepts with delight. Ben is on the verge of saying something to her when the telephone rings. It turns out to be a woman-friend of Lucy's, and Lucy settles down to enjoy a long gossip with her. After that, Ben thinks he can now bring the subject up, but the telephone rings again; this time it is a wrong number. Ben begins to get agitated, because he will soon have to leave, but all that Lucy can think of to calm him is to telephone for the correct time. Ben tries again to make Lucy listen to him, but inevitably the telephone interrupts him again. Preoccupied with this conversation, Lucy does not notice that Ben has left. Only when she has put the receiver down does she realize he is no longer there. Now the telephone rings yet again. This time it is Ben calling. The telephone is his only way of getting through to Lucy, if he is not going to give up trying to propose marriage. Lucy is delighted and asks Ben to telephone her every day.

The Telephone was premiered in a double-bill with Menotti's *The Medium* in keeping with the old practice of presenting a comic and serious opera together. Both operas were enormously successful and were equally well received when subsequently revived.

TENDER LAND, THE

Opera in three acts by Aaron Copland (1900–1990), to a libretto by Horace Everett. First performance: New York City Opera, 1 April 1954.

The action takes place on a small farm in the Midwest during the 1930s. Laurie Moss (soprano), who has until now been living at home with her overprotective mother (contralto) and grandfather (bass), is about to graduate from high school, when Martin (tenor) and Top (baritone), two casual labourers of doubtful morals, arrive at the farm. Laurie falls in love with Martin and wants to run away with him during the celebrations that follow her graduation. But Top persuades his friend not to do this, pointing out to him that their wandering life is not right for Laurie. So the two young men leave before dawn. Although disillusioned,

Laurie still decides to leave home in order to make a life for herself.

Commissioned by Rodgers and Hammerstein to mark the 30th anniversary of the League of Composers, *The Tender Land* is one of the most important American operas.

THAÏS

Opera in three acts and seven scenes by Jules Massenet (1842–1912), to a libretto by Louis Gallet from the novel by Anatole France. First performance: Paris, Opéra, 16 March 1894.

The action takes place in Egypt during the fourth century A.D. Athanaël (baritone), the Cenobite, decides to save the soul of Thaïs (soprano), a courtesan who is corrupting the city with the worship of Venus. Athanaël meets Thaïs in Alexandria at the house of the young hedonist Nicias (tenor) and persuades her to reflect on her dissolute life and on the true values to believe in. Moved by Athanaël's words, she decides to burn all her possessions and retire to a convent, where an abbess from Rome, Albine (mezzo-soprano), has created around herself a community of young women living a life of humility. And this is what she does. In the convent Thaïs finds redemption. But Athanaël is left sad and depressed. He cannot forget Thaïs's beauty. He dreams that she is dying and is so overwhelmed that he goes to see her again and arrives just in time to hear her last words. Thaïs recognizes him and thanks him for having saved her. Desperately, Athanaël speaks to her of his burning passion for her, but Thaïs, having found happiness in her detachment from earthly passions, dies.

At its first performance, *Thaïs* was an outstanding success and continues to be performed quite often. It contains passages of great beauty: Athanaël's invocation "Voilà donc la terrible cité," Thaïs's aria "Dis-moi que je suis belle," her subsequent duet with Athanaël and, above all, the famous Meditation for orchestra.

THIELEMANN, CHRISTIAN

(Berlin 1959)

German conductor. After studying music in Berlin, he began his career as répétiteur and assistant conductor at the Salzburg and Bayreuth Festivals. He made his debut as a conductor with the Zurich Opera in 1986 in Janáček's *Jenůfa*. He then appeared at the Vienna Staatsoper (Mozart's *Così fan tutte*, 1987), with the Genoa Opera in 1988 (Strauss's *Elektra* and Wagner's *Die Walküre*), at Covent Garden (*Jenůfa*, 1988) and at the Grand Théâtre in Geneva (*Kát'a Kabanová*, 1988). He is regarded as one of the most promising of the new generation of conductors.

THOMAS, AMBROISE

(Metz 1811–Paris 1896)

French composer. The son of a musician, he studied violin and piano as a child. He went on to attend the Paris Conservatoire, where his teachers were Kalkbrenner and Le Sueur. After his debut at the Opéra-Comique in 1837 with *La double échelle* he achieved success with *Le Caïd* (1849) and *Le songe d'une nuit d'été* (1850). The opera with which he finally made his name was *Mignon* (1866), consolidating his reputation with *Hamlet* (1868).

THOMAS, JESS FLOYD

(Hot Springs, South Dakota 1927)

American tenor. He studied with Otto Schulmann and made his debut in 1957 with San Francisco Opera as Fenton in *Falstaff*, following this with appearances in *Macbeth* and *Der Rosenkavalier*. From 1958, his career centered on Germany, where he built a reputation as a Wagner singer. His name was associated with the Bayreuth Festival (1961–76), the Vienna Staatsoper, the Deutsche Oper Berlin, the Munich Opera, the Metropolitan Opera in New York (where he sang in *Die Meistersinger von Nürnberg* in 1962) and other major international opera venues. In 1966 he appeared as Caesar in Samuel Barber's *Antony and Cleopatra* in the inaugural production at the new Metropolitan Opera House, Lincoln Center. He retired from the stage in 1982.

THREEPENNY OPERA, THE

See *Dreigroschenoper, Die*

TIEFLAND

(Lowland)

Opera in a prologue and two acts by Eugène d'Albert (1864–1932), to a libretto by Rudolf Lothar, based on the Catalan play Terra baixa *by Angel Guimerá. First performance: Prague, German Theater, 15 November 1903.*

Pedro (tenor) is a rough and simple shepherd living in the Pyrenees. Although happy with this kind of life, he longs to find a wife. Sebastiano (baritone), a wealthy, selfish, arrogant land-owner, persuades Pedro to leave the mountains: his plan for the shepherd is that he should settle in the lowlands, become a miller, and marry Marta (soprano), a poor young woman Sebastiano had found starving by the wayside and had subsequently made his mistress. Sebastiano imagines that by marrying an ignorant shepherd, Marta will continue to be accessible to him and

Poster for the premiere of *Thaïs* by Jules Massenet.

that he will be able to dampen the gossip that has made it difficult for him to marry a rich heiress. After marrying Pedro, Marta, who had tried to escape the marriage being forced on her, discovers that her shepherd husband's feelings for her are sincere, and her initial contempt for him gives way to love. She also realizes that Pedro does not know about her past life, and she dares not refer to it. But then comes the day when Sebastiano cruelly humiliates Pedro. Marta finally blurts out the truth and implores Pedro to avenge her. Pedro kills Sebastiano and then returns to his old life in the mountains with Marta, who is anxious to forget all about her sad and squalid past.

Tiefland is d'Albert's most famous opera and the only one that is not set in Germany.

TIPPETT, MICHAEL KEMP

(London 1905)

British composer. He studied at the Royal College of Music in London with Charles Wood and C.H. Kitson for composition and Adrian Boult and Malcolm Sargent for conducting. His first composition for the theater was the ballad opera *Robin Hood* (1934), but it was not until 1955, by which time Tippett had achieved a complete mastery of style, that he wrote the opera *The Midsummer Marriage*. This work, *King Priam* (1962), *The Knot Garden* (1970) and *The Ice Break* (1977) stand as significant landmarks in the history of British opera.

TITUS, ALAN

(New York 1945)

American baritone. He studied at the Colorado School of Music with Aksel Schiøtz and at the Juilliard School in New York with Hans Heinz. In 1969 he made his debut in Washington (Puccini's *La bohème*), returning there in September 1971 to sing the role of the Celebrant in Leonard Bernstein's *Mass*. From 1972 he appeared with New York City Opera and from 1976 with the Metropolitan Opera in New York (Strauss's *Ariadne auf Naxos*). His European debut came in 1973 in Amsterdam (Debussy's *Pelléas et Mélisande*), and appearances followed at the Aix-en-Provence Festival, the Paris Opéra, Frankfurt, among other venues. In 1992 he took part in Donizetti's *Il Duca d'Alba* at the Spoleto Festival.

TOCZYSKA, STEFANIA

(Grudziadz 1943)

Polish mezzo-soprano. She studied with Romuald Toczyski at the Gdansk Conservatory and was successful in a number of international singing competitions (Toulouse 1972, Paris 1973). She made her debut in *Carmen* in Gdansk (1974) and went on to sing with the Warsaw Opera. From the mid 1970s she sang at the main European opera houses, including the Vienna Staatsoper (*Un ballo in maschera*, 1978) and Munich (*Don Carlos*, 1979). Her appearances in the United States date from 1979: San Francisco (*La Gioconda* and *Roberto Devereux*, 1979), New York's Carnegie Hall (*Khovanshchina*, 1981) and Lyric Opera of Chicago (*Anna Bolena*, 1985). She sings regularly with the Metropolitan Opera in New York: *Khovanshchina* (1988), *Aida* (1989) and *Boris Godunov* (1990). Toczyska is an outstanding singer and performer of the principal roles in Italian and Russian opera.

TOKODY, ILONA

(Szeged 1953)

Hungarian soprano. She first studied singing at the Szeged Conservatory and then at the Liszt Academy in Budapest (1971). She made her debut at the Hungarian State Opera in 1973 and proved herself in international singing competitions. From 1978 she appeared with the Bratislava Opera and after that her international engagements gradually increased to include Covent Garden (1984), the Vienna Staatsoper and the San Francisco Opera. Despite a certain hardness in the upper register, Tokody is a singer of great character with very expressive phrasing.

The Bulgarian soprano Anna Tomowa-Sintow in Strauss's *Rosenkavalier*.

TOMLINSON, JOHN

(Accrington, Lancashire)

British bass. After studying at the Royal Manchester College of Music, he made his debut at the Glyndebourne Festival and went on to appear with Kent Opera. From 1974 to 1981 he sang with English National Opera and from 1976 at Covent Garden. His international career has taken him to San Francisco Opera (*Macbeth*, 1986), the Paris Opéra (*Boris Godunov*, 1988), the Bayreuth Festival (*Das Rheingold*, 1988) and other leading opera venues.

TOMOWA-SINTOW, ANNA

(Stara Zagora 1941)

Bulgarian soprano. She studied at the Conservatory in Sofia and made her debut in 1965 as Tatyana in *Eugene Onegin*. From 1967 until 1972 she sang with the Leipzig Opera, appearing in roles from a wide repertoire that included *Nabucco*, *Otello*, and *Manon Lescaut*. She was engaged by the Salzburg Festival in 1973 for the premiere production of Carl Orff's *De temporum fine comoedia*, then performed there regularly from 1976. Other leading venues included Covent Garden (*Così fan tutte*, 1975, and *Lohengrin*, 1977), the Vienna Staatsoper (*Le nozze di Figaro*, 1977), the Metropolitan Opera in New York (Mozart's *Don Giovanni*), La Scala, Milan (*Lohengrin*, 1981), and the Maggio Musicale Festival in Florence (*Der Rosenkavalier*, 1989). A singer of great refinement and musicianship, Tomowa-Sintow has won particular distinction for her performances in operas by Mozart and Richard Strauss.

TORQUATO TASSO

Opera in three acts by Gaetano Donizetti (1797–1848), to a libretto by Jacopo Ferretti, after Giovanni Rossini's play. First performance: Rome, Teatro Valle, 9 September 1833.

The poet Torquato Tasso (baritone) loves Eleonora (soprano), sister of Alfonso d'Este (bass), Duke of Ferrara. But their honourable feelings for each other are betrayed by intrigues at court, masterminded by the treacherous Roberto Gherardini (tenor), the Duke's secretary, and the courtier Gherardo (bass). As a result of these intrigues, Tasso is imprisoned. By the time he is set free again, Eleonora has been dead for some time.

Torquato Tasso mixes together dramatic and light roles, and is thus allied to the genre of *opera semiseria*. The figure of Tasso is given a high musical and dramatic profile and is one of the first great baritone roles, written by Donizetti for the talents of one of the greatest singers of the day, Giorgio Ronconi (1810–1890).

TORVALDO E DORLISKA

Opera in two acts by Gioachino Rossini (1792–1868), to a libretto by Cesare Sterbini. First performance: Rome, Teatro Valle, 26 December 1815.

The action takes place at the castle of Ordow. After wounding Torvaldo (tenor), a nobleman, the Duke imprisons Torvaldo's wife, Dorliska (soprano), with whom he is in love. The Duke leads her to believe that her husband is dead, but with the help of Giorgio (*buffo*), the castle keeper, Torvaldo manages to disguise himself and visit Dorliska. When she recognizes her husband, Dorliska's emotions get the better of her, and she accidentally gives Torvaldo away. As a result, the Duke puts Torvaldo in prison too, under sentence of death. The villagers, however, have grown tired of the Duke behaving like a tyrant, march on the castle, imprison the Duke and set Torvaldo and Dorliska free.

The *semiserio* aspects of this opera were not appreciated by the Roman audience which judged it a failure, despite the fact that the cast contained singers of the caliber of the tenor Domenico Donzelli (Torvaldo) and the bass Filippo Galli (Duke of Ordow). Not performed for many years, it was revived on the Italian network of Swiss Radio in a concert version (1992).

TOSCA

Opera in three acts by Giacomo Puccini (1858–1924), to a libretto by Giuseppe Giacosa and Luigi Illica, from the play by Victorien Sardou. First performance: Rome, Teatro Costanzi, 14 January 1900.

The action takes place in Rome in June 1800. Cesare Angelotti (bass), a consul of the former Roman republic, has escaped from the fortress of Castel Sant'Angelo. The fugitive's trail leads Baron Scarpia (baritone), chief of Rome's police, to the church of Sant'Andrea della Valle, where the painter Mario Cavaradossi (tenor) is working and has secretly helped Angelotti. Scarpia finds an empty food basket and a fan belonging to the Marchesa Attavanti, Angelotti's sister, and becomes convinced that Cavaradossi is involved with Angelotti's escape. At the church, where she has been visiting the painter at his work, Floria Tosca (soprano), a singer and Cavaradossi's mistress, is approached by Scarpia and shown the Marchesa's fan. This arouses her jealousy, and she hurries off to her lover's house, imagining she will surprise him there with the woman she assumes is her rival. What she does not know is that she is being followed by one of Scarpia's agents, Spoletta (tenor). Cavaradossi is arrested for having aided a fugitive from custody and is taken by Scarpia to Palazzo Farnese. Under interrogation, Cavaradossi denies everything, and Scarpia has him taken into an adjoining room to be tortured. Tosca arrives, summoned by Scarpia, and overhears her lover's cries of agony. Unable to bear it, she gives in and reveals Angelotti's hiding place to Scarpia. Cavaradossi is sentenced to death. Tosca begs Scarpia to show him clemency, saying that she is prepared to pay any price to save him. Scarpia promises to spare Cavaradossi's life if she will submit to his advances. In torment, she accepts Scarpia's terms. Scarpia issues an order seeming to indicate that the shooting of Cavaradossi be carried out with blank cartridges. After he has signed a document guaranteeing the couple safe conduct to leave Rome, Tosca stabs him to death. The scene changes to Castel Sant'Angelo, with only a short time left before Cavaradossi is due to be executed. Tosca arrives and tells him that the firing-squad he is about to face will only pretend to shoot him. The squad lines up, and the execution takes place. Then Tosca discovers in horror that Cavaradossi has actually been shot to death. Voices are heard close by. The

Above: *Torvaldo e Dorliska*, a *semiserio* opera in two acts by Gioachino Rossini.

Left: Luigi Illica, one of the two librettists of Giacomo Puccini's *Tosca*.

OPERA AND THE CINEMA

Opera proved attractive to film-makers from the very early days of the cinema: a film based on Gounod's *Faust* was produced in France in 1903, while another, on Puccini's *Manon Lescaut*, came out in Italy in 1909. In the United States, celebrated singers of *bel canto* were also appearing in film productions: in 1911, Lina Cavalieri and Lucien Muratore took part in a film version of *Manon Lescaut*; in 1915, Geraldine Farrar played the lead in *Carmen*, while Mary Garden in 1917 sang the role of Thaïs in a film based on Massenet's opera. These films, which were made in the "silent" era, were made by synchronizing the action on screen with a gramophone recording and "performing" the opera by miming the words – with the result that some roles could be taken by famous actors who were certainly not gifted singers: Mary Pickford, for example, sang the title role in *Madama Butterfly*, and Lilian Gish and John Gilbert were cast for the main parts in *La bohème* directed by King Vidor in 1926. With the advent of talking pictures, these productions increased, although actors still mimed the singing, and it was only in 1992, for a performance of *Tosca* recorded in Rome in the actual places where Puccini had set the opera, that the singers sang the work live. Between the 1930s and 1940s, there were a number of important achievements for opera on film, including Charpentier's *Louise* directed by Abel Gance and starring Grace Moore or a version of *Don Quichotte* (1934) with Fyodor Shalyapin to music by Ibert and directed by Pabst. Then came a whole series of films re-telling the stories of operas, like *Il sogno di Butterfly* (Butterfly's Dream, 1939) with Maria Cebotari and Tito Gobbi. Other famous names from the world of opera, like Gigli, Bechi, Melchior and Schipa had leading roles in films which had nothing to do with opera. In the years following the Second World War, a number of film directors made films of this sort, but operas themselves were very rarely filmed in their entirety and once again the opera singers who took part were joined by film stars: Gina Lollobrigida in *I pagliacci* (1948) alongside Galliano Masini and Tito Gobbi, and Sophia Loren in *La favorita* (1952) and *Aida* (1953), the latter dubbed with the singing voice of Renata Tebaldi. In America, the tenor and film actor Mario Lanza was enormously popular, starring in numerous successful films, such as *The Louisiana Fisherman*, *Old Heidelberg*, *Serenade* and, above all, *The Great Caruso* (1951), one of the most famous fictionalized biographies of the celebrated tenor. In the 1950s came film versions of actual opera-house productions, like that of the 1954 Paul Czinner production of Mozart's *Don Giovanni* and the famous production of *La bohème* by Zeffirelli with von Karajan conducting (1967). A number of other opera productions belong to this category, many of them by the theater director Jean-Pierre Ponnelle, who transferred many of his productions to the big scene (*Il barbiere di Siviglia*, *La Cenerentola*, etc.). Franco Zeffirelli has produced many well-known film versions of operas, such as *La traviata* and *Otello*. In the 1970s and 1980s, however, it became more common to film productions of operas in the opera house, a practice more in keeping with the style and nature of opera itself.

Above: A scene from Joseph Losey's film of *Don Giovanni*.

Right: The American soprano Julia Migenes, who starred in the cinema production of *Carmen* by Francesco Rosi.

guards have found Scarpia murdered and are coming for Tosca. She tears herself away from Cavaradossi's lifeless body and throws herself from the ramparts.

After the lyricism of *La bohème*, Puccini has created in *Tosca* a world of strong contrasts, dwelling particularly on cruelty and death (as in the musical motif he uses for the character of Scarpia). There is a wealth of invention in this music, and in the way in which it is required to keep pace with the hectic sequence of events. The disjointed and impassioned dialogue heightens the dramatic power of this opera, one of Puccini's most popular.

TOSCANINI, ARTURO

(Parma 1867–Riverdale, New York 1957)

Italian conductor. Originally a cellist at the Teatro Regio in Parma, he took over as conductor in *Aida* during a tour in Rio de Janiero in 1886. This launched him on a legendary conducting career. He conducted the premiere performances of Catalani's *Edmea*, Leoncavallo's *I pagliacci* and *Zazà*, Puccini's *La bohème*, *La fanciulla del West* and *Turandot*, Mascagni's *Le maschere*, Cilèa's *Gloria*, Giordano's *Madame Sans-Gêne*, Boito's *Nerone* and others, as well as the Italian premieres of *Götterdämmerung* and *Siegfried* and the American premieres of operas by Dukas, Wolf-Ferrari, Mussorgsky and Montemezzi. His name was principally associated with La Scala, Milan, where he made his debut in 1898 (in *Die Meistersinger von Nürnberg*), and with the Metropolitan Opera in New York, where he served as principal Italian conductor from 1908 to 1915. He left La Scala in 1929 in protest against the Fascist government in Italy, to return in 1946, after a sojourn in the United States.

TOTE STADT, DIE

(The Dead City)

Opera in three acts by Erich Wolfgang Korngold (1897–1957), to a libretto by "Paul Schott," a pseudonym used by the composer. First performance: simultaneously at the Stadttheater in Hamburg and the Stadttheater in Cologne, 4 December 1920.

The action takes place against the somber background of the city of Bruges, where Paul (tenor) has surrounded himself with all the things which remind him of Marie, his young wife, whose death he is now mourning. Frank (baritone), a friend of Paul's, has just returned to Bruges and finds Paul prostrate with grief. Little by little, however, Paul recovers: he has met Marietta, a woman who bears an astonishing resemblance to Marie. Enter Marietta (soprano), a dancer from Lille. She sings a song and begins to dance. This arouses strong feelings in Paul, who finds himself torn between the memory of his beloved Marie and the rekindling of his desire by Marietta. As he struggles with this inner conflict, Paul sinks into a dream-like state: he imagines experiencing his passion for Marietta to its fullest extent, and this means freeing himself forever of the memory of Marie. The dream seems to be about to come true when, in the room where he has spent a passionate night of love with Marietta, Paul hears the sound of a procession. Overcome with remorse, he falls to his knees, while Marietta mocks him and cruelly accuses him of hypocrisy and weakness. Paul flies into a rage and strangles her. At that moment, he wakes up. It has all been a dream, but now he feels free and decides to leave Bruges, the dead city.

The score of *Die Tote Stadt* displays a varied musical language, revealing the influence of both Puccini and Richard Strauss. A work of considerable charm, with many interesting touches, it skilfully conveys the story's decadent atmosphere.

TOTTOLA, ANDREA LEONE

(?Naples c.1760–1831)

Italian librettist, who wrote for Rossini (*La gazzetta*, *Mosè*, *Ermione*, *La donna del lago* and *Zelmira*) and for Donizetti (*La zingara*, *Il fortunato inganno*, *Alfredo il grande*, *Gabrielle di Vergy*, *Il giovedì grasso* and *Elisabetta al castello di Kenilworth*). He also wrote the texts for operas by Mercadante, Pacini, Bellini, Generali and Ricci.

TOURANGEAU, HUGUETTE

(Montreal 1938)

Canadian mezzo-soprano. A pupil of Herlingerová at the Quebec Conservatoire, she went on to complete her training in New York with the conductor Richard Bonynge,

An early twentieth-century postcard inspired by Puccini's *Tosca*.

with whom she was to appear frequently. In 1946 she won the Metropolitan Opera Auditions of the Air. She made her debut with Montreal Opera as Mercédès in Bizet's *Carmen*. After several tours with the Metropolitan Opera (1965), she appeared for the first time with New York City Opera (Bizet's *Carmen*). Engagements followed in Vancouver, Boston and Seattle. Tourangeau commands a variety of accents and outstanding expressive gifts, especially in the French repertoire.

TRAVIATA, LA

(The Wayward Woman)

Opera in three acts by Giuseppe Verdi (1813–1901), to a libretto by Francesco Maria Piave, after the novel La dame aux camélias *by Alexandre Dumas* fils *(1852). First performance: Venice, Teatro La Fenice, 6 March 1853.*

The action takes place in Paris around the year 1850. During a party at her luxurious home, Violetta Valéry (soprano), a courtesan, meets Alfredo Germont (tenor), a fervent admirer of hers. Germont is actually in love with Violetta and tells her of his feelings. She is disturbed by this and discovers that she too, for the first time in her life, is experiencing true love. Alfredo and Violetta leave Paris and live happily together in a house in the country. Their happiness is short-lived, however: Giorgio Germont (baritone), Alfredo's father, is so anxious to allay the scandal of this relationship, which is ruining the family's reputation, that he insists Violetta leave Alfredo. In a fit of jealousy, Alfredo bursts into the house of Flora Bervoix (mezzo-soprano), a friend of Violetta's. Here he finds Violetta in the company of Baron Duphol (baritone), her former protector, and accuses her of betraying him. Mindful of the promise she has made to Alfredo's father, she lies that she now loves Duphol. Incensed, Alfredo publicly insults Violetta, to the outrage of those present. The scene changes to Violetta's house. The consumption from which she had always suffered has become much worse. Before she dies, however, she is reunited with Alfredo, whose father finally told him the truth.

In *La traviata*, the third and last opera in Verdi's so-called "popular trilogy," the main character, as in *Rigoletto* and *Il trovatore*, overshadows the others. The psychological complexity of Violetta makes her an outstanding figure not only in this opera but in the context of Romantic theater as a whole. The modernity of the plot is just one of the features that helped Verdi to produce, from the very opening bars of the prelude, an extraordinarily lyrical score, capable of recreating in music the drama, feelings and sorrow of the story.

TREEMONISHA

Opera in three acts by Scott Joplin (1868–1917), to the composer's own libretto. Composed in 1908. First performance: Atlanta, Morehouse College, January 1972. Arranged and orchestrated by Gunther Schuller for the Houston Grand Opera, May 1975.

The action takes place in Arkansas, on a plantation surrounded by woodland, in 1884. Zodzetrick (tenor), a charlatan magician, is chased away by Treemonisha (soprano) after he has tried to sell a rabbit's paw to her mother Monisha (contralto). Zodzetrick attempts to win the young woman over, but Remus (tenor) explains that he will have no success in persuading her, as she is only one among them who has already fought and won other battles against superstition. The magician goes away, threatening that he will have his revenge. At a dance in the country held by the plantation workers, Monisha recalls a September morning in 1866 when they found a two-day old baby girl under the tree outside her hut, and how she and her husband, Ned (bass), adopted her and baptized her Tree-Monisha. The young woman herself and everyone else is completely taken aback, having always been under the impression that Treemonisha was Monisha and Ned's own daughter. Treemonisha thanks Monisha, whom she has loved as though she were her own mother, and then heads off to the woods with her friend Lucy (soprano). Here Treemonisha is abducted by Zodzetrick and his fellow quack magicians. They are on the point of throwing her into a large wasps' nest when a terrifying figure appears. They take fright and run away. The figure is actually Remus, disguised as a devil and wearing a grotesque scarecrow mask. While the magicians are rounded up, Remus and Treemonisha return to the village. Everyone wants the abductors

A scene from *La traviata* by Giuseppe Verdi in a Covent Garden production directed by Luchino Visconti.

punished, but Treemonisha asks that they be given a rebuke instead and then released. At this, the villagers unanimously proclaim Treemonisha their leader. Initially she hesitates, but then accepts and gives her first order, which is that everyone must start dancing.

Scott Joplin had *Treemonisha* published in 1911 but then fell seriously ill and was unable to see to the task of getting the opera staged. It was rediscovered in the 1970s and produced. A successful combination of numbers in true ragtime style and other features more reminiscent of traditional opera, the *Treemonisha* is a masterpiece of Afro-American music and theater.

TREIGLE, NORMAN

(New Orleans 1927–1975)

American bass. He studied in New Orleans, making his debut there in 1947 as Lodovico in Verdi's *Otello*. In 1953 he sang for the first time at New York City Opera and continued to appear there until 1972, performing an extremely wide-ranging repertoire, which included the great bass roles (Mefistofele, Boris, Padre Guardiano) and contemporary operas (he took the lead in the American premiere of Dallapiccola's *Il prigioniero*, 1951). Treigle's was a voice of great power which, together with his extraordinary presence on stage, contributed to his achievement as a celebrated interpreter of the character of Mephistopheles in the operas by Gounod and Boito.

TRISTAN UND ISOLDE

Opera in three acts by Richard Wagner (1813–1883), to the composer's own libretto. First performance: Munich, Hoftheater, 10 June 1865.

Tristan (tenor), equerry and nephew of King Marke (bass), is escorting Princess Isolde by ship to his uncle's court where she is to become the King's wife. Isolde had previously wanted her revenge on Tristan for killing her betrothed in combat, but now instead she falls in love with him. Tristan returns her love, but they are unable to admit to this mutual sentiment. Isolde orders her maid Brangäne (mezzo-soprano) to prepare the magic potions her mother had given her. She will share the suicide potion with Tristan. As the coast of Cornwall comes into view, Tristan goes to see the Princess. She accuses him of faint-heartedness but then invites him to drink from a cup of reconciliation. Tristan knows that the cup contains poison, but this does not deter him. However, Brangäne has replaced the suicide philter with another potion, which induces love. Inflamed by intense feelings, the pair look

at one another ecstatically, and then fall into each other's arms. The scene changes to the garden in front of King Marke's castle on a clear summer's night. Isolde, who is now married to the King, and Tristan are overcome with passion and surrender to the ecstasy of their feelings, not even noticing the dawn when it comes. As a result they are surprised by the King and his vassal Melot (tenor or

München.

Königl. Hof- und National-Theater.

Samstag den 10. Juni 1865.
Außer Abonnement.
Zum ersten Male:

Tristan und Isolde

von
Richard Wagner.

Personen der Handlung:

Tristan	Herr Schnorr von Carolsfeld.
König Marke	Herr Zottmayer.
Isolde	Frau Schnorr von Carolsfeld.
Kurwenal	Herr Mitterwurzer.
Melot	Herr Heinrich.
Brangäne	Fräulein Deinet.
Ein Hirt	Herr Simons.
Ein Steuermann	Herr Hartmann.

Schiffsvolk. Ritter und Knappen. Isolde's Frauen.

Textbücher sind, das Stück zu 12 kr., an der Kasse zu haben.

Regie: Herr Sigl.

Neue Decorationen:
Im ersten Aufzuge: Zeltartiges Gemach auf dem Verdeck eines Seeschiffes, vom K. Hoftheatermaler Herrn Angelo Quaglio.
Im zweiten Aufzuge: Park vor Isolde's Gemach, vom K. Hoftheatermaler Herrn Döll.
Im dritten Aufzuge: Burg und Burghof, vom K. Hoftheatermaler Herrn Angelo Quaglio.
Neue Costüme
nach Angabe des K. Hoftheater-Costümiers Herrn Seitz.

Der erste Aufzug beginnt um sechs Uhr, der zweite nach halb acht Uhr, der dritte nach neun Uhr

Preise der Plätze:

Eine Loge im I. und II. Rang	15 fl. — kr.
Ein Vorderplatz	2 fl. 24 kr.
Ein Rückplatz	2 fl. — kr.
Eine Loge im III. Rang	12 fl. — kr.
Ein Vorderplatz	2 fl. — kr.
Ein Rückplatz	1 fl. 36 kr.
Eine Loge im IV. Rang	9 fl. — kr.
Ein Vorderplatz	1 fl. 24 kr.
Ein Rückplatz	1 fl. 12 kr.
Ein Galerienoble-Sitz	2 fl. 24 kr.
Ein Parketsitz	2 fl. — kr.
Parterre	— fl. 48 kr.
Galerie	— fl. 24 kr.

Heute sind alle bereits früher zur ersten Vorstellung von Tristan und Isolde gelösten Billets giltig.

Die Kasse wird um fünf Uhr geöffnet.

Anfang um sechs Uhr, Ende nach zehn Uhr.

Der freie Eintritt ist ohne alle Ausnahme aufgehoben und wird ohne Kassabillet Niemand eingelassen.

Repertoire:
Sonntag den 11. Juni: (Im K. Hof- und National-Theater) Martha, Oper von Flotow.
Montag den 12. „ : (Im K. Hof- und National-Theater) Elisabeth Charlotte, Schauspiel von Paul Heyse.
Dienstag den 13. „ : (Im K. Hof- und National-Theater) Mit aufgehobenem Abonnement: Zum ersten Male wiederholt: Tristan und Isolde, von Richard Wagner.
Donnerstag den 15. „ : (Im K. Hof- und National-Theater) Lalla Roukh, Oper von Felicien David.

Der einzelne Zettel kostet 2 kr. Druck von Dr. C. Wolf & Sohn

baritone). The King is deeply aggrieved and condemns Tristan to exile, whereupon Tristan challenges Melot to a duel and allows himself to be hit by the vassal's sword. Now seriously wounded, Tristan lies beneath a tree outside his castle in Brittany, with his faithful groom Kurwenal (baritone) at his side watching over him. In his delirium, Tristan calls Isolde's name, and when he sees her ship coming towards him, he tears off his bandages and goes to meet her. Isolde takes him in her arms as he breathes his last. Another ship brings the King, who has come to forgive them after learning from Brangäne how she had switched the philters, and he wants to reunite the two lovers. But he arrives too late. Isolde sings her final lament for Tristan before falling, as though transfigured, across his body.

Early Celtic legends were the inspiration for the thirteenth-century poem by Gottfried von Strassburg which provided Wagner with the basis for the libretto he worked on in Zurich in 1857. He scored *Tristan und Isolde* between 1857 and 1859, first in Switzerland and later in Venice, where the composer had gone after the break-up of his liaison with Mathilde Wesendonk. The repercussions of this unfulfilled love, and Wagner's discovery of the pessimistic philosophy of Schopenhauer, are particularly in evidence in *Tristan und Isolde* and provide the basis for the work, its climax being the expression of longing for love and for death in the great duet in Act II. The fluidity of the music shows how Wagner had by now broken away from every known kind of dramatic structure, and makes this opera the starting-point for the whole of modern music.

TRITTICO, IL

(The Triptych)

Il Tabarro, Suor Angelica, Gianni Schicchi

Set of three operas by Giacomo Puccini (1858–1924), to libretti by Giuseppe Adami and Giovacchino Forzano. The three parts of the triptych are all operas in their own right and are not overtly linked to each other. First

Above: Model for the character of Germont in *La Traviata*, from the time of the opera.

Left: Playbill for the premier of *Tristan und Isolde* at the Hoftheater, Munich in 1865.

performance: New York, Metropolitan Opera House, 14 December 1918.

IL TABARRO

(The Cloak)

Libretto by Giuseppe Adami from the one-act play La Houppelande *by Didier Gold.*

The action takes place in Paris at the beginning of the century. An old barge moored on the River Seine is home to Michele (baritone) and his young wife, Giorgetta (soprano). Michele senses that his marriage is in trouble, and he begins to suspect that Giorgetta has a lover, Luigi, a young lighterman who tells Michele that he intends to leave the barge as soon as they reach Rouen. He can no longer bear the torment of a clandestine love, but Giorgetta asks him to stay on and arranges to see him that night, promising that she will signal to him with a lighted match as soon as she is free to meet him. When Luigi has left, Michele reappears and tries to rekindle in Giorgetta a memory from their past together, when he used to wrap her tenderly in his great cloak. Giorgetta, uneasy, replies evasively and then goes away. Left alone, Michele suppresses his anger, but pictures himself discovering his wife's lover and killing him. Deep in these somber thoughts, Michele lights his pipe, and Luigi, watching from a safe distance, thinks this is Giorgetta's signal and comes on board the barge. Michele guesses the truth, forces Luigi to confess and then strangles him, hiding the body in his cloak. Down below in the cabin, Giorgetta is seized by a strange premonition and comes up on deck, whereupon Michele lifts the cloak and shows her the face of her dead lover.

SUOR ANGELICA

(Sister Angelica)

Libretto by Giovacchino Forzano

The action takes place in a convent towards the end of the seventeenth century. For seven years Suor Angelica (soprano) has been living as a nun at the insistence of the noble family to which she belongs, in order that she may be absolved from the guilt of an illicit relationship as a result of which she gave birth to a son. Her aunt, the Princess (contralto), asks her to sign a document formally renouncing her right to part of the family inheritance and, in the course of their conversation, tells her in a cold and expressionless voice that her child is dead. Angelica is overtaken by such terrible despair that she takes poison, but during her agony she feels remorse and calls upon the Virgin Mary. She is answered by a heavenly choir and then the Virgin appears to her in radiant light, tenderly holding a child out to her as she lies dying.

GIANNI SCHICCHI

Libretto by Giovacchino Forzano, from an episode in Dante's Inferno.

The action takes place in Florence in 1299. The relatives of Buoso Donati, who has died a few hours ago, learn that the deceased has left the whole of his considerable fortune to the monks of Signa, outside Florence. In dismay, the family turns for help to Gianni Schicchi (baritone), who has a reputation for being astute. Schicchi duly comes up with a plan: he will impersonate the "dying" Buoso Donati and dictate a new last will and testament to the notary. Donati's relatives are enthusiastic about this idea, but when the will Schicchi dictates leaves most of the inheritance to himself, they are left speechless. As soon as the notary has left, they all turn on Schicchi, but he chases them all out of the house, which is now his. Rinuccio (tenor), the young Buoso Donati's young grandson, and Lauretta (soprano), Schicchi's daughter, who have been in love for some time, embrace tenderly.

Puccini's original idea for *Il trittico* was that the contrasting plots for the three operas would be taken from the three parts of Dante's *Divine Comedy*, the *Inferno*, *Purgatorio* and *Paradiso*, but in the end only one of them, *Gianni Schicchi*, was inspired by Dante. The notion of contrast remains, however: *Il tabarro* is a sordid and desperate story given full expression by the atmosphere of Puccini's music (the score shows how particularly aware he was of the new developments in contemporary music). *Suor Angelica*, on the other hand, is a tragedy which nevertheless leaves room for hope. The tenuous plot, devoid of drama and conflict, restricted Puccini's musical imagination. Only in the conversation scene between Suor Angelica and her aunt does the composer show the extent of his gifts as a dramatist. Unlike the other two works in the *Trittico*, it was an immediate success and received numerous performances.

A scene from *Suor Angelica*, one of the three operas making up Giacomo Puccini's *Il trittico*.

TROVATORE, IL

(The Troubadour)

Opera in four acts and eight scenes by Giuseppe Verdi (1813–1901), to a libretto by Salvatore Cammarano, after the Spanish tragedy El trovador *by Antonio García Gutiérrez. First performance: Rome, Teatro Apollo, 19 January 1853.*

The action takes place in Spain in the fifteenth century. Ferrando (bass), Captain of the Guard under the command of Count di Luna (baritone), tells how the Count's brother was seized as an infant and thrown in the fire by a gipsy woman seeking revenge after her own mother was accused of being a witch and burned at the stake. Leonora (soprano), lady-in-waiting to the Queen, confesses to her maid Inez (soprano) that she is in love with a troubadour who sang one night under her window. She now hears him again in the distance and leaves the castle in search of the singer. But on her way she meets Count di Luna. He too is in love with Leonora and, being jealous of the troubadour, whose name is Manrico (tenor), challenges him to a duel. Manrico emerges the winner but has been wounded and is lovingly cared for by the gipsy Azucena (mezzo-soprano), whom he believes to be his mother. He is in fact the brother of Count di Luna who was thought to have perished on the fire, but Azucena had been in such a state of turmoil and distraction that she had thrown her own son in the fire instead. Meanwhile comes news that Leonora, believing Manrico to be dead, has decided to enter a convent. Manrico arrives in time to rescue her and takes her with him. While Count di Luna is laying siege to the castle where Manrico and Leonora have taken refuge, he captures Azucena, and Ferrando recognizes her as the woman who had kidnapped the Count's brother. Azucena is condemned to die at the stake, and Manrico is captured and imprisoned while attempting to set her free. Leonora offers herself to the Count in exchange for Manrico's life. The Count accepts, but Leonora wants to remain faithful to Manrico and so takes poison. When she brings Manrico the news that he is about to be released, the poison takes effect and she dies in the troubadour's arms. Count di Luna is enraged and orders that Manrico be beheaded immediately. Only when the sentence has been carried out does Azucena reveal the terrible truth that Manrico was the Count's brother. Azucena thus has her revenge.

A supreme achievement, *Il trovatore* is the second opera in Verdi's ''popular trilogy'' (with *Rigoletto* and *La traviata*) and the most conventional in terms of plot. Verdi skilfully employs the music to outline the characters. While Manrico and Leonora may have some of the finest moments in the opera, they still manage to look rather stereotyped. Azucena, on the other hand, is a figure of great dramatic substance, in whom the contrast between a longing for revenge and feelings of heartbroken maternal love makes for a memorable character in Romantic opera.

TROYANOS, TATIANA

(New York 1938)

American mezzo-soprano. She studied singing with Hans J. Heinz and at the Juilliard School in New York. In 1963 she made her debut with New York City Opera in the American premiere of Britten's *A Midsummer Night's Dream*. She joined the Hamburg State Opera in 1965, appearing in 1969 in the role of Jeanne in the world premiere of Penderecki's *Diably z Loudun* (The Devils of Loudun). She scored a personal success in Aix-en-Provence as the Composer in Richard Strauss's *Ariadne auf Naxos* (1966) and at Covent Garden as Octavian in Strauss's *Der Rosenkavalier* (1967). In 1971 she took part in the Kennedy Center's inaugural production of Handel's *Ariodante* in Washington. She is one of the outstanding names associated with the Metropolitan Opera in New York, where she appeared in Mozart's *Così fan tutte* (1990), *Der Rosenkavalier* (1991) and the world premiere of Philip Glass's *The Voyage*. Troyanos has also performed in many other leading opera houses in the United States. With her powerful, supple voice and considerable range, combined with a remarkable stage presence, she has become one of the most celebrated singers of her generation, particularly admired for her performances in the operas of Richard Strauss.

TROYENS, LES

(The Trojans)

*Opera in two parts and five acts (*La prise de Troie*, The Capture of Troy, Acts I and II;* Les Troyens à Carthage*, The Trojans at Carthage, Acts III, IV and V) by Hector Berlioz (1803–1869), to the composer's own libretto after Virgil's* Aeneid*. First performance: Paris, Théâtre Lyrique, 4 November 1863 (Part Two only). Performance in German of the entire opera over two evenings, Karlsruhe, Hoftheater, 6 and 7 December 1890.*

The action takes place in Troy (Part One) and Carthage (Part Two). After laying siege to the city of Troy for ten years, the Greeks set sail for home, leaving behind on the beach a huge wooden horse. The Trojans take this to be an offering to Pallas Athene left by an army that has fled, and they decide to transport it into their city. Only Cassandre (mezzo-soprano) will not take part in the general

A scene from Giuseppe Verdi's *Il trovatore*.

rejoicing and instead predicts that fresh misfortunes will befall Troy, but her warning voice goes unheard. During the night, Énée (Aeneas, tenor) is wakened by sounds of battle and sees the ghost of Hector (bass) before him, urging him to escape. Troy is being set on fire and its people massacred by the Greeks. Énée flees with a few surviving Trojans while Cassandre, after inciting the women to commit suicide rather than fall into enemy hands, sets them an example by stabbing herself. The scene now changes to Carthage. As the Carthaginians celebrate the prosperity of their city, it is announced that a group of Trojans have landed. Then comes news that Carthaginian territory is being threatened by Numidian forces. The newly-arrived Énée offers to do battle with the enemy. He returns victorious, earning the gratitude of the Queen of Carthage, Didon (soprano), a feeling which soon develops into love. Énée loves Didon in return, but the gods are already pressing him to leave Carthage and head for Italy. Énée endeavours to convince Didon that they have no choice but to part. Didon tries in vain to make him stay, then hears that the Trojans have actually left and decides to die. After praying that her own descendants will one day wreak vengeance on the house of Énée, Didon stabs herself, but has a premonition that Rome will triumph, just before she dies.

Berlioz worked on the libretto of *Les Troyens* for several months, beginning in the spring of 1856, then continued composing and revising the score until 1860. The Opéra in Paris refused to stage the work, on the grounds that it was too ambitious in scale. Berlioz was forced to condense Part One into a summary prologue and to present Part Two, *Les Troyens à Carthage*, on its own. It was not exactly a resounding success, and the world had to wait until 1890, the year of the first performance of the complete opera, for his achievement to win recognition. The work has been staged quite frequently ever since. The last act of *Les Troyens à Carthage* has become particularly famous and is said to have been influenced by Purcell's *Dido and Aeneas*.

TSARSKAYA NEVESTA

(The Tsar's Bride)

Opera in four acts by Nicolai Rimsky-Korsakov (1844–1908), to a libretto by the composer, with one scene written by I.F. Tyumenev after a play by L.A. Mey. First performance: Moscow, Solodovnikov Theater, 3 November 1899.

Grigory Grigoryevich Gryaznoy (baritone) has seduced the young Lyubasha (mezzo-soprano) and taken her away from her parents to live with him. But one day he falls in love with the beautiful Marfa (soprano), daughter of Vassili Stepanovich Sobakin (bass), a wealthy merchant from Novgorod. Marfa is already engaged to Ivan Sergheyevich Lïkov (tenor), but Gryaznoy wants Marfa, no matter what it takes, and goes to consult the magician Dr Yelissey Bomelius (tenor) to ask him for a love potion. Lyubasha, who has overheard their conversation, gives herself to Bomelius on condition that he substitute a slow and deadly poison for the love philter. Unaware of the switch, Gryaznoy gives Marfa the poison. Then comes a *coup de théâtre*: a messenger from Ivan the Terrible brings word that the Tsar wants to marry Marfa. Ivan's orders are obeyed without question, but Marfa, after becoming Tsarina, is struck down by a slow and mysterious illness and dies. At first Gryaznoy accuses Lïkov of killing Marfa in a fit of jealous rage, but Lïkov is crazed with grief at her death. Eventually Lyubasha confesses to Gryaznoy, and he kills her. The Tsar's guards then take him away.

Although not one of the most successful of Rimsky-Korsakov's operas, *Tsarskaya Nevesta* reveals close links with the spirit of Russian folk music of which the composer was especially fond.

TUCKER, RICHARD

(New York 1913–Kalamazoo, Michigan 1975)

Stage name of Reuben Ticker, American tenor. He studied with the tenor Paul Althouse and with Angelo Canarutto. He made a successful debut at the Metropolitan Opera in New York in 1945 as Enzo in Ponchielli's *La Gioconda*, a role he repeated for his Italian debut at the Arena in Verona in 1947 alongside another debutante on that occasion, Maria Callas. Tucker's name became associated with the Metropolitan Opera, where he sang more than 600 performances from a repertoire which had Italian opera, and particularly Verdi, as its strongest suit. Radiant timbre, consistent delivery across the whole range, and a crowning quality to the voice in the upper register were Tucker's hallmarks, together with the considerable technique that enabled him to prolong his career (Halévy's *La Juive* in 1973, *Carmen* in 1975) and keep his voice more or less intact until shortly before his death.

TURANDOT

Opera in three acts by Giacomo Puccini (1858–1924), to a libretto by Giuseppe Adami and Renato Simoni from the fairy-tale

Above: A scence from *Les Troyens* by Berlioz, in a production at La Scala.

Right: Frontispiece to a selection of pieces from *Turandot* by Puccini. Designed by U. Brunelleschi.

drama by Carlo Gozzi. First performance: Milan, La Scala, 25 April 1926.

The action takes place in Peking. Princess Turandot has vowed that she will marry the suitor of noble blood who succeeds in solving three riddles; those who fail will be beheaded. Calàf (tenor), son of Timur (bass), the deposed king of Tartary, sees Turandot appear on the palace balcony, falls hopelessly in love with her and can think of nothing else but how to win her. Three courtiers, Ping (baritone), Pong (tenor) and Pang (tenor), Timur and the slave Liù (soprano), his faithful companion, try to dissuade Calàf, but to no avail. Calàf goes to the palace. The Emperor Altoum asks him to withdraw, but he firmly refuses to do so and faces the test. He solves the riddles one after the other and emerges triumphant. Turandot, humbled, begs the Emperor not to let her become a slave to this foreigner. Calàf generously offers to release her from her vow if she can discover his name. The guards bring Timur and Liù before Turandot and tell her that the two of them had been seen with Calàf earlier. Liù declares that she alone knows the Prince's name, and then, fearing that she will be tortured to reveal it, she stabs herself. Left alone with Turandot, Calàf reproaches her for her cruelty and then kisses her deeply. The Princess is disturbed by this and suddenly realizes that she has loved Calàf from the moment she first saw him. Only then does Calàf tell her who he is. Whereupon Turandot announces to the assembled courtiers that she has discovered the unknown Prince's name. It is Love.

Turandot was unfinished when Puccini died on 29 November 1924, having only composed as far as the death of Liù. The task of completing the score was entrusted to the composer Franco Alfano, although the opera's premiere at La Scala ended after Liù's aria "Tu che di gel sei cinta." *Turandot* is the most mature and accomplished of all Puccini's works, in addition to providing a retrospective overview of the composer's creative life. The orchestral writing is extraordinarily rich, with authentic Chinese motifs incorporated into the score along with elements deriving from modern music, including dissonances, polytonality and disquieting vocal and orchestral effects.

TURCO IN ITALIA, IL

(The Turk in Italy)

Opera in two acts by Gioachino Rossini (1792–1868), to a libretto by Felice Romani. First performance: Milan, La Scala, 14 August 1814.

The action takes place in a gipsy encampment, where the poet Prosdocimo (baritone) is seeking inspiration for a new play. Here he meets Geronio (*buffo*), a wealthy land-owner, and the young gipsy-woman Zaida (mezzo-soprano), who had previously been involved with a Turkish prince and is still in love with him. Then a Turkish prince actually arrives, on a visit to Italy. He has not long been on shore when he meets Fiorilla (soprano), the coquettish wife of Geronio. She invites Selim to have tea with her, which makes Geronio jealous. Meanwhile it transpires that Selim is the selfsame Turkish prince with whom Zaida is in love. This gives Prosdocimo great satisfaction, as he now has just the right plot for his new play, except that he intends to complicate it even more so as to make it even livelier. The ubiquitous poet starts out by causing a quarrel between Zaida and Fiorilla, and then, when he realizes that Fiorilla and Selim are planning to run away together during a masked ball, he warns Geronio and Zaida, and they arrive at the ball disguised as Selim and Fiorilla. After a giddy round of mistaken identities, order is restored. The old love between Zaida and Selim is rekindled, and Fiorilla goes back to Geronio. Prosdocimo is satisfied, because he has finished his play.

The successful libretto by Felice Romani helped to make *Il turco in Italia* one of the most original operas Rossini ever wrote. The idea of the plot operating on two levels is a clever dramatic device: on the one hand there is the action, made up of misunderstandings and intrigues, and on the other the figure of the poet, who both participates in the story and watches it unfold while himself pulling the strings.

Il turco in Italia, an opera in two acts by Gioachino Rossini.

TURN OF THE SCREW, THE

Opera in a prologue and two acts by Benjamin Britten (1913–1976), to a libretto by Myfanwy Piper, after the short story by Henry James. First performance: Venice, Teatro La Fenice, 14 September 1954.

The opera opens with the Prologue (tenor) describing how the story had originally been found handwritten on a yellowing sheet of paper. The guardian of two young orphans has such a busy life to attend to that he entrusts the care of the children to a Governess (soprano). The Governess arrives at Bly, a country house in East Anglia. She is welcomed by Mrs Grose, the housekeeper (soprano), and the children, Miles and Flora (treble and soprano). Some days later, the Governess sees a stranger one evening in the grounds of the house, and her description convinces the housekeeper that the figure was Peter Quint (tenor), a former servant at the house, who had exerted a diabolical influence over the children and the previous governess, Miss Jessel (soprano). Both are now dead, but the Governess and Mrs Grose realize the children are still under their control. There follows a series of episodes in which the Governess and the housekeeper make vain attempts to wrest Flora and Miles from the malign influence of the two ghosts. In desperation, the Governess decides to write to the children's guardian to tell him of these disturbing events. Prompted by Quint, Miles steals the letter from her desk. Then one night Flora suffers from terrible nightmares, and Mrs Grose takes her away to stay with her guardian. The Governess remains at Bly with Miles and, after a fearful struggle, manages to win the battle as Miles finally cries out the name of his persecutor, but the effort proves too much for him and he dies in the Governess's arms.

The plot of *The Turn of the Screw* has been divided up into 16 short but powerful scenes. The action is framed by a theme and 15 variations, each variation leading into the scene it has introduced. This structure is also an expression of the meaning of the opera's title, in that it consists of a theme that turns, like a screw, through the 15 variations of the various interludes which lead into the scenes to which they relate. Britten has reduced the orchestra to 13 instruments, which nonetheless achieve unusual richness of expression.

A sketch for *The Turn of the Screw* by Benjamin Britten, taken from the short story of the same name by Henry James.

U

UGO, CONTE DI PARIGI

Opera in two acts by Gaetano Donizetti (1797–1848), to a libretto by Felice Romani. First performance: Milan, La Scala, 13 March 1832.

The action takes place at the palace of Laon, where celebrations are being held in honour of the accession to the French throne of Luigi V (mezzo-soprano), son of the deposed king Lotario. But Prince Folco d'Anjou (baritone) does not join in the cries of jubilation that greet the new king. Instead he is heard cursing young Luigi and wishing on him the same fate as his father Lotario, who was hated throughout his reign by his Queen, Emma (soprano), and died as a result of her treachery. While Luigi is on his way to the cathedral, Bianca of Aquitaine (soprano), engaged to Luigi, tells her sister Adelia that she hates her husband-to-be and confesses her love for Count Ugo (tenor), regent until Luigi is crowned. Bianca's confession is all the more shocking to Adelia, because she herself loves and is loved by Ugo. Bianca asks to be allowed to leave the court, but Luigi accuses her of betraying him with Ugo. Ugo denies this, declaring that he is actually in love with another. Having admitted that she is in love with Ugo, Bianca wants to know the name of her rival, but Ugo will not reveal it. He is then imprisoned by Luigi, where Bianca visits him and begs him to flee with her. He says no, but the sudden appearance of Adelia gives away the secret of his love to Bianca, whereupon she swears that she will be avenged. Thus, while Ugo and Adelia are telling the King of their feelings for each other, Bianca, now aware that Ugo had received permission from Luigi to marry Adelia, decides to poison Luigi. As she is preparing the lethal potion, she hears the voice of Queen Emma, who is filled with remorse and asks to be pardoned for the wrongs she has done. Deeply moved by Emma's words, Bianca asks for her help. Emma assures her that no revenge is worth the agony and torment of the remorse that follows. But then voices are heard coming from the chapel where the wedding of Ugo and Adelia is taking place. Bianca's anger, apparently assuaged until that moment, now flares up again. Emma calls the guards, but Bianca, who has realized that she cannot win, takes the poison herself.

Ugo, conte di Parigi received its first performance during the 1831–32 La Scala season, which had already witnessed the premiere of Bellini's *Norma* on 26 December 1831, and the singers from *Norma* were retained to appear in this new Donizetti opera: Giuditta Pasta (Norma) in the role of Bianca, Giulia Grisi (Adalgisa) as Adelia, Domenico Donzelli (Pollione) singing Ugo, and Vincenzo Negrini (Oroveso) as Folco. The cast of *Ugo* was completed by Clorinda Corradi-Pantanelli in the *travesti* role of Luigi V and Felicità Baillou-Hillaret as Emma. Like that of *Norma*, the Donizetti premiere was a success, though there were a few dissenting voices. But whereas the success of *Norma* was to lead to triumph, *Ugo* was judged a fiasco after its second performance and was taken off after only five nights. Donizetti was extremely upset, as he had been convinced of the merit of his opera. In fact *Ugo* does contain passages of the highest quality, both musically and dramatically.

UHL, FRITZ

(Wien-Matzleinsdorf 1928)

Austrian tenor. A pupil of Elisabeth Rado in Vienna, he made his official debut in Graz in 1952 as Huon in Weber's *Oberon*. He rapidly emerged as one of the most gifted tenors of his generation. The silvery timbre of his voice and the crowning quality of his singing in the upper register won him acclaim in operas by Wagner and Richard Strauss. After being first tenor at the Munich Opera (Beethoven's *Fidelio*, 1956), he appeared as a guest artist at the Vienna Staatsoper (Wagner's *Parsifal*, 1961), San Francisco Opera (*Fidelio*, 1961), the Opéra in Paris (Berg's *Wozzeck*, 1967) and the Bayreuth Festival (from 1957). His greatest performances have included Loge in *Das Rheingold*, Siegmund in *Die Walküre*, Tristan in Wagner's *Tristan und Isolde* and two Strauss roles, the Emperor in *Die Frau ohne Schatten* and Bacchus in *Ariadne auf Naxos*.

ULFUNG, RAGNAR

(Oslo 1927)

Norwegian tenor. He studied music in Oslo and Milan, where he was a pupil of Minghetti. He made his debut at a concert in Oslo in 1950, and his stage debut followed two years later, again in Oslo, as Magadoff in Menotti's *The Consul*. In 1958 he joined the resident company of the Royal Opera, Stockholm, with which he continued to appear for a further 20 years, singing roles from an extremely varied repertoire, including Leoncavallo's *I pagliacci*, Verdi's *La traviata*, *Un ballo in maschera* and *Rigoletto*.

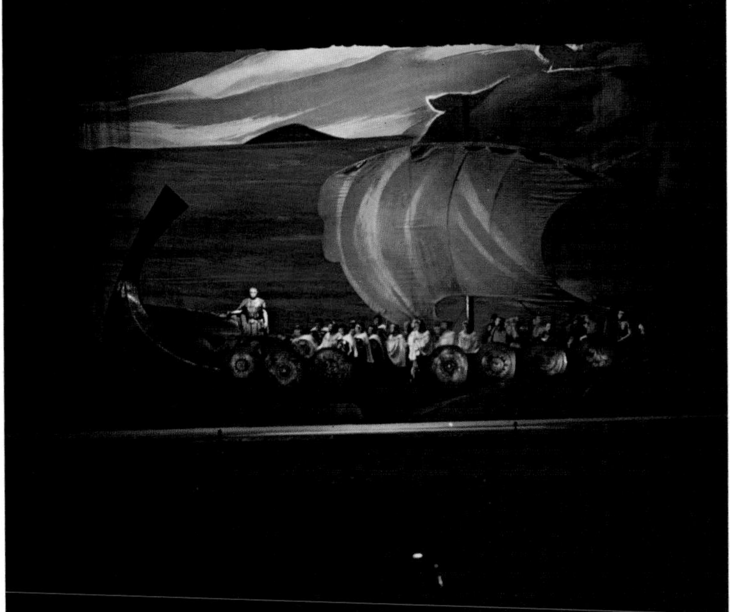

ULISSE

Opera in a prologue and two acts by Luigi Dallapiccola (1904–1975), to the composer's own libretto, after Homer's Odyssey. *First performance: Berlin, Deutsche Oper, 29 September 1968.*

Ulisse (baritone) resumes his long voyage after rejecting the promise of eternal youth held out to him by Calypso (soprano). But Poseidon is angry and causes him to be shipwrecked on the island of the Phaeacians. Here he is met by Nausicaa (soprano) and taken to the palace of her father, Alcinoo (bass). Ulisse reveals his identity and begins to recount his adventures since the fall of Troy: how he and his men landed on the island of the Lotus Eaters, where some of the sailors actually tasted that flower of oblivion and did not return to the ships, and how then he was detained by Circe (mezzo-soprano), who told him – as he finally took his leave of her – that he would never be able to find peace. Ulisse then tells of his journey into Hades, where he met his mother, Anticlea (soprano), and the soothsayer Tiresias (tenor), from whom he learned that his homecoming to Ithaca would be a bloody one. With Ulisse's story over, Alcinoo offers him an escort all the way to Ithaca. And so at last he reaches the island where, disguised as a beggar, he meets his son Telemaco (mezzo-soprano), from whom he learns of the outrages perpetrated by the Suitors surrounding his wife, Penelope. Accompanied by his son, Ulisse goes to the palace, flings off his cloak and to first the astonishment and then the horror of them all, takes up his bow and shoots the Suitors one by one. The scene changes and, as the prophecy had foretold, Ulisse is once again at sea, where he realizes sadly that in all his wanderings he has not found what he was looking for. In a sudden flash of revelation, he exclaims: ''Dear God! My heart and soul are no longer alone!''

In *Ulisse*, Dallapiccola draws on a host of literary sources both ancient and modern: Homer, Dante's *Divine Comedy*, Aeschylus's *Agamemnon*, Alfred Lord Tennyson's poem *Ulysses*, Gerhardt Hauptmann's *Der Bogen des Odysseus*, Thomas Mann's *Joseph und seine Brüder*, Cavafy's *Ithaka* and Joyce's *Ulysses*, as well as poems by Hölderlin and Machado. The result is the composer's personal reading of the nature of this Greek hero and his endless search, which leads him to the realization that peace and a sense of finality can only be found by experiencing the divine.

UNDINE

Opera in four acts by Gustav Albert Lortzing (1801–1851), to a libretto by the composer, after a tale by Friedrich de la Motte Fouqué. First performance: Magdeburg, Stadttheater, 21 April 1845.

The action takes place in 1452 in a fishing village and at the palace of Duke Henry. The knight Hugo von Ringstetten (tenor) is about to marry Undine (soprano). She is believed to be the daughter of Marthe (contralto) and Tobias (bass), two elderly fisherfolk, but in fact she is a nymph who was substituted for their real daughter by Kühleborn (baritone), Prince of the Waters. Meanwhile, Kühleborn is mingling with the guests and is present at the wedding. He declares that he has his doubts as to whether the young couple will be happy in love and resolves to take Undine back to the Kingdom of the Waters when Hugo ceases to love her. Undine reveals her true identity to Hugo and tells him that she will be able to keep her soul as long as she has his love, but that if this should ever die, she will change back into a nymph and will have to return to her Kingdom. The Duchess, Bertalda (soprano), who was in love with Hugo, is enraged to learn that her beloved has married someone else, yet she intends to win back his heart. Then Kühleborn announces publicly that Bertalda is the daughter of Marthe and Tobias and produces incontrovertible evidence of this. She is then compelled to leave the court. Now full of ideas as to how she might have her revenge, Bertalda manages to convince Hugo that he has been bewitched by Undine. In vain Undine reminds Hugo of his promises, but then Kühleborn appears and orders Undine to return to the Kingdom of the Waters. A short time later, Undine appears to Hugo in a dream, promising that she will return at midnight. Hugo orders that all the fountains and springs be covered with rocks to prevent Undine coming up through the water. But Veit (tenor), Hugo's equerry, is in such despair at the loss of his young mistress that he removes all the stones. As midnight strikes, Undine emerges from a fountain. Hugo is irresistibly attracted by the sight of her, even though it means that he must die. Undine opens her arms to him and the couple disappear together into the water.

Undine is one of the most important examples of German Romantic opera. It has a flowing melodic line, the orchestration is lively, and the excellence of the libretto ensures that the individual characters are well drawn. De La Motte-Fouqué's tale had already been used in a successful opera by E.T.A. Hoffmann (1816).

UPSHAW, DAWN

(New York 1960)

American soprano. She studied at the Manhattan School of Music, where she made her debut in 1963 singing the lead in the American premiere of Hindemith's *Sancta Susanna*. She went on to complete her training at the Metropolitan Opera school in New York. She has appeared at the Metropolitan since 1985, initially as second lead and then in more major roles.

The meeting with the Lotus Eaters, from Luigi Dallapiccola's *Ulisse*, in a production at La Scala.

V

VALDES, MAXIMIANO

(Santiago 1949)
Chilean conductor. After studying at the Conservatory in Santiago, in 1971 he moved to Italy, where he completed his training as a conductor at the Accademia di Santa Cecilia in Rome. He was assistant conductor at La Fenice in Venice (1976–80) and to Leonard Bernstein and Seiji Ozawa in Tanglewood (1977). After winning three international conducting competitions, that of the Rupert Foundation in 1978 and the Malko in Copenhagen and the Vittorio Gui in Florence, both in 1980, he appeared as guest conductor at opera houses and concert halls in Britain, France and Spain.

VALENTE, BENITA

(Delano, California 1939)
American soprano. She studied in Santa Barbara with Lotte Lehmann and Martial Singher and subsequently at the Curtis Institute in Philadelphia. Her career began with a concert as part of the Marlboro Festival in 1959, and from 1962 she began to sing in Europe. Her debut with the Metropolitan Opera in New York in 1963 as Pamina in Mozart's *Die Zauberflöte* (The Magic Flute) led to regular return appearances there from 1974, in *Rigoletto*, *La traviata*, Handel's *Rinaldo* and Mozart's *Idomeneo*. She has also been a guest artiste at numerous European opera houses (Zurich, Dortmund, Amsterdam).

VALENTINI-TERRANI, LUCIA

(Padua 1946)
Italian mezzo-soprano. After studying at the Conservatorio in Padua, she made her debut in 1969 at the Teatro Grande in Brescia, singing the lead in Rossini's *La Cenerentola*. In 1972 she took part in the Italian Radio competition for Rossini singers, on the strength of which she sang *La Cenerentola* at the Teatro Nuovo in Turin and at La Scala in Milan (1973), going on to appear in the same opera at leading international opera houses. Valentini-Terrani's qualities of timbre (a sumptuous and aristocratic middle register) and technique (a flawless mastery of passages requiring considerable vocal agility) prove a perfect combination for Rossini, and she has won particular acclaim not only in *La Cenerentola* but also in *L'italiana in Algeri* (which she first sang in 1971). She went on to tackle roles in Rossini's *opere serie*, including *Semiramide* (Teatro Regio, Turin, 1981), *Tancredi* (the Pesaro Festival, 1982), *La donna del lago* (Pesaro, 1983) and *Maometto II* (Pesaro, 1985). She also took part in the first production in modern times of Rossini's *Il viaggio a Reims* (Pesaro, 1984) and since the end of the 1970s has sung in *Werther* (Teatro Comunale, Florence, 1978), *Boris Godunov* (La Scala, 1979), *Falstaff* (Los Angeles and London, 1982), *Mignon* (Teatro Comunale, Florence, 1983) and *Carmen* (Bonn, 1986).

The Italian mezzo-soprano Lucia Valentini-Terrani.

VAMPYR, DER

(The Vampire)
Opera in two acts by Heinrich August Marschner (1795–1861), to a libretto by Wilhelm August Wohlbrück, after the story of the same name by John Polidori. First performance: Leipzig, Stadttheater, 29 March 1828.

Lord Ruthven (baritone), the Vampire of the title, is resuscitated by young Edgar Aubry (tenor) and asks Satan, lord of the vampires (speaking role), to grant him a little more time alive. His wish is granted, on the condition that he delivers to his Master three young brides or betrothed women. The first two, Ianthe (soprano), daughter of Sir Berkley (bass), and Emmy (soprano), engaged to George Dibdin (tenor), a young man in the service of Sir Humphrey Davenaut (bass), fall into his hands. But Malwina (soprano), Davenaut's daughter, who wants to remain faithful to her beloved Edgar, does not yield to Ruthven's advances, even though her father wants her to marry him. Edgar, bound to Ruthven by some mysterious pact, vainly entreats Sir Humphrey to postpone the marriage, then has no choice but to risk his own life and save Malwina by revealing that the man she is about to marry is a vampire. Just as the couple are about to be married, Ruthven's time alive granted him by Satan suddenly expires, whereupon he is struck by lightning and plunges down into Hell.

The premiere of *Der Vampyr* was a tremendous success, and the opera was equally well received outside Germany, with a 60-night run in London alone. It also earned the admiration of Wagner, who supplemented the score in 1833 with an aria he had written himself.

VAN ALLAN, RICHARD

(Nottingham 1935)

British bass. He studied in Birmingham and made his debut at Glyndebourne in 1964 as the Priest and an Armed Man in Mozart's *Die Zauberflöte* (The Magic Flute). From 1971 he sang regularly at Covent Garden, his first opera there being Puccini's *Turandot*. His name has been particularly associated since 1969 with the English National Opera, with whom he has appeared in *Don Giovanni*, *Boris Godunov*, *Don Carlos* and *Faust*. In addition to his active career in international opera and as a recording artist, Van Allan is also director of the National Opera Studio.

VANAUD, MARCEL

(Brussels 1953)

Belgian baritone. He studied music at the Royal Conservatoire in Brussels. After successes in numerous international competitions, he embarked on a career at the Opéra Royale de Wallonie, where he sang the title role in Gluck's *Orfeo*, Papageno in Mozart's *Die Zauberflöte* (The Magic Flute), Ourias (Gounod's *Mireille*) and Lescaut (Puccini's *Manon Lescaut*). In 1984 he made his American debut in Pittsburgh in Ravel's *L'enfant et les sortilèges* and went on to appear at New York City Opera in Bizet's *Les pêcheurs de perles* and Puccini's *Madama Butterfly*, as well as in Tulsa (*Don Carlos*, 1987) and Santa Fe (*Le nozze di Figaro*, 1987). He sang *Le nozze di Figaro* and *Le Comte Ory* at the Théâtre de la Monnaie in Brussels, singing the latter again at the Opéra in Paris. In 1991 he played the lead in Hindemith's opera *Cardillac* at the Maggio Musicale Festival in Florence.

VAN DAM, JOSÉ

(Brussels, 1940)

Belgian bass-baritone. Stage name of Joseph Van Damme. He studied at the Brussels Conservatoire with Frederic Anspach. After winning acclaim in singing competitions in Liège and Toulouse (1961), he made his debut at the Paris Opéra as Mercure in Berlioz's *Les Troyens*, returning there to sing Schaunard in Puccini's *La bohème*, Escamillo in Bizet's *Carmen* and Carlo V in Verdi's *Don Carlos*. He went on to join the resident companies of the Grand Théâtre in Geneva (1965–67) and the Deutsche Oper Berlin (1967–73). In 1968 came his Salzburg Festival debut (in Emilio de' Cavalieri's *La rappresentazione di Anima e di Corpo*), and it was there that Van Dam built a reputation for performances in Mozart's *Le nozze di Figaro* and *Die Zauberflöte* (The Magic Flute), Richard Strauss's *Salome* and Wagner's *Der fliegende Holländer* (The Flying Dutchman) and *Parsifal*. His international career took in the principal international opera houses (Covent Garden, La Scala, Milan, and the Metropolitan Opera in New York.) An artist of great personality with an extremely wide and varied repertoire, Van Dam has a particularly fine range and a rare sense of style, which have also enabled him to tackle baritone roles in French, German and Italian opera, from the eighteenth century (Rameau's *Dardanus*, Gluck's *Iphigénie en Tauride*, etc.) to contemporary works (he sang the lead in the world premiere of Messiaen's *Saint François d'Assise*, 1983).

VANESS, CAROL

(San Diego, California 1952)

American soprano. She studied music at the University of California and made her debut as Vitellia (Mozart's *La clemenza di Tito*) with San Francisco Opera (1977), following this with Cleopatra in Handel's *Giulio Cesare*, Mimi in Puccini's *La bohème* and Donna Anna in Mozart's *Don Giovanni*. In 1979 she appeared for the first time with New York City Opera as Donna Anna, repeating the role of Vitellia for her European debut in Bordeaux and going on to sing at the leading international opera houses, from Covent Garden (*La bohème*, 1982) to the Metropolitan Opera in New York (Handel's *Rinaldo*, 1982), the Salzburg Festival (*La clemenza di Tito*, 1988) and La Scala, Milan (Mozart's *Idomeneo*, 1990, and Gluck's *Iphigénie en Tauride*, 1992). Vaness has a sumptuous, flexible voice with a fine range. Her obvious musicianship and talents in performance have served her well not only in Mozart but also in operas by Verdi, Donizetti and Puccini.

VANESSA

Opera in four acts by Samuel Barber (1910–1981), to a libretto by Giancarlo Menotti. First performance: New York, Metropolitan Opera House, 15 January 1958.

The action takes place somewhere in "a northern country" around the year 1905 at Vanessa's house in a rural area. Vanessa (soprano), her mother, the Old Baroness (contralto), and Vanessa's niece Erika (mezzo-soprano) are awaiting the arrival of a guest. Vanessa is in a state of considerable agitation at the prospect of being reunited, after 20 years, with the man with whom she has always been in love, and is shocked when their visitor turns out not to be her beloved Anatol. He introduces himself as the son of Vanessa's lover, who is now dead, and he too is called Anatol (tenor). At first Vanessa reacts violently to the news and wants to send him away, but then she agrees that, since Anatol has made a long journey, he should stay the night. A month passes, and Anatol has still not left. Vanessa confides in Erika that despite the difference in their ages she feels she is in love with Anatol. Erika is deeply troubled

Left: The Belgian baritone JOSE VAN DAM

Above: The American soprano Carol Vaness.

by this revelation and when, on New Year's Eve, Vanessa and Anatol announce their engagement, she rushes out into the night. It is snowing heavily. Erika is found and she tells the Old Baroness that she is expecting Anatol's child. But she does not want Vanessa to know about it, and when Vanessa presses her to say what has been happening, Erika denies that she is pregnant. She does not want to destroy Vanessa's illusions, and as she watches the couple leave the house for the last time, she knows that now it is her turn to wait.

Vanessa represents a particularly key point in the history of American opera. It was the first work by an American composer to be staged at the Metropolitan Opera in New York for 24 years, and was a considerable success with audiences and critics alike. The *New York Times* hailed it as the best American opera yet presented at the Metropolitan, and the *Herald Tribune* compared Barber's orchestration to the work of Strauss for its impressive virtuosity. Much of the work's success was due to a prestigious cast of singers, which included Eleanor Steber, Rosalind Elias, Regina Resnik, Nicolai Gedda and Giorgio Tozzi, with Dimitri Mitropoulos conducting.

The soprano Julia Varady in the second act of Mozart's *Marriage of Figaro* in a production at La Scala.

VANZO, ALAIN

(Monte Carlo 1928)

French tenor and composer. He started singing at a very young age, and after being discovered in a competition for tenors in Cannes (1954), he began his career in supporting roles. His first major success was as the Duke of Mantua in Verdi's *Rigoletto* at the Opéra in Paris. He rose rapidly to become the greatest French tenor of his generation, with incomparable performances as Nadir in Bizet's *Les pêcheurs de perles*, Rodolfo in Puccini's *La bohème*, Don Ottavio in Mozart's *Don Giovanni* and Gérald in Delibes' *Lakmé*, but also as Werther, Des Grieux in Massenet's *Manon* and numerous other roles, including Robert in Meyerbeer's *Robert le diable*, one of the more recent performances for which he has won special acclaim (Paris, 1985). Although Vanzo's career has been centered mainly in France, he has also appeared at Covent Garden (Donizetti's *Lucia di Lammermoor*, 1961), Carnegie Hall in New York (Donizetti's *Lucrezia Borgia*, 1968), San Francisco (Gounod's *Faust*, 1971) and the Teatro dell'Opera in Rome (Bizet's *Carmen*, 1986). Vanzo's reputation rests not only on his beauty of timbre but also on his absolutely flawless delivery, which is consistent throughout the whole range from the lowest notes to a ringing upper register. His elegance of phrasing and considerable sensitivity in performance must also be acknowledged. He has written an operetta (*Le pêcheur d'étoiles*, Lille, 1972) and a theater work (*Les Chouans*, Avignon, 1982).

VARADY, JULIA

(Oradea 1941)

Romanian soprano who became a German citizen. After initially learning the violin, she studied singing at the Conservatories of Cluj and Bucharest. She made her debut with Cluj State Opera in 1960 and remained there for about ten years, appearing first in mezzo-soprano roles (Orfeo in Gluck's opera, Fenena in Verdi's *Nabucco*). In 1970 she joined the Frankfurt Opera, with which her first performance was as Antonia in Offenbach's *Les contes d'Hoffmann*. In 1971 her success as Vitellia in Mozart's *La clemenza di Tito* with the Bayerische Staatsoper in Munich launched her on an international career, which brought engagements from leading opera houses, although her name is most associated with the Bayerische Staatsoper and the other principal opera houses in Germany and Austria. Varady's firm voice and considerable gift as an actress have contributed to her convincing performances of an extremely wide and varied repertoire from Mozart to Verdi (*Macbeth*, *Nabucco*, *Il trovatore*), Puccini (*Madama Butterfly*, *Turandot*) and Richard Strauss (*Arabella*). In 1977 she married the baritone Dietrich Fischer-Dieskau.

VARVISO, SILVIO

(Zurich 1924)

Swiss conductor. He studied music at the Conservatory in Zurich and in Vienna, where he completed his training as a conductor with Clemens Krauss. In 1944 he made his opera house debut conducting Mozart's *Die Zauberflöte* (The Magic Flute) at St. Gallen. His next move was to Basle, where he conducted from 1950 to 1958 and also held the post of music director (from 1956). His international career included San Francisco (1959–61), the American premiere of Britten's opera *A Midsummer Night's Dream*, the Metropolitan Opera, New York (*Lucia di Lammermoor*, 1961), Covent Garden (from 1961), the Glyndebourne Festival (1962 and 1963) and the Bayreuth Festival (1969–74). He was also *Generalmusikdirektor* in Stuttgart (1972–80) and music director at the Paris Opéra (1980–81), and he regularly conducts the Royal Flemish Opera in Antwerp (Puccini's *Tosca*, Wagner's *Parsifal*, and Richard Strauss's *Der Rosenkavalier* in 1992).

VEASEY, JOSEPHINE

(London 1930)

British soprano. A pupil of Audrey Langford, she began her career in the chorus at Covent Garden (1948–50). In 1954 came her solo debut as the shepherd in Wagner's *Tannhäuser*. She went on to appear in more major roles, like Carmen, Princess Eboli in Verdi's *Don Carlos*, Octavian in Richard Strauss's *Der Rosenkavalier*, and from 1960, with the encouragement of Sir Georg Solti, the leading Wagner roles. She appeared at the Glyndebourne Festival in Massenet's *Werther* in 1969, at the Paris Opéra in the same year, at the Salzburg Easter Festival (1967–69) and at the Metropolitan Opera in New York. Veasey's fine timbre, range, precise delivery and excellent performance skills led to her being acclaimed as one of the greatest singers of her generation. She retired from the stage in 1982.

VĚC MAKROPULOS

(The Makropoulos Affair)

Opera in three acts by Léoš Janáček (1854–1928), to the composer's own libretto, after the play of the same name by Karel Capek. First performance: Brno, National Theater, 18 December 1926.

Emilia Marty (soprano), a celebrated singer at the Vienna Opera, takes part in a lawsuit concerning the estate of Baron Prus (baritone). Those contesting the will are Albert Gregor (tenor) and Jaroslav Prus (baritone), the Baron's son and nephew, respectively. Emilia astonishes everyone present with her knowledge of events which took place hundreds of years earlier. Quite how she is capable of this becomes clear when she reveals that she is the daughter of the Greek doctor Makropoulos, who had used her in his experiments to test an elixir that would prolong life. Using different aliases, Emilia has lived for 337 years, once entrusting the formula of this miraculous elixir to Baron Prus, whose mistress she had been. Now that the terrible document is once again in her possession, she could easily learn how the elixir was made, but her life has become such an intolerable burden, devoid of interest and without hope, that she offers it to anyone who will destroy it. Krista, the lawyer's daughter, takes it and burns it as Emilia is finally able to die.

Composed by Janáček between 1923 and 1925, *Věc Makropulos* shows the composer almost completely rejecting the Czech folk-music tradition. He handles the long legal arguments in the first part of the opera with a pared-down musical language and a "spoken" style. The dramatic final scene is strikingly powerful and effectively carries the whole weight of the score. Having dispensed with the themes of ordinary everyday life which had attracted and also perhaps restricted him in previous operas, Janáček is at last free to give full rein to his operatic gifts in the surreal outcome of the finale.

VEJZOVIC, DUNJA

(Zagreb 1943)

Croatian soprano. She studied at the Zagreb Academy of Music, the Conservatory in Stuttgart, the Salzburg Mozarteum and in Weimar. She began her career with the Zagreb Opera and then sang in Nuremberg and Frankfurt (1978–79). In 1979 she made her debut at the Bayreuth Festival as Kundry in Wagner's *Parsifal*, in which opera she subsequently appeared again at the Salzburg Easter Festival with Herbert von Karajan conducting. Vejzovic has also sung at the Vienna Staatsoper, the Paris Opéra (Cherubini's *Médée*, 1986), La Scala, Milan (Wagner's *Der fliegende Holländer*, The Flying Dutchman, 1988), and other major international opera houses.

VELTRI, MICHELANGELO

(Buenos Aires 1940)

Argentinian conductor of Italian origin. After studying piano, he began his professional life in music as répétiteur in various Argentinian opera houses and also took up conducting. He then moved to Europe, where he completed his training with Ettore Panizza in Milan (1965). Having decided on conducting as a career, he was soon appearing at major international opera houses, including La Scala, Milan (*Don Carlos*, 1970), the Vienna Staatsoper (1970) and, most notably, the Metropolitan Opera in New York, where he made his debut in 1971 and since 1983 has regularly conducted, mainly Italian opera.

VÊPRES SICILIENNES, LES

(The Sicilian Vespers)

Opera in five acts by Giuseppe Verdi (1813–1901), to a libretto by Eugène Scribe and Charles Duveyrier. First performance: Paris, Opéra, 13 June 1855.

The action takes place in Palermo, Sicily, in 1282. Guy de Montfort (baritone), the ruthless governor of Sicily, has charged Duke Frederick of Austria with treason and had him executed. The Duke's sister Hélène resolves to avenge his death and

Above: The Croatian soprano Dunja Vejzovic.

Left: A scene from *Věc Makropulos* (The Makropolous Affair) by Léoš Janáček.

joins forces with Sicilian patriots. She is in love with the young patriot Henri (tenor), and together they meet up with Jean Procida (bass), an exile who has secretly returned to Sicily. Procida reveals that Pierre d'Aragon is planning to intervene in Sicily if there are any signs of an uprising. Meanwhile, Montfort has discovered that Henri is his own son, sends for him and tells him who he is. Henri is stunned by the news, because he feels it will mean he must lose Hélène. That evening a ball is held. Procida informs Henri that there is a plot to assassinate Montfort. Henri protects his father. The conspirators are arrested, and Procida and Hélène are imprisoned in the fortress. Henri visits them there and defends his conduct by saying that as a son he owed it to his father to act as he did, but now wants to resume the struggle. Hélène reassures him of her love. Meanwhile, Montfort offers to save the prisoners if Henri will publicly acknowledge him as his father. Henri agrees, the prisoners are released, and the governor announces the marriage of his son to Hélène. The scene changes to the palace gardens, where preparations for the wedding are underway. Procida tells Hélène that the uprising will begin as soon as the bells are rung. Hélène shrinks in terror at the thought and does not want to go through with the ceremony, throwing Henri into despair. Montfort does not understand what is going on, assumes that the marriage is in trouble and reacts by ordering that the bells be rung at once to get the ceremony over more quickly. The opera ends with the start of the uprising.

Translated into Italian by Fusinato and Caimi, this opera was staged at the Teatro Ducale in Parma on 26 December 1855 and at La Scala, Milan, on 4 February 1856 with the title *Giovanna de Guzman*. Despite Verdi's strong reservations about the libretto, which he thought failed to integrate the love story and the historical context of the action and treated them almost as separate, the opera was an enormous success and earned the composer an invitation to go and live in Paris.

Right: Portrait of the young Giuseppe Verdi.

Above: *Les vêpres siciliennes* by Giuseppe Verdi at the Metropolitan Opera, New York.

VERDI, GIUSEPPE

(Roncole, Busseto 1813–Milan 1901)

Italian composer. Born to parents in extremely modest circumstances, Verdi initially had lessons with Pietro Baistrocchi, the organist in Roncole, and went on to study organ with the Busseto organist Fernando Provesi. After being refused entry to the Conservatorio in Milan, he studied privately with Vincenzo Lavigna, an opera composer who conducted from the harpsichord at La Scala, Milan. On the recommendation of the singer Giuseppina Strepponi and others who recognized the young composer's worth, the manager of La Scala decided to stage Verdi's first opera, *Oberto, Conte di San Bonifacio* (1839). The work's success led to Verdi being offered a contract to do three more operas. The first, *Un giorno di regno*, staged at La Scala in 1840, was a complete fiasco. As a result Verdi became so depressed that he considered giving up composing. However, Merelli encouraged him to persevere, so he came to write *Nabucco* (1842) and *I Lombardi alla prima crociata* (1843), both tremendous successes, which demonstrated beyond doubt that he was a composer of real stature. After these two operas for La Scala, Verdi wrote *Ernani* for La Fenice in Venice (1844). There followed a long and intensive period during which Verdi sought to develop a dramatic language of his own. Between 1844 and 1850 he received commissions from a number of Italian theaters which resulted in *I due Foscari*, *Giovanna d'Arco*, *Alzira*, *Attila*, *Macbeth*, *I masnadieri*, *Jérusalem* (a revised, French version of *I Lombardi*), *Il corsaro*, *La battaglia di Legnano* and *Luisa Miller*, the latter a work which shows the enormous progress Verdi had made in giving his characters and situations greater dramatic and psychological depth. After *Stiffelio* (1850), which Verdi revised in 1857 and renamed *Aroldo*, came the three great operas, *Rigoletto* (1851), *Il trovatore* (1853) and *La traviata* (1853), known as his Popular Trilogy. These works were followed by an enriching time of renewal in which the artistic choices he made were more precise and better worked out, with *Les vêpres siciliennes*, composed for the Paris Opéra (1855), *Simon Boccanegra* (1857, revised 1881), *Un ballo in maschera* (1859) and *La forza del destino* (1862), the last two constituting particularly important landmarks in the composer's output. Although it seemed after *Don Carlos* (1867) and *Aida* (1871) that Verdi's career as an opera composer was at an end, his gift for developing his style into something new yet again enabled him to write his great masterpieces *Otello* (1887) and finally *Falstaff* (1893), his witty but melancholy farewell to life.

VERRETT, SHIRLEY

(New Orleans 1931)
American soprano and mezzo-soprano. A pupil of Anna Fitziu in Chicago, she won a scholarship which enabled her to attend the Juilliard School in New York. She made her debut in 1957 in Yellow Springs (Ohio) in Britten's *The Rape of Lucretia*. In 1962 she sang Carmen at the Spoleto Festival, Ulrica at Covent Garden in Verdi's *Un ballo in maschera* (1966) and Elisabetta in Donizetti's *Maria Stuarda* at the Maggio Musicale Festival in Florence in 1967. Her debut at the Metropolitan Opera in New York was in 1968, and since then she has appeared at all the leading international houses. In the 1970s, having already won acclaim for her greatest roles of Eboli (*Don Carlos*), Carmen and Dalila (*Samson et Dalila*), she increased her repertoire with soprano roles, including Didon (Berlioz's *Les Troyens*), Lady Macbeth, Norma and Medea. As well as her vocal gifts, Verrett has been acclaimed for the noble sound of her singing, perfectly suited to the musical style of the roles she has tackled, and for outstanding stage presence.

VERSCHAEVE, MICHEL

(Malo-les-Bains 1955)
French baritone. He studied music at the Paris Conservatoire and completed his training at the École d'Art Lyrique of the Opéra in Paris. He specializes in seventeenth- and eighteenth-century opera and has sung Monteverdi (*Il ritorno d'Ulisse in patria*), Vivaldi (*L'incoronazione di Dario*), Rameau (*Dardanus*, *Zoroastre*, *Platée*) and Gluck (*Armide*).

VESTALE, LA

Opera in three acts by Gaspare Spontini (1774–1851), to a libretto by Étienne de Jouy. First performance: Paris, Opéra, 15 December 1807.

The young Roman general Licinio (tenor) returns to Rome in glory after his victories in Gaul and tells his friend Cinna (tenor) of the turmoil he is in. He is in love with Giulia (soprano), but she has become a vestal virgin in accordance with her father's dying wish. Giulia is also deeply affected by the hero's homecoming, the more so when the Chief Vestal (mezzo-soprano) insists that she be the one to place the laurel crown on Licinio's head during the victory celebrations. As she is crowning him, Giulia hears Licinio whispering words of love to her. The scene changes to the temple of Vesta, where Giulia watches over the sacred flame which must always be kept burning. Licinio arrives, and while they are singing of their passion the sacred flame, left unguarded, goes out. Cinna enters to announce the arrival of the priests and vestal virgins, which means Giulia must help Licinio to flee. The priests burst in. The High Priest (bass), discovering that the temple has been desecrated and the sacred flame allowed to go out, condemns Giulia to be buried alive. At the vestals' burial-place, a despairing Licinio confesses his guilt before the High Priest, but Giulia tries to exculpate him by swearing that she has never seen him before. Suddenly the sky goes dark, and a flash of lightning strikes the altar where Giulia had laid her veil. Vesta's verdict is clear: the sacred flame has been rekindled, and the goddess has pardoned her priestess. Now that she is no longer bound by her vows and there is no stain on her character, Giulia is free to be married to Licinio.

Maria Callas in *La Vestale* by Gaspare Spontini, at La Scala, Milan, 7 December 1954.

La vestale is Spontini's most expansive opera and the most important neo-classical work to come out of the First Empire. Although the characters seem somewhat stiff, resigned, and not capable of rebelling, allowing themselves rather to be pulled along by events, the opera has great qualities. The score is full of passion, Spontini's musical language is well-balanced, and the combination of instrumental tone-colours heralds the Romantic period.

VIAGGIO A REIMS, IL, OSSIA L'ALBERGO DEL GIGLIO D'ORO

(The Journey to Rheims, or The Inn of the Gilded Lily)
Opera in one act by Gioachino Rossini (1792–1868), to a libretto by Luigi Balocchi. First performance: Paris, Théâtre Italien, 19 June 1825.

On the eve of the coronation of Charles X of France, a group of holiday guests staying at the Gilded Lily, a hotel in Plombières where people come to take the waters, decides to set out together for Rheims to attend the new king's coronation. While Madama Cortese (soprano), the hotel proprietor, is busy giving instructions to her staff to do everything they can to help the guests on their way, the guests themselves become involved in a series of tragi-comic situations. The capricious and fashion-conscious Contessa di Folleville (soprano) faints when she finds out that her gowns were damaged when the coach carrying her wardrobe overturned. Then there are some amorous skirmishes between the beautiful Polish Marchesa Melibea (mezzo-soprano) and her suitors,

the Spanish general Don Alvaro (baritone) and the Russian general Conte di Libenskof (tenor). The poetess Corinna (soprano) is the object of desire for both Lord Sydney (bass) and Cavalier Belfiore (tenor). Also on the scene is Don Profondo (bass), a great connoisseur, and the German major Barone di Trombonok (bass), a music-lover. The various goings-on involving these characters are interrupted by the announcement that the journey to Rheims will have to be cancelled because there is not a single horse to be had in the whole of Plombières. However, Madama Cortese comforts her disappointed guests with the news that the people of Paris are making ready to welcome Charles X. The Contessa di Folleville offers everyone hospitality at her house. Happiness having been restored, the opera ends with a sumptuous banquet at which the holiday guests celebrate the coronation.

Il viaggio a Reims marks Rossini's Paris debut as an opera composer. The score shows him displaying his mastery of composition and expressiveness in music like wares in a shop-window, but it was quickly forgotten, and the music (some of which was used again by Rossini in *Le Comte Ory*) ended up in different archives. It was not until recently that the task of reconstructing the opera was undertaken by the musicologist Philip Gosset, paving the way for the opera to be revived in a series of performances in Pesaro in 1984.

VICKERS, JON

(Prince Albert, Saskatchewan 1926)

Stage name of Jonathan Stewart, Canadian tenor. He studied at the Conservatory in Toronto and with George Lambert. In 1954 he made his debut in Toronto with the Canadian Opera Company (in Verdi's *Rigoletto*) and continued to pursue his career in Canada until 1957, the year in which he made his debut at Covent Garden (Verdi's *Un ballo in maschera*). He remained at Covent Garden for many seasons, appearing in a vast repertoire of roles, which included Berlioz's *Les Troyens*, Cherubini's *Médée*, Bizet's *Carmen*, Beethoven's *Fidelio* and Saint-Saëns' *Samson et Dalila*. In 1958 he appeared for the first time at the Bayreuth Festival (Wagner's *Die Walküre*), and went on to perform at leading opera venues, including the Metropolitan Opera in New York (Leoncavallo's *I pagliacci*), La Scala, Milan (Beethoven's *Fidelio*, 1960), and the Salzburg Festival (Verdi's *Otello*, 1970–72). He was hailed one of the most outstanding interpreters of Florestan, Parsifal, Siegmund, Tristan, Samson and Peter Grimes.

Above: A scene from *Il viaggio a Reims* by Gioachino Rossini.

Right: The Canadian tenor Jon Vickers.

VIDA BREVE, LA

(The Brief Life)

Opera in two acts and four scenes by Manuel de Falla (1876–1946), to a libretto by Carlos Fernandez Shaw. First performance, in French: Nice, Théâtre du Casino, 1 April 1913.

The action takes place in Granada. While her grandmother (mezzo-soprano) feeds the birds, Salud (soprano) is waiting for her lover, Paco (tenor). He soon arrives, affectionate as ever. Salud's uncle Salvador (bass or bass-baritone) also appears. He tells Salud's grandmother that Paco is going to marry someone else, a wealthy young woman. At Paco's fiancée's house, the forthcoming wedding is being celebrated in fine style. Outside in the street, Salud listens in despair to the joyful singing and dancing. While her grandmother and uncle are cursing Paco, Salud sings a song Paco knows well and decides to see him again. The scene changes to the patio of the house, where Salud is telling Manuel (baritone), the bride-to-be's brother, the story of her relationship with Paco. Paco denies it all. When she hears these words, Salud collapses and dies of grief.

La vida breve, Falla's first opera, helped him to win the competition held in 1905 by the Real Academia de Bellas Artes in Madrid, but it was not staged until 1913 in Nice and subsequently in Paris. Its Spanish premiere in 1914 was a great success, despite the weak libretto.

VIIMEISET KIUSAUKSET

(The Last Temptations)

Opera in two acts by Joonas Kokkonen (b.1921), to a libretto by Lauri Kokkonen. First performance: Helsinki, Finnish National Opera, 1975.

The action takes place in Finland in the nineteenth century. On his death-bed Paavo Ruotsalainen (bass), wracked with

SPANISH OPERA

The birth of opera in Spain can be traced back to the year 1629 and *La selva sin amor*, which was composed anonymously to a text by Lope de Vega and provided the model for what in the second half of the century was to become the most typically Spanish form of theater, the *zarzuela*. At first described as *fiestas de zarzuela*, this musical genre is linked to the French *ballet de cour* and the English *masque*, two kinds of theater in which particular prominence is given to the spectacular element. The eighteenth century saw Italian opera predominating over all other forms of national theater in Spain as in most of the other European countries and enjoying the support of the Emperor Philip V, who had persuaded the famous *castrato* Farinelli to come to his Court. So it was that while the majority of Spanish composers, such as Martin y Soler (1754–1806), Terradellas (1713–1751) and Duran (?–c. 1791) adopted the style of Italian opera, a minority, among them Hita (1704–1787), Esteve (?–1794) and above all Mison (?–1776) started a new genre of theater, the *tonadilla*, allied to comic opera and the *intermezzo*. The first significant example of *tonadilla* is *La Mesonera y el Arriero* by Mison (1758); but this genre too (based on the *zarzuela*), was exposed to numerous foreign influences from the 1770s onwards and by the end of the century had taken on all the characteristics of Italian *opera buffa*. Among the most noted composers of *tonadilla* in this period, one especially, Manuel Garcia (1775–1832), head of one of the most distinguished families of Spanish musicians, is particularly prominent. A turning-point was reached in 1799 when the Italian language was banned, by royal decree, from all of Spain's opera houses with the exception of Barcelona. This helped Spanish opera to develop a stronger national identity in its own right, but did not eliminate the considerable influence which Italian and French opera both had on it, as a result of which Spanish opera continued to bear the unmistakeable imprint of its debt to the Italian model in its form and also in the way its libretti were put together. The survival of the Italian connection is well illustrated by the operas of Arriaga (1806–1826), Genovès (1806–1861) and Carnicer (1789–1855), one of the most illustrious of Spanish opera composers, who wrote *semi-seria* operas exclusively in Italian; Esclava (1807–1878), who was admired by Rossini; and Espin Guillén (1812–1882), one of the first composers of opera to draw on the folk music tradition in a more conspicuous way. The influence of folk music is basic to the nineteenth-century *zarzuela*, which developed, during that century, into two different types: the *gran zarzuela*, which continued to celebrate the French and Italian operatic styles, and the more typically Spanish *género chico* (or genre of comic one-act pieces), of which Gaztambide (1822–1870), Chapi (1851–1909), Vives (1871–1932) and Penella (1880–1939) were some of the most representative exponents as well as being opera composers (at the beginning of the twentieth century, the distinctions between these two genres were quite clear), but their names remained unknown outside Spain itself. Only the operas of Albéniz (*Pepita Jimenez*, 1896 and de Falla (*La vida breve*, *El Retablo de Maese Pedro* and *Atlantida*) have attracted international attention.

Above: Placido Domingo, a performer of *zarzuelas*.

Right: A scene from *La vida breve* by Manuel de Falla.

fever, calls out the name of Riitta, who has been dead for a long time. His present wife, Anna Loviisa (speaking role) and the maid Albertina (speaking role), do what they can to comfort him in his delirium, but he brusquely pushes them away, shouting that he wants to be on his own in the presence of God. Left alone, Paavo begins to hallucinate again, and gradually images of his past life and his youth appear to him. Paavo now relives the night he met Riitta (soprano), during a dance. Through Riitta, Paavo gets to know the smith Jaakko Högman (baritone), who persuades him to believe in some evangelical religious ideas. Paavo becomes a preacher, is quickly reduced to poverty, and goes to live with Riitta, whom he has since married, in the woods. The couple begin a harsh life together, struggling to survive against the forces of nature. But Paavo is also so taken up with his religious beliefs that he often leaves his family to go and preach. Riitta is driven to despair and threatens to kill him if he ever leaves her and their son Juhana (tenor) again without nourishment. In so saying, she throws an axe at him, which misses. A few days later, some women bring Riitta the news that Juhana has been found dead. Riitta cannot even find the strength to weep for her son, whereas the distraught Paavo cries out to God that this too is a punishment for his inadequacy. Three years go by, and Riitta is dying: she is at peace and thanks God for the joys he has given her. Paavo is deeply affected by the serenity with which his wife is preparing to die. Paavo returns to his preaching but experiences conflict and humiliation along the way. The opera ends with Paavo on his death-bed emerging from his delirious state. Now he too feels at peace and while his family, gathered round him, sing a hymn, he hears the voice of Riitta inviting him to come to her.

Viimeiset Kiusaukset is one of the greatest of Finnish operas. The success of the work's premiere led to more than 200 performances, and it was also staged by opera houses outside Finland. The plot is based on the real-life figure of Paavo Ruotsalainen (1777–1852), who, with his vision of a contemplative religion involving not dogma but a personal experience of the Divine, inspired a movement against certain religious stereotypes.

VILLAGE ROMEO AND JULIET, A

Opera in a prologue and three acts by Frederick Delius (1862–1934), to the composer's own libretto, based on a story by Gottfried Keller from the collection Die Leute von Seldwyla. *First performance, in German, with the title* Romeo und Julia auf dem Dorfe, *Berlin, Komische Oper, 21 February 1907.*

The scene is set in the Swiss village of Seldwyl. Two farmers, Manz (baritone) and Marti (bass), once the best of friends, start to argue over which of them is entitled to a piece of land located between their two properties. Their dispute goes on for so long that it eventually ruins them both. They each have one child, a son Sali (tenor) and a daughter Vrenchen (soprano), who have been fond of each other since they were very young, despite the feud between their two families. Sali and Vrenchen have continued to meet secretly, and with the onset of adulthood they discover that they love each other. For a time, the pair are tempted by the idea of joining a group of travellers who take life one day at a time, but then they come to see that their love is very different from the relationships these people are used to. Now they too have nowhere to go, are seen as undesirables, have no friends and are too poor to be able to marry. So they decide that if they cannot live together, they can at least die together, which they do, taking a boat out into the middle of the river and gradually sinking it as they hold each other.

Composed in 1901, *A Village Romeo and Juliet* is the most significant and celebrated of Delius's operas. It was staged in English at Covent Garden in London on 22 February 1910 and was a great success. The score, which bears the hallmark of Delius the symphonist, is distinctive for the considerable richness of its orchestral writing, and it is in fact through the orchestral rather than the vocal line that Delius unfolds the story and paints a portrait of the feelings and personalities of Sali and Vrenchen.

Frederick Delius, composer of *A Village Romeo and Juliet.*

VILLI, LE

Opera in two acts by Giacomo Puccini (1858–1924) to a libretto by Ferdinando Fontana. First performance: Milan, Teatro Dal Verme, 31 May 1884.

After celebrating his betrothal to Anna (soprano), Roberto (tenor) sets out for Mainz to collect the inheritance he has been left by an aunt. As he is leaving, Anna seeks his reassurance: she is troubled by premonitions which make her feel sad. In fact, Roberto falls in love with a *femme fatale* and forgets all about Anna. She waits for him for months and then dies of grief. Her spirit is transformed into one of the Villi (wilis), the ghosts of young women who have died of lovesickness after being abandoned. When Roberto is finally deserted by his new mistress, he returns to the village. Anna appears to him with the other Villi and he, thinking her to be alive, kisses her. He is then dragged into a wild dance, at the end of which he falls dead at Anna's feet.

The premiere of *Le Villi* was a resounding success, and the work earned the admiration of Verdi himself. A decidedly traditional opera in some respects, *Le Villi* nevertheless reveals Puccini's natural gift for handling dramatic scenes with a confidence.

VIOLANTA

Opera in one act by Erich Wolfgang Korngold (1897–1957), to a libretto by Hans Müller. First performance: Munich, Königlichen Hof- und Nationaltheater, 28 March 1916.

The action takes place in Venice during the fifteenth century at Carnival time. At the house of Simone Trovai (baritone), one of the Republic of Venice's military leaders, his wife, Violanta (soprano), is preoccupied by unhappy thoughts, even though outside her window the entire city is transported with delight at all the distractions of the Carnival. She has been in this somber mood ever since her sister Nerina was seduced and then deserted by Alfonso (tenor), prince of Naples, and committed suicide as a result, leaving Violanta obsessed by the desire to avenge her. Alfonso is now in Venice. Violanta tells her husband that she has managed to meet up with him and, without revealing her identity, has invited him to call on her that very evening. She then asks Simone if he will kill Alfonso for her. At first Simone refuses, but Violanta's hold over him prevails, and he agrees. Alfonso arrives after nightfall and Violanta continues her game of seduction until the moment arrives for her to take Alfonso by surprise, tell him who she really is, and unfold her plan for revenge. Alfonso's reaction is to cry out that a longing for death has always been part of his life, and now he asks her to go ahead at once and give the signal for him to be killed. Violanta is so shocked by his words that she entreats him to leave, but Alfonso senses that she loves him and begs her to forget the past and live this moment of love. As Violanta receives Alfonso's embraces, Simone comes in and hurls himself at Alfonso, but Violanta shields him and takes the fatal blow herself.

The first performance of *Violanta* was a triumph, and so was the follow-up on 10 April of the same year at the Vienna Staatsoper, in which the role of Violanta was sung by Maria Jeritza, for whom Korngold would later write the role of Marietta in *Die tote Stadt*. The work has an extraordinary dramatic intensity and shows the 17-year-old Korngold as already possessing considerable mastery in achieving richness of orchestral colour.

VISHNEVSKAYA, GALINA

(Leningrad 1926)

Russian soprano. A pupil of Vera Garina in Leningrad, she made her debut in 1944 with an operetta company. She became a member of the Bolshoi in Moscow in 1952, appearing in an extensive repertoire of roles drawn from not only Russian but also Italian and French opera. In 1955 she embarked on an international career, initially concentrating on countries in the Eastern bloc and from 1960 in the West, including performances at the Metropolitan Opera in New York (Verdi's *Aida* and Puccini's *Madama Butterfly*, 1961), Covent Garden (*Aida*, 1962) and La Scala, Milan (Tchaikovsky's *Pikovaya Dama*, Queen of Spades, 1964). After leaving Russia in 1974, she devoted most of her time to concerts and recitals but also appeared at the Metropolitan (1977), the Maggio Musicale Festival in Florence (1980) and the Opéra in Paris, where in 1982, she gave her farewell stage performance in Tchaikovsky's *Eugene Onegin*, although she reemerged in 1986 to sing in a production of Prokofiev's *Voyna i mir* (War and Peace) in Paris. The greatest Russian singer since the Second World War, Vishnevskaya had a beautiful voice of essentially operatic colouring. On the strength of her powerful talent and natural strengthening of the voice, she was also able to take on more markedly dramatic roles. She has worked as an opera producer, staging Rimsky-Korsakov's *Tsarskaya nevesta* (The Tsar's Bride) in Monte Carlo (1986) and at the Teatro dell'Opera in Rome (1987). She is married to the celebrated cellist and conductor Mstislav Rostropovich.

VIVALDI, ANTONIO

(Venice 1678–Vienna 1741)

Italian composer. His father, Giovanni Battista, was a cellist at St. Mark's in Venice. He was probably taught by Giovanni Legrenzi and Giovanni Battista Somis. Vivaldi was ordained a priest in 1703, but only a year later he was excused from saying Mass because he was suffering from a disease of the respiratory tract (most likely asthma or consumption). He composed some 50 operas, starting with *Ottone in Villa* (Vicenza, 1713), most of them staged in Venice but also in many other cities in Italy. They are all examples of *opera seria* and include *L'Orlando Furioso*, *La fida ninfa*, *La Griselda* , and *Catone in Utica*.

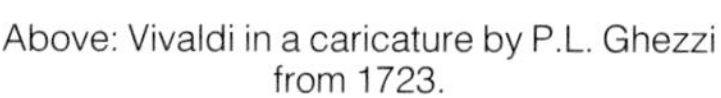

Above: Vivaldi in a caricature by P.L. Ghezzi from 1723.

Left: A scene from Vivaldi's opera *Farnace*.

"ANTONIO VIVALDI, OPERA COMPOSER AND IMPRESARIO"

After attending a performance in a Paris theater, an ambassador from Venice observed in astonishment: "Here the theaters are very different from ours – people come to them to listen and not to talk as we do in Italy." This comment bears witness to a practice which was particularly widespread in Italian opera houses during the eighteenth century and Vivaldi the theatrical impresario operated under these conditions. Venice, which could boast having opened Europe's first public theater in 1637, had as many as seven by the eighteenth century, among them the Teatro Sant'Angelo and the Teatro San Moisè, where Vivaldi staged so many of his operas. It should be remembered that the way in which theaters were organized at that time meant that the composer was certainly not seen as the most important person involved in an opera production; on the contrary, sometimes his name did not even appear – not only the singers but even the scenery-painter taking precedence over him. This being the situation, it is understandable that Vivaldi should have devoted so much to his energy to being an impresario, an activity to which he brought organizational skills and which became positively frenetic during the period of the Venice Carnival when the theaters were open and putting on daily performances. The output of the Venice theaters reached record levels (in Vivaldi's lifetime, more than 600 operas were staged in that city). The job of impresario was fraught with difficulties and the most unpredictable things would go wrong, causing Vivaldi a good deal of frustration: in 1737, for instance, he revised two of his operas for production in Ferrara. After he had sent the first opera to Ferrara, the theater manager, Bollani, immediately asked for the score of the other opera as well, but sent payment for only part of the fee which had been agreed on. Vivaldi sent several reminders to him for the balance and eventually accused him of incompetence and of not having understood how to manage money (Bollani engaged his singers not for their talent but because they had influential patrons). Vivaldi, on the other hand, was much more aware of what was required, as can be seen from a letter he wrote from Verona, where he had staged his opera *Catone in Utica*: this production had covered its costs over 600 performances and promised a handsome dividend for the remainder of the run. But he then advised against putting the opera on in Ferrara during Carnival: at that time of year, the overheads would be excessive, whereas in the summer, off season, he could name his price. Vivaldi's skill and success as an impresario did not save him from criticism, such as the salvo directed at him by Benedetto Marcello in his *Teatro alla Moda*. Referring to the custom of dedicating a composition to a monarch or patron, Marcello satirized Vivaldi's ostentatious style of dedication by declaring that he hereby "kissed, with great respect, the fleas on the paws of Your Excellency's dog." Quite apart from the personal or indrect gibes to which Vivaldi himself was being subjected, Marcello was endeavouring to draw attention to the state of Venetian opera in the first half of the eighteenth century when Vivaldi was active as a composer and impresario. It was a period in time when Venice audiences used to fail an opera (by whistling) not because of the music but if the singers gave bad performances. Vivaldi, especially in the years from 1732 to 1739, tried to go beyond the static nature of *opera seria* by using or resorting to a succession of arias and recitatives and achieving a greater richness of timbre.

Above: The monogram of Antonio Vivaldi.

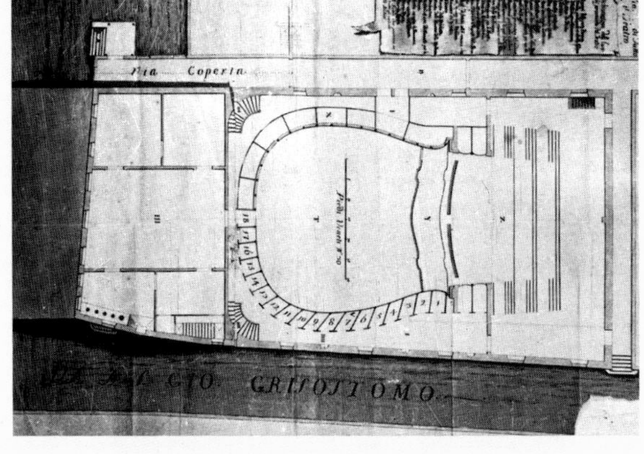

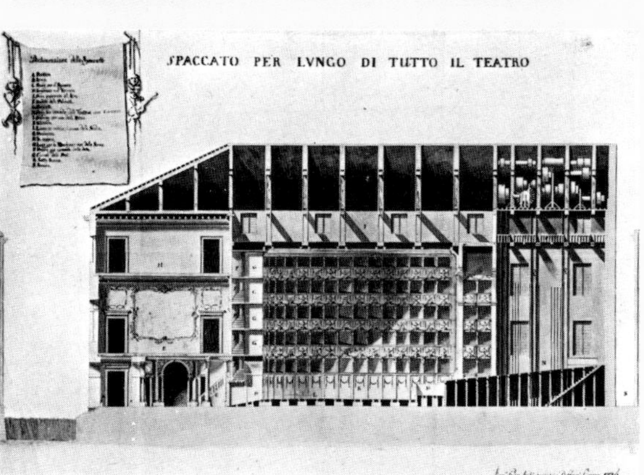

Right: Plan and cross-section by F. Pedro of Teatro San Giovanni Crisostomo, Venice.

VOGEL, SIEGFRIED
(Chemnitz, Karl Marx Stadt 1937)
German bass. He studied at the Dresden Hochschule (1955–56) and after completing his training at the Opera Studio attached to Dresden Opera, he made his debut there in 1959. He was contracted by the Berlin Staatsoper (then in East Berlin) in 1965 and made his mark mainly as a Mozart singer (Figaro, Leporello, Don Alfonso) but also in Wagner. With the Berlin Staatsoper company Vogel toured to various European cities, with appearances at the Paris Opéra (Beethoven's *Fidelio*, 1982, *Tannhäuser*, 1984, and *Tristan und Isolde*, 1985) and the Théâtre de la Monnaie in Brussels (*Don Giovanni*, 1980).

VOIGT, DEBORAH
(Chicago 1960)
American soprano. She won first prize at the International Tchaikovsky Competition in Moscow in 1990, the Verdi Competition in Busseto and the Rosa Ponselle Competition, and these successes launched her on a brilliant career. In 1991 she won great acclaim for her performance as Ariadne in Richard Strauss's *Ariadne auf Naxos* in Boston and as Amelia in Verdi's *Un ballo in maschera* in San Francisco (1990–91), the role in which she made her debut at the Metropolitan Opera in New York (1991). At the Metropolitan she has also appeared in Verdi's *Il trovatore* and again in *Ariadne auf Naxos* (1992–93) and she has sung Verdi's *Requiem* at Carnegie Hall. Her European engagements have included a Netherlands Radio production of Catalani's *La Wally*, Mascagni's *Il piccolo Marat*, and Korngold's *Die tote Stadt*, as well as recitals at the Théâtre du Châtelet in Paris and the Théâtre de la Monnaie in Brussels. Voigt's lyric soprano voice is particularly well suited to Wagner (*Lohengrin*, *Tannhäuser*) and Richard Strauss.

VOIX HUMAINE, LA
(The Human Voice)
Opera in one act by Francis Poulenc (1899–1963), to a text by Jean Cocteau. First performance: Paris, Théâtre de l'Opéra-Comique, 5 February 1959.

A woman is being deserted by her lover, who intends to marry someone else. The last conversation they have is by telephone. Of the two lovers, only the woman (soprano) is on stage. She experiences moments of deep tenderness, others of passion, sometimes even violence. The man on the other end of the phone remains unseen throughout, his existence hinted at only by the woman pausing to listen. Now and then this intense conversation is interrupted, but neither has the courage to say the last word and so let the feelings of despair and loss take over. At the end the woman, exhausted, grips the telephone and begs her lover to hang up, and the drama reaches its climax amid shouting and muffled words as the woman lets go of the receiver and it hits the floor.

In his *La voix humaine*, Poulenc stayed close to the text by Cocteau, who was enthusiastic about this operatic version of his original play. The work develops and probes the female psychology Poulenc had explored in his earlier opera *Les dialogues des Carmélites*. Having only one character in the cast enabled the composer to conduct that analysis with exceptional vigour.

VON HEUTE AUF MORGEN
(From Day to Day)
Opera in one act by Arnold Schoenberg (1874–1951) to a libretto by Max Blonda (pseudonym of Gertrud Kolisch Schoenberg). First performance: Frankfurt, Städtische Bühnen, 1 February 1930.

A husband (baritone) and wife (soprano) arrive home from a party. He has been strongly attracted to one of his wife's friends and praises the woman's wit, charm and modern style. His wife is stung into telling him in no uncertain terms that it is easy enough for a woman to retain her charm if she has no husband or children or home to think about. For his part, the husband dismisses as absurd the idea that there can be any comparison between a woman of the world and a superb housewife. The wife decides she is going to transform the way she behaves as a woman without delay: she gives herself the air of an expert seductress, neglects her son and the home, and accepts the attentions of a singer (tenor). The distraught husband has finally understood and is now afraid that he may lose the woman he loves. All of this happens in the space of a single night. Next morning

Above: The American soprano Deborah Voigt.

Left: The soprano Denise Duval in a scene from Poulenc's *La voix humaine*.

the wife changes back into her normal clothes and is once again her old self, the calm and efficient housewife. The singer and the wife's friend arrive and are disappointed to find that the husband and wife are no longer the independent, "modern" couple they had seemed to be before. Others may be ruled by fashion, says the husband, but we are moved by love.

Schoenberg worked on the composition of *Von Heute auf Morgen* between 1928 and 1929. Underneath the subtle irony present throughout the work lies the key theme of this opera, the relationship between outer and inner worlds, appearance and real substance, something the composer is clearly exploring in other operas, *Moses and Aaron*, for example. *Von Heute auf Morgen*, which features obvious musical allusions to popular music like waltzes and jazz, has its own moral: that which is supposedly modern and fashionable only exists from day to day.

VOYNA Y MIR

(War and Peace)

Opera in five acts and 13 scenes by Sergei Prokofiev (1891–1953), to a libretto by Prokofiev and Mira Mendelson-Prokofieva, from the novel by Leo Tolstoy. First performance: Leningrad, Maly Theater, 12 May 1946.

The action takes place in the early nineteenth century in Russia. The beautiful Natasha (soprano), daughter of Count Ilya Andreyevich Rostov (bass), has attracted Prince Andrei Bolkonsky (baritone), who admires her when she appears at the window of her room, then later sees her at a ball and realizes he is in love with her. But his father, old Prince Nikolai Bolkonsky (bass), treats Natasha coldly because she comes from a lower social order. Also secretly in love with Natasha is Count Pierre Bezhukhov (tenor), who is unhappily married to the unscrupulous Countess Hélène (mezzo-soprano). Her brother, the adventurer Anatole Kuragin (tenor), shocks Natasha by asking her to marry him and persuades her to run away with him. But Pierre reveals that Anatole is already married, and Anatole flees Moscow in a hurry, plunging Natasha into black despair, because she is convinced she has lost Andrei's love forever. Meanwhile, news reaches the capital that war has broken out with France. Andrei and Pierre join up so as to forget their love for Natasha and are determined to fight in the front lines, at Borodino. Andrei is seriously wounded and dies after telling Natasha he still loves her and learning from her that she still loves him. At the same time, Marshal Kutozov (bass), commander of the Russian army, orders his troops to retreat and decides to set fire to Moscow. In the end the French troops themselves withdraw, and many Russian prisoners, including Pierre, are set free. He hears of Andrei's death and that of his own wife and, filled with hope, sets out for Moscow, knowing that Natasha is there. The opera ends with the people of Moscow celebrating their victory.

The first performance of *War and Peace* was in a concert version at the Authors' Club in Moscow on 16 October 1944. The stage premiere followed in 1946, but this was not the complete work, only the first seven scenes. The complete opera, which was long and elaborate, had to wait until 31 March 1955 for its posthumous first stage performance in Leningrad. This huge score is wholly successful in transforming Tolstoy's novel and bringing out its key elements – the struggle of the Russian people against the invader and, at the same time, the lives and loves of the leading characters.

Above: The first act of *Voyna y Mir* (War and Peace) by Sergei Prokofiev in a 1964 production at the Bolshoi.

Right: The Austrian composer Arnold Schoenberg.

WÄCHTER, EBERHARD

(Vienna 1929–1992)

Austrian baritone. He received his musical education in Vienna, where he studied with Elisabeth Rado. In 1953 he made his debut at the Vienna Volksoper (as Silvio in Leoncavallo's *I pagliacci*). The following year he joined the Staatsoper company and simultaneously embarked on an international career, which led to appearances at Covent Garden (Mozart's *Le nozze di Figaro*, 1956), the Bayreuth Festival (Wagner's *Parsifal*, 1958), the Teatro dell'Opera in Rome (Wagner's *Tannhäuser*, 1960), the Salzburg Festival (Mozart's *Don Giovanni*, 1960), La Scala, Milan (*Le nozze di figaro*, 1960) and the Metropolitan Opera (*Tannhäuser*, 1961). His repertoire was extremely wide, from Mozart to Romantic opera, Richard Strauss (*Arabella*, *Capriccio*), Berg (*Wozzeck*) and Viennese light opera. One of the most renowned singers of his generation, Wächter's reputation rested on his musical discipline, softness of delivery and expressiveness of phrasing. He created the leading role in Dallapiccola's *Il prigioniero* (La Scala, 1962) and also sang in the premiere of von Einem's *Dantons Tod* (Staatsoper, 1963).

WAGNER RICHARD

(Leipzig 1813–Venice 1883)

German composer. Initially more interested in literature and philosophy, he came to music relatively late. His only formal music studies were at the Thomasschule in Leipzig in 1828, where he learned theory and counterpoint with Theodor Weinlig over a period of six months. He immediately devoted his energies to composition and in 1833 finished work on his first opera, *Die Feen* (The Fairies, produced in 1888). A year later came *Das Liebesverbot* (The Ban on Love, after Shakespeare's *Measure for Measure*, 1834). In 1837, while conducting in Riga, he wrote his first important work, *Rienzi* (Dresden, 1842). Around this time he went to Paris and London, Paris being where he began composing *Der fliegende Holländer* (The Flying Dutchman), which was staged in Dresden in 1843 and was the real starting-point of Wagner's dramatic art. Also in 1843 Wagner was appointed Kapellmeister in Dresden, a post he held for seven years, until 1849. This intensely productive period saw the composition of *Tannhäuser* (1845) and a start on *Lohengrin*. After he was accused of being a revolutionary, Wagner fled to Zurich and exile, and while there he made arrangements for the premiere of *Lohengrin*, which took place in Weimar in 1850 with his friend Franz Liszt conducting. He then set to work on drafting the text of the four-opera cycle *Der Ring des Nibelungen*, which he completed in 1852, before going on to write the music for *Das Rheingold* from 1853 to 1854, *Die Walküre* from 1854 to 1856, and the early scenes of *Siegfried* from 1856 to 1857. He interrupted work on the *Ring* for almost 12 years, during which he had a relationship with Mathilde Wesendonk (this led to the end of his marriage to Minna Planer) and composed *Tristan und Isolde* (1857–59). There followed an extended period of travel, to Venice (1858–59), Lucerne (1859) and Paris (where the second version of *Tannhäuser* was staged in 1861). He also began work on *Die Meistersinger von Nürnberg* (The Mastersingers) in 1861, completing it in 1867. King Ludwig II of Bavaria offered him financial support, which enabled him to continue with his career as a composer. Having also found emotional stability by marrying Cosima Liszt, daughter of Franz, Wagner had *Die Meistersinger* produced in Munich in 1868 and finished composing *Siegfried* (1869–71). He pressed ahead with *Götterdämmerung* (Twilight of the Gods), completing it in 1874 in Bayreuth, where he had moved in 1872. Under the patronage of Ludwig II, Bayreuth became the site of the theater built specially for the presentation of Wagner's operas. It was opened in 1875 with the first complete performance of the *Ring*. Now at the height of his fame, Wagner started work on the composition of *Parsifal*, which took him until 1882, the year in which it was first staged at Bayreuth. In the autumn of that year, he moved to Venice, where he died on 13 February 1883.

WALKER, SARAH

(Cheltenham, Gloucestershire 1943)

British mezzo-soprano. She made her debut at the Glyndebourne Festival as Ottavia (Monteverdi's *L'incoronazione di Poppea*) and as Giunone (Cavalli's *La Calisto*). She appeared regularly with the English National Opera in London (from 1972 onwards) and at Covent Garden (her first role there was Charlotte in Massenet's *Werther* in 1979). She has also sung at San Francisco Opera (since 1986) and the Metropolitan Opera, New York (Handel's *Samson* and *Giulio Cesare*, 1986 and 1988). Walker's voice is characterized by fine timbre and softness in delivery, and her outstanding technique has enabled her to tackle an extremely wide-ranging repertoire, both stylistically and vocally, from Monteverdi to Britten. She won particular acclaim for her performance as Elizabeth I in Britten's *Gloriana* (English National Opera, 1984).

Above: The Austrian baritone Eberhard Wächter.

Left: Richard Wagner.

WALLBERG, HEINZ

(Herringen 1923)

German conductor. He studied in Dortmund and Cologne and began his career in music as an instrumentalist with orchestras in Cologne and Dortmund. He then turned to conducting, initially in Munster, Trier and Hamburg, and then as music director in Augsburg (1954), Bremen (1955–61), Wiesbaden (1961–74) and Essen (1975–91). He conducted for Munich Radio (1975–82) as well as appearing at major opera and concert venues (including Covent Garden, the Bayreuth Festival and the Teatro Colón in Buenos Aires). Wallberg also made some important recordings, including Egk's *Peer Gynt*, Leoncavallo's *La bohème* and Weinberger's *Svanda dudák*.

WALLY, LA

Opera in four acts by Alfredo Catalani (1854–1893), to a libretto by Luigi Illica, after the novel Die Geyer-Wally *by Wilhelmine von Hillern. First performance: Milan, La Scala, 20 January 1892.*

The action takes place in the Northern Tyrol around the year 1800. In a village square, people are celebrating the birthday of old Stromminger (bass), the father of Wally (soprano). Some huntsmen put on a display in his honour, among them Walter (soprano), a faithful friend of Wally's, who sings a song, full of unhappy premonitions, written by Wally herself. The hunter Hagenbach (tenor) also makes his appearance and arrogantly relates his hunting exploits, until his behaviour provokes an argument with Stromminger. Wally intervenes to stop them. Stromminger promises Wally's hand in marriage to Gellner (baritone), but she is in love with Hagenbach and will have nothing to do with this, eventually leaving home rather than obey her father's wishes. The scene changes to the village where Wally has gone to live. It is a public holiday, and a celebration is taking place. Gellner and Hagenbach are among those present. Hagenbach is now engaged to Afra (mezzo-soprano), who has been offended by the jealous Wally, and Hagenbach decides to redress the balance on Afra's behalf (and at the same time show people how wrong they are to say that Wally is proud and unapproachable) by betting that he will manage to kiss her during the dancing. Unaware of this, Wally dances with Hagenbach, accepts his advances and kisses him. But when she realizes she has been tricked, she asks Gellner to kill Hagenbach, offering to marry him if he will do it. Gellner puts his plan into action and lies in wait for Hagenbach under cover of darkness, attacks him as he passes by and pushes him over a precipice. Wally is now worried for him, climbs down into the ravine and, with the help of local people who have come running to her aid, drags Hagenbach to safety and hands him back to Afra. Then she goes off into the mountains. Walter follows her and pleads with her to come back down with him because there is a real risk of an avalanche, but Wally lets him return down the mountain alone. Hagenbach now catches up with Wally and tells her that he loves her. The couple dream of being together for the rest of their lives, but they are caught up in a snowstorm, and an avalanche buries them.

La Wally is Catalani's last opera, written a year before his death. Undoubtedly the best as well as the most famous, this work is a confirmation of his distinctive style, combining the Italian opera tradition with Romanticism, as well as Wagnerian and French influences.

Right: The German conductor Bruno Walter.

Above: Sketch by E. Marchiolo for *La Wally* by Alfredo Catalani.

WALTER, BRUNO

(Berlin 1876–Los Angeles 1962)

Stage name of Bruno Schlesinger, German conductor. He studied at the Stern Conservatory in Berlin, appeared as a pianist at the age of nine and from 1889 onwards concentrated on conducting. He worked as a répétiteur in Cologne (1893–94), making his opera debut with Lortzing's *Der Waffenschmied* (The Armourer). He was engaged by the Hamburg Opera (1894–96) and went on to conduct in Breslau (1896–97), Riga (1899–1900) and Berlin (1900–1). In 1901 he joined the Vienna Staatsoper as an assistant to Gustav Mahler, who had become a close friend. He then moved from Vienna to Munich, where he was appointed *Generalmusikdirektor* (1913–22), and there in 1916 he conducted the premieres of Korngold's *Violanta* and

Der Ring des Polykrates, Pfitzner's *Palestrina* and Schreker's *Das Spielwerk und die Prinzessin*. He went on to be conductor at the Berlin Städtische Oper (1925–29) and the Leipzig Gewandhaus (1929–33). Compelled to leave Germany in 1933 because of the anti-semitic laws, he moved to Austria, where he played a major role at the Salzburg Festival and was from 1936 until 1938 *Generalmusikdirektor* at the Vienna Staatsoper. Germany's annexation of Austria in 1938 forced him to move to France, which he left when war broke out in 1939 in order to emigrate to the United States. He conducted regularly at the Metropolitan Opera in New York (1941–57) as well as at other leading opera houses and with the main American music establishments. After 1947 he also resumed his international career and made appearances in major European cities. Walter is acknowledged as one of the great conductors of the twentieth century, and his recorded performances of Mozart, Wagner and Richard Strauss are of primary importance.

WALTON, SIR WILLIAM

(Oldham 1902–Ischia 1983)

British composer. He studied at the Oxford Choir School but was mainly self-taught. He became established as one of the most prominent figures in the world of British contemporary music. Walton was an eclectic composer who attempted a variety of musical genres, including the music for Laurence Olivier's Shakespeare films (1944–54). He turned to opera in 1954 with *Troilus and Cressida*, in which the pervading spirit of Romanticism also influenced the musical structure of the work. This was in sharp contrast to Walton's second opera, *The Bear*,

performed at Aldeburgh in 1967, a stylistically brilliant "one-act extravaganza" abounding in musical parodies.

WARREN, LEONARD

(New York 1911–1960)

Stage name of Leonard Varenov, American baritone. Born of Russian parents who had emigrated to the United States, he studied with Sydney Dietsch and went on to complete his training in Rome and Milan (1938). He joined the Metropolitan Opera in New York in 1938, made his debut the following year as Paolo Albiani (Verdi's *Simon Boccanegra*) and continued to appear there for the rest of his life in 26 different roles and a total of 636 performances. Famous as a Verdi singer (*Macbeth*, *Simon Boccanegra*, *Rigoletto*) but also for his Scarpia (*Tosca*), Tonio (*I pagliacci*) and Barnaba (*La Gioconda*). Warren also appeared in South America (at the Teatro Colón in Buenos Aires and in Rio de Janiero) and at the opera houses of San Francisco (*Samson et Dalila*, *La forza del destino* and *Lucia di Lammermoor*) and Mexico City. The only operas he sang in Italy were *Otello* and *Rigoletto* at La Scala, Milan, in 1953. Warren was one of the great baritones of his generation, his reputation resting on a voice of great beauty, impressive range and consistent delivery in every register. He died on stage at the Metropolitan.

WATKINSON, CAROLYN

(Preston 1949)

British mezzo-soprano. After studying at the Royal College of Music in Manchester, she specialized in the baroque repertoire and took part in concerts with some of the leading Early Music ensembles, directed by Helmut Rilling, Jean-Claude Malgoire and Christopher Hogwood. Her appearances in opera have included Phèdre (Rameau's *Hippolyte et Aricie*) at Covent Garden and the Festival of Versailles in 1978 and Nerone (Monteverdi's *L'incoronazione di Poppea*) with Netherlands Opera, the Théâtre de la Monnaie in Brussels, the Spoleto Festival (1979) and La Fenice in Venice (1980). Watkinson has an outstanding voice, good technique and a gift for *coloratura* singing. She has also sung in Handel's *Ariodante* (La Scala, 1981) and appeared as Idamante in Mozart's *Idomeneo* (Salzburg Festival), as Dido (Purcell's *Dido and Aeneas*), in Gluck's *Orfeo ed Euridice* and Rossini's *Il barbiere di Siviglia* and *La Cenerentola*.

WATSON, LILLIAN

(London 1947)

British soprano. She studied at the Guildhall School of Music and the London Opera Center. From 1981 she sang regularly at Covent Garden. At the same time she was appearing with Welsh National Opera, English National Opera, Scottish Opera and in particular at the Glyndebourne Festival, where she made her name as a Mozart singer (Susanna in Mozart's *Le nozze di Figaro*, Despina in *Cosí fan tutte*). She also performed at the Salzburg Festival in Beethoven's *Fidelio* (1982–83), the Vienna Staatsoper, the Bayerische Staatsoper in Munich and the Paris Opéra, where she sang Blonde in Mozart's *Die Entführing aus dem Serail* (The Seraglio).

Left: The British soprano Carolyn Watkinson (on the left) in Handel's *Ariodante*.

Top: The British composer Sir William Walton.

WATTS, HELEN

(Haverfordwest, Pembrokeshire 1927)
Welsh contralto. She was a pupil of Caroline Hatchard and Frederick Jacobson and attended the Royal Academy of Music. She made her debut with the BBC in a concert performance of Gluck's *Orfeo ed Euridice* (1953). Much of her career has been devoted to concert repertoire, in particular Bach and Handel. Her appearances in opera have included Britten's *The Rape of Lucretia*, Ursula (Berlioz's *Béatrice et Bénédict*), Ino and Juno (Handel's *Semele*), Melo (Handel's *Sosarme*), the Witch (Purcell's *Dido and Aeneas*) and Aunt Jane (Vaughan Williams' *Hugh the Drover*). She has also sung Wagner at Covent Garden, as First Norn (1965–66) and Erda (1967–71) in the *Ring*.

WEBER, CARL MARIA VON

(Eutin, Lübeck 1786–London 1826)
German composer and conductor. He grew up in a theatrical environment (his father was a conductor and had founded a theater company made up of members of Weber's large family) and studied piano, singing and composition in Munich and Salzburg. After his early attempts at opera composition, he embarked on a conducting career, appearing in Breslau (1804–6), Karlsruhe (1806) and Stuttgart (1807), where he composed his first successful opera, *Silvana* (staged in Frankfurt in 1910). His appointments as opera director of the Deutsche Oper in Prague (1813–16) and the Deutsche Oper in Dresden (from 1817) contributed decisively to his development as an artist. During his time in Prague, and even more while in Dresden, Weber's opera composition reached a turning-point, out of which came *Der Freischütz* (1821), marking the beginning not only of his years of greatest accomplishment but also of the heyday of German Romantic opera. *Der Freischütz* was followed by *Die drei Pintos*, a work he started in 1821 but left unfinished. It was completed by Mahler and eventually staged in 1889. *Euryanthe* was written for the Kärtnertortheater in Vienna and first performed in 1823. The worsening of the tuberculosis from which Weber had been suffering for some time barely permitted him to compose *Oberon*, whose libretto presented him with considerable difficulties and features a number of spoken passages, in accordance with English taste at that time.

WEBER, PETER

(Vienna 1950)
Austrian baritone. He attended the Musikhochschule in Vienna and made his name between 1970 and 1978 in major singing competitions, which led to his being able to complete his training at the Vienna Staatsoper (1976–78), subsequently joining the company there (1978–80). Weber was also engaged by the Nuremberg Opera (1980–82) and embarked on an international career which brought him engagements not only in Germany and Austria but also at the Teatro dell'Opera in Rome (Strauss's *Salome*, 1988), the Glyndebourne Festival (Strauss's *Arabella*, 1989), the Grand Théâtre in Geneva, the Opéra in Paris and the Teatro Colón in Buenos Aires. Weber is one of the most renowned singers of Wagner (particularly for his Amfortas in *Parsifal* and Telramund in *Lohengrin*) and Strauss (especially the role of Jochanaan in *Salome*).

WEIDINGER, CHRISTINE

(Springville, New York 1946)
American soprano. After four seasons in secondary roles with the Metropolitan Opera, New York (1972–76), she left for Europe to expand her artistic career in Germany (Hamburg, Berlin, Frankfurt, Cologne) and went on to complete her training in Italy with Pietro Ferraris and Rodolfo Celletti. In 1989 she sang Armida (Handel's *Rinaldo*) at La Fenice in Venice, and in March of the following year made her debut at La Scala, Milan (as Vitellia in Mozart's *La clemenza di Tito*), returning there in December to sing Elettra in Mozart's *Idomeneo*, both with Riccardo Muti conducting. She has also sung at other opera houses in Italy (the Teatro Comunale in Bologna, the Teatro Bellini in Catania, etc.) and internationally, including the Vienna Staatsoper, the Nice Opera (*La clemenza di Tito*, 1991), the Marseille Opera (Donizetti's *Lucrezia Borgia*, 1992), the Liceu in Barcelona (Donizetti's *Anna Bolena*, 1992–93) and in the United States, where she returned to the Metropolitan as Rossini's Semiramide (1992–93).

Right: The American soprano Christine Weidinger in *La clemenza di Tito*, in a 1990 production at La Scala.

Above: The German composer and conductor Carl Maria von Weber.

WEIKERT, RALPH

(Sankt-Florian 1940)
Austrian conductor. After studying piano and conducting at the Conservatory in Linz, he attended the Vienna Academy of Music (1960). On the strength of his success in the International Nikolai Competition in Copenhagen (1965), he began his career as a conductor in Bonn (from 1968) and then went on to be first conductor with the Frankfurt Opera (1977–81) and the Zurich Opera (from 1983). He conducts regularly at the Metropolitan Opera, New York.

WEIKL, BERND

(Vienna 1942)
German baritone of Austrian origin. He studied at the Conservatory in Mainz (1962–65) and at the Hanover Musikhochschule (from 1965). He began his career with a concert in Berlin (1968) and made his opera debut at the Niedersächsiches Staatstheater in Hanover in 1968 as Ottokar in Weber's *Der Freischütz*, returning for further engagements there until 1970. He joined the company of the Deutsche Oper am Rheim in Düsseldorf (1970), at the same time embarking on an international career which led to appearances at the Bayreuth Festival (*Tannhäuser*, 1972), the Salzburg Easter Festival (Wagner's *Tristan und Isolde*, 1972), the Vienna Staatsoper (Rossini's *Il barbiere di Siviglia*, 1972), the Metropolitan Opera, New York (*Tannhäuser*, 1977), and La Scala, Milan (Verdi's *Falstaff*, 1980). Weikl's excellent technique leaves him in full command of his firm voice, hence his reputation as an outstanding actor and a performer of great musicianship. He has also sung in Strauss's *Die Frau ohne Schatten* (Metropolitan Opera, 1989), Wagner's *Die Meistersinger von Nürnberg* (La Scala, 1990; Metropolitan, New York, 1992–93) and Strauss's *Arabella* (La Scala, 1992).

WEILL, KURT

(Dessau 1900–New York 1950)
German composer, naturalized American. He studied privately with Albert Bing and then at the Berlin Hochschule für Musik, where he was a pupil of Engelbert Humperdinck. During the years 1920–23 he did further studies at the Prussian Academy of Arts in Berlin, where his teacher was Ferruccio Busoni. His early works for the theater include *Der Protagonist* (Dresden, 1926); *Royal Palace* (Berlin, 1927) and, best known of all, *Der Zar lässt sich photographieren* (The Tsar Has His Photograph Taken), staged in Leipzig in 1928. Weill's meeting with the playwright Bertolt Brecht led to the creation in 1928 of *Die Dreigroschenoper* (The Threepenny Opera), premiered with great success in Berlin with a cast headed by the singer Lotte Lenya, whom Weill married in 1926. A much more complex work, both dramatically and musically, is the opera *Aufstieg und Fall der Stadt Mahagonny* (Rise and Fall of the City of Mahagonny, Leipzig, 1930), unquestionably the most productive outcome of Weill's collaboration with Brecht. This partnership was to spawn two more works, the didactic drama *Der Jasager* (The Man Who Says Yes, Berlin, 1930) and the ballet *Singspiel* "spectacle in nine scenes," *Die sieben Todsünden* (The Seven Deadly Sins, Paris, 1931), which marked the last time Weill and Brecht worked together. At the same time Weill had been composing *Die Bürgschaft* (The Guarantee, Berlin, 1932), harshly attacked by the Nazi press, and *Der Silbersee* (The Silver Lake, Leipzig, 1933). The menacing advent of Nazism prompted the composer to leave Germany, and after spending some time in Paris (where *Die sieben Todsünden* was produced), he emigrated to the United States in 1935. There he wrote *Domestic Tragedy*, *Street Scene* (New York, 1947), *Musical Tragedy*, *Lost in the Stars* (New York, 1949) and other musical comedies and dramas for theaters on Broadway.

WELKER, HARTMUT

(Welbert, Rhineland 1941)
German baritone. After studying music studies in Essen (these were interrupted and resumed again in 1970), he made his debut in 1975 in Aix-La-Chapelle (Renato in Verdi's *Un ballo in maschera*). He then joined the resident companies at the opera houses in Karlsruhe and Berlin (Deutsche Oper). His international appearances have included the Paris Opéra (Wagner's *Tristan und Isolde*, 1985), the Vienna Staatsoper (Wagner's *Der fliegende Holländer*, The Flying Dutchman, 1985), La Scala, Milan (Strauss's *Die Frau ohne Schatten*, 1986), the Teatro Regio in Turin (Wagner's *Das Rheingold*, 1986, and Berg's *Wozzeck*, 1989), the Teatro Comunale in Bologna, the Teatro San Carlo in Naples

Top: The Italian singer Domenico Modugno in *Die Dreigroschenoper* (The Threepenny Opera) by Kurt Weill, in a 1973 production directed by Giorgio Strehler.

Left: The German baritone Bernd Weikl.

(*Fidelio*, 1987) and Lyric Opera of Chicago (Ponchielli's *La Gioconda*, 1987). Welker is also an exceptional stage performer.

WELTING, RUTH

(Memphis, Tennessee 1949)
American soprano. After studying music in New York and in Rome with Luigi Ricci, she made her debut at the age of 22 in 1971 with New York City Opera as Blonde in Mozart's *Die Entführung aus dem Serail* (The Seraglio) and subsequently appeared there regularly, as Oscar in Verdi's *Un ballo in maschera*, Gilda in Verdi's *Rigoletto* and Olympia in Offenbach's *Les contes d'Hoffmann*. Her international career took her to Covent Garden (from 1975, in *Un ballo in maschera*, *Il barbiere di Siviglia* and Strauss's *Ariadne auf Naxos*), San Francisco Opera, the Paris Opéra (*Ariadne auf Naxos*, 1983), the Teatro Comunale in Florence (Donizetti's *La fille du régiment*) and the Metropolitan Opera in New York (*Les contes d'Hoffman*, 1989 and 1992). With the crowning quality of her *coloratura* soprano voice and brilliant dramatic gifts, Welting is especially admired in such roles as that of Marie (*La fille du régiment*), Olympia (*Les contes d'Hoffman*), Philine (Thomas's *Mignon*) and Lakmé in the opera by Delibes.

WENKEL, ORTRUN

(Buttstädt 1942)
German mezzo-soprano. She studied music at the Franz Liszt Hochschule in Weimar and at the Staatlichen Hochschule in Frankfurt. In 1964 she began her artistic career with concert appearances, particularly in baroque repertoire, and sang at a number of international Early Music festivals. In 1971, after completing her training with Elsa Cavelti, she turned to opera, making her debut as Orfeo (Gluck's *Orfeo ed Euridice*) in Heidelberg. She has been a guest artiste with the Bayerische Staatsoper in Munich and appeared frequently at the Bayreuth Festival where she sang Erda and First Norn in the famous Boulez-Chéreau production of the *Ring*, and she has also performed in the *Ring* cycle at the Metropolitan, New York.

WERTHER

Opera in three acts and five scenes by Jules Massenet (1842–1912) to a libretto by Edouard Blau, Paul Milliet and Georges Hartmann, from Goethe's Die Leiden des jungen Werthers *(The Sorrows of Young Werther). First performance: Vienna, Hofoper, 16 February 1892.*

The action takes place near Frankfurt between July and December 1772. Charlotte (mezzo-soprano), daughter of the Burgomaster (bass or baritone), is getting ready to go to a ball in the village. Among the guests who have arranged to meet at Charlotte's house before going on to the ball together is Werther (tenor), a sensitive and melancholy young man. When Charlotte appears, he is visibly affected by her beauty. These two leave together to catch up with the others, who have gone on ahead. Later, when Charlotte and Werther return, the Burgomaster tells Charlotte that her fiancé Albert (baritone) is now home after a long absence. Charlotte confesses to Werther that she promised her dying mother that she would marry Albert. This

Above: A scene from *Werther* by Jules Massenet.

Right: The mezzo-soprano Marie Rennard, who sang the role of Charlotte in the first performance of *Werther* in 1892.

revelation leaves Werther in despair. The scene changes to the square in Wetzlar, where the local people, including Charlotte and Albert, who have been married now for just three months, are celebrating the Pastor's golden wedding. Werther, watching from a distance, is approached by Albert, who tells him how much he respects him for the honourable way in which he had renounced his own love for Charlotte. But Werther cannot find peace, and after a last desperate conversation with Charlotte, he decides to leave. Some time later, Charlotte is sadly rereading Werther's letters. No longer able to contain herself, she bursts into floods of tears. At that moment Werther enters, pale and debilitated by illness. He recites some lines by Ossian, and Charlotte is so moved that in a moment of weakness she allows Werther to kiss her. She quickly recovers herself and runs off, saying that this is farewell forever. When Werther too has left the house, Albert returns. He reads a letter from Werther in which Werther asks to borrow his pistols before leaving on a long journey. A servant delivers the pistols to Werther, but Charlotte fears there is going to be a tragedy and runs to her beloved. It is too late. Werther is lying on the ground, mortally wounded. In despair, Charlotte tells him she has loved him ever since they first met. Consoled by her words, Werther dies.

Werther enjoyed great success in its day and remains, after *Manon*, the most often performed of Massenet's operas. The highly romantic nature of the story was perfectly suited to the sensibility of a composer such as Massenet, who loved not only moments of passion in his music but also the subtle lyricism of a love melody.

WINBERGH, GÖSTA

(Stockholm 1943)

Swedish tenor. He studied singing in Stockholm with Martin Oehaman, Hjördis Schymberg and Erik Saedén. After completing his training at the Stockholm Opera School, he made his debut as Rodolfo (Puccini's *La bohème*) in Gothenburg. He then joined the resident company of the Royal Opera in Stockholm (1973–80) and also appeared at the Drottningholm Festival (*Così fan tutte*, *Don Giovanni*). Since 1980 he has pursued an international career, singing at the Glyndebourne Festival in Mozart's *Die Entführung aus dem Serail* (The Seraglio, 1980), as regular guest artist at the Zurich Opernhaus (from 1981), at the Grand Théâtre in Geneva (Strauss's *Salome*, 1983), the Salzburg Festival (Mozart's *Die Zauberflöte*, The Magic Flute, 1984), La Scala, Milan (*Die Zauberflöte*, 1985 and 1987; Donizetti's *L'elisir d'amore*, 1988; Mozart's *La clemenza di Tito* and *Idomeneo*, 1990; Gluck's *Iphigénie en Tauride*, 1992). Winbergh's fine voice and musicianship has brought him particular acclaim as a Mozart singer.

WINDGASSEN, WOLFGANG

(Annemasse, Haute-Savoie 1914–Stuttgart 1974)

German tenor. He made his debut in Pforzheim in 1941 (Alvaro in Verdi's *La forza del destino*). His career was interrupted by the war, but he resumed it in 1945 with the Stuttgart Opera, which he directed from 1972 until his death. In 1951 he appeared for the first time at the Bayreuth Festival (*Parsifal*) and sang there regularly, until 1970. As one of the most highly acclaimed of Wagner singers, Windgassen strengthened his reputation with appearances at leading international opera houses, including Covent Garden (1955), La Scala, Milan (1952), the Metropolitan Opera, New York (1957), and the Opéra in Paris (1966–68)

WINKLER, HERMANN

(Duisburg 1936)

German tenor. He studied at the Conservatory in Hanover and appeared at the opera houses in Bielefeld (where his debut was in Pfitzner's *Palestrina*) and Zurich. He made his name from performances at leading opera houses in Germany and Austria, from the Vienna Staatsoper to the Festivals at Munich and Bayreuth (Wagner's *Parsifal*) and Salzburg (Mozart's *Idomeneo* and Beethoven's *Fidelio*). His international career has taken him to the Opéra in Paris (Strauss's *Salome*, 1964), Lyric Opera of Chicago (Mozart's *Don Giovanni*, 1980), Covent Garden (Berg's *Wozzeck*, 1984) and the Teatro Comunale in Bologna (Wagner's *Das Rheingold*, 1987). In 1981 he sang in the first performance of Cerha's opera *Baal* at the Salzburg Festival.

WINZING, UTE

(Wuppertal 1936)

German soprano. She studied at the Wuppertal Conservatory and began her career with the Lübeck Opera (1968–71), the Wuppertal Opera (1971–76) and at the opera house in Hanover, where she made her name in Wagner and Strauss roles. She then pursued a brilliant international career with appearances at the Vienna Staatsoper, the Teatro Colón in Buenos Aires, the Opéra in Paris (*Die Walküre*, 1977, *Tristan und Isolde*, 1985) and the Metropolitan Opera, New York (Strauss's *Elektra*, 1984). Her repertoire also includes Beethoven's *Fidelio*, Wagner's *Parsifal*, Strauss's *Die Frau ohne Schatten* and Puccini's *Turandot*.

WIXELL, INGVAR

(Lulea 1931)

Swedish baritone. A pupil of Dagmar Gustafson at the Academy of Music in Stockholm, he made his debut in Gavle in 1952. In 1955 he sang Papageno in Mozart's *Die Zauberflöte* (The Magic Flute) at the Stockholm Rikstheater and subsequently joined the resident company at the Royal Opera (from 1956). From 1967 he made regular appearances with the Deutsche Oper in Berlin (still singing there as recently as 1989). Engagements followed at leading international opera

Above: The tenor Gösta Winbergh as Tamino in *Die Zauberflöte* (The Magic Flute).

venues, including the Bayreuth Festival (Wagner's *Lohengrin*, 1971), the Metropolitan Opera, New York (Verdi's *Rigoletto*, 1973), Covent Garden (*Simon Boccanegra*, 1971), the Salzburg Festival (Mozart's *Le nozze di Figaro*, 1966–68) and La Scala, Milan (Puccini's *Tosca*, 1980). His performing skills, musicianship and variety in phrasing have enabled him to build up an extremely wide repertoire from Mozart to Puccini (he has sung Scarpia in *Tosca* at the major international opera houses) and Strauss (*Salome*).

WOLF, HUGO

(Windischgraz, Styria, now Slovenj Gradec, Slovenia 1860–Vienna 1903)

Austrian composer. He began studying music with his father and then attended the Vienna Conservatory (1875). He left following differences with the director and continued his music studies by himself. After becoming a music critic (1884), he decided to devote all his energies to composition, especially *Lieder*, of which he was one of the greatest composers. He wrote one opera, *Der Corregidor* (1896), while a year later he set to work on another, *Manuel Venegas*, but a worsening of his mental illness interrupted its composition. He became a patient in an asylum in Vienna and died there five years later.

Above: The Swedish baritone Ingvar Wixell.

Right: The Italian composer Ermanno Wolf-Ferrari.

Top right: Sketch by O. Strnad for *Wozzeck* by Alban Berg.

WOLF-FERRARI, ERMANNO

(Venice 1876–1948)

Italian composer. He studied painting and music in Rome and then in Munich at the Akademie der Tonkunst, where his teacher was Josef Rheinberger. After periods in Milan and in the United States (1911–12), he settled in Venice and concentrated on composing. In 1939 he was offered a post teaching composition at the Salzburg Mozarteum and then spent time in Germany until 1946. After a brief stay in Zurich, he returned to Venice, where he died in 1948. His operas have links with the plays of Carlo Goldoni, several of whose comedies he used as libretti. Among the most successful of these were his musical versions of *Le donne curiose* (1903), *I quatro rusteghi* (1906), *La vedova scaltra* (1931) and *Il campiello* (1936), the last of which is considered to be his masterpiece. Although he stood apart from prevailing "realist" theories, he used unquestionably dramatic subjects for his operas *I gioielli della Madonna* (1911) and *Sly* (1927). Mention should also be made of his *Il segreto di Susanna* (1909), *L'amore medico* (1913) and *La dama boba* (1937). As well as his operas, Wolf-Ferrari wrote a number of symphonic and chamber works.

WOLFF, BEVERLY

(Georgia 1928)

American mezzo-soprano. After becoming an excellent trumpet player (she was first trumpet of the Atlanta Symphony Orchestra), she discovered her true vocation as a singer and attended the Philadelphia Academy of Vocal Arts. In 1952 she won the Youth Auditions of the Philadelphia Orchestra. In the same year she sang in a CBS Television production of Bernstein's *Trouble in Tahiti*, and in 1961 she made her debut with New York City Opera (as Cherubino in Mozart's *Le nozze di Figaro*), returning there to sing Sesto (Handel's *Giulio Cesare*, 1966), Sara (Donizetti's *Roberto Devereux*) and numerous other roles, including Adalgisa (Bellini's *Norma*) and Amneris (Verdi's *Aida*).

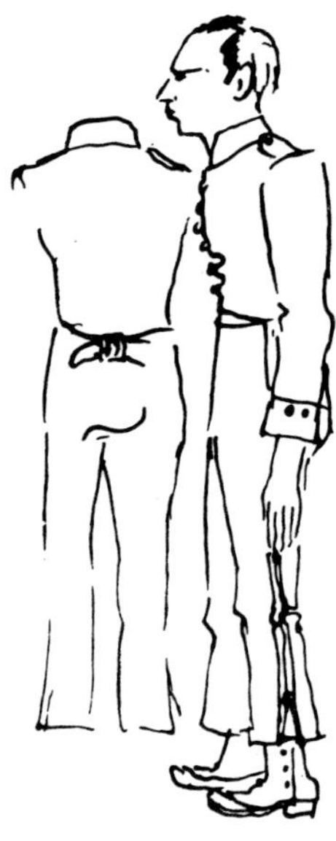

WOZZECK

Opera in three acts and 15 scenes by Alban Berg (1885–1935), to the composer's own libretto, after Georg Büchner's play Woyzeck. *First performance: Berlin, Staatsoper, 14 December 1925.*

The action takes place in Germany around the year 1836. Wozzeck (baritone) is working as a batman to the Captain (tenor), who misses no opportunity to lecture and chastise him because Wozzeck is living with a former prostitute, Marie (soprano), who has borne him a child. While out collecting wood with his friend Andres (tenor), Wozzeck is alarmed by strange sounds and visions. Still suffering from these hallucinations, he goes home to Marie. Wozzeck now suspects that Marie, who is attracted by the Drum Major (tenor), has become the latter's mistress. After losing control and shouting, Wozzeck hurries away to consult a half-mad Doctor (bass), who uses him as a guinea-pig in his experiments. Made suspicious again of Marie, this time by a pair of earrings she cannot explain but which are actually a gift from the Drum Major, and by some remarks made by the Captain and the Doctor, Wozzeck becomes increasingly convinced that Marie has betrayed him. He threatens her, and she reacts violently. The scene changes to a tavern where a group of soldiers and young men and

women are dancing, and Wozzeck catches sight of Marie with the Drum Major. While these two are dancing, a Fool (tenor) comes up to Wozzeck and whispers in his ear, "I smell blood." The same night, in the garrison guard's dormitory at the barracks, Wozzeck is mocked and beaten up by the Drum Major. By now consumed with jealousy, Wozzeck takes Marie to a pond, where he kills her in a mounting rage. Then he goes back to the tavern, and while the young men and women are dancing a polka, he makes advances to Margret (contralto), but when she discovers bloodstains on his clothes, she runs off in terror. Wozzeck hurries away from the tavern and returns to the pond side to look for the knife he had used to kill Marie. He finds it and throws it into the water, but then worries that it has not sunk deep enough and so wades in to throw it farther out and wash the blood off himself. But in his madness he believes the water to be blood and becomes so crazed by the thought that he drowns himself. Outside Marie's house, as the Child (treble), Marie's son, plays on his toy horse, the other children call out to him, "Your mother is dead." He does not understand and continues to ride his toy, then follows the others.

Berg attended a performance of Büchner's play *Woyzeck* at a Vienna theater and was so impressed by it that he decided to turn it into an opera. The task was long and laborious: it took him from 1914 to 1917 to complete the libretto and from 1917 to 1921 to write the music. It was not until 1925 that the opera was finally staged. Despite this protracted gestation period, the musical language of *Wozzeck* is extremely consistent and concise. Every page of the score is the result of Berg's thorough assimilation of the musical style which originated with Schoenberg, and which Berg's own imagination and poetic sensibility worked with and made his own. Rejecting the stylistic features of traditional opera, he does not yet make use of the 12-note row, choosing instead an atonal music not wholly devoid of tonal moments.

WUNDERLICH, FRITZ

(Kusel, Rhine Palatinate 1930–Heidelberg 1966)

German tenor. He first had music lessons with his father, a conductor, and his mother, a violinist. He then studied with Margarete von Winterfeld at the Musikhochschule in Freiburg, making his debut in the school's theater in 1954 as Tamino in Mozart's *Die Zauberflöte* (The Magic Flute). He was engaged by the Stuttgart Opera, with whom his first opera, in 1955, was again *Die Zauberflöte*. He went on to join the companies of the opera houses in Frankfurt (1958–60) and Munich (1960–66) and appeared from 1958 at the Salzburg Festival, at the Vienna Staatsoper (from 1962), Covent Garden (Mozart's *Don Giovanni*, 1965), the Edinburgh Festival (*Die Zauberflöte*, 1966) and the Maggio Musicale Festival in Florence (Mozart's *Die Entführung aus dem Serail*, The Seraglio, 1958). He took part in the first performances of Orff's *Oedipus der Tyrann* (Stuttgart, 1950) and Egk's *Die Verlobung in San Domingo* (Wedding at San Domingo, Munich, 1963). One of the most gifted German tenors of his generation with exceptional technique and musicianship, Wunderlich died young, as a result of a fall.

A scene from *Wozzeck* by Alban Berg, first performed in Berlin in 1925.

X Y Z

XERXES
See Serse

YAKAR, RACHEL
(Lyons 1938)
French soprano. A pupil of Germaine Lubin at the Paris Conservatoire, she made her debut in 1963 in Strasbourg. In 1964 she joined the Düsseldorf Opera, where she specialized in opera of the seventeenth and eighteenth centuries. Her repertoire, however, ranges much wider, and has included performances of Gilda (Verdi's *Rigoletto*) and Micaela (Bizet's *Carmen*) at the Opéra in Paris (1970), Donna Elvira (Mozart's *Don Giovanni*) in Munich (1974) and at Glyndebourne (1977) and Freia in Wagner's *Das Rheingold* at Bayreuth (1976). She has sung the role of Mélisande in Debussy's opera on several occasions. With her complete mastery of baroque ornamentation and her elegant, expressive phrasing, Yakar has given distinguished performances in operas by Monteverdi (*Orfeo* and *L'incoronazione di Poppea*), Lully (*Armide*), Leclair (*Scylla et Glaucus*), Rameau (*Les Indes galantes* and *Hippolyte et Aricie*) and Handel (*Admeto*).

YOUNG, BASIL ALEXANDER
(London 1920)
British tenor. He studied at the Royal College of Music in London and made his debut at the Edinburgh Festival in 1950 as Scaramuccio (Strauss's *Ariadne auf Naxos*). He sang at the Glyndebourne Festival (Mozart's *Così fan tutte*, 1953, etc.) and at Covent Garden in Smetana's *Prodaná nevěsta* (The Bartered Bride) in 1955, where he returned regularly in an extremely varied repertoire ranging from Monteverdi (*Orfeo*) and Handel (*Hercules* and *Tamerlano*) to Rossini (*Il barbiere di Siviglia*, *La Cenerentola*), Strauss (*Arabella*) and Stravinsky (*The Rake's Progress*). His reputation rests on outstanding stylistic gifts and skill in characterization.

ZAÏDE
Opera in two acts by Wolfgang Amadeus Mozart (1756–1791), to a libretto by Johann Andreas Schachtner after Das Serail, *a* Singspiel *with music by Joseph von Friebert. Mozart's score was composed in 1779 but left unfinished, and the opera was never performed.*

The action takes place in Turkey. A young nobleman, Gomatz (tenor), is taken prisoner by the Sultan Soliman (tenor), but the beauty and nobility of his appearance make him attractive to the Sultan's favourite, Zaïde (soprano), who decides to help him escape. Allazim (bass), one of the Sultan's servants, betrays his master by assisting the couple. But the plan fails, and all three are captured and sentenced to death. In a bid to save himself and his two companions, Allazim recounts the long story of how some time ago he had saved Soliman's life, and as a result it comes to light that Zaïde and Gomatz are the Sultan's own children. Soliman is much affected and orders them all to be released.

This opera was intended for Böhm's travelling opera company, in the hope that they could perform it in Vienna. The death of the Empress, however, prevented the work from being staged, and *Zaïde* was left unfinished (the overture and final chorus were missing). The subject had appealed to Mozart because it combined an exotic setting, which lent itself to a particular kind of musical colouring, with romantic situations, offering him the chance to explore a wide range of expressive possibilities. *Zaïde* can therefore be seen as a precursor of *Die Entführung aus dem Serail* (The Seraglio).

ZAIRA
Opera in two acts by Vincenzo Bellini (1801–1835), to a libretto by Felice Romani, from Voltaire's tragedy Zaïre. *First performance: Parma, Teatro Ducale, 16 May 1829.*

The action takes place in Jerusalem between the fourteenth and the sixteenth century. In the harem, the Sultan Orosmane (bass) is about to marry his favourite, Zaira (soprano), orphaned daughter of Christian parents. The vizir Corasmino (tenor), however, does not approve of the Sultan, a firm defender of the Islamic faith, marrying an infidel. A French knight, Nerestano (mezzo-soprano), arrives at the palace. Previously held prisoner by the Sultan, Nerestano had been released and sent to France to ransom Zaira (before Orosmane fell in love with her) and other French knights being held prisoner by the Sultan. Nerestano informs Orosmane that France is ready to negotiate for the prisoners' release. Orosmane announces he will free all the prisoners except two: the old prince Lusignano (baritone), whom the Sultan has condemned to death, and Zaira. But Zaira appeals to the Sultan to spare Lusignano, and he does so. Just as he is being set free, the old prince is overcome with emotion: he recognizes Nerestano and Zaira as his own children from many years ago, before he was separated from them never to hear of them again. He tells Zaira that he disapproves of her marrying the Sultan. Troubled by her father's stern words, Zaira sadly says goodbye to Nerestano as he prepares to return to France. Unseen, Corasmino watches them together, and when he sees them tenderly embrace, he suspects that they are lovers. Corasmino believes his suspicions are confirmed when, not long after this, Zaira asks Orosmane to postpone their wedding. Though unaware of what has been happening, the Sultan senses that Zaira is keeping something from him and is stunned when Corasmino brings him a letter in which Nerestano asks Zaira to meet him secretly. The vizir advises a distraught Orosmane to have the letter delivered to Zaira and keep a watch on her movements. Nerestano and Zaira meet, not knowing that Orosmane and Corasmino are lying in wait for them. Suddenly the Sultan comes rushing out of the darkness and stabs Zaira. As she dies, she tells him that Nerestano is her brother. In despair, Orosmane takes his own life.

Staged to mark the opening of the Teatro Ducale in Parma, *Zaira* was a disaster, despite the fact that the cast included the soprano Henriette Méric-Lalande (as Zaira), who had already sung the lead in Bellini's opera *La straniera*, and the bass Luigi Lablache (Orosmane). The composer himself had doubted that it would be a success: the opera had been written in too much of a hurry for Bellini to develop the characters and situations. He incorporated much of the musical material from *Zaira* into *I Capuleti e i Montecchi*, which was a great success the following year. *Zaira* itself has since proved that it possesses an enduring quality, clearly in evidence when the opera was revived at the Teatro Massimo Bellini in Catania in 1976 with Renata Scotto as Zaira and in 1990 with Katia Ricciarelli.

ZAJICK, DOLORA

(Reno, Nevada 1952)

American mezzo-soprano of Polish origin. She studied at the University of Nevada and with Ted Puffer, artistic director of Nevada Opera. She completed her music studies with Helen Vanni and Lou Galtiero at the Manhattan School of Music in New York. Winner of the 1982 International Tchaikovsky Competition in Moscow, she appeared with San Francisco Opera in 1986 as Azucena in Verdi's *Il trovatore*, a role she has sung at some of the leading international opera houses and also on her debut at the Metropolitan Opera in New York (1988), at Lyric Opera of Chicago (1988), the Vienna Staatsoper (1989) and the Maggio Musicale Festival in Florence (1990). A resident member of the company at the Metropolitan (*Aida*, 1989, *Don Carlos*, 1992, *Il trovatore*, 1992–93), she has also appeared at the Baths of Caracalla in Rome (*Aida*, 1988), the Arena in Verona (*Aida*, 1989, 1990 and 1992), the Teatro San Carlo in Naples (Cilèa's *Adriana Lecouvreur*, 1992), La Scala, Milan (*Don Carlos*, 1992), and other major international opera houses. As one of the finest of international opera singers, Zajick is admired for the range of her voice across the entire register, and her consistency in delivery, as well as for her considerable dramatic gifts.

ZAMPIERI, MARA

(Padua 1949)

Italian soprano. She studied at the Conservatorio in Padua and in 1972 won a singing competition in Pavia, the city in which she made her debut the same year. She won first prize in the 1975 Verdi Voices competition in Parma, and in 1976 appeared at the Teatro dell'Opera in Rome in Tchaikovsky's *Eugene Onegin*. During the 1977–78 season

Left: The American soprano Dolora Zajick in a scene from *Don Carlos* by Verdi, in a 1992 production at La Scala.

Above: The Italian soprano Mara Zampieri.

she sang at La Scala, Milan (Verdi's *I masnadieri, Un ballo in maschera, Il trovatore, Don Carlos*), in 1978 at the opera houses in Hamburg and Munich (*Don Carlos*), in 1979 at the Vienna Staatsoper (Mercadante's *Il giuramento*) and in 1980 at the Teatro San Carlo in Naples (Puccini's *Manon Lescaut*). Concentrating her career mainly in Germany and Austria, Zampieri compensates for a somewhat uneven delivery and technique by having a remarkable performing temperament in the more demanding dramatic soprano roles. Her more recent appearances have included Catalani's *La Wally* (Bregenz, 1990), Puccini's *La fanciulla del West* (La Scala, 1991), Verdi's *Macbeth* (Reggio Emilia, 1992), Verdi's *Don Carlos*, Strauss's *Salome* and Donizetti's *Maria Stuarda* (Vienna Staatsoper, 1992).

ZANCANARO, GIORGIO

(Verona 1939)
Italian baritone. In 1969 he won first prize in the Verdi Voices competition held in Busseto, which led to his 1970 debut as Riccardo (Bellini's *I puritani*) at the Teatro Nuovo in Milan. He then appeared at the major Italian opera houses until 1977, the year in which he sang in Verdi's *Il trovatore* in Hamburg, a performance which launched his international career. Engagements followed, from 1978, at Covent Garden (Verdi's *Don Carlos*, Giordano's *Andrea Chénier*, Donizetti's *Lucia di Lammermoor*) and with the San Francisco Opera (Gounod's *Faust*, 1977). He has made regular appearances there, in *Falstaff* (1981), in *Lucia di Lammermoor*, Puccini's *Madama Butterfly* (1986), Verdi's *Nabucco* (1987 and 1988), Mascagni's *Cavalleria rusticana* (1988), Rossini's *Guillaume Tell* (1988), Verdi's *Luisa Miller* (1989), *Les vêpres siciliennes* (1989) and *Attila* (1991). He has also sung at the Opéra in Paris (*Madama Butterfly*, 1983), the Vienna Staatsoper (from 1985), the Maggio Musicale Festival in Florence and a number of other international opera venues. Zancanaro's reputation is mainly based on his performances in Verdi operas, distinguished by fine timbre, consistency of delivery across the whole range, radiance in the upper register and impeccable thoroughness in matters of style.

Above: The Italian baritone Giorgio Zancanaro in Verdi's *Simon Boccanegra*.

Right: The composer Riccardo Zandonai.

ZANDONAI, RICCARDO

(Sacco di Rovereto 1883–Pesaro 1944)
Italian composer. He studied in Rovereto with Gianferrari and in Pesaro, where he was a pupil of Pietro Mascagni, with whom he did not enjoy good relations. He was noticed by the publisher Ricordi, who saw him as Puccini's successor, and his opera *Il grillo del focolare* (The Cricket on the Hearth) paved the way for a collaboration between Zandonai and Ricordi. Then came *Conchita* (1911), *Melenis* (1912) and *Francesca da Rimini* (1914), which remains his best-known opera and the one most often performed, followed by *La via della finestra* (1919), *Giulietta e Romeo* (1922), *I cavalieri di Ekebù* (1925), *Giuliano* (1928), *Una partita* (1933), *La farsa amorosa* (1933) and *Il bacio*, which he left unfinished and was completed by Meucci. Zandonai's vast musical output includes symphonic, chamber, sacred and film music.

ZAR LÄSST SICH PHOTOGRAPHIEREN, DER

(The Tsar Has His Photograph Taken)
Opera in one act by Kurt Weill (1900–1950), to a libretto by Georg Kaiser. First performance: Leipzig, Neues Theater, 18 February 1928.

The action takes place in Paris in 1914. The Tsar (baritone) is on a visit to the city, and a group of anarchists has planned to assassinate him. When they learn he is on his way to the studio of the well-known photographer, Angèle (soprano), to have his photograph taken, they abduct Angèle and replace her with a woman anarchist, the fake Angèle (soprano). But the Tsar is a formidable flatterer: he not only besieges the young woman with his attentions but even wants to take a picture of her. She then discovers that the police are about to arrive, and so as not to be caught and arrested, she and her fellow-conspirators have to abandon their plan and escape.

Der Zar boldly satirizes the power, method and content of anarchist conspiracies. It is developed along the lines of an operetta, with obvious references to silent films in its incredible situations and the immediacy of its humour.

ZAR UND ZIMMERMANN

(Tsar and Carpenter)

Opera in three acts by Gustav Albert Lortzing (1801–1851) to the composer's own libretto, after the play by Mélesville, Merle and Boirie. First performance: Leipzig, Stadttheater, 22 December 1837.

The action takes place in the coastal town of Saardam, Holland, in 1698. Under the name of Peter Michaelov, Tsar Peter I (baritone) has obtained employment in a naval dockyard in order to learn modern shipbuilding skills. Another Russian, the army deserter Peter Ivanov (tenor) is working in the same dockyard. He is in love with Marie (soprano), the niece of Van Bett (bass), the town Burgomaster, and confides in Michaelov. But the Tsar is troubled by his own problems: his envoy Admiral Lefort (bass) has just informed him that riots have broken out in Russia which threaten the country's security, and he must therefore return home at once. Van Bett, who has heard that one of the carpenters is a foreigner, will allow no one to leave the dockyard. He is then confused to learn from the British ambassador Lord Syndham (bass) that the Tsar is in Saardam incognito. The Burgomaster suspects Ivanov of being the Tsar, but the Marquis de Chateauneuf (tenor), the French envoy, has meanwhile discovered that Peter I has been posing as the carpenter Michaelov. An emissary (bass) arrives from Amsterdam bearing a decree that rules that any foreigner unable to give clear proof of identity is to be arrested. This pleases Van Bett, because now it will be possible to investigate the two Peters. Meanwhile Michaelov asks Marie to behave as though Ivanov is the Tsar, at least for an hour. In return, he will do what he can to ensure their happiness. Celebrations begin in honour of Saardam's illustrious guest, and then there is the sound of cannonfire from the quayside and the real Tsar is seen preparing to leave. Ivanov then opens a letter left by Michaelov and finds inside that he is appointed to the post of imperial superintendent and is granted permission to marry Marie. From on board ship, Peter offers his thanks for Saardam's warm hospitality while the crowds wave him goodbye.

The most famous of Lortzing's operas, *Zar und Zimmermann* has enjoyed enormous success since it was first performed and is a permanent fixture in German opera house repertories. The work's distinctive features include Lortzing's amusing characterization of Van Bett and an extremely accomplished melodic line. Wagner himself was definitely inspired by both this opera and the one which came after it, *Hans Sachs*, composed in 1840, when he came to write *Die Meistersinger von Nürnberg*. Van Bett became the model for Wagner's Beckmesser, the wise Tsar Peter was transformed into Hans Sachs, and the two lovers Peter and Marie provided the inspiration for Walther and Eva.

ZAUBERFLÖTE, DIE

(The Magic Flute)

Opera in two acts by Wolfgang Amadeus Mozart (1756–1791), to a libretto by Johann Emanuel Schikaneder. First performance: Vienna, Theater auf der Wieden, 30 September 1791.

The action takes place in an imaginary Ancient Egypt. The landscape is mountainous, and there is a temple in the near distance. Prince Tamino (tenor) enters, pursued by a serpent. The exertion has been too much for him, and he collapses unconscious. Three Ladies (two sopranos and a contralto) emerge from the temple, kill the serpent and then withdraw. Tamino recovers, is astonished to see the serpent lying there dead, and believes he owes his life to a strange-looking figure dressed in feathers, Papageno (baritone). Papageno does not

Drawing by L. Damiano for *Der Zar lässt sich photographieren* by Kurt Weill.

deny it but is promptly punished for telling such a lie by the three Ladies, who reappear and seal his mouth with a padlock. At the same time they show Tamino a portrait of Pamina (soprano), daughter of the Queen of the Night (soprano). Pamina is being held captive by Sarastro (bass), High Priest of Isis, and Tamino is so overcome by her beauty that he offers to rescue her. The Ladies then give him a flute that has magic powers, release Papageno's padlock and order him to accompany Tamino to Sarastro's palace. In order to avoid the advances of the Moor Monostatos (tenor), captain of the guard Pamina has attempted to escape, only to be recaptured by him. Monostatos flees in terror at the sight of Papageno, who then reveals to Pamina that he and a young prince have been sent by the Queen of the Night to set her free. Meanwhile, Tamino is being led through a wood by three Genii (two sopranos and a contralto) and reaches the temple of Isis, where a priest (bass) explains to him that Sarastro is not a cruel magician and has acted from the best of motives in removing Pamina from her mother's influence. When Sarastro appears, Pamina asks him to forgive her for trying to escape, and Sarastro declares he is ready to offer her in marriage to a knight who would be worthy of her, but he refuses to allow her to return to her mother. Tamino is brought in by Monostatos, and the two young people throw themselves into each other's arms, while Monostatos is punished. Tamino will have to undergo three ordeals, after which he will be able to join the ranks of the initiates and marry Pamina. The first is a test of silence: it means that when Pamina comes in, her beloved Tamino is not able to speak to her. She is so upset by this that she attempts to kill herself. The three Genii stay her hand, reassuring her that Tamino still loves her. Now Tamino has other tests to face, the ordeal by fire and the ordeal by water. Pamina is at his side and advises him to play the magic flute. This enables them to survive both ordeals. Papageno, who has had to confront the same trials as Tamino, also meets the woman he is destined to marry, Papagena (soprano). Meanwhile the Queen of the Night, Monostatos and the three Ladies try to gain entry to the temple to kill Sarastro, but they are driven back. The opera ends in the Temple of the Sun with Sarastro, surrounded by his priests and Tamino and Pamina, celebrating the victory of the Sun over darkness.

The plot of *Die Zauberflöte* brings together popular fairy-tale elements and themes drawn from the ideals and ceremonial of Freemasonry (of which Mozart and Schikaneder were disciples), which enriched the inner meaning of the work. At its premiere *Die Zauberflöte* was not understood, but later on audiences received it with increasing enthusiasm. Within a year the opera had enjoyed more than 100 performances, but Mozart had died not long after the first night.

Right: Papageno and Papagena in *Die Zauberflöte* (The Magic Flute) by Mozart.

Above: The ordeal by fire in *Die Zauberflöte* (The Magic Flute), in a production at La Scala.

ZAZÀ

Opera in four acts by Ruggero Leoncavallo (1857–1919), to the composer's own libretto, after the play of the same name by Simòn and Berton. First performance: Milan, Teatro Lirico, 10 November 1900.

The action takes place in France towards the end of the nineteenth century. Given her chance by the impresario Cascart (baritone), Zazà (soprano) is enjoying a triumphant success as a music-hall singer in a theater in Saint-Étienne. One evening she meets Milio Dufresne (tenor) there and falls in love with him, but he behaves coldly towards her. Zazà, however, succeeds in making him confess his feelings for her, which he had until then kept under control. Zazà and Milio become lovers, but then comes the day when Milio has to leave for America for a long sojourn. Time passes. Cascart tells Zazà he has seen Dufresne with another woman and advises her to resign herself to this and return to her career, which she had given up for love. But Zazà is mad with jealousy and wants to find out the truth. She goes to the other woman's house, where she sees enough to confirm Cascart's story of what had been going on, and her discovery is made all the more painful when she catches sight of little Totò (treble), Milio's daughter. Zazà knows that she can never destroy the happiness of a family and turns away in despair. Cascart tries in vain to comfort her. All that Zazà wants is to have a final talk with Milio. A turbulent meeting between them takes place. Zazà pretends to have told Milio's wife about their relationship, and Milio explodes with anger. He cruelly insults Zazà and makes it clear to her that he loves his wife. Faced with Milio's attitude, Zazà assures him that she was lying, his wife knows nothing, and so he can go back to her with a clear conscience. Dufresne is confused and wants to embrace Zazà, but she pushes him away.

Leoncavallo's most successful opera after *I pagliacci*, *Zazà* found a great advocate in the soprano Mafalda Favero, whose celebrated gifts as a singer and actress were well suited to such a demanding leading role.

ZEANI, VIRGINIA

(Solovastru, Transylvania 1928)

Stage name of Virginia Zehan, Romanian soprano, naturalized Italian. A pupil of Lucia Anghel and Lydia Lipowska in Bucharest, she went on to complete her training in Milan (1947). In 1948 she made her debut at the Teatro Duse in Bologna as Violetta (Verdi's *La traviata*), later to become one of her most highly acclaimed roles. She sang at the Teatro Comunale in Florence (Bellini's *I puritani*, 1952), La Scala, Milan (Handel's *Giulio Cesare*, 1956, the world premiere of Poulenc's *Les dialogues des Carmélites*, 1957), the Teatro San Carlo in Naples (Massenet's *Thaïs*, 1959), Covent Garden (*La traviata*, 1960), the Teatro dell'Opera in Rome (Verdi's *Otello*, 1962, Rossini's *Otello*, 1964) and at other major international opera houses, drawing on a vast repertoire, from roles for *coloratura* lyric soprano to Puccini (*Manon Lescaut*, *Tosca*, *Madama Butterfly*) and composers belonging to the so-called "Young School," including Mascagni (*Il piccolo Marat*), Giordano (*Fedora*) and Cilèa (*Adriana Lecouvreur*). She has also appeared in operas by Busoni (*Turandot*), Menotti (*Il console*) and other contemporary composers. Married to the bass Nicola Rossi-Lemeni, she retired from the stage in 1978 to devote herself to teaching.

ZEDDA, ALBERTO

(Milan 1928)

Italian conductor and musicologist. He studied music with Alceo Galliera, Antonino Votto and Carlo Maria Giulini and made his debut in Milan in 1956 conducting Rossini's *Il barbiere di Siviglia* for the Polytechnic Chamber Group of Milan. He has conducted at the principal opera houses in Italy and elsewhere (Covent Garden, Vienna Staatsoper, etc.). As a specialist in early nineteenth-century Italian opera, he has been particularly associated with Rossini. He has been responsible for critical editions of *Il barbiere di Siviglia*, *La Cenerentola*, *La gazza ladra* and *Semiramide*. He revised and presented *Semiramide* for the first time in its entirety at the Rossini Opera Festival in Pesaro (1992), where he held the post of artistic advisor. In 1992 he was appointed artistic director at La Scala, Milan.

ZEDNIK, HEINZ

(Vienna 1940)

Austrian tenor. He studied with Maria Wissman and at the Conservatory in Vienna, making his debut in 1964 as Trabucco in Verdi's *La forza del destino*. He joined the company of the Vienna Staatsoper and appeared in the world premieres of von Einem's *Der Besuch der alten Dame* (The Visit) in 1971, *Kabale und Liebe* (Love and Intrigue) in 1976 and Penderecki's *Die schwarze Maske* (The Black Mask) in 1986. He sings regularly at the Salzburg Festival (premiere of Berio's *Un re in ascolto*, 1984), the Bayreuth Festival (from 1970), the Metropolitan Opera in New York (from 1981), where he has performed the roles of Pedrillo in Mozart's *Die Entführung aus dem Serail* (The Seraglio, 1988) and Mime (Wagner's *Ring*, 1989–90 and 1992–93), and at other international opera venues. He has won particular acclaim for his outstanding gifts as a stage performer, notably in character roles (The Captain in Berg's *Wozzeck*, Mime and Loge in the *Ring*).

Left: Costume design for Papageno in *Die Zauberflöte* (The Magic Flute).

Above: Title page to the libretto of *Zazà* by Leoncavallo.

ZELMIRA

Opera in two acts by Gioachino Rossini (1792–1868), to a libretto by Andrea Leone Tottola, after the tragedy Zelmire *by de Belloy. First performance: Naples, Teatro San Carlo, 16 February 1822.*

Azor, having usurped the throne of Mytilene, has been murdered in his sleep by an unknown hand. The assassin was actually Prince Antenore (tenor), aided by his faithful servant Leucippo (bass). Antenore accuses the Princess Zelmira (soprano) of the crime and proclaims himself Azor's successor. Zelmira, daughter of the lawful king, Polidoro (bass), has already been blamed for the disappearance of her father and is now blamed for the death of Azor, who had invaded the kingdom because the Princess rejected his proposal of marriage in favour of Prince Ilo (tenor). But Zelmira is completely innocent: she has not killed her father but hidden him in the vaults where the ancient kings of Lesbos have their tombs. Ilo, who has been away from Lesbos for a long time and is therefore unaware of these serious developments, returns to Mytilene and is shocked by the accusations levelled at his wife. Antenore and Leucippo have meanwhile decided they will also kill Ilo and his son. But Zelmira has already taken the child to safety. Still troubled by what he has learned, and unable to find his son, Ilo is assailed by dark premonitions and, no longer able to cope with the emotional strain, collapses in a chair as though unconscious. Leucippo is keen to take advantage of this and attempts to stab Ilo, but Zelmira appears and wrests the dagger from Leucippo's grasp. Leucippo wakes Ilo and turns the charge of attempted murder on to Zelmira, who is still holding the dagger. Zelmira is put into prison, from where she sends her husband a message in which she professes her innocence and tells him that Polidoro is alive, but the letter is intercepted by Leucippo. Zelmira is released and followed, while the message is delivered to Ilo. Ilo goes down into the royal tombs and meets Polidoro, who leaves him in no doubt as to Zelmira's innocence and courage. Ilo goes off in search of help. Then Zelmira comes in, not realizing she is being shadowed by Antenore and Leucippo, and embraces her old father. At this point the pursuers reveal themselves and capture the pair. It seems as if all hope has run out for Zelmira and Polidoro when suddenly Ilo arrives with his forces, disarms and imprisons Antenore and Leucippo, is reunited with Zelmira and his son and restores Polidoro to the throne.

Zelmira is the last of Rossini's Neapolitan operas. Its was an outstanding success, for which some of the credit must go to the distinguished cast of singers, including Isabella Colbran (Zelmira), Giovanni David (Ilo) and Andrea Nozzari (Antenore). The fact that the libretto is rather too long is partly compensated for by the music, which contains some very inspired lyrical passages, such as the duet between Zelmira and Emma in Act I and the scene in the vaults in Act II with its incisive style and dramatic tension. The solo parts are very difficult, especially the tenor roles, and this is why *Zelmira* is seldom performed. The most recent revivals were in Venice in 1988 (concert version) and at the Teatro dell'Opera in Rome in 1989.

Top: A 1906 illustration for *Zolotoy Pyetushok* by Rimsky-Korsakov.

Above: The Austrian tenor Heinz Zednik.

ZENO, APOSTOLO

(Venice 1668–1750)

Italian librettist. A historian, critic and founder of a literary newspaper (1710–19), he turned his energies to the theater, writing numerous plays which were turned into operas by various composers, including Handel, Pergolesi and Vivaldi. His most famous works include *Griselda, Merope, Ifigenia in Aulide, Lucio Vero* and *Mitridate.*

ZIEGLER, DELORES

(Decatur, Georgia 1951)

American mezzo-soprano. She studied at the University of Tennessee and the Schubert Institute in Baden bei Wien. She made her debut in 1981 as Emilia (Verdi's *Otello*). After singing for two seasons at the opera house in Bonn, she appeared in 1983 for the first time at La Scala, Milan (Dorabella in Mozart's *Così fan tutte*, returning there regularly and appearing in Mozart's *Idomeneo* (1984 and 1990), Bellini's *I Capuleti e i Montecchi* (1987) and *Così fan tutte* again in 1989. She sang with New York City Opera (Strauss's *Ariadne auf Naxos*, 1983), the Glyndebourne Festival (*Così fan tutte*, 1984), the Vienna Staatsoper (*Idomeneo*, 1987) and the Maggio Musicale Festival in Florence (Strauss's *Der Rosenkavalier*, 1989). In 1990 came her debut at the Metropolitan Opera in New York (Gounod's *Faust*). She returned to the Metropolitan in 1991 to sing in *La clemenza di Tito*. A light mezzo-soprano with a good delivery technique, Ziegler has won recognition as a Mozart singer and in such roles as Octavian (*Der Rosenkavalier*), Romeo (*I Capuleti e i Montecchi*) and the Composer (*Ariadne auf Naxos*).

ZIMMERMANN, MARGARITA

(Buenos Aires 1942)

Argentinian mezzo-soprano of German origin. She studied music at the Conservatory in Buenos Aires and made her debut in a concert at the Teatro Colón, returning to sing in Bizet's *Carmen* (1974) and Ravel's *L'enfant et les sortilèges* (1975). In 1976 she completed her training by attending the courses held by the baritone Gérard Souzay in Aix-en-Provence and Geneva. The following year she resumed her association with the Teatro Colón (in Gluck's *Orfeo ed Euridice*, Purcell's *Dido and Aeneas*, etc.) as well as making her first appearances at international opera houses. These included the Théâtre de la Monnaie in Brussels (Mozart's *Le nozze di Figaro*, 1978), the Salzburg Festival (Mozart's *La betulia liberata*, 1978, *Idomeneo*, Bizet's *Carmen*, Saint-Saëns' *Samson et Dalila*), Covent Garden (*Le nozze di Figaro*, 1980), La Fenice in Venice (from 1981, Handel's *Agrippina*, Mozart's *Idomeneo*, Gluck's *Orfeo ed Euridice*, Massenet's *Don Quichotte*, etc.) and subsequently in San Francisco (Rossini's *Il barbiere di Siviglia*), the Paris Opéra (Bizet's *Carmen*), in Philadelphia (Massenet's *Werther*) and a number of other major venues. Zimmermann combines considerable acting ability and excellent vocal and stylistic gifts, which have enabled her to achieve outstanding results in opera, from Vivaldi (*Catone in Utica*) to Rossini (*Maometto II, Ermione*), Berlioz (*Les Troyens*) and Britten (*The Rape of Lucretia*).

ZOLOTOY PYETUSHOK

(The Golden Cockerel)

Opera in three acts by Nikolai Rimsky-Korsakov (1844–1908), to a libretto by Vladimir Belsky, after the story Skazka o zolotom pyetuske *by Pushkin. First performance: Moscow, Solodovnikov Theater, 7 October 1909.*

In the briefest of prologues, the Astrologer (tenor) announces a performance of a fable which may offer a lesson for life. King Dodon (bass) receives a gift of a golden cockerel (soprano) from the Astrologer. This bird is capable of keeping watch and singing or crowing to let the country know whether all is well or the people's safety is under threat. Time passes, and one day the cockerel is facing eastwards when it crows an alarm. In response, the King dispatches his sons Gvidon (tenor) and Afron (baritone) at the head of two armies, and then he too sets out. The two princes are bewitched by the Queen of Shemakha (soprano), as a result of which they kill each other. Then it is the King's turn to become enchanted by the voice and appearance of the Queen, and he sings and dances for her until she agrees to marry him. But the Astrologer intervenes. King Dodon had promised him a reward in return for his gift of the golden cockerel, and the Astrologer now asks for the Shemakhan Queen as his prize. The King refuses and strikes the Astrologer with his scepter, killing him. To avenge his master, the cockerel flies at Dodon and mortally wounds him. During the epilogue, the Astrologer reappears and explains to the audience that the opera was only make-believe, except for himself and the Shemakhan Queen, who are both real people.

Zolotoy pyetushok is a political satire in which the character of King Dodon is used to make the real-life Tsar Nicholas II look ridiculous. The opera was consequently vetoed by the censor, who ruled that it should not be staged. It was not until 1909, after the composer's death, that *Zolotoy pyetushok* could be produced (a number of adjustments having been made to the work). It proved to be a remarkable success.

ZYLIS-GARA, TERESA

(Landvarov, Vilnius 1935)

Polish soprano. A pupil of Olga Olghina at the Conservatory in Lódź, she made her debut in Kraków in 1956 in Moniuszko's *Halka* and Puccini's *Madama Butterfly*. She won a Bavarian Radio singing competition in 1960 and went on to appear at the opera houses in Dortmund (1962) and Düsseldorf (1965). Her international career has included Strauss's *Der Rosenkavalier* at the Glyndebourne Festival in 1965, Mozart's *Die Zauberflöte* (The Magic Flute) at the Teatro dell'Opera in Rome 1967, Verdi's *La traviata* at Covent Garden in 1968, Mozart's *Don Giovanni* at the Metropolitan Opera in New York in 1968 and *Don Giovanni* again at the Salzburg Festival in 1969 and 1977. Zylis-Gara's pure lyric soprano voice has been especially admired in operas by Mozart and Richard Strauss.

The American soprano Delores Ziegler.

ADAM, ADOLPHE (1803–1856)
Le postillon de Longjumeau (1836)
J. Anderson, J. Aler, F. Le Roux, J-P. Lafont/Ensemble Choral Jean Laforge, Orchestre Philharmonique de Monte-Carlo/T. Fulton.
2 CDs-EMI

AUBER, DANIEL-FRANÇOIS-ESPRIT (1782–1871)
La muette de Portici (1828)
J. Anderson, J. Aler, A. Kraus, J-P Lafont/Ensemble Choral Jean Laforge, Orchestre Philharmonique de Monte-Carlo/T. Fulton.
2 CDs-EMI

ADAMS, JOHN (b. 1947)
Nixon in China (1987)
S. Sylvan, J. Maddalena, T. Hammons, M. Opatz, S. Friedmann, M. Dry/St. Luke Choir, St. Luke Orchestra/E. de Waart
3 CDs-NONESUCH

ALBERT, EUGENE D' (1864–1932)
Tiefland (1903)
- I. Strauss, R. Schock, G. Feldhoff, I. Sardi/Rias Choir, Berlin Symphony Orchestra/H. Zanotelli.
  2 CDs-EURODISC
- E. Marton, R. Kollo, B. Weikl, K. Moll/Chorus and Orchestra of Bavarian Radio/M. Janowski.
  2 CDs-ACANTA

ALFANO, FRANCO (1876–1954)
Risurrezione (1904)
M. Olivero, G. Gismondo, A. Boyer, A. di Stasio, F. Cadoni/Chorus and Orchestra of Radiotelevisione italiana, Turin/E. Boncompagni.
2 CDs-LEGATO CLASSIC

BALFTE, MICHAEL (1808–1870)
The Bohemian Girl
N. Thomas, P. Power, B. Cullen, J. Del Carlo, T. German/Radio Telefis Eireann Philharmonic Choir, National Symphony Orchestra of Ireland/R. Bonynge.
2 CDs-ARGO

BARBER, SAMUEL (1910–1981)
Antony and Cleopatra (1966)
E. Hinds, J. Wells, R. Grayson, K. Cowdrick, J. Brunnell, E. Halfvarson/Westminster Choir, Spoleto Festival Orchestra/C. Badea.
2 CDs-NEW WORLD RECORDS
Vanessa (1958)
R. Elias, G. Tozzi, E. Steber, N. Gedda, R. Resnik/Chorus and Orchestra of the Metropolitan Opera House, New York/D. Mitropoulos.
2 CDs-RCA

BARTÓK, BÉLA (1881–1945)
A Kékszakállu herceg vára (1918)
- S. Sass, K Kovats/Philharmonia Orchestra/G. Solti.
  1 CD-DECCA
- E. Marton, S. Ramey/Hungarian State Symphony Orchestra/A. Fischer.
  1 CD-CBS

BEETHOVEN, LUDWIG VAN (1770–1827)
Fidelio (1814)
- R. Bampton, J. Peerce, H. Janssen. S. Belarsky, E. Steber, J. Laderoute, N. Moscona/NBC Chorus and NBC Symphony Orchestra/A. Toscanini.
  2 CDs-RAC
- G. Janowitz, R. Kollo, H. Sotin, M. Jungwirth, L. Popp, A. Dallapozza, D. Fischer-Dieskau/Vienna State Opera Chorus, Vienna Philharmonic Orchestra/L. Bernstein.
  2 CDs-DG
- H. Dernesch, J. Vickers, Z. Kéléman, K. Ridderbusch, H. Donath, H. Laubenthal, J. Van Dam, W. Hollweg/Chorus of the Deutsche Oper, Berlin, Berlin Philharmonic Orchestra/H. von Karajan.
  2 CDs-EMI

BELLINI, VINCENZO (1801–1835)
Beatrice di Tenda (1833)
J. Sutherland, C. Opthof, J. Veasey, L. Pavarotti/Ambrosian Opera Chorus, London Symphony Orchestra/R. Bonynge.
3 CDs-DECCA
Norma (1831)
- M. Callas, C. Ludwig, F. Corelli, N. Zaccaria/Chorus and Orchestra of La Scala, Milan/T. Serafin.
  3 CDs-EMI
- J. Sutherland, M. Horne, J. Alexander, R. Cross/London Symphony Orchestra and Chorus/R. Bonynge.
  3 CDs-DECCA
- M. Caballé, F. Cossotto, P. Domingo, R. Raimondi/Ambrosian Opera Chorus, London Philharmonic Orchestra/C.F. Cillario.
  3 CDs-RCA

I Capuleti e i Montecchi (1830)
R. Scotto, G. Aragall, L. Pavarotti/Chorus and Orchestra of La Scala, Milan/C. Abbado.
2 CDs-CGD
Bianca e Fernando (1826)
Y. Ok Shin, G. Kunde, A. Tomicich, H. Fu/Chorus and Orchestra of the Teatro Massimo Bellini, Catania/A. Licata.
2 CDs-NUOVA ERA
Il pirata (1827)
M. Caballé, B. Marti, P. Cappuccilli, R. Raimondi/Chorus and Orchestra of Radiotelevisione italiana, Rome/G. Gavazzeni.
2 CDs-EMI
I puritani (1835)
- J. Sutherland, L. Pavarotti, P. Cappuccilli, N. Ghiaurov/Chorus of the Royal Opera House, Covent Garden, London Symphony Orchestra/R. Bonynge.
  3 CDs-DECCA
- M. Devia, W. Matteuzzi, C. Robertson, P. Washington/Chorus and Orchestra of the Teatro Massimo Bellini, Catania/R. Bonynge.
  3 CDs-NUOVA ERA

La sonnambula (1831)
- M. Callas, N. Monti, N. Zaccaria/Chorus and Orchestra of La Scala, Milan/A. Votto.
  2 CDs-EMI
- J. Sutherland, L. Pavarotti, N. Ghiaurov/London Opera Chorus, National Philharmonic Orchestra/R. Bonynge.
  2 CDs-DECCA

La straniera (1829)
- R. Scotto, R. Cioni, E. Zilio, D. Trimarchi/Chorus and Orchestra of the Teatro Massimo, Palermo/N. Sanzogno.
  2 CDs-MELODRAM
- L. Aliberti, V. Bello, S. Mingardo, R. Frontali/Chorus and Orchestra of the Teatro Comunale Giuseppe Verdi, Trieste/G. Masini.
  2 CDs-RICORDI-FONIT CETRA

Zaira (1829)
K. Ricciarelli, S. Alaimo, R. Vargas, A. Papadjakou/Chorus and Orchestra of the Teatro Massimo G. Bellini, Catania/P. Olmi.
2 CDs-NUOVA ERA

BERG, ALBAN (1885–1935)
Lulu (1937)
- A. Silja, W. Berry, J. Hopfweiser, H. Hotter, B. Fassbaender/Vienna Philharmonic/C. von Dohnányi.
  2 CDs-DECCA
- T. Stratas, F. Mazura, K. Riegel, T. Blankenheim/Orchestre de l'Opéra de Paris/P. Boulez.
  3 CDs-DG

Wozzeck (1925)
- D. Fischer-Dieskau, E. Lear, K. C. Köhn, H. Melchert, G. Stolze, F. Wunderlich/Chorus and Orchestra of the Deutsche Oper Orchestra, Berlin/K. Böhm.
  3 CDs-DG (coupled with *Lulu*)
- F. Grundheber, H. Behrens, P. Langridge, H. Zednik, A. Haugland/Vienna State Opera Chorus/Vienna Philharmonic/C. Abbado.
  2 CDs-DG

BERLIOZ, HECTOR (1803–1869)
Béatrice et Benedict (1862)
S. Graham, J.L. Viala, S. McNair, C. Robbin, G. Cachemaille, G. Bacquier/Chorus and Orchestra of the Opéra de Lyon/J. Nelson.
2 CDs-ERATO
Benvenuto Cellini (1838)
N. Gedda, C. Eda-Pierre, J. Berbié, J. Bastin, R. Massard, R. Soyer/Chorus of the Royal Opera House, Covent Garden, BBC Symphony Orchestra/C. Davis.
3 CDs-PHILIPS
La damnation de Faust (1893)
- S. Danco, D. Poleri, M. Singher, D. Gramm/Choruses of the Harvard Glee Club and the Radcliffe Choral Society, Boston Symphony Orchestra/C. Münch.
  2 CDs-RCA
- J. Veasey, N. Gedda, J. Bastin, R. van Allan/Ambroasian Singers, London Symphony Orchestra/C. Davis.
  2 CDs-PHILIPS

Les Troyens (1890)

J. Veasey, J. Vickers, B. Lindholm, P. Glossop, H. Begg, A. Howells, R. Soyer/Chorus and Orchestra of the Royal Opera House, Covent Garden/C. Davis.
4 CDs-PHILIPS

BERNSTEIN, LEONARD
(1918–1990)
Candide (1956)
J. Hadley, J. Anderson, C. Ludwig, A. Green, N. Gedda, D. Jones, K. Ollmann/London Symphony Orchestra and Chorus/L. Bernstein.
2 CDs-DG
A Quiet Place (1983)
C. Ludgin, B. Morgan, J. Brandstetter, P. Kazaras, J. Kraft, T. Uppman/Austrian Radio Symphony Orchestra/L. Bernstein.
2 CDs-DG

BIZET, GEORGES (1838–1875)
Carmen (1875)
- (Guiraud version) L. Price, F. Corelli, M. Freni, R. Merrill/Vienna State Opera Chorus, Vienna Philharmonic Orchestra/H. von Karajan.
  3 CDs-RCA
- (with spoken recitatives) T. Troyanos, P. Domingo, K. Te Kanawa, J. Van Dam/J. Alldis Choir, London Philharmonic Orchestra/G. Solti.
  3 CDs-DECCA

Djamileh (1872)
L. Popp, F. Bonisolli, J-P. Lafont/Chorus and Orchestra of Bavarian Radio/L. Gardelli.
1 CD-ORFEO
La jolie fille de Perth (1867)
J. Anderson, A. Kraus, G. Quilico, J. Van Dam, M. Zimmerman, G. Bacquier/Chorus and Nouvel Orchestre Philharmonique de Radio France/M. Plasson.
Les pêcheurs de perles (1863)
A. Maliponte, A. Kraus, S. Bruscantini/Chamber Choir and Symphony Orchestra of the Teatro Liceo of Barcelona/C.F. Cillario.
2 CDs-BONGIOVANNI

BOIELDIEU, FRANÇOIS-ADRIEN (1775–1834)
La dame blanche (1825)
F. Louvay, M. Sénéchal, A. Doniat, J. Berbié, A. Legros/Raymond Saint Paul Symphony Orchestra and Chorus/P. Stol.
2 CDs-ACCORD

BOITO, ARRIGO (1842–1918)
Mefistofele (1868)
- N. Ghiaurov, M. Freni, M. Caballé, L. Pavarotti/London Opera Chorus, National Philharmonic Orchestra/O. de Fabritiis.
  3 CDs-DECCA
- S. Ramey, E. Marton. P. Domingo/Chorus of the Hungarian State Opera, Hungarian State Symphony Orchestra/G. Patané.
  2 CDs-SONY

Nerone (1924)
J.B. Nagy, J. Dene, L. Miller, I. Tokody, K. Takas/Hungarian Radio and Television Chorus, Hungarian State Opera Orchestra/E. Queler.
2 CDs-HUNGAROTON

BORODIN, ALEXANDER
(1833–1887)
Prince Igor
- I. Petrov, T. Tugarinova, V. Atlantov, A. Ejzen, A. Vedernikov, E. Obraztsova/Chorus and Orchestra of the Bolshoi Theater, Moscow/M. Ermler.
  3 CDs-CHANT DU MONDE
- B. Martinovich, S. Evstatieva, K. Kaludov, N. Ghiuselev, N. Ghiaurov, A. Miltcheva-Honova/Sofia Festival Chorus and Orchestra/E. Tchakarov.
  3 CDs-SONY

BRITTEN, BENJAMIN (1913–1976)
Albert Herring (1947)
P. Pears, A. Cantelo, S. Fisher, O. Brannigan/English Chamber Orchestra/B. Britten.
2 CDs-DECCA
Billy Budd (1951)
P. Glossop, P. Pears, M Langdon, J. Shirley-Quirk, B. Drake, D. Kelly/Ambrosian Opera Chorus, London Symphony Orchestra/B. Britten.
3 CDs-DECCA
Death in Venice (1973)
P. Pears, J. Shirley-Quirk, J. Bowman, K. Bower, N. Williams, P. Mckay/English Chamber Orchestra/S. Bedford.
2 CDs-DECCA
A Midsummer Night's Dream (1960)
E. Harwood, A. Deller, P. Pears, T. Hemsley, J. Veasey, H. Harper, O. Brannigan, J. Shirley-Quirk, H. Watts/Choirs of Downside and Emanuel Schools, London Symphony Orchestra/B. Britten.
2 CDs-DECCA
Peter Grimes (1945)
J. Vickers, H. Harper, J. Summers, E. Bainbridge, T. Cahill, J. Dobson, F. Robinson/Chorus and Orchestra of the Royal Opera House, Covent Garden/C. Davis.
2 CDs-PHILIPS
The Rape of Lucretia (1946)
P. Pears, H. Harper, J. Baker, B. Luxon, J. Shirley-Quirk, B. Drake/English Chamber Orchestra/B. Britten.
2 CDs-DECCA
The Turn of the Screw (1954)
P. Pears, J. Vyvyan, D. Hemmings, J. Cross, A. Mandikian/English Opera Group/B. Britten.
2 CDs-DECCA

BUSONI, FERRUCCIO (1866–1924)
Arlecchino, oder die Fenster (1917)
K. Gester, G. Evans, E. Malbin, I. Wallace, M. Dickie, F. Ollendorf/Glyndebourne Festival Chorus and Orchestra/J. Pritchard.
1 CD-THE OPERA SOCIETY
Doktor Faust (1925)
D. Fischer-Dieskau, K.C. Kohn, W. Cochran, A. de Ridder, H. Hillebrecht/Chorus and Orchestra of Bavarian Radio/F. Leitner.
3 CDs-DG
Turandot (1917)
M. Muszley, F. Uhl, C. Gillig, M. Geissler, G. Fehr, C. Owen, P. Kuen/Berne Chamber Choir, Berne Symphony Orchestra/O. Ackermann.
1 CD-FOYER

TCHAIKOVSKY, PETER ILYICH (1840–1893)
Eugene Onegin (1879)
T. Allen, M. Freni, N. Shicoff, A. S. von Otter, P. Burchuladze/Leipzig Radio Chorus/Dresden Staatskapelle Orchestra/J. Levine.
2 CDs-DG
Mazeppa (1884)
V. Valajtis, E. Nesterenko, T. Milaskina, I. Arkhipova, V. Piavko/Chorus and Orchestra of the Bolshoi Theatre, Moscow/F. Mansurov.
2 CDs-CHANT DU MONDE
Pikovaya Dama (The Queen of Spades, 1890)
V. Atlantov, M. Freni, S. Leiferkus, M. Forrester, D. Hvorostovsky/Festival Chorus, Boston Symphony Orchestra/S. Ozawa.
3 CDs-RCA

CAMPRA, ANDRÉ (1660–1744)
Tancrède (1702)
F. Le Roux, D. Evangelatos, C. Dubosc, P. Y. Le Maigat, G. Reinhart, D. Visse, C. Alliot-Lugaz/La Grande Ecurie et la Chambre du Roy/J.C. Malgoire.
2 CDs-ERATO

CASKEN, JOHN (b. 1949)
Golem (1991)
A. Clarke, J. Hall, P. Harrhy, R. Morris, C. Robson, P. Rozario, M. Thomas, P. Wilson/Music Projects London/R. Bernas.
2 CDs-VIRGIN

CATALANI, ALFREDO
(1854–1893)
Loreley (1890)
E. Suliotis, G. Cecchele, R. Talarico, P. Cappuccilli, A. Ferrin/Chorus and Orchestra of La Scala, Milan/G. Gavazzeni.
2 CDs-NUOVA ERA
La Wally (1892)
- R. Tebaldi, M. del Monaco, J. Diaz, P. Cappuccilli, S. Malagú/Coro Lirico, Turin, Monte Carlo Opera Orchestra/F. Cleva.
  2 CDs-DECCA
- E. Marton, F. Araiza, F. Ellero d'Artegna, A. Titus, J. Kaufmann/Chorus and Orchestra of Bavarian Radio/P. Steinberg.
  2 CDs-EURODISC

CAVALLI, PIER FRANCESCO (1602–1676)
Il Giasone (1649)
M. Chance, G. Banditelli, C. Dubosc, A. Mellon, D. Visse/Concerto Vocale/R. Jacobs.
3 CDs-HARMONIA MUNDI

CHABRIER, EMMANUEL
(1841–1894)
L'étoile (1877)
C. Alliot-Lugaz, G. Gautier, G. Bacquier, F. Le Roux, G. Raphanel, A. David, M. Damonte/Chorus and Orchestra of the Opéra de Lyon/J.E. Gardiner.
2 CDs-EMI

CHARPENTIER, GUSTAVE (1860–1956)
Louise (1900)
I. Cotrubas, P. Domingo, G. Bacquier, J. Berbié/ Ambrosian Opera Chorus, New Philharmonia/G. Prêtre.
3 CDs-CBS

CHARPENTIER, MARC-ANTOINE (1634–1704)
David et Jonathas (1688)
- P. Esswood, C. Alliot-Lugaz, P. Huttenlocher, R. Soyer, R. Jacobs/English Bach Orchestra/M. Corboz.
  2 CDs-ERATO
- G. Lesne, M. Zanetti, J-F. Gardeil, B. Delétre, J-P. Fouchécourt/Les Arts Florissants Vocal and Instrumental Ensemble/W. Christie.
  2 CDs-HARMONIA MUNDI

CHERUBINI, LUIGI (1760–1842)
Alí Babà (1833)
W. Ganzarolli, T. Stich-Randall, O. Santunione, A. Kraus, P. Montarsolo/Chorus and Orchestra of La Scala, Milan/N. Sanzogno.
2 CDs-NUOVA ERA
Lodiska (1791)
M. Devia, A. Corbelli, W. Shimell, T. Moser, F. Garbi/Chorus and Orchestra of La Scala, Milan/R. Muti.
2 CDs-SONY
Médée (1797)
M. Callas, M. Picchi, R. Scotto, M. Pirazzini, G. Modesti/Chorus and Orchestra of La Scala, Milan/T. Serafin.
2 CDs-EMI

CILEÀ, FRANCESCO (1866–1950)
Adriana Lecouvreur (1902)
R. Scotto, E. Obraztsova, P. Domingo, S. Milnes/ Ambrosian Opera Chorus, Philharmonia Orchestra/J. Levine.
2 CDs-CBS
L'Arlesiana (1897)
E. Zilio, M. Spacagna, P. Kelen/Hungarian State Chorus and Symphony Orchestra/C. Rosenkrans.
2 CDs-QUINTANA

CIMAROSA, DOMENICO (1749–1801)
La astuzie femminili (1794)
G. Sciutti, L. Alva. S. Bruscantini/Italian Radio Orchestra, Naples/M. Rossi.
2 CDs-MEMORIES
Il matrimonio segreto (1792)
E. Dara, D. Mazzucato, B. De Simone, A. Cicogna, M. R. Cosotti, V. Bainano/Orchestra Filarmonica Marchigiana/A. Cavallaro.
2 CDs-NUOVA ERA
Gli Orazi e i Curiazi (1796)
S. Alaimo, D. Dessí, K. Angeloni, M. Bolognesi/ Chorus of Opera Giocosa, San Remo Symphony Orchestra/M. De Bernart.
2 CDs-BONGIOVANNI

COPLAND, AARON (1900–1990)
The Tender Land (1954)
E. Comeaux, J. Hardy, M. Jette, L. Lehr, D. Dressen, J. Bohn/The Plymouth Orchestra and Chorus/P. Brunelle.
2 CDs-VIRGIN CLASSICS

CORNELIUS, PETER (1824–1874)
Der Barbier von Bagdad (1858)
S. Jurinac, G. Frick, R. Schock/Vienna Radio Chorus and Orchestra/H. Hollreiser.
2 CDs-MELODRAM

DARGOMYZHSKY, ALEXANDER (1813–1869)
Kamennyi gost (1872)
T. Milaskina, T. Sinyavskaya, V. Atlantov, V. Valaytis, A. Vedernikov/Orchestra of the Bolshoi Theater, Moscow/M. Ermler.
2 CDs-CHANT DU MOND

DEBUSSY, CLAUDE (1862–1918)
Pelléas et Mélisande (1902)
- R. Stilwell, F. von Stade, J. Van Dam, R. Raimondi, N. Denize/Chorus of the Deutsche Oper, Berlin, Berlin Philharmonic Orchestra/von Karajan.
  3 CDs-EMI
- F. Le Roux, M. Ewing, J. Van Dam, J.P. Courtis, C. Ludwig/Vienna State Opera Chorus and Vienna Philharmonic Orchestra/C. Abbado.
  2 CDs-DG

DELIBES, LEO (1836–1891)
Lakmé (1883)
J. Sutherland, A. Vanzo, G. Bacquier, J. Berbié, E. Belcourt/Chorus and Orchestra of the Opéra de Monte Carlo/R. Bonynge.
2 CDs-DECCA

DELIUS, FREDERICK (1862–1934)
A Village Romeo and Juliet (1901)
H. Field, A. Davies, B. Mora, S. Dean, T. Hampson/Schoenberg Choir/Orchestre de Radio France/C. Mackerras.
2 CDs-ARGO

DONIZETTI, GAETANO (1797–1848)
Alina, regina di Golconda (1828)
D. Dessí, R. Blake, P. Coni, A. Martin, A. Tabiadon/Arturo Toscanini Chorus and Orchestra/A. Allemandi.
2 CDs-NUOVA ERA
Anna Bolena (1830)
J. Sutherland, S. Mentzner, S. Ramey, J. Hadley/ Orchestra and Chorus of Welsh National Opera/R. Bonynge.
3 CDs-DECCA
L'assedio di Calais (1836)
D. Jones, C. Du Plessis, N. Focile, R. Smythe, E. Harrhy/G. Mitchell Choir, Philharmonia Orchestra/D. Parry.
2 CDs-OPERA RARA
Belisario (1836)
L. Gencer, G. Taddei, U. Grilli, M. Pecile, N. Zaccaria/Chorus and Orchestra of the Teatro La Fenice, Venice/G. Gavazzeni.
2 CDs-MELODRAM
Il campanello dello speziale (1836)
A. Baltsa, E. Dara, A. Romero, B.M. Casoni, C. Gaifa/Vienna State Opera Chorus, Vienna Symphony Orchestra/G. Bertini.
1 CD-CBS
Caterina Cornaro (1844)
M. Caballé, G. Aragall, R. Edwards, G. Howell/ Chorus and Orchestra of French Radio/ G. Masini.
2 CDs-RODOLPHE
Le convenienze ed inconvenienze teatrali (1827)
M.A. Peter, R. Scaltriti, S. Rigacci, D. Trimarchi, A. Cicogna/Chorus of the Teatro Rossini, Lugo, Arturo Toscanini Symphony Orchestra/B. Rigacci.
2 CDs-BONGIOVANNI
Don Pasquale (1844)
- M. Freni, s. Bruscantini, G. Winbergh, L. Nucci/ Ambrosian Singers, Philharmonia Orchestra/R. Muti.
  2 CDs-EMI
- L. Serra, E. Dara, A. Bertolo, A. Corbelli/Chorus and Orchestra of the Teatro Regio, Turin/B. Campanella.
  2 CDs-NUOVA ERA

Elisabetta al castello di Kenilworth (1829)
M. Devia, D. Mazzola, J. Kundlak, B. Anderson, C. Striuli/Chorus and Symphony Orchestra of Italian Radio, Milan/J. Latham-Koenig.
2 CDs-FONIT CETRA
L'elisir d'amore (1832)
J. Sutherland, L. Pavarotti, D. Cossa, S. Malas/ Ambrosian Singers, English Chamber Orchestra/R. Bonynge.
2 CDs-DECCA
La favorite (1840)
A. Tabiadon, G. Morino, P. Coni, A. Verducci/ Bratislava Philharmonic Chorus, Orchestra Internazionale d'Italia Opera/F. Luisi.
2 CDs-NUOVA ERA
- G. Sclachi, R. Massis, L. Canonici, G. Surjan/ Rai Chorus and Symphony Orchestra, Milan/D. Renzetti.
  3 CDs-RICORDI FONIT CETRA

La fille du régiment (1840)
- J. Sutherland, L. Pavarotti, M. Sinclair, S. Malas/Chorus and Orchestra of the Royal Opera House, Covent Garden/R. Bonynge.
  2 CDs-DECCA
- L. Serra, W. Matteuzzi, E. Dara, M. Tagliasacchi/Chorus and Orchestra of the Teatro Comunale, Bologna/B. Campanella.
  2 CDs-NUOVA ERA

Il furioso all'Isola di San Domingo (1833)
L Serra, L. Canonici, S. Antonucci, M. Picconi, E. Tandura, R. Coviello/Chorus and Orchestra of the Teatro Comunale, Genoa/M. De Bernart.
3 CDs-BONGIOVANNI
Gianni di Parigi (1839)
G. Morino, L. Serra, A. Romero, E. Zilio/Chorus and Symphony Orchestra of Italian Radio and Television Milan/C.F. Cillario.
2 CDs-NUOVA ERA
Lucia di Lammermoor (1835)
- M. Callas, G. Di Stefano, R. Panerai, N. Zacca-

ria/Chorus of La Scala, Milan and the Berlin Radio Symphony Orchestra/H. von Karajan.
2 CDs-EMI
- J. Sutherland, L. Pavarotti, S. Milnes, N. Ghiaurov/Chorus and Orchestra of the Royal Opera House, Covent Garden/R. Bonynge.
3 CDs-DECCA

Lucrezia Borgia (1833)
- M. Caballé, A. Kraus, E. Flagello, S. Verrett/RCA Italiana Chorus and Orchestra/J. Perlea.
2 CDs-RCA
- J. Sutherland, G. Aragall, I. Wixell, M. Horne/London Opera Chorus, National Philharmonic Orchestra/R. Bonynge.
2 CDs-DECCA

Maria di Rohan (1843)
M. Nicolesco, G. Morino, P. Coni, F. Franci/Bratislava Philharmonic Choir, Orchestra Internazionale d'Italia Opera/M. De Bernart.
2 CDs-NUOVA ERA

Maria Stuarda (1834)
J. Sutherland, L. Pavarotti, H. Tourangeau, J. Morris, R. Soyer/Chorus and Orchestra of the Teatro Comunale, Bologna/R. Bonynge.
2 CDs-DECCA

Poliuto (1848)
- F. Corelli, M. Callas, E. Bastianini, N. Zaccaria/Chorus and Orchestra of La Scala, Milan/A. Votto.
- N. Martinucci, E. Connell, R. Bruson, F. Federici/Chorus and Orchestra of the Teatro dell'Opera, Rome/J. Latham-Koenig.
2 CDs-NUOVA ERA

Roberto Devereux (1837)
L. Gencer, A. M. Rota, R. Bondino, P. Cappuccilli/Chorus and Orchestra of the Teatro San Carlo, Naples/M. Rossi.
2 CDs-HUNT

Torquato Tasso (1833)
S. Alaimo, L. Serra, R. Coviello, E. Palacio/Chorus and Orchestra of the Teatro Comunale, Genoa/M. De Bernart.
3 CDs-BONGIOVANNI

Ugo, Conte di Parigi (1831)
D. Jones, J. Price, Y. Kenny, M. Arthur, C. du Plessis, E. Harrhy/Geoffrey Mitchell Choir, New Philharmonia Orchestra/A. Francis.
3 CDs-OPERA RARA

DUKAS, PAUL (1865–1935)

Ariane et Barbe-Bleue (1907)
K. Ciesinski, G. Bacquier, M. Paunova, H. Schaer/Nouvel Orchestre Philharmonique de Radio France/A. Jordan.
2 CDs-ERATO

DVORÁK, ANTONÍN (1841–1904)

Rusalka (1901)
G. Benacková, R. Novak, V. Soukopova, W. Ochman/Prague Philharmonic Chorus, Czech Philharmonic Orchestra/V. Neumann.
3 CDs-SUPRAPHON

EINEM, GOTTFRIED VON (b. 1918)

Dantons Tod (1947)
W. Hollweg, K. Laki, T. Adam, H. Hierstermann, K. Rydl, H. Herger-Tuna/Chorus and Orchestra of Austrian Radio/L. Zagrosek.
2 CDs-ORFEO

ERKEL, FERENC (1810–1893)

Hunyadi László (1844)
S. Sass, D. Gulyas, I. Gati, J. Gregor/Hungarian Army Chorus, Hungarian State Opera Chorus and Orchestra/J. Kovacs.
3 CDs-HUNGAROTON

FALLA, MANUEL DE (1876–1946)

La vida breve (1905)
V. De Los Angeles, C. Cossutta, I. Rivadeneyra, A. M. Higueras/Spanish National Symphony Orchestra and Chorus/R. Frühbeck de Burgos.
1 CD-EMI

FLOTOW, FRIEDRICH VON (1812–1883)

Martha oder der Markt zu Richamond (1847)
A. Rothenberger, B. Fassbaender, N. Gedda, H. Prey/Chorus and Orchestra of Bavarian Radio/R. Heger.
2 CDs-EMI

FRANCHETTI, ALBERTO (1860–1942)

Cristoforo Colombo (1892)
R. Bruson, R. Scandiuzzi, R. Ragatzu, M. Berti, G. Pasino/Budapest Radio Chorus, Frankfurt Radio Symphony Orchestra/M. Viotti
3 CDs-KOCH SCHWANN

GAZZANIGA, GIUSEPPE (1743–1818)

Don Giovanni, ossia il convitato di pietra (1787)
J. Aler, E. Steinsky, P. Coburn, M. Kinzel, G. von Kannen, R. Swenson, J. Kaufmann, J. L. Chaignaud, A. Scharinger/Bavarian Radio Chorus, Munich Radio Orchestra/S. Soltesz. 2 CDs-ORFEO

GERSHWIN, GEORGE (1898–1937)

Porgy and Bess (1935)
W. White, L. Mitchell, H. Boatwright, F. Clemmens, F. Quivar, B. Hendricks/Cleveland Chorus and Orchesta/L. Maazel.
3 CDs-DECCA

GIORDANO, UMBERTO (1867–1948)

Andrea Chénier (1896)
- F. Corelli, A. Stella, M. Sereni/Chorus and Orchestra of the Teatro dell'Opera, Rome/G. Santini.
2 CDs-EMI
- P. Domingo, R. Scotto, S. Milnes/John Alldis Choir, National Philharmonic Orchestra/J. Levine.
2 CDs-RCA

Fedora (1898)
- M. Olivero, M. Del Monaco, L. Cappellino, T. Gobbi/Chorus and Orchestra of the Monte Carlo Opera/L. Gardelli.
2 CDs-DECCA
- E. Marton, J. Carreras, V. Kincses, J. Martin/Chorus and Orchestra of Hungarian Radio/G. Patané.
2 CDs-CBS

Madame Sans-Gêne (1915)
O. Santunione, F. Tagliavini, R. Capecchi, A. Misciano, M. Zanasi/Chorus and Orchestra of La Scala, Milan/G. Gavazzeni.
2 CDs-NUOVA ERA

GLASS, PHILIP (b. 1937)

Akhnaten (1984)
P. Esswood, M. Vargas, M. Liebermann, T. Hannula, H. Holzapfel, C.H.C. Hauptmann, D. Warrilow/Chorus and Orchestra of Stuttgart Opera/D. Russell Davies.
2 CDs-CBS

Einstein on the Beach (1976)
L Childs, S.M. Johnson, P. Mann, S. Sutton, P. Zukovsky/Philip Glass Ensemble/M. Riesman.
4 CDs-CBS

GLINKA, MIKHAIL IVANOVICH (1804–1857)

Ivan Susanin (1836)
- B. Christoff, T. Stich-Randall, M. Bugarinovich, N. Gedda/Belgrade Opera Chorus, Lamoureux Concerts Orchestra/I. Markevitch.
2 CDs-EMI

GLUCK, CHRISTOPH WILLIBALD (1714–1787)

Alceste (1767)
J. Norman, N. Gedda, B. Weikl, R. Gambill, T. Krause, S. Nimsgern/Chorus and Orchestra of Bavarian Radio/S. Baudo.
3 CDs-ORFEO

Iphigénie en Aulide (1774)
L. Dawson, A.S. von Otter, J. Van Dam, J. Aler, B. Deletré, G. Cachemaille/Monteverdi Choir, Orchestra of the Lyon Opera/J. E. Gardiner.
2 CDs-ERATO

Iphigénie en Tauride (1779)
D. Montague, J. Aler, T. Allen, R. Massis/Monteverdi Choir, Orchestra of the Lyon Opera/J.E. Gardiner.
2 CDs-PHILIPS

Echo et Narcisse (1779)
K. Streit, S. Boulin, D. Massell, P. Galliard/Hamburg State Opera Chorus, Concerto Köln/R. Jacobs.
2 CDs-HARMONIA MUNDI

Orfeo ed Euridice (1762)
- M. Horne, P. Lorengar, H. Donath/Chorus and Orchestra of the Royal Opera House, Covent Garden/G. Solti
2 CDs-DECCA
- A.S. von Otter, B. Hendricks, B. Fournier/Monteverdi Choir, Orchestra of the Lyon Opera/J.E. Gardiner.
2 CDs-EMI (sung in French, in the edition revised by Berlioz)

Paride e Elena (1770)
F. Bonisolli, I. Cotrubas, G. Fontana, S. Greenberg/

ORTF (French Radio) Chorus and Symphony Orchestra/L. Zagrosek.
2 CDs-ORFEO

GOLDMARK, KAROLY (1830–1915)

Die Königin von Saba (1875)
K. Takacs, S. Jerusalem, V. Kincses, S. Solyom-Nagy, L. Miller/Chorus and Orchestra of the Budapest State Opera/A. Fischer.
3 CDs-HUNGAROTON

GOUNOD, CHARLES (1818–1893)

Faust (1859)
F. Araiza, K. Te Kanawa, E. Nesterenko, A. Schmidt/Bavarian Radio Chorus and Symphony Orchestra/C. Davis.
3 CDs-PHILIPS
R. Leech, C. Studer, J. Van Dam, T. Hampson/Chorus and Orchestra of the Théâtre Capitole, Toulouse/M. Plasson.
3 CDs-EMI
Mireille (1864)
M. Freni, A. Vanzo, J. Van Dam, G. Bacquier/Chorus and Orchestra of the Théâtre Capitole, Toulouse/M. Plasson.
3 CDs-EMI
Roméo et Juliette (1867)
A. Kraus, C. Malfitano, G. Quilico, J. Van Dam, G. Bacquier/Chorus and Orchestra of the Théâtre Capitole, Toulouse/M. Plasson.
3 CDs-EMI

GRÉTRY, ANDRÉ MODESTE (1741–1813)

La caravane du Caire (1784)
G. Ragon, P. Huttenlocher, Guy De Mey, I. Poulenard, J. Bastin, V. Le Texier/Namur Chamber Choir, Ricercar Academy Orchestra/M. Minkowski.
2 CDs-RICERCAR

HANDEL, GEORGE FREDERICK (1685–1759)

Acis and Galatea (1718)
N. Burrowes, A. Rolfe-Johnson, M. Hill, W. White/English Baroque Solists/J.E. Gardiner.
2 CDs-ARCHIV
Agrippina (1709)
S. Bradshaw, W. Hill, L. Saffer, D. Minter, N. Isherwood/Cappella Savaria/N. McGegan.
3 CDs-HARMONIA MUNDI
Giulio Cesare in Egitto (1724)
J. Larmore, B. Schlick, M. Rorholm, D. Lee Ragin/Concerto Köln/R. Jacobs.
4 CDs-HARMONIA MUNDI
Il pastor fido (1712)
P. Esswood, K. Farkas, M. Lukin, G. Kallay/Savaria Vocal Ensemble, Cappella Savaria/N. McGegan.
2 CDs-HUNGAROTON
Serse (1738)
A. Terzian, D. Cole, S. Scumann-Halley, P. Atkinson, A. Teal, N. Anderson, R. Allen/Polish Radio Chamber Orchestra/A. Duczmal.
3 CDs-STUDIOS CLASSIQUE
Tamerlano (1724)
D.L. Ragin, N. Robson, N. Argenta, M. Chance, J. Findlay, R. Schirrer/English Baroque Soloists/J.E. Gardiner.
3 CDs-ERATO

HALÉVY, JACQUES FROMENTAL (1799–1862)

La Juive (1835)
J. Carreras, J. Varady, J. Anderson, D. Gonzales, F. Furlanetto/Ambrosian Singers, Philharmonia Orchestra/A. de Almeida.
3 CDs-PHILIPS

HAYDN, FRANZ JOSEPH (1732–1809)

L'infedeltà delusa (1773)
N. Argenta, L. Lootens, C. Prégardien, C. McFadden, G. Schwarz, S. Varcoe/La Petite Bande/S. Kuijken.
2 CDs-DEUTSCHE HARMONIA MUNDI

HENZE, HANS WERNER (b. 1926)

The Bassarids (1966)
K. Riegel, A. Schmidt, R. Tear, K. Armstrong/RIAS CHAMBER Choir, South German Radio Choir, Berlin Radio Symphony Orchestra/G. Albrecht.
2 CDs-SCHWANN
Boulevard Solitude (1952)
E. Vassilieva, J. Pruett, C.J. Falkmann, J-M. Salzmann, B. Brewer, D. Ottevaere/Lausanne Opera Chorus, Orchestre de Rencontres Musicales/I. Anguelov.
2 CDs-CASCAVELLE

HINDEMITH, PAUL (1895–1963)

Cardillac (1926)
D. Fischer-Dieskau, L. Kirschstein, D. Grobe, K.C. Kohn, E. Söderström/German Radio Choir, Cologne Radio Orchestra/J. Keilberth.
2 CDs-DG

HOLST, GUSTAV (1874–1934)

Savitri (1916)
F. Palmer, P. Langridge, S. Varcoe/City of London Symphony Orchestra/R. Hickox.
1 CD-HYPERION

HONEGGER, ARTHUR (1892–1955)

Jeanne d'Arc au bûcher (1938)
M. Keller, G. Wilson, P. Marie, F. Pollet, M. Command, N. Stutzmann, J. Aler/Choeur et Maîtrise de Radio France, Orchestre National de Frnace/S. Ozawa.
2 CDs-DG

HUMPERDINCK, ENGELBERT (1854–1921)

Hänsel und Gretel (1893)
- E. Grümmer, E. Schwarzkopf, J. Metternich, M. von Ilosvay, E. Schüroff, A. Felebermeyer/Choir of Loughton High School, London, Philharmonia Orchestra/H. von Karajan.
  2 CDs-EMI
- A.S. von Otter, B. Bonney, H. Schwarz, A. Schmidt, M. Lipovsek, B. Hendricks/Tölzer Knabenchor, Bavarian Radio Symphony Orchestra/J. Tate.
  2 CDs-EMI

JANÁCEK, LEÓS (1854–1928)

Jenufa (1904)
E. Söderström, E. Randova, W. Ochman, P. Dvorsky, L. Popp/Vienna State Opera Chorus, Vienna Philharmonic Orchestra/C. Mackerras.
2 CDs-DECCA
Káta Kabanová (1921)
E. Söderström, N. Kniplova, P. Dvorsky, V. Krejcik/Vienna State Opera Chorus, Vienna Philharmonic Orchestra/C. Mackerras.
2 CDs-DECCA
Príody lisky bystronsky (The cunning little vixen, 1924(
D. Jedlicka, E. Zikmundova, R. Novak, V. Krejcik, L. Popp, E. Randova/Vienna State Opera Chorus, Vienna Philharmonic Orchestra/C. Mackerras.
2 CDs-DECCA
Z mrtvého domu (From the House of the Dead, 1930)
D. Jedlicka, J. Janska, J. Zahradnicek, J. Soucek, I. Zidek/Vienna State Opera Chorus, Vienna Philharmonic Orchestra/C. Mackerras.
2 CDs-DECCA
Vec Makropulos (1926)
E. Söderström, P. Dvorsky, V. Krejcik, A. Czakova/Vienna State Opera Chorus, Vienna Philharmonic Orchestra/C. Mackerras.
2 CDs-DECCA

JOPLIN, SCOTT (1868–1917)

Treemonisha (1915)
C. Balthrop, C. Johnson, B. Allen, C. Rayam, B. Harney, D. Ranson, W. White/Houston Opera Chorus and Orchestra/G. Schuller.
2 CDs-DG

KODÁLY, ZOLTÁN (1882–1967)

Háry János (1926)
S. Solyom-Nagy, K. Takacs, J. Gregor, B. Poka, K. Meszöly/Hungarian State Opera Chorus and Orchestra/J. Ferencsik.
2 CDs-HUNGAROTON
Székely fonó (1932)
E. Andor, E. Komlossy, G. Melis, J. Simandy, S. Palcso/Hungarian Radio Chorus, Budapest Philharmonic Orchestra/J. Ferencsik.
2 CDs-HUNGAROTON

KORNGOLD, ERICH WOLFGANG (1897–1957)

Die tote Stadt (1920)
R. Kollo, C. Neblett, B. Luxon, H. Prey, R. Wagemann/Chorus and Orchestra of Bavarian Radio/E. Leinsdorf.
2 CDs-RCA
Violanta (1916)
E. Marton, S. Jerusalem, W. Berry, H. Laubenthal, R. Hesse/Chorus and Orchestra of Bavarian Radio/M. Janowski.
1 CD-CBS

KOKKONEN, JOONAS
(b. 1921)
Viimeiset kiusaukset (1975)
M. Talvela, R. Auvinen, S. Ruohonen, M. Lehtinen, M. Nordberg, L. M. Laaksonen/Chorus and Orchestra of the Savonlinna Festival/U. Söderblom.
2 CDs-FINLANDIA

LALO, EDOUARD-VICTOR-ANTOINE (1823–1892)
Le roi d'Ys (1888)
B. Hendricks, D. Ziegler, E. Villa, J-P. Courtis, M. Piquemal/Chorus and Orchestra of Radio France/A. Jordan.
2 CDs-ERATO

LEONCAVALLO, RUGGERO (1857–1919)
La bohème (1897)
F. Bonisolli, B. Weikl, A. Titus, A. Miltcheva, L. Popp/Bavarian Radio Chorus, Munich Radio Symphony Orchestra/H. Wallberg
2 CDs-ORFEO
I pagliacci (1892)
J. Carlyle, C. Bergonzi, G. Taddei, R. Panerai, U. Benelli/Chorus and Orchestra of La Scala, Milan/H. von Karajan.
3 CDs-DG (+ *Cavalleria rusticana*)
M. Caballé, P. Domingo, S. Milnes, B. McDaniel, L. Goeke/John Alldis Choir, London Symphony Orchestra/N. Santi.
2 CDs-RCA (+ *Il tabarro*)
Zaza (1900)
C. Petrella, E. Parker, G. Campora, T. Turtura/Symphony Orchestra and Chorus of Italian Radio (RAI), Turin/A. Silipigni.
2 CDs-NUOVA ERA

LISZT, FRANZ (1811–1886)
Don Sanche ou Le château d'amour (1825)
G. Garino, J. Hamari, I. Gati, K. Farkas, I. Komlosi/Chorus of Hungarian Radio, Hungarian State Opera Orchestra/T. Pal.
2 CDs-HUNGAROTON

LORTZING, GUSTAV ALBERT (1801–1851)
Undine (1845)
R.M. Pütz, N, Gedda, A. Rothenberger, H. Prey, P. Schreier/RIAS Chamber Choir, Berlin Radio Symphony Orchestra/R. Heger.
2 CDs-EMI

LULLY, JEAN-BAPTISTE
(1632–1687)
Atys (1676)
G.de Mey, G. Laurens, A. Mellon, J-F. Gardeil/Les Arts Florissants/W. Christie.
3 CDs-HARMONIA MUNDI

MARAIS, MARIN (1656–1728)
Alcyone (1706)
J. Smith, G. Ragon, P. Huttenlocher, V. Le Texier, S. Boulin, B. Deletré, J-J-P. Fouchécourt/Les Musiciens du Louvre/M. Minkowski.
3 CDs-ERATO

MARSCHNER, HEINRICH
(1795–1861)
Hans Heiling (1833)
T. Mohr, M. Hajossyova, E. Seniglova, M. Eklöf, K. Markus, L. Neshyba/Slovak Philharmonic Chorus and Orchestra/E. Körner.
2 CDs-MARCO POLO

MARTÍN Y SOLER, VICENTE (1754–1806)
Una cosa rara (1786)
M.A. Peters, E. Palacio, M. Figueras, G. Fabuel, I. Fresan, F. Belaza-Leoz, S. Palatachi, F. Garrigosa/Catalan Capella Reial, Concert des Nations/J. Savall.
3 CDs-ASTREE

MASCAGNI, PIETRO (1863–1945)
L'amico Fritz (1891)
L. Pavarotti, M. Freni, V. Sardinero, L. Didier/Chorus and Orchestra of the Royal Opera House, Covent Garden/G. Gavazzeni.
2 CDs-EMI
Cavalleria rusticana (1890)
- G. Di Stefano, M. Callas, R. Panerai/Chorus and Orchestra of La Scala, Milan/T. Serafin.
  3 CDs-EMI (+ *I pagliacci*)
- C. Bergonzi, F. Cossotto, G.G. Guelfi/Chorus and Orchestra of La Scala, Milan/H. von Karajan.
  3 CDs-DG (+ *I Pagliacci*)

Guglielmo Ratcliff (1895)
P.M. Ferraro, R. Mattioli, F. Mazzoli, G. Cominelli, M. Truccato Pace/Chorus and Symphony Orchestra of Italian Radio (RAI), Rome/A. La Rosa Parodi.
2 CDs-NUOVA ERA
Iris (1898)
I. Tokody, P. Domingo, J. Pons, B. Giaiotti/Bavarian Radio Chorus and Symphony Orchestra/G. Patané.
2 CDs-CBS
Lodoletta (1917)
M. Spacagna, P. Kelen, K. Szilagyi, L. Polgar, Z. Bazsinka/Hungarian Radio Orchestra and Chorus/C. Rosenkrans.
2 CDs-HUNGAROTON
Le maschere (1901)
A. Felle, V. La Scola, G. Sabbatini, M. Gallego, E. Dara, A. Romero, O. Di Credico, N. Portella/Chorus and Orchestra of the Teatro Comunale, Bologna/G. Gelmetti.
2 CDs-FONIT CETRA

MASSENET, JULES (1842–1912)
Cendrillon (1899)
F. von Stade, N. Gedda, J. Berbié, J. Bastin, R. Welting, T. Cahill, E. Bainbridge/Ambrosian Opera Chorus, Philharmonia Orchestra/J. Rudel.
2 CDs-CBS
Le Cid (1885)
G. Bumbry, P. Domingo, P. Plishka, E. Bergquist, A. Voketatis/Byrne Camp Chorale, New York Opera Orchestra/E. Queler.
2 CDs-CBS
Don Quichotte (1910)
N. Ghiaurov, R. Crespin, G. Bacquier/Chorus and Orchestra of the Suisse Romande/K. Kord.
2 CDs-DECCA
Esclarmonde (1889)
J. Sutherland, G. Aragall, C. Grant, H. Tourangeau, L. Quilico, R. Lloyd, R. Davies/John Alldis Choir, National Philharmonic Orchestra/R. Bonynge.
3 CDs-DECCA
Hérodiade (1881)
N. Denize, M. Channes, E. Blanc, J. Brazzi/Choeur et Orchestre Lyrique de Radio France/D. Lloyd-Jones.
2 CDs-RODOLPHE
Le jongleur de Notre-Dame (1902)
A. Vanzo, J. Bastin, M. Vento/Chorus and Orchestra of the Monte Carlo Opera/R. Boutry.
2 CDs-EMI (+ selection from *Thais*)
Manon (1884)
B. Sills, N. Gedda, G. Souzay, G. Bacquier/Ambrosian Opera Chorus, New Philharmonia Orchestra/J. Rudel.
2 CDs-EMI
Le roi de Lahore (1877)
L. Lima, J. Sutherland, S. Milnes, N. Ghiaurov, H. Tourangeau/London Opera Chorus, National Philharmonic Orchestra/R. Bonynge.
3 CDs-DECCA
Sapho (1897)
R. Doria, G. Sirera, G. Ory, A. Legros, E. Waisman/Stéphane Caillat Choir, Orchestre de la Garde Républicaine/R. Boutry.
2 CDs-BOURG
Thais (1894)
A. Esposito, R. Massard, J. Mollien, S. Michel, L. Lovano/Orchestre et Choeur Lyrique de Radio France/A. Wolff.
2 CDs-CHANT DU MONDE
Werther (1892)
A. Kraus, T. Troyanos, C. Barbaux, M. Manuguerra/Covent Garden Boys' Choir, London Philharmonic Orchestra/M. Plasson.
2 CDs-EMI

MAXWELL DAVIES, PETER (b. 1934)
The Martyrdom of St. Magnus (1977)
T. Dives, C. Gillet, P. Thomson, R. Morris, K. Thomas/Scottish Chamber Opera Ensemble/M. Rafferty.
1 CD-UNICORN

MÉHUL, ÉTIENNE-NICHOLAS (1763–1817)
Joseph en Egypte (1807)
L. Dale, F. Vassar, R. Massis/Intermezzo Choral Ensemble, Orchestre Régional Picardy/C. Bardon.
2 CDs-CHANT DU MONDE

MENOTTI, GIANCARLO (b. 1911)
Amahl and the Night Visitors (1951)
K. Yaghijan, M. King, J. McCollum, R. Cross, W. Patterson/NBC Orchestra and Chorus/H. Grossman.
1 CD-RCA
Goya (1986)
C. Hernandez, S. Guzman, D. Tonini, P. Daner, H. Bender, C. Tancredi/The Westminster Choir, Spo-

leto Festival Orchestra/S. Mercurio.
2 CDs-NUOVA ERA
The Telephone (1947)
A.V. Banks, G.L. Ricci/Orchestra da Camera di Milano/P. Vaglieri.
1 CD-NUOVA ERA

MERCADANTE, GIUSEPPE SAVERIO RAFFAELE (1795–1870)

Il Bravo (1839)
D. di Domenico, A. Tabiadon, J. Perry, S. Bertocchi, S. Antonucci/Slovak Philharmonic Choir, Bratislava, Orchestra Internazionale d'Italia/B. Aprea.
3 CDs-NUOVA ERA
Il giuramento (1837)
G. Colmagro, B. Wolff, P. Wells, M. Molese, S. Porzano, G. Novielli/Chorus and Orchestra of the Juilliard American Opera Center/T. Schippers.
2 CDs-MYTO

MEYERBEER, GIACOMO (1761–1864)

L'Africaine (1865)
S. Verrett, P. Domingo, E. Mandac, N. Mittlemann/ Chorus and Orchestra of San Francisco Opera/J. Perisson.
3 CDs-LEGATO CLASSICS
Il crociato in Egitto (1824)
I. Platt, Y. Kenny, D. Montague, D. Jones, B. Ford, L. Kitchen, U. Benelli/Geoffrey Mitchell Choir, Royal Philharmonic Orchestra/D. Parry.
4 CDs-OPERA RARA
Le prophète (1849)
M. Horne, R. Scotto, J. McCracken, J. Bastin, J. Hines, C. du Plessis/Ambrosian Opera Chorus, Royal Philharmonic Orchestra/H. Lewis.
4 CDs-CBS
Robert le diable (1831)
R. Scotto, G. Merighi, B. Christoff, S. Malagu, G. Manganotti, G. Antonini/Chorus and Orchestra of the Maggio Musicale Fiorentino/N. Sanzogno.
3 CDs-MELODRAM

MONIUSZKO, STANISLAW (1819–1872)

Halka (1848)
S. Woytowicz, W. Ochman, A. Hiolski, B. Ladysz, A. Saciuk/Cracow Radio Chorus, Polish Radio Orchestra/J. Semkov.
2 CDs-CHANT DU MONDE

MONTEVERDI, CLAUDIO (1567–1643)

L'incoronazione di Poppea (1642)
- E. Söderström, H. Donath, P. Esswood, C. Berberian, G. Luccardi, R. Hansmann, C. Gaifa, P. Langridge/Vienna Concentus Musicus/N. Harnoncourt.
  4 CDs-TELDEC

L'Orfeo (1607)
- L. Kozma, R. Hansmann, C. Berberian, M. van Egmond, E. Katanosake/Cappella Antiqua, Munich, Vienna Concentus Musicus/N. Harnoncourt.
  2 CDs-TELDEC
- A. Rolfe-Johnson, J. Baird, L. Dawson, A. S. von Otter, D. Montague/Monteverdi Choir, English Baroque Soloists/J. E. Gardiner.
  2 CDs-ARCHIV

Il ritorno d'Ulisse in patria (1640)
C. Prégardien, B. Fink, C. Högman, M. Hill, J. Taillon, D. Visse, M. Tucker, D. Thomas, G. de Mey/Concerto Vocale/R. Jacobs.
3 CDs-HARMONIA MUNDI

MOZART, WOLFGANG AMADEUS (1756–1791)

Apollo et Hyacinthus (1767)
C. Günther, S. Pratschske, M. Schäfer, C. Fliegner, P. Cieslewicz/Nice Baroque Ensemble/G. Schmidt-Gaden.
2 CDs-PAVANE
Ascanio in Alba (1771)
A. Baltsa, L. Sukis, E. Mathis, A. Augér, P. Schreier/Salzburg Chamber Choir, Orchestra of the Salzburg Mozarteum/L. Hager.
3 CDs-PHILIPS
Bastien und Bastienne (1768)
D. Oriesching, G. Nigl, D. Busch/Vienna Symphony Orchestra, U.C. Harrer.
1 CD-PHILIPS
La clemenza di Tito (1791)
- W. Krenn, T. Berganza, M. Casula, L. Popp, B. Fassbaender, T. Franc/Vienna State Opera Chorus and Orchestra/I. Kertesz.
  2 CDs-DECCA
- A. Rolfe-Johnson, J. Varady, A. S. von Otter, C. Robbin, S. McNair, C. Hauptmann/Monteverdi Choir, English Baroque Soloists/J.E. Gardiner.
  2 CDs-ARCHIV

Così fan tutte (1790)
- E. Schwarzkopf, C. Ludwig, H. Staffek, G. Taddei, A. Kraus, W. Berry/ London Philharmonic Chorus and Orchestra/K. Böhm.
  3 CDs-EMI
- M. Caballé, J. Baker, I Cotrubas, W. Ganzaroli, N. Gedda, R. van Allan/Chorus and Orchestra of the Royal Opera House, Covent Garden/C. Davis.
  3 CDs-PHILIPS

Don Giovanni (1787)
- E. Wächter, J. Sutherland, L. Alva, G. Frick, E. Schwarzkopf, G. Taddei, G. Sciutti, P. Cappuccilli/London Philharmonic Choir and Orchestra/C.M. Giulini.
  3 CDs-EMI
- W. Shimell, C. Studer, F. Lopardo, J-H. Rootering, C. Vaness, S. Ramey, S. Mentzer, N. de Carolis/Vienna State Opera Chorus, Vienna Philharmonic Orchestra/R. Muti.
  3 CDs-EMI

Die Entführung aus dem Serail (1782)
- E. Gruberova, K. Battle, G. Winbergh, H. Zednik, M. Talvela/Vienna State Opera Chorus, Vienna Philharmonic Orchestra/G. Solti.
  2 CDs-DECCA
- L. Orgonasova, C. Sieden, S. Olsen, U. Peper, C. Hauptmann/Monteverdi Choir, English Baroque Soloists/J.E. Gardiner.
  3 CDs-ARCHIV

La finta giardiniera (1775)
T. Moser, E. Gruberova, U. Heilmann, C. Margiono, M. Bacelli, D. Upshaw, A. Scharinger/ Vienna Concentus Musicus/N. Harnoncourt.
3 CDs-TELDEC
La finta semplice (1769)
B. Hendricks, S. Lorenz, D. Johnson, A. Murray, E. Lind, H-P. Blochwitz, A. Schmidt/C.P.E. Bach Chamber Orchestra/P. Schreier.
2 CDs-PHILIPS
Idomeneo re di Creta (1781)
- L. Pavarotti, A. Baltsa, E. Gruberova, L. Popp, L. Nucci/Vienna State Opera Chorus, Vienna Philharmonic Orchestra/J. Pritchard.
  3 CDs-DECCA
- A. Rolfe Johnson, A.S. von Otter, H. Martinpelto, S. McNair, N. Robson/Monteverdi Choir, English Baroque Soloists/J.E. Gardiner.
  3 CDs-ARCHIV

Lucio Silla (1772)
- A. Rolfe Johnson, L. Cuberli, A. Murray, C. Barbaux, B-M. Aruhn, A. van Baasbank/Chorus and Orchestra of the Théâtre La Monnaie, Brussels/S. Cambreling.
  3 CDs-RICERCAR
- P. Schreier, E. Gruberova, C. Bartoli, Y. Kenny, D. Upshaw/Schoenberg Choir, Vienna; Vienna Concentus Musicus/N. Harnoncourt.
  2 CDs-TELDEC

Mitridate re di Ponto (1770)
W. Hollweg, A. Auger E. Gruberova, A. Baltsa, I. Cotrubas, D. Kübler, C. Weidinger/Salzburg Mozarteum Orchestra/L. Hager.
3 CDs-PHILIPS
Le nozze di Figaro (1786)
- D. Fishcher-Dieskau, G. Janowitz, E. Mathis, H. Prey, T. Troyanos, P. Johnson, E. Wohlfahrt, P. Lagger/Chorus and Orchestra of the Deutsche Oper, Berlin/K. Böhm.
  3 CDs-DG
- A. Poell, L. Della Casa, H. Güden, C. Siepi, S. Danco, H. Rössel-Majden, F. Corena, M. Dickie/Vienna State Opera Chorus, Vienna Philharmonic Orchestra/E. Kleiber.
  3 CDs-DECCA

Il re pastore (1775)
S. McNair, A.M. Blasi, I. Vermillion, J. Hadley, C. Ahnsjö/Academy of St. Martin-in-the Fields/N. Marriner.
2 CDs-PHILIPS
Der Schauspieldirektor (1786)
J. Hamari, K. Laki, T. Hampson, H. van der Kamp/ Amsterdam Concertgebouw Orchestra/N. Harnoncourt.
1 CD-TELDEC (+ Salieri's *Prima la musica, poi le parole*).
Zaide (1779)
E. Mathis, P. Schreier, I. Wixell, W. Hollweg, D. Süss/Berlin Staatskapelle/B. Klee.
2 CDs-PHILIPS
Die Zauberflöte (The Magic Flute, 1791)
- M. Talvela, S. Burrows, D. Fischer-Dieskau, C. Deutekom, P. Lorengar, H. Prey, G. Stolze/ Vienna State Opera Chorus, Vienna Philharmonic Orchestra/G. Solti.
  3 CDs-DECCA
- S. Ramey, F. Araiza, C. Studer, K. Te Kanawa, O. Bär, J. Van Dam/Ambrosian Opera Chorus, Academy of St. Martin-in-the-Fields/N. Marriner.
  3 CDs-PHILIPS

MUSSORGSKY, MODEST
(1839–1881)
Boris Godunov (in the version by Rimsky-Korsakov, 1904)
- N. Ghiaurov, A. Maslennikov, M. Talvela, L. Spiess, G. Vishnevskaya/Choruses of Sofia Radio and the Vienna State Opera, Vienna Philharmonic Orchestra/H. von Karajan.
  3 CDs-DECCA
- (original version of 1872) A. Vedernikov, A. Sokolov, V. Matroin, V. Piavko, I. Arkhipova, A. Ejzen/Russian Radio Chorus and Orchestra/V. Fedoseyev.
  3 CDs-PHILIPS

Khovanshchina (1886)
- A. Haugland, V. Atlantov, V. Popov, A. Kotscherga, P. Burchuladze, M. Lipovsek/Slovak Philharmonic Chorus, Chorus and Orchestra of the Vienna State Opera/C. Abbado.
  (1883 version with additions) 3 CDs-DG
- N. Chiaurov, Z. Gadyev, N. Ghiuselev, K. Kaludov, A. Miltcheva/Chorus and Orchestra of the Sofia National Opera/E. Tchakarov.
  3 CDs-SONY (Shostakovich version, 1963)

NICOLAI, CARL OTTO
(1810–1849)
Die lustigen Weiber von Windsor (1849)
G. Frick, E. Gutstein, R-M. Pütz, G. Liz, E. Mathis, F. Wunderlich/Bavarian State Opera Chorus and Orchestra/R. Heger.
2 CDs-EMI

OFFENBACH, JACQUES
(1819–1880)
Les contes d'Hoffmann (post., 1881)
- P. Domingo, J. Sutherland, G. Bacquier/Chorus and Orchestra of the Suisse Romande/R. Bonynge.
  2 CDs-DECCA
- F. Araiza, E. Lind, J. Norman, C. Studer, S. Ramey, A.S. von Otter/Leipzig Radio Chorus, Dresden Staatskapelle Orchestra/J. Tate.
  3 CDs-PHILIPS

ORFF, CARL (1895–1982)
Die Kluge (1943)
- T. Stewart, G. Frick, L. Popp, R. Kogel, M. Schmidt, C. Nicolai/Munich Radio Orchestra/K. Eichhorn.
  2 CDs-EURODISC (+ *Der Mond*)

Der Mond (1939)
J. van Kesteren, H. Friedrich, R. Kogel, F. Gruber, B. Kusche, R. Grumbach, F. Crass/Bavarian Radio Chorus, Munich Radio Orchestra/K. Eichhorn.
2 CDs-EURODISC (+ *Die Kluge*)

PACINI, GIOVANNI (1796–1867)
Saffo (1840)
L. Gencer, L. Quilico, T. Del Bianco, F. Mattiucci/Chorus and Orchestra of the Teatro San Carlo, Naples/F. Capuana.
2 CDs-CGD HUNT

PAISIELLO, GIOVANNI
(1740–1816)
Il barbiere di Siviglia, ovvero La precauzione inutile (1782)
L. Cuberli, P. Visconti, E. Dara, A. Corbelli, D. Menicucci/Orchestra Filarmonica Romana/B. Campanella.
2 CDs-EUROPA MUSICA
Nina, ossia la pazza per amore (1789)
M. Bolgan, D. Bernardini, F. Musinu, F. Pediconi, G. Surjan/Chorus and Orchestra of the Teatro Massimo Bellini, Catania/R. Bonynge.
2 CDs-NUOVA ERA

PEPUSCH, JOHANN CHRISTOPH (1667–1752)
The Beggar's Opera (1728)
- N. Rogers, A. Jenkins, S. Minti, E. Fleet, M. Cable, J. Noble, V. Midgley/Chorus and Orchestra of the Accademia Monteverdiana/D. Stevens.
  2 CDs-KOCH SCHWANN
- J. Morris, K. Te Kanawa, J. Sutherland, A. Marks, A. Lansbury, S. Dean, A. Rolfe Johnson/National Philharmonic Orchestra/R. Bonynge.
  2 CDs-DECCA

PERGOLESI, GIOVAN BATTISTA (1710–1736)
Adriano in Siria (1734)
D. Dessí, J. Omilian, E. Di Cesare, G. Banditelli, S. Anselmi, L. Mazzaria/Orchestra dell'Opera di Camera, Rome/M. Panni.
3 CDs-BONGIOVANNI
Il Flaminio (1735)
G. Sica, D. Dessí, E. Zilio, F. Pediconi, M. Farruggia, V. Baiano, S. Pagliuca/Orchestra of the Teatro San Carlo, Naples/M. Panni.
3 CDs-RICORDI-FONIT CETRA
Lo frate 'nnamurato (1732)
A. Felle, N. Focile, A. Corbelli, B. De Simone, B. Manca di Nissa, N. Curiel, E. Norberg-Schulz, L. D'Intino, E. Di Cesare/Orchestra of La Scala, Milan/R. Muti.
3 CDs-EMI
La serva padrona (1733)
- R. Scotto, S. Bruscantini/I Virtuosi di Roma/R. Fasano.
  1 CD-RICORDI-FONIT CETRA
- K. Farkas, J. Gregor/Cappella Savaria/P. Nemeth.
  4 CDs-HUNGAROTON

PFITZNER, HANS (1869–1949)
Palestrina (1917)
N. Gedda, H. Donath, B. Fassbaender, D. Fischer-Dieskau, K. Ridderbusch, H. Prey, B. Weikl/Tölzerknabenchor and Bavarian Radio Chorus and Orchestra/R. Kubelik.
3 CDs-DG

PICCINNI, NICOLÒ (1728–1800)
La Cecchina, ossia La buona figliola (1760)
M.A. Peters, G. Morino, B. Praticò, A. Ruffini, G. Morigin, P. Spagnoli, S. Mingardo, M.C. Zanni/Orchestra Serenissima Pro Arte/B. Campanella.
2 CDs-MEMORIES-NUOVA ERA

PIZZETTI, ILDEBRANDO
(1880–1968)
L'assassinio nella cattedrale (1958)
N. Rossi Lemeni, V. Zeani, A.M. Rota, P. Montarsolo/Chorus and Symphony Orchestra of Italian Radio (RAI), Turin/I. Pizzetti.
2 CDs-STRADIVARIUS

PONCHIELLI, AMILCARE
(1834–1886)
La Gioconda (1876)
- M. Callas, F. Cossotto, P.M. Ferraro, P. Cappuccilli, I. Vinco/Chorus and Orchestra of La Scala, Milan/A. Votto.
  3 CDs-EMI
- R. Tebaldi, M. Horne, C. Bergonzi, R. Merrill, N. Ghiuselev/Chorus and Orchestra of the Accademia Nazionale di Santa Cecilia, Rome/L. Gardelli.
  3 CDs-DECCA

POULENC, FRANCIS (1899–1963)
Les dialogues des Carmélites (1957)
C. Dubosc, R. Gorr, R. Yakar, M. Dupuy, B. Fournier, J. Van Dam, J-L. Viala/Orchestre de l'Opéra de Lyon/K. Nagano.
2 CDs-VIRGIN CLASSICS
La voix humaine (1959)
J. Migenes/Orchestre National de France/G. Prêtre
1 CD-ERATO

PROKOFIEV, SERGEY SERGEYEVICH (1891–1953)
Lyubov k trem apelsinam (1921)
G. Bacquier, J-L. Viala, H. Perraguin, V. Le Texier, G. Gautier, D. Henry, M. Legrange, B. Fournier, C. Dubosc/Chorus and Orchestra of the Opéra de Lyon/K. Nagano.
2 CDs-VIRGIN CLASSICS
Igrok (1929)
A. Ognivtsiev, M. Kasrashvili, A. Maslennikov, D. Korolev, L. Vernigora, G. Borisova, V. Vlasov/Chorus and Orchestra of the Bolshoi Theater, Moscow/A. Lazarev.
2 CDs-OLYMPIA
Ognenny Angel (1953)
N. Secunde, S. Lorenz, H. Zednik. P. Salomaa, K. Moll, G. Zachrisson, B. Terfel, R. Lang/Ohlin Vocal Ensemble, Gothenburg Symphony Orchestra/N. Järvi.
2 CDs-DG

PUCCINI, GIACOMO (1858–1924)
La bohème (1896)
- R. Tebaldi, C. Bergonzi, E. Bastianini, G. D'Angelo/Orchestra and Chorus of the Accademia Nazionale di Santa Cecilia, Rome/T. Serafin.
  2 CDs-DECCA
- M. Frein, L. Pavarotti, R. Panerai, E. Harwood/Chorus of the Deutsche Oper, Berlin and Berlin Philharmonic Orchestra/H. von Karajan.
  2 CDs-DECCA

Edgar (1889)
R. Scotto, C. Bergonzi, G. Killebrew, V. Sardinero/New York City Opera Boys' Choir, New York Schola Cantorum, New York Opera Orchestra/E. Queler.
2 CDs-CBS
La fanciulla del West (1910)
- C. Neblett, P. Domingo, S. Milnes, G. Howell/Chorus and Orchestra of the Royal Opera House, Covent Garden/Z. Mehta.
  2 CDs-DG

M. Zampieri, P. Domingo, J. Pons, M. Chingari/Chorus and Orchestra of La Scala, Milan/L. Maazel.
2 CDs-SONY
Madama Butterfly (1904)
- R. Scotto, C. Bergonzi, A. Di Stasio, R. Panerai/Chorus and Orchestra of the Teatro dell'Opera, Rome/J. Barbirolli.
  2 CDs-EMI
- M. Freni, L. Pavarotti, C. Ludwig, R. Kerns/Vienna State Op-Opera Chorus, Vienna Philharmonic Orchestra/H. von Karajan.
  3 CDs-DECCA

Manon Lescaut (1893)
M. Caballé, P. Domingo, V. Sardinero/Ambrosian Opera Chorus, New Philharmonia Orchestra/B. Bartoletti.
2 CDs-EMI
M. Freni, P. Domingo, R. Bruson/Covent Garden Chorus, Philharmonia Orchestra/G. Sinopoli.
2 CDs-DG
La rondine (1917)
- A. Moffo, D. Barioni, M. Sereni, G. Sciutti, P. De Palma/RCA Italiana Chorus and Orchestra/F. Molinari-Pradelli.
  2 CDs-RCA
- K. Te Kanawa, P. Domingo, L. Nucci, M. Nicolesco, D. Rendall/Ambrosian Opera Chorus, London Symphony Orchestra/L. Maazel.
  2 CDs-CBS

Tosca (1900)
- M. Callas, G. Di Stefano, T. Gobbi/Chorus and Orchestra of La Scala, Milan/V. de Sabata.
  2 CDs-EMI
- L. Price, P. Domingo, S. Milnes/John Alldis Choir, New Philharmonia Orchestra/Z. Mehta.
  2 CDs-RCA

Il trittico (1918)
(*Il tabarro, Suor Angelica, Gianni Schicchi*)
I. Wixell, R. Scotto, P. Domingo – R. Scotto, M. Horne – T. Gobbi, I. Cotrubas, P. Domingo/Ambrosian Opera Chorus, New Philharmonia Orchestra/L. Maazel.
3 CDs-CBS
Turandot (1926)
- B. Nilsson, F. Corelli, R. Scotto, B. Giaiotti/Chorus and Orchestra of the Teatro dell'Opera, Rome/F. Molinari-Pradelli.
  2 CDs-EMI
- J. Sutherland, L. Pavarotti, M. Caballé, N. Ghiaurov/John Alldis Choir, London Philharmonic Orchestra/Z. Mehta.
  2 CDs-DECCA

Le villi (1884)
R. Scotto, P. Domingo, L. Nucci/Ambrosian Opera Chorus, National Philharmonic Orchestra/L. Maazel.
1 CD-CBS

PURCELL, HENRY (1659–1695)
Dido and Aeneas (1689)
- J. Norman, M. McLaughlin, P. Kern, T. Allen/English Chamber Orchestra and Chorus/R. Leppard.
  1 CD-PHILIPS
- A.S. von Otter, L. Dawson, N. Rogers, S. Varcoe/The English Concert/T. Pinnock.
  1 CD-ARCHIV

RAMEAU, JEAN-PHILIPPE (1683–1764)
Castor et Pollux (1737)
J. Scovotti, M. Schèle, Z. Vandersteene, R. Leanderson, N. Lerer, G. Souzay, J. Villesech/Stockholm Chamber Choir, Vienna Concentus Musicus/N. Harnoncourt.
3 CDs-TELDEC
Les Indes galantes (1735)
C. McFadden, J. Corréas, I. Poulenard, N. Rivenq, M. Ruggieri, H. Crook, B. Deletre, J-P. Fouchécourt/Les Arts Florissants/W. Christie.
3 CDs-HARMONIA MUNDI

PLATÉE (1745)
G. Ragon, J. Smith, G. de Mey, V. le Texier, G. Laurens, B. Deletre, V. Gens, M. Verschaeve/Emsemble Vocal Françoise Herr, Les Musiciens du Louvre/M. Minkowski.
2 CDs-ERATO

RAVEL, MAURICE (1875–1937)
L'enfant et les sortilèges (1925)
F. Ogéas, S. Gylma, J. Collard, J. Berbié, C. Herzog, H. Rehfuss, C. Maurane, M. Sénéchal/ORFT Chorus and National Orchestra/L. Maazel.
1 CD-DG
L'heure espagnole (1911)
J. Berbié, M. Sénéchal, J. Girardeau, G. Bacquier, J. Van Dam/Orchestre de l'Opéra de Paris/L. Maazel.
1 CD-DG

RESPIGHI, OTTORINO
(1879–1936)
Belfagor (1923)
L. Miller, S. Sass, G. Lamberti, L. Polgar, K. Takacs, M. Kalmar/Hungarian Radio Chorus, Hungarian State Symphony Orchestra/L. Gardelli.
2 CDs-HUNGAROTON
La fiamma (1934)
K. Takacs, S. Solyom-Nagy, P. Kelen, I. Tokody, T. Takacs, J. Gregor/Hungarian Radio Chorus, Hungarian State Symphony Orchestra/L. Gardelli.
3 CDs-HUNGAROTON

RICCI, FEDERICO AND LUIGI (1809–1877/1805–1859)
Crispino e la comare (1850)
R. Coviello, S. Lazzarini, D. Lojarro, S. Alaimo/Coro F. Cilea, Reggio Calabria, San Remo Symphony Orchestra/P. Carignani.
2 CDs-BONGIOVANNI

RIMSKY-KORSAKOV, NIKOLAI (1844–1908)
Skazaniye o Nevidimon Grade Kitezhe I Deve Fevronii (1907)
G. Kalinina, E. Raikov, V. Piavko, A. Vedernikov, M. Maslov/Orchestra Chorus of the Bolshoi Theatre, Moscow/E. Svetlanov.
3 CDs-CHANT DU MONDE
Tsarskaya nevesta (1899)
G. Vishnevskaya, I. Arkhipova, V. Atlantov, V. Valaitis, E. Nesterenko, A. Sokolov/Chours and Orchestra of the Bolshoi Theater, Moscow/F. Mansurov.
3 CDs-CHANT DU MONDE

ROSSINI, GIOACHINO
(1792–1868)
Adelaide di Borgogna (1817)
M. Dupuy, M. Devia, A. Caforio, A. Bertolo, E. Tandura, M. Farruggia, G. Fallisi/New Cambridge Chorus, Orchestra Filarmonica di Satu Mare/A. Zedda.
2 CDs-RICORDI-FONIT CETRA
Armida (1817)
G. Gasdia, W. Matteuzzi, B. Ford, C. Merritt, C.H. Workmann, F. Furlanetto/Ambrosian Opera Chorus, I Solisti Veneti/C. Scimone.
2 CDs-EUROPA MUSICA
Aureliano in Palmira (1813)
E. Di Cesare, D. Mazzola, L. D'Intino, N. Ciliento/Coro Cooperativa 'Artisti del Coro Associati'', Lucca, Orchestra Lirico Sinfonica del Teatro del Giglio, Lucca/G. Zami.
2 CDs-NUOVA ERA
Il barbiere di Siviglia (1816)
- L. Alva, T. Berganza, H. Prey, E. Dara, P. Montarsolo, S. Malagú/Ambrosian Opera Chorus, London Symphony Orchestra/C. Abbado.
  2 CDs-DG
- R. Blake, L. Serra, B. Pola, E. Dara, P. Montarsolo, N. Curiel/Chorus and Orchestra of the Teatro Regio, Turin/B. Campanella.
  2 CDs-NUOVA ERA

Bianca e Faliero (1819)
K. Ricciarelli, M. Horne, C. Merritt, G. Surjan/Prague Philharmonic Chorus, London Sinfonietta Opera Orchestra/D. Renzetti
3 CDs-RICORDI-FONIT CETRA
La cambiale di matrimonio (1810)
E. Dara, R. Frontali, S. Jeun, L. Canonici/Symphony Orchestra of Italian Radio (RAI), Turin/D. Renzetti.
1 CD-RICORDI-FONIT CETRA
La Cenerentola, ossia la bontà in trionfo (1817)
T. Berganza, M. Guglielmi, L. Zannini, L. Alva, R. Capecchi, P. Montarsolo, U. Trama/Scottish Opera Chorus, London Symphony Orchestra/C. Abbado.
2 CDs-DG
Ciro in Babilonia (1812)
D. Dessí, C. Calvi, E. Palacio, S. Antonucci, O. Ferraris, E. Cossutta, D. Serraiocco/Coro F. Cilea, Reggio Calabria, San Remo Symphony Orchestra/C. Rizzi.
2 CDs-CGD-HUNT
Le comte Ory (1828)
J. Aler, S. Jo, G. Cachemaille, D. Montague, G.

Quilico, R. Pierotti/Chorus and Orchestra of the Opéra de Lyon/J.E. Gardiner.
2 CDs-PHILIPS
La donna del lago (1819)
- M. Caballé, J. Hamari, F. Bonisolli, P. Bottazzo, P. Washington/Chorus and Symphony Orchestra of Italian Radio (RAI), Turin/P. Bellugi.
  2 CDs-MELODRAM
- K. Ricciarelli, L. Valentini Terrani, D. Gonzales, D. Raffanti, S. Ramey/Prague Philharmonic Choir, Chamber Orchestra of Europe/M. Pollini.
  3 CDs-RICORDI-FONIT CETRA

Elisabetta, regina d'Inghilterra (1815)
M. Caballé, V. Masterson, J. Carreras, U. Benelli/Ambrosian Singers, London Symphony Orchestra/G. Masini.
2 CDs-PHILIPS
Ermione (1819)
C. Gasdia, M. Zimmermann, C. Merritt, E. Palacio/Prague Philharmonic Chorus, Orchestre Philharmonique de Monte Carlo/C. Scimone.
2 CDs-ERATO
La gazza ladra (1817)
K. Ricciarelli, W. Matteuzzi, S. Ramey, B. Manca di Nissa, L. D'Intino, F. Furlanetto, R. Coviello/Prague Philharmonic Choir, Symphony Orchestra of Italian Radio (RIA), Turin/G. Gelmetti.
3 CDs-SONY
La gazzetta (1816)
G. Morigi, P. Barbacini, F. Federici, A. Cicogna, A. Ariostini/Coro F. Cilea, Reggio Calabria, Piacenza Symphony Orchestra/F. Luisi.
2 CDs-BONGIOVANNI
Guillaume Tell (1829)
- M. Freni, S. Milnes, L. Pavarotti, N. Ghiaurov, F. Mazzoli, J. Tomlinson/Ambrosian Opera Chorus, National Philharmonic Orchestra/R. Chailly.
  4 CDs-DECCA
- C. Studer, G. Zancanaro, C. Merritt, G. Surjan/Chorus and Orchestra of La Scala, Milan/R. Muti.
  4 CDs-PHILIPS

L'inganno felice (1812)
E. Cundari, F. Jacopucci, P. Montarsolo/A. Scarlatti Chorus and Orchestra of Italian Radio (RAI), Naples.
1 CD-AS-Disc
L'Italiana in Algeri (1813)
M. Horne, E. Palacio, S. Ramey, D. Trimarchi, K. Battle, N. Zaccaria/Prague Philharmonic Choir, I Solisti Veneti/C. Scimone.
2 CDs-ERATO
Maometto II (1820)
J. Anderson, M. Zimmermann, E. Palacio, S. Ramey, L. Dale/Ambrosian Opera Chorus, Philharmonia Orchestra/C. Scimone.
3 CDs-PHILIPS

Moïse et Pharaon (1827)
J. Gregor, A. Molnar, S. Solyom-Nagy, J.B. Nagy, M. Kalmar, J. Hamari/Hungarian Radio Chorus, Hungarian State Opera Orchestra/L. Gardelli.
3 CDs-HUNGAROTON
Mosè in Egitto (1818)
R. Raimondi, S. Nimsgern, S. Browne, J. Anderson, E. Palacio, Z. Gal, S. Fisichella/Ambrosian Opera Chorus, Philharmonic Orchestra/C. Scimone.
L'occasione fa il ladro (1812)
L. Serra, L. D'Intino, R. Gimenez, E. Gavazzi, J.P. Raftery, C. Desderi/Orchestra Giovanile Italiana/S. Accardo.
2 CDs-RICORDI-FONIT CETRA
Otello, ossia il Moro di Venezia (1816)
F. von Stade, J. Carreras, G. Pastine, S. Fisichella/Ambrosian Opera Chorus, Philharmonic Orchestra/J. Lopez Cobos.
2 CDs-PHILIPS
La pietra del paragone (1812)
B. Wolff, E. Bonazzi, A. Elgar, J. Reardon, J. Carreras, A. Foldi, J. Diaz, R. Murcell/The Clarion Concerts Chorus and Orchestra/N. Jenkins.
2 CDs-VANGUARD
La scala di seta (1812)
L. Serra, C. Bartoli, W. Matteuzzi, N. De Carolis, R. Coviello, O. Di Credico/Orchestra of the Teatro Comunale, Bologna/G. Ferro.
2 CDs-FONIT-CETRA
Semiramide (1823)
- J. Sutherland, M. Horne, J. Rouleau, J. Serge, S. Malas/Ambrosian Opera Chorus, London Symphony Orchestra/R. Bonynge.
  3 CDs-DECCA
- M. Caballé, M. Horne, S. Ramey, F. Araiza, D. Kavrakos/Chorus and Orchestra of the Aix-en-Provence Festival/J. Lopez Cobos. 3 CDs-LEGATO CLASSIC

Il Signor Bruschino (1813)
E. Dara, M. Devia, A. Rinaldi, E. Favano, D. Gonzales, A. Antoniozzi/Symphony Orchestra of Italian Radio (RAI), Turin/D. Renzetti.
2 CDs-RICORDI-FONIT-CETRA
Tancredi (1813)
M. Horne, L. Cuberli, E. Palacio, N. Zaccaria, P. Schuman, B. Manca di Nissa/Chorus and Orchestra of the Teatro La Fenice, Venice/R. Weikert.
3 CDs-RICORDI-FONIT-CETRA
Il turco in Italia (1814)
- M. Callas, N. Rossi-Lemeni, N. Gedda, M. Stabile, F. Calabrese, J. Giardino/Chorus and Orchestra of La Scala, Milan/G. Gavazzeni.
  2 CDs-EMI
- S. Jo, S. Alaimo, E. Fissore, R. Gimenez, A. Corbelli, S. Mentzer/Ambrosian Opera Chorus, The Academy of St Martin-inp-the-Fields/N. Marriner.
  2 CDs-PHILIPS

Il viaggio a Rheims (1825)
C. Gasdia, L. Valentini Terrani, L. Cuberli, K. Ricciarelli, E. Gimenez, F. Araiza, S. Ramey, R. Raimondi, E. Dara, L. Nucci/Prague Philharmonic Choir, The Chamber Orchestra of Europe/C. Abbado.
2 CDs-RICORDI-FONIT-CETRA
Zelmira (1822)
C. Gasdia, W. Matteuzzi, C. Merritt, B. Fink, J. Garcia/Ambrosian Singer, I Solisti Veneti/C. Scimone.
2 CDs-ERATO

ROUSSEL, ALBERT (1869–1937)
Padmâvatî (1923)
M. Horne, N. Gedda, J. Van Dam, J. Berbié, C. Burles/Orfeon Donastiarra Chorus, Orchestra of the Théâtre Capitol, Toulouse/M. Plasson.
2 CDs-EMI

SAINT-SAËNS, CAMILLE (1835–1921)
Henry VIII (1883)
P. Rouillon, M. Command, L. Vignon, A. Gabriel/Chorus of the Théâtre des Arts de Rouen, Orchestre Lyrique Français/A. Guingal.
3 CDs-CHANT DU MONDE
Samson et Dalila (1877)
- J. Vickers, R. Gorr, E. Blanc, A. Diakov/René Duclos Choir, Orchestre de l'Opéra de Paris/G. Prêtre.
  2 CDs-EMI
- P. Domingo, W. Meier, A. Fondary, S. Ramey/Chorus and Orchestra of the Opéra Bastille/M. W. Chung.
  2 CDs-EMI

SALIERI, ANTONIO (1750–1825)
Les Danaides (1784)
M. Marshall, D. Kavrakos, R. Gimenez, C. Bartha/Südfunk Chor, Stuttgart Radio Symphony Orchestra/G. Gelmetti.
2 CDs-EMI
Axur, re d'Ormus (1788)
A. Martin, C. Rayam, E. Mei, E. Nova, A. Vespasiani/Coro Guido d'Arezzo, Russe Philharmonic Orchestra/R. Clemencic.
3 CDs-NUOVA ERA
Prima la musica, poi le parole (1786)
M. Casula, K. Gamberucci, G. Polidori, G. Gatti/North Bohemian Philharmonic Chamber Orchestra/D. Sanfilippo.
2 CDs-BONGIOVANNI (with Scarlatti's *Lesbina e Adolfo*)

SCARLATTI, ALESSANDRO (1660–1725)
La Griselda (1721)
M. Freni, S. Bruscantini, L. Alva, V. Lucchetti, R. Panerai, C. Lavani/Chorus A. Scarlatti Chorus and Orchestra of Italian Radio (RAI), Naples/N. Sanzogno
2 CDs-MEMORIES

SCARLATTI, DOMENICO (1685–1757)
La Dirindina (1715)
G. Gatti, K. Gamberucci, G. Mari/Complesso da Camera dell'Associazione Filarmonica Umbra/F. Maestri.
1 CD-BONGIOVANNI

SCHMIDT, FRANZ (1874–1939)
Notre-Dame (1914)
G. Jones, K. Borris, J. King, H. Laubenthal, K. Moll, H. Welker/St. Hedwige Cathedral Choir, RIAS Chamber Choir, Berlin Radio Symphony Orchestra/C. Perick.
2 CDs-CAPRICCIO

SCHOENBERG, ARNOLD
(1874–1951)
Erwartung (1924)
A. Silja/Vienna Philharmonic Orchestra/C. Von Dohnanyi.
2 CDs-DECCA (+ Berg's *Wozzeck*).
Moses und Aron (1957)
F. Mazura, P. Langridge, B. Bonney, M. Zakai, D. Harper, A. Haugland/Chicago Symphony Chorus and Orchestra/G. Solti.
2 CDs-DECCA

SCHREKER, FRANZ (1878–1934)
Der Ferne Klang (1912)
G. Schnaut, T. Moser, S. Nimsgern, H. Helm, V. von Halem, B. Scherler/Berlin Radio Chorus and Orchestra/G. Albrecht.
2 CDs-CAPRICCIO

SCHUBERT, FRANZ (1797–1828)
Fierrabras (1897)
J. Protschka, K. Mattila, R. Holl, T. Hampson, R. Gambill, L. Polgar, C. Studer/A Schoenberg Choir of Vienna, Chamber Orchestra of Europe/C. Abbado.
2 CDs-DG

SCHUMANN, ROBERT
(1810–1856)
Genoveva (1850)
E. Moser, G. Schröter, P. Schreier, D. Fischer-Dieskau, S. Lorenz, S. Vogel/Berlin Radio Chorus, Leipzig Gewandhaus Orchestra/K. Masur.
2 CDs-BERLIN CLASSICS

SMETANA, BEDRICH (1824–1884)
Libuse (1881)
G. Benacková, V. Zitek, A. Svorc, L. M. Vodicka, K. Prusa, R. Tucek, E. Dépoltova, V. Soukoupova/ Prague National Opera Chorus and Orchestra/Z. Kosler.
3 CDs-SUPRAPHON
Prodaná nevesta (1866)
G. Benacková, P. Dvorsky, M. Kopp, R. Novak/ Prague Philharmonic Chorus and Orchestra/Z. Kosler.
3 CDs-SUPRAPHON

SHOSTAKOVICH, DMITRY DMITRIYEVICH
(1906–1975)
Katerina Izmaylova (1959)
G. Zipola, V. Gourov, A. Zagrebelny, S. Doubrovine, A. Istchenko/Kiev State Chorus and Orchestra/S. Tourtchak.
2 CDs-CHANT DU MONDE
Ledi Makbet Mtsenskago Uezda (1934)
G. Vishnevskaya, T. Valiakka, B. Finnilä, N. Gedda, W. Krenn/Ambrosian Opera Chorus, London Symphony Orchestra/M. Rostropovich.
2 CDs-EMI
Nos (1930)
E. Akhimov, B. Tarkhov, V. Belikh, B. Droujinine, A. Lomonossov, L. Sapeguina, L. Oukolova/Moscow Chamber Music Theater Chorus and Orchestra/G. Rozhdestvensky.
2 CDs-CHANT DU MONDE

SPOHR, LOUIS (1784–1859)
Jessonda (1823)
J. Varady, R. Behle, K. Moll, T. Moser, D. Fischer-Dieskau, P. Haage/Hamburg Opera Chorus, Hamburg State Philharmonic Orchestra/G. Albrecht.
2 CDs-ORFEO

SPONTINI, GASPARE (1774–1851)
Agnes von Hohenstaufen (1829)
M. Caballé, A. Stella, B. Prevedi, S. Bruscantini, G. Guelfi/Rome Symphony Chorus and Orchestra/R. Muti.
2 CDs-MEMORIES
Olympie (1819)
J. Varady, S. Toczyska, F. Tagliavini, D. Fischer-Dieskau, G. Fortune, J. Becker/Deutsche Oper Chorus, Berlin, and Berlin Radio Symphony Orchestra/G. Albrecht.
2 CDs-ORFEO
La vestale (1807)
R. Plowright, G. Pasino, F. Araiza, P. Lefebvre, F. De Grandis/Bavarian Radio Chorus, Munich Radio Symphony Orchestra/G. Kuhn.
2 CDs-ORFEO

STRAUSS, RICHARD (1864–1949)
Die Ägyptische Helena (1928)
G. Jones, M. Kastu, B. Hendricks, W. White, B. Finnilä, C. Rayam/Kenneth Jewell Chorale, Detroit Symphony Orchestra/A. Dorati.
2 CDs-DECCA
Arabella (1933)
- K. Te Kanawa, F. Grundheber, E. Gutstein, G. Fontana, P. Seiffert, H. Dernesch/Covent Garden Chorus and Orchestra/J. Tate.
  3 CDs-DECCA
- L. Della Casa, G. London, O. Edelmann, H. Güden, A. Dermota, I. Malaniuk, W. Kmentt, E. Wächter/Vieena Staatsoper Chorus, Vienna Philharmonic Orchestra/G. Solti.
  2 CDs-DECCA

Ariadne auf Naxos (1912)
- E. Schwarzkopf, R. Streich, R. Schock, I. Seefried, H. Prey, K. Dönch/Philharmonia Orchestra/H. von Karajan.
  2 CDs-EMI
- J. Norman, E. Gruberova, J. Varady, P. Frey, O. Bär, D. Fischer-Dieskau/Leipzig Gewandhaus Orchestra/K. Masur.
  2 CDs-PHILIPS

Capriccio (1942)
E. Schwarzkopf, E. Wächter, N. Gedda, D. Fischer-Dieskau, H. Hotter, C. Ludwig/Philharmonia Orchestra/W. Sawallisch.
2 CDs-EMI
Daphne (1938)
L. Popp, O. Wenkel, R. Goldberg, P. Schreier, K. Moll/Bavarian Radio Symphony Chorus and Orchestra/B. Haitink.
2 CDs-EMI
Elektra (1909)
- B. Nilsson, M. Collier, R. Resnik, T. Krause, G. Stolze/Vienna State Opera Chorus, Vienna Philharmonic Orchestra/G. Solit.
  2 CDs-DECCA
- H. Behrens, N. Secunde, C. Ludwig, J. Hynninen, R. Ulfung/Tanglewood Festival Chorus, Boston Symphony Orchestra/S. Ozawa.
  2 CDs-PHILIPS

Feuersnot (1901)
J. Varady, B. Weikl, H.D. Bader, H. Berger-Tuna/ Munich Radio Chous and Symphony Orchestra/H. Fricke.
2 CDs-PILZ
Die Frau ohne Schatten (1919)
- L. Rysanek, J. King, R. Hesse, W. Berry, B. Nilsson/Vienna State Opera Chorus and Orchestra/K. Böhm.
  3 CDs-DG
- J. Varady, P. Domingo, H. Behrens, J. Van Dam, R. Runkel/Vienna State Opera Chorus, Vienna Philharmonic Orchestra/G. Solit.
  3 CDs-DECCA

Friedenstag (1938)
R. Roloff, A Marc, T. Cook, K. Williams, R. Cassilly, J. Wood, P. Schmidt, P. van Derick/The Collegiate Chorale and Orchestra/R. Bass.
1 CD-KOCH INTERNATIONAL CLASSICS
Guntram (1894)
R. Goldberg, I. Tokody, S. Solyom-Nagy, I. Gati, J. Gregor/Hungarian Army Choir, Hungarian State Symphony Orchestra/E. Queler.
2 CDs-CBS
Intermezzo (1924)
L. Popp, D. Fischer-Dieskau, G. Fuchs, A. Dallapozza, K. Hirte, K. Moll/Bavarian Radio Orchestra/W. Sawallisch.
2 CDs-EMI
Die Liebe der Danae (1952)
P. Schöffler, J. Traxel, J. Gostic, L. Szemere, A. Kupper, A. Felbermayer, E. Réthy/Vienna State Opera Chorus, Vienna Philharmonic Orchestra/C. Krauss.
2 CDs-ORFEO
Der Rosenkavalier (1911)
E. Schwarzkopf, O. Edelmann, C. Ludwig, T. Stich-Randall, E. Wächter, N. Gedda/Philharmonic Chorus and Orchestra/H. von Karajan.
3 CDs-EMI
Salome (1905)
- H. Behrens, A Baltsa, J. Van Dam, K. W. Böhm, W. Ochman/Vienna Philharmonic/H. von Karajan.
  2 CDs-EMI
- C. Studer, L. Rysanek, H. Hiestermann, B. Terfel, C. Bieber/Deutsche Oper, Berlin/G. Sinopoli.
  2 CDs-GD

Die schweigsame Frau (1935)
T. Adam, A. Burmeister, J. Scovotti, W. Schöne, E. Büchner, T. Schmidt/Dresden State Opera Chorus, Dresden Staatskapelle Orchestra/M. Janowski.
3 CDs-EMI

STRAVINSKY, IGOR (1882–1971)

Mavra (1922)
S. Belinck, M. Simmons, P. Rideaut, S. Kolk/CBC Symphony Orchestra/I. Stravinsky.
1 CD-SONY
Oedipus Rex (1927)
– G. Shirely, S. Verrett, D. Gramm, C. Watson, L. Driscoll, J. Westbrook/Washington Society Chorus and Orchestra/I. Stravinsky.
1 CD-SONY
– V. Cole, A. S. von Otter, S. Estes, H. Sotin, N. Gedda, P. Chéreau/Swedish Radio Chorus, Ericson Chamber Choir, Swedish Radio Symphony Orchestra/E. P. Salonen.
1 CD-SONY
The Rake's Progress (1951)
– D. Garrad, J. Raskin, A. Young, J. Reardon, J. Manning, R. Sarfaty/S Sadler's Wells Chorus, Royal Philharmonic Orchestra/I.S.I. Stravinsky.
2 CDs-SONY
– S. Dean, C. Pope, P. Langridge, S. Ramey, A. Varnay, S. Walker/London Sinfonietta Chorus and Orchestra/R. Chailly.
2 CDs-DECCA

SZYMANOWSKI, KAROL (1882–1937)

Król Roger (1926)
F. Skulski, B. Zagorzanka, S. Kowalski, Z. Nikodem, J. Ostapiuk, R. Racewiz/Chorus and Orchestra of the Weikli Theatre, Warsaw/R. Satanowski.
2 CDs-KOCH SCHWANN

THOMAS, AMBROISE (1811–1896)

Hamlet (1868)
S. Milnes, J. Sutherland, J. Morris, B. Conrad, G. Winbergh/Welsh National Opera Orchestra and Chorus/R. Bonynge.
3 CDs-DECCA

TIPPETT, MICHAEL (1905)

King Priam (1962)
R. Tear, T. Allen, N. Bailey, F. Palmer, Y. Minton, P. Langridge, S. Robert, H. Harper/London Sinfonietta Chorus and Orchestra/D. Atherton
2 CDs-DECCA

VERDI, GIUSEPPE (1813–1901)

Aida (1871)
– L. Price, G. Bumbry, P. Domingo, S. Milnes, R. Raimondi/John Alldis Choir, London Symphony Orchestra/E. Leinsdorf
3 CDs-RCA
– M. Caballé, F. Cossotto, P. Domingo, P. Cappuccilli, N. Ghiaurov/Covent Garden Chorus, Philharmonia Orchestra/R. Muti.
3 CDs-EMI
Alzira (1845)
I. Cotrubas, F. Araiza, R. Bruson, J. H. Rootering/Bavarian Radio Chorus and Orchestra/L. Gardelli.
2 CDs-ORFEO
Aroldo (1857)
M. Caballé, G. Cecchele, J. Pons, V. Manno, L. Lebhery/New York Oratorio Society Choir, New York Opera Orchestra/E. Queler.
2 CDs-CBS
Attila (1846)
S. Ramey, C. Studer, G. Zancanaro, N. Shicoff, G. Surjan/Chorus and Orchestra of La Scala, Milan/R. Muti.
2 CDs-EMI
Un ballo in maschera (1859)
– C. Bergonzi, L. Price, R. Merrill, S. Verrett, R. Grist/RCA Italiana Chorus and Orchestra/E. Leinsdorf.
2 CDs-RCA
– L. Pavarotti, M. Price, R. Bruson, C. Ludwig, K. Battle/London Opera Chorus, National Philharmonic Orchestra/G. Solti.
2 CDs-DECCA
La battaglia di Legnano (1849)
J. Carreras, K. Ricciarelli, M. Manuguerra, N. Ghiuselev/Austrian Radio Chorus and Orchestra/L. Gardelli.
2 CDs-PHILIPS
Il corsaro (1848)
J. Carreras, C. Grant, J. Norman, M. Caballé, G. Mastromei/Ambrosian Singers, New Philharmonia Orchestra/L. Gardelli.
2 CDs-PHILIPS
Don Carlos (1867)
– P. Domingo, K. Ricciarelli, R. Raimondi, L. Nucci, L. Valentini Terrani, N. Chiaurov/Chorus and Orchestra of La Scala, Milan/C. Abbado.
4 CDs-DG
– C. Bergonzi, R. Tebaldi, N. Ghiaurov, D. Fischer-Dieskau, G. Bumbry, M. Talvela/G. Solti.
3 CDs-DECCA
– M. Sylvester, A. Millo, S. Ramey, V. Chernov, D. Zaijck, F. Furlanetto/Chorus and Orchestra of the Metropolitan Opera House, New York/J. Levine.
3 CDs-SON
I due Foscari (1844)
P. Cappuccilli, J. Carreras, K. Ricciarelli, S. Ramey/Chorus and Orchestra of Austrian Radio/L. Gardelli.
2 CDs-PHILIPS
Ernani (1844)
– P. Domingo, R. Bruson, M. Freni, N. Ghiaurov/Chorus and Orchestra of La Scala, Milan/R. Muti.
3 CDs-EMI
– V. La Scola, P. Coni, D. Dessí, M. Petusi/Bratislava Chamber Choir, Orchestra Internazional d'Italia/G. Carella.
2 CDs-NUOVA ERA
Falstaff (1893)
– G. Valdengo, H. Nelli, T. Stich-Randall, C. Elmo, A. Madasi, N. Merriman, F. Guarrara/Robert Shaw Chorale, NBC Symphony Orchestra/A. Toscanini.
2 CDs-RAC
– T. Gobbi, E. Schwarzkopf, A. Moffo, F. Barbieri, L. Alva, N. Merriman, R. Panerai/Philharmonia Orchestra/H. von Karajan.
2 CDs-EMI
La forza del destino (1862)
– L. Price, P. Domingo, S. Milnes, B. Giaiotti, G. Bacquier, F. Cossotto/John Alldis Choir, London Symphony Orchestra/J. Levine.
3 CDs-RCA
– M. Freni, P. Domingo, G. Zancanaro, P. Plishka, S. Bruscantini, D. Zajic/Chorus and Orchestra of La Scala, Milan/R. Muti.
3 CDs-EMI
Un giorno di regno, ossia il finto Stanislao (1840)
F. Cossotto, J. Norman, J. Carreras, I. Wixell, W. Canzarolli, V. Sardinero/Ambrosian Singers, Royal Philharmonic Orchestra/L. Gardelli.
2 CDs-PHILIPS
Giovanna d'Arco (1845)
P. Domingo, S. Milnes, M. Caballé/Ambrosian Opera Chorus, London Symphony Orchestra/J. Levine.
2 CDs-EMI
Jerusalem (1847)
L. Gencer, G. Aragall, E. Savoldi, G.G. Guelfi/Chorus and Orchestra of the Teatro La Fenice, Venice/G. Gavazzeni.
2 CDs-MELODRAM
I Lombardi alla prima crociata (1843)
– R. Scotto, L. Pavarotti, R. Raimondi, U. Grilli/Chorus and Orchestra of the Teatro dell'Opera, Rome/G. Gavazzeni.
2 CDs-MEMORIES
– C. Deutekom, P. Domingo, R. Raimondi, J. Lo Monaco/Ambrosian Singers, Royal Philharmonic Orchestra/L. Gardelli.
2 CDs-PHILIPS
Luisa Miller (1849)
– M. Caballé, L. Pavarotti, S. Milnes, A. Reynolds, B. Giaiotti, R. van Allan/London Opera Chorus, National Philharmonic Orchestra/P. Maag.
2 CDs-DECCA
– A. Millo, P. Domingo, V. Chernov, F. Quivar, J.H. Rootering, P. Plishka/Chorus and Orchestra of the Metropolitan Opera House, New York/J. Levine.
2 CDs-SONY
Macbeth (1847)
P. Cappuccilli, S. Verrett, P. Domingo, N. Ghiaurov/Chorus and Orchestra of La Scala, Milan/C. Abbado.
3 CDs-DG
I masnadieri (1847)
– R. Raimondi, C. Bergonzi, P. Cappuccilli, M. Caballé/Ambrosian Singers, New Philharmonia Orchestra/L. Gardelli.
2 CDs-PHILIPS
– S. Ramey, F. Bonisolli, M. Manuguerra, J. Sutherland/Chorus and Orchestra of Welsh National Opera/R. Bonynge.
2 CDs-DECCA
Nabucco (1842)
– M. Manuguerra, R. Scotto, N. Ghiaurov, V. Lucchetti, E. Obraztsova/Ambrosian Opera Chorus, Philharmonic Orchestra/R. Muti.
2 CDs-EMI
– P. Cappuccilli, G.Dimitrova, E. Nesterenko, P. Domingo, Lucia Valentini Terrani/Chorus and Orchestra of Deutsche Oper/G. Sinopli.
2 CDs-DG
Oberto, conte di San Bonifacio (1839)
R. Baldani, C. Bergonzi, R. Panerai, G. Dimitrova/Munich Radio Chorus and Orchestra/L. Gardelli.
2 CDs-ORFEO
Otello (1887)
– J. Vickers, L. Rysanek, T. Gobbi, F. Andreolli/

Chorus and Orchestra of the Teatro dell'Opera, Rome/T. Serafin.
2 CDs-RCA
- M. del Monaco, R. Tebaldi, A. Protti, N. Romanato/Vienna State Opera Chorus, Vienna Philharmonic Orchestra/H. von Karajan.
2 CDs-DECCA

Rigoletto (1851)
- C. Bergonzi, D. Fischer-Dieskau, R. Scotto, I. Vinco, F. Cossotto/Orchestra and Chorus of La Scala, Milan/R. Kubelik.
2 CDs-DG
- L. Pavarotti, S. Milnes, J. Sutherland, M. Talvela, H. Tourangeau/Ambrosian Opera Chorus, London Symphony Orchestra/R. Bonynge.
2 CDs-DECCA

Simon Boccanegra (1857)
- P. Cappuccilli, N. Ghiaurov, J. Van Dam, M. Freni, J. Carreras/Chorus and Orchestra of La Scala, Milan/C. Abbado.
2 CDs-DG
- R. Bruson, R. Scandiuzzi, G. De Angelis, M. Nicolesco, G. Sabbatini/Nikikai Chorus Group, Tokyo Symphony Orchestra/R. Paternostro.
2 CDs-CAPRICCIO

Stiffelio (1850)
J. Carreras, S. Sass, M. Manuguerra, W. Ganzarolli/Austrian Radio Chorus and Symphony Orchestra/L. Gardelli.
2 CDs-PHILIPS

La traviata (1853)
- M. Callas, G. Di Stefano, E. Bastianini/Chorus and Orchestra of La Scala, Milan/C.M. Giulini.
2 CDs-EMI
- R. Scotto, A. Kraus, R. Bruson/Ambrosian Opera Chorus, Philharmonia Orchestra/R. Muti.

Il trovatore (1853)
- S. Milnes, L. Price, F. Cossotto, P. Domingo, B. Giaiotti/Ambrosian Opera Chorus, New Philharmonia Orchestra/Z. Mehta.
2 CDs-RCA
- I. Wixell, J. Sutherland, M. Horne, L. Pavarotti, N. Ghiaurov/London Opera Chorus, National Philharmonic Orchestra/R. Bonynge.
2 CDs-DECCA

Les vêpres siciliennes (1855)
S. Milnes, P. Domingo, M. Arroyo, R. Raimondi/John Alldis Choir, New Philharmonia Orchestra/J. Levine.
3 CDs-RCA

VIVALDI, ANTONIO (1678–1741)

Catone in Utica (1737)
C. Gasdia, M. Schmiege, S. Rigacci, M. Zimmermann, L. Lendy, E. Palacio/I Solisti Veneti/C. Scimone.
2 CDs-ERATO

Il farnace (1727)
M. Dupuy, K. Angeloni, P. Malakova, D. Dessí, L. Rizzi, K. Gamberucci, R. Garazioti/San Remo Symphony Orchestra/M. De Bernart.
2 CDs-ARKADIA

Orlando Furioso (1727)
M. Horne, V. de los Angeles, L. Valentini Terrani, C. Gonzales, L. Kozma, S. Bruscantini, N. Zaccaria/Coro Amici della Polifonia, I Solisti Veneti/C. Scimone.
3 CDs-ERATO

WAGNER, RICHARD (1813–1883)

Die Feen (1888)
K. Moll, L.E. Gray, K. Lövaas, K. Laki, J. Alexander, J. Anderson, R. Hermann, J.H. Rootering, C. Studer/Bavarian Radio Chorus and Symphony Orchestra/W. Sawallisch.
3 CDs-ORFEO

Der fliegende Holländer (1843)
- G. London, L. Rysanek, G. tozzi, K. Liebl, R. Elias, R. Lewis/Covent Garden Chorus and Orchestra/A. Dorati.
2 CDs-DECCA
- J. Van Dam, D. Vejzovic, K. Moll, P; Hofmann, K. Borris, T. Moser/Vienna State Opera Chorus, Berlin Philharmonic Orchestra/H. von Karajan.
3 CDs-EMI

Das Liebesverbot (1836)
H. Imdhal, A. Dermota, K. Equiluz, H. Zadek, A. Steffek, C. Sorell/Chorus and Orchestra of Austrian Radio/R. Heger.
2 CDs-MELODRAM

Lohengrin (1850)
- J. Thomas, E. Grümmer, C. Ludwig, D. Fischer-Dieskau, G. Frick, O. Wiener/Vienna State Opera Chorus, Vienna Philharmonic Orchestra/R. Kempe.
3 CDs-EMI
- P. Domingo, J. Norman, E. Randova, S. Nimsgern, H. Sotin, Dietrich Fischer-Dieskau/Vienna State Opera Chorus, Vienna Philharmonic Orchestra/G. Solti.
4 CDs-DECCA

Die Meistersinger von Nürnberg (1868)
- O. Edelmann, H. Hopf, E. Schwarzkopf, E. Kunz, F. Dalberg, G. Unger, I. Malaniuk, H. Pflanzl/Bayreuth Festival Chorus and Orchestra/H. von Karajan.
4 CDs-EMI
- F. Frantz, R. Schock, E. Grümmer, B. Kusche, G. Frick, G. Unger, M. Höffgen, G. Neidlinger/Chorus of the Deutsche Oper, Berlin, Chorus of St. Hedwig's Cathedral, Berlin, Berlin Philharmonic Orchestra/R. Kempe.
4 CDs-EMI

Parsifal (1882)
- G. London, M. Talvela, H. Hotter, J. Thomas, G. Neidlinger, I. Dalis/Bayreuth Festival Chorus and Orchestra/H. Knappertsbusch.
4 CDs-PHILIPS
- J. Van Dam, V. von Halem, K. Moll, P. Hofmann, S. Nimsgern, D. Vejzovic/Chorus of the Deutsche Oper, Berlin/H. von Karajan.
4 CDs-DG

Rienzi der Letze der Tribunen (1842)
R. Kollo, S. Wennberg, T. Adam, N. Hillebrand, J. Martin, P. Schreier/Dresden State Opera Chorus, Dresden Staatskappell Orchestra/H. Hollreiser.
3 CDs-EMI

Der Ring des Nibelungen
(*Das Rheingold*, 1869/*Die Walküre*, 1870/ *Siegfried*, 1876/ *Götterdammerung*, 1874.)
- B. Nilsson, R. Grespin, K. Flagstad, D. Fischer-Dieskau, G. London, W. Windgassen, G. Neidlinger, G. Frick, H. Hotter/Vienna Philharmonic/G. Solti.
15 CDs-DECCA (also available as separate operas)
- H. Dernesch, R. Crespin, G. Janowitz, J. Vickers, T. Stewart, D. Fischer-Dieskau, M. Talvela, G. Stolze, K. Ridderbusch/Berlin Philharmonic/H. von Karajan.
15 CDs-DG (also available as separate operas)

Tannhäuser (1845)
- R. Kollo, H. Dernesch, C. Ludwig, V. Braun, H. Sotin/Vienna State Opera Chorus, Vienna Philharmonic Orchestra/G. Solti.
3 CDs-DECCA
- P. Domingo, C. Studer, A. Baltsa, A. Schmidt, M. Salminen/Covent Garden Chorus, Philharmonia Orchestra/G. Sinopoli.
3 CDs-DG

Tristan und Isolde (1865)
- L. Suthaus, K. Flagstad, D. Fischer-Dieskau, J. Greindl, B. Thebom/Covent Garden Chorus, Philharmonia Orchestra/W. Furtwaengler.
4 CDs-EMI
- J. Vickers, H. Dernesch, W. Berry, K. Ridderbusch, C. Ludwig/Chorus of the Deutsche Oper, Berlin/H. von Karajan.
4 CDs-EMI

WEBER, CARL MARIA VON (1786–1826)

Euryanthe (1823)
J. Norman, R. Hunter, N. Gedda, T. Krause, S. Vogel, R. Krahmer/Leipzig Radio Chorus, Dresden Staatskapelle/M. Janowski.
3 CDs-EMI

Der Freischütz (1821)
- E. Grümmer, L. Otto, R. Schock, K.C. Kohn, H. Prey/Chorus of the Deutsche Oper, Berlin, Berlin Philharmonic Orchestra/J. Keilberth
2 CDs-EMI
- G. Janowitz, E. Mathis, P. Schreier, T. Adam, B. Weikl, S. Vogel/Leipzig Radio Chorus, Dresden Staatskapelle Orchestra/C. Kleiber.
2 CDs-DG

Oberon (1826)
- D. Grobe, B. Nilsson, P. Domingo, H. Prey, J. Hamari, M. Schiml/Bavarian Radio Chorus and Orchestra/R. Kubelik.
2 CDs-DG
- G. Lakes, D. Voigt, B. Heppner, D. Croft, D. Ziegler, V. Livengood/Cologne Opera Chorus, Colonge Philharmonic Orchestra/J. Conlon.
2 CDs-EMI

WEILL, KURT (1900–1950)

Aufstieg und Fall der Stadt Mahagonny (1930)
- L. Lenya, G.Litz, H. Günther, G. Mund, F. Göllnitz, S. Roth, P. Markwort/Chorus and Orchestra of North West German Radio/W. Brückner-Rüggeberg.
2 CDs-CBS
- A. Silja, A. Schlemm, T. Lehrberger, K. Hirte, W. Neumann, F. Mayer/Cologne 'Pro Musica' Chorus, Cologne Radio Orchestra/J. Latham-Koenig.
2 CDs-CAPRICCIO

Die Dreigroschenoper (1928)

- L. Lenya, W. Trenk-Trebitsch, E. Shellow, J. von Koczian, W. Neuss/G Günther Arndt Choir, Senders Freies Orchestra, Berlin/W. Brückner-Rüggeberg.
  2 CDs-CBS
- U. Lemper, R. Kollo, M. Adorf, H. Dernesch, Milva, W. Reichmann, S. Tremper, R. Boyesn/ Rias Kammerchor, Rias Berlin Sinfonietta/J. Mauceri.
  1 CD-DECCA

Der Zar lässt sich photographieren (1928)
B. McDaniel, C. Pohl, T. Lehrberger, U. Tocha, M. Napier, H. Kruse/Chorus and Orchestra of Cologne Radio/Jan Latham-Koenig.
1 CD-CAPRICCIO

WOLF, HUGO (1860–1903)

Der Corregidor (1896)
H. Donath, D. Soffel, D. Fischer-Dieskau, W. Hollweg, K. Moll, V. von Halem/Rias Chorus and Symphony Orchestra, Berlin/G. Albrecht.
2 CDs-SCHWANN

WOLF-FERRARI, ERMANNO (1876–1948)

Il campiello (1936)
G. Devinu, M. Bolgan, D. Mazzuccato, C. De *Mola, U. Benelli, M.R. Cosotti, M. Comencini/ Chorus and Orchestra of the Teatro G. Verdi, Trieste/N. Bareza.*
2 CDs-RICORDI-FONIT CETRA

ZANDONAI, RICCARDO

(1883–1944)
Francesca da Rimini (1914)
R. Kabaivanska, F. Prandini, M. Manuguerra, W. Matteuzzi, P. De Palma/Bulgarian Radio Chorus and Orchestra/M. Arena.
2 CDs-RCA

PICTURE SOURCES

Giovanni Agostinucci; 233, 242. Amati Bacciardi: 22a, 41, 41, 62, 267a, 273a, 288, 306b, 326b. Archivio Fotografico Teatro alla Scala/Lelli & Masotti: 19, 34, 37, 63a, 76a, 78b, 83r, 85a, 87a, 95, 136a, 165a, 180a, 199b, 210b, 213a, 218a, 295a, 309, 336, 337b, 340a, 365b, 369b, 370b, 377b. Bisazza: 279. Maurizio Buscarino: 31a, 156a. Enzo Conte: 155. Alberto Dallatomasina: 20. De Rota: 214, 246a. Mike Evans: 217b. Gianfranco Fainello: 13, 103a, 224a, 239a, 374al. Corrado Maria Falsini: 102b, 318. Fayer: 8bl, 27a, 50b, 125b, 131, 137, 140a, 144, 147b, 152a, 154a, 163a, 163b, 167b, 169b, 171b, 188b, 194a, 197a, 207a, 208b, 210b, 218b, 219a, 225, 228, 240a, 244a, 248b, 253a, 255b, 296b, 297, 325b, 328a, 337a, 342, 344b, 367a, 371b, 377a, 380b, 382b. Inasaridse: 26b. Gabi Kahle/DGG: 168b. Anne Kirchbach: 26a. Fabio Lerisini: 30b. Magic-Vision: 245a. Marchiori: 39b, 48, 49a, 66b, 108, 126, 130b, 139b, 186a, 191, 220, 221b, 247, 312, 330a, 361b, 378a. Marco: 143a. Montanari-Marson: 244b, 292b. M. Montanari – L. Tazzari: 94a. Piccagliani: 21b. Piccardo e Rosso: 152b. Jorg Reichardt/DGG: 216, 335b. Luciano Romano: 24b, 53a, 55, 56b, 57, 59, 64, 83a, 89a, 105, 111, 120, 129, 140b, 229a, 251a, 259, 276b, 303, 307. V. Solowjow: 134b. Christian Steiner/DGG: 45b, 281a.
Illustrations in this book not listed above are from the Mondadori Archives, Milan.

The publishers wish to thank the following: Fedeli Opera International; Gianna Galli; Italartist; Jack Mastroianni of Columbia Artists Management; Stage Door Opera Management; Viviana Zampa and Enrico Tinchini of the Rossini Opera Festival; and all the operatic organizations and opera houses that have kindly supplied their own illustration material.